HUMAN PHYSIOLOGY
THE MECHANISMS OF BODY FUNCTION

McGraw-Hill, INC.

New York   St. Louis   San Francisco
Auckland   Bogotá   Caracas   Lisbon   London   Madrid
Mexico City   Milan   Montreal   New Delhi   San Juan   Singapore
Sydney   Tokyo   Toronto

SIXTH EDITION

HUMAN PHYSIOLOGY

THE MECHANISMS OF BODY FUNCTION

ARTHUR J. VANDER, M.D.

Professor Emeritus of Physiology
University of Michigan

JAMES H. SHERMAN, PH.D.

Associate Professor of Physiology
University of Michigan

DOROTHY S. LUCIANO, PH.D.

Formerly of the Department of Physiology
University of Michigan

HUMAN PHYSIOLOGY

THE MECHANISMS OF BODY FUNCTION

This book is printed on acid-free paper.

2 3 4 5 6 7 8 9 0 VNH   VNH   9 0 9 8 7 6 5 4

ISBN 0-07-066992-9

This book was set in New Caledonia by York Graphic
   Services, Inc.
The editors were Kathi M. Prancan and
   James W. Bradley;
the designer was Jo Jones;
the production supervisor was Paula Keller.
The photo editor was Mira Schachne.
The art editor was Arthur Ciccone.
New drawings were done by York Graphic Services,
   Inc.
New anatomical drawings were done by BioGraphics.
Von Hoffmann Press, Inc., was printer and binder.

Cover photograph by © Don Mason/The Stock Market.
Inset photographs, from top to bottom: © Scott
Camazine/Photo Researchers, Inc.; Dr. Dennis Kunkel/
PhotoTake, NYC, © Science Photo Library/Science
Source; and © Teri J. McDermott, M.A./PhotoTake.

The following illustrations were rendered by Deanne
McKeown, Uppercase Graphics, © 1990: Figures 1–1;
8–1; 8–35; 8–37; 8–38; 8–41; 9–6; 9–8; 9–12; 9–34;
9–37; 11–33; 11–34; 11–35; 11–36; 12–2A; 12–6;
12–8; 12–9; 12–10; 12–13; 13–7; 13–14B; 13–15;
14–13; 14–18; 14–19; 14–24; 14–30; 14–52; 14–54;
14–59; 15–4; 15–13; 15–26; 16–4; 17–14; 17–15;
17–16; 17–17; 17–31; and 19–12.

Library of Congress Cataloging-in-Publication Data

Vander, Arthur J., (date).
   Human physiology: the mechanisms of body function / Arthur J.
Vander, James H. Sherman, Dorothy S. Luciano.—6th ed.
      p.   cm.
   Includes bibliographical references and index.
   ISBN 0-07-066992-9 (acid-free paper)
   1. Human physiology.   I. Sherman, James H., (date).
II. Luciano, Dorothy S.   III. Title.
QP34.5.V36   1994
612—dc24   93-15950

INTERNATIONAL EDITION

When ordering this title, use ISBN 0-07-113761-0.

*To our parents,
and to Judy, Peggy, and Joe
without whose understanding
it would have been
impossible*

REFERENCES FOR FIGURE ADAPTATIONS

Berne, R. M., and N. M. Levy: "Cardiovascular Physiology," 6th edn., Mosby, St. Louis, 1992.

Bloom, F. E., A. Lazerson, and L. Hofstadter: "Brain, Mind, and Behaviour," Freeman, New York, 1985.

Carlson, B. M.: "Patten's Foundations of Embryology," 5th edn., McGraw-Hill, New York, 1988.

Chaffee, E. E., and I. M. Lytle: "Basic Physiology and Anatomy," 4th edn., Lippincott, Philadelphia, 1980.

Chapman, C. B., and J. H. Mitchell: *Sci. Amer.,* May, 1965.

Comroe, J. H.: "Physiology of Respiration," Year Book, Chicago, 1965.

Crosby, W. H.: *Hosp. Prac.,* February, 1987.

Curtis, B. A., S. Jacobson, and E. M. Marcus: "An Invitation to the Neurosciences," Saunders, Philadelphia, 1972.

Davis, H., and H. R. Silverman: "Hearing and Deafness," Holt, Rinehart, and Winston, New York, 1970.

Davson, H.: "The Eye," Vol. 1, 2d edn., Academic, New York, 1969.

Dowling, J. E., and B. B. Boycott: *Proc. R. Soc. Lond.,* **166:**80, 1966.

Erickson, G. F., D. A. Magoffin, C. A. Dyer, and C. Hofeditz: *Endocrine Reviews:* Summer, 1985.

Felig, P., and J. Wahren: *N. Eng. J. Med.,* **293:**1078 (1975).

Ganong, W. F.: "Review of Medical Physiology," 4th edn., Lange, Los Altos, Calif., 1969.

Gardner, E.: "Fundamentals of Neurology," 5th edn., Saunders, Philadelphia, 1968.

Golde, D. W., and Gasson, J. C.: *Sci. Amer.,* July, 1988.

Goodman, H. M.: "Basic Medical Endocrinology," Raven, New York, 1988.

Gray, H. M., A. Sette, and S. Buus (drawing by G. V. Kelvin): *Sci. Amer.,* November, 1989.

Guyton, A. C.: "Functions of the Human Body," 3d edn., Saunders, Philadelphia, 1969.

Hedge, G. A., H. D. Colby, and R. L. Goodman: "Clinical Endocrine Physiology," Saunders, Philadelphia, 1987.

Hoffman, B. F., and P. E. Cranefield: "Electrophysiology of the Heart," McGraw-Hill, New York, 1960.

Hubel, D. H., and T. N. Wiesel: *J. Physiol.,* **154:**572 (1960).

Hudspeth, A. J.: *Sci. Amer.,* January, 1983.

Kandel, E. R., and J. H. Schwartz: "Principles of Neural Science," 2d edn., Elsevier/North-Holland, New York, 1985.

Kappas, A., and A. P. Alvares: *Sci. Amer.,* June 1975.

Lambersten, C. J.: in P. Bard (ed.): "Medical Physiological Psychology," 11th edn., Mosby, St. Louis, 1961.

Lehninger, A. L.: "Biochemistry," Worth, New York, 1970.

Lentz, T. L.: "Cell Fine Structure," Saunders, Philadelphia, 1971.

Little, R. C.: "Physiology of the Heart and Circulation," 2d edn., Year Book, Chicago, 1981.

Maxwell, D. J., and M. Rethely: *TINS,* **10:**117 (1987).

Nauta, W. J. H., and M. Fiertag: "Fundamental Neuroanatomy," Freeman, New York, 1986.

Oldendorf, W. H.: *Hosp. Prac.,* **17:**143 (1982).

Olds, J.: *Sci. Am.,* October, 1956.

Pardo, J. V., P. J. Fox, and M. E. Raichle: *Nature,* **349:**61 (1991).

Patton, H. D., A. F. Fuchs, B. Hille, A. M. Scher, and R. Steiner: "Textbook of Physiology," Saunders, Philadelphia, 1989.

Rasmujssen, A. T.: "Outlines of Neuroanatomy," 2d edn., Wm. C. Brown, Dubuque, Ia., 1943.

Roberts, H. R., and J. N. Lozier (drawing by Ilil Arbil): *Hosp. Prac.* January, 1992.

Rushmer, R. F.: "Cardiovascular Dynamics," 2d edn., Saunders, Philadelphia, 1961.

Scales, W. E., A. J. Vander, M. B. Brown, and M. J. Kluger: *Am. J. Physiol.,* **65:**1840 (1988).

Snyder, S. H.: "Drugs and the Brain," Freeman, New York, 1986.

Tung, K.: Immunopathology and male infertility, *Hosp. Prac.,* June, 1988.

von Bekesy, G.: *Sci. Amer.,* August, 1957.

Wang, C. C., and M. I. Grossman: *Am. J. Physiol.,* **164:**527 (1951).

CONTENTS IN BRIEF

Preface xxi

1 A FRAMEWORK FOR HUMAN PHYSIOLOGY   1

PART ONE
BASIC CELL FUNCTIONS

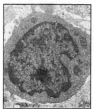

2 CHEMICAL COMPOSITION OF THE BODY   13

3 CELL STRUCTURE   39

4 MOLECULAR CONTROL MECHANISMS—PROTEIN AND DNA   55
SECTION A. BINDING SITES ON PROTEINS   56
SECTION B. GENETIC INFORMATION AND PROTEIN SYNTHESIS   63

5 ENERGY AND CELLULAR METABOLISM   83

6 MOVEMENT OF MOLECULES ACROSS CELL MEMBRANES   115

PART TWO
BIOLOGICAL CONTROL SYSTEMS

7 HOMEOSTATIC MECHANISMS AND CELLULAR COMMUNICATION   149

8 NEURAL CONTROL MECHANISMS   179
SECTION A. NEURAL TISSUE   181
SECTION B. MEMBRANE POTENTIALS   186
SECTION C. SYNAPSES   201
SECTION D. STRUCTURE OF THE NERVOUS SYSTEM   214

9 THE SENSORY SYSTEMS   233

10 HORMONAL CONTROL MECHANISMS   273

11 MUSCLE   303
SECTION A. SKELETAL MUSCLE   304
SECTION B. SMOOTH MUSCLE   338

12 CONTROL OF BODY MOVEMENT   349

13 CONSCIOUSNESS AND BEHAVIOR   369

PART THREE
COORDINATED BODY FUNCTIONS

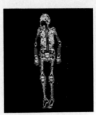

APPENDIX A. ANSWERS TO THOUGHT QUESTIONS   A-1
APPENDIX B. GLOSSARY   A-11
APPENDIX C. ENGLISH AND METRIC UNITS   A-43
APPENDIX D. ELECTROPHYSIOLOGY EQUATIONS   A-44
APPENDIX E. OUTLINE OF EXERCISE PHYSIOLOGY   A-45
APPENDIX F. INDEX OF CLINICAL APPLICATIONS
   IN THE TEXT   A-47
APPENDIX G. SUGGESTED READINGS   A-51

Index   *I1*

14 CIRCULATION   393
SECTION A. BLOOD   395
SECTION B. OVERALL DESIGN OF THE
   CARDIOVASCULAR SYSTEM   403
SECTION C. THE HEART   409
SECTION D. THE VASCULAR SYSTEM   429
SECTION E. INTEGRATION OF CARDIOVASCULAR
   FUNCTION: REGULATION OF SYSTEMIC ARTERIAL
   PRESSURE   450
SECTION F. CARDIOVASCULAR PATTERNS IN HEALTH
   AND DISEASE   460

15 RESPIRATION   473

16 THE KIDNEYS AND REGULATION OF WATER
   AND INORGANIC IONS   515
SECTION A. BASIC PRINCIPLES OF RENAL PHYSIOLOGY   517
SECTION B. REGULATION OF SODIUM, WATER, AND
   POTASSIUM BALANCE   529
SECTION C. CALCIUM REGULATION   546
SECTION D. HYDROGEN-ION REGULATION   552
SECTION E. DIURETICS AND KIDNEY DISEASE   557

17 THE DIGESTION AND ABSORPTION OF FOOD   561

18 REGULATION OF ORGANIC METABOLISM, GROWTH,
   AND ENERGY BALANCE   601
SECTION A. CONTROL AND INTEGRATION OF
   CARBOHYDRATE, PROTEIN, AND FAT METABOLISM   602
SECTION B. CONTROL OF GROWTH   624
SECTION C. REGULATION OF TOTAL-BODY ENERGY
   BALANCE AND TEMPERATURE   630

19 REPRODUCTION   647
SECTION A. GENERAL TERMINOLOGY AND CONCEPTS   648
SECTION B. MALE REPRODUCTIVE PHYSIOLOGY   651
SECTION C. FEMALE REPRODUCTIVE PHYSIOLOGY   661
SECTION D. THE CHRONOLOGY OF REPRODUCTIVE
   FUNCTION   692

20 DEFENSE MECHANISMS OF THE BODY   699
SECTION A. IMMUNOLOGY: DEFENSES AGAINST FOREIGN
   MATTER   700
SECTION B. NONIMMUNE METABOLISM OF FOREIGN
   CHEMICALS   738
SECTION C. HEMOSTASIS: THE PREVENTION OF BLOOD
   LOSS   741
SECTION D. RESISTANCE TO STRESS   751

CONTENTS

Preface xxi

1 A FRAMEWORK FOR PHYSIOLOGY 1

MECHANISM AND CAUSALITY 2
A SOCIETY OF CELLS 2
Cells: The Basic Units 2
Tissues 4
Organs and Organ Systems 4
THE INTERNAL ENVIRONMENT AND
HOMEOSTASIS 4
BODY-FLUID COMPARTMENTS 7
SUMMARY 8
KEY TERMS 9
REVIEW QUESTIONS 9

PART ONE
BASIC CELL FUNCTIONS

2 CHEMICAL COMPOSITION OF THE BODY 13

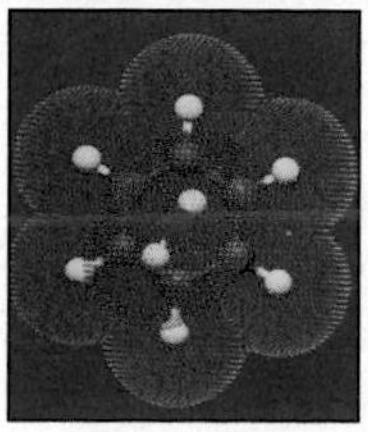

ATOMS 14
Atomic Number 14
Atomic Weight 15
Atomic Composition of the Body 15
MOLECULES 15
Covalent Chemical Bonds 15
Molecular Shape 16
IONS 17
POLAR MOLECULES 18
Hydrogen Bonds 19
Water 19
SOLUTIONS 20
Molecular Solubility 20
Concentration 22
Hydrogen Ions and Acidity 22
CLASSES OF ORGANIC MOLECULES 23
Carbohydrates 24
Lipids 25
Fatty acids 25
Triacylglycerols 25
Phospholipids 26
Steroids 26
Proteins 29
Amino acid subunits 29
Polypeptides 30
Primary protein structure 31
Protein conformation 31
Nucleic Acids 34
DNA 34
RNA 35
SUMMARY 36
KEY TERMS 38
REVIEW QUESTIONS 38

3 CELL STRUCTURE 39

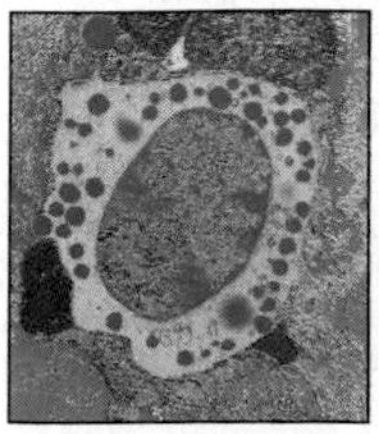

MICROSCOPIC OBSERVATIONS OF CELLS 40

CELL COMPARTMENTS 42
Membranes 43
Membrane structure 44
Membrane junctions 46
CELL ORGANELLES 48
Nucleus 48
Ribosomes 48
Endoplasmic Reticulum 48
Golgi Apparatus 49
Mitochondria 49
Lysosomes 50
Peroxisomes 51
Filaments 51
SUMMARY 53
KEY TERMS 54
REVIEW QUESTIONS 54

4 MOLECULAR CONTROL MECHANISMS: PROTEINS AND DNA **55**

SECTION A. BINDING SITES ON PROTEINS **56**
BINDING-SITE CHARACTERISTICS 56
Chemical Specificity 56
Affinity 57
Saturation 57
Competition 58
REGULATION OF BINDING-SITE
CHARACTERISTICS 59
Allosteric Modulation 60
Covalent Modulation 60
SECTION A SUMMARY 62
SECTION A KEY TERMS 62
SECTION A REVIEW QUESTIONS 62
SECTION B. GENETIC INFORMATION AND PROTEIN SYNTHESIS **63**
GENETIC CODE 63
PROTEIN SYNTHESIS 65
Transcription: mRNA Synthesis 65
Translation: Polypeptide Synthesis 67
Ribosomes 67
Transfer RNA 67
Protein assembly 67
Protein Secretion 70
Regulation of Protein Synthesis 72
REPLICATION AND EXPRESSION OF
GENETIC INFORMATION 73
Replication of DNA 73

Cell Division 73
Mutation 75
Recombinant DNA 77
CANCER 78
SECTION B SUMMARY 80
SECTION B KEY TERMS 81
SECTION B REVIEW QUESTIONS 81
CHAPTER 4 CLINICAL TERMS 81
CHAPTER 4 THOUGHT QUESTIONS 81

5 ENERGY AND CELLULAR METABOLISM **83**

CHEMICAL REACTIONS 84
Determinants of Reaction Rates 84
Reversible and Irreversible Reactions 85
Law of Mass Action 86
ENZYMES 86
Cofactors 87
REGULATION OF ENZYME-MEDIATED
REACTIONS 87
Substrate Concentration 88
Enzyme Concentration 88
Enzyme Activity 89
MULTIENZYME METABOLIC PATHWAYS 90
ATP AND CELLULAR ENERGY TRANSFER 91
The Role of ATP 91
Glycolysis 93
Krebs Cycle 96
Oxidative Phosphorylation 97
CARBOHYDRATE, FAT, AND PROTEIN
METABOLISM 100
Carbohydrate Metabolism 101
Carbohydrate catabolism 101
Glycogen storage 102
Glucose synthesis 103
Fat Metabolism 104
Fat catabolism 104
Fat synthesis 105
Protein and Amino Acid Metabolism 106
Fuel Metabolism Summary 110
ESSENTIAL NUTRIENTS 110
Vitamins 111
SUMMARY 111
KEY TERMS 113
REVIEW QUESTIONS 114
THOUGHT QUESTIONS 114

6 MOVEMENT OF MOLECULES ACROSS CELL MEMBRANES — 115

DIFFUSION — 116
Magnitude and Direction of Diffusion — 117
Speed of Diffusion — 117
Diffusion through Membranes — 119
Diffusion through the lipid bilayer — 119
Diffusion of ions through protein channels — 120
Role of electric forces on ion movements — 120
Regulation of diffusion through membranes — 122
MEDIATED-TRANSPORT SYSTEMS — 122
Facilitated Diffusion — 124
Active Transport — 124
Primary active transport — 127
Secondary active transport — 128
OSMOSIS — 131
Extracellular Osmolarity and Cell Volume — 135
ENDOCYTOSIS AND EXOCYTOSIS — 137
Endocytosis — 137
Exocytosis — 137
EPITHELIAL TRANSPORT — 138
Glands — 141
SUMMARY — 142
KEY TERMS — 144
REVIEW QUESTIONS — 144
THOUGHT QUESTIONS — 144

PART TWO
BIOLOGICAL CONTROL SYSTEMS

7 HOMEOSTATIC MECHANISMS AND CELLULAR COMMUNICATION — 149

GENERAL CHARACTERISTICS OF
HOMEOSTATIC CONTROL SYSTEMS — 150
Feedforward Regulation — 152
Acclimatization — 153
Biological Rhythms — 153
Aging and Homeostasis — 154

THE BALANCE CONCEPT AND CHEMICAL
HOMEOSTASIS — 155
COMPONENTS OF HOMEOSTATIC SYSTEMS — 157
Reflexes — 157
Local Homeostatic Responses — 158
Intercellular Chemical Messengers — 159
Eicosanoids — 160
RECEPTORS — 162
Regulation of Receptors — 163
SIGNAL TRANSDUCTION MECHANISMS
FOR PLASMA-MEMBRANE RECEPTORS — 164
Adenylyl Cyclase and Cyclic AMP — 166
Guanylyl Cylclase and Cyclic GMP — 170
Phospholipase C, Diacylglycerol, and Inositol
Trisphosphate — 170
Ion Channels Controlled by G Proteins — 171
Calcium as a Second Messenger — 172
SUMMARY — 174
KEY TERMS — 176
REVIEW QUESTIONS — 176
CLINICAL TERMS — 177
THOUGHT QUESTIONS — 177

8 NEURAL CONTROL MECHANISMS — 179

SECTION A. NEURAL TISSUE — 181
NEURAL GROWTH AND REGENERATION — 185
SECTION A SUMMARY — 186
SECTION A KEY TERMS — 186
SECTION A REVIEW QUESTIONS — 186
SECTION B. MEMBRANE POTENTIALS — 186
BASIC PRINCIPLES OF ELECTRICITY — 186
THE RESTING MEMBRANE POTENTIAL — 187
GRADED POTENTIALS AND ACTION
POTENTIALS — 191
Graded Potentials — 191
Action Potentials — 194
Ionic basis of the action potential — 194
Mechanism of ion-channel changes — 196
Threshold — 196
Refractory periods — 197
Action-potential propagation — 197
Initiation of action potentials — 198
SECTION B SUMMARY — 199
SECTION B KEY TERMS — 200
SECTION B REVIEW QUESTIONS — 200
SECTION C. SYNAPSES — 201
FUNCTIONAL ANATOMY OF SYNAPSES — 201
Excitatory Chemical Synapses — 203
Inhibitory Chemical Synapses — 203

ACTIVATION OF THE POSTSYNAPTIC CELL	203
SYNAPTIC EFFECTIVENESS	205
Modification of Synaptic Transmission by Drugs and Disease	207
NEUROTRANSMITTERS AND NEUROMODULATORS	207
Acetylcholine	208
Biogenic Amines	208
Norepinephrine and epinephrine	*211*
Serotonin	*211*
Amino Acid Neurotransmitters	211
Neuropeptides	212
Gases	212
SECTION C SUMMARY	213
SECTION C KEY TERMS	213
SECTION C REVIEW QUESTIONS	214
SECTION D. STRUCTURE OF THE NERVOUS SYSTEM	**214**
CENTRAL NERVOUS SYSTEM: SPINAL CORD	214
CENTRAL NERVOUS SYSTEM: BRAIN	215
Brainstem	215
Cerebellum	217
Forebrain	217
PERIPHERAL NERVOUS SYSTEM	221
Peripheral Nervous System: Afferent Division	222
Peripheral Nervous System: Efferent Division	222
Somatic nervous system	*222*
Autonomic nervous system	*222*
BLOOD SUPPLY, BLOOD-BRAIN BARRIER PHENOMENA, AND CEREBROSPINAL FLUID	229
SECTION D SUMMARY	230
SECTION D KEY TERMS	231
SECTION D REVIEW QUESTIONS	231
CHAPTER 8 CLINICAL TERMS	232
CHAPTER 8 THOUGHT QUESTIONS	232

Stimulus Location	241
Lateral inhibition	*242*
Stimulus Duration	243
Central Control of Afferent Information	244
SOMATIC SENSATION	245
Touch-Pressure	246
Sense of Movement and Posture	247
Temperature	247
Pain	248
VISION	249
Light	249
The Optics of Vision	249
Receptor Cells	252
Neural Pathways of Vision	254
Color Vision	256
Eye Movement	257
HEARING	257
Sound	258
Sound Transmission in the Ear	259
Hair Cells of the Organ of Corti	261
Neural Pathways in Hearing	263
VESTIBULAR SYSTEM	263
The Semicircular Canals	263
The Utricle and Saccule	265
Vestibular Information and Dysfunction	265
CHEMICAL SENSES	266
Taste	266
Smell	267
SUMMARY	267
KEY TERMS	270
REVIEW QUESTIONS	270
CLINICAL TERMS	270
THOUGHT QUESTIONS	271

9 THE SENSORY SYSTEMS 233

RECEPTORS	234
The Receptor Potential	235
NEURAL PATHWAYS IN SENSORY SYSTEMS	236
Sensory Units	236
Ascending Pathways	236
ASSOCIATION CORTEX AND PERCEPTUAL PROCESSING	238
Factors that Distort Perception	238
PRIMARY SENSORY CODING	240
Stimulus Type	240
Stimulus Intensity	240

10 HORMONAL CONTROL MECHANISMS 273

HORMONE STRUCTURES AND SYNTHESIS	276
Amine Hormones	276
Thyroid hormones	*276*
Adrenal medullary hormones and dopamine	*277*
Peptide Hormones	277
Steroid Hormones	278
Hormones of the adrenal cortex	*278*
Hormones of the gonads	*279*
HORMONE TRANSPORT IN THE BLOOD	280
HORMONE METABOLISM AND EXCRETION	281
MECHANISMS OF HORMONE ACTION	282
Hormone Receptors	282

Events Elicited by Hormone-Receptor Binding 283
   Effects of peptide hormones and catecholamines 283
   Effects of steroid and thyroid hormones 283
Pharmacological Effects of Hormones 283
TYPES OF INPUTS THAT CONTROL HORMONE SECRETION 284
   Control by Plasma Concentrations of Mineral Ions or Organic Nutrients 284
   Control by Neurons 284
   Control by Other Hormones 285
CONTROL SYSTEMS INVOLVING THE HYPOTHALAMUS AND PITUITARY 286
   Posterior Pituitary Hormones 286
   The Hypothalamus and Anterior Pituitary 287
   Anterior pituitary hormones 288
   Hypophysiotropic hormones 289
   Neural control of hypophysiotropic hormones 292
   Hormonal feedback control of the hypothalamus and anterior pituitary 292
   The role of "nonsequence" hormones on the hypothalamus and anterior pituitary 294
   A summary example: control of growth hormone secretion 294
CANDIDATE HORMONES 295
TYPES OF ENDOCRINE DISORDERS 296
   Hyposecretion 296
   Hypersecretion 296
   Hyporesponsiveness and Hyperresponsiveness 298
SUMMARY 298
KEY TERMS 300
REVIEW QUESTIONS 300
CLINICAL TERMS 301
THOUGHT QUESTIONS 301

11 MUSCLE **303**

SECTION A. SKELETAL MUSCLE **304**
STRUCTURE 304
MOLECULAR MECHANISMS OF CONTRACTION 307
Sliding-Filament Mechanism 307
Role of Troponin, Tropomyosin, and Calcium in Contraction 312
Excitation-Contraction Coupling 313
   Sarcoplasmic reticulum 314
Membrane Excitation: The Neuromuscular Junction 315

MECHANICS OF SINGLE-FIBER CONTRACTION 320
Twitch Contractions 321
Frequency-Tension Relation 322
Length-Tension Relation 323
Load-Velocity Relation 324
SKELETAL-MUSCLE ENERGY METABOLISM 324
Muscle Fatigue 326
TYPES OF SKELETAL-MUSCLE FIBERS 327
WHOLE-MUSCLE CONTRACTION 327
Control of Muscle Tension 329
Control of Shortening Velocity 330
Muscle Adaptation to Exercise 331
Lever Action of Muscles and Bones 332
Skeletal-Muscle Disease 334
   Muscle cramps 334
   Hypocalcemic tetany 334
   Muscular dystrophy 334
   Myasthenia gravis 334
SECTION A SUMMARY 335
SECTION A KEY TERMS 337
SECTION A REVIEW QUESTIONS 337
SECTION B. SMOOTH MUSCLE **338**
STRUCTURE 338
CONTRACTION AND ITS CONTROL 340
Cross-Bridge Activation 340
Sources of Cytosolic Calcium 341
Membrane Activation 341
   Spontaneous electrical activity 342
   Nerves and hormones 342
   Local factors 343
Types of Smooth Muscle 343
   Single-unit smooth muscle 344
   Multiunit smooth muscle 344
SECTION B SUMMARY 346
SECTION B KEY TERMS 346
SECTION B REVIEW QUESTIONS 346
CHAPTER 11 CLINICAL TERMS 346
CHAPTER 11 THOUGHT QUESTIONS 347

12 CONTROL OF BODY MOVEMENT **349**

MOTOR CONTROL HIERARCHY 350
Voluntary and Involuntary Actions 351
LOCAL CONTROL OF MOTOR NEURONS 352
Interneurons 352
Local Afferent Input 353
   Length-monitoring systems and the stretch reflex 354

Alpha-gamma coactivation   356
Tension-monitoring systems   357
Other local afferent input   357
THE BRAIN MOTOR CENTERS AND THE
DESCENDING PATHWAYS THEY
CONTROL   358
Cerebral Cortex   358
Subcortical and Brainstem Nuclei   359
Cerebellum   361
Descending Pathways   361
Corticospinal pathway   362
Noncorticospinal pathways   362
Summary comments on the descending
pathways   363
MUSCLE TONE   364
Abnormal Muscle Tone   364
MAINTENANCE OF UPRIGHT POSTURE
AND BALANCE   364
WALKING   365
SUMMARY   367
KEY TERMS   367
REVIEW QUESTIONS   368
CLINICAL TERMS   368
THOUGHT QUESTIONS   368

13 CONSCIOUSNESS AND BEHAVIOR   369

STATES OF CONSCIOUSNESS   370
Electroencephalogram   370
The Waking State   371
Sleep   371
Neural Substrates of States of Consciousness   372
Coma and Brain Death   374
CONSCIOUS EXPERIENCES   375
Directed Attention   375
Neural mechanisms for directed attention   375
Neural Mechanisms for Conscious Experiences   376
MOTIVATION AND EMOTION   377
Motivation   377
Chemical mediators   378
Emotion   378
ALTERED STATES OF CONSCIOUSNESS   379
Schizophrenia   379
The Affective Disorders: Depressions and
Manias   380
Psychoactive Drugs, Dependence, and
Tolerance   381
Dependence   381
Tolerance   382

LEARNING AND MEMORY   384
Memory   384
Working memory   384
Long-term memory   384
The Location of Memory   385
The Neural Basis of Learning and Memory   385
CEREBRAL DOMINANCE AND LANGUAGE   386
CONCLUSION   387
SUMMARY   388
KEY TERMS   389
REVIEW QUESTIONS   389
CLINICAL TERMS   389
THOUGHT QUESTIONS   389

PART THREE
COORDINATED BODY FUNCTIONS

14 CIRCULATION   393

SECTION A. BLOOD   395
PLASMA   396
THE BLOOD CELLS   396
Erythrocytes   396
Iron   398
Folic acid and vitamin B_{12} 398
Regulation of erythrocyte production   398
Anemia   399
Leukocytes   400
Platelets   402
Regulation of Blood Cell Production   402
SECTION A SUMMARY   403
SECTION A KEY TERMS   403
SECTION A REVIEW QUESTIONS   403
SECTION B. OVERALL DESIGN OF THE CARDIOVASCULAR
SYSTEM   404
PRESSURE, FLOW, AND RESISTANCE   408
SECTION B SUMMARY   408
SECTION B KEY TERMS   408
SECTION B REVIEW QUESTIONS   409
SECTION C. THE HEART   410
ANATOMY   410
Cardiac muscle   410
Innervation   411
Blood supply   411
HEARTBEAT COORDINATION   411
Cardiac Action Potentials   412
Sequence of Excitation   413
The Electrocardiogram   414

Excitation-Contraction Coupling 415
Refractory Period of the Heart 416
MECHANICAL EVENTS OF THE CARDIAC
  CYCLE 417
  Mid-to-Late Diastole 417
  Systole 419
  Early Diastole 420
  Pulmonary Circulation Pressures 420
  Heart Sounds 420
THE CARDIAC OUTPUT 421
  Control of Heart Rate 421
  Control of Stroke Volume 422
    Relationship between end-diastolic volume
      and stroke volume: Starling's law of the
      heart 422
    The sympathetic nerves 423
MEASUREMENT OF CARDIAC FUNCTION 427
SECTION C SUMMARY 427
SECTION C KEY TERMS 428
SECTION C REVIEW QUESTIONS 428
SECTION D. THE VASCULAR SYSTEM 429
ARTERIES 430
  Arterial Blood Pressure 430
  Measurement of Systemic Arterial Pressure 431
ARTERIOLES 432
  Local Controls 434
    Active hyperemia 434
    Flow autoregulation 435
    Reactive hyperemia 435
    Response to injury 435
  Extrinsic Controls 435
    Sympathetic nerves 435
    Parasympathetic nerves and other vasodilator
      nerves 436
    Hormones 436
  Endothelial Cells and Vascular Smooth Muscle 436
  Arteriolar Control in Specific Organs 437
CAPILLARIES 437
  Anatomy of the Capillary Network 439
  Velocity of Capillary Blood Flow 440
  Diffusion across the Capillary Wall: Exchanges
    of Nutrients and Metabolic End Products 440
  Bulk Flow across the Capillary Wall:
    Distribution of the Extracellular Fluid 442
VEINS 444
  Determinants of Venous Pressure 445
THE LYMPHATIC SYSTEM 446
  Mechanism of Lymph Flow 448
SECTION D SUMMARY 448
SECTION D KEY TERMS 449
SECTION D REVIEW QUESTIONS 449
SECTION E. INTEGRATION OF CARDIOVASCULAR
  FUNCTION: REGULATION OF SYSTEMIC ARTERIAL
  PRESSURE 450
BARORECEPTOR REFLEXES 455
  Arterial Baroreceptors 455
  Other Baroreceptors 456
  The Medullary Cardiovascular Center 456

Operation of the Baroreceptor Reflex 456
BLOOD VOLUME AND LONG-TERM
  REGULATION OF ARTERIAL PRESSURE 459
OTHER CARDIOVASCULAR REFLEXES AND
  RESPONSES 459
SECTION E SUMMARY 459
SECTION E KEY TERMS 460
SECTION E REVIEW QUESTIONS 460
SECTION F. CARDIOVASCULAR PATTERNS IN HEALTH
  AND DISEASE 460
HEMORRHAGE AND OTHER CAUSES
  OF HYPOTENSION 460
  Shock 462
THE UPRIGHT POSTURE 462
EXERCISE 463
  Maximal Oxygen Consumption and Training 465
HYPERTENSION 466
HEART FAILURE 468
CORONARY ARTERY DISEASE 469
SECTION F SUMMARY 471
SECTION F KEY TERMS 471
SECTION F REVIEW QUESTIONS 471
CHAPTER 14 CLINICAL TERMS 472
CHAPTER 14 THOUGHT QUESTIONS 472

15 RESPIRATION 473

ORGANIZATION OF THE RESPIRATORY
  SYSTEM 474
  The Airways 474
  Site of Gas Exchange: The Alveoli 476
  Relation of the Lungs to the Thoracic (Chest)
    Wall 476
  Pulmonary Pressures 477
VENTILATION AND LUNG MECHANICS 480
  Inspiration 481
  Expiration 482
  Lung Compliance 483
    Determinants of pulmonary compliance 483
  Airway Resistance 484
    Asthma 484
    Chronic obstructive lung disease 485
    The Heimlich maneuver 485
  Lung Volumes and Capacities 485
  Alveolar Ventilation 487
    Dead space 487
EXCHANGE OF GASES IN ALVEOLI AND
  TISSUES 488
  Partial Pressures of Gases 489
    Diffusion of gases in liquids 490

Alveolar Gas Pressures — 491
Alveolar-Blood Gas Exchange — 492
Matching of Ventilation and Blood Flow in Alveoli — 493
Gas Exchange in the Tissues — 493
TRANSPORT OF OXYGEN IN BLOOD — 494
Effect of P_{O_2} on Hemoglobin Saturation — 494
Effects of Blood P_{CO_2}, H^+ Concentration, Temperature, and DPG Concentration on Hemoglobin Saturation — 496
TRANSPORT OF CARBON DIOXIDE IN BLOOD — 497
TRANSPORT OF HYDROGEN IONS BETWEEN TISSUES AND LUNGS — 499
CONTROL OF RESPIRATION — 500
Neural Generation of Rhythmic Breathing — 500
Control of Ventilation by P_{O_2}, P_{CO_2}, and H^+ Concentration — 500
Control by P_{O_2} — 500
Control by P_{CO_2} — 502
Control by changes in arterial H^+ concentration not due to altered carbon dioxide — 504
Control of Ventilation During Exercise — 505
Increased P_{CO_2} as the stimulus? — 505
Decreased P_{O_2} as the stimulus? — 505
Increased H^+ concentration as the stimulus? — 505
Other factors — 505
Other Ventilatory Responses — 507
Protective reflexes — 507
Pain and emotion — 508
Voluntary control of breathing — 508
HYPOXIA — 508
Acclimatization to High Altitude — 508
NONRESPIRATORY FUNCTIONS OF THE LUNGS — 509
SUMMARY — 510
KEY TERMS — 512
REVIEW QUESTIONS — 512
CHAPTER 15 CLINICAL TERMS — 513
CHAPTER 15 THOUGHT QUESTIONS — 513

16 THE KIDNEYS AND REGULATION OF WATER AND INORGANIC IONS — 515

SECTION A. BASIC PRINCIPLES OF RENAL PHYSIOLOGY — 517
FUNCTIONS OF THE KIDNEYS — 517
STRUCTURE OF THE KIDNEYS AND URINARY SYSTEM — 517
BASIC RENAL PROCESSES — 520
Glomerular Filtration — 523
Forces involved in filtration — 523
Rate of glomerular filtration — 523
Tubular Reabsorption — 524
T_m-Limited Transport Mechanisms — 525
Reabsorption by Diffusion — 525
Tubular Secretion — 526
Metabolism by the Tubules — 526
The Concept of Renal Clearance — 526
MICTURITION — 527
SECTION A SUMMARY — 528
SECTION A KEY TERMS — 529
SECTION A REVIEW QUESTIONS — 529
SECTION B. REGULATION OF SODIUM, WATER, AND POTASSIUM BALANCE — 529
TOTAL-BODY BALANCE OF SODIUM AND WATER — 529
BASIC RENAL PROCESSES FOR SODIUM AND WATER — 530
Primary Active Sodium Reabsorption — 530
Coupling of Water Reabsorption to Sodium Reabsorption — 530
Urine Concentration: The Countercurrent Multiplier System — 532
RENAL SODIUM REGULATION — 535
Control of GFR — 536
Control of Sodium Reabsorption — 536
Aldosterone and the renin-angiotensin system — 536
Atrial natriuretic factor — 539
RENAL WATER REGULATION — 540
Baroreceptor Control of ADH Secretion — 540
Osmoreceptor Control of ADH Secretion — 541
A SUMMARY EXAMPLE: THE RESPONSE TO SWEATING — 541
THIRST AND SALT APPETITE — 542
POTASSIUM REGULATION — 542
Renal Regulation of Potassium — 543
SECTION B SUMMARY — 545
SECTION B KEY TERMS — 546
SECTION B REVIEW QUESTIONS — 546
SECTION C. CALCIUM REGULATION — 546
EFFECTOR SITES FOR CALCIUM HOMEOSTASIS — 547
Bone — 547
Kidneys — 548
Gastrointestinal Tract — 548
HORMONAL CONTROLS — 548
Parathyroid Hormone — 548
Vitamin D — 550
METABOLIC BONE DISEASES — 551
SECTION C SUMMARY — 551
SECTION C KEY TERMS — 551
SECTION C REVIEW QUESTIONS — 551
SECTION D. HYDROGEN-ION REGULATION — 552
SOURCES OF HYDROGEN-ION GAIN OR LOSS — 552

BUFFERING OF HYDROGEN IONS
IN THE BODY ... 552
INTEGRATION OF HOMEOSTATIC
CONTROLS ... 553
RENAL MECHANISMS ... 553
Bicarbonate Excretion ... 554
Addition of New Bicarbonate to the Plasma ... 554
Renal Responses to Acidosis and Alkalosis ... 555
CLASSIFICATION OF ACIDOSIS AND
ALKALOSIS ... 556
SECTION D SUMMARY ... 556
SECTION D KEY TERMS ... 557
SECTION D REVIEW QUESTIONS ... 557
SECTION E. DIURETICS AND KIDNEY DISEASE ... **557**
DIURETICS ... 557
KIDNEY DISEASE ... 558
Hemodialysis, Peritoneal Dialysis, and
Transplantation ... 559
SECTION E SUMMARY ... 560
CHAPTER 16 CLINICAL TERMS ... 560
CHAPTER 16 THOUGHT QUESTIONS ... 560

17 THE DIGESTION AND ABSORPTION OF FOOD ... **561**

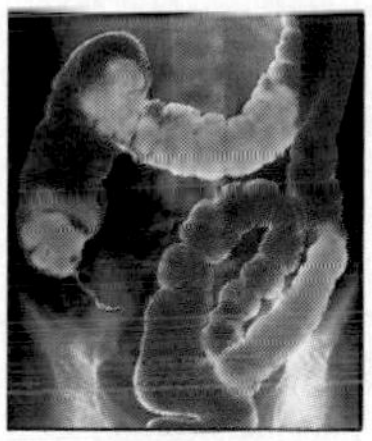

OVERVIEW: FUNCTIONS OF THE
GASTROINTESTINAL ORGANS ... 563
STRUCTURE OF THE GASTROINTESTINAL
TRACT WALL ... 567
DIGESTION AND ABSORPTION ... 569
Carbohydrate ... 569
Protein ... 571
Fat ... 571
Vitamins ... 573
Water and Minerals ... 574
REGULATION OF GASTROINTESTINAL
PROCESSES ... 575
Basic Principles ... 575
Neural regulation ... 575
Hormonal regulation ... 576
Phases of gastrointestinal control ... 578
Mouth, Pharynx, and Esophagus ... 578
Chewing ... 578
Saliva ... 578
Swallowing ... 578
Stomach ... 580
HCl secretion ... 581
Pepsin secretion ... 582
Gastric motility ... 583
Pancreatic Secretions ... 586
Bile Secretion ... 587

Small Intestine ... 590
Secretions ... 590
Motility ... 590
Large Intestine ... 591
Motility and defecation ... 592
PATHOPHYSIOLOGY OF THE
GASTROINTESTINAL TRACT ... 593
Ulcers ... 593
Vomiting ... 594
Gallstones ... 594
Lactose intolerance ... 595
Constipation and diarrhea ... 595
SUMMARY ... 596
KEY TERMS ... 598
REVIEW QUESTIONS ... 599
CLINICAL TERMS ... 599
THOUGHT QUESTIONS ... 600

**18 REGULATION OF ORGANIC METABOLISM, GROWTH,
AND ENERGY BALANCE** ... **601**

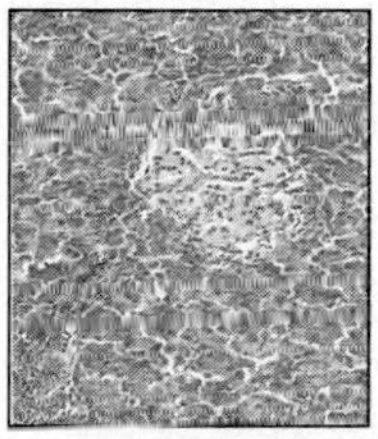

**SECTION A. CONTROL AND INTEGRATION OF
CARBOHYDRATE, PROTEIN, AND FAT METABOLISM** ... **602**
EVENTS OF THE ABSORPTIVE AND
POSTABSORPTIVE STATES ... 602
Absorptive State ... 603
Absorbed glucose ... 604
Absorbed triacylglycerols ... 605
Absorbed amino acids ... 605
Postabsorptive State ... 606
Sources of blood glucose ... 606
Glucose sparing (fat utilization) ... 607
ENDOCRINE AND NEURAL CONTROL OF
THE ABSORPTIVE AND POSTABSORPTIVE
STATES ... 607
Insulin ... 608
Effects on muscle and adipose tissue ... 609
Effects on liver ... 610
Effects of decreases in plasma insulin
concentration ... 611
Control of insulin secretion ... 611
Glucagon ... 613
Epinephrine and Sympathetic Nerves to Liver
and Adipose Tissue ... 614
Other Hormones ... 615
Cortisol ... 615
Growth hormone ... 616
Summary ... 616
FUEL HOMEOSTASIS IN EXERCISE AND
STRESS ... 617

DIABETES MELLITUS ... 618
HYPOGLYCEMIA AS A CAUSE OF SYMPTOMS ... 620
REGULATION OF PLASMA CHOLESTEROL ... 621
SECTION A SUMMARY ... 623
SECTION A KEY TERMS ... 624
SECTION A REVIEW QUESTIONS ... 624
SECTION B. CONTROL OF GROWTH ... **624**
BONE GROWTH ... 625
ENVIRONMENTAL FACTORS INFLUENCING
   GROWTH ... 625
HORMONAL INFLUENCES ON GROWTH ... 626
   Growth Hormone ... 626
   Thyroid Hormones ... 627
   Insulin ... 628
   Sex Hormones ... 628
   Cortisol ... 629
COMPENSATORY GROWTH ... 629
SECTION B SUMMARY ... 629
SECTION B KEY TERMS ... 629
SECTION B REVIEW QUESTIONS ... 630
**SECTION C. REGULATION OF TOTAL-BODY ENERGY
   BALANCE AND TEMPERATURE** ... **630**
BASIC CONCEPTS OF ENERGY
   EXPENDITURE AND CALORIC BALANCE ... 630
   Metabolic Rate ... 631
   Determinants of Metabolic Rate ... 631
      Basal metabolic rate ... *631*
      Thyroid hormones ... *632*
      Epinephrine ... *632*
      Food-induced thermogenesis ... *633*
      Muscle activity ... *633*
   Total-Body Energy Balance ... 633
   Control of Food Intake ... 634
   Obesity ... 636
   Eating Disorders: Anorexia Nervosa and Bulimia ... 637
REGULATION OF BODY TEMPERATURE ... 637
   Mechanisms of Heat Loss or Gain ... 638
   Temperature-regulating reflexes ... 638
      Control of heat production ... *639*
      *Control of heat loss by radiation and
         conduction* ... *640*
      Control of heat loss by evaporation ... *641*
      Integration of effector mechanisms ... *641*
   Temperature Acclimatization ... 641
      Acclimatization to heat ... *641*
      Acclimatization to cold ... *642*
   Fever ... 642
   Other Causes of Hyperthermia ... 644
      Exercise ... *644*
      Heat exhaustion and heat stroke ... *644*
SECTION C SUMMARY ... 645
SECTION C KEY TERMS ... 645
SECTION C REVIEW QUESTIONS ... 645
CHAPTER 18 CLINICAL TERMS ... 646
CHAPTER 18 THOUGHT QUESTIONS ... 646

19 REPRODUCTION 647

SECTION A. GENERAL TERMINOLOGY AND CONCEPTS ... **648**
GENERAL PRINCIPLES OF
   GAMETOGENESIS ... 649
SECTION A SUMMARY ... 651
SECTION A KEY TERMS ... 651
SECTION A REVIEW QUESTIONS ... 651
SECTION B. MALE REPRODUCTIVE PHYSIOLOGY ... **651**
ANATOMY ... 651
SPERMATOGENESIS ... 653
TRANSPORT OF SPERM ... 656
   Erection ... 657
   Ejaculation ... 658
HORMONAL CONTROL OF MALE
   REPRODUCTIVE FUNCTIONS ... 658
   Control of the Testes ... 658
   Testosterone ... 659
      Accessory reproductive organs ... *659*
      Secondary sex characteristics and growth ... *660*
      Behavior ... *660*
      Mechanism of action ... *660*
   Prolactin ... 660
SECTION B SUMMARY ... 660
SECTION B KEY TERMS ... 661
SECTION B REVIEW QUESTIONS ... 661
SECTION C. FEMALE REPRODUCTIVE PHYSIOLOGY ... **661**
ANATOMY ... 662
OVARIAN FUNCTION ... 663
   Oogenesis ... 663
   Follicle Growth ... 664
   Formation of the Corpus Luteum ... 666
   Ovarian Hormones ... 666
CONTROL OF OVARIAN FUNCTION ... 666
   Follicle Development and Estrogen Secretion
      during the Early and Middle Follicular Phase ... 668
   LH Surge and Ovulation ... 669
   The Corpus Luteum ... 670
UTERINE CHANGES IN THE MENSTRUAL
   CYCLE ... 671
OTHER EFFECTS OF ESTROGEN AND
   PROGESTERONE ... 672
ANDROGENS IN WOMEN ... 674
FEMALE SEXUAL RESPONSE ... 674
PREGNANCY ... 675
   Ovum Transport ... 675
   Sperm Transport and Capacitation ... 675
   Fertilization ... 675

Early Development, Implantation, and
Placentation 677
Hormonal and Other Changes during Pregnancy 680
Pregnancy sickness 681
Parturition 681
Lactation 684
Contraception 687
Infertility 690
SECTION C SUMMARY 690
SECTION C KEY TERMS 691
SECTION C REVIEW QUESTIONS 692
SECTION D. THE CHRONOLOGY OF REPRODUCTIVE
FUNCTION 692
SEX DETERMINATION 693
SEX DIFFERENTIATION 693
Differentiation of the Gonads 693
Differentiation of Internal And External
Genitalia 693
Sexual Differentiation of the Central Nervous
System 695
PUBERTY 695
MENOPAUSE 696
SECTION D SUMMARY 696
SECTION D KEY TERMS 697
SECTION D REVIEW QUESTIONS 697
CHAPTER 19 CLINICAL TERMS 697
CHAPTER 19 THOUGHT QUESTIONS 697

20 DEFENSE MECHANISMS OF THE BODY 699

SECTION A. IMMUNOLOGY: DEFENSES AGAINST FOREIGN
MATTER 700
CELLS MEDIATING IMMUNE DEFENSES 701
NONSPECIFIC IMMUNE DEFENSES 702
Defenses at Body Surfaces 703
Inflammation 703
Vasodilation and increased permeability
to protein 703
Chemotaxis 704
Killing by phagocytes 704
Complement 705
Tissue repair 706
Interferon 707
SPECIFIC IMMUNE DEFENSES 707
Overview 707
Lymphoid Organs and Lymphocyte Types 708
Lymphoid organs 708
Lymphocyte origins 710
Functions of B cells and T cells 710

Lymphocyte Receptors and Antigen
Presentation 711
B-cell receptors 712
T-cell receptors 712
Antigen Presentation to T Cells 713
Presentation to helper T cells 713
Presentation to cytotoxic T cells 714
NK Cells 715
Development of Immune Tolerance 716
Antibody-Mediated Immune Responses:
Defenses against Bacteria, Extracellular
Viruses, and Toxins 716
B-cell recognition and activation 716
Antibody secretion 717
The attack: effects of antibodies 718
Active and passive humoral immunity 720
Defenses against Virus-Infected Cells and
Cancer Cells 721
Role of cytotoxic T cells 721
Role of NK cells and activated macrophages 723
Immunotherapy against cancer 723
SYSTEMIC MANIFESTATIONS OF
INFECTION 723
FACTORS THAT ALTER THE BODY'S
RESISTANCE TO INFECTION 725
AIDS 726
Antibiotics 727
HARMFUL IMMUNE RESPONSES 728
Graft Rejection 728
Transfusion Reactions 728
Allergy (Hypersensitivity) 729
Immediate hypersensitivity 730
Autoimmune Disease 730
Excessive Inflammatory Reactions to Microbes 732
SECTION A SUMMARY 734
SECTION A KEY TERMS 736
SECTION A REVIEW QUESTIONS 737
SECTION B. NONIMMUNE METABOLISM OF FOREIGN
CHEMICALS 738
ABSORPTION 738
STORAGE SITES 738
EXCRETION 738
BIOTRANSFORMATION 740
SECTION B SUMMARY 740
SECTION B KEY TERMS 740
SECTION B REVIEW QUESTIONS 740
SECTION C. HEMOSTASIS: THE PREVENTION OF BLOOD
LOSS 741
FORMATION OF A PLATELET PLUG 741
BLOOD COAGULATION: CLOT FORMATION 742
ANTICLOTTING SYSTEMS 746
Factors that Oppose Clot Formation 746
The Fibrinolytic System 746
ANTICLOTTING DRUGS 748
SECTION C SUMMARY 749
SECTION C KEY TERMS 750
SECTION C REVIEW QUESTIONS 750

C H A P T E R

1

A FRAMEWORK
FOR HUMAN PHYSIOLOGY

MECHANISM AND CAUSALITY

A SOCIETY OF CELLS

Cells: The Basic Units

Tissues

Organs and Organ Systems

**THE INTERNAL ENVIRONMENT
AND HOMEOSTASIS**

BODY-FLUID COMPARTMENTS

SUMMARY

KEY TERMS

REVIEW QUESTIONS

One cannot meaningfully analyze the complex activities of the human body without a framework upon which to build, a set of viewpoints to guide one's thinking.

It is the purpose of this chapter to provide such an orientation to the subject of **human physiology**—the mechanisms by which the body functions.

MECHANISM AND CAUSALITY

The **mechanist view** of life holds that all phenomena, no matter how complex, are ultimately describable in terms of physical and chemical laws. In this view, which is that taken by physiologists, the human being is a machine—an enormously complex machine, but a machine nevertheless. In contrast, **vitalism** is the view that some "vital force" beyond physics and chemistry is required to explain life. The mechanist view has predominated in the twentieth century because virtually all information gathered from observation and experiment has agreed with it.

Physiologists should not be misunderstood when they sometimes say that "the whole is greater than the sum of its parts." This statement in no way implies a vital force but rather recognizes that *integration* of an enormous number of individual physical and chemical events occurring at all levels of organization is required for biological systems to function. Thus the scope of physiology is extremely broad. At one end of the spectrum, it includes the study of individual molecules—for example, how a particular protein's shape and electrical properties allow it to function as a channel for water movement into or out of a single cell. At the other end, it is concerned with complex processes that depend on the interplay of many widely separated organs in the body—for example, regulation of the amount of water in the entire body.

A common denominator of physiological processes is their contribution to survival. Unfortunately, it is easy to misunderstand the nature of this relationship. Consider, for example, the statement, "During exercise a person sweats because the body *needs* to get rid of the excess heat generated." This type of statement is an example of **teleology**, the explanation of events in terms of purpose, but it is not an explanation at all in the scientific sense of the word. It is somewhat like saying, "The furnace is on because the house needs to be heated." Clearly, the furnace is on not because it senses in some mystical manner the house's "needs," but because the temperature has fallen below the thermostat's set point and the electric current in the connecting wires has turned on the heater.

Is it not true that sweating serves a useful purpose because the excess heat, if not eliminated, might cause sickness or even death? Yes, it is, but this is totally different from stating that a need to avoid injury causes the sweating. The cause of the sweating is a sequence of events initiated by the increased heat generation: increased heat generation → increased blood temperature → increased activity of specific nerve cells in the brain → increased activity of a series of nerve cells → increased production of sweat by the sweat-gland cells. Each step occurs by means of physicochemical changes in the cells involved. In science, to explain a phenomenon is to reduce it to a causally linked sequence of physicochemical events. This is the scientific meaning of causality, of the word "because."

This is a good place to emphasize that causal chains can be not only long, as in the example just cited, but also multiple. In other words, one should not assume the simple relationship of one cause, one effect. We shall see that multiple factors often must interact to elicit a response. To take an example from medicine, cigarette smoking causes lung cancer, but the likelihood of cancer developing in a smoker depends on a variety of other factors, including the way that person's body processes the chemicals in cigarette smoke, the rate at which damaged molecules are repaired, and so on.

That a phenomenon is beneficial to a person, while not explaining the mechanism of the phenomenon, is of obvious interest and importance. Evolution is the key to understanding why most body activities do indeed appear to be purposeful, since those responses having survival value undergo natural selection. Throughout this book we emphasize how a particular process contributes to survival, but the reader must never confuse this survival value of a process with the explanation of the mechanisms by which the process occurs.

A SOCIETY OF CELLS

Cells: The Basic Units

The simplest structural units into which a complex multicellular organism can be divided and still retain the functions characteristic of life are called **cells**. One of the unifying generalizations of biology is that certain fundamental activities are common to almost all cells and represent the minimal requirements for maintaining cell integrity and life. Thus, a human liver cell and an amoeba are remarkably similar in their means of exchanging materials with their immediate environments, of obtaining energy from organic nutrients, of synthesizing complex molecules, and of duplicating themselves.

Each human organism begins as a single cell, the fertilized ovum, which divides to form two cells, each of which divides in turn, resulting in four cells, and so on. If cell multiplication were the only event occurring, the end result would be a spherical mass of identical cells. During development, however, each cell becomes specialized in the performance of a particular function, such as developing force and movement (muscle cells) or generating electric signals (nerve cells). The process of transforming an unspecialized cell into a specialized cell is known as **cell differentiation**.

In addition to differentiating, cells migrate to new locations during development and form selective adhesions with other cells to create multicellular structures. In this manner, the cells of the body are arranged in various combinations to form a hierarchy of organized structures. Differentiated cells with similar properties aggregate to form **tissues** (nerve tissue, muscle tissue, and so on), which combine with other types of tissues to form **organs** (the heart, lungs, kidneys, and so on), which are linked together to form **organ systems** (Figure 1-1).

About 200 distinct kinds of cells can be identified in the body in terms of differences in structure and function. When cells are classified according to the broad types of function they perform, however, four categories emerge: (1) muscle cells, (2) nerve cells, (3) epithelial cells, and (4) connective-tissue cells. In each of these functional categories, there are several cell types that perform variations of the specialized function. For example, there are three types of muscle cells—skeletal-, cardiac-, and smooth-muscle cells—all of which generate forces and produce movement but differ from each other in shape, in the mechanisms controlling their contractile activity, and in their location in the various organs of the body.

Muscle cells are specialized to generate the mechanical forces that produce force and movement. They may be attached to bones and produce movements of the limbs or trunk. They may be attached to skin, as for example, the muscles producing facial expressions, or they may enclose hollow cavities so that their contraction expels the contents of the cavity, as in the case of the pumping of the heart. Muscle cells also surround many of the tubes in the body—blood vessels, for example—and their contraction changes the diameter of these tubes.

Nerve cells are specialized to initiate and conduct electric signals, often over long distances. A signal may influence the initiation of new electric signals in other nerve cells, or it may influence secretion by a gland cell or contraction of a muscle cell. Thus, nerve cells provide a major means of controlling the activities of other cells.

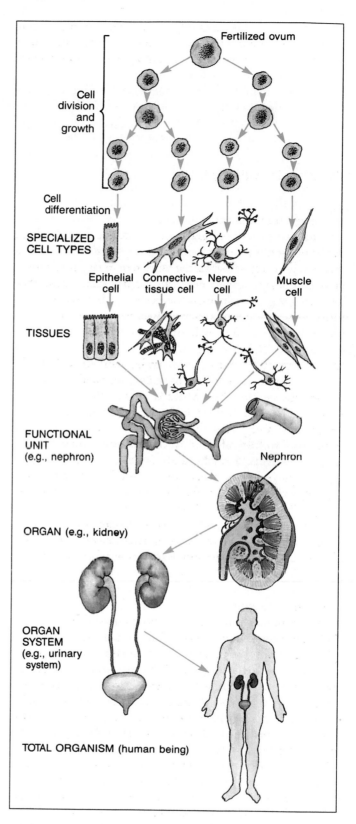

FIGURE 1-1

Levels of cellular organization.

Their activity also underlies such phenomena as consciousness, perception, and cognition.

Epithelial cells are specialized for the selective secretion and absorption of ions and organic molecules. They are located mainly at the surfaces that either cover the body or individual organs or else line the walls of various tubular and hollow structures within the body. Epithelial cells, which rest on a homogeneous noncellular material called the **basement membrane**, form the boundaries between compartments and function as selective barriers regulating the exchange of molecules across them. For example, the epithelial cells at the surface of the skin form a barrier that prevents most substances in the external environment from entering the body through the skin. Epithelial cells are also found in glands that form from the invagination of epithelial surfaces.

Connective-tissue cells, as their name implies, have as their major function connecting, anchoring, and supporting the structures of the body. These cells typically have a large amount of extracellular material between them. The cells themselves include those in the loose meshwork of cells and fibers underlying most epithelial layers, plus other types as diverse as fat-storing cells, bone cells, and red and white blood cells. Many connective-tissue cells secrete into the fluid surrounding them molecules that form a matrix consisting of various types of protein **fibers** embedded in a **ground substance** made of complex sugars, protein, and crystallized minerals. This matrix may vary in consistency from a semifluid gel, in loose connective tissue, to the solid crystalline structure of bone. These extracellular fibers include ropelike **collagen fibers**, which have a high tensile strength and resist stretching, rubber-band-like **elastin fibers**, and fine, highly branched **reticular fibers**.

Tissues

Most specialized cells are associated with other cells of a similar kind to form tissues. Corresponding to the four general categories of differentiated cells, there are four general classes of tissues: (1) **muscle tissue**, (2) **nerve tissue**, (3) **epithelial tissue**, and (4) **connective tissue**. It should be noted that the term "tissue" is frequently used in several ways. It is formally defined as just described, that is, as an aggregate of a single type of specialized cell. However, it is also commonly used to denote the general cellular fabric of any organ or structure, for example, kidney tissue or lung tissue, each of which in fact usually contains all four classes of tissue.

Organs and Organ Systems

Organs are composed of the four kinds of tissues arranged in various proportions and patterns: sheets, tubes, layers, bundles, strips, and so on. For example, the kidneys consist of (1) a series of small tubes, each composed of a single layer of epithelial cells; (2) blood vessels, whose walls contain varying quantities of smooth muscle and connective tissue; (3) nerve-cell extensions that end near the muscle and epithelial cells; and (4) a loose network of connective-tissue elements that are interspersed throughout the kidneys and also form enclosing capsules.

Many organs are organized into small, similar subunits often referred to as **functional units**, each performing the function of the organ. For example, the kidneys' 2 million functional units are termed nephrons (which contain the small tubes mentioned in the previous paragraph), and the total production of urine by the kidneys is the sum of the amounts formed by the individual nephrons.

Finally, we have the organ system, a collection of organs that together perform an overall function. For example, the kidneys, the urinary bladder, the tubes leading from the kidneys to the bladder, and the tube leading from the bladder to the exterior constitute the urinary system. There are 10 organ systems in the body. Their components and functions are given in Table 1-1.

To sum up, the human body can be viewed as a complex society of differentiated cells structurally and functionally combined and interrelated to carry out the functions essential to the survival of the organism. The individual cells constitute the basic units of this society, and almost all of these cells individually exhibit the fundamental activities common to all forms of life. Indeed, many of the cells can be removed and maintained in test tubes as free-living organisms (this is termed "in vitro," literally "in glass," as opposed to "in vivo," meaning "within the body").

There is a paradox in this analysis. If each cell performs the fundamental activities required for its own survival, what contributions do the organ systems make? How is it that the functions of the organ systems are essential to the survival of the organism when each individual cell seems capable of performing its own fundamental activities? The resolution of this paradox is found in the isolation of most of the cells of a multicellular organism from the environment surrounding the organism—the **external environment**—and the presence of an internal environment.

THE INTERNAL ENVIRONMENT AND HOMEOSTASIS

An amoeba and a human liver cell both obtain their energy by breaking down certain organic nutrients. The chemical reactions involved in this intracellular process are remarkably similar in the two types of cells and involve the utilization of oxygen and the production of carbon dioxide. The amoeba picks up oxygen directly from the fluid surrounding it (its external environment) and eliminates carbon dioxide into the same fluid. But how can

TABLE 1-1   ORGAN SYSTEMS OF THE BODY

System	Major organs or tissues	Primary functions
Circulatory	Heart, blood vessels, blood (Some classifications also include lymphatic vessels and lymph in this system.)	Transport of blood throughout the body's tissues
Respiratory	Nose, pharynx, larynx, trachea, bronchi, lungs	Exchange of carbon dioxide and oxygen; regulation of hydrogen-ion concentration
Digestive	Mouth, pharynx, esophagus, stomach, intestines, salivary glands, pancreas, liver, gallbladder	Digestion and absorption of organic nutrients, salts, and water
Urinary	Kidneys, ureters, bladder, urethra	Regulation of plasma composition through controlled excretion of salts, water, and organic wastes
Musculoskeletal	Cartilage, bone, ligaments, tendons, joints, skeletal muscle	Support, protection, and movement of the body; production of blood cells
Immune	White blood cells, lymph vessels and nodes, spleen, thymus, and other lymphoid tissues	Defense against foreign invaders; return of extracellular fluid to blood; formation of white blood cells
Nervous	Brain, spinal cord, peripheral nerves and ganglia, special sense organs	Regulation and coordination of many activities in the body; detection of changes in the internal and external environments; states of consciousness; learning; cognition
Endocrine	All glands secreting hormones: Pancreas, testes, ovaries, hypothalamus, kidneys, pituitary, thyroid, parathyroid, adrenal, intestinal, thymus, heart, and pineal	Regulation and coordination of many activities in the body
Reproductive	Male: Testes, penis, and associated ducts and glands Female: Ovaries, uterine tubes, uterus, vagina, mammary glands	Production of sperm; transfer of sperm to female Production of eggs; provision of a nutritive environment for the developing embryo and fetus; nutrition of the infant
Integumentary	Skin	Protection against injury and dehydration; defense against foreign invaders; regulation of temperature

the liver cell and all other internal parts of the body obtain oxygen and eliminate carbon dioxide when, unlike the amoeba, they are not in direct contact with the external environment—the air surrounding the body?

Figure 1-2 summarizes the exchanges of matter that occur in a person. Supplying oxygen is the function both of the respiratory system, which takes up oxygen from the external environment, and of the circulatory system, which distributes the oxygen to all parts of the body. In addition, the circulatory system carries the carbon dioxide generated by all the cells of the body to the lungs, which eliminate it to the exterior. Similarly, the digestive and circulatory systems working together make nutrients from the external environment available to all the body's cells. Wastes other than carbon dioxide are carried by the circulatory system from the cells that produced them to the kidneys and liver, which excrete them from the body. The kidneys also regulate the concentrations of water and

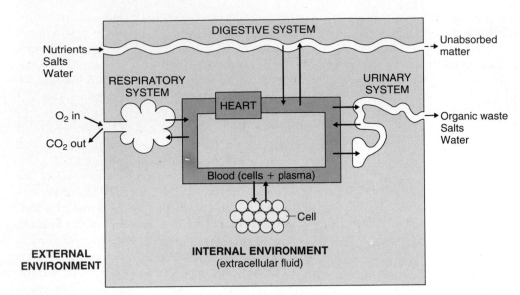

FIGURE 1-2

Exchanges of matter occur between the external environment and the circulatory system via the digestive, respiratory, and urinary systems. Extracellular fluid (plasma and interstitial fluid) is the internal environment of the body. The external environment is the air surrounding the body.

many essential minerals in the plasma. The nervous and hormonal systems coordinate and control the activities of all the other organ systems.

Thus the overall effect of the activities of organ systems is to create within the body an environment in which all cells can survive and function. This environment surrounding each cell is called the **internal environment**. The internal environment is not merely a theoretical physiological concept. It can be identified quite specifically in anatomical terms. The body's internal environment is the **extracellular fluid** (literally, "fluid outside the cells"), which bathes each cell (Figure 1-2).

In other words, the environment in which each cell lives is not the external environment surrounding the entire body but the local extracellular fluid surrounding that cell. It is from this fluid that the cells receive oxygen and nutrients and into which they excrete wastes. A multicellular organism can survive only as long as it is able to maintain the composition of its internal environment in a state compatible with the survival of its individual cells. In 1857, the French physiologist Claude Bernard clearly described the central importance of the extracellular fluid: "It is the fixity of the internal environment that is the condition of free and independent life. . . . All the vital mechanisms, however varied they may be, have only one object, that of preserving constant the conditions of life in the internal environment."

The concept that the composition of the internal environment is maintained relatively constant is known as **homeostasis**. Changes do occur, but the magnitudes of these changes are small and are kept within narrow limits. As emphasized by the twentieth-century American physiologist Walter B. Cannon, such stability can be achieved only through the operation of carefully coordinated physiological processes. The activities of the cells, tissues, and organs must be regulated and integrated with each other in such a way that any change in the extracellular fluid initiates a reaction to minimize the change. A collection of body components that functions to maintain a physical or chemical property of the internal environment relatively constant is termed a **homeostatic control system**.

The description at the beginning of this chapter of how sweating is brought about in response to increased heat generation is an example of a homeostatic control system in operation. Here is another: When, for any reason, the concentration of oxygen in the blood significantly decreases below normal, the nervous system detects the change and increases its output to the skeletal muscles responsible for breathing movements. The result is a compensatory increase in oxygen uptake by the body and a restoration of normal internal oxygen concentration.

To summarize, the total activities of every individual cell in the body fall into two categories: (1) Each cell performs for itself all those fundamental basic cellular processes—movement of materials across its membrane, extraction of energy, protein synthesis, and so on—that represent the minimal requirements for maintaining its individual integrity and life; and (2) each cell simultaneously performs one or more specialized activities that, in concert with the activities performed by the other cells of its tissue or organ system, contribute to the survival of the organism by helping maintain the stable internal environment required by all cells.

One more point should be made concerning basic cell activities: Because of our emphasis on homeostasis, we have introduced the principle of biological control in the context of the total body. You must realize, however, that the fundamental processes performed by any single cell are also carefully regulated by purely intracellular mechanisms. These determine, for example, which proteins a cell is to synthesize, how large the cell is to grow, and when it is to divide. Thus, an understanding of cellular physiology requires knowledge not only of the basic processes but also of the intracellular mechanisms that control them.

BODY-FLUID COMPARTMENTS

To reiterate, the internal environment can be equated with the extracellular fluid. What was not stated earlier is that extracellular fluid exists in two locations—surrounding cells and inside blood vessels. Approximately 80 percent of the extracellular fluid surrounds all the body's cells except the blood cells. Because it lies between cells, this 80 percent of the extracellular fluid is known as **intercellular fluid** or, more often, **interstitial fluid**. The remaining 20 percent of the extracellular fluid is the fluid portion of the blood, the **plasma**, in which the various blood cells are suspended.

As the blood (plasma plus suspended blood cells) is continuously circulated by the action of the heart to all parts of the body, the plasma exchanges oxygen, nutrients, wastes, and other metabolic products with the interstitial fluid surrounding the smallest of the blood vessels. Be-cause of the exchanges between plasma and interstitial fluid, concentrations of dissolved substances are virtually identical in the two fluids, except for protein concentration. With this major exception—higher protein concentration in plasma than in interstitial fluid—the entire extracellular fluid may be considered to have a homogeneous composition. In contrast, the composition of the extracellular fluid is very different from that of the **intracellular fluid**—the fluid inside the cells (the actual differences will be presented in Chapter 6, Table 6-1).

In essence, then, the fluids in the body are enclosed in "compartments." The volumes of the body-fluid compartments are summarized in Figure 1-3 in terms of water, since water is by far the major component of the fluids in each compartment. Water accounts for about 60 percent of normal body weight. Two-thirds of this water (28 L) is intracellular fluid. The remaining one-third (14 L) is extracellular, and as described above, 80 percent of this extracellular fluid is interstitial fluid (11 L) and 20 percent (3 L) is plasma.

Compartmentalization is an important general principle in physiology (we shall see in Chapter 2 that the inside of cells also is divided into compartments). Compartmentalization is achieved by barriers between the compartments, and the properties of the barriers determine the movements of substances between contiguous compartments. These movements in turn account for the differences in the compositions of the different compartments. In the case of the body-fluid compartments, the intracellu-

FIGURE 1-3

Fluid compartments of the body. Volumes are for a normal 70-kg man.

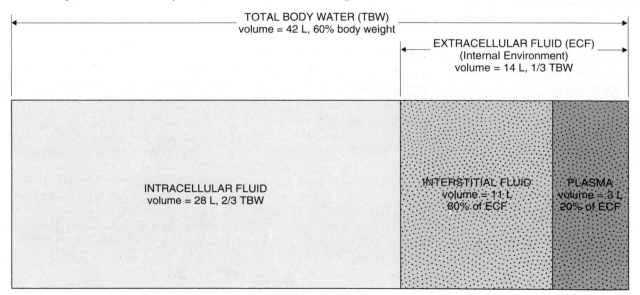

TOTAL BODY WATER (TBW)
volume = 42 L, 60% body weight

EXTRACELLULAR FLUID (ECF)
(Internal Environment)
volume = 14 L, 1/3 TBW

INTRACELLULAR FLUID
volume = 28 L, 2/3 TBW

INTERSTITIAL FLUID
volume = 11 L
80% of ECF

PLASMA
volume = 3 L
20% of ECF

lar fluid is separated from the extracellular fluid by molecular membranes that surround the cells. The properties of these membranes and how they account for the profound differences between intracellular and extracellular fluid are described in Chapter 6. In contrast, the two components of extracellular fluid—the interstitial fluid and the blood plasma—are separated by the cellular wall of the smallest blood vessels, the capillaries. How this barrier normally keeps 80 percent of the extracellular fluid in the interstitial compartment and restricts proteins mainly to the plasma is described in Chapter 14.

This completes our introductory framework. With it in mind, the overall organization and approach of this book should easily be understood. Because the fundamental features of cell function are shared by virtually all cells and because these features constitute the foundation upon which specialization develops, we devote the first part of the book to an analysis of basic cell physiology.

At the other end of the organizational spectrum, the final part of the book describes how coordinated functions (circulation, respiration, and so on) result from the precisely controlled and integrated activities of specialized cells grouped together in tissues and organs. The theme of these descriptions is that each function, with the obvious exception of reproduction, serves to keep some important aspect of the body's internal environment relatively constant. Thus, homeostasis, achieved by homeostatic control systems, is the single most important unifying idea to be kept in mind in Part 3.

The middle part of the book provides the principles and information required to bridge the gap between these two organizational levels, the cell and the body. Chapter 7 describes the basic characteristics of homeostatic control systems and the required cellular communications. The other chapters of Part 2 deal with the specific components of the body's control systems: nerve cells, muscle cells, and gland cells. Once familiar with this cast of major characters and the theme—the maintenance of a stable internal environment—the reader will be free to follow the specific plot lines—circulation, respiration, and so on—of Part 3.

SUMMARY

MECHANISM AND CAUSALITY

I. The mechanist view of life, the view taken by physiologists, holds that all phenomena are describable in terms of physical and chemical laws.

II. Vitalism holds that some additional force is required to explain the function of living organisms.

A SOCIETY OF CELLS

I. Cells are the simplest structural units into which a complex multicellular organism can be divided and still retain the functions characteristic of life.

II. Cell differentiation results in the formation of four categories of specialized cells.
   A. Muscle cells generate the mechanical activities that produce force and movement.
   B. Nerve cells initiate and conduct electric signals.
   C. Epithelial cells selectively secrete and absorb ions and organic molecules.
   D. Connective-tissue cells connect, anchor, and support the structures of the body.

III. Specialized cells associate with similar cells to form tissues: muscle tissue, nerve tissue, epithelial tissue, and connective tissue.

IV. Organs are composed of the four kinds of tissues arranged in various proportions and patterns; many organs contain multiple small similar functional units.

V. An organ system is a collection of organs that together perform an overall function.

THE INTERNAL ENVIRONMENT AND HOMEOSTASIS

I. The extracellular fluid surrounding a cell is the cell's internal environment.
   A. The function of organ systems is to maintain the internal environment relatively constant—homeostasis. This is achieved by homeostatic control systems.
   B. Each cell performs the basic cellular processes required to maintain its own integrity, plus specialized activities that help achieve homeostasis.

II. The body fluids are enclosed in compartments.
   A. The extracellular fluid is composed of the blood plasma and the fluid between cells—the interstitial fluid. Of the extracellular fluid, 80 percent is interstitial fluid and 20 percent is plasma.
   B. Interstitial fluid and plasma have essentially the same composition except that plasma contains a much higher concentration of protein.
   C. Extracellular fluid differs markedly in composition from the fluid inside cells—the intracellular fluid.
   D. Approximately one-third of body water is in the extracellular compartment, and two-thirds is intracellular.

E. The compositions of the compartments reflect the activities of the barriers separating them.

extracellular fluid
homeostasis
homeostatic control system
intercellular fluid

interstitial fluid
plasma
intracellular fluid

KEY TERMS

human physiology
mechanist view
vitalism
teleology
cells
cell differentiation
tissues
organs
organ systems
muscle cells
nerve cells
epithelial cells
basement membrane

connective-tissue cells
fibers
ground substance
collagen fibers
elastin fibers
reticular fibers
muscle tissue
nerve tissue
epithelial tissue
connective tissue
functional units
external environment
internal environment

REVIEW QUESTIONS

1. Describe the levels of cellular differentiation and state the four types of specialized cells and tissues.
2. List the 10 organ systems of the body and give one-sentence descriptions of their functions.
3. Contrast the two categories of functions performed by every cell.
4. Name two fluids that constitute the extracellular fluid. What are their relative proportions, and in what way do they differ from each other in composition?
5. State the relative volumes of water in the body-fluid compartments.

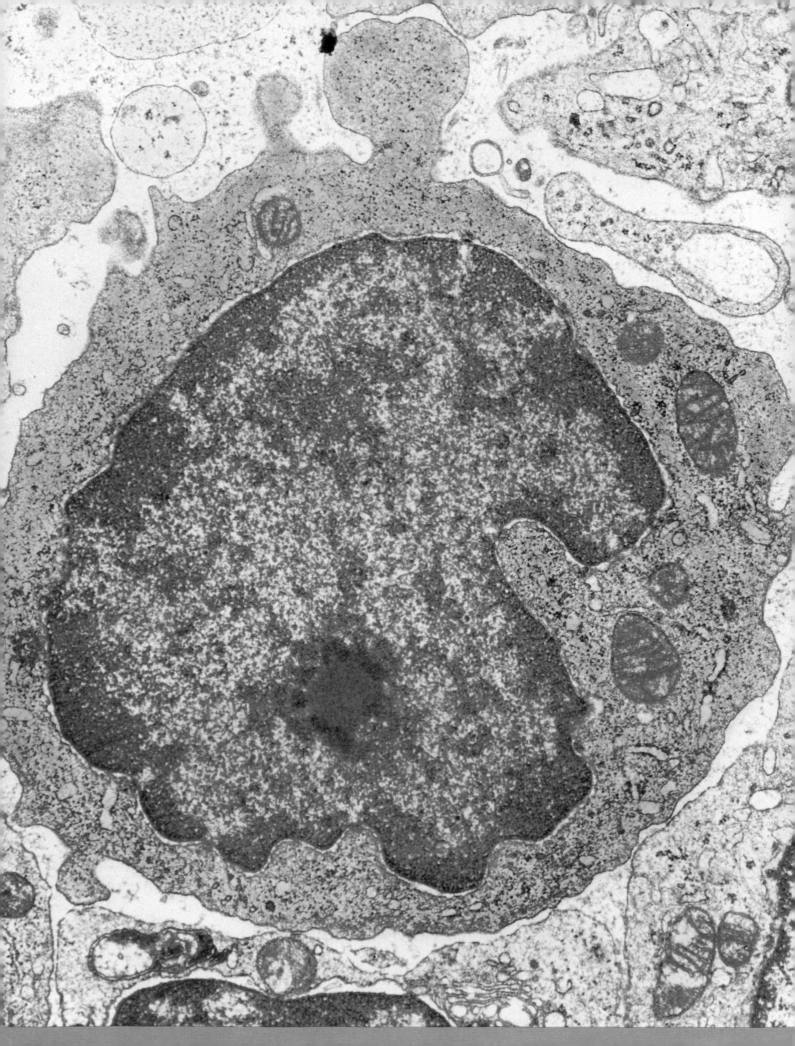

PART

ONE

BASIC
CELL
FUNCTIONS

CHAPTER 2   CHEMICAL COMPOSITION OF THE BODY   13
CHAPTER 3   CELL STRUCTURE   39
CHAPTER 4   MOLECULAR CONTROL MECHANISMS—
             PROTEIN AND DNA   55
                 SECTION A. BINDING SITES ON PROTEINS   56
                 SECTION B. GENETIC INFORMATION AND PROTEIN SYNTHESIS   63
CHAPTER 5   ENERGY AND CELLULAR METABOLISM   83
CHAPTER 6   MOVEMENT OF MOLECULES ACROSS CELL MEMBRANES   115

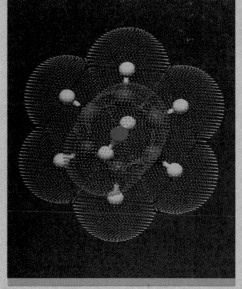

CHAPTER

2

CHEMICAL COMPOSITION
OF THE BODY

ATOMS

Atomic Number

Atomic Weight

Atomic Composition of the Body

MOLECULES

Covalent Chemical Bonds

Molecular Shape

IONS

POLAR MOLECULES

Hydrogen Bonds

Water

SOLUTIONS

Molecular Solubility

Concentration

Hydrogen Ions and Acidity

CLASSES OF ORGANIC MOLECULES

Carbohydrates

Lipids

Fatty Acids

Triacylglycerols

Phospholipids

Steroids

Proteins

Amino acid subunits

Polypeptides

Primary protein structure

Protein conformation

Nucleic Acids

DNA

RNA

SUMMARY

KEY TERMS

REVIEW QUESTIONS

toms and molecules are the chemical units of cell structure and function. In this chapter we describe the distinguishing characteristics of the major chemicals in the human body. The specific roles of these substances will be discussed in subsequent chapters. This chapter is, in essence, an expanded glossary of chemical terms and structures, and like a glossary, it should be consulted according to need.

ATOMS

The units of matter that form all chemical substances are called **atoms**. The smallest atom, hydrogen, is approximately 2.7 billionths of an inch in diameter. Each type of atom—carbon, hydrogen, oxygen, and so on—is called a **chemical element**. A one- or two-letter symbol is used as a shorthand identification of each chemical element. Although more than 100 chemical elements exist in the universe, only 24 (Table 2-1) are known to be essential for the structure and function of the human body.

The chemical properties of atoms can be described in terms of three subatomic particles—**protons**, **neutrons**, and **electrons** (Table 2-2). The protons and neutrons are confined to a very small volume at the center of an atom, the **atomic nucleus**, whereas the electrons revolve in orbits at various distances from the nucleus. This miniature-solar-system model of an atom is an oversimplification, but it is sufficient to provide a conceptual framework for understanding the chemical and physical interactions of atoms.

Each of these subatomic particles has a different electric charge: Protons have one unit of positive charge, electrons have one unit of negative charge, and neutrons are electrically neutral, having no electric charge. Since the protons are located in the atomic nucleus, the nucleus has a net positive charge equal to the number of protons it contains. The entire atom has no net electric charge however, because the number of negatively charged electrons orbiting the nucleus is equal to the number of positively charged protons in the nucleus.[1]

Protons and neutrons are approximately equal in mass and are about 1800 times heavier than an electron (Table 2-2). Thus, almost all the mass of an atom is located in its nucleus.

Atomic Number

Every atom of each chemical element contains a specific number of protons, and it is this number of protons that distinguishes one type of atom from another. This number is known as the **atomic number**. For example, hydrogen, the simplest atom, has an atomic number of 1, corresponding to its single proton, and calcium has an atomic number of 20, corresponding to its 20 protons. Since an atom is

TABLE 2-1   ESSENTIAL ELEMENTS IN THE BODY

Element	Symbol
Major elements: 99.3% of total atoms	
Hydrogen	H (63%)
Oxygen	O (26%)
Carbon	C (9%)
Nitrogen	N (1%)
Mineral elements: 0.7% of total atoms	
Calcium	Ca
Phosphorus	P
Potassium	K (Latin *kalium*)
Sulfur	S
Sodium	Na (Latin *natrium*)
Chlorine	Cl
Magnesium	Mg
Trace elements: less than 0.01% of total atoms	
Iron	Fe (Latin *ferrum*)
Iodine	I
Copper	Cu (Latin *cuprum*)
Zinc	Zn
Manganese	Mn
Cobalt	Co
Chromium	Cr
Selenium	Se
Molybdenum	Mo
Fluorine	F
Tin	Sn (Latin *stannum*)
Silicon	Si
Vanadium	V

---

[1]Although the number of neutrons in the nucleus of an atom is often equal to the number of protons, many chemical elements can exist in multiple forms—isotopes—distinguished by the number of neutrons they contain.

TABLE 2-2 CHARACTERISTICS OF MAJOR SUBATOMIC PARTICLES

Particle	Mass relative to electron mass	Electric charge	Location in atom
Electron	1	−1	Orbiting the nucleus
Proton	1836	+1	Nucleus
Neutron	1839	0	Nucleus

electrically neutral, the atomic number is also equal to the number of electrons in the atom.

Atomic Weight

Atoms have very little mass. A single hydrogen atom, for example, has a mass of only 1.67×10^{-24} g. The **atomic weight** scale is a scale that indicates an atom's mass relative to the mass of other atoms. This scale is based upon assigning the carbon atom a value of 12. On this scale a hydrogen atom has an atomic weight of approximately 1, indicating that it has one-twelfth the mass of a carbon atom; a magnesium atom, with an atomic weight of 24, has twice the mass of a carbon atom.[2] Since almost all the mass of an atom is due to its neutrons and protons, and since hydrogen, with a single proton, has an atomic weight of 1, the atomic weight of an atom is approximately equal to the sum of the number of protons and neutrons it contains. Its atomic weight is not exactly equal to this sum because electrons do have some mass and because protons and neutrons do not have exactly equal masses.

One **gram atomic mass** of a chemical element is the amount of the element in grams that is equal to the numerical value of its atomic weight. Thus, 12 g of carbon is 1 gram atomic mass of carbon, and 1 g of hydrogen is 1 gram atomic mass of hydrogen. *One gram atomic mass of any element contains the same number of atoms.* For example, 1 g of hydrogen contains 6×10^{23} atoms, and 12 g of carbon, whose atoms have 12 times the mass of a hydrogen atom, also has 6×10^{23} atoms.

Atomic Composition of the Body

Just four of the body's essential elements (Table 2-1)—hydrogen, oxygen, carbon, and nitrogen—account for over 99 percent of the atoms in the body.

---

[2]Since the atomic weight scale is a *ratio* of atomic masses, it has no units. The unit of atomic mass is known as a dalton [1 dalton (d) is equal to one-twelfth the mass of a single carbon atom]. Thus, carbon has an atomic weight of 12, and a single carbon atom has an atomic mass of 12 daltons.

The 7 essential mineral elements are the most abundant substances dissolved in the extracellular and intracellular fluids. Most of the body's calcium and phosphorus atoms, however, make up the solid matrix of bone tissue.

The 13 essential **trace elements** are present in extremely small quantities, but they are nonetheless essential for normal growth and function. For example, iron plays a critical role in the transport of oxygen by the blood. Additional trace elements will likely be added to this list as the chemistry of the body becomes better understood.

Many other elements, in addition to the 24 listed in Table 2-1, can be detected in the body. These elements enter through the foods we eat and the air we breathe but do not have any known essential chemical function. Some elements, for example, mercury, are not required for normal function and can be toxic.

MOLECULES

Two or more atoms bonded together make up a **molecule**. For example, a molecule of water contains two hydrogen atoms and one oxygen atom, which can be represented by H_2O. The atomic composition of glucose, a sugar, is $C_6H_{12}O_6$, indicating that the molecule contains 6 carbon atoms, 12 hydrogen atoms, and 6 oxygen atoms. Such formulas, however, do not indicate which atoms are linked to which in the molecule.

Covalent Chemical Bonds

The atoms in molecules are held together by chemical bonds, which are formed when electrons are transferred from one atom to another or are shared between two atoms. The strongest chemical bond between two atoms, a **covalent bond**, is formed when one electron in the outer electron orbit of each atom is shared between the two atoms. The atoms in most molecules found in the body are linked by covalent bonds.

The atoms of some elements can form more than one covalent bond and thus become linked simultaneously to two or more other atoms (Figure 2-1). Each type of atom has a characteristic number of covalent bonds it can form, which depends on the number of electrons present in its outermost electron orbit. The number of chemical bonds formed by the four most abundant atoms in the body are hydrogen, 1; oxygen, 2; nitrogen, 3; and carbon, 4. When the structure of a molecule is diagramed, each covalent bond is represented by a line indicating a pair of shared electrons. The covalent bonds of the four elements mentioned above can be represented as

H—   —O—   —N—   —C—

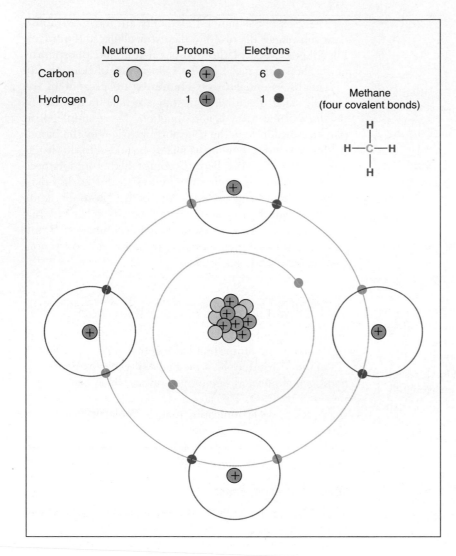

	Neutrons	Protons	Electrons
Carbon	6	6	6
Hydrogen	0	1	1

Methane
(four covalent bonds)

FIGURE 2-1
Each of the four hydrogen atoms in a molecule of methane, CH_4, forms a covalent bond with an atom of carbon by sharing its one electron with one of the electrons in the carbon atom. Each shared pair of electrons forms a covalent bond.

A molecule of water can be illustrated as

$$H\!-\!O\!-\!H$$

In some cases, two covalent bonds—a double bond—are formed between two atoms when two electrons from each atom are shared; an example of this is carbon dioxide (CO_2):

$$O\!=\!C\!=\!O$$

Note that in this molecule the carbon atom still forms four covalent bonds, and each oxygen atom only two.

Molecular Shape

When atoms are linked together, molecules with various shapes can be formed. Although we draw diagrammatic structures of molecules on flat sheets of paper, these molecules actually have a three-dimensional shape. When more than one covalent bond is formed with a given atom, the bonds are distributed about the atom in a pattern that may or may not be symmetrical (Figure 2-2).

Molecules are not rigid, inflexible structures. Within certain limits, the shape of a molecule can be changed without breaking the covalent bonds linking its atoms together. A covalent bond is like an axle around which the joined atoms can rotate. As illustrated in Figure 2-3, a sequence of six carbon atoms can assume a number of shapes as a result of rotations around various covalent bonds. As we shall see, the three-dimensional shape of molecules is one of the major factors governing molecular interactions.

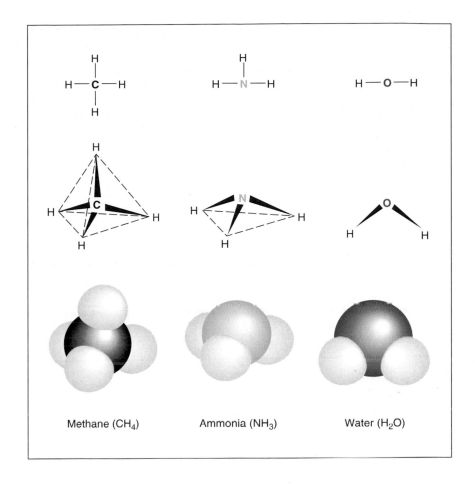

FIGURE 2-2
Geometrical configuration of covalent bonds around the carbon, nitrogen, and oxygen atoms bonded to hydrogen atoms.

Methane (CH₄)   Ammonia (NH₃)   Water (H₂O)

IONS

An atom is electrically neutral since it contains equal numbers of negative electrons and positive protons. If, however, an atom gains or loses one or more electrons, it acquires a net electric charge and becomes an **ion**. For example, when a sodium atom, which has 11 electrons, loses 1 electron, it becomes a sodium ion (Na^+) with a net positive charge; that is, it now has only 10 electrons but 11 protons. On the other hand, a chlorine atom, which has 17 electrons, can gain an electron and become a chloride ion (Cl^-) with a net negative charge—it now has 18 electrons but only 17 protons. Some atoms can gain or lose more than 1 electron to become ions with two or even three units of net electric charge, for example, calcium, Ca^{2+}.

Because of their ability to conduct electricity when dissolved in water, ions are collectively referred to as **electrolytes**. Hydrogen atoms and most mineral and trace element atoms readily form ions. The number of electrons an atom may gain or lose in becoming an ion is a specific characteristic of each type of atom. Table 2-3 lists the ionic forms of some of these elements. Ions that have a net positive charge are called **cations**; negatively charged ions are called **anions**.

The process of ion formation, known as ionization, can occur in single atoms or in atoms that are covalently linked in molecules. Within molecules two commonly encountered groups of atoms that undergo ionization are the **carboxyl group** (—COOH) and the **amino group** (—NH₂). The formulas for molecules containing such groups are written as R—COOH or R—NH₂, where R signifies the remaining portion of the molecule. The carboxyl group ionizes when the oxygen atom linked to the hydrogen atom captures the hydrogen atom's only electron to form a carboxyl ion (R—COO⁻) and releases a hydrogen ion (H^+):

$$R\text{---}COOH \rightleftharpoons R\text{---}COO^- + H^+$$

The amino group can bind a hydrogen ion to form an ionized amino group ($R\text{---}NH_3^+$):

$$R\text{---}NH_2 + H^+ \rightleftharpoons R\text{---}NH_3^+$$

The ionization of each of the above groups can be re-

TABLE 2-3 MOST FREQUENTLY ENCOUNTERED IONIC FORMS OF ELEMENTS

Atom	Chemical symbol	Ion	Chemical symbol	Electrons gained or lost
Hydrogen	H	Hydrogen ion	H^+	1 lost
Sodium	Na	Sodium ion	Na^+	1 lost
Potassium	K	Potassium ion	K^+	1 lost
Chlorine	Cl	Chloride ion	Cl^-	1 gained
Magnesium	Mg	Magnesium ion	Mg^{2+}	2 lost
Calcium	Ca	Calcium ion	Ca^{2+}	2 lost

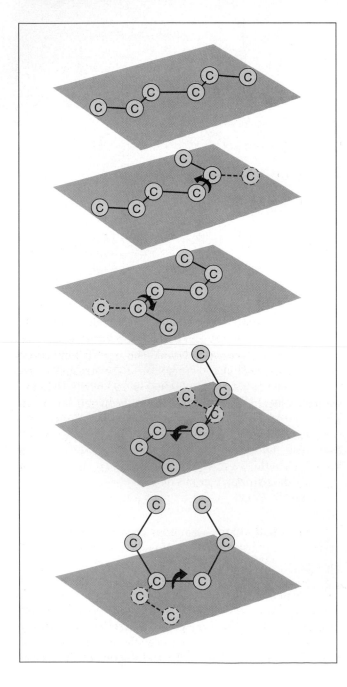

versed, as indicated by the double arrows; the ionized carboxyl group can combine with a hydrogen ion to form an un-ionized carboxyl group, and the ionized amino group can loose a hydrogen ion and become an un-ionized amino group.

POLAR MOLECULES

As we have seen, when the electrons of two atoms interact, the two atoms may share the electrons equally, forming an electrically neutral covalent bond, or one of the atoms may completely capture an electron from the other atom, forming an ion. Between these two extremes there exist covalent bonds in which the electrons are not shared equally between the two atoms but instead reside closer to one atom of the pair. This atom thus acquires a slight negative charge, while the other atom, having partly lost an electron, becomes slightly positive. Such bonds are known as **polar covalent bonds** (or, simply, polar bonds) since the atoms at each end of the bond have an opposite electric charge. Polar bonds do not have a *net* electric charge, as do ions, since they contain equal amounts of negative and positive charge. For example, the bond between hydrogen and oxygen in a **hydroxyl group** (—OH) is a polar covalent bond in which the oxygen is slightly negative and the hydrogen slightly positive.

$$\overset{(-)\quad(+)}{R—O—H}$$

The electric charge associated with the ends of a polar bond is considerably less than the charge of a fully ionized

FIGURE 2-3

Changes in molecular shape occur as portions of a molecule rotate around different carbon-carbon bonds, transforming the molecule's shape from a relatively straight chain into a ring.

TABLE 2-4   EXAMPLES OF NONPOLAR AND POLAR BONDS, AND IONIZED CHEMICAL GROUPS

Nonpolar bonds	$-\overset{\mid}{\underset{\mid}{C}}-H$	Carbon-hydrogen bond
	$-\overset{\mid}{\underset{\mid}{C}}-\overset{\mid}{\underset{\mid}{C}}-$	Carbon-carbon bond
Polar bonds	$\overset{(-)\quad(+)}{R-O-\!\!-H}$	Hydroxyl group (R—OH)
	$\overset{(-)\quad(+)}{R-S-\!\!-H}$	Sulfhydryl group (R—SH)
	$\underset{R-N-R}{\overset{H\;(+)}{\mid(-)}}$	Nitrogen-hydrogen bond
Ionized groups	$R-\overset{\overset{\displaystyle O}{\parallel}}{C}-O^{\ominus}$	Carboxyl group (R—COO⁻)
	$R-\overset{\overset{\displaystyle H}{\mid}}{\underset{\underset{\displaystyle H}{\mid}}{\overset{\oplus}{N}}}-H$	Amino group (R—NH₃⁺)
	$R-O-\overset{\overset{\displaystyle O}{\parallel}}{\underset{\underset{\displaystyle O}{\mid}}{\overset{\mid}{P}}}-O^{\ominus}$	Phosphate group (R—PO₄²⁻)

atom (for example, the oxygen in the polarized hydroxyl group has only about 13 percent of the negative charge associated with the oxygen in an ionized carboxyl group, R—COO⁻).

Atoms of oxygen and nitrogen, which have a relatively strong attraction for electrons, form polar bonds with hydrogen atoms; in contrast, the bond between carbon and hydrogen atoms and that between two carbon atoms are electrically neutral (Table 2-4).

A single molecule may contain nonpolar, polarized, and ionized bonds in different regions of the molecule. Molecules containing significant numbers of polar bonds or ionized groups are known as **polar molecules**, whereas molecules composed predominantly of electrically neutral bonds are known as **nonpolar molecules**. As we shall see, the physical characteristics of these two classes of molecules, especially their solubility in water, are quite different.

Hydrogen Bonds

The electrical attraction between a hydrogen atom in one polarized bond and an oxygen or nitrogen atom in a polarized bond of another molecule—or within the same molecule if the bonds are sufficiently separated from each other—forms a **hydrogen bond**. This type of bond is very weak, having only about 4 percent of the strength of the covalent bonds linking the hydrogen and oxygen within a water molecule (H_2O). These weak hydrogen bonds are represented in diagrams by dashed or dotted lines to distinguish them from stronger covalent bonds (Figure 2-4). Hydrogen bonds between and within molecules play an important role in molecular interactions and in determining the shape of large molecules.

Water

Hydrogen is the most numerous atom in the body, and water is the most numerous molecule. Out of every 100 molecules, 99 are water. The covalent bonds linking the two hydrogen atoms to the oxygen atom in a water molecule are polar. Therefore, the oxygen in water has a slight negative charge, and each hydrogen atom has a slight positive charge. The positively polarized regions near the hydrogen atoms of one water molecule are electrically attracted to the negatively polarized regions of the oxygen

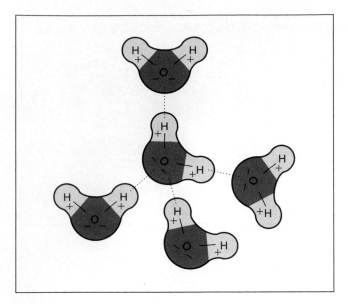

FIGURE 2-4

Five water molecules. Note that polarized covalent bonds link the hydrogen and oxygen atoms within each water molecule and that hydrogen bonds occur between adjacent water molecules. Hydrogen bonds are represented in diagrams by dashed or dotted lines, and covalent bonds by solid lines.

atoms in adjacent water molecules to form hydrogen bonds (Figure 2-4).

At body temperature, the hydrogen bonds between water molecules are continuously being formed and broken, accounting for the liquid state of water. If the temperature is lowered, hydrogen bonds are broken less frequently, and larger and larger clusters of water molecules are formed until at 0°C water freezes into a continuous crystalline matrix—ice.

Water molecules take part in many chemical reactions of the general type

$$R_1—R_2 \ + \ H—O—H \ \longrightarrow \ R_1—OH \ + \ H—R_2$$

In this reaction the covalent bond between R_1 and R_2 and the bond between a hydrogen atom and oxygen in water are broken and the hydroxyl group and hydrogen atom are transferred to R_1 and R_2, respectively. Reactions of this type are known as hydrolytic reactions or simply **hydrolysis**. Many large molecules in the body are broken down into smaller molecular units by hydrolysis.

SOLUTIONS

Substances dissolved in a liquid are known as **solutes**; the liquid in which they dissolve is the **solvent**. Solutes dissolve in a solvent to form a **solution**. Water is the most abundant solvent in the body, accounting for 60 percent of total body weight. A majority of the chemical reactions that occur in the body involve molecules that are dissolved in water—in either intracellular or extracellular fluid. But, not all molecules dissolve in water.

Molecular Solubility

In order to dissolve in water, a substance must be electrically attracted to water molecules. For example, table salt (NaCl) is a solid crystalline substance because of the strong electrical attraction between positive sodium ions and negative chloride ions. This strong attraction between two oppositely charged ions is known as an **ionic bond**. When a crystal of sodium chloride is placed in water, the polar water molecules are attracted to the charged sodium and chloride ions (Figure 2-5); the ions become surrounded by clusters of water molecules, allowing the sodium and chloride ions to separate from the salt crystal and enter the water, that is, to dissolve.

Molecules having a sufficient number of polar bonds and/or ionized groups will dissolve in water. Such molecules are said to be **hydrophilic**—water-loving. Thus, the presence in a molecule of ionized groups, such as carboxyl and amino groups, or of polar groups, such as hydroxyl groups, promotes solubility in water. In contrast, molecules composed predominantly of carbon and hydrogen are insoluble in water since their electrically neutral covalent bonds are not attracted to water molecules. These molecules are **hydrophobic**—water-fearing.

When nonpolar molecules are mixed with water, two phases are formed, as occurs when oil is mixed with water. The strong attraction between polar water molecules "squeezes" the nonpolar molecules out of the water phase. Such a separation is never 100 percent complete, however, and very small amounts of nonpolar solutes remain dissolved in the water phase. Although nonpolar molecules do not dissolve to any great extent in water, they do dissolve in nonpolar solvents, such as carbon tetrachloride.

Molecules that have a polar or ionized region at one end and a nonpolar region at the opposite end are called **amphipathic**—consisting of two parts. When mixed with water, amphipathic molecules form clusters, with their polar (hydrophilic) regions located at the surface of the cluster where they are attracted to the surrounding water molecules. The nonpolar (hydrophobic) ends are oriented toward the interior of the cluster (Figure 2-6). Such an arrangement provides the maximal interaction between water molecules and the polar ends of the amphipathic molecules. Nonpolar molecules can dissolve in the central nonpolar regions of these clusters and thus exist in aqueous solutions in far higher amounts than would otherwise be possible based on their low solubility in water. As we shall see, the orientation of amphipathic molecules plays an important role in the structure of cell membranes and in both the absorption of nonpolar molecules from the gastrointestinal tract and their transport in the blood.

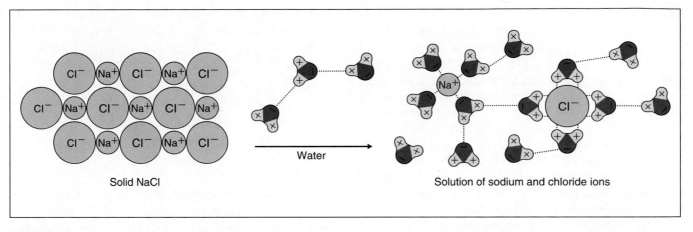

FIGURE 2-5

The ability of water to dissolve sodium chloride crystals depends upon the electrical attraction between the polar water molecules and the charged sodium and chloride ions.

FIGURE 2-6

In water, amphipathic molecules aggregate into spherical clusters. Their polar regions form hydrogen bonds with water molecules at the surface of the cluster.

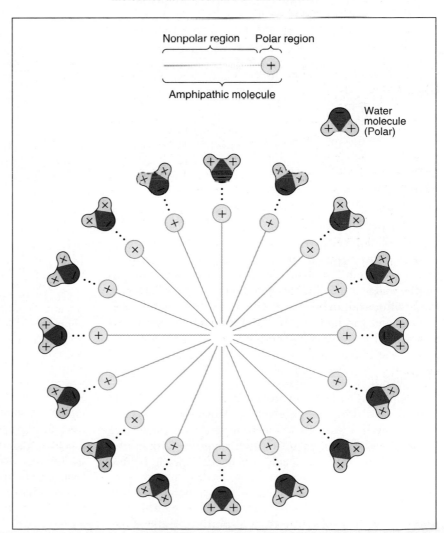

Concentration

Solute **concentration** is defined as the amount of the solute present in a unit volume of solution. The unit of volume in the metric system is a liter (L). (One liter equals 1.06 quarts. See Appendix C for English and metric units.) Smaller units are the milliliter (ml, or 0.001 liter) and the microliter (μl, or 0.001 ml). One measure of the amount of a substance is its mass given in grams. Its concentration in a solution can then be expressed as the number of grams of the substance present in one liter of solution (g/L).

A comparison of the concentrations of two different substances on the basis of the number of *grams* per liter of solution does not directly indicate how many *molecules* of each substance are present. For example, 10 g of compound X, whose molecules are heavier than those of compound Y, will contain fewer molecules than 10 g of compound Y. Concentrations in units of grams per liter are most often used when the chemical structure of the solute is unknown. When the structure of a molecule is known, concentrations are usually expressed as moles per liter, which provides a unit of concentration based upon the number of solute molecules in solution, as described next.

The **molecular weight** of a molecule is equal to the sum of the atomic weights of all the atoms in the molecule. For example, glucose ($C_6H_{12}O_6$) has a molecular weight of 180 ($6 \times 12 + 12 \times 1 + 6 \times 16 = 180$). One **mole** (mol) of a compound is the amount of the compound in grams equal to its molecular weight. A solution containing 180 g of glucose (1 mol) in 1 L of solution is said to be a 1 molar (abbreviated 1 M or 1 mol/L) solution of glucose. If 90 g of glucose is dissolved in enough water to produce 1 L of solution, the solution will have a concentration of 0.5 mol per liter (0.5 M). Just as 1 gram atomic mass of any element contains the same number of atoms, 1 mol (1 gram molecular mass) of any molecule has the same number of molecules—6×10^{23}. Thus, a 1 M solution of glucose contains the same number of solute molecules per liter as a 1 M solution of urea or any other substance.

The concentrations of solutes dissolved in the body fluids are much less than 1 M; many have concentrations in the range of millimoles per liter (1 mM = 0.001 M), while others are present at even smaller concentrations—micromoles per liter (1 μM = 0.000001 M) or nanomoles per liter (1 nM = 0.000000001 M).

Hydrogen Ions and Acidity

As mentioned earlier, a hydrogen atom consists of a single proton orbited by a single electron. A hydrogen ion (H^+), formed by the loss of the electron, is thus a single free proton. Hydrogen ions are formed when the proton of a hydrogen atom in a molecule is released, leaving behind its electron. Molecules that release hydrogen ions (protons) in solution are called **acids**, for example:

$$HCl \longrightarrow H^+ + Cl^-$$
Hydrochloric acid   Chloride

$$H_2CO_3 \rightleftharpoons H^+ + HCO_3^-$$
Carbonic acid   Bicarbonate

$$CH_3-\overset{\overset{\displaystyle OH}{|}}{\underset{\underset{\displaystyle H}{|}}{C}}-COOH \rightleftharpoons H^+ + CH_3-\overset{\overset{\displaystyle OH}{|}}{\underset{\underset{\displaystyle H}{|}}{C}}-COO^-$$
Lactic acid   Lactate

Conversely, any substance that can accept a hydrogen ion is termed a **base**. In the reactions above, bicarbonate and lactate are bases since they can combine with hydrogen ions (note the double arrows in the two reactions above). Bases will remove hydrogen ions from solution, lowering the hydrogen-ion concentration. It must be understood that the hydrogen-ion concentration of a solution refers only to the hydrogen ions that are free in solution and not to those that may be bound, for example, to amino groups ($R-NH_3^+$).

When hydrochloric acid is dissolved in water, 100 percent of its atoms separate to form hydrogen and chloride ions and do not recombine in solution (note the one-way arrow above). In the case of lactic acid, however, only a fraction of lactic acid molecules in solution release hydrogen ions at any instant. Therefore, if a 1 M solution of hydrochloric acid is compared with a 1 M solution of lactic acid, the hydrogen-ion concentration will be lower in the lactic acid solution than in the hydrochloric acid solution. Hydrochloric acid and other acids that are 100 percent ionized in solution are known as **strong acids**, whereas carbonic and lactic acids and other acids that do not completely ionize in solution are **weak acids**. The same principles apply to bases: Strong bases are 100 percent ionized in solution, whereas weak bases are only partially ionized.

The **acidity** of a solution refers to the *free* (unbound) hydrogen-ion concentration in the solution; the higher the hydrogen-ion concentration, the greater the acidity. The hydrogen-ion concentration is frequently expressed in terms of the **pH** of a solution, which is defined as the negative logarithm to the base 10 of the hydrogen-ion concentration (the brackets around the symbol for the hydrogen ion in the formula below indicate concentration):

$$pH = -\log[H^+]$$

Thus, a solution with a hydrogen-ion concentration of 10^{-7} M has a pH of 7, whereas a more acidic solution with a concentration of 10^{-6} M has a pH of 6. Note that as the acidity *increases,* the pH *decreases;* thus a change in pH from 7 to 6 represents a tenfold increase in the hydrogen-ion concentration.

Pure water has a hydrogen-ion concentration of $10^{-7}\ M$ (pH = 7.0) and is termed a **neutral solution**. **Alkaline solutions** have a lower hydrogen-ion concentration (a pH higher than 7.0), while those with a higher hydrogen-ion concentration (a pH lower than 7.0) are **acidic solutions**. The extracellular fluid of the body has a hydrogen-ion concentration of about $4 \times 10^{-8}\ M$ (pH = 7.4), with a normal range of about pH 7.35 to 7.45, and is thus slightly alkaline. Intracellular fluids have a slightly higher hydrogen-ion concentration than extracellular fluids.

As we saw earlier, the ionization of carboxyl and amino groups in various molecules in the body involves the release and uptake, respectively, of hydrogen ions. These groups behave as weak acids and bases. Increasing the free hydrogen ion concentration decreases the number of ionized carboxyl groups since it increases the probability that an ionized carboxyl group will bump into a hydrogen ion and combine with it.

$$R\text{—}COOH \rightleftharpoons R\text{—}COO^- + H^+$$

Lowering the hydrogen-ion concentration has the opposite effect.

Changes in the acidity of solutions containing molecules with carboxyl and amino groups alters the net electric charge on these molecules by shifting the ionization reaction to the right or left, as illustrated for the carboxyl group above. If the electric charge on a molecule is altered, its interaction with other molecules or with other regions within the same molecule is altered, and thus its functional characteristics are altered. In the extracellular fluid, hydrogen-ion concentrations beyond the tenfold pH range of 7.8 to 6.8 are incompatible with life if maintained for more than a brief period of time. Even small changes in the hydrogen-ion concentration can produce large changes in the activities of cells, as we shall see.

CLASSES OF ORGANIC MOLECULES

Because most naturally occurring carbon-containing molecules are found in living organisms, the study of these compounds became known as organic chemistry. (Inorganic chemistry is the study of non-carbon-containing molecules.) However, the chemistry of living organisms, biochemistry, now forms only a portion of the broad field of organic chemistry.

One of the properties of the carbon atom that makes life possible is its ability to form four covalent bonds with other atoms, in particular with other carbon atoms. Since carbon atoms can also combine with hydrogen, oxygen,

TABLE 2-5   MAJOR CATEGORIES OF ORGANIC MOLECULES IN THE BODY

Category	Percent of body weight	Majority of atoms	Subclass	Subunits
Carbohydrates	1	C, H, O	Monosaccharides (sugars)	
			Polysaccharides	Monosaccharides
Lipids	15	C, H	Triacylglycerols	3 fatty acids + glycerol
			Phospholipids	2 fatty acids + glycerol + phosphate + small charged nitrogen molecule
			Steroids	
Proteins	17	C, H, O, N	Peptides	Amino acids
			Proteins	Amino acids
Nucleic acids	2	C, H, O, N	DNA	Nucleotides containing the bases adenine, cytosine, guanine, thymine, the sugar deoxyribose, and phosphate
			RNA	Nucleotides containing the bases adenine, cytosine, guanine, uracil, the sugar ribose, and phosphate

nitrogen, and sulfur atoms, a vast number of compounds can be formed with relatively few chemical elements. Some of these molecules are extremely large (**macromolecules**), being composed of thousands of atoms. Such large molecules are formed by linking together hundreds of smaller molecules (subunits) and are thus known as **polymers** (many small parts). The structure of macromolecules depends upon the structure of the subunits, the number of subunits linked together, and the position along the chain of each type of subunit.

Most of the organic molecules in the body can be classified into one of four groups: carbohydrates, lipids, proteins, and nucleic acids (Table 2-5).

Carbohydrates

Although carbohydrates account for only about 1 percent of the body weight, they play a central role in the chemical reactions that provide cells with energy. Carbohydrates are composed of carbon, hydrogen, and oxygen atoms in the proportions represented by the general formula $C_n(H_2O)_n$, where n is any whole number. It is from this formula that this class of molecules gets its name, **carbohydrate**—water-containing (hydrated) carbon atoms. Linked to most of the carbon atoms in a carbohydrate are a hydrogen atom and a hydroxyl group:

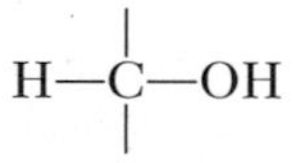

$$H-\overset{\displaystyle |}{\underset{\displaystyle |}{C}}-OH$$

Chemical groups containing nitrogen and phosphorus atoms may also be linked to this basic carbohydrate structure. The presence of numerous polar hydroxyl groups makes carbohydrates readily soluble in water.

Most carbohydrates taste sweet, and it is among the carbohydrates that we find the substances known as sugars. The simplest sugars are the **monosaccharides** (single-sweet), the most abundant of which is **glucose**, a six-carbon molecule ($C_6H_{12}O_6$) often called "blood sugar" because it is the major monosaccharide found in the blood.

There are two ways of representing the linkage between the atoms of a monosaccharide, as illustrated in Figure 2-7. The first is the conventional way of drawing the structure of organic molecules, but the second gives a better representation of the three-dimensional shape of monosaccharides. Five carbon atoms and an oxygen atom form a ring that lies in an essentially flat plane; the hydrogen and hydroxyl groups on each carbon lie above and below the plane of this ring. If one of the hydroxyl groups below the ring is shifted to a position above the ring, as shown in Figure 2-8, a different monosaccharide is produced.

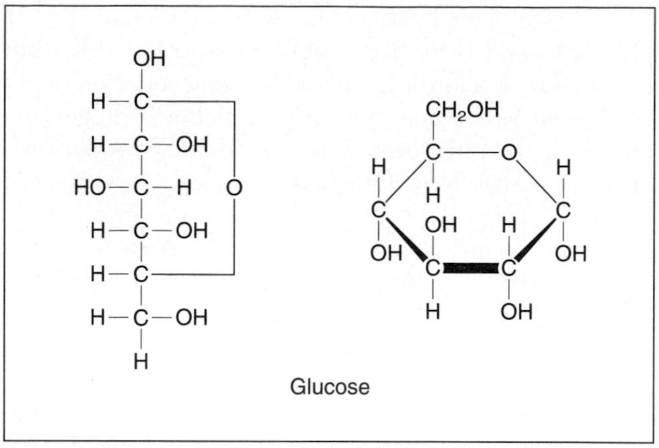

FIGURE 2-7

Two ways of diagramming the structure of the monosaccharide glucose.

Most monosaccharides in the body contain five or six carbon atoms and are called **pentoses** and **hexoses**, respectively. Larger carbohydrate molecules can be formed by linking a number of monosaccharides together. Carbohydrate molecules composed of two monosaccharides are known as **disaccharides**. **Sucrose** (table sugar) (Figure 2-9) is composed of two monosaccharides, glucose and fructose. The linking together of most monosaccharides involves the removal of a hydroxyl group from one monosaccharide and of a hydrogen atom from the other, giving rise to a molecule of water and linking the two sugars together through an oxygen atom. Conversely, hydrolysis of the disaccharide breaks this linkage by adding back the water and thus uncoupling the two monosaccharides. Additional disaccharides frequently encountered are maltose

FIGURE 2-8

The difference between the monosaccharides glucose and galactose has to do with whether the hydroxyl group at the position indicated lies above or below the plane of the ring.

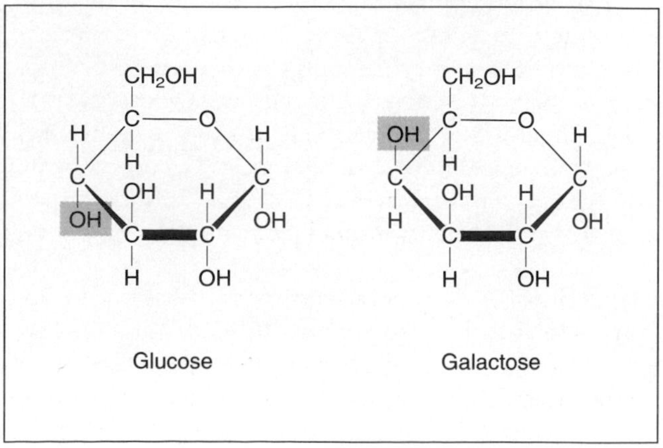

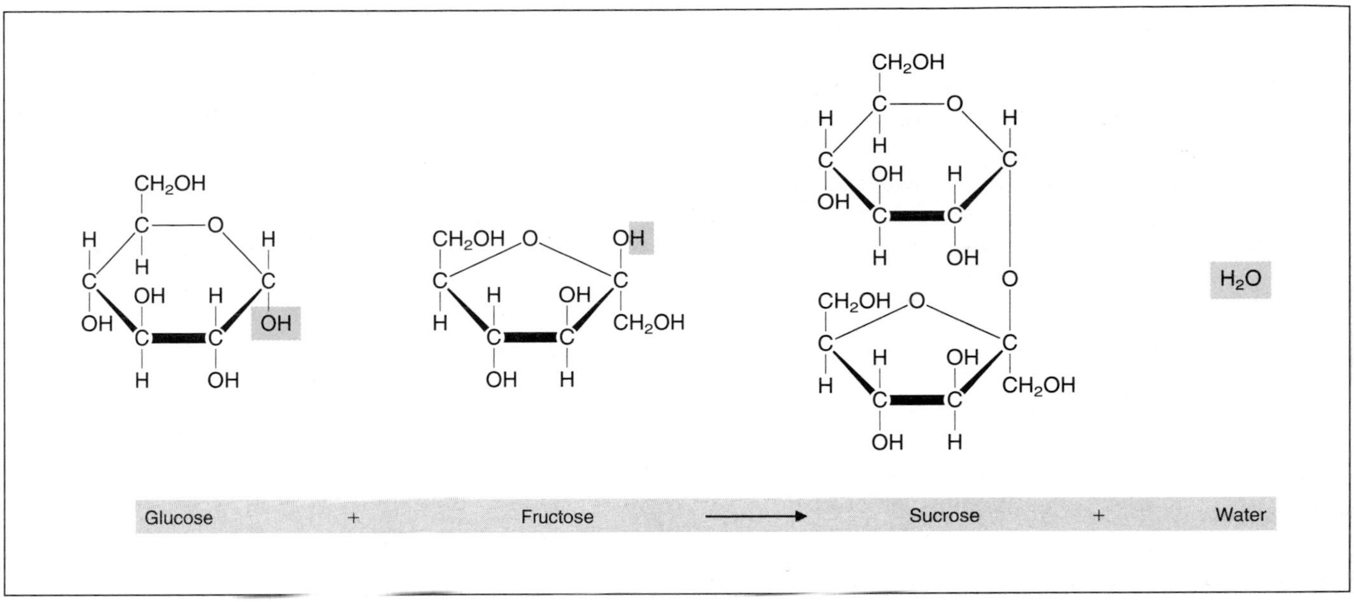

| Glucose | + | Fructose | ⟶ | Sucrose | + | Water |

FIGURE 2-9

Sucrose (table sugar) is a disaccharide formed by the linking together of two monosaccharides, glucose and fructose.

(glucose-glucose), formed during the digestion of large carbohydrate molecules in the intestinal tract, and lactose (glucose-galactose), present in milk.

When many monosaccharides are linked together to form large polymers, the molecules are known as **polysaccharides.** Starch, found in plant cells, and **glycogen** (Figure 2-10), present in animal cells and often called "animal starch," are examples of polysaccharides. Both of these polysaccharides are composed of thousands of glucose molecules linked together in long chains. They differ only in the degree of branching along the chain. Hydrolysis of these polysaccharides leads to release of the glucose subunits.

Lipids

Lipids are molecules composed predominantly of hydrogen and carbon atoms. Since these atoms are linked by neutral covalent bonds, lipids are nonpolar molecules and thus insoluble in water. It is this physical property of insolubility in water that characterizes this class of organic molecules. The lipids, which account for about 40 percent of the organic matter in the average body (15 percent of the body weight), can be divided into four subclasses: fatty acids, triacylglycerols, phospholipids, and steroids.

Fatty Acids. A **fatty acid** consists of a chain of carbon atoms with a carboxyl group at one end. Because fatty acids are synthesized in the body by the linking together of 2-carbon fragments, most fatty acids have an even number of carbon atoms, 16- and 18-carbon fatty acids being the most common. When all the carbons in a fatty acid chain are linked by single covalent bonds, the fatty acid is said to be a **saturated fatty acid.** Some fatty acids contain one or more double bonds, and these are known as **unsaturated fatty acids.** If one double bond is present, the fatty acid is said to be **monounsaturated**, and if more than one double bond, **polyunsaturated** (Figure 2-11). As we shall see, fatty acids can be found as subunits of triacylglycerols or phospholipids.

Some fatty acids can be altered to produce a special class of molecules that regulate a number of cell functions. As described in more detail in Chapter 7, these modified fatty acids—collectively termed **eicosanoids**—are derived from the 20-carbon, polyunsaturated fatty acid **arachidonic acid**.

Triacylglycerols. The **triacylglycerols** (also known as triglycerides) constitute the majority of the lipids in the body, and it is these molecules that are generally referred to simply as "fat." Triacylglycerols are formed by the linking together of **glycerol**, a three-carbon carbohydrate, with three fatty acids (Figure 2-11). Each of the three hydroxyl groups in glycerol is linked to the carboxyl group of a fatty acid by the removal of a molecule of water to form a triacylglycerol molecule. Animal fats generally contain a high proportion of saturated fatty acids, whereas vegetable fats contain more unsaturated fatty acids.

The three fatty acids in a molecule of triacylglycerol need not be identical; therefore, a variety of fats can be formed with fatty acids of different chain lengths and de-

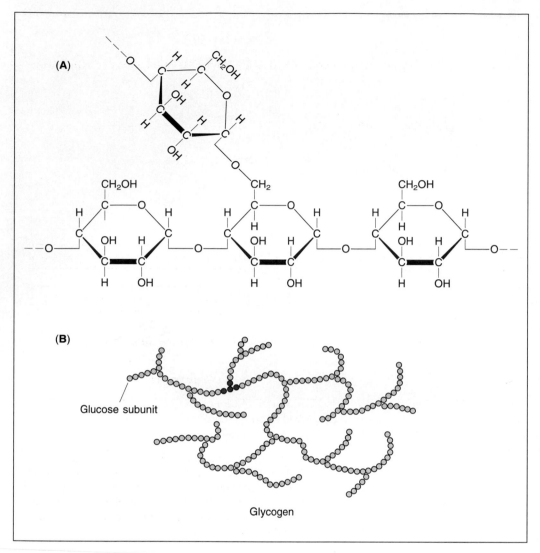

FIGURE 2-10

Many molecules of glucose linked end to end and at branch points form the branched-chain poly-saccharide glycogen (A), shown in diagrammatic form in B. The four red subunits in B correspond to the four glucose subunits in A.

grees of saturation. Hydrolysis of triacylglycerols releases the fatty acids from glycerol, and these products can then be utilized to provide energy for cell functions.

Phospholipids. Phospholipids are similar in overall structure to triacylglycerols, with one important difference. The third hydroxyl group of glycerol, rather than being attached to a fatty acid, is linked to phosphate. In addition, a small polar or ionized nitrogen-containing molecule is usually attached to this phosphate (Figure 2-11). These groups constitute a polar (hydrophilic) region at one end of the phospholipid molecule, whereas the fatty acid chains provide a nonpolar (hydrophobic) region at the opposite end. Therefore, these molecules are amphipathic. In water they become organized into clusters, with their polar ends being attracted to the water molecules.

Steroids. Steroids have a distinctly different structure from that of the other subclasses of lipid molecules. Four interconnected rings of carbon atoms form the skeleton of all steroids (Figure 2-12). A few polar hydroxyl groups may be attached to this ring structure, but they are not numerous enough to make a steroid water-soluble. Examples of steroids are cholesterol, cortisol from the adrenal glands, and female (estrogen) and male (testosterone) sex hormones secreted by the gonads.

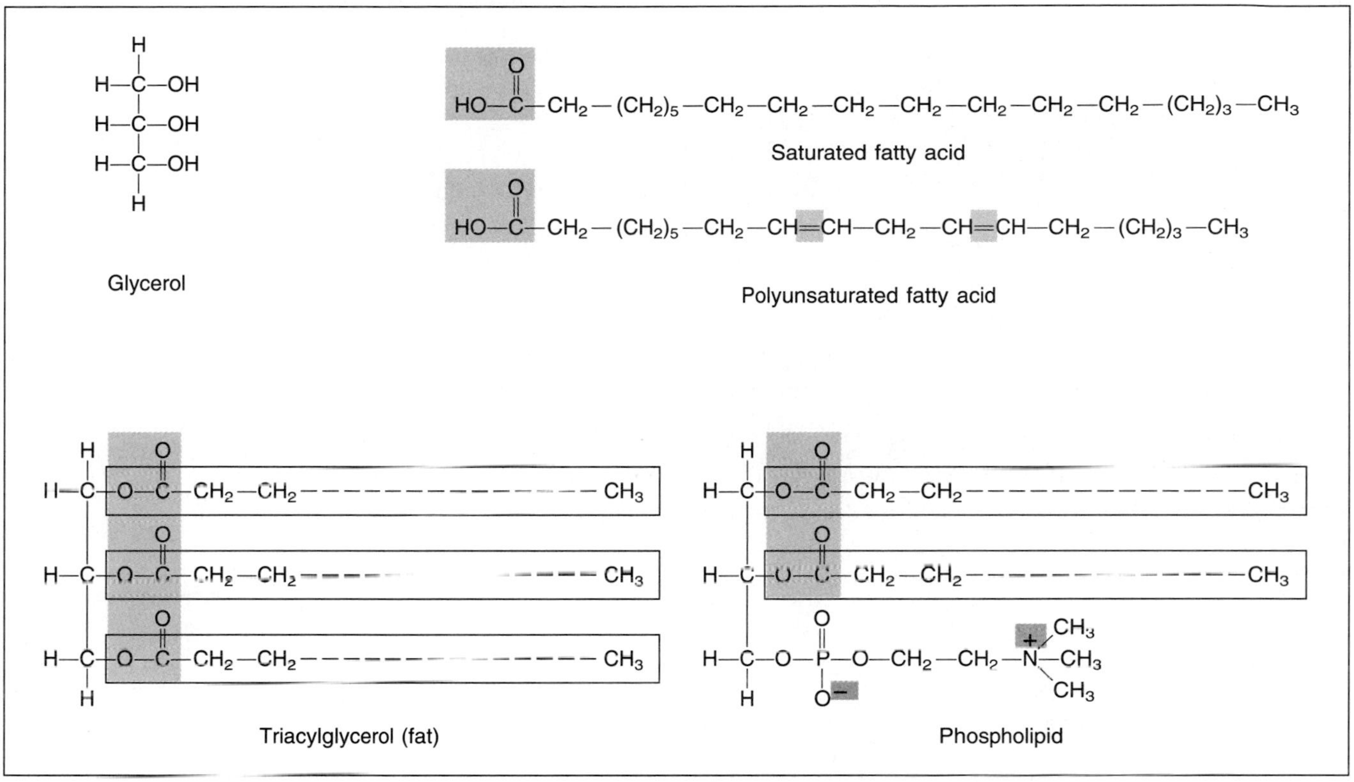

FIGURE 2-11

Glycerol and fatty acids are the major subunits that combine to form triacylglycerols and phospholipids.

FIGURE 2-12

Steroid ring structure, shown with all the carbon and hydrogen atoms in the rings and again without these atoms to emphasize the overall ring structure of this class of lipids. Different steroids have different types and numbers of chemical groups attached at various locations on the steroid ring, as shown by the example of the steroid cholesterol.

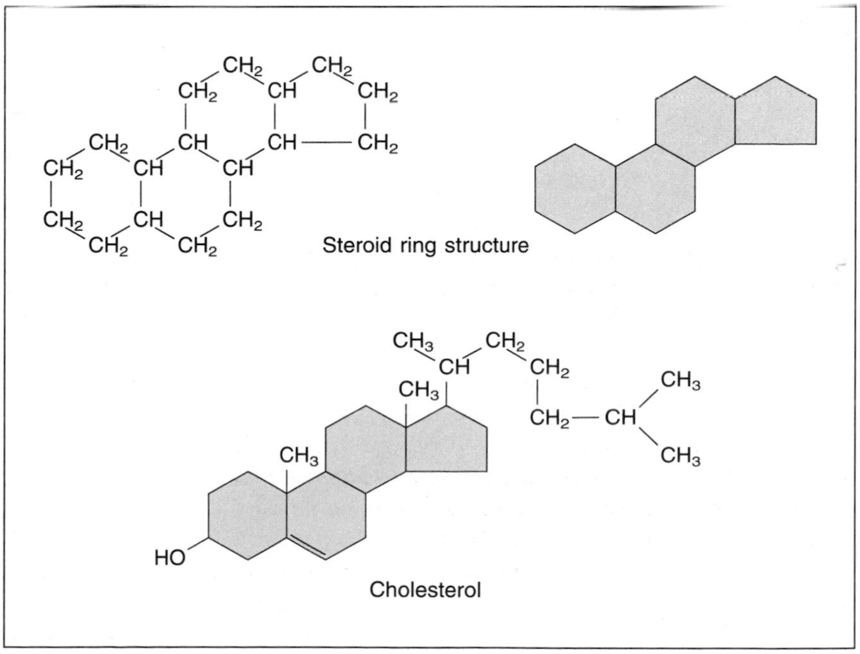

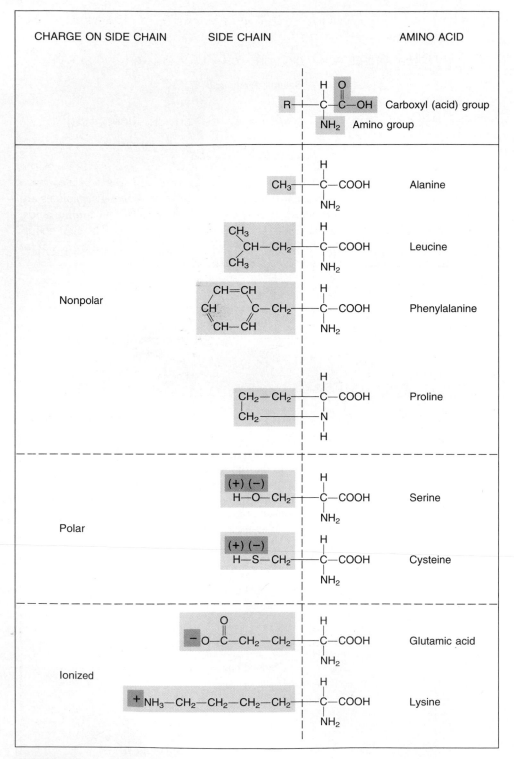

FIGURE 2-13

Structures of 8 of the 20 amino acids found in proteins. Note that proline does not have a free amino group, but it can still form a peptide bond.

Proteins

The term "**protein**" comes from the Greek *proteios* (of the first rank), which aptly describes their importance. These molecules, which account for about 50 percent of the organic material in the body (17 percent of the body weight), play critical roles in almost every physiological process. Proteins are composed of atoms of carbon, hydrogen, oxygen, and nitrogen, and small amounts of other elements, notably sulfur. They are macromolecules, often containing thousands of atoms, and like most large molecules, they are formed by the linking together of a large number of small subunits to form long chains.

Amino Acid Subunits.   The subunit of protein structure is an **amino acid**; thus, proteins are polymers of amino acids. Every amino acid (except one—proline) has an amino ($-NH_2$) and a carboxyl ($-COOH$) group linked to the terminal carbon atom in the molecule:

$$
\begin{array}{c}
\text{H} \\
| \\
\text{R}-\text{C}-\text{COOH} \\
| \\
\text{NH}_2
\end{array}
$$

The third bond of this terminal carbon atom is linked to a hydrogen atom, and the fourth to the remainder of the molecule, which is known as the **amino acid side chain** (R in the formula). The proteins of all living organisms are composed of the same set of 20 different amino acids, corresponding to 20 different side chains. The side chains may be nonpolar (8 amino acids), polar (7 amino acids), or ionized (5 amino acids) (Figure 2-13).

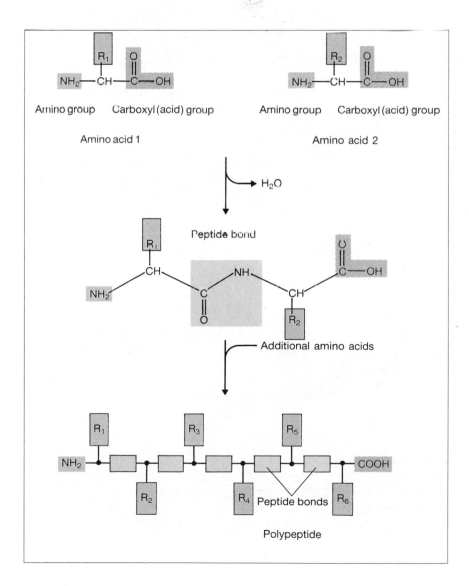

FIGURE 2-14

Linkage of amino acids by peptide bonds to form a polypeptide.

Polypeptides. Amino acids are joined together by linking the carboxyl group of one amino acid to the amino group of another. In the process, a molecule of water is formed (Figure 2-14). The bond formed between the amino and carboxyl groups is called a **peptide bond**, and it is a polar covalent bond. Note that when two amino acids are linked together, one end of the resulting molecule has a free amino group and the other has a free carboxyl group. Additional amino acids can be linked by peptide bonds to these free ends. A sequence of amino acids linked by peptide bonds is known as a **polypeptide**. The peptide bonds form the backbone of the polypeptide, and the side chain of each amino acid sticks out from the side of the chain. If the number of amino acids in a polypeptide is 50 or less, the molecule is known as a **peptide**; if the sequence is more than 50 amino acid units long, the polypeptide is known as a protein. The number 50 is arbitrary and has become the convention for distinguishing between large and small polypeptides.

After certain proteins have been synthesized, one or

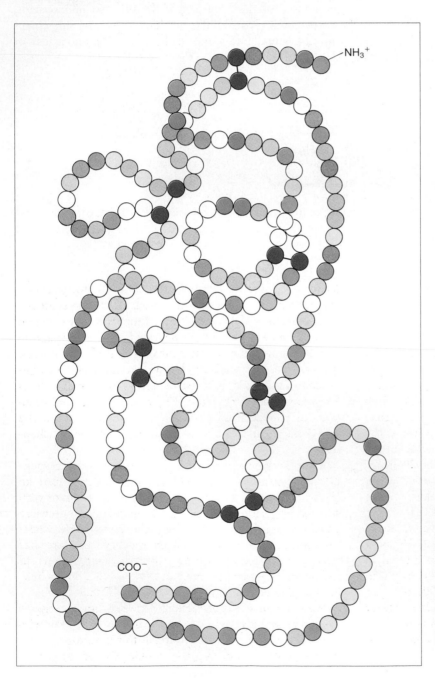

FIGURE 2-15

The position of each type of amino acid in a polypeptide chain and the total number of amino acids in the chain distinguish one polypeptide from another. The example shown above contains 223 amino acids; different types of amino acids are represented by different-colored circles. The bonds between different regions of the chain (red to red) represent covalent disulfide bonds between cysteine side chains.

FIGURE 2-16

Conformation of a protein molecule (myoglobin). Regions of alpha-helix conformation are interrupted at sites of bending by random coil conformations. (*Adapted from Albert L. Lehninger.*)

more monosaccharides are covalently attached to the side chains of specific amino acids (serine and threonine) to form a class of proteins known as **glycoproteins**.

Primary Protein Structure. Two variables determine the primary structure of a polypeptide: (1) the number of amino acids in the chain, and (2) the specific type of amino acid at each position along the chain (Figure 2-15). Each position along a polypeptide chain can be occupied by any one of the 20 different amino acids. Let us consider the number of different peptides that can be formed that have a sequence of three amino acids. Any one of the 20 different amino acids may occupy the first position in the sequence, any one of the 20 the second position, and any one of the 20 the third position, for a total of $20 \times 20 \times 20 = 20^3 = 8000$ possible sequences of three amino acids. If the peptide is 6 amino acids in length, $20^6 = 64,000,000$ possible combinations can be formed. Peptides that are only 6 amino acids long are still very small molecules compared to proteins, which may have sequences of 1000 or more amino acids. Thus, with 20 different amino acids an almost unlimited variety of polypeptides can be formed by altering both the amino acid sequence and the total number of amino acids in the chain.

Protein Conformation. The structure of a polypeptide is analogous to a string of beads, each bead representing a single amino acid (Figure 2-15). Moreover, since amino acids can rotate around their peptide bonds, a polypeptide chain is flexible and can be bent into a number of shapes, just as a string of beads can be twisted into many configurations. The three-dimensional shape of a molecule is known as its **conformation** (Figure 2-16). The conformations of peptides and proteins play a major role in the functioning of these molecules, as we shall see in Chapter 4.

Four factors determine the conformation of a polypeptide chain once the amino acid sequence has been formed: (1) hydrogen bonds between portions of the chain or with surrounding water molecules; (2) ionic bonds between polar and ionized regions along the polypeptide chain; (3) **van der Waals forces**, which are very weak forces of attraction between nonpolar (hydrophobic) regions in close proximity to each other; and (4) covalent bonds linking the side chains of two amino acids (Figure 2-17).

An example of the attractions between various regions along a polypeptide chain is the hydrogen bonds that can occur between the hydrogen linked to the nitrogen atom in one peptide bond and the double-bonded oxygen in

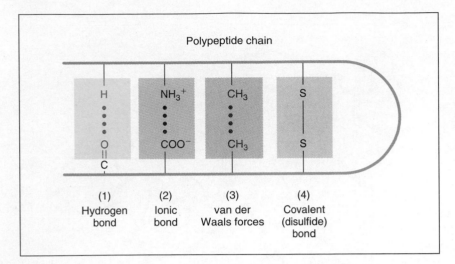

Polypeptide chain

(1) Hydrogen bond

(2) Ionic bond

(3) van der Waals forces

(4) Covalent (disulfide) bond

FIGURE 2-17

Factors that contribute to the folding of polypeptide chains and thus to their conformation are (1) hydrogen bonds between side chains or with surrounding water molecules, (2) ionic bonds between polar or ionized amino acid side chains, (3) weak van der Waals forces between nonpolar side chains, and (4) covalent bonds between side chains.

another peptide bond (Figure 2-18). Since peptide bonds occur at regular intervals along a polypeptide chain, the hydrogen bonds between them tend to force the polypeptide chain into a helical configuration known as an **alpha helix**. However, for several reasons, a given region of a polypeptide chain may not assume a helical shape. The sizes of the side chains and ionic bonds between oppositely charged ionized side chains can interfere with the coiling and distort the helix, producing shapes with no regularity. These uncoiled regions are known as **random coil** config-

urations and occur in regions where the polypeptide is bent (Figure 2-16).

Water plays an important role in determining the conformation of a polypeptide chain. When polypeptides are dissolved in water, the polarized and ionized regions of the molecule are attracted to the surrounding polar water molecules. This tends to force the polar and ionized side chains toward the surface of the molecule, orienting them toward the water, while the hydrophobic side chains tend to become located in the interior of the molecule, re-

FIGURE 2-18

Hydrogen bonds between regularly spaced peptide bonds can produce a helical configuration in a polypeptide chain.

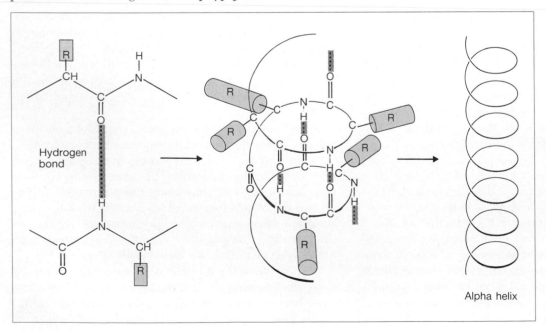

Alpha helix

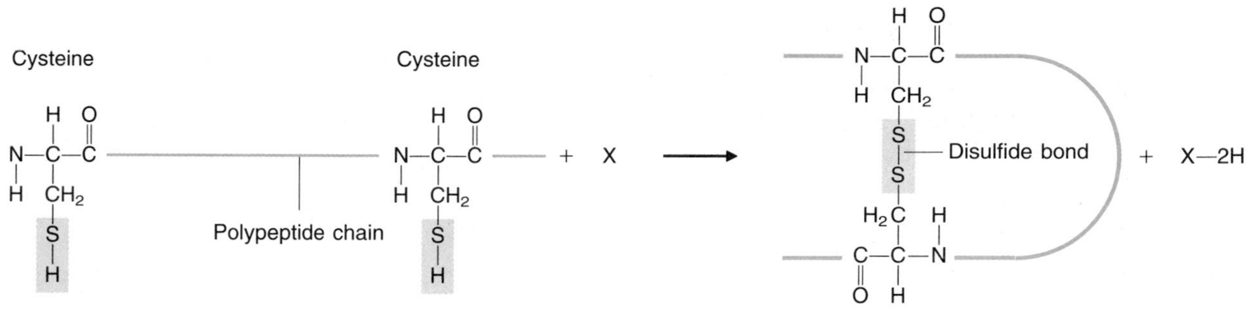

FIGURE 2-19

Formation of a disulfide bond between the side chains of two cysteine amino acids links two regions of the polypeptide together. The hydrogen atoms on the sulfhydryl groups of the cysteines are transferred to another molecule, X, during formation of the disulfide bond.

moved from contact with water. If they come close to each other, the hydrophobic side chains located in the interior of the protein are attracted by van der Waals forces as a result of the weak electromagnetic field that surrounds electrically neutral atoms.

Covalent bonds between certain side chains can distort the regular pattern of the alpha-helix conformation and can be used to link two polypeptides together. The side chain of the amino acid cysteine contains a sulfhydryl group (R—SH), which can react with a sulfhydryl group in another cysteine side chain to produce a **disulfide bond** (R—S—S—R), linking the two amino acid side chains together (Figure 2-19). Disulfide bonds form strong covalent bonds between portions of a polypeptide chain, in contrast to the weaker hydrogen and ionic bonds, which are more easily broken. Table 2-6 provides a summary of the types of bonding forces that contribute to the conformation of polypeptide chains. These same bonds are also involved in other intermolecular interactions, which will be described in later chapters.

TABLE 2-6 BONDING FORCES BETWEEN ATOMS AND MOLECULES

Bond	Strength	Characteristics	Examples
Hydrogen	Weak	Electrical attraction between polarized bonds, usually hydrogen and oxygen	Attractions between peptide bonds forming the alpha helix structure of proteins and between polar amino acid side chains contributing to protein conformation; attractions between water molecules
Ionic	Strong	Electrical attraction between oppositely charged ionized groups	Attractions between ionized groups in amino acid side chains contributing to protein conformation; attractions between ions in a salt
Van der Waals	Very weak	Attraction between nonpolar molecules and groups when very close to each other	Attractions between nonpolar amino acids in proteins contributing to protein conformation; attractions between lipid molecules
Covalent	Strong	Shared electrons between atoms	Most bonds linking atoms together to form molecules

A number of proteins contain more than one polypeptide chain. The same factors that influence the conformation of a single polypeptide also determine the interactions between the polypeptides in a multichain protein. Thus, the separate chains can be held together by interactions between various ionized, polar, and nonpolar side chains, as well as by disulfide covalent bonds between the chains. The polypeptide chains in a multichain protein may be identical or different. For example, hemoglobin, the protein that transports oxygen in the blood, is composed of four polypeptide chains, two of one kind and two of another.

The primary structures (amino acid sequences) of a large number of proteins are known, but three-dimensional conformations have been determined for only a few. Because of the multiple factors that can influence the folding of a polypeptide chain, it is not yet possible to predict accurately the conformation of a protein from its primary amino acid sequence.

Nucleic Acids

Nucleic acids account for only 2 percent of the body's weight, yet these molecules are extremely important because they are responsible for the storage, expression, and transmission of genetic information. It is the expression of genetic information that determines whether one is a human being or a mouse, or whether a cell is a muscle cell or a nerve cell.

There are two classes of nucleic acids, **deoxyribonucleic acid (DNA)** and **ribonucleic acid (RNA)**. DNA molecules store genetic information coded in terms of their repeating subunit structure, whereas RNA molecules are involved in the decoding of this information into instructions for linking together a specific sequence of amino acids to form a specific polypeptide chain. Both types of nucleic acids are polymers composed of linear sequences of repeating subunits. Each subunit, known as a **nucleotide**, has three components: a phosphate group, a sugar, and a ring of carbon and nitrogen atoms known as a base because it can accept hydrogen ions (Figure 2-20). The phosphate group of one nucleotide is linked to the sugar of the adjacent nucleotide to form a chain, with the bases sticking out from the side of the phosphate-sugar backbone (Figure 2-21).

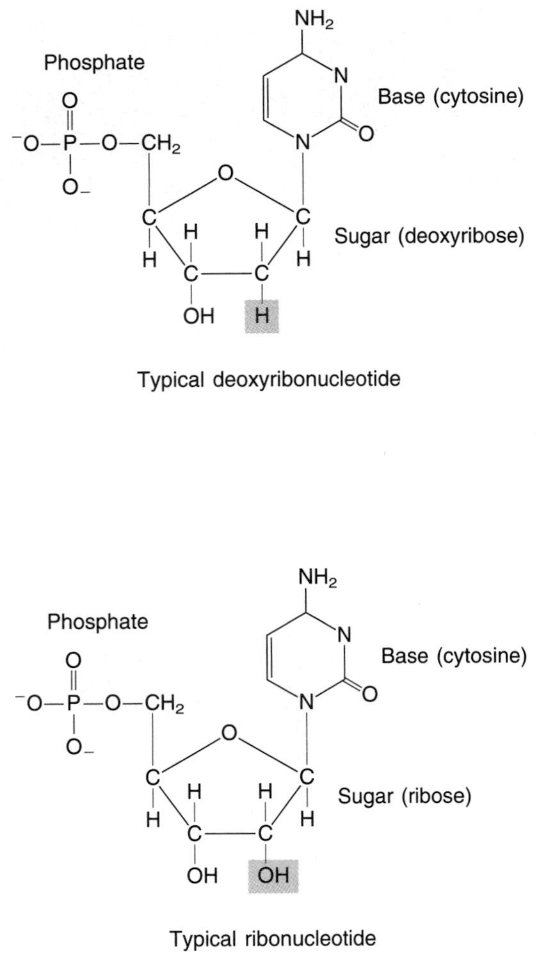

FIGURE 2-20

Nucleotide subunits of DNA and RNA. Nucleotides are composed of a sugar, a base, and phosphate. Deoxyribonucleotides present in DNA contain the sugar deoxyribose. The sugar in ribonucleotides, present in RNA, is ribose, which has an OH at the position that lacks this group in deoxyribose.

DNA. The nucleotides in DNA contain the five-carbon sugar **deoxyribose**; hence the name "deoxyribonucleic acid." Four different nucleotides are present in DNA, corresponding to the four different bases that can be linked to deoxyribose. These bases are divided into two classes: (1) the **purine** bases, **adenine** and **guanine**, which have double (fused) rings of nitrogen and carbon atoms; and

(2) the **pyrimidine** bases, **cytosine** and **thymine**, which have only a single ring (Figure 2-21).

A DNA molecule consists of not one but two chains of nucleotides coiled around each other in the form of a double helix (Figure 2-22). The two chains are held together by hydrogen bonds between purine and pyrimidine bases. This base pairing maintains a constant distance between

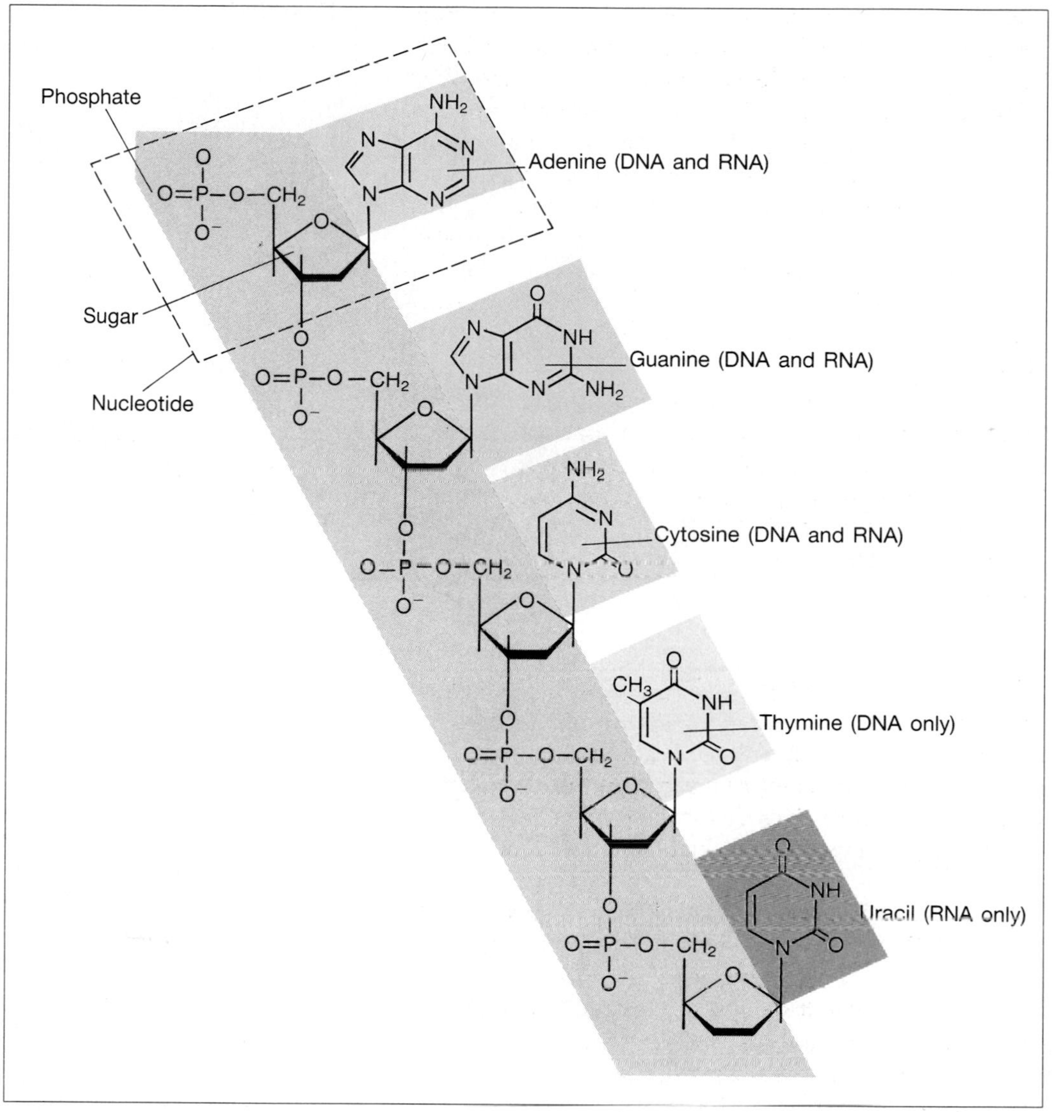

FIGURE 2-21
Phosphate-sugar bonds link nucleotides in sequence to form
nucleic acids. Note that the pyrimidine base thymine is found
only in DNA and uracil is present only in RNA.

the sugar-phosphate backbones of the two chains as they coil around each other. Specificity is imposed on the base pairings by the location of the hydrogen-bonding groups in the four bases (Figure 2-22). Three hydrogen bonds are formed between the purine guanine and the pyrimidine cytosine (G-C pairing), while only two hydrogen bonds can be formed between the purine adenine and the pyrimidine thymine (A-T pairing). As a result, G is always paired with

C, and A with T. In Chapter 4 we shall see how this specificity in base pairing provides the mechanism for duplicating and transferring genetic information.

RNA. The structure of RNA molecules differs in only a few respects from that of DNA (Table 2-7): (1) RNA consists of a single (rather than a double) chain of nucleotides; (2) in RNA, the sugar in each nucleotide is **ribose** rather

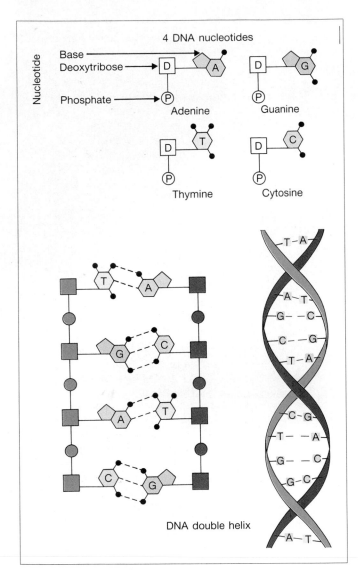

DNA double helix

FIGURE 2-22
Base pairings between two nucleotide chains form the double-helical structure of DNA. D and P represent deoxyribose and phosphate, which form the backbone of each polynucleotide chain. The four bases are indicated by A, T, C, and G.

than deoxyribose; and (3) the pyrimidine base thymine in DNA is replaced in RNA by the pyrimidine base **uracil** (U) (Figure 2-20), which can base-pair with the purine adenine (A-U pairing). The other three bases, adenine, guanine, and cytosine, are the same in both DNA and RNA. Although RNA contains only a single chain of nucleotides, portions of this chain can bend back upon itself and base-pair with other nucleotides in the same chain.

TABLE 2-7   COMPARISON OF DNA AND RNA COMPOSITION

	DNA	RNA
Nucleotide sugar	Deoxyribose	Ribose
Nucleotide bases		
Purines	Adenine	Adenine
	Guanine	Guanine
Pyrimidines	Cytosine	Cytosine
	Thymine	Uracil
Number of chains	Two	One

SUMMARY

ATOMS

I. Atoms are composed of three subatomic particles: positive protons and neutral neutrons, both located in the nucleus, and negative electrons revolving around the nucleus.

II. The atomic number is the number of protons in an atom, and because atoms are electrically neutral, it is also equal to the number of electrons.

III. The atomic weight of an atom is the ratio of an atom's mass relative to that of a carbon-12 atom. It is approximately equal to the number of protons plus neutrons.

IV. One gram atomic mass is the number of grams of an element equal to its atomic weight. One gram atomic mass of any element contains the same number of atoms—6×10^{23}.

V. The 24 elements essential for normal body function are listed in Table 2-1.

MOLECULES

I. Molecules are formed by linking atoms together.

II. A covalent bond is formed when two atoms share a pair of electrons. Each type of atom can form a characteristic number of covalent bonds: hydrogen forms one, oxygen two, nitrogen three, and carbon four.

III. Molecules have characteristic shapes, which can be altered within limits by the rotation of their atoms around covalent bonds.

IONS

I. When an atom gains or loses one or more electrons, it acquires a net electric charge and becomes an ion.

POLAR MOLECULES

I. In polar covalent bonds, one atom attracts the bonding electrons more than the other atom does.

II. The electrical attraction between hydrogen and the oxygen or nitrogen atom in a separate molecule or different region of the same molecule forms a hydrogen bond.

III. Water, a polar molecule, is attracted to other water molecules by hydrogen bonds.

SOLUTIONS

I. Substances dissolved in a liquid are solutes, and the liquid in which they are dissolved is the solvent. Water is the most abundant solvent in the body.

II. Substances that have polar or ionized groups dissolve in water by being electrically attracted to the polar water molecules.

III. In water, amphipathic molecules form clusters with the polar regions at the surface and the nonpolar regions in the interior of the cluster.

IV. The molecular weight of a molecule is the sum of the atomic weights of all its atoms. One mole of any substance is its weight in grams equal to its molecular weight and contains 6×10^{23} molecules.

V. Substances that release a hydrogen ion in solution are called acids. Those that accept a hydrogen ion are bases.

A. The acidity of a solution is determined by its free hydrogen-ion concentration; the greater the hydrogen-ion concentration, the greater the acidity.

B. The pH of a solution is the negative logarithm of the hydrogen-ion concentration. As the acidity of a solution increases, the pH decreases. Pure water has a pH of 7.0.

CLASSES OF ORGANIC MOLECULES

I. Carbohydrates are composed of carbon, hydrogen, and oxygen in the proportions $C_n(H_2O)_n$.

A. The presence of the polar hydroxyl groups makes carbohydrates soluble in water.

B. The most abundant monosaccharide in the body is glucose ($C_6H_{12}O_6$), which is stored in cells in the form of the polysaccharide glycogen.

II. Lipids lack polar and ionized groups, a characteristic that makes then insoluble in water.

A. Triacylglycerols are formed when fatty acids are linked to each of the three hydroxyl groups in glycerol.

B. Phospholipids contain two fatty acids linked to two of the hydroxyl groups in glycerol, with the third hydroxyl linked to phosphate, which in turn is linked to a small charged or polar compound. The polar and ionized groups at one end of phospholipids make these molecules amphipathic.

C. Steroids are composed of four interconnected rings, often containing a few polar hydroxyl groups.

III. Proteins, macromolecules composed primarily of carbon, hydrogen, oxygen, and nitrogen, are polymers of amino acids.

A. Nineteen of the 20 amino acids have an amino (—NH$_2$) and a carboxyl (—COOH) group linked to their terminal carbon atom.

B. Amino acids are linked together by peptide bonds between the carboxyl group of one amino acid and the amino group of the next.

C. The primary structure of a polypeptide chain is determined by (1) the number of amino acids in sequence, and (2) the type of amino acid at each position.

D. The factors that determine the conformation of a polypeptide chain are summarized in Figure 2-17.

E. Hydrogen bonds between peptide bonds along a polypeptide chain force much of the chain into an alpha helix.

F. The interactions of polar and ionized side chains with water tend to force these regions to the surface of the protein, leaving the nonpolar side chains to occupy the interior.

G. Covalent disulfide bonds can form between the sulfhydryl groups of cysteine side chains to hold regions of a polypeptide chain close to each other.

H. Some proteins have multiple polypeptide chains.

IV. Nucleic acids are responsible for the storage, expression, and transmission of genetic information.

A. Deoxyribonucleic acid (DNA) stores genetic information.

B. Ribonucleic acid (RNA) is involved in the decoding of the information coded in DNA into instructions for linking amino acids together to form proteins.

C. Both types of nucleic acids are polymers of nucleotides, each containing a phosphate group, a sugar, and a base of carbon, hydrogen and nitrogen atoms.

D. DNA contains the sugar deoxyribose and consists of two chains of nucleotides coiled around each other in a double helix. The chains are held together by hydrogen bonds between purine and pyrimidine bases in the two chains.

E. Base pairings in DNA always occur between guanine and cytosine and between adenine and thymine.

F. RNA consists of a single chain of nucleotides, containing the sugar ribose and three of the four bases found in DNA. The fourth base is the pyrimidine uracil rather than thymine. Uracil base-pairs with adenine.

KEY TERMS

atoms	neutral solution
chemical element	alkaline solutions
protons	acidic solutions
neutrons	macromolecules
electrons	polymers
atomic nucleus	carbohydrate
atomic number	monosaccharides
atomic weight	glucose
gram atomic mass	pentoses
trace elements	hexoses
molecule	disaccharides
covalent bond	sucrose
ion	polysaccharides
electrolytes	glycogen
cations	lipids
anions	fatty acid
carboxyl group	saturated fatty acid
amino group	unsaturated fatty acid
polar covalent bonds	monounsaturated fatty acid
hydroxyl group	polyunsaturated fatty acid
polar molecules	eicosanoids
nonpolar molecules	arachidonic acid
hydrogen bond	triacylglycerols
hydrolysis	glycerol
solutes	phospholipids
solvent	steroids
solution	protein
ionic bond	amino acid
hydrophilic	amino acid side chain
hydrophobic	peptide bond
amphipathic	polypeptide
concentration	peptide
molecular weight	glycoproteins
mole	conformation
acids	van der Waals forces
base	alpha helix
strong acids	random coil
weak acids	disulfide bond
acidity	nucleic acids
pH	deoxyribonucleic acid (DNA)

ribonucleic acid (RNA) pyrimidine
nucleotide cytosine
deoxyribose thymine
purine ribose
adenine uracil
guanine

REVIEW QUESTIONS

1. Describe the electric charge, mass, and location of the three major subatomic particles in an atom.
2. Which four atoms are the most abundant in the body?
3. Describe the distinguishing characteristics of the three classes of essential chemical elements found in the body.
4. How many covalent bonds can be formed by atoms of carbon, nitrogen, oxygen, and hydrogen?
5. What property of molecules allows them to change their three-dimensional shape?
6. Describe how an ion is formed.
7. Draw the structures of an ionized carboxyl group and an ionized amino group.
8. Describe the polar characteristics of a water molecule.
9. What determines a molecule's solubility or lack of solubility in water?
10. Describe the organization of amphipathic molecules in water.
11. What is the molar concentration of 80 g of glucose dissolved in sufficient water to make 2 L of solution?
12. What distinguishes a weak acid from a strong acid?
13. What effect does increasing the pH of a solution have upon the ionization of a carboxyl group? An amino group?
14. Name the four classes of organic molecules in the body.
15. Describe the three subclasses of carbohydrate molecules.
16. To which subclass of carbohydrates does each of the following molecules belong: glucose, sucrose, and glycogen?
17. What properties are characteristic of lipids?
18. Describe the subclasses of lipids.
19. Describe the linkage between amino acids to form a polypeptide chain.
20. What is the difference between a peptide and a protein?
21. What two factors determine the primary structure of a polypeptide chain?
22. Describe the types of interactions that determine the conformation of a polypeptide chain.
23. Describe the structure of DNA and of RNA.
24. Describe the characteristics of base pairings between nucleotide bases.

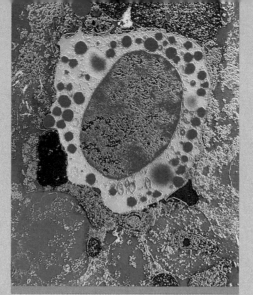

CHAPTER

3

CELL STRUCTURE

MICROSCOPIC OBSERVATIONS OF CELLS

CELL COMPARTMENTS

Membranes

Membrane structure

Membrane junctions

CELL ORGANELLES

Nucleus

Ribosomes

Endoplasmic Reticulum

Golgi Apparatus

Mitochondria

Lysosomes

Peroxisomes

Filaments

SUMMARY

KEY TERMS

REVIEW QUESTIONS

As we learned in Chapter 1, cells are the structural and functional units of all living organisms. The human body is composed of trillions of cells, each a microscopic compartment (Figure 3-1). In fact, the word "cell" means "a small chamber" (like a jail cell). In this chapter, we describe the structures present in most of the body's cells and state their functions. Subsequent chapters describe the mechanisms by which these structures perform their functions.

The cells of a mouse, a human being, and an elephant are all approximately the same size. An elephant is large because it has more cells, not because it has larger cells. A majority of the cells in a human being have diameters in the range of 10 to 20 μm, although cells as small as 2 μm and as large as 120 μm are present. A cell 10 μm in diameter is about one-tenth the size of the smallest object that can be seen with the naked eye; a microscope must therefore be used to observe cells and their internal structure.

MICROSCOPIC OBSERVATIONS OF CELLS

The smallest object that can be seen clearly under a microscope depends upon the wavelength of the radiation used to illuminate the specimen—the shorter the wavelength, the smaller the object that can be seen. With a **light microscope**, the smallest object that can be seen clearly is about 0.2 μm in diameter, and so this instrument can be used to see individual cells as well as some intracellular structure. However, an **electron microscope** is necessary to make visible the finer details of cellular structure.

An electron microscope uses electrons instead of light rays to form an image of a specimen. A beam of electrons can be focused by electromagnetic lenses, just as glass

FIGURE 3-1
Cellular organization of tissues, as illustrated by a portion of spleen. Oval, clear spaces in the micrograph are blood vessels. (*From Johannes A. G. Rhodin, "Histology: A Text and Atlas," Oxford University Press, New York, 1974.*)

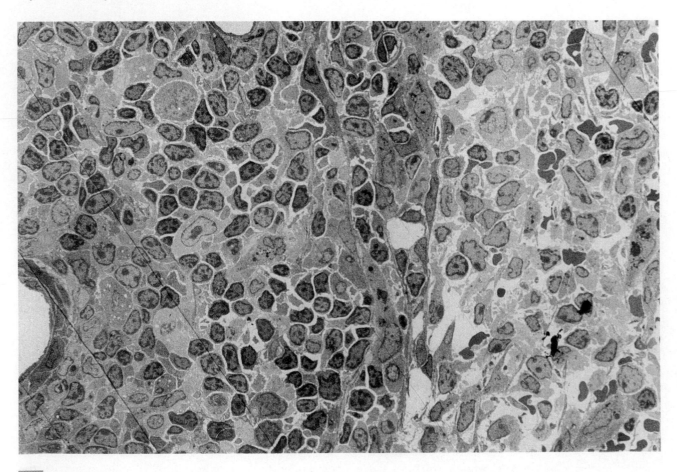

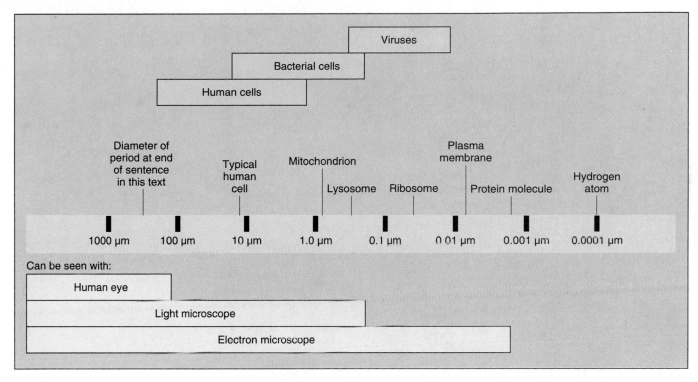

FIGURE 3-2

Size range of cell structures, plotted on a logarithmic scale. Typical sizes are given. Each component has a range of sizes around this typical value.

lenses focus a beam of light in a light microscope. A greater resolution is achieved by an electron microscope because electrons behave as waves with much shorter wavelengths than those of visible light. Cell structures as small as 0.002 μm can be resolved with an electron microscope. Very large molecules, such as proteins and nucleic acids, can be seen through an electron microscope, although the individual atoms that make up these large molecules are still beyond the limits of effective resolution. Typical sizes of cells and cellular components are illustrated in Figure 3-2.

Although *living* cells can be observed with a light microscope, this is not possible with an electron microscope. To form an image with an electron beam, most of the electrons must pass through the specimen, just as light passes through a specimen in a light microscope. However, electrons can penetrate only a short distance through matter; therefore, the observed specimen must be very thin. Cells must be specially prepared for observation in an electron microscope by being cut into thin sections, like slices of salami. Each section is on the order of 0.1 μm thick, which is about one-hundredth of the thickness of a typical cell.

Because electron micrographs (such as Figure 3-3) are images of very thin sections of a cell rather than of the whole cell, they can often be misleading. Structures that appear as separate objects in an electron micrograph may actually be continuous structures that are connected through a region lying outside the plane of the section. As an analogy, a thin section through a ball of string would appear as a collection of separate lines and disconnected dots even though the piece of string was originally continuous.

Cells have a variety of shapes. Most cells are surrounded by and anchored to neighboring cells, and such immobilized cells usually have a polyhedral shape (Figure 3-1). Specialized cells often have shapes that are related to the specific functions they perform. Extending from a nerve cell, for example, are one or more cylindrical processes, much like the branches of a tree, which are used to receive and transmit electric signals.

There are three types of biological units: **prokaryotic cells**, **eukaryotic cells**, and **viruses**. The cells in the human body, as well as in other multicellular animals and plants, are eukaryotic (true-nucleus) cells. These cells are distinguished by the presence of a nuclear membrane surrounding the cell nucleus and the presence of numerous membrane-bound organelles within the cell. Prokaryotic cells lack these membranous structures; bacteria make up the largest class of prokaryotic cells. Viruses have the simplest structure, consisting of only a nucleic acid molecule surrounded by a protein shell. Numerous infectious dis-

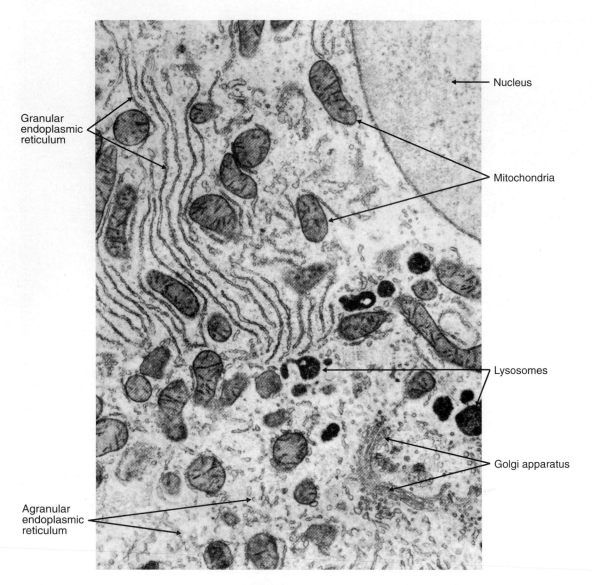

FIGURE 3-3

Electron micrograph of a thin section through a portion of a rat liver cell. [*From K. R. Porter, in T. W. Goodwin and O. Lindberg (eds.), "Biological Structure and Function," vol. 1, Academic Press, New York, 1961.*]

eases are caused by the invasion of multicellular organisms by prokaryotic cells and viruses (Chapter 20). This chapter describes the structure of eukaryotic cells only.

CELL COMPARTMENTS

Compare an electron micrograph of a section through a cell (Figure 3-3) with a diagrammatic illustration of a typical human cell (Figure 3-4). What is immediately obvious, from both the diagram and the electron micrograph, is the extensive structure inside the cell. A human

cell is not simply a chemical solution surrounded by a limiting barrier, the **plasma membrane**, which covers the cell surface. The cell interior is divided into a number of compartments also surrounded by membranes. These membrane-bound compartments, along with some particles and filaments, are known as **cell organelles** (little organs). Each cell organelle performs a specific function that contributes to the cell's survival.

The interior of a cell is divided into two regions: (1) the **nucleus**, a spherical or oval structure usually located near the center of the cell; and (2) the **cytoplasm**, the region that makes up all the interior of the cell except the nu-

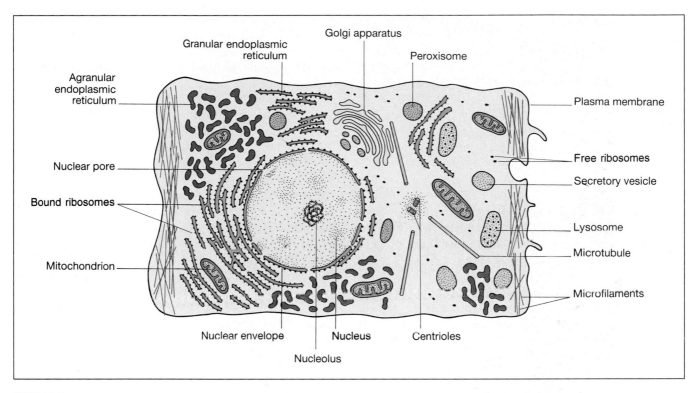

FIGURE 3-4

Structures found in most human cells.

cleus. The cytoplasm contains two components: (1) cell organelles other than the nucleus, and (2) the fluid surrounding these organelles and known as the **cytosol** (Figure 3-5). The term **intracellular fluid** refers to *all* the fluid inside a cell—in other words, cytosol plus the fluid inside all the organelles, including the nucleus. The chemical compositions of the fluids in these cell organelles differ from that of the cytosol. The cytosol is by far the largest intracellular fluid compartment.

Membranes

Membranes form a major structural element in human cells. They are found surrounding the entire cell (the plasma membrane) and enclosing most of the cell organelles. Although membranes perform a variety of functions, their most universal role is to act as a selective barrier to the passage of molecules, allowing some molecules to cross while excluding others. The plasma membrane regulates the passage of substances into and out of the cell, whereas the membranes surrounding cell organelles allow selective movement of substances between the organelles and the cytosol. One of the advantages of restricting the movements of molecules across membranes is that the products of chemical reactions can often be confined to specific cell organelles. As we shall see in Chapter 6, the hindrance offered by a membrane to the passage of sub-

stances can be altered to allow increased or decreased flow of molecules or ions across the membrane.

The plasma membrane, in addition to acting as a selective barrier, plays an important role in detecting chemical

FIGURE 3-5

Comparison of cytoplasm and cytosol. (A) Cytoplasm (the colored area) is the region that includes every point inside the cell except the interior of the nucleus. (B) Cytosol (the colored area) is the liquid that fills all of the cytoplasmic region except the interior of the cell organelles.

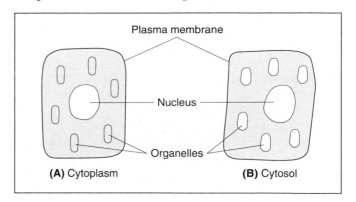

TABLE 3-1 FUNCTIONS OF PLASMA MEMBRANES

1. Regulate the passage of substances into and out of the cells
2. Detect chemical messengers arriving at the cell surface
3. Link adjacent cells together by membrane junctions
4. Anchor a variety of proteins, including intracellular and extracellular protein filaments involved in the generation and transmission of force, to the cell surface

signals from other cells, anchoring cells to adjacent cells, and providing sites for the attachment of protein filaments associated with the generation and transmission of force (Table 3-1).

Membrane Structure. All membranes consist of a double layer of lipid molecules in which proteins are embedded (Figure 3-6). The lipid layer prevents the movement of most polar or ionized molecules through the membrane, whereas the proteins provide pathways for the selective transfer of these substances through the lipid barrier.

The major membrane lipids are **phospholipids**. As described on page 26, these are amphipathic molecules.

One end has a charged region, and the remainder of the molecule, which consists of two long fatty acid chains, is nonpolar. The phospholipids in cell membranes are organized into a bimolecular layer with the nonpolar fatty acid chains located in the middle. The polar regions of the phospholipids are oriented toward the surfaces of the membrane as a result of their attraction to the polar water molecules in the extracellular fluid and cytosol.

There are no chemical bonds linking the phospholipids to each other or to the membrane proteins. Therefore, each molecule is free to move independently of the others. This results in considerable random lateral movement parallel to the surfaces of the bilayer. In addition, the long fatty acid chains can bend and wiggle back and forth. Thus, the lipid bilayer has the characteristics of a fluid, much like a thin layer of oil on a water surface. This fluidity makes the membrane quite flexible. Like a piece of cloth, membranes can be bent and folded but cannot be stretched without being torn. This flexibility, along with the fact that cells are filled with fluid, allows cells to undergo considerable changes in shape without disruption of their structural integrity.

The plasma membrane also contains **cholesterol** (about one molecule of cholesterol for each molecule of phospholipid), whereas intracellular membranes contain very little cholesterol. Cholesterol, a steroid, is slightly

FIGURE 3-6

(A) Electron micrograph of a human red-cell plasma membrane. Cell membranes are 6 to 10 nm thick, too thin to be seen without the aid of an electron microscope. In an electron micrograph a membrane appears as two dark lines separated by a light interspace. The dark lines correspond to the polar regions of the proteins and lipids, whereas the light interspace corresponds to the nonpolar regions of these molecules. [*From J. D. Robertson, in Michael Locke (ed.), "Cell Membranes in Development," Academic Press, New York, 1964.*] (B) Arrangement of the proteins and lipids in the membrane.

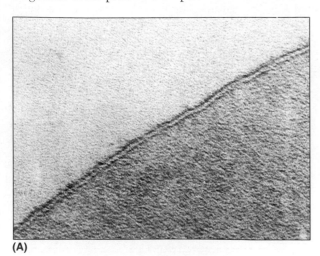

(A)

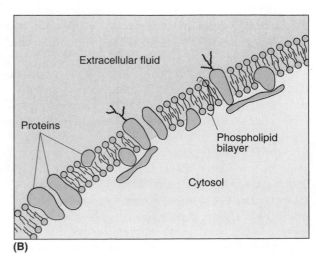

(B)

amphipathic because of a single polar hydroxyl group (Figure 2-12) on its nonpolar ring structure. Therefore, cholesterol, like the amphipathic phospholipids, is inserted into the lipid bilayer with its polar region at a bilayer surface and its nonpolar rings in the interior in association with the fatty acid chains. The cholesterol in the plasma membrane plays an important role in maintaining the fluidity of the lipid bilayer, preventing close association of the long fatty acid chains, which are attracted to each other by van der Waals forces (page 31). In the absence of cholesterol, these forces would tend to solidify the lipid bilayer.

There are two classes of membrane proteins: integral and peripheral membrane proteins. **Integral membrane proteins** are closely associated with the membrane lipids and cannot be extracted from the membrane without disrupting the lipid bilayer. Like the phospholipids, the integral proteins are amphipathic, having polar amino acid side chains located in one region of the molecule and nonpolar side chains clustered together in a separate region. Because they are amphipathic, integral proteins are arranged in the membrane with the same orientation as amphipathic lipids—the polar regions are at the surfaces in association with polar water molecules, and the nonpolar regions are in the interior in association with nonpolar fatty acid chains (Figure 3-7). Like the membrane lipids, many of the integral proteins can move laterally in the plane of the membrane, but others are immobilized because they are linked to a network of peripheral proteins located primarily at the cytoplasmic surface of the membrane.

Most integral proteins span the entire membrane and are referred to as "transmembrane" proteins. These proteins have two polar regions connected by a nonpolar segment that associates with the nonpolar regions of the lipids in the interior of the membrane. The polar regions of transmembrane proteins may extend far beyond the polar surface of the lipid bilayer. Some transmembrane integral proteins form channels through which ions or water can move across the membrane, whereas others are associated with the transmission of chemical signals across the membrane.

Peripheral membrane proteins are not amphipathic and do not associate with the nonpolar regions of the lipids in the interior of the membrane. They are located at the membrane surface where they are bound to the polar regions of the integral membrane proteins (Figure 3-7). Most of the peripheral proteins are located on the cytoplasmic surface of the plasma membrane rather than on the extracellular surface and are associated with such properties as cell shape and motility.

The plasma membrane also contains small amounts of carbohydrate covalently linked to some of the membrane lipids and proteins. These carbohydrates consist of short, branched chains of monosaccharides that extend from the cell surface into the extracellular fluid where they form a fuzzy, "sugar-coated" layer known as the **glycocalyx**. The carbohydrate portions of the membrane are all located at the extracellular surface. This is a second example of the asymmetrical distribution of membrane components, the first being the location of most peripheral proteins at the inner surface. In addition, the lipids in the outer half of the bilayer differ somewhat in kind and amount from those in the inner half, and, as we have seen, the proteins or portions of proteins on the outer surface differ from those on the inner surface. Many membrane functions are related to these asymmetries in chemical composition.

Although all membranes have the general structure described above, which has come to be known as the **fluid-mosaic model** (Figure 3-8), the proteins and, to a lesser extent, the lipids in the plasma membrane are dif-

FIGURE 3-7
Arrangement of integral and peripheral membrane proteins in association with a biomolecular layer of phospholipids. Dark-blue areas indicate the polar regions of integral membrane proteins.

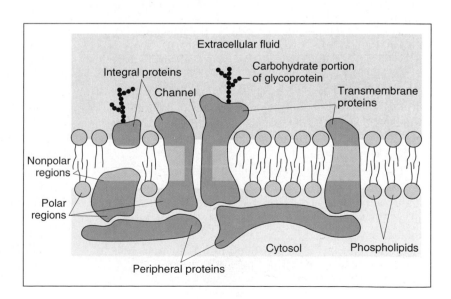

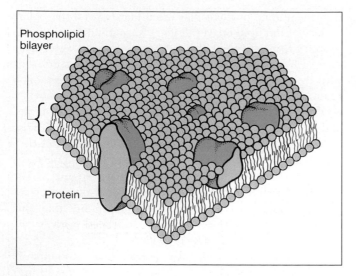

Phospholipid bilayer

Protein

FIGURE 3-8

Fluid-mosaic model of cell membrane structure. (*Redrawn from S. J. Singer and G. L. Nicholson, Science, 175:723. Copyright 1972 by the American Association for the Advancement of Science.*)

ferent from those in organelle membranes. Thus, the special functions of membranes, which depend primarily on the membrane proteins, are different in the various membrane-bound organelles and in the plasma membranes of different types of cells.

Membrane Junctions. In addition to providing a barrier to the movements of molecules between the intracellular and extracellular fluids, plasma membranes are involved in interactions between cells to form tissues. Some cells, particularly those of the blood, do not associate with other cells but remain as independent cells suspended in a fluid—the blood plasma in the case of blood cells. Most cells, however, are packaged into tissues and are not free to move around the body. But even the cells in a tissue are not packed so tightly that the adjacent cell surfaces are in direct contact with each other, except at certain specialized junctions. There usually exists a space of at least 20 nm between the opposing membranes of adjacent cells. This space is filled with extracellular fluid and provides the pathway for substances to pass between cells on their way to and from the blood.

The forces that organize cells into tissues and organs are poorly understood but depend, at least in part, on the ability of binding sites on the plasma membranes to recognize and associate with specific proteins that bind cells together.

Some tissues can be separated into individual cells by gentle procedures, such as shaking the tissues in a calcium-free medium. The absence of calcium ions decreases the ability of the cells to stick together, suggesting that the doubly charged Ca^{2+} may act as a link between cells by combining with negatively charged groups on adjacent cell surfaces. Many types of cells, however, require more drastic chemical procedures to separate them from their neighbors.

The electron microscope has revealed that many cells are physically joined by specialized types of membrane junctions known as desmosomes, tight junctions, and gap junctions.

Desmosomes (Figure 3-9A) consist of a region between two adjacent cells where the two opposed plasma membranes are separated by about 20 nm and have a dense accumulation of protein at each cytoplasmic membrane surface and in the space between the two membranes. In addition, fibers extend from the cytoplasmic surface into the cell and are linked to other desmosomes on the opposite side of the cell. The function of the desmosome is to hold adjacent cells firmly together in areas that are subject to considerable stretching, such as in the skin. The specialized area of the membrane in the region of a desmosome is usually disk-shaped, and these membrane junctions could be likened to rivets or spot welds.

A second type of membrane junction, the **tight junction** (Figure 3-9B), is formed when the extracellular surfaces of two adjacent plasma membranes are joined together so that there is no extracellular space between the adjacent cells. Unlike the desmosome, which is limited to a disk-shaped area of the membrane, the tight junction occurs in a band around the entire circumference of the cell. Tight junctions greatly restrict the movement of most organic molecules through the extracellular space between the joined cells, but they have a variable leakiness to small ions and water.

Most epithelial cells are joined by tight junctions. For example, epithelial cells cover the inner surface of the intestinal tract, where they come in contact with the digestion products in the cavity of the tract. During absorption, the products of digestion move across the epithelium and enter the blood. This transfer could take place by movement either through the extracellular space between the epithelial cells or through the epithelial cells themselves. Movement through the extracellular space is blocked by the tight junctions that encircle the cells near their luminal border. Thus, absorption of organic nutrients requires them to pass through cells, rather than between them. In this way the selective barrier properties of the plasma membrane can be used to control the types and amounts of absorbed substances. Figure 3-9D shows both a tight junction and a desmosome near the luminal border between two epithelial cells.

A third type of junction, the **gap junction**, contains protein channels linking the cytoplasms of adjacent cells (Figure 3-9C). In the region of the gap junction, the two

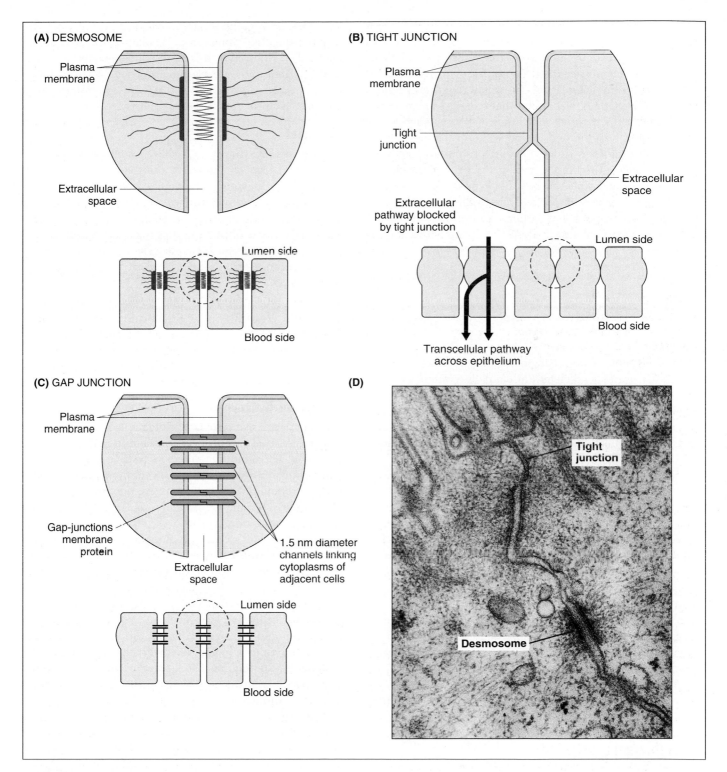

FIGURE 3-9

Three types of specialized membrane junctions: (A) desmosome, (B) tight junction, and (C) gap junction. (D) Electron micrograph of two intestinal epithelial cells joined by a tight junction near the luminal surface and a desmosome below the tight junction. [*Electron micrograph from M. Farquhar and G. E. Palade, Journal of Cell Biology, 17:375–412 (1963).*]

opposing plasma membranes come within 2 to 4 nm of each other, allowing proteins from the two membranes to become joined, thereby forming the walls of small channels. These channels extend across the gap between the cells, linking the cytoplasms. The small diameter of these channels (about 1.5 nm) limits what can pass between the connected cells to small molecules and ions, such as sodium and potassium, and excludes the exchange of large protein molecules. A variety of cell types possess gap junctions, including the muscle cells of the heart and smooth-muscle cells. As we shall see in Chapter 11, these gap junctions play a very important role in the transmission of electrical activity between certain types of muscle cells. In other cases, gap junctions coordinate the activities of adjacent cells by allowing chemical messengers to move from one cell to another.

CELL ORGANELLES

Nucleus

Almost all cells contain a single nucleus. (A few specialized types, for example, skeletal-muscle cells, contain multiple nuclei, while the mature red blood cell has none.) The primary function of the nucleus is the storage, transmission, and expression of genetic information used to synthesize the proteins that determine the structure and function of the cell (Chapter 4).

Surrounding the nucleus is a barrier, the **nuclear envelope**, composed of two membranes. At regular intervals along the surface of the nuclear envelope, the two membranes become joined to each other, forming the rims of circular openings known as **nuclear pores** (Figure 3-10). Molecules that regulate the expression of genetic information move between the nucleus and cytoplasm through these nuclear pores. Very large molecules, such as RNA and proteins, can move through the nuclear pores, but such movement is selective, that is, restricted to specific macromolecules. An energy-dependent process that alters the diameter of the pore in response to specific signals is involved in the transfer process.

Within the nucleus, DNA, in association with proteins, forms a fine network of threads, known as **chromatin**, that are coiled to a greater or lesser degree, producing the variations in the density of the nuclear contents seen in electron micrographs (Figure 3-10). When a cell divides, the chromatin threads become highly condensed to form **chromosomes**.

The most prominent organelle in the nucleus is the **nucleolus**, a highly coiled structure associated with numerous particles but not surrounded by a membrane. The nucleolus is composed of RNA and proteins associated with specific regions of DNA that contain the genes for forming the RNA found in particular cytoplasmic organelles called ribosomes. It is in the nucleolus that the subunits of ribosomes are assembled. These ribosomal subunits are transferred to the cytoplasm, where they combine to form functional ribosomes.

Ribosomes

Ribosomes are the sites at which protein molecules are synthesized from amino acids, using genetic information sent by RNA messenger molecules from DNA in the nucleus. Ribosomes are large particles, about 20 nm in diameter, each of which is composed of a large number of proteins and several RNA molecules (Chapter 4). Ribosomes are either bound to the organelle called granular endoplasmic reticulum (described next) or are found free in the cytoplasm.

The proteins synthesized on the free ribosomes are released into the cytosol, where they perform their functions. The proteins synthesized by ribosomes attached to the granular endoplasmic reticulum pass into the lumen of the reticulum from which they are transferred to yet another organelle, the Golgi apparatus.

Endoplasmic Reticulum

The most extensive cytoplasmic organelle is the network of membranes that forms the **endoplasmic reticulum** (Figure 3-11). The membranes enclose a space that is continuous throughout the network. The continuity of the endoplasmic reticulum is not obvious when examining a single electron micrograph because only a portion of the network is present in any one section.

Two forms of endoplasmic reticulum can be distinguished: **granular** (rough-surfaced) and **agranular** (smooth-surfaced). As noted above, the granular endoplasmic reticulum has ribosomes bound to its cytosolic surface, and it has a flattened-sac appearance. The outer membrane of the nuclear envelope also has ribosomes on its surface, and the space between the two nuclear envelope membranes is continuous with that of the granular endoplasmic reticulum. The agranular endoplasmic reticulum has no ribosomal particles on its surface and has a branched, tubular structure.

Both granular and agranular endoplasmic reticulum exist in the same cell. The relative amounts of the two types vary in different types of cells and even within the same cell during different periods of cell activity. Granular endoplasmic reticulum is involved in the packaging of proteins that are to be secreted by cells or distributed to other cell organelles (Chapter 6). The agranular endoplasmic reticulum is the site at which lipid molecules are synthesized (Chapter 5), and it also stores and releases calcium

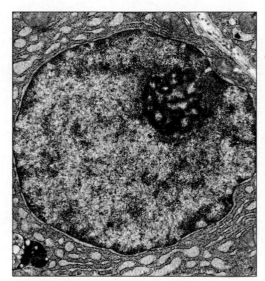

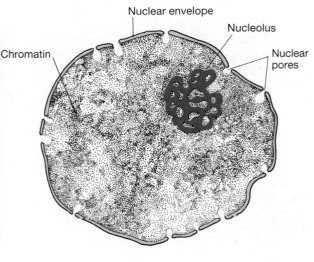

NUCLEUS

Structure: Largest organelle. Round or oval body located near cell center. Surrounded by nuclear envelope composed of two membranes. Envelope contains nuclear pores through which messenger molecules pass between the nucleus and the cytoplasm. No membrane-bound organelles are present in nucleus, which contains coiled strands of DNA known as chromatin, which condense to form chromosomes at the time of cell division.

Function: Stores and transmits genetic information in the form of DNA. Genetic information passes from the nucleus to the cytoplasm, where amino acids are assembled into proteins.

NUCLEOLUS

Structure: Densely stained filamentous structure within nucleus. Consists of proteins associated with DNA in regions where information concerning ribosomal proteins is being expressed.

Function: Forms subunits of ribosomal particles that move into the cytoplasm, where they function as sites of protein synthesis.

FIGURE 3-10
Components of cell nucleus. (*Electron micrograph courtesy of K. R. Porter.*)

ions involved in controlling various cell activities (Chapter 7).

Golgi Apparatus

The **Golgi apparatus** is a series of closely opposed, flattened membranous sacs that are slightly curved, forming a cup-shaped structure (Figure 3-12). Most cells have a single Golgi apparatus located near the nucleus, although some cells may have several. Associated with this organelle, particularly near its concave surface, are a number of approximately spherical, membrane-enclosed vesicles. The Golgi apparatus sorts the different types of proteins received from the granular endoplasmic reticulum into vesicles that will be delivered to various parts of the cell, including the plasma membrane where the protein contents of the vesicle are released to the outside of the cell. When proteins are secreted by cells, the vesicles that contain these proteins are known as **secretory vesicles**.

Mitochondria

Mitochondria (singular, *mitochondrion*) are primarily concerned with the chemical processes by which energy is made available to cells in the form of molecules of adenosine triphosphate (ATP) (Chapter 5). Most of the ATP

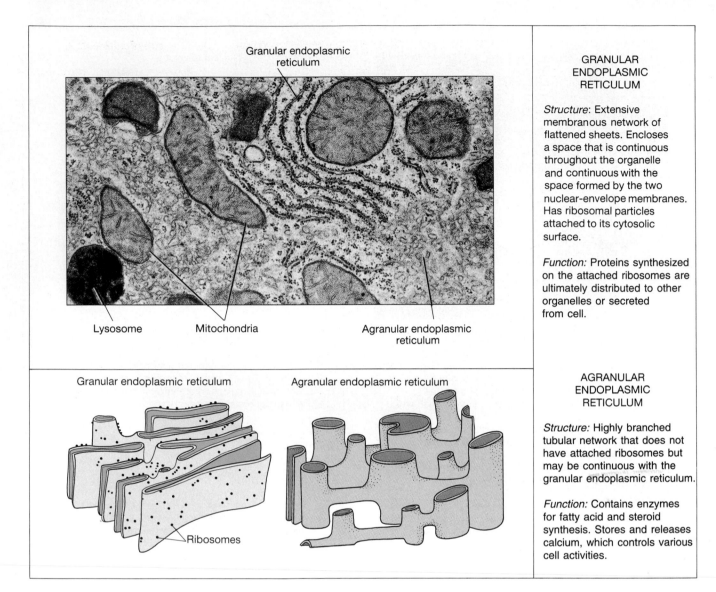

Granular endoplasmic reticulum

Lysosome   Mitochondria   Agranular endoplasmic reticulum

Granular endoplasmic reticulum   Agranular endoplasmic reticulum

Ribosomes

GRANULAR ENDOPLASMIC RETICULUM

Structure: Extensive membranous network of flattened sheets. Encloses a space that is continuous throughout the organelle and continuous with the space formed by the two nuclear-envelope membranes. Has ribosomal particles attached to its cytosolic surface.

Function: Proteins synthesized on the attached ribosomes are ultimately distributed to other organelles or secreted from cell.

AGRANULAR ENDOPLASMIC RETICULUM

Structure: Highly branched tubular network that does not have attached ribosomes but may be continuous with the granular endoplasmic reticulum.

Function: Contains enzymes for fatty acid and steroid synthesis. Stores and releases calcium, which controls various cell activities.

FIGURE 3-11

Endoplasmic reticulum. (*Electron micrograph from D. W. Fawcett, "The Cell: An Atlas of Fine Structure," W. B. Saunders, Philadelphia, 1966.*)

used by cells is formed in the mitochondria by a process that consumes oxygen and produces carbon dioxide.

Mitochondria are spherical or elongated, rodlike structures surrounded by an inner and an outer membrane (Figure 3-13). The outer membrane is smooth, whereas the inner membrane is folded into sheets or tubules, known as **cristae**, that extend into the inner compartment **(matrix)**. Mitochondria are found throughout the cytoplasm. Large numbers of them, as many as 1000, are present in cells that utilize large amounts of energy, whereas less active cells contain fewer.

Mitochondria have small amounts of DNA that contain the genes for the synthesis of some of the mitochondrial proteins. This DNA, which uses a slightly different genetic code than nuclear DNA (Chapter 4), was apparently acquired millions of years ago when a bacteria-like organism was engulfed by another cell and, rather than being destroyed, remained as a symbiotic organism within the cell.

Lysosomes

Lysosomes are spherical or oval organelles surrounded by a single membrane (Figure 3-11). A typical cell may con-

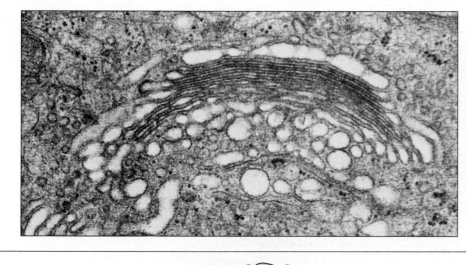

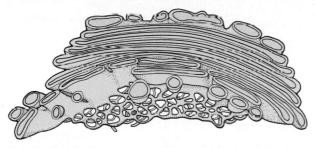

GOLGI APPARATUS

Structure: Series of cup-shaped, closely opposed, flattened, membranous sacs; associated with numerous vesicles. Generally, a single Golgi apparatus is located in central portion of cell near nucleus.

Function: Concentrates, modifies, and sorts newly synthesized proteins prior to their distribution, by way of the Golgi vesicles, to other organelles or their secretion from cell.

FIGURE 3-12

Golgi apparatus. (*Electron micrograph from W. Bloom and D. W. Fawcett, "Textbook of Histology," 9th ed. W. B. Saunders, Philadelphia, 1968.*)

tain several hundred lysosomes. The fluid within a lysosome is highly acidic and contains a variety of digestive enzymes. Lysosomes act as "cellular stomachs," breaking down bacteria and the debris from dead cells that have been engulfed by a cell. They may also break down cell organelles that have been damaged and are no longer functioning normally. They play an especially important role in the various specialized cells that make up the defense systems of the body (Chapter 20).

Peroxisomes

The structure of **peroxisomes** is similar to that of lysosomes, that is, oval bodies enclosed by a single membrane, but their chemical composition is quite different. Like mitochondria, peroxisomes consume oxygen, although in much smaller amounts, but this oxygen is not used in chemical reactions associated with ATP formation. Peroxisomes destroy certain products formed from oxygen, notably hydrogen peroxide, that can be quite toxic to cells—thus the organelles' name. In addition, the peroxisomes in

liver and kidney use the hydrogen peroxide formed to detoxify various ingested molecules.

Filaments

In addition to the membrane-enclosed organelles, the cytoplasm of most cells contains a variety of filaments. This filamentous network is referred to as the cell's **cytoskeleton** (Figure 3-14), and, like the bony skeleton of the body, it is associated with processes that maintain and change cell shape and produce cell movements.

There are four classes of filaments, based on their diameter and the types of protein they contain (Figure 3-15). In order of size, starting with the thinnest, they are (1) microfilaments, (2) intermediate filaments, (3) muscle thick filaments, and (4) microtubules. Microfilaments and microtubules can be rapidly assembled and disassembled, allowing a cell to change its cytoskeletal framework according to changing requirements. The other two types of filaments, once assembled, are less readily disassembled.

Microfilaments, which are composed of the contract-

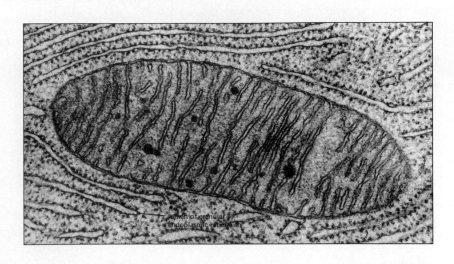

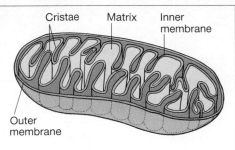

Cristae   Matrix   Inner membrane

Outer membrane

MITOCHONDRION

Structure: Rod- or oval-shaped body surrounded by two membranes. Inner membrane folds into matrix of the mitochondrion, forming cristae.

Function: Major site of ATP production, O_2 utilization, and CO_2 formation. Contains enzymes of Krebs cycle and oxidative phosphorylation.

FIGURE 3-13

Mitochondrion. (*Electron micrograph courtesy of K. R. Porter.*)

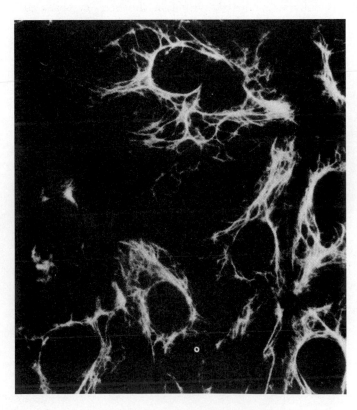

FIGURE 3-14

Cells stained to show the intermediate filament components of the cytoskeleton. [*From Roy A. Quinlan et al., Annals of the New York Academy of Sciences, 455:282–306 (1985).*]

ile protein **actin**, make up a major portion of the cytoskeleton in all cells. **Intermediate filaments** are most extensively developed in regions of cells that are subject to mechanical stress. **Muscle thick filaments**, composed of the contractile protein **myosin**, are found only in muscle cells. Individual molecules of myosin, however, are present in most nonmuscle cells where they are involved in producing forces associated with various cell movements.

Microtubules, which are composed of helical arrangements of the protein **tubulin**, are hollow tubes about 25 nm in diameter. They are the most rigid of the cytoskeletal filaments and are present in the long processes of nerve cells, where they provide the framework that maintains the processes' cylindrical shape. Microtubules are also associated with movements of parts of cells. For example, the spindle fibers responsible for separation of the

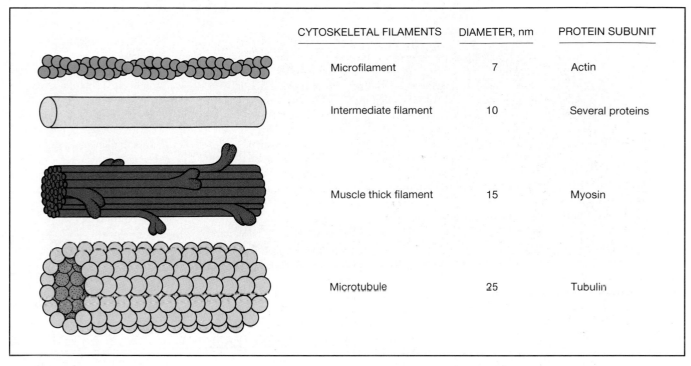

CYTOSKELETAL FILAMENTS	DIAMETER, nm	PROTEIN SUBUNIT
Microfilament	7	Actin
Intermediate filament	10	Several proteins
Muscle thick filament	15	Myosin
Microtubule	25	Tubulin

FIGURE 3-15

Cytoskeletal filaments associated with cell shape and motility.

chromosomes during cell division are composed of micro tubules, as are the **centrioles**, which are the organelles that generate the spindle fibers at the time of cell division (Figure 3-4).

The hairlike extensions—**cilia**—on the surface of some epithelial cells have a central core of microtubules, which produce the movements of the cilia. In hollow organs that are lined with ciliated epithelium, the cilia wave back and forth, propelling the luminal contents along the surface of the epithelium. Microtubules have also been implicated in the movements of organelles within the cytoplasm. The microtubules form tracks along which organelles are propelled by contractile proteins attached to the surface of the organelles.

SUMMARY

I. All living matter is composed of cells.

CELL COMPARTMENTS

I. Every cell is surrounded by a plasma membrane.

II. Within each cell are numerous membrane-bound compartments, nonmembranous particles, and filaments, known collectively as cell organelles.

III. A cell is divided into two regions, the nucleus and the cytoplasm, the latter composed of the cytosol and cell organelles other than the nucleus.

IV. The membranes that surround the cell and cell or-ganelles regulate the movements of molecules and ions into and out of the cell and its compartments.

A. Membranes consist of a bimolecular lipid layer, composed of phospholipids and cholesterol, in which proteins are embedded.

B. The lipid layer prevents the movement of most molecules through the membrane, while the proteins provide pathways for the selective entry of substances.

C. Integral membrane proteins are amphipathic proteins that often span the membrane, whereas peripheral membrane proteins are confined to the surfaces of the membrane.

V. Three types of membrane junctions link adjacent cells:
  A. Desmosomes link cells that are subject to considerable stretching.
  B. Tight junctions, found primarily in epithelial cells, limit the passage of molecules through the extracellular space between the cells.
  C. Gap junctions form channels between the cytoplasms of adjacent cells.

CELL ORGANELLES

I. The nucleus transmits and expresses genetic information.
  A. Threads of chromatin, composed of DNA and protein, condense to form chromosomes when a cell divides.
  B. The nucleolus is the site at which ribosomal subunits are formed.

II. Ribosomes, composed of RNA and protein, are the sites of protein synthesis.

III. The endoplasmic reticulum is a network of flattened sacs and tubules in the cytoplasm.
  A. Granular endoplasmic reticulum has attached ribosomes and is primarily involved in the packaging of proteins that are to be secreted by the cell.
  B. Agranular endoplasmic reticulum is tubular, lacks ribosomes, and is the site of lipid synthesis and calcium accumulation and release.

IV. The Golgi apparatus sorts the proteins that are synthesized on the rough endoplasmic reticulum and packages them into secretory vesicles.

V. Mitochondria are the major sites at which chemical energy is transferred to ATP.

VI. Lysosomes digest particulate matter that enters the cell.

VII. Peroxisomes break down certain toxic products formed from oxygen.

VIII. The cytoplasm contains a network of four types of filaments known as the cytoskeleton: (1) microfilaments, (2) intermediate filaments, (3) muscle thick filaments, and (4) microtubules.

KEY TERMS

light microscope	cell organelles
electron microscope	nucleus
prokarotic cells	cytoplasm
eukaryotic cells	cytosol
viruses	intracellular fluid
plasma membrane	phospholipids

cholesterol	Golgi apparatus
integral membrane proteins	secretory vesicles
peripheral membrane proteins	mitochondria
glycocalyx	mitochondrial cristae
fluid-mosaic model	mitochondrial matrix
desmosomes	lysosomes
tight junction	peroxisomes
gap junction	cytoskeleton
nuclear envelope	microfilaments
nuclear pores	actin
chromatin	intermediate filaments
chromosomes	muscle thick filaments
nucleolus	myosin
ribosomes	microtubules
endoplasmic reticulum	tubulin
granular endoplasmic reticulum	centrioles
agranular endoplasmic reticulum	cilia

REVIEW QUESTIONS

1. In terms of the size and number of cells, what makes an elephant larger than a mouse?

2. Identify the location of cytoplasm, cytosol, and intracellular fluid within a cell.

3. Identify the classes of organic molecules in cell membranes and describe the major contribution of each to membrane function.

4. Describe the orientation of the phospholipid molecules in a membrane.

5. Which plasma membrane components are responsible for membrane fluidity?

6. Describe the location and characteristics of integral and peripheral membrane proteins.

7. Describe the structure and function of the three types of junctions found between cells.

8. What function is performed by the nucleolus?

9. Describe the location and function of ribosomes.

10. Contrast the structure and functions of the granular and agranular endoplasmic reticulum.

11. What function is performed by the Golgi apparatus?

12. Describe the structure and primary function of mitochondria.

13. What functions are performed by lysosomes and peroxisomes?

14. List the four types of filaments associated with the cytoskeleton. Identify the structures in cells that are composed of microtubules.

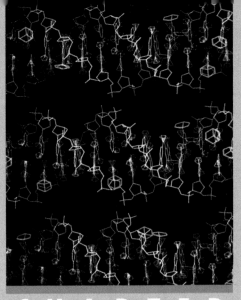

CHAPTER

4

MOLECULAR CONTROL MECHANISMS: PROTEINS AND DNA

SECTION A. BINDING SITES ON PROTEINS

BINDING-SITE CHARACTERISTICS

Chemical Specificity

Affinity

Saturation

Competition

REGULATION OF BINDING-SITE CHARACTERISTICS

Allosteric Modulation

Covalent Modulation

SECTION A SUMMARY

SECTION A KEY TERMS

SECTION A REVIEW QUESTIONS

SECTION B. GENETIC INFORMATION AND PROTEIN SYNTHESIS

GENETIC CODE

PROTEIN SYNTHESIS

Transcription: mRNA Synthesis

Translation: Polypeptide Synthesis

Ribosomes

Transfer RNA

Protein assembly

Protein Secretion

Regulation of Protein Synthesis

REPLICATION AND EXPRESSION OF GENETIC INFORMATION

Replication of DNA

Cell Division

Mutation

Recombinant DNA

CANCER

SECTION B SUMMARY

SECTION B KEY TERMS

SECTION B REVIEW QUESTIONS

CHAPTER 4 CLINICAL TERMS

CHAPTER 4 THOUGHT QUESTIONS

The outstanding accomplishment of twentieth-century biology has been the discovery of the chemical basis of heredity and its relationship to protein synthesis. Whether an organism is a human being or a mouse, has blue eyes or black, has light skin or dark, is determined by the proteins it possesses. Moreover, within an individual organism, muscle cells differ from nerve cells or epithelial cells or any other type of cell because of the types of proteins they contain and the functions performed by these proteins.

Crucial for an understanding of protein function is the fact that each protein has a unique shape, which determines its interaction with other molecules. In the first section of this chapter the relation between protein shape and function is described.

The hereditary information in each cell contains the instructions for synthesizing the cell's proteins. These instructions are coded into DNA molecules. The second section of this chapter describes the chemical basis of the genetic code and the decoding mechanisms that lead from DNA to protein synthesis.

Given that different cell types have different proteins and that the specifications for these proteins are coded in DNA, one might be led to conclude that different cell types contain different DNA molecules. However, such is not the case. All cells in the body, with the exception of sperm or eggs, receive the same genetic information when DNA molecules are duplicated and passed on to daughter cells at the time of cell division. Cells differ in structure and function because only a portion of the total genetic information common to all cells is used by any given cell to synthesize proteins. The last portion of this chapter describes some of the factors that govern the selective expression of genetic information, as well as the process by which DNA molecules are replicated and their genetic information passed on to daughter cells during cell division.

BINDING-SITE CHARACTERISTICS

The ability to bind various molecules and ions to specific sites on the surface of a protein forms the basis for the wide variety of functions performed by proteins. A **ligand** is any molecule or ion that is bound to the surface of a protein by forces other than covalent chemical bonds. These forces are either (1) attractions between oppositely charged ionic or polarized groups on the ligand and the protein, or (2) weaker attractions due to van der Waals forces between nonpolar regions on the two molecules (page 31). The region of a protein to which a ligand binds is known as a **binding site**. A protein may contain several binding sites, each specific for a particular ligand.

Chemical Specificity

The force of electrical attraction between oppositely charged regions on a protein and a ligand decreases markedly as the distance between them increases. The even weaker van der Waals forces act only between nonpolar groups that are very close to each other. Therefore, in order for a ligand to bind to a protein, the ligand must be close to the protein surface. This occurs when the shape of the ligand is complementary to the shape of the protein binding site, such that the two fit together like pieces of a jigsaw puzzle (Figure 4-1).

The binding between a ligand and a protein may be so specific that a binding site can bind only one type of ligand and no other. Such selectivity allows a protein to "identify" (by binding) one particular molecule in a solution containing hundreds of different molecules. This ability of a protein to bind specific ligands is known as **chemical specificity**, since the binding site determines the type of chemical that is bound.

In the previous chapter we described how the conformation of a protein is determined by the location of the various amino acids along the polypeptide chain. Accordingly, proteins with different amino acid sequences have different shapes and therefore differently shaped binding sites, each with its own chemical specificity. As illustrated in Figure 4-2, the amino acids that interact with a ligand at the binding site need not be adjacent to each other along the polypeptide chain since the folding of the protein may bring various segments of the molecule into juxtaposition.

Although some binding sites have a chemical specificity that allows them to bind only one type of ligand, other binding sites may be less specific and thus be able to bind a number of related ligands. For example, three different ligands can combine with the binding site of protein X in Figure 4-3 since a portion of each ligand is complementary to the shape of the binding site. In contrast, protein Y has a greater, that is, more limited, specificity and can bind only one of the three ligands.

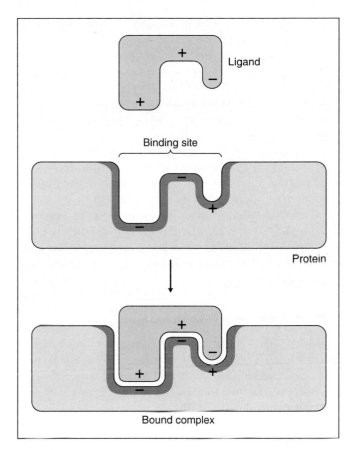

FIGURE 4-1

Complementary shapes of ligand and protein binding site determine the chemical specificity of binding.

Affinity

The strength of ligand-protein binding is a property of the binding site known as **affinity**. The affinity of a binding site for a ligand determines how likely it is that a bound ligand will leave the protein surface and return to its unbound state. Binding sites that tightly bind a ligand are called high-affinity binding sites; those to which the ligand is weakly bound are low-affinity binding sites.

Affinity and chemical specificity are two distinct, although closely related, properties of binding sites. Chemical specificity, as we have seen, depends only on the shape of the binding site, whereas affinity depends on the strength of the attraction between the protein and the ligand. Thus, different proteins may be able to bind the same ligand, that is, may have the same chemical specificity, but may have different affinities for that ligand. For example, a ligand may have a negatively charged ionized group that would bind strongly to a site containing a positively charged amino acid side chain but would bind less strongly (Figure 4-4) to a binding site having the same shape but no positive charge. In addition, the closer the

surfaces of the ligand and binding site to each other, the stronger the electrical or van der Waals attractions. Hence, the more closely the ligand shape matches the binding-site shape, the greater the affinity. In other words, shape can influence affinity as well as chemical specificity.

Saturation

In a solution containing both ligands and proteins, some ligands will bind to unoccupied binding sites on the proteins, while some of the bound ligands will come off. At any given time, a binding site will be either occupied or unoccupied. The term **saturation** refers to the fraction of binding sites that are occupied at any given time. When all the binding sites are occupied, the population of binding sites is 100 percent saturated. When half the available sites

FIGURE 4-2

Amino acids that interact with the ligand at a binding site need not be at adjacent sites along the polypeptide chain, as indicated in this model showing the three-dimensional folding of a protein. The unfolded polypeptide chain is shown below.

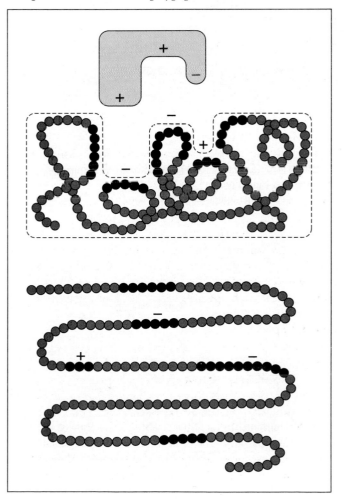

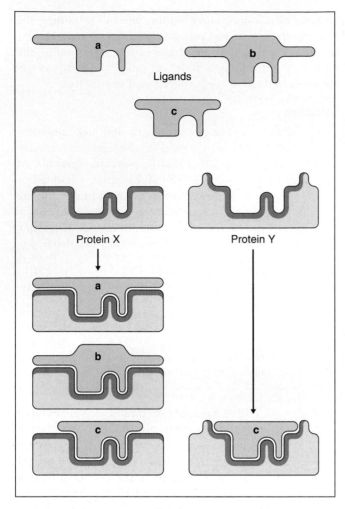

FIGURE 4-3

Protein X is able to bind all three ligands, which have similar chemical structures. Protein Y, because of the shape of its binding site, can bind only ligand c. Protein Y, therefore, has a greater chemical specificity than protein X.

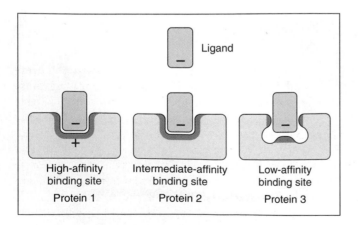

FIGURE 4-4

Three binding sites with the same chemical specificity for a ligand but different affinities.

are occupied, the system is 50 percent saturated, and so on. A *single* binding site would also be 50 percent saturated if it were occupied by a ligand 50 percent of the time.

The percent saturation of a binding site depends upon two factors: (1) the concentration of unbound ligand in the solution, and (2) the affinity of the binding site for the ligand.

The greater the ligand concentration, the greater the probability of a ligand molecule encountering an unoccupied binding site and becoming bound. Thus, the percent saturation of binding sites will increase with increasing ligand concentration until all the sites become occupied (Figure 4-5). Assuming that the ligand is a molecule that exerts a biological effect when it is bound to a protein, the magnitude of the effect would also increase with increasing numbers of bound ligands until all the binding sites were occupied. Further increases in ligand concentration would produce no further effect since there would be no additional sites to be occupied. To generalize, a continuous increase in the magnitude of a chemical stimulus (ligand concentration), which exerts its effects by binding to proteins, will produce an increased biological response up to the point where the protein binding sites become 100 percent saturated.

The second factor determining the percent of binding-site saturation is the affinity of the binding site. Collisions between molecules in a solution and a protein containing a bound ligand can dislodge a loosely bound ligand, just as tackling a football player may cause a fumble. If a binding site has a high affinity for a ligand, even a low ligand concentration will result in a high degree of saturation since, once bound to the site, the ligand is not easily dislodged. A low-affinity site, on the other hand, requires a much higher concentration of ligand to achieve the same degree of saturation (Figure 4-6) since any given ligand remains bound for a much shorter period of time, requiring more frequent encounters between unbound ligand and the binding site to keep the site occupied. One measure of binding-site affinity is the ligand concentration necessary to produce 50 percent saturation; the lower the ligand concentration required to produce 50 percent saturation, the greater the affinity of the binding site (Figure 4-6).

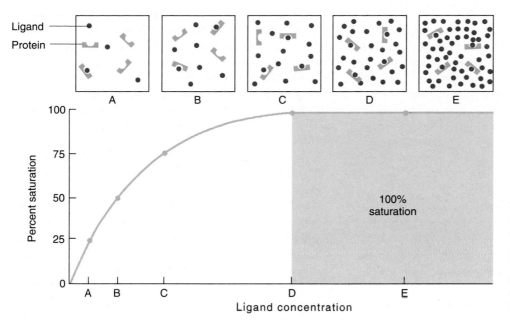

FIGURE 4-5

Increasing ligand concentration increases the number of binding sites occupied, that is, increases the percent saturation. At 100 percent saturation, all the binding sites are occupied, and further increases in ligand concentration do not increase the amount bound.

Competition

As we have seen, more than one type of ligand can bind to certain binding sites (Figure 4-3). In such cases **competition** occurs between the ligands for the same binding site.

FIGURE 4-6

When two different proteins, X and Y, are able to bind the same ligand, the protein with the higher-affinity binding site (protein Y) has more bound sites at any given ligand concentration until 100 percent saturation.

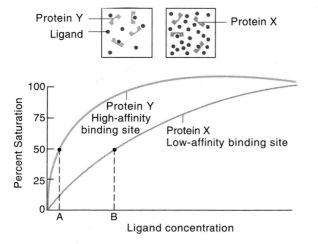

In other words, the presence of multiple ligands able to bind to the same binding site affects the percentage of binding sites occupied by any one ligand. If two competing ligands, A and B, are present, increasing the concentration of A will increase the amount of A that is bound, thereby decreasing the number of sites available for the binding of B and decreasing the amount of B that is bound.

As a result of competition, the biological effects of one ligand may be markedly diminished by the presence of another. For example, many drugs produce their effects by competing with the body's natural ligands for binding sites. By occupying the binding sites, the drug decreases the amount of natural ligand that can be bound.

REGULATION OF BINDING-SITE CHARACTERISTICS

Because proteins are associated with practically every cell function, the mechanisms for controlling these functions center on the control of protein activity. There are two ways of controlling protein activity: (1) Changing protein shape alters its binding of ligands; and (2) regulation of protein synthesis determines the types and amounts of proteins in a cell. The first type of regulation—control of protein shape—is discussed in this section, and the second—protein synthesis—in later sections.

Since a protein's shape depends on electrical attractions

between charged or polarized groups in various regions of a protein (page 31), a change in the charge distribution along a protein or in the polarity of the molecules immediately surrounding it will alter its shape. The two mechanisms used by cells to selectively alter protein shape are allosteric modulation and covalent modulation.[1] Before describing these mechanisms, however, it should be emphasized that most proteins are not subject to either allosteric or covalent modulation. Only certain key proteins are regulated by these mechanisms.

Allosteric Modulation

Whenever a ligand binds to a protein, the attracting forces between ligand and protein alter the protein's shape. For example, as a ligand approaches a binding site, these attracting forces can cause the surface of that binding site to bend into a shape that more closely approximates the shape of the ligand's surface.

Moreover, as the shape of a binding site changes during binding, it will produce changes in the shape of *other* regions of the protein outside that particular binding site, just as pulling on one end of a rope (the polypeptide chain) will cause the other end of the rope to move. Therefore, when a protein contains two binding sites, the binding of a ligand to one site can alter the shape of the second binding site and, hence, the binding characteristics of that site. This is termed **allosteric** (other shape) **modulation** (Figure 4-7), and such proteins are known as **allosteric proteins**.

One binding site on an allosteric protein, known as the **functional site** (also termed the active site), carries out the protein's physiological function. The other binding site is the **regulatory site**, and the ligand that binds to this site is known as a **modulator molecule** since its binding to the regulatory site allosterically modulates the shape and thus the activity of the functional site.

The regulatory site to which modulator molecules bind is the equivalent of a molecular switch that controls the functional site. In some allosteric proteins, the binding of the modulator molecule to the regulatory site turns *on* the functional site by changing its shape so that it can bind the functional ligand. In other cases, the binding of a modulator molecule turns *off* the functional site by preventing the functional site from bindings its ligand. In still other cases, binding of the modulator molecule may decrease or in-

crease the affinity of the functional site. For example, if the functional site is 50 percent saturated at a particular ligand concentration, the binding of a modulatory ligand that increases the affinity of the functional site may increase its saturation to 75 percent.

To summarize, the activity of a protein can be increased without changing the concentration of either the protein or the functional ligand. By controlling the concentration of the regulatory ligand, and thus the percent saturation of the regulatory site, the functional activity of an allosterically regulated protein has the potential of being altered over the entire range from 0 to 100 percent activity.

We have spoken thus far only of interactions between regulatory and functional binding sites. There is, however, a way that functional sites can influence each other in certain proteins. These proteins are composed of more than one polypeptide chain held together by electrical attractions between the chains. There may be only one binding site, a functional binding site, on each chain. The binding of a functional ligand to one of the chains, however, can result in an alteration of the functional binding sites in the other chains. This happens because the change in shape of the chain to which the ligand is bound induces a change in the shape of the other chains. This interaction between the functional binding sites of a multimeric protein is known as **cooperativity**. It can result in a progressive increase in the affinity for ligand binding as more and more of the sites become occupied. This occurs, for example, in the binding of oxygen to hemoglobin, a protein composed of four polypeptide chains, each containing one binding site for oxygen.

Covalent Modulation

A second way to alter the shape and therefore the activity of a protein is to covalently bind charged chemical groups to some of the protein's side chains. This is known as **covalent modulation**. In most cases a phosphate group, which has a net negative charge, is covalently attached by a chemical reaction called **phosphorylation**.

When one of the side chains in certain amino acids in a protein is phosphorylated, a negative charge is introduced into this region of the protein. This alters the distribution of electric forces in the protein, producing a change in protein conformation (Figure 4-7). If this conformational change affects a binding site, it will change the binding site's properties. Although the mechanism is completely different, the *effects* produced by covalent modulation are the same as those of allosteric modulation; that is, a functional binding site may be turned on or off or the affinity of the site for its ligand may be altered.

To reiterate, unlike allosteric modulation, which involves simple *binding* of modulator molecules, covalent modulation requires chemical reactions in which covalent bonds are formed. Most chemical reactions in the body are

---

[1]Two additional nonspecific factors that alter protein shape are (1) temperature, which alters the amount of kinetic energy available for breaking the electrostatic attractions between various regions of a protein; and (2) acidity, which alters the ionization of amino acid side chains. Because both these factors are maintained relatively constant in the body, they are not usually used to selectively regulate protein activity. Should large changes in temperature or acidity occur, however, as in disease, they can produce marked alterations in protein shape and thus in protein activity.

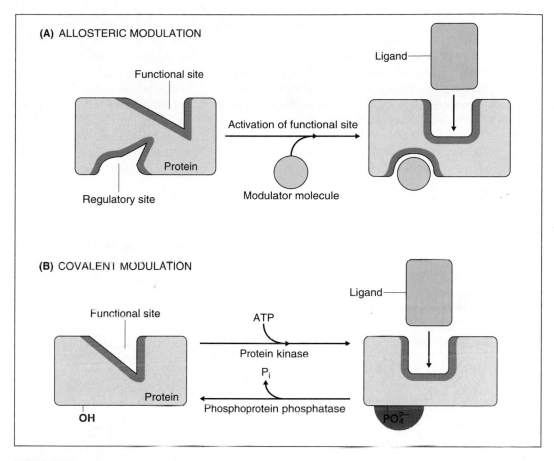

FIGURE 4-7

(A) Allosteric modulation. Binding of a modulator molecule at a regulatory site alters the shape of the functional site. (B) Covalent modulation. Phosphorylation of a hydroxyl group on an amino acid side chain in one region of the protein alters the shape of the functional site located in another region of the protein. The enzyme protein kinase catalyzes the phosphorylation of the protein, whereas a second enzyme, phosphoprotein phosphatase, removes the phosphate group, returning the protein to its original shape.

mediated by a special class of proteins known as **enzymes**, whose properties will be discussed in Chapter 5. For now, suffice it to say that enzymes accelerate the rate at which molecules called substrates are converted to different molecules called products. Any enzyme that mediates protein phosphorylation is called a **protein kinase**. These enzymes catalyze the transfer of phosphate from a molecule of adenosine triphosphate (ATP) (see Chapter 5) to a hydroxyl group present on the side chain of certain amino acids:

$$\text{Protein} + \text{ATP} \xrightarrow{\text{Protein kinase}} \text{protein—PO}_4^{2-} + \text{ADP}$$

The protein and ATP are the substrates for protein kinase, and the phosphorylated protein and ADP are the products of the reaction.

There is also a mechanism for removing the phosphate group and returning the protein to its original shape. This dephosphorylation is accomplished by a second enzyme known as **phosphoprotein phosphatase**:

$$\text{Protein—PO}_4^{2-} + \text{H}_2\text{O} \xrightarrow{\text{Phosphoprotein phosphatase}} \text{protein} + \text{HPO}_4^{2-}$$

Thus, two enzymes control a protein's activity by covalent modulation: one that adds phosphate and one that removes it.

Although most proteins contain amino acids capable of being phosphorylated, only those proteins that are substrates for specific protein kinases are actually phosphorylated. There are many protein kinases, each with specificities for different proteins, and several kinases may be present in the same cell. The chemical specificities of the phosphoprotein phosphatases are broader, and a single enzyme can dephosphorylate many different phosphorylated proteins. Moreover, unlike protein kinases, phosphoprotein phosphatases tend to be continuously active.

When a particular protein kinase is active, the rate of phosphorylation of the protein it acts upon exceeds that of dephosphorylation, and most of the protein molecules being covalently modulated are maintained in the phosphorylated state. Dephosphorylating such protein molecules requires only stopping the kinase reaction since the continuously active phosphoprotein phosphatase will remove the phosphate groups.

An important interaction between allosteric and covalent modulation results from the fact that protein kinases are themselves allosteric proteins and so can be controlled by modulator molecules. Thus, the process of covalent modulation is itself indirectly regulated by allosteric mechanisms. In addition, some allosteric proteins can also be modified by covalent modulation.

SECTION A SUMMARY

BINDING-SITE CHARACTERISTICS

   I. Ligands bind to proteins at sites that have shapes that are complementary to the ligand shape.
  II. Protein binding sites have the properties of chemical specificity, affinity, saturation, and competition.

REGULATION OF BINDING-SITE CHARACTERISTICS

   I. Protein activity in a cell can be controlled by regulating either the shape of the protein or the amount of protein synthesized.
  II. The binding of a modulator molecule to the regulatory site on an allosteric protein alters the shape of the functional binding site, thereby altering its binding characteristics and the activity of the protein. The activity of allosteric proteins is regulated by varying the concentrations of their modulator molecules.
 III. Protein kinase enzymes catalyze the addition of a phosphate group to the side chains of certain amino acids in a protein, changing the shape of the protein's binding site and thus altering the protein's activity by covalent modulation. A second enzyme is required to remove the phosphate group, returning the protein to its original state.

SECTION A KEY TERMS

ligand

binding site

chemical specificity
affinity
saturation
competition
allosteric modulation
allosteric proteins
functional site
regulatory site

modulator molecule
cooperativity
covalent modulation
phosphorylation
enzymes
protein kinase
phosphoprotein phosphatase

SECTION A REVIEW QUESTIONS

1. List the four characteristics of a protein binding site.
2. List the types of forces that hold a ligand on a protein surface.
3. What characteristics of a binding site determine its chemical specificity?
4. Under what conditions can a single binding site have a chemical specificity for more than one type of ligand?
5. What characteristics of a binding site determine its affinity for a ligand?
6. What two factors determine the percent saturation of a binding site?
7. Describe the mechanism responsible for competition in terms of the properties of binding sites.
8. What are two ways of controlling protein activity in a cell?
9. How is the activity of an allosteric protein modulated?
10. How does regulation of protein activity by covalent modulation differ from that by allosteric modulation?

GENETIC INFORMATION AND PROTEIN SYNTHESIS

GENETIC CODE

Molecules of DNA contain instructions, coded in the sequence of nucleotides, for the synthesis of proteins. A sequence of nucleotides containing the information that determines the amino acid sequence of a single polypeptide chain is known as a **gene**. A gene is thus a unit of hereditary information, and a single molecule of DNA contains many genes. The total collection of genes that specifies a particular organism's structure and function is known as its **genome**. The human genome contains between 50,000 and 100,000 genes.

As an example of the expression of genetic information, consider eye color, which is due to the presence of pigment molecules in certain cells in the eye. Sequences of enzyme-mediated reactions are required to synthesize these pigments, and the genes that determine eye color do so by coding for different enzymes in these pathways. Note that these genes do not contain any information about the chemical structure of the eye pigments. All they contain is the information required to synthesize the enzymes that mediate the formation of the pigments.

Within the human population a given gene exists in a number of slightly different nucleotide sequences that have resulted from mutations (see below). These variants of the same gene are known as **alleles**. At the time of conception the fertilized egg contains two copies of each of its genes,[2] one gene supplied by the mother's egg and the other allelic gene from the father's sperm. Both genes may have identical nucleotide sequences, in which case the individual is said to be **homozygous** for that particular gene, or the two genes may have slightly different nucleotide sequences (different alleles), in which case the individual is **heterozygous** for that gene.

The alleles of a particular gene can be classified as being either **dominant genes** or **recessive genes**, depending on the effects they have when present in a cell. A single copy of a dominant gene will cause the production of the protein coded for by that gene regardless of the protein coded for by its corresponding allelic gene. In the case of recessive genes, both alleles must code for the same protein (or no protein at all). For example, the gene that codes for the enzyme that leads to the production of black eye pigment is a dominant gene. If this gene is inherited from either the mother or the father, the child will have black eyes. In contrast, the gene for blue eyes is recessive, and a child must receive two copies of this gene, one from the mother and one from the father, to produce blue eyes.

Although DNA contains the information necessary for the synthesis of proteins, it does not itself participate *directly* in the assembly of protein molecules. Most of a cell's DNA is in the nucleus (a small amount is in the mitochondria), whereas most protein synthesis occurs in the cytoplasm. The transfer of information from DNA to the site of protein synthesis is the function of RNA molecules (page 35), whose synthesis is governed by the information in DNA. This mechanism for expressing genetic information occurs in all living organisms and is called the "central dogma" of molecular biology: Genetic information flows from DNA to RNA and then to protein:[3]

$$DNA \longrightarrow RNA \longrightarrow protein$$

Figure 4-8 summarizes the general pathway by which the information stored in DNA influences cell activity via protein synthesis.

As described on page 34, a molecule of DNA consists of two polynucleotide chains coiled around each other to form a double helix (see Figure 2-22). Each nucleotide contains one of four bases—adenine (A), guanine (G), cytosine (C), or thymine (T)—and each of these bases is specifically paired, A to T and G to C, with a base on the opposite chain of the double helix. Thus, both nucleotide chains contain a specifically ordered sequence of bases, one chain being complementary to the other.

The genetic language is similar in principle to a written

---

[2]Actually there are not two copies of every gene, only of most genes. Of the 23 pairs of chromosomes, one set, the sex chromosomes (see Chapter 19), do not contain corresponding copies of the same genes. In addition, some genes are present in multiple copies at different sites along a given DNA molecule.

---

[3]In some viruses, genetic information can be transferred from RNA to protein in the absence of DNA, while in other viruses the flow can be from RNA to DNA to RNA to protein.

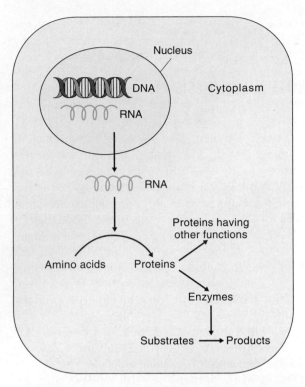

FIGURE 4-8

The expression of genetic information in a cell occurs through its transcription from DNA to RNA in the nucleus, followed by the translation of the RNA information into protein synthesis in the cytoplasm.

FIGURE 4-9

Relation between the sequence of triplet code words in one strand of DNA and the amino acid sequences of proteins that correspond to them. The names of the amino acids are abbreviated. Note that all three genes are part of the same DNA molecule, which may contain hundreds of genes in a linear sequence, each gene being composed of hundreds of sequential bases.

language, which consists of a set of symbols, such as α, β, δ, γ, forming an alphabet. The letters are arranged in specific sequences to form words, and the words are arranged in linear sequences to form sentences. The genetic language contains only four letters, corresponding to the four bases A, G, C, and T. The words are three-base sequences that specify particular amino acids; that is, each word in the genetic language is only three letters long. This is termed a triplet code. These triplets are arranged in a linear sequence along DNA, and the sequence of triplets specifying the structure of a single protein makes up a gene (Figure 4-9). A typical human gene may consist of a sequence of approximately 20,000 base pairs. Thus, a gene is equivalent to a sentence, and the entire collection of genes in a cell is equivalent to a book—the human genome.

The four bases in the DNA alphabet can be arranged in 64 different three-letter combinations ($4 \times 4 \times 4 = 64$). Thus, a triplet code actually provides more than enough words to code for 20 amino acids. It turns out, however, that not just 20, but 61 of the 64 possible triplets are used to specify amino acids. This means that a given amino acid is usually specified by more than one code word. For example, the four triplets C-C-A, C-C-G, C-C-T, and C-C-C all specify the same amino acid, glycine.

The three triplets that do not specify amino acids are known as **termination code words**. They perform the same function as does a period at the end of a sentence—they indicate that the end of a genetic message has been reached. The code word for the amino acid methionine does double duty by also indicating the beginning of the gene.

The **genetic code** is a universal language used by all living cells. For example, the code words for the amino acid tryptophan are the same in the DNA of a bacterium, an amoeba, a plant, and a human being. Although the same code words are used by all living cells, the messages

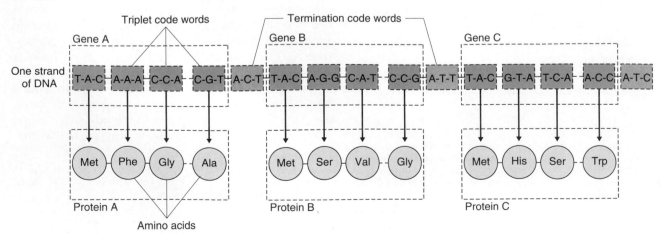

they spell out—the sequences of code words (the "sentences") that determine the amino acid sequences in proteins—are different in each organism. The universal nature of the genetic code supports the concept that all forms of life on earth evolved from a common ancestor.

PROTEIN SYNTHESIS

Molecules of DNA are too large to pass through the nuclear membrane into the cytoplasm. Yet it is in the cytoplasm, on ribosomes, that proteins are synthesized. Since DNA cannot leave the nucleus, a message carrying genetic information must pass from the nucleus to the cytoplasm. This message is carried by RNA molecules known as **messenger RNA (mRNA)**. The transfer of genetic information from DNA to protein thus occurs in two stages: First, the genetic message is passed from DNA to mRNA in the nucleus **(transcription)**; second, the message in mRNA passes from the nucleus to the cytoplasm where it is used to direct the assembly of the specific sequence of amino acids to form a particular protein **(translation)**.

Transcription: mRNA Synthesis

During transcription, the sequence of nucleotides in a gene in one of the DNA molecules is used to determine the sequence of nucleotides in mRNA corresponding to that gene. As described on page 35, ribonucleic acids are single-chain polynucleotides whose nucleotides differ from DNA in that they contain the sugar ribose (rather than deoxyribose) and the base uracil (rather than thymine). The other three bases—adenine, guanine, and cytosine—occur in both DNA and RNA. The pool of subunits used to synthesize mRNA are free (uncombined) ribonucleotides, each containing three phosphate groups (ribonucleotide triphosphates): ATP, GTP, CTP, and UTP.

In DNA, the two polynucleotide chains are linked together by hydrogen bonds (page 35) between specific pairs of bases—A pairing with T, and G with C. Transcription begins with the breakage of these hydrogen bonds so that a portion of the two chains of the DNA double helix separates (Figure 4-10). The bases in the exposed DNA nucleotides are then able to pair with the bases in the free ribonucleotide triphosphates. Free ribonucleotides containing adenine pair with any exposed thymine base in DNA. Likewise, free ribonucleotides containing G, C, or U pair with the exposed DNA bases C, G, and A, respectively. (Note that uracil, which is present in RNA but not DNA, pairs with the base adenine in DNA.) In this way, the nucleotide sequence in DNA acts as a template that determines the sequence of nucleotides in mRNA.

The aligned ribonucleotides are joined together by the enzyme **RNA polymerase**. This enzyme, which binds to a specific site on DNA just ahead of the gene to be transcribed, catalyzes both the splitting off of two of the three phosphate groups from each nucleotide and the covalent linkage of the RNA ribonucleotide to the next one in the sequence. RNA polymerase is active only when bound to DNA and will not link free ribonucleotides together (in what would be a random sequence) when they are not

FIGURE 4-10

Transcription of a gene from a single strand of DNA to mRNA.

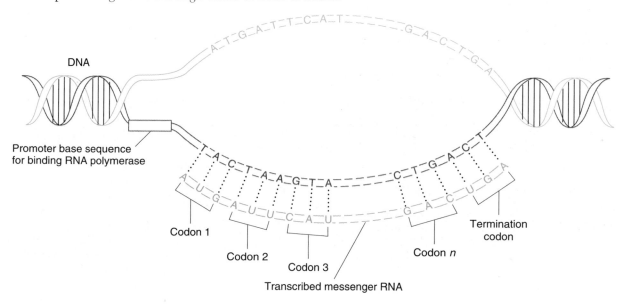

base-paired with DNA. DNA acts as a modulator molecule that allosterically activates RNA polymerase.

Since DNA consists of two strands of polynucleotides, both of which are exposed during transcription, it should theoretically be possible to form two different mRNA molecules, one from each strand. However, only one of the two potential mRNAs is ever formed. Which of the two DNA strands is used as the template for mRNA synthesis is determined by a specific sequence of nucleotides in DNA, called the **promoter**, located at the beginning of each gene (Figure 4-10). The promoter, to which RNA polymerase binds, is present in only one of the two DNA strands. Beginning at the promoter end of a gene, the RNA polymerase separates the two DNA strands as it moves along one strand, joining one ribonucleotide at a time to the growing mRNA chain until it reaches a termination code word at the end of the gene. This causes the RNA polymerase to release the newly formed mRNA.

In a given cell, the information in only a few of the thousands of genes present in DNA is transcribed into mRNA at any given time. Genes are transcribed only when RNA polymerase can bind to their promoter sites. Various mechanisms are used by cells either to block or to make accessible the promoter region of any particular gene. Such regulation of gene transcription provides a means of controlling the synthesis of specific proteins and thereby the activities of cells.

It must be emphasized that the base sequence in mRNA is not *identical* to that in the corresponding strand of DNA, since its formation depends on the pairing between complementary, not identical, bases (Figure 4-10). A three-base sequence in mRNA that specifies one amino acid is called a **codon**. Each codon is *complementary* to a three-base sequence in DNA. For example, the base sequence T-A-C in DNA corresponds to the codon A-U-G in mRNA.

Although the entire sequence of nucleotides in a gene is transcribed into a corresponding sequence of nucleotides in mRNA, only certain segments of the gene actually code for sequences of amino acids. These regions of the gene, known as **exons** (expression regions), are separated by noncoding sequences of nucleotides known as **introns** (intervening sequences). Before passing to the cytoplasm, a newly formed mRNA must undergo splicing (Figure 4-11) to remove the sequences that correspond to the DNA introns. Nuclear enzymes that identify specific nucleotide sequences at the beginning and end of each intron sequence remove the sequence from mRNA and splice the end of one exon-derived sequence to the beginning of another to form an mRNA with no intron-derived segments. In some cases, the exon-derived sequence from a single gene can be spliced together in several different ways, resulting in the formation of different mRNAs from the same gene and giving rise, in turn, to several different proteins.

The mRNAs formed as a result of RNA splicing are 75 to 90 percent shorter than the originally transcribed mRNA, meaning that 75 to 90 percent of the nucleotide

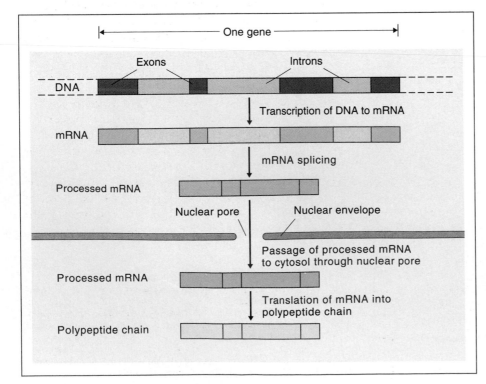

FIGURE 4-11

RNA splicing removes the noncoding sequences (corresponding to the introns in DNA) before the mRNA passes through the nuclear pores to the cytosol. The length of the intron and exon segments represent the relative lengths of the base sequences in these regions.

sequences in DNA are introns. What role such large amounts of "nonsense" DNA may perform is unclear.

Finally, it should be noted that not all genes give rise to mRNA and hence code for proteins. Some genes code for other RNA molecules that perform other functions in the process of protein synthesis, as described in the next sections.

Translation: Polypeptide Synthesis

Once transcribed and spliced, the mRNA moves through the pores in the nuclear envelope into the cytoplasm where it binds to a ribosome, the cell organelle that contains the enzymes and other components required for the translation of mRNA's coded message into protein. Before describing this assembly process, we must first present the structure of a ribosome as well as the characteristics of two additional types of RNA involved in protein synthesis.

Ribosomes. As described in Chapter 3, ribosomes are small granules (diameter about 23 nm) located in the cytoplasm, either suspended in the cytosol (free ribosomes) or attached to the surface of the endoplasmic reticulum (bound ribosomes). Proteins synthesized on free ribosomes are released into the cytosol, whereas those synthesized on bound ribosomes are inserted through the membrane of the endoplasmic reticulum and released into its lumen, from which they are either secreted by the cell or transferred to various other organelles (see below).

Each ribosome contains many proteins in association with a type of RNA known as **ribosomal RNA (rRNA)**. Ribosomal RNA is synthesized in the nucleus, with DNA again serving as a template for positioning the sequence of nucleotides in rRNA. The genes that code for rRNA, however, are associated with the nucleolus, which is also the site at which the protein and rRNA components of the ribosome are combined before passing into the cytoplasm.

Transfer RNA. How do individual amino acids identify the appropriate codons in mRNA during the process of translation? By themselves, free amino acids do not have the ability to bind to the bases in mRNA codons. This process of identification involves yet a third type of RNA, known as **transfer RNA (tRNA)**. Transfer RNA molecules are the smallest (about 80 nucleotides long) of the three types of RNA. The single chain of tRNA loops back upon itself, forming a structure resembling a cloverleaf with three loops (Figure 4-12).

Like mRNA and rRNA, tRNA is synthesized in the nucleus by base-pairing with DNA nucleotides at specific tRNA genes and then moves to the cytoplasm. The key to tRNA's role in protein synthesis is that it can combine with both a specific amino acid and a codon in ribosome-bound mRNA specific for that amino acid. This permits tRNA to act as the link between an amino acid and the mRNA codon for that amino acid.

Transfer RNA is covalently linked to an amino acid by an enzyme known as aminoacyl-tRNA synthetase. There are at least 20 different aminoacyl-tRNA synthetases, each of which catalyzes the linkage of a specific amino acid to a particular type of tRNA. The next step is to link the tRNA, bearing its attached amino acid, to the mRNA codon for that amino acid. As one might predict, this is achieved by base-pairing between tRNA and mRNA. A three-nucleotide sequence at the end of one of the loops of tRNA can base-pair with a complementary codon in mRNA. This tRNA triplet sequence is appropriately termed an **anticodon**. Figure 4-13 illustrates the binding between mRNA and a tRNA specific for the amino acid alanine. Note that alanine is covalently linked to one end of tRNA and does not itself bind to the anticodon region.

Protein Assembly. The individual amino acids linked to mRNA by tRNA must now be bound to each other by peptide bonds. Several ribosomal proteins and rRNA interact in a complex manner to identify the initial codon sequence in mRNA and to catalyze the formation of a peptide bond between the first and second amino acids in the peptide chain being synthesized.[4] This initial step is the slowest step in protein assembly, and the rate of protein synthesis can be regulated by factors that influence this initiation process.

Following the initiation of a protein's synthesis, the polypeptide chain is elongated by the successive addition of amino acids (Figure 4-13). A ribosome has two binding sites for tRNA. One holds the tRNA attached to the most recently added amino acid, and the other holds the tRNA containing the next amino acid to be added to the chain. Ribosomal enzymes catalyze the formation of a peptide bond between these two amino acids. Following the formation of the peptide bond, the tRNA at the first binding site is released from the ribosome, and the tRNA at the second site—now linked to the peptide chain—is transferred to the first binding site. The ribosome moves one codon space along the mRNA, making room for the binding of the next amino acid–tRNA molecule. This process is repeated over and over as each amino acid is added in succession to the growing peptide chain, at an average rate of two to three amino acids per second. When the ribo-

---

[4]Although rRNA accounts for the major portion of a cell's RNA, its precise function in the process of protein synthesis is still unclear. It is thought by some to be the remnant of an earlier stage in our evolutionary past in which RNA molecules acted as the major catalysts of chemical reactions in cells before being superseded in this role by protein enzymes. This role may be retained in the ribosome, where rRNA appears to be able to catalyze the formation of peptide bonds between the incoming amino acids and the growing polypeptide chain.

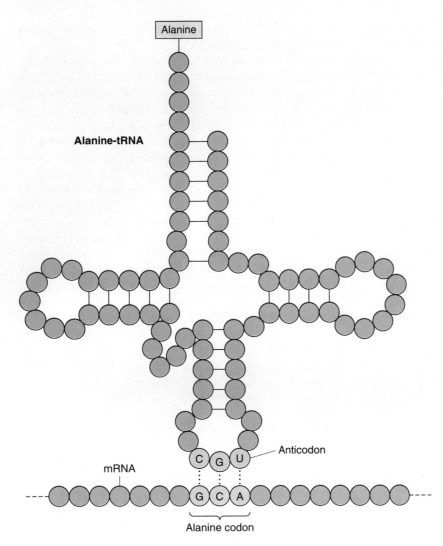

FIGURE 4-12

Base-pairing between the anticodon region of a tRNA molecule and the corresponding codon region of a mRNA molecule.

some reaches a termination codon in mRNA specifying the end of the protein, the link between the polypeptide chain and the last tRNA is broken, and the completed protein is released from the ribosome.

A single strand of mRNA can be used to synthesize many molecules of the protein because the mRNA is not destroyed during protein assembly. Moreover, while one ribosome is moving along a particular strand of mRNA, a second ribosome may become attached to the mRNA and begin the synthesis of a second identical protein molecule. Thus, a number of ribosomes, as many as 70, may be attached to the same strand of mRNA at any one time (Figure 4-14).

Molecules of mRNA do not, however, remain in the cytoplasm indefinitely. Eventually they are broken down into nucleotides by cytoplasmic enzymes. Therefore, if a gene corresponding to a particular protein ceases to be transcribed into mRNA, the synthesis of that protein will eventually slow down and cease as the mRNA is broken down.

The function of a protein, as we have noted, depends on its conformation, which determines its ability to bind specific ligands. A newly synthesized polypeptide comes off a ribosome as an essentially linear amino acid chain, which must then fold into its proper conformation. For some proteins this folding occurs spontaneously and is solely determined by the amino acid sequence of the proteins. For others, particularly large proteins, a number of other special proteins, known as **chaperones**, guide the folding of large segments of newly formed proteins into their proper conformations.

Finally, changes can occur in the structure of some polypeptide chains after their synthesis on a ribosome. Certain classes of proteins, the glycoproteins for example, are formed by the posttranslational addition of various carbohydrate groups to the protein. In other cases, specific peptide bonds in a large polypeptide are enzymatically broken to produce a number of shorter polypeptides, each of which may perform a different function. For example, as illustrated in Figure 4-15, five proteins can be derived

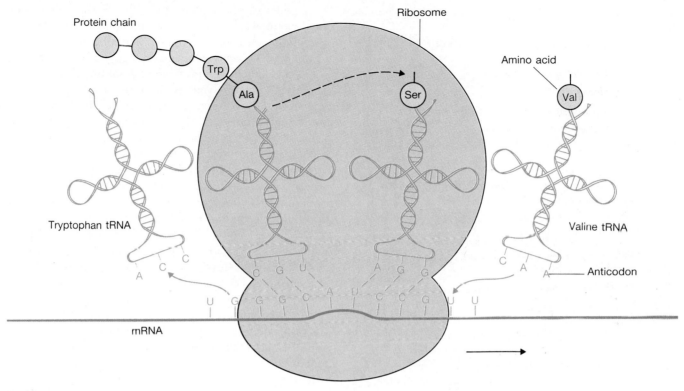

FIGURE 4-13

Sequence of events during the synthesis of a protein on the surface of a ribosome. The three-base anticodon of tRNA carrying one amino acid, for example, serine (ser), binds to the corresponding codon of mRNA, and the tRNA transfers its amino acid to the growing polypeptide chain. As the ribosome moves along the strand of mRNA, successive amino acids are added to the polypeptide chain.

FIGURE 4-14

Several ribosomes can simultaneously move along the same strand of messenger RNA, producing proteins in different states of assembly.

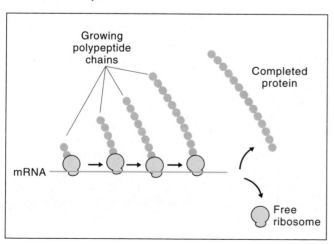

FIGURE 4-15

Posttranslational splitting of a protein can result in several proteins, each of which may perform a different function. All these proteins are derived from the same gene.

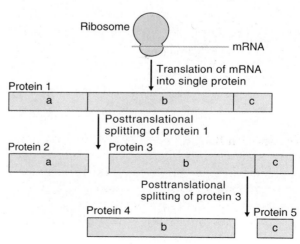

from the same mRNA as a result of posttranslational changes.

The steps leading from DNA to protein are summarized in Table 4-1.

Protein Secretion

A fact not stated earlier is that upon arriving in the cytoplasm from the nucleus, a molecule of mRNA binds to a *free* ribosome and begins the process of translating its message into a polypeptide chain. But during synthesis of the protein the ribosome may not remain free but may become attached to the endoplasmic reticulum. The first 15 to 30 amino acids to be linked together in the growing polypeptide chain determine the fate of the ribosome and where the protein's synthesis will be completed.

This initial portion of some protein chains is known as the **signal sequence** (or signal peptide). If there is no signal sequence at the beginning of the protein, synthesis is completed on the free ribosome and the protein is released into the cytosol. If there is a signal sequence, however, it acts as a ligand that binds to a site on the surface of the granular endoplasmic reticulum. By this mechanism ribosomes become attached to the reticulum. Once the mRNA, with its attached ribosome and growing polypeptide chain, is bound to the reticulum, the polypeptide chain is inserted through the reticulum membrane as additional amino acids are added to the polypeptide (Figure 4-16).

At the completion of its synthesis, the polypeptide with a signal sequence is either released into the lumen of the endoplasmic reticulum or remains inserted in the reticular membrane as a membrane protein. The mechanism by which the growing polypeptide chain passes through the reticulum membrane is unknown. This is the only stage along its route to the outside of the cell at which a protein that is to be secreted passes directly through a membrane.

Within the lumen of the endoplasmic reticulum, enzymes remove the signal sequence from most proteins, and so this portion is not present in the final protein. In addition, carbohydrate groups are added to these proteins by enzymes in the endoplasmic reticulum. Almost all proteins that are secreted are glycoproteins.

Following these modifications, portions of the reticulum membrane bud off, forming vesicles that contain the newly synthesized proteins. These vesicles migrate to the Golgi apparatus (Figure 4-16) and fuse with the Golgi membranes. Within the Golgi apparatus the protein undergoes still further modification. Some of the carbohydrates that were added in the granular endoplasmic reticulum are now removed and new groups added. These latter carbohydrate groups function as labels that can be recognized when the protein encounters various binding sites during the remainder of its trip through the cell.

While in the Golgi apparatus, the many different proteins that have been funneled into this organelle become sorted out according to their final destination. How this sorting takes place is largely unknown, but it involves selective binding of the proteins to different regions of the Golgi membrane.

Following modification and sorting, the proteins are packaged into vesicles that bud off the surface of the Golgi membrane. Some of the vesicles travel to the plasma membrane where they fuse with the membrane and release their contents to the extracellular fluid, a process

---

TABLE 4-1 EVENTS LEADING FROM DNA TO PROTEIN SYNTHESIS

Transcription

1. RNA polymerase binds to the promoter region of a gene and separates the two strands of the DNA double helix in the region of the gene to be transcribed.

2. Free ribonucleotide triphosphates base-pair with the deoxynucleotides in DNA.

3. The ribonucleotides paired with one strand of DNA are linked by RNA polymerase to form mRNA containing a sequence of bases complementary to one strand of the DNA base sequence.

4. mRNA splicing removes the intron regions of mRNA, which contain noncoding sequences, and splices together the exon regions, which code for specific amino acids.

Translation

5. Processed mRNA passes from the nucleus to the cytoplasm, where one end of the mRNA binds to a ribosome.

6. Free amino acids are linked to their corresponding tRNAs by aminoacyl-tRNA synthetase.

7. The three-base anticodon in an amino acid–tRNA complex pairs with the corresponding codon in the region of the mRNA bound to the ribosome.

8. The portion of the peptide that has already been synthesized (and is still attached to a tRNA bound to the ribosome) is now linked by a peptide bond to the amino acid on the tRNA next to it, thereby adding one more amino acid to the chain.

9. The tRNA that has been freed of the peptide chain is released from the ribosome.

10. The ribosome moves one codon step along mRNA.

11. Steps 7 to 10 are repeated over and over until the end of the mRNA message is reached.

12. The completed protein chain is released from the ribosome when the termination codon in mRNA is reached.

13. Chaperone proteins guide the folding of some proteins into their proper conformation.

14. In some cases, the protein undergoes posttranslational processing in which various chemical groups are attached to specific side chains or the protein is split into several smaller peptide chains.

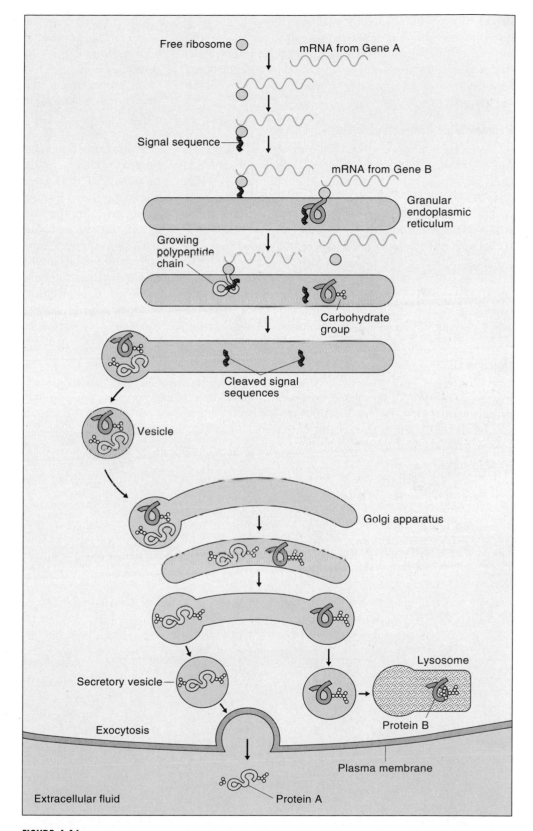

FIGURE 4-16

Pathway traveled by proteins that are to be secreted by cells or transferred to lysosomes.

known as exocytosis (Chapter 6). Other vesicles fuse with lysosome membranes, delivering digestive enzymes to the interior of this organelle. Where a particular vesicle goes, to the plasma membrane or to a lysosome, was determined by the sorting and "addressing" events that occurred in the Golgi apparatus.

Regulation of Protein Synthesis

As noted earlier, in any given cell only a small fraction of the 50,000 to 100,000 genes in the human genome are transcribed into mRNA and translated into proteins. Most genes are not transcribed because RNA polymerase is unable to bind effectively to the promoter sites of these genes. Thus, in order to transcribe a particular gene, something must happen that allows RNA polymerase to function at that gene's promoter site.

The key element in this process is the presence or absence of a group of proteins known as **transcription factors**, which can bind to specific regions of DNA and allow RNA polymerase to initiate transcription. A single tran-

scription factor can turn on the transcription of a number of genes that produce proteins related in function. Thus, there need not be a different transcription factor for each gene. Since any given cell is actively transcribing only a small proportion of the total genome, only a relatively small number of transcription factors need be produced by any given cell.

There still remains the problem of what turns on the genes for the transcription factors? Associated with the promoter regions of genes for transcription factors are proteins that can be activated by allosteric or covalent modulation in response to signals originating within the cell or reaching the cell via the extracellular fluid, for example, hormones. Modulation of these proteins allows RNA polymerase to initiate transcription of the gene leading to the formation of the particular transcription factor, which can then initiate the transcription of the other genes for which it is specific (Figure 4-17).

Once a gene's code has been transcribed into mRNA, the rate at which the corresponding protein is formed is

FIGURE 4-17

Control of gene transcription (gene A in diagram) by means of protein transcription factors that interact with RNA polymerase at specific promoter sites. A specific transcription factor may be formed in response to extracellular signals that initiate their transcription.

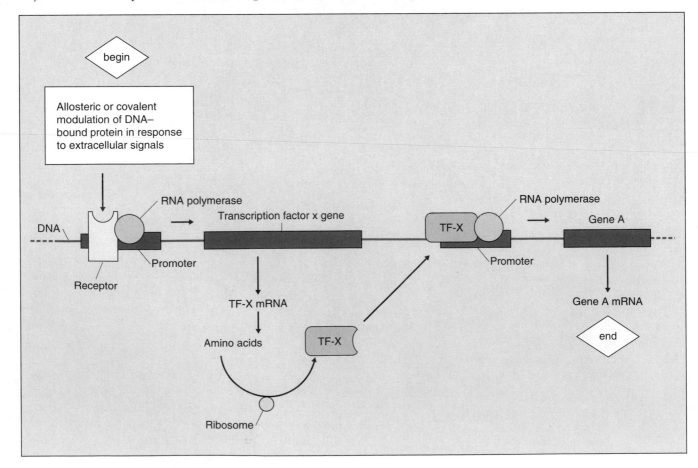

still subject to regulation at several stages between mRNA and the finished protein. For example, regulating the rate of mRNA breakdown will control the average time a molecule of mRNA remains in the cytoplasm and thus the number of protein molecules it forms. Finally, the translation process that occurs on the ribosome can be slowed down or speeded up. One or more of the above regulatory mechanisms may be involved in the synthesis of any given protein.

REPLICATION AND EXPRESSION OF GENETIC INFORMATION

The development of the human body from a single fertilized egg involves cell growth, division, and differentiation into specialized types such as nerve and muscle cells. The maintenance of structure and function in the adult also requires these same processes. Each process depends on the controlled synthesis of proteins, but cell division requires, in addition, the replication of DNA and the transmission of identical copies of this genetic information to each of the two resulting cells.

Replication of DNA

DNA is the only molecule in a cell able to duplicate itself without information from some other cell component. In contrast, as we have seen, RNA can only be formed using the information present in DNA, protein formation uses the information in mRNA, and all other molecules use the protein enzymes in metabolic pathways that determine the structure of the products formed.

DNA replication is, in principle, similar to the process whereby mRNA is synthesized. During DNA replication (Figure 4-18), the two strands of the double helix separate, but the exposed bases in *each* strand base-pair with free *deoxyribonucleotide* triphosphates present in the nucleus. The enzyme **DNA polymerase** then links the free nucleotides together, forming a new strand of DNA. The end result is two identical molecules of DNA, each called a "copy." In each copy, one strand of nucleotides is from the original DNA molecule and one strand has been newly synthesized.

Before cell division, the DNA molecules are replicated by the above process. One copy is passed on to each of the two new cells, termed **daughter cells**, when the cell divides. Thus, the daughter cells receive a copy of the same genetic information present in the parent cell.

Cell Division

Starting with a single fertilized egg, the first cell division produces 2 cells. When these daughter cells divide, they each produce 2 cells, giving a total of 4. These 4 cells

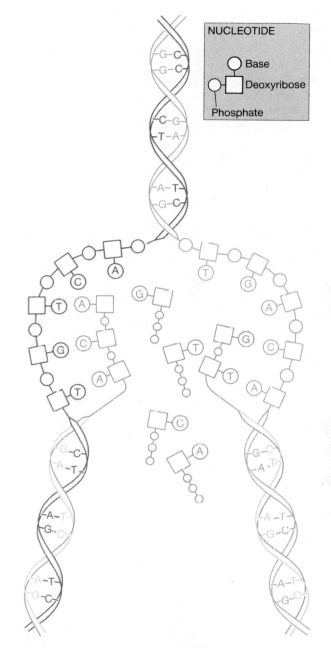

FIGURE 4-18

Replication of DNA involves the pairing of free deoxyribonucleotides with the bases of each DNA strand, giving rise to two new identical DNA molecules, each containing one old and one new polynucleotide strand.

produce a total of 8, and so on. Thus, starting from a single cell, 3 division cycles will produce 8 cells (2^3), 10 division cycles will produce $2^{10} = 1024$ cells, and 20 division cycles will produce $2^{20} = 1,048,576$ cells. If the development of the human body involved only cell division and growth without any cell death, only about 46 division cycles would be needed to produce all the cells in the adult body. However, large numbers of cells die during the course of development, and even in the adult many cells survive only a few days and are continually replaced by the division of existing cells.

The time between cell divisions varies considerably in different types of cells, and the most rapidly growing cells divide about once every 24 h. During most of this period, there is no visible evidence that the cell will divide. For example, in a 24-h division cycle, visible changes in cell structure begin to appear only 1 h before division. The period between the end of one division and the appearance of the structural changes that indicate the beginning of the next division is known as **interphase**. Since cell division takes only about 1 h, the cell spends most of its time in interphase, and most of the cell properties described in this book are properties of interphase cells.

One very important event related to subsequent cell division does occur during interphase, namely, the replication of DNA, which begins about 10 h before the first visible signs of division and lasts about 7 h. This period of the cell cycle is known as the S phase (synthesis) (Figure 4-19). Following the end of DNA synthesis there is a brief interval, G_2 (second gap), before the physical signs of cell division begin. The period from the end of cell division to the beginning of the S phase is the G_1 (first gap) phase of the cell cycle.

FIGURE 4-19

Phases of the cell cycle in a cell that divides every 24 h. A cell may leave the cell cycle and enter the G_0 phase in which division ceases unless it receives a specific signal to reenter the cycle.

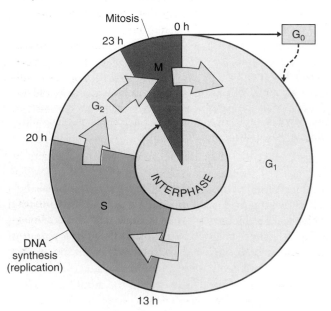

Cell division involves two processes: nuclear division (**mitosis**) and cytoplasmic division (**cytokinesis**). Although mitosis and cytokinesis are separate events, the term "mitosis" is often used in a broad sense to include the subsequent cytokinesis, and so the two events constitute the M phase (mitosis) of the cell cycle. Mitosis that is not followed by cytokinesis produces the multinucleated cells found in the liver, placenta, and some embryonic cells and cancer cells.

During most of interphase, DNA is dispersed throughout the nucleus in association with proteins called histones to form 46 extended nucleoprotein threads known as **chromatin** (Figure 4-20A). At the time of conception 23 of these chromatin threads were supplied by the mother's egg and 23 from one of the father's sperm. All 46 are duplicated during the S phase, and copies are passed on to each daughter cell during mitosis. When each of the 46 chromatin threads replicates, the result is two identical threads termed **sister chromatids**, which initially are joined together at one point known as the **centromere** (Figure 4-20B). In other words, there are now 46 pairs of sister chromatids. As a cell enters mitosis (Figure 4-20C), each chromatid pair becomes highly coiled and condensed, forming visible rod-shaped bodies known as **chromosomes** ("colored bodies," so named because of their intense staining by the dyes used to visualize structures under a microscope).

As the chromosomes condense, the nuclear membrane breaks down, and the chromosomes become linked, at their centromeres, to spindle fibers. The **spindle fibers**, composed of microtubules, generate the forces that divide the cell. Some of the spindle fibers extend between two **centrioles** (Figure 4-20C) located on opposite sides of the cell, while others connect the centrioles to the chromosomes. During the preceding interphase, at the time that DNA was replicating, the second centriole formed and the two centrioles moved to opposite sides of the nucleus and began to generate the spindle fibers. The spindle fibers and centrioles constitute the **mitotic apparatus**. A single centriole will pass to each of the daughter cells during cytokinesis.

As mitosis proceeds, the sister chromatids in each chromosome separate at the centromere and move toward the opposed centrioles (Figure 4-20D). Cytokinesis begins as the sister chromatids separate. The cell begins to constrict along a plane perpendicular to the axis of the mitotic apparatus, and constriction continues until the cell has been pinched in half, forming the two daughter cells (Figure 4-20E). Following cytokinesis, the spindle fibers dissolve, a nuclear envelope forms, and the chromatids uncoil in each daughter cell to form chromatin threads once again.

The forces producing the movements associated with mitosis and cytokinesis are generated by a family of contractile proteins similar to those producing the forces generated by muscle cells (see Chapter 11).

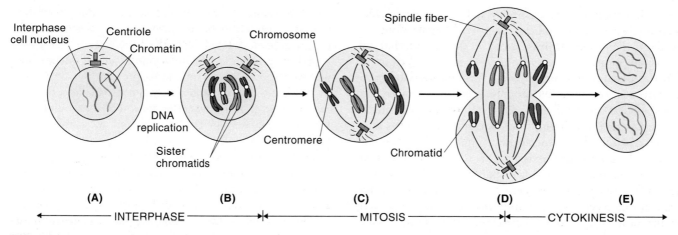

FIGURE 4-20

Mitosis and cytokinesis. (Only 4 of the 46 chromosomes in a human cell are illustrated.) (A) During interphase, chromatin exists in the nucleus as long, extended threads. (B) Prior to the onset of mitosis, DNA replicates, forming two sister chromatids that are joined at the centromere. A second centriole is also formed at this time. (C) As mitosis begins, the chromatids condense into chromosomes, which become attached to spindle fibers. (D) The two chromatids of each chromosome separate and move toward opposite poles of the cell as the cell divides (cytokinesis) into two daughter cells (E).

There are two classes of cells in the adult body with regard to the capacity to undergo cell division. Some cells proceed continuously through one cell cycle after another, while others do not normally divide. The first group constitutes the stem cells that provide a continuous supply of cells that differentiate into specialized cells to replace those that are continuously lost, such as blood cells, skin cells, and the cells lining the intestinal tract. The second class includes a number of differentiated, specialized cell types, such as nerve and striated muscle cells, that never divide once they have been formed. Such cells leave the cell cycle and enter a phase known as G_0 (Figure 4-19) in which they are prevented from progressing on to the next division. In some cases, however, a cell in the G_0 phase, upon receiving an appropriate signal, can reenter the cell cycle, begin replicating DNA, and proceed on to mitosis.

There are two critical control points in the cell cycle, at which special events must occur in order for a cell to progress to the next phase. One is at the boundary between G_1 and S, and again between G_2 and M. A group of **cell division cycle genes** (cdc genes) code for specific protein kinase enzymes that are essential for the cell to progress beyond its current phase in the cycle.

A protein, called **cyclin**, whose concentration progressively increases during interphase and then rapidly falls during mitosis, acts as a modulator molecule to activate the kinase enzymes produced by the cdc genes. Once activated, the kinase enzymes phosphorylate, and thus activate or inhibit, a variety of proteins involved in the division process, including an enzyme that digests cyclin and thus prepares the cell to begin the next division cycle.

Mutation

In order to form the 40 trillion cells of the adult human body, a minimum of 40 trillion individual cell divisions must occur.[5] Thus, the DNA in the original fertilized egg must be replicated at least 40 trillion times. Actually, many more than 40 trillion divisions occur during the growth of a fertilized egg into an adult human being since, as noted earlier, many cells die during development and are replaced by the division of existing cells.

If a secretary were to type the same manuscript 40 trillion times, one would expect to find some typing errors. Likewise, it is not surprising to find that during the duplication of DNA, errors occur that result in an altered sequence of bases and a change in the genetic message. What is amazing is that DNA can be duplicated so many times with relatively few errors.

A mechanism called **proofreading** corrects errors in the base sequence as it is being duplicated and is largely responsible for the low error rate observed during DNA replication. As described earlier, the replication process involves pairing between the base in a free deoxyribonucleotide and the appropriate complementary base in the old strand of DNA. DNA polymerase catalyzes the linking

---

[5]To be absolutely accurate, one less than 40 trillion cell divisions.

of the free nucleotide to the end of the new strand of DNA and then proceeds to the next nucleotide pair along the chain. If, however, an incorrect free nucleotide has become temporarily paired with a base in the old strand of DNA (for example, C pairing with A rather than its appropriate partner G), the DNA polymerase somehow "recognizes" this abnormal pairing and will not proceed in the linking of nucleotides until the abnormal pairing has been replaced. Note that in performing this proofreading, the DNA polymerase needs to identify only two configurations, the normal A-T and G-C pairing; any other combination halts polymerase activity. In this manner each nucleotide, as it is inserted into the new DNA chain, is checked for its appropriate complementarity to the base in the old chain.

Any alteration in the genetic message carried by DNA is known as a **mutation**. Factors in the environment that increase the mutation rate are known as **mutagens** and include certain chemicals and various forms of ionizing radiation, such as x-rays, cosmic rays, and atomic radiation. Most of these mutagens break chemical bonds in DNA so that incorrect pairing between bases occurs or the wrong base is incorporated when the broken bonds are reformed. Even in the absence of specific agents that increase the likelihood of mutations, the mutation rate is never zero.

The simplest type of mutation occurs when a single base is inserted at the wrong position in DNA. For example, the base sequence C-G-T forms the DNA code word for the amino acid alanine. If guanine (G) is replaced by adenine (A) in this sequence, it becomes C-A-T, which is the code word for valine.[6] It is during the replication of DNA, when free nucleotides are being incorporated into new strands of DNA, that incorrect base substitution is most likely to occur.

In a second type of mutation, large sections of DNA are deleted from the molecule or single bases are added or deleted. Such mutations may result in the loss of an entire gene or group of genes or may cause the misreading of a large sequence of bases. Figure 4-21 shows the effect of removing a single base on the reading of the genetic code. Since the code is read in sequences of three bases, the removal of one base not only alters the code word containing that base but also causes a misreading of all subsequent bases by shifting the reading sequence. Addition of

an extra base would cause a similar misreading. Such mutations result either in no protein being formed, if the gene has been deleted, or in the formation of a nonsense protein, a protein in which the amino acid sequence does not correspond to any functional protein.

Assume that a mutation has altered a single code word in a gene so that it now codes for a different amino acid, for example, alanine C-G-T changed to valine C-A-T. What effect does this mutation have upon the cell? The answer depends partly upon the type of gene and where in the gene the mutation has occurred. Although proteins are composed of many amino acids, the properties of a protein often depend upon only a very small region of the total molecule, such as the binding site of an enzyme. If the mutation does not alter the conformation of the binding site, there may be little or no change in the protein's properties. On the other hand, if the mutation alters the binding site, a marked change in the protein's properties may occur. Thus, if the protein is an enzyme, a mutation may change its affinity for a substrate or render it totally inactive.

If such a mutated enzyme is in a pathway supplying most of a cell's chemical energy, the loss of the enzyme *could* lead to the death of the cell. The story is more complex, however, since the cell contains a second gene for this enzyme, one which has not been mutated and is able to form an active enzyme. Thus, little or no change in cell function would result from this mutation. If both genes had mutations that rendered their products inactive, then no functional enzyme would be formed and the cell would die. In contrast, if the active enzyme were involved in the synthesis of a particular amino acid, and if the cell could obtain that amino acid from the extracellular fluid, the cell's functioning would not be impaired by the absence of the enzyme.

To generalize, a mutation may have any one of three effects upon a cell: (1) It may cause no noticeable change in the cell's functioning; (2) it may modify cell function but still be compatible with cell growth and replication; or (3) it may lead to cell death.

With one exception—cancer, to be described below—the malfunction of a single cell, other than a sperm or egg, as a result of a mutation usually has no significant effect because there are so many cells performing the same function in an organ. Unfortunately, the story is different when the mutation occurs in a sperm or egg since these cells combine to form the fertilized egg from which all the cells of a new individual will develop. In this case, the mutation will be passed on to *all* the cells in the body. Thus, mutations in the sperm or egg do not affect the individual in which they occur but do affect, often catastrophically, the child produced by these cells. Moreover, these mutations will also be passed on to some individuals in future generations descended from the individual carrying the original mutant gene.

---

[6]Because the genetic code has several different code words representing the same amino acid, a mutation in a single code word does not always alter the type of amino acid coded. We saw that substituting A for G in the alanine code word C-G-T produced the valine code word C-A-T. If, instead, the mutation caused cytosine C to be substituted for thymine T, the protein formed by the mutant gene would not be altered in amino acid sequence in spite of the change in base sequence because the new codon C-G-C is one of several that correspond to alanine.

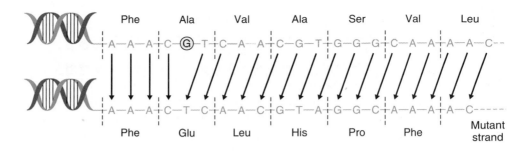

FIGURE 4-21

A deletion mutation caused by the loss of a single base G in one of the two DNA strands causes a misreading of all code words beyond the point of the mutation.

Inherited diseases resulting from gene mutation are termed ***inborn errors of metabolism***. An example is ***phenylketonuria***, a disorder that can lead to a form of mental retardation in children. Because of a single abnormal enzyme, these individuals are unable to convert the amino acid phenylalanine to the amino acid tyrosine at a normal rate. Phenylalanine is therefore diverted into other biochemical pathways in large amounts, giving rise to products that interfere with the normal activity of the nervous system. These products are also excreted in large amounts in the urine, accounting for the name of the disease. Fortunately, the symptoms of the disease can be prevented if the content of phenylalanine in the diet is restricted during childhood, thus preventing accumulation of the toxic products formed from phenylalanine.

Cells possess a number of enzymatic mechanisms for repairing DNA that has been damaged by chemical or physical trauma. Such abnormalities include breaks, loss of nucleotides, and formation of abnormal bases as a result of the loss or addition of chemical groups on the bases. These alterations result in abnormal molecular shapes that are recognized by the repair enzymes. These repair mechanisms all depend on the damage occurring in only one of the two DNA strands, so that the undamaged strand can provide the correct code for rebuilding the damaged strand. One set of repair enzymes identifies an abnormal region in one of the DNA strands. The enzymes then cut out the damaged segment, and DNA polymerase rebuilds the segment by base-pairing with the undamaged strand just as it did during DNA replication. Now, however, only a small segment of DNA is being replaced rather than the whole molecule. If adjacent regions in both strands of DNA are damaged, a permanent mutation is created which cannot be repaired by these mechanisms.

This repair mechanism is particularly important for long-lived cells, such as nerve and muscle cells, that do not divide and therefore do not replicate their DNA. This means that the same molecule of DNA in these cells must continue to function and maintain the stability of its genetic information for as long as the individual lives, which could be 100 years or even more.

Mutations contribute to evolution. Mutations may alter the activity of an enzyme in such a way that it is more, rather than less, active, or they may introduce an entirely new type of enzyme activity into a cell. If an organism carrying such a mutant gene is able to perform some function more effectively than an organism lacking the mutant gene, it has a better chance of surviving and passing the mutant gene on to its descendants. If the mutation produces an organism that functions less effectively than organisms lacking the mutation, the organism is less likely to survive and pass on the mutant gene. This is the principle of **natural selection**. Although any one mutation, if it is able to survive in the population, may cause only a very slight alteration in the properties of a cell, given enough time, a large number of small changes can accumulate to produce very large changes in the structure and function of an organism.

Recombinant DNA

Since a number of diseases are known to be the result of mutated genes, one approach to curing such diseases would be to replace the abnormal gene with a normal one. What was once a theoretical possibility is approaching the point of being a reality, at least under some circumstances. A tremendous number of technical problems must be solved before gene transfers become a practical approach to treating genetic diseases. First, the location of the normal gene on its chromosome must be identified, the gene isolated, its base sequence determined, and copies of the base sequence manufactured—a process known as **gene cloning**. Then a mechanism must be developed to insert copies of the normal gene into the DNA of mutated cells, forming **recombinant DNA**.

In the early 1970s, bacterial enzymes were discovered that split molecules of DNA in a unique manner. These enzymes, called **restriction nucleases**, identify specific nucleotide sequences, usually four to six nucleotides long, and in this region they cut DNA at a different site on each strand (Figure 4-22). Each of the cut strands has a short, exposed sequence of bases that are complementary to each other. If the DNA from two cells is cut by the same restriction nuclease, then a DNA fragment from one cell can base-pair with the complementary end of a DNA segment from a second cell. Another enzyme, known as a ligase, can then covalently link the two molecules of DNA

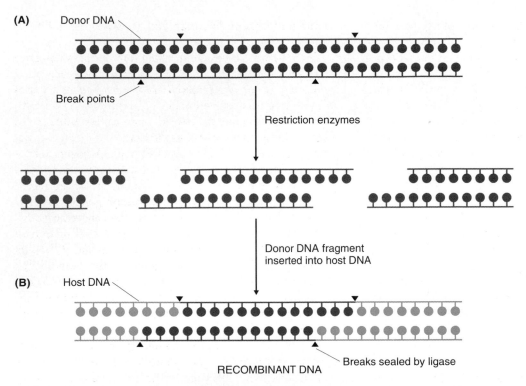

FIGURE 4-22

The basis of recombinant DNA. (A) Bacterial restriction enzymes break the two strands of DNA at different points, producing ends with exposed bases that are complementary to each other. (B) A segment of DNA containing one or more genes from one organism (donor) can be inserted into the DNA of another organism (host) by using these restriction enzymes to produce DNA segments whose ends can bind together.

together. By this procedure, DNA fragments (genes) from one cell can be inserted into the DNA from a second cell to form recombinant DNA.

The next step in replacing a mutated gene with a normal gene is to devise a means of inserting the recombinant DNA into a cell since a cell's plasma membrane is impermeable to these large DNA molecules. One method is to insert the gene into the nucleic acid of a virus and then infect cells with the altered virus. As will be described in Chapter 20, some viral nucleic acids become incorporated into the host's DNA and thus the virus acts as a carrier to get the recombinant DNA into the cell. When the recombinant DNA is inserted into a living cell, its genetic message is transcribed into mRNA along with the messages from the host's genes and then translated into protein.

It is hoped that techniques employing recombinant DNA may one day provide the ability to selectively replace mutant genes in humans with normal genes and thus provide a cure for genetic diseases. This recombinant DNA technology is already providing many practical benefits. For example, inserting the gene that codes for human insulin into bacterial DNA leads to the production of insulin by the bacteria. Large amounts of this protein hormone can then be produced and used to treat diabetic patients who are unable to synthesize their own insulin.

On the other hand, this technology bears potential hazards. For example, it would be theoretically possible to insert a gene that codes for a toxic protein into a harmless bacterium that commonly inhabits the human gastrointestinal tract and thereby produce a widespread epidemic.

CANCER

n an adult, the rates at which new cells in a tissue are formed and old cells die are in balance, producing a steady state in which the tissue does not increase in size. If the mechanisms regulating cell division are not functioning properly, however, the affected cells may produce new cells faster than old cells are removed, forming a growing mass of tissue known as a **tumor**. If the tumor cells remain localized and do not invade surrounding tissues, the tumor is said to be a **benign tumor**. If, however, the tumor cells grow into the surrounding tissues, disrupting their functions, and/or spread to other regions of the body, the tumor is said to be a *malignant tumor* and may lead to the death of the organism.

Malignant tumors are composed of *cancer cells*, which are cells that have lost the ability to respond to the normal mechanisms that regulate cell growth. Cancer cells are characterized by their capacity for unlimited multiplication and for their ability to break away from the parent tumor. They spread by way of the circulatory system to other parts of the body, where they form multiple tumor sites, a process known as *metastasis*.

Approximately 1200 Americans die each day from cancer. Fifty percent of all cancer deaths occur from cancers in three organs—the lung (28 percent), the colon (13 percent), and the breast (9 percent). About 90 percent of cancers develop in epithelial cells and are known as *carcinomas*. Those derived from connective tissue and muscle are called *sarcomas*, and those from blood cells are *leukemias* and *lymphomas*.

If a cancer is detected in the early stages of its growth, before it has metastasized, the tumor may be removed by surgery. Once it has metastasized to many organs, surgery is no longer possible. Drugs and radiation can be used to inhibit cell multiplication and destroy malignant cells, both before and after metastasis. Unfortunately these treatments also damage the growth of normal cells. Other treatments, which utilize the body's own immune defenses against cancer, are described in Chapter 20.

Any normal cell in the body may at some point undergo transformation to a malignant cell. A number of agents known as *carcinogens*, such as radiation, viruses, and certain chemicals, can induce the cancerous transformation of cells. These agents act mainly by altering or activating various genes associated with cell growth. Thus, mutagenic agents also tend to be carcinogenic. It is estimated that approximately 90 percent of all cancers are the result of environmental factors and life style.

The transformation of a normal cell into a cancer cell is a multistep process that involves altering not only the mechanisms that regulate cell replication but also those that control the invasiveness of the cell and its ability to subvert the body's defense mechanisms. (As will be discussed in Chapter 20, the body's defense system is normally able to detect and destroy most cancerous cells.) In most cases a cancer cell does not arise in its fully malignant form from a single mutation, but progresses through various stages from the benign to the malignant state as a result of successive mutations. The incidence of cancer increases with age as a result of the accumulation of these mutations. Some of the early stages of transformation result in changes in the cell's morphology, known as *dysplasia*, a precancerous state that can be detected by microscopic examination. At this stage the cell has not yet acquired a capacity for unlimited growth or an ability to invade surrounding tissues.

Over the last 20 years a growing number of genes have been identified that contribute to the cancerous state when they become mutated. These cancer-related genes fall into two classes: dominant and recessive. The dominant cancer-producing genes[7] are called *oncogenes* (Greek: *onkos,* mass, tumor—the branch of medicine that deals with cancer is known as oncology). Oncogenes arise as mutations of normal genes known as proto-oncogenes.

The second class of genes involved in cancer are recessive genes known as *tumor suppressor genes*. In their unmutated state these genes prevent the cancerous transformations produced by oncogenes. Mutation of one of the allelic pair of tumor suppressor genes inactivates its function but leaves a normal gene on the homologous chromosome that can still function to suppress tumor development. It is only when both alleles of the tumor suppressor genes have been mutated that the cell becomes cancerous.

Although a number of proto-oncogenes and tumor suppressor genes have been identified, little is currently known about how they function or how their altered function leads to uncontrolled growth. Some produce protein kinases that modulate the functions of other proteins, others produce transcription factors that control the transcription of specific genes, while still others produce proteins that act as binding sites for various regulatory molecules, such as growth factors. Thus, all cancer-related genes do not produce products with similar functions.

In addition to the mutations occurring in proto-oncogenes and tumor suppressor genes, a number of additional factors not related to mutations can influence the development of cancer. The normal growth of many types of cells is stimulated by various hormones and growth factors. Many cancer cells retain the ability to respond to these growth-promoting signals. These stimulating agents may also contribute to the progression of the tumor to a more malignant stage since rapidly dividing cells are more susceptible to mutations, which often occur during the process of replicating DNA. Thus, removing or inhibiting the actions of these stimulating agents can reduce the growth rates and progression of certain tumors. An example is the effect of estrogen on some forms of breast cancer.

Through a better understanding of the molecular processes that control both normal and abnormal growth, the means of combating cancerous growths may be found.

---

[7]Although dominant, and only a single copy of the mutated gene must be present, the full cancerous effects of the gene will not be expressed unless several other genes in the cell have also been mutated.

SECTION B SUMMARY

GENETIC CODE

I. Each individual inherits two copies of each gene, one from the mother and one from the father. These allelic genes can be classified as either dominant or recessive.

II. Genetic information is coded in the nucleotide sequence of DNA. A single gene contains either (a) the information that, via mRNA, determines the amino acid sequence in a specific protein, or (b) the information for forming rRNA or tRNA, which assists in protein assembly.

III. Genetic information is transferred from DNA to mRNA in the nucleus, and then mRNA passes to the cytoplasm, where its information is used to synthesize protein.

IV. The words in the DNA genetic code consist of a sequence of three nucleotide bases that specify a single amino acid. The sequence of triplet code words along a gene determines the sequence of amino acids in a protein. There can be more than one code word specifying a given amino acid.

PROTEIN SYNTHESIS

I. Protein synthesis involves (a) transcription of genetic information from DNA to mRNA, which occurs in the nucleus, and (b) translation of the information in mRNA into protein, which occurs in the cytoplasm on the surface of ribosomes. Table 4-1 summarizes the steps leading from DNA to protein and the role of tRNA.

II. Proteins secreted by cells pass through the sequence of steps illustrated in Figure 4-16.

III. The rate of protein synthesis can be regulated by controlling (a) transcription of a gene into mRNA, (b) splicing of mRNA, (c) stability of mRNA, and (d) translation of mRNA by ribosomes.

REPLICATION AND EXPRESSION OF GENETIC INFORMATION

I. When DNA replicates, exposed bases in each of the two unwound strands base-pair with bases of free deoxyribonucleotide triphosphates. DNA polymerase joins the nucleotides together to form a new strand of DNA.

II. When a cell divides, one copy of DNA passes to each daughter cell, so that both receive the same set of genetic instructions.

III. Cell division, consisting of nuclear division—mitosis—and cytoplasmic division—cytokinesis—lasts about 1 h.

IV. During interphase, DNA replicates, forming two identical sister chromatids joined by a centromere.

V. The main events of mitosis are:

A. The chromatids condense into highly coiled chromosomes.

B. The centromeres of each chromosome become attached to spindle fibers extending from the centrioles, which have migrated to opposite poles of the nucleus.

C. The two chromatids of each chromosome separate and move toward opposite poles of the cell as the cell divides into two daughter cells. Following cell division, the condensed chromatids uncoil into their extended interphase form.

VI. Entry into the S and M phases of the cell cycle is dependent on the activity of enzymes coded by cell division cycle genes. These enzymes are activated by cyclin.

VII. Proofreading mechanisms help prevent the introduction of errors during DNA replication.

VIII. Mutations occur when incorrect bases are inserted into new strands of DNA during replication or when single bases or large sections of DNA are added or deleted.

A. A mutation may (a) cause no noticeable change in a cell's function, (b) modify cell function but still be compatible with cell growth and replication, or (c) lead to the death of the cell.

B. Mutations occurring in egg or sperm cells will be passed on to all the cells on a new individual and possibly to some of the individuals in future generations.

IX. DNA repair mechanisms are important in preventing the accumulation of mutations, particularly in long-lived cells that do not divide.

X. With the use of bacterial enzymes, segments of DNA can be cut from the DNA of one cell and inserted into the DNA of another cell to form recombinant DNA. The recombinant DNA will then direct the synthesis of proteins coded by the donor DNA in the host cell.

XI. Cancer cells are characterized by their capacity for unlimited multiplication and their ability to metastasize to other parts of the body, forming multiple tumor sites.

A. Mutations in proto-oncogenes and tumor suppressor genes lead to cancer.

B. More than one mutation is necessary to cause the transformation of a normal cell into a cancer cell.

SECTION B KEY TERMS

gene	signal sequence
genome	transcription factors
alleles	DNA polymerase
homozygous	daughter cells
heterozygous	interphase
dominant genes	mitosis
recessive genes	cytokinesis
termination code words	chromatin
genetic code	sister chromatids
messenger RNA (mRNA)	centromere
transcription	chromosomes
translation	spindle fibers
RNA polymerase	centrioles
promoter	mitotic apparatus
codon	cell division cycle genes
exons	cyclin
introns	proofreading
ribosomal RNA (rRNA)	natural selection
transfer RNA (tRNA)	gene cloning
anticodon	recombinant DNA
chaperones	restriction nucleases

SECTION B REVIEW QUESTIONS

1. Describe the differences between a dominant and a recessive gene.

2. Summarize the direction of information flow during protein synthesis

3. Describe the way in which the genetic code in DNA specifies the amino acid sequence in a protein.

4. List the four nucleotides used to form mRNA.

5. Describe the main events that occur during the transcription of genetic information into mRNA.

6. List the components of a ribosome and identify the site of ribosomal subunit assembly.

7. Describe the role of tRNA in protein assembly.

8. Describe the events of protein translation that occur on the surface of a ribosome.

9. Describe the pathway that leads to the secretion of proteins from cells.

10. What is the function of the signal sequence of a protein?

11. List the ways in which regulation of protein synthesis can occur.

12. Describe the mechanism by which DNA is replicated.

13. Summarize the main events of mitosis and cytokinesis.

14. Describe the role of cell division cycle genes and the protein cyclin in controlling cell division.

15. How will the deletion of a single base in a gene affect the protein synthesized?

16. List the three effects that a mutation can have on a cell's function.

17. Describe the mechanism by which recombinant DNA is formed.

18. Describe the characteristics of a cancer cell.

19. Describe the difference between an oncogene and a tumor suppressor gene.

20. Describe how various environmental factors can increase the risk of cancer.

CHAPTER 4 CLINICAL TERMS

mutation	carcinomas
mutagens	sarcomas
inborn errors of metabolism	leukemias
phenylketonuria	lymphomas
tumor	carcinogens
benign tumor	dysplasia
malignant tumor	oncogenes
cancer cells	tumor suppressor genes
metastasis	

CHAPTER 4 THOUGHT QUESTIONS

(Answers are given in Appendix A.)

1. A variety of chemical messengers that normally regulate acid secretion in the stomach bind to proteins in the plasma membranes of the acid-secreting cells. Some of these binding reactions lead to increased acid secretion, and others inhibit its secretion. In what ways might a drug that inhibits acid secretion be acting on these cells?

2. In one type of diabetes the plasma concentration of the hormone insulin is normal, but the response of the cells to which insulin usually binds is markedly decreased. Suggest a reason for this in terms of the properties of protein binding sites.

3. Given the following substances in a cell and their effects on each other, predict the change in compound H that will result from an increase in compound A and diagram this sequence of changes.

Compound A is a modulator molecule that allosterically activates protein B.

Protein B is a protein kinase enzyme that activates protein C.

Protein C is an enzyme that converts substrate D to product E.

Compound E is a modulator molecule that allosterically inhibits protein F.

Protein F is an enzyme that converts substrate G to product H.

4. Shown below is the relation between the amount of acid secreted and the concentration of compound X, which stimulates acid secretion in the stomach by binding to a membrane protein. At a plasma concentration of 2 pM, compound X produces an acid secretion of 20 mmol/h.

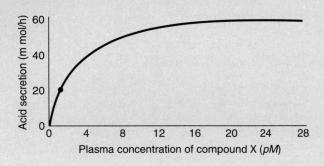

a. Specify two ways in which acid secretion by compound X could be increased to 40 mmol/h.

b. Why will increasing the concentration of compound X to 28 pM not produce more acid secretion than increasing the concentration of X to 18 pM?

5. What would be the consequences for protein regulation of a mutation that has led to the loss of phosphoprotein phosphatase from cells?

6. A base sequence in a portion of one strand of DNA is A-G-T-G-C-A-A-G-T-C-T. Predict:

a. The base sequence in the corresponding strand of DNA.

b. The base sequence in mRNA transcribed from the sequence shown.

7. The triplet code in DNA for the amino acid histidine is G-T-A. Predict the mRNA codon for this amino acid and the tRNA anticodon.

8. If a protein contains 100 amino acids, how many nucleotides will be present in the gene that codes for this protein?

9. Why will chemical agents that inhibit the polymerization of tubulin (Chapter 3, page 50) inhibit cell division?

10. Why are drugs that inhibit the replication of DNA potentially useful in the treatment of cancer? What are some of the limitations of such drugs?

CHAPTER
5

ENERGY AND CELLULAR METABOLISM

CHEMICAL REACTIONS

Determinants of Reaction Rates

Reversible and Irreversible Reactions

Law of Mass Action

ENZYMES

Cofactors

REGULATION OF ENZYME-MEDIATED REACTIONS

Substrate Concentration

Enzyme Concentration

Enzyme Activity

MULTIENZYME METABOLIC PATHWAYS

ATP AND CELLULAR ENERGY TRANSFER

The Role of ATP

Glycolysis

Krebs Cycle

Oxidative Phosphorylation

CARBOHYDRATE, FAT, AND PROTEIN METABOLISM

Carbohydrate Metabolism

Carbohydrate catabolism

Glycogen storage

Glucose synthesis

Fat Metabolism

Fat catabolism

Fat synthesis

Protein and Amino Acid Metabolism

Fuel Metabolism Summary

ESSENTIAL NUTRIENTS

Vitamins

SUMMARY

KEY TERMS

REVIEW QUESTIONS

THOUGHT QUESTIONS

housands of chemical reactions occur each instant throughout the body, this entire collection of reactions being termed **metabolism** (Greek: change). Metabolism includes the synthesis of the specific molecules required for cell structure and function, the breakdown of these molecules, and the provision of energy for cell functions. The synthesis of organic molecules by cells is called **anabolism**, and their breakdown, **catabolism**.

The body's organic molecules undergo continuous transformations as some molecules are broken down while others of the same type are being synthesized. Chemically, no person is the same at noon as at 8 o'clock in the morning since during even this short period much of the body's structure has been torn apart and replaced with newly syn-thesized molecules. In adults the body's composition is in a steady state in which the anabolic and catabolic rates for the synthesis and breakdown of most molecules are equal.

This chapter describes four aspects of metabolism: (1) the factors that determine the rates of chemical reactions; (2) the role of enzymes in accelerating chemical reactions and how enzyme activity can be controlled; (3) the biochemical pathways by which energy is obtained from the breakdown of carbohydrates, fats, and proteins; and (4) the pathways by which carbohydrates and fats are synthesized. (The pathway for protein synthesis was described in Chapter 4.) We begin by discussing the characteristics of chemical reactions because these concepts underlie all the other chapter topics.

CHEMICAL REACTIONS

hemical reactions involve (1) the breaking of chemical bonds in reactant molecules, followed by (2) the making of new chemical bonds to form the product molecules. In the chemical reaction in which carbonic acid is transformed into carbon dioxide and water, for example, two of the chemical bonds in carbonic acid are broken and the product molecules are formed by establishing two new bonds between different pairs of atoms:

$$
\underset{\substack{\uparrow \\ \text{Broken}}}{H-O}-\underset{\substack{\uparrow \\ \text{Broken}}}{\overset{\displaystyle \overset{O}{\parallel}}{C}}-O-H \longrightarrow \underset{\substack{\uparrow \\ \text{Formed}}}{O=\overset{\displaystyle \overset{O}{\parallel}}{C}} + \underset{\substack{\uparrow \\ \text{Formed}}}{H-O-H}
$$

$$
\underset{\substack{\text{Carbonic} \\ \text{acid}}}{H_2CO_3} \longrightarrow \underset{\substack{\text{Carbon} \\ \text{dioxide}}}{CO_2} + \underset{\text{Water}}{H_2O}
$$

Since the energy contents of the reactants and products are usually different, and because energy can neither be created nor be destroyed, energy must either be added or released during a chemical reaction. For example, the reaction in which carbonic acid breaks down into carbon dioxide and water occurs with the release of 4 kcal of energy per mole of products formed since carbonic acid has a higher energy content (155 kcal/mol) than the sum of the energy contents of carbon dioxide and water (94 + 57 = 151 kcal/mol).

The energy that is released appears as heat, the energy of increased molecular motion, which is measured in units of calories. One **calorie** (1 cal) is the amount of heat re-quired to raise the temperature of 1 g of water 1° on the Celsius scale. Energies associated with most chemical reactions are several thousand calories per mole and are reported as **kilocalories** (1 kcal = 1000 cal).

Determinants of Reaction Rates

The rate of a chemical reaction (in other words, how rapidly the products of the reaction are formed) can be determined by measuring the change in the concentration of reactants or products per unit of time. The faster the product concentration increases or the reactant concentration decreases, the greater the rate of the reaction. Four factors (Table 5-1) influence the reaction rate: reactant concentration, activation energy, temperature, and the presence of a catalyst.

The lower the concentration of reactants, the slower the reaction simply because there are fewer molecules available to react. Conversely, the higher the concentration of reactants, the faster the reaction rate.

Given the same initial concentrations of reactants, however, all reactions do not occur at the same rate. Each type of chemical reaction has its own characteristic rate, which depends upon what is called the activation energy for the

---

TABLE 5-1   DETERMINANTS OF CHEMICAL REACTION RATES

Reactant concentrations (higher concentrations: faster reaction rate)

Activation energy (higher activation energy: slower reaction rate)

Temperature (higher temperature: faster reaction rate)

Catalyst (increases reaction rate)

reaction. In order for a chemical reaction to occur, reactant molecules must acquire enough energy—the **activation energy**—to enter an activated state in which chemical bonds can be broken and formed. The activation energy does not alter the difference in energy content between the reactants and final products since this energy is released when the products are formed.

How do reactants acquire activation energy? In most of the metabolic reactions we will be considering, activation energy is obtained when reactants collide with other molecules. If the activation energy required for a reaction is large, then the probability of a given reactant molecule acquiring this amount of energy will be small, and the reaction rate will be slow. Thus, the higher the activation energy, the slower the rate of a chemical reaction.

Temperature is the third factor influencing reaction rates. The higher the temperature, the faster molecules move and thus the greater their impact when they collide. Therefore, one reason that increasing the temperature increases a reaction rate is that reactants have a better chance of acquiring sufficient activation energy from a collision. In addition, faster-moving molecules will collide more frequently.

A **catalyst** is a substance that interacts with a reactant in such a manner that it alters the distribution of energy between the chemical bonds of the reactant, the result being a decrease in the activation energy required to transform the reactant into product. Since less activation energy is required, a reaction will proceed at a faster rate in the presence of a catalyst. The chemical composition of a catalyst is not altered by the reaction, and thus a single catalyst molecule can be used over and over again to catalyze the conversion of many reactant molecules to products. Furthermore, a catalyst does not alter the difference in the energy contents of the reactants and products.

Reversible and Irreversible Reactions

Consider our previous example in which carbonic acid breaks down into carbon dioxide and water. The products of this reaction, carbon dioxide and water, can also recombine to form carbonic acid:

$$CO_2 \;+\; H_2O \;+\; 4\,\text{kcal/mol} \longrightarrow H_2CO_3$$
$$\text{94 kcal/mol}\quad\text{57 kcal/mol}\qquad\qquad\text{155 kcal/mol}$$

Since carbonic acid has a greater content than the sum of the energies contained in carbon dioxide and water, energy must be added to the latter molecules in order to form carbonic acid. (This 4 kcal of energy is *not* activation energy but is an integral part of the energy balance.) This energy can be obtained, along with the activation energy, through collisions with other molecules.

Thus, in every chemical reaction there are two reactions going on simultaneously: a reaction (we will call it "forward") in which reactants are converted to products, and one (we will call it "reverse") in which products are converted to reactants. The overall reaction is said to be a **reversible reaction**:

$$\text{Reactants} \underset{\text{Reverse}}{\overset{\text{Forward}}{\rightleftharpoons}} \text{Products}$$

As a reaction progresses, the rate of the forward reaction will decrease as the concentration of reactants decreases. Simultaneously the rate of the reverse reaction will increase as the concentration of the product molecules increases. Eventually the reaction will reach a state of **chemical equilibrium** in which the forward and reverse reaction rates are equal. At this point there will be no further change in the concentrations of reactants or products even though reactants will continue to be converted into products and products converted to reactants.

When chemical equilibrium has been reached, the concentration of products need not be equal to the concentration of reactants even though the forward and reverse reaction rates are equal. The ratio of product concentration to reactant concentration at equilibrium depends upon the amount of energy released or added during the reaction. This is because the greater the energy released, the smaller the probability that the product molecules will be able to obtain this energy and undergo the reverse reaction to re-form reactants. Therefore, in this case, the ratio of product to reactant concentration at chemical equilibrium will be large.

To be specific, if there is no difference in the energy contents of reactants and products, their concentrations will be equal at equilibrium. If only a small amount of energy is released, on the order of 1 kcal or less, the product concentration at equilibrium will be between 1 and 10 times the reactant concentration. When larger amounts of energy are released, for example, 4 kcal, the ratio of product to reactant molecules at equilibrium is about 1000 to 1.

Thus, although all chemical reactions are reversible to some extent, reactions that release large quantities of energy are said to be **irreversible reactions** in the sense that almost all of the reactant molecules have been converted to product molecules when chemical equilibrium is reached. A single arrow is used to indicate an irreversible reaction, and a double arrow for a reversible reaction. It must be emphasized that the energy released in a reaction determines the degree to which the reaction is reversible or irreversible. This energy is *not* the activation energy and it does *not* determine the reaction rate, which is governed by the four factors discussed earlier. The characteristics of reversible and irreversible reactions are summarized in Table 5-2.

TABLE 5-2   CHARACTERISTICS OF REVERSIBLE AND IRREVERSIBLE CHEMICAL REACTIONS

Reversible reactions	A + B $\rightleftharpoons$ C + D + small amount of energy
	At chemical equilibrium, product concentrations are only slightly higher than reactant concentrations.
Irreversible reactions	E + F $\longrightarrow$ G + H + large amount of energy
	At chemical equilibrium, almost all reactant molecules have been converted to product.

Law of Mass Action

The concentrations of reactants and products play a very important role in determining not only the rates of the forward and reverse reactions but also the direction in which the *net* reaction proceeds—whether products are accumulating or reactants are accumulating at a given time.

Consider the following reversible reaction that has reached chemical equilibrium:

$$\underset{\text{Reactants}}{A + B} \underset{\text{Reverse}}{\overset{\text{Forward}}{\rightleftharpoons}} \underset{\text{Products}}{C + D}$$

If at this point we increase the concentration of one of the reactants, the rate of the forward reaction will increase and lead to increased product formation. In contrast, increasing the concentration of one of the product molecules will drive the reaction in the reverse direction, increasing the formation of reactants. The direction in which the net reaction is proceeding can also be altered by *lowering* the concentration of one of the participants. Thus, lowering the concentration of one of the products will drive the net reaction in the forward direction since it will lower the rate of the reverse reaction without changing the rate of the forward reaction.

These effects of reactant and product concentrations on the direction in which the net reaction is proceeding are known as the **law of mass action**. Mass action is often a major determining factor controlling the direction in which metabolic pathways proceed.

ENZYMES

Most of the chemical reactions that occur in the body, if carried out in a test tube with only reactants and products present, would proceed at very low rates because they have high activation energies. In order to achieve the high reaction rates observed in living organisms, catalysts are required to lower the activation energy.

These particular catalysts are called enzymes (meaning "in yeast," since the first enzymes were discovered in yeast cells). Enzymes are protein molecules, and so an **enzyme** can be defined as a protein catalyst.[1]

To function, an enzyme must come into contact with reactants, which are called **substrates** in the case of enzyme-mediated reactions. The substrate becomes bound to the enzyme, forming an enzyme-substrate complex, which breaks down to release products and enzyme (Figure 5-1). The reaction between enzyme and substrate can be written:

$$\underset{\text{Substrate}}{S} + \underset{\text{Enzyme}}{E} \rightleftharpoons \underset{\substack{\text{Enzyme-}\\\text{substrate}\\\text{complex}}}{ES} \rightleftharpoons \underset{\text{Product}}{P} + \underset{\text{Enzyme}}{E}$$

At the end of the reaction, the enzyme is free to undergo the same reaction with additional substrate molecules. The overall effect is to accelerate the conversion of substrate into product, the enzyme acting as a catalyst.

The interaction between substrate and enzyme has all the characteristics described in Chapter 4 for the binding of a ligand to a binding site on a protein—specificity, affinity, competition, and saturation. The region of the enzyme to which the substrate binds is known as the enzyme's **active site** (a term equivalent to "binding site"). The shape of the enzyme in the region of the active site provides the basis for the enzyme's chemical specificity since the shape of the active site is complementary to the substrate's shape (Figure 5-1).

There are approximately 4000 different enzymes in a typical cell, each capable of catalyzing a different chemical reaction. Enzymes are generally named by adding the suffix *-ase* to the name of either the substrate or the type of reaction catalyzed by the enzyme. For example, the reaction in which carbonic acid is broken down into carbon dioxide and water is catalyzed by the enzyme carbonic anhydrase.

---

[1]Some RNA molecules possess catalytic activity, but the number of reactions they catalyze is very small, and so we shall restrict the term "enzyme" to protein catalysts.

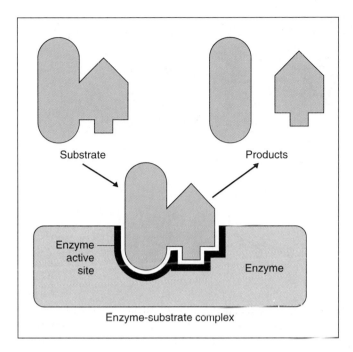

FIGURE 5-1
Binding of substrate to the active site of an enzyme catalyzes the formation of products.

The catalytic activity of an enzyme can be extremely large. For example, a single molecule of carbonic anhydrase can catalyze the conversion of about 100,000 substrate molecules to products in 1 s.

The major characteristics of enzymes are listed in Table 5-3.

TABLE 5-3 CHARACTERISTICS OF ENZYMES

1. An enzyme undergoes no net chemical change as a consequence of the reaction it catalyzes.
2. The binding of substrate to an enzyme's active site has all the characteristics—chemical specificity, affinity, competition, and saturation—of a ligand binding to a protein.
3. An enzyme increases the rate of a chemical reaction but does not cause a reaction to occur that would not occur in its absence.
4. An enzyme increases both the forward and reverse rates of a chemical reaction and thus does not change the chemical equilibrium that is finally reached. It only increases the rate at which equilibrium is achieved.
5. An enzyme lowers the activation energy of a reaction but does not alter the net amount of energy that is added to or released by the reactants in the course of the reaction.

Cofactors

Many enzymes are inactive in the absence of small amounts of other substances known as **cofactors**. In some cases, the cofactor is a trace metal (Chapter 2), such as magnesium, iron, zinc, or copper, and its binding to an enzyme alters the conformation of the enzyme so that the enzyme can interact with the substrate. Since only a few enzyme molecules need be present to catalyze the conversion of large amounts of substrate to product, very small quantities of these trace metals are sufficient to maintain enzymatic activity.

In other cases the cofactor is an organic molecule that directly participates as one of the substrates in the reaction being catalyzed, in which case the cofactor is termed a **coenzyme**. Enzymes that require coenzymes catalyze reactions in which a few atoms, for example, hydrogen, acetyl, or methyl groups, are either removed from or added to a substrate. For example:

$$R-2H + \text{coenzyme} \underset{\text{Enzyme}}{\rightleftharpoons} R + \text{coenzyme}-2H$$

What makes a coenzyme different from an ordinary substrate is the fate of the coenzyme. In our example, the two hydrogen atoms that are transferred to the coenzyme can then be transferred from the coenzyme to another substrate with the aid of a second enzyme. This second reaction converts the coenzyme back to its original form, which becomes available to accept two more hydrogen atoms (Figure 5-2). A single coenzyme molecule can be used over and over again to transfer molecular fragments from one reaction to another. Thus, as with metallic cofactors, only small quantities of coenzymes are necessary to maintain the enzymatic reactions in which they participate.

Coenzymes are derived from a special class of nutrients known as vitamins. **Vitamins** are organic substances that are required in small amounts for health but cannot be synthesized in the body from other nutrients and therefore must be supplied by the diet. The coenzymes nicotinamide adenine dinucleotide (**NAD$^+$**) and flavine adenine dinucleotide (**FAD**) (Figure 5-2) are derived from the B vitamins niacin and riboflavin, respectively, and as we shall see, play major roles in energy metabolism by transferring hydrogen from one substrate to another.

REGULATION OF ENZYME-MEDIATED REACTIONS

The rate of an enzyme-mediated reaction in the body depends on substrate concentration and on the concentration and activity (a term defined below) of the en-

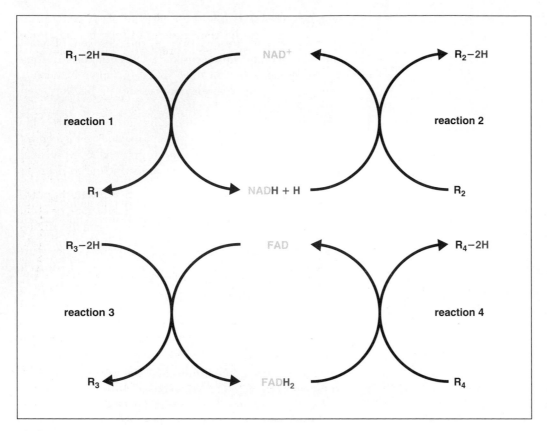

FIGURE 5-2

The coenzymes NAD^+ and FAD are used to transfer two hydrogen atoms from one reaction and donate them to a second reaction. In the process the hydrogen-free forms of the coenzymes are regenerated.

zyme that catalyzes the reaction. Since body temperature is normally maintained nearly constant, changes in temperature are not used directly to alter the rates of metabolic reactions. Increases in body temperature can occur during a fever, however, and around muscle tissue during exercise, and such increases in temperature increase the rates of all metabolic reactions in the affected tissues.

Substrate Concentration

Substrate concentration may be altered as a result of factors that alter the supply of a substrate from outside a cell. Thus, there may be changes in its blood concentration due, for example, to changes in diet or rate of substrate absorption from the intestinal tract. In addition, a substrate's entry into the cell through the plasma membrane can be controlled by mechanisms that will be discussed in Chapter 6. Intracellular substrate concentration can also be altered by reactions in a cell that either utilize the same substrate and thus tend to lower its concentration, or synthesize the substrate and thereby increase its intracellular concentration.

The rate of an enzyme-mediated reaction increases as the substrate concentration increases, as illustrated in Figure 5-3, until it reaches a maximal rate, which remains constant despite further increases in substrate concentration. The maximal rate is reached when the enzyme becomes saturated with substrate, that is, when the active site of every enzyme molecule is occupied by a substrate molecule.

Since coenzymes are substrates in certain enzyme reactions, changes in coenzyme concentration also affect reaction rates, as occurs with ordinary substrates.

Enzyme Concentration

At any substrate concentration, including saturating concentrations, the rate of an enzyme-mediated reaction can be increased by increasing the enzyme concentration. In most metabolic reactions, the substrate concentration is much greater than the small concentration of enzyme needed to catalyze the reaction. Therefore, if the number of enzyme molecules is doubled, twice as many active sites will be available to bind substrate, and twice as much sub-

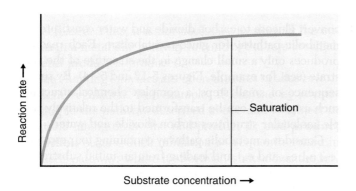

FIGURE 5-3

Rate of an enzyme-catalyzed reaction as a function of substrate concentration.

strate will be converted to product (Figure 5-4). Certain reactions proceed faster in some cells than in others because more enzyme molecules are present.

In order to change the concentration of an enzyme, either the rate of enzyme synthesis or the rate of enzyme breakdown must be altered. Since enzymes are proteins, this involves changing the rates of protein synthesis or breakdown. In Chapter 4 some of the mechanisms regulating protein synthesis were discussed; regulation of gene transcription is the primary mechanism for altering the synthesis and, hence, the concentrations of most enzymes. The substrate or product molecules of the reaction in which the enzyme takes part are often the molecules that lead to the activation or inhibition of gene transcription for the enzyme. Less is known about the factors controlling the selective breakdown of enzymes. Regardless of

whether altered synthesis or altered breakdown is involved, changing the concentration of enzymes is a relatively slow process, generally requiring several hours.

Enzyme Activity

In addition to changing the rate of enzyme-mediated reactions by changing the *concentration* of either substrate or enzyme, the rate can be altered by changing enzyme *activity*. Such a rate change occurs when the properties of the enzyme's active site are altered by either allosteric or covalent modulation (Chapter 4). Such modulation alters the rate at which the binding site converts substrate to product, or the affinity of the binding site for substrate, or both.

Figure 5-5 illustrates the effect of increasing the affinity of an enzyme's active site without changing the substrate (or enzyme) concentration. Provided the substrate concentration is less than the saturating concentration, the increased affinity of the enzyme's binding site will result in an increased number of active sites that contain bound substrate, and thus in the rate of the reaction.

The regulation of metabolism through the control of enzyme activity is an extremely complex process since, in many cases, the activity of an enzyme can be altered by more than one agent (Figure 5-6). The modulator molecules that *allosterically* alter enzyme activities are product molecules produced by other reactions in the cell. The result is that the overall rates of metabolism can be adjusted to meet various metabolic demands, as will be illustrated in the next section. In contrast, *covalent* modulation of enzyme activity is usually mediated by the activity of protein kinase enzymes (enzymes that phosphorylate specific proteins—Chapter 4) in response to various chemical signals received by a cell, for example, in response to a

FIGURE 5-4

Rate of an enzyme-catalyzed reaction as a function of substrate concentration at two enzyme concentrations: A and 2A. Enzyme concentration 2A is twice the enzyme concentration of A, resulting in a reaction that proceeds twice as fast at any substrate concentration.

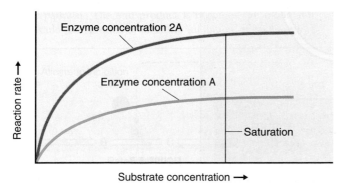

FIGURE 5-5

At a constant substrate concentration, increasing the affinity of an enzyme for its substrate by allosteric or covalent modulation increases the rate of the enzyme-mediated reaction. Note that increasing the enzyme's affinity does not increase the *maximal* rate of the enzyme-mediated reaction.

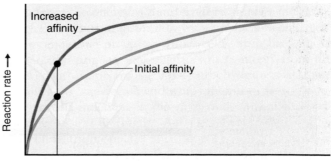

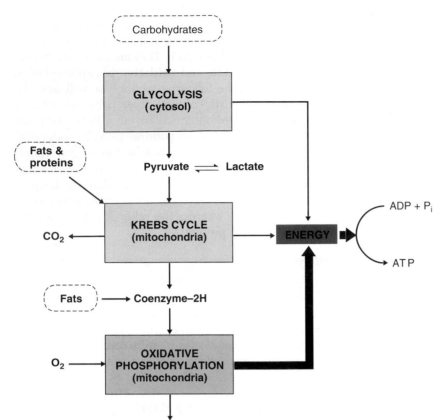

FIGURE 5-11

Pathways linking the energy released from the catabolism of fuel molecules to the formation of ATP. For simplicity, this figure does not show that glycolysis also provides some coenzyme-2H molecules to oxidative phosphorylation.

The first *formation* of ATP in glycolysis occurs during reaction 7 when a phosphate group is transferred from 1,3-bisphosphoglycerate to ADP to form ATP. This mechanism of forming ATP is known as **substrate level phosphorylation** since the phosphate group is transferred from a substrate molecule to ADP. Since, as stressed above, two intermediates exist at this step, reaction 7 produces two molecules of ATP, one from each of them. As we shall see, this mechanism is quite different from that used during oxidative phosphorylation in which *free* inorganic phosphate is coupled to ADP to form ATP.

A similar substrate level phosphorylation of ADP occurs during reaction 10, where again two molecules of ATP are formed. Thus, reactions 7 and 10 generate a total of four molecules of ATP for every molecule of glucose entering the pathway. There is a net gain, however, of only two molecules of ATP during glycolysis because of the two molecules of ATP used in the earlier reactions 1 and 3.

The end product of glycolysis, pyruvate, can proceed in one of two directions, depending on the availability of molecular oxygen, which, as we stressed earlier, is *not* utilized in any of the glycolytic reactions themselves. If oxygen is present, that is, if **aerobic** conditions exist, pyruvate enters the Krebs cycle and is broken down into carbon dioxide, as described in the next section. In contrast, in the absence of oxygen (**anaerobic** conditions), pyruvate is converted to **lactate** by a single enzyme-mediated reaction.[3] In this reaction (Figure 5-13) two hydrogen atoms derived from NADH + H$^+$ are transferred to pyruvate to form lactate. These hydrogens were originally added to NAD$^+$ during glycolysis in reaction 6, and so the coenzyme NAD$^+$ shuttles hydrogen between the two reactions during anaerobic glycolysis. The *overall* reaction, therefore, for anaerobic glycolysis is

$$\text{Glucose} + 2\,\text{ADP} + 2\,\text{P}_i \longrightarrow$$
$$2\,\text{lactate} + 2\,\text{ATP} + 2\,\text{H}_2\text{O} \quad (5\text{-}2)$$

Recall that under aerobic conditions pyruvate is not converted to lactate but rather enters the Krebs cycle. Therefore, the mechanism just described for regenerating NAD$^+$ from NADH + H$^+$ by forming lactate no longer occurs. Instead, as we shall see, the NADH + H$^+$ formed in reaction 6 is reconverted to NAD$^+$ by the transfer of its hydrogens to oxygen during oxidative phosphorylation.

---

[3]In some microorganisms, yeast cells for example, pyruvate is converted under anaerobic conditions to carbon dioxide and alcohol rather than to lactate. This process is known as fermentation and forms the basis for the production of alcohol from cereal grains that are rich in carbohydrates.

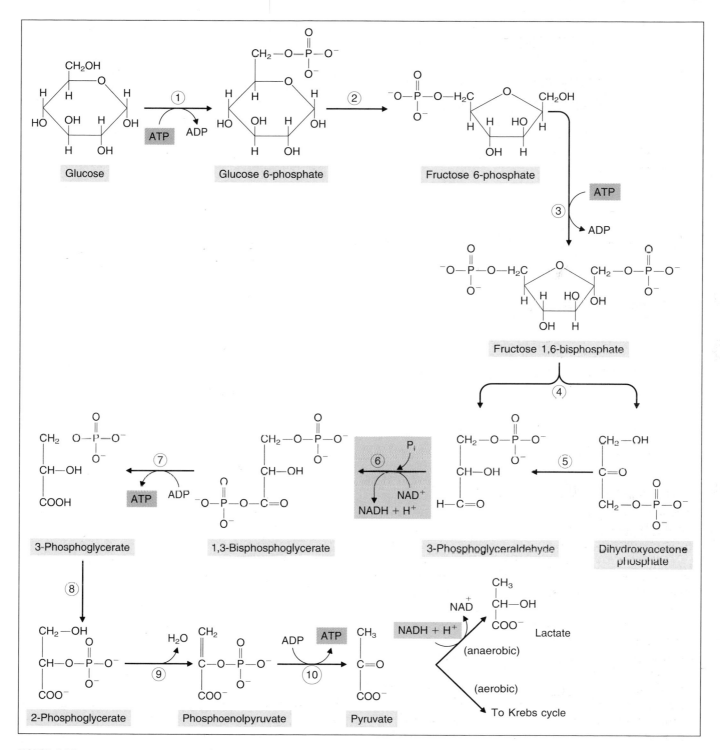

FIGURE 5-12

Glycolytic pathway. Under anaerobic conditions there is a net synthesis of two molecules of ATP for every molecule of glucose that enters the pathway. Two molecules of ATP are used in reactions 1 and 3. Reactions 4 and 5 combined produce two molecules of 3-phosphoglyceraldehyde, each of which yields two molecules of ATP, one at step 7 and one at step 10. Thus, in glycolysis, there is a total of four ATP produced and two consumed.

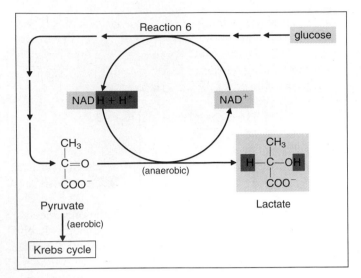

FIGURE 5-13

Under anaerobic conditions the coenzyme NAD^+ utilized in the glycolytic reaction 6 (Figure 5-12) is regenerated when it transfers its hydrogen atoms to pyruvate during the formation of lactate.

In most cells, the amount of ATP produced by glycolysis is much smaller than the amount formed by the other two ATP-generating pathways—the Krebs cycle and oxidative phosphorylation. There are special cases, however, in which glycolysis supplies most, and even all, of a cell's ATP. For example, erythrocytes contain the enzymes for glycolysis but have no mitochondria, which are required for the other pathways. All of their ATP production occurs, therefore, by glycolysis. Certain types of skeletal muscles contain considerable amounts of glycolytic enzymes but have few mitochondria. During intense muscle activity,

glycolysis provides most of the ATP in these cells and is associated with the production of large amounts of lactate. Despite these exceptions most cells do not have sufficient concentrations of glycolytic enzymes or enough glucose to provide, by glycolysis alone, the high rates of ATP production necessary to meet their energy requirements and thus are unable to function under anaerobic conditions.

Our discussion of glycolysis has focused upon glucose as the major carbohydrate entering the glycolytic pathway. However, other carbohydrates such as fructose, derived from the disaccharide sucrose (table sugar), and galactose, from the disaccharide lactose (milk sugar), can also be catabolized by glycolysis since these carbohydrates are converted into several intermediates that participate in the early portion of the glycolytic pathway.

Table 5-4 summarizes the major characteristics of glycolysis.

Krebs Cycle

The Krebs cycle, named in honor of Hans Krebs who worked out the intermediate steps in this pathway (also known as the **citric acid cycle** or **tricarboxylic acid cycle**) is the second of the three pathways involved in fuel catabolism and ATP production. It utilizes molecular fragments formed during carbohydrate, protein, and fat breakdown, and it produces carbon dioxide, hydrogen atoms bound to coenzymes, and small amounts of ATP. The enzymes for this pathway are located in the mitochondria. Most of these enzymes are soluble enzymes in the inner mitochondrial compartment (the matrix—page 50).

The primary molecule entering at the beginning of the Krebs cycle is **acetyl coenzyme A** (acetyl CoA):

$$CH_3 - \overset{\displaystyle O}{\overset{\displaystyle \|}{C}} - S - R$$

TABLE 5-4 CHARACTERISTICS OF GLYCOLYSIS

Entering substrates	Glucose and other monosaccharides
Enzyme location	Cytosol
Net ATP production	2 ATP formed directly per molecule of glucose entering pathway
	Can be produced in the absence of oxygen (anaerobically)
Coenzyme production	2 NADH + H$^+$ formed under aerobic conditions
Final products	Pyruvate—under aerobic conditions
	Lactate—under anaerobic conditions
Net reaction	
Aerobic:	Glucose + 2 ADP + 2 P$_i$ + 2 NAD$^+$ $\longrightarrow$
	2 pyruvate + 2 ATP + 2 NADH + 2 H$^+$ + 2 H$_2$O
Anaerobic:	Glucose + 2 ADP + 2 P$_i$ $\longrightarrow$ 2 lactate + 2 ATP + 2 H$_2$O

Coenzyme A (CoA), a precursor of acetyl CoA, is derived from the B vitamin pantothenic acid, and its primary function is to transfer the two-carbon acetyl group from one molecule to another.[4] These acetyl groups come either from pyruvate, which as we have just seen is the end product of glycolysis, or from the breakdown of fatty acids and some amino acids, as we shall see in a later section. Pyruvate, upon entering mitochondria from the cytosol, undergoes the following reaction to produce acetyl CoA:

$$Pyruvate + CoA + NAD^+ \longrightarrow$$
$$acetyl\ CoA + CO_2 + NADH + H^+ \quad (5\text{-}3)$$

Note that this reaction produces the first molecule of CO_2 we have seen formed thus far in the pathways of fuel catabolism, and that hydrogen atoms have been transferred to NAD^+. We will make use of this latter fact later.

The Krebs cycle begins with the transfer of the acetyl group of acetyl CoA to the four-carbon molecule, oxaloacetate, to form the six-carbon molecule, citrate (Figure 5-14). At the third step in the cycle one molecule of CO_2 is produced, and again at the fourth step. Thus, two carbon atoms entered the cycle in the form of the acetyl group attached to CoA and now two carbons (although not the same ones) have left in the form of CO_2. Note also that the oxygen that appears in the CO_2 is not derived from molecular oxygen but from the carboxyl groups of Krebs-cycle intermediates.

In the remainder of the cycle, the four-carbon molecule formed in reaction 4 is modified through a series of reactions to produce the four-carbon molecule oxaloacetate, which becomes available to accept another acetyl group and repeat the cycle.

Now we come to a very crucial fact: In addition to producing carbon dioxide, intermediates in the Krebs cycle donate hydrogen atoms to the coenzymes NAD^+ and FAD. Two hydrogen atoms are transferred to NAD^+ in each of steps 3, 4, and 8, and to FAD in reaction 6. These hydrogens will be transferred from the coenzymes to oxygen in the next stage of fuel metabolism, oxidative phosphorylation. Since oxidative phosphorylation is necessary for regeneration of the hydrogen-free form of these coenzymes, the Krebs cycle can operate only under aerobic conditions. There is no pathway in the mitochondria that can remove the hydrogen from these coenzymes under anaerobic conditions.

So far we have said nothing of how the Krebs cycle contributes to the formation of ATP. In fact, the Krebs cycle directly produces only one high-energy nucleotide triphosphate. This occurs during reaction 5 in which inorganic phosphate is transferred to guanosine diphosphate (GDP) to form guanosine triphosphate (GTP). The hydrolysis of GTP, like that of ATP, can provide energy for some energy-requiring reactions. In addition, the energy in GTP can be transferred to ATP by the reaction

$$GTP + ADP \rightleftharpoons GDP + ATP$$

This reaction is reversible, and the energy in ATP can be used to form GTP from GDP when additional GTP is required for this molecule's roles in protein synthesis and signal transduction (Chapter 7).

To reiterate, the formation of GTP is the only mechanism by which ATP is directly formed within the Krebs cycle. Why, then, is the Krebs cycle so important? Because the hydrogen atoms transferred in the cycle to the coenzymes are used in the next pathway, oxidative phosphorylation, to form large amounts of ATP. The net result of the catabolism of one acetyl group from acetyl CoA by way of the Krebs cycle can be written:

$$Acetyl\ CoA + 3\ NAD^+ + FAD + GDP +$$
$$P_i + 2\ H_2O \longrightarrow 2\ CO_2 + CoA + 3\ NADH +$$
$$3\ H^+ + FADH_2 + GTP \quad (5\text{-}4)$$

Table 5-5 summarizes the characteristics of the Krebs-cycle reactions.

One more point should be noted: Although the major function of the Krebs cycle is the provision of hydrogen atoms to the oxidative phosphorylation pathway, some of the intermediates in the cycle can be used to synthesize organic molecules, especially several types of amino acids, required by cells. Oxaloacetate is one of the intermediates used in this manner. When a molecule of oxaloacetate is removed from the Krebs cycle in the process of forming amino acids, it is not available to combine with the acetate fragment of acetyl CoA at the beginning of the cycle. Thus, there must be a way of replacing the oxaloacetate and other Krebs-cycle intermediates that are consumed in synthetic pathways. Carbohydrates provide one source of oxaloacetate replacement by the following reaction, which converts pyruvate into oxaloacetate (contrast this reaction to Equation 5-3):

$$Pyruvate + CO_2 + ATP \longrightarrow$$
$$oxaloacetate + ADP + P_i \quad (5\text{-}5)$$

Certain amino acid derivatives, as we shall see, also can be used to form oxaloacetate and other Krebs-cycle intermediates.

Oxidative Phosphorylation

Oxidative phosphorylation provides the third, and quantitatively most important, mechanism by which energy de-

---

[4]Coenzyme A can also transfer other small carbon fragments such as succinate, as occurs in reaction 5 of the Krebs cycle.

TABLE 5-7 AEROBIC YIELD OF ATP FROM GLUCOSE CATABOLISM

Pathway		ATP per glucose	Percent of total ATP
Glycolysis (cytosol), substrate phosphorylation		2	5
Krebs cycle (mitochondria), 2 GTP to 2 ATP		2	5
Oxidative phosphorylation (mitochondria)		32 or 34	90
1. 2 NADH + 2 H$^+$ from glycolysis:	4 or 6 ATP		
2. 2 NADH + 2 H$^+$ from pyruvate to acetyl CoA:	6 ATP		
3. 6 NADH + 6 H$^+$ from Krebs cycle:	18 ATP		
4. 2 FADH$_2$ from Krebs cycle:	4 ATP		
Total		36 or 38	100

In the absence of oxygen, only 2 molecules of ATP can be formed by the breakdown of glucose to lactate. This yield represents only 2 percent of the energy stored in glucose. Thus, the evolution of aerobic metabolic pathways greatly increased the amount of energy available to a cell from glucose catabolism. For example, if a muscle consumed 38 molecules of ATP during a contraction, this amount of ATP could be supplied by the breakdown of 1 molecule of glucose in the presence of oxygen or 19 molecules of glucose under anaerobic conditions.

It is important to note, however, that although only 2 molecules of ATP are formed per molecule of glucose under anaerobic conditions, large amounts of ATP can still be supplied by the glycolytic pathway if large amounts of glucose are broken down to lactate. This is not an efficient utilization of fuel energy, but it does permit continued ATP production under anaerobic conditions, such as occur during intense exercise (Chapter 9).

Glycogen Storage. A small amount of glucose can be stored in the body to provide a reserve supply for use during those periods when glucose is not being absorbed into the blood from the intestinal tract. It is stored in the form of the polysaccharide **glycogen**, mostly in skeletal muscles and the liver.

Glycogen is synthesized from glucose by the pathway illustrated in Figure 5-17. The enzymes for both glycogen synthesis and glycogen breakdown are located in the cytosol. The first step, the transfer of phosphate from a molecule of ATP to glucose, forming glucose 6-phosphate, is the same as the first step in glycolysis. Thus glucose 6-phosphate can either be broken down to pyruvate or be incorporated into glycogen.

Note that, as indicated by the bowed arrows in Figure 5-17, different enzymes are used to synthesize and break down glycogen. The existence of two pathways containing enzymes that are subject to both covalent and allosteric modulation provides a mechanism for regulating the flow of glucose to and from glycogen. When an excess of glucose is available to a liver or muscle cell, the enzymes in

FIGURE 5-17
Pathways for glycogen synthesis and breakdown. Each bowed arrow indicates an irreversible reaction that requires one enzyme to catalyze the reaction in the forward direction and a separate enzyme (or enzymes) for the reverse reaction.

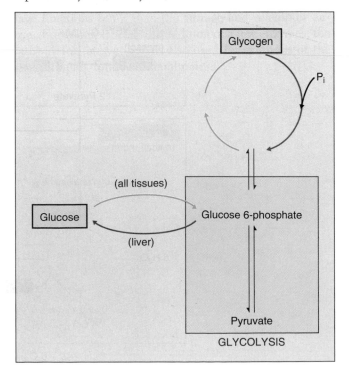

the glycogen synthesis pathway are activated, by the chemical signals described in Chapter 18, and the enzyme that breaks down glycogen is simultaneously inhibited. This combination leads to the net storage of glucose in the form of glycogen. When less glucose is available, the reverse combination of enzyme stimulation and inhibition occurs, and there is a net breakdown of glycogen to glucose 6-phosphate.

Two paths are available to the glucose 6-phosphate formed from the breakdown of glycogen: (1) In most cells, including skeletal muscle, glucose 6-phosphate enters the glycolytic pathway and, in the presence of oxygen, the pyruvate formed passes into the mitochondria where it is broken down into carbon dioxide and water; (2) in liver cells, glucose 6-phosphate can be converted to free glucose by removal of the phosphate group, and glucose is then able to pass out of the cell into the blood and become available to be used as fuel by other cells (Chapter 18).

Glucose Synthesis. In addition to being formed in the liver from the breakdown of glycogen, glucose can be synthesized in the liver and kidneys from intermediates derived from the breakdown of other classes of fuel molecules. This process of generating new molecules of glucose is known as **gluconeogenesis**. The major input to gluconeogenesis is pyruvate, formed from lactate and from several amino acids during protein breakdown. In addition, glycerol derived from the hydrolysis of triacylglycerols can be converted into glucose via a pathway that does not involve pyruvate.

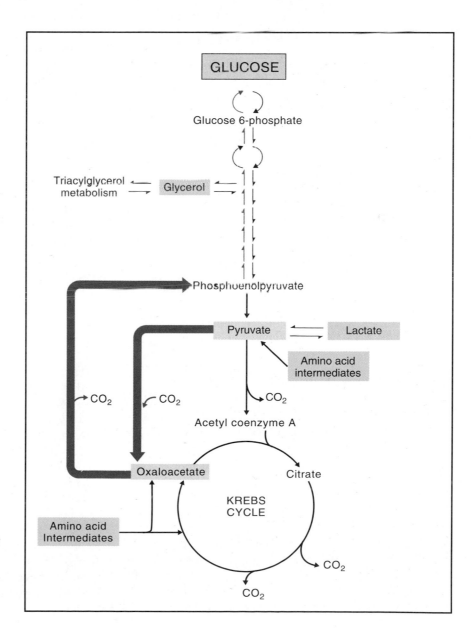

FIGURE 5-18

Gluconeogenic pathway by which pyruvate, lactate, glycerol, and various amino acid intermediates can be converted into glucose in the liver. Note the points at which each of these precursors, supplied by the blood, enters the pathway.

The pathway for gluconeogenesis in the liver and kidneys (Figure 5-18) makes use of many but not all of the enzymes used in glycolysis because most of these enzyme reactions are reversible. However, reactions 3 and 10 (Figure 5-12) are irreversible, and additional enzymes are required, therefore, to form glucose from pyruvate. Pyruvate is converted to phosphoenolpyruvate by a series of mitochondrial reactions in which CO_2 is added to pyruvate to form the four-carbon Krebs-cycle intermediate oxaloacetate. [In addition to being an important intermediary step in gluconeogenesis, this reaction (Equation 5-5) provides a pathway for replacing Krebs-cycle intermediates, as described earlier.] An additional series of reactions leads to the transfer of a four-carbon intermediate derived from oxaloacetate out of the mitochondria and its conversion to phosphoenolpyruvate in the cytosol. Phosphoenolpyruvate then reverses the steps taken in glycolysis back to the level of reaction 3, in which a different enzyme from that used in glycolysis is required to convert fructose 1,6-bisphosphate to fructose 6-phosphate. From this point on the reactions are again reversible, leading to glucose 6-phosphate, which can be converted to glucose or stored as glycogen.

Since energy is released during the glycolytic breakdown of glucose to pyruvate in the form of heat and ATP generation, energy must be added to reverse this pathway. A total of six ATP are consumed in the reactions of gluconeogenesis. Thus, as with most anabolic reactions, energy must be expended to synthesize glucose, whereas energy is released during glucose breakdown.

Since many of the same enzymes are used in glycolysis and gluconeogenesis, the question arises as to what controls the direction of metabolic flow through this series of enzymes. What conditions determine whether glucose is broken down to pyruvate or whether pyruvate is converted into glucose? The answer lies in the concentrations of glucose or pyruvate in a cell and in the allosteric control of the enzymes that occur at the irreversible steps in the pathway, a control exerted via various hormones (Chapter 18).

Fat Metabolism

Fat Catabolism. Triacylglycerol (fat) consists of three fatty acids linked to glycerol (page 25). Fat accounts for the major portion (approximately 80 percent) of the energy stored in the body (Table 5-8). Under resting conditions, approximately half the energy used by such tissues as muscle, liver, and kidneys is derived from the catabolism of fatty acids.

Although most cells store small amounts of fat, the majority of the body's fat is stored in specialized cells known as **adipocytes**. Almost the entire cytoplasm of these cells is filled with a single large fat droplet. Clusters of adipocytes form **adipose tissue**, most of which is located in

TABLE 5-8   FUEL CONTENT OF A 70-KG PERSON

	Total-body content, kg	Energy content, kcal/g	Total-body energy content	
			kcal	%
Triacylglycerols	15.6	9	140,000	78
Proteins	9.5	9	38,000	21
Carbohydrates	0.5	4	2,000	1

deposits underlying the skin. The function of adipocytes is to synthesize and store triacylglycerols during periods of food uptake and then, when food is not being absorbed from the intestinal tract, to release fatty acids and glycerol into the blood from which they can be taken up and used by other cells to provide the energy for ATP formation. The factors controlling fat storage and release from adipocytes will be described in Chapter 18. Here we will emphasize the pathway by which fatty acids are catabolized by most cells to provide the energy for ATP synthesis, and the pathway for the synthesis of fatty acids from other fuel molecules.

Figure 5-19 shows the pathway for fatty acid catabolism, which is achieved by enzymes present in the mitochondrial matrix. The breakdown of a fatty acid is initiated by linking a molecule of coenzyme A to the carboxyl end of the fatty acid. This initial step is accompanied by the breakdown of ATP to AMP and two P_i. Since the terminal phosphates of both ATP and ADP are high-energy bonds, the energy released in this reaction is equivalent to that released when two ATP are hydrolyzed to two ADP and two P_i. Thus, although only one ATP is used in the reaction, the energy cost is equivalent to two ATP.

The coenzyme A derivative of the fatty acid then proceeds through a series of reactions, known as **beta oxidation**, which split off a molecule of acetyl coenzyme A from the end of the fatty acid and transfer two pairs of hydrogen atoms to coenzymes, one pair to FAD and the other to NAD^+. These coenzymes then enter the oxidative phosphorylation pathway, $NADH + H^+$ forming three molecules of ATP, and $FADH_2$ forming two, for a total of five ATP.

When the terminal acetyl coenzyme A is split from the fatty acid, another coenzyme A is added (ATP is not required for this step), and the sequence is repeated. Each passage through this sequence shortens the fatty acid chain by two carbon atoms until all the carbon atoms have been transferred to coenzyme A. As we saw on page 97, the acetyl coenzyme A molecules then enter the Krebs

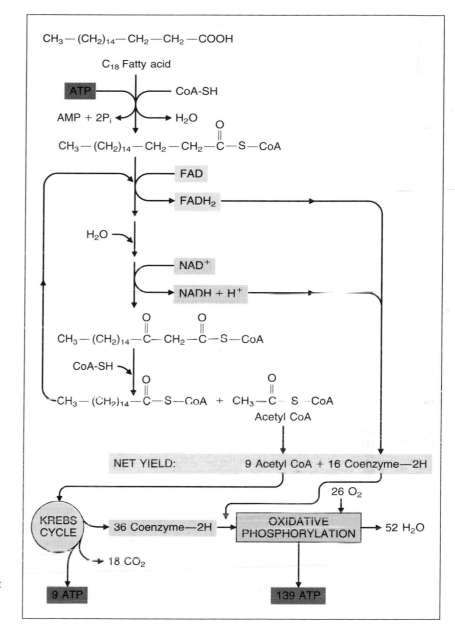

FIGURE 5-19

Pathway of fatty acid catabolism, which takes place in the mitochondria. The energy equivalent of two ATP is consumed at the start of the pathway.

cycle, each two-carbon fragment producing 2 molecules of CO_2 and ultimately 12 molecules of ATP via the Krebs cycle and oxidative phosphorylation.

How much ATP is formed as a result of the total catabolism of a fatty acid? Most fatty acids in the body contain 14 to 22 carbons, 16 and 18 being most common. The catabolism of one 18-carbon saturated fatty acid yields 146 ATP molecules (Table 5-9). In contrast, the catabolism of one glucose molecule yields a maximum of 38 ATP molecules. Thus, taking into account the difference in molecular weight of the fatty acid and glucose, it turns out that the amount of ATP formed from the catabolism of a gram of fat is about $2\frac{1}{2}$ times greater than the amount of ATP pro-

duced by catabolizing one gram of carbohydrate. If an average person stored most of his or her fuel as carbohydrate rather than as fat, body weight would have to be approximately 30 percent greater in order to store the same amount of usable energy, and the person would consume more energy moving this extra weight around. Thus, a major step in fuel economy occurred when animals evolved the ability to store fuel as fat. In contrast, plants store almost all their fuel as carbohydrate (starch).

Fat Synthesis. The synthesis of fatty acids occurs by reactions that are almost the reverse of those that degrade them. However, the enzymes in the synthetic pathway are

stant in spite of variations in salt and water intake and loss, thereby preventing damage to cells that would occur from excessive swelling or shrinkage.

If cells are placed in a solution of nonpenetrating solutes having an osmolarity of 300 m*Osm,* they will neither swell nor shrink since the water concentrations in the intra- and extracellular fluid are the same and the solutes cannot leave or enter. Such solutions are said to be **isotonic** (Figure 6-21), defined as having the same concentration of *nonpenetrating* solutes as normal extracellular fluid. Solutions containing less than 300 mOsm of nonpenetrating solutes (**hypotonic** solutions) will cause cells to swell because water will diffuse into the cell from its higher concentration in the extracellular fluid. Solutions containing greater than 300 m*Osm* of nonpenetrating solutes (**hypertonic** solutions) will cause cells to shrink as water diffuses out of the cell into the fluid with a lower water concentration. Note that the concentration of *nonpenetrating* solutes in a solution, not the total osmolarity, determines its tonicity—hypotonic, isotonic, or hypertonic.

In contrast, another set of terms—**isoosmotic, hyperosmotic,** and **hypoosmotic**—denotes simply the osmolarity of a solution relative to that of normal extracellular fluid without regard for whether the solute is penetrating or nonpenetrating. The two sets of terms are therefore not synonymous. For example, a 1-L solution containing 300 mOsmol of nonpenetrating NaCl and 100 mOsmol of urea, which can cross plasma membranes, would have a total osmolarity of 400 m*Osm* and would be hyperosmotic. It would, however, still be an isotonic solution, and so cells immersed in it would not shrink or swell. The reason is that urea will diffuse into the cells and reach the same concentration as the urea in the extracellular solution, and thus both the intracellular and extracellular solutions will have the same osmolarity (400 m*Osm*), and there will be no difference in the water concentration across the membrane and thus no change in cell volume.

Table 6-3 provides a comparison of the various terms used to describe the osmolarity of solutions. All hypoosmotic solutions are also hypotonic, whereas a hyperosmotic solution can be hypertonic, isotonic, or hypotonic.

The tonicity of solutions injected into the body is of great importance in medicine. Such solutions usually consist of an isotonic solution of NaCl (150 m*M* NaCl—isotonic saline) or an isotonic solution of glucose (5% dextrose solution). Injecting a drug dissolved in such solutions will not produce changes in cell volume, whereas injection

TABLE 6-3	TERMS REFERRING TO THE SOLUTE OSMOLARITY AND TONICITY OF SOLUTIONS
Isoosmotic	A solution containing 300 mOsmol/L of solute, regardless of its composition of membrane-penetrating and nonpenetrating solutes
Hyperosmotic	A solution containing greater than 300 mOsmol/L of solutes, regardless of the composition of membrane-penetrating and nonpenetrating solutes
Hypoosmotic	A solution containing less than 300 mOsmol/L of solutes, regardless of the composition of membrane-penetrating and nonpenetrating solutes
Isotonic	A solution containing 300 mOsmol/L of nonpenetrating solutes, regardless of the concentration of membrane-penetrating solutes that may be present
Hypertonic	A solution containing greater than 300 mOsmol/L of nonpenetrating solutes, regardless of the concentration of membrane-penetrating solutes that may be present
Hypotonic	A solution containing less than 300 mOsmol/L of nonpenetrating solutes, regardless of the concentration of membrane-penetrating solutes that may be present

of the same drug dissolved in pure water, a hypotonic solution, will produce cell swelling, perhaps to the point that plasma membranes will rupture, destroying cells.

ENDOCYTOSIS AND EXOCYTOSIS

In addition to diffusion and mediated transport, there is another pathway by which substances can enter or leave cells, one that does not require the molecules to pass through the structural matrix of the membrane. When living cells are observed under a light microscope, regions of the plasma membrane can be seen to fold into the cell, forming small pockets that pinch off to produce intracellular membrane-bound vesicles that enclose a small volume of extracellular fluid. This process is known as **endocytosis** (Figure 6-22). A similar process in the reverse direction, known as **exocytosis**, occurs when membrane-bound vesicles in the cytoplasm fuse with the plasma membrane and release their contents to the outside of the cell.

Endocytosis

Several varieties of endocytosis can be identified. When the vesicle simply encloses a small volume of extracellular fluid, as described above, the process is known as **fluid endocytosis**. In other cases, specific molecules in the extracellular fluid bind to the plasma membrane and are carried into the cell along with the extracellular fluid when the membrane invaginates. This is known as **adsorptive endocytosis**. In addition to taking in trapped extracellular fluid, adsorptive endocytosis leads to selective concentration in the vesicle of the material bound to the membrane. Both fluid and adsorptive endocytosis are often referred to as **pinocytosis** (cell drinking). A third type of endocytosis

FIGURE 6-22

Endocytosis and exocytosis.

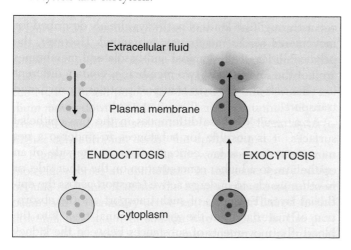

occurs when large particles, such as bacteria and debris from damaged tissues, are engulfed by the plasma membrane. In this form of endocytosis, known as **phagocytosis** (cell eating), the membrane folds around the surface of the particle so that little extracellular fluid is enclosed within the vesicle. While most cells undergo pinocytosis, only a few special cells carry out phagocytosis.

In most cells, fluid endocytosis occurs continuously, whereas adsorptive endocytosis and phagocytosis are stimulated by the binding of specific molecules or particles to the cell surface. Endocytosis of any kind requires metabolic energy in the form of ATP, although the molecular mechanisms by which this energy is coupled to membrane movements during endocytosis are unknown.

What is the fate of the endocytotic vesicles once they have entered the cell? In some cases they pass through the cytoplasm and fuse with the plasma membrane on the opposite side of the cell, releasing their contents to the extracellular space (Figure 6-23). This provides a pathway for transferring large molecules, such as proteins, across the cells that separate two compartments, for example, blood and interstitial fluid. A similar process allows small amounts of protein to be moved across the intestinal epithelium.

In most cells, however, endocytotic vesicles fuse with the membranes of lysosomes (Figure 6-23), organelles that contain digestive enzymes that break down large molecules such as proteins, polysaccharides, and nucleic acids. The fusion of the endocytotic vesicle with the lysosomal membrane exposes the contents of the vesicle to these digestive enzymes. The phagocytosis of bacteria and their destruction by the lysosomal digestive enzymes is one of the body's major defense mechanisms against germs (Chapter 20).

Endocytosis removes a small portion of the membrane from the cell surface. In cells that have a great deal of endocytotic activity, more than 100 percent of the plasma membrane may be internalized in an hour, yet the membrane surface area remains constant. This is because the membrane is replaced at about the same rate by vesicle membrane that fuses with the plasma membrane during exocytosis.

Exocytosis

Exocytosis performs two functions for cells: (1) It provides a way to replace portions of the plasma membrane that have been removed by endocytosis and, in the process, to add new membrane components; and (2) it provides a route by which membrane-impermeable molecules synthesized by cells can be released (secreted) into the extracellular fluid.

How are substances that are to be secreted by exocytosis packaged into vesicles? The story for protein synthesis and packaging into vesicles was described in Chapter 4.

KEY TERMS

plasma membrane	osmole
diffusion	osmotic pressure
flux	nonpenetrating solutes
net flux	isotonic
diffusion equilibrium	hypotonic
permeability constant k_p	hypertonic
channels	isoosmotic
membrane potential	hyperosmotic
electrochemical difference	hypoosmotic
channel gating	endocytosis
voltage-sensitive channels	exocytosis
mechanosensitive channels	fluid endocytosis
transporters	adsorptive endocytosis
mediated transport	pinocytosis
facilitated diffusion	phagocytosis
active transport	luminal membrane
primary active transport	basolateral membrane
secondary active transport	paracellular pathway
cotransport	transcellular pathway
countertransport	exocrine gland
osmosis	endocrine gland
osmolarity	hormones

REVIEW QUESTIONS

1. What determines the direction in which net diffusion of a nonpolar molecule will occur?

2. In what ways can the net solute flux between two compartments separated by a permeable membrane be increased?

3. Why are membranes more permeable to nonpolar molecules than to most polar and ionized molecules?

4. Ions diffuse across cell membranes by what pathway?

5. When considering the diffusion of ions across a membrane, what driving force, in addition to the ion concentration gradient, must be considered?

6. What factors can alter the opening and closing of protein channels in a membrane?

7. Describe the mechanism by which a mediated-transport protein moves a solute from one side of a membrane to the other.

8. What determines the magnitude of a mediated-transport flux across a membrane?

9. What characteristics distinguish diffusion from facilitated diffusion?

10. What characteristics distinguish facilitated diffusion from active transport?

11. Contrast the mechanism by which energy is coupled to a transport protein during (a) primary active transport, and (b) secondary active transport.

12. Describe the direction in which sodium ions and a transported solute move during cotransport and countertransport.

13. How can the concentration of water in a solution be decreased?

14. If two solutions having different osmolarities are separated by a water-permeable membrane, why will there be a change in the volumes of the two compartments if the membrane is impermeable to the solutes, but no change in volume if the membrane is permeable to solute?

15. To which solution must pressure be applied to prevent the osmotic flow of water across a membrane separating a solution of high osmolarity and a solution of lower osmolarity?

16. Why do sodium and chloride ions in the extracellular fluid and potassium ions in the intracellular fluid behave as if they are nonpenetrating solutes?

17. What is the osmolarity of the extracellular fluid? Of the intracellular fluid?

18. What change in cell volume will occur when a cell is placed in a hypotonic solution? In a hypertonic solution?

19. Under what conditions will a hyperosmotic solution be isotonic?

20. Endocytotic vesicles deliver their contents to which parts of a cell?

21. How do the mechanisms for actively transporting glucose and sodium across an epithelium differ?

22. By what mechanism does the active transport of sodium lead to the osmotic flow of water across an epithelium?

23. What is the difference between an endocrine gland and an exocrine gland?

THOUGHT QUESTIONS

(Answers are given in Appendix A.)

1. In two cases (A and B), the concentrations of solute X in two 1-L compartments separated by a membrane through which X can diffuse are

	Concentration of X, mM	
Case	Compartment 1	Compartment 2
A	3	5
B	32	30

a. In what direction will the net flux take place in case A and in case B?

b. When diffusion equilibrium is reached, what will be the concentration of solute in each compartment in case A and in case B?

c. Will A reach diffusion equilibrium faster, slower, or at the same rate as B?

2. When the extracellular concentration of the amino acid alanine is increased, the flux of the amino acid leucine into a cell is decreased. How might this observation be explained?

3. If an active-transport protein has a lower affinity for the transported solute on the extracellular surface of the plasma membrane than on the intracellular surface, in what direction will there be a net transport of the solute across the membrane? (Assume that the rate of protein conformational change is the same in both directions.)

4. Why will inhibition of ATP synthesis by a cell lead to a decrease in secondary active transport?

5. Given the following solutions, which has the lowest water concentration? Which two are isoosmotic?

	Concentration, mM			
Solution	Glucose	Urea	NaCl	CaCl$_2$
A	20	30	150	10
B	10	100	20	50
C	100	200	10	20
D	30	10	60	100

6. Assume that a membrane separating two compartments is permeable to urea but not permeable to NaCl. If compartment 1 contains 200 mmol/L of NaCl and 100 mmol/L of urea and compartment 2 contains 100 mmol/L of NaCl and 300 mmol/L of urea, which compartment will have increased in volume when osmotic equilibrium is reached?

7. What will happen to cell volume if a cell is placed in each of the following solutions?

	Concentration, mM	
Solution	NaCl (nonpenetrating)	Urea (penetrating)
A	150	100
B	100	150
C	200	100
D	100	50

8. Characterize each of the solutions in question 7 as to whether it is isotonic, hypotonic, hypertonic, hypoosmotic, or hyperosmotic.

9. By what mechanism might an increase in intracellular sodium concentration lead to an increase in exocytosis?

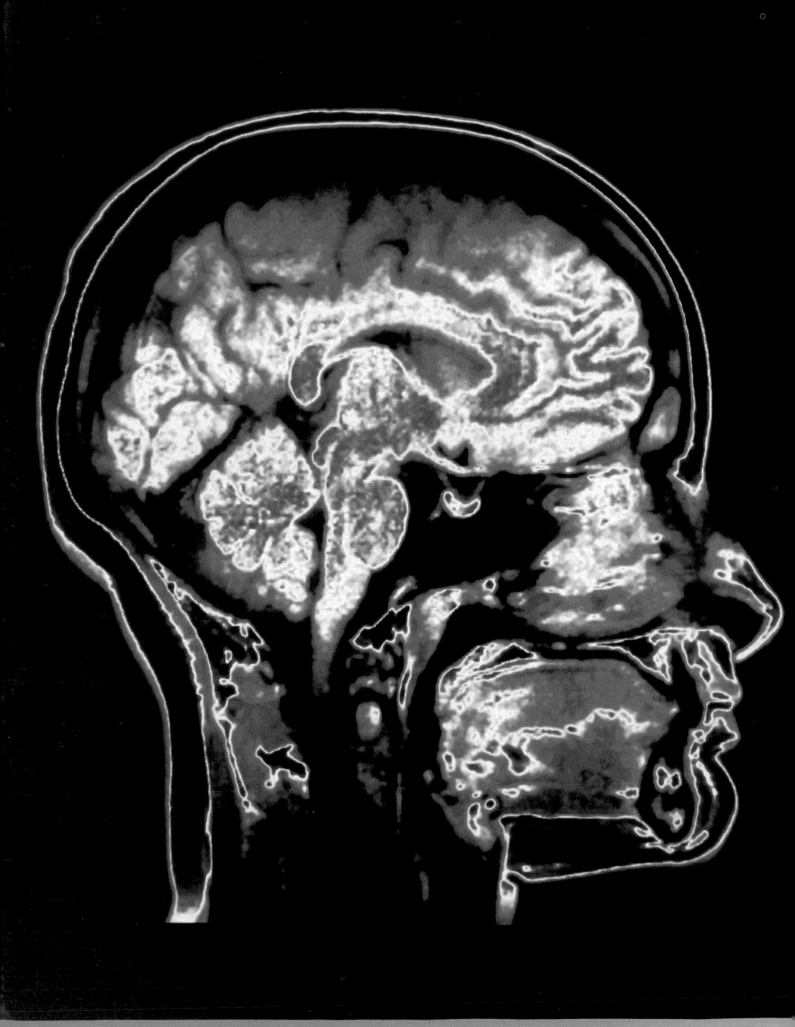

PART

TWO

BIOLOGICAL CONTROL SYSTEMS

CHAPTER 7   HOMEOSTATIC MECHANISMS AND
             CELLULAR COMMUNICATION   149
CHAPTER 8   NEURAL CONTROL MECHANISMS   179
             SECTION A. NEURAL TISSUE   181
             SECTION B. MEMBRANE POTENTIALS   186
             SECTION C. SYNAPSES   201
             SECTION D. STRUCTURE OF THE NERVOUS SYSTEM   214
CHAPTER 9   THE SENSORY SYSTEMS   233
CHAPTER 10   HORMONAL CONTROL MECHANISMS   273
CHAPTER 11   MUSCLE   303
             SECTION A. SKELETAL MUSCLE   304
             SECTION B. SMOOTH MUSCLE   338
CHAPTER 12   CONTROL OF BODY MOVEMENT   349
CHAPTER 13   CONSCIOUSNESS AND BEHAVIOR   369

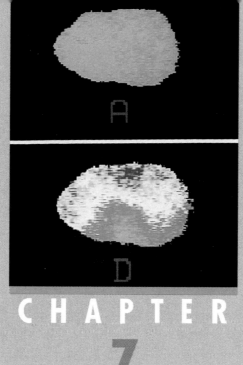

CHAPTER
7

HOMEOSTATIC MECHANISMS AND CELLULAR COMMUNICATION

GENERAL CHARACTERISTICS OF HOMEOSTATIC CONTROL SYSTEMS

Feedforward Regulation

Acclimatization

Biological Rhythms

Aging and Homeostasis

THE BALANCE CONCEPT AND CHEMICAL HOMEOSTASIS

COMPONENTS OF HOMEOSTATIC SYSTEMS

Reflexes

Local Homeostatic Responses

Intercellular Chemical Messengers

   Eicosanoids

RECEPTORS

Regulation of Receptors

SIGNAL TRANSDUCTION MECHANISMS FOR PLASMA-MEMBRANE RECEPTORS

Adenylyl Cyclase and Cyclic AMP

Guanylyl Cyclase and Cyclic GMP

Phospholipase C, Diacylglycerol, and Inositol Trisphosphate

Ion Channels Controlled by G Proteins

Calcium as a Second Messenger

SUMMARY

KEY TERMS

REVIEW QUESTIONS

CLINICAL TERMS

THOUGHT QUESTIONS

art 2 provides the information needed to bridge the gap between the cell physiology discussed in Part 1 and the coordinated body functions described in Part 3. This chapter begins that process by amplifying the concept of homeostasis first presented in Chapter 1 and describing the general characteristics of homeostatic control systems. The operation of these systems requires that cells be able to communicate with each other, often over long distances. We shall see that much of this intercellular communication is mediated by chemical messengers that interact with their target cells by means of specific proteins—receptors—on the cells. Finally, these interactions trigger, *within* the target cells, sequences of chemical events that culminate in the cells' response to the messenger.

GENERAL CHARACTERISTICS OF HOMEOSTATIC CONTROL SYSTEMS

s described in Chapter 1, the activities of cells, tissues, and organs must be regulated and integrated with each other in such a way that any change in the extracellular fluid initiates a reaction to minimize the change. **Homeostasis** denotes the relatively stable conditions of the internal environment that result from these compensating regulatory responses performed by **homeostatic control systems**.

Consider the regulation of body temperature. Our subject is a resting, lightly clad man in a room having a temperature of 20°C and moderate humidity. His internal body temperature is 37°C, and he is losing heat to the external environment because it is at a lower temperature. However, the chemical reactions occurring within the cells of his body are producing heat at a rate equal to the rate of heat loss. Under these conditions, the body undergoes no net gain or loss of heat and the body temperature remains constant. The system is said to be in a **steady state**, defined as a system in which a particular variable (temperature, in this case) is not changing, but energy (in this case, heat) must be added continuously to maintain the variable constant. Steady states differ from equilibria, in which a particular variable is not changing but no input of energy is required to maintain the constancy. The steady-state temperature in our example is known as the **operating point** (also termed the set point) of the thermoregulatory system.

This example illustrates a crucial generalization about homeostasis: Stability of an internal environmental variable is achieved by the balancing of inputs and outputs. In this case, the variable—body temperature—remains constant because metabolic heat production (input) equals heat loss from the body (output).

Now we lower the temperature of the room rapidly, say to 5°C, and keep it there. This immediately increases the loss of heat from our subject's warm skin, upsetting the dynamic balance between heat gain and loss. The body temperature therefore starts to fall. Very rapidly, however, a variety of homeostatic responses occur to limit the fall (Figure 7-1). First, the blood vessels to the skin narrow, reducing the amount of warm blood flowing through the skin and thus reducing heat loss. At a room temperature of 5°C, however, blood vessel constriction is not able to eliminate completely the extra heat loss from the skin. Our subject curls up in order to reduce the surface area of skin available for heat loss. This helps a bit, but excessive heat loss still continues and body temperature keeps falling, although at a slower rate. He has a strong desire to put on more clothing, for "voluntary" behavioral responses are often crucial components in homeostasis, but no clothing is available. Clearly, then, if excessive heat loss (output) cannot be prevented, the only way of restoring the balance between heat input and output is to increase input, and this is precisely what occurs. He begins to shiver, and the chemical reactions responsible for the muscular contractions that constitute shivering produce large quantities of heat.

Indeed, heat production may transiently exceed heat loss so that body temperature begins to go back toward the value existing before the room temperature was lowered. It eventually stabilizes at a temperature *a bit below this original value*; at this new steady state, heat input and heat output are again equal to each other. Here is another crucial generalization about homeostasis: Stability of an internal environmental variable depends not upon the absolute magnitudes of opposing inputs and outputs, but only upon the balance between them.

The thermoregulatory system just described is an example of a **negative-feedback** system, in which an increase or decrease in the variable being regulated brings about responses that tend to move the variable in the direction opposite ("negative" to) the direction of the original change. Thus, in our example, the *decrease* in body temperature led to responses that tended to *increase* the body temperature, that is, move it toward its original value.

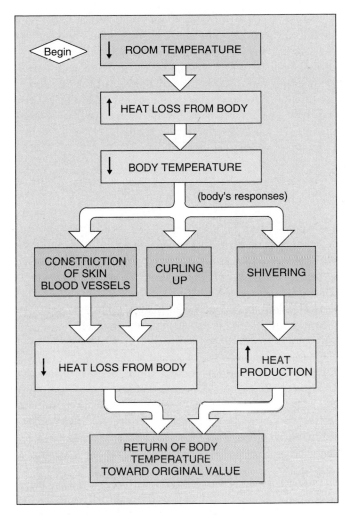

FIGURE 7-1

A homeostatic control system. This system maintains body temperature relatively constant when room temperature decreases. This diagram is typical of those used throughout the remainder of this book to illustrate homeostatic systems, and several conventions should be noted. The "begin" sign indicates where to start. The arrows next to each term denote increases or decreases. The arrows connecting any two terms in the figure denote cause and effect; that is, an arrow can be read as "causes" or "leads to" (for example, decreased room temperature "leads to" increased heat loss from the body). In general, one should add the words "tends to" in thinking about these cause-and-effect relationships. For example, decreased room temperature tends to cause an increase in heat loss from the body, and curling up tends to cause a decrease in heat loss from the body. Qualifying the relationship in this way is necessary because variables like heat production and heat loss are under the influence of many factors, some of which oppose each other.

Negative-feedback control systems are the most common homeostatic mechanisms in the body, but there is another type of feedback known as **positive feedback** in which an initial disturbance in a system sets off a train of events that increase the disturbance even further. Thus positive feedback does not favor stability and often abruptly displaces a system away from its steady-state operating point. As we shall see, several important positive-feedback relationships occur in the body, blood clotting being one example.

Much of the sequence of events shown in Figure 7-1 is familiar, of course, since the ultimate responses—decreased skin temperature, curling up, and shivering—are visible. But what about the internal workings underlying them? First, what initiated the signals in the nerves to the blood vessels and the muscles that shiver? These nerves are controlled by centers in the brain, which are in turn controlled by signals coming from small groups of temperature-sensitive nerve cells in various parts of the body. The chain of events can be summarized: Decreased internal body temperature → increased activity of temperature sensitive nerve cells → increased activity of a series of nerve cells in the central nervous system, the last of which stimulate contraction of skeletal muscles (to produce shivering) and smooth muscles in the skin blood vessels (to reduce skin blood flow).

A third generalization about homeostasis follows from the preceding description of system components and the nature of negative feedback: Homeostatic control systems cannot maintain *complete* constancy of the internal environment in the face of persistent change in the external environment but can only minimize changes (Figure 7-2). Imagine for the moment that the body's responses to a cold environment really did return body temperature completely to 37°C. What would happen to the output of the first component, the temperature-sensitive nerve cells — the "detectors"? Recall that it was the drop in internal body temperature that elicited the change in output from these detectors in the first place. If the body temperature were to return completely to its original value, so would the output of the detectors, and the entire sequence of events would stop. The blood vessels would stop constricting, shivering would cease, and body temperature would once again fall since the compensations would no longer be present. In other words, as long as the exposure to cold continues, some decrease in body temperature must persist to serve as a signal to maintain the responses. Such a signal is termed an **error signal**.

Just how big the error signal is in a control system depends on the magnitude of the external change, the sensitivity of the detectors, the efficiency of the connections between the system's components, and the responsiveness of the final apparatus in the control system. The temperature-regulating systems of the body are extremely sensitive, so that body temperature normally varies by only about 1°C even in the face of marked changes in the external environment.

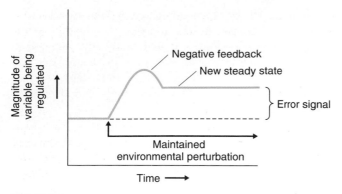

FIGURE 7-2

Negative-feedback control systems cannot return the regulated variable to its original value as long as the environmental perturbation persists. The deviation from the original value is called the error signal.

Inherent in the last sentence is another generalization about homeostasis: Even in reference to one individual, thus ignoring variation among persons, any regulated variable in the body cannot be assigned a single "normal" value but has a more-or-less narrow range of normal values, depending on external conditions. The more precise the homeostatic mechanisms for regulating a variable are, the narrower is the range. Thus, the concept of homeostasis is an ideal, since total constancy of the internal environment can never be achieved.

As we have seen, perturbations in the external environment can displace a variable from its preexisting operating point. In addition, we now recognize that the operating points for many regulated variables can be physiologically altered or *reset*; that is, the values which the homeostatic control systems are "trying" to maintain relatively constant can be altered. A common example is fever, the increase in body temperature that occurs in response to infection and which is analogous to raising the setting of your house's thermostat. The homeostatic control systems regulating body temperature are still functioning during a fever, but they maintain the temperature at a higher value. We shall see in Chapter 20 that this regulated rise in body temperature is adaptive for fighting the infection. The resetting of a set point that occurs for other variables is also adaptive in some cases, but in others it reflects the clashing demands of different regulatory systems.

The example of fever may have left the impression that operating points are reset only in response to external stimuli, in this case the presence of bacteria, but such is not the case. Indeed, as described in the next section, the operating points for many regulated variables change on a rhythmical basis every day; for example, the operating point for body temperature is higher during the day than at night.

One more generalization should be noted: It is not possible for everything to be maintained relatively constant by homeostatic mechanisms. In our example, body temperature was maintained constant, but only because large changes occurred in skin blood flow and skeletal-muscle contraction. Moreover, because so many properties of the internal environment are closely interrelated, it is often possible to maintain one property relatively constant only by moving others farther from their usual values. This is what we meant earlier by "clashing demands."

The generalizations we have given concerning homeostatic control systems are summarized in Table 7-1.

Feedforward Regulation

Another type of regulatory process frequently used in conjunction with negative-feedback systems is feedforward. Let us give an example of feedforward and then define it. The temperature-sensitive nerve cells that trigger negative-feedback regulation of body temperature when body temperature begins to fall are located *inside* the body. In addition, there are temperature-sensitive nerve cells in the skin, and these cells, in effect, monitor *outside* temperature. When outside temperature falls, as in our example, these nerve cells immediately detect the change and relay this information to the brain, which then sends out signals to the blood vessels and muscles, resulting in heat conservation and increased heat production. In this manner com-

---

TABLE 7-1   SOME IMPORTANT GENERALIZATIONS ABOUT HOMEOSTATIC CONTROL SYSTEMS

1. Stability of an internal-environmental variable is achieved by balancing inputs and outputs. It is not the absolute magnitudes of the inputs and outputs that matter but the balance between them.

2. In negative-feedback systems, a change in the variable being regulated brings about responses that tend to move the variable in the direction opposite the original change, that is, back toward the initial value.

3. Homeostatic control systems cannot maintain complete constancy of any given feature of the internal environment. Therefore, any regulated variable will have a more-or-less narrow range of normal values depending on the external-environmental conditions.

4. The operating point of some variables regulated by homeostatic control systems can be reset, that is, physiologically raised or lowered.

5. It is not possible for everything to be maintained relatively constant by homeostatic control systems. There is a hierarchy of importance, such that the constancy of certain variables is altered markedly to maintain others relatively constant.

pensatory thermoregulatory responses are activated *before* the colder outside temperature can cause the internal body temperature to fall. Thus, **feedforward** regulation anticipates changes in a regulated variable (internal body temperature in the example), improves the speed of the body's homeostatic responses, and minimizes fluctuations in the level of the variable being regulated.

Acclimatization

The term **adaptation** denotes a characteristic that favors survival in specific environments. Homeostatic control systems are inherited biological adaptations. An individual's ability to adapt to a particular environmental stress is not fixed, however, but can be enhanced, with no change in genetic endowment, by prolonged exposure to that stress. This type of adaptation is known as **acclimatization**.

Let us take sweating in response to heat exposure as an example and perform a simple experiment. On day 1 we expose a person for 30 min to a high temperature and ask her to do a standardized exercise test. Body temperature rises, and sweating begins after a certain period of time. The sweating provides a mechanism for increasing heat loss from the body and thus tends to minimize the rise in body temperature in a hot environment. The volume of sweat produced under these conditions is measured. Then, for a week, our subject enters the heat chamber for 1 or 2 h per day and exercises. On day 8, the sweating rate is again measured during the same exercise test performed on day 1; the striking finding is that the subject begins to sweat earlier and much more profusely than she did on day 1. Accordingly, her body temperature does not rise to nearly the same degree.

The subject has become acclimatized to the heat; that is, she has undergone an adaptive change induced by exposure to the heat and is now better adapted to heat exposure. In a sense, acclimatization may be viewed as an environmentally induced improvement in the functioning of an already existing genetically based homeostatic system. Up to some maximal limit, repeated or prolonged exposure to a particular environmental stress enhances the responsiveness of the system to that type of stress.

Heat acclimatization is completely reversible. If the daily exposures to heat are discontinued, the sweating rate of our subject will revert to the preacclimatized value within a relatively short time. If an acclimatization is induced very early in life, however, at the **critical period** for development of a structure or response, it is termed a **developmental acclimatization** and may be irreversible. For example, the barrel-shaped chests of natives of the Andes Mountains represent not a genetic difference between them and their lowland compatriots but rather an irreversible acclimatization induced during the first few years of their lives by their exposure to the low-oxygen environment of high altitude. The altered chest size remains even though the individual moves to a lowland environment later in life and stays there. Lowland persons who have suffered oxygen deprivation from heart or lung disease during their early years show precisely the same chest shape.

Biological Rhythms

A striking characteristic of many body functions is the rhythmical changes they manifest. The most common type is the **circadian rhythm**, which cycles approximately once every 24 h. Waking and sleeping, body temperature, hormone concentrations in the blood, the excretion of ions into the urine, and many other functions undergo circadian variation (Figure 7-3). Other cycles have much longer periods, the menstrual cycle (approximately 28 days) being the most well known.

A crucial point concerning most body rhythms is that they are *internally* driven. Environmental factors do not drive the rhythm but rather provide the timing cues important for **entrainment** (that is, setting of the actual hours) of the rhythm. A classic experiment will clarify this distinction.

Subjects were put in experimental chambers that completely isolated them from the external environment. For the first few days, they were exposed to a 24-h rest-activity cycle in which the room lights were turned on and off at the same time each day. Under these conditions, their sleep-wake cycles were 24 h long. Then, all environmental time cues were eliminated, and the individuals were allowed to control the lights themselves. Immediately, their sleep-wake patterns began to change. On the average, bedtime began about 30 min later *each day* and so did wake-up time. Thus a sleep-wake cycle persisted in the complete absence of environmental cues, and such a rhythm is called a **free running rhythm**. In this case it was approximately 25 h rather than 24; that is, cues are required to entrain a circadian rhythm to 24 h.

One more point should be mentioned: By altering the duration of the light-dark cycles, sleep-wake cycles can be entrained to any value between 23 and 27 h, but shorter or longer durations cannot be entrained; instead, the rhythm continues to free-run. Because of this, the bodies of people whose work causes them to adopt sleep-wake cycles longer than 27 h are never able to make the proper adjustments and achieve stable rhythms. The result is symptoms similar to those of jet lag, to be described later.

The light-dark cycle is the most important environmental time cue in our lives but not the only one. Others include external environmental temperature, meal timing, and many social cues. Thus, if several people were undergoing the experiment just described in isolation from each other, their free-runs would be different, but if they were all in the same room, one person would be dominant and set the cycle for the others.

Environmental time cues also function to phase-shift rhythms, in other words, to reset the internal clock. Thus if

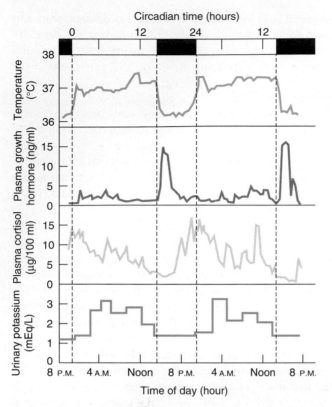

FIGURE 7-3

Circadian rhythms of several physiological variables in a human subject with room lights on (open bars at top) for 16 h and off (black bars at top) for 8 h. As is usual in dealing with rhythms, we have used a 24-h clock in which both 0 and 24 designate midnight and 12 designates noon. Cortisol is a hormone secreted by the adrenal glands. *(Adapted from Moore-Ede and Sulzman.)*

What is the neural basis of body rhythms? In the part of the brain called the hypothalamus are several specific collections of nerve cells that function as the principal **pacemaker** (time clock) for circadian rhythms. How they "keep time" independent of any external environmental cues is not really understood. The input the pacemaker receives from the eyes and many other parts of the nervous system mediates the entrainment effects exerted by the external environment.

What have biological rhythms to do with homeostasis? They add a "predictive" component to homeostatic control systems, in effect a feedforward response operating without detectors. The negative-feedback homeostatic responses we described earlier in this chapter are corrective responses, in that they are initiated *after* the steady state of the individual has been perturbed. In contrast, biological rhythms enable homeostatic mechanisms to be utilized immediately and automatically by activating them at times when a challenge is *likely* to occur but before it actually does occur. For example, there is a rhythm in the urinary excretion of potassium such that excretion is high during the day and low at night; this makes sense since we ingest potassium in our food during the day, not at night when we are asleep. Therefore, the total amount of potassium in the body fluctuates less than if the rhythm did not exist.

It should not be surprising that rhythms have effects on the body's resistance to various **stresses**. Indeed, certain diseases have characteristic rhythms. For example, heart attacks are almost twice as common in the first hours after waking, and asthma frequently flares at night. Insights about these rhythms have already been incorporated into therapy; for example, once-a-day timed-release pills for asthma are taken at night and deliver a high dose of medication between midnight and 8 A.M. Perhaps the most striking application in medicine of the growing information about rhythms is in the treatment of **cancer**. Many drugs used in cancer chemotherapy kill only dividing cells; since cancer cells generally divide rapidly, they are preferentially destroyed. However, the drugs also injure normal tissues and organs consisting of cells that divide rapidly, leading to toxic side effects such as diarrhea caused by damage to the intestinal lining. It is known that intestinal cells divide most slowly during the evening, and so by delivering the drug only at this time a much larger dose of drug can be given with less toxicity to these normal cells.

Aging and Homeostasis

Aging represents the operation of a distinct process that is distinguishable from those diseases such as heart disease frequently associated with aging. Whether these diseases are themselves promoted by the aging process or simply occur over the same time frame is not known.

Aging is associated with a decrease in the number of cells in the body, due to some combination of decreased

one jets west or east to a different time zone, the sleep-wake cycle and other circadian rhythms slowly shift to the new light-dark cycle. These shifts take time, however, and the disparity between external time and internal time is one of the causes of the symptoms of *jet lag*—disruption of sleep, gastrointestinal disturbances, decreased vigilance and attention span, and a general feeling of malaise. Similar symptoms occur in workers on permanent or rotating night shifts. Such individuals generally do not adapt to these schedules even after several years because they are exposed to the usual outdoor light-dark cycle (normal indoor lighting is too dim to function as a good entrainer). In recent experiments, night-shift workers were exposed to extremely bright indoor lighting while they worked and 8 h of total darkness during the day while they slept. This schedule produced total adaptation to the night-shift work within 5 days.

cell division and increased cell death, and to malfunction of many of the cells that remain. The immediate cause of these changes is probably an interference in the function of the cells' macromolecules—DNA, RNA, and cell proteins—and in the flow of information between these macromolecules. The crucial question, unanswered at present, concerns what causes these changes. One theory places the blame on progressive accumulation of damage to the macromolecules, while the other hypothesizes that cellular senescence is actually programmed in our genes; that is, that certain genes responsible for the aging process become activated as one grows older.

The physiological manifestations of aging are a gradual deterioration in the function of virtually all tissues and organ systems and in the capacity of the body's homeostatic systems to respond to environmental stresses. However, it is difficult to sort out the extent to which any particular age-related change is due to aging itself and the extent to which it is secondary to disease and lifestyle changes. For example, until recently it was believed that the functioning of the nervous system markedly deteriorates as a result of aging per se, but this view is now being seriously questioned. It seems to have been based on studies of the performance of individuals with age-related diseases. More recent studies of people without such diseases do document changes—loss of memory, increased difficulty in learning new tasks, a decrease in the speed of processing by the brain, loss of brain mass—but these changes are modest, and most brain functions considered to underlie intelligence seem to remain relatively intact.

To take another example, a similar reevaluation of changes in heart function with age has suggested that much of the decrease in the ability of the heart to pump blood at rest and during exercise in older people may be the result of disease and lifestyle changes (decreased physical activity, for example) rather than to the aging process itself. In contrast, the 30 to 40 percent decrease (somewhat less in women) in the mass and strength of limb muscles that occurs in men between 30 and 80 years of age is due to aging changes per se. Physically active individuals have greater strength at any given age, compared to inactive persons, but the rate of decline with age is similar.

THE BALANCE CONCEPT AND CHEMICAL HOMEOSTASIS

Many homeostatic systems are concerned with the balance of a chemical component. Figure 7-4 is a generalized schema of the possible pathways involved in the balance of a chemical substance. The **pool** occupies a position of central importance in the balance sheet. It is the body's readily available quantity of the particular substance and is frequently identical to the amount present in the extracellular fluid. The pool receives substances from and contributes them to all the pathways.

The pathways on the left of the figure are sources of net gain to the body. A substance may enter the body through the gastrointestinal (GI) tract or the lungs. Alternatively, a substance may be synthesized by cells within the body from other materials.

The pathways on the right of the figure are causes of net loss from the body. A substance may be lost in the urine, feces, expired air, or menstrual fluid, as well as from the surface of the body as skin, hair, nails, sweat, and tears. The substance may also be chemically altered and thus removed by metabolism.

The central portion of the figure illustrates the distribution of the substance within the body. The substance may

FIGURE 7-4

Balance diagram for a chemical substance.

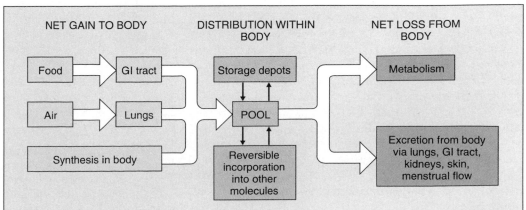

be taken from the pool and accumulated in storage depots, as for example the accumulation of fat in adipose tissue. Conversely, it may leave the storage depots to reenter the pool. Finally, the substance may be incorporated reversibly into some other molecular structure such as fatty acids into membranes or iodine into thyroxine. Incorporation is reversible in that the substance is liberated again whenever the more complex molecule is broken down. This pathway is also distinguished from storage in that the latter has no function other than the passive one of storage, whereas the incorporation of the substance into other molecules produces new molecules with specific functions.

It should be recognized that not every pathway of this generalized schema is applicable to every substance. For example, mineral electrolytes such as sodium cannot be synthesized, do not normally enter through the lungs, and cannot be removed by metabolism.

The orientation of Figure 7-4 illustrates two important generalizations concerning the balance concept: (1) Total-body balance depends upon the rates of net gain and net loss to the body; and (2) the pool concentration depends not only upon total-body balance but also upon exchanges of the substance within the body.

For any chemical, three states of total-body balance are possible (Table 7-2): (1) Loss exceeds gain, so that the total amount of the substance in the body decreases and the person is said to be in **negative balance**; (2) gain exceeds loss, so that the total amount of the substance in the body increases and the person is said to be in **positive balance**; and (3) gain equals loss, and the person is in **stable balance**.

Clearly a stable balance can be upset by alteration of the amount being gained or lost in any single pathway in the schema; for example, severe negative water balance can be caused by increased sweating. Conversely, stable balance can be restored by homeostatic control of water intake and output.

Let us take sodium as an example. The control systems for sodium balance have as their targets the kidneys, and

TABLE 7-2	THREE STATES OF TOTAL-BODY BALANCE OF A CHEMICAL SUBSTANCE
Negative balance:	Loss exceeds gain
Positive balance:	Gain exceeds loss
Stable balance:	Loss equals gain

the systems operate by inducing the kidneys to excrete into the urine an amount of sodium approximately equal to the amount ingested daily. In this example, we assume for simplicity that all sodium loss from the body occurs via the urine. Now imagine a person with a daily intake and excretion of 7 g of sodium and a stable amount of sodium in her body (Figure 7-5). On day 2 of our experiment, the subject changes her diet so that her daily sodium consumption rises to 15 g and remains there indefinitely. On this same day, the kidneys excrete into the urine somewhat more than 7 g of sodium but certainly not all the ingested 15 g. The result is that some excess sodium is retained in the body on that day; that is, the person goes into *positive* sodium balance. The kidneys do somewhat better on day 3, but it is probably not until day 4 or 5 that they are excreting 15 g. From this time on, output from the body once again equals input and sodium balance is once again *stable*.

But, and this is an important point, although again in stable balance, the woman has perhaps 2 to 3 percent more sodium in her body than was the case when she was in stable balance ingesting 7 g.[1] It is this 2 to 3 percent extra sodium that constitutes the continuous error signal to the control systems driving the kidneys to excrete 15 g/day

---

[1]Note that a large percentage change in intake (>100 percent) causes only a small change (2 to 3 percent) in total body content before the new steady state is reached. In other words, the percentage change in the regulated variable is small compared to the percentage change in the altered input.

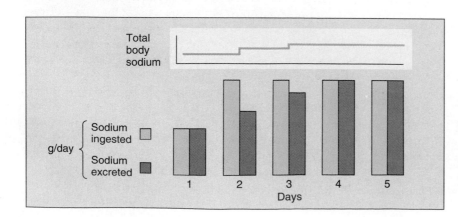

FIGURE 7-5

Effects of a continued change in the amount of sodium ingested on sodium excretion and total-body sodium balance. A stable sodium balance is reattained by day 4 but with some gain of total-body sodium.

rather than 7 g/day. An increase of 2 to 3 percent does not seem large, but it has been hypothesized that this small gain might facilitate the development of high blood pressure in some persons.

COMPONENTS OF HOMEOSTATIC SYSTEMS

Reflexes

The thermoregulatory systems we used as an example earlier in the chapter and many of the body's other homeostatic control systems belong to the general category of stimulus-response sequences known as reflexes. Although in some reflexes we are aware of the stimulus and/or the response, many reflexes regulating the internal environment occur without any conscious awareness.

In the most narrow sense of the word, a **reflex** is an involuntary, unpremediated, unlearned "built-in" response to a stimulus. Examples of such reflexes include pulling one's hand away from a hot object or shutting one's eyes as an object rapidly approaches the face. There are also many responses, however, that appear to be automatic and stereotyped but are actually the result of learning and practice. For example, an experienced driver performs many complicated acts in operating a car. To the driver these motions are, in large part, automatic, stereotyped, and unpremediated, but they occur only because a great deal of conscious effort was spent learning them. We shall refer to such reflexes as **learned** or **acquired**. In general, most reflexes, no matter how basic they may appear to be, are subject to alteration by learning; that is, there is often no clear distinction between a basic reflex and one with a learned component.

The pathway mediating a reflex is known as the **reflex arc**, and its components are shown in Figure 7-6.

A **stimulus** is defined as a detectable change in the internal or external environment, such as a change in temperature, potassium concentration, or blood pressure. A **receptor** detects the environmental change; we referred to the receptor as a detector earlier. A stimulus acts upon a receptor to produce a signal that is relayed to an **integrating center**. The pathway traveled by the signal between the receptor and the integrating center is known as the **afferent pathway** (the general term afferent means "to carry to," in this case the integrating center).

An integrating center often receives signals from many receptors, some of which may be responding to quite different types of stimuli. Thus, the output of an integrating center reflects the net effect of the total afferent input; that is, it represents an integration of numerous bits of information.

The output of an integrating center is sent to the last component of the system, a device whose change in activ-

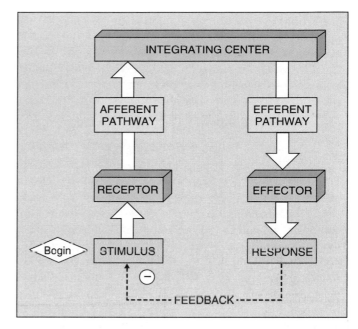

FIGURE 7-6

General components of a reflex arc that functions as a negative-feedback control system. The response of the system has the effect of counteracting or eliminating the stimulus. This phenomenon of negative feedback is emphasized by the minus sign in the feedback loop.

ity constitutes the overall response of the system. This component is known as an **effector**. The information going from an integrating center to an effector is like a command directing the effector to alter its activity. The pathway along which this information travels is known as the **efferent pathway** (the general term "efferent" means "to carry away from," in this case away from the integrating center).

Thus far we have described the reflex arc as the sequence of events linking a stimulus to a response. If the response produced by the effector causes a decrease in the magnitude of the stimulus that triggered the sequence of events, then the reflex incorporates negative feedback and we have a typical homeostatic control system. Not all reflexes incorporate such feedback. For example, the smell of food stimulates the secretion of a hormone by the stomach, but this hormone does not eliminate the smell of food (the stimulus).

To illustrate the components of a homeostatic reflex arc, let us use Figure 7-7 to apply these terms to thermoregulation. The temperature receptors are the endings of certain nerve cells in various parts of the body. They generate electric signals in the nerve cells at a rate determined by the temperature. These electric signals are conducted by the nerve fibers—the afferent pathway—to a specific part of the brain—the integrating center—which in turn

occurs. Cells exposed for a prolonged period to very low concentrations of a messenger may come to have many more receptors for that messenger, thereby developing increased sensitivity to it. For example, days after the nerves to a muscle are cut, thereby eliminating the neurotransmitter released by those nerves, the muscle will contract in response to amounts of experimentally injected neurotransmitter much smaller than those to which an innervated muscle can respond.

Up-regulation and down-regulation are made possible because there is a continuous degradation and synthesis of receptors. The main cause of down-regulation of plasma-membrane receptors is as follows: The binding of a messenger to its receptor stimulates the internalization of the complex; that is, the complex is taken into the cell by endocytosis (an example of receptor-mediated endocytosis, Chapter 6); this increases the rate of receptor degradation inside the cell. Thus, at high hormone concentrations, the number of plasma-membrane receptors of that type gradually decreases.

The opposite events also occur. The cell may contain stores of receptors bound in intracellular vesicles, and these are available for insertion into the plasma membrane via exocytosis (Chapter 6).

Down-regulation and up-regulation are physiological responses, but there also are many disease processes in which the number of receptors or their affinity for messenger becomes abnormal. The result is unusually large or small responses to any given level of messenger. For example, the disease called *myasthenia gravis* is due to destruction of the skeletal muscle receptors for acetylcholine, the neurotransmitter that normally causes contraction of the muscle in response to nerve stimulation; the result is muscle weakness or paralysis.

SIGNAL TRANSDUCTION MECHANISMS FOR PLASMA-MEMBRANE RECEPTORS

We have moved, in this chapter, from the broad organismic concept of homeostasis to the mechanisms by which cells communicate with one another. Now we move into the cell and describe the mechanisms by which the binding of a chemical messenger—hormone, neurotransmitter, or paracrine agent—to a receptor causes the cell to respond to the messenger. A note on terminology is appropriate here: For reasons that will be clear very soon, all these messengers, which reach the cell from the extracellular fluid, are termed **first messengers**.

The combination of messenger with receptor causes a change in the conformation of the receptor. This event, known as **receptor activation**, is always the initial step

leading to the cell's ultimate responses to the messenger, which can be (1) changes in the permeability, transport properties, or electrical state of the cell's plasma membrane; (2) changes in the cell's metabolism; (3) changes in the cell's secretory activity; and (4) changes in the contractile activity, if the cell is a muscle cell.

Despite the seeming variety of these ultimate responses, there is a common denominator: They are all due directly to alterations of particular cell proteins. Let us take a few examples of messenger-induced responses, all of which are described fully in subsequent chapters. Generation of electric signals in nerve cells reflects the altered conformation of membrane proteins constituting ion channels through which substances can diffuse between extracellular fluid and intracellular fluid. Changes in the rate of glucose secretion by the liver reflect the altered activity and concentration of enzymes in the metabolic pathways for glucose synthesis. Muscle contraction results from the altered conformation of contractile proteins.

To repeat, receptor activation by a messenger is only the first step leading to the cell's ultimate response (contraction, secretion, and so on) to that messenger. The sequences of events, however, between receptor activation and the responses may be very complicated and are termed **signal transduction mechanisms**. The "signal" is the receptor activation, and "transduction" denotes the process by which a stimulus is transformed into a response. The question is: How does receptor activation influence the cell's internal components, which may be located far from the receptor?

Signal transduction mechanisms differ at the very outset for the lipid-soluble and lipid-insoluble messengers since, as described earlier, the receptors for these two broad chemical classes of messenger are in different locations. The receptors for lipid-soluble messengers are intracellular; when activated, these receptors act in the nucleus as modulators of gene transcription. Because lipid-soluble messengers are all hormones, we shall delay further description of this mechanism to Chapter 10 and restrict the present discussion to the much larger number of messengers that are lipid-insoluble and bind to receptors on the cell's plasma membrane. On the basis of the signal transduction mechanisms used, plasma-membrane receptors can be classified into the types listed in Table 7-5.

The first type of plasma-membrane receptor signal transduction mechanism listed in Table 7-5 is the simplest mechanism since no molecules other than the receptor are involved. The protein complex that acts as receptor forms an ion channel, and activation of the receptor by a messenger causes the channel to open. The opening results in an increase in the net diffusion across the plasma membrane of the ion or ions specific to the channel (Figure 7-12). As we shall see in Chapter 8, such a change in ion diffusion is associated with an electric signal in the membrane, and

TABLE 7-5 CLASSIFICATION OF PLASMA-MEMBRANE RECEPTORS BASED ON THE SIGNAL TRANSDUCTION MECHANISMS THEY USE

1. Receptors that themselves function as ion channels

2. Receptors that themselves function as protein kinases, specifically as tyrosine kinases

3. Receptors that activate G proteins, which in turn act upon effector proteins in the plasma membrane. The effector proteins include:

    a. Adenylyl cyclase (leads to the formation of cyclic AMP)

    b. Guanylyl cyclase (leads to the formation of cyclic GMP)

    c. Phospholipase C (leads to the formation of diacylglycerol and inositol trisphosphate)

    d. Ion channels

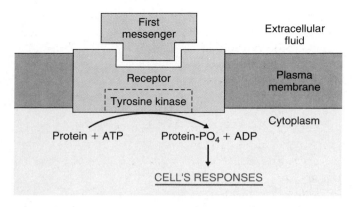

FIGURE 7-13

Signal transduction mechanism in which the receptor complex itself can function as a protein kinase, specifically as a tyrosine kinase. Activation of the receptor activates the tyrosine kinase, which then phosphorylates cellular proteins, and these proteins participate in reactions leading to the cell's response.

this signal is an essential event in the cell's response to the messenger.

The second plasma-membrane signal transduction mechanism listed in Table 7-5, like the first, has the receptor playing a dual role, in this case functioning as an enzyme (rather than an ion channel) as well as a receptor. A portion of the protein complex that constitutes the receptor has the ability to function as a **protein kinase**, the general term for any enzyme that phosphorylates other proteins by transferring to them a phosphate group from ATP. As described in Chapter 4, introduction of the phosphate group changes the activity of the protein, often itself an enzyme. Accordingly, the sequence of events is as follows: A messenger binds to the extracellular surface of the

receptor, and this changes the conformation of the receptor so that its enzyme portion, located at its cytoplasmic surface, is activated and phosphorylates specific cytosolic and plasma-membrane proteins, including itself (Figure 7-13). Phosphorylation causes these proteins to alter their activity, and this brings about the response of the cell.[3]

Now for a very important point: As we shall see in the rest of this chapter, there are many different types of protein kinases involved in signal transduction mechanisms, each protein kinase being able to phosphorylate only certain proteins. It will be necessary to keep these different protein kinases straight. The receptors we described in the previous paragraph all function as **tyrosine kinases**, protein kinases that phosphorylate specifically the tyrosine portions of proteins. The messengers that use these receptors are almost all involved in growth and development.

The third category of plasma-membrane receptors listed in Table 7-5 is by far the largest, including approximately 100 distinct receptors. These receptors, upon activation, interact with one or more plasma-membrane proteins belonging to the family known as **G proteins**. (The term "G protein" includes all those proteins, regardless of location, that avidly bind guanine nucleotides with high affinity, and the plasma-membrane G proteins therefore encompass only a subset of G proteins.) The mechanism by which receptor activation leads to plasma-membrane G-protein activation is illustrated in Figure 7-14.

To repeat, in G-protein-dependent signal transduction, all the activated receptor does is activate a G protein, and

FIGURE 7-12

Signal transduction mechanism in which the receptor complex itself contains an ion channel. The first messenger, which reaches the cell from the extracellular fluid, is a hormone, neurotransmitter, paracrine agent, or autocrine agent. Activation of the receptor causes the ion channel portion of the receptor to open.

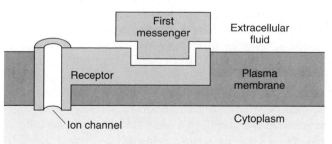

---

[3]As described in Chapter 4, protein phosphatases do the reverse of protein kinases. These enzymes also participate in signal transduction mechanisms, but their roles are much less understood than those of the protein kinases.

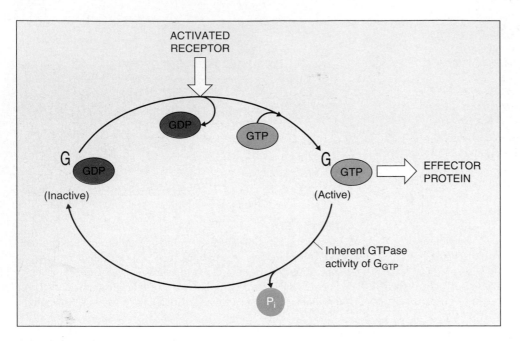

FIGURE 7-14

Biochemistry of plasma-membrane G proteins (the GTPase cycle). G proteins bind guanine nucleotides—both guanosine diphosphate (GDP) and guanosine triphosphate (GTP)—with high affinity, and the conformation of the G protein is different, depending upon which of the two nucleotides is bound to it. In the basal or inactive state, G proteins bind GDP. When a receptor that can couple to a G protein is activated by a first messenger, the receptor interacts with the G protein, causing the G protein to give up its bound GDP and bind GTP instead. This binding of GTP activates the G protein, which allows the G protein to interact in turn with effector proteins in the membrane and modulate these proteins' activity (Figure 7-15). This entire sequence is transient since the activated G protein has GTPase activity and splits off inorganic phosphate from itself to return to its GDP-bound inactive state, ready to reenter the cycle again by interacting with activated receptor.

the G protein takes over from there (Figure 7-15). It interacts with still other plasma-membrane proteins, called **effector proteins**, which are either ion channels or enzymes, and these effector proteins mediate the next step in the sequence of events leading to the cell's response (secretion, contraction, and so on). In essence, then, the G protein serves to "couple" a receptor to an effector protein in the plasma membrane, and the effector protein then takes over. We shall see in subsequent sections that the action of the effector protein is to cause a change in membrane potential and/or to yield **second messengers**, substances that serve as a direct relay from *the plasma membrane*—where the entire receptor, G protein, effector protein sequence has occurred—to the biochemical machinery *inside* the cell. Now you can see why the term "first messenger" is used to denote the original chemical messenger—hormone, neurotransmitter, or paracrine agent—that combines with the receptor.

Several features of the G-protein system help explain how a single first messenger can initiate a very complex cellular response. First, there are at least 16 distinct

plasma-membrane G proteins, and a single receptor type may be associated with more than one type of G protein. Second, each of these G proteins may couple to more than one type of the many plasma-membrane effector proteins. Thus, a messenger-activated receptor, via its G-protein couplings, can call into action a variety of effector proteins, which in turn induce a variety of cellular events, to which we now turn. We will present only those pathways considered most important at present.

Adenylyl Cyclase and Cyclic AMP

The sequence of events for the most widely distributed plasma-membrane effector protein and its second messenger is illustrated in Figure 7-16. Activation of the receptor by the binding of first messenger allows the receptor to couple to a G protein known as **G_s protein** (the subscript s denotes "stimulatory"; for orientation, we give the actual names of the involved G proteins in this system but will abandon this practice in subsequent sections). This binding causes G_s protein to activate its effector protein, the membrane enzyme called **adenylyl cyclase**. The acti-

FIGURE 7-15

Flow of information in G-protein-dependent signal transduction. Subsequent sections of this chapter describe the specific effector proteins and second messengers. For simplicity, this figure does not show that a receptor can interact with more than a single type of G protein and that a G protein can interact with more than a single type of effector protein.

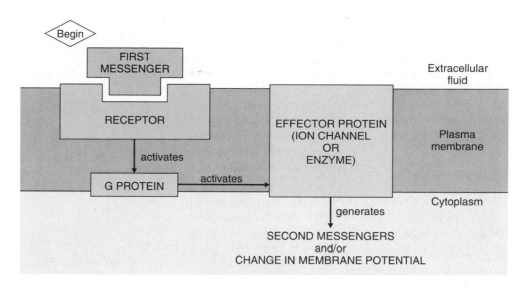

FIGURE 7-16

Cyclic-AMP second-messenger system. Combination of the first messenger—hormone, neurotransmitter, or paracrine agent—with its specific receptor permits the receptor to bind to the membrane G protein termed G_s. This protein in turn binds to adenylyl cyclase, activating it and causing it to catalyze the formation of cyclic AMP (cAMP) inside the cell. This cAMP activates cAMP-dependent protein kinase, which then phosphorylates specific proteins in the cell, thereby triggering the biochemical reactions leading ultimately to the cell's response. Not shown in the figure is the existence of another regulatory protein, G_i, with which certain receptors can react to cause inhibition of adenylyl cyclase.

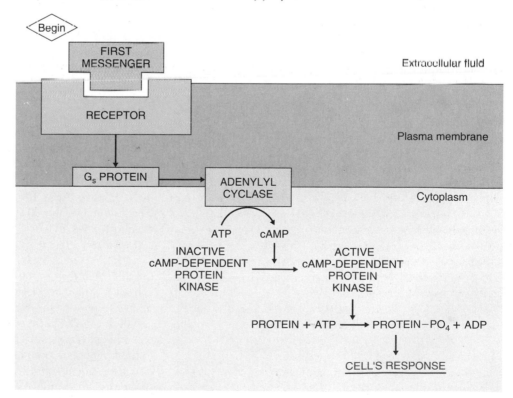

vated adenylyl cyclase, whose catalytic site is located on the cytosolic surface of the plasma membrane, then catalyzes the conversion of some cytosolic ATP molecules to **cyclic 3',5'-adenosine monophosphate**, called simply **cyclic AMP (cAMP)**. Cyclic AMP then diffuses throughout the cell to trigger the sequences of events leading to the cell's ultimate response to the first messenger. In this manner, cAMP is acting as a second messenger. Its action is terminated by its breakdown to noncyclic AMP, a reaction catalyzed by the enzyme **phosphodiesterase** (Figure 7-17).

What does cyclic AMP actually do inside the cell? It activates an enzyme known as **cAMP-dependent protein kinase** (also termed protein kinase A). In other words, the event common to the sequences initiated by cAMP is acti-

FIGURE 7-17

Structure of ATP, cAMP, and AMP, the last resulting from enzymatic alteration of cAMP.

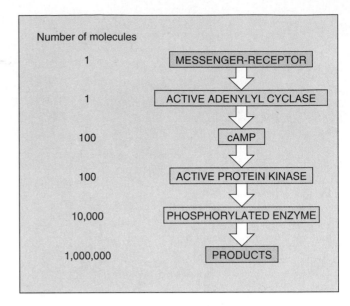

FIGURE 7-18

Example of amplification in the cAMP system. By means of an enzyme cascade, a single messenger-receptor complex ultimately leads to the generation of a very large number of product molecules. (Actually, there is another amplification step not shown in the figure, namely, the ability of a single activated receptor to activate more than one G_s protein, the G protein that will activate adenylyl cyclase.)

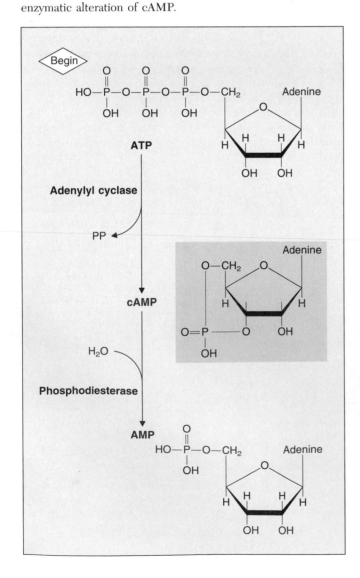

vation of this particular protein kinase. As defined above, protein kinases phosphorylate other proteins—often enzymes—by transferring a phosphate group to them. The change in the activity of the protein owing to its phosphorylation by cAMP-dependent protein kinase brings about the response of the cell (secretion, contraction, and so on). This is the second time—and it will not be the last—that we have invoked a protein kinase in the action of a receptor; earlier we pointed out how some receptors can themselves act as protein kinases of the tyrosine kinase type. The cAMP-dependent protein kinase is completely distinct from these tyrosine kinases and has different protein substrates.

In essence, then, the activation of adenylyl cyclase by G_s protein initiates a chain, or "cascade," of events in which proteins are converted in sequence from inactive to active forms. Figure 7-18 illustrates the benefit of such a cascade. While it is active, a single enzyme molecule is capable of transforming into product not one but many substrate molecules, let us say 100. Therefore, one active molecule of adenylyl cyclase may catalyze the generation of 100 cAMP molecules. At each of the two subsequent enzyme-activation steps in our example, another hundredfold amplification occurs. Therefore, the end result is that a single molecule of the first messenger could theoretically trigger the generation of 1 million product molecules. This fact helps to explain how hormones and other messengers can be effective at extremely low extracellular concentrations.

How can activation of a single molecule, cAMP-dependent protein kinase, by cAMP be an event common to the great variety of biochemical sequences and cell responses initiated by cAMP-generating messengers? The answer is that cAMP-dependent protein kinase has a large number of distinct substrates; that is, it can phosphorylate a large number of different proteins (Figure 7-19). This allows activated cAMP-dependent protein kinase to have multiple actions within a single cell and different actions in different cells. For example, epinephrine, a hormone that utilizes the cAMP pathway, acts on fat cells to cause both glycogen breakdown (mediated by one phosphorylated enzyme) and triacylglycerol breakdown (mediated by another phosphorylated enzyme). In other cells, in contrast, there are other substrates for cAMP-dependent protein kinase, and so cAMP generation in these cells induced by a first messenger will yield responses different from those of fat cells.

Another source of variety is that, whereas phosphorylation mediated by cAMP-dependent protein kinase *activates* certain enzymes, it *inhibits* others. For example, the enzyme catalyzing the rate-limiting step in glycogen synthesis is inhibited by phosphorylation, which explains how epinephrine inhibits glycogen synthesis at the same time that it stimulates glycogen breakdown (Figure 7-20).

In summary, the biochemistry of cAMP-dependent protein kinase and its substrates (the proteins it phosphorylates) explains how a single molecule, cAMP, can produce so many different effects. It must be reemphasized that the ability of a cell to respond at all to a cAMP-generating first messenger depends upon the presence of specific receptors for that messenger in the plasma membrane and upon the presence within the cell of proteins that can be phosphorylated by cAMP-dependent protein kinase.

Not mentioned previously is the fact that receptors for some first messengers, upon activation by their messengers, cause adenylyl cyclase to be *inhibited*, resulting in less, rather than more, generation of cAMP. This occurs because these receptors interact with a different G protein, known as **G_i protein** (the subscript i denotes "inhibitory"), and activation of G_i protein causes inhibition of adenylyl cyclase. The result is to decrease the concentration of cAMP in the cell and thereby to decrease the phosphorylation of key proteins inside the cell.

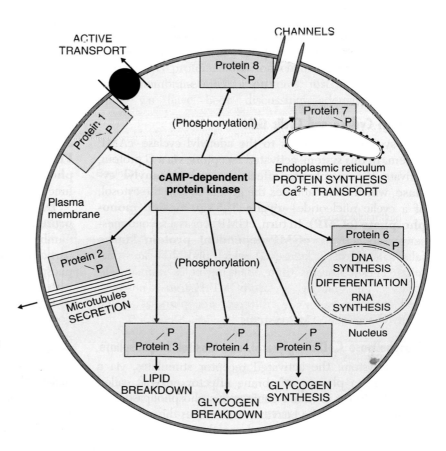

FIGURE 7-19

The variety of cellular responses induced by cAMP is due to the fact that cAMP-dependent protein kinase can phosphorylate many different proteins, activating them or inhibiting them. Our designations of the proteins being phosphorylated as 1, 2, and so on, are arbitrary. For clarity, the generation of cAMP and its activation of cAMP-dependent kinase are not shown in this figure (see Figure 7-16).

guanylyl cyclase, and phospholipase C. A receptor, once activated by a first messenger, activates in turn a particular G protein, which then interacts with an ion channel, causing it to open or close and thereby altering the net diffusion across the plasma membrane of the ion or ions specific to that channel (Figure 7-22). The overall result is an electric signal in the plasma membrane, that is, a change in the membrane potential. In addition, when calcium channels are opened, there occurs a significant increase in cytosolic calcium concentration, with consequences to be described in the subsequent section on calcium.

The situation described in the previous paragraph is known as *direct* G-protein gating of plasma-membrane ion channels because the G protein interacts directly with the channel (the term "gating" denotes control of the opening or closing of a channel). All the events occur in the plasma membrane and are independent of second messengers. Now we emphasize how this phenomenon differs from *indirect* gating of plasma-membrane ion channels by G proteins. Look back at Figure 7-19, and you will see that cAMP-dependent protein kinase can phosphorylate a plasma-membrane ion channel, thereby causing it to open. Since, as we have seen, the sequence of events leading to activation of cAMP-dependent protein kinase proceeds through G_s protein, it should be clear that the opening of this channel is *indirectly* dependent on that G protein. To generalize, the indirect gating of ion channels by G proteins utilizes a second-messenger pathway (cAMP, DAG, and so on) for the opening (or closing) of the channel.

Table 7-6 lists the three ways we have described by which receptor activation by a first messenger leads to opening or closing of ion channels. You might be wondering at this point what the adaptive value is of having multiple pathways. One thing that is affected is the time required for the response: When the channel is part of the receptor, the channel will open most rapidly (in about 1 ms), direct gating by G proteins takes longer (about 300 ms), and indirect gating by G proteins takes still longer (seconds) because of the required second-messenger processes. These time differences are particularly important for the functioning of the nervous system, as we shall see in Chapters 8 and 9.

TABLE 7-6 SUMMARY OF MECHANISMS BY WHICH RECEPTOR ACTIVATION INFLUENCES CHANNELS

1. The ion channel is part of the receptor.
2. A G protein directly gates the channel.
3. A G protein gates the channel indirectly via a second messenger.

Calcium as a Second Messenger

In our descriptions of the signal transduction pathways involving either IP_3 or gating of calcium channels by G proteins, we ended up with an increase in cytosolic calcium and stated that we would eventually describe the signficance of this increase for the rest of the signal transduction pathway. That is the subject of this section—how the calcium ion (Ca^{2+}) functions as a second messenger in a great variety of cellular responses to stimuli, both chemical (first messenger) and electrical.

The physiology of calcium as a second messenger requires an analysis of two broad questions: (1) How do stimuli cause the cytosolic calcium concentration to increase? and (2) How does the increased calcium concentration elicit the cells' responses? Note that, for simplicity, our two questions are phrased in terms of an *increase* in cytosolic concentration. There are, in fact, first messengers that elicit a *decrease* in cytosolic calcium concentration and therefore a decrease in calcium's second-messenger effects. As you read the next paragraph, therefore, keep in mind that cytosolic calcium concentration can be decreased by an event opposite that being described (for example, closing a calcium channel rather than opening it). Now for the answer to the first question.

The regulation of cytosolic calcium concentration is described in Chapter 6. In brief, by means of active-transport systems in the plasma membrane and cell organelles, this ion is maintained at an extremely low concentration in the cytosol. Accordingly, there is always a large electrochemical difference favoring diffusion of calcium into the cytosol via calcium channels in both the plasma membrane and endoplasmic reticulum. A stimulus to the cell can alter this steady state by influencing the active transport systems and/or the ion channels, resulting in a change in cytosolic calcium concentration.

The three ways that receptor activation by a first messenger can do this are summarized in the top part of Table 7-7. (1) The receptor activates a G protein that either directly or indirectly, via a second messenger, opens a *plasma-membrane* calcium channel; (2) via the phospholipase C pathway, IP_3 is generated and opens calcium channels in the membranes of the *endoplasmic reticulum*. (Note that in this last sequence IP_3 is acting as a second messenger to mobilize yet another second messenger—calcium); (3) a second messenger (cAMP, for example) is generated that leads to inhibition of the active transport of calcium out of the cytosol. These three mechanisms for increasing cytosolic calcium concentration, which all depend on receptor activation by a first messenger, are not mutually exclusive. On the contrary, several are often triggered simultaneously by the same first messenger (Figure 7-22).

This section has thus far dealt exclusively with receptor-initiated sequences of events. This is a good place, how-

TABLE 7-7 CALCIUM AS A SECOND MESSENGER

Mechanisms by which stimulation of a cell leads to an increase in cytosolic Ca^{2+} concentration:

1. Receptor activation by a first messenger
   a. Plasma-membrane calcium channels open as a result of direct or indirect gating by G proteins.
   b. Calcium is released from the endoplasmic reticulum; this is mediated by inositol trisphosphate (IP_3) generated from the breakdown of membrane phospholipid.
   c. Active calcium transport out of the cell is inhibited by a second messenger.
2. Opening of voltage-sensitive calcium channels

Mechanisms by which an increase in cytosolic Ca^{2+} concentration induces the cell's responses:

1. Calcium binds to calmodulin. On binding calcium, the calmodulin changes shape, which allows it to combine with a large variety of enzymes and other proteins, activating them or inhibiting them in turn. Many of these enzymes are protein kinases.
2. Calcium combines with calcium-binding intermediary proteins other than calmodulin. These proteins then act in a manner analogous to calmodulin.
3. Calcium combines with and alters response proteins directly, without the intermediation of any specific calcium-binding protein.

ever, to emphasize that there are calcium channels in the plasma membrane that are opened directly by an *electric* stimulus to the membrane (Chapter 6). Calcium can act as a second messenger, therefore, in response not only to chemical stimuli acting via receptors, but to electric stimuli acting via voltage-sensitive calcium channels as well.

Now we turn to the second question posed in the second paragraph of this section: How does the increased cytosolic calcium concentration elicit the cell's responses (bottom of Table 7-7)? The common denominator of calcium's actions is its ability to bind tightly and specifically to various cytosolic calcium-binding proteins. One of the most important of these is a protein found in virtually all cells and known as **calmodulin** (Figure 7-23). On binding with calcium, calmodulin changes shape, and this allows it to combine with a large variety of enzymes and other proteins, activating them or inhibiting them. At this point, the story for calcium-activated calmodulin becomes, at least in part, analogous to that for cAMP, cGMP, and DAG, in that several of the many proteins influenced by calmodulin are protein kinases. Activation or inhibition of **calmodulin-**

dependent protein kinases leads, via phosphorylation, to activation or inhibition of proteins involved in the cell's ultimate responses to the first messenger—contraction, secretion, and so on.

Calmodulin is not, however, the only intracellular protein that is influenced by calcium. Several other proteins bind calcium and then influence other proteins in turn. In still other cases, the calcium binds to proteins immediately involved in the cell's responses, without the intermediation of any other calcium-binding protein.

This concludes our description of signal transduction mechanisms, and Tables 7-5 through 7-8 together present an overview of these mechanisms. The five second mes-

FIGURE 7-23

Calcium, calmodulin, and the calmodulin-dependent protein kinase system. The mechanisms for increasing cytosolic calcium concentration are summarized in Figure 7-22 and the top of Table 7-7.

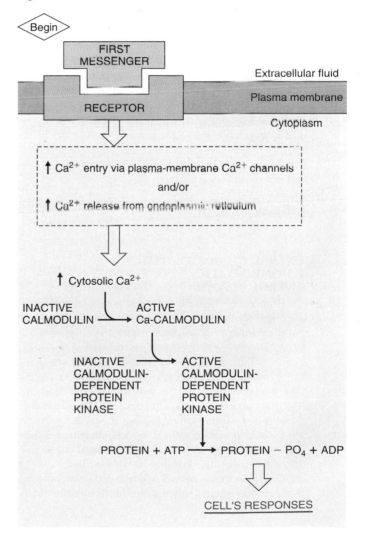

calcium channels can influence cytosolic calcium concentration.

B. Calcium binds to one of several intracellular proteins, most often calmodulin. Calcium-activated calmodulin activates or inhibits many proteins, including calmodulin-dependent protein kinases.

KEY TERMS

homeostasis
homeostatic control systems
steady state
operating point
negative feedback
positive feedback
error signal
feedforward
adaptation
acclimatization
critical period
developmental acclimatization
circadian rhythm
entrainment
free-running rhythms
pacemaker
pool
negative balance
positive balance
stable balance
reflex
learned reflex
acquired reflex
reflex arc
stimulus
receptor (in reflex)
integrating center
afferent pathway
effector
efferent pathway
hormone
endocrine gland
local homeostatic response
target cell
neurotransmitter
neurohormone
paracrine agents
autocrine agents
eicosanoids
arachidonic acid
cyclic endoperoxides
prostaglandins
thromboxanes
leukotrienes
phospholipase A_2

cyclooxygenase
lipoxygenase
receptors (for messengers)
specificity
saturation
competition
antagonists
agonists
down-regulation
up-regulation
first messengers
receptor activation
signal transduction mechanisms
protein kinase
tyrosine kinases
G proteins
effector proteins
second messengers
G_s protein
adenylyl cyclase
cyclic 3′,5′-adenosine monophosphate
cyclic AMP (cAMP)
phosphodiesterase
cAMP-dependent protein kinase
G_i protein
guanylyl cyclase
cyclic 3′,5′-guanosine monophosphate (cGMP)
cGMP-dependent protein kinase
phospholipase C
phophatidylinositol bisphosphate (PIP_2)
diacylglycerol (DAG)
inositol trisphosphate (IP_3)
protein kinase C
calmodulin
calmodulin-dependent protein kinases

REVIEW QUESTIONS

1. Describe five important generalizations about homeostatic control systems.

2. Contrast negative-feedback systems and positive-feedback systems.

3. Contrast feedforward and negative feedback.

4. How do error signals develop and why are they essential for maintaining homeostasis?

5. Describe the conditions under which acclimatization occurs. In what period of life might an acclimatization be irreversible? Are acclimatizations passed on to a person's offspring?

6. Under what conditions do circadian rhythms become free-running?

7. How do phase shifts occur?

8. What are the important environmental time cues for entrainment of body rhythms?

9. What are the physiological manifestations of aging?

10. Draw a figure illustrating the balance concept in homeostasis.

11. What are the three possible states of total-body balance of any chemical?

12. List the components of a reflex arc.

13. What is the basic difference between a local homeostatic response and a reflex?

14. List the general categories of intercellular messengers.

15. Describe two types of intercellular communication that do not depend on chemical messengers.

16. Draw a figure illustrating the various pathways for eicosanoid synthesis.

17. What is the chemical nature of receptors? Where are they located?

18. Explain why different types of cells may respond differently to the same chemical messenger.

19. Describe how the metabolism of receptors can lead to down-regulation or up-regulation.

20. What is the first step in the action of a messenger on a cell?

21. Classify plasma-membrane receptors according to the signal transduction mechanisms they use.

22. What is the result of opening a membrane ion channel?

23. What kind of protein kinase activity is expressed by some receptors upon activation?

24. Describe the functioning of plasma-membrane G proteins and their relationship to membrane effector proteins and second messengers.

25. Draw a diagram describing the adenylyl cyclase–cAMP system.

26. What are the analogies between the cAMP and cGMP systems?

27. What are the two products released from PIP_2 by the action of phospholipase C? Contrast their actions.

28. Contrast direct and indirect gating of ion channels by G proteins.

29. What are the four mechanisms by which first messengers elicit an increase in cytosolic calcium concentration? What are the sources of the calcium in each mechanism?

30. How does the calcium-calmodulin system function?

31. List five second messengers and four types of protein kinases that participate in signal transduction. Which second messenger influences which protein kinase, directly or indirectly?

CLINICAL TERMS

jet lag	nonsteroidal anti-inflammatory drugs
stresses	(NSAIDs)
cancer	myasthenia gravis
aspirin	

THOUGHT QUESTIONS

(Answers are given in Appendix A.)

1. A person's plasma potassium concentration (a homeostatically regulated variable) is 4 mmol/L when she is eating 150 mmol of potassium per day. One day she doubles her potassium intake and continues to eat that amount indefinitely. At the new steady state, do you think her plasma potassium concentration is more likely to be 8, 4.4, or 4 mmol/L? (The answer to this question requires no knowledge about potassium, only the ability to reason about homeostatic control systems.)

2. Eskimos have a remarkable ability to work in the cold without gloves and not suffer decreased skin blood flow. Does this prove that there is a genetic difference between Eskimos and other people with regard to this characteristic?

3. Patient A is given a drug that blocks the synthesis of all eicosanoids, whereas patient B is given a drug that blocks the synthesis of leukotrienes but none of the other eicosanoids. What are the enzymes most likely blocked by these drugs?

4. Certain nerves to the heart release the neurotransmitter norepinephrine. If these nerves are removed in experimental animals, the heart becomes extremely sensitive to the administration of a drug that is an agonist of norepinephrine. Explain why in terms of receptor physiology.

5. A particular hormone is known to elicit, completely by way of the cyclic AMP system, six different responses in its target cell. A drug is found that eliminates one of these responses but not the other five. Which of the following, if any, could the drug be blocking: the hormone's receptors, G_s protein, adenylyl cyclase, or cyclic AMP?

6. If a drug were found that blocked all calcium channels directly linked to G proteins, would this eliminate the role of calcium as a second messenger?

7. What are DAG and calcium-activated calmodulin analogous to in the cAMP system?

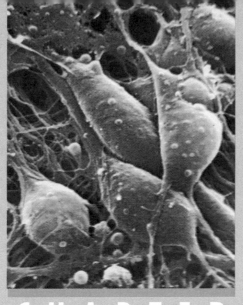

C H A P T E R

8

NEURAL CONTROL MECHANISMS

SECTION A. NEURAL TISSUE

NEURAL GROWTH AND REGENERATION

SECTION A SUMMARY

SECTION A KEY TERMS

SECTION A REVIEW QUESTIONS

SECTION B. MEMBRANE POTENTIALS

BASIC PRINCIPLES OF ELECTRICITY

THE RESTING MEMBRANE POTENTIAL

GRADED POTENTIALS AND ACTION POTENTIALS

Graded Potentials

Action Potentials

Ionic basis of the action potential

Mechanism of ion-channel changes

Threshold

Refractory periods

Action-potential propagation

Initiation of action potentials

SECTION B SUMMARY

SECTION B KEY TERMS

SECTION B REVIEW QUESTIONS

SECTION C. SYNAPSES

FUNCTIONAL ANATOMY OF SYNAPSES

Excitatory Chemical Synapses

Inhibitory Chemical Synapses

ACTIVATION OF THE POSTSYNAPTIC CELL

SYNAPTIC EFFECTIVENESS

Modification of Synaptic Transmission by Drugs
and Disease

NEUROTRANSMITTERS AND NEUROMODULATORS

Acetylcholine

Biogenic Amines

Norepinephrine and epinephrine

Serotonin

Amino Acid Neurotransmitters

Neuropeptides

Gases

NEUROEFFECTOR COMMUNICATION

SECTION C SUMMARY

SECTION C KEY TERMS

SECTION C REVIEW QUESTIONS

SECTION D. STRUCTURE OF THE NERVOUS SYSTEM

CENTRAL NERVOUS SYSTEM: SPINAL CORD

CENTRAL NERVOUS SYSTEM: BRAIN

Brainstem

Cerebellum

Forebrain

PERIPHERAL NERVOUS SYSTEM

Peripheral Nervous System: Afferent Division

Peripheral Nervous System: Efferent Division

Somatic nervous system

Autonomic nervous system

BLOOD SUPPLY, BLOOD-BRAIN BARRIER PHENOMENA, AND CEREBROSPINAL FLUID

SECTION D SUMMARY

SECTION D KEY TERMS

SECTION D REVIEW QUESTIONS

CHAPTER 8 CLINICAL TERMS

CHAPTER 8 THOUGHT QUESTIONS

Along with the body's other communication system, the endocrine system, the nervous system regulates many internal functions and also organizes and controls the activities we know collectively as human behavior. These activities include not only such easily observed acts as smiling and walking but also experiences such as feeling angry, being motivated, having an idea, or remembering a long-past event. These experiences, which we attribute to the "mind," are related to the integrated activities of nerve cells in as yet unidentified ways.

The various parts of the nervous system are interconnected, but for convenience they can be divided into two parts: (1) the **central nervous system (CNS)**, composed of the brain and spinal cord; and (2) the **peripheral nervous system**, consisting of the nerves, which extend from the brain and spinal cord out to all points of the body (Figure 8-1). For example, branches of the peripheral nervous system go from the base of the spine to the tips of the toes and, although they are not shown in Figure 8-1, from the base of the brain to the internal organs.

In this chapter we are concerned with the components common to all neural mechanisms: the structure of individual nerve cells, the mechanisms underlying neural function, and the basic organization and major divisions of the nervous system.

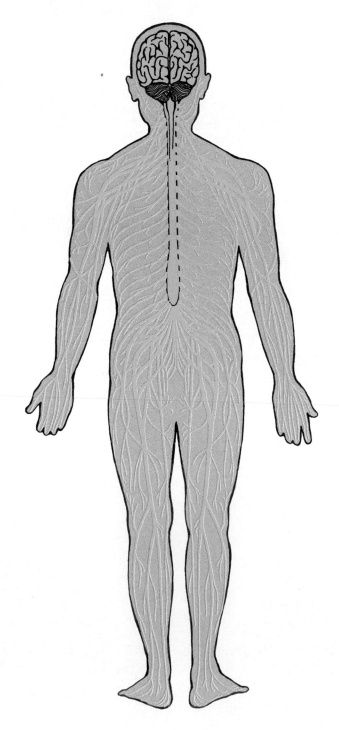

FIGURE 8-1

The central nervous system (violet) and the peripheral nervous system (blue). Some of the peripheral nerves connect with the brain (these nerves are not shown) and others with the spinal cord.

The basic unit of the nervous system is the individual nerve cell—the **neuron**. Nerve cells operate by generating electric signals and passing them from one part of the cell to another and by releasing chemical messengers to communicate with other cells.

Neurons occur in a variety of sizes and shapes; nevertheless, as shown in Figure 8-2, most of them contain four parts: (1) the cell body, (2) the dendrites, (3) the axon, and (4) the axon terminals.

As in other types of cells, a neuron's **cell body** contains the nucleus and ribosomes and thus has the genetic information and machinery necessary for protein synthesis. The **dendrites** form a series of highly branched outgrowths from the cell body. They and the cell body are the sites of most of the specialized junctions where signals are received from other neurons, the dendrites being vastly more important in this role than the cell body. The dendrites (an average neuron may have as many as 10,000) increase the cell's receptive surface area and thereby increase its capacity to communicate with other neurons.

The **axon**, sometimes also called a **nerve fiber**, is a single long extension from the cell body. The portion of the axon closest to the cell body plus the part of the cell body where the axon is joined is known as the **initial segment**. The initial segment is where the electric signals are generated that then propagate away from the cell body along the axon. The axon may have branches, called **collaterals**, along its course, and near their ends both the axon and the collaterals undergo further branching. The greater the degree of branching of the axon, the greater the cell's sphere of influence. Each branch ends in an **axon terminal**, which is responsible for releasing chemical messengers from the axon. These messengers diffuse to the cell contacted by the terminal. In addition, some neurons release their chemical messengers from a series of bulging areas along the axon known as **varicosities**.

FIGURE 8-2

(A) Diagrammatic representation of a neuron. The proportions shown here are misleading because the axon may be 5000 to 10,000 times longer than the cell body is wide. The neuron shown here is a multipolar neuron, but there are several other types, one of which has no axons. (B) A neuron as observed through a microscope. The axon terminals cannot be seen at this magnification.

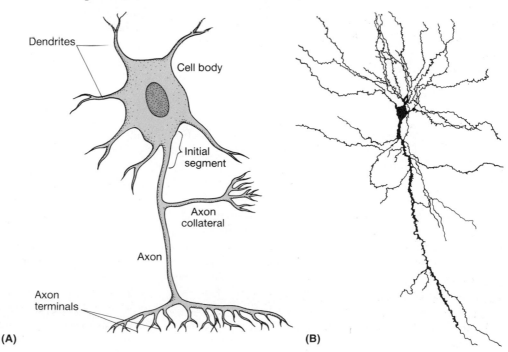

(A)   (B)

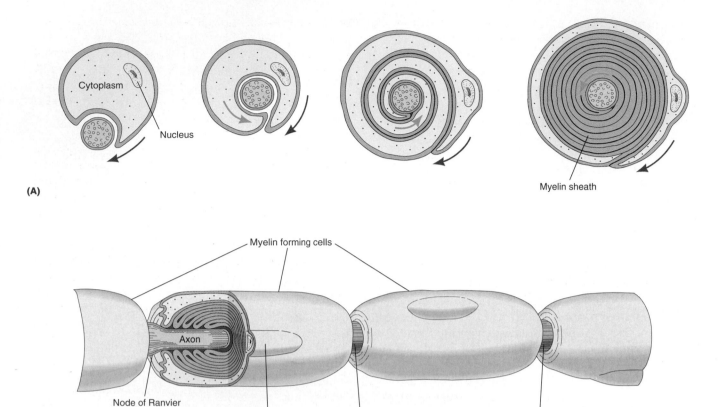

FIGURE 8-3

(A) Cross section of an axon in successive stages of myelinization. The myelin-forming cell may migrate around the axon, trailing successive layers of its plasma membrane (red arrows). Alternatively, it may add to its tip, which lies against the axon, so that the tip is pushed around the axon, burrowing under the layers of myelin that are already formed (green arrows). The latter process must be used in the central nervous system where each myelin-forming cell may send branches to as many as 40 axons. (B) The myelin-forming cells are separated by a small space, the node of Ranvier (also called neurofibril node).

The axons of some neurons are covered by **myelin** (Figure 8-3), a fatty, membranous sheath consisting of layers of plasma membrane and formed by nearby supporting cells which wrap their plasma membranes around the axon. In the central nervous system these cells are the oligodendroglia, and in the peripheral nervous system they are the **Schwann cells**. The spaces between the myelin-forming cells where the axon's plasma membrane is exposed to extracellular fluid are the **nodes of Ranvier**. Myelin speeds up passage of the electric signal along the axon and conserves energy, as will be discussed later.

In order to maintain the structure and function of the cell axon, particularly when it is long, diverse organelles and materials must be moved from the cell body, where they are made, to the axon and its terminals. This movement is termed **axon transport**.

Axon transport of certain materials also occurs in the opposite direction, from the axon terminals to the cell body. This permits growth factors and other chemical signals picked up at the terminals to affect the neuron's morphology, biochemistry, and connectivity. This is also the route by which toxins, such as tetanus toxin, and herpes and polio viruses taken up by the peripheral nerve terminals enter the central nervous system.

Neurons can be divided into three functional classes: afferent neurons, efferent neurons, and interneurons. **Afferent neurons** convey information from the tissues and organs of the body *into* the central nervous system, **effer-**

ent neurons transmit electric signals *from* the central nervous system out to effector cells (muscle or gland cells), and **interneurons** connect afferent and efferent neurons within the central nervous system[1] (Figure 8-4).

At their ends farthest from the central nervous system, afferent neurons have receptors that respond to various physical or chemical changes in their environment by causing electric signals to be generated in the neuron. The receptor may be a specialized ending of the neuron or a separate cell closely associated with it. The afferent neurons propagate these electric signals from the receptors into the brain or spinal cord. (Recall from Chapter 7 that the term "receptor" has two totally distinct meanings, the one defined here and the other referring to the specific proteins with which a chemical messenger combines to exert its effects on a target cell; both types of receptors will be referred to frequently in this chapter.)

Afferent neurons are atypical in that they have no dendrites and only a single process, considered to be an axon.

Shortly after leaving the cell body, the axon divides. One branch, the peripheral process, ends at the receptors, and the other branch, the central process, enters the central nervous system to form junctions with other neurons. Note in Figure 8-4 that both the cell body and the long peripheral process of the axon are *outside* the central nervous system and that only part of the relatively short central process enters the brain or spinal cord.

The cell bodies and dendrites of efferent neurons are within the central nervous system, but the axons extend out into the periphery. The axons of both the afferent and efferent neurons, except for the small part in the brain or spinal cord, form the **nerves** of the peripheral nervous system.

Interneurons lie entirely within the central nervous system. They account for about 99 percent of all neurons and have a wide range of physiological properties, shapes, chemistries, and functions. As a rough estimate, for each afferent neuron entering the central nervous system, there are about 10 efferent neurons and about 200,000 interneurons. The number of interneurons interposed between certain afferent and efferent neurons varies according to the complexity of the action. The knee-jerk reflex elicited by tapping below the kneecap has no interneurons, for there the afferent neurons end directly on the efferent

---

[1]We use the term "interneuron" in its broadest sense. Some authors, however, limit its use to those nerve cells that have only a local action because they have a relatively short axon that remains in a given part of the nervous system. In that scheme, neurons within the central nervous system that have long axons are called projection neurons.

FIGURE 8-4

Three classes of neurons. Note that the interneurons form the connections between afferent and efferent neurons and lie entirely within the CNS. The dendrites, which function as an extension of the neuron cell body, are not shown. The arrows indicate the direction of transmission of neural activity. The stylized neurons in this figure show the conventions that we will use throughout this book for the different parts of neurons.

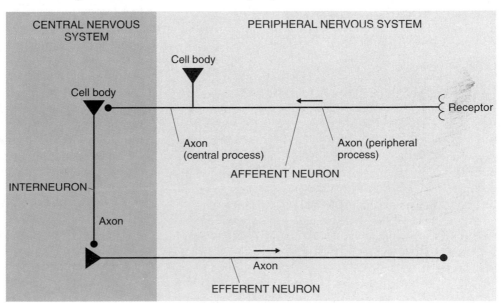

neurons. In contrast, stimuli invoking memory or language may involve millions of interneurons.

Interneurons serve as integrators within networks of neurons because their output reflects the balance of inputs they receive from the thousands of active neurons that impinge upon them. Interneurons also serve as signal changers or gatekeepers, changing, for example, an excitatory input into a inhibitory output or into no output at all. The mechanisms used by interneurons to achieve these functions will be discussed at length throughout this chapter.

Characteristics of the three functional classes of neurons are summarized in Table 8-1.

The anatomically specialized junction between two neurons where one neuron alters the activity of another is called a **synapse**.[2] At most synapses, a signal is transmitted from one neuron to another by chemical messengers known as **neurotransmitters**, a term that also includes the chemicals by which efferent neurons communicate

---

[2]The term "synapse" is also used sometimes for the junction between a neuron and an effector (muscle or gland) cell. In this book, we use the term "neuroeffector junction" for this site.

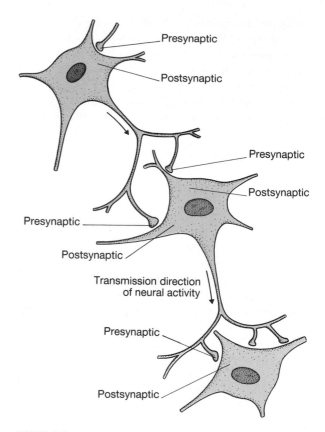

FIGURE 8-5

A neuron postsynaptic to one cell can be presynaptic to another.

with effector cells. The neurotransmitter released from one neuron alters the receiving neuron by binding with a specific membrane receptor on the receiving neuron. (The reader is cautioned one last time not to confuse this use of the term "receptor" with the receptors mentioned above that are on or associated with afferent neurons.)

Synapses generally occur between the axon terminal of one neuron and the dendrite or cell body of a second. In certain areas, however, synapses also occur between two dendrites, between a dendrite and a cell body, or between an axon terminal and a second axon terminal. A neuron conducting signals toward a synapse is called a **presynaptic neuron**, whereas a neuron conducting signals away from a synapse is a **postsynaptic neuron**. Figure 8-5 shows how, in a multineuronal pathway, a single neuron can be postsynaptic to one group of cells and presynaptic to another.

A postsynaptic neuron may have thousands of synaptic junctions on the surface of its dendrites and cell body, so that signals from many presynaptic neurons can affect it. Certain neurons in the brain receive more than 100,000 synaptic inputs.

TABLE 8-1   THREE CLASSES OF NEURONS

I. Afferent neurons
   A. Transmit information into the central nervous system from receptors at their peripheral endings
   B. Are mostly (that is, the cell body and the long peripheral process of the axon) outside the central nervous system; only the short central process of the axon enters the central nervous system
   C. Have no dendrites

II. Efferent neurons
   A. Transmit information out of the central nervous system to effector cells (muscles or glands)
   B. Are mostly (that is, the cell body, dendrites, and a small segment of the axon) in the central nervous system; most of the axon is outside the central nervous system

III. Interneurons
   A. Function as integrators and signal changers
   B. Integrate groups of afferent and efferent neurons into reflex circuits
   C. Lie entirely within the central nervous system
   D. Account for 99 percent of all neurons

Only about 10 percent of the cells in the central nervous system are neurons, and the neurons occupy about 50 percent of the volume of the central nervous system. The remainder are **glial cells** (also termed neuroglia). Glial cells branch but not as extensively as the neurons do.

As noted earlier, one type of glial cell, the oligodendroglia, forms the myelin covering of axons in the central nervous system.

A second type of glial cell, the astroglia, has multiple functions. They help regulate the composition of the extracellular fluid in the central nervous system because they remove potassium ions and neurotransmitters from the extracellular fluid around synapses. They also help sustain the neurons metabolically—for example, by providing glucose and removing ammonia. In the embryo, astroglia guide neurons as they migrate during neural development, and they stimulate the neurons' growth and the formation of their axons and dendrites by secreting growth factors. In addition, astroglia have many neuron-like characteristics, such as receptors for certain neurotransmitters, ion channels, and the capability of generating electrical responses. Thus, it has been suggested that glia take part in information signaling in the brain.

NEURAL GROWTH AND REGENERATION

The elaborate networks of nerve-cell processes that characterize the nervous system are remarkably similar in all human beings and depend upon the outgrowth of specific axons to specific targets. The mechanisms that guide the development of the brain and spinal cord are today under intense investigation by neuroscientists.

Development of the nervous system in the embryo begins with a series of divisions of precursor cells termed neuroblasts. After the last cell division, each cell, now called a neuron, migrates to its final location and begins to develop a spatial orientation, sending out processes that will become the axon and dendrites. A specialized enlargement, the growth cone, forms the tip of each extending process and is involved in finding the correct route and final target for the process.

As the cell process grows, it is guided along the surfaces of other cells, most commonly glial cells. Which particular route is followed depends in part on the presence of glycoproteins, known as cell adhesion molecules (CAMs), that provide recognition markers on the membranes of early neurons and other embryonic cells. Neuronal development is also influenced by chemical messengers that affect growth, such as **nerve growth factor**, in the extracellular region immediately surrounding the growth cone.

Once the target of the advancing growth cone is reached, synapses are formed. The synapses must be used, however, to transmit activity before their final maturation occurs. During these intricate early stages of neural development, alcohol and other drugs, radiation, and viruses can exert effects that cause permanent damage to the fetal nervous system.

A normal—although unexpected—aspect of development of the nervous system occurs after growth and projection of the axons. Many of the newly formed neurons and synapses are *destroyed*. In fact, as many as 50 to 70 percent of neurons die in some regions of the developing nervous system! Why this seemingly wasteful process occurs is unknown.

Although the basic shape of existing neurons in the mature central nervous system does not change, the creation and removal of synaptic contacts begun during fetal development continues at a slower pace throughout life as part of normal growth, learning, and aging.

Division of neuron precursors is essentially complete before birth, and no new neurons are formed to replace those that die. Damaged neurons can repair themselves, however, and significant function may be regained, provided that the damage occurs outside the central nervous system and does not affect the neuron cell body. After repairable injury, the segment of the axon now separated from the cell body degenerates. The proximal part of the axon (the stump still attached to the cell body) then gives rise to a growth cone, which grows out to the effector organ so that in some cases function is restored.

In contrast, damage to axons within the central nervous system is followed by attempts at sprouting, but no significant regeneration of the axon occurs across the damaged site, and there are no well-documented reports of function return. Mature neurons of the central nervous system are capable of regrowing processes when isolated in tissue culture, but some property of their environment in vivo, such as inhibitory factors from nearby oligodendroglia, prevents this from happening in the body.

Researchers are attempting to create artificial tubes of Schwann-cell membrane or even fetal amniotic membrane to provide an environment that will support axonal regeneration in the central nervous system. Attempts are also being made to restore function to damaged or diseased brains by the implantation of pieces of fetal brain or of tissues, such as the patient's own adrenal medulla (part of the adrenal glands, which are situated above the kidneys), that synthesize and secrete neurotransmitters.

This completes our discussion of neural tissue. We now turn to the mechanisms by which neurons and synapses function, beginning with the electrical properties that underlie all these events.

SECTION A SUMMARY

The nervous system is divided into two parts: The central nervous system comprises the brain and spinal cord, and the peripheral nervous system consists of nerves extending from the CNS.

I. The basic unit of the nervous system is the nerve cell, or neuron.
   A. The cell body and dendrites receive information from other neurons.
   B. The axon (nerve fiber), which may be covered with sections of myelin separated by nodes of Ranvier, transmits information to other neurons or effector cells.
II. Neurons are classified in three ways:
   A. Afferent neurons transmit information *into* the CNS from receptors at their peripheral endings.
   B. Efferent neurons transmit information *out of* the CNS to effector cells.
   C. Interneurons lie entirely within the CNS and form circuits with other interneurons or connect afferent and efferent neurons.
III. Information is transmitted across a synapse by a neurotransmitter, which is released by a presynaptic neuron and combines with receptors on a postsynaptic neuron.
IV. The CNS also contains glial cells, which sustain the neurons metabolically, form myelin, and serve as guides for the neurons during development.

NEURAL GROWTH AND REGENERATION

I. Neurons develop from precursor cells, migrate to their final location, and send out processes to their target cells.
II. Cell division to form new neurons is completed by birth.
III. After degeneration of a severed axon, damaged peripheral neurons can regrow the axon to their target organ. Damaged neurons of the CNS do not regenerate or restore function.

SECTION A KEY TERMS

central nervous system (CNS)	nodes of Ranvier
peripheral nervous system	axon transport
neuron	afferent neurons
cell body	efferent neurons
dendrites	interneurons
axon	nerves
nerve fiber	synapse
initial segment	neurotransmitters
collaterals	presynaptic neuron
axon terminal	postsynaptic neuron
varicosities	glial cells
myelin	nerve growth factor
Schwann cells	

SECTION A REVIEW QUESTIONS

1. Describe the direction of information flow through a neuron; through a network consisting of afferent neurons, efferent neurons, and interneurons.
2. Contrast the two uses of the word "receptor."

SECTION

B

MEMBRANE POTENTIALS

BASIC PRINCIPLES OF ELECTRICITY

As we have seen, many molecules have a net electric charge due to such components as the negative carboxyl group RCOO$^-$ and the positive amino group RNH$_3^+$. Moreover, most of the mineral elements, such as sodium, potassium, and chloride, are present in solution as ions (Na$^+$, K$^+$, and Cl$^-$).

With the exception of water, the major chemical substances in the extracellular fluid are, as discussed in Chapter 6, sodium and chloride ions, whereas the intracellular fluid contains high concentrations of potassium ions and ionized organic molecules, particularly proteins and phosphate compounds. Since many charged particles are found both inside and outside cells, it is not surprising that electrical phenomena resulting from the distribution of these charged particles play a significant role in cell function.

Like charges repel each other; that is, positive charge repels positive charge, and negative charge repels negative charge. In contrast, an electric force draws positively and negatively charged substances together.

When oppositely charged particles come together, the electric force of attraction moving them can be used to perform work. Conversely, to separate opposite charges, energy must be used to overcome this attractive force. Thus, separated electric charges of opposite sign have the potential of doing work if they are allowed to come together. This potential is called an **electric potential** or, because it is determined by the difference in charge between two points, a **potential difference**, which we shall often shorten to **potential**. The units of electric potential are volts, but since the total charge that can be separated in most biological systems is very small, the potential differences are small and are measured in millivolts (1 mV = 0.001 V).

The movement of electric charge is called a **current**. The electric force between charges tends to make them flow, producing a current. If the charges are of opposite sign, the current brings them toward each other; if the charges are alike, the current increases the separation between them. The amount of charge that moves—in other words, the current—depends on the potential difference between the charges and on the nature of the material through which they are moving. The hindrance to electric charge movement is known as the **resistance**. The relationship between current I, voltage E (for electric potential difference), and resistance R is given by **Ohm's law**:

$$I - \frac{E}{R}$$

Materials that have a high electrical resistance are known as insulators, whereas materials having a low resistance are conductors.

Water that contains dissolved ions is a relatively good conductor of electricity because the ions can carry the current. As we have seen, the intracellular and extracellular fluids contain numerous ions and can therefore carry current. Lipids, however, contain very few charged groups and cannot carry current. Therefore, the lipid layers of the plasma membrane are regions of high electrical resistance separating two water compartments—the intracellular fluid and the extracellular fluid—of low resistance.

THE RESTING MEMBRANE POTENTIAL

All cells under resting conditions have a potential difference across their plasma membranes oriented with the inside of the cell negatively charged with respect

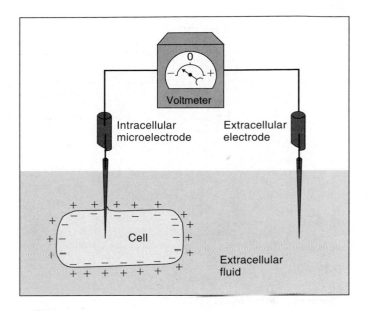

FIGURE 8-6

The potential difference across a plasma membrane as measured by an intracellular microelectrode.

to the outside (Figure 8-6). This potential is the **resting membrane potential**.

By convention, extracellular fluid is assigned a voltage of zero, and the polarity (positive or negative) of the membrane potential is stated in terms of the sign of the excess charge on the inside of the cell. For example, if the intracellular fluid has an excess of negative charge and the potential difference across the membrane has a magnitude of 70 mV, we say that the membrane potential is −70 mV.

The magnitude of the resting membrane potential varies from about −5 to −100 mV, depending upon the type of cell (in neurons, it is generally in the range of −40 to −75 mV). As we shall see, the membrane potential of some cells can change rapidly in response to stimulation, an ability of key importance in their functioning.

The resting membrane potential can be accounted for by the fact that there is a small excess of negative ions inside the cell and an excess of positive ions outside. The excess negative charges inside are electrically attracted to the excess positive charges outside the cell, and vice versa. Thus, the excess charges (ions) collect in a thin shell at the inner and outer surfaces of the plasma membrane (Figure 8-7), whereas the bulk of the intracellular and extracellular fluids are electrically neutral. Unlike the diagrammatic representation in Figure 8-7, the number of positive and negative charges that have to be separated across a membrane to account for the potential is an infinitesimal fraction of the total number of charges within the cell.

The magnitude of the resting membrane potential is determined mainly by two factors: (1) the difference in ion concentrations of the intracellular and extracellular fluids,

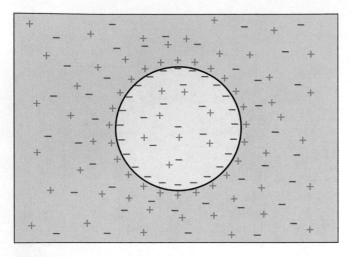

FIGURE 8-7

The excess of positive charges outside the cell and the excess of negative charges inside collect close to the plasma membrane. In reality, these excess charges are only a very small fraction of the total number of ions inside and outside the cell.

and (2) differences in membrane permeability to the different ions, which reflect the number of open channels for the different ions in the plasma membrane. The rest of this section analyzes how these two factors operate.

The concentrations of sodium, potassium, and chloride ions in the extracellular and intracellular fluids of a nerve cell are listed in Table 8-2. Although this table appears to contradict our earlier assertion that the bulk of the intra- and extracellular fluids are electrically neutral, there are many other ions, such as Mg^{2+}, Ca^{2+}, H^+, HCO_3^-, HPO_4^{2-}, SO_4^{2-}, amino acids, and proteins, in both fluid compartments. Sodium, potassium, and chloride ions, however, are present in the highest concentrations and therefore generally play the most important roles in generation of the resting membrane potential. Note that the sodium and chloride concentrations are lower inside the cell than outside, and that the potassium concentration is

greater inside. As we mentioned in Chapter 6, the concentration differences for sodium and potassium are due to the action of a plasma-membrane active-transport system, which pumps sodium out of the cell and potassium into it. We will see later the reason for the chloride distribution.

To understand how such concentration differences for sodium and potassium create membrane potentials, let us consider the situation in Figure 8-8. The assumption in this model is that the membrane contains potassium channels but no sodium channels. *Initially*, compartment 1 contains 0.15 *M* NaCl and compartment 2 contains 0.15 *M* KCl. There is no potential difference across the membrane because the two compartments contain equal numbers of positive and negative ions; that is, they are electrically neutral. The positive ions are different—sodium versus potassium—but the *total* numbers of positive ions in the two compartments are the same, and each positive ion is balanced by a chloride ion.

The initial state will not, however, last. Because of the potassium channels, potassium will diffuse down its concentration gradient from compartment 2 into compartment 1. After a few potassium ions have moved into compartment 1, that compartment will have an excess of positive charge, and compartment 2 will have an excess of

FIGURE 8-8

Generation of a diffusion potential across a membrane that contains only potassium channels. Arrows represent ion movements.

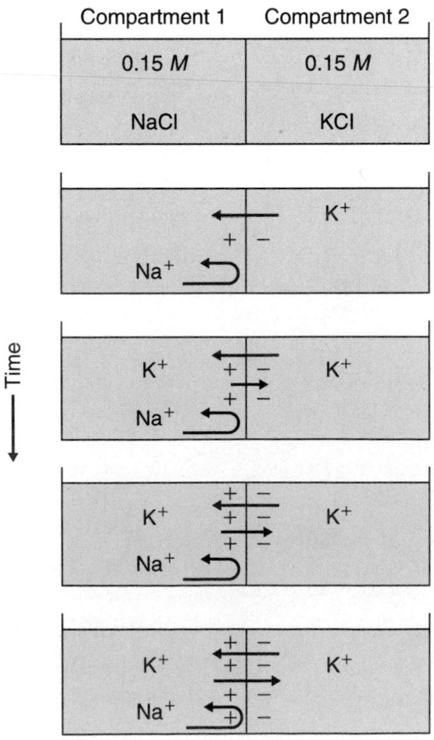

TABLE 8-2	DISTRIBUTION OF MAJOR IONS ACROSS THE PLASMA MEMBRANE OF A TYPICAL NERVE CELL	
	Concentration, mmol/L	
Ion	**Extracellular**	**Intracellular**
Na^+	150	15
Cl^-	110	10
K^+	5	150

negative charge. Thus, a potential difference will exist across the membrane.

Now we introduce a second factor that can cause net movement of ions across a membrane: an electric potential. As compartment 1 becomes increasingly positive and compartment 2 increasingly negative, the membrane potential difference begins to influence the movement of the potassium ions. They are attracted by the negative charge of compartment 2 and repulsed by the positive charge of compartment 1.

As long as the flux due to the potassium concentration gradient is greater than the flux due to the membrane potential, there will be net movement of potassium from compartment 2 to compartment 1, and the membrane potential will increase. Compartment 1 will become more and more positive until the potential eventually produces a flux equal but opposite the flux due to the concentration gradient. The membrane potential at which these two fluxes become equal in magnitude but opposite in direction is called the **equilibrium potential** for that type of ion. At the equilibrium potential for an ion there is no net movement of the ion because the opposing fluxes are equal, and the potential will undergo no further change.

The value of the equilibrium potential for any type of ion depends on the concentration gradient for that ion across the membrane. If the concentrations on the two sides were equal, the flux due to the concentration gradient would be zero and the equilibrium potential would also be zero. The larger the concentration gradient, the larger the equilibrium potential since a larger electrically driven movement of ions would be required to balance the larger movement due to the concentration difference.

If the membrane separating the two compartments is replaced with one that contains only sodium channels, a parallel situation will occur (Figure 8-9). A sodium equilibrium potential will eventually be established, but compartment 2 will be *positive* with respect to compartment 1, at which point net movement will cease.

Thus, the equilibrium potential for one ion species can be different in magnitude and sometimes even in direction from those for other ion species, depending on the concentration gradients for each ion. Given the concentration gradient, the equilibrium potential for any ion can be calculated (by means of the Nernst equation, Appendix D).

When more than one ion species can diffuse across the membrane, the permeabilities and concentration gradients for all the ions must be considered when accounting for the membrane potential. For a given concentration gradient, the greater the membrane permeability to an ion species, the greater the contribution that ion species will make to the membrane potential. Given the concentration gradients and membrane permeabilities for several ion species, the potential of a membrane permeable to these species can be calculated (by the Goldman equation, Appendix D).

It is not difficult to move from these hypothetical examples to a nerve cell at rest where (1) the potassium concentration is much greater inside the nerve cell than outside (Figure 8-10A) and the sodium concentration profile is just the opposite (Figure 8-11A); and (2) the plasma membrane contains about 50 to 75 times more open potassium channels than open sodium channels. Given the actual potassium and sodium concentration differences, one can calculate that the potassium equilibrium potential will be approximately −90 mV (Figure 8-10B) and the sodium equilibrium potential about +60 mV (Figure 8-11B).

Since the membrane is permeable, to some extent, to both potassium and sodium, the resting membrane potential cannot be equal to either of these two equilibrium potentials. Because the membrane is so much more permeable to potassium than to sodium, however, the resting potential will be much closer to the potassium equilibrium potential.

In other words, a potential is generated across the plasma membrane largely because of the movement of potassium down its concentration gradient through open potassium channels, so that the inside of the cell becomes negative with respect to the outside. The experimentally measured resting membrane potential is *not* equal to the potassium equilibrium potential, however, because a small number of sodium channels are open in the resting state, and some sodium ions continually move into the cell, canceling the effect of an equivalent number of potassium ions simultaneously moving out.

Thus, at a resting potential of −70 mV, a typical value for neurons, neither sodium nor potassium is at its equilibrium potential, and so there is net movement through ion channels of sodium into the cell and potassium out. If such net ion movements occur, why does the concentration of

FIGURE 8-9

Generation of a diffusion potential across a membrane that contains only sodium channels. Arrows represent ion movements.

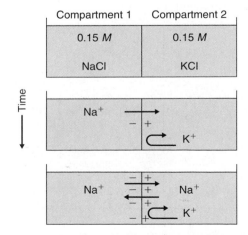

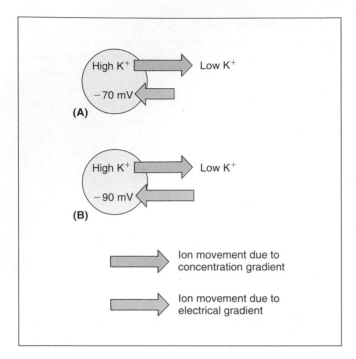

FIGURE 8-10

Forces acting on potassium when the membrane of a neuron is at (A) the resting potential (−70 mV, inside negative), and (B) the potassium equilibrium potential (−90 mV, inside negative).

FIGURE 8-11

Forces acting on sodium when the membrane of a neuron is at (A) the resting potential (−70 mV, inside negative), and (B) the sodium equilibrium potential (+60 mV, inside positive).

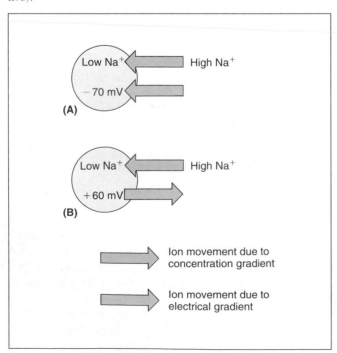

intracellular sodium not progressively increase and that of intracellular potassium decrease? The reason is that active-transport mechanisms in the plasma membrane utilize energy derived from cellular metabolism to pump the sodium back out of the cell and the potassium back in. Actually, the pumping of these ions is linked because they are both transported by the Na,K-ATPase pumps in the membrane (page 127).

In a resting cell, the number of ions moved by the pump equals the number of ions that move in the opposite direction through channels in the membrane down their concentration and/or electrical gradients (Figure 8-12), and therefore the concentrations of sodium and potassium in the cell do not change. As long as the concentration gradients remain fixed and the ion permeabilities of the plasma membrane do not change, the electric potential across the resting membrane will remain constant.

Thus far, we have described the membrane potential as due purely and directly to the passive movement of ions down their electrical and concentration gradients, the concentration gradients having been established by membrane pumps. There is, however, another component to the membrane potential, reflecting the *direct* separation of charge across the membrane by the transport of ions by the membrane Na,K-ATPase pump. If the pump were to move equal numbers of sodium and potassium ions across the membrane in opposite directions, it would not contribute directly to the separation of charge and all the charge separation would result from ion diffusion. If equal numbers of ions are not moved, however, the pump does separate charge and contributes directly to the membrane potential. It is known in this case as an **electrogenic pump**.

The Na,K-ATPase pump is, in fact, electrogenic since it moves three sodium ions out of the cell for every two potassium ions that it brings in. This unequal transport of positive ions directly makes the inside of the cell more negative than it would be from ion diffusion alone. In most cells (but by no means all), however, the electrogenic contribution to the membrane potential is quite small. It must be reemphasized that, even when the electrogenic contribution of the Na,K-ATPase pump is small, the pump makes an essential *indirect* contribution to the membrane potential because it maintains the concentration gradients down which the ions diffuse to produce most of the charge separation that makes up the potential.

We have not yet dealt with chloride ions. The plasma membranes of many cells have chloride channels and do not contain chloride-ion pumps. Therefore, in these cells the membrane potential, set up by all the interactions just described, acts on chloride ions. The inside negativity moves chloride out of the cell, and the chloride concentration outside the cell becomes higher than that inside. This concentration gradient, however, produces a diffusion of chloride back into the cell that exactly opposes the move-

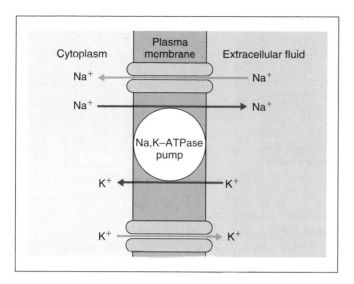

FIGURE 8-12

Movements of sodium and potassium ions across the plasma membrane of a resting neuron. The passive movements (blue arrows) are exactly balanced by the active transport (red arrows) of the ions in the opposite direction.

ment out because of the electric potential. Thus, chloride concentrations shift until the equilibrium potential for chloride is equal to the resting membrane potential, and chloride makes no contribution to the magnitude of the membrane potential.

In contrast, some cells have an active-transport system that moves chloride out of the cell. In these cells, the membrane potential is not at the chloride equilibrium potential, and net chloride diffusion *into* the cell contributes to the excess negative charge inside the cell; that is, it increases the magnitude of the membrane potential.

Most of the negative charge in neurons is accounted for, however, not by chloride ions but by negatively charged organic molecules, such as proteins. Unlike chloride, these molecules do not readily cross the plasma membrane but remain inside the cell, where their charge contributes to the total negative charge within the cell.

GRADED POTENTIALS AND ACTION POTENTIALS

Transient changes in the membrane potential from its resting level produce electric signals that can alter cell activities. Such changes are the most important way that nerve cells process and transmit information. These signals occur in two forms: graded potentials and action potentials. Graded potentials are important in signaling over short distances, whereas action potentials are the long-distance signals of nerve and muscle membranes.

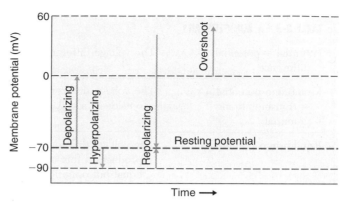

FIGURE 8-13

Depolarizing, repolarizing, hyperpolarizing, and overshoot changes in membrane potential.

Adjectives such as "membrane," "resting," "action," and "graded" define the conditions under which the potential is measured or the way it develops (Table 8-3).

The terms "depolarize," "hyperpolarize," and "repolarize" will be used to describe the direction of changes in the membrane potential relative to the resting potential (Figure 8-13). The membrane is said to be **depolarized** when its potential is less negative (closer to zero) than the resting level. The membrane is **hyperpolarized** when the potential is more negative than the resting level. When a membrane potential that has been either depolarized or hyperpolarized returns toward the resting value, it is said to be **repolarizing**. **Overshoot** refers to a reversal of the membrane-potential polarity, that is, when the inside of a cell becomes positive.

Graded Potentials

Graded potentials are changes in membrane potential that are confined to a relatively small region of the plasma membrane and die out within 1 to 2 mm of their site of origin. They can occur in either a depolarizing or hyperpolarizing direction (Figure 8-14A), and they are usually produced by some stimulus, that is, by a specific change in the cell's environment acting on a specialized region of the membrane. They are called "graded potentials" because the magnitude of the potential change is variable (graded) and is related to the magnitude of the stimulus (Figure 8-14B). We shall encounter a number of graded potentials, which are given various names related to the location of the potential or to the function it performs: receptor potentials, synaptic potentials, end-plate potentials, pacemaker potentials.

Whenever a graded potential occurs, charge flows between the place of origin of the potential and adjacent regions of the plasma membrane, which are at the resting

dients of sodium and potassium would gradually disappear and action potentials could no longer be generated. As might be expected, cellular accumulation of sodium and loss of potassium are prevented by the continuous action of the membrane Na,K-ATPase pumps.

It may seem foolish to let sodium move into the neuron and then pump it back out, but sodium movement into the cell creates the electric signal necessary for communication between parts of the cell, and pumping sodium out restores the concentration gradient so that, in response to a new stimulus, sodium will enter the cell and create another signal.

Mechanism of Ion-channel Changes. In the above section, we described the various phases of the action potential as due to the opening and/or closing of ion channels. What causes these changes? The very first part of the depolarization, as we shall see later, is due to local current. Once depolarization starts, the depolarization itself causes sodium channels to open. In light of our discussion of the ionic basis of membrane potentials, it is very easy to confuse the cause-and-effect relationships of this last statement. Earlier we pointed out that an increase in sodium permeability *causes* membrane depolarization; now we are saying that depolarization *causes* an increase in sodium permeability. Combining these two distinct causal relationships yields the positive-feedback cycle (Figure 8-18) responsible for the depolarizing phase of the action potential: Depolarization opens sodium channels so that the membrane permeability to sodium increases. Because of increased sodium permeability, sodium diffuses into the cell; this addition of positive charge to the cell further depolarizes the membrane, which in turn produces a still greater increase in sodium permeability, which in turn causes. . . .

Ion channels, such as these sodium channels, that can be opened or closed by changes in membrane potential

FIGURE 8-18

Positive-feedback relation between membrane depolarization and increased sodium permeability, which leads to the rapid depolarizing phase of the action potential.

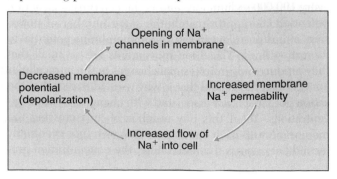

are called voltage-sensitive ion channels (page 122). The potassium channels that open during an action potential are also voltage-sensitive. In fact, their opening is triggered by the same depolarization that opens the sodium channels, but the potassium-channel opening is slightly delayed.

What about the inactivation of the voltage-sensitive sodium channels that opened during the rising phase of the action potential? This is the result of a change in the conformation of the proteins that constitute the channel.

The generation of action potentials is prevented by *local anesthetics* such as procaine hydrochloride (Novocaine) and lidocaine (Xylocaine) because these drugs prevent opening of the sodium channels in response to depolarization. Without action potentials, afferent signals generated in the periphery—in response to injury, for example—cannot reach the brain and give rise to the sensation of pain.

Although we have discussed only sodium and potassium channels, in some regions of nerve-cell membrane and in various nonneural cells calcium channels open in response to membrane depolarization. In these cases, calcium diffusion into the cell through these voltage-sensitive channels is responsible for generating action potentials. These are generally prolonged action potentials, and the inward calcium diffusion couples membrane excitability to events within the cell, explaining some of the special properties of these cells.

Threshold. Not all stimulus-induced depolarizations trigger the positive-feedback relationship that leads to an action potential. Action potentials occur only when the membrane is depolarized enough (and therefore enough sodium channels are open) so that sodium entry exceeds potassium exit. In other words, action potentials occur only when the *net* movement of positive charge through ion channels is inward. The membrane potential at which the *net* movement of ions through the ion channels first changes from outward to inward is the **threshold**, and stimuli that are just strong enough to depolarize the membrane to this level are **threshold stimuli** (Figure 8-19).

The threshold of most excitable membranes is about 15 mV less negative inside than the resting membrane potential. Thus, if the resting potential of a neuron is −70 mV, the threshold potential may be −55 mV. Stimuli must depolarize the membrane by at least 15 mV in order to initiate the positive feedback that produces an action potential. At depolarizations less than threshold, outward potassium movement still exceeds sodium entry and the positive-feedback cycle cannot get started despite the increase in sodium entry. In such cases, the membrane will return to its resting level as soon as the stimulus is removed, and no action potential is generated. These weak depolarizations are **subthreshold potentials**, and the stimuli that cause them are **subthreshold stimuli**.

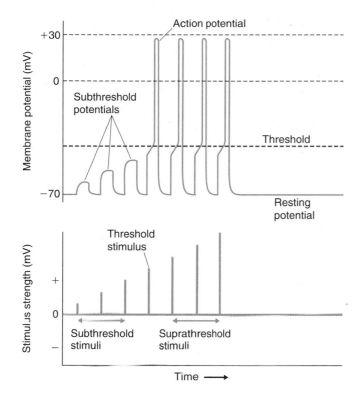

FIGURE 8-19

Changes in the membrane potential with increasing strength of depolarizing stimulus. When the membrane potential reaches threshold, action potentials are generated. Increasing the stimulus strength above threshold level does not cause larger action potentials. (The afterhyperpolarization has been omitted from this figure for clarity.)

Just like threshold stimuli, stimuli of more than threshold magnitude (**suprathreshold stimuli**) also elicit action potentials, but as can be seen in Figure 8-19, the action potentials resulting from such stimuli have exactly the same amplitude as those caused by threshold stimuli. This is explained by the fact that once threshold is reached, membrane events are no longer dependent upon stimulus strength. The depolarization continues on to generate an action potential because the positive-feedback cycle is operating. Action potentials either occur maximally or do not occur at all. Another way of saying this is that action potentials are **all-or-none**.[3]

The firing of a gun is a mechanical analogy that shows the principle of all-or-none behavior characteristic of nerve axons. The magnitude of the explosion and the velocity at which the bullet leaves the gun do not depend on how hard the trigger is squeezed. Either the trigger is pulled hard enough to fire the gun, or it is not; one cannot fire a gun halfway.

Because of this all-or-none nature, a single action potential cannot convey information about the magnitude of the stimulus that initiated it. How then does one distinguish between a loud noise and a whisper, a light touch and a pinch? This information, as we shall see, depends in part upon the number of action potentials transmitted per unit of time, that is, frequency, and not upon their size.

Refractory Periods. How soon after firing an action potential can an excitable membrane fire a second one? During the action potential, a second stimulus—no matter how strong—will not produce a second action potential, and the membrane is said to be in its **absolute refractory period**. Following this period, there is an interval during which a second action potential can be produced, but only if the stimulus strength is considerably greater than threshold. This is the **relative refractory period**, which can last 10 to 15 ms or longer. If a threshold depolarization outlasts the relative refractory period, an additional action potential will be fired.

Refractory periods reflect the fact that after an action potential, time is required to restore the proteins of the voltage-sensitive ion channels to their original resting conformation. Both refractory periods correspond to times of residual sodium inactivation and increased potassium permeability. A suprathreshold stimulus can cause an action potential during the relative refractory period when a threshold stimulus cannot because the suprathreshold stimulus opens more sodium channels so there is a greater chance that sodium entry will exceed potassium exit, triggering the positive feedback cycle illustrated in Figure 8-18.

The refractory periods limit the number of action potentials that can be produced by an excitable membrane in a given period of time. Most nerve cells respond at frequencies of up to 100 action potentials per second, and some may produce much higher frequencies for brief periods of time.

Action-potential Propagation. Once generated, one particular action potential does not itself travel along the membrane. Rather, the local current produced by one action potential is great enough to serve as the stimulus that depolarizes the adjacent membrane to its threshold potential. The sodium positive-feedback cycle takes over, and a new action potential occurs there.

The new action potential then produces local currents of its own, which depolarize the region adjacent to it, producing yet another action potential at the next site, and so on to cause **action-potential propagation** along the length of the membrane. Because each action potential depends on the sodium-feedback cycle of the membrane

---

[3]There is a qualification: The action potential fires maximally if it fires at all, but its maximal amplitude depends on the electrical and chemical conditions across the membrane and upon the state of the membrane. For example, if extracellular sodium concentration is reduced, the action potential will be smaller than usual because of the reduced concentration gradient that drives sodium into the cell.

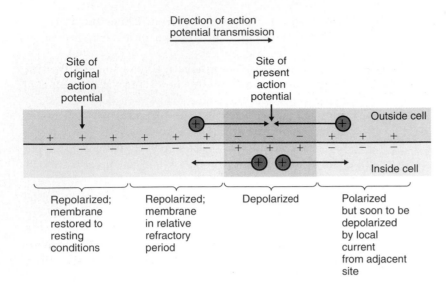

Direction of action potential transmission →

Site of original action potential

Site of present action potential

Outside cell

Inside cell

Repolarized; membrane restored to resting conditions

Repolarized; membrane in relative refractory period

Depolarized

Polarized but soon to be depolarized by local current from adjacent site

FIGURE 8-20

Propagation of an action potential along a plasma membrane.

where the action potential is occurring, the action potential arriving at the end of the membrane is virtually identical in form to the initial one. Thus, action potentials are not conducted decrementally as are graded potentials.

Because the membrane areas that have just undergone an action potential are refractory and cannot immediately undergo another, the only direction of action-potential propagation is away from a region of membrane that has recently been active (Figure 8-20).

If the membrane through which the action potential must travel is not refractory, excitable membranes are able to conduct action potentials in either direction, the direction of propagation being determined by the stimulus location. For example, the action potentials in skeletal muscle cells are initiated near the middle of these cylindrical cells and propagate toward the two ends. In most nerve cells, however, action potentials are initiated at one end of the cell and propagate toward the other end, for reasons to be described in the next section. The propagation ceases when the action potential reaches the end of an axon.

The velocity with which an action potential propagates along a membrane depends upon fiber diameter and whether or not the fiber is myelinated. The larger the fiber diameter, the faster the action potential propagates. This is because a larger fiber offers less resistance to local current, and so adjacent regions of the membrane are brought to threshold faster.

Myelin is an insulator that makes it more difficult for charge to flow between intra- and extracellular fluid compartments. Moreover, the concentration of sodium channels in the myelinated region of axons is low. Therefore, action potentials do not occur along the sections of membrane covered by myelin. Rather, they occur only at the nodes of Ranvier where the myelin coating is interrupted and the concentration of sodium channels is high. Thus,

action potentials literally jump from one node to the next as they propagate along a myelinated fiber, and for this reason this method of propagation is called **saltatory conduction** (Latin *saltare*, to leap).

Propagation via saltatory conduction is faster than propagation in nonmyelinated fibers of the same axon diameter because less charge leaks out through the myelin-covered section of the membrane (Figure 8-21). Thus, more charge arrives at the node adjacent to the active node, and an action potential is generated there sooner than if the myelin were not present.

Conduction velocities range from about 0.5 m/s (1 mi/h) for small-diameter, unmyelinated fibers to about 100 m/s (225 mi/h) for large-diameter, myelinated fibers. At 0.5 m/s, an action potential travels from the head to the toe of an average-size person in about 4 s; at a velocity of 100 m/s, it would take about 0.02 s.[4]

Initiation of Action Potential. In afferent neurons, the initial depolarization to threshold is achieved by a graded potential generated in the receptors at the peripheral ends of the neurons, in other words, at the ends farthest from the central nervous system, and where the nervous system functionally encounters the outside world. In all other neurons, the depolarization to threshold is due either to a graded potential generated by synaptic input to the neuron or to a spontaneous change in the neuron's membrane potential, known as a **pacemaker potential**. How synaptic potentials are produced is the subject of the next sec-

---

[4]The actual time required for a signal to travel from the head to the toe is slightly longer because there are no single nerve fibers leading from the head to the toe. Synapses must be crossed, each synapse contributing a slight delay.

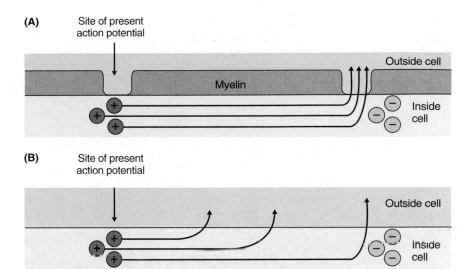

FIGURE 8-21

Current direction during an action potential in (A) a myelinated and (B) an unmyelinated axon.

tion. The production of receptor potentials is discussed in Chapter 9.

Spontaneous generation by pacemaker potentials occurs in the absence of any identifiable external stimulus and is an inherent property of certain neurons (and other excitable cells, including certain smooth-muscle and cardiac-muscle cells). In these cells, the ion channels in the plasma membrane open and close by intrinsic mechanisms,[5] the net effect being a graded depolarization of the membrane—the pacemaker potential. If threshold is reached, an action potential occurs; the membrane then repolarizes and again begins to depolarize (Figure 8-22). There is no stable, resting membrane potential in such cells because of the continuous change in membrane permeability. The rate at which the membrane depolarizes to threshold determines the action-potential frequency. Pacemaker potentials are implicated in many rhythmical behaviors, such as breathing, the heartbeat, and movements within the walls of the stomach and intestines.

FIGURE 8-22

Action potentials resulting from pacemaker potentials.

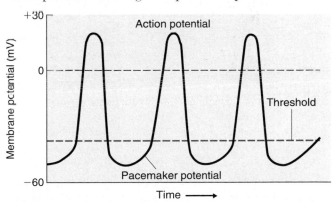

---

[5]For example, in one case, the depolarizing phase of the pacemaker potential occurs because calcium enters the cell through voltage-sensitive calcium channels, some of which are open at the cell's resting potential. The cytosolic calcium concentration rises, and this causes calcium-sensitive potassium channels to open. As potassium flows out through these channels, the membrane repolarizes and most of the calcium channels close. As the membrane calcium pumps restore cytosolic calcium to resting levels, the potassium channels close. Once the resting state is achieved, the cycle begins anew.

SECTION B SUMMARY

THE RESTING POTENTIAL

I. Membrane potentials are generated by the diffusion of ions and are determined by (a) the ionic concentration differences across the membrane, and (b) the membrane's relative permeability to ions.

A. Plasma membrane Na,K-ATPase pumps maintain intracellular sodium concentration low and potassium high.

B. In almost all resting cells, the plasma membrane is much more permeable to potassium than to sodium, and so the membrane potential is close to the potassium equilibrium potential, that is, the inside is negative relative to the outside.

C. The Na,K-ATPase pumps also contribute directly a small component of the potential because they are electrogenic.

GRADED POTENTIALS AND ACTION POTENTIALS

I. Neurons signal information by graded potentials and action potentials.

II. Graded potentials are local potentials whose magnitude can vary and that die out within 1 or 2 mm of their site of origin.

III. An action potential (AP) is a rapid change in the membrane potential during which the potential rapidly depolarizes and repolarizes. In neurons the potential reverses and the membrane becomes positive inside. APs provide long-distance transmission of information through the nervous system.

A. APs occur in excitable membranes because these membranes contain voltage-sensitive sodium channels, which open as the membrane depolarizes, causing a positive feedback toward the sodium equilibrium potential.

B. The action potential is ended as the sodium channels close and additional potassium channels open, which restores the resting conditions.

C. Depolarization of excitable membranes triggers action potentials only when the membrane potential exceeds a threshold potential.

D. Regardless of the size of the stimulus, if the membrane reaches threshold, the APs generated are all the same size.

E. A membrane is refractory for a brief time even though stimuli that were previous effective are applied.

F. APs are propagated from one site to another along a membrane without any change in size.

G. In a myelinated nerve fiber, action potentials manifest saltatory conduction.

H. APs can be initiated by receptors at the ends of afferent neurons, by synapses, or in some cells, by pacemaker potentials.

SECTION B KEY TERMS

electric potential	action potentials
potential difference	excitable membranes
potential	excitability

current	afterhyperpolarization
resistance	threshold
Ohm's law	threshold stimuli
resting membrane	subthreshold potentials
potential	subthreshold stimuli
equilibrium potential	suprathreshold stimuli
electrogenic pump	all-or-none
depolarized	absolute refractory period
hyperpolarized	relative refractory period
repolarizing	action-potential
overshoot	propagation
graded potentials	saltatory conduction
decremental	pacemaker potential

SECTION B REVIEW QUESTIONS

1. Describe the way that negative and positive charges interact and the potential that exists between separated charges.

2. Contrast the abilities of intracellular and extracellular fluids and membrane lipid to conduct electric current.

3. Draw a simple cell; indicate where the concentrations of Na^+, K^+, and Cl^- are high and low and the electric potential difference across the membrane when the cell is at rest.

4. Explain the conditions that give rise to the resting membrane potential. What effect does membrane permeability have on this potential? What is the role of the Na,K-ATPase membrane pumps on the membrane potential? Is this role direct or indirect?

5. Which two factors determine the magnitude of the resting membrane potential?

6. Explain why the resting membrane potential is not equal to the potassium equilibrium potential.

7. Draw a graded potential and an action potential on a graph of membrane potential versus time. Indicate zero membrane potential, resting membrane potential, and threshold potential; indicate when the membrane is depolarized, hyperpolarized, and repolarizing.

8. List at least eight differences between graded potentials and action potentials.

9. Describe the ionic basis of an action potential; include the role of voltage-sensitive channels and the positive-feedback cycle.

10. Explain threshold and the relative and absolute refractory periods in terms of the ionic basis of the action potential.

11. Describe the propagation of an action potential. Contrast this event in myelinated and unmyelinated axons.

12. List three ways in which action potentials can be initiated in neurons.

SECTION

SYNAPSES

As defined earlier, a synapse is an anatomically specialized junction between two neurons, at which the electrical activity in one neuron, the presynaptic neuron, influences the electrical activity in the second, postsynaptic cell. Anatomically, synapses include parts of the presynaptic and postsynaptic neurons and, for most synapses, the extracellular space between these two cells.

When active, synapses can increase or decrease the activity in a postsynaptic neuron by producing a brief, graded potential there. The membrane potential of a postsynaptic neuron is brought closer to threshold at an **excitatory synapse**, and it is either driven farther from threshold or stabilized at its present level at an **inhibitory synapse**.

Thousands of synapses from many different presynaptic cells can affect a single postsynaptic cell (**convergence**), and a single presynaptic cell can send branches to affect many other postsynaptic cells (**divergence**, Figure 8-23).

The level of excitability of a postsynaptic cell at any moment, that is, how close its membrane potential is to threshold, depends on the number of synapses active at any one time and the number that are excitatory or inhibitory. If the membrane of the postsynaptic neuron reaches threshold, it will generate an action potential that is propagated along the axon to the terminal branches, which diverge to influence the excitability of other neurons. Because the output of a neuron reflects the sum of all the incoming signals arriving in the form of excitatory and in-

hibitory synaptic inputs, neurons function as integrators, as described in Chapter 7.

FUNCTIONAL ANATOMY OF SYNAPSES

There are two types of synapses: **electric** and **chemical**. At electric synapses, the plasma membranes of the pre- and postsynaptic cells are joined by gap junctions (page 46). These allow the local currents resulting from action potentials in the presynaptic neuron to flow directly into the postsynaptic cell, depolarizing the membrane to threshold and thus initiating an action potential in the postsynaptic cell. Electric synapses are rare in the mammalian nervous system, and we shall discuss the much more common chemical synapse.

Figure 8-24 shows the structure of a single typical chemical synapse. Note that in actuality the size and shape

FIGURE 8-24

Diagram of a synapse. The "dust" in the synaptic cleft represents not neurotransmitters but rather a fibrillar substance that lies within the cleft.

FIGURE 8-23

Convergence of neural input from many neurons onto a single neuron and divergence of output from a single neuron onto many others. Presynaptic neurons are shown in orange, and postsynaptic neurons in brown.

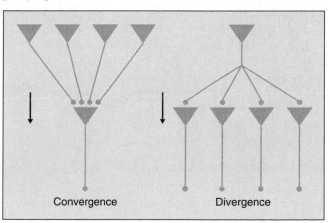

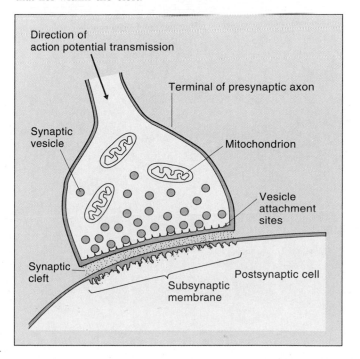

of the pre- and postsynaptic elements can vary greatly (Figure 8-25). The axon of the presynaptic neuron ends in a slight swelling, the axon terminal, and the postsynaptic membrane under the axon terminal is usually thickened. A 10- to 20-nm extracellular space, the **synaptic cleft**, separates the pre- and postsynaptic neurons and prevents *direct* propagation of the current from the presynaptic neuron to the postsynaptic cell. Instead, signals are transmitted across the synaptic cleft by means of a chemical messenger—a neurotransmitter—released from the presynaptic axon terminal. Sometimes, more than one neurotransmitter may be simultaneously released from an axon, in which case the additional neurotransmitter is called a **cotransmitter**.

The neurotransmitter in terminals is stored in membrane-bound **synaptic vesicles**. When an action potential in the presynaptic neuron reaches the end of the axon and depolarizes the axon terminal, voltage-sensitive calcium channels in the membrane open, and calcium diffuses into the axon terminal from the extracellular fluid. The increase in calcium ions in the terminal causes some of the synaptic vesicles to fuse with specific vesicle-attachment sites on the inner surface of the presynaptic plasma membrane and liberate the vesicle contents into the synaptic cleft by the process of exocytosis.

Once released from the axon terminal, small quantities of neurotransmitter—and cotransmitter, if there is one—diffuse across the cleft, and a fraction of these molecules bind to receptor sites on the plasma membrane of the postsynaptic cell (the fate of the others will be described later). The activated receptor may itself contain an ion channel, or it may act indirectly, via a G protein, on ion channels. In either case, the result of the binding of neurotransmitter to receptor is the opening or closing of specific ion channels in the postsynaptic plasma membrane. These channels belong, therefore, to the classes of channels whose function is controlled by receptors, as discussed in Chapter 7 and are distinct from voltage-sensitive channels.

Although Figure 8-25 shows a few exceptions, in general the neurotransmitter is stored on the presynaptic side of the synaptic cleft, whereas receptor sites are on the postsynaptic side. Therefore, chemical synapses operate in only one direction. One-way conduction across synapses causes action potentials to be transmitted along a given multineuronal pathway in one direction.

There is a delay between the arrival of an action potential at a presynaptic terminal and the membrane-potential changes in the postsynaptic cell. It lasts about 1 ms and is called the **synaptic delay**. It can be accounted for by the time required for calcium to enter the axon terminal, for the synaptic vesicles to fuse with the plasma membrane and release their neurotransmitter, and for the neurotransmitter to diffuse across the synaptic cleft.

The ion channels in the postsynaptic membrane return to their resting state when the neurotransmitter is no longer bound to the receptor. Neurotransmitters may be removed because (1) they are chemically transformed into an ineffective substance; (2) they diffuse away from the receptor site; or (3) they are actively transported back into the axon terminal or, in some cases, into nearby glial cells.

The two kinds of chemical synapses—excitatory and inhibitory—are differentiated by the effects the neurotransmitter has on the postsynaptic cell. Whether the effect is inhibitory or excitatory depends on the type of signal transduction mechanism brought into operation when the neurotransmitter binds to a receptor and the type of channel the receptor influences.

Excitatory Chemical Synapses

At an excitatory synapse, the postsynaptic response to the neurotransmitter is a depolarization, bringing the mem-

FIGURE 8-25
Variety of synaptic associations made upon a fiber of an ascending pathway in the spinal cord. Dendrites are shaded green, and axon terminals purple. (A) Simple axodendritic connection, which may include (B) one or more presynaptic synapses or (C) an arrangement known as a synaptic triad. (D) Synaptic arrangement ending on a spine extending from the postsynaptic cell. Such spines are common in the CNS and are thought to play a role in learning. The arrows indicate the direction of synaptic transmission. (*Redrawn from Maxwell and Rethelyi.*)

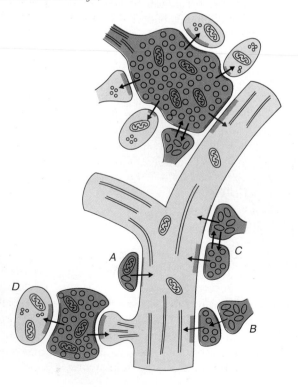

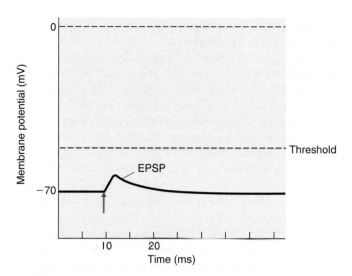

FIGURE 8-26

Excitatory postsynaptic potential (EPSP). Stimulation of the presynaptic neuron is marked by the arrow.

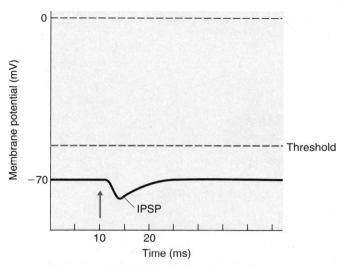

FIGURE 8-27

Inhibitory postsynaptic potential (IPSP). Stimulation of the presynaptic neuron is marked by the arrow.

brane potential closer to threshold. Here the usual effect of the activated receptor on the postsynaptic membrane is to open postsynaptic-membrane ion channels that are permeable to sodium, potassium, and other small, positively charged ions. These ions then are free to move according to the electrical and chemical gradients across the membrane.

Recall that there is both an electrical and a concentration gradient driving sodium into the cell, whereas in the case of potassium, the electrical gradient is opposed by the concentration gradient. Opening channels to all small positively charged ions, therefore, results in the simultaneous movement of a relatively small number of potassium ions out of the cell and a larger number of sodium ions into the cell. Thus, the *net* movement of positive ions is into the postsynaptic cell, and this slightly depolarizes it. This potential change is called an **excitatory postsynaptic potential** (**EPSP**, Figure 8-26).

The EPSP is a graded potential that spreads decrementally away from the synapse by local current. Its only function is to bring the membrane potential of the postsynaptic neuron closer to threshold.

Inhibitory Chemical Synapses

At inhibitory synapses, any potential change in the postsynaptic neuron is a hyperpolarizing graded potential called an **inhibitory postsynaptic potential** (**IPSP**, Figure 8-27). Alternatively, there may be no IPSP but rather *stabilization* of the membrane potential at its existing value. In either case, activation of an inhibitory synapse lessens the likelihood that the cell will depolarize to threshold and generate an action potential.

At an inhibitory synapse the activated receptors on the postsynaptic membrane open chloride or, sometimes, potassium channels; sodium channels are not affected. In cells that actively transport chloride ions out of the cell, the chloride equilibrium potential (−80 mV) is more negative than the resting potential. As chloride channels open, chloride enters the cell, producing a hyperpolarization; that is, an IPSP. In cells in which the equilibrium potential for chloride is equal to the resting membrane potential, a rise in chloride ion permeability increases chloride's influence on the membrane potential. This in turn makes it more difficult for other ion types to affect the potential and results in a stabilization of the membrane at the resting level without producing a hyperpolarization.

Increased potassium permeability also produces an IPSP. On page 189 it was noted that if a cell membrane were permeable only to potassium ions, the resting membrane potential would equal the potassium equilibrium potential; that is, the resting membrane potential would be −90 mV instead of −70 mV. Thus, with an increased potassium permeability, more potassium ions leave the cell and cause a hyperpolarization.

ACTIVATION OF THE POSTSYNAPTIC CELL

A feature that makes postsynaptic integration possible is that, in most neurons, one excitatory synaptic event by itself is not enough to cause threshold to be reached in the postsynaptic neuron. For example, a single EPSP in a neuron that goes to skeletal muscle is estimated

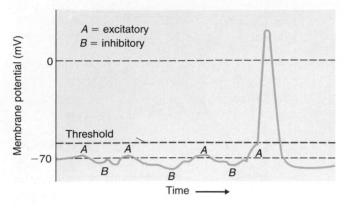

FIGURE 8-28

Intracellular recording from a postsynaptic cell during episodes when (A) excitatory synaptic activity predominates and the cell is facilitated, and (B) inhibitory synaptic activity dominates.

to be only 0.5 mV, whereas changes of about 15 mV are necessary to depolarize the membrane to threshold. This being the case, an action potential can be initiated only by the combined effects of many excitatory synapses.

Of the thousands of synapses on any one neuron, probably hundreds are active simultaneously or close enough in time so that the effects can add together. The membrane potential of the neuron at any moment is, therefore, the resultant of all the synaptic activity affecting it at that time. There is a depolarization of the membrane toward threshold when excitatory synaptic input predominates, and either a hyperpolarization or stabilization when inhibitory input predominates (Figure 8-28).

Let us perform a simple experiment to see how two EPSPs, two IPSPs, or an EPSP plus an IPSP interact (Figure 8-29). Assume there are three synaptic inputs to the postsynaptic cell: The synapses from axons A and B are

excitatory, and the synapse from axon C is inhibitory. There are laboratory stimulators on axons A, B, and C so that each can be activated individually. An electrode is placed in the cell body of the postsynaptic neuron and connected to record the membrane potential. In part 1 of the experiment, we shall test the interaction of two EPSPs by stimulating axon A and then, after a short time, stimulating it again. Part 1 of Figure 8-29 shows that no interaction occurs between the two EPSPs. The reason is that the change in membrane potential associated with an EPSP is fairly short-lived. Within a few milliseconds (by the time we stimulate axon A for the second time), the postsynaptic cell has returned to its resting condition.

In part 2, we stimulate axon A for the second time *before* the first EPSP has died away; the second synaptic potential adds to the previous one and creates a greater depolarization than from one synapse alone. This is called **temporal summation** since the input signals arrive at the same cell at different times. The potentials summate because there are a greater number of open ion channels and, therefore, a greater flow of positive ions into the cell. In part 3, axon B is stimulated alone to determine its response, and then axons A and B are stimulated simultaneously. The two EPSPs that result also summate in the postsynaptic neuron; this is called **spatial summation** since the two inputs occurred at different locations on the same cell. The interaction of multiple EPSPs through ongoing spatial and temporal summation can increase the inward flow of positive ions and bring the membrane to threshold so that action potentials are initiated (part 4).

So far we have tested only the patterns of interaction of excitatory synapses. What happens if an excitatory and an inhibitory synapse are activated so that their effects occur in the postsynaptic cell simultaneously? Since EPSPs and IPSPs are due to oppositely directed local currents, they tend to cancel each other, and there is little or no change

FIGURE 8-29

Interaction of EPSPs and IPSPs at the postsynaptic neuron. Arrows indicate time of stimulation.

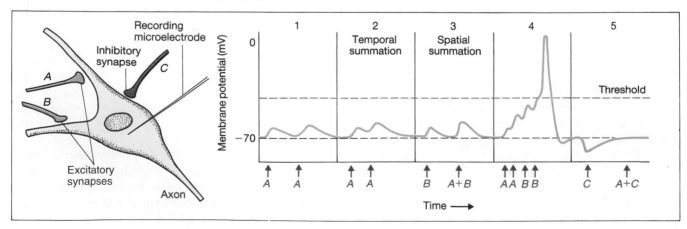

in membrane potential (Figure 8-29, part 5). Inhibitory potentials can also show spatial and temporal summation.

As described above, the postsynaptic membrane is depolarized at an activated excitatory synapse and either hyperpolarized or stabilized at an activated inhibitory synapse. Via the local-current mechanisms described earlier, the plasma membrane of the entire postsynaptic cell body and the initial segment reflect these changes. It becomes slightly depolarized during activation of an excitatory synapse and slightly hyperpolarized or stabilized during activation of an inhibitory synapse (Figure 8-30).

In the above examples, we referred to the threshold of the postsynaptic neuron as though it were the same for all parts of the cell. However, different parts of the neuron have different thresholds. In many cells the initial segment has a threshold that is lower, that is, much closer to the resting potential than the threshold of the cell body and dendrites. In these cells the initial segment reaches

FIGURE 8-30

Comparison of excitatory and inhibitory synapses, showing current direction through the postsynaptic cell following synaptic activation. (A) Current through the postsynaptic cell is away from the excitatory synapse, depolarizing the cell. (B) Current through the postsynaptic cell is toward an inhibitory synapse, hyperpolarizing the cell.

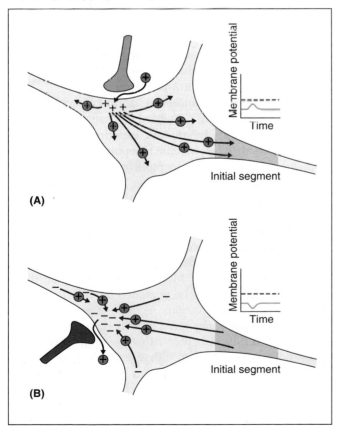

threshold first whenever enough EPSPs summate, and the resulting action potential is initiated and then propagated from this point down the axon.

The fact that the initial segment usually has the lowest threshold explains why the location of individual synapses on the postsynaptic cell is important. A synapse located near the initial segment will produce a greater voltage change there than will a synapse on the outermost branch of a dendrite because it will expose the initial segment to a larger local current. In fact, some dendrites are so long that they use propagated action potentials over portions of their length to convey information about the synaptic events occurring at their endings to the initial segment of the cell.

Postsynaptic potentials last much longer than action potentials do. In the event that cumulative EPSPs cause the initial segment to still be depolarized to threshold after an action potential has been fired and the refractory period is over, a second action potential will occur. In fact, as long as the membrane is depolarized to threshold, action potentials will continue to fire. Neuronal responses almost always occur in bursts of action potentials rather than as single isolated events.

This discussion has no doubt left the impression that one neuron can influence another only at a synapse. This view requires qualification. Under certain circumstances, local currents from one neuron may directly affect the membrane potential of nearby neurons. This phenomenon is particularly important in areas of the central nervous system that contain a high density of unmyelinated neuronal processes.

SYNAPTIC EFFECTIVENESS

ndividual synaptic events—whether excitatory or inhibitory—have been presented as though their effects are constant and reproducible. Actually, the variability in postsynaptic potentials following any particular presynaptic input is enormous. The effect of a given synapse can be influenced by both presynaptic and postsynaptic mechanisms (Table 8-5), as described in the next section.

A presynaptic terminal does not secrete a constant amount of neurotransmitter every time it is activated. One reason for this is as follows. Calcium that has entered the terminal during previous action potentials is normally removed by being pumped out of the cell or (temporarily) into intracellular organelles. If the calcium removal systems are not able to keep up with entry, as can occur during high-frequency stimulation, calcium concentration in the terminal and hence the amount of neurotransmitter released upon subsequent stimulation will be greater than normal. The greater the amount of neurotransmitter rethe other hand, more often bring about biochemical changes in neurons, often via G proteins coupled to second-messenger systems. These changes, which can occur over minutes, hours, or even days, include alterations in enzyme activity or, by way of influences on RNA transcription, in protein synthesis. Thus, neurotransmitters are involved in rapid communication, whereas neuromodulators tend to be associated with slower events such as learning, development, motivation states, or even some sensory or motor activities.

Table 8-6 lists some substances generally accepted as neurotransmitters or neuromodulators.[6] In Chapter 10 you will see that some of these substances also are secreted by endocrine glands and function as hormones.

For simplicity's sake, in the following discussion of several major chemical messengers in the nervous system, we use the term "neurotransmitter" in a general sense, realizing that sometimes the messenger may more appropriately be described as a neuromodulator. A note on terminology should be included here: Neurons are often referred to as _____ergic, where the blank is the type of neurotransmitter released by the neuron. For example, "dopaminergic" applies to neurons that release the neurotransmitter dopamine, and "cholinergic" to those that release acetylcholine.

Acetylcholine

Acetylcholine (ACh) is synthesized from choline and acetyl coenzyme A in the cytoplasm of synaptic terminals and is stored in synaptic vesicles. After it is released and activates receptors on the postsynaptic membrane, the concentration of ACh at the postsynaptic membrane is reduced (thereby stopping receptor activation) by an enzyme, **acetylcholinesterase**. This enzyme is located on the pre- and postsynaptic membranes and rapidly destroys ACh, releasing choline. The choline is then actively transported back into the axon terminals where it is reused in the synthesis of new ACh. The acetylcholine concentration at the receptors is also reduced by simple diffusion away from the site and eventual breakdown of the molecule by an enzyme in the blood.

Some acetylcholine receptors respond to the drug nicotine and, therefore, have come to be known as **nicotinic receptors**. Others are stimulated by the mushroom poison muscarine; they are called **muscarinic receptors**.

Acetylcholine is a major neurotransmitter in the peripheral nervous system (page 180) and is also present in the brain. The cell bodies of the brain's cholinergic neurons are concentrated in relatively few areas, but their axons are widely distributed. Fibers that release acetylcholine are called **cholinergic** fibers.

One cholinergic system in the brain (Figure 8-33) plays a major role in learning and memory. Neurons associated with this system degenerate in people with **Alzheimer's disease**, a brain disease that is usually age-related and is the most common cause of declining intellectual function in late life, affecting 10 to 15 percent of people over age 65 and 50 percent of people over age 85. Because of the degeneration of cholinergic neurons, this disease is associated with a decreased amount of ACh in certain areas of the brain and a loss of the postsynaptic neurons that would have responded to it.[7] These defects are presumably related to the declining language and perceptual abilities, confusion, and memory loss that characterize Alzheimer's victims. The exact causes of this disease are unknown.

Biogenic Amines

The **biogenic amines** are neurotransmitters that are synthesized from amino acids and contain an amino group ($R-NH_2$). Amino acids themselves also function as neurotransmitters and fit this chemical type, but neurophysiologists traditionally put them into a category of their own. The most common biogenic amines in the nervous system are dopamine, norepinephrine, serotonin, and histamine. Epinephrine, another biogenic amine, is not a common neurotransmitter in the nervous system but is the major _hormone_ secreted by the adrenal medulla, a gland that is activated by the peripheral nervous system, as will be discussed later.

Dopamine, **norepinephrine**, and **epinephrine** all contain a catechol ring (a six-sided carbon ring with two adjacent hydroxyl groups) and an amine group; thus they are called **catecholamines**. The catecholamines are formed from the amino acid tyrosine and share the synthetic pathway shown in Figure 8-34, which begins with the uptake of tyrosine by the axon terminals. Depending on the enzymes present in the terminals, the neurotransmitter ultimately released may be any one of the three catecholamines. Release of catecholamines from the presynaptic terminals is strongly modulated by receptors on the presynaptic terminals.

After activation of the receptors on the postsynaptic cell, the catecholamine concentration in the synaptic cleft declines mainly because the catecholamine is actively transported back into the axon terminal. As we shall see in Chapter 13, the drug cocaine interferes with the reuptake of dopamine and, therefore, increases its concentration in the synaptic cleft.

---

[6]All these substances have not met all the criteria to be classified as "established" neurotransmitters or neuromodulators, and some are more properly considered "candidates." We shall not distinguish between them.

[7]The loss of ACh-containing neurons in the base of the forebrain is one of the most consistent characteristics of Alzheimer's disease, but many other neurotransmitter systems also degenerate.

TABLE 8-6 CLASSES OF SOME OF THE CHEMICALS KNOWN OR PRESUMED TO BE NEUROTRANSMITTERS OR NEUROMODULATORS

1. Acetylcholine (ACh)

2. Biogenic amines
    Catecholamines
        Dopamine (DA)
        Norepinephrine (NE)
        Epinephrine (Epi)
    Serotonin (5-hydroxytryptamine, 5-HT)
    Histamine

3. Amino acids
    Excitatory amino acids
        Glutamate
        Aspartate
    Inhibitory amino acids
        Gamma-aminobutyric acid (GABA)
        Glycine
        Taurine

4. Neuropeptides
    Endogenous opioids (endorphin, enkephalins, dynorphins)   Prolactin
    Substance P   Bombesin
    Somatostatin   Motilin
    Vasoactive intestinal peptide (VIP)   Peptide histidine isoleucine (PHI)
    Cholecystokinin   Peptide histidine methionine (PHM)
    Neurotensin   Secretin
    Insulin   Neuropeptide Y (NPY)
    Gastrin   Peptide YY
    Glucagon   Pancreatic polypeptide
    Thyrotropin releasing hormone (TRH)   Growth hormone releasing hormone (GHRH)
    Gonadotropin releasing hormone (GnRH)   Neurokinin A (substance K)
    Adrenocorticotropic hormone (ACTH)   Neurokinin B
    Angiotensin II   Interferon
    Bradykinin   Interleukin 1 (IL-1)
    Vasopressin (antidiuretic hormone, ADH)   Thymosin
    Oxytocin   Galanin
    Epidermal growth factor   Calcitonin gene-related peptide (CGRP)

5. Miscellaneous
    Gases
        Nitric oxide
        Carbon monoxide
    Nucleotides
        Adenosine
        Adenosine triphosphate (ATP)
    Steroids
        Aldosterone
        Cortisol and other glucocorticoids
        Progesterone
        Estrogens (17β-estriol)
        Testosterone
    Prostaglandins (prostaglandin E)

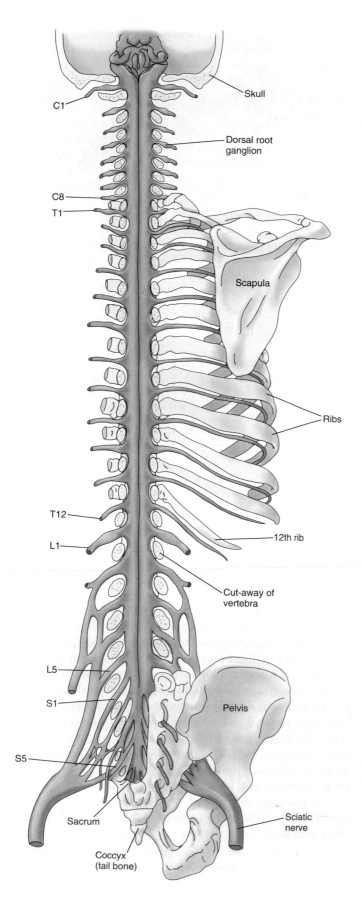

C1

Skull

Dorsal root
ganglion

C8

T1

Scapula

Ribs

T12

12th rib

L1

Cut-away of
vertebra

L5

S1

Pelvis

S5

Sacrum

Sciatic
nerve

Coccyx
(tail bone)

FIGURE 8-36

Dorsal view of the spinal cord. Parts of the skull and verte-brae have been cut away. In general, the 8 cervical nerves (C) control the muscles and glands and receive sensory input from the neck, shoulder, arm, and hand. The 12 thoracic nerves (T) are associated with the chest and abdominal walls. The 5 lumbar nerves (L) are associated with the hip and leg, and the 5 sacral nerves (S) are associated with the genitals and lower digestive tract. *(Redrawn from FUNDAMENTAL NEUROANATOMY by Walle J. H. Nauta and Michael Fiertag. Copyright © 1986 by W. H. Freeman and Co. Reprinted by permission.)*

ical for regulation of the internal environment. Some of the fibers from these two branches continue to the cere-bral cortex, which is thought to be that part of the brain having the greatest mental capacity and influence over social behavior. These ascending reticular pathways affect such things as wakefulness and the direction of attention to specific events.

The reticular formation also gives rise to connections with the cerebellum and the spinal cord. The fibers that descend to the spinal cord form the reticulospinal path-ways. They influence activity in both the efferent and af-ferent neurons. There is considerable interaction between the reticular pathways that go up to the forebrain, down to the spinal cord, and to the cerebellum. For example, all three components function in controlling muscle activity.

Some reticular-formation neurons are clustered to-gether, forming certain of the brainstem nuclei and inte-grating centers. These include the cardiovascular, respira-tory, swallowing, and vomiting centers, all of which are discussed in subsequent chapters. The reticular formation also has nuclei important in eye-movement control and the reflex orientation of the body in space.

In addition, the brainstem contains nuclei involved in processing information for 10 of the 12 pairs of **cranial nerves**. These are the peripheral nerves that connect with the brain and innervate the muscles, glands, and sensory receptors of the head as well as many organs in the tho-racic and abdominal cavities (Table 8-7).

Information can pass through the brainstem in two ways: (1) **long neural pathways**, which carry information directly between the brain and spinal cord or between the forebrain and brainstem; and (2) **multineuronal** or **mul-tisynaptic pathways** (Figure 8-39). As their name sug-gests, the multineuronal pathways are made up of many neurons and many synaptic connections. Since synapses are the sites where new information can be integrated into neural messages, there are many opportunities for neural processing along the multineuronal pathways. The long pathways, on the other hand, consist of chains of only a few sequentially connected neurons. Because the long pathways contain few synapses, there is little opportunity for alteration in the information they transmit.

FIGURE 8-37

The spinal cord and six divisions of the brain.

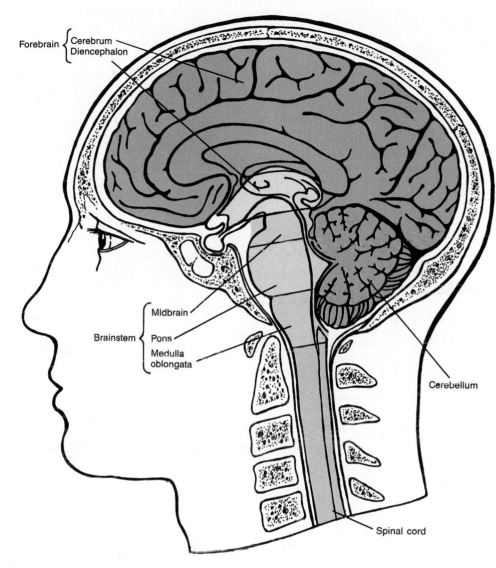

Forebrain { Cerebrum
Diencephalon

Brainstem { Midbrain
Pons
Medulla oblongata

Cerebellum

Spinal cord

FIGURE 8-38

The four interconnected ventricles of the brain.

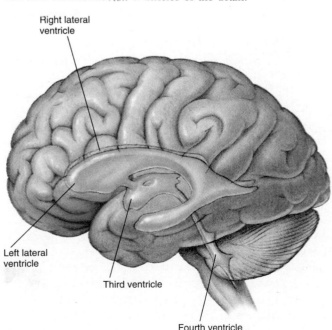

Right lateral ventricle

Left lateral ventricle

Third ventricle

Fourth ventricle

Cerebellum

The cerebellum, chiefly involved with the control of skeletal muscle functions, consists of an outer layer of cells, the cerebellar cortex, and several deeper cell clusters, the cerebellar nuclei. It is connected to the brainstem by the cerebellar peduncles. Although the cerebellum does not initiate voluntary movements, it is an important center for coordinating and learning movements and for controlling posture and balance. In order to carry out these functions, the cerebellum receives information from the muscles and joints, skin, eyes and ears, viscera, and the parts of the brain involved in control of movement.

Forebrain

The central core of the forebrain is formed by the diencephalon. It is covered by the second component of the forebrain, the cerebrum, which consists of the right and left **cerebral hemispheres** and certain other structures on the underside of the brain.

The cerebral hemispheres (Figure 8-40) consist of the

TABLE 8-7   THE CRANIAL NERVES

Name	Fibers	Comments
I. Olfactory nerve	Afferent	Tract of brain; not true nerve. Carries input from receptors in olfactory (smell) epithelium.
II. Optic nerve	Afferent	Tract of brain; not true nerve. Carries input from receptors in eye.
III. Oculomotor nerve	Efferent	Innervates skeletal muscles that move eyeball up, down, and medially and raise upper eyelid; innervates smooth muscles that constrict pupil and alter lens shape for near and far vision.
	Afferent	Transmits information from receptors in muscles.
IV. Trochlear nerve	Efferent	Innervates skeletal muscles that move eyeball downward and laterally.
	Afferent	Transmits information from receptors in muscle.
V. Trigeminal nerve	Efferent	Innervates skeletal chewing muscles.
	Afferent	Transmits information from receptors in skin; skeletal muscles of face, nose, and mouth; and teeth sockets.
VI. Abducens nerve	Efferent	Innervates skeletal muscles that move eyeball laterally.
	Afferent	Transmits information from receptors in muscle.
VII. Facial nerve	Efferent	Innervates skeletal muscles of facial expression and swallowing; innervates nose, palate, and lacrimal and salivary glands.
	Afferent	Transmits information from taste buds in front of tongue and mouth.
VIII. Vestibulocochlear nerve	Afferent	Transmits information from receptors in ear.
IX. Glossopharyngeal nerve	Efferent	Innervates skeletal muscles involved in swallowing and parotid salivary gland.
	Afferent	Transmits information from taste buds at back of tongue and receptors in auditory-tube skin.
X. Vagus nerve	Efferent	Innervates skeletal muscles of pharynx and larynx and smooth muscle and glands of thorax and abdomen.
	Afferent	Transmits information from receptors in thorax and abdomen.
XI. Accessory nerve	Efferent	Innervates neck skeletal muscles.
XII. Hypoglossal nerve	Efferent	Innervates tongue skeletal muscles.

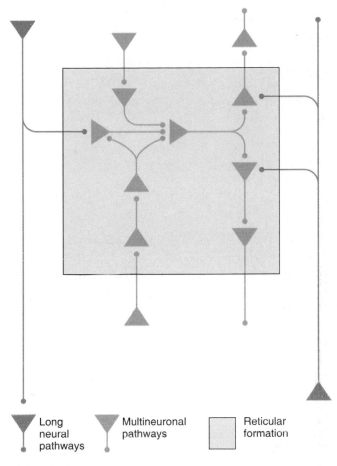

Long
neural
pathways

Multineuronal
pathways

Reticular
formation

FIGURE 8-39

Relationship of long neural pathways and multineuronal (multisynaptic) pathways to the reticular formation.

cerebral cortex, an outer shell of gray matter, plus underlying nuclei and the many nerve fibers that bring information into the cerebrum, carry information out, and interconnect the neurons in the cerebrum. The hemispheres, although largely separated by a longitudinal division, are connected to each other by bundles of nerve fibers known as commissures, the **corpus callosum** being the largest (Figure 8-40). Areas within a hemisphere are connected to each other by association fibers, not shown in the figure.

The cortex of each hemisphere is divided into four **lobes**: the **frontal**, **parietal**, **occipital**, and **temporal** (Figure 8-41). It averages only 3 mm in thickness but accounts for 46 percent of the cerebrum's volume. The cortex is highly folded, which increases the area available for cortical neurons without increasing appreciably the volume of the brain. Its cells are arranged most often in six layers, a distinguishing trait of the cortex. The cortical neurons are of two basic types: pyramidal cells (named for the shape of their cell bodies) and nonpyramidal cells. The

pyramidal cells form the major output cells of the cortex, sending their axons to other parts of the cortex and to other parts of the central nervous system.

The cerebral cortex is the most complex integrating area of the nervous system. It is necessary for the bringing together of basic afferent information into meaningful

TABLE 8-8 SUMMARY OF FUNCTIONS OF THE MAJOR PARTS OF THE BRAIN

I. Brainstem
   A. Contains fibers passing between spinal cord, forebrain, and cerebellum
   B. Contains the reticular formation and its integrating centers for cardiovascular and respiratory activity (Chapters 14 and 15)
   C. Contains nuclei for most of the cranial nerves
II. Cerebellum
   A. Coordinates movements, including those for posture and balance (Chapter 12)
   B. Participates in some forms of learning (Chapter 13)
III. Cerebral hemispheres
   A. Contains the cerebral cortex, which participates in perception (Chapter 9), the generation of skilled movements (Chapter 12), reasoning, learning, and memory (Chapter 13)
   B. Contains subcortical nuclei, which participate in coordination of skeletal-muscle activity (Chapter 12)
   C. Contains interconnecting fiber pathways
IV. Thalamus
   A. Is a synaptic relay station for sensory pathways on their way to the cerebral cortex (Chapter 9)
   B. Participates in control of skeletal-muscle coordination (Chapter 12)
V. Hypothalamus
   A. Regulates anterior pituitary gland (Chapter 10)
   B. Regulates water balance (Chapter 16)
   C. Participates in regulation of autonomic nervous system (Chapters 8 and 18)
   D. Regulates eating and drinking behavior (Chapter 18)
   E. Regulates reproductive system (Chapters 10 and 19)
   F. Reinforces certain behaviors (Chapter 13)
   G. Generates and regulates circadian rhythms (Chapters 7, 9, 10, and 18)
   H. Regulates body temperature (Chapter 18)
   I. Participates in generation of emotional behavior (Chapter 13)
VI. Limbic system
   A. Participates in generation of emotions and emotional behavior (Chapter 13)
   B. Plays essential role in most kinds of learning (Chapter 13)

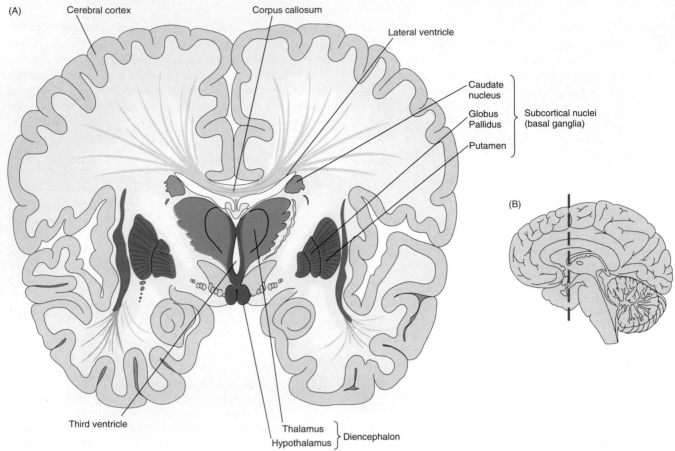

(A) Cerebral cortex

Corpus callosum

Lateral ventricle

Caudate nucleus

Globus Pallidus

Putamen

Subcortical nuclei (basal ganglia)

(B)

Third ventricle

Thalamus

Hypothalamus

Diencephalon

FIGURE 8-40

(A) Coronal (side-to-side) section of the brain, with the thalamus shaded in blue–green and the hypothalamus shaded in violet. (B) The dashed line indicates the location of the cross section in A.

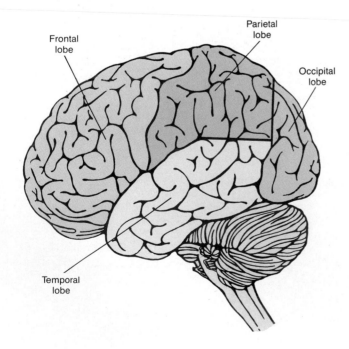

Frontal lobe

Parietal lobe

Occipital lobe

Temporal lobe

FIGURE 8-41

A lateral view of the brain. The outer layer of the forebrain (the cortex) is divided into four lobes, as shown.

perceptual images and for the ultimate refinement of control over the systems that govern the movement of the skeletal muscles. Nerve fibers enter the cortex from a variety of places but particularly from the thalamus, from other regions of the cortex, and from the brainstem reticular formation. Some of the input fibers convey information about specific events in the environment, whereas others are more concerned with controlling levels of cortical excitability, determining states of arousal, and directing attention to specific stimuli.

The **subcortical nuclei** form other areas of gray matter that lie deep within the cerebral hemispheres. Predominant among them are the **basal ganglia**, which play an important role in the control of movement and posture and in more complex aspects of behavior. In other parts of the forebrain, axons predominate, their whitish myelin coating distinguishing them as white matter.

The diencephalon, the second component of the forebrain, contains two major parts: the thalamus and the hypothalamus (Figure 8-40). The **thalamus**, which lies at the center of the brain, is a large cluster of nuclei that serves as a synaptic relay station and important integrating center for most inputs to the cortex.

The **hypothalamus** (Figure 8-40), which lies below the thalamus, is a tiny region that accounts for less than 1 percent of the brain's weight. Yet it is crucial to homeostatic regulation and is a principal site for regulating the behavior essential to the survival of the individual and the species. The integration achieved by the hypothalamus often involves correlation of neural and endocrine functions. Indeed, the hypothalamus appears to be the single most important control area for regulation of the internal environment. It lies directly above the pituitary gland, an important endocrine structure, attached to it by a stalk.

An area of the forebrain that includes both gray and white matter is the **limbic system**. This is an interconnected group of brain structures, taking in portions of frontal-lobe cortex, temporal lobe, thalamus, and hypothalamus, as well as the circuitous fiber pathways that connect them (Figure 8-42). The limbic system is associated with learning, emotional experience and behavior, and a wide variety of visceral and endocrine functions. Besides being connected with each other, the parts of the limbic system are connected with many other parts of the central nervous system.

The functions of the major parts of the brain are listed in Table 8-8 on page 219.

PERIPHERAL NERVOUS SYSTEM

Nerve fibers in the peripheral nervous system transmit signals between the central nervous system and

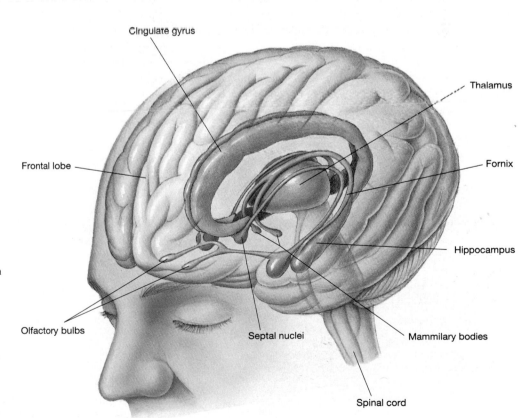

FIGURE 8-42

Structures of the limbic system are shown shaded in violet in this partially transparent view of the brain. *(Redrawn from BRAIN, MIND AND BEHAVIOR by Floyd E. Bloom and Arlyne Lazerson. Copyright © 1985, 1988 by Educational Broadcasting Corporation. Reprinted by permission of W. H. Freeman and Co.)*

Cingulate gyrus

Thalamus

Frontal lobe

Fornix

Hippocampus

Olfactory bulbs

Septal nuclei

Mammilary bodies

Spinal cord

all other parts of the body. As noted earlier, the nerve fibers are grouped into bundles called nerves. The peripheral nervous system consists of 43 pairs of nerves: 12 pairs of cranial nerves and 31 pairs that connect with the spinal cord as the spinal nerves. The cranial nerves and a summary of the information they transmit were listed in Table 8-7.

Each nerve fiber is surrounded by a Schwann cell. Some of the fibers are wrapped in layers of Schwann-cell membrane, and these tightly wrapped membranes form a myelin sheath (Figure 8-3). Other fibers are unmyelinated.

A nerve contains nerve fibers that are the axons of efferent neurons or afferent neurons. Accordingly, fibers in a nerve may be classified as belonging to the **efferent** or the **afferent division** of the peripheral nervous system (Table 8-9). All the spinal nerves contain both afferent and efferent fibers, whereas some of the cranial nerves (the optic nerves from the eyes, for example) contain only afferent fibers.

Peripheral Nervous System: Afferent Division

As noted earlier, afferent neurons convey information from receptors at their peripheral endings to the central nervous system. The long part of their axon is outside the central nervous system and is part of the peripheral nervous system. Afferent neurons are sometimes called primary afferents or first-order neurons because they are the first cells entering the central nervous system in the synaptically linked chains of neurons that handle incoming information.

Peripheral Nervous System: Efferent Division

Recall that efferent neurons carry signals from the central nervous system out to muscles or glands. The efferent division of the peripheral nervous system is more complicated than the afferent, being subdivided into a **somatic nervous system** and an **autonomic nervous system**. These terms are somewhat misleading because they suggest additional nervous systems distinct from the central and peripheral systems. Keep in mind that the terms refer simply to the efferent division of the peripheral nervous system.

TABLE 8-9   DIVISIONS OF THE PERIPHERAL NERVOUS SYSTEM

I. Afferent division
II. Efferent division
   A. Somatic nervous system
   B. Autonomic nervous system
      1. Sympathetic division
      2. Parasympathetic division

TABLE 8-10   DIFFERENCES BETWEEN SOMATIC AND AUTONOMIC NERVOUS SYSTEMS

Somatic
1. Consists of a single neuron between central nervous system and effector organ
2. Innervates skeletal muscle
3. Can lead only to muscle excitation

Autonomic
1. Has two-neuron chain (connected by synapse) between central nervous system and effector organ
2. Innervates smooth and cardiac muscle, glands, and GI neurons
3. Can lead to excitation or inhibition of effector cells

The simplest distinction between the somatic and autonomic systems is that the neurons of the somatic division innervate skeletal muscle, whereas the autonomic neurons innervate smooth and cardiac muscle, glands, and neurons in the gastrointestinal tract. Other differences are listed in Table 8-10.

Somatic Nervous System.   The somatic portion of the efferent division of the peripheral nervous system is made up of all the nerve fibers going from the central nervous system to skeletal-muscle cells. The cell bodies of these neurons are located in groups in the brainstem or spinal cord. Their large-diameter, myelinated axons leave the central nervous system and pass without any synapses to skeletal-muscle cells. The neurotransmitter released by these neurons is acetylcholine. Because activity in the somatic neurons leads to contraction of the innervated skeletal-muscle cells, these neurons are often called **motor neurons**. Excitation of motor neurons leads only to the *contraction* of skeletal-muscle cells; there are no somatic neurons that inhibit the muscles.

Autonomic Nervous System.   The efferent innervation of all tissues other than skeletal muscle is by way of the autonomic nervous system. In the case of the gastrointestinal tract, the autonomic nervous system innervates the neurons that are part of the **enteric nervous system**, a specialized nerve network in the wall of the intestinal tract, which regulates the glands and smooth muscles found there. The enteric nervous system is considered by some to be a specialized part of the autonomic nervous system and does not have all of the characteristics discussed below. It will be discussed in Chapter 17.

In the autonomic nervous system, the groups of axons between the central nervous system and the effector cells

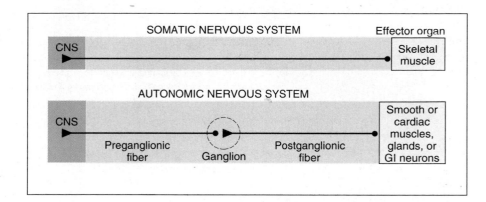

FIGURE 8-43
Efferent division of the peripheral nervous system. Overall plan of the somatic and autonomic nervous systems.

consist of two neurons and one synapse (Figure 8-43). (This is in contrast to the single neuron of the somatic system.) The first neuron has its cell body in the central nervous system. The synapse between the two neurons is outside the central nervous system, in a cell cluster called an **autonomic ganglion**. The nerve fibers passing between the central nervous system and the ganglia are called **preganglionic fibers**; those passing between the ganglia and the effector cells are **postganglionic fibers**.

Anatomical and physiological differences within the autonomic nervous system are the basis for its further subdivision into **sympathetic** and **parasympathetic** components. The nerve fibers of these components leave the central nervous system at different levels—the sympathetic fibers from the thoracic and lumbar (chest) regions of the spinal cord and the parasympathetic fibers from the brain and the sacral portion of the spinal cord (lower back, Figure 8-44). Therefore, the sympathetic division is also called the thoracolumbar division, and the parasympathetic, the craniosacral division.

The two divisions of the autonomic nervous system also differ in the location of ganglia. Most of the sympathetic ganglia lie close to the spinal cord and form the two chains of ganglia—one on each side of the cord—known as the **sympathetic trunks** (Figure 8-44). Other sympathetic ganglia, called collateral ganglia—the celiac, superior mesenteric, and inferior mesenteric ganglia—lie far away from the spinal cord, closer to the innervated organ (Figure 8-44). In contrast, the parasympathetic ganglia lie within the organs innervated by the postganglionic neurons.

The anatomy of the sympathetic nervous system can be confusing. Preganglionic sympathetic *fibers* leave the spinal cord only between the first thoracic and third lumbar segments, whereas sympathetic *trunks* extend the entire length of the cord—from the cervical levels high in the neck down to the sacral levels. The "extra" ganglia in the sympathetic trunks receive preganglionic fibers from the thoracolumbar regions because some of the preganglionic fibers, once in the sympathetic trunks, turn to travel up-

ward or downward for several segments before forming synapses with postganglionic neurons (Figure 8-45, numbers 1 and 4). The ganglia at the cervical levels are the superior cervical, middle cervical, and stellate ganglia (Figure 8-44). Other possible paths taken by the sympathetic fibers are shown in Figure 8-45, numbers 2, 3, and 5.

The anatomical arrangements in the sympathetic nervous system to some extent tie the entire system together so it can act as a single unit, although small segments of the system can still be regulated independently. Furthermore, the ganglia can act either as automatic relay stations with practically no change in the information they transmit to the effector organ or as important integrating centers capable of generating individualized responses. The parasympathetic system, in contrast, is made up of relatively independent components. Thus, overall autonomic responses, made up of many small parts, are quite variable and finely tailored to the specific demands of any given situation.

In both sympathetic and parasympathetic divisions, the major neurotransmitter released between pre- and postganglionic fibers is acetylcholine (Figure 8-46). In the parasympathetic division, the major neurotransmitter between the postganglionic fiber and the effector cell is also acetylcholine. In the sympathetic division, the major transmitter between the postganglionic fiber and the effector cell is usually norepinephrine. We stress "major" and "usually" because acetylcholine is released by some sympathetic postganglionic endings. Moreover, one or more cotransmitters are usually stored and released with the autonomic transmitters; these include ATP, dopamine, and several of the neuropeptides. These substances, however, play a smaller role in sympathetic nervous system activity than norepinephrine does.

Recall that the somatic efferent nerve fibers are also cholinergic. Thus, the neurons in the entire efferent nervous system are either cholinergic or adrenergic (Figure 8-46).

Many of the drugs that stimulate or inhibit various com-

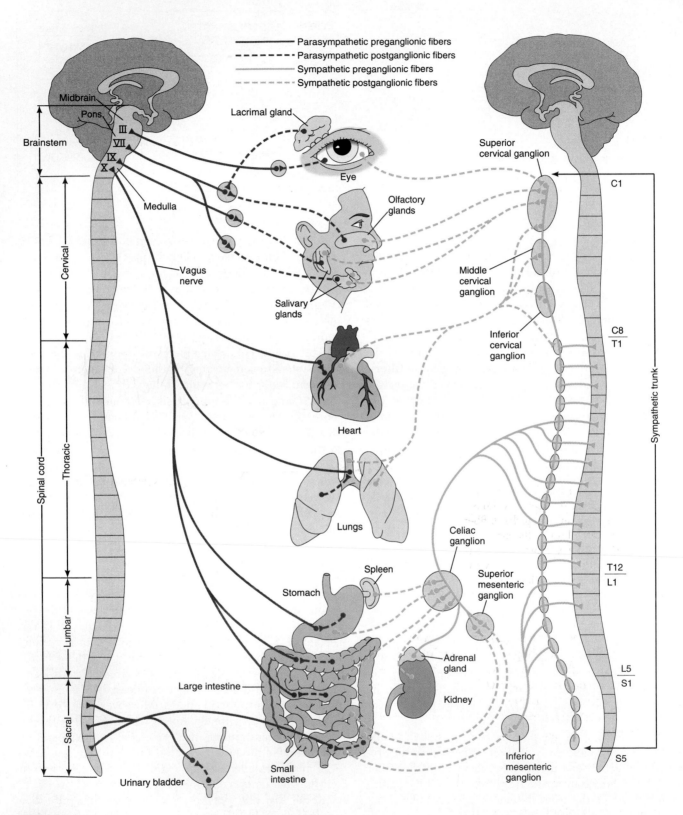

FIGURE 8-44

The parasympathetic (left) and sympathetic (right) divisions of the autonomic nervous system. The celiac, superior mesenteric, and inferior mesenteric ganglia are collateral ganglia. Only the sympathetic trunk on the right side of the spinal cord is shown, although another exists on the left. Not shown are the fibers passing to the liver, blood vessels, and skin glands from the sympathetic trunk.

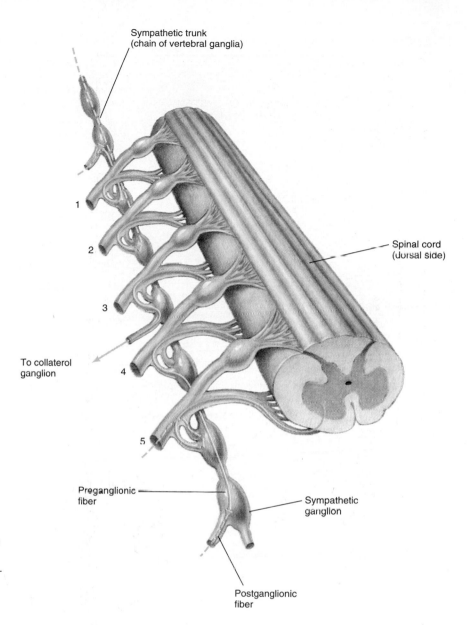

Sympathetic trunk
(chain of vertebral ganglia)

1

2

3

Spinal cord
(dorsal side)

To collateral
ganglion

4

5

Preganglionic
fiber

Sympathetic
ganglion

Postganglionic
fiber

FIGURE 8-45

Relationship between a sympathetic trunk and the spinal cord. (1 through 5) Various courses that preganglionic sympathetic fibers (solid lines) may take through the sympathetic trunk. Dashed lines represent postganglionic fibers. A mirror image of this exists on the opposite side of the spinal cord.

ponents of the autonomic nervous system affect receptors for acetylcholine and norepinephrine. Recall that there are several types of receptors for each neurotransmitter (Table 8-11). The great majority of acetylcholine receptors on autonomic postganglionic neurons are nicotinic receptors. In contrast, the acetylcholine receptors on smooth-muscle, cardiac-muscle, and gland cells are muscarinic receptors. To complete the story of the peripheral cholinergic receptors, it should be emphasized that the cholinergic receptors on the neuromuscular junctions of skeletal-muscle fibers, innervated by the *somatic* motor neurons, not autonomic neurons, are nicotinic receptors.

One set of postganglionic neurons in the sympathetic division never develops axons; instead, upon activation by preganglionic axons, the cells of this "ganglion" release their transmitters into the bloodstream (Figure 8-46). This "ganglion," called the **adrenal medulla**, therefore functions as an endocrine gland whose secretion is controlled by the sympathetic preganglionic nerve fibers. It releases a mixture of about 80 percent epinephrine and 20 percent norepinephrine into the blood (plus small amounts of other substances, such as dopamine, ATP, and some of the neuropeptides). These substances, properly called hormones rather than neurotransmitters in this circumstance, are transported via the blood to receptor sites on effector cells sensitive to them. The receptor sites may be the same adrenergic receptors that are located near the release sites of sympathetic postganglionic neurons and that are normally activated by the norepinephrine released from these neurons, or the receptor sites may be located at places that are not near the neurons and therefore activated only by the circulating epinephrine or norepinephrine.

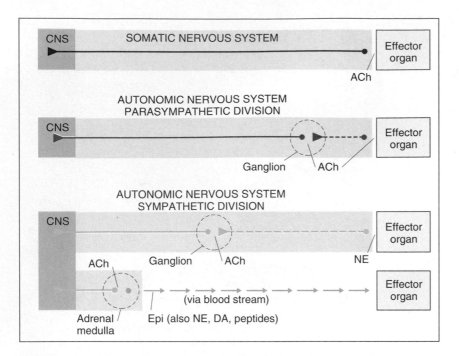

FIGURE 8-46

Transmitters used in the various components of the peripheral nervous system. In a few cases (to be described later) sympathetic neurons release a transmitter other than norepinephrine. ACh, Acetylcholine; NE, norepinephrine; Epi, epinephrine, DA, dopamine.

TABLE 8-11 CLASSES OF RECEPTORS FOR ACETYLCHOLINE, NOREPINEPHRINE, AND EPINEPHRINE

I. Receptors for acetylcholine
   A. Nicotinic receptors
      On postganglionic neurons in the autonomic ganglia
      At neuromuscular junctions of skeletal muscle
      On some central nervous system neurons
   B. Muscarinic receptors
      On smooth muscle
      On cardiac muscle
      On gland cells
      On some central nervous system neurons
      On some neurons of autonomic ganglia (although the great majority of receptors at this site are nicotinic)

II. Receptors for norepinephrine and epinephrine
      On smooth muscle
      On cardiac muscle
      On gland cells
      On some central nervous system neurons

Table 8-12 is a reference list of the effects of the autonomic nervous system, which will be described in subsequent chapters. Note that the heart and many glands and smooth muscles are innervated by both sympathetic and parasympathetic fibers; that is, they receive **dual innervation**. Whatever effect one division has on the effector cells, the other division frequently (but not always) has the opposite effect.

Dual innervation by nerve fibers that cause opposite responses provides a very fine degree of control over the effector organ—it is like equipping a car with both an accelerator and a brake. One can slow the car simply by decreasing the pressure on the accelerator; however, the combined effects of releasing the accelerator and applying the brake provide faster and more accurate control. Analogously, the sympathetic and parasympathetic divisions are usually activated reciprocally; that is, as the activity of one division is increased, the activity of the other is decreased.

A helpful generalization is that the sympathetic system increases its response under conditions of stress. Indeed, a full-blown sympathetic response is called the **fight-or-flight response**, describing the situation of an animal forced to challenge an attacker or run from it. Activity of the parasympathetic system, on the other hand, increases with vegetative, housekeeping functions, such as digestion.

Autonomic responses usually occur without conscious control or awareness, as though they were indeed autonomous (in fact, the autonomic nervous system has been called the "involuntary" nervous system). However, it is wrong to assume that this is always the case, for it has been shown that discrete visceral or glandular responses can be learned and thus, to this extent, voluntarily controlled.

TABLE 8-12   SOME EFFECTS OF AUTONOMIC NERVOUS SYSTEM ACTIVITY

Effector organ	Sympathetic effect		Parasympathetic effect[†]
	Receptor type[°]		
Eyes			
Iris muscles	Alpha$_1$	Contracts radial muscle (widens pupil)	Contracts sphincter muscle (makes pupil smaller)
Ciliary muscle	Beta$_2$	Relaxes (flattens lens for far vision)	Contracts (allows lens to become more convex for near vision)
Heart			
SA node	Beta$_1$	Increases heart rate	Decreases heart rate
Atria	Beta$_1$	Increases contractility	Decreases contractility
AV node	Beta$_1$	Increases conduction velocity	Decreases conduction velocity
Ventricles	Beta$_1$	Increases contractility	Decreases contractility slightly
Arterioles			
Coronary	Alpha$_{1,2}$	Constricts	Dilates
	Beta$_2$	Dilates	
Skin	Alpha$_{1,2}$	Constricts	—[‡]
Skeletal muscle	Alpha[§]	Constricts	—
	Beta$_2$	Dilates	
Abdominal viscera	Alpha$_1$	Constricts	—
	Beta$_2$	Dilates	
Salivary glands	Alpha$_{1,2}$	Constricts	Dilates
Veins	Alpha$_1$	Constricts	
	Beta$_2$	Dilates	
Lungs			
Bronchial muscle	Beta$_2$	Relaxes	Contracts
Bronchial glands	Alpha$_1$	Inhibits secretion	Stimulates secretion
	Beta$_2$	Stimulates secretion	
Salivary glands	Alpha$_1$	Stimulates K^+ and H_2O secretion	Stimulates K^+ and H_2O secretion
	Beta[§]	Stimulates enzyme secretion	
Stomach			
Motility, tone	Alpha$_{1,2}$ Beta$_2$	Decreases	Increases
Sphincters	Alpha$_1$	Contracts	Relaxes
Secretion	§	Inhibits (?)	Stimulates

(continued)

TABLE 8-12 (*continued*)

Effector organ	Sympathetic effect		Parasympathetic effect[†]
	Receptor type[°]		
Intestine			
Motility	Alpha$_{1,2}$	Decreases	Increases
	Beta$_{1,2}$	Decreases	
Sphincters	Alpha$_1$	Contracts (usually)	Relaxes (usually)
Secretion	Alpha$_2$	Inhibits	Stimulates
Gallbladder	Beta$_2$	Relaxes	Contracts
Liver	§	Glycogenolysis Gluconeogenesis	—
Pancreas			
Exocrine glands	Alpha[§]	Inhibits secretion	Stimulates secretion
Endocrine glands	Alpha$_2$	Inhibits insulin secretion	Stimulates insulin secretion
Fat cells	Alpha[§] Beta$_1$	Increases fat breakdown	
Kidneys	Beta$_1$	Increases renin secretion	—
Urinary bladder			
Bladder wall	Beta$_2$	Relaxes	Contracts
Sphincter	Alpha$_1$	Contracts	Relaxes
Uterus	Alpha$_1$	Contracts in pregnancy	Variable
	Beta$_2$	Relaxes	
Reproductive tract (male)	Alpha$_1$	Ejaculation	Erection
Skin			
Muscles causing hairs to stand erect	Alpha$_1$	Contracts	—
Sweat glands	Alpha$_1$	Localized secretion	Generalized secretion
Lacrimal glands	Alpha[§]	Secretion	Secretion

[°]Note that in many effector organs, there are both alpha-adrenergic and beta-adrenergic receptors. Activation of these receptors may produce either the same or opposing effects. For simplicity, except for the arterioles and a few other cases, only the dominant sympathetic effect is given when the two receptors oppose each other.

[†]These effects are all mediated by muscarinic receptors.

[‡]A dash means these cells are not innervated by this branch of the autonomic nervous system.

[§]The specific receptor type is undetermined.

Table adapted from "Goodman and Gilman's The Pharmacological Basis of Therapeutics," Alfred Goodman Gilman, Theodore W. Rall, Alan S. Nies, and Palmer Taylor, eds., 8th edn., Pergamon Press, New York, 1990.

BLOOD SUPPLY, BLOOD-BRAIN BARRIER PHENOMENA, AND CEREBROSPINAL FLUID

Usually, glucose is the only substrate metabolized by the brain to supply its energy requirements, and most of the energy from the oxidative breakdown of glucose is transferred to ATP. The brain's glycogen stores being negligible, it is completely dependent upon a continuous blood supply of glucose. Also essential is a blood supply of oxygen for oxidative phosphorylation. Although the adult brain is only 2 percent of the body weight, it receives 15 percent of the total blood supply to support its high oxygen utilization. If the oxygen supply is cut off for 4 to 5 min or if the glucose supply is cut off for 10 to 15 min, brain damage will occur. In fact, the most common form of brain damage is caused by a stoppage of the blood supply to a region of the brain, which results in a *stroke*. The cells in the region deprived of nutrients cease to function and die.

The exchange of substances between blood and extracellular fluid in the central nervous system is different from the more-or-less unrestricted diffusion of nonprotein substances from blood to extracellular fluid in the other organs of the body. A complex group of **blood-brain barrier** mechanisms closely controls both the kinds of substances that enter the extracellular fluid of the brain and the rate at which they enter. These mechanisms regulate the chemical composition of the extracellular fluid of the brain and minimize the ability of many harmful substances to reach the neurons.

The blood-brain barrier resides within the cells—endothelial cells—that line the brain capillaries (capillaries are the smallest blood vessels and the major vessels across which substances pass between the blood and tissue fluids). In brain capillaries the edges of adjacent endothelial cells abut against each other, and the cells are completely sealed together by continuous tight junctions. This means that all substances entering or leaving the brain must pass through the two plasma membranes and cytoplasm of the endothelial cells (Figure 8-47) rather than between the cells. Capillaries in certain areas of the brain lack a blood-brain barrier, but these areas account for less than 1 percent of the brain volume.

The blood-brain barrier has both anatomical structures and physiological transport systems that handle different classes of substances in different ways; thus, the barrier is said to be selective. For example, substances that dissolve readily in the lipid components of the plasma membranes enter the brain quickly. This characteristic of the blood-brain barrier explains some drug actions, as can be seen from the following scenario: Morphine differs chemically from heroin only in that morphine has two hydroxyl

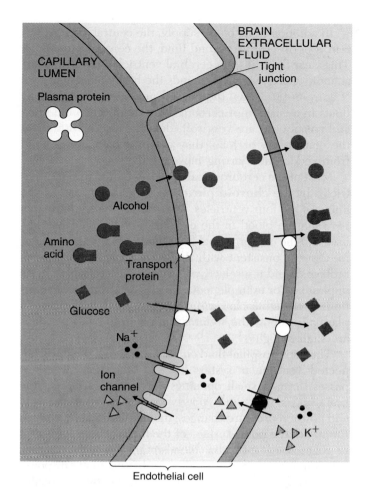

FIGURE 8-47

A diagram of the blood-brain barrier, which is formed by the endothelial cells that line the brain capillaries. (*Redrawn from Oldendorf.*)

groups where heroin has two acetyl groups ($-COCH_3$). This small difference renders morphine highly lipid-insoluble and heroin highly lipid-soluble. Thus, heroin crosses the blood-brain barrier more readily than morphine. As soon as heroin enters the brain, however, enzymes remove the acetyl groups from heroin and change it to morphine. The morphine, highly insoluble in lipid, is then effectively trapped in the brain where it continues to exert its effect. Some other drugs that have rapid effects in the central nervous system because of their high lipid solubility are the barbiturates, nicotine, caffeine, and alcohol.

Many substances that do not dissolve readily in lipids, such as glucose and other important substrates of brain metabolism, nonetheless enter the brain quite rapidly, by combining with membrane transport proteins. Similar transport systems also move surplus substances out of the brain and into the blood, preventing the buildup of molecules that could interfere with brain function.

function of the graded potential is to trigger action potentials. (Turn to Figure 8-14 to review the properties of graded potentials.)

As long as the afferent neuron remains depolarized to threshold, action potentials continue to fire and propagate along the afferent neuron. With greater depolarizations, threshold is reached faster and the frequency of action potentials is greater, up to a limit.[1] Therefore, the magnitude of the graded potential determines the action-potential frequency in the afferent neuron. Although the graded-potential amplitude is a determinant of action-potential *frequency,* it does not determine action-potential *magnitude.* Since the action potential is all-or-none, its magnitude is independent of the strength of the initiating stimulus.

Factors that control the magnitude of the receptor potential include stimulus strength, rate of change of stimulus application, temporal summation of successive receptor potentials (Figure 8-14), and **adaptation**, which is a decrease in the frequency of action potentials in an afferent neuron despite maintenance of the stimulus at constant strength.

Adaptation of an afferent neuron can be seen in Figure 9-3. We shall see the significance of adaptation later when we discuss the coding of stimulus duration.

NEURAL PATHWAYS IN SENSORY SYSTEMS

The afferent neurons form the first link in a sensory pathway. A **sensory pathway** is made up of a group of neuron chains, each chain consisting of three or more neurons connected end to end by synapses. The chains in a given pathway run parallel to each other in the central nervous system and carry information to that part of the brain responsible for conscious recognition of the information.

---

[1]The action-potential frequency is limited by the refractory period. Recall from Chapter 8 that during the absolute refractory period, no further action potentials can be generated, and during the relative refractory period, threshold is raised and the membrane must be depolarized more than usual to generate action potentials.

FIGURE 9-3

Action potentials in a single afferent nerve fiber showing adaptation to a stimulus of constant strength.

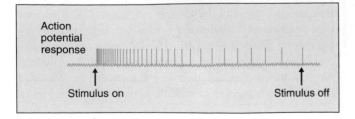

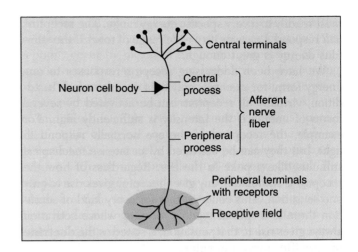

FIGURE 9-4

Sensory unit and receptive field.

tion, generally accepted to be the cerebral cortex. Sensory pathways are called **ascending pathways** because they go to the brain.

Sensory Units

A single afferent neuron with all its receptor endings makes up a **sensory unit**. In a few cases, the afferent neuron has a single receptor, but generally the peripheral end of an afferent neuron divides into many fine branches, each terminating at a receptor.

The portion of the body that, when stimulated, leads to activity in a particular afferent neuron is called the **receptive field** for that neuron (Figure 9-4). Receptive fields of neighboring afferent neurons overlap so that stimulation of a single point activates several sensory units; activation of a single sensory unit almost never occurs. As we shall see, the degree of overlap varies in different parts of the body.

Ascending Pathways

The central processes of the afferent neurons synapse upon interneurons in the brain or spinal cord. The central processes diverge to terminate on several, or many, interneurons (Figure 9-5A) and converge so that the processes of many afferent neurons terminate upon a single interneuron (Figure 9-5B). The interneurons upon which the afferent neurons synapse are termed second-order neurons, and these in turn synapse with third-order neurons, and so on, until the information reaches the cerebral cortex.

Some of the pathways convey information about only a single type of sensory information. Thus, one pathway may be influenced only by information from mechanoreceptors, whereas another may be influenced only by information from thermoreceptors. The ascending pathways in the

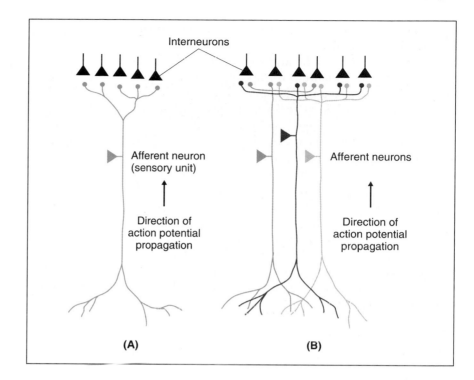

FIGURE 9-5

(A) Divergence of afferent neuron terminals. (B) Convergence of input from several afferent neurons onto single interneurons.

spinal cord and brain that carry information about single types of stimuli are known as the **specific ascending pathways**. The specific pathways, except for the olfactory pathways (which go to parts of the limbic system), pass to the brainstem and thalamus, and the final neurons in the pathways go from there to different areas of the cerebral cortex.

The specific ascending pathways that transmit information from **somatic receptors**, that is, the receptors in the framework or outer walls of the body, including skin, skeletal muscle, tendons, and joints, go to the **somatosensory cortex**, a strip of cortex that lies in the parietal lobe of the brain just behind the junction of the parietal and frontal lobes (Figure 9-6). The specific pathways from the eyes go

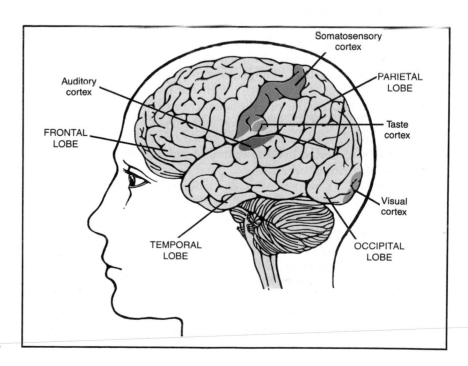

FIGURE 9-6

Primary sensory areas of the cerebral cortex.

PRIMARY SENSORY CODING

The sensory systems code four aspects of a stimulus: stimulus type, intensity, location, and duration.

Stimulus Type

Another term for stimulus type, that is, heat, cold, sound, or pressure, for example, is stimulus **modality**. Modalities can be divided into submodalities: Cold and warm are submodalities of temperature, whereas salt, sweet, bitter, and sour are submodalities of taste. The specific receptor type activated by a stimulus plays the primary role in coding the stimulus modality.

As mentioned earlier, a given receptor type is particularly sensitive to one stimulus modality because of the signal transduction mechanisms and ion channels incorporated in the receptor's plasma membrane. For example, receptors for vision, which contain pigment molecules whose shape is transformed by light, have intracellular mechanisms by which changes in the pigment molecules alter the activity of membrane ion channels and generate a neural signal. Receptors in the skin have neither light-sensitive molecules nor plasma-membrane ion channels that can be affected by them; thus, receptors in the eyes respond to light and those in the skin do not.

All the receptors of an afferent neuron are preferentially sensitive to the same type of stimulus. For example, they are all sensitive to cold or all to pressure. Adjacent sensory units may be sensitive to different types of stimuli. Since the receptive fields for different modalities overlap, a single stimulus—let us say an ice cube on the skin—can give rise simultaneously to the sensations of touch and temperature.

Regardless of the stimulus type and the receptors that respond to that particular stimulus, however, all information from receptors is transmitted in afferent neurons and throughout the central nervous system in the form of graded potentials and action potentials.

Stimulus Intensity

How is a strong stimulus distinguished from a weak one when the information about both stimuli is relayed by action potentials, which are all the same size? Action-potential *frequency* in a single afferent nerve fiber is one way, since increased stimulus strength means a larger receptor potential and a higher frequency of action-potential firing. A record of an experiment in which increased stimulus intensity is reflected in increased action-potential frequency in a single afferent nerve fiber is shown in Figure 9-9.

As stimulus strength increases, receptors on other branches of the same afferent neuron also begin to respond. The action potentials generated by these receptors propagate along the branches to the main afferent nerve fiber and add to the train of action potentials there (Figure 9-10).

In addition to increasing the firing frequency in a single afferent neuron, stronger stimuli usually affect a larger area and activate similar receptors on the endings of *other* afferent neurons. For example, when one touches a surface lightly with a finger, the area of skin in contact with the surface is small, and only receptors in that skin area are stimulated. Pressing down firmly increases the area of skin

FIGURE 9-9

Action potentials from the afferent fiber leading from a pressure receptor as the receptor is subjected to pressures of different magnitudes.

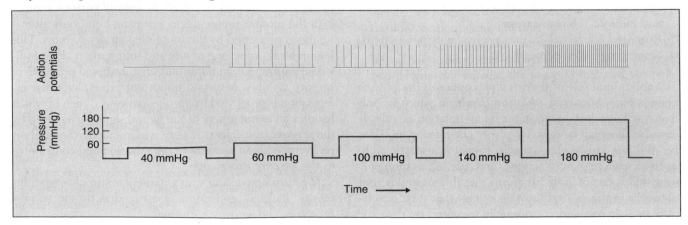

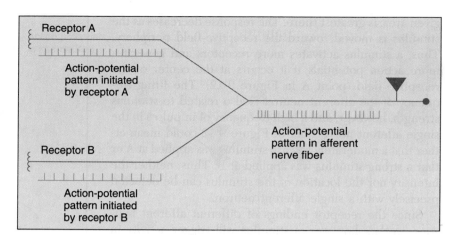

FIGURE 9-10

Simultaneous activation of two receptors in a sensory unit increases the number of action potentials transmitted along the afferent neuron. If, however, the main branch of the neuron is refractory because of just having transmitted an action potential, the transmission of further action potentials may be blocked for a brief time.

stimulated. This "calling in" of receptors on additional afferent neurons is known as **recruitment** or, sometimes, as spatial summation (*not* synaptic spatial summation).

Stimulus Location

A third type of information to be signaled is the location of the stimulus, in other words, where the stimulus is being applied. (It should be noted that in vision, hearing, and smell, stimulus location is interpreted as arising from the site from which the stimulus *originated* rather than the place on our body where the stimulus was actually *applied*. For example, we interpret the sight and sound of a barking dog as occurring in that furry thing on the other side of the fence rather than to a specific region of our eyes and ears. More will be said of this later; we deal here with the senses in which the stimulus is located to a site on the body.)

The main factor coding stimulus location is the site of the stimulated receptor. The precision (**acuity**) with which one stimulus can be located and differentiated from an adjacent one depends upon the amount of convergence of neuronal input in the specific ascending pathways. The greater the convergence, the less the acuity. Other factors affecting acuity are the size of the receptive field covered by the single sensory unit and the amount of overlap of nearby receptive fields. For example, it is easy to discriminate between two adjacent stimuli (two-point discrimination) applied to the skin on a finger, where the sensory units are small and the overlap considerable. It is harder to do so on the back, where the sensory units are large and widely spaced. Locating sensations from the internal organs is less precise than from the skin because there are fewer afferent neurons in the internal organs and each has a larger receptive field.

It is fairly simple to see why a stimulus to a neuron that has a small receptive field can be located more precisely than a stimulus to a neuron with a large receptive field (Figure 9-11). The fact is, however, that even in the

former case one cannot distinguish exactly where within a receptive field a stimulus has been applied. One can only tell that the afferent neuron has been activated. This is where receptive-field overlap aids stimulus localization even though, intuitively, overlap would seem to "muddy" the image. Let us examine more closely how overlap improves stimulus localization.

An afferent neuron responds most vigorously to stimuli applied at the center of its receptive field because the receptor density, that is, the number of receptors in a

FIGURE 9-11

The information from neuron A indicates the stimulus location more precisely than does that from neuron B because A's receptive field is smaller.

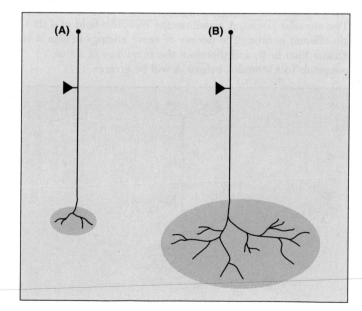

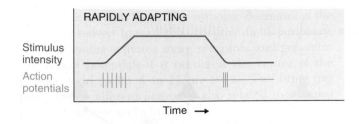

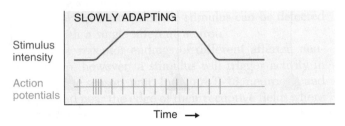

FIGURE 9-16

Rapidly and slowly adapting receptors. The top line (red) indicates application of the stimulus, and the bottom line (green), the action potential firing of the afferent nerve fiber from the receptor.

Some receptors adapt so rapidly that they fire only a single action potential at the onset of a stimulus, while others respond at the beginning of the stimulus and again at its removal. The rapid fading of the sensation of our clothes pressing on our skin is due to rapidly adapting receptors.

Slowly adapting receptors (or tonic receptors) maintain their response at or near the initial level of firing regardless of the stimulus duration (Figure 9-16). These receptors signal slow changes or prolonged events, such as occur in the joint and muscle receptors that participate in the maintenance of upright posture when we are standing or sitting for long periods of time.

Central Control of Afferent Information

All sensory information is subject to extensive control at the various synaptic junctions along the ascending pathways before it reaches higher levels of the central nervous system. Much of the incoming information is reduced or even abolished by inhibition from collaterals from other neurons in ascending pathways—an example being lateral inhibition, discussed earlier—or by pathways descending downward from higher regions. The reticular formation and cerebral cortex in particular control much afferent information via descending pathways. The inhibitory controls may be exerted directly by synapses on the axon terminals of the primary afferent neurons (an example of presynaptic inhibition, introduced in Chapter 8) or indirectly via interneurons that affect other neurons in the sensory pathways via inhibitory synapses (Figure 9-17).

In some cases, for example pain pathways, the afferent input is continuously, that is, tonically, inhibited to some degree. This provides the flexibility of either removing the inhibition (disinhibition) so as to allow a greater degree of signal transmission or of increasing the inhibition so as to block the signal more completely.

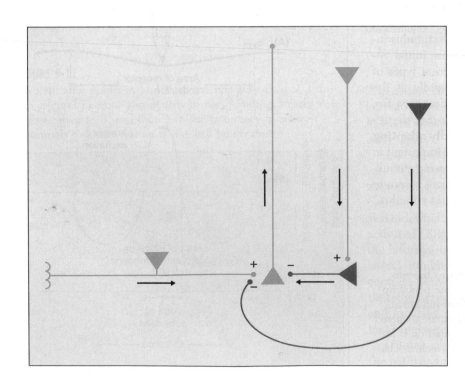

FIGURE 9-17

Descending pathways may control sensory information by directly inhibiting the central terminals of the afferent neuron (an example of presynaptic inhibition) or via an interneuron that affects the ascending pathway by inhibitory synapses. Neurons ending in excitatory synapses are green; those ending in inhibitory synapses are red. Arrows indicate the direction of action-potential transmission.

This completes our general introduction to sensory system pathways and coding. We now present the individual systems, covering the somatic sensations and vision in greater detail than the others because they serve as good models for the principles of sensory system organization that appear in all the sensory systems. These principles are (1) a specific sensory pathway codes for the particular modality being discussed; (2) information is organized such that initial processing of the various modalities occurs in different parts of the brain; (3) the ascending pathways are crossed so that sensory information is processed by the side of the brain opposite the side of the body that was stimulated; and (4) in addition to other synaptic relay points, all ascending pathways, except for those involved in taste, synapse in the thalamus.

SOMATIC SENSATION

Sensation from the skin, body walls, muscles, bones, tendons, and joints is termed **somatic sensation** and is initiated by a variety of somatic receptors (Figure 9-18). Some respond to mechanical stimulation of the skin, hairs,

and underlying tissues, whereas others respond to temperature changes and some chemical changes. Activation of somatic receptors gives rise to the sensations of touch, pressure, warmth, cold, pain, and awareness of the position of the body parts and their movement. (Visceral sensations, which arise in the organs of the thoracic and abdominal cavities, originate in the same kinds of receptors that give rise to somatic sensations. Only the receptor locations differ.)

Each sensation is associated with a specific receptor type. In other words, there are distinct receptors for heat, cold, touch, pressure, limb position or movement, and pain. After entering the central nervous system, the afferent nerve fibers from the somatic receptors synapse on neurons that form the specific ascending pathways going primarily to the somatosensory cortex via the brainstem and thalamus. They also synapse on interneurons that give rise to the nonspecific pathways. The location of some important ascending pathways is shown in a cross section of the spinal cord (Figure 9-19A), and two are diagrammed in Figure 9-19B and C.

Note that the pathways cross from the side at which the afferent neurons enter the central nervous system to the opposite side in the spinal cord (Figure 9-19B) or brain-

FIGURE 9-18

Skin receptors. Some nerve fibers, usually those with little or no myelin, have free nerve terminals not related to any apparent receptor structures. These terminals are sensitive to stimuli that give rise to pain and temperature. Thicker, myelinated axons, on the other hand, end in receptors that can be quite complex, for example, the lamellated (Pacinian) corpuscle, the tactile (Meissner's and Merkel's) corpuscles, and the corpuscle of Ruffini. These are all mechanoreceptors, sensitive to displacement of the skin: The Pacinian corpuscles are especially sensitive to vibration and other rapid changes, the Meissner corpuscle to slow flutter, and the corpuscles of Ruffini and Merkel disks to sustained pressure. One afferent fiber connects to only one type of receptor so that the information coded by the different receptor types is kept separate.

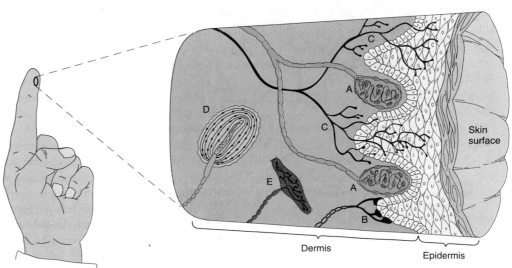

A – Tactile (Meissner's) corpuscle
B – Tactile (Merkle's) corpuscles
C – Free terminal
D – Lamellated (Pacinian) corpuscle
E – Ruffini corpuscle

Warmth receptors respond to temperatures between 30 and 43°C with an increased discharge rate upon warming, whereas receptors for cold are stimulated by temperatures between 35 and 20°C and increase their discharge rate upon cooling. It is not known how heat or cold alters the endings of the thermosensitive afferent neurons to generate receptor potentials.

Pain

A stimulus that causes (or is on the verge of causing) tissue damage usually elicits a sensation of pain. Pain differs from the other somatosensory modalities in that such emotions as fear and anxiety and feelings of unpleasantness are experienced along with the perceived sensation. Also, a painful stimulus can evoke a reflex escape or withdrawal response as well as a gamut of physiological changes similar to those elicited during fear, rage, and aggression. These changes, mediated by the sympathetic nervous system, include increased heart rate and blood pressure, greater secretion of epinephrine into the bloodstream, increased blood glucose concentration, decreased gastric motility, decreased blood flow to the viscera and skin, dilation of the pupils, and sweating. In other words, the stimuli that give rise to pain result in a sensory experience *plus* a reaction to it.

Probably more than any other type of sensation, pain can be altered by past experiences, suggestion, emotions (particularly anxiety), and the simultaneous activation of other sensory modalities. Thus, the level of pain is not solely a physical property of the stimulus as, for example, shape is. Instead, painfulness depends in part on the subjective opinion of the person receiving the stimulus.

The receptors, known as **nociceptors**, whose stimulation gives rise to pain are located at the ends of small unmyelinated or lightly myelinated afferent neurons. These receptors have high thresholds and respond to intense mechanical and thermal stimulation or to irritant chemicals. Chemicals such as H^+, K^+, histamine, bradykinin, and prostaglandins released from nearby damaged tissue may depolarize nociceptor nerve endings, initiating action potentials in the afferent nerve fibers.

In addition, these chemicals may alter the nociceptors themselves so that their threshold is decreased and their response to later painful stimuli is increased. They may even fire spontaneously. This increase in sensitivity to painful stimuli, known as **hyperalgesia**, can last hours after the original stimulus is over. Inhibition of prostaglandin production at the stimulation site by aspirin and aspirin-like drugs (Chapter 7) partially accounts for their effectiveness in the relief of hyperalgesia.

The primary afferents coming from nociceptors synapse on interneurons after entering the central nervous system. Substance P is one of the transmitters released at this site. Pain information is mediated by three ascending pathways that together are known as the **anterolateral system**. They convey information that leads to both the localization of pain and its affective component.

Reflecting the diverse influences on pain perception, neurons in the central-nervous-system pain pathways are subject to both short- and long-term changes in excitability and show a high degree of plasticity, or alterability. Thus, a neuron may or may not respond to a given nociceptive input, depending on the circumstances, and stimuli that are not normally painful may become so.

The activation of interneurons by incoming nociceptive afferents may lead to the phenomenon of **referred pain**, in which the sensation of pain is experienced at a site other than the injured or diseased part. For example, during a heart attack, pain is often experienced in the left arm. This type of referred pain occurs because both visceral and somatic afferents often converge on the same interneurons in the pain pathways. Excitation of the somatic afferent fibers is the more usual source of afferent discharge, so we "refer" the location of receptor activation to the somatic source even though, in the case of visceral pain, the perception is incorrect.

Electrical stimulation of specific areas of the central nervous system can produce a profound reduction in pain, a phenomenon called **stimulation-produced analgesia**, by inhibiting pain pathways. Parts of the thalamus, central region of the brainstem, and spinal cord at the level of entry of the active nociceptor afferents have all been electrically stimulated with some success in alleviating pain.

Analgesia occurs from such stimulation because descending pathways that originate in these brain areas selectively inhibit the transmission of information originating in nociceptors. The descending axons end at lower brainstem and spinal levels on interneurons in the pain pathways as well as on the synaptic terminals of the afferent nociceptor neurons themselves. Some of the neurons in these inhibitory pathways release or are sensitive to certain endogenous opioids (Chapter 8). Thus, infusion of morphine, which stimulates opioid receptors, into the spinal cord at the level of entry of the active nociceptor fibers can provide relief in many cases of intractable pain. This is separate from morphine's effect on the brain.

Transcutaneous electric nerve stimulation, or **TENS**, in which the painful site itself or the nerves leading from it are stimulated by electrodes placed on the surface of the skin, is often useful in lessening pain. TENS works because the stimulation of nonpain, low-threshold afferent fibers (for example, the fibers from touch receptors) leads to inhibition of neurons in the pain pathways. We often apply our own type of TENS therapy when we rub or press hard on a painful area, utilizing the fact that pathways activated by the touch receptors add inhibitory synaptic input to the pain pathways.

Under certain circumstances **acupuncture** prevents or

alleviates pain. During acupuncture analgesia, needles are introduced into specific parts of the body to stimulate afferent fibers, which causes analgesia in the same way as TENS. The endogenous opioid neurotransmitters may be involved in acupuncture analgesia.

Stimulation-produced analgesia, TENS, and acupuncture work by exploiting the body's built-in mechanisms that control pain.

VISION

The eyes are composed of an optical portion, which focuses the visual image on the receptor cells, and a neural component, which transforms the visual image into a pattern of neural discharges. The receptors of the eye are sensitive only to that tiny portion of the vast spectrum of electromagnetic radiation that we call visible light (Figure 9-21).

Light

Radiant energy is described in terms of wavelengths and frequencies. The **wavelength** is the distance between two successive wave peaks of the electromagnetic radiation (Figure 9-22). Wavelengths can vary from several kilometers at the long-wave radio end of the spectrum to minute fractions of a millimeter at the γ-ray end. The **frequency**, or the number of cycles per second, of the radiation wave varies inversely with wavelength. Those wavelengths capable of stimulating the receptors of the eye—the **visible spectrum**—are between 400 and 700 nm. Light of different wavelengths in this band is perceived as having different colors.

The Optics of Vision

A light wave can be represented by a line drawn in the direction in which the wave is traveling. Light waves are propagated in all directions from every point of a visible object. Before an accurate image of the object is achieved, these divergent light waves must pass through an optical system that focuses them back into a point. In the eye, the image of the object being viewed is focused upon the **retina**, a thin layer of neural tissue lining the back of the eyeball (Figure 9-23). The retina contains the light-sensitive receptor cells of the eye.

The **lens** and **cornea** of the eye are the optical systems that focus an image upon the retina. At a boundary between two substances, such as the cornea and the air, light rays are bent so that they travel in a new direction. The cornea plays a larger role than the lens in focusing light rays because the rays are bent more in passing from air into the cornea than they are when passing into and out of the lens or any other transparent structure of the eye.

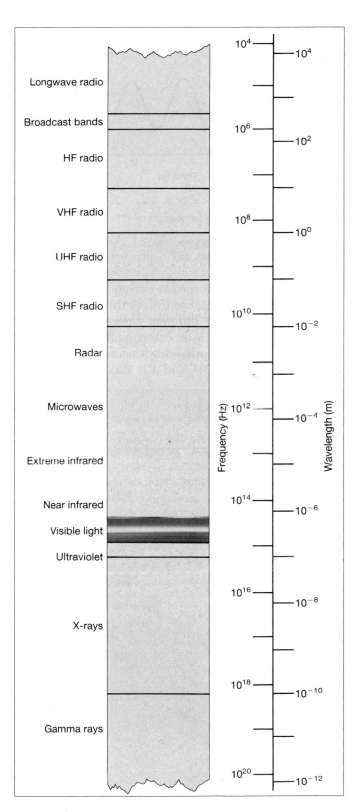

FIGURE 9-21
Electromagnetic spectrum.

all other retinal neurons produce only graded potentials. The axons of the ganglion cells form the output from the retina—the optic nerve, or cranial nerve II—which leads into the brain. The two optic nerves meet at the base of the brain to form the optic chiasm, where some of the fibers cross to the opposite side of the brain, providing both cerebral hemispheres with input from each eye.

Optic nerve fibers project to several structures in the brain, the largest number passing to the **lateral geniculate nucleus** in the thalamus (Figure 9-31), where the information from P and M ganglion cells is kept distinct. In addition to the input from the retina, many neurons of the lateral geniculate nucleus also receive input from the brainstem reticular formation and input relayed back from the visual cortex. These nonretinal inputs can control the transmission of information from the retina to the visual cortex and may be involved in the ability to shift attention between vision and the other sensory modalities or between different objects in the visual field.

The lateral geniculate nucleus sends action potentials on to the visual cortex, the primary visual area of cerebral cortex (Figure 9-6). The visual cortex has several subdivisions, each representing the complete **visual field**, that part of the visual world that stimulates the retina at any given time. Just as in the somatosensory system, the visual cortex on one side of the brain receives input from the opposite visual field. For example, the visual cortex in the left cerebral hemisphere receives information about what is out in the visual world on the right side of the head. The relay of information from the retina to the various areas of the visual cortex follows a precise point-to-point projection pattern so that adjacent retinal regions project to adjacent regions in each subdivision of the visual cortex.

The separate functions of cells, which began in the retina, are maintained in the visual cortex. In fact, an important aspect of lateral geniculate function is to separate and relay different kinds of visual information from the retina to different cortical zones. Thus, most neurons in one subdivision of the visual cortex are responsive only to stimuli oriented in a particular direction in the visual field, a property important in elaboration of the form of an object. The neurons in another subdivision are most responsive to movement of an object across the visual field. Furthermore, other neuronal groups may respond best to color, and others only to input from both eyes, an important clue to depth perception. Again, the functional differences between various areas of the visual cortex are determined by the input these areas receive from the distinct classes of ganglion cells.

Some of the information is kept separate even after it leaves the visual cortex. For example, some pathways transmit information from the visual cortex to the temporal lobe, where the identification of objects in the visual field is processed—analyzing the "what" of the visual stimulus. Other pathways travel to the parietal lobe, where information about the location of objects in the visual field is processed—analyzing the "where" of the visual stimulus. Output from both the temporal and parietal lobes then passes to the frontal cortex, which uses the visual information, for example, in directing actions. Thus, different aspects of visual information are carried in parallel pathways and are processed simultaneously in a number of independent ways in different parts of the cerebral cortex before they are reintegrated to produce the conscious sensation of sight.

Note that the cells of the visual pathways are organized to handle information about line, contrast, movement, and color. They do not, however, form a picture in the brain. Rather, they form a spatial and temporal pattern of electrical activity.

We mentioned that a substantial number of fibers of the visual pathway project to regions of the brain other than the visual cortex. For example, visual information is transmitted to the **suprachiasmatic nucleus**, which lies just above the optic chiasm and plays a major role in a variety of circadian behaviors, as described in Chapter 7. This nucleus functions as a "biological clock," and information about diurnal cycles of light intensity is used to synchronize this neuronal clock. Other visual information is passed to the brainstem and cerebellum, where it is used in the coordination of eye and head movements, fixation of gaze, and constriction of the pupils.

Color Vision

The colors we perceive are related to the wavelengths of light that are reflected, absorbed, or transmitted by the pigments in the objects of our visual world. For example, an object appears red because shorter wavelengths, which would be perceived as blue, are absorbed by the object, while the longer wavelengths, perceived as red, are reflected to excite the photopigment of the retina most sensitive to red. Light perceived as white is a mixture of all wavelengths, and black is the absence of all light.

Color vision begins with activation of the photopigments in the cone receptor cells. Human retinas have three kinds of cones, which contain red-, green-, or blue-sensitive photopigments. As their names imply, these pigments absorb and hence respond optimally to light of different wavelengths. Because the red pigment is actually more sensitive to the wavelengths that correspond to yellow, this pigment is sometimes called the yellow photopigment.

Although each type of cone is excited most effectively by light of one particular wavelength, it responds to other wavelengths as well. Thus, for any given wavelength, the three cone types are excited to different degrees (Figure 9-32). For example, in response to light of 530-nm wavelength, the green cones respond maximally, the red cones less, and the blue cones not at all. Our sensation of color

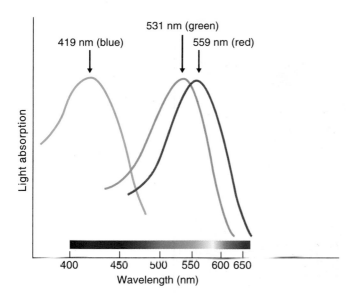

FIGURE 9-32

The sensitivities of the photopigments in the three types of cones in the normal human retina. Action potential frequency in the optic nerve is directly related to absorption of light by a photopigment.

depends upon the relative outputs of these three types of cone cells and their comparison by higher-order cells in the visual system.

The pathways for color vision follow those described in Figure 9-31. The M-type ganglion cells respond to a broad band of wavelengths. In other words, they receive input from all three types of cones, and they signal not specific color but general brightness. P-type ganglion cells code

FIGURE 9-33

Response of a single opponent color ganglion cell to blue, red, and white lights. (*Redrawn from Hubel and Wiesel.*)

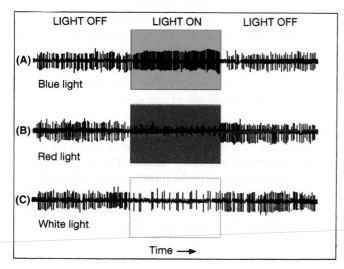

specific colors. These latter cells are also called **opponent color cells** because they have an excitatory input from one type of cone receptor and an inhibitory input from another. For example, the cell in Figure 9-33 increases its rate of firing when the retina is stimulated by a blue light but decreases it when a red light replaces the blue. The cell gives a weak response when stimulated with a white light because the light contains both blue and red wavelengths. Other more complicated patterns also exist. Opponent cells are also found in the lateral geniculate nucleus and visual cortex.

At high light intensities, as in daylight vision, most people—92 percent of the male population and over 99 percent of the female population—have normal color vision. People with the most common kind of **color blindness** lack either the red or green cone pigments and, as a result, have trouble perceiving red versus green.

Eye Movement

The cones are most concentrated in a specialized area of the retina known as the **fovea centralis** (Figure 9-23), and images focused there are seen with the greatest acuity. In order to focus the most important point in the visual image, the fixation point, on the fovea and keep it there, the eyeball must be able to move. Six skeletal muscles attached to the outside of each eyeball (Figure 9-34) control its movement. These muscles perform two basic movements, fast and slow.

The fast movements, called **saccades**, are small, jerking movements that rapidly bring the eye from one fixation point to another to allow a sweeping search of the visual field. In addition, saccades move the visual image over the receptors, thereby preventing adaptation. Saccades also occur during certain periods of sleep when the eyes are closed and may be associated with "watching" the visual imagery of dreams.

Slow eye movements are involved both in tracking visual objects as they move through the visual field and during compensation for movements of the head. The control centers for these compensating movements obtain their information about head movement from the vestibular system, which will be described shortly. Control systems for the other slow movements of the eyes require the continuous feedback of visual information about the moving object.

HEARING

The sense of hearing is based on the physics of sound and the physiology of the external, middle, and inner ear, the nerves to the brain, and the brain parts involved in processing acoustic information.

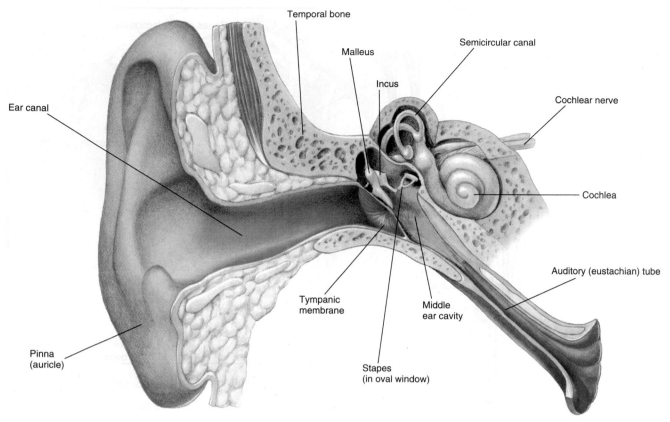

FIGURE 9-36

The human ear. In this and the following drawing, violet indicates the outer ear, green the middle ear, and blue the inner ear. The malleus, incus, and stapes are bones even though they are colored green in this figure to indicate that they are components of the middle ear compartment. The end of the auditory tube is normally closed, but it opens temporarily during muscle movements of the pharynx.

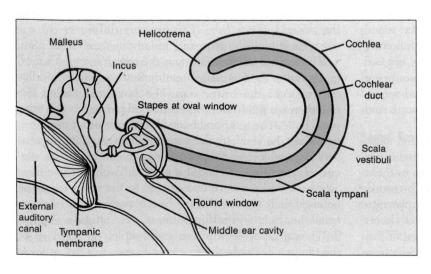

FIGURE 9-37

Relationship between the middle ear bones and the cochlea. Movement of the stapes against the membrane covering the oval window sets up pressure waves in the fluid-filled scala vestibuli. These waves cause vibration of the cochlear duct and the basilar membrane. Some of the pressure is transmitted around the helicotrema directly into the scala tympani.

(the **oval window**) separating the middle and inner ear (Figure 9-38).

The *total* force of a sound wave applied to the tympanic membrane is transferred to the oval window, but because the oval window is so much smaller than the tympanic membrane, the *force per unit area* (that is, the pressure) is increased 15 to 20 times. Additional advantage is gained through the lever action of the middle-ear bones. The amount of energy transmitted to the inner ear can be lessened by the contraction of two small muscles in the middle ear that alter the tension of the tympanic membrane and the position of the stapes in the oval window. These muscles help to protect the delicate receptor apparatus of the inner ear from continuous intense sound stimuli and improve hearing over certain frequency ranges.

The entire system described thus far has been concerned with the transmission of sound energy into the cochlea, where the receptor cells are located. The cochlea is almost completely divided lengthwise by a fluid-filled membranous tube, the **cochlear duct**, which follows the cochlear spiral (Figure 9-37).

On either side of the cochlear duct are fluid-filled compartments: the **scala vestibuli**, which is on the side of the cochlear duct that ends at the oval window; and the **scala tympani**, which is below the cochlear duct and ends in a second membrane-covered opening to the middle ear, the round window. The scala vestibuli and scala tympani meet at the end of the cochlear duct at the helicotrema (Figure 9-37).

As the sound waves in the ear canal push on the tympanic membrane, the chain of middle-ear bones presses the stapes against the membrane covering the oval window, causing it to bow into the scala vestibuli and back out

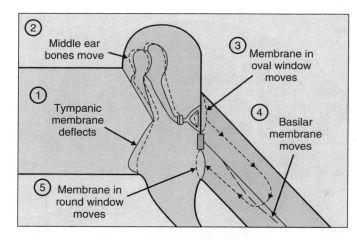

FIGURE 9-39

Transmission of sound vibrations through the middle and inner ear. (*Redrawn from Davis and Silverman.*)

(Figure 9-39), creating waves of pressure there. The wall of the scala vestibuli is largely bone, but there are two paths by which the pressure waves can be dissipated. One path is to the helicotrema, where the waves pass around the end of the cochlear duct into the scala tympani and back to the round-window membrane, which is then bowed out into the middle-ear cavity. However, most of the pressure is transmitted from the scala vestibuli across the cochlear duct.

One side of the cochlear duct is formed by the **basilar membrane** (Figure 9-40), to which is attached the **organ of Corti** (also called the spiral organ), which contains the ear's sensitive receptor cells. Pressure waves crossing the cochlear duct cause the basilar membrane to vibrate.

The region of maximal displacement of the basilar membrane varies with the frequency of the sound source. The properties of the membrane nearest the middle ear are such that this region vibrates most easily, that is, undergoes the greatest movement, in response to high-frequency (high-pitched) tones. As the frequency of the sound is lowered, vibration waves travel out along the membrane for greater distances. Progressively more distant regions of the basilar membrane vibrate maximally in response to progressively lower tones.

Hair Cells of the Organ of Corti

The receptor cells of the organ of Corti, the **hair cells**, are mechanoreceptors that have hairlike **stereocilia** protruding from one end (Figure 9-40C). The hair cells transform the pressure waves in the cochlea into receptor potentials. Movements of the basilar membrane stimulate the hair cells because they are attached to the membrane. The greatest stimulation of the hair cells occurs wherever displacement of the basilar membrane is greatest. Thus, indi-

FIGURE 9-38

Diagrammatic representation showing that the middle ear bones act as a piston against the fluid of the inner ear. (*Redrawn from von Bekesy.*)

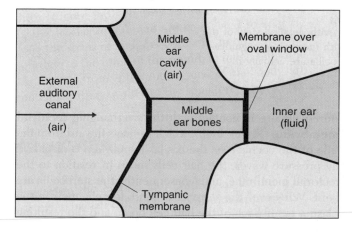

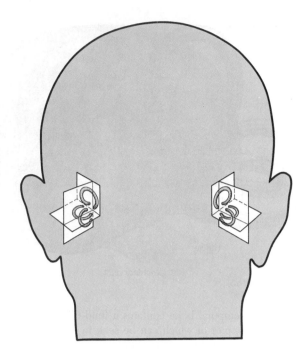

FIGURE 9-42
Relation of the two sets of semicircular canals.

FIGURE 9-43
(A) Organization of a cupula and ampulla. (B) Relation of the cupula to the ampulla when the head is at rest and when it is accelerating.

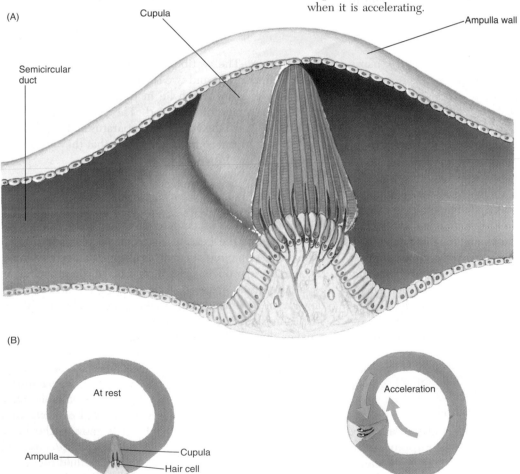

inertia tends to retain its original position, that is, to be "left behind." Thus, the moving ampulla is pushed against the stationary fluid, which causes bending of the cilia, stimulation of the hair cells, and release of a chemical transmitter that activates the nerve terminals synapsing with the hair cells.

At a constant velocity, the duct fluid begins to move at the same rate as the rest of the head, and the cilia slowly return to their resting position. For this reason, the hair cells are stimulated only during *changes* in the rate of motion, that is, during acceleration or deceleration, of the head.

The speed and magnitude of rotational head movements determine the way in which the cilia are bent and the hair cells stimulated. Each receptor has one direction of maximum sensitivity, and when its cilia are bent in this direction, the receptor cell depolarizes. When the cilia are bent in the opposite direction, the cell hyperpolarizes (Figure 9-44). The frequency of action potentials in the afferent nerve fibers that synapse with the hair cells is related to both the amount of force bending the cilia on the receptor cells and to the direction in which this force is applied.

The Utricle and Saccule

The utricle and saccule provide information about *linear* acceleration and changes in head position relative to the forces of gravity. The receptor cells here, too, are mechanoreceptors sensitive to the displacement of projecting hairs. The patch of hair cells in the utricle is nearly horizontal in a standing person, and that in the saccule is vertical.

The cilia are covered by a gelatinous substance in which tiny stones, or otoliths, made up of calcium carbonate crystals are embedded, making the gelatinous substance heavier than the surrounding fluid. In response to any linear acceleration, the gelatinous-otolithic material changes its position, pulled by gravitational forces against the hair cells so that the cilia are bent and the receptor cells stimulated.

Vestibular Information and Dysfunction

Information about hair-cell stimulation is relayed from the vestibular apparatus to the brainstem via cranial nerve VIII, the same nerve that carries acoustic information. It is transmitted via a multineuronal pathway to the parietal lobe to an area adjacent to the somatosensory cortex. Vestibular information is integrated with information from the joints, tendons, and skin, leading to the sense of posture and movement.

Vestibular information is used in three ways. One is to control eye muscles so that, in spite of changes in head position, the eyes can remain fixed on the same point. **Nystagmus**, a repetitive, back-and-forth movement of the

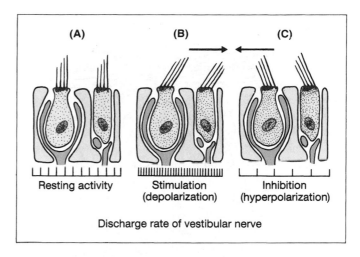

FIGURE 9-44

Relationship between position of hairs and activity in afferent neurons. (A) Resting activity. (B) Movement of hairs in one direction increases the action potential frequency in the afferent nerve activated by the hair cell. (C) Movement in the opposite direction decreases the rate relative to the resting state. (*Redrawn from Wersall, Gleisner, and Lundquist.*)

eyes, can occur in response to vestibular input in normal people but can also be a pathological sign.

The second use of vestibular information is in reflex mechanisms for maintaining upright posture. The vestibular apparatus plays a role in the support of the head during movement, orientation of the head in space, and reflexes accompanying locomotion. Very few postural reflexes depend primarily on input from the vestibular system, however, despite the fact that the vestibular organs are sometimes called the sense organs of balance.

The third use of vestibular information is, after relay via the thalamus to the cortex, in providing conscious awareness of the position and acceleration of the body.

An unexpected combination of inputs from the vestibular system and other sensory systems can induce **vertigo**, defined as an illusion of movement, which is often accompanied by feelings of nausea and lightheadedness. Some people, for example, experience the sensation of falling, nausea, and dizziness when they are in high places looking down to the ground. **Motion sickness** also involves the vestibular system, as when one is on a boat in rough weather and linear and rotational accelerations occur in an unpredicted way.

Ménière's disease is a disorder involving the vestibular system and is associated with episodes of abrupt and often severe dizziness, ringing in the ears, and bouts of hearing loss. It is due to an increased pressure of the fluid in the membranous duct system of the inner ear. The dizziness occurs because the inputs from the two ears are not bal-

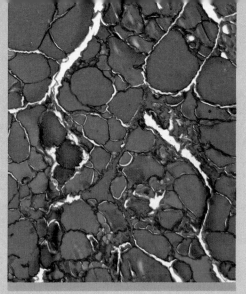

C H A P T E R

10

HORMONAL CONTROL MECHANISMS

HORMONE STRUCTURES AND SYNTHESIS

Amine Hormones

    Thyroid hormones

    Adrenal medullary hormones and dopamine

Peptide Hormones

Steroid Hormones

    Hormones of the adrenal cortex

    Hormones of the gonads

HORMONE TRANSPORT IN THE BLOOD

HORMONE METABOLISM AND EXCRETION

MECHANISMS OF HORMONE ACTION

Hormone Receptors

Events Elicited by Hormone-Receptor Binding

    Effects of peptide hormones and catecholamines

    Effects of steroid and thyroid hormones

Pharmacological Effects of Hormones

TYPES OF INPUTS THAT CONTROL HORMONE SECRETION

Control by Plasma Concentrations of Mineral Ions or Organic Nutrients

Control by Neurons

Control by Other Hormones

CONTROL SYSTEMS INVOLVING THE HYPOTHALAMUS AND PITUITARY

Posterior Pituitary Hormones

The Hypothalamus and Anterior Pituitary

    Anterior pituitary hormones

    Hypophysiotropic hormones

    Neural control of hypophysiotropic hormones

    Hormonal feedback control of the hypothalamus and anterior pituitary

    The role of "nonsequence" hormones on the hypothalamus and anterior pituitary

    A summary example: Control of growth hormone secretion

CANDIDATE HORMONES

TYPES OF ENDOCRINE DISORDERS

Hyposecretion

Hypersecretion

Hyporesponsiveness and Hyperresponsiveness

SUMMARY

KEY TERMS

REVIEW QUESTIONS

CLINICAL TERMS

THOUGHT QUESTIONS

nuity with each other; however, they do form a system in the functional sense. The reader may be puzzled to see listed as endocrine glands some organs—the heart, for instance—that clearly have other functions. The explanation is that, in addition to the cells that carry out the organ's other functions, the organ also contains cells that secrete hormones.

Note also in Table 10-1 that the hypothalamus, a part of the brain, is considered part of the endocrine system too. This is because the chemical messengers released by certain neuron terminals in both the hypothalamus and its extension, the posterior pituitary, do not function as neurotransmitters affecting adjacent cells but rather enter the blood and are carried to sites of action elsewhere. As pointed out in Chapter 7, hormones released from neuron terminals are referred to as **neurohormones**.

Table 10-1 demonstrates that there are a large number of endocrine glands and hormones. One way of describing the physiology of the individual hormones is to present all relevant material, gland by gland, in a single chapter. In keeping with our emphasis on hormones as messengers in homeostatic control mechanisms, however, we have chosen to describe the physiology of specific hormones and the glands that secrete them in subsequent chapters, in the context of the control systems in which they participate. For example, pancreatic hormones are described in Chapter 18 on organic metabolism, parathyroid hormone in Chapter 16 in the context of calcium metabolism, and so on.

The aims of the present chapter are therefore limited to presenting (1) the general principles of endocrinology, that is, a structural and functional analysis of hormones in general that transcends individual glands; and (2) an analysis of the hypothalamus-pituitary hormonal system. The control systems for the hormones of this particular system are so interconnected that they are best described as a unit to lay the foundation for subsequent descriptions in other chapters.

Before we turn to these analyses, however, several additional general points should be made concerning Table 10-1. One phenomenon evident from this table is that a single gland may secrete multiple hormones. The usual pattern in such cases is that a single cell type secretes only one hormone, so that multiple hormone secretion reflects the presence of different endocrine cell types in the same gland. In a few cases, however, a single cell may secrete more than one hormone.

Another point of interest illustrated by Table 10-1 is that a particular hormone may be produced by more than one type of endocrine gland. For example, somatostatin is secreted by endocrine cells in both the gastrointestinal tract and the pancreas and is also one of the hormones secreted by the hypothalamus.

HORMONE STRUCTURES AND SYNTHESIS

Hormones fall into three chemical classes: (1) amines, (2) peptides and proteins, and (3) steroids.

Amine Hormones

The **amine hormones** are all derivatives of the amino acid tyrosine. They include the thyroid hormones, epinephrine and norepinephrine (produced by the adrenal medulla), and dopamine (produced by the hypothalamus and posterior pituitary).

Thyroid Hormones. The **thyroid gland** is located in the lower part of the neck wrapped around the front of the trachea (windpipe). It secretes three hormones, but the two iodine-containing amine hormones shown in Figure 10-1—**thyroxine (T_4)** and **triiodothyronine (T_3)**—are collectively known as the **thyroid hormones (TH)**. The third hormone, a peptide called calcitonin, is not included in subsequent references to thyroid hormones.

Iodine is an essential element that functions as a component of T_4 and T_3. Most of the iodine ingested in food is absorbed, by active transport, into the blood from the gastrointestinal tract, in the process being converted to the ionized form, iodide. Iodide then leaves the blood and is actively transported into the thyroid cells. Once in the gland, the iodide is converted back to iodine, which is then used, along with tyrosine, for hormone synthesis.

The thyroid hormones are stored in the thyroid gland, incorporated by peptide bonds into molecules of the protein called **thyroglobulin**. Hormone secretion occurs by enzymatic splitting of T_4 and T_3 from the thyroglobulin and the entry of the freed hormones into the blood. T_4 is secreted in much larger amounts than is T_3. However, a variety of tissues, particularly the liver and kidneys, convert most of this T_4 into T_3 by enzymatic removal of one iodine atom, and this constitutes the major source of plasma T_3. This is an important point because T_3 is a much more active hormone than is T_4.

Virtually every tissue in the body is affected by the thyroid hormones. These effects, which are described in

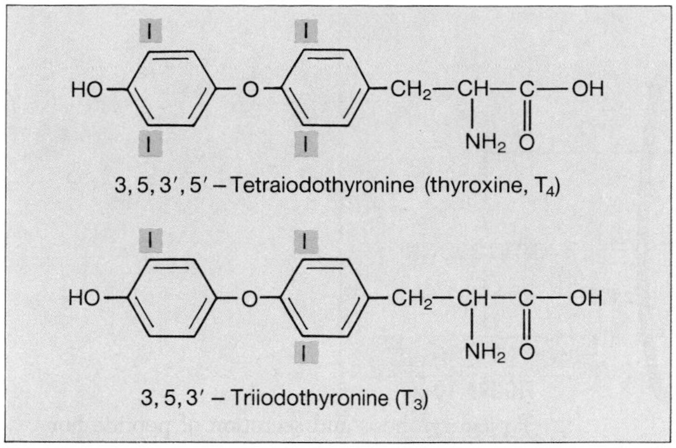

FIGURE 10-1

Chemical structures of the thyroid hormones, thyroxine and triiodothyronine. The two molecules differ by only one iodine atom, a difference noted in the abbreviations T_3 and T_4.

Chapter 18, include regulation of metabolic rate, growth, and brain development and function.

Adrenal Medullary Hormones and Dopamine. There are two adrenal glands, one on the top of each kidney. Each **adrenal gland** constitutes two distinct endocrine glands, an inner **adrenal medulla**, which secretes amine hormones, and a surrounding **adrenal cortex**, which secretes steroid hormones. As described in Chapter 8, the adrenal medulla is really a modified sympathetic ganglion whose cell bodies do not send out nerve fibers but instead release their secretions into the blood, thereby fulfilling a criterion for an endocrine gland.

The adrenal medulla secretes mainly two amine hormones, **epinephrine (E)** and **norepinephrine (NE)**, which constitute, with **dopamine (DA)**, the chemical family of **catecholamines**. The structures and pathways for synthesis of the catecholamines were described in Chapter 8, when these three substances were dealt with as neurotransmitters. In humans, the adrenal medulla secretes approximately four times more epinephrine than norepinephrine.[1] Epinephrine and norepinephrine exert actions similar to those of the sympathetic nerves. These effects are described in various chapters and summarized in Chapter 20 in the section on stress.

The adrenal medulla also secretes small amounts of dopamine and several substances other than catechol-

amines, but whether any of these adrenal secretions other than epinephrine and norepinephrine actually serve hormonal functions is unknown.

In contrast, as described below, the dopamine secreted by cells in two other sites—the hypothalamus and the posterior pituitary—does function as a hormone.

Peptide Hormones

The great majority of all hormones are either peptides or proteins. They range in size from small peptides having only three amino acids to small proteins (some of which are glycoproteins). For convenience, we shall follow a common practice of endocrinologists and refer to all these hormones as **peptide hormones**.

In many cases, they are initially synthesized, on the ribosomes of the endocrine cells, as larger proteins known as preprohormones, which are then cleaved to **prohormones** by proteolytic enzymes in the granular endoplasmic reticulum of the cell (Figure 10-2). The prohormone is then packaged into secretory vesicles by the Golgi apparatus of the cell. In this process, the prohormone is cleaved to yield the active hormone and other peptide chains found in the prohormone. Therefore, when the cell is stimulated to release the contents of the secretory vesicles by exocytosis, the other peptides are cosecreted with the hormone. In certain cases they, too, may exert hormonal effects. In other words, instead of just one peptide hormone, the cell may be secreting multiple peptide hormones that differ in their effects on target cells.

The direct stimulus of secretory-vesicle exocytosis in peptide-producing endocrine cells, as in neurons, is an increase in cytosolic calcium concentration. The source of the calcium during cell stimulation is either the extracellular fluid or the agranular endoplasmic reticulum. Many of the stimuli directly or indirectly cause some degree of plasma-membrane depolarization—sometimes even action potentials—which opens voltage-sensitive calcium channels in the plasma membrane and allows diffusion of calcium into the cell.

Capillaries supplying peptide-secreting endocrine glands are generally quite leaky to proteins, and so, once released into the extracellular fluid by exocytosis, peptide hormones diffuse between the capillary endothelial cells to enter the blood.

One more point about peptide hormones: As mentioned in Chapters 7 and 8, many peptides serve as both neurotransmitters (or neuromodulators) and as hormones. For example, most of the hormones secreted by the endocrine glands in the gastrointestinal tract are also produced by neurons in the brain where they function as neurotransmitters. It is important to recognize the separation of function here: Because of the blood-brain barrier, the gastrointestinal hormones circulating in the blood cannot gain entry to the brain and activate the receptors normally acti-

---

[1]Yet under basal conditions, the plasma concentration of norepinephrine is much higher than that of epinephrine; the source of most of this circulating norepinephrine is not the adrenal medulla but neurotransmitter that has been released from postganglionic sympathetic neurons and entered the blood.

vous system. However, one large group of hormones—those secreted by the hypothalamus and its extension, the posterior pituitary—are under the direct control not of autonomic neurons but of neurons in the brain itself (Figure 10-12). This category will be described in detail later in this chapter.

Control by Other Hormones

In many cases, the secretion of a particular hormone is directly controlled by the blood concentration of another hormone. As we shall see, there are often complex sequences in which the only function of the first few hormones in the sequence is to stimulate the secretion of the next one. A hormone that stimulates the secretion of another hormone is often referred to as a **tropic hormone**. The tropic hormones usually stimulate not only secretion but the growth of the gland as well.

CONTROL SYSTEMS INVOLVING THE HYPOTHALAMUS AND PITUITARY

The **pituitary gland** (or hypophysis) lies in a pocket of bone at the base of the brain (Figure 10-13), just below the brain area called the **hypothalamus**. The pituitary is connected to the hypothalamus by a stalk (the infundibulum) containing nerve fibers and small blood vessels. In adult human beings, the pituitary gland is composed of two adjacent lobes—the **anterior pituitary** (toward the front of the head) and the **posterior pituitary** (toward the back of the head)—each of which is a more-or-less distinct gland.[3] The anterior pituitary and its part of the stalk are termed the adenohypophysis, and the posterior pituitary with its part of the stalk is the neurohypophysis.

The posterior pituitary is an outgrowth of the hypothalamus and is neural tissue. The axons of two well-defined clusters of hypothalamic neurons pass down the infundibulum and end within the posterior pituitary in close proximity to capillaries (the smallest of blood vessels) (Figure 10-13).

In contrast to the neural connections between the hypothalamus and *posterior* pituitary, there are no important neural connections between the hypothalamus and *anterior* pituitary. There is, however, an unusual *blood-vessel* connection (Figure 10-13B). The capillaries at the base of the hypothalamus (the **median eminence**) recombine into the **hypothalamo-pituitary portal vessels**—the

term "portal" denotes vessels that connect distinct capillary beds. The hypothalamo-pituitary portal vessels pass down the stalk connecting the hypothalamus and pituitary and enter the anterior pituitary where they drain into a second capillary bed, the anterior pituitary capillaries. Thus, the hypothalamo-pituitary portal vessels offer a local route for blood flow directly from the hypothalamus to the anterior pituitary.

As shown in Figure 10-13B, the hypothalamo-pituitary portal vessels are not the only portal-type vessels involving the anterior pituitary. A second group—termed the short portal vessels—carries some blood directly from the posterior pituitary to the anterior pituitary. It must be emphasized that the short portal vessels carry only a small portion of the blood leaving the posterior pituitary, the rest going by a different set of vessels directly to the heart. With one important exception to be described in the next section, the short portal vessels will not be mentioned again in this book.

Posterior Pituitary Hormones

Earlier we stressed that the posterior pituitary is really a neural extension of the hypothalamus (Figure 10-13). The term "posterior pituitary hormones" is somewhat of a misnomer, therefore, since the hormones are not synthesized in the posterior pituitary itself but in the hypothalamus, specifically in the cell bodies of the hypothalamic neurons whose axons pass through the infundibulum and end in the posterior pituitary. Only one hormone is produced by any particular neuron. Enclosed in small vesicles, the hormone moves down the neural axons to accumulate at the axon terminals in the posterior pituitary. In response to an action potential in the axon, the hormone is released into the capillaries and carried away by the blood returning to the heart.

The two well-established posterior pituitary hormones are **oxytocin** and **vasopressin** (the latter is also known as **antidiuretic hormone**, or **ADH**). Vasopressin participates in the control of water excretion by the kidneys and of blood pressure (Chapters 14 and 16). Oxytocin acts on the breasts and uterus (Chapter 19).

Recent studies indicate that there are probably two other posterior pituitary hormones—the catecholamine dopamine and an as yet unidentified substance termed **prolactin releasing factor (PRF)**. Dopamine and PRF help control secretion of a hormone—prolactin—from the *anterior* pituitary (see below); this is the one case in which the short portal vessels described in the previous section are known to be important—they provide a route directly from the posterior pituitary to the anterior pituitary.

Vasopressin, oxytocin, and dopamine are also produced in other areas of the brain and serve in these locations as neurotransmitters or neuromodulators.

---

[3]In many mammalian species an intermediate lobe is found between the anterior and posterior portions of the pituitary, but this is not the case in humans.

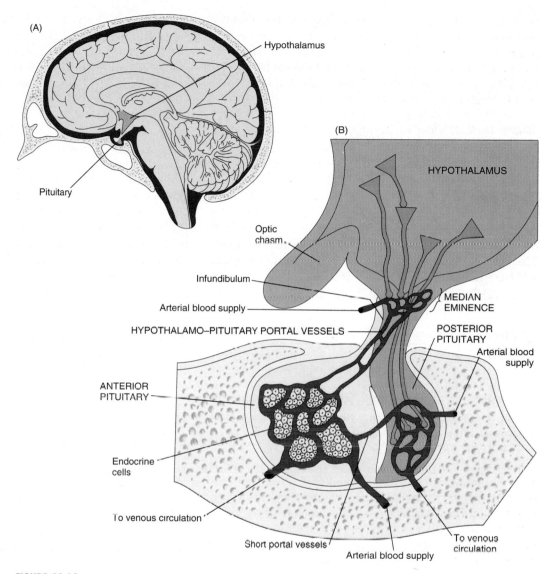

FIGURE 10-13

(A) Relation of the pituitary gland to the brain and hypothalamus. (B) Neural and vascular connections between the hypothalamus and pituitary. Some hypothalamic neurons run down the infindibulum to end in the posterior pituitary, whereas others end in the median eminence. Almost the entire blood supply of the anterior pituitary comes via the hypothalamo-pituitary portal vessels, which originate in the median eminence. The short portal vessels, which originate in the posterior pituitary, carry only a small fraction of the blood leaving the posterior pituitary and supply only a small fraction of the blood supplying the anterior pituitary.

The Hypothalamus and Anterior Pituitary

Hypothalamic neurons, in addition to producing the hormones released from the *posterior* pituitary, secrete other hormones that control, in large part, the secretion of all the *anterior* pituitary hormones. These other hypothalamic hormones are collectively termed **hypophysio-tropic hormones** (recall that another name for the pituitary is hypophysis); they are also commonly called hypothalamic releasing hormones. One more word about terminology is appropriate: "Hypophysiotropic hormones" denotes only those hormones from the *hypothalamus* that influence the anterior pituitary. We shall see later that nonhypothalamic hormones also can influence the anterior pituitary, but they are not categorized as hypophysiotropic hormones.

With one exception, each of the hypophysiotropic hormones is the beginning of a sequence of three hormones: (1) A hypophysiotropic hormone controls the secretion of (2) an anterior pituitary hormone, which controls the secretion of (3) a hormone from some other endocrine gland (Figure 10-14). This last hormone then acts on its target cells. We begin our description of these sequences in the middle, that is, with the anterior pituitary hormones, because the names and actions of the hypophysiotropic hormones are all based on the names of the anterior pituitary hormones.

Before proceeding, however, we must emphasize that the hypophysiotropic hormones are the *major* but not the *sole* controllers of anterior pituitary function. Hormones produced in locations other than the hypothalamus also exert important effects on hormone secretion by the anterior pituitary.

Anterior Pituitary Hormones. As shown in Table 10-1, the anterior pituitary secretes at least eight hormones, but only six have well-established functions. All peptides, these six "classical" hormones are **follicle-stimulating hormone (FSH)**, **luteinizing hormone (LH)**, **growth hormone (GH)**, **thyroid-stimulating hormone (TSH,** thyrotropin), **prolactin,** and **adrenocorticotropic hormone (ACTH,** corticotropin). Each of the last four is probably secreted by a distinct cell type in the anterior pituitary, whereas FSH and LH, collectively termed **gonadotropic hormones** because they stimulate the gonads, are both secreted by the same cells.

What about the other two peptides—β-lipotropin and β-endorphin—secreted by the anterior pituitary? They are initially synthesized as part of the large **pro-opiomelanocortin** molecule (Figure 10-15), which is then cleaved in the cell to form ACTH and other peptides, including **β-lipotropin**. The latter molecule is cleaved, in turn, to form the powerful opioid **β-endorphin**. Then β-lipotropin and β-endorphin, and perhaps other cleavage products as well, are cosecreted from the anterior pituitary along with ACTH. The functions of circulating β-lipotropin and β-endorphin are not presently known, but some possibilities are described in Chapters 9 and 13.

The target organs and major functions of the six classical anterior pituitary hormones are summarized in Figure 10-16. Note that the only major function of two of the six is to stimulate secretion of other hormones: Thyroid-stimulating hormone induces secretion of thyroid hormones—thyroxine and triiodothyronine—from the thyroid; adrenocorticotropic hormone, meaning "hormone that stimulates the adrenal cortex," stimulates the secretion of cortisol by that gland.

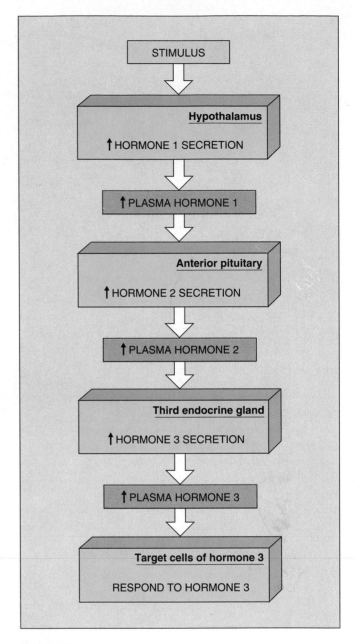

FIGURE 10-14

Typical sequential pattern by which a hypothalamic hormone controls the secretion of an anterior pituitary hormone, which in turn controls the secretion of a hormone by a third endocrine gland. As will be described later (Figures 10-20 through 10-23), the second and third hormones in the sequence usually also exert feedback effects on the sequence.

Three other anterior pituitary hormones also stimulate secretion of another hormone but have an additional function as well: Follicle-stimulating hormone and luteinizing hormone stimulate secretion of the sex hormones—

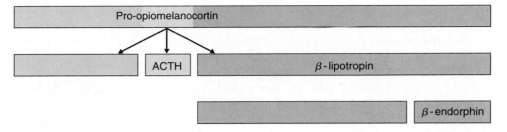

FIGURE 10-15

After its synthesis in the anterior pituitary, the pro-opiomelanocortin molecule is successively cleaved to yield ACTH and other peptides, the most important of which is β-endorphin, an endogenous opiod. The other peptides are cosecreted with ACTH. For simplicity, several of the peptides resulting from the cleavages have not been named in the figure; they are represented by empty boxes.

estradiol, progesterone, and testosterone—by the gonads and, in addition, regulate the growth and development of sperm and ova. Growth hormone stimulates the liver and many other body cells to secrete a growth-promoting peptide hormone known as **insulin-like growth factor I (IGF-I**, also called somatomedin C) and, in addition, exerts direct effects on the metabolism of protein, carbohydrate, and lipid by various organs and tissues (Chapter 18).

Prolactin is unique among the anterior pituitary hormones in that it does not exert major control over the secretion of a hormone by another endocrine gland. Rather, its most important action is to stimulate develop-

ment of the mammary glands and milk production by direct effects upon the breasts. In the male, prolactin may facilitate several components of reproductive function.

It should be emphasized that many, perhaps all, of the anterior pituitary hormones are also secreted by cells elsewhere in the body and may, in those other sites, exert functions (as neurotransmitters, neuromodulators, or paracrine agents) quite different from those summarized in Figure 10-16.

Hypophysiotropic Hormones. As stated above, secretion of the anterior pituitary hormones is largely regulated

FIGURE 10-16

Targets and major functions of the six classical anterior pituitary hormones.

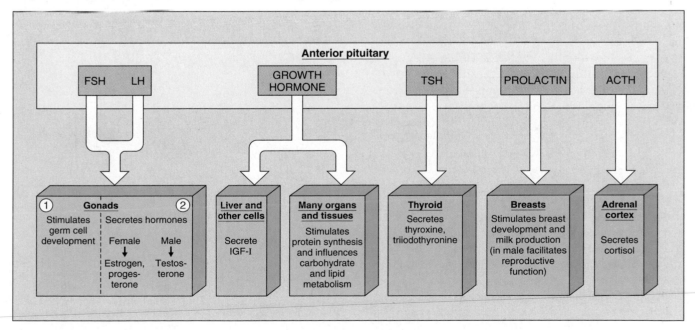

by hormones produced by the hypothalamus and collectively called hypophysiotropic hormones. These hormones are secreted by neurons that originate in diverse areas of the hypothalamus and terminate in the median eminence around the capillaries that are the origins of the hypothalamo-pituitary portal vessels. The generation of action potentials in these neurons causes them to release their hormones, which enter the capillaries and are carried to the anterior pituitary by the hypothalamo-pituitary portal vessels (Figure 10-17). There they act upon the various anterior pituitary cells to control their hormone secretions.

Thus, these hypothalamic neurons secrete hormones in a manner identical to that described previously for the hypothalamic neurons whose axons end in the posterior pituitary. In both cases the hormones are made in hypothalamic neurons, pass down axons to the neuron terminals, and are released in response to action potentials in the neurons. The crucial differences, however, between the two systems need emphasizing: (1) The axons of the hypothalamic neurons that secrete the posterior pituitary hormones leave the hypothalamus and end in the posterior pituitary, whereas those that secrete the hypophysiotropic hormones remain in the hypothalamus, ending in its median eminence. (2) Most of the posterior pituitary capillaries, into which the posterior pituitary hormones are secreted, immediately drain into the main bloodstream, which carries the hormones to the heart to be distributed to the entire body.[4] In contrast, the capillaries entered by the hypophysiotropic hormones in the median eminence of the hypothalamus do not directly join the main bloodstream but empty into the hypothalamo-pituitary portal vessels, which provide a direct route to the anterior pituitary (from which the blood then returns to the heart). Thus, the anterior pituitary is uniquely exposed to plasma concentrations of the hypophysiotropic hormones much higher than those existing in systemic arterial plasma.

There are multiple discrete hypophysiotropic hormones, each secreted by a particular group of hypotha-

---

[4]Some blood, as described earlier in the text, does go directly to the anterior pituitary via a set of "short portal vessels" connecting the posterior and anterior pituitaries.

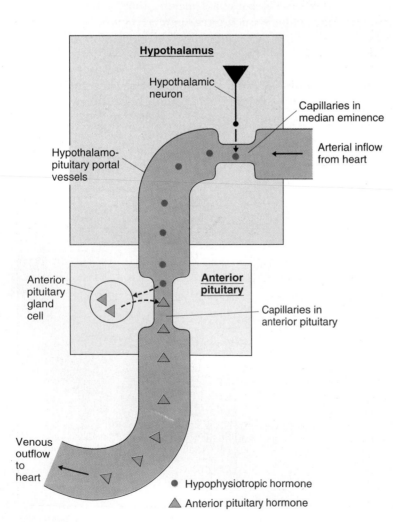

FIGURE 10-17

Hormone secretion by the anterior pituitary is controlled by hypophysiotropic hormones released by hypothalamic neurons and reaching the anterior pituitary by way of the hypothalamo-pituitary portal vessels.

lamic neurons and influencing the release of one or more of the anterior pituitary hormones. For simplicity, Figure 10-18 and this chapter summarize only those hypophysiotropic hormones that are known to play important roles and whose structures have been identified.[5] Each is named according to an anterior pituitary hormone whose secretion it controls; for example, the secretion of growth hormone is stimulated by **growth hormone releasing hormone (GHRH)**, and the secretion of ACTH is stimulated by **corticotropin releasing hormone (CRH)**.[6]

---

[5]A variety of other substances, some of which have not yet been identified, very likely function as hypophysiotropic hormones, but their precise contributions remain to be determined.

[6]Interestingly, the hypothalamic neurons that secrete CRH cosecrete vasopressin, which also stimulates ACTH secretion. Thus vasopressin is secreted not only by neurons that end in the posterior pituitary but also by neurons that end in the median eminence.

As shown in Figure 10-18, at least two of the hypophysiotropic hormones do not cause *release* of anterior pituitary hormones but rather *inhibit* their release. One of them inhibits secretion of growth hormone and is most commonly called **somatostatin (SS)**. The other—dopamine (also termed, in this location, prolactin inhibiting hormone)—inhibits secretion of prolactin. Here is a potential source of confusion: We mentioned earlier in this chapter that dopamine is released from the *posterior pituitary* and is therefore a posterior pituitary hormone; now we have stated that dopamine is also released from the median eminence of the hypothalamus and is therefore also a hypophysiotropic hormone. This should reinforce the generalization, made several times already, that a single hormone is often produced in multiple sites.

As also shown in Figure 10-18, there is not a strict one-to-one correspondence of hypophysiotropic hormone and anterior pituitary hormone. For one thing, in at least three

FIGURE 10-18

Major known hypophysiotropic hormones and their effects on the anterior pituitary.

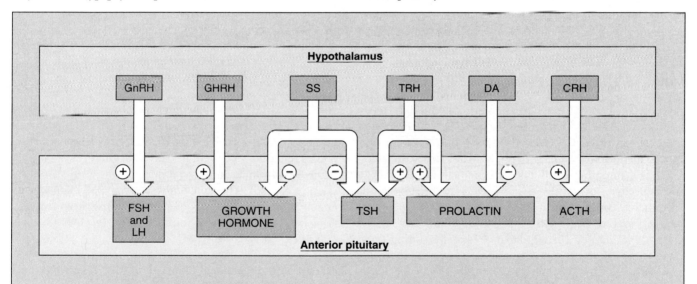

Major, known hypophysiotropic hormones	Effect on anterior pituitary
Corticotropin releasing hormone (CRH)	Stimulates secretion of ACTH
Thyrotropin releasing hormone (TRH)	Stimulates secretion of TSH and prolactin
Growth hormone releasing hormone (GHRH)	Stimulates secretion of GH
Somatostatin (SS, also known as growth hormone release inhibiting hormone, GIH)	Inhibits secretion of GH and TSH (and possibly several other hormones)
Gonadotropin releasing hormone (GnRH)	Stimulates secretion of LH and FSH
Dopamine (DA, also known as prolactin release inhibiting hormone, PIH)°	Inhibits secretion of prolactin

°Dopamine is a catecholamine; all the other hypophysiotropic hormones are peptides.

cases, a hypophysiotropic hormone influences the secretion of more than one anterior pituitary hormone: (1) **gonadotropin releasing hormone (GnRH)** stimulates the secretion of both FSH and LH, (2) **thyrotropin releasing hormone (TRH)** stimulates the secretion not only of TSH but of prolactin as well, and (3) somatostatin inhibits the secretion not only of growth hormone but also of TSH.[7]

The cases described in the previous paragraph are of a single hypophysiotropic hormone controlling more than one anterior pituitary hormone, but Figure 10-18 also shows that in at least three cases—growth hormone, TSH and prolactin—secretion of a single anterior pituitary hormone is controlled by more than one hypophysiotropic hormone. Moreover, the several hypophysiotropic hormones involved may exert opposing effects. Thus, as we have seen, the secretion of growth hormone is controlled by two hypophysiotropic hormones—somatostatin, which inhibits its release, and growth hormone releasing hormone, which stimulates it. In such multiple-control cases, the anterior pituitary response depends upon the relative amounts of the opposing hormones released by the hypothalamic neurons, as well as upon the relative sensitivities of the anterior pituitary to them.

Control of prolactin secretion offers a further example of this generalization. As shown in Figure 10-18, the hypothalamus secretes two established hypophysiotropic hormones—TRH and dopamine—that influence prolactin secretion. TRH stimulates prolactin secretion (just as it does TSH secretion), whereas dopamine inhibits it. In addition, not shown in the figure, there is evidence for at least one other, as-yet-unidentified, hypophysiotropic hormone, distinct from TRH, that stimulates prolactin secretion. The important point is that under basal conditions the inhibitory hormone—dopamine—is dominant over all stimulatory inputs from the hypothalamus (and elsewhere), and so prolactin secretion is quite low. As described in Chapter 19, this balance changes during pregnancy and lactation, and prolactin secretion increases markedly.

With one exception, all the known hypophysiotropic hormones are peptides. These peptides all also occur in locations other than the hypothalamus, particularly in other areas of the central nervous system, where they function as neurotransmitters or neuromodulators, and in the gastrointestinal tract. The one hypophysiotropic hormone that is not a peptide is dopamine. As described earlier, this substance is a member of the catecholamine family.

---

[7]Somatostatin can also inhibit several other anterior pituitary hormones, although whether these inhibitory effects are physiological is still not clear.

Figure 10-19 summarizes the information presented in Figures 10-16 and 10-18 to demonstrate the full sequences controlled by the hypothalamus.

Given that the hypophysiotropic hormones control anterior pituitary function, we must now ask: What controls secretion of the hypophysiotropic hormones? Some of the neurons that secrete hypophysiotropic hormones may possess spontaneous activity, but the firing of most of them requires neuronal and hormonal input. First, let us deal with the neuronal input.

Neural Control of Hypophysiotropic Hormones. The hypothalamus receives synaptic input, both stimulatory and inhibitory, from virtually all areas of the central nervous system, and specific neural pathways influence secretion of the individual releasing hormones. A large number of neurotransmitters, including the catecholamines, acetylcholine, and β-endorphin, are used at the synapses on the hormone-secreting hypothalamic neurons, and this explains why the secretion of the hypophysiotropic hormones can be altered by drugs that influence these neurotransmitters.

Figure 10-20 illustrates one example of the role of neural input to the hypothalamus. Corticotropin releasing hormone (CRH), secreted by the hypothalamus, stimulates the anterior pituitary to secrete ACTH, which in turn stimulates the adrenal cortex to secrete cortisol. A wide variety of stresses, both physical and emotional, act via neural pathways to the hypothalamus to increase CRH secretion and, hence, ACTH and cortisol secretion, markedly above basal values. Thus, stress is the common denominator of reflexes leading to increased cortisol secretion. Cortisol then functions to facilitate an individual's response to stress. Even in an unstressed person, however, the secretion of cortisol varies in a highly stereotyped manner during a 24-h period because neural rhythms within the central nervous system also impinge upon the hypothalamic neurons that secrete CRH.

Hormonal Feedback Control of the Hypothalamus and Anterior Pituitary. A prominent feature of each of the hormonal sequences initiated by the hypophysiotropic hormones is negative feedback exerted upon the hypothalamo-pituitary system by one or more of the hormones in the sequence. For example, in the CRH-ACTH-cortisol sequence (Figure 10-20), the final hormone—cortisol—acts upon the hypothalamus to reduce secretion of CRH by causing a decrease in the frequency of action potentials in the neurons secreting CRH. In addition, cortisol acts directly on the anterior pituitary to reduce the response of the ACTH-secreting cells to CRH. Thus, by a double-barreled action, cortisol exerts a negative-feedback control over its own secretion.

Such a system is effective in dampening hormonal re-

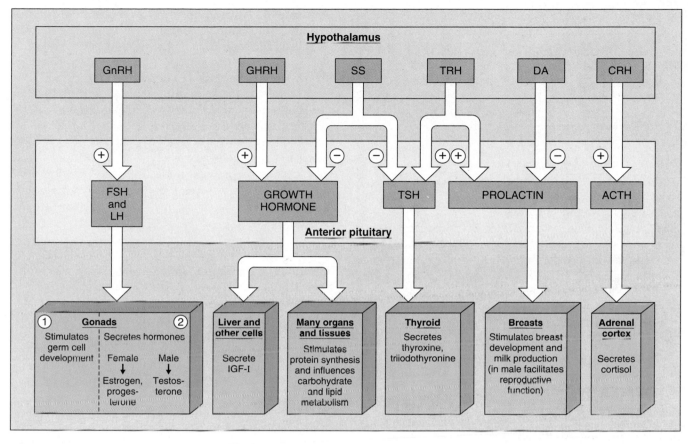

FIGURE 10-19

A combination of Figures 10-16 and 10-18 summarizes the hypothalamic anterior-pituitary system.

sponses, that is, in limiting the extremes of hormone secretory rates. For example, when a painful stimulus elicits increased secretion of CRH, ACTH, and cortisol, the resulting elevation in plasma cortisol concentration feeds back to inhibit the hypothalamus and anterior pituitary. Therefore, cortisol secretion does not rise as much as it would without these negative feedbacks.

Another adaptive function of these negative feedbacks is that they maintain the plasma concentration of the final hormone in a sequence relatively constant whenever a primary change occurs in the metabolism of that hormone. An example of this is shown in Figure 10-21 for cortisol.

Another example is provided by the TRH-TSH-TH system. The thyroid hormones (TH) exert a feedback inhibition on the hypothalamo-pituitary system, mainly by decreasing the response of TSH-secreting cells to the stimulatory effects of TRH. Since iodine is essential for the synthesis of TH, individuals with iodine deficiencies tend to have a deficient production of TH. The resulting decrease in plasma TH concentration relieves some of the feedback inhibition TH exerts on the pituitary. Therefore, more TSH is secreted in response to the TRH coming from the hypothalamus, and the increased plasma TSH

stimulates the thyroid gland to enlarge and to utilize more efficiently whatever iodine is available (the enlarged gland is known as *iodine-deficient goiter*). In this manner, plasma TH concentration can be kept quite close to normal.

The situations described above for cortisol and the thyroid hormones, in which the hormone secreted by the third endocrine gland in a sequence exerts a negative-feedback effect over the anterior pituitary and/or hypothalamus, is known as a **long-loop negative feedback** (Figure 10-22). This type of feedback exists for each of the five three-hormone sequences initiated by a hypophysiotropic hormone.

Long-loop feedback cannot exist for prolactin since this is the one anterior pituitary hormone that does not have major control over another endocrine gland; that is, it does not participate in a three-hormone sequence. Nonetheless, there is negative feedback in the prolactin system, for this hormone itself acts upon the hypothalamus to influence the secretion of at least one—dopamine—of the hypothalamic hormones that control its secretion. This influence of an anterior pituitary hormone on the hypothalamus is known as a **short-loop negative feedback** (Figure

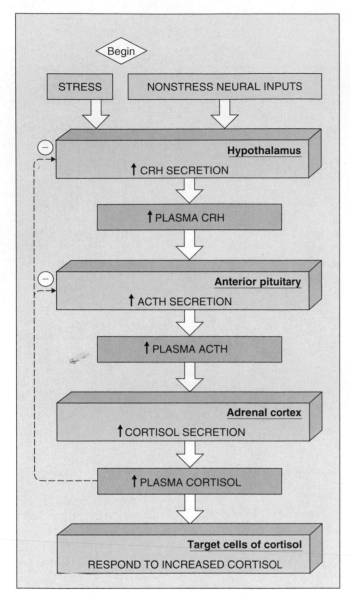

FIGURE 10-20

CRH-ACTH-cortisol sequence. The "stress" input to the hypothalamus is via neural pathways. Cortisol exerts a negative feedback control over the system by acting on (1) the hypothalamus to inhibit CRH secretion and (2) the anterior pituitary to reduce responsiveness to CRH. Not shown is that vasopressin and other messengers released both by hypothalamic neurons and by peripheral tissues also act on the anterior pituitary to stimulate ACTH secretion. The common denominator of many of the effects of cortisol is to increase plasma glucose concentration and to facilitate a person's responses to stress (Chapters 18 and 20).

10-22). Several anterior pituitary hormones (growth hormone, for example) other than prolactin also exert such feedback on the hypothalamus.

The Role of "Nonsequence" Hormones on the Hypothalamus and Anterior Pituitary. It must be emphasized that there are many hormonal influences, both stimulatory and inhibitory, on the secretion of hormones by the hypothalamus and/or anterior pituitary other than those that fit the feedback patterns just described. In other words, a hormone that is not itself in a particular hormonal sequence may nevertheless exert important influences on the secretion of the hypothalamic or anterior pituitary hormones in that sequence. For example, estrogen markedly enhances the secretion of prolactin by the anterior pituitary, even though estrogen secretion is not controlled by prolactin. Thus, one should not view these sequences as isolated units.

A Summary Example: Control of Growth Hormone Secretion. The three-hormone sequences beginning in the hypothalamus can be extremely complex, incorporating multiple sites of feedback, both long-loop and short-loop, as well as other hormones not in the sequence. Purely for the sake of illustrating this complexity, we describe here the control of growth hormone secretion (Figure 10-23), building upon the information already presented in this chapter.

Recall from Figure 10-18 that the secretion of GH by the anterior pituitary is controlled mainly by two hormones from the hypothalamus: (1) somatostatin, which inhibits GH secretion; and (2) GHRH, which stimulates it. With such a dual control system, the rate of GH secretion at any moment reflects the relative amounts of simultaneous stimulation by GHRH and inhibition by somatostatin. For example, as shown in Figure 10-9, very little growth hormone is secreted during the day in nonstressed persons who are eating normally, and whether this reflects a very low secretion of GHRH or a very high secretion of somatostatin is not yet clear. Similarly, a large number of physiological states (exercise, stress, fasting, a low plasma glucose concentration, and sleep) stimulate growth hormone secretion by decreasing the secretion of somatostatin and/or increasing that of GHRH.

As shown in Figures 10-16 and 10-19, growth hormone stimulates the secretion of another hormone, IGF-I, from the liver and many other target cells of GH. This makes possible a variety of feedbacks by which an increase in plasma GH results in inhibition of GH secretion (Figure 10-23): (1) a short-loop negative feedback exerted by GH on the hypothalamus, and (2) a long-loop negative feedback exerted by IGF-I on the hypothalamus. Both of these feedbacks operate by inhibiting secretion of GHRH and/or stimulating secretion of somatostatin, the result in either case being less stimulation of GH secretion. In addition, (3) IGF-I also acts directly on the pituitary to inhibit the stimulatory effect of GHRH on GH secretion; again, the result is decreased GH secretion.

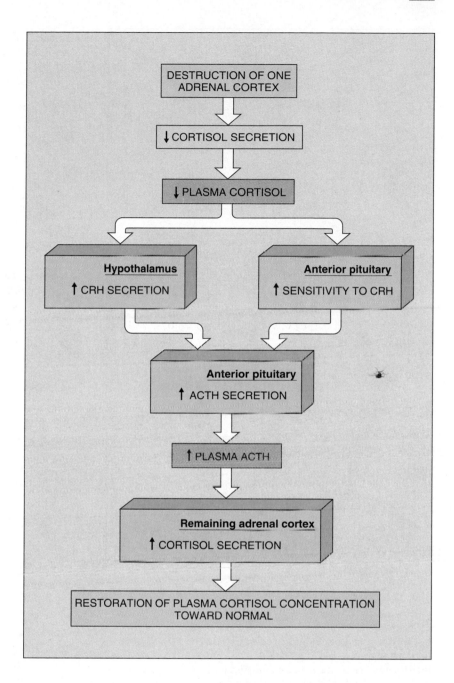

FIGURE 10-21

Example of how negative feedback in a hormonal sequence helps maintain the plasma concentration of the final hormone when disease-induced changes in hormone secretion occur. The same analysis would apply if the original reduction in plasma cortisol were due to excessive metabolism of cortisol rather than deficient secretion.

Finally, the secretion of growth hormone is influenced by several other hormones not in the sequence, for example, by the sex hormones. Some of these hormones may affect the sequence indirectly by altering the release of somatostatin and/or GHRH from the hypothalamus, whereas others may act directly upon the anterior pituitary.

CANDIDATE HORMONES

Many substances, termed **candidate hormones**, are suspected of being hormones in humans but are not considered classical hormones for one of two rea-

sons: Either (1) their functions have not been conclusively documented; or (2) they have well-documented functions as paracrine and autocrine agents, but it is not certain that they ever reach additional target cells via the blood, an essential criterion for classification as a hormone. This second category includes certain of the eicosanoids (Chapter 7) and a large number of what are called growth factors (Chapter 18) that are secreted by multiple cell types and stimulate specific cells to differentiate and undergo cell division.

A substance that fits the first category described above is the amino acid derivative **melatonin**, which is synthesized from serotonin. This candidate hormone is produced by the **pineal gland** (also known as the pineal body), an

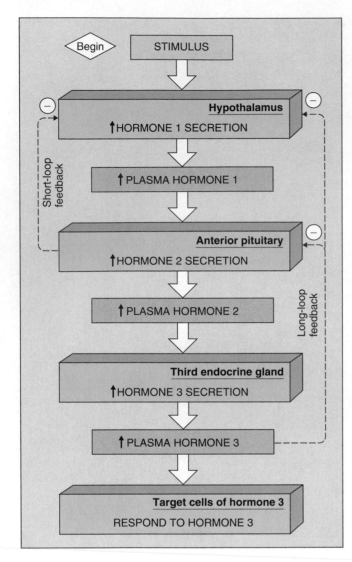

FIGURE 10-22

Short-loop and long-loop feedbacks. Long-loop feedback is exerted on the hypothalamus and/or anterior pituitary by the third hormone in the sequence. Short-loop feedback is exerted by the anterior pituitary hormone on the hypothalamus. A third type of negative feedback, not shown in the figure, is that the action of hormone 3 may eliminate the original stimulus for the secretion of hormone 1.

outgrowth from the roof of the diencephalon of the brain (see Figure 8-37). The function of melatonin and the pineal gland in humans, in contrast to several other animals, is uncertain. Its secretion is stimulated by sympathetic postganglionic neurons that constitute the last link in a neuronal chain primarily triggered by receptors in the eyes responding to the prevailing light-dark environment. Melatonin secretion, therefore, undergoes a marked 24-h cycle, being high at night and low during the day, and melatonin probably influences a variety of body rhythms.

Its relationship to **seasonal affective disorder** ("winter depression"), its ability to reduce the symptoms of jet lag, and its possible role in the onset of puberty are all being studied.

TYPES OF ENDOCRINE DISORDERS

Most endocrine disorders fall into one of three categories: (1) too little hormone (**hyposecretion**), (2) too much hormone (**hypersecretion**), and (3) reduced response of the target cells (**hyporesponsiveness**). The phrases "too little hormone" and "too much hormone" here mean "too little" or "too much" for any given physiological situation. For example, as we shall see, insulin secretion decreases during fasting, and this decrease is an adaptive physiological response, not too little insulin. In contrast, insulin secretion should increase after eating, and if its increase is less than normal, this is too little hormone secretion.

Hyposecretion

An endocrine gland may be secreting too little hormone because the gland is not able to function normally. This is termed **primary hyposecretion**. Examples of primary hyposecretion include (1) genetic absence of a steroid-forming enzyme, leading to decreased cortisol secretion, and (2) dietary deficiency of iodine, leading to decreased secretion of thyroid hormones. There are many other causes—infections, toxic chemicals, and so on—all having the common denominator of damaging the endocrine gland.

In contrast to primary hyposecretion, a gland may be secreting too little hormone not because the gland is abnormal but because there is not enough of its tropic hormone. This is termed **secondary hyposecretion**. For example, there may be nothing wrong with the thyroid gland, but it may be secreting too little thyroid hormone because the secretion of TSH by the anterior pituitary is abnormally low. Thus, the hyposecretion by the thyroid gland in this case is secondary to inadequate secretion by the anterior pituitary.

This example raises the next question applicable to any of the other anterior pituitary hormones as well: Is the hyposecretion of TSH primary, that is, due to a defect in the anterior pituitary, or is it secondary to a hypothalamic defect causing too little secretion of TRH? If the latter were true, then we would have the following sequence: primary hyposecretion of TRH leading to secondary hyposecretion of TSH leading to secondary hyposecretion of TH.

In diagnosing the presence of hyposecretion, a basic measurement to be made is the concentration of the

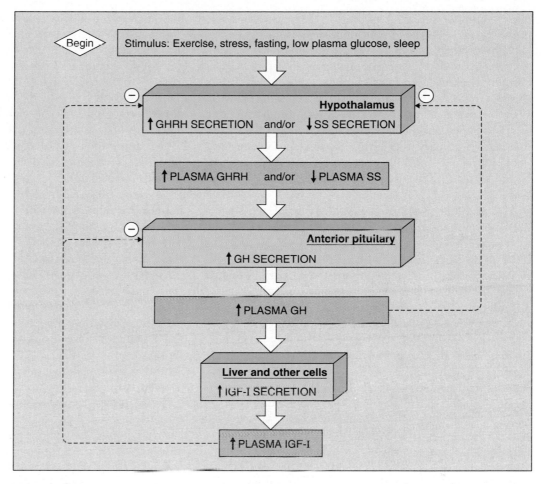

FIGURE 10-23

Hormonal pathways controlling the secretion of growth hormone (GH) and insulin-like growth factor I (IGF-I). At the hypothalamus, the minus sign (−) denotes that the input inhibits the secretion of growth hormone releasing hormone (GHRH) and/or stimulates the release of somatostatin (SS). Not shown in the figure is that several hormones (for example, the thyroid hormones) influence growth hormone secretion via effects on the hypothalamus and/or anterior pituitary.

hormone in either plasma or urine. The finding of a low concentration will not distinguish between primary and secondary hyposecretion, however. To do this, the concentration of the relevant tropic hormone must also be measured. Thus, in our example, if the hyposecretion of TH is secondary to hyposecretion of TSH, then the plasma concentrations of both will be decreased. If the hyposecretion of TH is primary, then TH concentration will be decreased and TSH concentration will be increased because of less negative-feedback inhibition by TH over TSH secretion.

Another diagnostic approach is to attempt to stimulate the gland in question by administering either its tropic hormone or some other substance known to elicit increased secretion. The increase in hormone secretion elicited by the stimulus will be normal if the original hyposecretion is secondary, but less than normal if primary hyposecretion is the problem.

The most common means of treating hormone hyposecretion is to administer the hormone that is missing or present in too small amounts. In cases of secondary hyposecretion, there is a choice since at least two hormones are involved. In our example, the TH deficiency could theoretically be eliminated by administering either TH or TSH.

Hypersecretion

A hormone can also undergo either **_primary hypersecretion_** (the gland is secreting too much of the hormone on its own) or **_secondary hypersecretion_** (there is excessive stimulation of the gland by its tropic hormone). One of the most common causes of primary hypersecretion is the presence of a hormone-secreting endocrine-cell tumor.

The diagnosis of primary versus secondary hypersecretion of a particular hormone is analogous to that of hyposecretion. The concentrations of the hormone and, if relevant, its tropic hormone are measured in plasma or urine. If both concentrations are elevated, then the hormone in question is being secondarily hypersecreted. If the hypersecretion is primary, there will be a decreased concentration of the tropic hormone because of negative feedback by the high concentration of the hormone being hypersecreted.

When an endocrine tumor is the cause of hypersecretion, it can often be removed surgically or destroyed with radiation. In many cases hypersecretion can also be blocked by drugs that inhibit the hormone's synthesis. Alternatively, the situation can be treated with drugs that do not alter the hormone's secretion but instead block the hormone's actions on its target cells.

Hyporesponsiveness and Hyperresponsiveness

In some cases, the endocrine system may be dysfunctioning even though there is nothing wrong with hormone secretion. The problem is that the target cells do not respond normally to the hormone. This condition is termed hyporesponsiveness. An important example of a disease resulting from hyporesponsiveness, in this case to insulin, is the major form of diabetes mellitus ("sugar diabetes").

One cause of hyporesponsiveness is either a lack or deficiency of receptors for the hormone. For example, certain men have a genetic defect manifested by the absence of receptors for dihydrotestosterone, the form of testosterone active in many target cells. In such men, these cells are unable to bind dihydrotestosterone, and the result is lack of development of certain male characteristics, just as though the hormone were not being produced.

In a second type of hyporesponsiveness the receptors for a hormone may be normal, but some event occurring after the hormone binds to receptors may be defective. For example, the activated receptor might be unable to stimulate formation of cyclic AMP or open a plasma-membrane channel.

A third cause of hyporesponsiveness applies to hormones that require metabolic activation by some other tissue after secretion. There may be a lack or deficiency of the enzymes that catalyze the activation. For example, some men secrete testosterone normally and have normal receptors for dihydrotestosterone but are missing the enzyme that converts testosterone to dihydrotestosterone. The result is the same as in the case in which there are no dihydrotestosterone receptors.

In situations characterized by hyporesponsiveness to a hormone, the plasma concentration of the hormone in question is normal or elevated, but the response to administered hormone is diminished.

Finally, in a few cases *hyperresponsiveness* to a hormone can occur and cause problems. For example, the thyroid hormones cause an up-regulation of the beta-adrenergic receptors for epinephrine, and so a primary or secondary hyperthyroidism causes in turn a hyperresponsiveness to epinephrine.

SUMMARY

I. The endocrine system is one of the body's two major communications systems. It consists of all the glands that secrete hormones, which are chemical messengers carried by the blood from the endocrine glands to target cells elsewhere in the body.

HORMONE STRUCTURES AND SYNTHESIS

I. The amine hormones are the iodine-containing thyroid hormones—thyroxine and triiodothyronine—and the catecholamines secreted by the adrenal medulla, the hypothalamus, and the posterior pituitary.

II. The majority of hormones are peptides, many of which are synthesized as larger molecules, which are then cleaved.

III. Steroid hormones are produced from cholesterol by the adrenal cortex and the gonads, and by the placenta during pregnancy.

A. The most important steroid hormones produced by the adrenal cortex are the mineralocorticoid aldosterone, the glucocorticoid cortisol, and two androgens.

B. The ovaries produce mainly estradiol and progesterone, and the testes mainly testosterone.

HORMONE TRANSPORT IN THE BLOOD

I. Peptide hormones and catecholamines circulate dissolved in the plasma water, but steroid and thyroid hormones circulate mainly bound to plasma proteins.

HORMONE METABOLISM AND EXCRETION

I. The liver and kidneys are the major organs that remove hormones from the plasma by metabolizing or excreting them.

II. The peptide hormones and catecholamines are rapidly removed from the blood, whereas the steroid and thyroid hormones are removed more slowly.

III. After their secretion, some hormones are metabolized to more active molecules in their target cells or other organs.

MECHANISMS OF HORMONE ACTION

I. The receptors for steroid and thyroid hormones are inside the target cells; those for the peptide hormones and catecholamines are on the plasma membrane.

II. Hormones can cause up-regulation and down-regulation of their own receptors and those of other hormones. The induction of one hormone's receptors by another hormone increases the first hormone's effectiveness and may be essential to permit the first hormone to exert its effects.

III. Receptors activated by peptide hormones and catecholamines utilize one or more of the signal transduction mechanisms available to plasma membrane receptors; the result is altered activity of proteins in the cell.

IV. Intracellular receptors activated by steroid and thyroid hormones combine with DNA in the nucleus and induce the transcription of DNA into mRNA; the result is increased synthesis of particular proteins.

V. In pharmacological doses, hormones can have effects not seen under ordinary circumstances.

TYPES OF INPUTS THAT CONTROL HORMONE SECRETION

I. The secretion of a hormone may be controlled by the plasma concentration of an ion or nutrient that the hormone regulates, by neural input to the endocrine cells, and by a tropic hormone.

II. The autonomic nervous system is the neural input controlling many hormones, but the hypothalamic and posterior pituitary hormones are controlled by neurons in the brain.

CONTROL SYSTEMS INVOLVING THE HYPOTHALAMUS AND PITUITARY

I. The pituitary gland, comprising the anterior pituitary and the posterior pituitary, is connected to the hypothalamus by a stalk containing nerve fibers and blood vessels.

II. The nerve fibers, which originate in the hypothalamus and terminate in the posterior pituitary, secrete oxytocin, vasopressin, dopamine, and a prolactin releasing factor.

III. The anterior pituitary secretes growth hormone (GH), thyroid-stimulating hormone (TSH), adrenocorticotropic hormone (ACTH), prolactin, and two gonadotropic hormones—follicle-stimulating hormone (FSH) and luteinizing hormone (LH). The functions of these hormones are summarized in Figure 10-16.

IV. The anterior pituitary also produces β-lipotropin and β-endorphin along with ACTH, all being portions of the parent pro-opiomelanocortin molecule.

V. Secretion of the anterior pituitary hormones is controlled mainly by hypophysiotropic hormones secreted into capillaries in the median eminence of the hypothalamus and reaching the anterior pituitary via the portal vessels connecting the hypothalamus and anterior pituitary. The actions of the hypophysiotropic hormones on the anterior pituitary are summarized in Figure 10-18.

VI. The secretion of each hypophysiotropic hormone is controlled by neuronal and hormonal input to the hypothalamic neurons producing it.
A. In each of the three-hormone sequences beginning with a hypophysiotropic hormone, the third hormone exerts a long-loop, negative-feedback effect on the secretion of the hypothalamic and/or anterior pituitary hormone.
B. The anterior pituitary hormone may exert a short-loop, negative-feedback inhibition of the hypothalamic releasing hormone(s) controlling it.
C. Hormones not in a particular sequence can also influence secretion of the hypothalamic and/or anterior pituitary hormones in that sequence.

CANDIDATE HORMONES

I. Substances that are suspected of functioning as hormones but have not yet been proven to do so are called candidate hormones.

II. Melatonin is a hormone secreted with a 24-h rhythm by the pineal gland, an outgrowth of the diencephalon, but its functions in humans are uncertain.

TYPES OF ENDOCRINE DISORDERS

I. Endocrine disorders may be classified as hyposecretion, hypersecretion, and target-cell hyporesponsiveness or hyperresponsiveness.

A. Primary disorders are those in which the defect is in the cells that secrete the hormone.
B. Secondary disorders are those in which there is too much or too little tropic hormone.
C. Hyporesponsiveness is due to an alteration in the receptors for the hormone, to disordered postreceptor events, or to failure of normal metabolic activation of the hormone in those cases requiring such activation.

II. These disorders can be distinguished by measurements of the hormone and any tropic hormones under both basal conditions and during experimental stimulation or suppression of the hormone's secretion.

KEY TERMS

endocrine system
endocrine glands
hormones
target cells
neurohormones
amine hormones
thyroid gland
thyroxine (T_4)
triiodothyronine (T_3)
thyroid hormones (TH)
iodine
thyroglobulin
adrenal gland
adrenal medulla
adrenal cortex
epinephrine (E)
norepinephrine (NE)
dopamine (DA)
catecholamines
peptide hormones
prohormones
steroid hormones
gonads
aldosterone
mineralocorticoid
cortisol
glucocorticoids
androgens
testosterone
estradiol
progesterone
up-regulation
down-regulation
permissiveness
tropic hormone
pituitary gland
hypothalamus
anterior pituitary
posterior pituitary

median eminence
hypothalamo-pituitary portal vessels
oxytocin
vasopressin
antidiuretic hormone (ADH)
prolactin releasing factor (PRF)
hypophysiotropic hormones
follicle-stimulating hormone (FSH)
luteinizing hormone (LH)
growth hormone (GH)
thyroid-stimulating hormone (TSH)
prolactin
adrenocorticotropic hormone (ACTH)
gonadotropic hormones
pro-opiomelanocortin
β-lipotropin
β-endorphin
insulin-like growth factor I (IGF-I)
growth hormone releasing hormone (GHRH)
corticotropin releasing hormone (CRH)
somatostatin (SS)
gonadotropin releasing hormone (GnRH)
thyrotropin releasing hormone (TRH)
long-loop negative feedback
short-loop negative feedback
candidate hormones
melatonin
pineal gland

REVIEW QUESTIONS

1. What are three general chemical classes of hormones?
2. What essential nutrient is needed for synthesis of the thyroid hormones?
3. Which catecholamine is secreted in the largest amount by the adrenal medulla?
4. What are the major hormones produced by the adrenal cortex? By the testes? By the ovaries?
5. Which classes of hormones are carried in the blood mainly as unbound, dissolved hormone? Mainly bound to plasma proteins?
6. Do protein-bound hormones cross capillary walls?
7. Which organs are the major sites of hormone excretion and metabolic transformation?
8. How do the rates of metabolism and excretion differ for the various classes of hormones?
9. What must some hormones undergo after their secretion to become activated?
10. Contrast the locations of receptors for the various classes of hormones.
11. How do hormones influence the concentrations of their own receptors and those of other hormones? How does this explain permissiveness in hormone action?
12. Describe the sequence of events when steroid or thyroid hormones bind to their receptors.
13. Describe the sequence of events when peptide or catecholamine hormones bind to their receptors.
14. What are the four types of direct inputs to endocrine glands controlling hormone secretion?
15. How does control of hormone secretion by plasma mineral ions and nutrients achieve negative-feedback control of these substances?
16. What roles does the autonomic nervous system play in controlling hormone secretion?
17. What groups of hormones receive input from neurons located in the brain rather than in the autonomic nervous system?
18. Describe the anatomical relationships between the hypothalamus and the pituitary.
19. Name the two well-established posterior pituitary hormones and describe their site of synthesis and mechanism of release. Name two other posterior pituitary hormones.
20. List the six well-established anterior pituitary hormones and their functions; list two other anterior pituitary hormones and their biochemical origin.
21. List the major hypophysiotropic hormones and the hormone(s) whose release each controls.
22. What kinds of inputs control secretion of the hypophysiotropic hormones?
23. Diagram the CRH-ACTH-cortisol system.
24. What is the difference between long-loop and short-loop negative feedback in the hypothalamo-anterior pituitary system?
25. How would you distinguish between primary and secondary hyposecretion of a hormone? Between hyposecretion and hyporesponsiveness?

CLINICAL TERMS

pharmacological effects
iodine-deficient goiter
seasonal affective disorder
hyposecretion
hypersecretion
hyporesponsiveness

primary hyposecretion
secondary hyposecretion
primary hypersecretion
secondary hypersecretion
hyperresponsiveness

THOUGHT QUESTIONS

(Answers are given in Appendix A.)

1. In an experimental animal the sympathetic preganglionic fibers to the adrenal medulla are cut. What happens to the plasma concentration of epinephrine at rest and during stress?

2. During pregnancy there is an increase in both the production (by the liver) and the plasma concentration of the major plasma binding protein for the thyroid hormones (TH). This causes a sequence of events involving feedback that results in an increase in the plasma concentration of TH but no evidence of hyperthyroidism. Describe the sequence of events.

3. A child shows the following symptoms: deficient growth, failure to show sexual development, decreased ability to respond to stress. What is the most likely source of all these symptoms?

4. If all the neural connections between the hypothalamus and pituitary were severed, the secretion of which pituitary hormones would be affected? Which pituitary hormones would not be affected?

5. An antibody to a peptide combines with the peptide and renders it nonfunctional. If an animal were given an antibody to somatostatin, the secretion of which anterior pituitary hormones would change and in what direction?

6. A drug that blocks the action of norepinephrine is injected directly into the hypothalamus of an experimental animal, and the secretion rates of several anterior pituitary hormones are observed to change. How is this possible, since norepinephrine is not a hypophysiotropic hormone?

7. A person is receiving very large doses of a cortisol-like drug to treat her arthritis. What happens to her secretion of cortisol?

8. A person with symptoms of hypothyroidism (for example, sluggishness and intolerance to cold) is found to have abnormally low plasma concentrations of T_4, T_3, and TSH. After an injection of TRH the plasma concentrations of all three hormones increase. Where is the site of the defect leading to the hypothyroidism?

CHAPTER

11

MUSCLE

SECTION A. SKELETAL MUSCLE

STRUCTURE

MOLECULAR MECHANISMS OF CONTRACTION

Sliding-Filament Mechanism

Role of Troponin, Tropomyosin, and Calcium in Contraction

Excitation-Contraction Coupling

   Sarcoplasmic reticulum

Membrane Excitation: The Neuromuscular Junction

MECHANICS OF SINGLE-FIBER CONTRACTION

Twitch Contractions

Frequency-Tension Relation

Length-Tension Relation

Load-Velocity Relation

SKELETAL-MUSCLE ENERGY METABOLISM

Muscle Fatigue

TYPES OF SKELETAL-MUSCLE FIBERS

WHOLE-MUSCLE CONTRACTION

Control of Muscle Tension

Control of Shortening Velocity

Muscle Adaptation to Exercise

Lever Action of Muscles and Bones

Skeletal-Muscle Disease

   Muscle cramps

   Hypocalcemic tetany

   Muscular dystrophy

   Myasthenia gravis

SECTION A SUMMARY

SECTION A KEY TERMS

SECTION A REVIEW QUESTIONS

SECTION B. SMOOTH MUSCLE

STRUCTURE

CONTRACTION AND ITS CONTROL

Cross-Bridge Activation

Sources of Cytosolic Calcium

Membrane Activation

   Spontaneous electrical activity

   Nerves and hormones

   Local factors

Types of Smooth Muscle

   Single-unit smooth muscle

   Multiunit smooth muscle

SECTION B SUMMARY

SECTION B KEY TERMS

SECTION B REVIEW QUESTIONS

CHAPTER 11 CLINICAL TERMS

CHAPTER 11 THOUGHT QUESTIONS

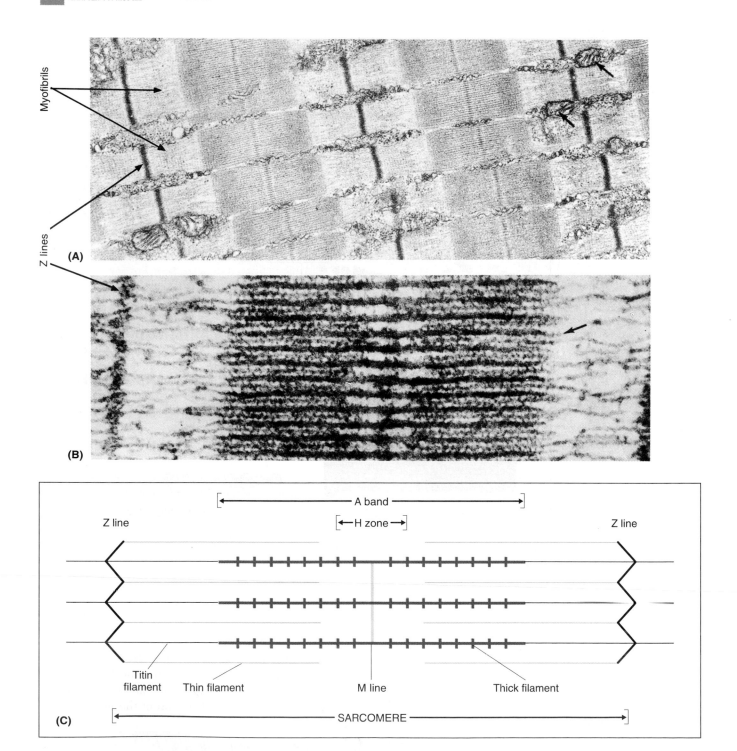

FIGURE 11-5

(A) Numerous myofibrils in a single skeletal-muscle fiber (arrows in upper right corner indicate mitochondria located between the myofibrils). (B) High magnification of a single sarcomere within a single myofibril (arrow at the right of A band indicates end of a thick filament). (C) Arrangement of the thick and thin filaments in the single sarcomere shown in B.

(A)

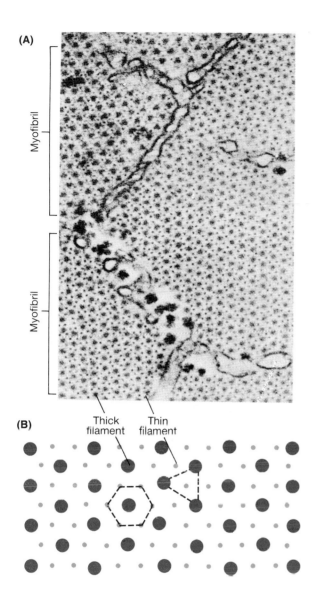

(B)

FIGURE 11-6

(A) Electron micrograph of a cross section through six myofibrils in a single skeletal-muscle fiber. [*From H. E. Huxley, J. Mol. Biol., 37:507–520 (1968).*] (B) Hexagonal arrangements of the thick and thin filaments in the overlap region in a single myofibril. Six thin filaments surround each thick filament and three thick filaments surround each thin filament.

the A band toward the center of the sarcomere, thereby shortening the sarcomere (Figure 11-9). One stroke of a cross bridge produces only a very small movement of a thin filament relative to a thick filament. While the force-generating mechanism remains active, however, the cross bridges repeat their swiveling motion many times, resulting in large displacements of the filaments, each displacement being made up of a series of the small steps.

Let us look more closely at these events. A muscle fiber's ability to generate force and movement depends on the interactions of the two so-called contractile proteins—myosin in the thick filaments and actin in the thin filaments—and the energy provided by ATP. Actin is a globular protein that polymerizes to form the two intertwined helical chains (Figure 11-10) that make up the core of the thin filaments. Myosin has a globular end attached to a long tail (Figure 11-11). The tails lie along the axis of the thick filament, and the globular heads extend out to the sides, forming the cross bridges. Each globular head contains a binding site for actin and an enzymatic site—an ATPase—that catalyzes the hydrolysis of ATP to ADP and inorganic phosphate, releasing the chemical energy stored in ATP.

FIGURE 11-7

High-magnification electron micrograph in the filament-overlap region near the middle of a sarcomere. Cross bridges between the thick and thin filaments can be seen at regular intervals along the filaments. [*From H. E. Huxley and J. Hanson, in G. H. Bourne (ed.), "The Structure and Function of Muscle," Vol. 1, Academic Press, New York, 1960.*]

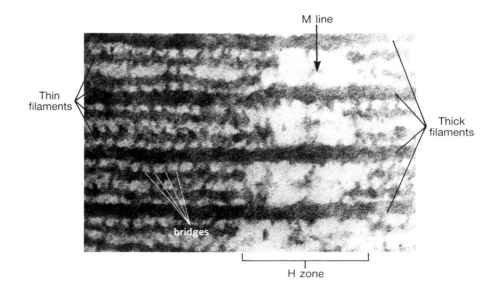

MECHANICS OF SINGLE-FIBER CONTRACTION

The force exerted on an object by a contracting muscle is known as muscle **tension**, and the force exerted on the muscle by the weight of an object is the **load**. Muscle tension and load are opposing forces. Whether or not force generation leads to fiber shortening depends on the relative magnitudes of the tension and the load. In order for muscle fibers to shorten and therefore move a load, muscle tension must become and remain slightly greater than the opposing load.

When a muscle develops tension but does not shorten (or lengthen), the contraction is said to be **isometric** (constant length). Such contractions occur when the muscle supports a load in a constant position or attempts to move an otherwise supported load that is greater than the tension developed by the muscle. A contraction in which the load on a muscle remains constant but the muscle is shortening is said to be **isotonic** (constant tension).

A third type of contraction is a **lengthening contraction**. This occurs when an unsupported load on a muscle is greater than the tension being generated by the cross bridges. In this situation, the load pulls the muscle to a longer length in spite of the opposing force being produced by the cross bridges. Such lengthening contractions occur when an object being supported by muscle contractions is lowered, such as occurs when you sit down from a standing position or walk down a flight of stairs. It must be emphasized that in these situations the lengthening of muscle fibers is not an active process produced by the contractile proteins but a consequence of the external forces being applied to the muscle. In the absence of external forces, a fiber will only *shorten* when stimulated; it will never lengthen. All three types of contractions—isometric, isotonic, and lengthening—occur in the natural course of muscle activity in the body.

During each type of contraction the cross bridges repeatedly go through the four steps of the cross-bridge cycle illustrated in Figure 11-12. During step 2 of an isotonic contraction, the cross bridges bound to actin move to their angled positions, causing shortening of the sarcomeres. In contrast, during an isometric contraction, the bound cross bridges are unable to move the thin filaments because of the load on the muscle fiber, but they do exert a force on the thin filaments—isometric tension. During a lengthening contraction, the cross bridges in step 2 are pulled toward the Z lines by the load while still bound to actin. The events of steps 1, 3, and 4 are the same in all three types of contractions. Thus, the chemical changes in the contractile proteins during each type of contraction are the same. The end result of shortening, no length change, or lengthening is determined by the magnitude of the load on the muscle.

Figure 11-20 illustrates the general method of recording isotonic and isometric contractions. During an isotonic contraction, the distance the muscle shortens as a function of time is recorded. The shortening distance is measured by a pen attached to the muscle and leaves a trace on a moving strip of paper as the muscle contracts and relaxes. During an isometric contraction, the force (tension) generated by the muscle as a function of time is measured by attaching the muscle at one end to a rigid support and at the other end to an electronic force-sensing device that controls the movement of a pen in proportion to the force exerted.

FIGURE 11-20

Methods of recording (A) isotonic and (B) isometric muscle contractions.

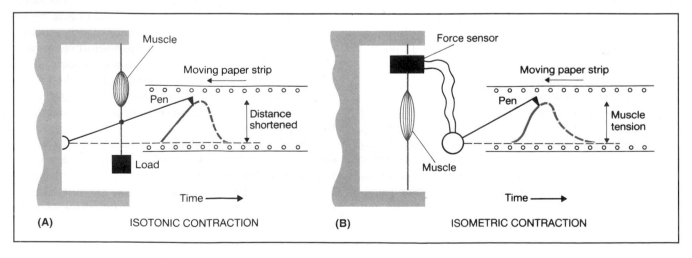

Contraction terminology and recording methods apply to both single fibers and whole muscles. We first describe the mechanics of single-fiber contractions and later discuss the factors controlling the mechanics of whole-muscle contraction.

Twitch Contractions

The mechanical response of a muscle fiber to a single action potential is known as a **twitch**. Figure 11-21 shows the main features of an isometric twitch. Following the action potential, there is an interval of a few milliseconds, known as the **latent period**, before the tension in the muscle fiber begins to increase. During this latent period, the processes associated with excitation-contraction coupling (page 313) are occurring. The time interval from the beginning of tension development at the end of the latent period to the peak tension in an isometric contraction is the **contraction time**. Not all skeletal-muscle fibers have the same contraction time. Some fast fibers have contraction times as short as 10 ms, whereas slower fibers may take 100 ms or longer.

Comparing an isotonic twitch with an isometric twitch in the same muscle fiber, one can see from Figure 11-22 that the time between the action potential and the beginning of shortening in an isotonic twitch is longer than the latent period in an isometric contraction, while the duration of the mechanical event—shortening—is briefer than the duration of force generation in an isometric twitch. Moreover, the characteristics of an isotonic twitch depend upon the magnitude of the load being lifted (Figure 11-23). At heavier loads the delay before shortening is longer, but the velocity of shortening (distance shortened per unit of time), the duration of the twitch, and the distance shortened all decrease.

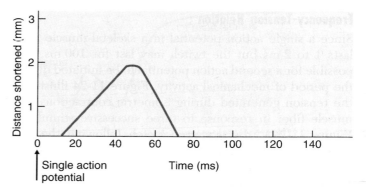

FIGURE 11-22

An isotonic twitch of a skeletal-muscle fiber following a single action potential.

Let us look more closely at the sequence of events in an isotonic contraction. Following excitation the cross bridges begin to develop force, but shortening does not begin until the muscle tension just exceeds the load on the fiber. Thus, before shortening, there is a period of isometric contraction during which the tension increases. (A similar period of isometric contraction occurs at the end of an isotonic contraction, as the tension becomes less than the load.) The heavier the load, the longer it takes for the tension to increase to the value of the load, where shortening will begin. If the load on a fiber is increased, eventually a load will be reached that the muscle is unable to lift, the velocity and distance of shortening will be zero, and the contraction will become completely isometric. At still higher loads, if the load is otherwise unsupported, the muscle fiber will lengthen, in spite of maximal cross-bridge force—a lengthening contraction.

FIGURE 11-21

An isometric twitch of a skeletal-muscle fiber following a single action potential.

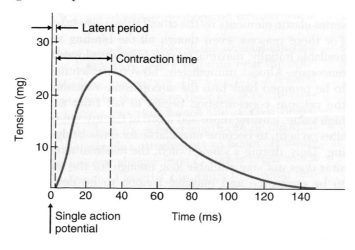

FIGURE 11-23

Isotonic twitches with different loads. The distance shortened, velocity of shortening, and duration of shortening all decrease with increased load, whereas the latent period increases with increasing load.

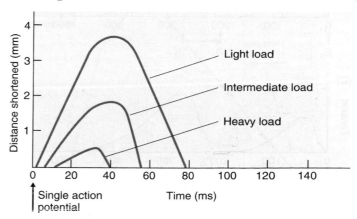

CHAPTER
12

CONTROL OF BODY MOVEMENT

FIGURE 12-1

The hierarchical organization of the neural system controlling body movement. All the skeletal muscles of the body are controlled by motor neurons. Sensorimotor cortex includes those parts of the cerebral cortex that act together to control skeletal-muscle activity.

cal structures are located in pa[...] and in the cerebellum, subcort[...] (Figure 12-2A and B). These str[...] terconnections.

As the neurons in the middle [...] receiving input from the comma[...] neously receive afferent inforr[...] the muscles, tendons, joints, s[...] and eyes) about the starting pos[...] is to be "commanded" to move[...] is integrated by neurons of the [...] chy with the signals from the c[...] middle level of the hierarchy c[...] that is, the pattern of neural ac[...] the desired movement.

The information determined [...] then transmitted via **descendir**[...] level of the motor control hie[...] which the motor neurons to the [...] or spinal cord. This level of the [...] minant of exactly which motor[...]

The motor programs are co[...] the course of most movements[...] gram is implemented and the a[...] brain regions concerned with r[...] level of the hierarchy contin[...] stream of updated information[...]

MOTOR CONTROL HIERARCHY
Voluntary and Involuntary Actions
LOCAL CONTROL OF MOTOR NEURONS
Interneurons
Local Afferent Input
Length-monitoring systems and the stretch reflex
Alpha-gamma coactivation
Tension-monitoring systems
Other local afferent input
**THE BRAIN MOTOR CENTERS AND THE
DESCENDING PATHWAYS THEY CONTROL**
Cerebral Cortex
Subcortical and Brainstem Nuclei
Cerebellum

Descending Pathways
Corticospinal pathway
Noncorticospinal pathways
Summary comments on the descending pathways
MUSCLE TONE
Abnormal Muscle Tone
**MAINTENANCE OF UPRIGHT POSTURE
AND BALANCE**
WALKING
SUMMARY
KEY TERMS
REVIEW QUESTIONS
CLINICAL TERMS
THOUGHT QUESTIONS

Carrying out a coordinate[...] process involving nerve[...] sider the events associated wi[...] an object. The fingers are fir[...] reach around the object, and[...] The degree of extension will[...] object (Is it a golf ball or a s[...] flexion will depend upon it[...] bowling ball or a balloon?).[...] elbow, and shoulder are ex[...] clined forward, the exact mo[...] object's position relative to[...] The shoulder, elbow, and w[...] port first the weight of the[...] added weight of the object. [...] ture is maintained despite th[...] balance.

The building blocks for[...] **units**, each comprising one [...] the skeletal-muscle fibers[...] (page 316). It is through [...] motor units that all skeletal [...] is controlled.

All the motor neurons fo[...] **motor neuron pool** for the[...]

MOTOR CONTROL HIERAR[...]

Throughout the CNS, th[...] ling skeletal muscles a[...] fashion—the **motor contr**[...] each level having a limited [...] portant to realize that we ar[...] archy, not an anatomical [...] nervous system that are in[...] ment and posture, howeve[...] nections that it is nearly i[...] function to a given brain a[...] archical model is meant to[...]

Note that many contrac[...] cles—particularly the mus[...] port—are isometric, and e[...] during these contractions,[...] following discussions the[...] ment" includes these isom[...] keep in mind throughout[...]

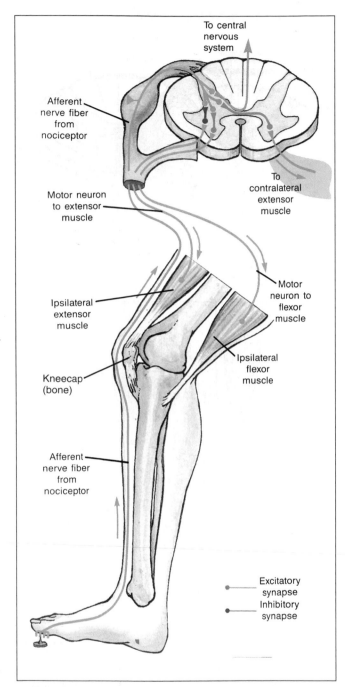

FIGURE 12-9

In response to pain, the ipsilateral flexor's motor neuron is stimulated (flexion reflex). In the case illustrated, the opposite limb is extended (crossed-extensor reflex) to support the body's weight. Arrows indicate direction of action potential transmission.

support more of the body's weight as the hurt foot is raised from the ground by flexion.

The local motor control systems are also affected by information from joint receptors. These inputs are all polysynaptic.

THE BRAIN MOTOR CENTERS AND THE DESCENDING PATHWAYS THEY CONTROL

As emphasized in our model, the motor neurons and interneurons at the local levels of motor control are influenced by descending pathways, and these pathways are themselves controlled by various motor centers in the brain (Figure 12-1).

Cerebral Cortex

The cerebral cortex plays a critical role in both the planning and ongoing control of normal voluntary movements, functioning in both the highest and middle levels of the motor control hierarchy. The term **sensorimotor cortex** is used to include all those parts of the cerebral cortex that act together in the control of muscle movement. A large number of nerve fibers that give rise to some of the descending pathways come from two areas of sensorimotor cortex on the posterior part of the frontal lobe: the **primary motor cortex** (sometimes called simply the **motor cortex**) and the **premotor area** (Figure 12-10). Other areas of sensorimotor cortex are the **supplementary motor cortex**, which lies on the surface of the frontal lobe where the cortex folds down between the two hemispheres (Figure 12-10B), the **somatosensory cortex**, and parts of the **parietal-lobe association cortex** (Figure 12-10A and B).

Neurons in the primary motor cortex mainly contribute directly to movements involving the use of individual muscle groups, such as those that move a single finger. In general, the location of the neurons in the motor cortex varies with the parts of the body they serve. As one starts at the top of the brain and moves down along the side (A to B in Figure 12-11), the cortical neurons affecting movements of the toes and feet are at the top, followed by neurons controlling leg, trunk, arm, hand, fingers, neck, and face.

The size of the representation of each of the individual body parts in Figure 12-12 is proportional to the amount of cortex devoted to its control. Clearly, the cortical areas representing the hand and face are the largest. The great number of cortical neurons for innervation of the hand and face is one factor responsible for the fine degree of motor control that can be exerted over those parts. The more delicate the function of any muscle, the more nearly one-to-one the relationship between cortical neurons and the muscle's motor units. Even with the finest control, however, there is still much convergence of input onto each motor neuron so that losing one cortical neuron never causes the loss of control of a motor neuron.

Moving anteriorly (C to D in Figure 12-11) in the cortex, primary motor cortex gives way to the premotor area,

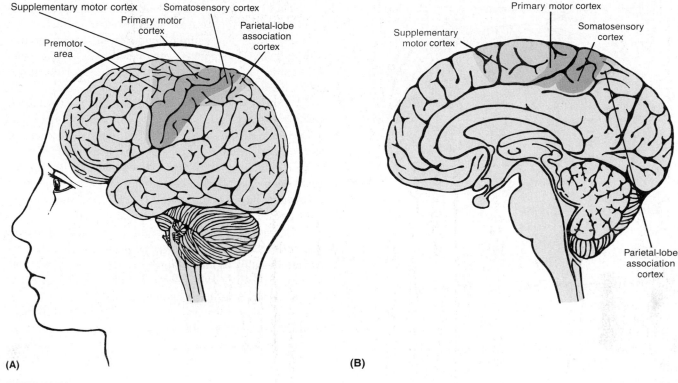

FIGURE 12-10

(A) The major motor areas of cerebral cortex. (B) Midline view of the brain showing the supplementary motor cortex, which lies in the part of the cerebral cortex that is folded down between the two cerebral hemispheres. Other cortical motor areas also extend onto this area. The premotor, supplementary motor, primary motor, somatosensory, and parietal-lobe association cortexes together make up the sensorimotor cortex.

whose neurons are involved in more complicated motor functions such as a change in the force or velocity of a movement, a change from one task to another, a movement made in response to visual control or a spoken command, two-handed coordination, and postural support for a wide variety of detailed movements.

The premotor area is also an important gateway for relaying processed information from other regions of the cerebral cortex and from other parts of the brain to the primary motor cortex or directly to the descending pathways. Some of this relayed information comes, for example, from the parietal-lobe association areas that process signals from sensory systems to indicate the body's position in space and the direction in which the body must be moved to achieve the desired goal.

We have described the primary motor cortex and premotor areas as giving rise, either directly or indirectly, to pathways descending to the motor neurons. As we have stated, however, these neurons are part of the middle hierarchical level and are not the prime *initiators* of movement. They are simply a tremendously important relay and integrative station.

Starting about 55 ms before voluntary muscle activity begins, a distinct wave of electrical activity, known as the **motor potential**, occurs within the primary motor cortex, signifying neuronal excitement there. About 800 ms before this, however, a different wave, the **readiness potential**, can be recorded from electrodes on the scalp. It arises in the supplementary motor cortex (Figure 12-10B), although other brain regions, particularly the association areas of the parietal and frontal lobes, also contribute to it. The readiness potential is the earliest detectable sign of "getting ready" to make a voluntary motion and is an indication of activity at the highest hierarchical level.

In the short time between the termination of the readiness potential and the beginning of the motor potential, subcortical mechanisms become active, and it is to these areas of the middle-level motor control system that we now turn.

Subcortical and Brainstem Nuclei

A dozen or so highly interconnected structures lie within the cerebrum beneath the cerebral cortex and in the brainstem, and they interact with the cortex to control movements. Their influence is transmitted to the motor neurons both by pathways that go back to the cerebral cortex and by descending pathways that arise directly from some of the brainstem nuclei.

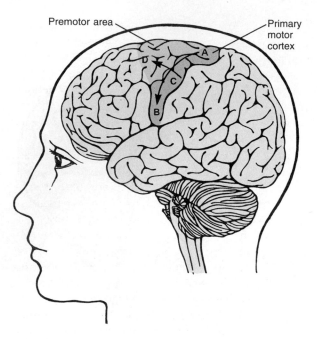

FIGURE 12-11

Primary motor cortex and the premotor area. Arrows A-B and C-D are explained in the text.

It is not known to what extent, if any, these structures act at the highest level of the motor control hierarchy, but they definitely play a prominent role in the hierarchy's middle level. They convert the overall plan or goal of an action into programs that determine the specific movements needed to accomplish that action.

Prominent among the subcortical nuclei are the paired **basal ganglia** (Figure 12-2B). In contrast to most other components of the motor control system, which transmit via excitatory synapses, the basal ganglia are characterized by their inhibitory influences. They seem to select appropriate components from the excitatory repertoire and suppress antagonistic or unwanted behaviors so that desired patterns of motor activity can be maintained.

This role explains the defects in motor control associated with individuals who have the inadequately functioning basal ganglia of **_Parkinson's disease_**. These individuals have difficulty establishing new behaviors because it is difficult for them to stop ongoing activity. Thus, if walking, they tend to keep walking; if seated, they tend to remain seated. A common set of other symptoms evolve, including a tremor that is most prominent at rest; a change in facial

FIGURE 12-12

Representation of the body in primary motor cortex. Note the disproportionately large areas devoted to control of the hands and facial muscles. Within the hand area, however, no one area exclusively controls the movement of a single finger, and there is much overlap between adjacent finger regions.

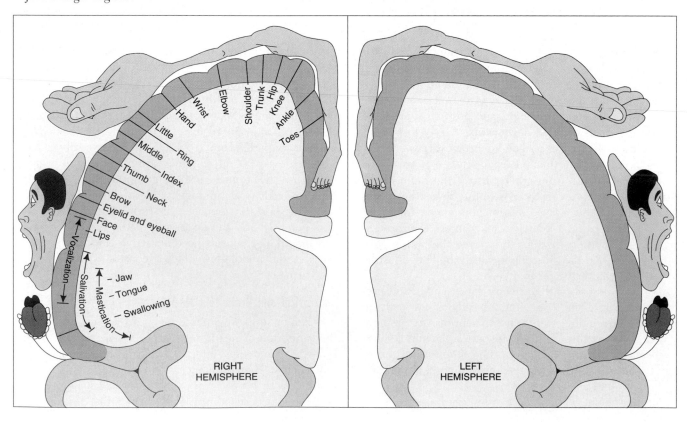

expression resulting in a masklike, unemotional appearance; muscular rigidity; a shuffling gait with loss of arm swing; and a stooped and unstable posture.

Although the symptoms of Parkinson's disease reflect inadequate functioning of the basal ganglia, the initial defect arises in neurons of the **substantia nigra** ("black substance"), a subcortical nucleus that gets its name from the dark pigment in its cells. These neurons, which degenerate in Parkinson's disease, project to the basal ganglia where they normally liberate the neurotransmitter dopamine from their axon terminals. As substantia nigra neurons degenerate, the amount of dopamine they deliver to the basal ganglia is reduced and the basal ganglia function decreases.

One drug used to treat Parkinson's disease is L-dopa, a precursor of dopamine. L-Dopa enters the bloodstream, crosses the blood-brain barrier, and is converted to dopamine (dopamine itself is not used as medication because it cannot cross the blood-brain barrier). The newly formed dopamine activates the receptors in the basal ganglia and relieves the symptoms of the disease. Another drug used to slow the progress of the disease is deprenyl, which inhibits the brain enzyme that breaks down dopamine so that more of the neurotransmitter reaches the neurons in the basal ganglia. Still highly controversial is an experimental treatment for Parkinson's disease that involves the transplantation into (or onto) the basal ganglia of either fetal neurons that synthesize dopamine or genetically engineered cells that form tyrosine hydroxylase, the enzyme that drives dopamine production (see Figure 8-34).

In addition to the role played by the basal ganglia in posture and movement, they serve in intellectual function and possibly in learning motor tasks.

Cerebellum

The cerebellum is behind the brainstem, as can be seen in Figure 12-2A. It exerts a very important influence on posture and movement, but it does not exert this influence *directly* by pathways that descend to the motor neurons. Rather, the cerebellum affects motor behavior by means of input to brainstem nuclei and (by way of the thalamus) to regions of the sensorimotor cortex.

The cerebellum's role in motor functioning, at least in part, is to perform the critical task of comparing information about what the muscles *should* be doing with information about what they actually *are* doing. To achieve this, the cerebellum receives information both from the sensorimotor cortex (relayed via brainstem nuclei) and from the vestibular system, eyes, ears, skin, muscles, joints, and tendons, that is, from the major receptors affected by movement. If there is a discrepancy between the intended movement and the actual one, the cerebellum sends an error signal to the motor cortex and subcortical centers to modify the central motor programs, correct the ongoing movement, and ensure that future movements of the same kind will be performed more accurately. In fact, the cerebellum plays an important role in the learning of motor skills. The cerebellum serves another crucial function, that of regulating the timing of the complex muscle actions required for even the simplest motor act.

The role of the cerebellum in programming movements can best be appreciated when seeing the absence of this function in individuals with cerebellar disease who cannot perform movements smoothly. If they try to touch an object, their movements are jerky and accompanied by oscillating, to-and-fro tremors that become more marked as the hand approaches the object and continue for a few moments after the object has been reached (called **dysmetria**). They cannot start or stop movements quickly or easily. If, for example, they are asked to rotate the wrist over and back rapidly, their motions are slow and irregular. Moreover, they cannot easily combine the movements of several joints into a single smooth, coordinated motion. To move the arm, they might first move the shoulder, then the elbow, and finally the wrist.

Unstable posture is another symptom characteristic of cerebellar dysfunction. For example, persons with cerebellar damage walk awkwardly, with the feet well apart, and they have such difficulty maintaining balance that their gait appears drunken. A final symptom involves difficulty in learning new motor skills, and individuals with cerebellar dysfunction find it hard to modify movements in response to new situations. Cerebellar damage does not cause paralysis, which indicates that the cerebellum is not responsible for *initiating* movements.

Descending Pathways

The influence exerted by the various brain regions on posture and movement has to be relayed by descending pathways to the motor neurons and the interneurons that affect them. The pathways are of two types: the corticospinal pathways which, as their name implies, originate in the cerebral cortex; and a second group which we shall call the noncorticospinal pathways, which originate in the brainstem.

Descending fibers from both types of descending pathways may end at synapses on alpha and gamma motor neurons, but most end on interneurons that affect the alpha motor neurons either directly or via still other interneurons. Sometimes, as mentioned earlier, these are the same interneurons that are used by reflex arcs, thereby ensuring that the descending signals are fully integrated with local information before the activity of the motor neurons is altered. The ultimate effect of the descending pathways on the alpha motor neurons may be excitatory or inhibitory.

Some of the descending fibers affect *afferent* systems. They do this via (1) presynaptic synapses on the terminals of afferent neurons as these fibers enter the central nervous system, or (2) synapses on interneurons in the ascending pathways. The overall effect of this descending input to afferent systems is to limit their influence on either the local or brain motor control areas, thereby altering the importance of a particular bit of afferent information or sharpening its focus. Because of this descending (motor) control over ascending (sensory) information, there is clearly no real functional separation of the motor and sensory systems.

Corticospinal Pathway. The nerve fibers of the **corticospinal pathways**, as mentioned before, have their cell bodies in the cerebral cortex, specifically, in the sensorimotor regions, and terminate in the spinal cord. The corticospinal pathways are also called the **pyramidal tracts**, or **pyramidal system** (perhaps because of their shape as they pass along the surface of the medulla oblongata or because they were formerly thought to arise solely from the pyramidal cells of the motor cortex). In the medulla oblongata, near the junction of the spinal cord and brain-

FIGURE 12-13

The corticospinal pathway. Most of these fibers cross in the brainstem to descend in the opposite side of the spinal cord. Arrows indicate direction of action potential propagation. (*Adapted from Gardner.*)

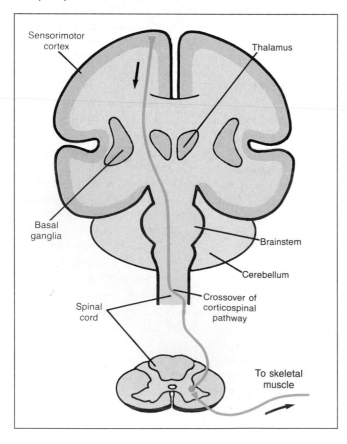

stem, most of the corticospinal fibers cross the spinal cord to descend on the opposite side (Figure 12-13). Thus, the skeletal muscles on the left side of the body are controlled largely by neurons in the right half of the brain, and vice versa.

As the corticospinal fibers descend through the brain from the cerebral cortex, they are accompanied by fibers of the **corticobulbar pathway** (bulbar means "pertaining to the brainstem"), a pathway that begins in the sensorimotor cortex and ends in the brainstem. The corticobulbar fibers control, directly or indirectly via interneurons, the motor neurons that innervate muscles of the eye, face, tongue, and throat. These fibers are the main source of control for voluntary movement of the muscles of the head and neck, whereas the corticospinal fibers serve this function for the muscles of the rest of the body. For convenience, we shall henceforth include the corticobulbar pathway in the general term "corticospinal pathways."

Axons of single corticospinal neurons influence motor neurons of several muscles, and neurons from a wide area of the sensorimotor cortex converge (page 201) on a single motor neuron. The extensive convergence suggests that the activity of each motor neuron is influenced by more than one of the brain motor control centers.

The corticospinal pathways serve rapid, fine movements of the distal extremities, such as those made when an object is manipulated by the fingers. After damage to the corticospinal pathways, all movements are slower and weaker, individual finger movements are absent, and it is difficult to release a grip.

Noncorticospinal Pathways. Axons descending from neurons in the brainstem also form pathways that descend into the spinal cord to influence motor neurons. These pathways were previously referred to as the extrapyramidal system to distinguish them from the corticospinal (pyramidal) pathways, but this is now in disfavor. No new general term has been adopted for these pathways that descend from the brainstem, and for convenience we shall refer to them collectively as the noncorticospinal pathways.

Axons of some of the noncorticospinal pathways cross from their side of origin in the brainstem to affect muscles on the opposite side of the body, and others remain uncrossed. In the spinal cord the fibers of the noncorticospinal pathways form distinct clusters, named according to their sites of origin. For example, the vestibulospinal pathway descends to the spinal cord from the vestibular nuclei in the brainstem, whereas the reticulospinal pathway descends from neurons in the brainstem reticular formation.

The noncorticospinal pathways are especially important in the control of upright posture, balance, and walking. These pathways are anatomically suited to invoke the large groups of muscles characteristic of postural support in three ways: (1) They generally exert greater influence on motor neurons that control muscles in the neck, trunk, and upper part of the limbs than on motor neurons that control muscles in the fingers and toes; (2) as they descend through the spinal cord, they give rise to collateral branches that affect motor neurons at many levels of the cord; and (3) rather than ending on interneurons that are part of the local reflex arcs, as corticospinal neurons generally do, fibers of the noncorticospinal descending pathways are apt to end on interneurons that send long branches that interconnect different levels of the spinal cord.

Summary Comments on the Descending Pathways. In general, the corticospinal neurons have greater influ-

ence over motor neurons that control muscles involved in fine, isolated movements, particularly those of the fingers and hands. The noncorticospinal descending pathways are more involved with coordination of the large muscle groups used in the maintenance of upright posture, in locomotion, and in head and body movements when turning toward a specific stimulus.

There is, however, much interaction between the descending pathways. For example, some fibers of the corticospinal pathway end on interneurons that play important roles in posture, whereas fibers of the noncorticospinal descending pathways sometimes end directly on the alpha motor neurons to control discrete muscle movements. Because of this redundancy, loss of function resulting from

---

TABLE 12-2   SOME CHARACTERISTICS OF MOTOR CONTROL SYSTEMS

1. Even though it seems obvious to think of the motor system as controlling the contraction of *muscles*, much of the motor system functions more in determining the components of *actions* as they are needed to achieve a purpose or goal. This can be said in another way. The central nervous system knows more about movements than it knows about muscles. Thus, to take a book from a shelf, more of the motor control system is involved with calculating the direction the arm must move and how far than with selecting which motor neurons to activate and when.

2. Before descending pathways can activate specific motor neurons, a great deal of neural activity takes place in the brain. Whether the intention of an action arises from within the brain (I think I'll study now so I won't have to do it later) or as an outside stimulus (the telephone rings and I answer it), the intention has to be translated into the direction and distance the body must be moved. This translation process is completed gradually by many components of the brain's motor system acting simultaneously, each component adding a special contribution.

3. The motor control system must select from a variety of ways of achieving the purpose, since most motor acts can be executed in many ways with different sets of muscles. A simple example of this is a rat trained to press a lever whenever a light flashes. Depending upon its original position in the cage, its movements can be quite varied. If the rat is to the left of the lever, it moves to the right; if it is to the right, it moves to the left. If its paw is on the floor, it raises the paw; if its paw is above the lever, it lowers the paw.

4. The brain operates pretty much as a whole in producing movement; that is, many brain structures are involved.

5. The motor cortex is unable to generate coordinated

voluntary movements without input from the subcortical motor centers.

6. Not all voluntary movements are channeled through the motor cortex. For example, tongue movements during speech are controlled by special speech areas (Chapter 13).

7. A given set of muscles can be controlled by several neural systems, and the central nervous system can select from them to execute a movement.

8. Movements that involve learning, movements to be made in response to an expected signal, highly skilled movements that have become almost automatic—all these are controlled by different components of the motor control systems.

9. The limbic system (emotion and motivation) plays an important role in motor control (we are all aware that it is usually difficult to make well-controlled, detailed movements when in a highly emotional state).

10. The motor cortex is more important in controlling skilled, accurate movements than in producing automatic or rhythmical ones.

11. Movements performed to achieve a specific task are variable and seemingly inconsequential. For example, it usually does not matter whether you comb your hair with the right or left hand. It is the end result that matters, but only the intervening acts or movements can be programmed by the nervous system

12. In certain circumstances a spinal reflex, for example, the flexion reflex, can override a command from a higher hierarchical level, for example, "extend leg to bear body's weight."

13. Movements are generally accompanied by changes in posture and alterations in sensory input. Anticipatory adjustments are made to prevent loss of balance and to compensate for the changed sensory information.

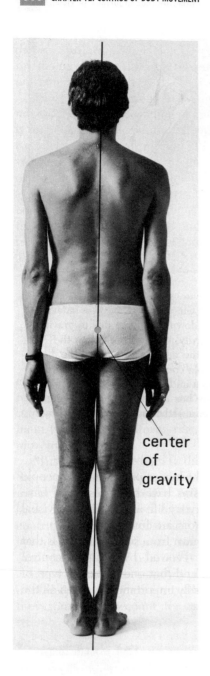
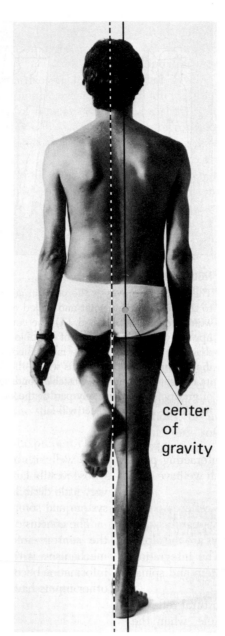

center
of
gravity

center
of
gravity

FIGURE 12-15
Postural changes with stepping. (Left) Normal standing posture. The line of the center of gravity falls directly between the two feet. (Right) As the left foot is raised, the whole body leans to the right so that the center of gravity shifts over the right foot.

with each other, as in walking or running. In such cases, spinal pattern generators utilize reciprocal innervation so that when the extensor muscles are activated on one side of the body, to bear the body's weight, the contralateral extensors are inhibited to allow that limb to flex and swing forward.

Although the central pattern generators can bring about the rhythmical movement of a limb in the absence of afferent information, such input normally does contribute substantially to locomotion by acting on the generators and indirectly on the motor neurons themselves. This afferent information ensures that the output of the central pattern generator is optimally adapted to the environment. For example, if the limb movement should be slowed by external factors, as in wading through water, the afferent signals prevent a premature flexion of the limb.

The central pattern generators are also affected by the descending pathways, both during the initiation of activity and during ongoing activity. Such input helps adjust the movement to the person's goals and to the environment, adding influence from the eyes, vestibular apparatus, and ears. For example, depending upon commands from the descending pathways, the two limbs may be operated together, as in jumping, instead of reciprocally. One attractive hypothesis is that the brain can control stereotyped behaviors such as locomotion simply by activating the appropriate central pattern generators by way of the descending pathways.

SUMMARY

Skeletal muscles are controlled by their motor neurons. All the motor neurons that control a given muscle form a motor neuron pool.

MOTOR CONTROL HIERARCHY

The neural systems that control body movements are arranged in a motor control hierarchy.

I. The highest level determines the general intention of an action.

II. The middle level specifies the postures and movements needed to carry out the intended action and, taking account of sensory information that indicates the body's position, establishes a motor program.

III. The lowest level determines which motor neurons will be activated.

IV. As the movement progresses, information about what the muscles are doing is fed back to the motor control centers, which make any needed program corrections.

V. Actions are voluntary when we are aware of what we are doing and why, or when we are paying attention to the action or its purpose.

VI. Almost all actions have conscious and unconscious components.

LOCAL CONTROL OF MOTOR NEURONS

I. Most input to motor neurons is from local interneurons, which themselves receive input from peripheral receptors, descending pathways, and other interneurons.

II. Muscle length and changes in length are monitored by muscle-spindle stretch receptors.
   A. Activation of these receptors initiates the stretch reflex, in which motor neurons of ipsilateral antagonists are inhibited and those of synergists are activated.
   B. Tension on the stretch receptors is maintained during muscle contraction by gamma efferent activation of the spindle muscle fibers.
   C. Alpha and gamma motor neurons are often coactivated.

III. Muscle tension is monitored by Golgi tendon organs, which, via interneurons, activate inhibitory synapses on motor neurons of the contracting muscle and excitatory synapses on motor neurons of ipsilateral antagonists.

IV. The flexion reflex excites the ipsilateral flexor muscles and inhibits the ipsilateral extensors. The crossed-extensor reflex excites the contralateral extensor muscles during excitation of the ipsilateral flexors.

THE BRAIN MOTOR CENTERS AND THE DESCENDING PATHWAYS THEY CONTROL

I. The location of the neurons in the motor cortex varies with the part of the body the neurons serve.

II. A motor potential occurs in the motor cortex before muscle activation occurs. This is preceded by a readiness potential produced by the supplementary motor cortex 800 ms before any electrical activity in the motor cortex begins.

III. The basal ganglia help determine the direction, force, and speed of movements.

IV. The cerebellum coordinates posture and movement and plays a role in motor learning.

V. The corticospinal pathways pass directly from the sensorimotor cortex to motor neurons in the spinal cord (or in the brainstem, in the case of the corticobulbar pathways) or to nearby interneurons.
   A. In general, neurons on one side of the brain control muscles on the other side of the body.
   B. Corticospinal pathways serve predominately fine, precise movements.
   C. Some corticospinal fibers affect the transmission of information in afferent pathways.

VI. Other (noncorticospinal) pathways arise in the brainstem and are involved in the coordination of large groups of muscles used in posture and locomotion.

VII. There is some duplication of function between the two descending pathways.

MUSCLE TONE

I. Hypertonia, as seen in spasticity, rigidity, spasms, and cramps, usually occurs with disorders of the descending pathways.

II. Hypotonia can be seen with cerebellar disease or, more commonly, with disease of the alpha motor neurons or muscle.

MAINTENANCE OF UPRIGHT POSTURE AND BALANCE

I. To maintain balance, the body's center of gravity must be kept over the body's base.

II. The stretch and crossed-extensor reflexes are postural reflexes.

WALKING

I. Central pattern generators bring about the cyclical, alternating movements of locomotion.

II. The pattern generators are affected by feedback and motor programs.

hallucinations, especially "hearing" voices, and delusions, such as the belief that one has been chosen for a special mission or is being persecuted by others. Schizophrenics become withdrawn, show little empathy for others, and experience inappropriate moods. They also experience abnormal motor behavior, which can range from total immobilization **(catatonia)** to wild, purposeless activity.

Two patterns of the disease exist, one in which the patients have mainly so-called positive symptoms (delusions and hallucinations, for example), and the other in which they show mainly negative symptoms (emotional unresponsiveness, withdrawal, few movements or gestures, loss of drive, depressed mood). Those with the positive symptoms respond better to drug therapy, and those having negative symptoms are apt to show more abnormalities in brain structure.

As compared to normal people, some schizophrenics have smaller brains and a decreased number of neurons, particularly in the frontal lobes and the part of the temporal lobes that houses the hippocampus and amygdala (Figure 13-10). These abnormalities are usually greater in the left hemisphere of the brain.

Schizophrenia is a fairly common disease. It can appear gradually, often during adolescence in an otherwise bright and normal person, or it can occur suddenly after a single precipitating event. Despite extensive research, the causes of schizophrenia remain unclear, although the disease is known to have a genetic component: Whereas 1 percent of the general population will develop the disease, 10 to 16 percent of people having a schizophrenic parent will themselves become schizophrenic.

The most widely accepted explanation for schizophrenia is the **dopamine hypothesis**, which suggests that increased stimulation of dopamine receptors at least partially explains the symptoms of the disease. This hypothesis is supported by the fact that drugs that alter schizophrenia influence transmission at dopamine-mediated synapses. Thus, the symptoms are made worse by amphetamine-like drugs, which are dopamine agonists, and the most therapeutically beneficial drugs used in treating schizophrenia block dopamine receptors.

Abnormalities in neurotransmitter function in the brains of schizophrenics are, however, not *directly* due to dopamine. Rather, in some schizophrenics at least, abnormalities are found in the glutamate systems, which are closely related to dopaminergic systems, and in serotonin levels.

The Affective Disorders: Depressions and Manias

The term **affect** refers to the external expression of inner emotions. Whereas schizophrenia is largely a disease with disordered thought, the **affective disorders** are characterized by serious, prolonged disturbances of mood. The affective disorders include the **depressions**, the **manias**, and swings between these two states, the **bipolar affec-**

tive disorders. In the depressive disorders, the prominent feature is a pervasive sadness, loss of interest or pleasure, and feelings of worthlessness. The essential features of the manias are elated mood, sometimes with euphoria (that is, an exaggerated sense of well being), overconfidence, and irritability. Along with schizophrenia, the affective disorders form the major psychiatric illnesses today. The causes of mood disorders are not known.

Depression can be triggered by stressful events, it can accompany other mental or medical disorders, or it can arise spontaneously. Although the biochemical basis of depression is unknown, it is associated with abnormally low levels of certain neurotransmitters in the brain. Serotonin is the major neurotransmitter implicated, although norepinephrine may be involved as well, and the major antidepressant drugs alter the functioning of one or the other of these substances or both of them.

The classical antidepressant drugs are of two types. The **tricyclic antidepressant drugs**, such as Elavil and Pamelor, interfere with serotonin and/or norepinephrine uptake by presynaptic endings. The **monoamine oxidase inhibitors** interfere with the enzyme responsible for the breakdown of these same two neurotransmitters. A newer class of antidepressant drugs, of which Prozac is an example, selectively inhibits serotonin reuptake by presynaptic terminals. In all three cases, the result is an *increased* concentration of serotonin and/or norepinephrine in the extracellular fluid at synapses. Since the reuptake inhibitors show beneficial effects only after several weeks of treatment, their therapeutic effects must be due to a compensatory change in response to the elevated levels of transmitter and not directly to the increased neurotransmitter levels.

In depressed (or manic) persons for whom drug therapy has proved ineffective or is contraindicated, **electroconvulsive therapy (ECT)** is often effective. As the name suggests, electricity is used to induce a convulsion, or seizure, the patient being under anesthesia and prepared with a muscle relaxant to minimize convulsions. A series of ECT treatments alters neurotransmitter function, for example, by causing a down-regulation of certain postsynaptic receptors. It is unclear whether serotonin receptors are involved in these changes. The finding that beta-adrenergic and muscarinic acetylcholine receptors are also down-regulated after ECT raises the possibility that it might be the *balance* between the various transmitter systems that is important in depression rather than functional alterations involving only a single transmitter.

The major drug used in treating manic or bipolar affective disorder is lithium carbonate. It is highly specific, normalizing both the manic and depressing moods of bipolar disorders and slowing down thinking and motor behavior without causing sedation. In addition, it decreases the severity of the swings between mania and depression that occur in the bipolar disorders. In some cases, lithium is even effective in depression not associated with manias.

Lithium is thought to interfere with the formation of members of the inositol phosphate family and, therefore to decrease the postsynaptic neurons' response to neurotransmitters that utilize this second-messenger pathway (Chapter 7).

Psychoactive Drugs, Dependence, and Tolerance

In the previous sections, we mentioned several drugs used to combat altered states of consciousness. Psychoactive drugs are also used as "street drugs" in a deliberate attempt to elevate mood (euphorigens) and produce unusual states of consciousness ranging from meditational states to hallucinations. Virtually all the psychoactive drugs exert their actions either directly or indirectly by altering neurotransmitter-receptor interactions. For example, cocaine blocks the reuptake of serotonin and the catecholamine neurotransmitters, particularly dopamine, into the presynaptic axon terminal. As mentioned on page 211, psychoactive drugs are often chemically similar to neurotransmitters such as serotonin, dopamine (Figure 13-11), and norepinephrine, and they interact with the receptors activated by these transmitters.

Dependence. *Drug dependence*, the term now preferred for addiction, has two facets that may occur either together or independently: (1) a psychological dependence that is experienced as a craving for a drug and an inability to stop using the substance at will; and (2) a physical dependence that requires one to take the drug to avoid *withdrawal*, that is, the unpleasant symptoms that occur with cessation of drug use.

Drug dependence has not been defined to everyone's satisfaction. Regardless, most agree that the definition should include the following concepts: (1) Drug dependence is characterized by the tendency toward a progressive increase in consumption of the drug; and (2) it is characterized by a persistent tendency to relapse to use of the substance even after abstinence has been achieved and withdrawal symptoms are no longer in evidence.

Different substances have different potentials for pro-

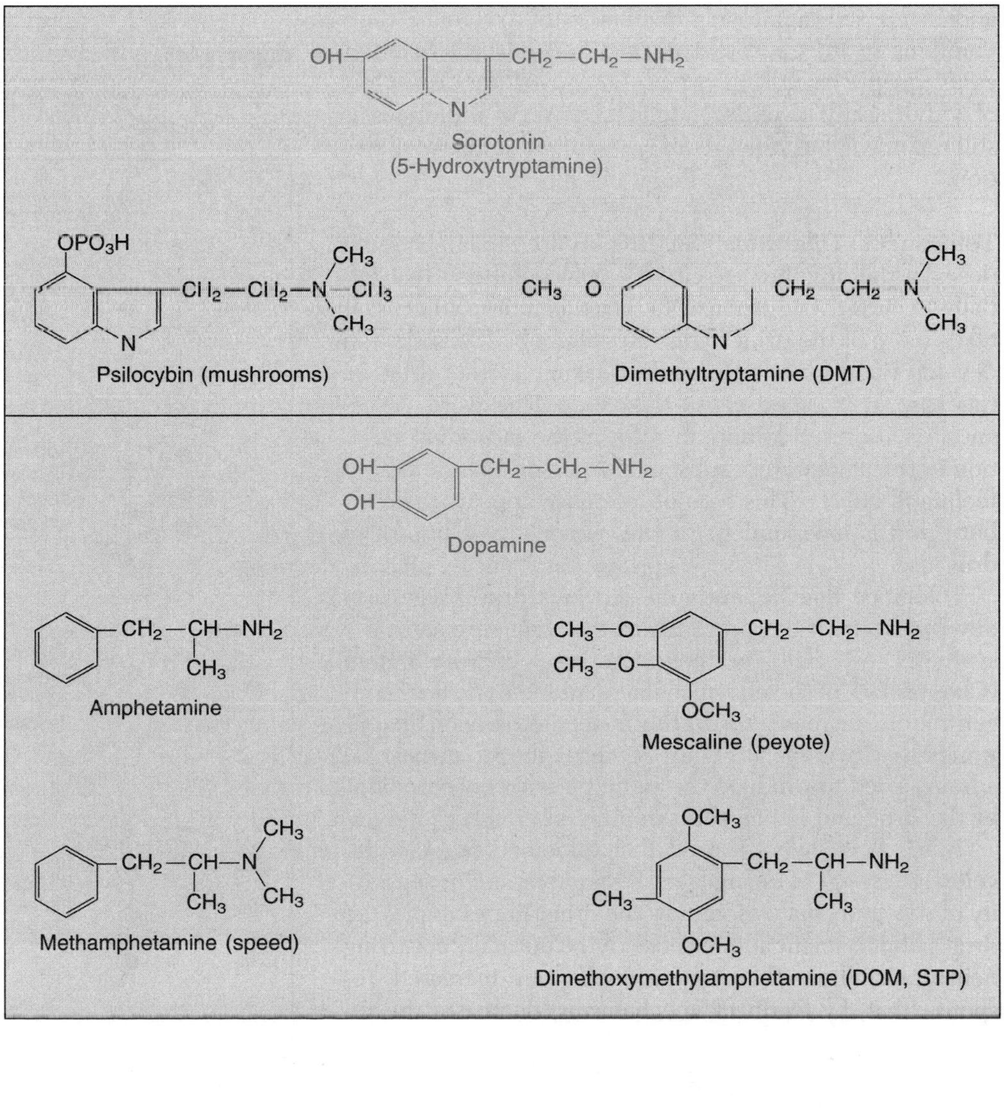

FIGURE 13-11

Molecular similarities between neurotransmitters (blue type) and some euphorigens (black type). At high doses, these euphorigens can cause hallucinations.

These events could also explain withdrawal symptoms. When the drug is stopped (abstinence), the receptors receive neither the drug nor the normal neurotransmitter for some time since the neurotransmitter synthesis and release have been inhibited by previous prolonged drug use. This results in the physical symptoms of withdrawal. Withdrawal symptoms disappear as neurotransmitter release returns to normal levels.

Tolerance may also be due to changes in the postsynaptic cells. For example, concentrations of calcium and cAMP may change in response to continued drug usage.

LEARNING AND MEMORY

Learning is the acquisition and storage of information as a consequence of experience. It is measured by an increase in the likelihood of a particular behavioral response to a stimulus. Generally, rewards or punishments, as mentioned earlier, are crucial ingredients of learning, as is contact with and manipulation of the environment. **Memory** is the relatively permanent storage form of the learned information.

The neural circuits that connect a sensory event with a learned behavioral response to that event must have been altered in some way to support the learning. This change is called the **memory trace**. For example, if an animal learns to blink its eye in response to a tone, the learning can only be explained by some molecular or cellular change in the neural circuits between the ear and the motor neurons that control the eye muscles. It is important to note that the memory trace is the only part of those circuits that shows the training-induced behavioral changes. Just where the memory trace occurs and what form it takes are the paramount questions in the study of learning. We shall discuss them after a brief description of memory itself.

Memory

Depending on how long a memory lasts, it is designated as either **working memory**, a limited-capacity, short-term memory that lasts seconds to minutes, or **long-term memory**, which lasts hours, days, or years. The process of transferring memories from the working to the long-term form is called **memory consolidation** (Figure 13-13). When stored information suddenly becomes relevant and is retrieved from long-term memory, it returns to working memory, where it is accessed.

Working Memory. Working memory consists of the set of things we are paying attention to at any one time. It incorporates (1) the attention-focusing mechanisms that have been directed to a specific object, (2) the visual image or language-based information that is associated with that object, and (3) relevant stored data that have been retrieved from long-term memory. In working memory, information is simultaneously processed and stored.

The operations of working memory are carried out in the frontal lobes of the cerebral cortex, where discrete regions seem to be specialized for dealing with specific kinds of information. Thus, one area of the frontal cortex encodes information about the location of objects, whereas a different area encodes information about the objects' color, size, and shape.

Dopamine is one of the most important neurotransmitters in the operation of working memory.

The component of working memory that focuses attention is essential for many memory-based skills. The longer the span of attention in working memory, the better the chess player, the greater the ability to reason, and the better a student is at understanding complicated sentences and drawing inferences from texts. Conversely, the specific memory deficit in victims of Alzheimer's disease, a condition marked by serious memory losses, may be in this attention-focusing component of working memory.

Long-Term Memory. After their existence in working memory, memories may either fade away or be consolidated into long-term memories. Which of these two events happens depends on factors such as attention, motivation, and the levels of various neurotransmitters and hormones. For example, at specific synaptic sites within the brain, increasing levels of GABA decreases memory consolidation, whereas increasing brain levels of glutamate, acetylcholine, and norepinephrine enhance it. The hormones epinephrine, ACTH, and vasopressin also affect the retention of learned experiences. These hormones are normally released in response to stressful or even mildly stimulating experiences, suggesting that the hormonal consequences of our experiences affect our memories of them.

Two of the opioid peptides, enkephalin and endorphin, interfere with learning and memory, particularly when the lesson involves a painful stimulus. They may inhibit learning simply because they decrease the emotional (fear, anxiety) component of the painful experience associated with the learning situation, thereby decreasing the motivation necessary for learning to occur.

Memories can be consolidated very rapidly, sometimes after just one trial, and they can be retained over extended periods. Information can be retrieved from long-term memory stores after long periods of disuse, and the common notion that memory, like muscle, atrophies with lack of use is not always true. Also, unlike working memory, long-term memory has a seemingly unlimited capacity because people's memories never seem to be so full that they cannot learn something new.

Long-term memories are of two kinds: procedural and declarative. **Procedural memories** are those involved in

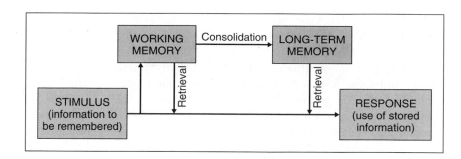

FIGURE 13-13

Events involved in learning and retrieving information.

remembering how to do something, such as ride a bike, whereas **declarative memories** are involved in remembering facts and events, for example, someone's name. Individuals can suffer from severe deficits in declarative memory but have intact procedural memory. One case study describes a pianist who learned a new piece to accompany a singer at a concert but had no recollection the following morning of having performed the composition. He could remember *how* to play the music but could not remember having done so.

The Location of Memory

Most researchers agree that memory traces are laid down in specific neural systems throughout the brain and that different types of memory tasks utilize different systems. For even a simple memory task, such as trying to recall a certain word from a previously seen word list, different specific parts of the brain are activated in sequence. It is as though there are several small "processors" linked together in a memory system for that type of memory task.

The structures most involved in declarative memories are the hippocampus (Figure 13-10) and the areas of the cerebral cortex that are closely associated with the limbic system. The cerebral cortex is essential for declarative memories. The hippocampus and the cerebral cortex that overlies it pull information together from the individual sites activated in the cerebral cortex during the working-memory phase that together represents an entire memory episode. The finding that people in whom the hippocampus has been destroyed are unable to form new declarative memories supports the importance of the hippocampus in memory functions.

Although the hippocampus is essential during early phases of learning, its role is temporary. Eventually, declarative memories are stored at other sites that are independent of the hippocampus.

The cerebellum is necessary for procedural learning, and the amygdala seems to be necessary for learning to avoid pain.

The Neural Basis of Learning and Memory

Working memory and long-term memory have different neural mechanisms. Conditions such as coma, deep anesthesia, electroconvulsive shock, and insufficient blood sup-

ply to the brain, all of which interfere with the electrical activity of the brain, interfere with working memory. Thus, it is assumed that working memory exists in the form of ongoing graded or action potentials. Working memory is interrupted when a person becomes unconscious from a blow on the head, and memories are abolished for all that happened for a variable period of time before the blow, so-called **retrograde amnesia**. (**Amnesia** is defined as the loss of memory.) Working memory is also susceptible to external interference, such as an attempt to learn conflicting information. On the other hand, long-term memory can survive deep anesthesia, trauma, or electroconvulsive shock, all of which disrupt the normal patterns of neural conduction in the brain.

As stated earlier, memory consolidation involves cellular or molecular changes in one or more neurons, and these changes constitute the memory trace. The changes are initiated by electrical activity in the neurons during working memory. This activity, in turn, causes alterations in synaptic effectiveness (pages 205–207) or even in the formation of new synapses.

One model for memory consolidation is **long-term potentiation (LTP)**, in which certain synapses undergo a long-lasting increase in their effectiveness when they are heavily used. This increased efficacy, which results in increased firing in the *postsynaptic* cell, can last minutes, hours, or even weeks. Although LTP occurs at many excitatory synapses in the central nervous system, it takes place most prominently in the hippocampus which, as we have just seen, is essential during the early phases of learning.

Learning is also associated with increased transmitter release from the *presynaptic* neuron. The postsynaptic cell must therefore inform the presynaptic cell in some way about its increased activity; in other words, information must move backward across the synapse. Candidates for this retrograde messenger are arachidonic acid, nitric oxide, and carbon monoxide because these compounds readily cross cell membranes and can diffuse back to the presynaptic neuron. Resulting changes in Ca^{2+} permeability alter the amount of neurotransmitter released from the presynaptic terminal in response to action potentials in the terminal. These changes can be long-lasting. Such changes occur in invertebrate systems during memory formation and probably occur in the human brain as well.

SUMMARY

Consciousness includes states of consciousness and conscious experiences.

STATES OF CONSCIOUSNESS

I. The electroencephalogram provides one means of defining the state of consciousness.
   A. Electric currents in the cerebral cortex due predominately to summed postsynaptic potentials are recorded as the EEG.
   B. Slower EEG waves correlate with less responsive behaviors.
   C. Rhythm generators in the thalamus are probably responsible for the wavelike nature of the EEG.
   D. EEG is used to diagnose brain disease and damage.
II. Alpha rhythms and, during EEG arousal, beta rhythms characterize the EEG of an awake person.
III. Slow-wave sleep progresses from stage 1 (faster, lower-amplitude waves) through stage 4 (slower, higher-amplitude waves) and then back again, followed by an episode of REM (paradoxical) sleep. There are generally four or five of these cycles per night.
IV. In the hypothalamus and brainstem, sleep-producing and arousal centers interact to cause the progressive sleep phases. The overall sleep-wake cycling is controlled by the suprachiasmatic nucleus in the hypothalamus. The hypothalamic centers use prostaglandins as neurotransmitters, whereas the brainstem centers use norepinephrine, serotonin, dopamine, and acetylcholine.

CONSCIOUS EXPERIENCES

I. Brain structures involved in directed attention determine which brain areas gain temporary predominance in the ongoing stream of conscious experience.
II. Conscious experiences might occur because a set of neurons temporarily functions together, the neurons comprising the set changing as the focus of attention changes.

MOTIVATION AND EMOTION

I. Behaviors that satisfy homeostatic needs are primary motivated behaviors. Behavior not related to homeostasis is a result of secondary motivation.
   A. Repetition of a behavior indicates that it is rewarding, and avoidance of a behavior indicates it is punishing.
   B. Lateral portions of the hypothalamus are involved in reward.
   C. Norepinephrine, dopamine, and enkephalin are transmitters in the brain pathways that mediate motivation and reward.

II. Two aspects of emotion, inner emotions and emotional behavior, can be distinguished. The limbic system integrates inner emotions and behavior.

ALTERED STATES OF CONSCIOUSNESS

I. Schizophrenics manifest either mainly positive or negative symptoms. Hyperactivity in brain dopaminergic systems is implicated in the disease.
II. The affective disorders are caused, at least in part, by disturbances in transmission at brain synapses mediated by dopamine or norepinephrine.
III. Many psychoactive drugs, which are often chemically related to neurotransmitters, result in drug dependence, withdrawal, and tolerance. These drug use patterns may result from homeostatic attempts to keep the transmitter-receptor interaction at a constant level.

LEARNING AND MEMORY

I. Depending on how long it lasts, memory is designated as working or long-term memory.
   A. Working memory has limited capacity, is short term, and depends on functioning brain electrical activity.
   B. After registering in working memory, facts either fade away or are consolidated in long-term memory, depending on attention, motivation, and various hormones.
   C. Long-term memory, of which there are two forms—procedural and declarative—has an unlimited capacity and is not destroyed by procedures that temporarily interrupt ongoing brain electrical activity.
II. Memory traces are cellular or molecular changes specific to different memories.
III. Learning is enhanced after subjects are exposed to enriched environments. The enhancement is presumably due to the brain neural and chemical development that follows such exposure.

CEREBRAL DOMINANCE AND LANGUAGE

I. The two cerebral hemispheres differ anatomically, chemically, and functionally. In 90 percent of the population, the left hemisphere is superior at producing language and in performing other tasks that require rapid changes over time.
II. After damage to the dominant hemisphere, some language function can be acquired by the opposite hemisphere—the younger the patient, the greater the transfer of function.

CONCLUSION

I. Many brain units are involved in the performance of even simple mental tasks.

11. Each unit is localized to a specific brain area, but, because many units are involved, widely distributed brain areas take part in mental tasks.

KEY TERMS

states of consciousness	emotions
conscious experiences	inner emotions
electroencephalogram (EEG)	emotional behavior
alpha rhythm	affect
beta rhythm	learning
EEG arousal	memory
slow wave sleep	memory trace
REM sleep	working memory
paradoxical sleep	long-term memory
preoptic area	memory consolidation
directed attention	procedural memories
orienting response	declarative memories
preattentive processing	long-term potentiation
habituation	plasticity
motivations	Wernicke's area
primary motivated behavior	Broca's area
brain self-stimulation	

REVIEW QUESTIONS

1. State the two criteria used to define one's state of consciousness.
2. What type of neural activity is recorded as the EEG?
3. Draw EEG records that show alpha and beta rhythms, the stages of slow-wave sleep, and REM sleep. Indicate the characteristic wave frequencies of each.
4. Using four characteristics, distinguish slow-wave sleep from REM sleep.
5. Briefly describe the neural mechanisms that determine the states of consciousness.
6. Name the criteria used to distinguish brain death from coma.
7. Describe the orienting response as a form of directed attention.
8. State two criteria that determine whether an experience will be conscious.
9. List the effects that unconscious processes can have on mental experiences.
10. Distinguish primary from secondary motivated behavior.
11. Explain how rewards and punishments are anatomically related to emotions.

12. Explain what brain self-stimulation can tell about emotions and rewards and punishments.
13. Name two neurotransmitters that mediate the brain reward systems.
14. Distinguish inner emotions from emotional behavior. Name the brain areas involved in each.
15. Describe the role of the limbic system in emotions.
16. Name the neurotransmitters involved in schizophrenia and the affective disorders.
17. Describe a mechanism that could explain tolerance and withdrawal.
18. Distinguish working memory from long-term memory and explain the relationship between them.
19. Name three factors that influence memory consolidation.
20. Explain how we can say that basic neural units are "strictly localized to specific parts of the brain" and yet say that "mental tasks are not performed by any single area of the brain."

CLINICAL TERMS

epilepsy	tricyclic antidepressant
sleep apnea	drugs
narcolepsy	monoamine oxidase
African sleeping sickness	inhibitors
brain death	electroconvulsive
altered states of	therapy (ECT)
consciousness	drug dependence
schizophrenia	withdrawal
catatonia	tolerance
dopamine hypothesis	cross-tolerance
affective disorders	retrograde amnesia
depressions	amnesia
manias	aphasias
bipolar affective disorders	

THOUGHT QUESTIONS

(Answers are given in Appendix A.)

1. Explain why patients given drugs to treat Parkinson's disease (pages 360–361) sometimes develop symptoms similar to those of schizophrenia.
2. Explain how clinical observations of individuals with various aphasias help physiologists understand the neural basis of language.

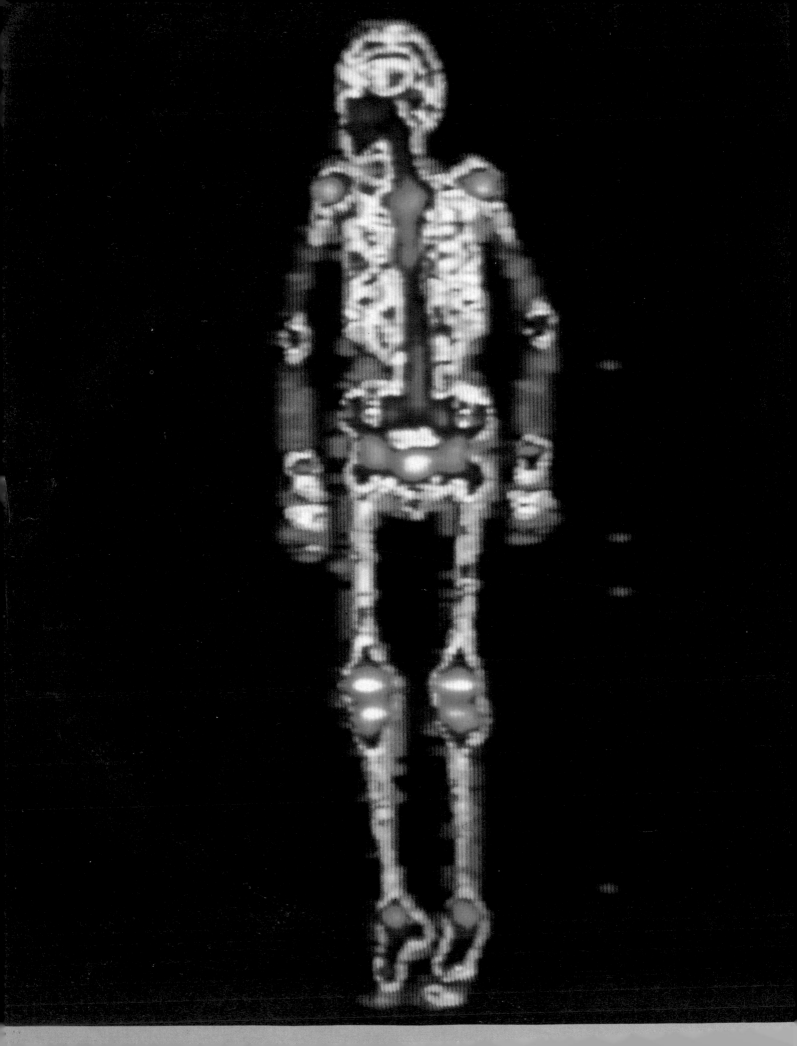

PART THREE

COORDINATED BODY FUNCTIONS

CHAPTER 14   CIRCULATION   393
              SECTION A. BLOOD   395
              SECTION B. OVERALL DESIGN OF THE
                         CARDIOVASCULAR SYSTEM   403
              SECTION C. THE HEART   409
              SECTION D. THE VASCULAR SYSTEM   429
              SECTION E. INTEGRATION OF CARDIOVASCULAR
                         FUNCTION: REGULATION OF SYSTEMIC
                         ARTERIAL PRESSURE   450
              SECTION F. CARDIOVASCULAR PATTERNS IN HEALTH
                         AND DISEASE   460
CHAPTER 15   RESPIRATION   473
CHAPTER 16   THE KIDNEYS AND REGULATION OF WATER
              AND INORGANIC IONS   515
              SECTION A. BASIC PRINCIPLES OF
                         RENAL PHYSIOLOGY   517

SECTION B. REGULATION OF SODIUM, WATER, AND POTASSIUM   529

SECTION C. CALCIUM REGULATION   546

SECTION D. HYDROGEN-ION REGULATION   552

SECTION E. DIURETICS AND KIDNEY DISEASE   557

CHAPTER 17   THE DIGESTION AND ABSORPTION OF FOOD   561

CHAPTER 18   REGULATION OF ORGANIC METABOLISM, GROWTH, AND ENERGY BALANCE   601

SECTION A. CONTROL AND INTEGRATION OF CARBOHYDRATE, PROTEIN, AND FAT METABOLISM   602

SECTION B. CONTROL OF GROWTH   624

SECTION C. REGULATION OF TOTAL BODY ENERGY BALANCE AND TEMPERATURE   630

CHAPTER 19   REPRODUCTION   647

SECTION A. GENERAL TERMINOLOGY AND CONCEPTS   648

SECTION B. MALE REPRODUCTIVE PHYSIOLOGY   651

SECTION C. FEMALE REPRODUCTIVE PHYSIOLOGY   661

SECTION D. THE CHRONOLOGY OF REPRODUCTIVE FUNCTION   692

CHAPTER 20   DEFENSE MECHANISMS OF THE BODY   699

SECTION A. IMMUNOLOGY: DEFENSES AGAINST FOREIGN MATTER   700

SECTION B. NONIMMUNE METABOLISM OF FOREIGN CHEMICALS   738

SECTION C. HEMOSTASIS: THE PREVENTION OF BLOOD LOSS   741

SECTION D. RESISTANCE TO STRESS   751

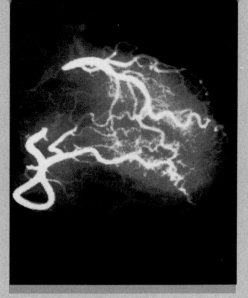

CHAPTER

14

CIRCULATION

SECTION A. BLOOD

PLASMA

THE BLOOD CELLS

Erythrocytes

 Iron

 Folic acid and vitamin B$_{12}$

 Regulation of erythrocyte production

 Anemia

Leukocytes

Platelets

Regulation of Blood Cell Production

SECTION A SUMMARY

SECTION A KEY TERMS

SECTION A REVIEW QUESTIONS

SECTION B. OVERALL DESIGN OF THE CARDIOVASCULAR SYSTEM

PRESSURE, FLOW, AND RESISTANCE

SECTION B SUMMARY

SECTION B KEY TERMS

SECTION B REVIEW QUESTIONS

SECTION C. THE HEART

ANATOMY

Cardiac Muscle

 Innervation

 Blood supply

HEARTBEAT COORDINATION

Cardiac Action Potentials

Sequence of Excitation

The Electrocardiogram

Excitation-Contraction Coupling

Refractory Period of the Heart

MECHANICAL EVENTS OF THE CARDIAC CYCLE

Mid-Diastole to Late Diastole

Systole

Early Diastole

Pulmonary Circulation Pressures

Heart Sounds

THE CARDIAC OUTPUT

Control of Heart Rate

Control of Stroke Volume

 Relationship between end-diastolic volume and stroke volume: Starling's law of the heart

 The sympathetic nerves

MEASUREMENT OF CARDIAC FUNCTION

SECTION C SUMMARY

SECTION C KEY TERMS

SECTION C REVIEW QUESTIONS

SECTION D. THE VASCULAR SYSTEM

ARTERIES

Arterial Blood Pressure

Measurement of Systemic Arterial Pressure

ARTERIOLES

Local Controls

Active hyperemia

Flow autoregulation

Reactive hyperemia

Response to injury

Extrinsic Controls

Sympathetic nerves

Parasympathetic nerves and other vasodilator nerves

Hormones

Endothelial Cells and Vascular Smooth Muscle

Arteriolar Control in Specific Organs

CAPILLARIES

Anatomy of the Capillary Network

Velocity of Capillary Blood Flow

Diffusion across the Capillary Wall: Exchanges of Nutrients and Metabolic End Products

Bulk Flow across the Capillary Wall: Distribution of the Extracellular Fluid

VEINS

Determinants of Venous Pressure

THE LYMPHATIC SYSTEM

Mechanism of Flow

SECTION D SUMMARY

SECTION D KEY TERMS

SECTION D REVIEW QUESTIONS

SECTION E. INTEGRATION OF CARDIOVASCULAR FUNCTION: REGULATION OF SYSTEMIC ARTERIAL PRESSURE

BARORECEPTOR REFLEXES

Arterial Baroreceptors

Other Baroreceptors

The Medullary Cardiovascular Center

Operation of the Baroreceptor Reflex

BLOOD VOLUME AND LONG-TERM REGULATION OF ARTERIAL PRESSURE

OTHER CARDIOVASCULAR REFLEXES AND RESPONSES

SECTION E SUMMARY

SECTION E KEY TERMS

SECTION E REVIEW QUESTIONS

SECTION F. CARDIOVASCULAR PATTERNS IN HEALTH AND DISEASE

HEMORRHAGE AND OTHER CAUSES OF HYPOTENSION

Shock

THE UPRIGHT POSTURE

EXERCISE

Maximal Oxygen Consumption and Training

HYPERTENSION

HEART FAILURE

CORONARY ARTERY DISEASE

SECTION F SUMMARY

SECTION F KEY TERMS

SECTION F REVIEW QUESTIONS

CHAPTER 14 CLINICAL TERMS

CHAPTER 14 THOUGHT QUESTIONS

eyond a distance of a few cell diameters, diffusion—the random movement of substances from a region of high concentration to one of low concentration—is not sufficiently rapid to meet the metabolic requirements of cells. For multicellular organisms to evolve to a size larger than a microscopic cluster of cells, some mechanism other than diffusion was needed to transport molecules rapidly over the long distances between internal cells and the body's surface and between the various specialized tissues and organs. This problem was solved in the animal kingdom by the **circulatory system**, which comprises the blood, the set of interconnected tubes (**blood vessels** or **vascular system**) through which the blood flows, and a pump (the **heart**) that produces this flow. The heart and blood vessels together are termed the **cardiovascular system**.

SECTION

BLOOD

lood is composed of cells and a liquid, **plasma**, in which they are suspended. The cells are the **erythrocytes** (red blood cells), the **leukocytes** (white blood cells), and the **platelets**, which are not complete cells but cell fragments. More than 99 percent of the cells are erythrocytes, which are the oxygen-carrying cells of the blood. The leukocytes protect against infection and cancer. The platelets function in blood clotting. In the cardiovascular system, the constant motion of the blood keeps all the cells well dispersed throughout the plasma.

The **hematocrit** is defined as the percentage of total blood volume that is erythrocytes. It is determined by centrifuging (spinning at high speed) a sample of blood, the erythrocytes being forced to the bottom of the centrifuge tube and the plasma to the top, the leukocytes and platelets forming a very thin layer between them (Figure 14-1). The normal hematocrit is approximately 45 percent in men and 42 percent in women.

The total blood volume of an average person is approximately 5.5 L. If we take the hematocrit to be 45 percent, then

$$\text{Total erythrocyte volume} = 0.45 \times 5.5 \text{ L} = 2.5 \text{ L}$$

Therefore,

$$\text{Plasma volume} = 5.5 \text{ L} - 2.5 \text{ L} = 3.0 \text{ L}$$

This last calculation ignores the volume occupied by the leukocytes and platelets because it is normally so small.

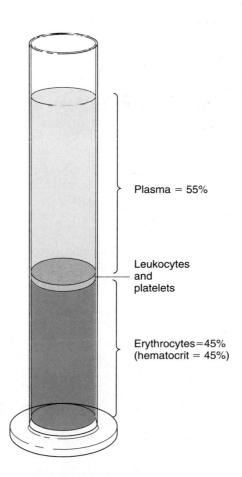

Plasma = 55%

Leukocytes and platelets

Erythrocytes=45% (hematocrit = 45%)

FIGURE 14-1
If a blood-filled capillary tube is centrifuged, the erythrocytes become packed in the lower portion, and the percentage of blood that is erythrocytes can be determined. This is called the hematocrit. The leukocytes and platelets form a very thin layer, known as a buffy coat, between the plasma and red cells. Its presence explains why, in this example, the value for plasma determined by this method is actually slightly less than 55 percent.

PLASMA

Plasma, the liquid portion of the blood, consists of a large number of organic and inorganic substances dissolved in water (Table 14-1). Most **plasma proteins** can be classified, according to certain physical and chemical reactions, into three broad groups: the **albumins** and **globulins**, which have many overlapping functions summarized in Table 14-1 and described in relevant chapters, and **fibrinogen**, which functions in blood clotting (Chapter 20). The albumins are by far the most abundant of these three groups and are synthesized by the liver.

It must be emphasized that the plasma proteins normally are not taken up by cells. Cells use plasma amino acids, not plasma proteins, to make their own proteins. Accordingly, plasma proteins must be viewed quite differently from most of the other organic constituents of plasma, which use the plasma as a vehicle for transport but are used by cells. The plasma proteins perform their functions in the plasma itself or in the interstitial fluid.

Serum is plasma from which fibrinogen and other proteins involved in clotting have been removed as a result of clotting.

In addition to the organic solutes—proteins, nutrients, and metabolic waste products—plasma contains a variety of mineral electrolytes. Note in Table 14-1 that these ions constitute much less of the weight of plasma than the proteins do but in most cases have much higher molar concentrations. This is because molarity is a measure not of *weight* but of *number* of molecules or ions per unit volume. Thus, there are many more ions than protein molecules, but the protein molecules are so large that a very small number of them greatly outweighs the much larger number of ions.

The characteristic straw color of plasma is due largely to a waste product of hemoglobin breakdown called **bilirubin**, which will be described in a later section.

THE BLOOD CELLS

Erythrocytes

Erythrocytes have the shape of a biconcave disk, that is, a disk thicker at the edge than in the middle, like a doughnut with a center depression on each side instead of a hole (Figure 14-2). Their shape and small size (7 μm in diameter) impart to them a high surface-to-volume ratio, so that oxygen and carbon dioxide can rapidly diffuse to and from the interior of the cell. The plasma membrane of erythrocytes contains specific polysaccharides and proteins that differ from person to person, and these confer upon the blood its so-called type, or group. Our description of blood groups is best delayed until Chapter 20, where it can be

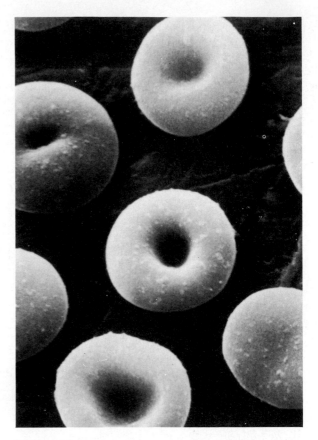

FIGURE 14-2

Scanning electron micrograph of erythrocytes. (*From R. G. Kessel and C. Y. Shih, "Scanning Electron Microscopy in Biology," Springer-Verlag, New York, 1974, p. 265.*)

done in the context of the immune responses that occur in so-called transfusion reactions.

Erythrocytes contain the protein **hemoglobin**, which binds oxygen taken in by the lungs. Each erythrocyte contains 200 to 300 million hemoglobin molecules, which constitute approximately one-third of the total weight of the erythrocyte. Each hemoglobin molecule is made up of four subunits bound together. Each subunit consists of a molecular group known as **heme** and a polypeptide attached to the heme. The four polypeptides of a hemoglobin molecule are collectively called **globin**. Each of the four heme groups in a hemoglobin molecule (Figure 14-3) contains one atom of iron (Fe), which can bind one molecule of oxygen. Thus, a single hemoglobin molecule can bind four molecules of oxygen. The average concentration of hemoglobin in blood is 14 g/dl in women and 16 g/dl in men. Hemoglobin is not the only heme-containing protein in the body; the other major ones are the cytochromes (Chapter 5).

The site of erythrocyte production is the soft interior of bones called **bone marrow**, specifically the "red" bone

TABLE 14-1   CONSTITUENTS OF PLASMA

Constituent	Amount/concentration	Major functions
Water	93% of plasma weight	Medium for carrying all other constituents
Electrolytes (inorganic)	Total < 1% of plasma weight	Keep H_2O in extracellular compartment; act as buffers; function in membrane excitability and blood clotting
Na^+	145 mM	
K^+	4 mM	
Ca^{2+}	2.5 mM	
Mg^{2+}	1.5 mM	
Cl^-	103 mM	
HCO_3^-	24 mM	
Phosphate (mostly HPO_4^{2-})	1 mM	
SO_4^{2-}	0.5 mM	
Proteins	Total — 7% of plasma weight, 7.3 g/100 ml (2.5 mM)	Provide nonpenetrating solutes of plasma; act as buffers; bind and transport other plasma constituents (lipids, hormones, vitamins, metals, etc.); clotting factors; enzymes; enzyme precursors; antibodies (immune globulins); hormones
Albumins	4.5 g/100 ml	
Globulins	2.5 g/100 ml	
Fibrinogen	0.3 g/100 ml	Blood clotting
Gases		
CO_2	2 ml/100 ml (1 mM)	No function; a waste product
O_2	0.2 ml/100 ml (0.1 mM)	Oxidative metabolism
N_2	0.9 ml/100 ml (0.5 mM)	No function
Nutrients		
Glucose and other carbohydrates	100 mg/100 ml (5.6 mM)	
Total amino acids	40 mg/100 ml (2 mM)	
Total lipids	500 mg/100 ml (7.5 mM)	
Cholesterol	150–250 mg/100 ml (4–7 mM)	
Individual vitamins	0.0001–2.5 mg/100 ml (0.00005–0.1 mM)	
Individual trace elements	0.001–0.3 mg/100 ml (0.0001–0.01 mM)	
Waste products		
Urea (from protein)	34 mg/100 ml (5.7 mM)	
Creatinine (from creatine)	1 mg/100 ml (0.09 mM)	
Uric acid (from nucleic acids)	5 mg/100 ml (0.3 mM)	
Bilirubin (from heme)	0.2–1.2 mg/100 ml (0.003–0.018 mM)	
Individual hormones	0.000001–0.05 mg/100 ml (10^{-9}–10^{-6} mM)	

marrow. As differentiation occurs, these cells begin to produce hemoglobin but then ultimately lose their nuclei and organelles. Young erythrocytes in the bone marrow still contain a few ribosomes, which produce a weblike (reticular) appearance when treated with special stains, an appearance that gives these young erythrocytes the name **reticulocyte**. Normally, only mature erythrocytes, which have lost these ribosomes, leave the bone marrow and enter the general circulation. In the presence of unusually rapid erythrocyte production, however, many reticulocytes do enter the blood.

Because erythrocytes lack nuclei and organelles, they can neither reproduce themselves nor maintain their normal structure for very long. The average life span of an

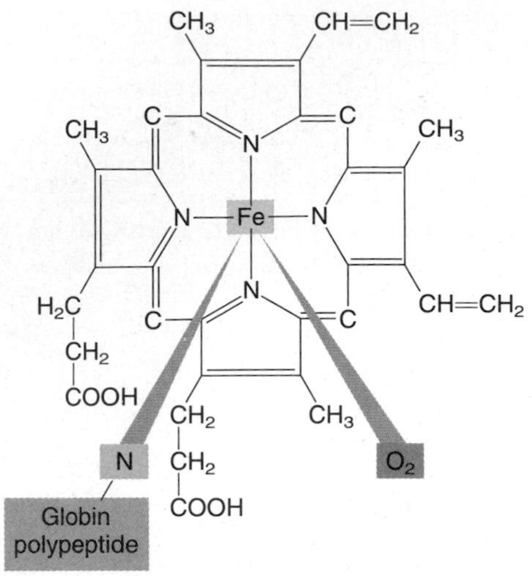

FIGURE 14-3

Heme. Oxygen binds to the iron atom (Fe). Heme attaches to a polypeptide chain by a nitrogen atom to form one subunit of hemoglobin. Four of these subunits bind to each other to make a single hemoglobin molecule.

erythrocyte is approximately 120 days, which means that almost 1 percent of the body's erythrocytes are destroyed and must be replaced every day. This amounts to 100 billion cells per day! Erythrocyte destruction normally occurs in the spleen and the liver. As will be described below, most of the iron released in the process is conserved. The major breakdown product of heme is bilirubin, which, as noted above, gives plasma its color (the fate of this substance will be described in Chapter 17).

The production of erythrocytes requires the usual nutrients needed to synthesize any cell: amino acids, lipids, and carbohydrates. In addition, both iron and certain growth factors, including folic acid and vitamin B_{12}, are essential.

Iron. As noted above, **iron** is the element to which oxygen binds within an erythrocyte. Small amounts of iron are lost via the urine, feces, sweat, and cells sloughed from the skin. In addition, women lose a similar amount via menstrual blood. In order to remain in iron balance, the amount of iron lost from the body must be replaced by ingestion of iron-containing foods—particularly rich sources are meat, liver, shellfish, egg yolk, beans, nuts, and cereals. A significant upset of iron balance can result either in *iron deficiency*, leading to inadequate hemoglobin production, or in an excess of iron in the body, with serious toxic effects.

The homeostatic control of iron balance resides primarily in the intestinal epithelium, which actively absorbs iron from ingested food. Only a small fraction of ingested iron is normally absorbed, but what is more important, this

fraction is increased or decreased, in a negative-feedback manner, depending upon the state of the body's iron balance. These fluctuations are mediated by changes in the iron content of the intestinal epithelium (Chapter 17): The more iron in the body, the more in the intestinal epithelium, and the less new iron will be absorbed.

A buffer against iron deficiency is the considerable body store of iron, mainly in the liver, bound up in a protein called **ferritin**. About 50 percent of the total body iron is in hemoglobin, 25 percent is in heme-containing proteins (mainly the cytochromes) in other cells of the body, and 25 percent is in liver ferritin. Moreover, the recycling of iron is very efficient (Figure 14-4): As old erythrocytes are destroyed in the spleen and liver, their iron is released into the plasma and bound to an iron-transport protein called **transferrin**. Almost all of this iron is delivered by transferrin to the bone marrow to be incorporated into new erythrocytes. On a much lesser scale, other organs and tissues, some cells of which are continuously dying and being replaced, release iron from their cytochromes into the plasma and take up iron from it, transferrin serving as the carrier.

Folic Acid and Vitamin B_{12}. **Folic acid**, a vitamin found in large amounts in leafy plants, yeast, and liver, is required for synthesis of the pyrimidine thymine. It is, therefore, essential for the formation of DNA, and hence for normal cell division. When this vitamin is not present in adequate amounts, impairment of cell division occurs throughout the body but is most striking in rapidly proliferating cells, including erythrocyte precursors. Thus, fewer erythrocytes are produced when folic acid is deficient.

Production of normal erythrocyte numbers also requires extremely small quantities (one-millionth of a gram per day) of a cobalt-containing molecule, **vitamin B_{12}** (also called **cobalamin**), since this vitamin is required for the action of folic acid. Vitamin B_{12} is found only in animal products, and strictly vegetarian diets may be deficient in it. Also, as described in Chapter 17, the absorption of vitamin B_{12} from the gastrointestinal tract requires a protein, called **intrinsic factor**, which is secreted by the stomach; lack of this protein also causes vitamin B_{12} deficiency. Unlike folic acid, vitamin B_{12} is also needed for myelin formation, so a variety of neurological symptoms may accompany the poor erythrocyte production when vitamin B_{12} is deficient.

Regulation of Erythrocyte Production. In a normal person, the total volume of circulating erythrocytes remains remarkably constant because of reflexes that regulate the bone marrow's production of these cells. In the previous section, we stated that iron, folic acid, and vitamin B_{12} must be present for normal erythrocyte produc-

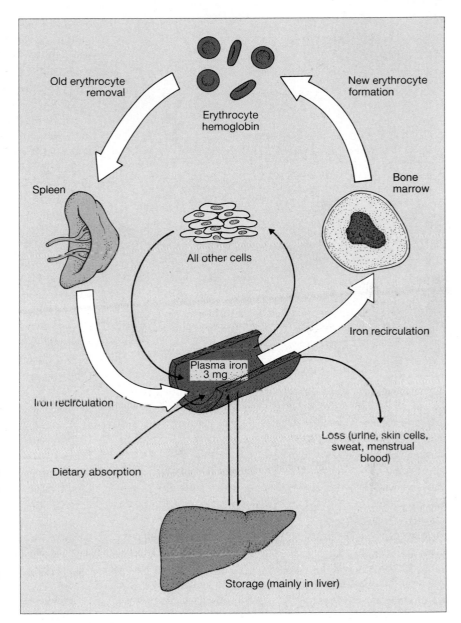

FIGURE 14-4

Summary of iron balance. The thickness of the arrows corresponds approximately to the amount of iron involved. In the steady state, the rate of gastrointestinal iron absorption and the rate of iron loss via urine, skin, and menstrual flow are equal. The rate of absorption is the major homeostatically controlled process. Recirculation of erythrocyte iron is very important because it involves 20 times more iron per day than is absorbed and excreted. (*Adapted from Crosby.*)

tion. However, none of these substances constitutes the signal that *regulates* production rate.

The direct control of erythrocyte production (erythropoiesis) is exerted mainly by a hormone called **erythropoietin**, which is secreted into the blood by capillary endothelial cells in the kidneys (and, to a much lesser extent, the liver). Erythropoietin acts on the bone marrow to stimulate the proliferation of erythrocyte progenitor cells and their differentiation into erythrocytes.

Erythropoietin is normally secreted in relatively small amounts, which stimulate the bone marrow to produce erythrocytes at a rate adequate to replace the usual loss. The erythropoietin secretion rate can be increased markedly above basal values, the stimulus being a decreased oxygen delivery to the kidneys. As a result of the increase

in erythropoietin secretion, plasma erythropoietin concentration, erythrocyte production, and the oxygen-carrying capacity of the blood all increase; therefore, oxygen delivery to the tissues returns toward normal (Figure 14-5).

Testosterone also stimulates the release of erythropoietin. This may account, at least in part, for the higher hemoglobin concentration in men than in women.

Anemia. Defined as (1) a decrease in the total number of erythrocytes, each having a normal quantity of hemoglobin, or (2) a diminished concentration of hemoglobin per erythrocyte, or (3) a combination of both, *anemia* has a wide variety of causes, summarized in Table 14-2.

The last disease—*sickle-cell anemia*—mentioned in Table 14-2 is due to a genetic mutation that causes substi-

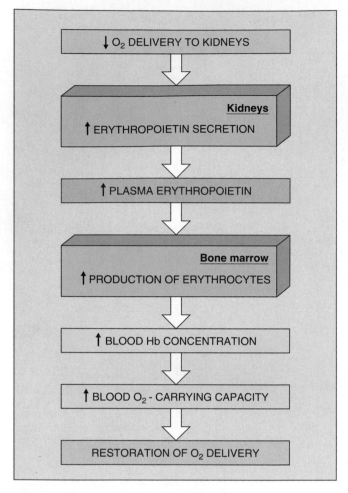

FIGURE 14-5

Reflex by which a decreased oxygen delivery to the kidneys increases erythrocyte production via increased erythropoietin secretion. Situations that trigger this reflex include insufficient pumping of blood by the heart, lung disease, anemia (a decrease in number of erythrocytes or in hemoglobin concentration), and exposure to high altitude. The exact mechanism by which a decreased oxygen delivery stimulates erythropoietin secretion by the renal endothelial cells is unclear.

TABLE 14-2 MAJOR CAUSES OF ANEMIA

1. Dietary deficiencies of iron, vitamin B_{12} (***pernicious anemia***), or folic acid
2. Bone marrow failure due to toxic drugs or cancer
3. Blood loss from the body (***hemorrhage***) leading to iron deficiency
4. Inadequate secretion of erythropoietin in kidney disease
5. Excessive destruction of erythrocytes (for example, ***sickle-cell anemia***)

---

tution of one wrong amino acid in a particular portion of globin. At the low oxygen concentrations existing in many capillaries, the abnormal hemoglobin molecules interact with each other to form fiber-like structures that distort the erythrocyte membrane and cause the cell to form sickle shapes or other bizarre forms. This results both in the blockage of capillaries, with consequent tissue damage and pain, and in the destruction of the deformed erythrocytes, with consequent anemia.

Laboratory evaluation of anemia starts with analysis of a blood sample for the concentration of hemoglobin, the number of erythrocytes, and the average cell size. Average cell size is particularly useful since it correlates well with several common types of anemia. For example, ***microcytosis*** (small cells) most commonly occurs in iron deficiency, ***normocytosis*** (normal-sized cells) accompanies acute blood loss, and ***macrocytosis*** (large cells) is characteristic of vitamin B_{12} or folic acid deficiency. Macrocytosis is due to delayed cell division because of a DNA deficiency.

Finally, there also exist conditions in which the problem is just the opposite of anemia, namely, too many erythrocytes; this is termed ***polycythemia***.

Leukocytes

If one adds appropriate dyes to a drop of blood and examines it under a microscope, the various leukocyte types (Table 14-3) can be seen clearly (Figure 14-6). They are classified according to their structure and affinity for various dyes.

TABLE 14-3 NUMBERS AND DISTRIBUTIONS OF ERYTHROCYTES, LEUKOCYTES, AND PLATELETS IN NORMAL HUMAN BLOOD

Total erythrocytes = 5,000,000 per mm^3 of blood

Total leukocytes = 7000 per mm^3 of blood

  Percent of total leukocytes:

    Polymorphonuclear granulocytes

      Neutrophils 50–70

      Eosinophils 1–4

      Basophils 0.1

    Monocytes 2–8

    Lymphocytes 20–40

Total platelets = 250,000 per mm^3 of blood

The name **polymorphonuclear granulocytes** refers to the three types of leukocytes with multilobed nuclei and abundant membrane-bound granules. The granules of one group take up the red dye eosin, thus giving the cells their name **eosinophils**. Cells of a second group have an affinity for a blue dye termed a "basic" dye and are called

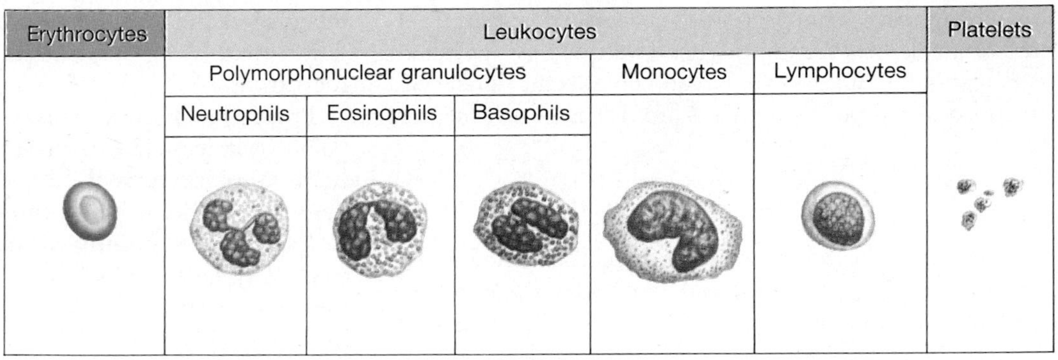

Erythrocytes	Leukocytes						Platelets
	Polymorphonuclear granulocytes			Monocytes	Lymphocytes		
	Neutrophils	Eosinophils	Basophils				

FIGURE 14-6
Normal blood cell types.

basophils. The granules of the third group have only little affinity for either dye and are therefore called **neutrophils**. Neutrophils are by far the most abundant type of leukocyte.

A fourth type of leukocyte is the **monocyte**, which is somewhat larger than the granulocyte and has an oval or horseshoe-shaped nucleus and relatively few cytoplasmic granules. The final class of leukocytes is the **lymphocyte**, which contains scanty cytoplasm and, like the monocyte, a relatively large nucleus.

Like the erythrocytes, all types of leukocytes are produced in the bone marrow. In addition, monocytes and

FIGURE 14-7
Production of blood cells by the bone marrow. For simplicity, no attempt has been made to differentiate the appearance of the various precursors (*Adapted from Golde and Gasson.*)

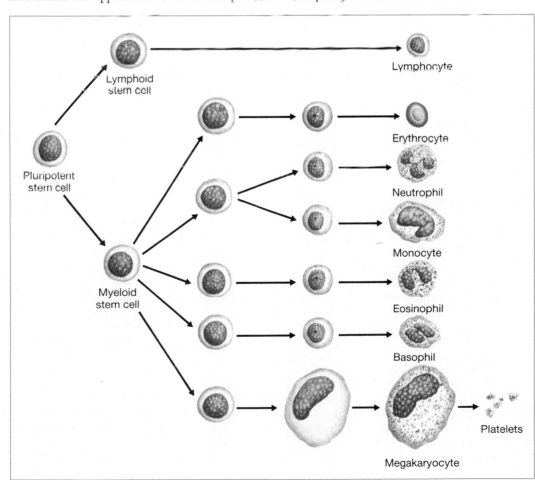

many lymphocytes undergo further development and cell division in tissues outside the bone marrow, as described in Chapter 20. These events and the specific leukocyte functions in the body's defenses are discussed in Chapter 20.

Platelets

The circulating platelets are colorless cell fragments that contain numerous granules and are much smaller than erythrocytes. Platelets are produced when the cytoplasm of large bone marrow cells, termed **megakaryocytes**, becomes pinched off and enters the circulation. Platelet functions in blood clotting are described in Chapter 20.

Regulation of Blood Cell Production

In children, the marrow of most bones produces blood cells. By adulthood, however, only the bones of the chest, the base of the skull, and the upper portions of the limbs remain active. The bone marrow in an adult weighs almost as much as the liver, and it produces cells at an enormous rate.

All blood cell types are descended from a single population of bone marrow cells called **pluripotent stem cells**, which are undifferentiated cells capable of giving rise to precursors (progenitors) of any of the individual cell types (Figure 14-7). When a pluripotent stem cell divides, its two daughter cells either remain pluripotent stem cells or become committed to a particular developmental pathway—what governs this "decision" is not known. The first branching yields lymphoid stem cells, which give rise to the lymphocytes, and myeloid stem cells, the progenitors of all the other types. At some point, the proliferating offspring of the myeloid stem cells become committed to differentiate along only one path, for example, into erythrocytes.

Production of the various cells is stimulated at multiple points by at least 12 protein hormones collectively termed **hematopoietic growth factors (HGFs)**. Erythropoietin, described above, is one such hormone. Another group of HGFs are called **colony-stimulating factors (CSFs)** because they were originally discovered to stimulate the formation of colonies derived from individual bone marrow progenitors. The major effects of the CSFs are to stimulate the cell lines leading to granulocytes and monocytes. Still another group of HGFs belong to the family of hormones called **interleukins** for their ability to mediate communication between leukocytes, as described in Chapter 20.

The physiology of the HGFs is very complex since there are so many of them and since any given HGF often is produced by a variety of cell types throughout the body and exerts actions other than stimulating blood-cell production in the bone marrow. There are, moreover, many interactions of the HGFs on particular bone marrow cells and processes. For example, although erythropoietin is the major stimulator of erythropoiesis, at least 10 other HGFs cooperate in the process. Finally, the HGFs also enhance the function of blood cells after these cells' release from the bone marrow into the blood.

The administration of specific HGFs is proving to be of considerable clinical importance. Examples are the use of erythropoietin in persons with a deficiency of this hormone due to kidney disease, and the use of granulocyte CSF to stimulate granulocyte production in individuals whose bone marrow has been damaged.

SECTION A SUMMARY

I. Blood is composed of cells (erythrocytes, leukocytes, and platelets) and plasma, the liquid in which the cells are suspended.

II. Plasma contains proteins (albumins, globulins, and fibrinogen), nutrients, metabolic end products, hormones, and mineral electrolytes.

III. Erythrocytes, which make up more than 99 percent of blood cells, contain hemoglobin, an oxygen-binding protein consisting of heme and globin. Oxygen binds to the iron in heme.

    A. Erythrocytes are produced in the bone marrow and destroyed in the spleen and liver.

    B. Iron, folic acid, and vitamin B_{12} are essential for erythrocyte formation.

    C. The hormone erythropoietin, which is produced by the kidneys in response to low oxygen supply, stimulates erythrocyte differentiation and production by the bone marrow.

    D. Anemia can be caused not only by a deficiency of iron, vitamin B_{12}, or folic acid but also by bone marrow failure, excessive blood loss, excessive destruction of erythrocytes, and an erythropoietin deficiency.

IV. The leukocytes include three types of polymorphonuclear granulocytes (neutrophils, eosinophils, and basophils), monocytes, and lymphocytes.

V. Platelets are cell fragments essential for blood clotting.

VI. Blood cells are descended from stem cells in the bone marrow. Their production is controlled by hematopoietic growth factors.

SECTION A KEY TERMS

circulatory system	iron
blood vessels	ferritin
vascular system	transferrin
heart	folic acid
cardiovascular system	vitamin B_{12}
blood	cobalamin
plasma	intrinsic factor
erythrocytes	erythropoietin
leukocytes	polymorphonuclear
platelets	granulocytes
hematocrit	eosinophils
plasma proteins	basophils
albumins	neutrophils
globulins	monocytes
fibrinogen	lymphocytes
serum	megakaryocytes
bilirubin	pluripotent stem cells
hemoglobin	hematopoietic growth factors
heme	(HGFs)
globin	colony-stimulating factors
bone marrow	(CSFs)
reticulocytes	interleukins

SECTION A REVIEW QUESTIONS

1. Give average values for total blood volume, erythrocyte volume, plasma volume, and hematocrit.

2. Which is the most abundant class of plasma protein?

3. Which solute has the highest concentration in plasma?

4. Describe the structure of hemoglobin.

5. Summarize the production, life span, and destruction of erythrocytes.

6. What are the routes of iron gain, loss, and distribution, and how is iron recycled when erythrocytes are destroyed?

7. Describe the control of erythropoietin secretion and the effect of this hormone.

8. State the relative proportions of erythrocytes and leukocytes in blood.

9. Diagram the derivation of the different blood cell lines.

10. List the different hematopoietic growth factors.

SECTION

B

OVERALL DESIGN OF THE CARDIOVASCULAR SYSTEM

The rapid flow of blood throughout the body is produced by pressures created by the pumping action of the heart. This type of flow is known as **bulk flow** because all constituents of the blood move in one direction together. The extraordinary degree of branching of blood vessels ensures that almost all cells in the body are within a few cell diameters of at least one of the smallest branches, the capillaries. Nutrients and metabolic end products move between capillary blood and the interstitial fluid by *diffusion*. Movements between the interstitial fluid and cell interior are by diffusion and medicated transport.

At any given moment, approximately 5 percent of the total circulating blood is flowing through the capillaries. Yet it is this 5 percent that is performing the ultimate functions of the entire cardiovascular system: the supplying of nutrients and the removal of metabolic end products. All other components of the system subserve the overall aim of getting adequate blood flow through the capillaries. This point should be kept in mind as we describe these components.

As discovered by the British physiologist William Harvey in 1628, the cardiovascular system forms a circle, so that blood pumped out of the heart through one set of vessels returns to the heart via a different set. There are actually two circuits (Figure 14-8), both originating and terminating in the heart, which is divided longitudinally into two functional halves. Each half contains two chambers: an **atrium** and a **ventricle**. The atrium on each side empties into the ventricle on that side, but there is no direct communication between the two atria or the two ventricles.

Blood is pumped via one circuit (the **pulmonary cir-**

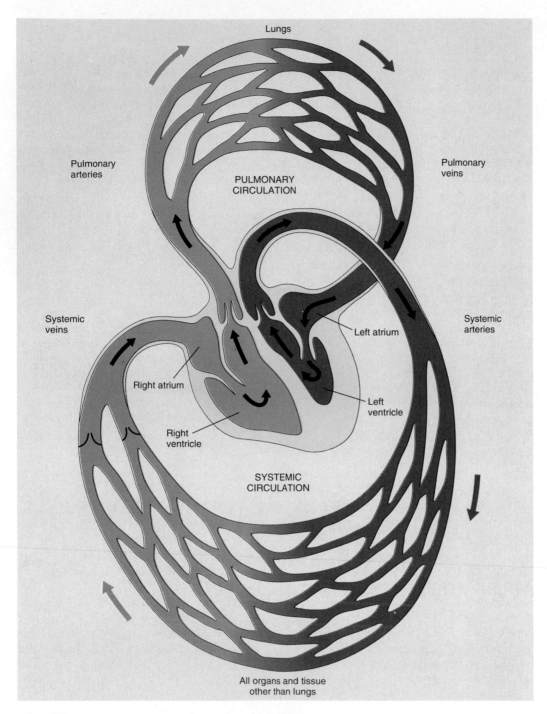

FIGURE 14-8

The systemic and pulmonary circulations. The pulmonary circulation pumps blood through the lungs, and the systemic circulation supplies all other organs and tissues. As depicted by the color change from blue to red, blood is fully oxygenated as it flows through the lungs and then loses some oxygen (red to blue) as it flows through the other organs and tissues. For simplicity, the arteries and veins leaving and entering the heart are depicted as single vessels; in reality, this is true for the arteries but not for the veins (see Figure 14-9).

culation) from the right ventricle through the lungs and then to the left atrium. It is then pumped through the **systemic circulation**, from the left ventricle through all the tissues of the body except the lungs and then to the right atrium. In both circuits, the vessels carrying blood away from the heart are called **arteries**, and those carrying blood from either the lungs or all other parts of the body (peripheral organs and tissues) back to the heart are called **veins**.

In the systemic circuit, blood leaves the left ventricle via a single large artery, the **aorta** (Figure 14-9). The systemic arteries come off the aorta, dividing into progressively smaller branches. The smallest arteries branch into **arterioles**, which branch into a huge number of very small vessels—the **capillaries**, which unite to form larger-diameter vessels—**venules**. The arterioles, capillaries, and venules are collectively termed the **microcirculation**.

The venules in the systemic circulation then unite to form larger vessels, the veins. The veins from the various peripheral organs and tissues unite to produce two large veins, the **inferior vena cava**, which collects blood from the lower portion of the body, and the **superior vena cava**, which collects blood from the upper half of the body. It is via these two veins that blood is returned to the right atrium.

The pulmonary circulation is composed of a similar circuit. Blood leaves the right ventricle via a single large artery, the **pulmonary trunk**, which divides into two **pulmonary arteries**, one supplying the right lung and the other the left. In the lungs, the arteries continue to branch, ultimately forming capillaries that unite into venules and then veins. The blood leaves the lungs via four **pulmonary veins**, which empty into the left atrium.

As blood flows through the lung capillaries, it picks up oxygen supplied to the adjacent lung air sacs by breathing. Therefore, the blood in the pulmonary veins, left heart, and systemic arteries has a high oxygen content. As this blood flows through the capillaries of peripheral tissues

FIGURE 14-9

Blood leaves each of the ventricles via a single artery, the pulmonary trunk from the right ventricle and the aorta from the left ventricle. [Because the aorta and pulmonary trunk cross each other before emerging from the heart (Figure 14-13), one gets the mistaken impression that the aorta arises from the right ventricle and pulmonary trunk from the left ventricle.] Blood enters the right atrium via two large veins, the superior vena cava and inferior vena cava; it enters the left atrium via four pulmonary veins.

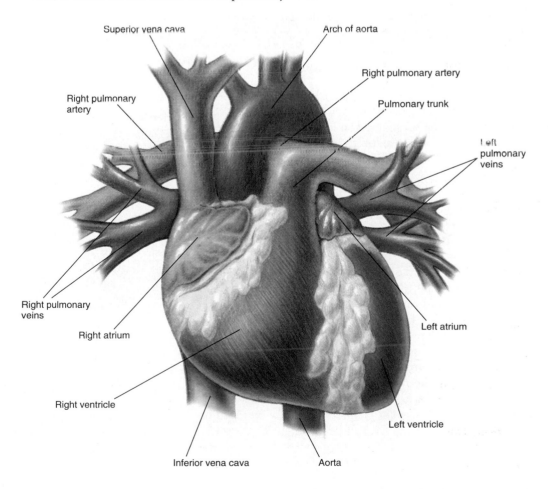

	Rest ml/min
Brain	750 (13%)
Heart	250 (4%)
Muscle	1200 (20%)
Skin	500 (9%)
Kidney	1100 (20%)
Abdominal organs	1400 (24%)
Other	600 (10%)
Total	5800

FIGURE 14-10

Distribution of systemic blood flow to the various organs and tissues of the body at rest. (*Adapted from Chapman and Mitchell.*)

and organs, some of this oxygen leaves the blood to enter and be used by cells, resulting in the lower oxygen content of systemic venous blood.

As shown in Figure 14-8, blood can pass from the systemic veins to the systemic arteries only by first being pumped through the lungs. Thus all the blood returning from the body's peripheral organs and tissues via the systemic veins is oxygenated before it is pumped back to them.

It must be emphasized that the lungs receive all the blood pumped by the right heart, whereas each of the peripheral organs and tissues receives only a fraction of the blood pumped by the left ventricle. For reference, the typical distribution of the blood pumped by the left ventricle in an adult at rest is given in Figure 14-10.

Finally, there are several exceptions, notably the liver and kidneys, to the usual anatomical pattern described in this section for the systemic circulation, and these will be presented in the relevant chapters dealing with those organs.

PRESSURE, FLOW, AND RESISTANCE

The last task in this survey of the design of the cardiovascular system is to introduce the concepts of pressure, flow, and resistance. Throughout the system, blood flow (*F*) is always from a region of higher pressure to one of lower pressure. The term "pressure" refers to the force exerted by the blood. The pressure exerted by a fluid is often termed a **hydrostatic pressure**. The units for the rate of flow are volume per unit time, usually liters per minute (L/min). The units for the pressure difference (ΔP) driving the flow are millimeters of mercury (mmHg) because historically blood pressure was measured by determining how high a column of mercury could be driven by the blood pressure.

It must be emphasized that it is not the absolute pressure at any point in the cardiovascular system that determines flow rate, but the *difference* in pressure between the relevant points (Figure 14-11).

Knowing only the pressure difference between two points will not tell you the flow rate, however. For this, you also need to know the **resistance (*R*)** to flow, that is, how difficult it is for blood to flow between two points at any given pressure difference. Resistance is the measure of the friction that impedes flow. The basic equation relating these variables is

$$F = \frac{\Delta P}{R} \qquad (14\text{-}1)$$

FIGURE 14-11

Flow between two points within a tube is proportional to the pressure difference between the points. The flows in these two identical tubes are the same because the pressure differences are the same.

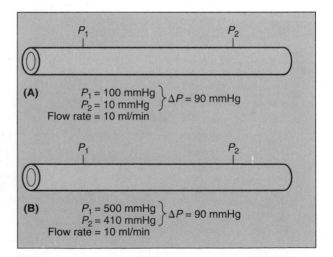

In words, flow rate is directly proportional to pressure difference and inversely proportional to resistance. This equation applies not only to the cardiovascular system but to any system in which liquid or air flows through tubes.

Resistance cannot be directly measured but is calculated from the directly measured F and ΔP. For example, in Figure 14-11 the resistances in both examples can be calculated to be 90 mmHg $\div$ 10 ml per minute = 9 mmHg/ml per minute.

This example illustrates how resistance can be *calculated*, but what is it that actually *determines* the resistance?[1] One determinant is the fluid property known as **viscosity**, which is a measure of the friction between adjacent layers of a flowing fluid; the greater the friction, the greater the viscosity. The other determinants of resistance are the tube's length and radius, which determine the amount of friction between the fluid and the tube wall. The following equation defines the contributions of these three determinants:

$$ R = \frac{\eta L}{r^4}\, \frac{8}{\pi} \qquad (14\text{-}2) $$

where η = fluid viscosity
L = tube length
r = inside radius of the tube
$8/\pi$ = a constant

In other words, resistance is directly proportional to both the fluid viscosity and tube length, and inversely proportional to the fourth power of the radius, that is, the radius multiplied by itself four times.[2]

Blood viscosity is not fixed but increases as hematocrit increases, and changes in hematocrit, therefore, can have important effects on the resistance to flow in certain situations. Under most physiological conditions, however, the hematocrit and, hence, viscosity of blood is relatively constant and does not play a role in the *control* of resistance.

Similarly, since the lengths of the blood vessels remain constant in the body, length is also not a factor in the control of resistance. In contrast, as we shall see, tube radius does not remain constant, and so tube radius—the $1/r^4$ term in our equation—is the most important determinant of changes in resistance. Just how important changes in radius can be is illustrated in Figure 14-12: Decreasing

---

[1]This distinction between how a thing is measured (or calculated) and its determinants may seem confusing to the reader. By standing on a scale you *measure* your weight, but your weight is not *determined* by the scale but rather by how much you eat, exercise, and so on.

[2]Substituting the determinants of R, as given in Equation 14-2, for R in Equation 14-1 gives the so-called Poiseuille equation, the full expression of the determinants of flow.

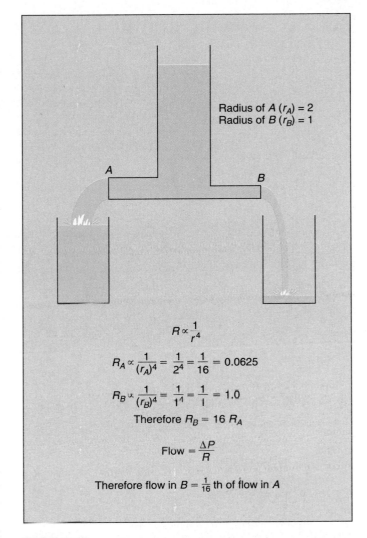

FIGURE 14-12
Effect of tube radius (r) on resistance (R) and flow.

the radius of a tube *twofold* increases its resistance *sixteenfold*. If ΔP is held constant in this example, flow through the tube decreases sixteenfold since $F = \Delta P/R$.

This completes our introductory survey of the cardiovascular system. We now turn to a description of its components and their control. In so doing, we might very easily lose sight of the forest for the trees if we do not persistently ask of each section: How does this component of the circulation contribute to adequate blood flow through the capillaries of the various organs or to an adequate exchange of materials between blood and cells? Referring to the summary in Table 14-4 as you read the description of each component will help you keep focused on this question.

TABLE 14-4 THE CARDIOVASCULAR SYSTEM

Component	Function
Heart	
Atria	Chambers through which blood flows from veins to ventricles. Atrial contraction adds to ventricular filling but is not essential.
Ventricles	Chambers whose contractions produce the pressures that drive blood through the pulmonary and systemic vascular systems and back to the heart.
Vascular system	
Arteries	Low-resistance tubes conducting blood to the various organs with little loss in pressure. They also act as pressure reservoirs for maintaining blood flow during ventricular relaxation.
Arterioles	Major sites of resistance to flow; responsible for the pattern of blood-flow distribution to the various organs; participate in the regulation of arterial blood pressure.
Capillaries	Sites of nutrient, waste product, and fluid exchange between blood and tissues.
Venules	Sites of nutrient, waste product, and fluid exchange between blood and tissues.
Veins	Low-resistance conduits for blood flow back to the heart. Their capacity for blood is adjusted so as to facilitate this flow.

SECTION B SUMMARY

I. The cardiovascular system consists of two circuits: the pulmonary circulation, from the right ventricle to the lungs and then to the left atrium; and the systemic circulation, from the left ventricle to all organs and tissues other than the lungs and then to the right atrium.

II. Arteries carry blood away from the heart, and veins carry blood to the heart.

   A. In the systemic circuit, the large artery leaving the left heart is the aorta, and the large veins emptying into the right heart are the superior and inferior venae cavae. The analogous vessels in the pulmonary circulation are the pulmonary trunk and the four pulmonary veins.

   B. The microcirculation consists of the vessels between arteries and veins—the arterioles, capillaries, and venules.

III. Flow between two points in the cardiovascular system is directly proportional to the pressure difference between the points and inversely proportional to the resistance: $F = \Delta P/R$

IV. Resistance is directly proportional to the viscosity of a fluid and to the length of the tube. It is inversely proportional to the fourth power of the tube's radius, which is the major variable controlling changes in resistance.

SECTION B KEY TERMS

bulk flow	venules
atrium	microcirculation
ventricle	inferior vena cava
pulmonary circulation	superior vena cava
systemic circulation	pulmonary trunk
arteries	pulmonary arteries
veins	pulmonary veins
aorta	hydrostatic pressure
arterioles	resistance (R)
capillaries	viscosity

SECTION B REVIEW QUESTIONS

1. State the formula relating flow, pressure difference, and resistance.
2. What are the three determinants of resistance?

ANATOMY

The heart is a muscular organ enclosed in a fibrous sac, the **pericardium**, and located in the chest (thorax). The narrow space between the pericardium and the heart is filled with a watery fluid that serves as a lubricant as the heart moves within the sac.

The walls of the heart are composed primarily of cardiac-muscle cells and are termed the **myocardium**. The inner surface of the walls, that is, the surface in contact with the blood within the cardiac chambers, is lined by a thin layer of cells known as **endothelial cells** or **endothelium**. (As we shall see, endothelial cells line not only the heart chambers but the entire vascular system as well.)

As noted earlier, the human heart is divided into right and left halves, each consisting of an atrium and a ventricle. Located between the atrium and ventricle in each half of the heart are the **atrioventricular (AV) valves**, which permit blood to flow from atrium to ventricle but not from ventricle to atrium (Figure 14-13). The right AV valve is called the **tricuspid valve**, and the left is called the **mitral valve**.

The opening and closing of the AV valves is a passive process resulting from pressure differences across the valves. When the blood is moving from atrium to ventricle, the valves are pushed open, but when a ventricle contracts, its AV valve is forced closed when the pressure of the blood in the ventricle becomes greater than that in the atrium. Blood is therefore forced into the pulmonary trunk from the right ventricle and into the aorta from the left ventricle, but blood does not normally move back into the atria.

To prevent the AV valves from being pushed up into the atrium, the valves are fastened to muscular projections **(papillary muscles)** of the ventricular walls by fibrous strands (chordae tendinae). The papillary muscles do *not* open or close the valves. They act only to limit the valves' movements and prevent them from being everted.

The opening of the right ventricle into the pulmonary trunk and of the left ventricle into the aorta are also regulated by valves, the **pulmonary** and **aortic valves** (Figure 14-13). These valves permit blood to flow into the arteries during ventricular contraction but prevent blood from moving in the opposite direction during ventricular relaxation. Like the AV valves, these valves act in a purely pas-

FIGURE 14-13

Diagrammatic section of the heart. The arrows indicate the direction of blood flow.

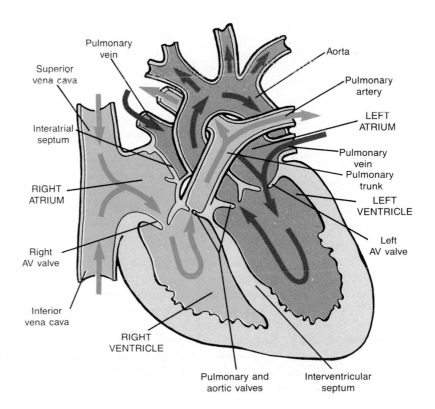

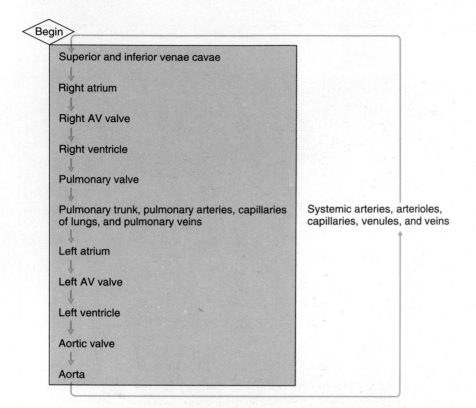

Begin

Superior and inferior venae cavae
↓
Right atrium
↓
Right AV valve
↓
Right ventricle
↓
Pulmonary valve
↓
Pulmonary trunk, pulmonary arteries, capillaries of lungs, and pulmonary veins
↓
Left atrium
↓
Left AV valve
↓
Left ventricle
↓
Aortic valve
↓
Aorta

Systemic arteries, arterioles, capillaries, venules, and veins

FIGURE 14-14

Path of blood flow through the entire cardiovascular system. All the structures within the colored box are located in the chest.

sive manner. Their being open or closed depends upon the pressure differences across them.

There are no valves at the entrances of the superior and inferior venae cavae (plural of vena cava) into the right atrium, and of the pulmonary veins into the left atrium. However, atrial contraction pumps very little blood back into the veins because atrial contraction compresses the veins at their site of entry into the atria, increasing the resistance to backflow. Actually, a little blood is ejected back into the veins, and this accounts for the venous pulse that can often be seen in the neck veins when the atria are contracting.

Figure 14-14 summarizes the path of blood flow through the entire cardiovascular system.

Cardiac Muscle

The cardiac-muscle cells of the myocardium are arranged in layers that are tightly bound together and completely encircle the blood-filled chambers. When the walls of a chamber contract, they come together like a squeezing fist and exert pressure on the blood they enclose.

Cardiac muscle combines properties of both skeletal and smooth muscle (Chapter 11). The cells are striated (Figure 14-15) as the result of an arrangement of thick myosin and thin actin filaments similar to that of skeletal muscle. Cardiac-muscle cells are considerably shorter than

skeletal-muscle fibers, however, and have several branching processes. Adjacent cells are joined end to end at structures called intercalated disks, within which are desmosomes that hold the cells together and to which the myofibrils are attached. Adjacent to the intercalated disks are gap junctions, similar to those in many smooth muscles.

Approximately 1 percent of the cardiac-muscle fibers have specialized features that are essential for normal heart excitation. They constitute a network known as the **conducting system** of the heart and are in contact with the other cardiac-muscle fibers via gap junctions. The conducting system initiates the heartbeat and helps spread the impulse rapidly throughout the heart.

One final point about the cardiac-muscle cells should be noted: Certain cells in the atria secrete the family of peptide hormones collectively called atrial natriuretic factor, described in Chapter 16.

Innervation. The heart receives a rich supply of sympathetic and parasympathetic nerve fibers, the latter contained in the vagus nerves. The sympathetic postganglionic fibers release primarily norepinephrine, and the parasympathetics release primarily acetylcholine. The receptors for norepinephrine on cardiac muscle are mainly beta-adrenergic (of the beta$_1$ subtype). The hormone epinephrine, from the adrenal medulla, combines with the same

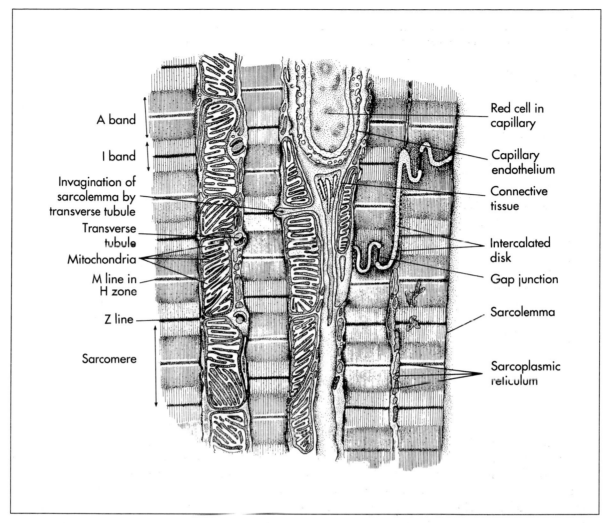

FIGURE 14-15

Diagram of an electron micrograph of cardiac muscle. (*From R. M. Berne and M. N. Levy.*)

receptors as norepinephrine and exerts the same actions on the heart. The receptors for acetylcholine are of the muscarinic type.

Blood Supply. The blood being pumped through the heart chambers does not exchange nutrients and metabolic end products with the myocardial cells. They, like the cells of all other organs, receive their blood supply via arteries that branch from the aorta. The arteries supplying the myocardium are the **coronary arteries**, and the blood flowing through them is termed the **coronary blood flow**. The coronary arteries exit from the very first part of the aorta and lead to a branching network of small arteries, arterioles, capillaries, venules, and veins similar to those in all other organs.

HEARTBEAT COORDINATION

Contraction of cardiac muscle, like that of other muscle types, is triggered by depolarization of the plasma membrane of the cells making up the muscle. As described earlier, myocardial cells are connected to each other by gap junctions. These allow action potentials to spread from one cell to another. Thus, the initial excitation of one myocardial cell results in excitation of all cells. This initial depolarization normally arises in a small group of conducting-system cells, the **sinoatrial (SA) node**, located in the right atrium near the entrance of the superior vena cava. The action potential then spreads from the SA node throughout the heart in a manner that causes first the atria and then the ventricles to contract.

Note that peak ventricular and aortic pressures are reached before the end of ventricular ejection; that is, these pressures start to fall during the last part of systole despite continued ventricular contraction. This is because the strength of ventricular contraction and rate of blood ejection diminish during the last part of systole as shown by the ventricular volume curve, and the ejection rate is less than the rate at which blood is leaving the aorta. Accordingly, the volume and therefore the pressure in the aorta begin to decrease.

Early Diastole

Diastole begins as ventricular contraction and ejection stop and the ventricular muscle begins to relax. Immediately, ventricular pressure falls significantly[5] below aortic pressure, and the aortic valve closes. However, at this time, ventricular pressure still exceeds atrial pressure, so that the AV valve also remains closed. This early diastolic phase—isovolumetric ventricular relaxation—ends as ventricular pressure falls below atrial pressure, the AV valve opens, and rapid ventricular filling begins.

The ventricle's previous contraction compressed the elastic elements of this chamber in such a way that the ventricle actually tends to recoil outward once systole is over. This expansion, in turn, lowers ventricular pressure more rapidly than would otherwise occur—and may even create a negative pressure in the ventricle—which enhances filling. Thus, some energy is stored within the myocardium during contraction, and its release during the subsequent relaxation aids filling.

The fact that ventricular filling is almost complete during early diastole is of the greatest importance. It ensures that filling is not seriously impaired during periods when the heart is beating very rapidly and the duration of diastole and therefore total filling time are reduced. However, when rates of approximately 200 beats/min or more are reached, filling time does become inadequate, and the volume of blood pumped during each beat is decreased. The significance of this will be described in the section on exercise.

Early ventricular filling also explains why the conduction defects that eliminate the atria as efficient pumps do not seriously impair ventricular filling, at least in otherwise normal individuals at rest. One example of this is *atrial fibrillation*, a state in which the atria contract in a continuous and completely disordered manner and so fail to serve as effective pumps. Thus, the atrium may be conveniently viewed as merely a continuation of the large veins.

---

[5]The word "significantly" is used in this sentence because, in reality, left ventricular pressure is already slightly less than aortic pressure during late systole, despite the fact that ejection is still occurring. The physical explanation of this pressure "reversal" in late systole is beyond the scope of this book.

Pulmonary Circulation Pressures

The pressure changes in the right ventricle and pulmonary arteries are qualitatively similar to those just described for the left ventricle and aorta (Figure 14-26). There are striking quantitative differences, however. Typical pulmonary artery systolic and diastolic pressures are 24 and 8 mmHg, respectively, compared to systemic arterial pressures of 120 and 70 mmHg. Thus, the pulmonary circulation is a low-pressure system, for reasons to be described in a later section. This difference is clearly reflected in the ventricular architecture, the right ventricular wall being much thinner than the left (Figure 14-27). Despite its lower pressure during contraction, however, the right ventricle ejects the same amount of blood as the left.

Heart Sounds

Two sounds, termed **heart sounds**, stemming from cardiac contraction are normally heard through a stethoscope placed on the chest wall. The first sound, a soft low-pitched *lub*, is associated with closure of the AV valves at the onset of systole (Figure 14-25); the second, a louder *dup*, is associated with closure of the pulmonary and aortic valves at the onset of diastole. These sounds, which result from vibrations caused by the closing valves, are perfectly normal, but other sounds, known as **heart murmurs**, are frequently a sign of heart disease.

Murmurs can be produced by blood flowing rapidly in the usual direction through an abnormally narrowed valve (*stenosis*), by blood flowing backward through a damaged leaky valve (*insufficiency*), or by blood flowing between

FIGURE 14-26

Pressures in the right ventricle and pulmonary artery during the cardiac cycle. This figure is done on the same scale as Figure 14-25 to facilitate comparison. The pressure profiles are qualitatively identical in the pulmonary and systemic circuits, but the pressures are much lower in the former.

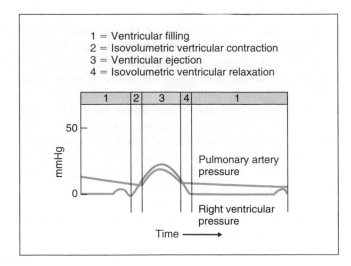

1 = Ventricular filling
2 = Isovolumetric vertricular contraction
3 = Ventricular ejection
4 = Isovolumetric ventricular relaxation

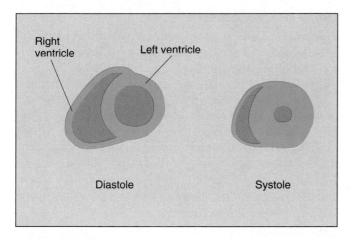

FIGURE 14-27
Cross section of the ventricular walls to illustrate the changes that occur during contraction. The view is from above, with the atria removed.

the two atria or two ventricles via a small hole in the wall separating them.

The exact timing and location of the murmur provide the physician with a powerful diagnostic clue. For example, a murmur heard throughout systole suggests a stenotic pulmonary or aortic valve, an insufficient AV valve, or a hole in the interventricular septum. In contrast, a murmur heard during diastole suggests a stenotic AV valve or an insufficient pulmonary or aortic valve.

THE CARDIAC OUTPUT

The volume of blood pumped by *each* ventricle per minute is called the **cardiac output (CO)**, usually expressed as liters per minute. It is also the volume of blood flowing through *either* the systemic *or* the pulmonary circuit per minute.

The cardiac output is determined by multiplying the heart rate (HR)—the number of beats per minute—and the stroke volume (SV), the blood volume ejected by each ventricle with each beat:

$$CO = HR \times SV$$

Thus, if each ventricle has a rate of 72 beats/min and ejects 70 ml of blood with each beat, the cardiac output is

$$CO = 72 \text{ beats/min} \times 0.07 \text{ L/beat} = 5.0 \text{ L/min}$$

These values are approximately normal for a resting adult. Since, by coincidence, total blood volume is also approximately 5 L, this means that essentially all the blood is

pumped around the circuit once each minute. During periods of exercise in well-trained athletes, the cardiac output may reach 35 L/min.

The following description of the factors that alter the two determinants of cardiac output—heart rate and stroke volume—applies in all respects to both the right and left heart since stroke volume and heart rate are the same for both under steady-state conditions. It must also be emphasized that heart rate and stroke volume do not always change in the same direction. For example, as we shall see, stroke volume decreases following blood loss while heart rate increases. These changes produce opposing effects on cardiac output.

Control of Heart Rate

Rhythmical beating of the heart at a rate of approximately 100 beats/min will occur in the complete absence of any nervous or hormonal influences on the SA node. This is the inherent autonomous discharge rate of the SA node. The heart rate may be much lower or higher than this, however, since the SA node is normally under the constant influence of nerves and hormones.

As mentioned earlier, a large number of parasympathetic and sympathetic postganglionic fibers end on the SA node. Activity in the parasympathetic (vagus) nerves causes the heart rate to decrease, whereas activity in the sympathetic nerves increases the heart rate. In the resting state, there is considerably more parasympathetic activity to the heart than sympathetic, and so the normal resting heart rate is well below the inherent rate of 100 beats/min.

Figure 14-28 illustrates how sympathetic and parasympathetic activity influences SA-node function. Sympathetic stimulation increases the slope of the pacemaker potential,

FIGURE 14-28
Effects of sympathetic and parasympathetic nerve stimulation on the slope of the pacemaker potential of an SA-nodal cell. Note that parasympathetic stimulation not only reduces the slope of the pacemaker potential but also causes the membrane potential to be more negative before the pacemaker potential begins. (*Adapted from Hoffman and Cranefield.*)

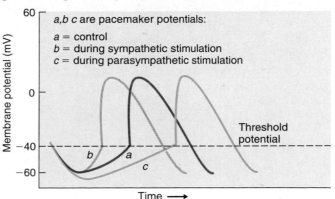

causing the SA-node cells to reach threshold more rapidly and the heart rate to increase. Stimulation of the parasympathetics has the opposite effect: The slope of the pacemaker potential decreases, threshold is reached more slowly, and heart rate decreases. Parasympathetic stimulation also hyperpolarizes the plasma membrane of the SA-node cells so that the pacemaker potential starts from a lower value.

How do the neurotransmitters released by the autonomic neurons cause these changes in the pacemaker potential? They do so by opening or closing ion channels for sodium and potassium. For example, one action of acetylcholine, the parasympathetic neurotransmitter, is to increase the number of open potassium channels, which tends to hold the membrane potential closer to the potassium equilibrium potential.

Factors other than the cardiac nerves can also alter heart rate. Epinephrine, the main hormone liberated from the adrenal medulla, speeds the heart by acting on the same beta-adrenergic receptors in the SA node as does neurally released norepinephrine. The heart rate is also sensitive to changes in body temperature, plasma electrolyte concentrations, and hormones other than epinephrine. These factors are normally of lesser importance, however. Figure 14-29 summarizes the major determinants of heart rate.

As stated in the section on innervation, sympathetic and parasympathetic neurons innervate other parts of the conducting system as well as the SA node. Thus, sympathetic stimulation not only speeds the SA node but increases conduction through the AV node. Parasympathetic stimulation, in contrast, decreases the rate of spread of excitation along almost the entire conducting system of the heart.

Control of Stroke Volume

The second variable that determines cardiac output is stroke volume, the volume of blood ejected by each ventricle during each contraction. As emphasized earlier, the ventricles never completely empty themselves of blood during contraction. Therefore, a more forceful contraction can produce an increase in stroke volume. Changes in the force of contraction can be produced by a variety of factors, but two are dominant under most physiological conditions: (1) changes in the end-diastolic volume, that is, the volume of blood in the ventricles just before contraction; and (2) changes in the magnitude of sympathetic nervous system input to the ventricles.

Relationship Between End-diastolic Volume and Stroke Volume: Starling's Law of the Heart. It is possible to study the characteristics of an isolated heart by using what is called a heart-lung preparation (Figure 14-30). Tubes are placed in the heart and blood vessels of an anesthetized animal so that blood flows from the first part of the aorta into a blood-filled reservoir and from there into the right atrium. The blood is then pumped by the right heart via the lungs into the left heart, from which it is returned to the reservoir.

A key feature of this preparation is that the pressure causing blood flow *into* the heart can be altered simply by raising or lowering the reservoir. This is analogous to altering the systemic venous and right atrial pressures to cause changes in the quantity of blood entering the right ventricle during diastole. Thus, when the reservoir is raised, the pressure is raised, and ventricular filling increases, thereby increasing end-diastolic volume. The important finding is that the ventricle, now distended with more blood, re-

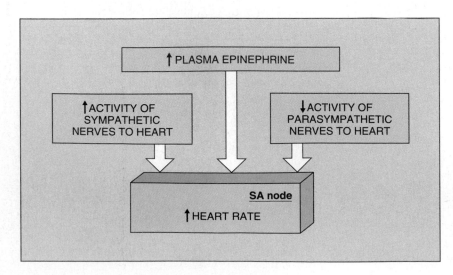

FIGURE 14-29
Major factors that influence heart rate. All effects are exerted upon the SA node. The figure shows how heart rate is increased; reversal of all the arrows in the boxes would illustrate how heart rate is decreased.

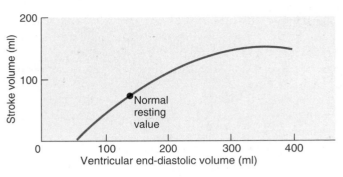

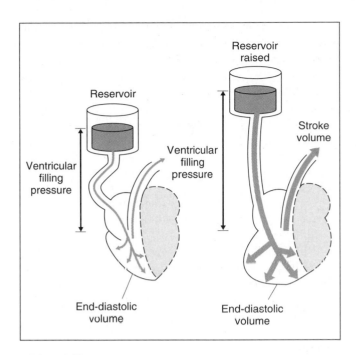

FIGURE 14-30

Experiment for demonstrating the relationship between ventricular end-diastolic volume and stroke volume (Starling's law of the heart). When the reservoir is raised, the pressure that causes ventricular filling is increased, and more blood enters the ventricle. This stretches the ventricular muscle, which responds with a stronger contraction.

FIGURE 14-31

Relationship between ventricular end-diastolic volume and stroke volume (Starling's law of the heart). The data were obtained by progressively increasing ventricular filling pressure with a heart-lung preparation. The horizontal axis could have been labeled "sarcomere length," and the vertical "contractile force." In other words, this is a length-tension curve.

sponds with a more forceful contraction. The net result is a new steady state in which end-diastolic volume and stroke volume are both increased. The British physiologist Ernest Henry Starling described this relationship between end-diastolic volume and force of contraction, and it is termed **Starling's law of the heart**.[6] A typical response curve obtained by progressively increasing end-diastolic volume is shown in Figure 14-31.

This characteristic of cardiac muscle is analogous to the length-tension relationship described for skeletal muscle in Chapter 11. End-diastolic volume acts as the preload for ventricular muscle, determining how stretched the ventricular sarcomeres are just before contraction. However, the major mechanism accounting for the increased contraction with increasing stretch is different for cardiac muscle than for skeletal muscle. For as yet unclear reasons, the affinity of troponin for calcium is increased with increasing length of the cardiac-muscle cells. Thus, at any given cytosolic calcium concentration, more calcium will bind to troponin as the muscle is stretched, thereby leading to a stronger contraction.

The significance of the intrinsic mechanism represented by Starling's law of the heart should be apparent: When the flow of blood from the veins into the heart, termed **venous return**, increases, this automatically forces an increase in cardiac output by distending the ventricle and increasing stroke volume. One important function of this relationship is maintaining the equality of right and left cardiac outputs. Should the right heart, for example, suddenly begin to pump more blood than the left, the increased blood flow to the left ventricle would automatically produce an equivalent increase in left ventricular output. This ensures that blood will not accumulate in the lungs.

The Sympathetic Nerves. Sympathetic nerves are distributed not only to the conducting system but to the entire myocardium. The effect of the sympathetic mediator norepinephrine, acting on beta-adrenergic receptors, is to increase ventricular **contractility**, defined as the strength of contraction *at any given end-diastolic volume*. Plasma epinephrine, acting on these same receptors, also increases myocardial contractility. Thus, the increased force of contraction and stroke volume resulting from sympathetic-nerve stimulation or epinephrine is *independent* of a change in end-diastolic ventricular volume.

Note that a change in contraction force due to increased end-diastolic volume (Starling's law) does *not* reflect increased contractility. Increased contractility is specifically defined as an increased contraction force *at any given* end-diastolic volume.

The relationship between Starling's law and the cardiac sympathetic nerves as measured in a heart-lung prepara-

[6]It is also called the Frank-Starling mechanism in recognition of Otto Frank, who was one of the first to identify the relationship.

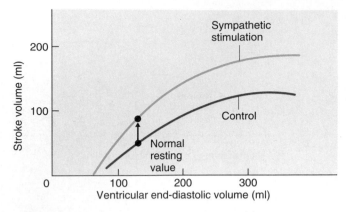

FIGURE 14-32

Effects on stroke volume of stimulating the sympathetic nerves to the heart. Stroke volume is increased at any given end-diastolic volume; that is, the sympathetic stimulation has increased ventricular contractility.

tion is illustrated in Figure 14-32. The red line is the same as the line shown in Figure 14-31. The blue line was obtained for the same heart during sympathetic-nerve stimulation. Starling's law still applies, but during nerve stimulation the stroke volume is greater at any given end-diastolic volume. In other words, the increased contractility leads to a more complete ejection of the end-diastolic ventricular volume.

FIGURE 14-33

Effects of sympathetic stimulation on ventricular contraction and relaxation. Note that both the rate of force development and the rate of relaxation are increased, as is the maximal force developed. All these changes reflect an increased contractility.

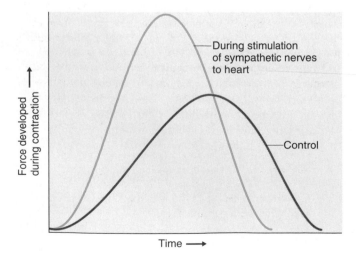

One way of quantitating contractility is as the **ejection fraction (EF)**, defined as the ratio of stroke volume (SV) to end-diastolic volume (EDV):

$$EF = \frac{SV}{EDV}$$

Expressed as a percentage, the ejection fraction normally averages 67 percent under resting conditions. Increased contractility causes an increased ejection fraction.

Not only does enhanced sympathetic-nerve activity to the myocardium cause the contraction to be more powerful, it also causes both the contraction and relaxation of the ventricles to occur more quickly (Figure 14-33). These latter effects are quite important since, as described earlier, increased sympathetic activity to the heart also increases heart rate. As heart rate increases, the time available for diastolic filling decreases, but the quicker contraction and relaxation induced simultaneously by the sympathetic neurons partially compensate for this problem by permitting a larger fraction of the cardiac cycle to be available for filling.

At the level of the contractile apparatus, two processes account for the increased contractility induced by norepinephrine and epinephrine. One is an increase in the number of actin-myosin cross-bridge attachments, resulting from an increased cytosolic calcium concentration. The other is an increase in the rate of cross-bridge cycling during a contraction. The cellular mechanisms by which these changes are brought about are summarized in Figure 14-34. This figure also describes the cause of the increased rate of relaxation associated with increased contractility.

In contrast to the sympathetic nerves, the parasympathetic nerves to the ventricles normally have only a small effect on contractility.

Table 14-5 summarizes the effects of the autonomic nerves on cardiac function.

In summary (Figure 14-35), the two major controllers of stroke volume are a mechanism (Starling's law) dependent upon changes in end-diastolic volume and a mechanism that is mediated by the cardiac sympathetic nerves and circulating epinephrine and that causes increased ventricular contractility. The contribution of each of these two mechanisms in specific physiological situations is described in later sections.

A summary of the major factors that determine cardiac output is presented in Figure 14-36, which combines the information of Figures 14-29 and 14-35.

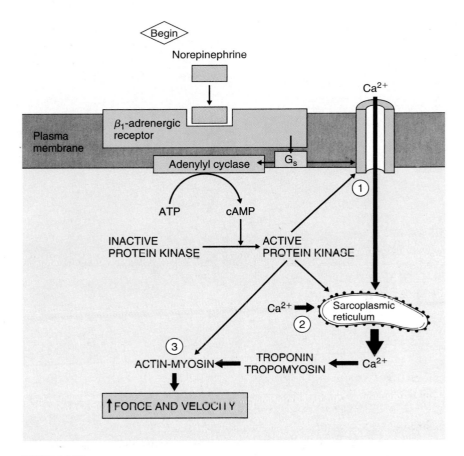

FIGURE 14-34

Mechanisms by which norepinephrine and epinephrine alter cardiac contractility and relaxation. Norepinephrine binds to beta$_1$-adrenergic receptors in the plasma membrane of the myocardial cells, and this causes the receptor to activate a G$_s$ protein. This G protein has two distinct effects: it directly opens slow calcium channels in the plasma membrane, and it activates membrane-bound adenylyl cyclase. The latter effect results in an increase in intracellular cAMP, which activates cAMP-dependent protein kinase, which in turn phosphorylates and thereby activates at least three proteins: (1) a plasma-membrane protein that opens slow calcium channels; (2) a sarcoplasmic-reticulum protein that stimulates the ATP-dependent calcium-uptake pump in this organelle; and (3) myosin. These three phosphorylated proteins plus the direct G-protein opening of calcium channels then mediate the observed effects: (1) In the plasma membrane a greater number of slow calcium channels open during excitation, which permits more calcium to enter the cell and stimulate the sarcoplasmic reticulum to release still more calcium—the result is an increase in the number of actin-myosin cross-bridge attachments leading to more force development. (2) The sarcoplasmic reticulum protein stimulates the active transport of calcium into the sarcoplasmic reticulum, thereby increasing this organelle's calcium stores and the amount of calcium released into the cytosol during subsequent excitations. The increased rate of calcium pumping from the cytosol back into the sarcoplasmic reticulum after contraction is over also explains why norepinephrine speeds cardiac relaxation. (3) Phosphorylation of myosin causes an increase in the rate at which the cross bridges cycle. The result is an increase in the velocity of the contraction, that is, the rate of tension development per unit time.

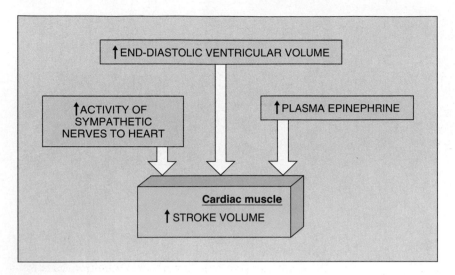

FIGURE 14-35
Major factors that directly influence stroke volume. The figure as drawn shows how stroke volume is increased. A reversal of all arrows in the boxes would illustrate how stroke volume is decreased.

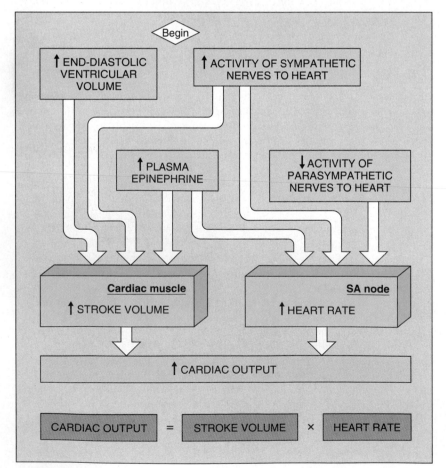

FIGURE 14-36
Major factors determining cardiac output (an amalgamation of Figures 14-29 and 14-35).

TABLE 14-5   EFFECTS OF AUTONOMIC NERVES ON THE HEART

Area affected	Sympathetic nerves	Parasympathetic nerves
SA node	Increased heart rate	Decreased heart rate
AV node	Increased conduction rate	Decreased conduction rate
Atrial muscle	Increased contractility	Decreased contractility
Ventricular muscle	Increased contractility	Decreased contractility (minor)

MEASUREMENT OF CARDIAC FUNCTION

Cardiac output in human beings can be measured by a variety of methods. Moreover, recent advances now make possible two- and three-dimensional images of the heart throughout the entire cardiac cycle. For example, in *echocardiography*, the most commonly used visualization technique, ultrasonic sound is beamed at the heart and returning echos are electronically plotted by computer to produce continuous images of the heart. This technique can detect abnormal functioning of cardiac valves or contractions of the cardiac walls and can be used to measure ejection fraction.

Echocardiography is a noninvasive technique because everything used remains external to the body. Other visualization techniques are invasive. One, *cardiac angiography*, requires the temporary placement of a thin flexible tube (catheter) into the heart, via an artery or vein, under fluoroscopy. A dye is then injected through the catheter during high-speed x-ray filming. This technique is useful not only for evaluating cardiac function but also for identifying narrowed coronary arteries.

SECTION C SUMMARY

ANATOMY

I. The atrioventricular (AV) valves prevent flow from the ventricles back into the atria.

II. The pulmonary and aortic valves prevent backflow from the pulmonary trunk into the right ventricle and from the aorta into the left ventricle.

III. Cardiac-muscle cells are joined by gap junctions that permit action potentials to be conducted from cell to cell.

IV. The myocardium also contains specialized muscle cells that constitute the conducting system of the heart, initiating the cardiac action potentials and speeding their spread through the heart.

HEARTBEAT COORDINATION

I. Cardiac-muscle cells must undergo action potentials for contraction to occur.

A. The rapid depolarization of the action potential in atrial and ventricular cells (other than those in the conducting system) is due mainly to a positive-feedback increase in sodium permeability.

B. Following the initial rapid depolarization, the membrane remains depolarized (the plateau phase) almost the entire duration of the contraction because of prolonged entry of calcium into the cell through slow plasma-membrane channels.

II. The SA node generates the current that leads to depolarization of all other cardiac-muscle cells.

A. The SA node manifests a pacemaker potential, which brings its membrane potential to threshold and initiates an action potential.

B. The impulse spreads from the SA node throughout both atria and to the AV node, where a small delay occurs. The impulse then passes in turn into the bundle of His, right and left bundle branches, Purkinje fibers, and non-conducting-system ventricular fibers.

III. Calcium, mainly released from the sarcoplasmic reticulum (SR), functions as the excitation-contraction coupler in cardiac muscle, as in skeletal muscle, by combining with troponin.

A. The major signal for calcium release from the SR

is calcium entering across the plasma membrane during the action potential.

   B. The amount of calcium released does not usually saturate all troponin binding sites, and so the number of active cross bridges can be increased if cytosolic calcium is increased still further.

IV. Cardiac muscle cannot undergo summation of contractions because it has a very long refractory period.

MECHANICAL EVENTS OF THE CARDIAC CYCLE

I. The cardiac cycle is divided into systole (ventricular contraction) and diastole (ventricular relaxation).

   A. At the onset of systole, ventricular pressure rapidly exceeds atrial pressure, and the AV valves close. The aortic and pulmonary valves are not yet open, however, and so no ejection occurs during this isovolumetric ventricular contraction.

   B. When ventricular pressures exceed aortic and pulmonary trunk pressures, the aortic and pulmonary valves open, and ventricular ejection of blood occurs.

   C. When the ventricles relax at the beginning of diastole, the ventricular pressures fall significantly below those in the aorta and pulmonary trunk, and the aortic and pulmonary valves close. Because the AV valves are also still closed, no change in ventricular volume occurs during this isovolumetric ventricular relaxation.

   D. When ventricular pressures fall below the pressures in the right and the left atria, the AV valves open, and the ventricular filling phase of diastole begins.

   E. Filling occurs very rapidly at first so that atrial contraction, which occurs at the very end of diastole, usually adds only a small amount of additional blood to the ventricles.

II. The amount of blood in the ventricles just before systole is the end-diastolic volume. The volume remaining after ejection is the end-systolic volume, and the volume ejected is the stroke volume.

III. Pressure changes in the systemic and pulmonary circulations have similar patterns, but the pulmonary pressures are much lower.

IV. The first heart sound is due to the closing of the AV valves, and the second to the closing of the aortic and pulmonary valves.

THE CARDIAC OUTPUT

I. The cardiac output is the volume of blood pumped by each ventricle and equals the product of heart rate and stroke volume.

   A. Heart rate is increased by stimulation of the sympathetic nerves to the heart and by epinephrine; it is decreased by stimulation of the parasympathetic nerves to the heart.

   B. Stroke volume is increased by an increase in end-diastolic volume (Starling's law of the heart) and by an increase in contractility due to sympathetic-nerve stimulation or to epinephrine.

SECTION C KEY TERMS

pericardium	P wave
myocardium	QRS complex
endothelial cells	T wave
endothelium	refractory period
atrioventricular (AV) valves	cardiac cycle
tricuspid valve	systole
mitral valve	diastole
papillary muscles	isovolumetric ventricular
pulmonary valve	contraction
aortic valve	ventricular ejection
conducting system	stroke volume
coronary arteries	isovolumetric ventricular
coronary blood flow	relaxation
sinoatrial (SA) node	ventricular filling
slow channels	end-diastolic volume
pacemaker potential	end-systolic volume
automaticity	heart sounds
heart rate	cardiac output (CO)
atrioventricular (AV) node	Starling's law of
bundle of His	the heart
right and left bundle	venous return
branches	contractility
Purkinje fibers	ejection fraction (EF)
electrocardiogram (ECG)	

SECTION C REVIEW QUESTIONS

1. List the structures through which blood passes from the systemic veins to the systemic arteries.

2. Contrast and compare cardiac muscle with skeletal and smooth muscle.

3. Describe the autonomic innervation of the heart, including the types of receptors involved.

4. Draw a ventricular action potential. Describe the changes in membrane permeability that underlie the potential changes.

5. Contrast action potentials in ventricular cells with SA-node action potentials. What is the pacemaker potential due to, and what is its inherent rate? By what mechanism does the SA node function as the pacemaker for the entire heart?

6. Describe the spread of excitation from the SA node through the rest of the heart.

7. Draw and label a normal ECG. Relate the P, QRS, and T waves to the ventricular action potential.

8. Describe the sequence of events leading to excitation-contraction coupling in cardiac muscle.

9. What prevents the heart from undergoing summation of contractions?

10. Draw a diagram of the pressure changes in the left ventricle and aorta throughout the cardiac cycle. Show when the valves open and close, when the heart sounds occur, and the pattern of ventricular ejection.

11. Contrast the pressures in the right ventricle and pulmonary trunk with those in the left ventricle and aorta.

12. What causes heart murmurs in diastole? In systole?

13. Write the formula relating cardiac output, heart rate, and stroke volume; give normal values for a resting adult.

14. Describe the effects of the sympathetic and parasympathetic nerves on heart rate. Which is dominant at rest?

15. What are the two major factors influencing force of contraction?

16. Draw a curve illustrating Starling's law of the heart.

17. Describe the effects of the sympathetic nerves on cardiac muscle during contraction and relaxation.

18. Draw a family of curves relating end-diastolic volume and stroke volume during different levels of sympathetic stimulation.

19. Summarize the effects of the autonomic nerves on the heart.

20. Draw a flow diagram summarizing the factors determining cardiac output.

SECTION

THE VASCULAR SYSTEM

The functional and structural characteristics of the blood vessels change with successive branching. Yet the entire cardiovascular system, from the heart to the smallest capillary, has one structural component in common, a smooth, single-celled layer of endothelial cells, or endothelium, which lines the inner (blood-contacting) surface of the vessels. Capillaries consist only of endothelium, whereas all other vessels have, in addition, layers of connective tissue and smooth muscle. Endothelial cells have a large number of active functions. These are summarized for reference in Table 14-6 and are described in relevant sections of this chapter or subsequent chapters.

We have previously described the pressures in the aorta and pulmonary arteries during the cardiac cycle. Figure 14-37 illustrates the pressure changes that occur along the rest of the systemic and pulmonary vascular systems. Text sections below dealing with the individual vascular segments will describe the reasons for these changes in pressure. For the moment, note only that by the time the blood has completed its journey back to the atrium in each circuit, virtually all the pressure originally generated by the ventricular contraction has been dissipated. The reason pressure at any point in the vascular system is less than that at an earlier point is that the blood vessels offer resistance to the flow from one point to the next.

TABLE 14-6 FUNCTIONS OF ENDOTHELIAL CELLS

1. Serve as a physical lining of heart and blood vessels

2. Secrete substances that act on adjacent vascular smooth muscle; these include the vasodilators, prostacyclin and endothelium-derived relaxing factor (EDRF), and the vasoconstrictor endothelin-1

3. Mediate angiogenesis (new capillary growth)

4. Regulate transport of macromolecules and other substances between plasma and interstitial fluid

5. Undergo contractile activity, which regulates capillary permeability

6. Influence vascular smooth-muscle proliferation in the disease atherosclerosis

7. Secrete substances that regulate platelet clumping, clotting, and anticlotting (Chapter 20)

8. Synthesize active hormones from inactive precursors (Chapter 16)

9. Extract or degrade hormones and other mediators (Chapter 15)

10. Function similarly to macrophages during immune responses (Chapter 20)

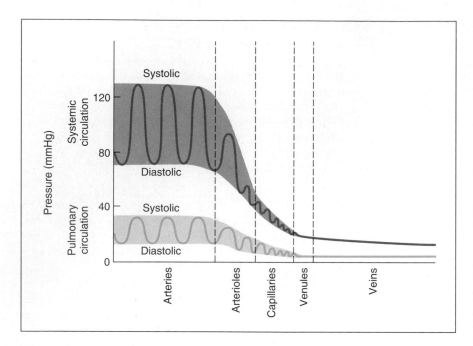

FIGURE 14-37
Pressures in the vascular system.

FIGURE 14-38
Movement of blood into and out of the arteries during the cardiac cycle. The lengths of the arrows denote relative quantities flowing into and out of the arteries and remaining in the arteries during systole. During systole, less blood leaves the arteries than enters from the heart, and so blood is retained in the arteries, stretching their walls. During diastole, the stretched walls recoil passively, and the blood retained in the arteries during the previous systole is driven out of the arteries.

ARTERIES

The aorta and other systemic arteries have thick walls containing large quantities of elastic tissue. Although they also have smooth muscle, arteries can be viewed most conveniently as elastic tubes. Because the arteries have large radii, they serve as low-resistance tubes conducting blood to the various organs. Their second major function, related to their elasticity, is to act as a "pressure reservoir" for maintaining blood flow through the tissues during diastole, as described below.

Arterial Blood Pressure

What are the factors determining the pressure within an elastic container, such as a balloon filled with water? The pressure inside the balloon depends on (1) the volume of water, and (2) how easily the balloon walls can be stretched. If the walls are very stretchable, large quantities of water can be added with only a small rise in pressure. Conversely, the addition of a small quantity of water causes a large pressure rise in a balloon that is difficult to stretch. The term used to denote how easily a structure can be stretched is **compliance**:

$$\text{Compliance} = \frac{\Delta \text{ volume}}{\Delta \text{ pressure}}$$

The *higher* the compliance of a structure, the *more easily* it can be stretched.

These principles can be applied to an analysis of arterial blood pressure. The contraction of the ventricles ejects

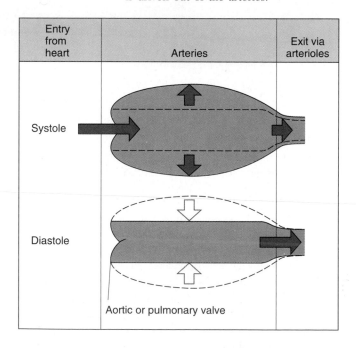

blood into the pulmonary and systemic arteries during systole. If a precisely equal quantity of blood were to flow simultaneously out of the arteries, the total volume of blood in the arteries would remain constant and arterial pressure would not change. Such is not the case, however. As shown in Figure 14-38, a volume of blood equal to only about one-third the stroke volume leaves the arteries during systole. The rest of the stroke volume remains in the arteries during systole, distending them and raising the arterial pressure. When ventricular contraction ends, the stretched arterial walls recoil passively, like a stretched

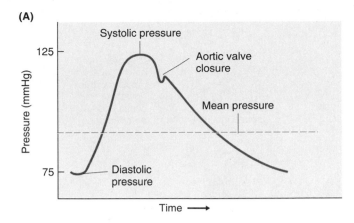

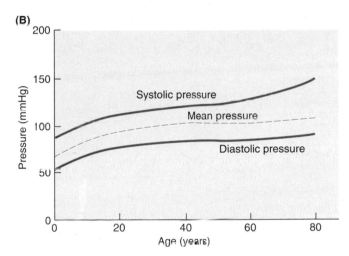

FIGURE 14-39

(A) Typical arterial pressure fluctuations during the cardiac cycle. (B) Changes in arterial pressure with age. (*Adapted from Guyton.*)

rubber band being released, and blood continues to be driven into the arterioles during diastole. As blood leaves the arteries, the arterial volume and therefore the arterial pressure slowly fall, but the next ventricular contraction occurs while there is still adequate blood in the arteries to stretch them partially. Therefore, the arterial pressure does not fall to zero.

The aortic pressure pattern shown in Figure 14-39A is typical of the pressure changes that occur in all the large systemic arteries. The maximum pressure reached during peak ventricular ejection is called **systolic pressure (SP)**. The minimum pressure occurs just before ventricular ejection begins and is called **diastolic pressure (DP)**. Arterial pressure is generally recorded as systolic/diastolic, that is, 125/75 mmHg in our example (see Figure 14-39B for average values in people of different ages).

The difference between systolic pressure and diastolic pressure (125 − 75 = 50 mmHg in the example) is called

the **pulse pressure**. It can be felt as a pulsation or throb in the arteries of the wrist or neck with each heartbeat. During diastole, nothing is felt over the artery, but the rapid rise in pressure at the next systole pushes out the artery wall, and it is this expansion of the vessel that produces the detectable throb.

The two most important factors determining the magnitude of the pulse pressure, that is, how much greater systolic pressure is than diastolic, are (1) stroke volume, and (2) arterial compliance. Specifically, the pulse pressure produced by a ventricular ejection will be greater if the volume of blood ejected is increased or if the arteries are less compliant. This last phenomenon occurs in arteriosclerosis, the "hardening" of the arteries that progresses with age and accounts for the increasing pulse pressure seen so often in older people.

It is evident from Figure 14-39A that arterial pressure is continuously changing throughout the cardiac cycle. The *average* pressure (**mean arterial pressure, MAP**) in the cycle is not merely the value halfway between systolic pressure and diastolic pressure because diastole usually lasts longer than systole. The true mean arterial pressure can be obtained by complex methods, but for most purposes it is approximately equal to the diastolic pressure plus one-third of the pulse pressure (SP − DP):

$$MAP = DP + \tfrac{1}{3}(SP - DP)$$

Thus, in our example, MAP = 75 + ⅓(50) = 92 mmHg. The MAP is the most important of the pressures described because it is the pressure driving blood into the tissues averaged over the entire cardiac cycle. We can say mean "arterial" pressure without specifying to which artery we are referring because the aorta and other large arteries have such large diameters that they offer only negligible resistance to flow, and the mean pressures are therefore similar everywhere in the large arteries.

One additional important point should be made: We have stated that arterial compliance is an important determinant of *pulse* pressure, but for complex reasons, compliance does *not* influence the *mean* arterial pressure. Thus, for example, a person with a low arterial compliance (due to atherosclerosis) but an otherwise normal cardiovascular system will have a large pulse pressure but a normal mean arterial pressure.

Measurement of Arterial Pressure

Both systolic and diastolic blood pressure are readily measured in human beings with the use of a sphygmomanometer. An inflatable cuff is wrapped around the upper arm, and a stethoscope is placed in a spot on the arm just below the cuff and beneath which the major artery to the lower arm runs.

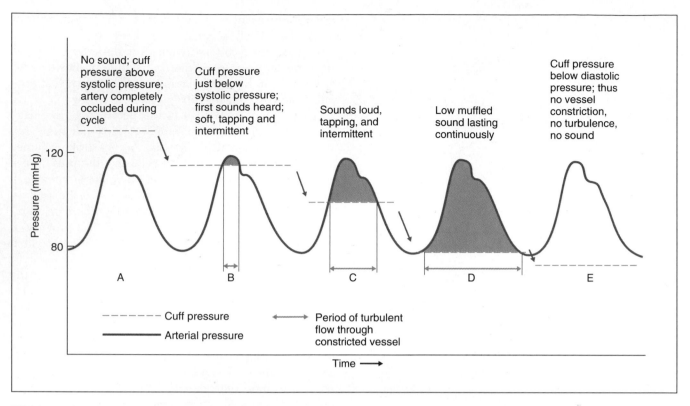

No sound; cuff pressure above systolic pressure; artery completely occluded during cycle

Cuff pressure just below systolic pressure; first sounds heard; soft, tapping and intermittent

Sounds loud, tapping, and intermittent

Low muffled sound lasting continuously

Cuff pressure below diastolic pressure; thus no vessel constriction, no turbulence, no sound

A B C D E

– – – – – Cuff pressure

———— Arterial pressure

←——→ Period of turbulent flow through constricted vessel

Time ——→

FIGURE 14-40

Sounds heard through a stethoscope while the cuff pressure of a sphygmomanometer is gradually lowered. Sounds are first heard at systolic pressure, and they disappear at diastolic pressure.

The cuff is then inflated with air to a pressure greater than systolic blood pressure (Figure 14-40). The high pressure in the cuff is transmitted through the tissue of the arm and completely compresses the artery under the cuff, thereby preventing blood flow through the artery. The air in the cuff is then slowly released, causing the pressure in the cuff and on the artery to drop. When cuff pressure has fallen to a value just below the systolic pressure, the artery opens slightly and allows blood flow for this brief time. During this interval, the blood flow through the partially compressed artery occurs at a very high velocity because of the small opening and the large pressure difference across the opening. The high-velocity blood flow is turbulent and produces vibrations that can be heard through the stethoscope. Thus, the pressure, measured on the manometer attached to the cuff, at which sounds are first heard as the cuff pressure is lowered is identified as the systolic blood pressure.

As the pressure in the cuff is lowered further, the duration of blood flow through the artery in each cycle becomes longer. When the cuff pressure reaches the diastolic blood pressure, all sound stops, because flow is now continuous and nonturbulent through the open artery.

Thus, diastolic pressure is identified as the cuff pressure at which sounds disappear.

It should be clear from this description that the sounds heard during measurement of blood pressure are *not* the same as the heart sounds described earlier, which are due to closing of cardiac valves.

ARTERIOLES

The arterioles play two major roles: (1) The arterioles in individual organs are responsible for determining the relative blood flows to those organs, and (2) the arterioles, as a whole, are a major factor in determining mean arterial pressure. The first function will be described in this section, and the second in the section on control of blood pressure.

Figure 14-41 illustrates the major principles of blood-flow distribution in terms of a simple model, a fluid-filled tank with a series of compressible outflow tubes. What determines the rate of flow through each exit tube? As stated in Section B of this chapter,

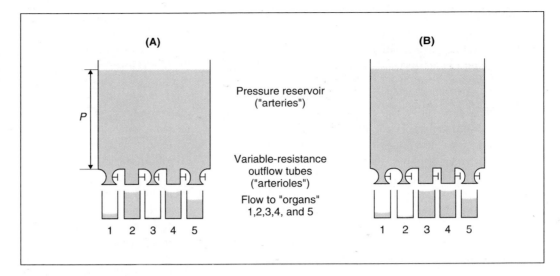

FIGURE 14-41

Physical model of the relationship between arterial pressure, arteriolar radius in different organs, and blood-flow distribution. In (A), blood flow is high through tube 2 and low through tube 3, whereas just the opposite is true for (B). This shift in blood flow was achieved by constricting tube 2 and dilating tube 3.

$$F = \frac{\Delta P}{R}$$

Since the driving pressure (the height of the fluid column in the tank) is identical for each tube, differences in flow are completely determined by differences in the resistance to flow offered by each tube. The lengths of the tubes are approximately the same, and the viscosity of the fluid is constant; therefore, differences in resistance offered by the tubes are due solely to differences in their radii. Obviously, the widest tubes have the greatest flows. If we equip each outflow tube with an adjustable cuff, we can obtain various combinations of flows.

This analysis can now be applied to the cardiovascular system. The tank is analogous to the arteries, which serve as a pressure reservoir, the major arteries themselves being so large that they contribute little resistance to flow. Therefore, all the large arteries of the body can be considered a single pressure reservoir.

The arteries branch within each organ into progressively smaller arteries, which then branch into arterioles. The smallest arteries are narrow enough to offer significant resistance to flow, but the still narrower arterioles are the major sites of resistance in the vascular tree and are therefore analogous to the outflow tubes in the model. This explains the large decrease in mean pressure—from about 90 mmHg to 35 mmHg—as blood flows through the arterioles (Figure 14-37). Pulse pressure also diminishes to the point that flow beyond the arterioles, that is, through capillaries and veins, is no longer pulsatile.

Like the model's outflow tubes, the arteriolar radii in individual organs are subject to independent adjustment. The blood flow through any organ is given by the following equation, assuming for simplicity that the venous pressure, the other component of the pressure gradient, is zero:

$$F_{organ} = \frac{MAP}{R_{organ}}$$

Since the MAP, the driving force for flow through each organ, is identical throughout the body, differences in flows between organs depend entirely on the relative resistances offered by the arterioles of each organ. Arterioles contain smooth muscle, which can either relax and cause the vessel radius to increase (**vasodilation**) or contract and decrease the vessel radius (**vasoconstriction**). Thus the pattern of blood-flow distribution depends upon the degree of arteriolar smooth-muscle contraction within each organ and tissue.

Arteriolar smooth muscle possesses a large degree of spontaneous activity, that is, contraction independent of any neural, hormonal, or paracrine input. This spontaneous contractile activity, which is submaximal, is called **myogenic tone** (also termed intrinsic or basal tone). It sets a baseline level of contraction that can be increased or decreased by external signals, such as neurotransmitters. These signals act by inducing changes in the muscle cell's cytosolic calcium concentration (see Chapter 11 for a description of excitation-contraction coupling in smooth muscle). An increase in contractile force above the vessel's myogenic tone causes vasoconstriction, whereas a decrease in contractile force causes vasodilation. The mechanisms controlling these changes in arteriolar resistance fall into two general categories: (1) local controls, and (2) extrinsic (or reflex) controls.

Local Controls

The term **local controls** denotes mechanisms independent of nerves or hormones by which organs and tissues alter their own arteriolar resistances, thereby self-regulating their blood flows. This self-regulation includes the phenomena of active hyperemia, flow autoregulation, reactive hyperemia, and local responses to injury.

Active Hyperemia. Most organs and tissues manifest an increased blood flow **(hyperemia)** when their metabolic activity is increased (Figure 14-42); this is termed **active hyperemia.** For example, the blood flow to exercising skeletal muscle increases in direct proportion to the increased activity of the muscle. Active hyperemia is the direct result of arteriolar dilation in the more active organ or tissue. The vasodilation does not depend upon the presence of nerves or hormones but is a locally mediated response by which an increased rate of activity in an organ or tissue automatically produces an increased blood flow to that organ or tissue.

The factors acting upon arteriolar smooth muscle in active hyperemia to cause it to relax are local chemical changes in the extracellular fluid surrounding the arterioles. These result from the increased metabolic activity in

the cells near the arterioles. The relative contributions of the various factors implicated vary, depending upon the organs involved and on the duration of the increased activity. Therefore, we shall only name but not quantify some of these local chemical changes that occur in the extracellular fluid: decreased oxygen concentration; increased concentrations of carbon dioxide, hydrogen ion, and metabolites such as adenosine; increased concentration of potassium as a result of enhanced potassium movement out of muscle cells during the more frequent action potentials; increased osmolarity resulting from the increased breakdown of high-molecular-weight substances; increased concentrations of eicosanoids (Chapter 7); and, in some glands, increased concentration of a peptide known as **bradykinin.** This last substance is generated locally from a circulating protein, **kininogen,** by the action of an enzyme, **kallikrein,** secreted by the active gland cells.

Changes in all these chemical factors have been shown to cause arteriolar dilation under controlled experimental conditions, and they all probably contribute to the active-hyperemia response in one or more organs. It is likely, moreover, that additional important local factors remain to be discovered. It must be emphasized once more that all these chemical changes in the extracellular fluid act locally upon the arteriolar smooth muscle, causing it to relax. No nerves or hormones are involved.

It should not be too surprising that active hyperemia is most highly developed in muscle and glands, which show the widest range of normal metabolic activities in the body. It is highly efficient, therefore, that their supply of

FIGURE 14-42

Local control of organ blood flow. Decreases in metabolic activity or increases in blood pressure would produce changes opposite those shown here.

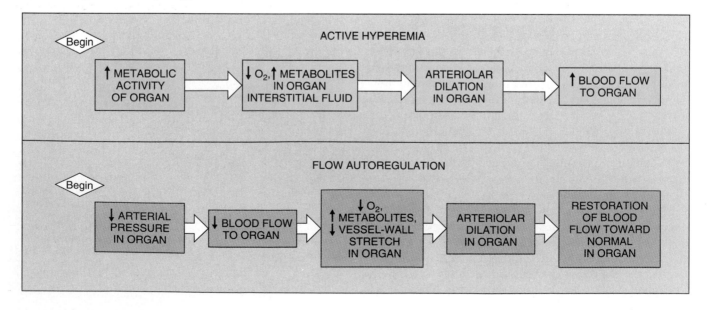

blood be primarily determined locally. Active hyperemia also provides a local mechanism for adjusting flow *within* an organ when different regions of the organ undergo different degrees of metabolic activity.

Flow Autoregulation. During active hyperemia, increased metabolic activity of the tissue or organ is the initial event leading to local vasodilation. However, locally mediated changes in arteriolar resistance may also occur when a tissue or organ suffers a change in its blood supply resulting from a change in blood pressure (Figure 14-42). The change in resistance is in the direction of maintaining blood flow nearly constant in the face of the pressure change and is therefore termed **flow autoregulation**. For example, when arterial pressure in an organ is reduced, say, because of a partial occlusion in the artery supplying the organ, local controls cause arteriolar vasodilation, which tends to maintain flow relatively constant.

What is the mechanism of flow autoregulation? One mechanism is the same metabolic factors described for active hyperemia. When an arterial pressure reduction lowers blood flow to an organ, the supply of oxygen to the organ is diminished and the local extracellular oxygen concentration decreases. Simultaneously, the extracellular concentrations of carbon dioxide, hydrogen ion, and metabolites all increase because they are not removed by the blood as fast as they are produced. Also, eicosanoid synthesis is increased by still unclear stimuli. Thus, the local metabolic changes occurring during decreased blood supply at constant metabolic activity are similar to those that occur during increased metabolic activity. This is because both situations reflect an initial imbalance between blood supply and level of cellular metabolic activity. Note then that the vasodilations of active hyperemia and of flow autoregulation in response to low arterial pressure differ not in their major mechanisms—local metabolic factors—but in the event—altered metabolism or altered blood pressure—that brings these mechanisms into play.

Flow autoregulation is not limited to circumstances in which arterial pressure goes down. The opposite events may occur when, for various reasons, arterial pressure increases: The initial increase in flow due to the increase in pressure removes the local vasodilator chemical factors faster than they are produced and increases the local concentration of oxygen. This causes the arterioles to constrict, thereby maintaining local flow relatively constant in the face of the increased pressure.

Although our description has emphasized the role of local *chemical* factors in flow autoregulation, it should be noted that another mechanism also participates in this phenomenon in certain tissues and organs. Some arteriolar smooth muscle responds directly to increased stretch, caused by increased arterial pressure, by contracting to a greater extent. Conversely, decreased stretch, due to decreased arterial pressure, causes this vascular smooth muscle to decrease its tone. These direct responses of arteriolar smooth muscle to stretch are termed **myogenic responses**. They are due to stretch-dependent changes in calcium movement into the smooth-muscle cells.

Reactive Hyperemia. When an organ or tissue has had its blood supply completely occluded, a profound transient increase in its blood flow occurs as soon as the occlusion is released. This phenomenon, known as **reactive hyperemia**, is essentially an extreme form of flow autoregulation. During the period of no blood flow, the arterioles in the affected organ or tissue dilate, owing to the local factors described above. Blood flow, therefore, is very great through these wide-open arterioles as soon as the occlusion to arterial inflow is removed.

Response to Injury. Tissue injury causes a variety of substances to be released locally from cells or generated from plasma precursors. These substances make arteriolar smooth muscle relax and cause vasodilation in an injured area. This phenomenon, part of the general process known as inflammation, will be described in detail in Chapter 20.

Extrinsic Controls

Sympathetic Nerves. Most arterioles receive a rich supply of sympathetic postganglionic nerve fibers. These neurons release norepinephrine,[7] which combines with alpha-adrenergic receptors on the vascular smooth muscle to cause vasoconstriction.

Note that the receptors for norepinephrine on arterioles are alpha-adrenergic, whereas those for norepinephrine on heart muscle, including the conducting system, are mainly beta-adrenergic. This permits the use of beta-adrenergic antagonists to block the actions of norepinephrine on the heart but not the arterioles, and vice versa for alpha-adrenergic antagonists.

Control of the sympathetic nerves can also be used to produce vasodilation. Since the sympathetic nerves are seldom completely quiescent but discharge at some finite rate, which varies from organ to organ, they always cause some degree of tonic constriction in addition to the vessels' myogenic tone. Dilation can be achieved by *decreasing* the rate of sympathetic activity below the basal level.

The skin offers an excellent example of the processes. At room temperature, skin arterioles are already under the

---

[7]There is one possible exception to the generalization that sympathetic nerves to arterioles release norepinephrine. In some mammalian species, a second group of sympathetic (not parasympathetic) nerves to the arterioles in skeletal muscle release acetylcholine, which causes arteriolar dilation and increased blood flow. The only known function of these vasodilator fibers is in the response to exercise or stress. Because their existence in human beings is questionable, we shall not deal with them here.

influence of a moderate rate of sympathetic discharge. An appropriate stimulus—fear or loss of blood, for example—causes reflex enhancement of this sympathetic discharge, and the arterioles constrict further. In contrast, an increased body temperature reflexly inhibits the sympathetic nerves to the skin, the arterioles dilate, and the skin flushes. This generalization cannot be stressed too strongly: Control of the sympathetic constrictor nerves to arteriolar smooth muscle can accomplish either vasodilation or vasoconstriction.

In contrast to active hyperemia and flow autoregulation, the primary functions of sympathetic nerves to blood vessels are concerned not with the coordination of local metabolic needs and blood flow but with reflexes. The most common reflex employing these nerves, as we shall see, is that which regulates arterial blood pressure by influencing arteriolar resistance throughout the body. Other reflexes redistribute blood flow to achieve a specific function (for example, to increase heat loss from the skin).

Parasympathetic Nerves and Other Vasodilator Nerves. Acetylcholine, the major parasympathetic neurotransmitter, is a vasodilator, but with few exceptions—notably the blood vessels supplying the external genitals—there is little important parasympathetic innervation of arterioles. Under study, however, are the possible physiological roles of a group of autonomic nerves that release neurotransmitters other than norepinephrine or acetylcholine and cause vasodilation.

Hormones. Epinephrine, like norepinephrine released from sympathetic nerves, can combine with alpha-adrenergic receptors on arteriolar smooth muscle and cause vasoconstriction. The story is more complex, however, because many arteriolar smooth-muscle cells possess beta-adrenergic receptors as well as alpha-adrenergic receptors, and combination of epinephrine with these beta-adrenergic receptors causes the muscle cells to relax rather than contract (Figure 14-43).

In most vascular beds, the existence of beta-adrenergic receptors is of little if any importance since they are greatly outnumbered by the alpha-adrenergic receptors. The arterioles in skeletal muscle are an important exception, however, because they have large numbers of beta-adrenergic receptors. Circulating epinephrine therefore usually causes dilation in this vascular bed.

Another hormone important for arteriolar control is angiotensin II, which directly constricts most arterioles and also increases the activity of the sympathetic nervous system. This peptide is part of the renin-angiotensin system, which will be described fully in Chapter 16.

Yet another important hormone that causes arteriolar constriction is vasopressin, which, as described in Chapter 10, is released into the blood by the posterior pituitary gland. The functions of vasopressin will also be described more fully in Chapter 16.

Finally, the hormone secreted by the atria—atrial natriuretic factor—is a potent vasodilator. Whether this hormone, whose actions on the kidneys are described in Chapter 16, plays a widespread role in control of arterioles is unsettled.

Endothelial Cells and Vascular Smooth Muscle

It should be clear from the preceding discussion that a large number of substances can induce the contraction or relaxation of vascular smooth muscle. Many substances do

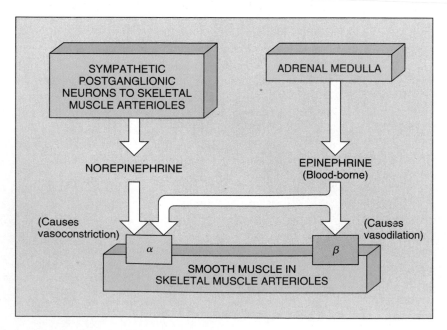

FIGURE 14-43

Effects of sympathetic nerves and plasma epinephrine on the arterioles in skeletal muscle. After its release from neuron terminals, norepinephrine diffuses to the arterioles, whereas epinephrine—a hormone—is blood-borne. Note that activation of alpha-adrenergic receptors and beta-adrenergic receptors produces opposing effects. For simplicity, norepinephrine is shown binding only to alpha-adrenergic receptors; it also can bind to beta-adrenergic receptors on the arterioles, but this occurs to a lesser extent.

so by acting *directly* on the smooth muscle, but others act *indirectly* via the endothelial cells adjacent to the smooth muscle. Endothelial cells, in response to these latter substances as well as certain mechanical stimuli, secrete several paracrine agents, which then diffuse to the adjacent vascular smooth muscle and induce either relaxation or contraction, resulting in vasodilation or vasoconstriction, respectively.

One vasodilator released by endothelial cells is the eicosanoid **prostacyclin**, the actions of which will be described further in Chapter 20 in the context of blood clotting. A second, very important vasodilator released by endothelial cells is **endothelium-derived relaxing factor (EDRF)**, which is actually nitric oxide (formed in the endothelial cells from arginine). EDRF is released continuously in significant amounts by endothelial cells in the arterioles and contributes to arteriolar vasodilation in the basal state, but its secretion is rapidly and markedly increased in response to a large number of the chemical mediators involved in both reflex and local control of arterioles. For example, EDRF release is stimulated by bradykinin and histamine, substances produced locally during inflammation.

Endothelial cells in *arteries* can also secrete EDRF, in response to the mechanical shear stress that accompanies high blood-flow rate. The EDRF causes the arterial vascular smooth muscle to relax and the artery to dilate. This "flow-induced arterial vasodilation," which is independent of internal pressure and should be distinguished from *arteriolar* flow autoregulation, may be important in optimizing the supply of blood to tissues.

One of the *vasoconstrictor* substances released by endothelial cells in response to certain mechanical and chemical stimuli is **endothelin-1**, which belongs to a family of peptide paracrine agents secreted in various organs and tissues. The physiological role of this potent vasoconstrictor is presently unknown.

Arteriolar Control in Specific Organs

Figure 14-44 summarizes the factors that determine arteriolar radius. The importance of local and reflex controls varies from organ to organ, and Table 14-7 lists for reference the key features of arteriolar control in specific organs.

CAPILLARIES

As mentioned at the beginning of Section B, at any given moment, approximately 5 percent of the total circulating blood is flowing through the capillaries, and it is this 5 percent that is performing the ultimate function of the entire cardiovascular system—the exchange of nutrients and metabolic end products. (Some exchange also occurs in the venules, which can be viewed as extensions of capillaries.)

The capillaries permeate almost every tissue of the body. Since most cells are no more than 0.01 cm from a capillary, diffusion distances are very small, and exchange is highly efficient. There are an estimated 25,000 mi of capillaries in an adult, each individual capillary being only about 1 mm long with an inner diameter of 5 μm, just wide enough for an erythrocyte to squeeze through. (For comparison, a human hair is about 100 μm in diameter.)

The essential role of capillaries in tissue function has stimulated many questions concerning how capillaries develop and grow (**angiogenesis**). For example, how do tumors stimulate growth of new capillaries, and what turns

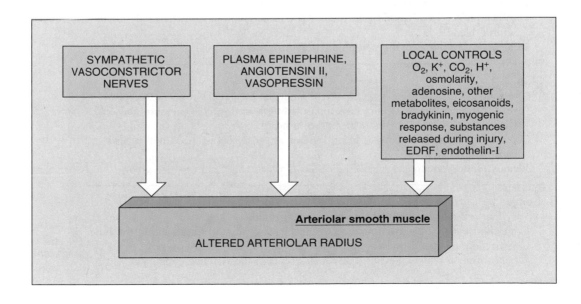

FIGURE 14-44
Major factors affecting arteriolar radius.

Blood flow through capillaries depends very much on the state of the other vessels that constitute the microcirculation (Figure 14-46). Thus, vasodilation of the arterioles supplying the capillaries causes increased capillary flow, whereas arteriolar vasoconstriction reduces capillary flow. In addition, in some tissues and organs blood does not enter capillaries directly from arterioles but from vessels, called **metarterioles**, which connect arterioles to venules. Metarterioles are transitional vessels in that they retain, like arterioles, scattered smooth-muscle cells. The site at which a capillary exits from a metarteriole is surrounded by a ring of smooth muscle, the **precapillary sphincter**, which relaxes or contracts in response to local metabolic factors. When contracted, the precapillary sphincter closes the entry to the capillary completely. The more active the tissue, the more precapillary sphincters are open at any moment and the more capillaries in the network are receiving blood. Precapillary sphincters may also exist at the site of capillary exit from arterioles.

Velocity of Capillary Blood Flow

Figure 14-47 illustrates a simple mechanical model of a series of 1-cm-diameter balls being pushed down a single tube that branches into narrower tubes. Although each tributary tube has a smaller cross section than the wide tube, the sum of the tributary cross sections is much greater than that of the wide tube. Let us assume that in the wide tube each ball moves 3 cm/min. If the balls are 1 cm in diameter and they move two abreast, six balls leave the wide tube per minute and enter the narrow tubes, and six balls leave the narrow tubes per minute. At what speed does each ball move in the small tubes? The answer is *1 cm/min*.

This example illustrates the following important principle: When a continuous stream moves through consecutive sets of tubes, the velocity of flow decreases as the sum of the cross-sectional areas of the tubes increases. This is precisely the case in the cardiovascular system (Figure 14-48). The blood velocity is very great in the aorta, slows progressively in the arteries and arterioles, and then slows markedly as the blood passes through the huge cross-sectional area of the capillaries. The velocity of flow then progressively increases in the venules and veins because the cross-sectional area decreases.

Diffusion Across the Capillary Wall: Exchanges of Nutrients and Metabolic End Products

There are three basic mechanisms by which substances move across the capillary walls in most organs and tissues to enter or leave the interstitial fluid: diffusion, vesicle transport, and bulk flow. Mediated transport constitutes a fourth mechanism in the capillaries of the brain.

FIGURE 14-47

Relationship between total cross-sectional area and flow velocity. The total cross-sectional area of the small tubes is three times greater than that of the large tube. Accordingly, velocity of flow is one-third as great in the small tubes.

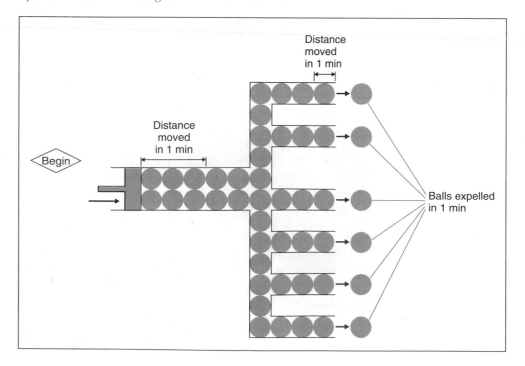

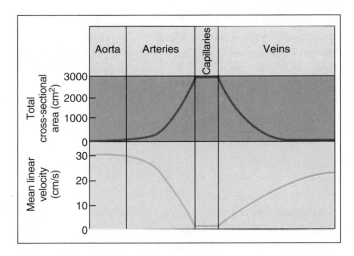

FIGURE 14-48

Relationship between total cross-sectional area and flow velocity in the systemic circulation (*Adapted from Lytle.*)

In all capillaries, excluding those in the brain, the first of these mechanisms—diffusion—constitutes the only important means by which net movement of nutrients, oxygen, and metabolic end products occurs across capillary walls. As described in the next section, there is some movement of these substances by bulk flow, but it is of negligible importance.

The factors determining diffusion rates were described in Chapter 6. Lipid-soluble substances, including oxygen and carbon dioxide, easily diffuse through the plasma membranes of the capillary endothelial cells. In contrast, ions and polar molecules are poorly soluble in lipid and must pass through small water-filled channels in the endothelial lining. One location of these channels is the intercellular clefts, that is, the narrow water-filled spaces between adjacent cells.[8] Another set of water-filled channels is provided by the fused-vesicle channels that penetrate the endothelial cells. The presence of water-filled channels in the capillary walls causes the permeability of ions and small polar molecules to be quite high, although still much lower than that of lipid-soluble molecules.

The intercellular clefts are, however, too small to allow the passage of proteins, but some protein can diffuse through the fused-vesicle channels, which are larger. Protein may also cross by endocytosis of plasma at the luminal border and movement of the vesicle across the endothelial cell, with exocytosis of its contents at the interstitial side. Although these various mechanisms do provide a means

for protein movement from plasma to interstitial fluid, such movement is quite small in most organs.

Variations in the size of the water-filled channels account for the great differences in the "leakiness" of capillaries in different organs. At one extreme are the "tight" capillaries of the brain, which have no intercellular clefts, only tight junctions. Therefore, water-soluble substances, even those of low molecular weight, can gain access to or exit from brain interstitial space only by carrier-mediated transport through the blood-brain barrier (Chapter 8).

At the other end of the spectrum are liver capillaries, which have large intercellular clefts as well as holes within the endothelial cells so that even protein molecules can readily pass. This is important because one of the major functions of the liver is the synthesis of plasma proteins and the metabolism of protein-bound substances, both of which must be able to enter or leave the blood.

The leakiness of capillaries in most organs and tissues lies between these extremes of brain and liver capillaries.

What is the sequence of events involved in transfers of materials between capillaries and cells? Tissue cells do not exchange material *directly* with blood; the fluid surrounding the cells—the interstitial fluid—acts as intermediary. Therefore, nutrients diffuse first across the capillary wall into the interstitial fluid, from which they gain entry to cells. Conversely, metabolic end products move across the tissue cells' plasma membranes into interstitial fluid, from which they diffuse into the plasma.

Transcapillary diffusion gradients for oxygen, nutrients, and metabolic end products occur as a result of cellular utilization or production of the substance. Let us take two examples: glucose and carbon dioxide in muscle. Glucose is continuously transported from interstitial fluid into the muscle cells by carrier-mediated transport mechanisms and utilized there. The removal of glucose from interstitial fluid lowers the interstitial-fluid glucose concentration below the glucose concentration in capillary plasma and creates the gradient for diffusion of glucose from the capillary into the interstitial fluid.

Simultaneously, carbon dioxide is continuously produced by muscle cells and diffuses into the interstitial fluid. This causes the carbon dioxide concentration in interstitial fluid to be greater than that in capillary plasma, producing a gradient for carbon dioxide diffusion from the interstitial fluid into the capillary. Note that in both examples metabolism of the substance is the event that ultimately establishes the transcapillary diffusion gradients.

If a tissue is to increase its metabolic rate, it must obtain more nutrients from the blood and eliminate more metabolic end products. One mechanism for achieving this is active hyperemia. The second important mechanism is to increase diffusion gradients between plasma and tissue: Increased cellular utilization of oxygen and nutrients lowers their tissue concentrations, while increased produc-

---

[8]Except in the kidney, the basement membrane offers no diffusion barrier, and so we ignore it in this discussion of diffusion.

tion of carbon dioxide and other end products raises their tissue concentrations. In both cases the substance's trans-capillary concentration difference is increased, which increases the rate of diffusion.

Bulk Flow Across the Capillary Wall: Distribution of the Extracellular Fluid

To repeat, the exchange of nutrients, oxygen, and metabolic end products across most capillaries occurs almost entirely by diffusion. At the same time these diffusional exchanges are occurring, another completely distinct process is taking place across the capillary: the bulk flow of protein-free plasma. The function of this process is *not* exchange of materials but rather distribution of the extracellular fluid. As described in Chapter 1, extracellular fluid comprises the blood plasma and the interstitial fluid. Normally, there is approximately three times more interstitial fluid than plasma, 10 L vs. 3 L in a 70-kg person. This distribution is not fixed, however, and the interstitial fluid functions as a reservoir that can supply fluid to the plasma or receive fluid from it.

As described in the previous section, the capillary wall is highly permeable to water and to almost all plasma solutes, except plasma proteins. Therefore, in the presence of a hydrostatic pressure difference across it, the capillary wall behaves like a porous filter through which protein-free plasma (**ultrafiltrate**) moves by bulk flow from capillary plasma to interstitial fluid through the water-filled channels. The concentrations of all the plasma solutes except protein are virtually the same in the filtering fluid as in plasma.

The magnitude of the bulk flow is directly proportional to the difference between the capillary blood pressure and the interstitial-fluid pressure. Normally, the former is much larger than the latter. Therefore, a considerable hydrostatic pressure difference exists to filter protein-free plasma out of the capillaries into the interstitial fluid, the protein remaining behind in the plasma.

Why then does all the plasma not filter out into the interstitial space? The explanation was first presented by Starling—the same scientist who expounded the law of the heart that bears his name—and depends upon the principle of osmosis. In Chapter 6 we described how a net movement of water occurs across a semipermeable membrane from a solution of high water concentration to a solution of low water concentration, that is, from a region with a low concentration of solute to which the membrane is impermeable (nonpermeating solute) to a region of high nonpermeating solute concentration. Moreover, this osmotic flow of water "drags" along with it any dissolved solutes to which the membrane is highly permeable (permeating solute). Thus, a difference in water concentration secondary to different concentrations of *nonpermeating*

solute on the two sides of a membrane can result in the movement of a solution containing both water and permeating solutes in a manner similar to the bulk flow produced by a hydrostatic pressure difference. Units of pressure can be used in expressing this osmotic flow across a membrane.

This analysis can now be applied to capillary-fluid movements. The plasma within the capillary and the interstitial fluid outside it contain large quantities of low-molecular-weight permeating solutes (also termed **crystalloids**), for example, sodium, chloride, and glucose. Since the capillary lining is highly permeable to all these crystalloids, their concentrations in the two solutions are essentially identical.[9] Accordingly, no significant water concentration difference is caused by the presence of the crystalloids. In contrast, the plasma proteins (also termed **colloids**), being essentially nonpermeating, have a very low concentration in the interstitial fluid. This difference in protein concentration between plasma and interstitial fluid means that the water concentration of the plasma is lower than that of interstitial fluid, inducing an osmotic flow of water from the interstitial compartment into the capillary. Since the crystalloids in the interstitial fluid move along with the water, osmotic flow of fluid, like flow driven by a hydrostatic pressure difference, does not alter their concentrations in either plasma or interstitial fluid.

A key word in this last sentence is "concentrations." Because the interstitial fluid and plasma have identical crystalloid concentrations to start with, a transfer of fluid across the capillary wall does not change the crystalloid concentrations in either location. However, the *amount* of water (the *volume*) and the *amount* of crystalloids in the two locations do change. Thus, an increased filtration of fluid from plasma to interstitial fluid increases the volume of the interstitial fluid and decreases the volume of the plasma, even though no changes in crystalloid concentrations occur.

In summary (Figure 14-49A), two opposing forces act to move fluid across the capillary wall: (1) The difference between capillary blood hydrostatic pressure and interstitial-fluid hydrostatic pressure favors the filtration out of the capillary, and (2) the water concentration difference between plasma and interstitial fluid, which results from differences in protein concentration, favors the flow of interstitial fluid into the capillary. Accordingly, the movements of fluid depend directly upon four variables: capillary hydrostatic pressure, interstitial hydrostatic pressure, plasma protein concentration, and interstitial-fluid protein concentration. These four factors are termed the **Starling forces**.

[9]As we have seen, there are small concentration differences for substances that are consumed or produced by the cells. These tend, however, to cancel each other out.

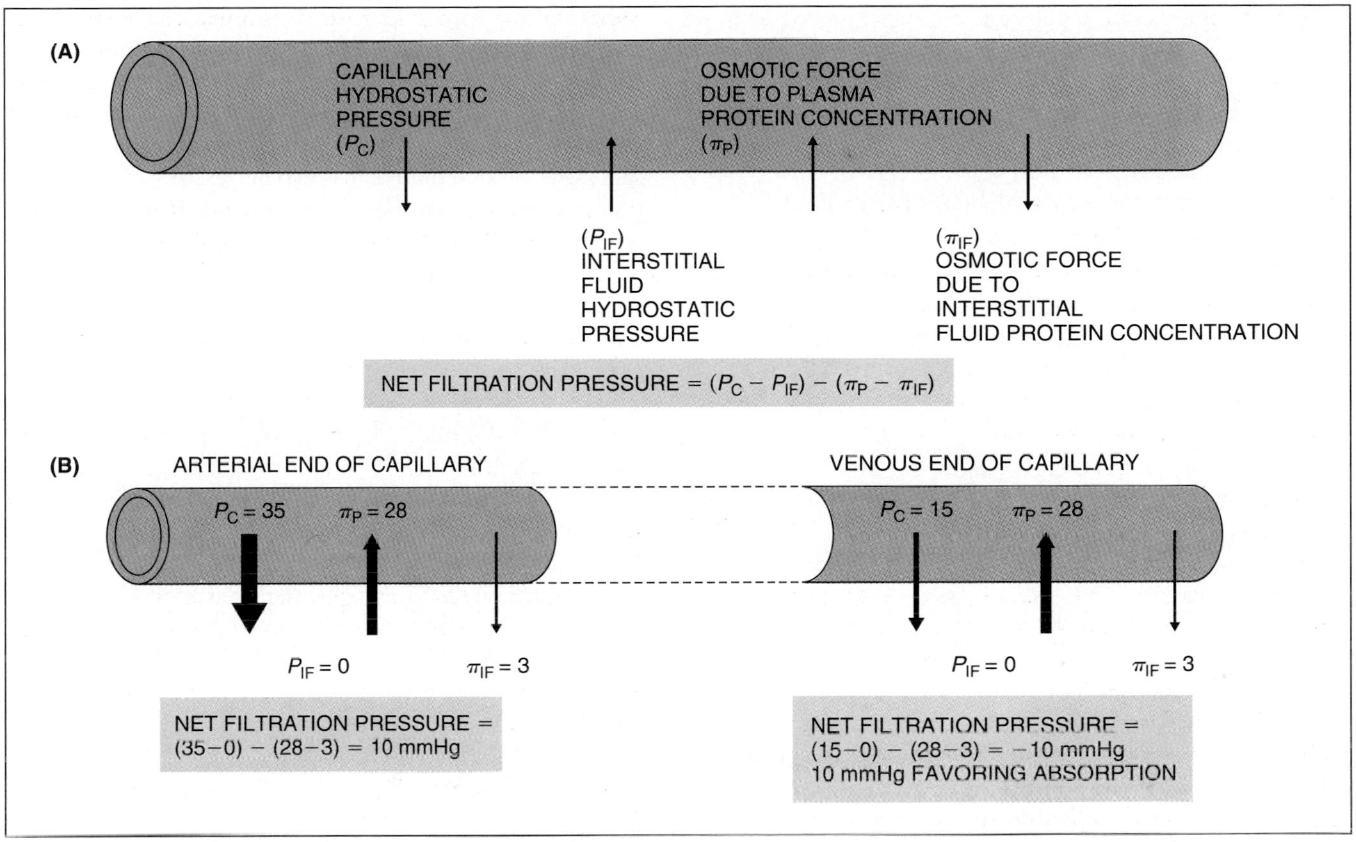

FIGURE 14-49

(A) The four factors determining fluid movement across capillaries. (B) Quantitation of forces causing filtration at the arteriolar end of the capillary and absorption at the venous end. Arrows in (B) denote magnitude of forces. No arrow is shown for interstitial fluid hydrostatic pressure (P_{IF}) because it is zero.

We may now consider this movement quantitatively in the systemic circulation (Figure 14-49B). Much of the arterial blood pressure has already been dissipated as the blood flows through the arterioles, so that pressure at the beginning of the capillary (the part closest to the arteriole) is about 35 mmHg. Since the capillary also offers resistance to flow, the pressure continuously decreases to approximately 15 mmHg at the end of the capillary (the part farthest from the arteriole). The interstitial pressure is very low, and we shall assume it to be zero.[10] The plasma protein concentration would produce an osmotic flow of water equivalent to that produced by a hydrostatic pressure of 28 mmHg. The interstitial protein concentration would produce a flow of water equivalent to that produced by a hydrostatic pressure of 3 mmHg. Therefore, the difference in protein concentrations induces a flow of fluid into the capillary equivalent to that produced by a hydrostatic pressure difference of $28 - 3 = 25$ mmHg.

Thus, in the beginning of the capillary the hydrostatic pressure difference across the capillary wall (35 mmHg) is greater than the opposing osmotic force (25 mmHg), and a net movement of fluid out of the capillary (**filtration**) occurs. In the end of the capillary, however, the osmotic force (25 mmHg) is greater than the hydrostatic pressure difference (15 mmHg), and fluid moves into the capillary (**absorption**). The result is that the early and late capillary events tend to cancel each other out. For the aggregate of capillaries in the body, however, there is a small net filtration of approximately 4 L/day (this number does not include the capillaries in the kidneys). The fate of this fluid will be described in the section on the lymphatic system.

This analysis of capillary fluid dynamics at the arterial and venous ends of the capillary has been somewhat oversimplified. It is very likely that many individual capillaries manifest only net filtration or net absorption along their

---

[10]The exact value of interstitial hydrostatic pressure remains highly controversial. Many physiologists believe that it is not zero but is actually subatmospheric. The outcome of this controversy will not, however, alter the basic concepts being presented here.

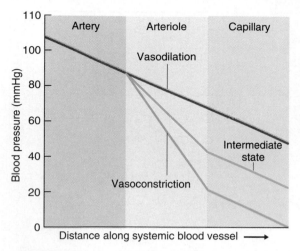

FIGURE 14-50

Effects of arteriolar vasodilation or vasoconstriction in an organ on capillary blood pressure in that organ.

entire lengths because the arterioles supplying them are either so dilated or so constricted that a capillary hydrostatic pressure above or below 25 mmHg exists along the entire length of the capillary.

The last paragraph illustrates the very important point that capillary pressure in any vascular bed is subject to physiological regulation, mediated mainly by changes in the resistance of the arterioles in that bed. As shown in Figure 14-50, dilating the arterioles in a particular vascular bed raises capillary pressure because less pressure is lost overcoming resistance between the arteries and the capillaries. Because of the increased capillary pressure, filtration is increased, and more protein-free fluid is lost to the interstitial fluid. In contrast, marked arteriolar constriction produces decreased capillary pressure and hence net movement of interstitial fluid into the vascular compartment.

It is this ability to change capillary pressure that determines the distribution of the extracellular-fluid volume between the cardiovascular and interstitial compartments. For example, when blood volume is low, as following a hemorrhage, the resulting decrease in capillary pressure causes net movement of interstitial fluid into the capillaries and helps expand the blood volume.

It should be stated again that capillary filtration and absorption play no significant role in the exchange of nutrients and metabolic end products between capillary and tissues. The reason is that the total quantity of a substance, such as glucose or carbon dioxide, moving into or out of a capillary as a result of net bulk flow is extremely small in comparison with the quantities moving by net diffusion.

Finally, this analysis of capillary fluid dynamics has been in terms of the systemic circulation. Precisely the same Starling forces apply to the capillaries in the pulmonary circulation, but the values of the four variables differ. In particular, because the pulmonary circulation is a low-resistance, low-pressure circuit, the normal pulmonary capillary pressure—the major force favoring movement of fluid out of the pulmonary capillaries into the interstitium—is only 15 mmHg. Therefore, normally net absorption of fluid occurs all along lung capillaries.

VEINS

Blood flows from capillaries into venules and then into veins. Some exchange of materials occurs between the interstitial fluid and the venules. Indeed, permeability to macromolecules is often greater for venules than for capillaries, particularly in damaged areas.

The veins outside the chest, the **peripheral veins**, contain valves that permit flow only toward the heart. Why are these valves necessary if the pressure gradient created by cardiac contraction pushes blood only toward the heart anyway? The answer will be given below.

The veins are the last set of tubes through which blood flows on its way back to the heart. In the systemic circulation the force driving this venous return is the pressure difference between the peripheral veins and the right atrium.[11] Most of the pressure imparted to the blood by the heart is dissipated by resistance as blood flows through the arterioles, capillaries, and venules so that pressure in the first portion of the peripheral veins is only 5 to 10 mmHg. The right atrial pressure is close to 0 mmHg, so that the total driving pressure for flow from the peripheral veins to the right atrium is only 5 to 10 mmHg. This is adequate because of the low resistance to flow offered by the veins, which have large diameters. Thus, a major function of the veins is to act as low-resistance conduits for blood flow from the tissues to the heart.

In addition to their function as low-resistance conduits, the veins perform a second important function: Their diameters are reflexly altered in response to changes in blood volume, thereby maintaining peripheral venous pressure and venous return to the heart. In a previous section, we emphasized that the rate of venous return to the heart is a major determinant of end-diastolic ventricular volume and thereby stroke volume. Thus, we now see that peripheral venous pressure is an important determinant of stroke volume.

---

[11] The blood in the right atrium and large veins of the thorax constitutes a single "pool"—the central venous pool. The pressure in this pool—the central venous pressure—is easily measured, and it is customary to substitute this pressure for right atrial pressure when dealing with venous return. However, to avoid potential confusion, we have not adopted this convention.

Determinants of Venous Pressure

The factors determining pressure in any elastic tube are, as we know, the volume of fluid within it and the compliance of its wall. Accordingly, total blood volume is one important determinant of venous pressure since, at any given moment, most blood is in the veins. The walls of veins are thinner and much more compliant than those of arteries. Thus, veins can accommodate large volumes of blood with a relatively small increase in internal pressure. Approximately 60 percent of the total blood volume is present in the systemic veins at any given moment (Figure 14-51), but the venous pressure averages less than 10 mmHg. In contrast, the systemic arteries contain less than 15 percent of the blood, at a pressure of approximately 100 mmHg.

The walls of the veins contain smooth muscle innervated by sympathetic neurons. Stimulation of these neurons releases norepinephrine, which causes contraction of the venous smooth muscle, decreasing the diameter and compliance of the vessels and raising the pressure within

FIGURE 14-51

Distribution of the total blood volume in different parts of the cardiovascular system. (*Adapted from Guyton.*)

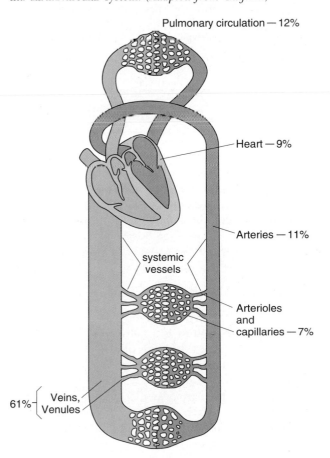

Pulmonary circulation — 12%

Heart — 9%

Arteries — 11%

systemic vessels

Arterioles and capillaries — 7%

61% Veins, Venules

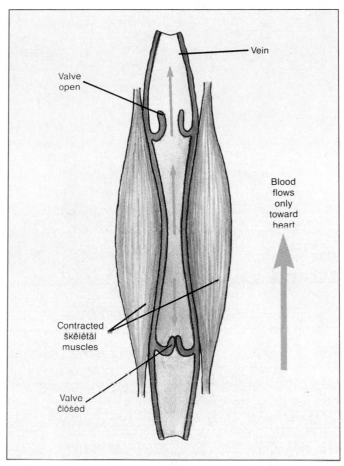

FIGURE 14-52

The skeletal muscle pump. During muscle contraction, venous diameter decreases and venous pressure rises. The resulting increase in blood flow can occur only toward the heart because the valves in the veins are forced closed by any backward flow.

them. Increased venous pressure drives more blood out of the veins into the right heart.

Two other mechanisms, in addition to contraction of venous smooth muscle, can increase venous pressure and facilitate venous return. These mechanisms are the **skeletal-muscle pump** and the **respiratory pump**. During skeletal-muscle contraction, the veins running through the muscle are partially compressed, which reduces their diameter and forces more blood back to the heart. Now we can describe a major function of the peripheral-vein valves: When the skeletal-muscle pump raises venous pressure locally, the valves permit blood flow only toward the heart and prevent flow back toward the tissues (Figure 14-52).

The respiratory pump is somewhat more difficult to visualize. As will be described in Chapter 15, during inspira-

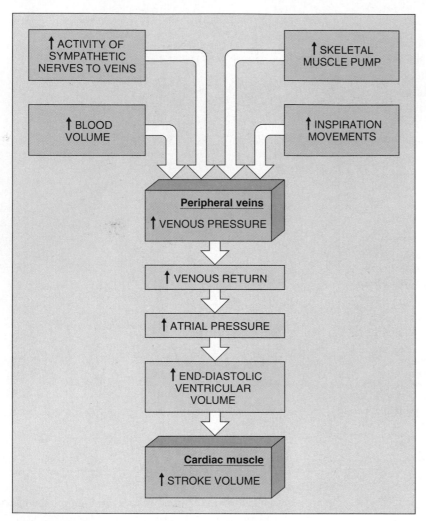

FIGURE 14-53

Major factors determining peripheral venous pressure and, hence, venous return and stroke volume. The figure shows how venous pressure and stroke volume are increased. Reversing the arrows in the boxes would indicate how these can be decreased. The effects of increased inspiration on end-diastolic ventricular volume are actually quite complex, and for the sake of simplicity, they are shown only as increasing venous pressure.

tion of air, the diaphragm descends, pushes on the abdominal contents, and increases abdominal pressure. This pressure increase is transmitted passively to the intraabdominal veins. Simultaneously, the pressure in the thorax *decreases,* thereby decreasing the pressure in the intrathoracic veins and right atrium. The net effect of the pressure changes in the abdomen and thorax is to increase the pressure difference between the peripheral veins and the heart. Accordingly, venous return is enhanced during inspiration (expiration would reverse this effect if it were not for the venous valves). The larger the inspiration, the greater the effect. Thus, breathing deeply and frequently, as in exercise, helps blood flow from the peripheral veins to the heart.

One might get the (incorrect) impression from these descriptions that venous return and cardiac output are independent entities. However, any change in venous return, due say to the skeletal-muscle pump, almost immediately causes equivalent changes in cardiac output, largely through the operation of Starling's law. Venous return and

cardiac output therefore must be identical except for very brief periods of time.

In summary (Figure 14-53), the effects of venous smooth-muscle contraction, the skeletal-muscle pump, and the respiratory pump are to facilitate return of blood to the heart and thereby to enhance cardiac output.

THE LYMPHATIC SYSTEM

The **lymphatic system** is a network of small organs (lymph nodes) and tubes (**lymphatic vessels** or simply "lymphatics") through which **lymph**—a fluid derived from interstitial fluid—flows. The lymphatic system is not technically part of the cardiovascular system, but it is described in this chapter because its vessels constitute a route for the movement of interstitial fluid to the cardiovascular system (Figure 14-54).

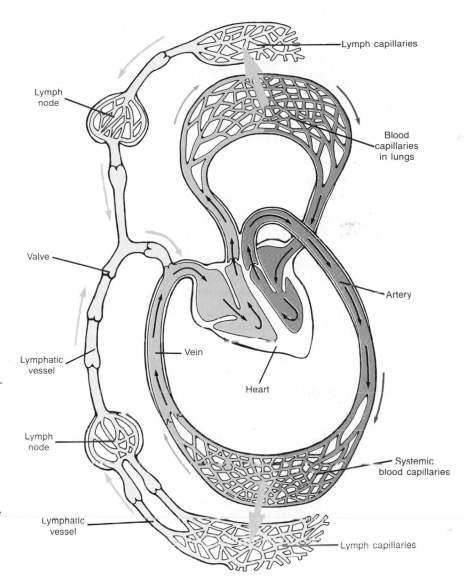

FIGURE 14-54

The lymphatic system (yellow) in relation to the cardiovascular system (blue and red). The lymphatic system is a one-way system from interstitial fluid to the cardiovascular system. The excess fluid that filters from the blood capillaries into the interstitial fluid enters the lymph capillaries and flows through the lymphatic vessels and the nodes along them. Many lymphatic vessels arise in the systemic organs and the lungs, and each has multiple lymph nodes. All the lymphatic vessels converge into large lymphatic vessels that empty into the systemic circulation via the systemic veins.

Present in the interstitium of virtually all organs and tissues are numerous **lymphatic capillaries** that are completely distinct from blood vessel capillaries. Like the latter, they are tubes made of only a single layer of endothelial cells, but they have large water-filled channels that are permeable to all interstitial-fluid constituents, including protein. The lymphatic capillaries are the first of the lymphatic vessels, for unlike the blood vessel capillaries, no tubes flow into them.

Small amounts of interstitial fluid continuously enter the lymphatic capillaries at rates determined by the interstitial pressure. Now known as lymph, the fluid flows from the lymphatic capillaries into the next set of lymphatic vessels, which converge to form larger and larger lymphatic vessels. Ultimately, the entire network ends in two large lymphatic vessels that drain into veins in the lower neck. Valves at these junctions permit only one-way flow from

lymphatic vessels into veins. Thus, the lymphatic vessels carry interstitial fluid to the cardiovascular system. At various points, the lymph flows through lymph nodes, the function of which is described in Chapter 20.

The movement of interstitial fluid to the cardiovascular system via the lymphatics is very important because, as noted earlier, the amount of fluid filtered out of all the blood vessel capillaries (except those in the kidneys) exceeds that reabsorbed by approximately 4 L each day. This 4 L is returned to the blood via the lymphatic system. In the process, the small amounts of protein that leak out of blood vessel capillaries into the interstitial fluid are also returned to the cardiovascular system.

Failure of the lymphatic system, due for example to occlusion by infectious organisms (as in the disease **elephantiasis**) allows the accumulation of excessive interstitial fluid. The result can be massive swelling of the involved area. The accumulation of interstitial fluid for whatever cause (others are described in the section on heart failure) is termed *edema*.

As will be described in Chapter 17, the lymphatic system also provides the pathway by which fat absorbed from the gastrointestinal tract reaches the blood. The lymphatics also, unfortunately, are often the route by which cancer cells spread from their area of origin to other parts of the body.

Mechanism of Lymph Flow

In large part, the lymphatic vessels propel the lymph within them by their own contractions. The smooth muscle in the wall of the lymphatics exerts a pumplike action by inherent rhythmical contractions. Since the lymphatic vessels have valves similar to those in veins, these contractions produce a one-way flow toward the points at which the lymphatics enter the circulatory system. The lymphatic vessel smooth muscle is responsive to stretch, so when

there is no accumulation of interstitial fluid, and hence no entry of lymph into the lymphatics, the smooth muscle is inactive. As lymph formation increases, however, say as a result of increased fluid filtration out of blood vessel capillaries, the increased lymph entering the lymphatics stretches the walls and triggers rhythmical contractions of the smooth muscle, the rate and force of which depend on the degree of stretch. This constitutes a negative-feedback mechanism for adjusting the rate of lymph flow to the rate of lymph formation and thereby helps prevent edema formation.

Moreover, the smooth muscle of the lymphatic vessels is innervated by sympathetic neurons, and excitation of these neurons in various physiological states such as exercise may contribute to increased lymph flow.

Lymph flow can also be enhanced by forces external to the lymphatic vessels. These include the same external forces we described for veins—the skeletal-muscle and respiratory pumps.

SECTION D SUMMARY

ARTERIES

I. The arteries function as low-resistance conduits and as pressure reservoirs for maintaining blood flow to the tissues during ventricular relaxation.

II. The difference between maximal arterial pressure (systolic pressure) and minimal arterial pressure (diastolic pressure) during a cardiac cycle is the pulse pressure.

III. Mean arterial pressure can be estimated as diastolic pressure plus one-third pulse pressure.

ARTERIOLES

I. Arterioles, the major site of resistance to flow in the vascular system, play a major role in determining both mean arterial pressure and the distribution of flows to the various organs and tissues.

II. Arteriolar resistance is determined by local factors and by reflex neural and hormonal input.
   A. Local factors that change with the degree of metabolic activity cause the arteriolar vasodilation and increased flow of active hyperemia.
   B. Flow autoregulation, a change in resistance that maintains flow constant in the face of a change in blood pressure, is due to local metabolic factors and to arteriolar myogenic responses to stretch.
   C. The sympathetic nerves are the only innervation of most arterioles and cause vasoconstriction via alpha-adrenergic receptors.
   D. Epinephrine causes vasoconstriction or vasodilation, depending on the proportion of alpha- and beta-adrenergic receptors in the organ.

   E. Angiotensin II and vasopressin cause vasoconstriction.
   F. Some vasodilator inputs act by releasing endothelium-derived relaxing factor from endothelial cells.

III. Arteriolar control in specific organs is summarized in Table 14-7.

CAPILLARIES

I. Capillaries are the site of exchange of nutrients and waste products between blood and tissues.

II. Capillary blood flow is determined by the resistance of the arterioles supplying the capillaries and by the number of open precapillary sphincters.

III. Blood flows through the capillaries more slowly than in any other part of the vascular system because of the huge cross-sectional area of the capillaries.

IV. Diffusion is the mechanism by which nutrients and waste products exchange between capillary plasma and interstitial fluid.
   A. Lipid-soluble substances move across the entire endothelial wall, whereas ions and polar molecules move through water-filled intercellular clefts or fused-vesicle channels.
   B. Plasma proteins move across most capillaries only very slowly, either by diffusion or vesicle transport.
   C. The diffusion gradient for a substance across capillaries arises as a result of cell utilization or production of the substance. Increased metabolism increases the diffusion gradient and increases the rate of diffusion.

V. Bulk flow of protein-free plasma or interstitial fluid across capillaries determines the distribution of extra-cellular fluid between these two fluid compartments.
A. Filtration from plasma to interstitial fluid is favored by the hydrostatic pressure difference between the capillary and the interstitial fluid. Absorption from interstitial fluid to plasma is favored by the plasma protein concentration difference between the plasma and the interstitial fluid.
B. Filtration and absorption do not change the concentrations of crystalloids in the plasma and interstitial fluid because these substances move together with water.
C. There is normally a small excess of filtration over absorption.

VEINS

I. Veins serve as low-resistance conduits for venous return.
II. Veins are very compliant and contain most of the blood in the vascular system.
A. Their diameters are reflexly altered by sympathetically mediated vasoconstriction or vasodilation so as to maintain venous pressure and venous return.
B. The skeletal-muscle pump and respiratory pump increase venous pressure locally and enhance venous return. Venous valves permit the pressure to produce only flow toward the heart.

THE LYMPHATIC SYSTEM

I. The lymphatic system provides a one-way route for movement of interstitial fluid to the cardiovascular system.
II. Lymph returns the excess fluid filtered from the blood vessel capillaries, as well as the protein that leaks out of the blood vessel capillaries.
III. Lymph flow is driven mainly by contraction of smooth muscle in the lymphatic vessels but also by the skeletal-muscle pump and the respiratory pump.

SECTION D KEY TERMS

compliance	kallikrein
systolic pressure (SP)	flow autoregulation
diastolic pressure (DP)	myogenic responses
pulse pressure	reactive hyperemia
mean arterial pressure (MAP)	prostacyclin
vasodilation	endothelium-derived
vasoconstriction	relaxing factor
myogenic tone	(EDRF)
local controls	endothelin-1
hyperemia	metarterioles
active hyperemia	angiogenesis
bradykinin	angiogenic factors
kininogen	intercellular clefts
fused-vesicle channels	peripheral veins
precapillary sphincter	skeletal-muscle pump
ultrafiltrate	respiratory pump
crystalloids	lymphatic system
colloids	lymphatic vessels
Starling forces	lymph
filtration	lymphatic capillaries
absorption	

SECTION D REVIEW QUESTIONS

1. Draw the pressure changes along the systemic and pulmonary vascular systems during the cardiac cycle.
2. What are the two functions of the arteries?
3. What are normal values for systolic, diastolic, and mean arterial pressures? How is mean arterial pressure estimated?
4. What are the three factors that determine pulse pressure?
5. What denotes systolic and diastolic pressure in the measurement of arterial pressure with a sphygmomanometer?
6. What are the major sites of resistance in the systemic vascular system?
7. What are two functions of arterioles?
8. Write the formula relating flow through an organ to (a) mean arterial pressure, and (b) the resistance to flow offered by that organ.
9. List the chemical factors thought to mediate active hyperemia.
10. Name the mechanism other than chemical factors that contributes to flow autoregulation.
11. What is the only autonomic innervation of most arterioles? What are the major adrenergic receptors influenced by these nerves? How can control of sympathetic nerves to arterioles achieve either dilation or constriction?
12. Name three hormones that influence arterioles and describe their effects.
13. Draw a flow diagram summarizing the factors affecting arteriolar radius.
14. What are the relative velocities of flow through the various segments of the vascular system?
15. Contrast diffusion and bulk flow. Which is the mechanism of exchange of nutrients, oxygen, and metabolic end products across the capillary wall?
16. What is the only solute to have significant concentration differences across the capillary wall? How does this difference influence water concentration?
17. What four variables determine flow of fluid across the capillary wall? Give representative values for each of them in the systemic capillaries.
18. How do changes in local arteriolar resistance influence local capillary pressure?
19. What is the relationship between cardiac output and venous return in the steady state? What is the force driving venous return?

20. Contrast the compliances and blood volumes of the veins and arteries.

21. What three factors influence venous pressure?

22. Approximately how much fluid is returned to the blood by the lymphatics each day?

23. Describe the forces that cause lymph flow.

SECTION

E

INTEGRATION OF CARDIOVASCULAR FUNCTION: REGULATION OF SYSTEMIC ARTERIAL PRESSURE

In Chapter 7 we described the fundamental ingredients of all reflex control systems: (1) the internal-environmental variable being maintained relatively constant, (2) receptors sensitive to changes in this variable, (3) afferent pathways from the receptors, (4) an integrating center that receives and integrates the afferent inputs, (5) efferent pathways from the control center, (6) effectors "directed" by the efferent pathways to alter their activities. The result is a change in the level of the regulated variable. The control and integration of cardiovascular function will be described in these terms.

The major cardiovascular variable being regulated is the mean arterial blood pressure in the systemic circulation. This should not be surprising since this pressure is the driving force for blood flow through all the organs except the lungs. Maintaining it is therefore a prerequisite for ensuring adequate blood flow to these organs.

The mean systemic arterial pressure is the arithmetic product of two factors: (1) the cardiac output and (2) the **total peripheral resistance (TPR)**, which is the sum of the resistances to flow offered by all the systemic blood vessels:

Mean systemic arterial pressure
(MAP)

= cardiac output × total peripheral resistance
(CO) (TPR)

The reason these two factors set the mean systemic arterial pressure is because they determine the average volume of blood in the systemic arteries over time, and it is this blood volume that causes the pressure.

That the volume of blood pumped into the arteries per unit time—the cardiac output—is one of the two direct determinants of mean arterial blood volume and hence mean arterial pressure should come as no surprise. That the total resistance of the blood vessels to flow—the TPR—is the other determinant may not be so intuitively obvious

but can be illustrated by using the model introduced in Figure 14-41.

As shown in Figure 14-55 a pump pushes fluid into a container at the rate of 1 L/min. At steady state, fluid also leaves the container via outflow tubes at a total rate of 1 L/min. Therefore, the height of the fluid column (ΔP), which is the driving pressure for outflow, remains stable. We then disturb the steady state by loosening the cuff on outflow tube 1, increasing its radius, reducing its resistance, and increasing its flow. The total outflow for the system immediately becomes greater than 1 L/min, and more fluid leaves the reservoir than enters from the pump. Therefore, the volume and hence the height of the fluid column begin to decrease until a new steady state between inflow and outflow is reached. In other words, at any given pump input, a change in *total* outflow resistance must produce changes in the volume and hence the height (pressure) in the reservoir.

This analysis can be applied to the cardiovascular system by again equating the pump with the heart, the reservoir with the arteries, and the outflow tubes with various arteriolar beds. As described earlier, most of the vascular resistance in the systemic circulation is supplied by the arterioles, and so we usually equate total peripheral resistance with arteriolar resistance. An analogy to opening outflow tube 1 is exercise: During exercise, the skeletal-muscle arterioles dilate, thereby decreasing resistance. If the cardiac output and the arteriolar diameters of all other vascular beds were to remain unchanged, the increased runoff through the skeletal-muscle arterioles would cause a decrease in systemic arterial pressure.

It must be reemphasized that it is the *total* arteriolar resistance that influences systemic arterial blood pressure. The *distribution* of resistances among organs is irrelevant in this regard. Figure 14-56 illustrates this point. On the right, outflow tube 1 has been opened, as in the previous example, while tubes 2 to 4 have been simultaneously tightened. The increased resistance offered by tubes 2 to 4 compensates for the decreased resistance offered by tube

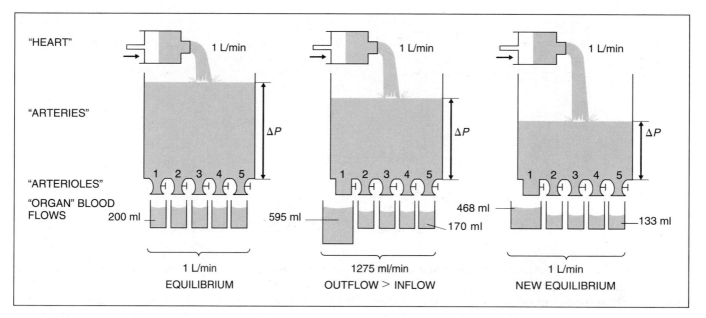

FIGURE 14-55

Dependence of arterial blood pressure upon total arteriolar resistance. Dilating one arteriolar bed affects arterial pressure and organ blood flow if no compensatory adjustments occur. The middle panel is a transient state before the new steady state occurs.

1; therefore total resistance remains unchanged, and reservoir pressure is unchanged. Total outflow remains 1 L/min, although the distribution of flows is such that flow through tube 1 is increased, that of tubes 2 to 4 is decreased, and that of tube 5 is unchanged.

Applied to the systemic circulation, this process is anal-

ogous to altering the distribution of systemic vascular resistances. When the skeletal-muscle arterioles (tube 1) dilate during exercise, the *total* resistance of the systemic circulation can still be maintained if arterioles constrict in other organs, such as the kidneys, gastrointestinal tract, and skin (tubes 2 to 4). In contrast, the brain arterioles

FIGURE 14-56

Compensation for dilation in one bed by constriction in others. When outflow tube 1 is opened, outflow tubes 2 to 4 are simultaneously tightened so that total outflow resistance, total runoff rate, and reservoir pressure all remain constant.

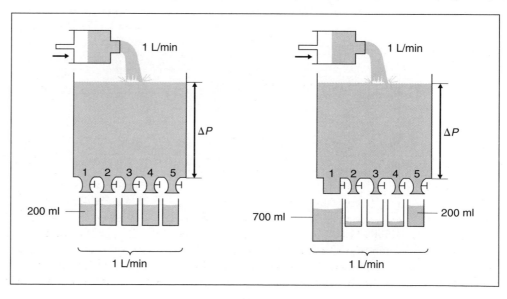

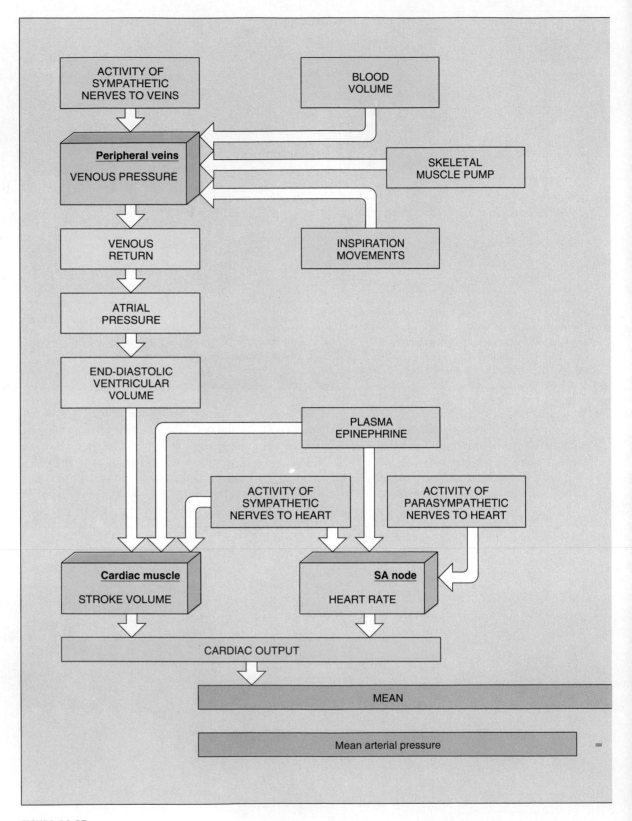

FIGURE 14-57

Summary of factors that determine systemic arterial pressure, an amalgamation of Figures 14-36, 14-44, and

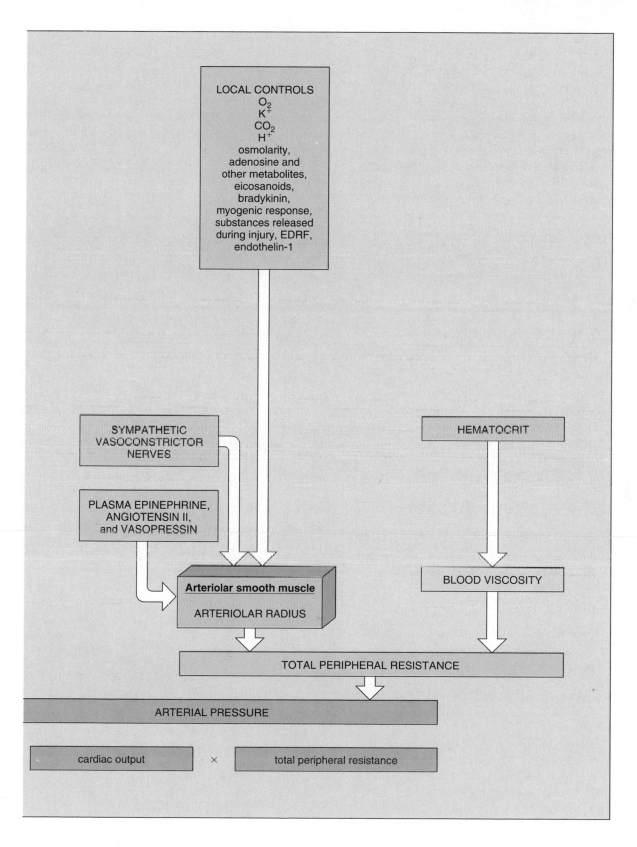

14-53, with the addition of the effect of hematocrit on resistance.

(tube 5) remain unchanged, ensuring constant brain blood supply.

This type of resistance juggling can maintain total resistance only within limits, however. Obviously if tube 1 opens very wide, even total closure of the other tubes cannot prevent total outflow resistance from falling. We shall see that this is actually the case during exercise.

We have thus far explained in an intuitive way why cardiac output (CO) and total peripheral resistance (TPR) are the two variables that set mean systemic arterial pressure. This intuitive approach, however, does not explain specifically why MAP is the *arithmetic product* of CO and TPR. This relationship can be derived formally from the basic equation relating flow, pressure, and resistance:

$$F = \frac{\Delta P}{R}$$

Rearranging terms algebraically, we have

$$\Delta P = FR$$

Because the systemic vascular system is a continuous series of tubes, this equation holds for the entire system, that is, from the arteries to the right atrium. Therefore, the ΔP term is mean systemic arterial pressure (MAP) minus the pressure in the right atrium, F is the cardiac output (CO), and R is the total peripheral resistance (TPR):

$$MAP - \text{right atrial pressure} = CO \times TPR$$

Since the pressure in the right atrium is very close to 0 mmHg, we can drop this term and we are left with the equation presented earlier:

$$MAP = CO \times TPR$$

This equation is the fundamental equation of cardiovascular physiology. An analogous equation can also be applied to the pulmonary circulation:

$$\text{Mean pulmonary arterial pressure} = CO \times \text{total pulmonary vascular resistance}$$

These equations provide a way to integrate almost all the information presented in this chapter. For example, we can now explain why mean pulmonary arterial pressure is much lower than mean systemic arterial pressure. The cardiac output through the pulmonary and systemic arteries is, of course, the same. Therefore, the pressures can differ only if the resistances differ. Thus, the pulmonary vessels offer much less resistance to flow than do the systemic vessels. In other words, the total pulmonary vascular resistance is lower than the total peripheral resistance.

Figure 14-57 presents the grand scheme of factors that determine mean systemic arterial pressure.[12] None of this information is new, all of it having been presented in previous figures. A change in only a single variable will produce a change in mean systemic arterial pressure by altering either cardiac output or total peripheral resistance. For example, Figure 14-58 illustrates how the decrease in

---

[12]Any model of a system as complex as the circulatory system must, of necessity, be an oversimplification. One basic deficiency in our model is that its chain of causal links is entirely unidirectional (from top to bottom in Figure 14-57), whereas in fact there are also important causal interactions in the reverse direction. A reader interested in delving further into these complex interactions and feedback loops should consult the more advanced works listed in Appendix G.

FIGURE 14-58

Sequence of events by which a decrease in blood volume leads to a decrease in mean arterial pressure.

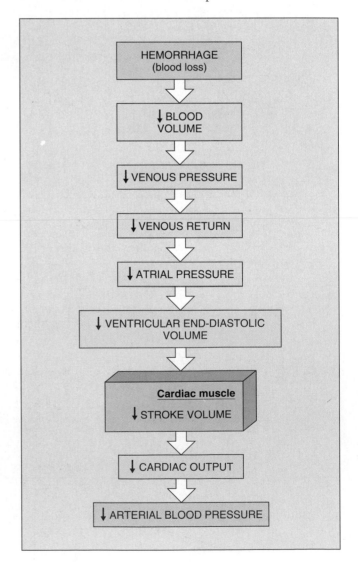

blood volume occurring during hemorrhage leads to a decrease in mean arterial pressure.

Conversely, any deviation in arterial pressure, such as that occurring during hemorrhage, will elicit reflexes so that cardiac output and/or total peripheral resistance will be changed in the direction required to minimize the initial change in arterial pressure.

In the short term—seconds to hours—these homeostatic adjustments are brought about by reflexes termed the baroreceptor reflexes. They utilize mainly changes in the activity of the autonomic nerves supplying the heart and blood vessels, as well as changes in the secretion of the hormones—epinephrine, angiotensin II, and vasopressin—that influence these structures. Over longer time spans, the baroreceptor reflexes become less important, and factors controlling blood volume play a dominant role in determining blood pressure.

BARORECEPTOR REFLEXES

Arterial Baroreceptors

It is only logical that the reflexes that homeostatically regulate arterial pressure originate primarily with arterial receptors that respond to changes in pressure. High in the neck, each of the two major vessels supplying the head, the common carotid arteries, divides into two smaller arteries. At this division, the wall of the artery is thinner than usual and contains a large number of branching, vinelike nerve endings (Figure 14-59). This portion of the artery is called the **carotid sinus**. Its nerve endings are highly sensitive to stretch or distortion. Since the degree of wall stretching is directly related to the pressure within the artery, the carotid sinuses serve as pressure receptors (**baroreceptors**). An area functionally similar to the carotid sinuses is found in the arch of the aorta and is termed the **aortic arch baroreceptor**. The two carotid sinuses and the aortic arch baroreceptor constitute the **arterial baroreceptors**. Afferent neurons from them travel to the brain and provide input to the neurons of cardiovascular control centers there.

Action potentials recorded in single afferent fibers from the carotid sinus demonstrate the pattern of baroreceptor response (Figure 14-60). In this experiment the pressure in the carotid sinus is artificially controlled so that the pressure is either steady or pulsatile, that is, varying as usual between systolic and diastolic pressure. At a particular steady pressure, for example, 100 mmHg, there is a certain rate of discharge by the neuron. This rate can be increased by raising the arterial pressure, or it can be decreased by lowering the pressure. Thus, the rate of discharge of the carotid sinus is directly proportional to the mean arterial pressure.

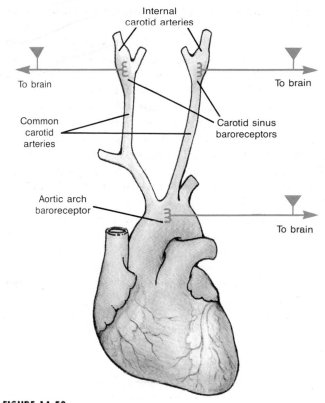

FIGURE 14-59
Locations of arterial baroreceptors.

If the experiment is repeated using the same mean pressures as before but allowing pressure pulsations, it is found that at any given mean pressure, the larger the pulse pressure, the faster the rate of firing by the carotid sinus. This responsiveness to pulse pressure adds a further ele-

FIGURE 14-60
Effect of changing mean arterial pressure (MAP) on the firing of action potentials by afferent neurons from the carotid sinus. This experiment is done by pumping blood through an isolated carotid sinus so as to be able to set the pressure inside it at any value desired.

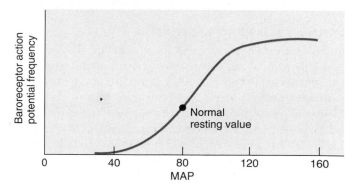

ment of information to blood pressure regulation, since small changes in factors such as blood volume may cause changes in arterial pulse pressure with little or no change in mean arterial pressure.

Other Baroreceptors

The large systemic veins, the pulmonary vessels, and the walls of the heart also contain baroreceptors, most of which function in a manner analogous to the arterial baroreceptors. By keeping brain cardiovascular control centers constantly informed about changes in the systemic venous, pulmonary, atrial, and ventricular pressures, these other baroreceptors provide feedforward and a further degree of regulatory sensitivity. Thus, a slight decrease in ventricular pressure may reflexly increase the activity of the sympathetic nervous system even before the change lowers cardiac output and arterial pressure far enough to be detected by the arterial baroreceptors.[13]

The Medullary Cardiovascular Center

The primary integrating center for the baroreceptor reflexes is a diffuse network of highly interconnected neurons in the brainstem medulla oblongata called the **medullary cardiovascular center**. The neurons in this center receive input from the various baroreceptors. This input determines the outflow from the center along axons that terminate upon the cell bodies and dendrites of the vagus (parasympathetic) neurons to the heart and the sympathetic neurons to the heart, arterioles, and veins. When the arterial baroreceptors *increase* their rate of discharge, the result is a *decrease* in sympathetic outflow to the heart, arterioles, and veins, and an *increase* in parasympathetic outflow to the heart (Figure 14-61). A decrease in baroreceptor firing rate results in just the opposite pattern.

As parts of the baroreceptor reflexes, angiotensin II generation and vasopressin secretion are also altered so as to help restore blood pressure. Thus, a decreased pressure elicits increased plasma concentrations of both these hormones, which raise arterial pressure by constricting arterioles. For simplicity, however, we focus in the rest of this chapter only on the sympathetic nervous system when discussing reflex control of arterioles. The roles of angiotensin II and vasopressin will be described in Chapter 16.

Operation of the Baroreceptor Reflex

Our description of the baroreceptor reflex is now complete. If arterial pressure decreases as during a hemorrhage (Figure 14-62), this causes the discharge rate of the carotid sinus and aortic arch baroreceptors to decrease. Fewer impulses travel up the afferent nerves to the medullary cardiovascular center, and this induces (1) increased heart rate because of increased sympathetic activity to the

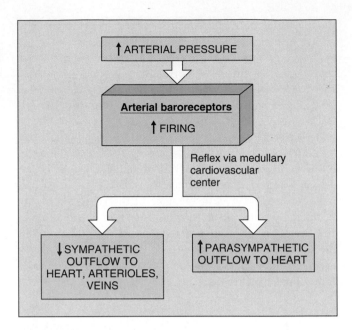

FIGURE 14-61
Neural components of the arterial baroreceptor reflex. When the initial change is a decrease in arterial pressure, all the arrows in the boxes would be reversed.

heart and decreased parasympathetic activity, (2) increased myocardial contractility because of increased sympathetic activity to the heart, (3) arteriolar constriction because of increased sympathetic activity to the arterioles and increased plasma concentrations of angiotensin II and vasopressin, and (4) increased venous constriction because of increased sympathetic activity to the veins. The net result is an increased cardiac output (increased heart rate and stroke volume), increased total peripheral resistance (arteriolar constriction), and return of blood pressure toward normal.

An increase in arterial blood pressure for any reason causes *increased* firing of the arterial baroreceptors, which reflexly induces a compensatory *decrease* in cardiac output and total peripheral resistance.

Having emphasized the great importance of this baroreceptor reflex, we must now add an equally important qualification. The baroreceptor reflex functions primarily as a *short-term* regulator of arterial blood pressure. It is activated instantly by any blood pressure *change* and attempts to restore blood pressure rapidly toward normal. Yet, if arterial pressure deviates from its normal operating point for more than a few days—recent experiments suggest even less time may be required—the arterial baroreceptors adapt to this new pressure, that is, they have a decreased frequency of action-potential firing at any given pressure. Thus, in patients who have chronically elevated blood pressure, the baroreceptors continue to oppose minute-to-minute changes in blood pressure, but at the higher level.

---

[13]One of these reflexes, termed the Bainbridge reflex, works in the opposite direction. By this reflex, an increased atrial pressure reflexly elicits an increased heart rate.

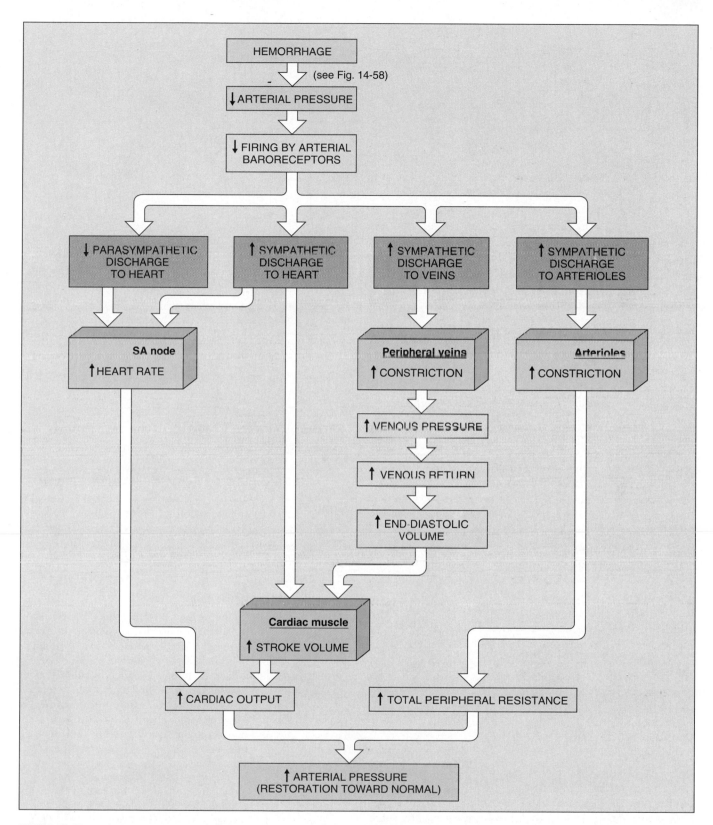

FIGURE 14-62

Arterial baroreceptor reflex compensation for hemorrhage. Hemorrhage causes a decrease in arterial pressure by causing decreases, in turn, of blood volume, venous pressure, venous return, atrial pressure, ventricular end-diastolic pressure, stroke volume, and cardiac output. The compensatory mechanisms do not restore arterial pressure completely to normal. Beyond the initial decrease in arterial pressure, all arrows signifying increases or decreases are relative to the state immediately following the hemorrhage but before reflex compensation begins. For simplicity, we have not shown the fact that plasma angiotensin II and vasopressin are also reflexly increased and help constrict arterioles.

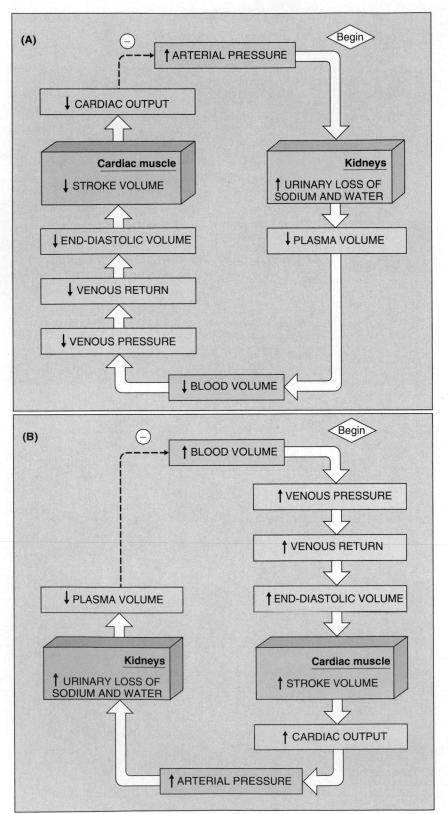

FIGURE 14-63

Causal reciprocal relationships between arterial pressure and blood volume. (A) An increase in arterial pressure due, for example, to an increased cardiac output induces a decrease in blood volume by promoting fluid excretion by the kidneys, which tends to restore arterial pressure to its original value. (B) An increase in blood volume due, for example, to altered kidney function induces an increase in arterial pressure, which tends to restore blood volume to its original value by promoting fluid excretion by the kidneys. Because of these relationships, blood volume is a major determinant of arterial pressure.

BLOOD VOLUME AND LONG-TERM REGULATION OF ARTERIAL PRESSURE

The fact that the baroreceptors adapt to prolonged changes in arterial pressure means that the baroreceptor reflex cannot *set* long-term arterial pressure. The major factor for long-term regulation is the blood volume. As described earlier, blood volume is a major determinant of arterial pressure because it influences in turn venous pressure, venous return, end-diastolic volume, stroke volume, and cardiac output. Thus, an increased blood volume increases arterial pressure. But the opposite causal chain also exists—an increased arterial pressure reduces blood volume (more specifically, the plasma component of the blood volume) by increasing the excretion of salt and water by the kidneys.

Figure 14-63 illustrates how these two causal chains constitute a negative-feedback loop that determines both blood volume and arterial pressure. If, for whatever reason, the blood *pressure* goes up as the initial event, this will cause a decreased blood volume, which will tend to bring the blood pressure back down. If, for whatever reason, the blood *volume* goes up as the initial event, this will raise the blood pressure, which will tend to bring the blood volume back down. The important point is this: Because arterial pressure influences blood volume but blood volume also influences arterial pressure, blood pressure can stabilize, in the long run, only at a value at which blood volume is also stable. Accordingly, blood volume changes are the single most important determinant, long term, of blood pressure.

OTHER CARDIOVASCULAR REFLEXES AND RESPONSES

Stimuli acting upon receptors other than baroreceptors can initiate reflexes that cause changes in arterial pressure. For example, the following stimuli all cause an increase in blood pressure: decreased arterial oxygen concentration, increased arterial carbon dioxide concentration, decreased brain blood flow, increased intracranial pressure, and pain originating in the skin (in contrast, pain originating in the viscera or joints may cause marked *decreases* in arterial pressure).

Many physiological states such as eating and sexual activity are also associated with changes in blood pressure. New techniques of noninvasive monitoring have allowed blood pressure to be taken while people go about normal daily activities. For example, attending business meetings raises mean blood pressure by 20 mmHg, walking increases it 10 mmHg, and sleeping lowers it 10 mmHg. Mood also has a significant effect on blood pressure, which tends to be lower when people reported that they are happy than when they are angry or anxious.

These changes are triggered by input from receptors or higher brain centers to the medullary cardiovascular center or, in some cases, to pathways distinct from these centers. For example, certain neurons in the cerebral cortex and hypothalamus synapse directly on the sympathetic neurons in the spinal cord, bypassing the medullary center altogether.

Thus, there is a marked degree of flexibility and integration in the control of blood pressure. For example, by stimulating electrically a discrete area of the hypothalamus of an experimental animal, all the usually observed neurally mediated cardiovascular responses to an acute emotional situation can be elicited. Stimulation of other brain sites elicits cardiovascular changes appropriate to the maintenance of body temperature, feeding, or sleeping. It seems that such outputs are "preprogrammed." The complete pattern can be released by a natural stimulus that initiates the flow of information to the appropriate controlling brain center.

SECTION E SUMMARY

I. Mean arterial pressure, the primary regulated variable in the cardiovascular system, equals the product of cardiac output and total peripheral resistance.

II. The factors that determine cardiac output and total peripheral resistance are summarized in Figure 14-57.

BARORECEPTOR REFLEXES

I. The primary baroreceptors are the arterial baroreceptors—the two carotid sinuses and the aortic arch. Nonarterial baroreceptors are located in the systemic veins, pulmonary vessels, and walls of the heart.

II. The firing rates of the arterial baroreceptors are proportional to mean arterial pressure and to pulse pressure.

III. An increase in firing of the arterial baroreceptors due to an increase in pressure causes, by way of the medullary cardiovascular center, an increase in parasympathetic outflow to the heart and a decrease in sympathetic outflow to the heart, arterioles, and veins. The result is a decrease in cardiac output and total peripheral resistance and, hence, a decrease in mean arterial pressure. The opposite occurs when the initial change is a decrease in arterial pressure.

BLOOD VOLUME AND LONG-TERM REGULATION OF ARTERIAL PRESSURE

I. The baroreceptor reflexes are short-term regulators of arterial pressure but adapt to a maintained change in pressure.

II. The most important long-term regulator of arterial pressure is the blood volume

SECTION E KEY TERMS

total peripheral resistance (TPR)
carotid sinus baroreceptors

aortic arch baroreceptor
arterial baroreceptors
medullary cardiovascular center

SECTION E REVIEW QUESTIONS

1. Write the equation relating mean arterial pressure to cardiac output and total peripheral resistance.

2. What variable accounts for mean pulmonary arterial pressure being lower than mean systemic arterial pressure?

3. Draw a flow diagram illustrating the factors that determine mean arterial pressure.

4. Identify the receptors, afferent pathways, integrating center, efferent pathways, and effectors in the arterial baroreceptor reflex.

5. When the arterial baroreceptors decrease or increase their rate of firing, what changes in autonomic outflow and cardiovascular function occur?

6. Describe the role of blood volume in the long-term regulation of arterial pressure.

SECTION

CARDIOVASCULAR PATTERNS IN HEALTH AND DISEASE

HEMORRHAGE AND OTHER CAUSES OF HYPOTENSION

The term **hypotension** means a low blood pressure, regardless of cause. The decrease in blood volume caused by hemorrhage produces hypotension by the sequence of events shown previously in Figure 14-58. The most serious consequences of hypotension are reduced blood flow to the brain and cardiac muscle.

The immediate counteracting response to hemorrhage is the baroreceptor reflex, previously summarized in Figure 14-62. Figure 14-64, which shows how five variables change over time when there is a decrease in blood volume, adds a further degree of clarification. The values of factors changed as a *direct* result of the hemorrhage—stroke volume, cardiac output, and mean arterial pressure—are restored by the baroreceptor reflex *toward,* but not *to* normal. In contrast, values not altered directly by the hemorrhage but only by the *reflex response* to hemorrhage—heart rate and total peripheral resistance—are increased above their prehemorrhage values. The increased peripheral resistance results from increases in sympathetic outflow to the arterioles in many vascular beds but not those of the heart and brain. Thus, skin blood flow may decrease markedly because of arteriolar vasocon-

striction—this is why the skin becomes cold and pale. Kidney and intestinal blood flow also decrease.

A second important type of compensatory mechanism (one not shown in Figure 14-62) involves the movement of interstitial fluid into capillaries. This occurs because both the drop in blood pressure and the increase in arteriolar constriction decrease capillary hydrostatic pressure, thereby favoring absorption of interstitial fluid (Figure 14-65). Thus, the initial event blood loss and decreased

TABLE 14-8 FLUID SHIFTS AFTER HEMORRHAGE

		Percent of normal value	
	Normal	Immediately after hemorrhage	18 h after hemorrhage
Total blood volume, ml	5000	80	98
Erythrocyte volume, ml	2300	80	80
Plasma volume, ml	2700	80	113

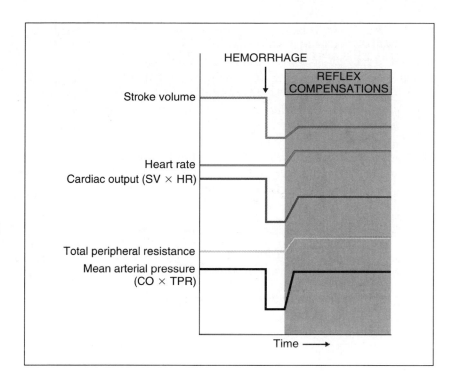

FIGURE 14-64

Five simultaneous graphs showing the time course of cardiovascular effects of hemorrhage. Note that the entire decrease in arterial pressure immediately following hemorrhage is secondary to the decrease in stroke volume and, hence, cardiac output. This figure emphasizes the relativeness of the "increase" and "decrease" arrows of Figure 14-62. All variables shown are increased relative to the state immediately following the hemorrhage, but not necessarily to the state prior to the hemorrhage.

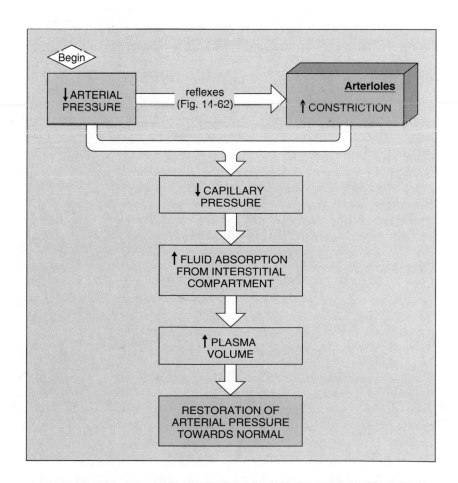

FIGURE 14-65

Mechanisms compensating for blood loss by movement of interstitial fluid into the capillaries.

blood volume—is in large part compensated for by the movement of interstitial fluid into the vascular system. Indeed, 12 to 24 h after a moderate hemorrhage, the blood volume may be restored virtually to normal by this mechanism (Table 14-8). At this time the entire restoration of blood volume is due to expansion of the plasma volume.

The early compensatory mechanisms for hemorrhage, the baroreceptor reflexes and interstitial fluid absorption, are highly efficient, so that losses of as much as 1.5 L of blood—approximately 30 percent of total blood volume—can be sustained with only slight reductions of mean arterial pressure or cardiac output.

We must emphasize that absorption of interstitial fluid only *redistributes* the extracellular fluid. Ultimate *replacement* of the fluid lost involves the control of fluid ingestion and kidney function. Both processes are described in Chapter 16. Replacement of the lost erythrocytes requires stimulation of erythropoiesis by erythropoietin. These replacement processes require days to weeks in contrast to the rapidly occurring reflex compensations described in Figure 14-62.

Loss of large quantities of cell-free extracellular fluid rather than whole blood can also cause hypotension. This type of fluid loss may occur via the skin, as in severe sweating or burns, via the gastrointestinal tract, as in diarrhea or vomiting, or via unusually large urinary losses. Regardless of the route, the loss of fluid decreases circulating blood volume and produces symptoms and compensatory cardiovascular changes similar to those seen in hemorrhage.

Hypotension may be caused by events other than blood or fluid loss. One such cause is strong emotion, during which hypotension can cause fainting. Somehow, the higher brain centers involved with emotions inhibit sympathetic activity and enhance parasympathetic activity, resulting in a markedly decreased arterial pressure and brain blood flow. This whole process is usually transient. It should be noted that the fainting that sometimes occurs in a person donating blood is usually due to hypotension brought on by emotion, not the blood loss, since losing 0.5 L of blood will not itself cause serious hypotension in normal individuals.

Massive liberation of chemicals that relax arteriolar smooth muscle may also cause hypotension by reducing total peripheral resistance. An important example is the hypotension that occurs during severe allergic responses.

Treatment of patients with hypotension in ways commonly favored by the uninformed, namely, administering alcohol and covering the person with mounds of blankets, is not appropriate. Both alcohol and excessive body heat cause dilation of skin arterioles, thus lowering total peripheral resistance and decreasing arterial blood pressure still further.

Shock

The term *shock* denotes any situation in which a decrease in blood flow to the organs and tissues damages them. The most common cause of shock is severe hemorrhage, and arterial pressure is usually, but not always, low in shock. The cardiovascular system, especially the heart, suffers damage if shock is prolonged. As the heart deteriorates, cardiac output declines even more and shock becomes progressively worse and ultimately irreversible, even though blood transfusions and other appropriate therapy may temporarily restore blood pressure.

Just as hemorrhage is not the only cause of hypotension and decreased cardiac output, so it is not the only cause of shock. Loss of fluid other than blood, excessive release of vasodilators as in allergy and infection, loss of neural tone to the cardiovascular system, and extensive bodily damage can all lead to severe reductions of tissue blood flow and the positive-feedback cycles culminating in irreversible shock.

THE UPRIGHT POSTURE

A decrease in the *effective* circulating blood volume occurs in the circulatory system when going from a lying, horizontal position to a standing, vertical one. Why this is so requires an understanding of the action of gravity upon the long, continuous columns of blood in the vessels between the heart and the feet.

The pressures we have given in previous sections of this chapter are for an individual in the horizontal position, in which all blood vessels are at approximately the same level as the heart. In this position, the weight of the blood produces negligible pressure. In contrast, when a person is vertical, the intravascular pressure everywhere becomes equal to the pressure generated by cardiac contraction *plus* an additional pressure equal to the weight of a column of blood from the heart to the point of measurement. In an average adult, for example, the weight of a column of blood extending from the heart to the feet amounts to 80 mmHg. In a foot capillary, therefore, the pressure increases from 25 (the pressure resulting from cardiac contraction) to 105 mmHg, the extra 80 mmHg being due to the weight of the column of blood.

This increase in pressure due to gravity influences the effective circulating blood volume. The increased hydrostatic pressure that occurs in the legs when a person is quietly standing pushes outward on the highly distensible vein walls, causing marked distension. The result is pooling of blood in the veins; that is, much of the blood emerging from the capillaries simply goes into expanding the veins rather than returning to the heart. Simultaneously, the increase in capillary pressure caused by the gravitational force produces increased filtration of fluid out of the capillaries into the interstitial space. This accounts for the fact that our feet swell during prolonged standing. The combined effects of venous pooling and increased capillary filtration reduce the *effective* circulating blood volume very similarly to the effects caused by a mild hemorrhage. The ensuing decrease in arterial pressure causes reflex compensatory adjustments similar to those shown in Figure 14-62 for hemorrhage.

One way to offset the effects of gravity is to contract the skeletal muscles in the legs. These contractions produce intermittent, complete emptying of the leg veins so that uninterrupted columns of venous blood from the heart to the feet no longer exist (Figure 14-66). The result is a decrease in both venous distension and pooling plus a marked reduction in capillary hydrostatic pressure and fluid filtration out of the capillaries.

Soldiers may faint while standing at attention for long periods of time because they have minimal contractions of the leg muscles. Here fainting may be considered adaptive in that the venous and capillary pressure changes induced by gravity are eliminated once the person is prone. The pooled venous blood is mobilized, and the filtered fluid is absorbed back into the capillaries. Thus, the wrong thing to do to a person who has fainted for whatever reason is to hold him or her upright.

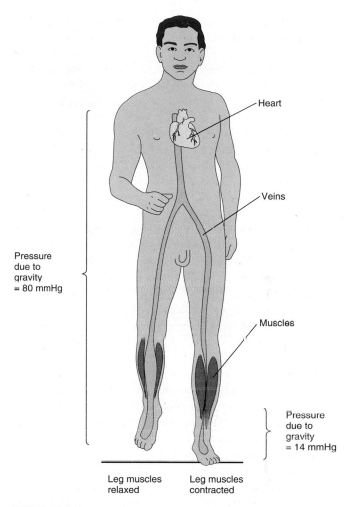

FIGURE 14-66

Role of contraction of the leg skeletal muscles in reducing capillary pressure and filtration in the upright position. The skeletal muscle contraction compresses the veins, causing intermittent emptying so that the columns of blood are interrupted. The venous pooling is exaggerated in this figure for purposes of illustration.

EXERCISE

During exercise, cardiac output may increase from a resting value of 5 L/min to a maximal value of 35 L/min in trained athletes. The distribution of this cardiac output during strenuous exercise is illustrated in Figure 14-67. As expected, most of the increase in cardiac output goes to the exercising muscles, but there are also increases in flow to skin, required for dissipation of heat, and to the heart, required for the additional work performed by the heart in pumping the increased cardiac output. The increases in flow through these three vascular beds are the result of arteriolar dilation in them. In both skeletal and cardiac muscle, the dilation is mediated by local metabolic factors, whereas the dilation in skin is achieved by a decrease in the firing of the sympathetic neurons to the skin. At the same time that arteriolar dilation is occurring in these beds, arteriolar constriction—manifested as decreased blood flow in Figure 14-67—is occurring in the kidneys and gastrointestinal organs, secondary to increased activity of the sympathetic neurons supplying them.

Dilation of arterioles in skeletal muscle, cardiac muscle, and skin causes a decrease in total peripheral resistance to blood flow. This decrease is partially offset by constriction of arterioles in other organs. Such "resistance juggling," however, is quite incapable of compensating for the huge dilation of the muscle arterioles, and the net result is a marked decrease in total peripheral resistance.

What happens to arterial blood pressure during exercise? As always, the mean arterial pressure is simply the arithmetic product of cardiac output and total peripheral resistance. During most forms of exercise (Figure 14-68 illustrates the case for mild exercise), the cardiac output tends to increase somewhat more than the total peripheral

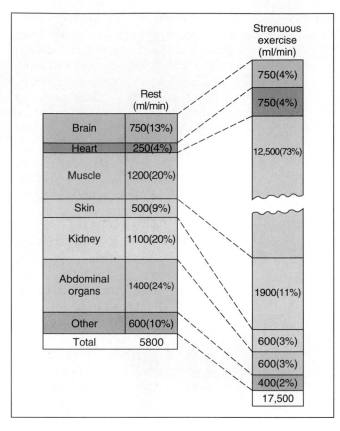

FIGURE 14-67

Distribution of the systemic cardiac output at rest and during strenuous exercise. The values at rest were previously presented in Figure 14-10. (*Adapted from Chapman and Mitchell.*)

resistance decreases, so that mean arterial pressure usually increases slightly.

The cardiac output increase during exercise is caused by a combination of greater sympathetic activity and less parasympathetic activity to the heart (which of these two autonomic changes is more important varies in different types of exercise). The increases in heart rate are usually much greater than those of stroke volume. Note in Figure 14-68 that, in our example, the increased stroke volume occurs without change in end-diastolic ventricular volume. Accordingly, the increased stroke volume in this case cannot be ascribed to Starling's law but is due completely to the increased contractility induced by the cardiac sympathetic nerves.

It would be incorrect to leave the impression that altered autonomic activity to the heart is sufficient to account for the elevated cardiac output that occurs in exercise. The fact is that cardiac output can be increased to high levels only if venous return to the heart is simultaneously increased to the same degree. Otherwise, the shortened filling time resulting from the high heart rate would

lower end-diastolic volume and stroke volume (Starling's law). Therefore, factors promoting venous return during exercise are extremely important. They are (1) increased activity of the skeletal-muscle pump, (2) increased depth and frequency of inspiration, (3) sympathetically mediated increase in venous tone, and (4) greater ease of blood flow from arteries to veins through the dilated skeletal-muscle arterioles.

During vigorous exercise, in contrast to the mild exercise illustrated in Figure 14-68, these four factors may be so powerful that venous return is enhanced enough to cause an *increase* in end-diastolic ventricular volume. Under such conditions, stroke volume is further enhanced above what it would have been from increased contractility alone.

What are the control mechanisms by which the cardiovascular changes in exercise are elicited? As described previously, dilation of arterioles in skeletal and cardiac muscle once exercise is underway represents active hyperemia secondary to local metabolic factors within the muscle. But what drives the enhanced sympathetic outflow to most

FIGURE 14-68

Summary of cardiovascular changes during mild exercise.

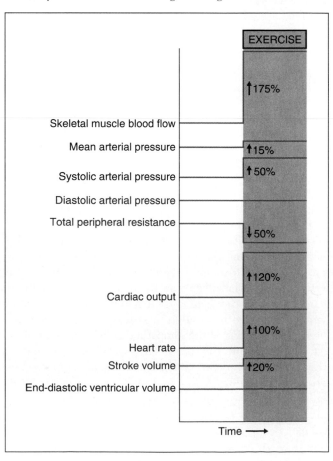

other arterioles, the heart, and the veins and the decreased parasympathetic outflow to the heart? The control of this autonomic outflow during exercise offers an excellent example of what we earlier referred to as a preprogrammed pattern, modified by continuous afferent input. One or more discrete control centers in the brain are activated during exercise, and according to this "central command," descending pathways from these centers to the appropriate autonomic preganglionic neurons elicit the firing pattern typical of exercise. Indeed, these centers begin to "direct traffic" even before the exercise begins, since a person just about to begin exercising already manifests many of the changes in cardiac and vascular function.

Once exercise is underway, local chemical changes in the muscle develop unless there is a perfect matching between flow and metabolic demands, and these changes activate chemoreceptors in the muscle. Afferent input from these receptors goes to the medullary cardiovascular center and facilitates the output reaching the autonomic neurons from higher brain centers (Figure 14-69). The result is a further increase in heart rate, myocardial contractility, and vascular resistance in the nonactive organs. Such a system permits a fine degree of matching between cardiac pumping and total oxygen and nutrients required by the exercising muscles. Mechanoreceptors in the exercising muscles are also stimulated and provide input to the medullary cardiovascular center.

Finally, what role do the arterial baroreceptors play? Knowing that the mean and pulsatile pressures rise during exercise, you might assume that these baroreceptors would try to lower them by eliciting a pattern of autonomic responses opposite that coming from central command and the muscle chemoreceptors. This does not occur, however, because another component of the central neural command is to "reset" the arterial baroreceptors upward as exercise begins.

Table 14-9 summarizes the changes that occur during moderate endurance exercise, that is, exercise that involves large muscle groups for an extended period of time.

Maximal Oxygen Consumption and Training

As the magnitude of any endurance exercise increases, oxygen consumption also increases in exact proportion until a point is reached when it fails to rise despite a further increment in work load. This is known as **maximal oxygen consumption** ($\dot{V}_{O_2max}$). After $\dot{V}_{O_2max}$ has been reached, work can be increased and sustained only very briefly by anaerobic metabolism in the exercising muscles.

Theoretically, $\dot{V}_{O_2max}$ could be limited by the cardiac output, the respiratory system's ability to deliver oxygen to the blood, or the exercising muscle's ability to use oxygen. In fact, in normal people, cardiac output is the factor that determines $\dot{V}_{O_2max}$. With increasing work load (Figure 14-

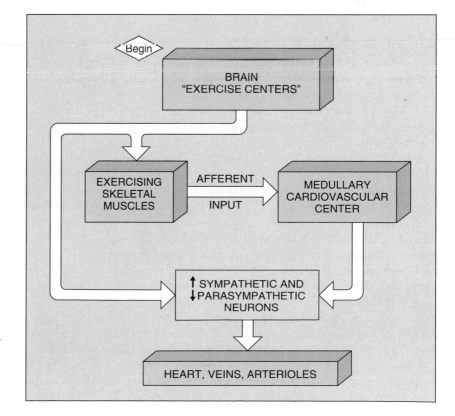

FIGURE 14-69

Control of the autonomic nervous system during exercise. The primary outflow to the sympathetic and parasympathetic neurons is via pathways from "exercise centers" in the brain, pathways parallel to those going to the exercising muscles. Afferent input from chemoreceptors in these muscles also influences the autonomic neurons by way of the medullary cardiovascular center.

TABLE 14-9 CARDIOVASCULAR CHANGES IN MODERATE ENDURANCE EXERCISE

Variable	Change	Explanation
Cardiac output	Increases	Heart rate and stroke volume both increase.
Heart rate	Increases	Sympathetic-nerve activity to the SA node increases, and parasympathetic nerve activity decreases.
Stroke volume	Increases	Contractility increases due to increased sympathetic-nerve activity to the ventricular myocardium.
Total peripheral resistance	Decreases	Resistance in heart and skeletal muscles decreases more than resistance in other vascular beds increases.
Mean arterial pressure	Increases	Cardiac output increases more than total peripheral resistance decreases.
Pulse pressure	Increases	Stroke volume and velocity of ejection of the stroke volume increase.
End-diastolic volume	Unchanged	Filling time is decreased by the high heart rates, but this is compensated for by the factors favoring venous return—venoconstriction, skeletal-muscle pump, and increased inspiratory movements.
Blood flow to heart and skeletal muscle	Increases	Active hyperemia occurs in both vascular beds, mediated by local metabolic factors.
Blood flow to skin	Increases	Sympathetic nerves to skin vessels are inhibited reflexly by the increase in body temperature.
Blood flow to viscera	Decreases	Sympathetic nerves to the abdominal organs and the kidneys are stimulated.
Blood flow to brain	Unchanged	Autoregulation of brain arterioles maintains constant flow despite the increased mean arterial pressure.

70) heart rate increases progressively and markedly until it reaches a maximum. Stroke volume increases much less and tends to level off when 75 percent of $\dot{V}_{O_2max}$ has been reached (it actually starts to go back down in elderly people). The major factors responsible for limiting the rise in stroke volume are (1) the very rapid heart rate, which decreases diastolic filling time, and (2) inability of the peripheral factors favoring venous return—skeletal-muscle pump, respiratory pump, venoconstriction, arteriolar dilation—to increase ventricular filling further during the very short time available.

A person's $\dot{V}_{O_2max}$ is not fixed at any given value but can be altered by the habitual level of physical activity. For example, prolonged bed rest may decrease maximal exercise capacity by 25 percent, whereas intense long-term physical training may increase it by a similar amount. To be effective, the training must be of an endurance type. We are still uncertain of the most effective relative combinations of intensity and duration, but, as an example, jogging 20 to 30 min three times weekly at 5 to 8 mi/h definitely produces some training effect in most people.

This training effect is manifested at rest as an increased stroke volume and decreased heart rate with no change in cardiac output. At $\dot{V}_{O_2max}$, the trained individual has an increased cardiac output due entirely to an increased maximal stroke volume, since maximal heart rate is not altered by training (Figure 14-70). The increase in stroke volume is due to a combination of (1) effects on the heart—increased cardiac muscle mass and increased ventricular contractility, and (2) peripheral effects—increased blood volume and increases in the number of blood vessels in skeletal muscle, which increase muscle blood flow and venous return. Training also increases the concentrations of oxidative enzymes and mitochondria in the exercised muscles.

HYPERTENSION

Hypertension is defined as a chronically increased systemic arterial pressure. The dividing line between normal pressure and hypertension is set at approximately 140/90 mmHg.

Theoretically, hypertension could result from an increase in cardiac output or in total peripheral resistance,

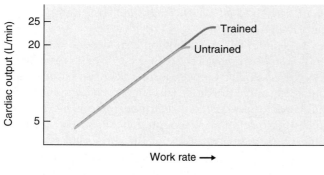

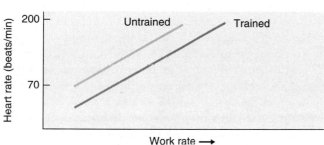

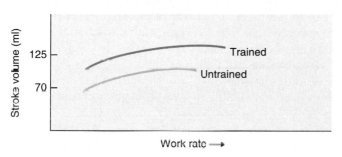

FIGURE 14-70

Changes in cardiac output, heart rate, and stroke volume with increasing work in untrained and trained persons.

or both. In reality, however, the major abnormality in most cases of well-established hypertension is increased total peripheral resistance, caused by abnormally reduced arteriolar radius.

What causes the arteriolar constriction? In only a small fraction of cases is the cause known. For example, diseases that damage a kidney or decrease its blood supply are often associated with **renal hypertension**; the cause of the hypertension may be increased release of renin from the kidney, with subsequent increased generation of the potent vasoconstrictor angiotensin II. However, for more than 95 percent of individuals with hypertension, the cause of the arteriolar constriction is unknown. Hypertension of unknown cause is called **primary hypertension** (formerly essential hypertension).

Many hypotheses have been proposed to explain the increased arteriolar constriction of primary hypertension. At present, much evidence suggests that excessive sodium retention is a contributing factor in genetically predisposed persons. Although this relationship remains controversial, it is certainly true that many individuals with hypertension show a drop in blood pressure after being on low-sodium diets or receiving drugs, termed **diuretics**, that cause increased sodium loss via the urine. Low dietary intake of calcium has also been implicated as a possible contributor to primary hypertension, but this, too, remains controversial. Obesity is a definite risk factor for primary hypertension, and weight reduction and exercise are frequently effective in causing some reduction of blood pressure in overweight sedentary persons with hypertension. Cigarette smoking, too, is a definite risk factor.

Hypertension causes a variety of problems. One of the organs most affected is the heart. Because the left ventricle in a hypertensive person must chronically pump against an increased arterial pressure, it develops an adaptive increase in muscle mass. In the early phases of the disease, this helps maintain the heart's function as a pump. With time, however, changes in the organization and properties of myocardial cells occur, and these result in diminished contractile function and heart failure. The presence of hypertension also enhances the development of atherosclerosis and heart attacks (see below), kidney damage, and rupture of a cerebral blood vessel, which causes localized brain damage—a **stroke**.

In addition to diuretics, four other classes of drugs, all of which reduce peripheral resistance, are in common use for treating hypertension: (1) blockers of beta-adrenergic receptors, (2) blockers of calcium channels, (3) blockers of the formation of angiotensin II, and (4) drugs that act either on the brain or outside the brain to antagonize the sympathetic nervous system.

That drugs that block beta-adrenergic receptors *reduce* total peripheral resistance by *dilating* arterioles should come as a surprise to the reader: Since beta-adrenergic receptors in the arterioles mediate dilation, one would deduce that blockage of these receptors should cause arteriolar constriction. Clearly, the beta-adrenergic receptors on the *blood vessels* are not the critical ones being blocked in the treatment of hypertension, and the explanation of the decrease in resistance is uncertain.[14]

The calcium-channel blockers reduce the entry of calcium into vascular smooth-muscle cells, causing them to contract less strongly.

As will be described in Chapter 16, the final step in the formation of angiotensin II, a vasoconstrictor, is mediated by an enzyme called angiotensin-converting enzyme.

---

[14]One hypothesis is as follows. As described in Chapter 16, sympathetic nerves act via beta-adrenergic receptors to stimulate the secretion of renin, with subsequent generation in the plasma of angiotensin II. Blockade of these receptors would therefore result in a lower plasma concentration of this potent vasoconstrictor.

Drugs that block this enzyme therefore reduce the concentration of angiotensin II in plasma, which causes arteriolar dilation.

The antagonists of the sympathetic nervous system reduce sympathetically mediated stimulation of arteriolar smooth muscle.

HEART FAILURE

The heart may fail as a pump for many reasons. Two examples are pumping against a chronically elevated arterial pressure in hypertension and structural damage due to decreased coronary blood flow. It has become standard practice to separate persons with *heart failure* (also termed congestive heart failure) into two categories: (1) those with systolic dysfunction (problems with ventricular ejection), and (2) those with diastolic dysfunction (problems with ventricular filling). In fact, however, most persons with heart failure have elements of both categories.

A decreased contractility is often the hallmark of heart failure. As shown in Figure 14-71, the failing heart shifts downward to a lower Starling curve, that is, to a lower stroke volume at any given end-diastolic volume. When this occurs, a number of compensatory mechanisms come into play; these are quite similar to the reflex responses generated by a fall in blood pressure. For one thing, a reflex increase in sympathetic outflow to the heart helps to increase contractility back toward normal and also raises

heart rate, both of which contribute to a restoration of cardiac output.

A second reflex compensation is to increase ventricular end-diastolic volume. The sequence of events is as follows: Decreased cardiac output causes a decrease in mean and pulsatile arterial pressure. This triggers reflexes, including the baroreceptor reflexes, that induce the kidneys to reduce their excretion of sodium and water. The retained fluid then causes expansion of the extracellular volume, increasing venous pressure, venous return, and end-diastolic ventricular volume—thus tending to restore stroke volume toward normal. Thus, the heart in failure is generally distended with blood, as are the veins and capillaries, the major cause being an increase, sometimes massive, in plasma volume. It must be recognized, however, that if the ventricle becomes too distended, its force of contraction decreases and the situation worsens.

Even before this overdistension is reached, however, there is an undesirable result of the elevated venous pressure: the formation of edema. Why does an increased venous pressure cause edema? The capillaries, of course, drain via venules into the veins, and so when venous pressure increases, the capillary pressure also increases and causes increased filtration of fluid out of the capillaries into the interstitial fluid. Swelling of the legs and feet is usually prominent, but the engorgement occurs elsewhere as well.

Failure of the left ventricle leads to *pulmonary edema*, which is the accumulation of fluid in the interstitial spaces of the lung or in the air spaces themselves. This impairs gas exchange. The reason for such accumulation is that the relatively ineffective left ventricle *temporarily* fails to pump blood to the same extent as the right ventricle, and so the volume of blood in all the pulmonary vessels increases. The resulting engorgement of pulmonary capillaries raises the capillary pressure above its normally very low value, causing increased filtration out of the capillaries. This situation usually worsens at night: During the day, because of the patient's upright posture, fluid accumulates in the legs; then the fluid is slowly absorbed when the patient lies down at night, thus expanding the plasma volume and precipitating an attack of pulmonary edema.

The treatment for heart failure is easily understood in terms of its pathophysiology: (1) The precipitating cause, for example, hypertension, should be corrected if possible; (2) ventricular contractility can be increased by a drug known as *digitalis*, which acts by increasing cytosolic calcium in the myocardial cells; (3) fluid accumulation contributing to edema can be minimized by salt restriction and the use of diuretics; (4) vasodilator drugs can be used to lower peripheral resistance and hence the arterial blood pressure (afterload) against which the failing heart must pump. (Peripheral resistance is usually excessively elevated in heart failure because of reflex increases in both

FIGURE 14-71

Relationship between end-diastolic ventricular volume and stroke volume in normal and failing hearts. The normal curve is that shown previously in Figure 14-31. The failing heart can still eject an adequate stroke volume if the sympathetic activity to it is increased or if the end-diastolic volume increases, that is, if the ventricle becomes more distended.

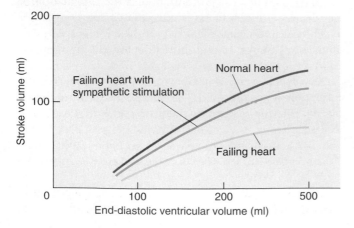

TABLE 14-10 MAJOR CAUSES OF EDEMA

Physiological Event	Cause of edema
Increased arterial pressure secondary to increased cardiac output°	Increased capillary pressure, leading to increased filtration
Local arteriolar dilation, as in exercise or inflammation	Increased capillary pressure, leading to increased filtration.
Increased venous pressure, as in heart failure or venous obstruction	Increased capillary pressure, leading to increased filtration
Decreased plasma protein concentration, as in liver disease (decreased protein production), kidney disease (loss of protein in the urine), or protein malnutrition	Decreased force for osmotic absorption across capillary. Therefore, *net* filtration is increased.
Increased interstitial fluid protein concentration resulting from increased capillary permeability to protein (as in inflammation)	Decreased force for osmotic absorption across capillary. Therefore, *net* filtration is increased.
Obstruction of lymphatic vessels, as in infection by filaria roundworms (elephantiasis)	Fluid filtered from the blood capillaries into the interstitial compartment is not carried away. Protein also accumulates in the interstitial fluid.

°In contrast, if arterial pressure is elevated because of increased total peripheral resistance, edema may not occur; the capillary pressure may not be elevated because the increased arteriolar resistance causing the increased arterial pressure will prevent most of that increase in pressure from reaching the capillaries.

sympathetic outflow to arterioles and in the plasma concentrations of the two major hormonal vasoconstrictors— angiotensin II and vasopressin.)

The mechanism of action of digitalis offers an excellent review of cellular calcium metabolism. Digitalis inhibits Na,K-ATPase in the myocardial plasma membranes, leading to an increase in cytosolic sodium concentration. This decreases the gradient for sodium-calcium exchange across the plasma membranes, thereby decreasing calcium exit and increasing cytosolic calcium concentration.

In closing this section it should be emphasized that there are causes of edema other than heart failure and lymphatic malfunction described earlier. They are all understandable as imbalances in the Starling forces and are listed in Table 14-10.

CORONARY ARTERY DISEASE

We have seen that the myocardium does not extract oxygen and nutrients from the blood within the atria and ventricles but depends upon its own blood supply via the coronary arteries. In **coronary artery disease**, changes (to be described below) in one or more of the coronary arteries causes insufficient coronary blood flow. The result may be myocardial damage in the affected region and, if severe enough, death of that portion of the heart—a **myocardial infarction (heart attack)**. Many patients with coronary artery disease experience recurrent short-lived episodes of inadequate coronary blood flow, usually during exertion or emotional tension, before ultimately suffering a heart attack. The chest pain associated with these episodes is called **angina pectoris** (or, more commonly, simply angina).

The symptoms of myocardial infarction include prolonged chest pain, often radiating to the left arm, nausea, vomiting, sweating, weakness, and shortness of breath. Diagnosis is made by ECG changes typical of infarction and by measurement of certain enzymes in plasma. These enzymes are present in cardiac muscle and leak out into the blood when the muscle is damaged; they include particular variants of creatine phosphokinase (CPK) and lactate dehydrogenase (LDH).

Of the approximately 1.5 million heart attack victims in the United States each year, three-fourths are admitted to a hospital, where they can be given advanced care, and more than 80 percent of these people survive the attack and are discharged. Unfortunately, the other one-fourth of heart attacks occur with so little immediate warning that the victim has no opportunity to reach a hospital before the heart stops. These sudden cardiac deaths are due mainly to **ventricular fibrillation**, an abnormality in impulse condition triggered by the damaged myocardial cells and resulting in continuous disorganized ventricular contractions that are ineffective in producing flow. (Note that ventricular fibrillation is fatal, whereas atrial fibrillation, as described earlier in this chapter, generally causes only minor problems.) Many of these individuals can be saved if modern emergency resuscitation procedures are applied immediately after the attack. This treatment is **cardiopulmonary resuscitation (CPR)**, a repeated series of mouth-to-mouth respirations and chest compressions that circulate a small amount of blood to the brain, heart, and other vital organs when the heart has stopped. CPR is then followed by definitive treatment, including defibrillation, a procedure in which electric current is passed through the heart to try to halt the abnormal electrical activity causing the fibrillation. CPR is a potentially life-saving procedure that is easily learned in a few hours of training at readily available courses sponsored by the Red Cross and other groups.

The major cause of coronary artery disease is the presence of atherosclerosis in these vessels. **Atherosclerosis** is a disease characterized by a thickening of the portion of the arterial vessel wall closest to the lumen with (1) large numbers of abnormal smooth-muscle cells and (2) deposits of cholesterol and other substances. The mechanisms by which atherosclerosis reduces coronary blood flow is as follows: The extra muscle cells and various deposits in the wall bulge into the lumen of the vessel and increase resistance to flow. This is progressive, sometimes leading ultimately to complete occlusion. Total occlusion is usually caused, however, by the formation of a blood clot **(coronary thrombosis)** in the narrowed atherosclerotic artery, and this triggers the heart attack.

The processes that lead to atherosclerosis are complex and still not completely understood. But it is known that cigarette smoking, high plasma cholesterol concentration, hypertension, diabetes, a sedentary life style, and stress can increase the incidence and the severity of the atherosclerotic process. These are all termed, therefore, "risk factors" for coronary artery disease, and prevention of this disease focuses on eliminating or minimizing them.[15] The

control of plasma cholesterol concentration is described in Chapter 18.

The chronic treatment of coronary artery disease and angina with drugs can be understood in terms of physiological concepts described in this chapter. First, vasodilator drugs such as nitroglycerin[16] help in the following way: They dilate the coronary arteries and the systemic arterioles; the arteriolar effect lowers total peripheral resistance, thereby lowering arterial blood pressure and the work the heart must expend in ejecting blood. Second, beta-adrenergic blocking agents may be used to lower the arterial pressure, but more importantly, they block the effects of the sympathetic nerves on the heart; the result is reduced myocardial work, and hence oxygen demand because both heart rate and contractility are reduced. Third, calcium-channel blockers also reduce myocardial work by reducing myocardial contractility. Calcium-channel blockers are also coronary and general vasodilators, and they prevent abnormal electrical rhythms that can lead to ventricular fibrillation. How a blockage of calcium channels may achieve each of these effects should be understandable from previous descriptions of the roles of calcium in excitation-contraction coupling in cardiac and smooth muscle. Fourth, drugs that prevent or reverse clotting are also very important in the treatment (and prevention) of heart attacks. Use of these drugs is described in Chapter 20.

There are several surgical treatments for coronary artery disease after the area of narrowing or occlusion is identified by cardiac angiography (described earlier in this chapter). **Coronary angioplasty** is the passing of a catheter with a balloon at its tip into the occluded artery and then expanding the balloon. This enlarges the lumen by stretching the vessel and breaking up abnormal tissue deposits. A second surgical technique is **coronary bypass,** in which an area of occluded coronary artery is removed and replaced with a new vessel, often a vein taken from elsewhere in the patient's body. Tubes made of synthetic materials may also be used.

We do not wish to leave the impression that atherosclerosis attacks only the coronary vessels, for such is not the case. Many arteries of the body are subject to this same occluding process, and whenever the atherosclerosis becomes severe, the resulting symptoms reflect the decrease in blood flow to the specific area. For example, occlusion of a cerebral artery due to atherosclerosis and its associated blood clotting can cause localized brain damage—a stroke (recall that rupture of a cerebral vessel, as in hypertension, is the other cause of stroke). Persons with atherosclerotic cerebral vessels may also suffer reversible neurologic deficits, known as **transient ischemic attacks**

---

[15]Regular exercise is protective against heart attacks for a variety of reasons. It induces (1) increased diameter of coronary arteries, (2) decreased severity of hypertension and diabetes, (3) decreased plasma cholesterol concentration with simultaneous increase in the plasma concentration of a cholesterol-carrying lipoprotein thought to be protective against atherosclerosis, and (4) improved ability to dissolve blood clots.

[16]Nitroglycerin is a vasodilator because it is converted to nitric oxide, which as described in the text is actually EDRF.

(TIAs), lasting minutes to hours, without actually experiencing a stroke at the time.

Finally, it should be noted that both myocardial infarcts and strokes due to occlusion may result from the breaking off of a fragment of a blood clot or fatty deposit that then lodges downstream, completely blocking a smaller vessel. The fragment is termed an **embolus**, and the process is **embolism**.

SECTION F SUMMARY

HEMORRHAGE AND OTHER CAUSES OF HYPOTENSION

I. The physiological responses to hemorrhage are summarized in Figures 14-62, 14-64, and 14-65.

II. Hypotension can be caused by loss of body fluids, by strong emotion, and by liberation of vasodilator chemicals.

III. Shock is any situation in which blood flow to the tissues is low enough to cause damage to them.

THE UPRIGHT POSTURE

I. In the upright posture, gravity acting upon unbroken columns of blood reduces venous return by increasing vascular pressures in the veins and capillaries in the limbs.

   A. The increased venous pressure distends the veins, causing venous pooling, and the increased capillary pressure causes increased filtration out of the capillaries.

   B. These effects are minimized by contraction of the skeletal muscles in the legs.

EXERCISE

I. The cardiovascular changes that occur in endurance-type exercise are illustrated in Figures 14-67 and 14-68.

II. The changes are due to active hyperemia in the exercising skeletal muscles and heart, to increased sympathetic outflow to the heart, arterioles, and veins, and to decreased parasympathetic outflow to the heart.

III. The increase in cardiac output depends not only on the autonomic influences on the heart but on factors that help increase venous return.

IV. Training can increase a person's maximal oxygen consumption by increasing maximal stroke volume and hence cardiac output.

HYPERTENSION

I. Hypertension is usually due to increased total peripheral resistance resulting from increased arteriolar constriction.

II. More than 95 percent of hypertension is termed primary in that the cause of the increased arteriolar constriction is unknown.

HEART FAILURE

I. Heart failure can occur when a decreased cardiac contractility causes cardiac output to be inadequate.

II. This leads to fluid retention by the kidneys and formation of edema because of increased capillary pressure.

III. Pulmonary edema can occur when the left ventricle fails.

CORONARY ARTERY DISEASE

I. Insufficient coronary blood flow can cause damage to the heart.

II. Acute death from a heart attack is usually due to ventricular fibrillation.

III. The major cause of reduced coronary blood flow is atherosclerosis, an occlusive disease of arteries.

IV. Persons may suffer intermittent attacks of angina pectoris without actually suffering a heart attack at the time of the pain.

V. Atherosclerosis can also cause strokes and symptoms of inadequate blood flow in other areas.

SECTION F KEY TERMS

maximal oxygen consumption ($\dot{V}_{O_2max}$)

SECTION F REVIEW QUESTIONS

1. Draw a flow diagram illustrating the reflex compensation for hemorrhage.

2. What happens to plasma volume and interstitial-fluid volume following a hemorrhage?

3. What causes hypotension during a severe allergic response?

4. How does gravity influence effective blood volume?

5. Describe the role of the skeletal-muscle pump in decreasing capillary filtration.

6. List the directional changes that occur during exercise for all relevant cardiovascular variables. What are the specific efferent mechanisms that bring about these changes?

7. What factors enhance venous return during exercise?

8. Diagram the control of autonomic outflow during exercise.

9. What is the limiting cardiovascular factor in endurance exercise?

10. What changes in cardiac function occur at rest and during exercise as a result of endurance training?

11. What is the abnormality in most cases of established hypertension?

12. Describe two mechanisms for raising stroke volume in heart failure.

13. How does heart failure lead to edema?

14. Name four risk factors for atherosclerosis.

CHAPTER 14 CLINICAL TERMS

iron deficiency	renal hypertension
anemia	primary hypertension
pernicious anemia	diuretics
hemorrhage	stroke
sickle-cell anemia	heart failure
microcytosis	pulmonary edema
normocytosis	digitalis
macrocytosis	coronary artery disease
polycythemia	myocardial infarction
AV conduction	heart attack
disorders	angina pectoris
atrial fibrillation	ventricular fibrillation
heart murmurs	cardiopulmonary resuscitation
stenosis	(CPR)
insufficiency	atherosclerosis
echocardiography	coronary thrombosis
cardiac angiography	coronary angioplasty
elephantiasis	coronary bypass
edema	transient ischemic attacks
hypotension	(TIAs)
shock	embolus
hypertension	embolism

CHAPTER 14 THOUGHT QUESTIONS

(Answers are given in Appendix A.)

1. A person is found to have a hematocrit of 35 percent. Can you conclude from this that there is a decreased volume of erythrocytes in the blood?

2. Which would cause a greater increase in resistance to flow—a doubling of blood viscosity or a halving of tube radius?

3. If all plasma-membrane calcium channels in contractile cardiac-muscle cells were blocked with a drug, what would happen to the muscle's action potentials and contraction.

4. A person with a heart rate of 40 has no P waves but normal QRS complexes on the ECG. What is the explanation?

5. A person has a left ventricular systolic pressure of 180 mmHg and an aortic systolic pressure of 110 mmHg. What is the explanation?

6. A person has a left atrial pressure of 20 mmHg and a left ventricular pressure of 5 mmHg during ventricular filling. What is the explanation.

7. A patient is taking a drug that blocks beta-adrenergic receptors. What changes in cardiac function will the drug cause?

8. What is the mean arterial pressure in a person whose diastolic and systolic pressure are, respectively, 160 and 100 mmHg?

9. A person is given a drug that doubles the blood flow to her kidneys but does not change the mean arterial pressure. What must the drug be doing?

10. A blood vessel removed from an experimental animal dilates when exposed to acetylcholine. After the endothelium is scraped from the lumen of the vessel, it no longer dilates in response to this mediator. Explain.

11. A person is accumulating edema throughout the body. Average capillary pressure is 25 mmHg, and lymphatic function is normal. What is the most likely cause of the edema.

12. A person's cardiac output is 7 L/min and mean arterial pressure is 140 mmHg. What is the person's total peripheral resistance?

13. The following data are obtained for an experimental animal before and after a drug. Before: heart rate = 80 beats/min, and stroke volume = 80 ml/beat. After: heart rate = 100 beats/min, and stroke volume = 64 ml/beat. Total peripheral resistance remains unchanged. What has the drug done to mean arterial pressure?

14. When the nerves from all the arterial baroreceptors are cut in an experimental animal, what happens to mean arterial pressure?

15. What happens to the hematocrit within several hours after a hemorrhage?

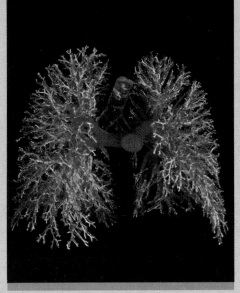

C H A P T E R
15

RESPIRATION

ORGANIZATION OF THE RESPIRATORY SYSTEM
The Airways
Site of Gas Exchange: The Alveoli
Relation of the Lungs to the Thoracic (Chest) Wall
Pulmonary Pressures
VENTILATION AND LUNG MECHANICS
Inspiration
Expiration
Lung Compliance
    Determinants of lung compliance
Airway Resistance
    Asthma
    Chronic obstructive pulmonary disease
    The Heimlich maneuver
Lung Volumes and Capacities
Alveolar Ventilation
    Dead space
EXCHANGE OF GASES IN ALVEOLI AND TISSUES
Partial Pressures of Gases
    Diffusion of gases in liquids
Alveolar Gas Pressures
Alveolar-Blood Gas Exchange
Matching of Ventilation and Blood Flow in Alveoli
Gas Exchange in the Tissues
TRANSPORT OF OXYGEN IN BLOOD
Effect of P_{O_2} on Hemoglobin Saturation
Effects of Blood P_{CO_2}, H^+ Concentration, Temperature,
    and DPG on Hemoglobin Saturation

TRANSPORT OF CARBON DIOXIDE IN BLOOD
**TRANSPORT OF HYDROGEN IONS BETWEEN
TISSUES AND LUNGS**
CONTROL OF RESPIRATION
Neural Generation of Rhythmical Breathing
Control of Ventilation by P_{O_2}, P_{CO_2}, and H^+ Concentration
    Control by P_{O_2}
    Control by P_{CO_2}
    *Control by changes in arterial H^+ concentration not due
        to altered carbon dioxide*
Control of Ventilation During Exercise
    Increased P_{CO_2} as the stimulus?
    Decreased P_{O_2} as the stimulus?
    Increased H^+ concentration as the stimulus?
    Other factors
Other Ventilatory Responses
    Protective reflexes
    Pain and emotion
    Voluntary control of breathing
HYPOXIA
Acclimatization to High Altitude
NONRESPIRATORY FUNCTIONS OF THE LUNGS
SUMMARY
KEY TERMS
REVIEW QUESTIONS
CLINICAL TERMS
THOUGHT QUESTIONS

Respiration has two quite different meanings: (1) utilization of oxygen in the metabolism of organic molecules by cells, as described in Chapter 5, and (2) the exchanges of oxygen and carbon dioxide between an organism and the external environment. The second meaning is the subject of this chapter.

Our cells obtain most of their energy from chemical reactions involving oxygen. In addition, cells must be able to eliminate carbon dioxide, the major end product of oxidative metabolism. A unicellular organism can exchange oxygen and carbon dioxide directly with the external environment, but this is obviously impossible for most cells of a complex organism like a human being. Therefore, the evolution of large animals required the development of a specialized system—the respiratory system—to exchange oxygen and carbon dioxide for the entire animal with the external environment.

The **respiratory system** comprises those structures involved in the exchange of gases between the blood and external environment: the lungs (**pulmonary** is the adjectival form of "lungs"), the series of tubes leading to the lungs, and the chest structures responsible for moving air into and out of the lungs during breathing.

In addition to the provision of oxygen and elimination of carbon dioxide, the respiratory system serves other functions, as listed in Table 15-1 and discussed in this chapter.

TABLE 15-1 FUNCTIONS OF THE RESPIRATORY SYSTEM

1. Provides oxygen
2. Eliminates carbon dioxide
3. Regulates the blood's hydrogen-ion concentration (pH)
4. Forms speech sounds (phonation)
5. Defends against microbes
6. Influences arterial concentrations of chemical messengers by removing some from pulmonary capillary blood and producing and adding others to this blood
7. Traps and dissolves blood clots

ORGANIZATION OF THE RESPIRATORY SYSTEM

There are two lungs, the right and left, each divided into several lobes. The lungs of an adult consist mainly of tiny air-containing sacs called **alveoli** (singular, **alveolus**), which number approximately 300 million and are the sites of gas exchange with the blood. The **airways** are all the tubes through which air flows between the external environment and the alveoli.

Inspiration is the movement of air from the external environment through the airways into the alveoli during breathing. **Expiration** is movement in the opposite direction. An inspiration and an expiration constitute a respiratory cycle. During the entire respiratory cycle, the right ventricle of the heart pumps blood through the capillaries surrounding each alveolus. At rest, in a normal adult, approximately 4 L of environmental air enters and leaves the alveoli per minute, while 5 L of blood, the entire cardiac output, flows through the pulmonary capillaries. During heavy exercise, the air flow can increase thirty- to fortyfold, and the blood flow five- to sixfold. The alveolar air and capillary blood are separated from each other by extremely thin membranes, across which oxygen and carbon dioxide diffuse.

The Airways

During inspiration air passes through either the nose (the most common site) or mouth into the **pharynx** (throat), a passage common to the routes followed by air and food (Figure 15-1). The pharynx branches into two tubes, one (the esophagus) through which food passes to the stomach, and the other, the **larynx,** which is part of the airways. The larynx houses the **vocal cords,** two folds of elastic tissue stretched horizontally across its lumen. The flow of air past the vocal cords causes them to vibrate,

---

TABLE 15-2 FUNCTIONS OF THE CONDUCTING ZONE OF THE AIRWAYS

1. Provides a low-resistance pathway for air flow; resistance is physiologically regulated by changes in contraction of airway smooth muscle and by physical forces acting upon the airways.
2. Defends against microbes and other toxic chemicals and foreign matter; cilia, mucus, and phagocytes perform this function.
3. Warms and moistens the air.
4. Phonates (vocal cords).

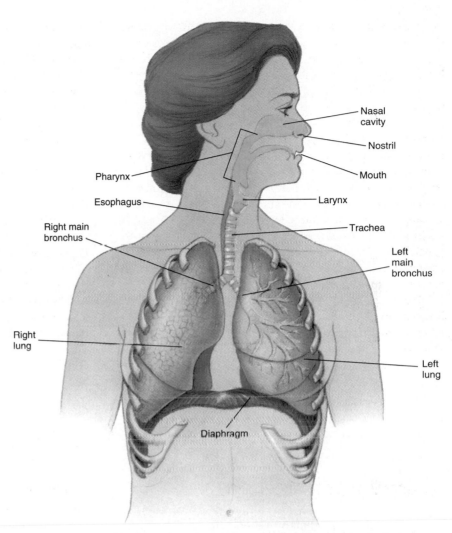

FIGURE 15-1

Organization of the respiratory system. The ribs have been removed in front, and the left lung is shown in cross-section.

producing sounds. The nose, mouth, pharynx, and larynx are termed the upper airways.

The larynx opens into a long tube, the **trachea,** which in turn branches into two **bronchi** (singular, **bronchus**), one of which enters each lung. Within the lungs, there are more than 20 generations of branchings, each resulting in narrower, shorter, and more numerous tubes, the names of which are summarized in Figure 15-2. The walls of the trachea and bronchi contain cartilage, which gives them their cylindrical shape and supports them. The first airway branches that no longer contain cartilage are termed **bronchioles.** Alveoli first begin to appear, attached to the walls, in the bronchioles called respiratory bronchioles, and their number increases in the alveolar ducts (Figure 15-2) until the airways end in grapelike clusters of alveoli (Figure 15-3).

The airways beyond the larynx can be divided into two zones: (1) the **conducting zone**—from the top of the trachea to the beginning of the respiratory bronchioles—which contains no alveoli and across which gas exchange with the blood does not occur (Table 15-2); and (2) the **respiratory zone**—from the respiratory bronchioles on down—which contains alveoli and across which gas exchange occurs.

The blood vessels supplying the lung generally accompany the airways and also undergo numerous branchings. The smallest of these vessels branch into networks of capillaries that richly supply the alveoli (Figure 15-3).

The epithelial surfaces of the airways, to the end of the respiratory bronchioles, contain cilia that constantly beat toward the pharynx. They also contain glands and individual epithelial cells that secrete mucus. Particulate matter, such as dust contained in the inspired air, sticks to the mucus, which is continually and slowly moved by the cilia to the pharynx and then swallowed. This mucus escalator is important to keep the lungs clear of particulate matter and the many bacteria that enter the body on dust particles. Ciliary activity can be inhibited by many noxious agents. For example, smoking a single cigarette can immobilize the cilia for several hours.

Adequate function of the mucus escalator depends not only on ciliary action but also on the secretion by the airway epithelium of a watery fluid upon which the mucus can ride freely. The production of this fluid requires active

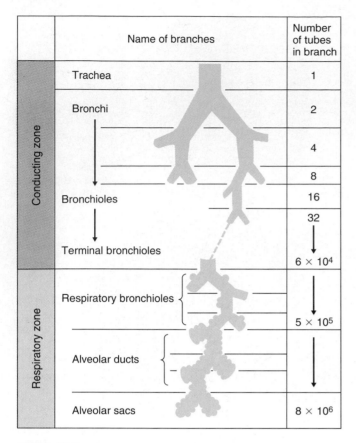

Name of branches	Number of tubes in branch
Conducting zone	
Trachea	1
Bronchi	2
	4
	8
Bronchioles	16
	32
Terminal bronchioles	6×10^4
Respiratory zone	
Respiratory bronchioles	5×10^5
Alveolar ducts	
Alveolar sacs	8×10^6

FIGURE 15-2
Airway branching.

secretion of chloride into the lumen of the airways, and this process is impaired in the genetic disease called *cystic fibrosis,* which is the most common lethal genetic disease of Caucasians and is characterized by the presence of a thick, dehydrated mucus layer. The impaired chloride secretion is due to a defect in the activation of chloride channels.

A second protective mechanism against infection is provided by cells, present in the airways (and alveoli) and termed macrophages, that engulf inhaled particles and bacteria and thus keep them from gaining access to other lung cells or from entering the blood. These cells are also injured by cigarette smoke and air pollutants.

Site of Gas Exchange: The Alveoli

The alveoli are tiny hollow sacs whose open ends are continuous with the lumens of the airways (Figures 15-2 and 15-4A). Typically, the air in two alveoli is separated by a single alveolar wall (Figure 15-4A). The air-facing surface(s) of the wall are lined by a continuous layer, one cell thick, of epithelial cells, most of which are the flat **type I alveolar cells.**

The alveolar walls contain capillaries, the endothelial linings of which are separated from the alveolar epithelial lining by only a basement membrane and a very thin interstitial space containing interstitial fluid and a loose meshwork of connective tissue (Figure 15-4B). Indeed, in places, the interstitial space may be absent altogether, and the basement membranes of the alveolar-surface epithelium and the capillary-wall endothelium may fuse. Thus the blood within an alveolar-wall capillary is separated from the air within the alveolus by only an extremely thin barrier (0.2 μm, compared with the 7-μm diameter of an average red blood cell). The total surface area of alveoli in contact with capillaries is approximately 75 m^2 (roughly the size of a tennis court and 40 times greater than the external body surface area). This extensive area, as well as the thinness of the barrier, permits the rapid exchange of large quantities of oxygen and carbon dioxide.

In addition to the type I alveolar cells, the alveolar epithelium contains smaller numbers of thicker specialized cells (**type II alveolar cells**) (Figure 15-4B) that produce a detergent-like substance, surfactant, to be discussed below. The alveolar walls also contain macrophages and other connective-tissue cells that function in the lung's defense mechanisms. Finally, the alveolar surfaces in contact with the air are moist.

In some of the alveolar walls there are pores that permit the flow of air between alveoli. This route can be very important when the airway leading to an alveolus is occluded by disease, since some air can still enter the alveolus by way of the pores between it and adjacent alveoli.

Relation of the Lungs to the Thoracic (Chest) Wall

The lungs, like the heart, are situated in the **thorax,** the compartment of the body between the neck and abdomen. "Thorax" and "chest" are synonyms, even though common usage often assumes that "chest" refers only to the front of the thorax. The thorax is a closed compartment, bounded at the neck by muscles and connective tissue and completely separated from the abdomen by a large dome-shaped sheet of skeletal muscle, the **diaphragm.** The wall of the thorax is formed by the spinal column, the ribs, the breastbone (sternum), and the muscles that lie between the ribs (the **intercostal muscles**). The thoracic wall also contains large amounts of elastic connective tissue.

Each lung is surrounded by a completely closed sac, the **pleural sac,** consisting of a thin sheet of cells called **pleura.** The two pleural sacs, one on each side of the midline, are completely separate from each other. The relationship between a lung and its pleural sac can be visualized by imagining what happens when one pushes a fist into a balloon (Figure 15-5): The arm represents the major bronchus leading to the lung, the fist is the lung, and the balloon is the pleural sac. The fist becomes coated by one surface of the balloon. In addition, the balloon is pushed back upon itself so that its opposite surfaces lie close together. The pleural surface coating the lung (the visceral

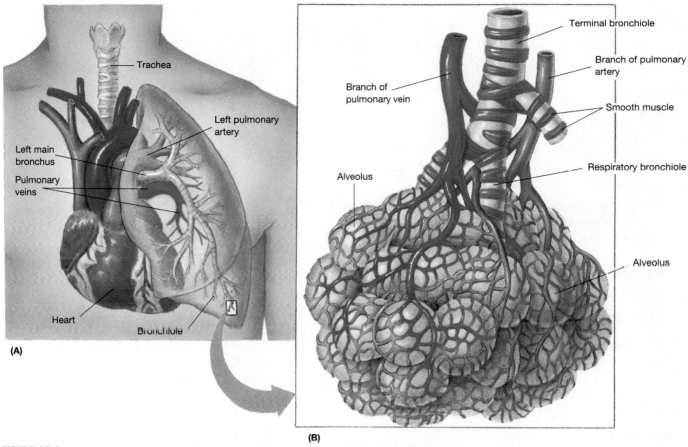

FIGURE 15-3

Relationships between blood vessels and airways. (A) The lung appears transparent so that the relationships can be seen. The airways beyond the bronchiole are too small to be seen. (B) An enlargement of a small section of 15-3A to show the continuation of the airways and the clusters of alveoli at their ends. Virtually the entire lung, not just the surface, consists of such clusters.

pleura) is firmly attached to the lung. Similarly, the outer layer (parietal pleura) is attached to and lines the interior thoracic wall and diaphragm. The two layers of pleura are so close to each other that normally they are always in virtual contact, but they are *not* attached to each other. Rather, they are separated by an extremely thin layer of **intrapleural fluid,** the total volume of which is only a few milliliters. The intrapleural fluid lubricates the outer surface of the lungs. More important, as we shall see, pressure changes in the intrapleural fluid cause the lung surface and thoracic wall to move in and out together during breathing.

Pulmonary Pressures

An important point for the discussion that follows is that both the lungs and the thoracic wall are elastic structures. If they are either stretched or compressed by some force, they will recoil, that is, return to their original sizes and positions when the force is removed.

The volume of the lungs and thorax at the end of an unforced expiration is determined only by passive elastic forces since no significant contractions of the respiratory muscles are occurring. The volume of air in the lungs at this time is known as the **functional residual capacity.** The following simple observation reveals that this position reflects a balance point between opposed forces.

In certain kinds of surgery, the chest wall ("chest wall" and "thoracic wall" are synonyms) is opened and the parietal pleura cut, exposing the fluid-filled intrapleural space. The lung is not cut, yet on the side of the incision the lung collapses immediately to a smaller volume. Simultaneously, the chest wall on that side moves outward. The behavior of the lung shows that as long as the chest wall is intact, some force must be acting to stretch the lung and that this force is eliminated when the chest is opened. The observations also show that the intact chest wall is normally partially pulled inward (compressed) by some force resulting from the presence of the lung within it. In other

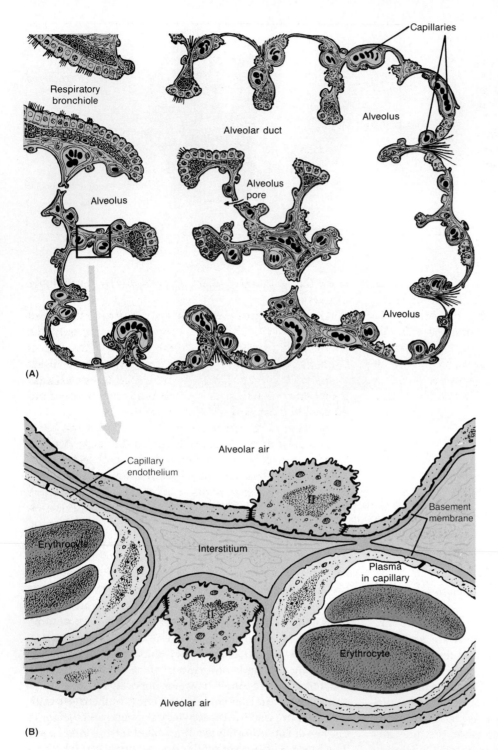

FIGURE 15-4

(A) Cross section through an area of the respiratory zone. There are 18 alveoli in this figure, only 4 of which are labelled. Two frequently share a common wall. (*From R. O. Greep and L. Weiss, "Histology," 3d edn., McGraw-Hill, New York, 1973.*) (B) Schematic enlargement of a portion of an alveolar wall. I = nucleus of a type I cell; II = nucleus of a type II cell. (*Adapted from Gong and Drage.*)

words, the lungs and chest wall would move away from each other, the lungs to recoil inward and the chest wall to pop outward, except that forces exist that keep them from doing so. We now turn to the nature of these forces and how they result in a stable equilibrium when the lung is at functional residual capacity.

Figure 15-6 illustrates the situation that normally exists at the end of an unforced expiration, when no respiratory muscle contraction is occurring and no air is flowing. All pressures in the respiratory system, as in the cardiovascular system, are given relative to **atmospheric pressure**—the pressure of the air surrounding the body (760 mmHg at sea level). The pressure within the alveoli is the **alveolar pressure** (P_{alv}, also termed intrapulmonary pressure).

FIGURE 15-5

Relationship of lungs, pleura, and thoracic wall, shown as analogous to pushing a fist into a fluid-filled balloon. Note that there is no communication between the right and left intrapleural fluids. For purposes of illustration, in this figure and other similar ones in this chapter, the volume of intrapleural fluid is greatly exaggerated; it normally consists of an extremely thin layer of fluid between the pleura membrane lining the inner surface of the thoracic wall and that lining the surface of the lungs.

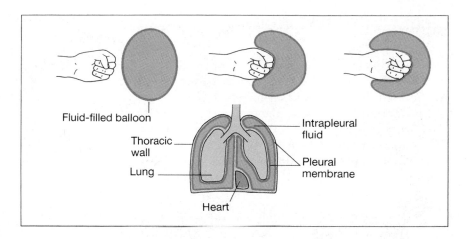

Between breaths it is 0 mmHg; that is, it is the same as atmospheric pressure. The pressure in the intrapleural fluid is the **intrapleural pressure (P_{ip})** or intrathoracic pressure. Between breaths it is approximately 4 mmHg less than atmospheric pressure, that is, −4 mmHg.[1] There is therefore a pressure difference of 4 mmHg [0 − (−4) = 4] across the lung wall. This pressure difference is known as the **transpulmonary pressure,** and it is the force that

---

[1]Physiologists usually express pressures in the respiratory system in cmH_2O rather than mmHg; we have chosen, for simplicity, not to do this (for reference, 1 cmH_2O = 1.3 mmHg).

FIGURE 15-6

Alveolar (P_{alv}), intrapleural (P_{ip}), and transpulmonary ($P_{alv} - P_{ip}$) pressures at the end of an unforced expiration. The transpulmonary pressure exactly opposes the elastic recoil of the lung, and the lung volume (and chest wall) remain stable. The lung volume at this time is the functional residual capacity.

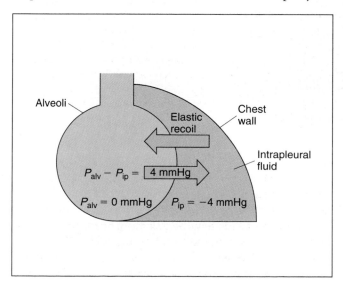

holds the *lungs* open, that is, keeps the stretched lungs from collapsing.

At the same time there is also a pressure difference of 4 mmHg keeping the *chest wall* from moving out: The atmospheric pressure against the outside of the wall is 0 mmHg, and the intrapleural pressure against the inside of the wall is −4 mmHg; the difference is 4 mmHg directed inward and opposing the tendency of the compressed thoracic wall to move outward.

We have so far not described how it is that the intrapleural pressure is subatmospheric. As the lungs (tending to move inward from their stretched position) and the thoracic wall (tending to move outward from its compressed position) move ever so slightly away from each other, there occurs an infinitesimal enlargement of the fluid-filled intrapleural space between them. But fluid cannot expand the way air can, and so even this tiny enlargement of the intrapleural space—so small that the pleural surfaces still remain in contact with each other—drops the intrapleural pressure below atmospheric pressure. In this way, the elastic recoil of both the lung and chest wall creates the subatmospheric intrapleural pressure that keeps them from moving apart more than a tiny amount.

Why the lung collapses when the chest wall is opened should now be apparent. When the chest wall is pierced, atmospheric air rushes through the wound into the intrapleural space (a phenomenon called **pneumothorax**), and the intrapleural pressure goes from −4 mmHg to 0 mmHg. The transpulmonary pressure acting to hold the lung open is thus eliminated, and the stretched lung collapses. At the same time, the chest wall moves outward because there is no longer a difference in pressure between the external environment and the intrapleural space to keep the chest wall compressed.

As we shall see in the next section, the magnitudes of the alveolar, intrapleural, and transpulmonary pressures vary during breathing and directly cause the changes in lung size that occur during inspiration and expiration.

VENTILATION AND LUNG MECHANICS

An inventory of steps involved in respiration (Figure 15-7) is provided for orientation before beginning the detailed descriptions of each step.

Ventilation is defined as the exchange of air between the atmosphere and alveoli. Like blood, air moves by *bulk flow*, from a region of high pressure to one of low pressure. We saw in Chapter 14 that bulk flow can be described by the equation

$$F = \frac{\Delta P}{R}$$

That is, flow (F) is proportional to the pressure difference (ΔP) between two points and inversely proportional to the resistance (R). For air flow into or out of the lungs, the relevant pressures are the alveolar pressure and the pressure at the nose and mouth, normally atmospheric pressure (P_{atm}):

$$F = \frac{P_{atm} - P_{alv}}{R}$$

Air moves into and out of the lungs because the alveolar pressure is made alternately less than and greater than atmospheric pressure (Figure 15-8). These alveolar pressure changes are caused, as we shall see, by changes in the dimensions of the lungs. To describe these changes, we need to learn one more basic concept. As stated by **Boyle's law** (Figure 15-9), at constant temperature the relationship between the pressure exerted by a fixed number of gas molecules in a container and the volume of the

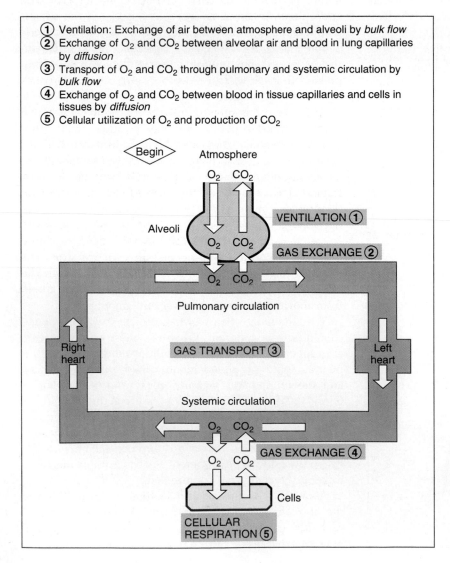

① Ventilation: Exchange of air between atmosphere and alveoli by *bulk flow*
② Exchange of O_2 and CO_2 between alveolar air and blood in lung capillaries by *diffusion*
③ Transport of O_2 and CO_2 through pulmonary and systemic circulation by *bulk flow*
④ Exchange of O_2 and CO_2 between blood in tissue capillaries and cells in tissues by *diffusion*
⑤ Cellular utilization of O_2 and production of CO_2

FIGURE 15-7

The steps of respiration.

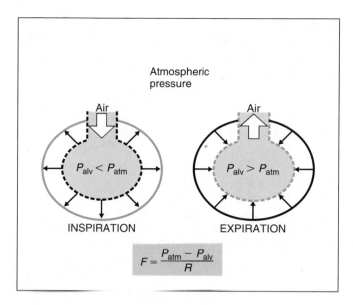

FIGURE 15-8

Relationships required for ventilation. When the alveolar pressure (P_{alv}) is less than atmospheric pressure (P_{atm}), air enters the lungs. Flow (F) is directly proportional to the pressure difference and inversely proportional to airway resistance (R). Black lines show lung's position at beginning of inspiration or expiration, and blue lines at end.

FIGURE 15-9

Boyle's law: The pressure exerted by a constant number of gas molecules in a container is inversely proportional to the volume of the container, that is, P is proportional to $1/V$.

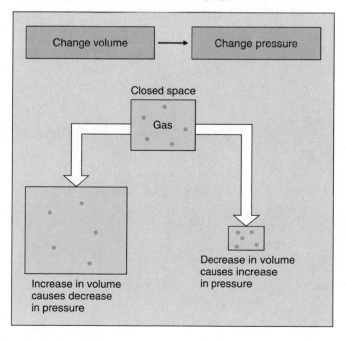

container is as follows: An increase in the volume of the container decreases the pressure of the gas, whereas a decrease in container volume increases the pressure.

Inspiration

Figures 15-10 and 15-11 summarize the events during normal inspiration at rest. Just before inspiration begins, that is, at functional residual capacity, the respiratory muscles are relaxed, and no air is flowing because the alveolar pressure is 0 mmHg, that is, the same as atmospheric pressure. As described earlier, the intrapleural pressure at this point is subatmospheric (-4 mmHg), and the transpulmonary pressure ($P_{alv} - P_{ip}$) is 4 mmHg.

Inspiration is initiated by the neurally induced contraction of the diaphragm and the inspiratory intercostal muscles.[2] The diaphragm is the most important inspiratory muscle during normal quiet breathing. When activation of the nerves to it causes it to contract, its dome moves downward into the abdomen, enlarging the thorax. Simultaneously, activation of the nerves to the inspiratory intercostal muscles causes them to contract, leading to an upward and outward movement of the ribs and a further increase in thoracic size. As the thorax enlarges, the thoracic wall moves ever so slightly further away from the lung surface, and the intrapleural fluid pressure becomes even more subatmospheric than it was between breaths. This increases the transpulmonary pressure, which forces the lung to expand.

Thus, when the inspiratory muscles increase the thoracic dimensions, the lungs are also forced to enlarge virtually to the same degree because of the change in intrapleural pressure. The enlargement of the lung causes an increase in the sizes of the alveoli throughout the lung. Therefore, by Boyle's law, the pressure within the alveoli drops to less than atmospheric. This produces the difference in pressure ($P_{alv} < P_{atm}$) that causes a bulk flow of air from the atmosphere through the airways into the alveoli. By the end of the inspiration, the pressure in the alveoli again equals atmospheric pressure.[3]

---

[2]It has generally been assumed that the intercostal muscles involved in inspiration are the external intercostal muscles, whereas the internal intercostals are used in active expiration. However, because there is some controversy over this view, we shall simply refer to inspiratory and expiratory intercostals; that is, we shall use functional rather than anatomical terms. It should also be noted that additional muscles, termed the accessory muscles of inspiration, may be brought into play during labored inspiration. These muscles act both on the upper ribs to enlarge the upper thorax and on the sternum to move it forward and upward.

[3]It should be noted that the analysis of Figure 15-11 treats the lungs as a single alveolus. The fact is that there are significant regional differences in alveolar, intrapleural, and transpulmonary pressures throughout the lungs and thoracic cavity. These differences are due mainly to the effects of gravity. They are of great importance in determining the distribution of inspired air throughout the lung.

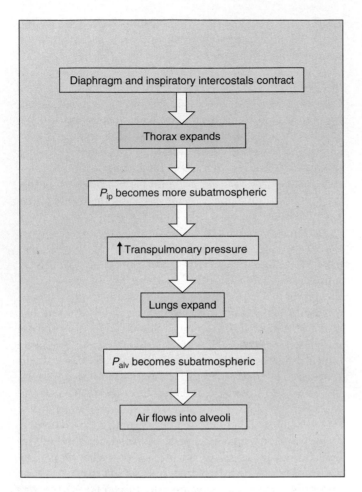

FIGURE 15-10
Sequence of events during inspiration. Figure 15-11 illustrates these events quantitatively.

Expiration

Figures 15-11 and 15-12 summarize the sequence of events during expiration. At the end of inspiration, the nerves to the diaphragm and inspiratory intercostal muscles cease firing, and so these muscles relax. The lungs and chest wall *passively* return to their original dimensions. As the lungs shrink, air in the alveoli becomes temporarily compressed so that, by Boyle's law, alveolar pressure exceeds atmospheric. Therefore, air flows from the alveoli through the airways out into the atmosphere. Thus, expiration at rest is completely passive, depending only upon the relaxation of the inspiratory muscles and recoil of the stretched lungs.

FIGURE 15-11

Summary of alveolar, intrapleural, and transpulmonary pressure changes and air flow during inspiration and expiration of 500 ml of air. The transpulmonary pressure is the gray area between the alveolar pressure and intrapleural pressure. Note that normal atmospheric pressure (760 mmHg) has a value of zero on the respiratory pressure scale. Note also that the transpulmonary pressure exactly opposes the elastic recoil of the lungs at the end of both inspiration and expiration.

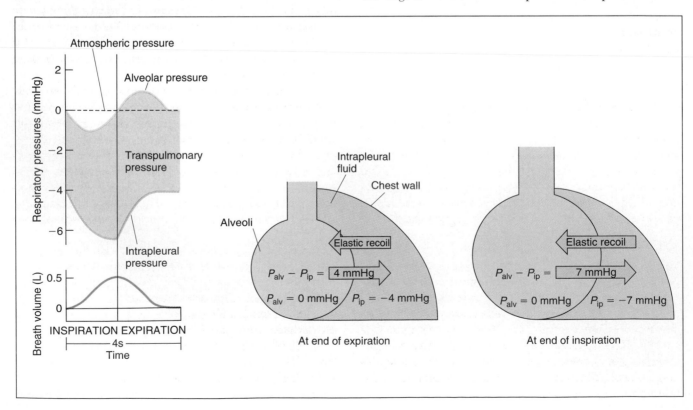

$$C_L = \frac{\Delta V_L}{\Delta(P_{alv} - P_{ip})}$$

Thus, the higher the lung compliance, the easier it is to expand the lungs at any given transpulmonary pressure. A low lung compliance means that a greater-than-normal transpulmonary pressure must be developed across the lung wall to produce a given amount of lung expansion. In other words, when lung compliance is low, intrapleural pressure must be made more subatmospheric than usual during inspiration to achieve lung expansion. This requires more vigorous contractions of the diaphragm and inspiratory intercostal muscles. Thus, the less compliant the lung, the more energy is required for a given amount of expansion. Persons with low lung compliance therefore tend to breathe shallowly and must compensate by breathing rapidly.

Determinants of Lung Compliance. There are two major determinants of lung compliance. One is the stretchability of the lung tissues, particularly its elastic connective tissues. Thus a thickening of the lung tissues decreases lung compliance. However, the single most important determinant of lung compliance is not the stretchability of the lung *tissues*, but the surface tension at the air-water interfaces within the alveoli. As noted earlier, the surfaces of the alveolar cells are moist, and so they can be pictured as air-filled sacs lined with water. At an air-water interface, the attractive forces between the water molecules, known as **surface tension,** make the water lining like a stretched balloon that constantly tries to shrink and resists further stretching. Thus, expansion of the lung requires energy not only to stretch the connective tissue of the lung but also to overcome the surface tension of the water layer lining the alveoli.

Indeed, the surface tension of pure water is so great that were the alveoli lined with pure water, lung expansion would require exhausting muscular effort and the lungs would tend to collapse. It is extremely important, therefore, that the type II alveolar cells produce a detergent-like substance known as pulmonary **surfactant,** which markedly reduces the cohesive forces between water molecules on the alveolar surface. Therefore, surfactant lowers the surface tension and increases lung compliance (Table 15-3).

Surfactant is a complex of both lipids and proteins, but its major component is a phospholipid, which forms a monomolecular layer between the air and water at the alveolar surface. The amount tends to decrease when breaths are small and constant. A deep breath, which people normally intersperse frequently in their breathing pattern, stimulates the type II cells to replenish the surfactant. This is why patients who have had thoracic or abdominal surgery and are breathing shallowly because of the pain must be urged to take occasional deep breaths.

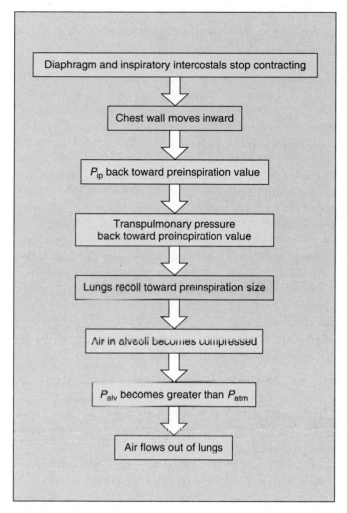

FIGURE 15-12

Sequence of events during expiration.

Under certain conditions, during exercise, for example, expiration of larger volumes is achieved by contraction of the expiratory intercostal muscles and the abdominal muscles, which *actively* decreases thoracic dimensions. The expiratory intercostal muscles insert on the ribs in such a way that their contraction pulls the chest wall in. Contraction of the abdominal muscles increases intraabdominal pressure and forces the diaphragm up into the thorax.

Lung Compliance

To reiterate, the degree of lung expansion at any instant is proportional to the transpulmonary pressure, that is, the difference between the alveolar pressure and the intrapleural pressure. But just how much any given transpulmonary pressure expands the lung depends upon the stretchability, or compliance, of the lung. **Lung compliance (C_L)** is defined as the magnitude of the change in lung volume (ΔV_L) produced by a given change in the transpulmonary pressure:

TABLE 15-3 SOME IMPORTANT FACTS ABOUT PULMONARY SURFACTANT

1. Pulmonary surfactant is a phospholipid bound to a protein.
2. It is secreted by type II alveolar cells.
3. It lowers surface tension of the water layer at the alveolar surface, which increases lung compliance, that is, makes the lungs easier to expand.
4. Its concentration decreases when breaths are small and constant.

A striking example of what occurs when surfactant is deficient is the disease known as ***respiratory-distress syndrome of the newborn,*** which is the second leading cause of death in premature infants, in whom the surfactant-synthesizing cells may be too immature to function adequately. Because of low lung compliance, the infant is able to inspire only by the most strenuous efforts, which may ultimately cause complete exhaustion, inability to breathe, lung collapse, and death. Normal maturation of the surfactant-synthesizing apparatus is facilitated by several hormones, particularly cortisol, the secretion of which is increased late in pregnancy. Accordingly, administration of cortisol late in pregnancy to a woman who is likely to deliver prematurely provides an important means of preventing this disease. Another important therapy is the administration of exogenous surfactant to the newborn infant via the trachea.

Airway Resistance

As previously stated, the volume of air that flows into or out of the alveoli per unit time is directly proportional to the pressure difference between the atmosphere and alveoli and inversely proportional to the resistance to flow offered by the airways:

DARCY'S law

$$F = \frac{P_{atm} - P_{alv}}{R}$$

What factors determine airway resistance? Resistance is (1) directly proportional to the magnitude of the frictional interactions between the flowing gas molecules, that is, the viscosity of the air, which is much less than that of blood; (2) directly proportional to the length of the airway; and (3) inversely proportional to the fourth power of the airway radius. These factors are analogous to those determining resistance in the circulatory system. Resistance in the respiratory tree, just as in the circulatory tree, is largely controlled by the radius of the airways.

Resistance to air flow is normally so small that very small pressure differences suffice to produce large vol-umes of air flow. As we have seen (Figure 15-11), the average atmosphere-to-alveoli pressure difference during a normal breath at rest is less than 1 mmHg; yet, approximately 500 ml of air is moved by this tiny difference.

Airway radii and therefore resistance are affected by physical, neural, and chemical factors. One important physical factor is the transpulmonary pressure, which exerts a distending force on the airways, just as on the alveoli. This is a major factor keeping the smaller airways—those without cartilage to support them—from collapsing. Because, as we have seen, transpulmonary pressure increases during inspiration, airway radius is larger and airway resistance is smaller when the lungs are expanded than when they are at functional residual capacity.

A second physical factor holding the airways open is the connective tissue fibers that attach to the airway exteriors and, because of their arrangement, continuously pull outward on the sides of the airways. This is termed **lateral traction**. Since these fibers become stretched as the lungs expand, they help pull the airways open even more during inspiration. Thus, both the transpulmonary pressure and lateral traction act in the same direction.

Such physical factors also explain why the airways become narrower and airway resistance increases during a forced expiration. Indeed, because of increased airway resistance, there is a limit as to how much one can increase the air flow rate during a forced expiration no matter how intense the effort.

In addition to these physical factors, a variety of chemical factors can influence airway smooth muscle and thereby airway resistance. The most important of these, along with the physical factors, are summarized in Table 15-4.

One might wonder why we have presented all these physical and chemical factors that *can* influence airway resistance when we earlier stated that airway resistance is *normally* so low that it is no impediment to air flow. The reason is that, under *abnormal* circumstances, changes in these factors may cause serious increases in airway resistance. Asthma and chronic obstructive pulmonary disease provide important examples.

Asthma. ***Asthma*** is a disease characterized by intermittent attacks in which airway smooth muscle contracts, increasing airway resistance enough to impair ventilation. More mucus may also be secreted by the airways, and this mucus may be abnormally thick, leading to a further increase in airway resistance secondary to mucous plugs. The basic defect in asthma is inflammation of the airways, the causes of which vary from person to person and include, among others, allergy and virus infections. The important point is that the underlying inflammation causes the airway smooth muscle to be hyperresponsive and to contract strongly when, depending upon the individual, he

TABLE 15-4	MAJOR FACTORS INFLUENCING THE AIRWAY RESISTANCE

Physical factors

Airways are held open by transpulmonary pressure and by lateral traction. Because of these factors, they open wider during inspiration and may collapse during forced expiration.

Airways may be partially or totally occluded by mucus accumulation.

Neuroendocrine agents

Parasympathetic nerves constrict (neurotransmitter = acetylcholine).

Circulating epinephrine dilates (action is on beta-adrenergic receptors).

Noncholinergic, nonadrenergic nerves dilate (neurotransmitter = vasoactive intestinal peptide).

Paracrine agents

Histamine constricts.

Several eicosanoids, notably the leukotrienes, constrict.

Several eicosanoids dilate.

or she exercises, is under emotional stress, is exposed to cold air, cigarette smoke, inhaled irritants, and certain drugs. The therapy for asthma is twofold—to reduce the inflammation with so-called anti-inflammatory drugs (such as adrenal glucocorticoids, Chapter 20), and to overcome the excessive airway smooth-muscle contraction with bronchodilator drugs, that is, drugs that relax the airways. The latter drugs work by influencing the neuroendocrine and paracrine effects on the airways summarized in Table 15-4. For example, some bronchodilator drugs mimic the action of epinephrine on beta-adrenergic receptors.

Chronic Obstructive Pulmonary Disease. The term *chronic obstructive pulmonary disease* refers to emphysema or chronic bronchitis or a combination of the two. These diseases, which cause severe difficulties not only in breathing but in oxygenation of the blood, are among the major causes of disability and death in the United States. In contrast to asthma, increased smooth-muscle contraction is *not* the cause of airway obstruction in these diseases.

Emphysema is characterized by destruction of the alveolar walls and consequently a marked enlargement of the alveolar air spaces and loss of pulmonary capillaries. These changes impair gas exchange, as will be described later. In addition, the small airways—those from the terminal bronchioles on down—are reduced in number and have atrophied walls. How all these changes occur is still poorly understood, but it is hypothesized that the lung

undergoes self-destruction by proteolytic enzymes secreted by leukocytes in the lung. Cigarette smoking, perhaps by stimulating the release of these enzymes, is by far the most important cause of emphysema. Air pollution and hereditary factors also play a role in some patients.

The airway obstruction in emphysema is due to collapse of the airways. To understand this, recall that two physical factors passively holding the airways open are the transpulmonary pressure and the lateral traction of connective-tissue fibers attached to the airway exteriors. Both of these factors are diminished in emphysema because of the destruction of the lung elastic tissues, and so the airways collapse.

Chronic bronchitis is characterized by excessive mucus production in the bronchi and chronic inflammatory changes in the small airways. The cause of obstruction is accumulation of mucus in the airways and thickening of the inflamed airways. The same agents listed above—smoking, for example—that cause emphysema also cause chronic bronchitis. That is why the two diseases frequently coexist.

The Heimlich Maneuver. The *Heimlich maneuver* is used to aid persons choking on foreign matter caught in the upper airways. A sudden increase in abdominal pressure is produced as the rescuer's fists, placed against the victim's abdomen slightly above the navel and well below the tip of the sternum, are pressed into the abdomen with a quick upward thrust (Figure 15-13). The increased abdominal pressure forces the diaphragm upward into the thorax, reducing thoracic size and, by Boyle's law, increasing alveolar pressure. The forceful expiration produced by the increased alveolar pressure expels the object caught in the respiratory tract.

Lung Volumes and Capacities

The volume of air entering the lungs during a single inspiration is normally approximately equal to the volume leaving on the subsequent expiration and is called the **tidal volume**. The tidal volume during normal quiet breathing—termed the resting tidal volume—is approximately 500 ml.

After expiration of a resting tidal volume, the lungs still contain air. Recall that this volume is termed the functional residual capacity; it amounts to approximately 2500 ml (Figure 15-14). In other words, at rest, the 500 ml of air inspired with each breath adds to and mixes with 2500 ml of air already in the lungs, and then 500 ml of the total is expired. Through maximal active contraction of the expiratory muscles, it is possible to expire 1500 ml of the 2500 ml remaining after the resting tidal volume has been expired; this additional volume is termed the **expiratory reserve volume**. Even after a maximal active expiration, approximately 1000 ml of air still remains in the lungs and is termed the **residual volume**.

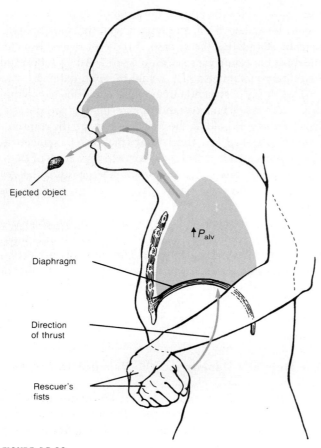

FIGURE 15-13

The Heimlich maneuver. The rescuer's fists are placed against the victim's abdomen. A quick upward thrust of the fists causes elevation of the diaphragm and a forceful expiration because of an increased P_{alv}. As this expired air is forced through the trachea and larynx, the foreign object in the airway is expelled.

Let us return to the situation in which a person is breathing at rest and see how much inspiration can be increased from this point. The volume of air that can be inspired over and above the resting tidal volume is called the **inspiratory reserve volume** and amounts to approximately 3000 ml of air (Figure 15-14). Thus, someone inspiring maximally after a resting expiration will inspire 500 ml, the resting tidal volume, plus another 3000 ml, the inspiratory reserve volume, for a total of 3500 ml. On the subsequent expiration, this air is all expelled.

A useful clinical measurement is the **vital capacity**, the maximal volume of air that a person can expire after a maximal inspiration. Under these conditions, the person is expiring the resting tidal volume and inspiratory reserve volume just inspired, followed by the expiratory reserve volume (Figure 15-14). In other words, the vital capacity is the sum of these three volumes.

A variant on this method is the *forced vital capacity (FVC)*, in which the person takes a maximal inspiration and then exhales maximally *as fast as possible;* thus the name, "forced" vital capacity. For several reasons the FVC may differ somewhat from the value obtained in an "unforced" vital capacity measurement. But, most important, the apparatus used to measure FVC also measures the volume expired after 1 s [the *forced expiratory volume in 1 s (FEV$_1$)*]. Normal individuals can expire approximately 80 percent of the FVC in 1 s.

These measurements are useful diagnostic tools. For example, people with obstructive lung diseases (increased airway resistance) typically have a FEV$_1$ which is less than 80 percent of the FVC because it is difficult for them to expire air rapidly through the narrowed airways. In contrast to obstructive lung diseases, *restrictive lung diseases* are characterized by normal airway resistance but

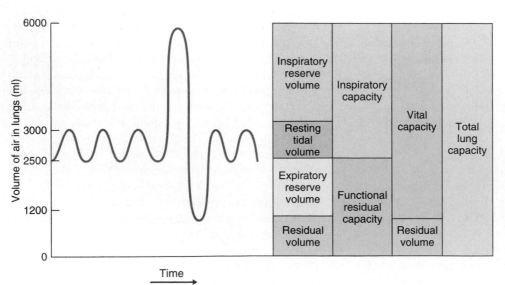

FIGURE 15-14

Lung volumes and capacities recorded on a spirometer, an apparatus for measuring inspired and expired volumes. When the subject inspires, the pen moves up; with expiration, it moves down. The capacities are the sums of two or more lung volumes. The lung volumes are the four distinct components of total lung capacity. (Note that residual volume and total lung capacity cannot be measured with a spirometer.)

impaired respiratory movements because of abnormalities in the lung tissue, the pleura, the chest wall, or the neuromuscular machinery. Restrictive lung diseases are characterized by a reduced vital capacity but a normal FEV_1/FVC ratio.

Alveolar Ventilation

The total ventilation per minute, termed the **minute ventilation**, is equal to the tidal volume multiplied by the respiratory rate:

Minute ventilation (ml/min) =
tidal volume (ml/breath) × respiratory rate (breaths/min)

For example, at rest, a normal person moves approximately 500 ml of air in and out of the lungs with each breath and takes 10 breaths each minute. The minute ventilation is therefore 500 ml/breath × 10 breaths/min = 5000 ml of air per minute. However, because of dead space, not all this air is available for exchange with the blood.

Dead Space. The conducting airways have a volume of about 150 ml. Exchanges of gases with the blood occur only in the alveoli and not in this 150 ml of the airways. Picture, then, what occurs during expiration of a tidal volume, which in this instance is 450 ml: The 450 ml of air is forced out of the alveoli and through the airways. Approximately 300 ml of this alveolar air is exhaled at the nose or mouth, but approximately 150 ml still remains in the airways at the end of expiration. During the next inspiration (Figure 15-15), 450 ml of air flows into the alveoli, but the first 150 ml entering the alveoli is not atmospheric air but the 150 ml left behind from the last breath. Thus, only 300 ml of new atmospheric air enters the alveoli during the inspiration. At the end of inspiration, 150 ml of fresh air fills the conducting airways, but no gas exchange with the blood can occur there. At the next expiration, this fresh air will be washed out and again replaced by old alveolar air, thus completing the cycle. The end result is that 150 ml of the 450 ml of atmospheric air entering the respiratory system during each inspiration never reaches the alveoli but is merely moved in and out of the airways. Because these airways do not permit gas exchange with the blood, the space within them is termed the **anatomic dead space**.

Thus the volume of fresh air entering the alveoli during each inspiration equals the tidal volume minus the volume of air in the anatomic dead space. For the previous example:

Tidal volume = 450 ml

Anatomic dead space = 150 ml

Fresh air entering alveoli in one inspiration =
450 ml − 150 ml = 300 ml

To determine how much fresh air enters the alveoli per minute, we simply multiply the volume of fresh air entering the alveoli per breath by the breathing frequency (set at 12 breaths/min in our example):

300 ml/breath × 12 breaths/min = 3600 ml/min

This total, the volume of fresh air entering the alveoli per minute, is called the **alveolar ventilation**:

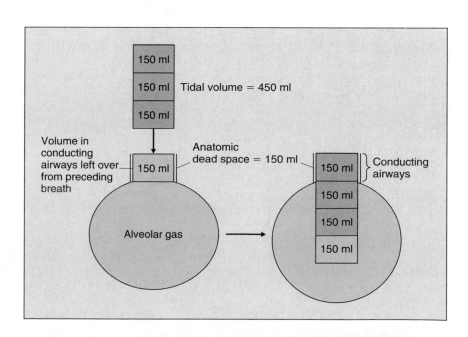

FIGURE 15-15
Effects of anatomic dead space on alveolar ventilation. Anatomic dead space is the volume of the conducting airways.

Alveolar ventilation =
$$(\text{tidal volume} - \text{dead space}) \times \text{frequency}$$

The value calculated for alveolar ventilation may be somewhat confusing because it seems to indicate that, in our example, only 3600 ml of gas enters and leaves the alveoli in each minute. This is not true—the total is 5400 ml (12 × 450), but only 3600 ml is fresh air; the rest, of course, is the air from the anatomic dead space.

What is the significance of the anatomic dead space and alveolar ventilation? Since only that portion of inspired air that enters the alveoli, that is, the alveolar ventilation, is useful for gas exchange with the blood, the magnitude of the alveolar ventilation is of much greater significance than is the minute ventilation, as can be demonstrated readily by data in Table 15-5.

In this experiment, subject A breathes rapidly and shallowly, B normally, and C slowly and deeply. Each subject has exactly the same minute ventilation; that is, each is moving the same amount of air in and out of the lungs per minute. Yet, when we subtract the anatomic-dead-space ventilation from the minute ventilation, we find marked differences in alveolar ventilation. Subject A has no alveolar ventilation and would become unconscious in several minutes, whereas C has a considerably greater alveolar ventilation than B, who is breathing normally. The important deduction to be drawn from this example is that increased *depth* of breathing is far more effective in elevating alveolar ventilation than is an equivalent increase in breathing *rate*. Conversely, a decrease in depth can lead to a critical reduction in alveolar ventilation. This is because a fixed volume of *each* tidal volume goes to the dead space. If the tidal volume decreases, the fraction of the tidal volume going to the dead space increases until, as in subject A, it may represent the entire tidal volume. On the other hand, any increase in tidal volume goes entirely toward increasing alveolar ventilation. These concepts have important physiological implications. Most situations that produce an increased ventilation, such as exercise, reflexly call forth a relatively greater increase in breathing depth than rate.

The anatomic dead space is not the only type of dead space. Some fresh inspired air is not used for gas exchange with the blood even though it reaches the alveoli because some alveoli, for various reasons, have little or no blood supply. This volume of air is known as **alveolar dead space**. It is quite small in normal persons but may be very large in several kinds of lung disease. As we shall see, it is minimized by local mechanisms that match air and blood flows. The sum of the anatomic and alveolar dead space is known as the **physiologic dead space**.

EXCHANGE OF GASES IN ALVEOLI AND TISSUES

We have now completed our discussion of the lung mechanics that produce alveolar ventilation, but this is only the first step in the respiratory process. Oxygen must move across the alveolar membranes into the pulmonary capillaries, be transported by the blood to the tissues, leave the tissue capillaries and enter the extracellular fluid, and finally cross plasma membranes to gain entry into cells. Carbon dioxide must follow a similar path in reverse.

In the steady state, the volume of oxygen that leaves the tissue capillaries and is consumed by the body cells per unit time is exactly equal to the volume of oxygen added to the blood in the lungs during the same time period. Similarly, the rate at which carbon dioxide is produced by the body cells and enters the systemic blood is identical to the rate at which carbon dioxide leaves the blood in the lungs and is expired.

The relative amounts of oxygen consumed by cells and carbon dioxide produced depend primarily upon which nutrients are being used for energy. The ratio CO_2 produced/O_2 consumed is known as the **respiratory quotient (RQ)**. On a mixed diet the RQ is approximately 0.8, that is, 8 molecules of CO_2 are produced for every 10 molecules of O_2 consumed.[4]

---

[4]The RQ is 1 for carbohydrate, 0.7 for fat, and 0.8 for protein.

TABLE 15-5 EFFECT OF BREATHING PATTERNS ON ALVEOLAR VENTILATION

Subject	Tidal volume, ml/breath	×	Frequency, breaths/min	=	Minute ventilation, ml/min	Anatomic dead-space ventilation, ml/min	Alveolar ventilation, ml/min
A	150		40		6000	150 × 40 = 6000	0
B	500		12		6000	150 × 12 = 1800	4200
C	1000		6		6000	150 × 6 = 900	5100

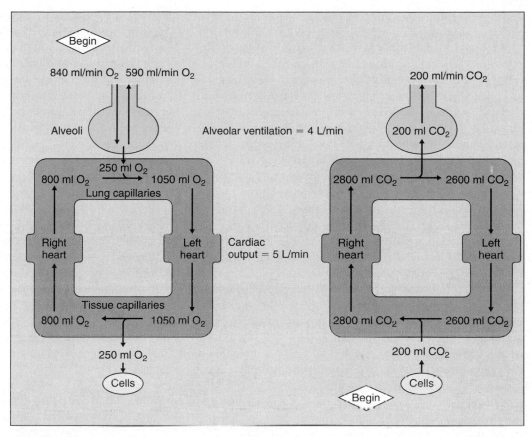

FIGURE 15-16

Summary of oxygen and carbon dioxide exchanges between atmosphere, lungs, blood, and tissues during 1 min. It is assumed that RQ = 0.8. Note that the values for oxygen and carbon dioxide in blood are *not* the values per liter of blood but rather the amounts transported per minute in the cardiac output (5 L normally). Thus, the volume of oxygen in 1 L of arterial blood is approximately 1000 ml O_2 divided by 5 L of blood = 200 ml O_2/L.

Figure 15-16 presents typical exchange values during 1 min for a person at rest, assuming a cellular oxygen consumption of 250 ml/min, a carbon dioxide production of 200 ml/min, an alveolar ventilation (supply of fresh air to the alveoli) of 4000 ml/min, and a cardiac output of 5000 ml/min.

Since only 21 percent of the atmospheric air is oxygen, the total oxygen entering the alveoli is 21 percent of 4000 ml, or 840 ml/min. Of this inspired oxygen, 250 ml crosses the alveoli into the pulmonary capillaries, and the remaining 590 ml is exhaled. This 250 ml of oxygen is carried away by 5 L of blood per minute—the cardiac output. Note, however, in Figure 15-16 that blood entering the lungs already contains large quantities of oxygen (the adaptive value of this seeming inefficiency will be described later), to which the new 250 ml is added. The blood then flows from the lungs to the left heart and is pumped by the left ventricle through the tissue capillaries, where 250 ml of oxygen leaves the blood to be taken up and utilized by cells. The quantities of oxygen added to the blood in the lungs and removed in the tissues are identical.

As shown by Figure 15-16, the story reads in reverse for carbon dioxide. There is already a good deal of carbon dioxide in systemic arterial blood; to this is added an additional 200 ml, the amount produced by the cells, as blood flows through tissue capillaries. This additional amount is eliminated as blood flows through the lungs.

Blood pumped by the heart carries oxygen and carbon dioxide between the lungs and tissues by bulk flow, but diffusion is responsible for the net movement of these molecules between the alveoli and blood, and between the blood and the cells of the body. Understanding the mechanisms involved in these diffusional exchanges depends upon some basic chemical and physical properties of gases, which we will now discuss.

Partial Pressures of Gases

Gas molecules undergo continuous random motion. These rapidly moving molecules exert a pressure, the magnitude of which is increased by anything that increases the rate of movement. The pressure a gas exerts is proportional to (1) the temperature (because heat increases the sp which molecules move) and (2) the concentration of the gas, that is, the number of molecules per unit volume.

As stated by **Dalton's law**, in a mixture of gases, the pressure exerted by each gas is independent of the pressure exerted by the others. This is because gas molecules are normally so far apart that they do not interfere with each other. Since each gas in a mixture behaves as though no other gases are present, the total pressure of the mixture is simply the sum of the individual pressures. These individual pressures, termed **partial pressures**, are denoted by a P in front of the symbol for the gas. For example, the partial pressure of oxygen is represented by P_{O_2}. Net diffusion of a gas will occur from a region where its partial pressure is high to a region where it is low.

Atmospheric air consists primarily of nitrogen (approximately 79 percent) and oxygen (approximately 21 percent), with very small quantities of water vapor, carbon dioxide, and inert gases. The sum of the partial pressures of all these gases is termed atmospheric pressure or barometric pressure. It varies in different parts of the world as a result of differences in altitude (it also varies with local weather conditions), but at sea level it is 760 mmHg. Since the partial pressure of any gas in a mixture is the fractional concentration of that gas times the total pressure of all the gases, the P_{O_2} of atmospheric air is $0.21 \times 760 \text{ mmHg} = 160 \text{ mmHg}$ at sea level.

Diffusion of Gases in Liquids. When a liquid is exposed to air containing a particular gas, molecules of the gas will enter the liquid and dissolve in it. Suppose, for example, that a closed container contains both water and gaseous oxygen. Oxygen molecules from the gas phase constantly bombard the surface of the water, some entering the water and dissolving. Since the number of molecules striking the surface is directly proportional to the P_{O_2} of the gas phase, the number of molecules entering the water is also directly proportional to the P_{O_2}. As long as the P_{O_2} in the gas phase is higher than the P_{O_2} in the liquid, there will be a net diffusion of oxygen into the liquid. Diffusion equilibrium will be reached when the P_{O_2} in the liquid is equal to the P_{O_2} in the gas phase, and there will be no further net diffusion between the two phases.

Conversely, if a liquid containing a dissolved gas at high partial pressure is exposed to a lower partial pressure of that same gas in a gas phase, gas molecules will diffuse from the liquid into the gas phase until the partial pressures in the two phases become equal.

The exchanges *between* gas and liquid phases described in the last two paragraphs are precisely the phenomena occurring between alveolar air and pulmonary capillary blood. In addition, dissolved gas molecules also diffuse *within* a liquid from a region of higher partial pressure to a region of lower partial pressure, an effect that underlies

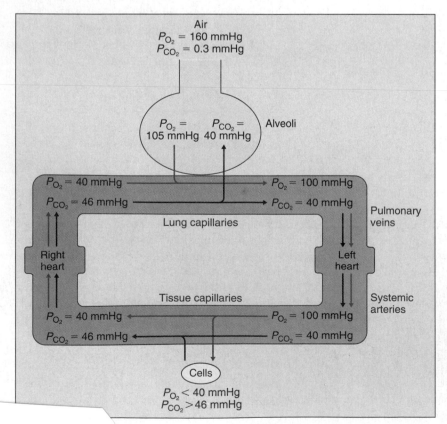

FIGURE 15-17

Partial pressures of carbon dioxide and oxygen in inspired air at sea level and various places in the body. Note that the P_{O_2} in the systemic arteries is shown as identical to that in the pulmonary veins; actually, for reasons described in the text, the arterial value should be slightly less, but we have ignored this for the sake of clarity.

the exchange of gases between cells, extracellular fluid, and capillary blood throughout the body.[5]

With these basic gas properties as the foundation, we can now discuss the diffusion of oxygen and carbon dioxide across alveolar, capillary, and plasma membranes. The pressures of these gases in air and in various sites of the body are given in Figure 15-17 for a resting person at sea level. We start our discussion with the *alveolar* gas pressures because their values set those of systemic arterial blood. This fact cannot be emphasized too strongly: In normal persons, the alveolar P_{O_2} and P_{CO_2} determine the systemic arterial P_{O_2} and P_{CO_2}.

Alveolar Gas Pressures

Normal alveolar gas pressures are P_{O_2} = 105 mmHg and P_{CO_2} = 40 mmHg. (We do not deal with nitrogen, even though it is the most abundant gas in the alveoli, because nitrogen is biologically inert under normal conditions and does not undergo any net exchange across the lung walls.) Compare these values with the gas pressures in the air being breathed: P_{O_2} = 160 mmHg and P_{CO_2} = 0.3 mmHg, a value so low that we will simply assume it to be zero. The alveolar P_{O_2} is lower than atmospheric P_{O_2} because some of the oxygen in the air entering the alveoli leaves them to enter the pulmonary capillaries. Alveolar P_{CO_2} is higher than atmospheric P_{CO_2} because carbon dioxide enters the alveoli from the pulmonary capillaries.

The factors that determine the precise value of alveolar P_{O_2} are (1) the P_{O_2} of atmospheric air, (2) the rate of cellular oxygen consumption, and (3) the alveolar ventilation. Although there are equations for calculating the alveolar

---

[5]The *concentration* of a gas in a liquid is proportional not only to the partial pressure of the gas but also to the solubility of the gas in the liquid; the more soluble the gas, the greater will be its concentration at any given partial pressure. Thus, if a liquid is exposed to two different gases at the same partial pressures, at equilibrium the *partial pressures* of the two gases will be identical in the liquid but the *concentrations* of the gases in the liquid will differ, depending upon their solubilities in that liquid.

gas pressures from these variables, we will describe the interactions in a more qualitative manner (Table 15-6).

First, breathing air having a low P_{O_2}, as at a high altitude, results in a low alveolar P_{O_2} since fewer molecules of oxygen are present in the air flowing into the alveoli. In contrast, administration of a high-oxygen gas mixture to a person increases alveolar P_{O_2}.

Next, consider the effects on the alveolar gas pressures of changing the alveolar ventilation but not the oxygen consumption (Figure 15-18). Suppose that the alveolar ventilation is larger than the usual 4 L/min because a resting person is deliberately breathing rapidly and deeply, but that the cellular oxygen utilization is unchanged at 250 ml/min. Under these conditions, the 250 ml of oxygen that leaves the alveoli each minute to enter the blood and be supplied to cells is a smaller fraction of the oxygen supplied by the alveolar ventilation. Therefore, steady-state alveolar P_{O_2} is higher; that is, it more closely approximates atmospheric air than usual. At the same time, the alveolar P_{CO_2} is lower than usual because the still normal amount of carbon dioxide (200 ml) entering the alveoli from the blood is diluted more than usual by the larger alveolar ventilation.

In contrast, a reduced alveolar ventilation in a person with normal cellular oxygen utilization and carbon dioxide production will result in a lower alveolar P_{O_2} and a higher alveolar P_{CO_2}.

Next, consider the effects of increasing cellular oxygen utilization and carbon dioxide production at constant alveolar ventilation. In this case, a larger fraction of the oxygen in the alveolar ventilation will leave the alveoli to enter the pulmonary capillaries; therefore, alveolar P_{O_2} will decrease. At the same time, the larger amount of carbon dioxide entering the alveoli from the blood will be diluted less than usual by the alveolar ventilation; therefore, the alveolar P_{CO_2} will increase.

Finally, consider the effects on the alveolar gas pressures of increasing cellular oxygen utilization and carbon

---

TABLE 15-6 EFFECTS OF VARIOUS CONDITIONS ON ALVEOLAR GAS PRESSURES

Condition	Alveolar P_{O_2}	Alveolar P_{CO_2}
Breathing air with low P_{O_2}	Decreases	No change°
↑Alveolar ventilation and unchanged metabolism	Increases	Decreases
↓Alveolar ventilation and unchanged metabolism	Decreases	Increases
↑Metabolism and unchanged alveolar ventilation	Decreases	Increases
Proportional increases in metabolism and alveolar ventilation	No change	No change

°Breathing air with low P_{O_2} has no direct effect on alveolar P_{CO_2}. However, as described later in the text, people in this situation will reflexly increase their ventilation and that will lower P_{CO_2}.

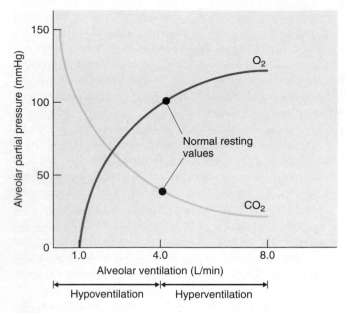

FIGURE 15-18

Effects of increasing or decreasing alveolar ventilation on alveolar partial pressures in a person having a constant metabolic rate (cellular oxygen consumption and carbon dioxide production). Note that alveolar P_{O_2} approaches zero when alveolar ventilation is about 1 L/min. At this point all the oxygen entering the alveoli crosses into the blood, leaving virtually no oxygen in the alveoli.

dioxide production while simultaneously increasing alveolar ventilation in an exact proportion. The result is that the gas pressures remain unchanged. This is the situation in modest exercise.

This last example emphasizes that, at any particular atmospheric P_{O_2}, it is the *ratio* of oxygen consumption to alveolar ventilation (that is, O_2 consumption/alveolar ventilation) that determines alveolar P_{O_2}—the *higher* the ratio, the *lower* the alveolar P_{O_2}. Alveolar P_{CO_2} is also determined by the ratio of carbon dioxide production to alveolar ventilation (that is, CO_2 production/alveolar ventilation); the *higher* the ratio, the *higher* the alveolar P_{CO_2}.

Two terms that denote the relationship between alveolar ventilation and metabolism can now be defined. For reasons that need not concern us here, these definitions are in terms of carbon dioxide rather than oxygen. **Hypoventilation** exists when there is an *increase in the ratio* of CO_2 production to alveolar ventilation. In other words, a person is said to be hypoventilating if his alveolar ventilation cannot keep pace with his carbon dioxide production. The result is that alveolar P_{CO_2} increases. **Hyperventilation** exists when there is a *decrease in the ratio* of CO_2 production to alveolar ventilation, that is, when alveolar ventilation is actually too great for the amount of carbon dioxide being produced. The result is that alveolar P_{CO_2} decreases.

Alveolar-Blood Gas Exchange

The blood that enters the pulmonary capillaries is, of course, systemic venous blood pumped to the lungs via the pulmonary arteries. Having come from the tissues, it has a high P_{CO_2} (46 mmHg in a normal person at rest) and a low P_{O_2} (40 mmHg) (Table 15-7). The differences in the partial pressures of oxygen and carbon dioxide on the two sides of the alveolar-capillary membrane result in the net diffusion of oxygen from alveoli to blood and of carbon dioxide from blood to alveoli. As this diffusion occurs, the capillary blood P_{O_2} rises and its P_{CO_2} falls. The net diffusion of these gases ceases when the capillary partial pressures become essentially equal to those in the alveoli.

In a normal person, the rates at which oxygen and carbon dioxide diffuse are so rapid and the blood flow through the capillaries so slow that complete equilibrium is reached well before the end of the capillaries (Figure 15-19). Only during the most strenuous exercise, when blood flows through the lung capillaries very rapidly, is there insufficient time for complete equilibration.

Thus, the blood that leaves the pulmonary capillaries to return to the heart and be pumped into the systemic arteries has essentially the same P_{O_2} and P_{CO_2} as alveolar air. (They are not exactly the same, for reasons given later.) Accordingly, the factors described in the previous section—atmospheric P_{O_2}, cellular oxygen consumption and carbon dioxide production, and alveolar ventilation—determine the alveolar gas pressures, which then determine the systemic arterial gas pressures.

Given that diffusion between alveoli and pulmonary capillaries normally achieves complete equilibrium, the more capillaries participating in this process, the more total oxygen and carbon dioxide can be exchanged. Many of the pulmonary capillaries are normally closed at rest. During exercise, these capillaries open and receive blood, thereby enhancing gas exchange. The mechanism by which this occurs is a simple physical one; the pulmonary circulation at rest is at such a low pressure that the pressure in many capillaries is inadequate to keep them open, but the increased cardiac output of exercise raises pulmonary vascular pressures, which opens these capillaries.

The diffusion of gases between alveoli and capillaries may be impaired in a number of ways, resulting in inade-

TABLE 15-7 NORMAL GAS PRESSURES IN SYSTEMIC BLOOD

	Venous	**Arterial**	**Alveoli**
P_{O_2}	40 mmHg	100 mmHg°	105 mmHg°
P_{CO_2}	46 mmHg	40 mmHg	40 mmHg

°The reason that the arterial P_{O_2} and alveolar P_{O_2} are not exactly the same is described later in the text.

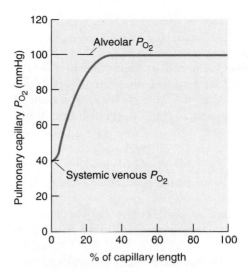

FIGURE 15-19

Complete equilibration of blood P_{O_2} with alveolar P_{O_2} along the length of the pulmonary capillaries.

quate oxygen diffusion into the blood, particularly during exercise when the time for equilibration is reduced. For one thing, the surface area of the alveoli in contact with pulmonary capillaries may be decreased. In lung infections or pulmonary edema, for example, some of the alveoli may become filled with fluid. Diffusion may also be impaired if the alveolar walls become thickened, as for example in the disease (of unknown cause) called **diffuse interstitial fibrosis.** Very importantly, diffusion problems in the lung are restricted to oxygen and do not affect elimination of carbon dioxide, which is much more diffusible than oxygen.

Matching of Ventilation and Blood Flow in Alveoli

The major disease-induced cause of inadequate oxygen movement between alveoli and pulmonary capillary blood is mismatching of the air supply and blood supply in individual alveoli.

The lungs are composed of approximately 300 million discrete alveoli, each capable of receiving carbon dioxide from, and supplying oxygen to, the pulmonary capillary blood. To be most efficient, the right proportion of alveolar air flow (ventilation) and capillary blood flow (perfusion) should be available to each alveolus. Any mismatching is termed **ventilation-perfusion inequality.**

Even in normal persons there are factors, the most important of which is gravity, that cause ventilation and perfusion to be somewhat out of proportion to each other in parts of the lung. In disease states, regional changes in lung compliance, airway resistance, and vascular resistance can cause marked ventilation-perfusion inequalities. The extremes of this phenomenon are easy to visualize: (1) There may be ventilated alveoli with no blood supply at all (as defined earlier, this is alveolar dead space), or

(2) there may be blood flowing through areas of lung that have no ventilation (this is termed a **shunt**). But the inequality need not be all-or-none to be quite significant.

A striking example of ventilation-perfusion inequality is provided by emphysema. First, because of the destruction of lung tissue in this disease, as well as the obstruction of airways, some areas of lung may receive large amounts of air while others receive little or none. Second, there is also a maldistribution of blood flow because capillaries are lost when the alveolar walls are destroyed.

What is the effect of ventilation-perfusion inequalities on gas exchange? The major effect is to lower the P_{O_2} of systemic arterial blood. Indeed, there is enough ventilation-perfusion inequality in normal people to cause the arterial P_{O_2} to be about 5 mmHg less than it would otherwise be. (This is the major explanation of the fact, given earlier, that the P_{O_2} of systemic arterial blood is normally 5 mmHg less than that of average alveolar air.)

Carbon dioxide elimination is also impaired by ventilation-perfusion inequality but, for complex reasons, not to the same degree as oxygen uptake. Nevertheless, severe ventilation-perfusion inequalities in disease can lead to some elevation of arterial P_{CO_2}.

There are several local homeostatic responses within the lungs to minimize the mismatching of ventilation and blood flow. One of the most important operates on the blood vessels to alter blood-flow distribution. If an alveolus is receiving too little air relative to its blood supply, the P_{O_2} in the alveolus and its surrounding area will be low. This decreased P_{O_2} causes vasoconstriction of the small pulmonary blood vessels. (Note that this local effect of oxygen on *pulmonary* blood vessels is precisely the opposite of that exerted on *systemic* arterioles.) The net effect is to supply less blood to poorly ventilated areas and more blood to well-ventilated areas.

Gas Exchange in the Tissues

As the systemic arterial blood enters capillaries throughout the body, it is separated from the interstitial fluid by only the thin capillary wall, which is highly permeable to both oxygen and carbon dioxide. The interstitial fluid in turn is separated from intracellular fluid by cells' plasma membranes, which are also quite permeable to oxygen and carbon dioxide. Metabolic reactions occurring within cells are constantly consuming oxygen and producing carbon dioxide. Therefore, as shown in Figure 15-17, intracellular P_{O_2} is lower and P_{CO_2} higher than in blood. As a result, there is a net diffusion of oxygen from blood into cells and a net diffusion of carbon dioxide from cells into blood. In this manner, as blood flows through systemic capillaries, its P_{O_2} decreases and its P_{CO_2} increases. This accounts for the systemic venous blood values shown in Figure 15-17 and Table 15-7.

The mechanisms that enhance diffusion of oxygen and

carbon dioxide between cells and blood when a tissue increases its metabolic activity were discussed in Chapter 14.

In summary, the supply of new oxygen to the alveoli and the consumption of oxygen in the cells create P_{O_2} gradients that produce net diffusion of oxygen from alveoli to blood in the lungs and from blood to cells in the rest of the body. Conversely, the production of carbon dioxide by cells and its elimination from the alveoli via expiration create P_{CO_2} gradients that produce net diffusion of carbon dioxide from cells to blood in the rest of the body and from blood to alveoli in the lungs.

TRANSPORT OF OXYGEN IN BLOOD

Table 15-8 summarizes the oxygen content of systemic arterial blood (we shall henceforth refer to systemic arterial blood simply as arterial blood). Each liter normally contains the number of oxygen molecules equivalent to 200 ml of pure gaseous oxygen at atmospheric pressure. The oxygen is present in two forms: (1) dissolved in the plasma and erythrocyte water, and (2) reversibly combined with hemoglobin molecules.

The amount of oxygen dissolved in blood is directly proportional to the P_{O_2} of the blood. Because oxygen is relatively insoluble in water, only 3 ml can be dissolved in 1 L of blood at the normal arterial P_{O_2} of 100 mmHg. The other 197 ml of oxygen in a liter of arterial blood, more than 98 percent of the oxygen content in the liter, is carried in the erythrocytes reversibly bound to hemoglobin.

As described in Chapter 14, hemoglobin is a protein composed of four polypeptide chains, each of which contains a single atom of iron. It is the iron atom to which a molecule of oxygen binds. Thus, each hemoglobin molecule can bind four molecules of oxygen. However, for simplicity, the equation for the reaction between oxygen and hemoglobin is usually written in terms of a single polypeptide-heme chain of a hemoglobin molecule:

$$O_2 + Hb \rightleftharpoons HbO_2 \qquad (15\text{-}1)$$

Thus this chain can exist in one of two forms—**deoxyhemoglobin** (**Hb**) and **oxyhemoglobin** (**HbO$_2$**). In a blood sample containing many hemoglobin molecules, the fraction of all the hemoglobin in the form of oxyhemoglobin is expressed as the **percent hemoglobin saturation**:

$$\text{Percent saturation} = \frac{\text{amount of } O_2 \text{ on Hb}}{\text{maximal possible amount}} \times 100$$

For example, if 40 percent of all the hemoglobin in a blood sample is oxyhemoglobin, the sample is said to be 40 percent saturated.

What factors determine the percent hemoglobin saturation? By far the most important is the blood P_{O_2}. Thus, the P_{O_2} determines not only the concentration of oxygen dissolved in the blood but also the amount that binds to hemoglobin. In this regard one more point deserves strong emphasis: The total amount of oxygen carried by hemoglobin in blood depends not only on the percent saturation of hemoglobin but also on how much hemoglobin is in each liter of blood. For example, if a person's blood contained only half as much hemoglobin per liter as normal, then at any given P_{O_2} the oxygen content of the blood would be only half as much. Thus, in the equation above, the denominator—"maximal possible amount"—is determined by the concentration of hemoglobin and is called the **oxygen-carrying capacity** of the blood.

Effect of P_{O_2} on Hemoglobin Saturation

From inspection of Equation 15-1 and the law of mass action, one can see that raising the blood P_{O_2} should increase the combination of oxygen with hemoglobin. The quantitative relationship between these variables is shown in Figure 15-20, which is called an **oxygen-hemoglobin dissociation curve**. (The term "dissociate" means "to separate," in this case oxygen from hemoglobin; it could just as well have been called an oxygen hemoglobin association curve.) The curve is S-shaped because, as stated earlier, each hemoglobin molecule contains four subunits; each subunit can combine with one molecule of oxygen, and the reactions of the four subunits occur sequentially, with each combination facilitating the next one. This is an example of cooperativity, as described in Chapter 4. Note that the curve has a steep slope between 10 and 60 mmHg P_{O_2} and a relatively flat portion (or plateau) between 70 and 100 mmHg P_{O_2}. Thus, the extent to which hemoglobin combines with oxygen increases very rapidly from 10 to 60 mmHg, so that at a P_{O_2} of 60 mmHg, 90 percent of the total hemoglobin is combined with oxygen. From this point on, a further increase in P_{O_2} produces only a small increase in oxygen binding.

TABLE 15-8   OXYGEN CONTENT OF SYSTEMIC ARTERIAL BLOOD AT SEA LEVEL

1 liter (L) arterial blood contains

3 ml	O_2 physically dissolved (1.5%)
197 ml	O_2 bound to hemoglobin (98.5%)
Total 200 ml	O_2

Cardiac output = 5 L/min

O_2 carried to tissues/min = 5 L/min × 200 ml O_2/L
= 1000 ml O_2/min

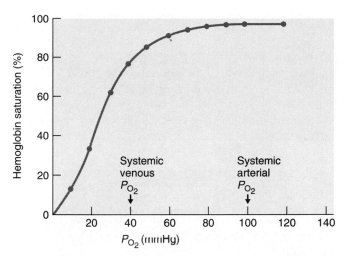

FIGURE 15-20

Oxygen-hemoglobin dissociation curve. This curve applies to blood at 37°C and a normal arterial hydrogen-ion concentration. At any given blood hemoglobin concentration, the vertical axis could also have plotted oxygen content, in milliliters of oxygen. At 100 percent saturation, the amount of hemoglobin in normal blood carries 200 ml of oxygen. (*Adapted from Comroe.*)

The importance of this plateau at higher P_{O_2} values is as follows. Many situations, including high altitude and cardiac or pulmonary disease, are characterized by a moderate reduction in alveolar and therefore arterial P_{O_2}. Even if the P_{O_2} fell from the normal value of 100 to 60 mmHg, the total quantity of oxygen carried by hemoglobin would decrease by only 10 percent since hemoglobin saturation is still close to 90 percent at a P_{O_2} of 60 mmHg. The plateau therefore provides an excellent safety factor in the supply of oxygen to the tissues.

The plateau also explains another fact: In a normal person at sea level, raising the alveolar (and therefore the arterial) P_{O_2} either by hyperventilating or by breathing 100 percent oxygen adds very little additional oxygen to the blood. A small additional amount dissolves, but because hemoglobin is already almost completely saturated with oxygen at the normal arterial P_{O_2} of 100 mmHg, it simply cannot pick up any more oxygen when the P_{O_2} is elevated beyond this point. (This applies only to normal people at sea level. If the person initially has a low arterial P_{O_2} because of lung disease or high altitude, then there would be a great deal of deoxyhemoglobin initially present in the arterial blood. Therefore, raising the alveolar and thereby the arterial P_{O_2} would result in significantly more oxygen carriage.)

We now retrace our steps and reconsider the movement of oxygen across the various membranes, this time including hemoglobin in our analysis. It is essential to recognize that the oxygen bound to hemoglobin does *not* contribute directly to the P_{O_2} of the blood. Only dissolved oxygen does so. Therefore, oxygen diffusion is governed only by the dissolved portion, a fact that permitted us to ignore hemoglobin in discussing transmembrane partial pressure gradients. However, the presence of hemoglobin plays a critical role in determining the *total amount* of oxygen that will diffuse, as illustrated by a simple example (Figure 15-21).

Two solutions separated by a semipermeable membrane contain equal quantities of oxygen, the gas pressures are equal, and no net diffusion occurs. Addition of hemoglobin to compartment B destroys this equilibrium because much of the oxygen combines with hemoglobin. Despite the fact that the total quantity of oxygen in compartment B is still the same, the number of dissolved oxygen molecules has decreased. Therefore, the P_{O_2} of compartment B is less than that of A, and so net diffusion of oxygen occurs from A to B. At the new equilibrium, the oxygen pressures are once again equal, but almost all the oxygen is in compartment B and is combined with hemoglobin.

Let us now apply this analysis to capillaries of the lungs and tissues (Figure 15-22). The plasma and erythrocytes entering the lungs have a P_{O_2} of 40 mmHg. As we can see from Figure 15-20, hemoglobin saturation at this P_{O_2} is 75 percent. Oxygen then diffuses from the alveoli, because of its higher P_{O_2} (105 mmHg), into the plasma. This increases plasma P_{O_2} and induces diffusion of oxygen into the erythrocytes, elevating erythrocyte P_{O_2} and causing increased combination of oxygen and hemoglobin. The vast prepon-

FIGURE 15-21

Effect of added hemoglobin on oxygen distribution between two compartments containing a fixed number of oxygen molecules and separated by a semipermeable membrane. At the new equilibrium, the P_{O_2} values are again equal to each other but lower than before the hemoglobin was added. However, the total oxygen, in other words, that dissolved plus that combined with hemoglobin, is now much higher on the right side of the membrane. (*Adapted from Comroe.*)

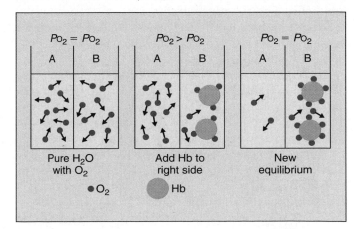

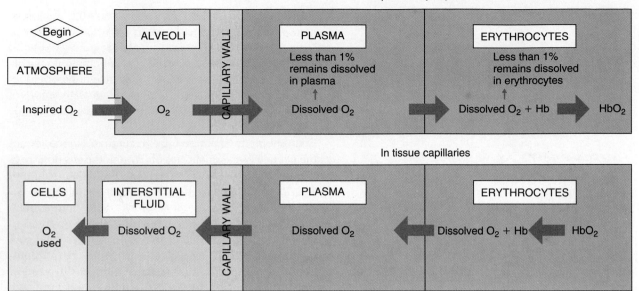

FIGURE 15-22

Oxygen movement in the lungs and tissues. Movement of inspired air into the alveoli is by bulk flow; all movement across membranes is by diffusion.

derance of the oxygen diffusing into the blood from the alveoli does not remain dissolved but combines with hemoglobin. Therefore, the blood P_{O_2} normally remains less than the alveolar P_{O_2} until hemoglobin is virtually 100 percent saturated. Thus the diffusion gradient favoring oxygen movement into the blood is maintained despite the very large transfer of oxygen.

In the tissue capillaries, the procedure is reversed: As the blood enters the capillaries, plasma P_{O_2} is greater than interstitial fluid P_{O_2}, and net oxygen diffusion occurs out of the capillary from the plasma. Plasma P_{O_2} is now lower than erythrocyte P_{O_2}, and oxygen diffuses out of the erythrocyte into the plasma. The lowering of erythrocyte P_{O_2} causes the dissociation of some of the oxygen from hemoglobin, thereby liberating oxygen. Simultaneously, the oxygen that had diffused into the interstitial fluid is moving into cells along the concentration gradient generated by cellular utilization of oxygen. The net result is a transfer of large quantities of oxygen from hemoglobin into cells purely by diffusion.

To repeat, in most tissues under resting conditions, hemoglobin is still 75 percent saturated as the blood leaves the tissue capillaries. This fact underlies an important automatic mechanism by which cells can obtain more oxygen whenever they increase their activity. An exercising muscle consumes more oxygen, thereby lowering its tissue P_{O_2}. This increases the blood-to-tissue P_{O_2} gradient and hence the diffusion of oxygen from blood to cell. In turn, the resulting reduction in erythrocyte P_{O_2} causes additional dissociation of hemoglobin and oxygen. Because of these

gradient changes, an exercising muscle can extract almost all the oxygen from its blood supply. This process is so effective because it takes place in the steep portion of the oxygen-hemoglobin dissociation curve. Of course, an increased blood flow to the muscles also contributes greatly to the increased oxygen supply.

Effects of Blood P_{CO_2}, H^+ Concentration, Temperature, and DPG Concentration on Hemoglobin Saturation

At any given P_{O_2}, a variety of other factors influence the degree of hemoglobin saturation: blood P_{CO_2}, H^+ concentration, temperature, and the concentration of a substance—DPG—produced by the erythrocytes. As illustrated in Figure 15-23, an increase in any of these factors causes the dissociation curve to shift to the right, which means that at any given P_{O_2} hemoglobin has less affinity for oxygen. In contrast, a decrease in any of these factors causes the dissociation curve to shift to the left, which means that, at any given P_{O_2}, hemoglobin has a greater affinity for oxygen.

The effects of increased P_{CO_2}, H^+ concentration, and temperature are continuously exerted on the blood in tissue capillaries, because each of these factors is higher in tissue-capillary blood than in arterial blood. The P_{CO_2} is increased because of the carbon dioxide entering the blood from the tissues. For reasons to be described later, the H^+ concentration is elevated because of the elevated P_{CO_2}. The temperature is increased because of the heat produced by tissue metabolism. Therefore, hemoglobin exposed to this elevated blood P_{CO_2}, H^+ concentration,

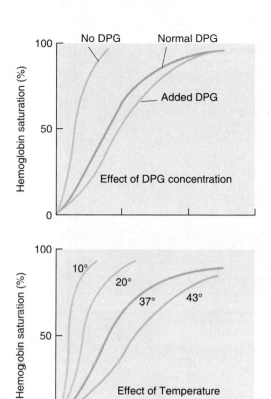

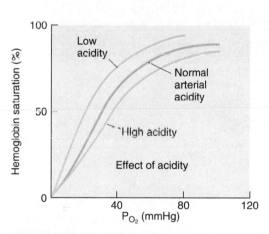

FIGURE 15-23

Effects of DPG concentration, temperature, and acidity on the relationship between P_{O_2} and hemoglobin saturation. (*Adapted from Comroe.*)

What is the mechanism by which these factors influence hemoglobin's affinity for oxygen? Carbon dioxide and hydrogen ions do so by combining with the hemoglobin and altering its molecular configuration. Thus, these effects are a form of allosteric modulation, described in Chapter 4. An elevated temperature also decreases hemoglobin's affinity for oxygen by altering its molecular configuration.

Erythrocytes contain large quantities of the substance **2,3-diphosphoglycerate (DPG)**, which is present in only trace amounts in other mammalian cells. DPG, which is produced by the erythrocytes during glycolysis, binds reversibly with hemoglobin, causing it to have a lower affinity for oxygen (Figure 15-23). The net result is that whenever DPG levels are increased, there is enhanced unloading of oxygen from hemoglobin as blood flows through the tissues. Such an increase in DPG concentration is triggered by a variety of conditions associated with inadequate oxygen supply to the tissues and helps to maintain oxygen delivery. Examples include anemia and exposure to high altitude.

TRANSPORT OF CARBON DIOXIDE IN BLOOD

As noted earlier, carbon dioxide is much more soluble in water than is oxygen, and so more dissolved carbon dioxide than dissolved oxygen is carried in blood. Even so, only a small amount of blood carbon dioxide is transported in this way.

Some of the carbon dioxide molecules, after dissolving in the blood, can also react reversibly with the amino groups of proteins, particularly hemoglobin, to form **carbamino compounds**:

$$RNH_2 + CO_2 \rightleftharpoons RNHCOOH$$

For simplicity, this reaction with hemoglobin is often written as

$$CO_2 + Hb \rightleftharpoons HbCO_2 \qquad (15\text{-}2)$$

But most of the carbon dioxide molecules, after dissolving in the blood, are converted to bicarbonate:

$$CO_2 + H_2O \underset{\text{Carbonic anhydrase}}{\rightleftharpoons} \underset{\text{Carbonic acid}}{H_2CO_3} \rightleftharpoons \underset{\text{Bicarbonate}}{HCO_3^- + H^+}$$

$$(15\text{-}3)$$

The first reaction in Equation 15-3 is rate-limiting and is catalyzed by the enzyme **carbonic anhydrase**, which is present in the erythrocytes but not in the plasma. Car-

and temperature as it passes through the tissue capillaries has its affinity for oxygen decreased and therefore it gives up even more oxygen than it would have if the decreased tissue-capillary P_{O_2} had been the only operating factor.

The more active a tissue is, the greater its P_{CO_2}, H^+ concentration, and temperature. This causes hemoglobin to release more oxygen, at any given P_{O_2}, during passage through the tissue's capillaries, thereby providing the more active cells with additional oxygen.

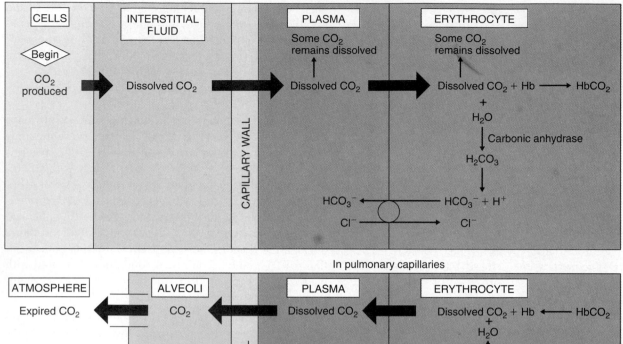

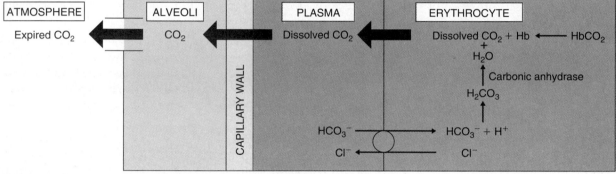

FIGURE 15-24

Summary of CO_2 movement. All movement across membranes is by diffusion. Note that most of the CO_2 entering the blood in the tissues ultimately is converted to HCO_3^-. This occurs almost entirely in the erythrocytes because the carbonic anhydrase is located there, but most of the HCO_3^- then moves out of the erythrocytes into the plasma in exchange for chloride ions (the "chloride shift"). See Figure 15-25 for the fate of the hydrogen ions generated in the erythrocytes.

bonic acid dissociates into a bicarbonate ion and a hydrogen very rapidly without any enzyme assistance.

Because carbon dioxide undergoes these various reactions in blood, it is customary to add up the amounts of dissolved carbon dioxide, bicarbonate, and carbon dioxide in carbamino form and call this sum the **total blood carbon dioxide**.

Metabolism, in a resting person, generates about 200 ml of carbon dioxide per minute. When arterial blood flows through tissue capillaries, this volume of carbon dioxide diffuses from the tissues into the blood. Let us review, with the addition of a few more important facts, the reactions that this carbon dioxide undergoes after it enters the blood (Figure 15-24).

1. A small fraction (10 percent) of the carbon dioxide entering the blood remains physically dissolved in the plasma and erythrocytes.

2. Another fraction (30 percent) reacts directly with hemoglobin to form the carbamino compound, $HbCO_2$. This process is facilitated because much of the oxyhemoglobin becomes deoxyhemoglobin as blood flows through the tissues, and deoxyhemoglobin reacts more readily with carbon dioxide than does oxyhemoglobin.

3. Most of the carbon dioxide (60 percent) is converted to bicarbonate and hydrogen ions (Equation 15-3).[6] This occurs mainly in the erythrocytes because they contain the carbonic anhydrase required for the reactions to go

---

[6]The 60 percent figure might seem to conflict with the fact that bicarbonate constitutes 90 percent of the carbon dioxide content of arterial blood. There is no conflict, however. The *new* carbon dioxide added to blood in tissue capillaries does not distribute among carbamino and bicarbonate in the same proportions as those already present in *arterial blood*. The reason is that the concentration of deoxyhemoglobin is much higher in the *tissue capillary blood* than arterial blood and is available for binding carbon dioxide to form carbamino.

quickly. Once formed, most of the bicarbonate moves out of the erythrocytes into the plasma via a transporter that exchanges one bicarbonate for one chloride ion (this is called the "chloride shift"). The reactions described in Equation 15-3 also explain why, as mentioned earlier, the H^+ concentration in tissue capillary blood and systemic venous blood is higher than that of the arterial blood and increases as metabolic activity increases. The fate of these hydrogen ions will be discussed in the next section.

Just the opposite events occur as systemic venous blood flows through the lung capillaries (Figure 15-24). Because the blood P_{CO_2} is higher than alveolar P_{CO_2}, a net diffusion of CO_2 from blood into alveoli occurs. This loss of carbon dioxide from the blood lowers the blood P_{CO_2} and drives these reactions to the left: HCO_3^- and H^+ combine to give H_2CO_3, which then dissociates to CO_2 and H_2O. Similarly, $HbCO_2$ generates Hb and free CO_2. Normally, as fast as this CO_2 is generated from HCO_3^- and H^+ and from $HbCO_2$, it diffuses into the alveoli. In this manner, all the CO_2 delivered into the blood in the tissues now is delivered into the alveoli, from which it is eliminated from the body during expiration.

TRANSPORT OF HYDROGEN IONS BETWEEN TISSUES AND LUNGS

To repeat, as blood flows through the tissues, a fraction of oxyhemoglobin loses its oxygen to become deoxyhemoglobin, while simultaneously a large quantity of carbon dioxide enters the blood and undergoes the reactions that generate bicarbonate and hydrogen ions. What happens to these hydrogen ions? Deoxyhemoglobin has a much greater affinity for H^+ than does oxyhemoglobin, and so it binds (buffers) most of the hydrogen ions (Figure 15-25). Indeed, deoxyhemoglobin is often abbreviated HbH rather than Hb to denote its binding of H^+. In effect, the reaction is $HbO_2 + H^+ = HbH + O_2$.

In this manner only a small number of the hydrogen ions generated in the blood remain free. This explains why the acidity of venous blood is only slightly greater than that of arterial blood. The pH of arterial blood is 7.4, and that of venous blood is 7.36. (Remember than pH goes down as H^+ concentration goes up.) Thus, hemoglobin's ability to buffer hydrogen ions is crucial for preventing large and potentially damaging changes in blood acidity.

As the venous blood passes through the lungs, all these reactions are reversed. Deoxyhemoglobin becomes converted to oxyhemoglobin and, in the process, releases the hydrogen ions it had picked up in the tissues. The hydrogen ions react with bicarbonate to give carbon dioxide and water, and the carbon dioxide diffuses into the alveoli to

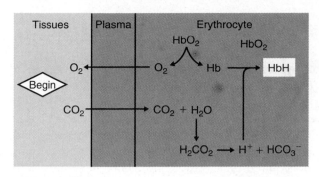

FIGURE 15-25
Binding of hydrogen ions by hemoglobin as blood flows through tissue capillaries. This reaction is facilitated because deoxyhemoglobin, formed as oxygen comes off hemoglobin, has a greater affinity for hydrogen ions than does oxyhemoglobin. For this reason, Hb and HbH are both abbreviations for deoxyhemoglobin.

be expired. Normally all the hydrogen ions that are generated from the reaction of carbon dioxide and water in the tissue capillaries recombine with bicarbonate to form carbon dioxide and water in the pulmonary capillaries. Therefore, none of these hydrogen ions appear in the arterial blood.

But what if the person is hypoventilating or has a lung disease that prevents normal elimination of carbon dioxide? Not only would arterial P_{CO_2} rise as a result but so would arterial H^+ concentration. Increased arterial H^+ concentration due to carbon dioxide retention is termed **respiratory acidosis**. Conversely, hyperventilation would lower the arterial values of both P_{CO_2} and H^+ concentration—a **respiratory alkalosis**.

In the course of describing the transport of oxygen, carbon dioxide, and H^+ in blood, we have presented multiple factors that influence the binding of these substances by hemoglobin. They are all summarized in Table 15-9.

TABLE 15-9 EFFECTS OF VARIOUS FACTORS ON HEMOGLOBIN

The affinity of hemoglobin for oxygen is decreased by:

1. Increased hydrogen-ion concentration
2. Increased P_{CO_2}
3. Increased temperature
4. Increased DPG concentration

The affinity of hemoglobin for both hydrogen ions and carbon dioxide is decreased by increased P_{O_2}.

CONTROL OF RESPIRATION

Neural Generation of Rhythmical Breathing

Like cardiac muscle, the inspiratory muscles normally contract rhythmically, that is, alternately contract and relax. The origins of these contractions, however, are quite different. Certain cardiac-muscle cells have automaticity, and the nerves to the heart merely alter this inherent rate but are not required for cardiac contraction. In contrast, the diaphragm and intercostal muscles consist of skeletal muscle, which cannot contract unless stimulated to do so by nerves. Thus, breathing depends entirely upon cyclical respiratory muscle excitation by the motor nerves to the diaphragm and the intercostal muscles. Destruction of these nerves or the areas from which they originate, as in *poliomyelitis*, for example, results in paralysis of the respiratory muscles and death, unless some form of artificial respiration can be instituted.

Inspiration is initiated by a burst of action potentials in the nerves to the inspiratory muscles. Then the action potentials cease, the inspiratory muscles relax, and expiration occurs as the elastic lungs recoil. In situations when expiration is facilitated by contraction of expiratory muscles, the nerves to these muscles, which were quiescent during inspiration, begin firing during expiration.

By what mechanism are nerve impulses to the respiratory muscles alternately increased and decreased? Automatic control of this neural activity resides primarily in neurons in the medulla oblongata, the same area of brain that contains the major cardiovascular control centers. (For the rest of this chapter we shall refer to the medulla oblongata simply as the medulla.) In several areas of the medulla, clusters of neurons discharge in synchrony with inspiration and cease discharging during expiration. These neurons are called **medullary inspiratory neurons**. They provide, through either direct or interneuronal connections, the rhythmical input to the motor neurons innervating the inspiratory muscles.

Just how the brain generates alternating cycles of firing and quiescence in the medullary inspiratory neurons remains unclear. It is possible that the inspiratory neurons, or neurons that synapse upon them, are pacemaker neurons, that is, that they have inherent automaticity and rhythmicity. However, most experts believe that even though such pacemakers might play a role, a much more complex model is required to explain the on-off cycle of the neuronal output.

The medullary inspiratory neurons also receive a rich synaptic input from neurons in various areas of the pons, the part of the brainstem just above the medulla. This input modulates the output of the medullary inspiratory neurons and may help terminate inspiration by inhibiting them.

Another cutoff signal for inspiration comes from **pulmonary stretch receptors**, which lie in the airway smooth-muscle layer and are activated by lung inflation. Action potentials in the afferent nerve fibers from them travel to the brain and inhibit the medullary inspiratory neurons. This is known as the Hering-Breuer inflation reflex. Thus, feedback from the lungs helps to terminate inspiration. However, the threshold of these receptors in human beings is very high, and this pulmonary stretch receptor reflex plays a role in setting respiratory rhythm only under conditions of very large tidal volumes, as in exercise.

One last point about the medullary inspiratory neurons should be made: They are quite sensitive to depression by drugs, especially barbiturates and morphine, and death from an overdose of these drugs is often secondary to a cessation of ventilation.

Control of Ventilation by P_{O_2}, P_{CO_2}, and H^+ Concentration

Respiratory rate and tidal volume are not fixed but can be increased or decreased over a wide range. For simplicity, we shall describe the control of total ventilation without discussing whether rate or depth makes the greater contribution to the change.

There are many inputs to the medullary inspiratory neurons, but the most important for the involuntary control of ventilation are from peripheral chemoreceptors and central chemoreceptors.

The **peripheral chemoreceptors**, located high in the neck at the bifurcation of the common carotid arteries and in the thorax on the arch of the aorta (Figure 15-26), are called the **carotid** and **aortic bodies.** In both locations they are quite close to, but distinct from, the arterial baroreceptors described in Chapter 14. Of the two groups of peripheral chemoreceptors, the carotid bodies are by far the more important. They are composed of epithelium-like cells and neuron terminals in intimate contact with the arterial blood. Afferent nerve fibers arising from these terminals pass to the brainstem, where they influence ultimately the medullary inspiratory neurons. The peripheral chemoreceptors are sensitive to changes in the arterial P_{O_2}, H^+ concentration, and P_{CO_2}.

The **central chemoreceptors** are located in the medulla and provide synaptic input to the medullary inspiratory neurons. They respond to changes in the H^+ concentration of the brain's extracellular fluid. As we shall see, such changes occur particularly when the blood P_{CO_2} is altered.

The stimuli for the central and peripheral chemoreceptors are summarized in Table 15-10.

Control by P_{O_2}. Figure 15-27 illustrates an experiment in which healthy subjects breath low-P_{O_2} gas mixtures for several minutes. The experiment is performed in a way

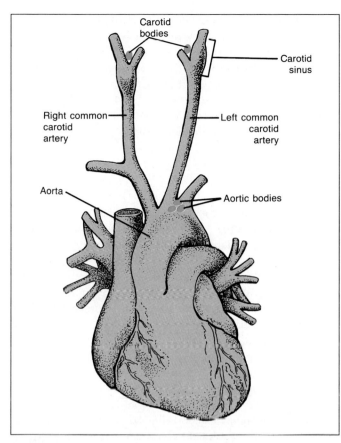

FIGURE 15-26

Location of the carotid and aortic bodies. Note that the carotid body is quite close to the carotid sinus, the major arterial baroreceptor. Both right and left common carotid bifurcations contain a carotid sinus and a carotid body.

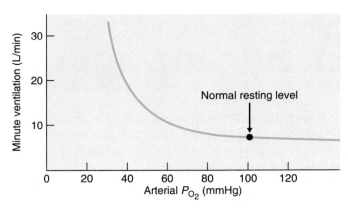

FIGURE 15-27

The effect on ventilation of breathing low-oxygen mixtures. The arterial P_{CO_2} was maintained at 40 mmHg throughout the experiment.

FIGURE 15-28

Sequence of events by which a low arterial P_{O_2} causes hyperventilation, which maintains alveolar (and, hence, arterial) P_{O_2} at a value higher than would exist if the ventilation had remained unchanged.

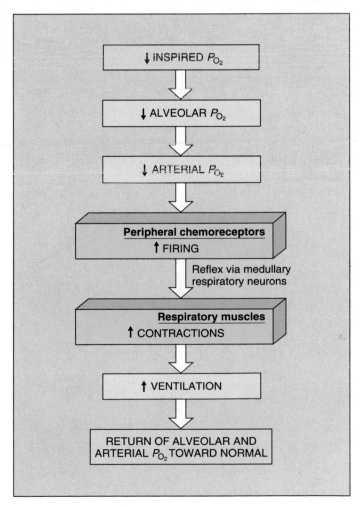

TABLE 15-10   STIMULI FOR THE CENTRAL AND PERIPHERAL CHEMORECEPTORS

Peripheral chemoreceptors—that is, carotid bodies and aortic bodies—respond to changes in the *arterial blood*. They are stimulated by:

1. Decreased P_{O_2}
2. Increased hydrogen-ion concentration
3. Increased P_{CO_2}, mainly via associated changes in hydrogen-ion concentration

Central chemoreceptors—that is, located in the medulla oblongata—respond to changes in the *brain interstitial fluid*. They are stimulated by increased P_{CO_2}, via associated changes in hydrogen-ion concentration. (See Equation 15-3.)

that keeps arterial P_{CO_2} constant so that the pure effects of changing only P_{O_2} can be studied. Little increase in ventilation is observed until the oxygen content of the inspired air is reduced enough to lower arterial P_{O_2} to 60 mmHg. Beyond this point, any further reduction in arterial P_{O_2} causes a marked reflex hyperventilation.

This reflex is mediated by the peripheral chemoreceptors (Figure 15-28). The low arterial P_{O_2} increases the rate at which the receptors discharge, resulting in an increased number of action potentials traveling up the afferent nerve fibers and stimulating the medullary inspiratory neurons. The resulting increase in ventilation provides more oxygen to the alveoli and minimizes the drop in alveolar and arterial P_{O_2} produced by the low-P_{O_2} gas mixture.

It may seem surprising that we are so insensitive to smaller reductions in arterial P_{O_2}, but look again at the oxygen-hemoglobin dissociation curve (Figure 15-20). Total oxygen carriage by the blood is not really reduced very much until the arterial P_{O_2} falls below 60 mmHg. Therefore, increased ventilation would not result in very much more oxygen being added to the blood until that point is reached.

To reiterate, the peripheral chemoreceptors respond to decreases in arterial P_{O_2}, as occurs in lung disease or exposure to high altitude. However, the peripheral chemoreceptors are *not* stimulated in situations in which there are modest reductions in the *oxygen content* of the blood but no change in arterial P_{O_2}. An example of this is anemia, where there is a decrease in the amount of hemoglobin present in the blood (Chapter 14) but no decrease in arterial P_{O_2} because the concentration of dissolved oxygen in the blood is normal. This same analysis holds true when oxygen content is reduced by the presence of carbon monoxide, a gas that has an extremely high affinity for the oxygen binding sites in hemoglobin and reduces the amount of oxygen combined with hemoglobin by competing for these sites. Since carbon monoxide does not affect the amount of oxygen that can dissolve in blood, the arterial P_{O_2} is unaltered, and no increase in peripheral chemoreceptor output occurs.

Control by P_{CO_2} That an increase in arterial P_{CO_2} plays an important role in the control of ventilation can be demonstrated by a simple experiment in which subjects breath air containing variable quantities of carbon dioxide. The presence of carbon dioxide in the inspired air causes an elevation of alveolar P_{CO_2} and thereby an elevation of arterial P_{CO_2}. As can be seen in Figure 15-29, increased P_{CO_2} markedly stimulates ventilation, an increase of 2 to 5 mmHg in alveolar P_{CO_2} causing a 100 percent increase in ventilation.

Thus, unlike the case for lowered P_{O_2}, even the slightest change in arterial P_{CO_2} is associated with a significant reflex change in ventilation. Experiments like this have documented that small changes in arterial P_{CO_2} are resisted by the reflex mechanisms controlling ventilation to a greater degree than are equivalent changes in arterial P_{O_2}. An increase in arterial P_{CO_2} due, say, to lung disease results in stimulation of ventilation to promote the elimination of carbon dioxide. Conversely, a decrease in arterial P_{CO_2} below normal levels removes some of the stimulus for ventilation, thereby reducing ventilation and allowing metabolically produced carbon dioxide to accumulate and return the P_{CO_2} to normal. In this manner, the arterial P_{CO_2} is stabilized at the normal value of 40 mmHg.

The pathways by which changes in the arterial P_{CO_2} result in changes in ventilation include both the peripheral and central chemoreceptors. Before looking at the specific reflexes, we must emphasize that the ability of changes in arterial P_{CO_2} to control ventilation reflexly is largely due to associated changes in H^+ concentration (Equation 15-3).[7]

Figure 15-30 summarizes the pathways by which increased arterial P_{CO_2} stimulates ventilation. For one thing, the peripheral chemoreceptors are stimulated by the increased arterial H^+ concentration resulting from the increased P_{CO_2}. At the same time, because carbon dioxide diffuses rapidly across the membranes separating capillary blood and brain tissue, the increase in arterial P_{CO_2} causes a rapid identical increase in brain extracellular fluid P_{CO_2}. This increased P_{CO_2} increases brain extracellular fluid

FIGURE 15-29

Effects on respiration of increasing arterial P_{CO_2} achieved by adding carbon dioxide to inspired air.

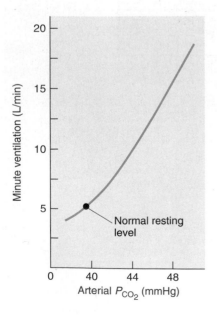

---

[7]An increased P_{CO_2} exerts some direct stimulation of the peripheral chemoreceptors, but this is very small compared to its indirect effects via changes in hydrogen-ion concentration.

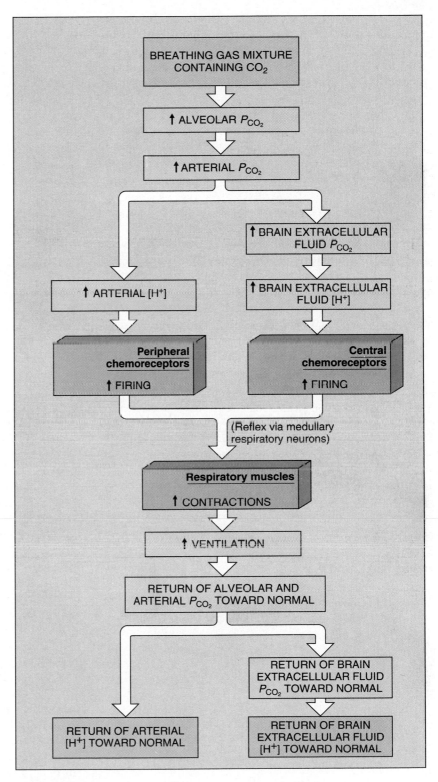

FIGURE 15-30

Pathways by which increased arterial P_{CO_2} stimulates ventilation. Note that the peripheral chemoreceptors are stimulated by an *increase* in H^+ concentration, whereas they are stimulated by a *decrease* in P_{O_2} (Fig. 15-28).

H^+ concentration, which stimulates the central chemoreceptors. Inputs from both the peripheral and central chemoreceptors stimulate the medullary inspiratory neurons to increase ventilation. The end result is a return of arterial and brain extracellular fluid P_{CO_2} and H^+ concentration toward normal.

Of the two sets of receptors involved in this reflex response to elevated P_{CO_2}, the central chemoreceptors are the more important, accounting for about 70 percent of the stimulus to ventilation. Contrast this to the low-oxygen reflex, which is mediated only by the peripheral chemoreceptors.

It should also be noted that the effects of increased P_{CO_2} and decreased P_{O_2} not only exist as independent inputs to the medulla but manifest synergistic interactions as well. Acute ventilatory response to combined low P_{O_2} and high P_{CO_2} is considerably greater than the sum of the individual responses.

Throughout this section, we have described the *stimulatory* effects of carbon dioxide on ventilation via *reflex* input to the medulla, but *very high* levels of carbon dioxide have just the opposite effect and may be lethal. This is because such concentrations of carbon dioxide act *directly* on the medulla to *inhibit* the respiratory neurons by an anesthesia-like effect. Symptoms caused by increased blood P_{CO_2} include severe headaches, restlessness, and dulling or loss of consciousness. The accompanying increased H^+ concentration also causes serious problems.

Control by Changes in Arterial H^+ Concentration Not Due to Altered Carbon Dioxide. We have seen that retention or excessive elimination of carbon dioxide

FIGURE 15-31

Changes in ventilation in response to an elevation of plasma hydrogen-ion concentration, produced by the administration of lactic acid. (*Adapted from Lambertsen.*)

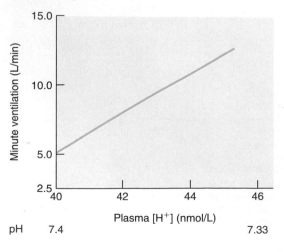

FIGURE 15-32

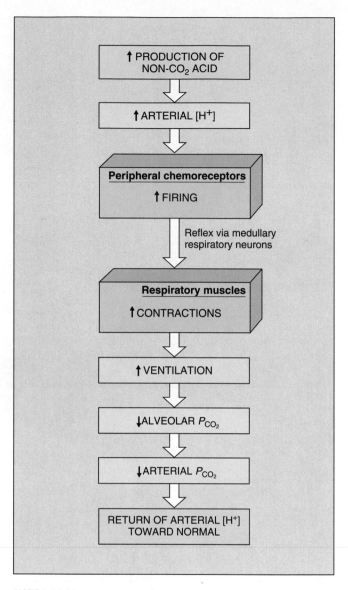

Reflexly induced hyperventilation minimizes the change in arterial hydrogen-ion concentration when acids are produced in excess in the body. Note that under such conditions, arterial P_{CO_2} is reflexly reduced below its normal value.

causes respiratory acidosis and respiratory alkalosis, respectively. There are, however, many normal and pathological situations in which a change in arterial H^+ concentration is due to some cause other than a primary change in P_{CO_2}. These are termed **metabolic acidosis** when H^+ concentration is increased, and **metabolic alkalosis** when it is decreased. In such cases, the peripheral chemoreceptors play the major role in altering ventilation.

For example, increased addition of lactic acid to the blood, as in strenuous exercise, causes hyperventilation almost entirely by stimulation of the peripheral chemoreceptors (Figures 15-31 and 15-32). The central chemoreceptors are only minimally stimulated in this case because brain H^+ concentration is increased to only a small extent, at least early on, by the hydrogen ions generated from the lactic acid. This is because hydrogen ions penetrate the blood-brain barrier very slowly. Contrast this with how easily carbon dioxide penetrates the blood-brain barrier and changes brain H^+ concentration.

The converse of the above situation is also true: When arterial H^+ concentration is lowered by any means other than by a reduction in P_{CO_2} (for example, by loss of hydrogen ions from the stomach in vomiting), ventilation is reflexly depressed because of decreased peripheral chemoreceptor output.

The adaptive value such reflexes have in regulating arterial H^+ concentration should be evident (Figure 15-32). The hyperventilation induced by a metabolic acidosis lowers arterial P_{CO_2}, which lowers arterial H^+ concentration back toward normal. Similarly, hypoventilation induced by a metabolic alkalosis results in an elevated arterial P_{CO_2} and a restoration of H^+ concentration toward normal. Notice that when a change in arterial H^+ concentration due to some acid unrelated to carbon dioxide influences ventilation via the peripheral chemoreceptors, P_{CO_2} is displaced from normal. This is a reflex that regulates arterial H^+ concentration at the expense of changes in arterial P_{CO_2}.

Figure 15-33 summarizes the control of ventilation by P_{O_2}, P_{CO_2}, and H^+ concentration.

Control of Ventilation During Exercise

During exercise, the alveolar ventilation may increase as much as twentyfold. On the basis of our three variables—P_{O_2}, P_{CO_2}, and H^+ concentration—it might seem easy to explain the mechanism that induces this increased ventilation. Unhappily, such is not the case.

Increased P_{CO_2} as the Stimulus? It would seem logical that, as the exercising muscles produce more carbon dioxide, blood P_{CO_2} would increase. This is true, however, only for systemic *venous* blood but not for arterial blood. Therefore, the reflex mechanisms by which increased arterial P_{CO_2} increases ventilation are *not* brought into play.

The reader might well wonder why arterial P_{CO_2} does not increase during exercise. Recall two facts from the section on alveolar gas pressures: (1) Alveolar P_{CO_2} sets arterial P_{CO_2}, and (2) alveolar P_{CO_2} is determined by the *ratio* of carbon dioxide production to alveolar ventilation. During exercise, the alveolar ventilation increases in exact proportion to the increased carbon dioxide production, and so alveolar and therefore arterial P_{CO_2} do not change. Indeed, for reasons described below, in very strenuous exercise the alveolar ventilation increases relatively more

than carbon dioxide production. In other words, the person hyperventilates, and thus alveolar and systemic arterial P_{CO_2} actually decrease (Figure 15-34).

Decreased P_{O_2} as the Stimulus? The story is similar for oxygen: although systemic venous P_{O_2} decreases during exercise, alveolar P_{O_2} and hence systemic arterial P_{O_2} usually remain unchanged. This is because cellular oxygen consumption and alveolar ventilation increase in exact proportion to each other (Figure 15-34).[8]

This is a good place to remind you of an important point made in Chapter 14: In normal individuals, ventilation is not the limiting factor in endurance exercise, cardiac output is. Ventilation can, as we have just seen, increase enough to maintain arterial P_{O_2}.

Increased H^+ Concentration as the Stimulus? Since the arterial P_{CO_2} does not change during moderate exercise and decreases in severe exercise, there is no accumulation of excess H^+ resulting from carbon dioxide accumulation. However, during strenuous exercise, there *is* an increase in arterial H^+ concentration (Figure 15-34), but for quite a different reason, namely, generation and release of lactic acid into the blood. This change in H^+ concentration is responsible, in part, for stimulating the hyperventilation of severe exercise.

We are left with the fact that we do not know what input stimulates ventilation during most exercise. Our "big three"—decreased arterial P_{O_2}, increased arterial P_{CO_2}, and increased arterial H^+ concentration do not occur and, therefore, cannot be the stimuli.

Other Factors. Many receptors in joints and muscles are stimulated by the physical movements that accompany muscle contraction. It is quite likely that afferent pathways from these receptors play a significant role in stimulating respiration during exercise. Thus, the mechanical events of exercise help to coordinate alveolar ventilation with the metabolic requirements of the tissues.

An increase in body temperature also frequently occurs as a result of increased physical activity and contributes to stimulation of alveolar ventilation. Body temperature also increases in many situations other than exercise, and when it does, it stimulates ventilation. Thus, people with fever show increased ventilation.

Epinephrine and norepinephrine are also respiratory stimulants. The increased plasma concentrations of these

---

[8]The hyperventilation of very strenuous exercise *raises* alveolar P_{O_2}, just as it lowers alveolar P_{CO_2}, but for a variety of reasons, the increase in alveolar P_{O_2} is not accompanied by an increase in arterial P_{O_2}. Indeed, especially in highly conditioned athletes, the arterial P_{O_2} may decrease somewhat during strenuous exercise and may also contribute to stimulation of ventilation.

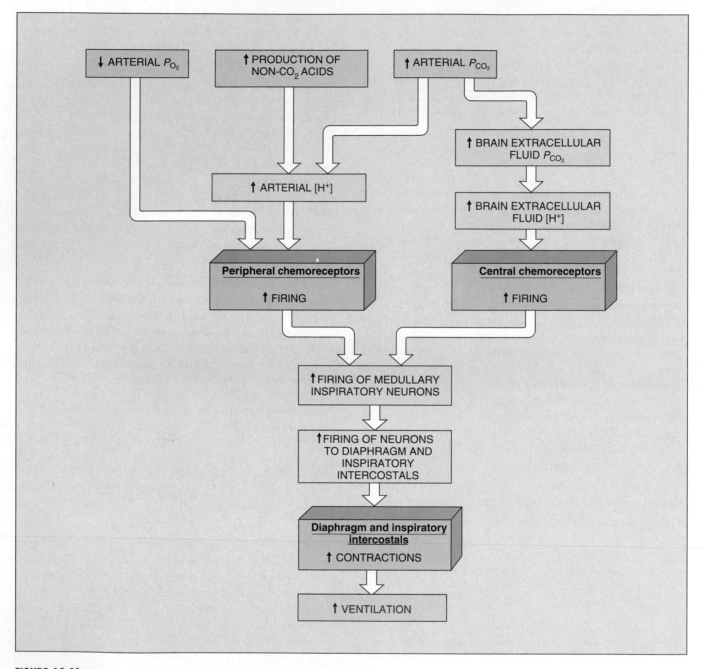

FIGURE 15-33

This is a combination of portions of Figures 15-28, 15-30, and 15-32, in order to summarize the chemical inputs that stimulate ventilation. When arterial P_{O_2} increases or when P_{CO_2} or hydrogen-ion concentration decreases, ventilation is reflexly decreased.

catecholamines with exercise probably contributes to the increased ventilation.[9]

Higher brain centers also influence ventilation during

exercise. Branches come off the axons descending from the brain to motor neurons supplying exercising muscles, and these branches influence the neurons that control the respiratory muscles.

Finally, there may be an important learned component to the ventilatory response to exercise. As shown in Figure 15-35, there is an abrupt increase—within seconds—in ventilation at the onset of exercise and an equally abrupt decrease at the end. Clearly, these changes occur too rap-

[9]Another plasma constituent, the concentration of which increases during exercise, is potassium, because of leakage from the exercising muscles. It is possible, though unproven, that this increased plasma potassium concentration stimulates ventilation, acting via the peripheral chemoreceptors.

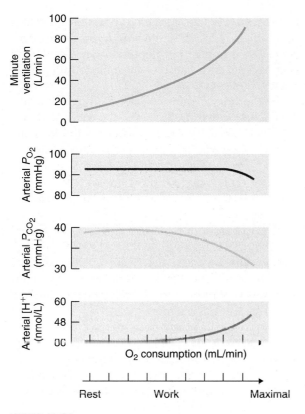

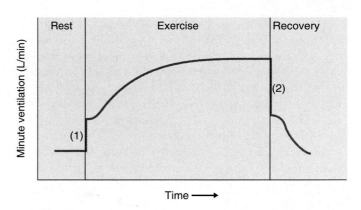

FIGURE 15-35

Ventilation changes during exercise. Note (1) the abrupt increase at the onset of exercise and (2) the equally abrupt but larger decrease at the end of the exercise.

idly to be explained by alteration of chemical constituents of the blood or altered body temperature. They probably represent a conditioned response mediated by neural input to the respiratory centers.

Figure 15-36 summarizes various factors that influence ventilation during exercise.

Other Ventilatory Responses

Protective Reflexes. A group of responses protect the respiratory system against irritant materials. Most familiar are the cough and the sneeze reflexes which originate in receptors located between airway epithelial cells. The re-

FIGURE 15-34

The effect of exercise on ventilation, arterial gas pressures, and hydrogen-ion concentration. (*Adapted from Comroe.*)

FIGURE 15-36

Summary of factors that stimulate ventilation during exercise. The possibility that *oscillatory* changes in P_{O_2}, P_{CO_2}, or H$^+$ concentration occur, in the absence of unchanged levels of these variables, and play a role has been proposed but remains unproven. Presently unknown factors also play important roles.

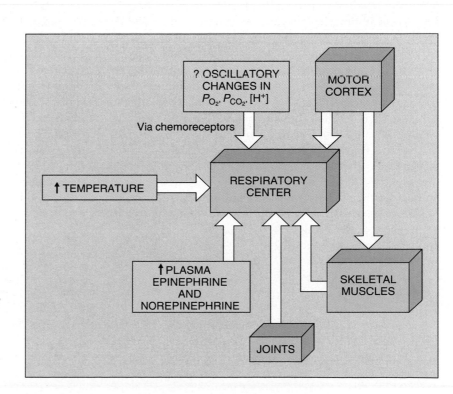

ceptors for the sneeze reflex are in the nose or pharynx, and those for cough are in the trachea. When these receptors are stimulated, the medullary respiratory neurons cause reflexly a deep inspiration and a violent expiration. In this manner, particles can be literally exploded out of the respiratory tract. The cough reflex is inhibited by alcohol, which may contribute to the susceptibility of alcoholics to choking and pneumonia.

Another example of a protective reflex is the immediate cessation of respiration which is frequently triggered when noxious agents are inhaled. Chronic smoking causes a loss of this reflex.

Pain and Emotion. Painful stimuli anywhere in the body can produce reflex stimulation of the respiratory neurons. Emotional states are also often accompanied by marked alterations in respiration, as evidenced by the rapid breathing that characterizes fright, anxiety, and many similar emotions. In addition, movement of air in or out of the lungs is required for such involuntary expressions of emotion as laughing and crying. In such situations, the descending pathways from higher brain centers are the controlling input.

Voluntary Control of Breathing. Although we have discussed in detail the involuntary nature of most respiratory reflexes, it is quite obvious that considerable voluntary control of respiratory movements exists. Voluntary control is accomplished by descending pathways from the cerebral cortex to the motor neurons of the respiratory muscles. This voluntary control of respiration cannot be maintained when the involuntary stimuli, such as an elevated P_{CO_2} or H^+ concentration, become intense. An example is the inability to hold one's breath for very long.

The opposite of breath-holding—deliberate hyperventilation—lowers alveolar and arterial P_{CO_2} and increases P_{O_2}. Unfortunately, swimmers sometimes voluntarily hyperventilate immediately before underwater swimming to be able to hold their breath longer. We say "unfortunately" because the low P_{CO_2} may still permit breath-holding at a time when the exertion is lowering the arterial P_{O_2} to levels that can cause unconsciousness and lead to drowning.

Besides the obvious forms of voluntary control, respiration must also be controlled during such complex actions as speaking and singing.

HYPOXIA

Hypoxia is defined as a deficiency of oxygen at the tissue level. There are many potential causes of hypoxia, but they can be classed in four general categories:

(1) **hypoxic hypoxia** (also termed **hypoxemia**), in which the arterial P_{O_2} is reduced; (2) **anemic hypoxia,** in which the arterial P_{O_2} is normal but the total oxygen *content* of the blood is reduced because of inadequate numbers of erythrocytes, deficient or abnormal hemoglobin, or competition for the hemoglobin molecule by carbon monoxide; (3) **ischemic hypoxia** (also called hypoperfusion hypoxia), in which blood flow to the tissues is too low; and (4) **histotoxic hypoxia**, in which the quantity of oxygen reaching the tissues is normal but the cell is unable to utilize the oxygen because a toxic agent—cyanide, for example—has interfered with the cell's metabolic machinery.

The primary causes of hypoxic hypoxia in disease are listed in Table 15-11. Exposure to the reduced P_{O_2} of high altitude also causes hypoxia but is not a "disease." The brief summaries in Table 15-11 provide a review of many of the key aspects of respiratory physiology and pathophysiology described in this chapter.

This table also emphasizes that some of the diseases that produce hypoxia also produce carbon dioxide retention and an increased arterial P_{CO_2} (**hypercapnea**). In such cases, treating only the oxygen deficit by administering oxygen may constitute inadequate therapy because it does nothing about the hypercapnea.[10]

Acclimatization to High Altitude

Atmospheric pressure progressively decreases as altitude increases. Thus, at the top of Mt. Everest (approximately 29,000 ft or 9000 m), the atmospheric pressure is 253 mmHg (recall that it is 760 mmHg at sea level). The air is still 21 percent oxygen, which means that the P_{O_2} is 53 mmHg, that is, 0.21×253 mmHg. Obviously, the alveolar and arterial P_{O_2} must decrease as one ascends unless pure oxygen is breathed.

The effects of oxygen lack vary from one individual to another, but most people who ascend rapidly to altitudes above 10,000 ft experience some degree of **mountain sickness.** This disorder consists of breathlessness, heart palpitations, headache, nausea, vomiting, insomnia, fatigue, and impairment of mental processes. Much more serious is the appearance, in some individuals, of life-threatening pulmonary edema.[11]

Over the course of several days, the symptoms of mountain sickness disappear, although maximal physical

---

[10]Indeed, such therapy may be dangerous. The primary respiratory drive in such patients is the hypoxia, since for several reasons the response to an increased P_{CO_2} may be lost in chronic situations; the administration of pure oxygen may cause such patients to stop breathing entirely.

[11]The cause of the pulmonary edema is still unclear. It may be due to increased permeability to protein and/or increased hydrostatic pressure in the pulmonary capillaries. Decreased active fluid absorption by the alveolar epithelial cells may also play a role.

TABLE 15-11 CAUSES OF A DECREASED ARTERIAL P_{O_2} (HYPOXIC HYPOXIA) IN DISEASE

1. **Hypoventilation** may be caused (a) by a defect anywhere along the respiratory control pathway, from the medulla through the respiratory muscles, (b) by severe thoracic cage abnormalities, and (c) by major obstruction of the upper airway. The hypoxemia of hypoventilation is always accompanied by an increased arterial P_{CO_2}.

2. **Diffusion impairment** results from thickening of the alveolar membranes or a decrease in their surface area. In turn, it causes failure of equilibration of blood P_{O_2} with alveolar P_{O_2}. Often it is apparent only during exercise. Arterial P_{CO_2} is either normal, since carbon dioxide diffuses more readily than oxygen, or reduced, if the hypoxemia reflexly stimulates ventilation.

3. A **Shunt** is an abnormality of the cardiovascular system or lungs that causes blood to bypass ventilated alveoli in passing from the right heart to the left heart. The most common causes are cardiac defects that permit blood to flow directly from the right heart to the left heart. Arterial P_{CO_2} generally does not rise since the effect of the shunt on it is counterbalanced by the increased ventilation reflexly stimulated by the hypoxemia.

4. **Ventilation-perfusion inequality** is by far the most common cause of hypoxemia. It occurs in chronic obstructive lung diseases and many other lung diseases. Arterial P_{CO_2} may be normal or increased, depending upon how much ventilation is reflexly stimulated.

TABLE 15-12 ACCLIMATIZATION TO THE HYPOXIA OF HIGH ALTITUDE

1. The peripheral chemoreceptors stimulate ventilation.

2. Erythropoietin, secreted by the kidneys, stimulates erythrocyte synthesis, resulting in increased erythrocyte and hemoglobin concentration of blood.

3. DPG increases and shifts the hemoglobin dissociation curve to the right, facilitating oxygen unloading in the tissues.

4. Increases in capillary density, mitochondria, and muscle myoglobin occur, all of which increase oxygen transfer.

5. The peripheral chemoreceptors stimulate an increased loss of sodium and water in the urine. This reduces plasma volume, resulting in a concentration of the erythrocytes and hemoglobin in the blood.

capacity remains reduced. Acclimatization to high altitude is achieved by the compensatory mechanisms given below. The highest villages permanently inhabited by people are in the Andes at 19,000 ft (5700 m). These villagers work quite normally, and the only major precaution they take is that the women come down to lower altitudes during late pregnancy.

In response to hypoxia, oxygen supply to the tissues is maintained in the five ways summarized in Table 15-12. It should be noted that the DPG effect is not always adaptive and may be maladaptive. This is because, at very high altitudes, a right shift in the curve impairs oxygen *loading* in the lungs, an effect that outweighs any benefit from facilitation of *unloading* in the tissues. Indeed, many high-altitude species such as the llama have a left-shifted curve, indicating an adaptive value for this factor.

Finally, it should be noted that the responses to high altitude are essentially the same as the responses to hypoxia from any other cause. Thus, a person with severe hypoxia from lung disease may show many of the same changes—increased hematocrit, for example—as a high-altitude sojourner.

NONRESPIRATORY FUNCTIONS OF THE LUNGS

The lungs have a variety of functions in addition to their roles in gas exchange and regulation of H^+ concentration. Most notable are the influences they have on the arterial concentrations of a large number of biologically active substances. Many substances—neurotransmitters and paracrine agents, for example—released locally into interstitial fluid may diffuse into capillaries and thus make their way into the systemic venous system. The lungs partially or completely remove some of these substances from the blood and thereby prevent them from reaching other locations in the body via the arteries. The cells that perform this function are the endothelial cells lining the pulmonary capillaries.

In contrast, the lungs may also produce and add new substances to the blood. Some of these substances play local regulatory roles within the lungs, but if produced in large enough quantity, they may diffuse into the pulmonary capillaries and be carried to the rest of the body. For example, inflammatory responses (Chapter 20) in the lung may lead, via excessive release of potent chemicals such as histamine, to profound alterations of systemic blood pressure or flow. In at least one case, the lungs contribute a hormone, angiotensin II, to the blood (Chapter 16).

Finally, the lungs also act as a "sieve" that traps and dissolves small blood clots generated in the systemic circulation, thereby preventing them from reaching the systemic arterial blood where they could occlude blood vessels in other organs.

3. A patient is being artificially ventilated by a machine during surgery at a rate of 20 breaths/min and a tidal volume of 250 ml/breath. Assuming a normal anatomic dead space of 150 ml, is this patient receiving an adequate alveolar ventilation?

4. Why must a person floating on the surface of the water and breathing through a snorkel increase his tidal volume and/or breathing frequency if alveolar ventilation is to remain normal?

5. A normal person breathing room air voluntarily increases her alveolar ventilation twofold and continues to do so until new steady-state alveolar gas pressures for oxygen and carbon dioxide are reached. Are the new values higher or lower than normal?

6. A person has an alveolar P_{O_2} of 105 mmHg and an arterial P_{O_2} of 80 mmHg. Could hypoventilation, say, due to respiratory muscle weakness, produce these values?

7. A person's alveolar membranes have become thickened enough to moderately decrease the rate at which gases diffuse across them at any given partial pressure differences. Will this person necessarily have a low arterial P_{O_2} at rest? During exercise?

8. A person is breathing 100 percent oxygen. How much will the oxygen content (in milliliters per liter of blood) of the arterial blood increase compared to when the person is breathing room air?

9. Which of the following have higher values in systemic venous blood than in systemic arterial blood: plasma P_{CO_2}, erythrocyte P_{CO_2}, plasma bicarbonate concentration, erythrocyte bicarbonate concentration, plasma hydrogen-ion concentration, erythrocyte hydrogen-ion concentration, erythrocyte carbamino concentration, erythrocyte chloride concentration, plasma chloride concentration?

10. If the spinal cord were severed where it joins the brainstem, what would happen to respiration?

11. The peripheral chemoreceptors are denervated in an experimental animal, and the animal then breathes a gas mixture containing 10 percent oxygen. What changes occur in the animal's ventilation? What changes occur when this denervated animal is given a mixture of air containing 21 percent oxygen and 5 percent carbon dioxide to breathe?

12. Patients with severe uncontrolled diabetes mellitus produce large quantities of certain organic acids. Can you predict the ventilation pattern in these patients and whether their arterial P_{O_2} and P_{CO_2} increase or decrease?

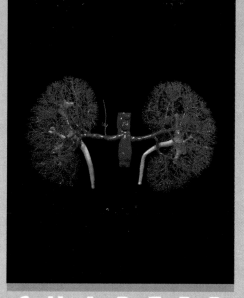

CHAPTER

16

THE KIDNEYS AND REGULATION OF WATER AND INORGANIC IONS

SECTION A. BASIC PRINCIPLES OF RENAL PHYSIOLOGY

FUNCTIONS OF THE KIDNEYS

STRUCTURE OF THE KIDNEYS AND URINARY SYSTEM

BASIC RENAL PROCESSES

Glomerular Filtration

Forces involved in filtration

Rate of glomerular filtration

Tubular Reabsorption

T_m-limited transport mechanisms

Reabsorption by diffusion

Tubular Secretion

Metabolism by the Tubules

The Concept of Renal Clearance

MICTURITION

SECTION A SUMMARY

SECTION A KEY TERMS

SECTION A REVIEW QUESTIONS

SECTION B. REGULATION OF SODIUM, WATER, AND POTASSIUM BALANCE

TOTAL-BODY BALANCE OF SODIUM AND WATER

BASIC RENAL PROCESSES FOR SODIUM AND WATER

Primary Active Sodium Reabsorption

Coupling of Water Reabsorption to Sodium Reabsorption

Urine Concentration: The Countercurrent Multiplier System

RENAL SODIUM REGULATION

Control of GFR

Control of Sodium Reabsorption

Aldosterone and the renin-angiotensin system

Atrial natriuretic factor

RENAL WATER REGULATION

Baroreceptor Control of ADH Secretion

Osmoreceptor Control of ADH Secretion

A SUMMARY EXAMPLE: THE RESPONSE TO SWEATING

THIRST AND SALT APPETITE

POTASSIUM REGULATION

Renal Regulation of Potassium

SECTION B SUMMARY

SECTION B KEY TERMS

SECTION B REVIEW QUESTIONS

SECTION C. CALCIUM REGULATION

EFFECTOR SITES FOR CALCIUM HOMEOSTASIS

Bone

Kidneys

Gastrointestinal Tract

HORMONAL CONTROLS

Parathyroid Hormone

Vitamin D

METABOLIC BONE DISEASES

SECTION C SUMMARY

SECTION C KEY TERMS

SECTION C REVIEW QUESTIONS

SECTION D. HYDROGEN-ION REGULATION

SOURCES OF HYDROGEN-ION GAIN OR LOSS

BUFFERING OF HYDROGEN IONS IN THE BODY

INTEGRATION OF HOMEOSTATIC CONTROLS

RENAL MECHANISMS

Bicarbonate Excretion

Addition of New Bicarbonate to the Plasma

Renal Responses to Acidosis and Alkalosis

CLASSIFICATION OF ACIDOSIS AND ALKALOSIS

SECTION D SUMMARY

SECTION D KEY TERM

SECTION D REVIEW QUESTIONS

SECTION E. DIURETICS AND KIDNEY DISEASE

DIURETICS

KIDNEY DISEASE

Hemodialysis, Peritoneal Dialysis, and Transplantation

SECTION E SUMMARY

CHAPTER 16 CLINICAL TERMS

CHAPTER 16 THOUGHT QUESTIONS

This chapter deals with how the water and inorganic-ion composition of the internal environment are homeostatically regulated. The kidneys play the central role in these processes, but other organs participate too, for example, bone in the regulation of calcium. Most people assume that the kidneys' sole job is to eliminate wastes and poisons from the body, but that is only one of their tasks. Indeed, their prime function is to balance the body's water and inorganic ions so as to maintain stable concentrations of these substances in the extracellular fluid. Altering urinary excretion is the means to this balancing function.

Regulation of the total-body balance of any substance can be studied in terms of the balance concept described in Chapter 7. Theoretically, a substance can appear in the body either as a result of ingestion or as a product of metabolism. On the loss side, a substance can be excreted from the body or can be metabolized. Therefore, if the quantity of any substance in the body is to be maintained at a nearly constant level over a period of time, the total amounts ingested and produced must equal the total amounts excreted and metabolized.

Reflexes that alter excretion, specifically excretion via the urine, constitute the major mechanisms that regulate the body balances of water and many of the inorganic ions determining the properties of the extracellular fluid. The extracellular concentrations of these ions are given in Chapter 6, Table 6-1. We will first describe how the kidneys work in general and then apply this information to how they process specific substances—sodium, water, potassium, and so on—and participate in reflexes that regulate these substances. It should be noted, however, that the kidneys are not important regulators of *all* inorganic substances. In particular, the body balances of many of the trace elements, such as zinc and iron, are regulated mainly by control of gastrointestinal absorption of the element or by control of its excretion in the bile by the liver, as described in Chapter 17.

SECTION

BASIC PRINCIPLES OF RENAL PHYSIOLOGY

FUNCTIONS OF THE KIDNEYS

The kidneys process blood by removing substances from it and, in a few cases, by adding substances to it. In so doing they perform a variety of functions, as summarized in Table 16-1. The major function is to regulate the water content, mineral composition, and acidity of the body by excreting each substance in an amount adequate to achieve total-body balance and maintain normal concentrations in the extracellular fluid.

A second renal (the adjective denoting kidney) function is the excretion of metabolic **waste products**, so termed because they serve no function. These include **urea** from protein; **uric acid** from nucleic acids; **creatinine** from muscle creatine; the end products of hemoglobin breakdown, which give urine much of its color; and many others.

A third renal function is the excretion, in the urine, of some foreign chemicals—drugs, pesticides, food additives, and so on—and their metabolites.

In addition to their excretory functions, the kidneys act as endocrine glands, secreting at least three hormones: erythropoietin (Chapter 14), renin, and the active form of vitamin D. These last two hormones are discussed in this chapter. (To avoid confusion it should be noted that renin is part of a hormonal system called the renin-angiotensin system; renin functions, as we shall see, as an enzyme in

this system, but it is customary to refer to it as a "hormone.")

Finally, during prolonged fasting, the kidneys synthesize glucose from amino acids and other precursors and release it into the blood; this is termed **gluconeogenesis.** The kidneys can supply as much glucose to the blood as the liver does at such times (Chapter 18).

STRUCTURE OF THE KIDNEYS AND URINARY SYSTEM

The kidneys are paired organs that lie in the back of the abdominal wall but not actually in the abdominal cavity. They are retroperitoneal, meaning they are just behind the lining—the peritoneum—of this cavity.

Each kidney is composed of approximately 1 million functional units bound together by small amounts of connective tissue, which contains blood vessels, nerves, and lymphatics. One such unit, or **nephron**, is shown in Figure 16-1. Each nephron consists of (1) an initial filtering component called the **renal corpuscle**, and (2) a **tubule** that extends out from the renal corpuscle. The renal corpuscle forms a filtrate from blood that is free of cells and proteins. This filtrate then leaves the renal corpuscle and enters the tubule, where it is processed before exiting the kidney as urine. Let us describe the anatomy of these two structures, beginning with the renal corpuscle.

Systemic arterial blood enters each kidney via a renal artery, which then divides into progressively smaller branches. Each of the smallest arteries gives off, at right angles to itself, a series of arterioles, the **afferent arterioles**. Each of the afferent arterioles conducts blood to a compact tuft of interconnected capillary loops called the **glomerulus** (plural *glomeruli*) (also termed the **glomerular capillaries** (Figure 16-2). The glomerulus protrudes into a balloon-like hollow capsule—**Bowman's capsule**. The combination of the glomerulus and Bowman's capsule constitutes the renal corpuscle.[1]

TABLE 16-1 FUNCTIONS OF THE KIDNEYS

1. Regulation of water and inorganic-ion balance
2. Removal of metabolic waste products from the blood and their excretion in the urine
3. Removal of foreign chemicals from the blood and their excretion in the urine
4. Secretion of hormones:
   a. Erythropoietin, which controls erythrocyte production (Chapter 14)
   b. Renin, which controls formation of angiotensin, which influences blood pressure and sodium balance (this chapter)
   c. 1,25-Dihydroxyvitamin D_3, which influences calcium balance (this chapter)
5. Gluconeogenesis

---

[1]Until recently, renal physiologists have not used the term "renal corpuscle" but rather have used "glomerulus" to denote the combination of capillary tuft and Bowman's capsule, and the term *glomerular capillaries* to refer to the tuft alone. However, a standard nomenclature introduced in 1988 has recommended the usage adopted in this text.

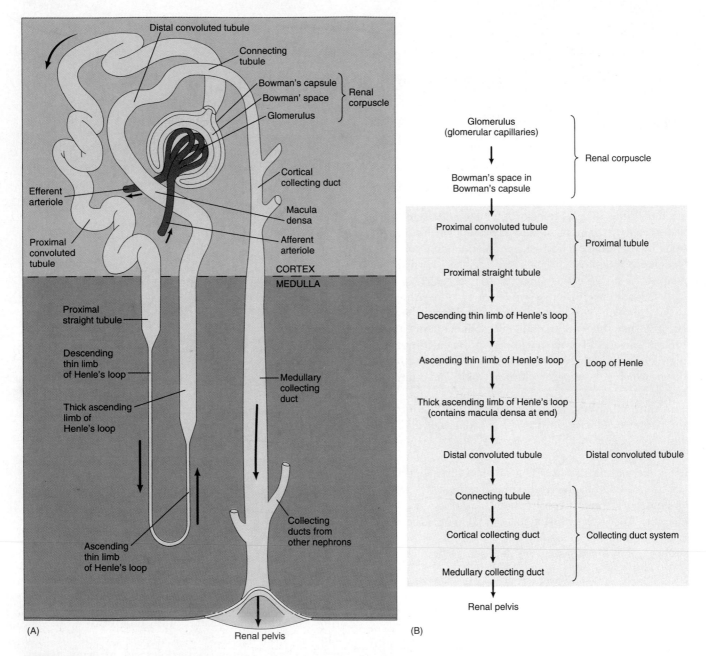

FIGURE 16-1

Basic structure of a nephron. (A) Anatomical organization. The macula densa is not a distinct segment but a plaque of cells in the ascending loop of Henle where the loop passes between the arterioles supplying its renal corpuscle of origin. The orange (outer) area is the cortex and the dark pink (inner) the medulla. (B) Consecutive segments of the nephron. All segments in the screened area are parts of the renal tubule; the terms enclosed in braces are the most commonly used combination terms for several consecutive segments.

One way of visualizing the relationships within the renal corpuscle is to imagine a loosely clenched fist—the glomerulus—punched into a balloon—Bowman's capsule. The part of Bowman's capsule in contact with the glomerulus becomes pushed inward but does not make contact with the opposite side of the capsule. Accordingly, a fluid-filled space—**Bowman's space**—exists within the capsule, and it is into this space that fluid filters from the glomerulus. Blood in the glomerulus is separated from the fluid in Bowman's space by a filtration barrier consisting of three layers: (1) the single-celled capillary endothelium, (2) the single-celled epithelial lining of Bowman's capsule,

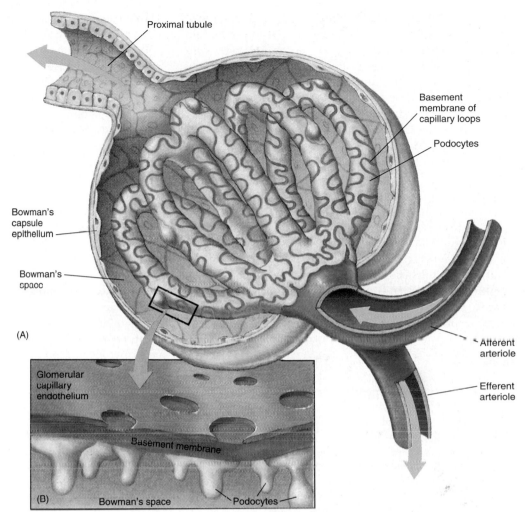

FIGURE 16-2

(A) Anatomy of the renal corpuscle. (B) Cross section of the three corpuscular membranes—capillary endothelium, basement membrane (BM), and epithelium (podocytes) of Bowman's capsule.

and (3) the noncellular proteinaceous layer of basement membrane between the endothelium and epithelium. The epithelial cells in this region are quite different from the simple flattened cells that line the rest of Bowman's capsule (the part of the "balloon" not in contact with the "fist") and are called **podocytes**. They have an octopus-like structure in that they possess a large number of extensions, or foot processes, which are embedded in the basement membrane. During filtration, fluid moves between these foot processes.

Extending out from Bowman's capsule is the nephron tubule, the lumen of which is continuous with Bowman's space. Throughout its course, the tubule is composed of a single layer of epithelial cells resting on a basement membrane. The epithelial cells differ in structure and function along the tubule's length, and 10 to 12 distinct segments are presently recognized (Figure 16-1). It is possible, however, to group two or more contiguous tubular segments when discussing function, and we shall follow this practice. Accordingly, the segment of the tubule that drains Bow-

man's capsule is the **proximal tubule** (comprising the proximal convoluted tubule and the proximal straight tubule of Figure 16-1). The next portion of the tubule is the **loop of Henle**, which is a sharp hairpin-like loop consisting of a **descending limb** coming from the proximal tubule and an **ascending limb** leading to the next tubular segment, the **distal convoluted tubule**. [In nephrons with long loops (Figure 16-1), the ascending limb is subdivided into an initial thin segment and a subsequent thick segment; in short loops there is no thin segment.] Fluid flows from the distal convoluted tubule into the **collecting duct system**, the first portion of which is the **connecting tubule**, followed by the **cortical collecting duct** and then the **medullary collecting duct**. The connecting tubule is so similar in function to the cortical collecting duct that, in subsequent discussions, we will not describe its function separately.

The many specific functions of these tubular segments will be described in the course of this chapter. We shall see that the proximal tubule is the major site for processing not only the organic constituents of the fluid filtered at the renal corpuscles but a large fraction of the water and inorganic constituents as well. The loop of Henle is involved in producing a concentrated urine. The collecting duct system is the "fine-tuning" portion of the tubule; it is the target for the major hormones that act on the kidneys, and in response to these hormones it makes the final adjustments to the urine.

From Bowman's capsule to the end of the connecting tubule, each of the nephrons is completely separate from the others. This separation ends when the tubules merge to form the cortical collecting ducts. The result of additional joining from this point on is that the completed urine drains into the kidney's central cavity, the **renal pelvis**, via only several hundred large medullary collecting ducts.

There are important regional differences in the kidney (Figures 16-1 and 16-3). The outer portion is the **renal cortex**, and the inner portion the **renal medulla**. The cortex contains all the renal corpuscles. The loops of

FIGURE 16-3

Section of a human kidney. For clarity, the nephron illustrated to show nephron orientation is not to scale—its outline would not be clearly visible without a microscope. The outer kidney, which contains all the renal corpuscles, is the cortex, and the inner kidney is the medulla. In the medulla, the loops of Henle and the collecting ducts run parallel to each other, giving the medulla a striped appearance. The medullary collecting ducts drain into the renal pelvis.

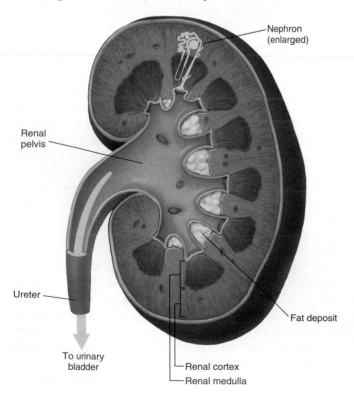

Nephron (enlarged)

Renal pelvis

Ureter

To urinary bladder

Renal cortex

Renal medulla

Fat deposit

Henle extend from the cortex for varying distances down into the medulla, through which also course the medullary collecting ducts on their way to the renal pelvis. The nephrons, termed juxtamedullary nephrons, that originate in renal corpuscles near the cortex-medulla junction have long loops that extend the entire length of the medulla.

The renal pelvis is continuous with the **ureter**, the tube that passes from the kidney to the **urinary bladder**, where urine is temporarily stored. During urination urine is eliminated from the bladder via the **urethra**, the tube leading from the bladder to the external world (Figure 16-4).

To return to the kidney blood vessels: The capillaries of each glomerulus do not lead directly to a vein. Instead, they recombine to form another arteriole, the **efferent arteriole**, through which blood leaves the glomerulus. In the great majority of cases, each efferent arteriole soon divides into a second set of capillaries, the **peritubular capillaries**, which branch profusely to form a network surrounding all portions of the tubule in the cortex. The peritubular capillaries then eventually rejoin to form the veins by which blood leaves the kidney. In contrast, the blood from some efferent arterioles (those from renal corpuscles in the innermost portion of the cortex) flows into capillary-like vessels, termed the **vasa recta**, which do not supply blood to cortical structures but instead enter and supply the medulla.

One additional anatomical detail involving both the tubule and the arterioles must be mentioned. Near its end, the ascending limb of the loop of Henle passes between and contacts the afferent and efferent arterioles of its glomerulus (Figure 16-1). At this point there is a plaque of cells in the ascending limb called the **macula densa**. In the region of contact, the wall of the afferent arteriole contains secretory cells known as **juxtaglomerular (JG) cells** (also termed granular cells). The combination of macula densa and juxtaglomerular cells is known as the **juxtaglomerular apparatus (JGA)** (this term should be distinguished from the juxtaglomerular *cells* defined in the previous sentence) (Figure 16-5). The juxtaglomerular cells secrete the hormone renin; the control of this process and the participation of the macula densa in it will be described later.

BASIC RENAL PROCESSES

U rine formation begins with **glomerular filtration**, the bulk flow of protein-free plasma from the glomerular capillaries through the combined membranes of the renal corpuscle—capillary endothelium, basement membrane, and epithelial cells (podocytes) of Bowman's

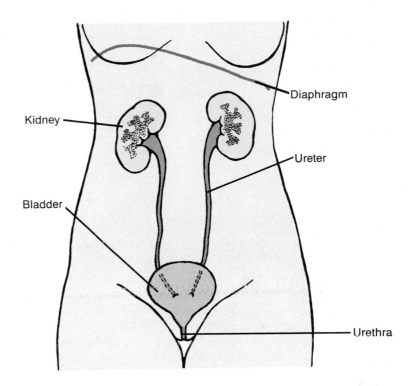

FIGURE 16-4

Urinary system in a woman. The urine, formed by the kidneys, flows from the kidneys through the ureters into the bladder, from which it is eliminated via the urethra. In the male, the urethra passes through the penis (Chapter 19).

capsule—and into Bowman's space. This fluid, now called the **glomerular filtrate**, contains all the substances, except protein, present in plasma and in virtually the same concentrations they have in plasma.

The filtrate contains almost no protein because the corpuscular membranes (specifically the basement mem-

FIGURE 16-5

Anatomy of the juxtaglomerular apparatus. The juxtaglomerular cells are specialized cells in the wall of the afferent arteriole and secrete the hormone renin. The macula densa is a group of cells located near the end of the thick ascending limb of Henle's loop as this segment passes between the arterioles supplying its renal corpuscle of origin.

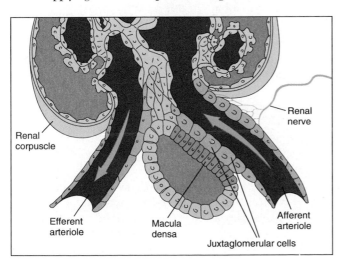

brane and podocytes) restrict the movement of such high-molecular-weight substances. Size is not the only reason for protein restriction; the filtration channels in the corpuscular membranes are negatively charged and so oppose the movement of plasma proteins, which are also negatively charged. In addition, the corpuscular membranes normally completely prevent any movement of blood cells from the glomerulus to Bowman's space.

The urine that eventually enters the renal pelvis is quite different from the glomerular filtrate because, as the filtrate flows from Bowman's space through the tubule, its composition is altered. This change occurs by two processes, tubular reabsorption and tubular secretion (Figure 16-6). The tubule is intimately associated with the peritubular capillary network, a relationship that permits transfer of materials between peritubular blood and the lumen of the tubule. When the direction of transfer is from tubular lumen to peritubular capillary plasma, the process is called **tubular reabsorption**, or simply reabsorption. Movement in the opposite direction, that is, from peritubular plasma to tubular lumen, is called **tubular secretion**, or simply secretion.

"Tubular reabsorption" and "tubular secretion" denote only the direction of the transfer, not the mechanism, which is diffusion for some substances and mediated transport for others. In the latter case the transport processes are in the plasma membranes of the tubular epithelial cells, and this explains the common use of the phrases "the tubule secretes" and "the tubule reabsorbs."

To summarize: *The amount of any substance excreted in*

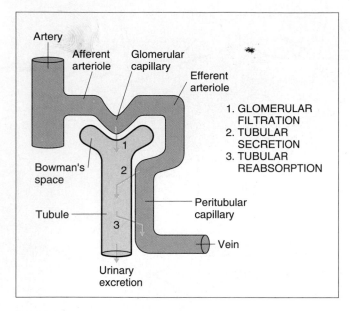

FIGURE 16-6

The three basic components of renal function. This figure is to illustrate only the directions of reabsorption and secretion, not specific sites or order of occurrence. Depending on the particular substance, reabsorption and secretion can occur at various sites along the tubule.

the urine is equal to the amount filtered plus the amount secreted minus the amount reabsorbed. Not all these processes apply to any given substance. To emphasize general principles, the renal handling of three hypothetical substances is illustrated in Figure 16-7. Approximately 20 percent of the plasma that enters the glomerular capillaries is filtered into Bowman's space. This filtrate, which contains

X, Y, and Z in the same concentrations as in the plasma remaining in the capillaries, enters the proximal tubule and begins its flow through the rest of the tubule. Simultaneously, the remaining 80 percent of the plasma, with its X, Y, and Z, leaves the glomerular capillaries via the efferent arteriole and enters the peritubular capillaries.

The tubule can secrete 100 percent of the peritubular-capillary X into the tubular lumen but cannot reabsorb X. Thus, by the combination of filtration and tubular secretion, all the plasma that originally entered the renal artery loses all of its substance X, which leaves the body via the urine.

The tubule can reabsorb but not secrete Y and Z. The amount of Y reabsorption is small, so that much of the filtered material is not reabsorbed and escapes from the body. But for Z the reabsorptive mechanism is so powerful that all the filtered Z is transported back into the plasma. Therefore, no Z is lost from the body. Hence, for Z the processes of filtration and reabsorption have canceled each other out, and the net result is as though Z had never entered the kidney.

For each substance in plasma, a particular combination of filtration, tubular reabsorption, and tubular secretion applies. The critical point is that, for many substances, the rates at which the processes proceed are subject to physiological control. What would be the effect, for example, if the Y-filtration rate were increased by some physiological mechanism or its reabsorption rate decreased? Either change would mean that more Y would be lost from the body via the urine. By triggering such changes in filtration, reabsorption, or secretion whenever the plasma concentration of a substance changes from normal, homeostatic mechanisms can regulate the substance's plasma concentration.

FIGURE 16-7

Renal handling of three hypothetical substances X, Y, and Z. X is filtered and secreted but not reabsorbed. Y is filtered, and a fraction is then reabsorbed. Z is filtered and is completely reabsorbed.

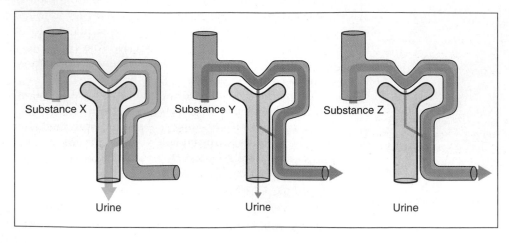

Glomerular Filtration

As stated above, the glomerular filtrate, that is, the fluid in Bowman's space, is essentially protein-free and contains all other substances present in plasma in virtually the same concentrations as in plasma. The only exceptions to the last part of this generalization are certain low-molecular-weight substances that would otherwise be filterable but are bound to proteins and therefore are not filtered. For example, half of the plasma calcium and virtually all of the plasma fatty acids are bound to protein.

Forces Involved in Filtration. Glomerular filtration, like filtration across any capillary, is a bulk-flow process. As described in Chapter 14, capillary filtration is determined by opposing forces: The hydrostatic pressure difference across the capillary wall favors filtration, while the protein concentration difference across the wall creates an osmotic force that opposes filtration. This also applies to the glomerular capillaries, as summarized in Figure 16-8.

The pressure of the blood in the glomerular capillaries averages 60 mmHg.[2] This is higher than in other capillaries of the body because the nephron afferent arterioles, having relatively large diameters, offer less resistance than most arterioles, and so more of the arterial pressure is transmitted to the capillaries. This glomerular capillary hydrostatic pressure is a force favoring filtration.

The fluid in Bowman's space exerts a hydrostatic pressure of 15 mmHg, and this opposes filtration into the space. A second opposing force results from the presence of protein in the glomerular capillary plasma and its virtual absence in Bowman's space. This unequal distribution of protein (similar to that across other capillaries in the body) causes the water concentration of the plasma to be less than that of the fluid in Bowman's space. This difference in water concentration favors an osmotic flow of fluid—water plus all the low-molecular-weight solutes—from Bowman's space into the glomerular capillary, a flow equivalent to that produced by a pressure difference of 27 mmHg.

Thus, as can be seen from Figure 16-8, the **net glomerular filtration pressure**, that is, the algebraic sum of the three relevant forces, is approximately 18 mmHg. This pressure initiates urine formation by forcing an essentially protein-free filtrate of plasma out of the glomeruli and into Bowman's space and thence down the tubule into the renal pelvis.

Rate of Glomerular Filtration. The volume of fluid filtered from the glomeruli into Bowman's space per unit time is known as the **glomerular filtration rate (GFR)**. The glomerular capillaries are so much more permeable to

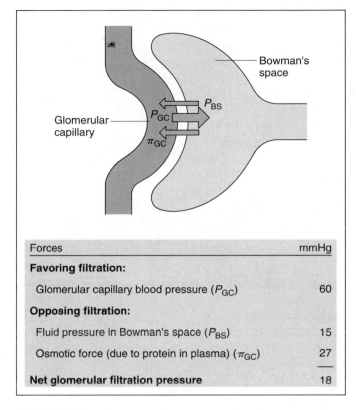

Forces	mmHg
Favoring filtration:	
Glomerular capillary blood pressure (P_{GC})	60
Opposing filtration:	
Fluid pressure in Bowman's space (P_{BS})	15
Osmotic force (due to protein in plasma) (π_{GC})	27
Net glomerular filtration pressure	18

FIGURE 16-8

Forces involved in glomerular filtration. The symbol π denotes an osmotic force due to differences in solute and hence water concentration. The difference in solute concentration is due solely to the presence of protein in plasma but not in Bowman's space, since the filtrate is essentially protein-free plasma. The rate at which fluid is filtered—the glomerular filtration rate—averages 180 L/day.

fluid than, say, a muscle or skin capillary, that the net filtration pressure of 18 mmHg causes massive filtration. In a 70-kg person, the volume filtered into Bowman's space averages 180 L/day (125 ml/min)! Contrast this figure with the net filtration of fluid across all the other capillaries in the body—4 L/day, as described in Chapter 14.

There are several implications of this remarkable filtration rate. First, in order to form such a huge volume of filtrate, the kidneys must receive a large share of the cardiac output. Each moment the kidneys receive about 20 to 25 percent of the blood pumped by the left ventricle even though the kidneys account for only about 1 percent of body weight. Second, when we recall that the total volume of plasma in the cardiovascular system is approximately 3 L, it follows that the entire plasma volume is filtered by the kidneys about 60 times a day. This opportunity to process such huge volumes of plasma enables the kidneys to regulate the constituents of the internal environment rapidly and to excrete large quantities of waste products.

It is possible to measure the total amount of any non-

---

[2]Glomerular capillary pressure cannot be directly measured in humans, and this figure is the best educated guess from work on experimental animals.

protein substance (assuming also that the substance is not bound to protein) filtered into Bowman's space by multiplying the GFR by the plasma concentration of the substance. This amount is called the **filtered load** of the substance. For example, if the GFR is 180 L/day and plasma glucose concentration is 1 g/L, than 180 L/day × 1 g/L = 180 g/day is the filtered load of glucose.

Once we know the filtered load of the substance we can compare it to the amount of the substance excreted and tell whether the substance undergoes net tubular reabsorption or net secretion. Whenever the quantity of a substance excreted in the urine is less than the filtered load, tubular reabsorption must have occurred. Conversely, if the amount excreted in the urine is greater than the filtered load, tubular secretion must have occurred. Such measurements have played an important role in determining which substances undergo tubular reabsorption or tubular secretion.

Tubular Reabsorption

Many filterable plasma components are either absent from the urine or present in smaller quantities than were filtered at the renal corpuscle. This fact alone is sufficient to prove that these substances undergo tubular reabsorption. An idea of the magnitude and importance of these reabsorptive mechanisms can be gained from Table 16-2, which summarizes data for a few plasma components that that undergo filtration and reabsorption.

The values in Table 16-2 are typical for a normal person on an average diet. There are at least three important conclusions to be drawn from this table: (1) The filtered loads are enormous, generally larger than the amount of the substances in the body. For example, the body contains about 40 L of water, but the volume of water filtered each day is, as we have seen, 180 L. (2) Reabsorption of waste products is relatively incomplete, for example, only 44 percent in the case of urea, so that large fractions of their filtered loads are excreted in the urine. (3) Reabsorption of most useful plasma components, for example, water, inorganic ions, and organic nutrients, is relatively complete, so that the amounts excreted in the urine represent very small fractions of the filtered loads.

In this last regard an important distinction should be made between reabsorptive processes that can be controlled physiologically and those that cannot. The reabsorption rates of most organic nutrients, for example, glucose, are always very high and are not physiologically regulated, and so the filtered loads of these substances are normally completely reabsorbed, none appearing in the urine. For these substances, like substance Z in our earlier example, it is as though the kidneys do not exist since the kidneys do not eliminate them from the body at all. Therefore, the kidneys do not help *regulate* the plasma concentrations of these organic nutrients, that is, minimize changes from their normal plasma levels. Rather, the kidneys merely maintain whatever plasma concentrations already exist, generally the result of hormonal regulation of nutrient metabolism (Chapter 18).

In contrast, the reabsorptive rates for water and many ions, although also very high, are regulatable. Consider what happens when a person drinks a lot of water. Within 1 to 2 h, all the excess water has been excreted in the urine, chiefly, as we shall see, as the result of decreased renal tubular reabsorption of water, and water balance is restored to normal. The critical point is that the rates at which water and the inorganic ions are reabsorbed, and therefore the rates at which they are excreted, are subject to physiological control.

Tubular reabsorption is a process fundamentally different from glomerular filtration. The latter occurs completely by bulk flow, with water and all low-molecular-weight solutes moving together. In contrast, there is relatively little bulk flow across the epithelial cells of the tubule from lumen to interstitial fluid, so that reabsorption is not by mass movement. Rather, the reabsorption of some substances is by diffusion, while that of others requires more-or-less distinct mediated transport systems. The phrase "more-or-less distinct" denotes the fact that, as we shall see, the reabsorption of different substances is often linked.

Reference to Figure 16-9 highlights the fact that there are two potential routes for reabsorptive movement from lumen to interstitium. The first is by diffusion *between* tubular cells, that is, across the tight junctions connecting the cells. The second route is *through* the cells: The reabsorbed substance must first cross the **luminal membrane** (separating the lumen from the cell interior), then diffuse through the cytosol of the cell, and finally cross the **basolateral membrane** (which begins at the tight junctions and constitutes the plasma membrane of the sides and base of the cell). This latter route is termed *transcellular* epithelial transport, and its mechanisms were described in Chapter 6 and should be reviewed at this time. Suffice it to point out here that if the movement across

Substance	Amount filtered per day	Amount excreted per day	Percent reabsorbed
TABLE 16-2	**AVERAGE VALUES FOR SEVERAL COMPONENTS THAT UNDERGO FILTRATION AND REABSORPTION**		
Water, L	180	1.8	99.0
Sodium, g	630	3.2	99.5
Glucose, g	180	0	100
Urea, g	54	30	44

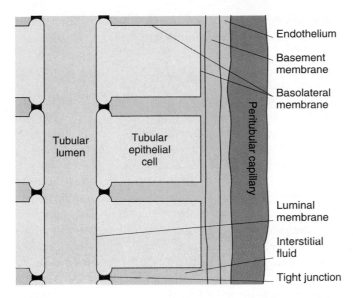

FIGURE 16-9

Diagrammatic representation of tubular epithelium. The basement membrane of the tubule is a homogeneous proteinaceous structure that plays no significant role in transport and will not be shown in subsequent figures illustrating transport in this chapter.

either the luminal membrane or the basolateral membrane is active, then the entire process is termed active.

Regardless of which route the reabsorbed substance takes to reach the interstitial fluid, movement from this fluid into the peritubular capillaries is by a combination of diffusion and bulk flow.[3]

T_m-Limited Transport Mechanisms.

Many of the active reabsorptive systems in the renal tubule have a limit, termed a **transport maximum (T_m)**, to the amounts of material they can transport per unit time, because the membrane proteins responsible for the transport become saturated. An important example is the active transport process for glucose, located in the proximal tubule. As noted earlier, normal persons do not excrete glucose in their urine because all filtered glucose is reabsorbed. Indeed, even by eating an extremely carbohydrate-rich meal, normal persons cannot raise their plasma glucose concentrations high enough to exceed the renal glucose T_m. In contrast, in people with diabetes mellitus, a disease in which the hormonal control of the plasma glucose concentration is defective (Chapter 18), the plasma glucose concentration and thus the filtered load become so high that

the glucose T_m is exceeded and glucose does appear in the urine (glucosuria). In other words, the kidneys' ability to reabsorb glucose is perfectly normal in diabetes, but the tubules cannot reabsorb the markedly increased filtered load.

The pattern described for glucose is also true for a large number of other organic nutrients. For example, most amino acids and water-soluble vitamins are filtered in large amounts each day, but almost all these filtered molecules are reabsorbed by the proximal tubule. If for some reason the plasma concentration becomes high enough, however, reabsorption of the filtered load will not be as complete, and the substance will appear in larger amounts in the urine. Thus, persons ingesting very large quantities of vitamin C manifest progressive increases in their plasma concentrations of vitamin C until the filtered load exceeds the tubular reabsorptive T_m for this substance, and any additional ingested vitamin C is excreted in the urine.

Reabsorption by Diffusion. Urea reabsorption provides an example of passive reabsorption by diffusion. An analysis of urea concentrations in the tubule will help elucidate the mechanism. Because the corpuscular membranes are freely filterable to urea, the urea concentration in the fluid within Bowman's space is the same as that in the plasma. Then, as this fluid flows through the proximal tubule, water reabsorption occurs (by mechanisms to be described later), increasing the concentrations of tubular-fluid solutes that, like urea, are not being reabsorbed by active transport. The result is that the tubular-fluid urea concentration becomes greater than the peritubular-plasma urea concentration. Accordingly, urea diffuses down this concentration gradient from tubular lumen to peritubular capillary. Urea reabsorption is thus a passive process dependent upon the reabsorption of water. As noted earlier, this process causes reabsorption of about 50 percent of the filtered urea.[4]

Reabsorption by diffusion is also of considerable importance for many foreign organic chemicals. The plasma membranes of the tubular epithelium, like all plasma membranes, are primarily lipid, and so lipid-soluble substances can penetrate them fairly readily. Recall from Chapter 6 that one of the major determinants of lipid solubility is the polarity of a molecule; the less polar, the more lipid-soluble. Many drugs and environmental pollutants (DDT, for example) are nonpolar and therefore highly lipid-soluble. This makes their excretion from the body via the urine difficult since they are filtered at the renal cor-

---

[3]Bulk flow occurs from interstitial fluid into peritubular capillaries because the hydrostatic pressure in the capillary is low and the protein concentration is high. This combination produces a net filtration pressure favoring bulk flow into the capillary.

[4]You might logically ask why there should be *any* reabsorption of a waste product like urea. Put another way, is there any adaptive value in not excreting the entire filtered load of this substance? The answer is probably no, and the partial reabsorption simply reflects an inevitable consequence of the easy diffusibility of urea through plasma membranes.

puscle but then reabsorbed by diffusion as water reabsorption causes their intratubular concentrations to increase. The body does have a way of making these substances more excretable, however. The liver transforms them to more polar metabolites, which, because of their reduced lipid solubility, diffuse across the tubular wall poorly and are therefore not reabsorbed but rather excreted.

Tubular Secretion

Tubular secretory processes, by which substances move from peritubular capillaries into the tubular lumen, constitute a second pathway into the tubule, the first being glomerular filtration. The most important substances secreted by the tubules are hydrogen ions and potassium, and the mechanisms by which they are secreted are described in the sections on these substances.

The kidney is also able to secrete a large number of organic ions, some of which are normally occurring metabolites such as choline and creatinine, while others are foreign chemicals, penicillin, for example.

Metabolism by the Tubules

Although renal physiologists have traditionally listed glomerular filtration, tubular reabsorption, and tubular secretion as the three basic renal processes, a fourth process—metabolism by the cells of the tubule—is of considerable importance for many substances. The cells of the renal tubules are able to synthesize certain substances, notably ammonium, which are then added to the luminal fluid and excreted. Why the cells would make something just to have it excreted will be made clear when we discuss the role of ammonium in the regulation of plasma hydrogen-ion concentration. The cells are also capable of catabolizing certain organic substances, peptides, for example, taken up from either the tubular lumen or peritubular capillaries. Catabolism eliminates these substances from the body as surely as if they had been excreted in the urine.

The Concept of Renal Clearance

A useful way of quantitating renal function is in terms of clearance. The renal **clearance** of any substance is the *volume of plasma* from which that substance is completely cleared by the kidneys per unit time. Every substance has its own distinct clearance value, but the units are always in volume of plasma per unit time. The basic clearance formula for any substance S is

$$\text{Clearance of S} = \frac{\text{mass of S excreted per unit time}}{\text{plasma concentration of S}}$$

Since the mass of S excreted per unit time is equal to the urine concentration of S multiplied by the urine volume during that time, the formula becomes

$$C_S = \frac{U_S V}{P_S}$$

where C_S = clearance of S
U_S = urine concentration of S
V = urine volume per unit time
P_S = plasma concentration of S

Let us take the particularly important example of a polysaccharide named **inulin** (not insulin). This substance is not normally present in the body, but we will administer it intravenously to a person at a rate sufficient to maintain plasma concentration constant at 4 mg/L. Urine collected over a 1-h period has a volume of 0.1 L and an inulin concentration of 300 mg/L; thus, inulin excretion equals 0.1 L/h × 300 mg/L, or 30 mg/h. From a variety of experiments it is known that inulin is filterable at the renal corpuscle but is not reabsorbed, secreted, or metabolized by the tubule. Therefore, the mass of inulin *excreted* in our experiment—30 mg/h—must be equal to the mass *filtered* over that same time period (Figure 16-10). How much plasma had to be completely cleared of its inulin to supply this 30 mg/h? We simply divide 30 mg/h by the plasma concentration, 4 mg/L, to obtain the volume cleared—7.5 L/h. In other words, we are calculating the inulin clearance (C_{In}) from the measured urine volume per time (V), urine inulin concentration (U_{In}), and plasma inulin concentration (P_{In}):

$$\begin{aligned} C_{In} &= \frac{U_{In} V}{P_{In}} \\ &= \frac{300 \text{ mg/L} \times 0.1 \text{ L/h}}{4 \text{ mg/L}} \\ &= 7.5 \text{ L/h} \end{aligned}$$

Now for the crucial point: Since inulin is filterable at the renal corpuscle but is not reabsorbed, secreted, or metabolized by the tubule, its clearance must equal the volume of plasma originally filtered; that is, C_{In} is equal to GFR.

It is important to realize that the clearance of *any* substance handled by the kidneys' in the same way as inulin—filtered, but not reabsorbed, secreted, or metabolized—would equal the GFR. Unfortunately, there are no substances normally present in the plasma that meet these criteria. Because inulin must be administered, it is usually used as a research tool rather than a routine clinical measurement. For clinical purposes, the **creatinine clearance** (C_{Cr}) is commonly used to *approximate* the GFR as

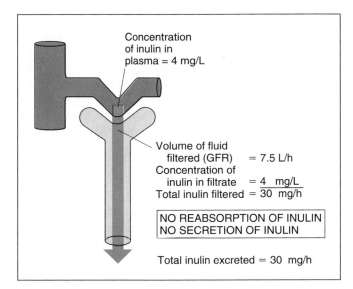

FIGURE 16-10
Example of renal handling of inulin, a substance that is filtered by the renal corpuscles, but is neither reabsorbed nor secreted by the tubule. Therefore, the mass of inulin excreted per unit time is equal to the mass filtered during the same time period, and as explained in the text, the clearance of inulin is equal to the glomerular filtration rate.

follows. The waste product creatinine produced by muscle is filtered at the renal corpuscle and does not undergo reabsorption. It does undergo a small amount of secretion, however, so that some plasma is cleared of its creatinine by secretion. Accordingly, the C_{Cr} overestimates the GFR but is close enough to be highly useful.

The leads to an important generalization: When the clearance of any substance is greater than the GFR, as measured by the inulin clearance, that substance must undergo tubular secretion. Look back now at our hypothetical substance X (page 522): X is filtered, and all the X that escapes filtration is secreted; no X is reabsorbed. Accordingly, all the plasma that enters the kidney per unit time is cleared of its X, and the clearance of X is therefore a measure of renal plasma flow. A substance that is handled like X is the organic anion para-aminohippurate (PAH), which is used for this purpose (unfortunately, like inulin, it must be administered).

One more example is needed: What is the clearance of glucose (C_G) in normal people? The answer is 0 ml/min. As stated earlier, no glucose is normally excreted in the urine; accordingly, the numerator of the clearance equation is 0 and C_G is 0. This leads to another important generalization: When the clearance of a filterable substance is less than the GFR, as measured by the inulin clearance, that substance must undergo reabsorption. For a substance that undergoes only partial reabsorption, so-dium, for example, the clearance value will not be zero but will still be less than the inulin clearance.

MICTURITION

Urine flow through the ureters to the bladder is propelled by contractions of the ureter-wall smooth muscle. The urine is stored in the bladder and intermittently ejected during urination, termed **micturition**.

The bladder is a balloon-like chamber with walls of smooth muscle collectively termed the **detrusor muscle**, the contraction of which squeezes on the urine in the lumen to produce urination. That part of the detrusor muscle at the base (or "neck") of the bladder where the urethra begins functions as a sphincter—the **internal urethral sphincter**. Because of its anatomical orienta-

FIGURE 16-11
Micturition reflex. As the bladder fills with urine, stimulation of the stretch receptors in the bladder walls causes reflex stimulation of the parasympathetic nerves to the bladder and inhibition of the motor nerves to the external urethral sphincter. The result is bladder contraction and sphincter relaxation. Not shown in the figure is the fact that ascending pathways triggered by the stretch receptors act upon higher brain-centers to give the awareness of bladder fullness and the desire to urinate. Descending input from these higher centers acts on the efferent neurons, as described in the text, to allow voluntary initiation or delay of micturition.

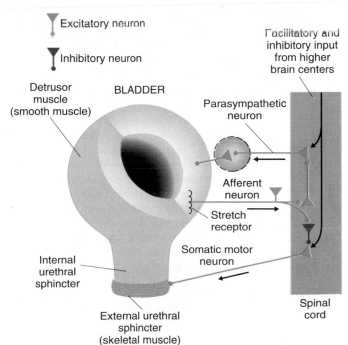

TABLE 16-3   AVERAGE DAILY WATER GAIN AND LOSS IN ADULTS

Intake	
Drunk	1200 ml
In food	1000 ml
Metabolically produced	350 ml
Total	2550 ml
Output	
Insensible loss (skin and lungs)	900 ml
Sweat	50 ml
In feces	100 ml
Urine	1500 ml
Total	2550 ml

strual flow constitutes a fifth potential source of water loss in women. The loss of water by evaporation from the skin and the lining of respiratory passageways is a continuous process, often referred to as **insensible water loss**, because the person is unaware of its occurrence. Additional water can be made available for evaporation from the skin by the production of sweat. Normal gastrointestinal loss of water in feces is generally quite small but can be severe in diarrhea. Gastrointestinal loss can also be large in vomiting.

Table 16-4 is a summary of total-body balance for sodium chloride. The excretion of sodium and chloride via the skin and gastrointestinal tract is normally quite small but may increase markedly during severe sweating, vomiting, or diarrhea.

Hemorrhage can also result in loss of large quantities of both salt and water.

Under normal conditions, as can be seen from Tables 16-3 and 16-4, salt and water losses exactly equal salt and water gains, and no net change in body salt and water occurs. As we stated at the beginning of this chapter, this matching of losses and gains is primarily the result of regulation of urinary loss, which can be varied over an extremely wide range. For example, urinary water excretion can vary from approximately 0.4 L/day to 25 L/day, depending upon whether one is lost in the desert or partici-

TABLE 16-4   DAILY SODIUM CHLORIDE INTAKE AND LOSS

Intake	
Food	10.50 g
Output	
Sweat	0.25 g
Feces	0.25 g
Urine	10.00 g
Total	10.50 g

pating in a beer-drinking contest. Similarly, some individuals ingest 20 to 25 g of sodium chloride per day, whereas a person on a low-salt diet may ingest only 50 mg. The normal kidney can readily alter its excretion of salt over this range to match loss with gain.

We will first present the basic renal processes—filtration and reabsorption—for sodium and water and then describe the homeostatic reflexes that influence these processes. The renal processing of chloride is usually coupled directly or indirectly to that of sodium, and so we shall have little more to say about chloride even though it is the most abundant anion in the extracellular fluid.

BASIC RENAL PROCESSES FOR SODIUM AND WATER

Being of low molecular weight and not bound to protein, both sodium and water freely filter from the glomerular capillaries into Bowman's space. They both undergo considerable reabsorption—normally more than 99 percent (Table 16-2)—but no secretion. Most renal energy utilization goes to accomplish this enormous reabsorptive task. The bulk of sodium and water reabsorption—about two-thirds—occurs in the proximal tubule, but the major hormonal controls of reabsorption are exerted on the collecting ducts. The mechanisms of sodium and water reabsorption can be summarized by two generalizations: (1) Sodium reabsorption is a primary active process occurring in all four major tubular segments—the proximal tubule, loop of Henle, distal convoluted tubule, and collecting duct; and (2) water reabsorption is by diffusion and is dependent upon sodium reabsorption.

Primary Active Sodium Reabsorption

The reabsorption of sodium and water occurs largely by the mechanisms of transcellular epithelial transport described in Chapter 6. The key feature throughout the tubule is the primary active transport of sodium, via basolateral-membrane Na,K-ATPase pumps, out of the cells and into the interstitial fluid (Figure 16-12). This active transport keeps the intracellular concentration of sodium low compared to the luminal concentration, and so sodium diffuses out of the lumen into the tubular epithelial cells. As summarized in Figures 16-12 and 16-13, the precise mechanism of this passive sodium movement across the luminal membrane varies from segment to segment of the tubule depending upon which channels and/or transporters are present in their luminal membranes.

Coupling of Water Reabsorption to Sodium Reabsorption

How does active sodium reabsorption lead to passive water reabsorption? The movement of sodium from the

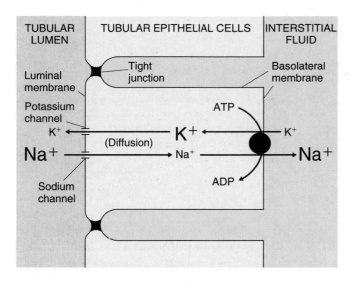

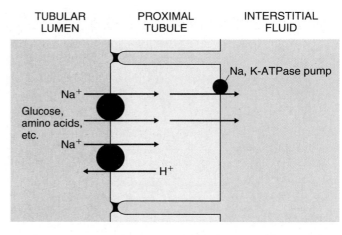

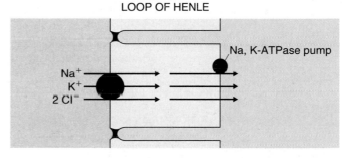

FIGURE 16-12

Mechanism of sodium reabsorption in the cortical collecting duct. The sizes of the letters for Na^+ and K^+ denote high and low concentrations of these ions. Na,K-ATPase pumps in the epithelial cell's basolateral membrane actively transport sodium out of the cell. This produces a low cytosolic sodium concentration, relative to that of the tubular lumen, and this concentration gradient causes the diffusion of Na^+ across the luminal membrane through sodium channels. (In addition to this concentration gradient favoring diffusion, there is an electrical gradient—not shown in the figure—because the cell interior is negative relative to the lumen.) Note that the K^+ pumped into the cell across the basolateral membrane diffuses into the tubular lumen through K^+ channels in the luminal membrane. Thus, as described later in the text, the *reabsorption* of sodium by the cortical collecting duct is associated with the *secretion* of potassium by this tubular segment.

tubular lumen to the interstitial fluid across the epithelial cells lowers the osmolarity, that is, *raises* the water concentration, of the luminal fluid (see Chapter 6 for a review of osmolarity and water concentration). It simultaneously raises the osmolarity, that is, *lowers* the water concentration, of the interstitial fluid adjacent to the epithelial cells. The difference in water concentration between lumen and interstitial fluid causes net diffusion of water from the lumen across the tubular cells' plasma membranes and/or tight junctions into the interstitial fluid. From there, water, sodium, and everything else in the interstitial fluid move together by bulk flow into peritubular capillaries as the final step in reabsorption (Figure 16-14).

Water movement across the tubular epithelium can occur, however, only if the epithelium is permeable to water. No matter how large its concentration gradient, water cannot cross an epithelium impermeable to it. Water permeability varies from tubular segment to segment. The water permeability of the proximal tubule is always very

FIGURE 16-13

Sodium reabsorption in tubular segments other than the cortical collecting duct. The essential points for these segments are: (1) Sodium movement across the basolateral membrane is, as in the cortical collecting duct (Figure 16-12), always via active Na,K-ATPase pumps; (2) the luminal entry step for sodium is always downhill (passive) but is via carrier-mediated transport systems rather than through channels, as is the case in the cortical collecting duct; (3) these luminal transporters simultaneously achieve *secondary active* cotransport of glucose, amino acids, potassium, and chloride into the cell or countertransport of hydrogen ion into the lumen. The cotransported substances then move passively (the mechanisms are not shown in the figure) across the basolateral membrane into the interstitial fluid and thence into peritubular capillaries. Thus, sodium reabsorption achieves the reabsorption of all these cotransported substances. This explains, for example, why the proximal tubule is the only site of glucose reabsorption—it is the only site that has the luminal-membrane Na/glucose cotransporter. The origin of the hydrogen ions countertransported with sodium is described later in the chapter.

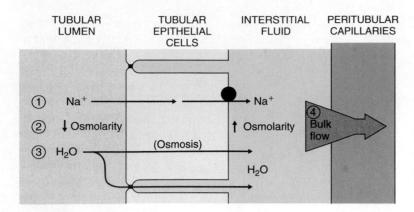

FIGURE 16-14

Coupling of water and sodium reabsorption. (1) Reabsorption of sodium creates (2) a difference in osmolarity between lumen and interstitial fluid, which causes (3) the diffusion of water in the same direction either through the cell or across the tight junctions. (4) Movement of both solute and water from interstitial fluid into peritubular capillaries occurs by bulk flow.

high, and so water molecules are reabsorbed by this segment almost as rapidly as sodium ions. As a result, the proximal tubule always reabsorbs sodium and water in the same proportions.

We will describe the water permeability of the next tubular segments—the loop of Henle and distal convoluted tubule—later. Now for the really crucial point: The water permeability of the last portions of the tubules—the collecting ducts—can be high or low because it is subject to physiological control, the only tubular segments under such control.

The major determinant of this controlled permeability, and hence of water reabsorption in the collecting ducts, is a peptide hormone secreted by the posterior pituitary and known as **antidiuretic hormone (ADH)** or **vasopressin**.[5] ADH stimulates production of cyclic AMP in the epithelial cells of the collecting ducts, and this second messenger then induces, by a sequence of events, the insertion into the luminal membrane of proteins that function as water channels. Accordingly, in the presence of a high plasma concentration of ADH, the water permeability of the collecting ducts is very great, water reabsorption is maximal, and the final urine volume is small—less than 1 percent of the filtered water. In the absence of ADH, the water permeability of the collecting ducts is very low, and very little water is reabsorbed from these sites.[6] Therefore, a large volume of water remains behind in the tubule to be excreted in the urine, which is hypoosmotic, that is, has an osmolarity much lower than that of plasma. This increased urine excretion resulting from low

ADH is termed **water diuresis** ("**diuresis**" simply means a large urine flow from any cause). In a subsequent section we will describe the reflexes that control ADH secretion.

The disease ***diabetes insipidus***, which is distinct from diabetes mellitus or "sugar diabetes," illustrates what happens when the ADH system is disrupted. People with this disease have lost the ability to produce ADH, usually as a result of damage to the hypothalamus. Thus, the permeability to water of the collecting ducts is low and unchanging regardless of the state of the body fluids, and diabetes insipidus is characterized by a constant water diuresis—as much as 25 L/day. In most cases, the flow can be restored to normal by the administration of ADH.

Note that in water diuresis, there is an increased urine flow but not an increased solute excretion. In all other cases of diuresis, termed **osmotic diuresis**, the increased urine flow (increased water excretion) is the result of a primary increase in solute excretion. For example, failure to reabsorb sodium normally will cause not only increased sodium excretion but increased water excretion as well since, as we have seen, water reabsorption is absolutely dependent on solute reabsorption. Another example of osmotic diuresis occurs in patients with uncontrolled marked diabetes *mellitus*: In this case, the glucose that escapes reabsorption because of the huge filtered load pulls out water into the urine with it. We shall talk more about the consequences of this in Chapter 18.

From what has been said so far about sodium-water coupling, one might logically, but wrongly, conclude that even in the presence of maximal amounts of ADH, the kidneys would be unable to excrete a hyperosmotic urine, that is, one with an osmolarity greater than that of plasma. For this to occur, relatively more water must be reabsorbed than sodium, but how can this happen when water reabsorption is always secondary to sodium reabsorption? The answer is given in the rest of this section.

Urine Concentration: The Countercurrent Multiplier System

The ability of the kidneys to produce hyperosmotic urine is a major determinant of one's ability to survive without

---

[5]Throughout this chapter, we use the name "antidiuretic hormone" in keeping with the action of this hormone on the kidney. Its other name, "vasopressin," which is becoming its "official" label, reflects the fact, noted in Chapter 14, that this hormone can also exert a direct vasoconstrictor action on arterioles, resulting in elevated total peripheral resistance and thereby increased arterial blood pressure.

[6]What makes the luminal plasma membranes of these tubular segments, in contrast to most plasma membranes, so impermeable to water in the absence of the water channels induced by ADH is not known.

water. The human kidney can produce a maximal urinary concentration of 1400 mOsmol/L, almost five times the osmolarity of plasma, which is 300 mOsmol/L. The typical daily excretion of urea, sulfate, phosphate, other waste products, and ions amounts to approximately 600 mOsmol. Therefore, the minimal volume of urine water in which this mass of solute can be dissolved equals

$$\frac{600 \text{ mOsmol/day}}{1400 \text{ mOsmol/L}} = 0.444 \text{ L/day}$$

This volume of urine is known as the **obligatory water loss**. The loss of this minimal volume of urine (it would be somewhat lower if no food were available) contributes to dehydration when a person is deprived of water intake.

Urinary concentration takes place as the tubular fluid flows through the medullary collecting ducts. The interstitial fluid surrounding these ducts is very hyperosmotic, and in the presence of ADH water therefore diffuses out of the ducts into the interstitial fluid and thence into the blood vessels of the medulla. The key question is: How did the medullary interstitial fluid become hyperosmotic?

The complex process that sets up this interstitial hyperosmolarity is called the **countercurrent multiplier system** and takes place in the loops of Henle. These loops, like the collecting ducts, extend into the medulla, and the long loops from the juxtamedullary nephrons extend to its very tip. The fluid in a loop flows first in one direction—down the descending limb—and then in the opposite direction—up the ascending limb; thus the name "countercurrent."

First let us explain the principle of countercurrent multiplication with a model that has some features of the loop of Henle but is simpler to visualize (Figure 16-15). Then we will move to the more complex real-life situation. Our model is a hairpin-loop tube through which flows a sodium chloride solution that enters the loop at an osmolarity of 300 mOsmol/L. The ascending limb actively cotransports sodium and chloride into the descending limb and is relatively impermeable to water, so that little water can follow the salt. The pump can achieve a maximal osmolarity difference of 200 mOsmol/L across the loop. Let us look at what occurs under conditions of tubular flow, simplifying the analysis by assuming that fluid flow along the tubule and ion pumping occur in discontinuous out-of-phase steps. Think of it as a series of snapshots of the loop.

We begin (A) by allowing the entire loop to fill with fluid having an osmolarity of 300 mOsmol/L. Then we stop the flow and allow the pumps all along the ascending loop to operate so that the osmolarity in the entire ascending limb falls to 200 mOsmol/L and that of the descending limb rises to 400 mOsmol/L (B). Then we restart the flow (C) until new 300-mOsmol/L fluid fills the top half of the descending limb; this new fluid of course pushes the entire

fluid column in front of it down, around, and up, so that an equal volume of 200-mOsmol/L fluid is forced out the top of the ascending limb. Again flow is stopped and the pumps begin operating until once again they have established a 200-mOsmol/L difference across the tubule (D). The sequence is repeated once more (E and F), this time allowing only half as much new 300-mOsmol/L fluid to enter the descending limb as in step C.

The critical point emerges after this last cycle is completed: Even though only a 200-mOsmol/L difference exists across the loop *at each level*, a 275-mOsmol/L difference exists *from the top of the descending loop to the bottom*. In other words, the 200-mOsmol/L difference generated at each level by the pumps has been *multiplied* along the length of the tubule by the countercurrent system. With continued small cycles of the system, the multiplication would have been much greater than the extra 75 mOsmol/L shown here.

We can now apply this model to the loop of Henle. Because the proximal tubule always reabsorbs sodium and water in the same proportions, the fluid entering the descending limb from the proximal tubule is the same as plasma—300 mOsmol/L. The Na,K,2Cl cotransporters in the *ascending* limb (Figure 16-13) actively cotransport sodium and chloride (we shall ignore the potassium) into the medullary interstitial fluid.[7] The ascending limb is relatively impermeable to water, so that little water follows the salt. Note the major difference between the previous model and the loop of Henle: The pumps in the ascending limb do not transport sodium and chloride into the descending limb but rather into the interstitial fluid surrounding the tubules.

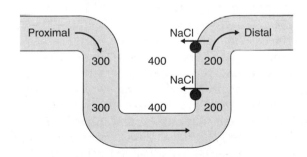

The *descending* limb, in contrast to the ascending limb, does not pump sodium chloride and is highly permeable to water. Therefore, there is a net diffusion of water out of the descending limb into the more concentrated intersti-

---

[7]These transporters probably exist only in the thick segment of the ascending limb. How sodium and chloride move across the epithelial cells of the thin segment is not known with certainty. For simplicity, we have treated the entire ascending limb as though it had the characteristics of the thick portion.

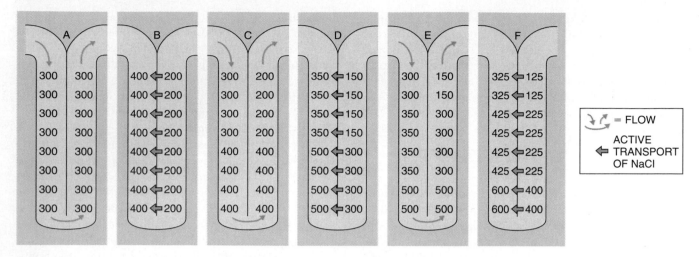

FIGURE 16-15

Model to illustrate the basic principle of countercurrent multiplication. The ascending limb actively transports sodium chloride into the descending limb. The transport process and the flow of fluid through the loop actually occur continuously but have been separated into discontinuous steps for purposes of illustration.

tial fluid until the osmolarities inside this limb and in the interstitial fluid are again equal. The interstitial osmolarity is maintained at 400 mOsmol/L during this equilibration because the ascending limb continues to pump sodium chloride to maintain the 200-mOsmol/L difference between it and the interstitial fluid.

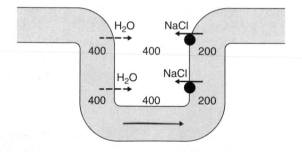

Thus, the osmolarities of the descending limb and interstitial fluid become equal, and both are 200 mOsmol/L higher than that of the ascending limb. This is the essence of the system: The loop countercurrent multiplier causes the interstitial fluid of the medulla to become concentrated. It is this hyperosmolarity that will draw water out of the collecting ducts and concentrate the urine.

When we allow flow in this system, as in our simpler model, the result is the same (Figure 16-16): Multiplication of the osmolarity difference from 200 mOsmol/L at any given level to a much higher value—1400 mOsmol/L in this case—at the bend in the loop. It should be emphasized that the active sodium chloride transport mechanism in the ascending limb is the essential component of the

entire system. Without it, the countercurrent flow would have no effect whatever on loop and interstitial concentrations.

Now we have our concentrated medullary interstitial fluid, but we must still follow the fluid *within* the tubules from the loop of Henle through the distal convoluted tubule and into the collecting duct, using Figure 16-16 as our guide. The countercurrent multiplier system concentrates the descending-loop fluid, but then it redilutes it in the ascending loop so that the fluid entering the distal convoluted tubule is actually more dilute than the plasma (hypoosmotic). This situation persists throughout the distal convoluted tubule, since this tubular segment, like the ascending loop, actively transports sodium chloride out of the tubule but is relatively impermeable to water. Thus, hypoosmotic fluid then enters the cortical collecting duct.

As noted earlier, here in the collecting duct is where ADH increases tubular permeability to water. In other words, ADH does not influence water reabsorption in the earlier parts of the tubule and so, regardless of the plasma concentration of this hormone, the fluid entering the cortical collecting duct is always hypoosmotic. From here on, however, ADH is crucial. In the presence of high levels of ADH, water reabsorption occurs, by diffusion, from the hypoosmotic fluid in the cortical collecting duct until the fluid in this segment becomes isoosmotic to plasma, that is, until it is once again at 300 mOsmol/L.

This isoosmotic tubular fluid then enters and flows along the medullary collecting ducts. Under the influence of ADH, the medullary collecting ducts are also highly permeable to water, which diffuses out of the ducts into

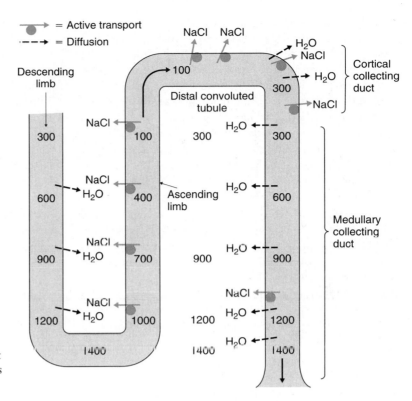

FIGURE 16-16
Generation of an interstitial fluid osmolarity gradient by the renal countercurrent multiplier system and its role in the formation of hyperosmotic urine.

the medullary interstitial fluid as a result of the high osmolarity set up there by the loop countercurrent multiplier system. This water then enters the medullary capillaries (recall that these are the vasa recta) and is carried out of the kidneys by the venous blood. Water reabsorption occurs all along the lengths of the medullary collecting ducts so that, in the presence of ADH, the fluid at the end of these ducts has essentially the same osmolarity as the interstitial fluid surrounding the bend in the loops, that is, at the bottom of the medulla. By this means, the final urine is hyperosmotic.[8] By retaining as much water as possible, the kidneys compensate for a body water deficit.

In contrast, when plasma ADH concentration is low, both the cortical and medullary collecting ducts become relatively impermeable to water. Therefore, fluid in the cortical collecting ducts does not reequilibrate with cortical peritubular plasma, and, even more important, the high medullary interstitial osmolarity set up by the loop is ineffective in inducing water movement out of the medullary collecting ducts. As a result, a large volume of hypoosmotic urine is excreted, thereby compensating for an excess of water in the body.

---

[8]We have presented here only the absolutely essential components of the countercurrent multiplier system. It is actually much more complex and includes a unique role for the vasa recta, nonhomogeneity of the thin and thick segments of the ascending loop, and a contribution from urea as well as sodium and chloride. The interested reader can consult the suggested readings for this chapter listed in Appendix G.

RENAL SODIUM REGULATION

Now we turn to the reflexes that play upon the basic renal processes for sodium and, in the next section, water to regulate their excretion. In normal individuals, urinary sodium excretion is reflexly increased when there is a sodium excess in the body and reflexly decreased when there is a sodium deficit. These reflexes are so precise that total-body sodium normally varies by only a few percent despite a wide range of sodium intakes and the sporadic occurrence of large losses via the skin and gastrointestinal tract.

Since sodium is freely filterable from the glomerular capillaries into Bowman's space and actively reabsorbed but not secreted, the amount of sodium excreted in the urine represents the resultant of two processes:

Sodium excreted = sodium filtered − sodium reabsorbed

The body is able to reflexly adjust sodium excretion by changing both processes. Thus, when total-body sodium decreases for any reason, sodium excretion is reflexly decreased below normal levels by lowering the GFR and raising sodium reabsorption.

Most of these reflexes are initiated by various cardiovascular baroreceptors, such as the carotid sinus. As described in Chapter 14, baroreceptors respond to pressure changes within the cardiovascular system and initiate reflexes that regulate these pressures. The reason that regulation of cardiovascular pressures by baroreceptors simultaneously achieves regulation of total-body sodium is that these variables are closely correlated, as described in the next paragraph.

Because sodium is the major extracellular solute, changes in total-body sodium result in similar changes in extracellular volume. Now, since extracellular volume comprises plasma volume and interstitial volume, plasma volume is also significantly affected by total-body sodium. We saw in Chapter 14 that plasma volume is in turn an important determinant of the pressures in the veins, cardiac chambers, and arteries. Thus, the chain linking total-body sodium to cardiovascular pressures is completed: Low total-body sodium leads to low plasma volume, which leads to low cardiovascular pressures, which, via baroreceptors, initiate reflexes that (1) restore the cardiovascular pressures via direct actions on the cardiovascular system (Chapter 14), and (2) simultaneously lower GFR and increase sodium reabsorption. These latter events decrease sodium excretion, thereby retaining sodium in the body and preventing further decreases in plasma volume and cardiovascular pressures. Increases in total-body sodium have the the reverse reflex effects.

Control of GFR

Figure 16-17 summarizes the major mechanisms by which a lower total-body sodium, as caused by diarrhea, for example, elicits a decrease in GFR. The key event—a reduced glomerular capillary pressure—occurs both as a direct consequence of a lowered arterial pressure in the kidneys and, more importantly, as a result of baroreceptor reflexes acting on the afferent arterioles. Note that the latter are simply the basic baroreceptor reflexes described in Chapter 14, where it was pointed out that a decrease in cardiovascular pressures causes reflex vasoconstriction in many areas of the body.

Conversely, an increased GFR is elicited when an increased total-body sodium level causes increased plasma volume, and this increased GFR contributes to the increased renal sodium loss that returns extracellular volume to normal.[9]

Control of Sodium Reabsorption

As far as long-term regulation of sodium excretion is concerned, the control of sodium reabsorption is more important than the control of GFR. The major factor determining the rate of tubular sodium reabsorption is the hormone aldosterone.

---

[9]In addition to being acted upon by this neural reflex control of GFR, the renal blood vessels are affected by several hormones. Moreover, the kidneys have the ability to self-regulate their own GFR (and blood flow). These mechanisms are described in the suggested readings for this chapter listed in Appendix G.

Aldosterone and the Renin-Angiotensin System. The adrenal cortex produces a steroid hormone, **aldosterone**, which stimulates sodium reabsorption by the cortical collecting ducts. By the time this portion of the tubule has been reached, almost all (approximately 98 percent) of the filtered sodium has already been reabsorbed by earlier tubular segments. Aldosterone then controls the reabsorption of this last remaining sodium. When this hormone is completely absent, virtually all of this sodium (equivalent to 35 g of sodium chloride per day) will not be reabsorbed but is excreted. When aldosterone is present in large quantities, essentially all of the remaining sodium will be reabsorbed and none excreted. In a normal person, the amounts of aldosterone produced and sodium excreted lie somewhere between these extremes, varying reflexly with the amount of sodium ingested.

Aldosterone, like other steroids, acts by inducing the synthesis of proteins in its target cells, in this case proteins involved in sodium transport—for example, proteins that function as sodium channels in the luminal membrane and proteins that constitute the Na,K-ATPase pumps. (By this same mechanism, aldosterone also stimulates sodium transport into the blood from the lumens of both the large intestine and the ducts carrying fluid from the sweat glands and salivary glands. In this manner, less sodium is lost in the feces and from the surface of the skin in sweat.)

The secretion of aldosterone is controlled, in part, by reflexes involving the kidneys, specifically the juxtaglomerular apparatus, and a hormonal complex called the **renin-angiotensin system**. As mentioned in the section on renal anatomy, the juxtaglomerular cells of the juxtaglomerular apparatus synthesize and secrete into the blood a protein known as **renin**. This protein acts as an enzyme to split off a small polypeptide, **angiotensin I**, from a large plasma protein, **angiotensinogen** (Figure 16-18). Angiotensin I then undergoes further cleavage to form **angiotensin II**. This conversion is mediated by an enzyme known as **angiotensin converting enzyme**, which is found in very high concentration on the luminal surface of capillary endothelial cells, particularly those in the lung. Thus, most conversion of angiotensin I to angiotensin II occurs as blood flows through the lungs. Angiotensin II is a potent stimulator of aldosterone secretion and constitutes a major input to the adrenal cortex controlling the production and release of this hormone.

FIGURE 16-17 (*opposite*)
Direct and reflex pathways by which the GFR and hence sodium and water excretion are decreased when plasma volume decreases. The reflex pathway, initiated by baroreceptors in large veins, the atria, and the carotid sinuses and aortic arch, is much more effective in lowering GFR than is the direct effect on the kidneys of the lowered arterial pressure.

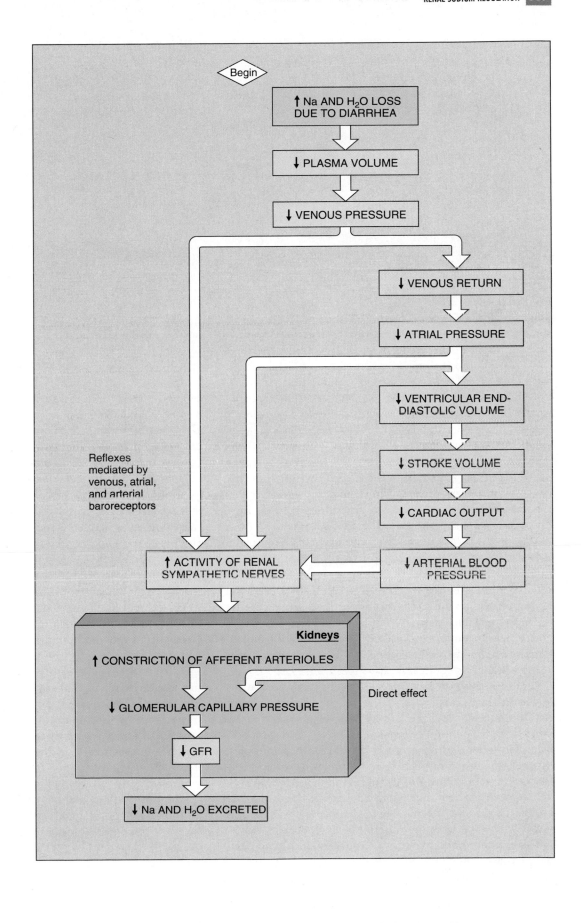

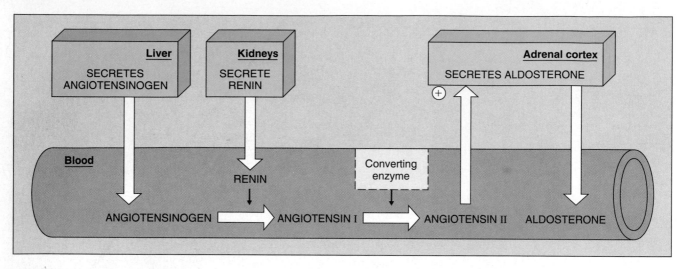

FIGURE 16-18

Summary of the renin-angiotensin-aldosterone system. Converting enzyme is located on the surface of capillary endothelial cells, particularly in the lungs. Renin is the rate-limiting factor in the system.

What determines the plasma concentration of angiotensin II? Angiotensinogen is synthesized by the liver and is always present in the blood. Angiotensin converting enzyme is also always present in amounts adequate to convert all angiotensin I to angiotensin II. Therefore, the rate-limiting factor in angiotensin II formation is the concentration of plasma renin, which in turn depends upon the rate of renin secretion by the kidneys. The critical question now becomes: What controls renin secretion?

There are at least three distinct inputs to the juxtaglomerular cells: (1) the renal sympathetic nerves, (2) *intrarenal* baroreceptors, and (3) the macula densa. That the renal sympathetic nerves constitute one important input makes excellent sense teleologically, since a reduction in body sodium and plasma volume lowers blood pressure and, via baroreceptors external to the kidneys, triggers increased sympathetic discharge to the juxtaglomerular cells, stimulating renin release (Figure 16-19).

The other two inputs for controlling renin release—intrarenal baroreceptors and the macula densa—are totally contained within the kidneys and require no external neuroendocrine input. As noted earlier, the juxtaglomerular cells are located in the walls of the afferent arterioles; they are themselves sensitive to the pressure within these arterioles, and so function as **intrarenal baroreceptors**. When renal arterial (and hence arteriolar) pressure decreases, as would occur when extracellular volume is down, these cells secrete more renin (Figure 16-19). Thus, normally, the juxtaglomerular cells respond simultaneously to the combined effects of sympathetic input, triggered by baroreceptors *external* to the kidneys, and to their own pressure sensitivity.

The second completely internal input to the juxtaglomerular cells is via the macula densa, which, as noted ear-lier, is located near the ends of the ascending loops of Henle. The macula densa senses the sodium and/or chloride concentration in the fluid flowing past it, a decreased salt concentration causing increased renin secretion. For several reasons, including a decrease in GFR and hence tubular flow rate, macula densa sodium and chloride concentrations tend to decrease when a person's arterial pressure is decreased. This input therefore also signals for increased renin release at the same time that the sympathetic nerves and intrarenal baroreceptor are doing so (Figure 16-19).[10]

By helping to regulate sodium balance, and thereby plasma volume, the renin-angiotensin system contributes to the control of arterial blood pressure. However, this is not the only way in which it influences arterial pressure. Recall from Chapter 14 that angiotensin II is a potent constrictor of arterioles and that this effect on peripheral resistance increases arterial pressure. Abnormal increases in the activity of the renin-angiotensin system (as occurs, for example, when a renal artery becomes partially occluded) can contribute to the development of **hypertension** (high blood pressure) via both the sodium-retaining and arteriole-constricting effects. It should not be surprising, therefore, that certain individuals suffering from hypertension are treated with drugs that block the renin-angiotensin system. One such group of drugs (termed ***angiotensin converting enzyme [ACE] inhibitors***) blocks the action of angiotensin converting enzyme, thus preventing the generation of angiotensin II.

---

[10]In addition to its control of renin release, the macula densa has another quite distinct function: It participates in control of its own nephron's GFR. See suggested readings listed in Appendix G.

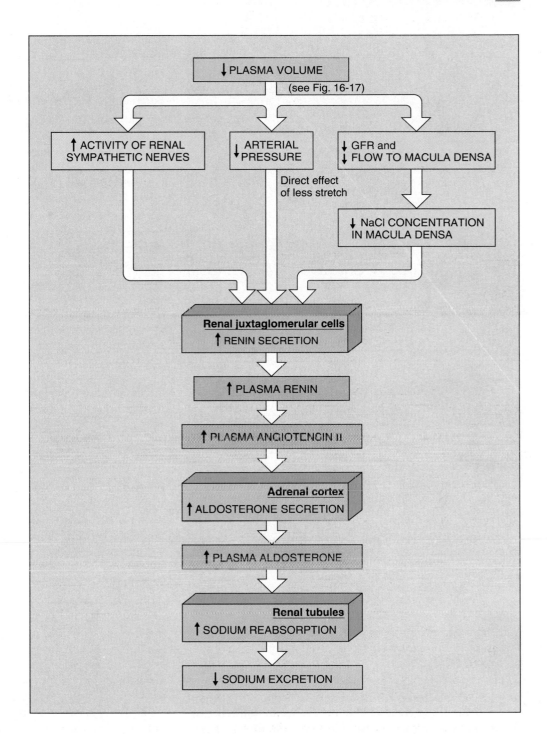

FIGURE 16-19

Pathways by which decreased plasma volume leads, via the renin-angiotensin system and aldosterone, to increased sodium reabsorption and hence decreased sodium excretion.

Atrial Natriuretic Factor.   Although aldosterone is the most important controller of sodium reabsorption, a variety of other factors also play roles, including the renal nerves (which act directly on the tubules to stimulate sodium reabsorption) and a variety of other hormones. The most important of these is the peptide hormone known as **atrial natriuretic factor (ANF)**, which is synthesized and secreted by cells in the cardiac atria. ANF acts on the kidneys to inhibit sodium reabsorption. It also acts on the renal blood vessels to increase GFR, which further contributes to increased sodium excretion. As would be predicted, the secretion of ANF is increased when there is an excess of sodium in the body, the stimulus being an increase in atrial distention (Figure 16-20).

This completes our survey of the control of sodium excretion, which depends upon the control of two renal variables—the GFR and sodium reabsorption. The latter is controlled by the renin-angiotensin-aldosterone hormone system and by other factors, including atrial natriuretic factor. The reflexes that control both GFR and sodium reabsorption are essentially reflexes that regulate blood pressure since they are most frequently initiated by changes in arterial or venous pressures.

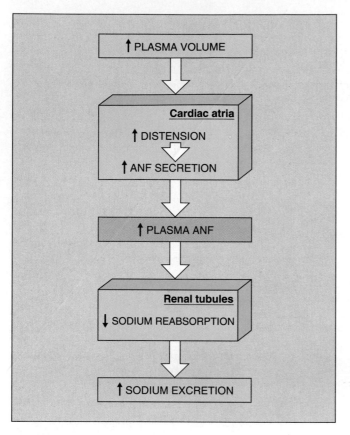

FIGURE 16-20

Atrial natriuretic factor in the *direct* control of sodium reabsorption and hence sodium excretion. ANF exerts several other effects not shown in the figure: (1) it inhibits the secretion of renin and of aldosterone and this leads *indirectly* to decreased sodium reabsorption; (2) by actions on the renal blood vessels, it also increases GFR, which further contributes to increased sodium excretion.

RENAL WATER REGULATION

Water excretion, like sodium excretion, is the difference between the volume of water filtered (the GFR) and the volume reabsorbed. Accordingly, the baroreceptor-initiated GFR-controlling reflexes described in the previous section tend to have the same effects on water excretion as on sodium excretion. As in the case of sodium, however, the major regulated determinant of water excretion is not GFR, but instead the rate of water reabsorption. As we have seen, this is determined by ADH, and so total-body water is regulated mainly by reflexes that alter the secretion of this hormone.

As described in Chapter 10, ADH is produced by a discrete group of hypothalamic neurons whose axons termi-

nate in the posterior pituitary, from which ADH is released into the blood. The most important of the inputs to these neurons are from baroreceptors and osmoreceptors.

Baroreceptor Control of ADH Secretion

We have seen that a decreased extracellular volume, due say to diarrhea or hemorrhage, reflexly calls forth, via the renin-angiotensin system, an increased aldosterone secretion. The new fact is that decreased extracellular volume also triggers increased ADH secretion. This increased ADH increases the water permeability of the collecting ducts, more water is reabsorbed and less is excreted, and so water is retained in the body to help stabilize the extracellular volume.

This reflex is mediated by neural input to the ADH-secreting cells from several baroreceptors in the cardiovascular system (Figure 16-21). The baroreceptors decrease their rate of firing with the decreased cardiovascular pressures that occur when blood volume decreases. When fewer impulses are transmitted from the baroreceptors via afferent neurons and ascending pathways to the hypothalamus, the result is increased ADH secretion. Conversely, increased cardiovascular pressures cause more firing by the baroreceptors, resulting in a decrease in ADH secretion.

FIGURE 16-21

Baroreceptor pathway by which ADH secretion is decreased when plasma volume is increased. The greater plasma volume raises cardiovascular pressures, which stimulate baroreceptors and thereby inhibit ADH secretion. The opposite events (an increase in ADH secretion) occur when plasma volume decreases, as during hemorrhage.

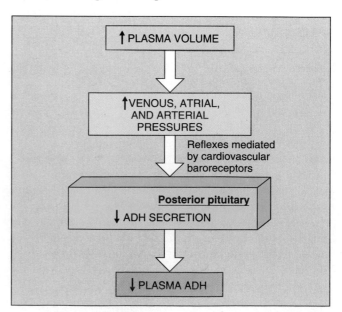

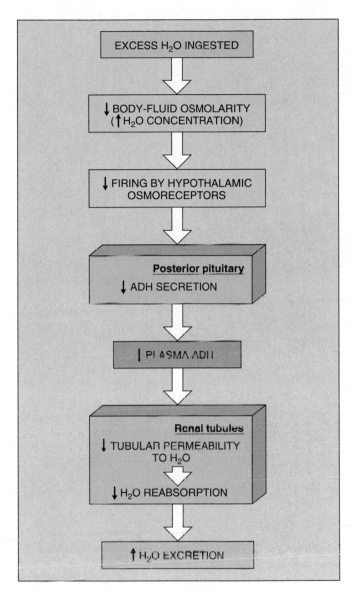

FIGURE 16-22
Osmoreceptor pathway by which ADH secretion is lowered and water excretion raised when excess water is ingested. The opposite events (a decrease in ADH secretion) occur when osmolarity increases, as during water deprivation.

Osmoreceptor Control of ADH Secretion

We have seen how changes in extracellular volume simultaneously elicit reflex changes in the excretion of *both* sodium *and* water. This is adaptive since the situations causing extracellular volume alterations are very often associated with loss or gain of both sodium and water in approximately proportional amounts. In contrast, we shall see now that changes in total-body water in which no change in total-body sodium occurs are compensated for by altering water excretion without altering sodium excretion.

The major change caused by water loss or gain out of proportion to sodium loss or gain is a change in osmolarity of the body fluids. The reason this is a key point is that, under conditions of predominantly water gain or loss, the receptors that initiate the reflexes controlling ADH secretion are **osmoreceptors** in the hypothalamus, receptors responsive to changes in osmolarity.

Take, as an example, a person drinking 2 L of sugar-free soft drink, which contains little sodium or other solute, in a short time. The excess water lowers the body-fluid osmolarity, which reflexly inhibits ADH secretion via the hypothalamic osmoreceptors (Figure 16-22). As a result, water permeability of the collecting ducts becomes very low, water is not reabsorbed from these segments, and a large volume of hypoosmotic urine is excreted. In this manner, the excess water is eliminated.

At the other end of the spectrum, when the osmolarity of the body fluids is increased, say, because of water deprivation, ADH secretion is reflexly increased via the osmoreceptors, water reabsorption by the collecting ducts is increased, and a very small volume of highly concentrated urine is excreted. In this manner, the kidneys retain water in excess of solute and reduce the body-fluid osmolarity toward normal.

We have now described two afferent pathways controlling the ADH-secreting hypothalamic cells, one from baroreceptors and one from osmoreceptors. To add to the complexity, these cells receive synaptic input from many other brain areas, so that ADH secretion, and therefore urine volume and concentration, can be altered by pain, fear, and a variety of drugs. For example, alcohol is a powerful inhibitor of ADH release, and this probably accounts for much of the increased urine volume produced following the ingestion of alcohol, a urine volume well in excess of the volume of beverage consumed.

A SUMMARY EXAMPLE: THE RESPONSE TO SWEATING

Figure 16-23 shows the factors that control renal sodium and water excretion in response to severe sweating. Sweat is a hypoosmotic solution containing mainly water, sodium, and chloride. Therefore, sweating causes both a decrease in extracellular volume and an increase in body-fluid osmolarity. The renal retention of water and sodium helps to compensate for the water and salt lost in the sweat.

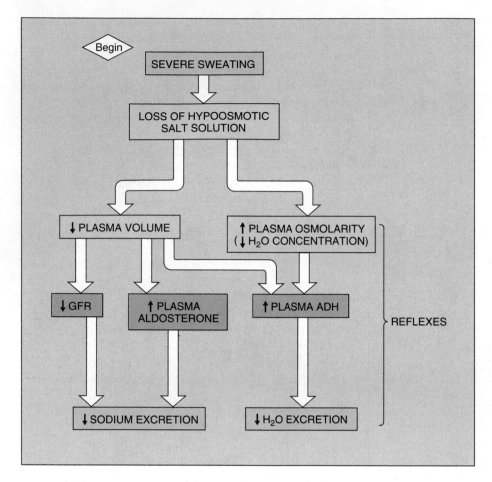

FIGURE 16-23

Pathways by which sodium and water excretion are decreased in response to severe sweating. This figure is an amalgamation of Figs. 16-17, 16-19, and the reverse of 16-21 and 16-22.

THIRST AND SALT APPETITE

Now we turn to the other component of any balance—control of intake. Deficits of salt and water must eventually be compensated for by ingestion of these substances, for the kidneys cannot create new sodium ions or water; they can only minimize their excretion until ingestion replaces the losses.

The subjective feeling of thirst, which drives one to obtain and ingest water, is stimulated both by a lower extracellular volume and a higher plasma osmolarity (Figure 16-24). Note that these are precisely the same two changes that stimulate ADH production, and the osmoreceptors and atrial baroreceptors that control ADH secretion are identical to those for thirst. The brain centers that receive input from these receptors and mediate thirst are located in the hypothalamus, very close to those areas that produce ADH.

Another influencing factor is angiotensin II, which stimulates thirst by a direct effect on the brain. Thus, the renin-angiotensin system helps regulate not only sodium

balance but water balance as well and constitutes one of the pathways by which thirst is stimulated when extracellular volume is decreased.

There are still other pathways controlling thirst. For example, dryness of the mouth and throat causes profound thirst, which is relieved by merely moistening them. Some kind of "metering" of water intake by the gastrointestinal tract also occurs, but its nature remains a mystery.

Although the analog of thirst for sodium, **salt appetite**, is an important component of sodium homeostasis in most mammals, its contribution to everyday sodium homeostasis in normal human beings is probably slight.

POTASSIUM REGULATION

Potassium is, as we have seen, the most abundant intracellular ion. Although only 2 percent of total-body potassium is in the extracellular fluid, the potassium concentration in this fluid is extremely important for the function of excitable tissues, notably nerve and muscle. Recall

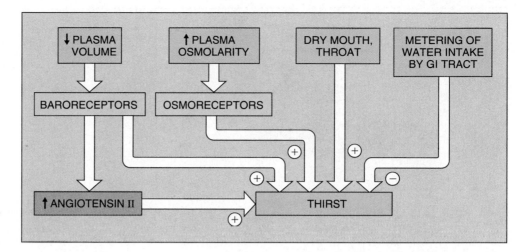

FIGURE 16-24

Inputs reflexly controlling thirst. Psychosocial factors and conditioned responses are not shown.

(Chapter 8) that the resting-membrane potentials of these tissues are directly related to the relative intracellular and extracellular potassium concentrations. An increase in extracellular potassium concentration depolarizes plasma membranes, triggering action potentials and often rendering the membrane inexcitable afterward. In the heart this may cause serious abnormalities of heart rhythm, ***arrythmias***. Conversely, lowering the external potassium concentration hyperpolarizes plasma membranes. Therefore, early manifestations of potassium depletion are weakness of skeletal muscles, because of decreased firing of action potentials, and abnormalities of cardiac-muscle conduction and rhythm.

Total-body potassium balance is analogous to that of sodium in that a normal person remains in balance by daily excreting an amount of potassium in the urine equal to the amount ingested minus the amounts eliminated in the feces and sweat. Also, like sodium, potassium losses via sweat and the gastrointestinal tract are normally quite small, although large quantities can be lost during vomiting or diarrhea. The control of renal function is the major mechanism by which body potassium is regulated.

Renal Regulation of Potassium

Potassium is freely filterable from the glomerular capillaries into Bowman's space, and most of this filtered potassium is then reabsorbed by the proximal tubule and loop of Henle. In contrast, the cortical collecting ducts can *secrete* potassium, and changes in potassium *excretion* are due mainly to changes in potassium secretion by this tubular segment.

Thus, during potassium depletion, when the homeostatic response is to minimize potassium loss, there is no potassium secretion by the cortical collecting ducts, and only the small amount of filtered potassium that escaped reabsorption upstream is excreted. In all other situations, to the small amount of potassium not reabsorbed by the proximal tubule and loop of Henle is added a variable amount of potassium secreted by the cortical collecting ducts, an amount necessary to maintain total-body balance (Figure 16-25). The mechanism of this potassium secretion was illustrated in Figure 16-12 in the context of sodium reabsorption.

FIGURE 16-25

Simplified model of the basic renal processing of potassium. Net reabsorption always occurs in the proximal tubule and loop of Henle, but the collecting ducts can show either net reabsorption or net secretion. Usually, net secretion occurs in these ducts (specifically in the cortical collecting duct), as in this figure. In a person who is potassium-depleted, however, net reabsorption occurs in the collecting ducts.

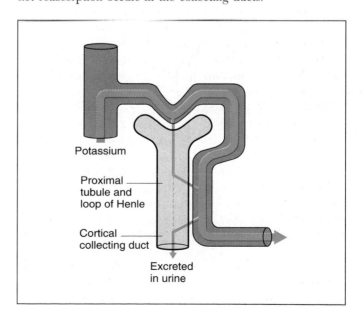

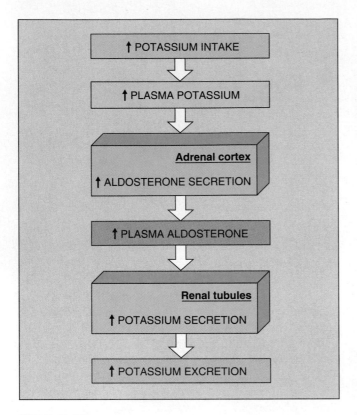

FIGURE 16-26

Pathway by which an increased potassium intake induces greater potassium excretion mediated by aldosterone.

One of the most important factors altering potassium secretion is aldosterone, which in addition to stimulating sodium reabsorption by the cortical collecting duct, increases potassium secretion by it. One of the major mechanisms by which it does so was mentioned earlier—recall that aldosterone stimulates the production of basolateral Na,K-ATPase pumps.

The reflex by which an excess or deficit of potassium controls aldosterone production is completely different from the reflex initiated by changes in extracellular volume. The latter constitutes the complex pathway discussed earlier involving renin and angiotensin. The former is much simpler (Figure 16-26): The aldosterone-secreting cells of the adrenal cortex are sensitive to the potassium concentration of the extracellular fluid bathing them. Thus, an increased intake of potassium leads to an increased extracellular potassium concentration, which in turn directly stimulates aldosterone production by the adrenal cortex. The resulting increased plasma aldosterone concentration increases potassium secretion and thereby eliminates the excess potassium from the body.

Conversely, a lowered extracellular potassium concentration decreases aldosterone production and thereby re-

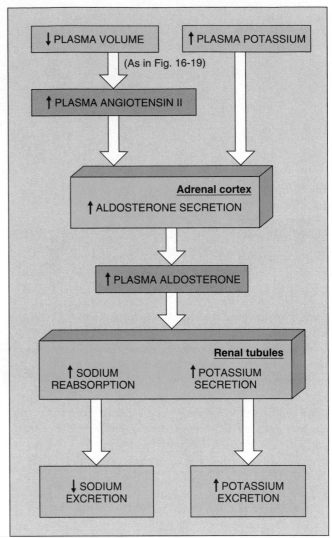

FIGURE 16-27

Summary of the control of aldosterone and its effects on sodium reabsorption and potassium secretion. The fact that a single hormone regulates both sodium and potassium excretion raises the question of potential conflicts between homeostasis of the two ions. For example, if a person were sodium-deficient and therefore secreting large amounts of aldosterone, the potassium-secreting effects of this hormone would tend to cause some potassium loss even though potassium balance were normal to start with. Normally, such conflicts cause only minor imbalances because there are a variety of other counteracting controls of sodium and potassium excretion.

duces potassium secretion. Less potassium than usual is excreted in the urine, thus helping to restore the normal extracellular concentration.

The control and major renal tubular effects of aldosterone are summarized in Figure 16-27.

SECTION B SUMMARY

TOTAL-BODY BALANCE OF SODIUM AND WATER

I. The body gains sodium and chloride by ingestion and loses them via the skin (in sweat), gastrointestinal tract, and urine.

II. The body gains water via ingestion and internal production, and it loses water via urine, the gastrointestinal tract, and evaporation from the skin and respiratory tract (as insensible loss and sweat).

III. For both water and sodium, the major homeostatic control point for maintaining a stable balance is renal excretion.

BASIC RENAL PROCESSES FOR SODIUM AND WATER

I. Sodium is freely filterable at the glomerulus, and its reabsorption is a primary active process dependent upon Na,K-ATPase pumps in the basolateral membranes of the tubular epithelium.

II. Sodium entry into the cell from the tubular lumen is always passive. Depending on the tubular segment, it is either through channels or by cotransport or countertransport with other substances.

III. Sodium reabsorption creates an osmotic difference across the tubule, which drives water reabsorption.

IV. Water reabsorption is independent of the posterior pituitary hormone antidiuretic hormone (ADH) until the collecting ducts, the water permeability of which is increased by this hormone. A large volume of dilute urine is produced when plasma ADH concentration, and hence water reabsorption by the collecting ducts, is low.

V. A small volume of concentrated urine is produced by the renal countercurrent multiplier system when plasma ADH concentration is high.

   A. The active transport of sodium chloride by the ascending loop of Henle is independent of ADH and causes a progressive concentration of the interstitial fluid of the medulla but a dilution of the luminal fluid.

   B. ADH increases the permeability of the cortical collecting ducts to water, and so water is reabsorbed by this segment until the luminal fluid is isoosmotic to cortical interstitial fluid.

   C. The luminal fluid then enters and flows through the medullary collecting ducts, and the concentrated medullary interstitium causes water to move out of these ducts, made highly permeable to water by ADH. The result is concentration of the collecting duct fluid and the urine.

RENAL SODIUM REGULATION

I. Sodium excretion is the difference between the amount of sodium filtered and the amount reabsorbed.

II. GFR, and therefore the filtered load of sodium, are controlled by baroreceptor reflexes. Decreased vascular pressures cause decreased baroreceptor firing and hence reflexly increased sympathetic outflow to the renal arterioles, resulting in vasoconstriction and decreased GFR.

III. The major control of tubular sodium reabsorption is the adrenal cortical hormone aldosterone, which stimulates sodium reabsorption in the cortical collecting ducts.

IV. The renin-angiotensin system is one of the major controllers of aldosterone secretion.

   A. Renin, the rate-limiting variable in the renin-angiotensin system, is secreted by the juxtaglomerular cells of the kidney juxtaglomerular apparatus and catalyzes, in the blood, the formation of angiotensin I from circulating angiotensinogen produced by the liver. Angiotensin I is then cleaved by angiotensin converting enzyme to yield angiotensin II, which acts on the adrenal cortex to stimulate aldosterone secretion.

   B. When extracellular volume decreases, renin secretion is stimulated by three inputs: (1) stimulation of the renal sympathetic nerves to the juxtaglomerular cells by baroreceptor reflexes; (2) pressure decreases sensed by the juxtaglomerular cells, themselves acting as intrarenal baroreceptors; and (3) a signal generated by low sodium or chloride concentration in the macula densa.

V. Atrial natriuretic factor, secreted by cells in the cardiac atria in response to atrial distention, inhibits sodium reabsorption and also increases GFR.

RENAL WATER REGULATION

I. Water excretion is the difference between the amount of water filtered and the amount reabsorbed.

II. GFR regulation via the baroreceptor reflexes plays some role in regulating water excretion, but the major control is via ADH-mediated control of water reabsorption.

III. ADH secretion by the posterior pituitary is controlled by cardiovascular baroreceptors and by osmoreceptors in the hypothalamus.

   A. Via the baroreceptor reflexes, a low extracellular volume stimulates ADH secretion and a high extracellular volume inhibits it.

   B. Via the osmoreceptors, a high body-fluid osmolarity stimulates ADH secretion and a low osmolarity inhibits it.

THIRST AND SALT APPETITE

I. Thirst is stimulated by a variety of inputs, including baroreceptors, osmoreceptors, and angiotensin II.

TABLE 16-6 SUMMARY OF MAJOR HORMONAL INFLUENCES ON BONE MASS*

Hormones that favor bone formation and increased bone mass

Insulin
Growth hormone
Insulin-like growth factor I (IGF-I)
Estrogen
Testosterone
1,25-Dihydroxyvitamin D_3 (influences only mineralization, not matrix)
Calcitonin

Hormones that favor increased bone resorption and decreased bone mass

Parathyroid hormone
Cortisol
Thyroid hormones (T_4 and T_3)

---

*The effects of all hormones except 1,25-dihydroxyvitamin D_3 are ultimately due to a hormone-induced alteration of the balance between the activities of the osteoblasts and osteoclasts. This altered balance is not always the result of a *direct* action of the hormone on these cells, however, but may result *indirectly* from some other action of the hormone. For example, large amounts of cortisol depress intestinal absorption of calcium, which in turn causes reduced plasma calcium, increased parathyroid hormone secretion, and stimulation of osteoclasts by parathyroid hormone.

---

reason, it nonetheless has important influences on bone mass and plasma calcium concentration.

Kidneys

About 60 percent of plasma calcium is filterable at the renal corpuscle (the rest is bound to plasma protein), and most of this filtered calcium is reabsorbed. There is no tubular secretion of calcium. Accordingly, the urinary excretion of calcium is the difference between the amount filtered and the amount reabsorbed. Like that of sodium, the control of calcium excretion is exerted mainly on reabsorption; that is, reabsorption is reflexly decreased when plasma calcium concentration goes up for whatever reason, and reflexly increased when plasma calcium goes down.

In addition, as we shall see, the renal handling of phosphate plays a role in the regulation of extracellular calcium. Phosphate, too, is handled by a combination of filtration and reabsorption, the latter being hormonally controlled.

Gastrointestinal Tract

The absorption of sodium, water, and potassium from the gastrointestinal tract normally approximates 100 percent.

There is some homeostatic control of these processes, but it is relatively unimportant and so we ignored it. In contrast, a considerable amount of ingested calcium is not absorbed from the intestine and simply leaves the body along with the feces. Moreover, the active-transport system that moves this ion from intestinal lumen to blood is under important hormonal control. Accordingly, there can be large regulated increases or decreases in the amount of calcium absorbed. These changes markedly affect total-body calcium and plasma calcium concentration.

HORMONAL CONTROLS

The two major hormones that homeostatically regulate plasma calcium concentration are parathyroid hormone and the active form of vitamin D, called 1,25-dihydroxyvitamin D_3. (Another hormone, calcitonin, which is secreted by the thyroid gland, has long been thought to help regulate plasma calcium, but present evidence indicates that this hormone plays only a minor role in this regard.)

Parathyroid Hormone

All three of the effector sites described above are subject, directly or indirectly, to control by a protein hormone called **parathyroid hormone**, produced by the parathyroid glands. These glands are embedded in the surface of the thyroid gland but are distinct from it. Parathyroid hormone production is controlled by the plasma calcium concentration. Decreased plasma calcium concentration stimulates parathyroid hormone secretion, and an increased plasma calcium concentration does just the opposite. Extracellular calcium concentration acts directly upon the parathyroid glands without any intermediary hormones or nerves.

Parathyroid hormone exerts at least four distinct effects influencing calcium homeostasis (Figure 16-29):

1. It increases the resorption of bone, which results in the movement of calcium (and phosphate) from bone into extracellular fluid.
2. It stimulates the activation of vitamin D (see below), and this latter hormone then increases intestinal absorption of calcium.
3. It increases renal tubular calcium reabsorption, thus decreasing urinary calcium excretion.
4. It reduces the tubular reabsorption of phosphate, thus raising its urinary excretion and lowering its extracellular concentration.

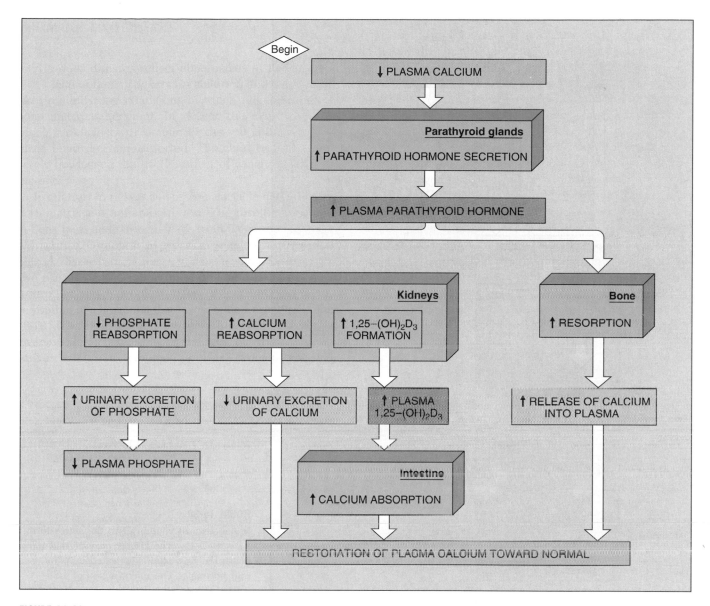

FIGURE 16-29

Reflexes by which a reduction in plasma calcium concentration is restored toward normal via the actions of parathyroid hormone. See Figure 16-30 for a description of $1,25\text{-}(OH)_2D_3$.

The adaptive value of the first three is straightforward: They all tend to increase extracellular calcium concentration, thus compensating for the decreased concentration that originally stimulated parathyroid hormone secretion. The adaptive value of the fourth effect for calcium regulation requires further explanation as follows.

Parathyroid hormone, by stimulating bone resorption, causes both calcium and phosphate to be released from bone into the extracellular fluid. If the extracellular phosphate concentration were to increase as a result of this release, further movement of calcium from bone would be retarded because a high extracellular phosphate level causes calcium and phosphate to be deposited on bone and other tissues. Therefore, it is adaptive that parathyroid hormone also decreases tubular reabsorption of phosphate, thus permitting excess phosphate to be eliminated in the urine.

Vitamin D

The term **vitamin D** denotes a group of closely related chemicals involved in absorption of ingested calcium by the intestine. **Vitamin D_3** is formed by the action of ultraviolet radiation (from sunlight, usually) on a substance—

Metabolic reactions are highly sensitive to the hydrogen-ion concentration of the fluid in which they occur. This sensitivity is due to the influence on enzyme function exerted by hydrogen ions, which change the shapes of proteins. Accordingly, the hydrogen-ion concentration of the extracellular fluid is closely regulated. (At this point the reader might want to review the section on hydrogen ions, acidity, and pH in Chapter 2.)

This regulation can be viewed in the same way as the balance of any other ion, that is, as the matching of gains and losses. When loss exceeds gain, the arterial plasma hydrogen-ion concentration goes down (pH goes above 7.4), and this is termed an *alkalosis*. When gain exceeds loss, the arterial plasma hydrogen-ion concentration goes up (pH goes below 7.4), and this is termed an *acidosis*.

SOURCES OF HYDROGEN-ION GAIN OR LOSS

Table 16-7 summarizes the major routes for gains and losses of hydrogen ion. First, as described in Chapter 15, a huge quantity of CO_2 is generated daily as the result of oxidative metabolism and yields hydrogen ions via the reactions

$$CO_2 + H_2O \underset{\text{Carbonic anhydrase}}{\rightleftharpoons} H_2CO_3 \rightleftharpoons HCO_3^- + H^+$$

$$(16\text{-}1)$$

TABLE 16-7   SOURCES OF HYDROGEN-ION GAIN OR LOSS

Gain

1. Generation of hydrogen ions from CO_2
2. Production of phosphoric and sulfuric acids from the metabolism of protein and other organic molecules
3. Gain of hydrogen ions due to loss of bicarbonate in diarrhea or other nongastric GI fluids
4. Gain of hydrogen ions due to loss of bicarbonate in the urine

---

Loss

1. Loss of hydrogen ions in vomitus
2. Loss of hydrogen ions in the urine

This source does not normally constitute a net gain of hydrogen ions, however, since all the hydrogen ions generated via these reactions during passage of blood through the tissues are reincorporated into water when the reactions are reversed during passage of blood through the lungs (Chapter 15). Net retention of CO_2, however, as occurs in hypoventilation or respiratory disease, will result in a net gain of hydrogen ions. Conversely, net loss of CO_2, which occurs in hyperventilation, causes net elimination of hydrogen ions.

The body also produces acids, both organic and inorganic, from sources other than CO_2. These include phosphoric acid and sulfuric acid, generated mainly by the catabolism of proteins, and several organic acids. In the United States, where the diet is high in protein, people normally have a net daily production of 40 to 80 mmol of these acids. In addition, under certain conditions (described later) large amounts of other acids can be produced.

A third potential source of net body gain or loss of hydrogen ion is gastrointestinal secretions leaving the body. Vomitus contains a high concentration of hydrogen ions and so constitutes a source of net loss. In contrast, the other gastrointestinal secretions are alkaline, that is, contain very little hydrogen ion but a concentration of bicarbonate higher than exists in plasma. Loss of these fluids, as in diarrhea, constitutes in essence a body gain of hydrogen ions. This is an extremely important point: Given the mass action relationship shown in Equation 16-1, the loss of a bicarbonate ion from the body has virtually the same net result as gaining a hydrogen ion because loss of the bicarbonate causes the reaction to be driven to the right, thereby generating a hydrogen ion. Similarly, the gain of a bicarbonate by the body has virtually the same net result as losing a hydrogen ion.

Finally, the kidneys constitute the fourth source of net hydrogen-ion gain or loss; that is, the kidneys can either remove hydrogen ions from the plasma or add them. How they do so will be described later.

BUFFERING OF HYDROGEN IONS IN THE BODY

Any substance that can reversibly bind hydrogen ions is called a **buffer**. Between their generation in the body and their elimination, most hydrogen ions are buffered by extracellular and intracellular buffers. The normal extracellular-fluid pH of 7.4 corresponds to a hydrogen-ion concentration of only 0.00004 mmol/L. Without buffering, the daily turnover rate of the 40 to 80 mmol of H^+ produced by our diet would cause huge changes in body-fluid hydrogen-ion concentration. The general form of buffering reactions is

$$Buffer^- + H^+ \rightleftharpoons HBuffer \qquad (16\text{-}2)$$

HBuffer is a weak acid in that it can exist as the undissociated molecule (HBuffer) or can dissociate to $Buffer^-$ plus H^+. When the H^+ concentration increases for whatever reason, the reaction is forced to the right and more H^+ is bound by $Buffer^-$ to form HBuffer. For example, when H^+ concentration is increased because of increased production of lactic acid, some of the hydrogen ions combine with the body's buffers, and so the hydrogen-ion concentration does not increase as much as it otherwise would have. Conversely, when H^+ concentration decreases because of the loss of hydrogen ions or the addition of alkali, Equation 16-2 proceeds to the left and H^+ is released from HBuffer. In this manner, the body buffers stabilize H^+ concentration against changes in either direction.

The major extracellular buffer is the CO_2-HCO_3^- system summarized in Equation 16-1. This system also plays some role in buffering within cells, but the major intracellular buffers are phosphates and proteins. An example of the latter is hemoglobin, as described in Chapter 15.

You must recognize that buffering does not eliminate hydrogen ions from the body or add them to the body; it only keeps them "locked-up" until balance can be restored, which is the subject of the rest of this section.

INTEGRATION OF HOMEOSTATIC CONTROLS

The kidneys are ultimately responsible for balancing hydrogen-ion gains and losses so as to maintain plasma hydrogen-ion concentration relatively constant. Thus, they eliminate the excess hydrogen ions generated in the body during the normal catabolism of proteins and organic acids. Moreover, should there be an additional net gain of hydrogen ions due to hypoventilation or respiratory malfunction, increased metabolic production from sources other than CO_2, or loss of alkaline gastrointestinal secretions, the kidneys would increase their elimination of hydrogen ions from the body so as to restore balance. Alternatively, should there be a net loss of hydrogen ions from the body due to hyperventilation or vomiting, the kidneys would replenish these hydrogen ions.

Although the kidneys are the ultimate hydrogen-ion balancers, the respiratory system also plays a very important homeostatic role. We have pointed out that hypoventilation, respiratory malfunction, and hyperventilation can *cause* a hydrogen-ion *imbalance*; now we emphasize that when a hydrogen-ion imbalance is due to a *nonrespiratory cause*, then ventilation is *reflexly* altered so as to help compensate for the imbalance. We described this phenomenon in Chapter 15 (Figure 15-32): An elevated arterial hydrogen-ion concentration stimulates ventilation, and this reflex hyperventilation causes reduced arterial P_{CO_2}, and hence, by mass action, reduced hydrogen-ion concentration. Alternatively, a decreased plasma hydrogen-ion concentration inhibits ventilation, thereby raising arterial P_{CO_2} and therefore hydrogen-ion concentration.

Thus, the respiratory system and kidneys work together. The respiratory response to altered plasma hydrogen-ion concentration is very rapid (minutes) and keeps this concentration from changing too much until the more slowly responding kidneys (hours to days) can actually eliminate the imbalance. Of course, if the respiratory system is the actual *cause* of the hydrogen-ion imbalance, then the kidneys are the sole homeostatic responder. By the same token, malfunctioning kidneys can create a hydrogen-ion imbalance by eliminating too little or too much hydrogen ion from the body, and then the respiratory response is the only one operating.

RENAL MECHANISMS

We have spoken of the kidneys eliminating hydrogen ions from the body or replenishing them. *The kidneys perform this task by altering plasma bicarbonate concentration.* The key to understanding how altering plasma bicarbonate concentration regulates plasma hydrogen-ion concentration was stated earlier: The excretion of a bicarbonate in the urine increases the plasma hydrogen-ion concentration just as if a hydrogen ion had been added to the plasma. Similarly, the addition of a *new* bicarbonate to the plasma lowers the plasma hydrogen-ion concentration just as if a hydrogen ion had been removed from the plasma.

Thus, when there is a lowering of plasma hydrogen-ion concentration (alkalosis) for whatever reason, the kidneys' homeostatic response is to excrete large quantities of bicarbonate in the urine. This raises plasma hydrogen-ion concentration back toward normal. In contrast, in response to a rise in plasma hydrogen-ion concentration (acidosis), the kidneys do not excrete bicarbonate in the urine, but instead kidney tubular cells *produce new bicarbonate* and add it to the plasma. This lowers the plasma hydrogen-ion concentration back toward normal.

Let us now look at the basic mechanisms by which bi-

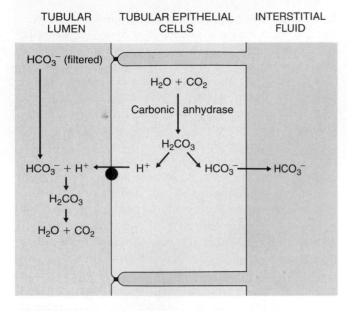

TUBULAR LUMEN	TUBULAR EPITHELIAL CELLS	INTERSTITIAL FLUID

FIGURE 16-31

Reabsorption of bicarbonate is achieved by tubular hydrogen-ion secretion. Start this figure inside the cell, with the combination of CO_2 and H_2O to form H_2CO_3, a reaction catalyzed by the enzyme carbonic anhydrase. The H_2CO_3 immediately dissociates to yield H^+ and bicarbonate (HCO_3^-). The HCO_3^- moves down its concentration gradient across the basolateral membrane into the interstitial fluid and then into the blood. Simultaneously the H^+ is secreted into the lumen, *but it is not excreted.* Instead, it combines with a *filtered* HCO_3^- and generates CO_2 and H_2O (both of which can diffuse into the cell and be used for another cycle of hydrogen-ion generation). The overall result is that the bicarbonate filtered from the plasma at the renal corpuscle has disappeared but its place in the plasma has been taken by the bicarbonate that was produced inside the cell, and so no net change in plasma bicarbonate concentration has occurred. It may seem inaccurate to refer to this process as bicarbonate "reabsorption," since the bicarbonate that appears in the peritubular plasma is not the same bicarbonate ion that was filtered. Yet the overall result is, in effect, the same as if the filtered bicarbonate had been more conventionally reabsorbed like a sodium or potassium ion. These events occur in both the proximal tubule and cortical collecting duct, but the mechanisms by which hydrogen ions cross the luminal membrane differ in the two segments. In the cortical collecting duct, shown here, the hydrogen ions are transported by a primary H-ATPase pump, whereas in the proximal tubule they move mainly by Na/H countertransport (Fig. 16-13).

carbonate excretion or addition of new bicarbonate to the plasma is achieved.

Bicarbonate Excretion

Bicarbonate is completely filterable at the renal corpuscles and undergoes marked tubular reabsorption in the proxi-

mal tubules and the collecting ducts. Bicarbonate can also be secreted into the lumen of at least one tubular segment. Therefore,

$$HCO_3^- \text{ excretion} = HCO_3^- \text{ filtered} + HCO_3^- \text{ secreted} - HCO_3^- \text{ reabsorbed}$$

For simplicity, we can ignore the secretion of bicarbonate (because it is always quantitatively much less than tubular reabsorption) and treat bicarbonate excretion as the difference between filtration and reabsorption.

Bicarbonate reabsorption is an active process, but it is not accomplished in the conventional manner of simply having an active pump for bicarbonate ions at the luminal or basolateral membrane of the tubular cells. Instead, bicarbonate reabsorption requires the tubular secretion of hydrogen ions, which combine in the lumen with filtered bicarbonates. Figure 16-31 and its legend describe the sequence of events.

Addition of New Bicarbonate to the Plasma

It is essential to note in Figure 16-31 that bicarbonate reabsorption is absolutely dependent on the secretion of hydrogen ions from the tubular cells into the lumen. As long as there are still significant amounts of filtered bicarbonate in the lumen, almost all secreted hydrogen ions will combine with it. But what happens to any secreted hydrogen ions once the bicarbonate has all been reabsorbed and is no longer available in the lumen to combine with hydrogen ions?

The answer, illustrated in Figure 16-32, is that the extra secreted hydrogen ions combine in the lumen with a filtered *nonbicarbonate* buffer, usually HPO_4^{2-}. The hydrogen ion is then excreted in the urine as part of an $H_2PO_4^-$ ion (other filtered buffers can also participate but HPO_4^{2-} is the most important). Now for the critical point: Note in Figure 16-32 that, under these conditions, the bicarbonate generated within the tubular cell by the carbonic anhydrase reaction and entering the plasma constitutes a *net gain* of bicarbonate by the plasma, not merely a replacement for a filtered bicarbonate. Thus, when a secreted hydrogen ion combines in the lumen with a buffer other than bicarbonate, the overall effect is not merely one of bicarbonate conservation, as in Figure 16-31, but rather of addition to the plasma of a new bicarbonate. This raises the bicarbonate concentration of the plasma and alkalinizes it.[11]

There is a second mechanism by which the tubules con-

[11]Why do significant numbers of hydrogen ions combine with filtered nonbicarbonate buffers like phosphate only after the filtered bicarbonate has all been reabsorbed? The main reason is that there is such a large load of filtered bicarbonate compared to that of filtered nonbicarbonate buffers.

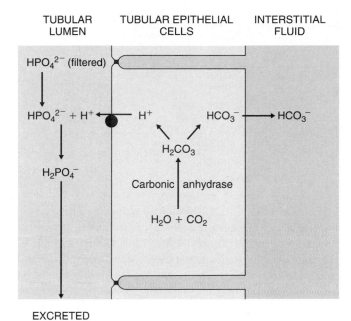

TUBULAR LUMEN   TUBULAR EPITHELIAL CELLS   INTERSTITIAL FLUID

EXCRETED

FIGURE 16-32

Renal contribution of new HCO_3^- to the plasma, as achieved by tubular secretion of H^+. The process of intracellular H^+ and HCO_3^- generation, with H^+ movement into the lumen and HCO_3^- into the plasma, is identical to that shown in Fig. 16-31. Once in the lumen, however, the H^+ combines with filtered phosphate (HPO_4^{2-}) rather than filtered HCO_3^- and is excreted. Therefore, the HCO_3^- that moves from the cell into the plasma does not merely replace "old" filtered HCO_3^-, as in Figure 16-31 but results in the addition of *new* HCO_3^- to the plasma.

tribute new bicarbonate to the plasma—one that involves not hydrogen-ion secretion but rather the renal production and secretion of ammonium (NH_4^+) (Figure 16-33). Tubular cells, mainly those of the proximal tubule, take up glutamine from both the glomerular filtrate and peritubular plasma and, by a series of steps, metabolize it. In the process, both NH_4^+ and bicarbonate are formed inside the cells. The NH_4^+ is actively secreted (via Na^+/NH_4^+ countertransport) into the lumen and excreted, while the bicarbonate moves into the peritubular capillaries and constitutes new plasma bicarbonate.[12]

---

[12]A comparison of Figures 16-32 and 16-33 demonstrates that the overall result—renal contribution of new bicarbonate to the plasma—is the same regardless of whether it is achieved by (1) H^+ secretion and excretion on nonbicarbonate buffers such as phosphate (Figure 16-32), or (2) by glutamine metabolism with NH_4^+ excretion (Figure 16-33). It is convenient, therefore, to view the latter case as representing H^+ excretion "bound" to NH_3, just as the former case constitutes H^+ excretion bound to nonbicarbonate buffers. Thus, the amount of H^+ excreted in the urine in these two forms is a measure of the amount of new bicarbonate added to the plasma by the kidneys. Indeed, "urinary H^+ excretion" and "renal contribution of new bicarbonate to the plasma" are really two sides of the same coin and are synonomous phrases.

Renal Responses to Acidosis and Alkalosis

Three events occur when the kidneys are responding homeostatically to an acidosis: (1) Enough hydrogen ions are secreted to reabsorb all the filtered bicarbonate; (2) additional hydrogen ions are secreted, and this contributes new bicarbonate to the plasma as these hydrogen ions are excreted bound to nonbicarbonate urinary buffers such as HPO_4^{2-}; and (3) tubular glutamine metabolism and ammonium excretion are enhanced, which also contributes new bicarbonate to the plasma. The net result of these three events is that plasma bicarbonate is increased, thereby compensating for the acidosis.

In contrast, when the kidneys are responding homeostatically to an alkalosis, (1) their rate of hydrogen-ion secretion is inadequate to reabsorb all the filtered bicarbonate, so that significant amounts of bicarbonate are excreted in the urine and there is little or no excretion of hydrogen ions on nonbicarbonate urinary buffers; and (2) simultaneously, tubular glutamine metabolism and ammonium excretion are decreased so that little or no new bicarbonate is contributed to the plasma from this source. The net result is that the plasma bicarbonate concentration is decreased, thereby compensating for the alkalosis.

Clearly, these homeostatic responses require that the rate of both hydrogen-ion secretion and glutamine metabolism be subject to reflex control. The specific pathways

FIGURE 16-33

Renal contribution of new HCO_3^- to the plasma, as achieved by renal metabolism of glutamine and excretion of ammonium (NH_4^+). Compare this figure to Figure 16-32. This process occurs mainly in the proximal tubule.

TUBULAR LUMEN   TUBULAR EPITHELIAL CELLS   INTERSTITIAL FLUID

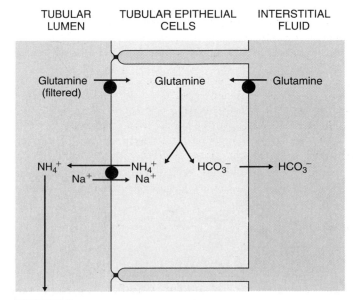

EXCRETED

**TABLE 16-8   CHANGES IN THE ARTERIAL CONCENTRATIONS OF HYDROGEN ION, BICARBONATE, AND CARBON DIOXIDE
IN ACID-BASE DISORDERS**

Primary disorder	H^+	HCO_3^-	CO_2	Cause of HCO_3^- change	Cause of CO_2 change
Respiratory acidosis	↑	↑	↑	} Renal compensation	} Primary abnormality
Respiratory alkalosis	↓	↓	↓		
Metabolic acidosis	↑	↓	↓	} Primary abnormality	} Reflex ventilatory compensations
Metabolic alkalosis	↓	↑	↑		

that bring about these rate changes are very complex and can be found in the recommended further readings listed in Appendix G.

CLASSIFICATION OF ACIDOSIS AND ALKALOSIS

To repeat, acidosis refers to any situation in which the hydrogen-ion concentration of arterial plasma is elevated; alkalosis denotes a reduction. All such situations fit into two distinct categories (Table 16-8): (1) *respiratory acidosis* or *alkalosis*, (2) *metabolic acidosis* or *alkalosis*.

Respiratory acidosis results from failure of the lungs to eliminate carbon dioxide as fast as it is produced. Respiratory alkalosis occurs when carbon dioxide is eliminated faster than it is produced. As described earlier, the imbalance of arterial hydrogen-ion concentrations in such cases is completely explainable in terms of mass action. Thus, the hallmark of a respiratory acidosis is an elevation in both arterial P_{CO_2} and hydrogen-ion concentration; that of respiratory alkalosis is a reduction in both.

Metabolic acidosis or alkalosis includes all situations other than those in which the primary problem is respiratory. Some common causes of metabolic acidosis are excessive production of lactic acid during severe exercise or

hypoxia, or of ketone bodies in uncontrolled diabetes mellitus or fasting (described in Chapter 18). Metabolic acidosis can also result from excessive loss of bicarbonate, as in diarrhea. A frequent cause of metabolic alkalosis is persistent vomiting, with its associated loss of hydrogen ions as HCl from the stomach.

What is the arterial P_{CO_2} in metabolic acidosis or alkalosis? Since, by definition, metabolic acidosis and alkalosis must be due to something other than excess retention or loss of carbon dioxide, you might have predicted that arterial P_{CO_2} would be unchanged, but such is not the case. As emphasized earlier in this chapter, the elevated hydrogen-ion concentration associated with metabolic acidosis reflexly stimulates ventilation and lowers arterial P_{CO_2}. By mass action this helps restore the hydrogen-ion concentration toward normal. Conversely, a person with metabolic alkalosis will reflexly have ventilation inhibited. The result is a rise in arterial P_{CO_2} and, by mass action, an associated restoration of hydrogen-ion concentration toward normal.

To reiterate, the plasma P_{CO_2} changes in metabolic acidosis and alkalosis are not the *cause* of the acidosis or alkalosis but are the *result* of compensatory reflex responses to nonrespiratory abnormalities. Thus, in metabolic, as opposed to respiratory conditions, the arterial plasma P_{CO_2} and hydrogen-ion concentration go in opposite directions, as summarized in Table 16-8.

SECTION D SUMMARY

SOURCES OF HYDROGEN-ION GAIN OR LOSS

I. Total-body balance of hydrogen ions is the result of both metabolic production of these ions and of net gains or losses via the gastrointestinal tract and urine (Table 16-7).

II. A stable balance is achieved by regulation of urinary losses.

BUFFERING OF HYDROGEN IONS IN THE BODY

I. Buffering is a means of minimizing changes in hy-

drogen-ion concentration by combining these ions reversibly with anions such as bicarbonate and intracellular proteins.

II. The major extracellular buffering system is the CO_2-HCO_3^- system, and the major intracellular buffers are proteins and phosphates.

INTEGRATION OF HOMEOSTATIC CONTROLS

I. The kidneys and the respiratory system are the homeostatic regulators of plasma hydrogen-ion concentration.

II. The kidneys are the ultimate balancers of body hydrogen-ion balance.

III. A decrease in arterial plasma hydrogen-ion concentration causes reflex hypoventilation, which raises arterial P_{CO_2} and, hence, raises plasma hydrogen-ion concentration toward normal. An increase in plasma hydrogen-ion concentration causes reflex hyperventilation, which lowers arterial P_{CO_2} and, hence, lowers hydrogen-ion concentration toward normal.

RENAL MECHANISMS

I. The kidneys maintain a stable plasma hydrogen-ion concentration by regulating plasma bicarbonate concentration. They can either excrete bicarbonate or contribute new bicarbonate to the blood.

II. Bicarbonate is reabsorbed when hydrogen ions, generated in the tubular cells by a process catalyzed by carbonic anhydrase, are secreted into the lumen and combine with filtered bicarbonate. The secreted hydrogen ions are not excreted in this situation.

III. In contrast, when the secreted hydrogen ions combine in the lumen with filtered phosphate or other non-bicarbonate buffer, they are excreted and the kidneys have contributed new bicarbonate to the blood.

IV. The kidneys also contribute new bicarbonate to the blood when they produce and excrete ammonium.

CLASSIFICATION OF ACIDOSIS AND ALKALOSIS

I. Acid-base disorders are categorized as respiratory or metabolic.

A. Respiratory acidosis is due to retention of carbon dioxide, and respiratory alkalosis to excessive elimination of carbon dioxide.

B. All other causes of acidosis or alkalosis are termed metabolic and reflect gain or loss, respectively, of hydrogen ions from a source other than carbon dioxide.

SECTION D KEY TERM

buffer

SECTION D REVIEW QUESTIONS

1. What are the sources of gain and loss of hydrogen ions in the body?
2. List the body's major buffer systems.
3. Describe the role of the respiratory system in the regulation of hydrogen-ion concentration.
4. How does the tubular secretion of hydrogen ions occur and how does it achieve bicarbonate reabsorption?
5. How does hydrogen-ion secretion contribute to the renal contribution of new bicarbonate to the blood. What determines whether a secreted hydrogen ion will achieve these events or will instead cause bicarbonate reabsorption?
6. How does the metabolism of glutamine by the tubular cells contribute new bicarbonate to the blood and ammonium to the urine?
7. How do the kidneys respond to the presence of an acidosis or alkalosis?
8. Classify the four types of acid-base disorders according to plasma hydrogen-ion concentration, bicarbonate concentration, and P_{CO_2}.

SECTION

DIURETICS AND KIDNEY DISEASE

DIURETICS

Drugs used clinically to increase the volume of urine excreted are known as **_diuretics_**. Such agents act by inhibiting the reabsorption of sodium, along with chloride and/or bicarbonate, resulting in increased excretion of these ions. Since water reabsorption is dependent upon sodium reabsorption, water reabsorption is also reduced, resulting in increased water excretion.

Diuretics are among the most commonly used medications. For one thing, they are used to treat diseases characterized by renal retention of salt and water. In normal individuals, the mechanisms for controlling total-body sodium are so precise that sodium balance does not vary by more than a few percent despite marked changes in dietary intake or in losses due to sweating, vomiting, or diarrhea. In several types of diseases, however, sodium balance becomes deranged by the failure of the kidneys to excrete sodium normally. Sodium excretion may fall virtually to zero despite continued sodium ingestion, and the person may retain huge quantities of sodium and water, leading to abnormal expansion of the extracellular fluid and formation of edema. Diuretics are used to prevent or reverse this renal retention of sodium and water.

The most common example of this phenomenon is **_con-_**

TABLE 16-9   CLASSES OF DIURETICS

Class	Mechanism	Major site affected
Carbonic anhydrase inhibitors	Inhibit secretion of hydrogen ion; this causes less reabsorption of sodium and bicarbonate.	Proximal tubules
Loop diuretics	Inhibit Na,K,2Cl cotransport in luminal membrane.	Ascending loops of Henle
Thiazides	Inhibit Na,Cl cotransport in luminal membrane.	Distal convoluted tubules
Potassium-sparing diuretics	Inhibit action of aldosterone.	Cortical collecting ducts
	Block sodium channels in luminal membrane.	Cortical collecting ducts

gestive heart failure (Chapter 14). A person with a failing heart manifests (1) a decreased GFR, and (2) increased aldosterone secretion, both of which contribute to the virtual absence of sodium from the urine. The net result is extracellular volume expansion and formation of edema. The sodium-retaining responses are triggered by the lower cardiac output—a result of cardiac failure—and the resulting decrease in arterial pressure.

Another disease in which diuretics are frequently employed is hypertension (Chapter 14). It is still unclear why the decrease in body sodium and water resulting from the diuretic-induced excretion of these substances brings about arteriolar dilation and a lowering of the blood pressure.

As summarized in Table 16-9, clinically used diuretics are classified according to the mechanisms by which they inhibit ion reabsorption. Figures 16-12 and 16-13 should be used in conjunction with this table to visualize the mechanisms. Except for one category, the potassium-sparing diuretics, all diuretics not only increase sodium excretion but also cause increased potassium excretion, an unwanted side effect.

KIDNEY DISEASE

The term "kidney disease" is no more specific than "car trouble," since many diseases affect the kidneys. Bacteria, allergies, congenital defects, kidney stones, tumors, and toxic chemicals are some possible sources of kidney damage. Obstruction of the urethra or a ureter may cause injury as the result of a buildup of pressure and may predispose the kidneys to bacterial infection.

Disease can attack the kidneys at any age. Experts estimate that there are at present more than 3 million undetected cases of kidney infection in the United States and that 25,000 to 75,000 Americans die of kidney failure each year.

Although many diseases of the kidney are self-limited and produce no permanent damage, others progress if untreated. The end stage of progressive diseases, regardless of the nature of the damaging agent—bacteria, toxic chemical, and so on—is a shrunken, nonfunctioning kidney. Similarly, the symptoms of profound renal malfunction are relatively independent of the damaging agent and are collectively known as **uremia**, laterally, "urine in the blood."

The severity of uremia depends upon how well the impaired kidneys are able to preserve the constancy of the internal environment. Assuming that the person continues to ingest a normal diet containing the usual quantities of nutrients and electrolytes, what problems arise? The key fact to keep in mind is that the kidney destruction markedly reduces the number of functioning nephrons. Accordingly, the many substances that gain entry to the tubule entirely or primarily by *filtration* are excreted in diminished amounts. In addition, the excretion of potassium and hydrogen ion is impaired because there are too few nephrons capable of normal tubular *secretion*. The buildup of all these substances—water, ions, and toxic waste products—in the blood causes many of the problems of uremia.

The remarkable fact is how large the safety factor is in renal function. In general, the kidneys are still able to perform their regulatory function quite well as long as 10 percent of the nephrons are functioning. This is because these remaining nephrons undergo alterations in function—filtration, reabsorption, and secretion—so as to compensate for the missing nephrons. For example, each remaining nephron increases its rate of potassium secretion so that the total amount of potassium excreted by the kidneys can be maintained at normal levels. The limits of regulation are restricted, however. To use potassium as our example again, if someone with severe renal disease were to go on a diet high in potassium, the remaining nephrons might not be able to secrete enough potassium to prevent potassium retention.

To take another example, the diseased kidney is unable to concentrate urine normally, which should not be surprising given the complex interactions required for normal functioning of the countercurrent multiplier system. Whereas water balance can be maintained by diseased kidneys when the person is ingesting reasonable quantities of water, the kidneys may not be able to reduce urine volume adequately to avoid dehydration if the individual is water-deprived.

As noted earlier, the glomerular filtrate and, hence, the urine are essentially protein-free. Certain diseases cause the renal corpuscles to become leaky to protein, however, and considerable amounts of protein are therefore filtered. Some of this protein is reabsorbed, but much may be excreted in the urine.

Other problems arise in uremia because of abnormal secretion of the hormones produced by the kidneys. Thus, decreased secretion of erythropoietin results in anemia. Decreased ability to form $1,25\text{-}(OH)_2D_3$ results in deficient absorption of calcium from the gastrointestinal tract, with a resulting decrease in plasma calcium and inadequate bone calcification. Both of these hormones are now available for administration to patients with uremia.

The problem with renin, the third of the renal hormones, is rarely too little secretion but rather too much secretion by the juxtaglomerular cells of the damaged kidneys. The result is increased plasma angiotensin II concentration and the development of **renal hypertension**.

Hemodialysis, Peritoneal Dialysis, and Transplantation

As described above, failing kidneys reach a point when they can no longer excrete water and ions at rates that maintain body balances of these substances, nor can they excrete waste products as fast as they are produced. Dietary alterations can minimize these problems, for example, by lowering potassium intake and thereby reducing the amount of potassium to be excreted, but such alterations cannot eliminate the problems. The techniques used to perform the kidneys' excretory functions are hemodialysis and peritoneal dialysis. The general term "dialysis" means to separate substances using a membrane.

The artificial kidney is an apparatus that utilizes a process termed **hemodialysis** to remove excess substances from the blood. During hemodialysis, blood is pumped from one of the patient's arteries through tubing that is bathed by a large volume of fluid. The tubing then conducts the blood back into the patient by way of a vein. The tubing is generally made of cellophane that is highly permeable to most solutes but relatively impermeable to protein and completely impermeable to blood cells—characteristics quite similar to those of capillaries. The bath fluid is a salt solution with ionic concentrations similar to or lower than those in normal plasma. As blood flows through the tubing, the concentrations of nonprotein plasma solutes tend to reach diffusion equilibrium with those of the solutes in the bath fluid. For example, if the plasma potassium concentration of the patient is above normal, potassium diffuses out of the blood across the cellophane tubing and into the bath fluid. Similarly, waste products and excesses of other substances also diffuse into the bath and thus are eliminated from the body.

Patients with acute reversible renal failure may require hemodialysis for only days or weeks. Patients with chronic irreversible renal failure require treatment for the rest of their lives, however, unless they receive a renal transplant. Such patients undergo hemodialysis several times a week, often at home.

Another way of removing excess substances from the blood is **peritoneal dialysis**, which uses the lining of the patient's own abdominal cavity (peritoneum) as a dialysis membrane. Fluid is injected, via a needle inserted through the abdominal wall, into this cavity and allowed to remain there for hours, during which solutes diffuse into the fluid from the person's blood. The dialysis fluid is then removed by reinserting the needle and is replaced with new fluid. This procedure can be performed several times daily by a patient who is simultaneously doing normal activities.

The treatment of choice for most patients with permanent renal failure is kidney transplantation. Rejection of the transplanted kidney by the recipient's body is a potential problem with transplants, but great strides have been made in reducing the frequency of rejection (Chapter 20). Many people who might benefit from a transplant do not receive one because a kidney is not available. Presently, the major source of kidneys for transplanting is recently deceased persons, and improved public understanding should lead to many more individuals giving permission in advance to have their kidneys and other organs used following their death.

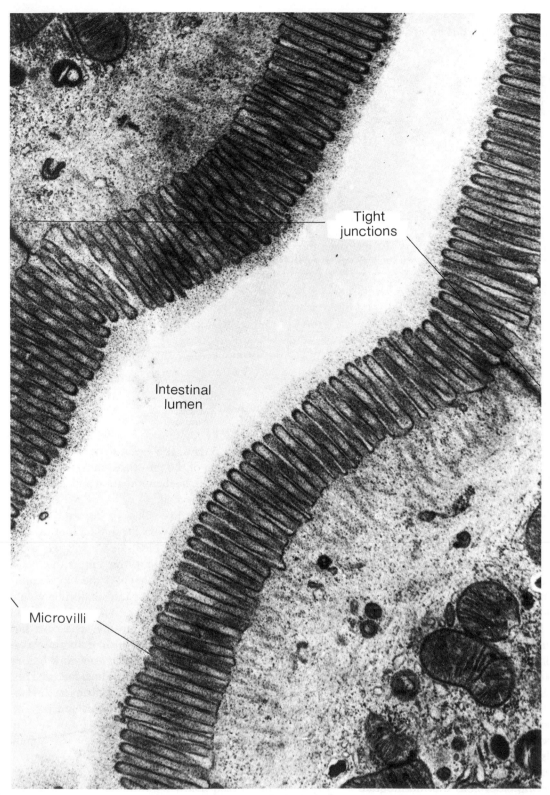

FIGURE 17-8

Microvilli on the surface of intestinal epithelial cells. [*From D. W. Fawcett, J. Histochem. Cytochem. 13:75–91 (1965). Courtesy of Susumo Ito.*]

(table sugar) and lactose (milk sugar) (Table 17-2). Only small amounts of monosaccharides are normally present in the diet. Cellulose and certain other complex polysaccharides found in vegetable matter cannot be broken down by the enzymes in the small intestine. These polysaccharides, collectively referred to as **fiber**, are passed on to the large intestine, where they are partially metabolized by bacteria.

Starch digestion by salivary amylase begins in the mouth and continues in the upper part of the stomach before amylase is destroyed by gastric acid. Starch digestion is completed in the small intestine by pancreatic amylase. The products produced by both amylases are the disaccharide maltose and a mixture of short, branched chains of glucose molecules. These products, along with ingested sucrose and lactose, are then broken down into monosaccharides—glucose, galactose, and fructose—by enzymes located on the brush-border membranes of the small intestine epithelial cells. These monosaccharides are then transported across the intestinal epithelium into the blood. Fructose crosses the epithelium by facilitated diffusion, while glucose and galactose undergo secondary active transport coupled to sodium (page 128). Most of the ingested carbohydrate is digested and absorbed within the first 20 percent of the small intestine.

Protein

Only 40 to 50 g of protein is required by a normal adult to supply essential amino acids and replace the amino acid nitrogen converted to urea. A typical American diet contains about 125 g of protein per day. In addition, a large amount of protein, in the form of enzymes and mucus, is secreted into the gastrointestinal tract or enters it via the disintegration of epithelial cells. Regardless of source, most of the protein in the lumen is broken down into amino acids and absorbed by the small intestine.

Proteins are broken down to peptide fragments in the stomach by pepsin, and in the small intestine by **trypsin** and **chymotrypsin**, which are secreted by the pancreas. These fragments are further digested to free amino acids by **carboxypeptidase**, secreted by the pancreas, and by **aminopeptidase**, located on the luminal epithelial membranes of the small intestine. These last two enzymes split off amino acids from the carboxyl and amino ends of the peptide chains, respectively.

The free amino acids then undergo secondary active transport coupled with sodium across the intestinal wall. Short chains of two or three amino acids are also actively absorbed.[2] This is in contrast to carbohydrate absorption, in which molecules larger than monosaccharides are not absorbed. As with carbohydrates, protein digestion and absorption are largely completed in the upper portion of the small intestine.

Small amounts of intact proteins are able to cross the intestinal epithelium and gain access to the interstitial fluid. They do so by a combination of endocytosis and exocytosis. The absorptive capacity for intact proteins is much greater in infants than in adults, and antibodies (proteins involved in the immunological defense system of the body) secreted into the mother's milk can be absorbed by the infant, providing some immunity until the infant can produce its own antibodies.

Fat

Fat intake ranges from about 25 to 160 g/day in a typical American diet; most is in the form of triacylglycerols. Fat digestion occurs almost entirely in the small intestine. The major digestive enzyme in this process is pancreatic **lipase**, which catalyzes the splitting of bonds linking fatty acids to the first and third carbon atoms of glycerol, producing two free fatty acids and a monoglyceride as products:

$$\text{Triacylglycerol} \xrightarrow{\text{Lipase}} \text{monoglyceride} + 2 \text{ fatty acids}$$

The triacylglycerols entering the small intestine are insoluble in water and aggregate into large lipid droplets. Since pancreatic lipase is a water-soluble enzyme, its digestive action can take place only at the *surface* of a lipid droplet. Therefore, if most of the ingested lipids remained in large lipid droplets, the rate of lipid digestion would be very slow. The rate of digestion is, however, substantially increased by dividing the large lipid droplets into a number of much smaller droplets, each about 1 mm in diameter, thereby increasing their surface area and accessibility to lipase action. This process is known as emulsification,

TABLE 17-2 CARBOHYDRATES IN FOOD		
Class	**Examples**	**Made up of**
Polysaccharides	Starch	Glucose
	Cellulose	Glucose
	Glycogen	Glucose
Disaccharides	Sucrose	Glucose-fructose
	Lactose	Glucose-galactose
	Maltose	Glucose-glucose
Monosaccharides	Glucose	
	Fructose	
	Galactose	

[2]Amino acids are actually absorbed at a greater rate when present in small peptides than as free amino acids. This has practical applications when adequate levels of nutrients must be supplied to patients with various GI disorders.

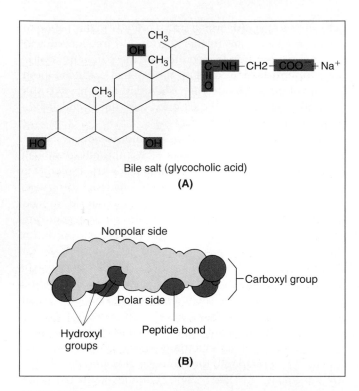

FIGURE 17-9

Structure of bile salt. (A) Chemical formula of glycocholic acid, one of several bile salts secreted by the liver (polar groups in color). (B) Three-dimensional structure of a bile salt, showing its polar and nonpolar surfaces.

and the resulting suspension of small lipid droplets is an **emulsion**.

The emulsification of fat requires (1) mechanical disruption of the large fat droplets into smaller droplets; and (2) an emulsifying agent, which acts to prevent the smaller droplets from reaggregating back into large droplets. The mechanical disruption is provided by contractile activity, occurring in the lower portion of the stomach and in the small intestine, which acts to grind and mix the luminal contents. Phospholipids in food and phospholipids and bile salts secreted in the bile provide the emulsifying agents.

Phospholipids are amphiphatic molecules (Chapter 2) consisting of two nonpolar fatty acid chains attached to glycerol, with a charged phosphate group located on glycerol's third carbon. Bile salts are formed from cholesterol in the liver and are also amphiphatic (Figure 17-9). The nonpolar portions of the phospholipids and bile salts associate with the nonpolar interior of the lipid droplets, leaving the polar portions exposed at the water surface. There they repel other lipid droplets that are similarly coated with these emulsifying agents, thereby preventing their reaggregation into larger fat droplets (Figure 17-10).

Although digestion is speeded up by emulsification, absorption of the insoluble products of the lipase reaction would still be very slow if it were not for a second action of the bile salts, the formation of **micelles**, which are similar in structure to emulsion droplets but are much smaller, 4 to 7 nm in diameter. Micelles consist of bile salts, fatty acids, monoglycerides, and phospholipids all clustered together with the polar ends of each molecule oriented toward the micelle's surface and the nonpolar portions forming the micelle's core. Also included in the core of the micelle are small amounts of nonpolar, fat-soluble vitamins.

How do micelles increase absorption? Although fatty acids and monoglycerides have an extremely low solubility in water, a few molecules do exist in solution and are free to diffuse across the plasma membranes of the epithelial cells lining the small intestine. Micelles, containing the products of fat digestion, are continuously breaking down and re-forming. When a micelle breaks down, its contents are released into the solution and become available to dif-

FIGURE 17-10

Emulsification of fat by bile salts and phospholipids.

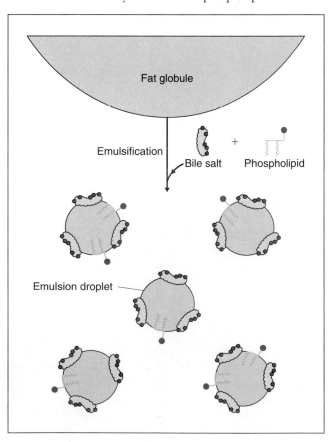

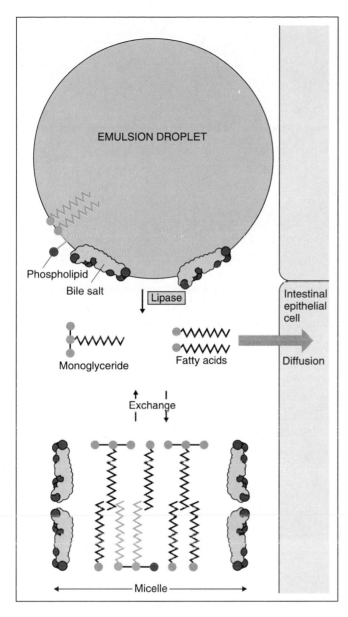

FIGURE 17-11

The products of fat digestion by lipase are held in solution in the micellar state, combined with bile salts and phospholipids. The micellar contents rapidly exchange with the free products in aqueous solution, which are able to diffuse into intestinal epithelial cells.

fuse across the intestinal lining. As the concentration of free lipids falls, because of their diffusion out of the lumen, more lipids shift out of the micelles into the free phase (Figure 17-11). Thus, the micelles provide a means of keeping most of the insoluble fat digestion products in solution, while at the same time replenishing the small amount of products that are free in solution as they diffuse into the intestinal epithelium. Note that it is not the mi-

celle that is absorbed but rather the lipids that are free in solution.

Although fatty acids and monoglycerides are the molecules that enter the epithelial cells from the intestinal lumen, it is triacylglycerol that is released on the other side of the cell into the interstitial fluid. In other words, during their passage through the epithelial cells, fatty acids and monoglycerides are resynthesized into triacylglycerols. This occurs in the agranular endoplasmic reticulum, where the enzymes for triacylglycerol synthesis are located. Within this organelle, the resynthesized fat aggregates into small droplets coated with an amphipathic protein that performs an emulsifying function similar to that of a bile salt.

The exit of these fat droplets from the cell follows the same pathway as a secreted protein (page 70). Vesicles containing the droplet pinch off the endoplasmic reticulum, are processed through the Golgi apparatus, and eventually fuse with the plasma membrane, releasing the fat droplet into the interstitial fluid. These small, extracellular fat droplets are known as **chylomicrons**. Chylomicrons contain, in addition to triacylglycerols, other lipids (including phospholipids, cholesterol, and fat-soluble vitamins) that have been absorbed by the same process that led to fatty acid and monoglyceride absorption.

The chylomicrons released from the epithelial cells pass into the lacteals rather than into the capillaries. The chylomicrons cannot enter the capillaries because a basement membrane (an extracellular glycoprotein layer) at the outer surface of the capillary provides a barrier to the large chylomicrons, which are about 1 μm in diameter. The lacteals do not have basement membranes and have very large slit pores between their endothelial cells. Thus, the chylomicrons can pass through the lacteal wall into the lymph. The lymph from the small intestine, as from everywhere else in the body, eventually empties into systemic veins. In Chapter 18 we describe how the lipids in the circulating blood chylomicrons are made available to the cells of the body.

Figure 17-12 summarizes the pathway taken by fat in moving from the intestinal lumen into the lymphatic system.

Vitamins

Most vitamins undergo little enzymatic modification during digestion and absorption. Digestion of food particles releases the vitamins, transferring them to a soluble form in which they can be absorbed.

The fat-soluble vitamins—A, D, E, and K—follow the pathway for fat absorption described in the previous section. They are solubilized in micelles. Thus, any interference with the secretion of bile or the action of bile salts in the intestine decreases the absorption of the fat-soluble vitamins.

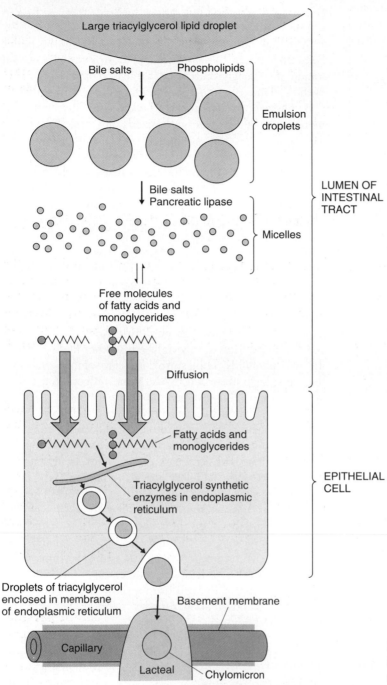

Large triacylglycerol lipid droplet

Bile salts   Phospholipids

Emulsion droplets

Bile salts
Pancreatic lipase

Micelles

LUMEN OF INTESTINAL TRACT

Free molecules of fatty acids and monoglycerides

Diffusion

Fatty acids and monoglycerides

EPITHELIAL CELL

Triacylglycerol synthetic enzymes in endoplasmic reticulum

Droplets of triacylglycerol enclosed in membrane of endoplasmic reticulum

Basement membrane

Capillary

Lacteal   Chylomicron

FIGURE 17-12

Summary of fat absorption across the walls of the small intestine.

Most water-soluble vitamins are absorbed by diffusion or carrier-mediated transport. However, one—vitamin B_{12}—is a very large, charged molecule. In order to be absorbed, vitamin B_{12} must first bind to a protein, known as **intrinsic factor**, produced by the acid-secreting cells in the stomach. The resulting complex then binds to specific sites on the epithelial cells in the lower portion of the ileum, where vitamin B_{12} is absorbed. As described on page 398, vitamin B_{12} is required for erythrocyte formation, and deficiencies result in *pernicious anemia*. This form of anemia may occur when the stomach either has

been removed (as, for example, to treat ulcers or gastric cancer) or fails to secrete intrinsic factor. Since the absorption of vitamin B_{12} occurs in the lower part of the ileum, removal of this segment because of disease can also result in pernicious anemia.

Water and Minerals

Water is the most abundant substance in chyme. Approximately 9000 ml of ingested and secreted fluid enters the small intestine each day, but only 1500 ml is passed on to the large intestine since 80 percent of the fluid is absorbed in the small intestine. The epithelial membranes of the small intestine are very permeable to water. Therefore, net water diffusion occurs across the epithelium whenever a water concentration difference is established by the active absorption of solutes (page 139).

Sodium ions account for much of the actively transported solutes because they constitute the most abundant solute in chyme. Sodium absorption is a primary active process, using the Na,K-ATPase pumps in a manner similar to that for renal tubular sodium reabsorption (Chapter 16).

Chloride and bicarbonate ions move with the sodium ions and contribute another large fraction of the absorbed solute. Other minerals present in smaller concentrations, such as potassium, magnesium, and calcium, are also absorbed, as are trace elements such as iron, zinc, and iodide. Consideration of the transport processes associated with all these is beyond the scope of this book, and we shall briefly consider as an example the absorption of only one of them—iron.

Only about 10 percent of ingested iron is absorbed into the blood each day. Iron ions are actively transported into intestinal epithelial cells, where most of them are incorporated into ferritin, the protein-iron complex that functions as an intracellular iron store (page 398). The absorbed iron that does not bind to ferritin is released on the blood side and bound to the plasma protein, transferrin, in which form it circulates throughout the body (page 398). Most of the iron bound to ferritin is released back into the intestinal lumen when the intestinal cells disintegrate at the tip of the villus and is excreted in the feces.

Iron absorption depends on the body's iron content. When body stores are ample, the increased concentration of free iron in the plasma and intestinal epithelial cells leads to an increased transcription of the ferritin protein and thus an increased storage of iron as ferritin. This reduces the amount of iron available for release into the blood. When the body stores drop, for example, when there is a loss of hemoglobin during hemorrhage, the production and hence the concentration of intestinal ferritin decrease; therefore, the amount of iron bound to intestinal ferritin decreases, thereby increasing the unbound iron available for release into the blood.

Once iron has entered the blood, the body has very little means of excreting it and it will accumulate in tissues. Although the control mechanisms for iron absorption just described tend to maintain the iron content of the body fairly constant, a large ingestion of iron can overwhelm them, leading to an increased deposition of iron in tissues and producing toxic effects. Some people have genetically defective control mechanisms and therefore absorb toxic amounts of iron even when ingestion is normal. This condition is termed *hemochromatosis*.

Iron absorption also depends on the type of food ingested. This is because iron binds to many negatively charged ions in food that can retard its absorption. For example, iron in ingested liver is much more absorbable than iron in egg yolk since the latter contains phosphates that bind the iron to form an insoluble complex.

The absorption of iron is typical of that of most trace metals in several respects: (1) Cellular storage proteins and plasma carrier proteins are involved; and (2) the control of absorption, rather than urinary excretion, is the major mechanism for the homeostatic control of the body's content of the trace metal.

REGULATION OF GASTROINTESTINAL PROCESSES

Unlike control systems that regulate variables in the internal environment, the control mechanisms of the gastrointestinal system regulate conditions in the lumen of the tract. With few exceptions, like those for trace metals, these control mechanisms are governed not by the nutritional state of the body, but rather by the volume and composition of the luminal contents.

Basic Principles

Gastrointestinal reflexes are initiated by a relatively small number of luminal stimuli: (1) distension of the wall by the luminal contents; (2) chyme osmolarity (total solute concentration); (3) chyme acidity; and (4) chyme concentrations of specific digestion products—monosaccharides, fatty acids, peptides, and amino acids. These stimuli act on receptors located in the wall of the tract—mechanoreceptors, osmoreceptors, and chemoreceptors—to trigger reflexes that influence the effectors—the muscle layers in the wall of the tract and the exocrine glands that secrete substances into its lumen.

Neural Regulation. The gastrointestinal tract has its own local nervous system, known as the **enteric nervous system**, in the form of two nerve networks, the myenteric plexus and the submucous plexus (Figure 17-6). These neurons either synapse with other neurons in the plexus or end near smooth muscles and glands. Many axons leave the myenteric plexus and synapse with neurons in the submucous plexus, and vice versa, so that neural activity in one plexus influences the activity in the other. Moreover, stimulation at one point in the plexus can lead to impulses that are conducted both up and down the tract. Thus, for example, stimuli in the upper part of the small intestine may affect smooth muscle and gland activity in the stomach as well as in the lower part of the intestinal tract.

The enteric nervous system contains adrenergic and cholinergic neurons as well as neurons that release other neurotransmitters, many of which are small peptides. ATP and nitric oxide have also been found to play major roles in the enteric nervous system as neurotransmitters and neuromodulators.

Many of the effectors mentioned earlier are at the ends of neurons that are part of the enteric nervous system. This permits neural reflexes that are completely within the tract, that is, independent of the central nervous system (CNS). In addition, nerve fibers from both the sympathetic and parasympathetic branches of the autonomic nervous system enter the intestinal tract and synapse with neurons in both plexuses. Via these pathways, the CNS can influence the motility and secretory activity of the gastrointestinal tract.

Thus, two types of neural reflex arcs exist (Figure 17-13): (1) **short reflexes** from receptors through the nerve plexuses to effector cells; and (2) **long reflexes** from receptors in the tract to the CNS by way of afferent nerves and back to the nerve plexuses and effector cells by way of the autonomic nerve fibers. Some controls are mediated either solely by short reflexes or solely by long reflexes, whereas other controls use both.

Finally, it should be noted that not all neural reflexes are initiated by signals *within* the tract. The sight or smell of food and the emotional state of an individual can have significant effects on the gastrointestinal tract, effects that are mediated by the CNS via autonomic neurons.

Hormonal Regulation. The hormones that control the gastrointestinal system are secreted mainly by endocrine cells scattered throughout the epithelium of the stomach and small intestine; that is, these cells are not clustered into discrete organs like the thyroid or adrenal glands. One surface of each endocrine cell is exposed to the lumen of the gastrointestinal tract. At this surface, various chemical substances in the chyme stimulate the cell to release its

hormones from the opposite, blood side of the cell. Although some of these hormones can also be detected in the lumen and may therefore be acting locally as paracrine agents, most of the gastrointestinal hormones reach their target cells via the circulation.

Several dozen substances are currently being investigated as possible gastrointestinal hormones, but only four —**secretin, cholecystokinin (CCK), gastrin,** and **glucose-dependent insulinotropic peptide (GIP)**[3]—have met all the criteria for true hormones. They, as well as several candidate hormones, also exist in the CNS and in gastrointestinal plexus neurons, where they function as neurotransmitters or neuromodulators.

Table 17-3, which summarizes the major characteristics of the four established GI hormones, not only serves as a reference for future discussions but also illustrates two generalizations: (1) Each hormone participates in a feedback control system that regulates some aspect of the luminal environment, and (2) each hormone affects more than one type of target cell.

These two generalizations can be illustrated by CCK. The presence of fatty acids in the small intestine triggers CCK secretion from the duodenum into the blood. Circulating CCK then stimulates secretion by the pancreas of digestive enzymes, including lipase, which digests fat. CCK also causes the gallbladder to contract, delivering to the intestine the bile salts required for fat digestion and absorption. As fat is digested and absorbed, the stimulus (fatty acids in the lumen) for CCK release is removed.

In many cases, a single effector cell contains receptors for more than one hormone, as well as receptors for neu-

---

[3]GIP was originally called gastric inhibitory peptide.

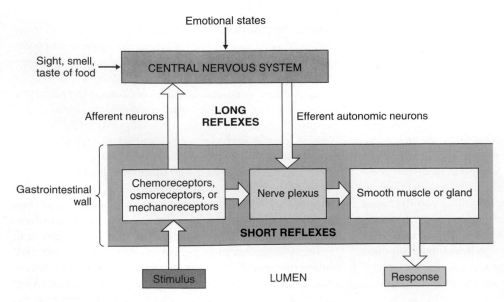

FIGURE 17-13

Long and short neural reflex pathways initiated by stimuli in the gastrointestinal tract. The long reflexes utilize neurons that link the central nervous system to the gastrointestinal tract.

TABLE 17-3 PROPERTIES OF GASTROINTESTINAL HORMONES

	Gastrin	CCK	Secretin	GIP
Structure	Peptide	Peptide	Peptide	Peptide
Endocrine cell location	Antrum of stomach	Small intestine	Small intestine	Small intestine
Stimuli for hormone release	Amino acids, peptides in stomach; parasympathetic nerves	Amino acids, fatty acids in small intestine	Acid in small intestine	Glucose, fat in small intestine
Stimuli inhibiting hormone release	Acid in stomach lumen			

Target-Cell Responses

	Gastrin	CCK	Secretin	GIP
Stomach				
Acid secretion	Stimulates		Inhibits	
Growth	Stimulates			
Pancreas				
Bicarbonate secretion		Potentiates secretin's actions	Stimulates	
Enzyme secretion		Stimulates		
Insulin secretion				Stimulates
Growth	Stimulates	Stimulates	Stimulates	
Liver				
Bicarbonate secretion		Potentiates secretin's actions	Stimulates	
Gallbladder		Stimulates		
Sphincter of Oddi		Relaxes		
Small intestine	Stimulates ileum; inhibits ileocecal sphincter			
Growth	Stimulates			
Large intestine	Stimulates mass movement			

rotransmitters and paracrine agents, with the result that a variety of inputs can affect the cell's response. One such group of interactions is the phenomenon known as **potentiation**, an example of which is the interaction between secretin and CCK. Secretin strongly stimulates pancreatic bicarbonate secretion, whereas the hormone CCK is a weak stimulus of bicarbonate secretion. Both hormones together, however, stimulate pancreatic bicarbonate secretion more strongly than would be predicted by the sum of the individual stimulatory effects of CCK and secretin. This is because CCK potentiates the effect of secretin. One of the consequences of potentiation is that small

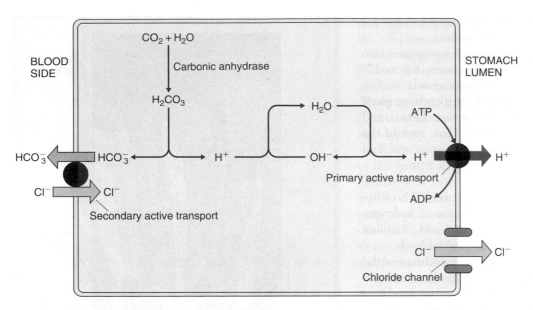

FIGURE 17-18

Secretion of hydrochloric acid by parietal cells. The hydrogen ions secreted into the lumen by primary active transport are derived from the breakdown of water molecules, leaving hydroxyl ions (OH^-) behind. These hydroxyl ions are neutralized by combination with other hydrogen ions generated by the reaction between carbon dioxide and water, a reaction catalyzed by the enzyme carbonic anhydrase, which is present in high concentrations in parietal cells. The bicarbonate ions formed by this reaction move out of the parietal cell on the blood side, in exchange for chloride ions.

ample, ingestion of large amounts of calcium can stimulate acid secretion. Both regular and decaffeinated coffee increase acid secretion, but the stimulatory ingredient has not been identified.[5]

We now come to the intestinal phase of acid secretion control, the phase in which stimuli in the early portion of the small intestine reflexly influence acid secretion by the stomach. First, high acidity in the duodenum triggers reflexes that inhibit gastric acid secretion. This reflex is beneficial for the following reason. The digestive activity of enzymes and bile salts in the small intestine is strongly inhibited by acidic solutions, and this reflex ensures that acid secretion by the stomach will be reduced whenever chyme entering the small intestine from the stomach contains so much acid that it cannot be rapidly neutralized by the bicarbonate-rich fluids simultaneously secreted into the intestine by the liver and pancreas.

A high acidity of duodenal chyme is not the only factor triggering reflex inhibition of gastric acid secretion. Distension, hypertonic solutions, and solutions containing amino acids, fatty acids, or monosaccharides also do so. Thus, the extent to which acid secretion is inhibited during the intestinal phase varies, depending upon the volume and composition of the meal, but the net result is the same—balancing the secretory activity of the stomach with the digestive and absorptive capacities of the small intestine.

The inhibition of gastric acid secretion during the intestinal phase is mediated by short and long neural reflexes and by hormones that inhibit either parietal-cell acid secretion or gastrin secretion. The hormones released by the intestinal tract that inhibit gastric activity are collectively called **enterogastrones** and include secretin, CCK, and additional unidentified hormones.

Pepsin Secretion. Pepsin is secreted by chief cells in an inactive precursor form known as pepsinogen. The high acidity in the stomach's lumen alters the shape of pepsinogen, exposing its active site so that this site can act on other pepsinogen molecules to break off a small chain of amino acids from their ends. This cleavage converts pepsinogen to a fully active form, pepsin (Figure 17-19). The activation of pepsin is thus an autocatalytic, positive-feedback process.

The synthesis and secretion of pepsinogen, followed by its intraluminal activation to pepsin, provides an example

[5] Acid secretion can also be altered by several paracrine agents, especially histamine and prostaglandins. Histamine, released from the stomach mucosa, can produce a marked increase in parietal-cell acid secretion (indeed, histamine is often administered clinically to measure the maximal acid-secreting capacity of the stomach), but its physiological role in the normal control of acid secretion remains unclear.

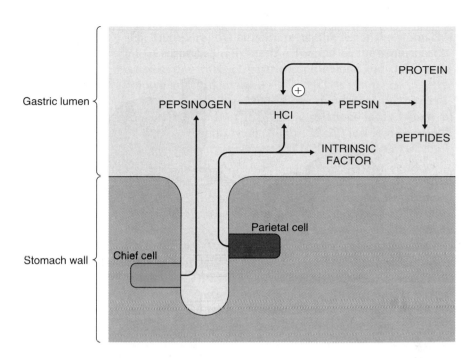

Gastric lumen

Stomach wall

FIGURE 17-19

Conversion of pepsinogen to pepsin in the lumen of the stomach.

of a process that occurs with many other secreted enzymes in the gastrointestinal tract. Because these enzymes are synthesized in inactive forms, collectively referred to as **zymogens**, any substrates that these enzymes might be able to act upon *inside* the cell producing them are protected from digestion, thus preventing damage to the cells.

Pepsin is active only in the presence of a high H^+ concentration. It becomes inactive, therefore, when it enters the small intestine, where the hydrogen ions are neutralized by the bicarbonate ions secreted into the small intestine.

The primary pathway for stimulating pepsinogen secretion is input to the chief cells from the nerve plexuses. During the cephalic, gastric, and intestinal phases, most of the factors that stimulate or inhibit acid secretion exert the same effect on pepsinogen secretion. Thus, pepsinogen secretion parallels acid secretion.

Pepsin is not *essential* for protein digestion since in its absence, as occurs in some pathological conditions, protein can be completely digested by enzymes in the small intestine. In fact the only *absolutely required* substance produced by the stomach is intrinsic factor secreted by the parietal cells, which we saw is essential for adequate absorption of vitamin B_{12}.

Gastric Motility. An empty stomach has a volume of only about 50 ml, and the diameter of its lumen is only slightly larger than that of the small intestine. When a meal is swallowed, however, the smooth muscles in the fundus and body relax before the arrival of food, allowing the stomach's volume to increase to as much as 1.5 L with little increase in pressure. This is called **receptive relaxa-**

tion and is mediated by the parasympathetic nerves with coordination by the swallowing center in the brain.

As in the esophagus, the stomach's primary contractile activity produces peristaltic waves. Each wave begins in the body of the stomach and produces only a ripple as it proceeds toward the antrum, a contraction too weak to produce much mixing of the luminal contents with acid and pepsin. As the wave approaches the larger mass of wall muscle surrounding the antrum, however, it produces a more powerful contraction, which both mixes the luminal contents and closes the **pyloric sphincter**, a ring of smooth muscle and connective tissue between the antrum and the duodenum (Figure 17-20). The pyloric sphincter is normally relaxed and closes only upon arrival of a peristaltic wave. As a consequence of sphincter closing, only a small amount of chyme is expelled into the duodenum with each wave, and most of the antral contents are forced backward toward the body of the stomach, thereby contributing to the mixing activity of this region.

What is responsible for producing gastric peristaltic waves? Their rhythm (three per minute) is generated by pacemaker cells in the longitudinal smooth-muscle layer that undergo spontaneous depolarization-repolarization cycles (slow waves) known as the **basic electrical rhythm** of the stomach. These slow waves are conducted through gap junctions along the stomach's longitudinal muscle layer and also induce similar slow waves in the overlying circular muscle layer. In the absence of neural or hormonal input, however, these depolarizations are too small to cause the muscle membranes to reach threshold and fire action potentials. Excitatory neurotransmitters and hormones act upon the muscle to further depolarize the

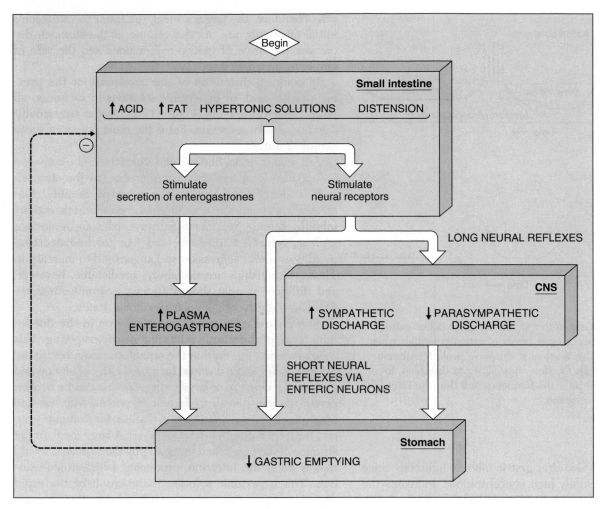

FIGURE 17-22

Intestinal-phase pathways inhibiting gastric emptying.

blood volume and produce circulatory complications. The large distension of the intestine by the entering fluid can also trigger vomiting in these patients. All these symptoms produced by the rapid entry of large quantities of ingested material into the small intestine are known as the ***dumping syndrome***.

Pancreatic Secretions

The exocrine portion of the pancreas secretes bicarbonate ions and a number of digestive enzymes into ducts that converge into the pancreatic duct, the latter joining the common bile duct from the liver just before entering the duodenum (Figure 17-4). The enzymes are secreted by gland cells at the pancreatic end of the duct system, whereas bicarbonate ions are secreted by the epithelial cells lining the early portions of the duct system itself (Figure 17-23).

The mechanism of bicarbonate secretion is analogous to that of hydrochloric acid secretion by the stomach, ex-

cept that the directions of hydrogen-ion and bicarbonate-ion movement are reversed. Hydrogen ions are actively transported out of the duct cells and released into the blood, while bicarbonate ions are secreted into the duct lumen.

The enzymes secreted by the pancreas, following activation, digest fat, polysaccharides, proteins, and nucleic acids to fatty acids, sugars, amino acids, and nucleotides, respectively. A partial list of these enzymes and their activities is given in Table 17-5. Most of the proteolytic enzymes are secreted in inactive forms (zymogens) and then activated in the duodenum by other enzymes.[6] A key step in this process is mediated by **enterokinase**, which is embedded in the luminal plasma membrane of the intesti-

---

[6]Several of the pancreatic enzymes, such as amylase and lipase, are secreted in their active forms but require additional factors, such as ions and bile salts encountered in the intestinal lumen, to produce maximal activity.

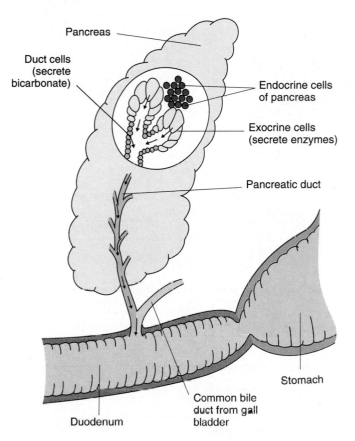

Pancreas

Duct cells
(secrete
bicarbonate)

Endocrine cells
of pancreas

Exocrine cells
(secrete enzymes)

Pancreatic duct

Stomach

Common bile
duct from gall
bladder

Duodenum

FIGURE 17-23

Structure of the pancreas. The gland areas are shown greatly enlarged relative to the entire pancreas and ducts.

nal epithelium. It is a proteolytic enzyme that splits off a peptide from pancreatic **trypsinogen**, forming the active enzyme trypsin. Trypsin is a proteolytic enzyme, and once activated, it activates the other pancreatic zymogens by splitting off peptide fragments (Figure 17-24). This func-

tion is in addition to trypsin's role in digesting ingested protein.

Pancreatic secretion increases during a meal, mainly as a result of stimulation by the hormones secretin and CCK (Table 17-3). Secretin is the primary stimulant for bicarbonate secretion, whereas CCK mainly stimulates enzyme secretion. (As noted earlier on page 577, CCK potentiates the action of secretin.)

Since the function of pancreatic bicarbonate is to neutralize the acid entering the duodenum from the stomach, it is appropriate that the major stimulus for secretin release is increased acidity in the duodenum. In analogous fashion, since CCK stimulates the secretion of digestive enzymes, including those for fat and protein digestion, it is appropriate that the stimuli for its release are fatty acids and amino acids in the duodenum. Thus, the organic nutrients in the small intestine initiate, via hormonal reflexes, the secretions involved in their own digestion.[7]

Although about 75 percent of the pancreatic exocrine secretions are controlled by stimuli arising from the intestinal phase of digestion, cephalic and gastric stimuli, by way of the parasympathetic nerves to the pancreas, also play a role. Thus, the taste of food or the distension of the stomach by food, will lead to increased pancreatic secretion. Figures 17-25 and 17-26 summarize the main factors controlling pancreatic secretion.

Bile Secretion

As stated earlier, bile is secreted by cells in the liver into a number of small ducts, the **bile canaliculi** (Figure 17-27), which converge to form the common hepatic duct (Figure

---

[7]As the amount of trypsin in the small intestine increases, the rate of CCK release decreases, and thus pancreatic enzyme secretion decreases. This negative feedback is probably the result of trypsin's digestion of a protein required for CCK secretion.

TABLE 17-5 PANCREATIC ENZYMES		
Enzyme	**Substrate**	**Action**
Trypsin, chymotrypsin, elastase	Proteins	Breaks peptide bonds in proteins to form peptide fragments
Carboxypeptidase	Proteins	Splits off terminal amino acid from carboxyl end of protein
Lipase	Fat	Splits off two fatty acids from triacylglycerols, forming free fatty acids and monoglycerides
Amylase	Polysaccharide	Splits polysaccharides into glucose and maltose
Ribonuclease, deoxyribonuclease	Nucleic acids	Splits nucleic acids into free mononucleotides

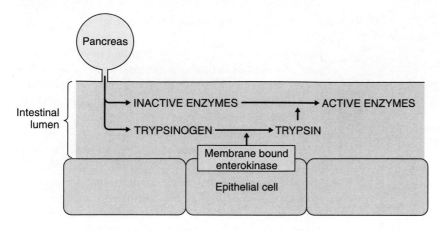

FIGURE 17-24

Activation of pancreatic enzyme precursors in the small intestine.

FIGURE 17-26

Hormonal regulation of pancreatic enzyme secretion.

FIGURE 17-25

Hormonal regulation of pancreatic bicarbonate secretion.

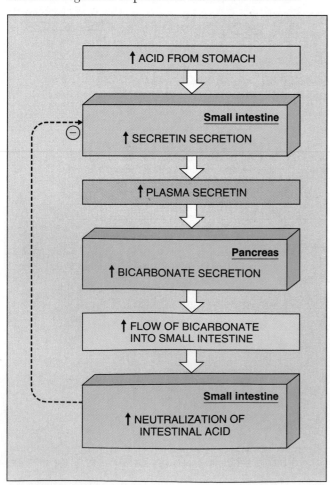

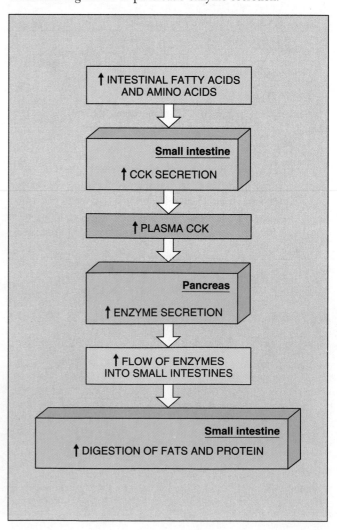

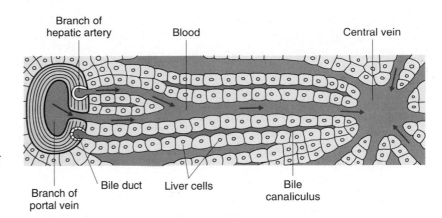

FIGURE 17-27

A small section of the liver showing location of bile canaliculi and ducts with respect to blood and liver cells. (*Adapted from Kappas and Alvares.*)

17-4). Bile contains six major ingredients: (1) bile salts, (2) cholesterol, (3) lecithin (a phospholipid), (4) bicarbonate ions and other salts, (5) bile pigments and small amounts of other metabolic end products, and (6) trace metals. The first three ingredients are synthesized in the liver and help solubilize fat in the small intestine. Bicarbonate ions neutralize acid in the duodenum, and the fifth and sixth categories represent substances extracted from the blood by the liver and excreted via the bile.

From the standpoint of gastrointestinal function, the most important components of bile are the bile salts. During the digestion of a fatty meal, most of the bile salts entering the intestinal tract via the bile are absorbed in the ileum (the last segment of the small intestine) and returned via the portal vein to the liver, where they are once again secreted into the bile. This recycling pathway from the intestine to the liver and back to the intestine via the bile duct is known as the **enterohepatic circulation** (Figure 17-28). A small amount of the bile salts are not recycled, however, but are lost in the feces. The liver synthesizes new bile salts from cholesterol to replace them.

In addition to synthesizing bile salts from cholesterol, the liver also secretes cholesterol into the bile. [This process, followed by excretion of cholesterol in the feces, is one of the mechanisms by which cholesterol homeostasis is maintained (Chapter 18).] Cholesterol is insoluble in water, and its solubility in the bile is achieved by its incorporation into micelles. (Gallstones, consisting of precipitated cholesterol, will be discussed at end of the chapter.)

The **bile pigments** are substances formed when the heme portions of hemoglobin are broken down during the destruction of old or damaged erythrocytes in the spleen and liver. The predominant bile pigment is **bilirubin**. Hepatic cells extract bilirubin from the blood and actively secrete it into the bile. It is bilirubin that gives bile its yellow color. After entering the intestinal tract via the bile, bilirubin is modified by bacterial enzymes to form the brown pigments that give feces their characteristic color. During their passage through the intestinal tract some of

the bile pigments are absorbed into the plasma and are eventually excreted in the urine, giving urine its yellow color.

Like pancreatic secretions, the components of bile are secreted by two different cell types. The bile salts, cholesterol, lecithin, and bile pigments are secreted by **hepatocytes** (liver cells), whereas most of the bicarbonate-rich salt solution is secreted by the epithelial cells lining the bile ducts. The salt solution secreted by the bile ducts, just like that secreted by the pancreas, is stimulated by secretin in response to the presence of acid in the duodenum.

FIGURE 17-28

Enterohepatic circulation of bile salts.

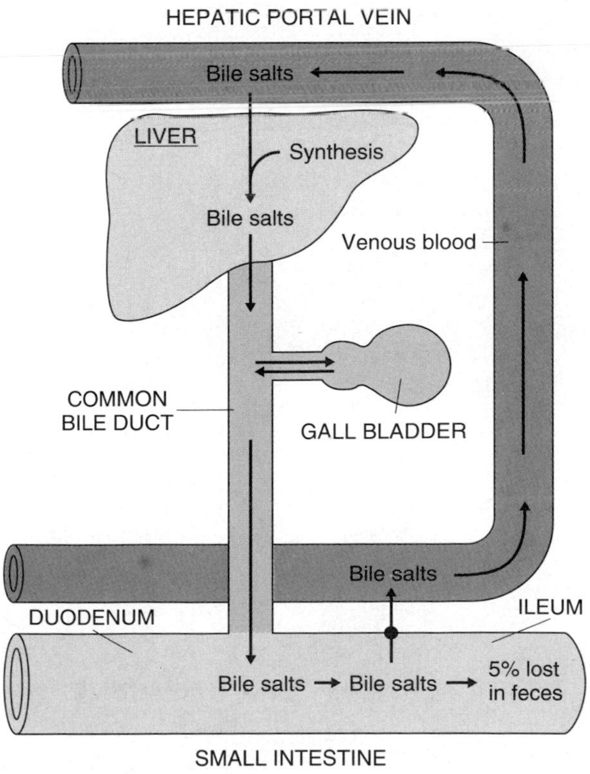

Although bile secretion is greatest during and just after a meal, some bile is always being secreted by the liver. Surrounding the bile duct at the point where it enters the duodenum is a ring of smooth muscle known as the **sphincter of Oddi**. When this sphincter is closed, the dilute bile secreted by the liver is shunted into the gallbladder and becomes concentrated as salt and water are absorbed. During a meal, the gallbladder contracts, emptying concentrated bile into the small intestine. The higher plasma concentration resulting from increased absorption of the bile salts from the intestine leads to an increased rate of bile salt secretion by the liver. Bile salt secretion is controlled by the concentration of bile salts in the blood—the greater the plasma concentration of bile salts, the greater their secretion into the bile canaliculi.

Shortly after the beginning of a fatty meal, the sphincter of Oddi relaxes, and the smooth muscles in the wall of the gallbladder contract, discharging concentrated bile into the duodenum. The signal for gallbladder contraction and sphincter relaxation is the intestinal hormone CCK—appropriately so, since a major stimulus for this hormone's release is the presence of fat in the duodenum. (It is from this ability to cause contraction of the gallbladder that cholecystokinin received its name: *chole,* bile; *cysto,* bladder; *kinin,* to move). Figure 17-29 summarizes the factors controlling the entry of bile into the small intestine.

FIGURE 17-29

Regulation of bile entry into the small intestine.

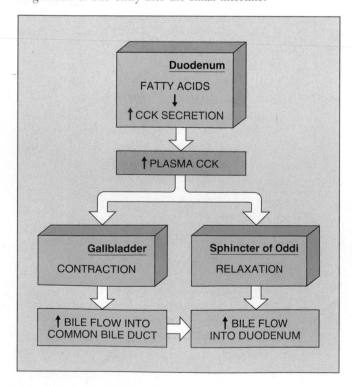

Small Intestine

Secretions. Approximately 2000 ml of fluid is *secreted* from the blood into the lumen by the walls of the small intestine each day. A much larger volume, contributed by the salivary, gastric, hepatic, and pancreatic secretions as well as ingested water, is simultaneously absorbed—from the lumen into the blood—so that normally there is an overall net absorption of water from the small intestine.

One of the reasons for water movement into the lumen is that the intestinal epithelium secretes a number of mineral ions, notably sodium, chloride, and bicarbonate ions into the lumen, and water moves with these ions. As stated earlier, another reason for water movement into the lumen is that the chyme entering the small intestine from the stomach may be hypertonic because of a high concentration of solutes in the meal and because digestion breaks down large molecules into many more small molecules. This hypertonicity causes the osmotic movement of water from the isotonic plasma into the intestinal lumen.

As noted above, the intestinal epithelium secretes not only water but also a number of mineral ions. The continuous disintegration of the intestinal epithelium and the secretion of mucus provide additional sources of material entering the lumen of the small intestine.

Motility. In contrast to the peristaltic waves that sweep over the stomach, the most common motion of the small intestine during a meal is a stationary contraction and relaxation of intestinal segments, with little apparent net movement toward the large intestine (Figure 17-30). Each contracting segment is only a few centimeters long, and the contraction lasts a few seconds. The chyme in the lumen of a contracting segment is forced both up and down the intestine. This rhythmical contraction and relaxation of the intestine, known as **segmentation**, produces a continuous division and subdivision of the intestinal contents, thoroughly mixing the chyme in the lumen and bringing it into contact with the intestinal wall.

These segmenting movements are initiated by electrical activity generated by pacemaker cells in the longitudinal smooth-muscle layer. Like the slow waves in the stomach, this intestinal basic electrical rhythm produces oscillations in smooth-muscle membrane potential that, if threshold is reached, trigger action potentials causing muscle contraction. The frequency of segmentation is set by the frequency of the intestinal basic electrical rhythm, but unlike the stomach, which normally has a single rhythm, the intestinal rhythm varies along the length of the intestine, each successive region having a slightly lower frequency than the one above. For example, segmentation in the duodenum occurs at a frequency of about 12 contractions/min, whereas in the terminal portion of the ileum the rate is only 9 contractions/min. Segmentation produces, there-

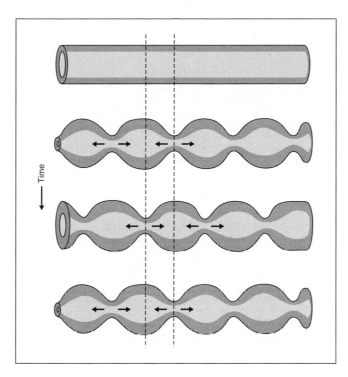

FIGURE 17-30
Segmentation movements of the small intestine in which segments of the intestine contract and relax in a rhythmical pattern but do not undergo peristalsis. This is the pattern encountered during a meal which mixes the luminal contents.

fore, a slow migration of the intestinal contents toward the large intestine because more chyme is forced downward, on the average, than upward.

The intensity of segmentation can be altered by hormones, the enteric nervous system, and autonomic nerves; parasympathetic activity increases the force of contraction, and sympathetic stimulation decreases it. As is true for the stomach, these inputs produce changes in the force of smooth-muscle contraction but do not significantly change the frequencies of the basic electrical rhythms.

After most of a meal has been absorbed, the segmenting contractions cease and are replaced by a pattern of peristaltic activity known as the **migrating motility complex**. Beginning in the lower portion of the stomach, repeated waves of peristaltic activity travel only a short distance (about 2 ft) along the small intestine and then die out. This short segment of peristaltic activity slowly migrates down the small intestine, taking about 2 h to reach the large intestine. By the time the migrating motility complex reaches the end of the ileum, new waves are beginning in the upper portion of the intestinal tract and the process is repeated. Upon the arrival of a meal in the stomach, the migrating motility complex rapidly ceases and is replaced by segmentation.

The migrating motility complex moves into the large intestine any undigested material still remaining in the small intestine and also prevents bacteria from remaining in the small intestine long enough to grow and multiply. In diseases in which there is an aberrant migrating motility complex, bacterial overgrowth in the small intestine can become a major problem.

A rise in the plasma concentration of a candidate intestinal hormone, called **motilin**, is thought to initiate the migrating motility complex, while the patterns of contractile activity during segmentation and peristalsis are coordinated by the enteric nervous system. The mechanisms of motilin action and the control of its release are unclear.

Mild distension of the intestine produces a contraction of the smooth muscle on the oral side of the distension and relaxation of the smooth muscle on the anal side. This pattern of activity, known as the **law of the intestine**, is mediated by neurons in the myenteric plexus and promotes movement of the luminal contents toward the large intestine.

The contractile activity in various regions of the small intestine can be altered by reflexes initiated at different points along the gastrointestinal tract. For example, segmentation intensity in the ileum increases during periods of gastric emptying, and this is known as the **gastroileal reflex**. Large distensions of the intestine, injury to the intestinal wall, and various bacterial infections in the intestine lead to a complete cessation of motility, the **intestino-intestinal reflex**.

A person's emotional state can also affect the contractile activity of the intestine, and therefore the rate of chyme propulsion and mixing. Fear tends to decrease motility, whereas hostility increases it, although, as with gastric motility, these intestinal responses vary greatly in different individuals. They are mediated via autonomic nerves to the intestine.

As much as 500 ml of air may be swallowed during a meal. Most of this air travels no farther than the esophagus, from which it is eventually expelled by belching. Some of the air reaches the stomach, however, and is passed on to the intestines, where its percolation through the chyme as the intestinal contents are mixed produces gurgling sounds that are often quite loud.

Large Intestine

The large intestine is a tube 2.5 in. in diameter and about 4 ft long. Its first portion, the **cecum**, forms a blind-ended pouch from which extends the **appendix**, a small finger-like projection having no known function (Figure 17-31). The colon consists of three relatively straight segments—the ascending, transverse, and descending portions. The terminal portion of the descending colon is S-shaped, forming the sigmoid colon, which empties into a relatively straight segment, the **rectum**, which ends at the anus.

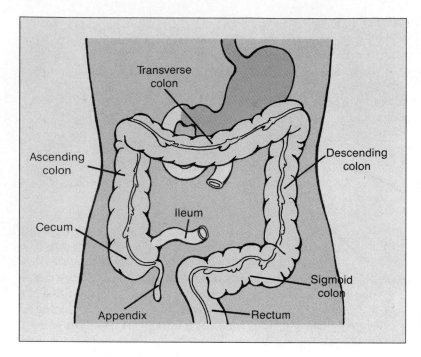

FIGURE 17-31

The large intestine (colon) and rectum.

Although the large intestine has a greater diameter than the small intestine, its epithelial surface area is far less than that of the small intestine, since the colon is about half as long as the small intestine, its surface is not convoluted, and its mucosa lacks villi. The secretions of the colon are scanty, lack digestive enzymes, and consist mostly of mucus. The primary function of the large intestine is to store and concentrate fecal material before defecation.

Chyme enters the colon through the **ileocecal sphincter**. This sphincter is normally closed, but after a meal, when the gastroileal reflex increases ileal contractions, it relaxes each time the terminal portion of the ileum contracts, allowing chyme to enter the large intestine. Distension of the colon, on the other hand, produces a reflex contraction of the sphincter, preventing fecal material from moving back into the small intestine.

About 1500 ml of chyme enters the colon from the small intestine each day. This material is derived largely from the secretions of the lower small intestine since most of the ingested food has been absorbed before reaching the large intestine. Absorption by the colon accounts for only about 4 percent of the material entering the gastrointestinal tract.

The primary absorptive process in the large intestine is the active transport of sodium from lumen to blood, with the accompanying osmotic absorption of water. If fecal material remains in the large intestine for a long time, almost all the water is absorbed, leaving behind hard fecal pellets. There is normally a net movement of potassium

from blood into the colon lumen, and severe depletion of total-body potassium can result when large volumes of fluid are excreted in the feces. There is also net movement of bicarbonate ions into the lumen, and loss of this bicarbonate in patients with prolonged diarrhea can cause the blood to become acidic.

The large intestine also absorbs some of the products (vitamins, for example) synthesized by the bacteria inhabiting this region. Although this source of vitamins generally provides only a small part of the normal daily requirement, it may make a significant contribution when dietary vitamin intake is low. An individual who depends on colonic absorption of vitamins may become vitamin-deficient if treated with antibiotics that inhibit many species of colonic bacteria as well as disease-causing bacteria.

Other bacterial products include gas (**flatus**), which is a mixture of nitrogen and carbon dioxide, with small amounts of hydrogen, methane, and hydrogen sulfide. Bacterial fermentation of undigested polysaccharides produces these gases in the colon at the rate of about 400 to 700 ml/day. Certain foods, beans, for example, contain large amounts of carbohydrates that cannot be digested by intestinal enzymes but are readily metabolized by bacteria in the large intestine, producing large amounts of gas.

Motility and Defecation. Contractions of the circular smooth muscle in the colon produce a segmentation motion with a rhythm considerably slower (one every 30 min) than that in the small intestine. Because of the slow propulsion of the colonic contents, material entering the colon from the small intestine remains for about 18 to 24 h. This provides time for bacteria to grow and multiply. Three to four times a day, generally following a meal, a wave of intense contraction, known as a **mass movement**, spreads rapidly over the colon toward the rectum. This usually coincides with the gastroileal reflex. Unlike a peristaltic wave, in which the smooth muscle at each point relaxes after the wave of contraction has passed, the smooth muscle of the colon remains contracted for some time after a mass movement.

The **anus,** the exit from the rectum, is normally closed by the **internal anal sphincter**, which is composed of smooth muscle, and the **external anal sphincter**, composed of skeletal muscle under voluntary control. The sudden distension of the walls of the rectum produced by the mass movement of fecal material into it initiates the **defecation reflex**, which is mediated primarily by the external nerves to the terminal end of the large intestine. The reflex response consists of a contraction of the rectum, relaxation of the internal anal sphincter, contraction initially of the external anal sphincter, and increased peristaltic activity in the sigmoid colon. Eventually, a pressure is reached in the rectum that triggers *relaxation* of the external anal sphincter, allowing the feces to be expelled.

The conscious urge to defecate, mediated by stretched mechanoreceptors, accompanies distension of the rectum. Brain centers can, however, via descending pathways to somatic nerves to the external anal sphincter, override the reflexive signals that eventually would relax the sphincter, thereby keeping the external sphincter closed and allowing a person to delay defecation. In this case the smooth muscle in the walls of the rectum relaxes, and the urge to defecate subsides until the next mass movement propels more feces into the rectum, increasing its volume and again initiating the defecation reflex. Voluntary control of the external anal sphincter is learned during childhood. Spinal-cord damage can lead to a loss of voluntary control over defecation.

Defecation is normally assisted by a deep inspiration, followed by closure of the glottis and contraction of the abdominal and thoracic muscles, producing an increase in abdominal pressure that is transmitted to the contents of the large intestine and rectum. This maneuver also causes a rise in intrathoracic pressure, which leads to a transient rise in blood pressure followed by a fall in pressure as the venous return to the heart is decreased. The cardiovascular changes resulting from excessive strain during defecation may precipitate a stroke or heart attack in individuals with cardiovascular disease.

About 150 g of feces, consisting of about 100 g of water and 50 g of solid material, is normally eliminated each day. The solid matter is mostly bacteria, undigested polysaccharides, bile pigments, cholesterol, and small amounts of electrolytes, particularly potassium.

PATHOPHYSIOLOGY OF THE GASTROINTESTINAL TRACT

Since the end result of gastrointestinal function is the absorption of nutrients, salts, and water, most malfunctions of this organ system affect either the nutritional state of the body or its salt and water content. The following provide a few examples of disordered gastrointestinal function.

Ulcers

Considering the high concentration of acid and pepsin secreted by the stomach, it is natural to wonder why the stomach does not digest itself. Several of the factors that protect the walls of the stomach from being digested are: (1) The surface of the mucosa is lined with cells that secrete a slightly alkaline mucus, which forms a thin layer over the luminal surface. Both the protein content of mucus and its alkalinity neutralize hydrogen ions in the immediate area of the epithelium. Thus, mucus forms a chemical barrier between the highly acid contents of the lumen and the cell surface. (2) In addition, the tight junctions between the epithelial cells lining the stomach restrict the diffusion of hydrogen ions into the underlying tissues. (3) Also, these epithelial cells are replaced every few days by new cells arising by the division of cells within the gastric pits.

Yet these protective mechanisms can prove inadequate, and erosions (***ulcers***) of the gastric surface occur. Ulcers can occur not only in the stomach but also in the lower part of the esophagus and in the duodenum. Indeed, duodenal ulcers are about 10 times more frequent than gastric ulcers, affecting about 10 percent of the U.S. population. Damage to blood vessels in the tissues underlying the ulcer may cause bleeding into the gastrointestinal lumen. On occasion, the ulcer may penetrate the entire wall, resulting in leakage of the luminal contents into the abdominal cavity.

Ulcer formation involves breaking the mucosal barrier and exposing the underlying tissue to the corrosive action of acid and pepsin, but it is not always clear what produces the initial damage to the barrier. Although acid is essential for ulcer formation, it is not necessarily the primary factor that breaks the mucosal barrier. Many patients with ulcers have normal or even subnormal rates of acid secretion. However, reducing the level of acid and pepsin secretion, either by the use of drugs that inhibit acid secretion or by cutting the parasympathetic (vagus) nerves to the stomach, promotes healing and tends to prevent the reoccurrence of ulcers.

Many factors—genetic susceptibility, drugs, alcohol, bile salts, and excessive secretion of acid and pepsin—

may contribute to ulcer formation. The major factor, however, may be the presence of a bacterium, *Helicobacter pylori,* that is present in the stomachs of a majority of patients with ulcers or **gastritis** (inflammation of the stomach's walls). Suppression of this bacterium with antibiotics often leads to healing of the damaged mucosa.

Despite popular notions that ulcers are due to emotional stress and despite the existence of a pathway (the parasympathetic nerves) for mediating stress-induced increases in acid secretion, the role of stress in producing ulcers remains unclear. Once the ulcer has been formed, however, emotional stress can aggravate it by increasing acid secretion.

Vomiting

Vomiting is the forceful expulsion of the contents of the stomach and upper intestinal tract through the mouth. Like swallowing, vomiting is a complex reflex coordinated by a region in the brainstem medulla oblongata, in this case known as the **vomiting center**. Neural input to this center from receptors in many different regions of the body can initiate the vomiting reflex. For example, excessive distension of the stomach or small intestine, various substances acting upon chemoreceptors in the intestinal wall or in the brain, increased pressure within the skull, rotating movements of the head (motion sickness), intense pain, and tactile stimuli applied to the back of the throat can all initiate vomiting.

What is the adaptive value of this reflex? Obviously, the removal of ingested toxic substances before they can be absorbed is of benefit. Moreover, the nausea that usually accompanies vomiting may have the adaptive value of conditioning the individual to avoid the future ingestion of foods containing such toxic substances. Why other types of stimuli, such as those producing motion sickness, have become linked to the vomiting center is not clear.

Vomiting is usually preceded by increased salivation, sweating, increased heart rate, pallor, and feelings of nausea. The events leading to vomiting begin with a deep inspiration, closure of the glottis, and elevation of the soft palate. The abdominal muscles then contract, raising the abdominal pressure, which is transmitted to the stomach's contents. The lower esophageal sphincter relaxes, and the high abdominal pressure forces the contents of the stomach into the esophagus. This initial sequence of events can occur repeatedly without expulsion via the mouth and is known as *retching*. Vomiting occurs when the abdominal contractions become so strong that the increased intrathoracic pressure forces the contents of the esophagus through the upper esophageal sphincter.

Vomiting is also accompanied by strong contractions in the upper portion of the small intestine, contractions that tend to force some of the intestinal contents back into the stomach from which they can be expelled. Thus, some bile may be present in the vomitus.

Excessive vomiting can lead to large losses of the water and salts that normally would be absorbed in the small intestine. This can result in severe dehydration, upset the body's salt balance, and produce circulatory problems due to a decrease in plasma volume. The loss of acid from vomiting lowers blood acidity.

Gallstones

As described earlier, bile contains not only bile salts but also cholesterol and phospholipids, which are water-insoluble and are maintained in soluble form in the bile as micelles. When the concentration of cholesterol in the bile becomes too high in relation to the concentrations of phospholipid and bile salts, cholesterol crystallizes out of solution, forming **gallstones**. This can occur if the liver secretes excessive amounts of cholesterol or if the cholesterol becomes overly concentrated in the gallbladder as a result of salt and water absorption. Although cholesterol gallstones are the most frequently encountered gallstones in the Western world, the precipitation of bile pigments can also occasionally be responsible for gallstone formation.

Why some individuals develop gallstones and others do not is still unclear. Women, for example, have about twice the incidence of gallstone formation as men, and Native Americans have a very high incidence compared with other ethnic groups in the United States.

If a gallstone is small, it may pass through the common bile duct into the intestine with no complications. A larger stone may become lodged in the opening of the gallbladder, causing contractile spasms of the smooth muscle and pain. A more serious complication arises when a gallstone lodges in the common bile duct, thereby preventing bile from entering the intestine. The absence of bile in the intestine decreases the rate of fat digestion and absorption, so that approximately half of ingested fat is not digested and passes on to the large intestine and eventually appears in the feces. Furthermore, bacteria in the large intestine convert some of this fat into fatty acid derivatives that alter salt and water movements, leading to a net flow of fluid into the large intestine. The result is diarrhea and increased fluid loss.

Since the duct from the pancreas joins the common bile duct just before it enters the duodenum, a gallstone that becomes lodged at this point prevents both bile and pancreatic secretions from entering the intestine. This results in failure both to neutralize acid and to digest most organic nutrients, not just fat, adequately. The end result is severe nutritional deficiencies.

The buildup of pressure in a blocked common bile duct inhibits further secretion of bile. As a result, bilirubin, which is normally secreted into the bile from the blood, accumulates in the blood and diffuses into tissues, where it produces the yellowish coloration of the skin and eyes known as *jaundice*.

It should be emphasized, however, that bile duct obstruction is not the only cause of jaundice. Bilirubin accumulation in the blood can occur if hepatocytes are damaged by liver disease and therefore fail to secrete bilirubin into the bile. It can also occur if the level of bilirubin in the blood exceeds the capacity of the normal liver to secrete it, as in diseases that result in an increased breakdown of red blood cells—hemolytic jaundice. At birth, the liver's capacity to secrete bilirubin is not fully developed. This may result in jaundice during the first few days of life, but the jaundice normally clears spontaneously. Excessive accumulation of bilirubin during the neonatal period, as occurs, for example, with hemolytic disease of the newborn (Chapter 20), carries a risk of bilirubin-induced neurological damage at a time when a critical consolidation of the nervous system is occurring.

Lactose Intolerance

Lactose is the major carbohydrate in milk. It cannot be absorbed directly but must first be digested into its components—glucose and galactose—which are readily absorbed by active transport. Lactose is digested by the enzyme **lactase**, which is embedded in the plasma membranes of intestinal epithelial cells. Lactase is present at birth, but in approximately 25 percent of white Americans and in most northern Europeans its concentration then declines when the child is between 18 and 36 months old. In those individuals with decreased lactase, ingested lactose is not completely digested and some remains in the small intestine, leading to a condition known as *lactose intolerance*.

Since the absorption of water requires prior absorption of solute to provide an osmotic gradient, the unabsorbed lactose in persons with lactose intolerance prevents some of the water from being absorbed. This lactose-containing fluid is passed on to the large intestine, where bacteria digest the lactose. They then metabolize the released monosaccharides, producing large quantities of gas (which distends the colon, producing pain) and organic products that inhibit active ion absorption. This causes fluid movement into the lumen of the large intestine, producing diarrhea. The response to milk ingestion by adults whose lactase levels have diminished during development varies from mild discomfort to severely dehydrating diarrhea,

according to the volume of milk and milk products ingested and the amount of lactase present in the intestine.

Constipation and Diarrhea

Many people have a mistaken belief that, unless they have a bowel movement every day, the absorption of toxic substances from fecal material in the large intestine will somehow poison them. Attempts to identify such toxic agents in the blood following prolonged periods of fecal retention have been unsuccessful, and there appears to be no physiological necessity for having bowel movements at frequent intervals. Whatever maintains a person in a comfortable state is physiologically adequate, whether this means a bowel movement after every meal, once a day, or only once a week.

On the other hand, there often are symptoms—headache, loss of appetite, nausea, and abdominal distension—that may arise when defecation has not occurred for several days or even weeks, depending on the individual. These symptoms of **constipation** are caused not by toxins but by distension of the rectum. In addition, the longer fecal material remains in the large intestine, the more water is absorbed and the harder and drier the feces become, making defecation more difficult and sometimes painful. Thus, constipation tends to promote constipation.

Decreased motility of the large intestine is the primary factor causing constipation. This often occurs in the elderly or may result from damage to the colon's enteric nervous system. Emotional stress can also decrease the motility of the large intestine.

One of the factors increasing colonic motility, and thus opposing the development of constipation, is distension of the large intestine. As noted earlier, dietary fiber (cellulose and other complex polysaccharides) is not digested by the enzymes in the small intestine and is passed on to the large intestine, where its bulk produces distension and thereby increases motility. Bran and most fruits and vegetables are examples of foods that have a relatively high fiber content.

Laxatives, agents that increase the frequency or ease of defecation, act through a variety of mechanisms. Thus, fiber provides a natural laxative. Some laxatives, such as mineral oil, simply lubricate the feces, making defecation easier and less painful. Others contain magnesium and aluminum salts, which are poorly absorbed and therefore lead to water retention in the intestinal tract. Still others, such as castor oil, stimulate the motility of the colon and alter ion transport across the wall, thus indirectly affecting water movement.

Excessive use of laxatives in an attempt to maintain a preconceived notion of regularity leads to a decreased responsiveness of the colon to normal defecation-promoting signals. In such cases, a long period without defecation may occur following cessation of laxative intake, appearing to confirm the necessity of taking laxatives to promote regularity.

Diarrhea is characterized by an increased fecal water content and weight (greater than 200 g/day) and may be accompanied by an increased frequency of defecation. Diarrhea results from decreased fluid absorption, increased fluid secretion, or both. The increased motility that accompanies diarrhea probably does not cause the diarrhea (by decreasing the time available for fluid absorption) but rather is a result of the distension produced by increased luminal fluid.

A number of bacterial, protozoan, and viral diseases of the intestinal tract cause diarrhea. In many cases they do so by releasing substances that either alter ion-transport processes in the epithelial membranes or damage the epithelial barriers by direct penetration into the mucosa. As described earlier, the presence of unabsorbed solutes in the lumen, resulting from decreased digestion or absorption, also results in retained fluid and diarrhea.

The major consequences of severe diarrhea are decreased blood volume, potassium depletion, and metabolic acidosis, resulting from the excessive fecal loss of water and sodium, potassium, and bicarbonate ions. Untreated diarrhea is a major cause of death in children in underdeveloped countries. In most cases of childhood diarrhea prevention of severe dehydration can be achieved by ingesting a simple solution containing salt and glucose. The active absorption of these solutes is accompanied by absorption of water, which replaces the fluid lost by diarrhea.

SUMMARY

I. The gastrointestinal system transfers organic nutrients, minerals, and water from the external environment to the internal environment. The four processes used to accomplish this function are (a) digestion, (b) secretion, (c) absorption, and (d) motility.
   A. The system is designed to maximize the absorption of most nutrients, not to regulate the amount absorbed.
   B. The system does not play a major role in the removal of waste products from the internal environment.

OVERVIEW: FUNCTIONS OF THE GASTROINTESTINAL ORGANS

I. The names and functions of the gastrointestinal organs are summarized in Figure 17-3.
II. Each day the gastrointestinal tract secretes about 3.5 times more fluid into the lumen than is ingested. Only about 1 percent of the luminal contents is excreted in the feces.

STRUCTURE OF THE GASTROINTESTINAL TRACT WALL

I. The structure of the wall of the gastrointestinal tract is summarized in Figure 17-6.
   A. The area available for absorption in the small intestine is greatly increased by the folding of the intestinal wall, the presence of villi, and microvilli on the surface of the epithelial cells.
   B. The epithelial cells lining the intestinal tract are continuously replaced by new cells arising from mitosis.
   C. The venous blood from the small intestine, containing absorbed nutrients other than fat, passes to the liver via the hepatic portal vein before returning to the heart. Fat is absorbed into the lymphatic vessels (lacteals) in each villus.

DIGESTION AND ABSORPTION

I. Starch is digested by amylases secreted by the salivary glands and pancreas, and the resulting products, as well as ingested disaccharides, are digested to monosaccharides by enzymes in the membranes of epithelial cells in the small intestine.
   A. The monosaccharides are then absorbed by secondary active transport.
   B. Some polysaccharides, such as cellulose, cannot be digested and pass to the large intestine, where they are metabolized by bacteria.
II. Proteins are broken down into small peptides and amino acids, which are absorbed by secondary active transport in the small intestine.
   A. The breakdown of proteins to peptides is catalyzed by pepsin in the stomach and primarily by the pancreatic enzymes trypsin and chymotrypsin in the small intestine.
   B. Peptides are broken down into amino acids by pancreatic carboxypeptidase and intestinal aminopeptidase.
III. The digestion and absorption of fat by the small intestine requires mechanisms that solubilize the fat and its digestion products.
   A. Large fat globules leaving the stomach are emulsified in the small intestine by bile salts and phospholipids secreted by the liver.
   B. Lipase from the pancreas digests fat at the surface of the emulsion droplets, forming fatty acids and monoglycerides.
   C. These water-insoluble products of lipase action,

when combined with bile salts, form micelles that are in equilibrium with the free molecules.

D. Free fatty acids and monoglycerides diffuse across the luminal membranes of epithelial cells, within which they are enzymatically recombined to form triacylglycerol, which is released as chylomicrons from the blood side of the cell by exocytosis.

E. The released chylomicrons enter lacteals in the intestinal villa and pass, by way of the lymphatic system, to the venous blood returning to the heart.

IV. Fat-soluble vitamins are absorbed by the same pathway used for fat absorption. Most water-soluble vitamins are absorbed in the small intestine by diffusion or carrier-mediated transport. Vitamin B_{12} is absorbed in the ileum after combining with intrinsic factor secreted by the stomach.

V. Water is absorbed from the small intestine by osmosis following the active absorption of solutes, primarily sodium chloride.

REGULATION OF GASTROINTESTINAL PROCESSES

I. Most gastrointestinal reflexes are initiated by luminal stimuli: (a) distension, (b) osmolarity, (c) acidity, and (d) digestion products.

A. Neural reflexes are mediated by short reflexes in the enteric nervous system and by long reflexes involving afferent and efferent neurons to and from the CNS.

B. Gastrin, secretin, CCK, and GIP are secreted by endocrine cells scattered throughout the epithelium of the stomach (gastrin) and small intestine (secretin, CCK, and GIP). Their properties are summarized in Table 17-3.

C. The three phases of gastrointestinal regulation—cephalic, gastric, and intestinal—are named for the location of the stimulus that initiates the response.

II. Chewing breaks up food into particles suitable for swallowing but is not essential for the eventual digestion and absorption of food.

III. Salivary secretion is stimulated by food in the mouth acting reflexly via chemoreceptors and pressure receptors. Both sympathetic and parasympathetic stimulation increase salivary secretion.

IV. Food moved into the pharynx by the tongue initiates swallowing, which is coordinated by the swallowing center in the brainstem medulla oblongata.

A. Food is prevented from entering the trachea by inhibition of respiration and by closure of the glottis.

B. The upper esophageal sphincter relaxes as food is moved into the esophagus and then closes.

C. Food is moved through the esophagus toward the stomach by peristaltic waves. The lower esophageal sphincter remains open throughout swallowing.

D. If food does not reach the stomach with the first peristaltic wave, distension of the esophagus will initiate secondary peristalsis.

V. The factors controlling acid secretion by parietal cells in the stomach are summarized in Table 17-4.

VI. Pepsinogen, secreted by the gastric chief cells in response to most of the same reflexes that control acid secretion, is converted to the active proteolytic enzyme pepsin in the stomach's lumen by acid and by pepsin itself.

VII. Peristaltic waves sweeping over the stomach become stronger in the antrum, where most mixing occurs. With each wave, only a small portion of the stomach's contents are expelled into the small intestine through the pyloric sphincter.

A. The basic electrical rhythm generated by gastric smooth muscle determines gastric peristaltic wave frequency. Contraction strength depends on the frequency of action potentials triggered by the slow waves.

B. The larger a meal, the faster the stomach empties initially. Distension of the small intestine, and fat, acid, or hypertonic solutions in the intestinal lumen inhibit gastric emptying.

VIII. The exocrine portion of the pancreas secretes digestive enzymes and bicarbonate ions, which reach the duodenum through the pancreatic duct.

A. The bicarbonate ions neutralize acid entering the small intestine from the stomach.

B. Most proteolytic enzymes, including trypsin, are secreted by the pancreas in inactive forms. Trypsin is activated by enterokinase located on the membranes of the small intestine cells and in turn activates the other inactive enzymes.

C. The hormone secretin, released from the small intestine in response to increased luminal acidity, stimulates bicarbonate secretion. CCK is released from the small intestine in response to the products of fat and protein digestion, and stimulates pancreatic enzyme secretion.

IX. The liver secretes bile, the major ingredients of which are bile salts, cholesterol, lecithin, bicarbonate ions, bile pigments, and trace metals.

A. Bile salts undergo continuous enterohepatic recirculation. The liver also synthesizes new bile salts to replace those lost in the feces.

B. The greater the bile salt concentration in the hepatic portal blood, the greater the rate of bile secretion.

C. Bilirubin, the major bile pigment, is a breakdown product of hemoglobin and is absorbed

BASIC CONCEPTS OF ENERGY EXPENDITURE AND CALORIC BALANCE

Metabolic Rate

Determinants of Metabolic Rate

Basal metabolic rate

Thyroid hormones

Epinephrine

Food-induced thermogenesis

Muscle activity

Total-Body Energy Balance

Control of Food Intake

Obesity

Eating Disorders: Anorexia Nervosa and Bulimia

REGULATION OF BODY TEMPERATURE

Mechanisms of Heat Loss or Gain

Temperature-Regulating Reflexes

Control of heat production

Control of heat loss by radiation and conduction

Control of heat loss by evaporation

Integration of effector mechanisms

Temperature Acclimatization

Acclimatization to heat

Acclimatization to cold

Fever

Other Causes of Hyperthermia

Exercise

Heat exhaustion and heat stroke

SECTION C SUMMARY

SECTION C KEY TERMS

SECTION C REVIEW QUESTIONS

CHAPTER 18 CLINICAL TERMS

CHAPTER 18 THOUGHT QUESTIONS

Chapter 5 introduced the concepts of energy and of organic metabolism at the level of the individual cell. This chapter deals with a variety of topics that are concerned in one way or another with those same concepts, but for the entire body. First we describe how the metabolic pathways for carbohydrate, fat, and protein are controlled so as to provide a continuous source of energy to the various tissues and organs at all times. The next topic is how the metabolic changes that underlie body growth occur and are controlled. Finally, we describe the determinants of total-body energy balance in terms of energy intake and output and how the body temperature—a measure of the heat content of the body—is regulated.

SECTION

A

CONTROL AND INTEGRATION OF CARBOHYDRATE, PROTEIN, AND FAT METABOLISM

EVENTS OF THE ABSORPTIVE AND POSTABSORPTIVE STATES

Mechanisms have evolved for survival during alternating periods of plenty and fasting. We speak of two functional states or periods: the **absorptive state**, during which ingested nutrients are entering the blood from the gastrointestinal tract, and the **postabsorptive state**, during which the gastrointestinal tract is empty of nutrients and energy must be supplied by the body's own stores. Since an average meal requires approximately 4 h for complete absorption, our usual three-meals-a-day pattern places us in the postabsorptive state during the late morning and afternoon and almost the entire night. We shall refer to going more than 24 h without eating as fasting.

During the absorptive period, some of the ingested nutrients supply the energy needs of the body, and the remainder are added to the body's energy stores, to be called upon during the next postabsorptive period. Total-body energy stores are adequate for the average person to easily withstand a fast of many weeks (provided that water is available).

Figures 18-1 and 18-2 summarize the major pathways to be described in this chapter. Although they may appear formidable at first glance, they should present little difficulty after we have described the component parts, and

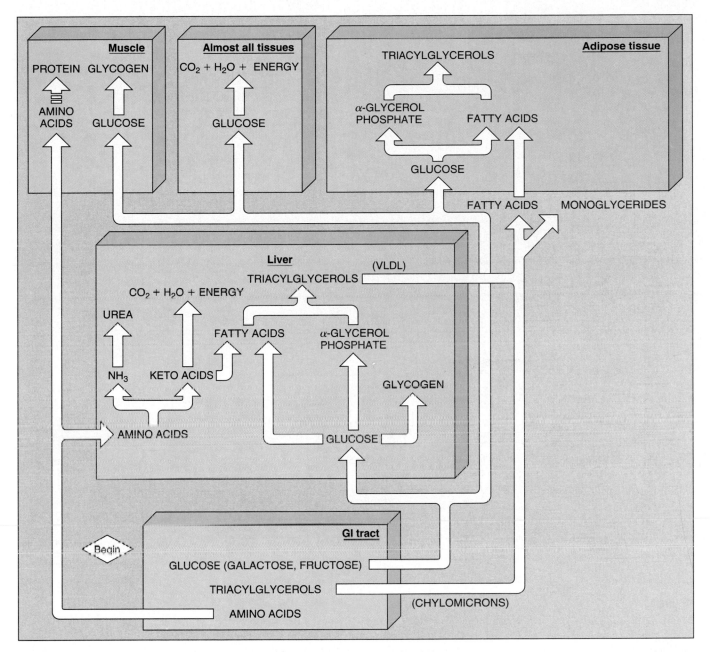

FIGURE 18-1

Major metabolic pathways of the absorptive state. The monoglycerides formed by the action of lipoprotein lipase in the adipose-tissue capillaries are not taken up by the adipose-tissue cells but circulate to the liver for further metabolism. The arrow from amino acids to protein in muscle is dashed to denote the fact that excess amino acids are not *stored* as protein (see text). Urea, formed in the liver, enters the blood and is excreted by the kidneys. All arrows between boxes denote carriage of the substance via the blood. VLDL = very low density lipoproteins.

these figures should be referred to constantly during the following discussion.

Absorptive State

We shall assume, for this discussion, that an average meal contains all three of the major nutrients—carbohydrate, protein, and fat, the carbohydrate constituting most of the meal's energy content (calories). Recall from Chapter 17 that carbohydrate and protein are absorbed primarily as monosaccharides and amino acids, respectively, into the blood supplying the gastrointestinal tract. The blood leaves the gastrointestinal tract to go directly to the liver

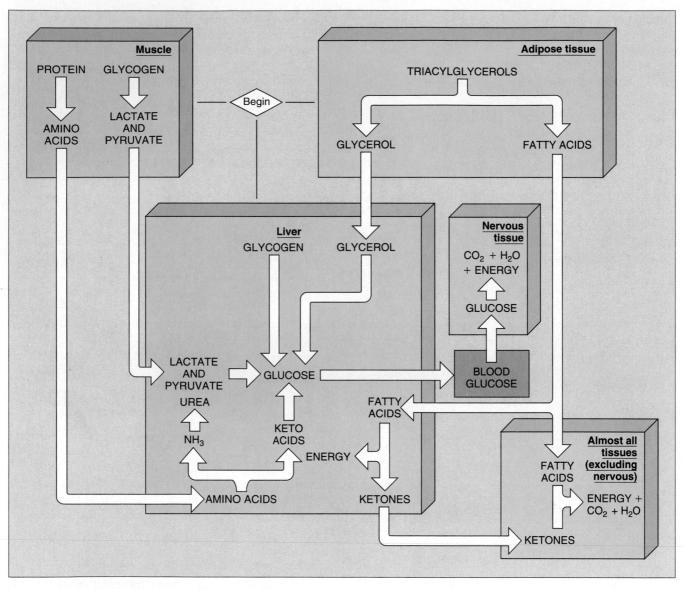

FIGURE 18-2

Major metabolic pathways of the postabsorptive state. The central focus is regulation of the blood glucose concentration. All arrows between boxes denote carriage of the substance via the blood. Urea, formed in the liver, enters the blood and is excreted by the kidneys.

by way of the hepatic portal vein, allowing the liver to alter the nutrient composition of the blood before it returns to the heart to be pumped to the rest of the body. In contrast to carbohydrate and amino acids, fat is absorbed into the lymph, as triacylglycerols in chylomicrons; the lymph then drains into the systemic venous system. Thus, the liver does not get first crack at absorbed fat.

Absorbed Glucose. Some of the carbohydrate absorbed from the gastrointestinal tract is galactose and fructose, but since these sugars are either converted to glucose by the liver or enter essentially the same metabolic pathways

as does glucose, we shall simply refer to absorbed carbohydrate as glucose.

As shown in Figure 18-1, a fraction of the absorbed glucose enters the liver cells. This is a very important point: During the absorptive period there is net *uptake* of glucose by the liver. We shall describe the fate of this glucose in a moment.

Of the absorbed glucose that does not enter liver cells, a very large fraction enters most other body cells and is catabolized to carbon dioxide and water, providing the energy for ATP formation (Chapter 5). Indeed, and this is a key point, glucose is the body's major energy source during the absorptive state. In this regard, it should be recognized that skeletal muscle makes up the majority of body mass and is the major consumer of metabolic fuel, even at rest.

Skeletal muscle not only catabolizes glucose during the absorptive phase but converts some of the glucose to the polysaccharide glycogen, which is then stored in the muscle.

Yet another fraction of absorbed glucose enters adipose-tissue cells (adipocytes) where some, as in muscle, is catabolized for energy. The most important fate, however, of glucose in adipocytes during the absorptive phase is its transformation to both α-glycerol phosphate and fatty acids, which are then linked together to form triacylglycerols.

We now return to the absorbed glucose that enters the liver: As shown in Figure 18-1, it is either stored as glycogen, as in skeletal muscle, or transformed to α-glycerol phosphate and fatty acids, which are then used to synthesize triacylglycerols, as in adipose tissue. Some of this fat synthesized from glucose in the liver is stored there, but most is packaged, along with specific proteins, into molecular aggregates of lipids and proteins. These aggregates are secreted by the liver cells and enter the blood. They are called **very-low-density lipoproteins (VLDL)** because they contain much more fat than protein, and fat is less dense than protein. The synthesis of VLDL by liver cells occurs by processes similar to those for synthesis of chylomicrons by intestinal mucosal cells, as described in Chapter 17.

Once in the bloodstream, VLDL complexes, being quite large, do not readily penetrate capillary walls. Instead, their triacylglycerols are hydrolyzed mainly to monoglycerides (glycerol linked to one fatty acid chain) and fatty acids by the enzyme **lipoprotein lipase** located on the blood-facing surface of the capillary endothelium. The capillaries of most tissues and organs contain lipoprotein lipase, but those in adipose tissue are particularly rich in this enzyme. The fatty acids generated by this enzyme's action in adipose tissue diffuse across the capillary wall and into the adipocytes. There they combine with α-glycerol phosphate, supplied by glucose metabolites, to form triacylglycerols once again. Thus, most of the fatty acids in the VLDL triacylglycerol originally synthesized from glucose by the *liver* end up being stored in triacylglycerol in *adipose tissue*. (The monoglycerides released into the blood by the action of lipoprotein lipase in adipose tissue do not enter the adipocytes but circulate to the liver where they are metabolized.)

To summarize, the major fates of glucose during the absorptive phase are utilization for energy, storage as glycogen in liver and skeletal muscle, and storage as fat in adipose tissue.

Absorbed Triacylglycerols. As noted earlier, almost all ingested fat is absorbed as chylomicrons into the lymph, which flows into the systemic circulation. The biochemical processing of these chylomicron triacylglycerols in plasma is quite similar to that just described for VLDL produced by the liver. The fatty acids of plasma chylomicrons are released, mainly within adipose tissue capillaries, by the action of endothelial lipoprotein lipase, and the released fatty acids then enter adipocytes and combine with α-glycerol phosphate, synthesized from glucose metabolites, to form triacylglycerols.

The importance of glucose for triacylglycerol synthesis in adipocytes cannot be overemphasized. Adipocytes do not have the enzyme required for phosphorylation of glycerol, and so α-glycerol phosphate can be formed in these cells only from glucose metabolites and not from glycerol or any other fat metabolites.

In contrast, there are three major sources of the fatty acids found in adipose-tissue triacylglycerol: (1) glucose that enters adipose tissue and is converted to fatty acids; (2) glucose that is converted in liver to VLDL triacylglycerols, which are transported via the blood to the adipose tissue; and (3) ingested triacylglycerols transported to adipose tissue in chylomicrons. Sources 2 and 3 require the action of lipoprotein lipase to release the fatty acids from the circulating triacylglycerols.

This description has emphasized the *storage* of ingested fat. For simplicity, we have not shown in Figure 18-1 that a fraction of the ingested fat is not stored but is oxidized during the absorptive state by various organs to provide energy. The relative amounts of carbohydrate and fat used for energy during the absorptive period depend largely on the content of the meal.

Absorbed Amino Acids. A minority of the absorbed amino acids enter liver cells. They are used to synthesize a variety of proteins, including liver enzymes and plasma proteins, or they are converted to carbohydrate-like intermediates known as **keto acids** by removal of the amino group (deamination, Chapter 5). The amino groups are used to synthesize urea, which is excreted by the kidneys.

The keto acids generated by deamination are *not* converted to glucose during the absorptive phase, unlike the situation to be described for the postabsorptive phase. However, they can enter the Krebs tricarboxylic acid cycle and be catabolized to provide energy for the liver cells, or they can be converted to fatty acids, thereby participating in fat synthesis by the liver.

Most ingested amino acids are not taken up by the liver cells but enter other cells (Figure 18-1), where they may be used to synthesize proteins. We have simplified the diagram by showing "nonliver" amino acid uptake only by muscle, because muscle contains by far the largest amount of body protein. It should be emphasized, however, that all cells require a constant supply of amino acids for protein synthesis and participate in the dynamics of protein metabolism.

Protein synthesis is represented by a *dashed* line in the muscle box in Figure 18-1 to call attention to an important fact: There is a net synthesis of protein during the absorptive period, but this basically just replaces the proteins catabolized during the postabsorptive period. In other words, excess amino acids are not *stored* as protein in the sense that glucose is stored as glycogen or that both glucose and fat are stored as fat. Rather, ingested amino acids in excess of those needed to maintain a stable protein turnover are merely converted to carbohydrate or fat. Therefore, eating large amounts of protein does not in itself cause increases in body protein. This discussion does not apply to growing children, who manifest a continuous increase in body protein, or to adults who are actively building body mass as, for example, by weightlifting.

Nutrient metabolism during the absorptive period is summarized in Table 18-1.

Postabsorptive State

As the absorptive period ends, net synthesis of glycogen, fat, and protein ceases, and net catabolism of all these substances begins to occur. The overall significance of these events can be understood in terms of the essential problem during the postabsorptive period: No glucose is being absorbed from the intestinal tract, yet the plasma glucose concentration must be maintained because the brain normally utilizes only glucose for energy. Too low a plasma glucose concentration can result in alterations of neural activity ranging from subtle impairment of mental function to coma and even death.

The events that maintain plasma glucose concentration fall into two categories: (1) reactions that provide sources of blood glucose, and (2) glucose sparing because of fat utilization.

TABLE 18-1   SUMMARY OF NUTRIENT METABOLISM DURING THE ABSORPTIVE PERIOD

1. Energy is provided primarily by absorbed carbohydrate.
2. There is net uptake of glucose by the liver.
3. Some carbohydrate is stored as glycogen in liver and muscle, but most carbohydrate and fat in excess of that utilized for energy are stored mainly as fat in adipose tissue.
4. There is some synthesis of body proteins, but much dietary protein is utilized for energy or converted to fat.

Sources of Blood Glucose.   The sources of blood glucose during the postabsorptive period are as follows (Figure 18-2):

1. **Glycogenolysis**, the hydrolysis of glycogen stores, occurs in the liver and skeletal muscle. In the liver, glucose is formed by this process and enters the blood. Hepatic glycogenolysis, a rapidly occurring event, is the first line of defense maintaining plasma glucose concentration. Its role, however, is relatively short-lived for the following reason: After the absorptive period is completed, the normal liver contains less than 100 g of glycogen; at 4 kcal/g, the subsequent breakdown of all this glycogen would provide 400 kcal, enough to fulfill an average person's total caloric need for only 4 h. Moreover, this is an overestimate since liver glycogen stores never become fully depleted even during prolonged fasting.

   Glycogenolysis also occurs in skeletal muscle, which contains approximately the same amount of glycogen as the liver. However, muscle, unlike liver, lacks the enzyme necessary to form glucose from the glucose 6-phosphate formed during glycogenolysis (Chapter 5). The glucose 6-phosphate undergoes glycolysis within the muscle to yield pyruvate and lactate. These substances are liberated into the blood, circulate to the liver, and are converted into glucose, which can then leave the liver cells to enter the blood. Thus, muscle glycogen contributes to the blood glucose indirectly via the liver.

2. The catabolism of triacylglycerols, a process termed **lipolysis**, yields glycerol and fatty acids. The major site of lipolysis is adipose tissue, and the glycerol and fatty acids then enter the blood. The glycerol reaching the liver is converted to glucose. Thus, an important source of glucose during the postabsorptive period is the glycerol released when adipose-tissue triacylglycerol is broken down.

3. A few hours into the postabsorptive period protein becomes the major source of blood glucose. Large quantities of protein in muscle and, to a lesser extent, other tissues can be catabolized without serious cellular malfunction. There are, of course, limits to this process, and continued protein loss during a prolonged fast ultimately means functional disintegration, sickness, and death. Before this point is reached, however, protein breakdown can supply large quantities of amino acids, particularly alanine, that enter the blood and are picked up by the liver, which converts them, via the keto acid pathway, to glucose.

We have now described the synthesis of glucose from pyruvate, lactate, glycerol, and amino acids. Synthesis from any of these precursors is known as **gluconeogene-**

sis, that is, new formation of glucose. During a 24-h fast, gluconeogenesis provides approximately 180 g of glucose. The liver is not the only organ capable of gluconeogenesis; the kidneys also perform gluconeogenesis, but mainly during a prolonged fast. In such a fast the kidneys may contribute as much glucose as the liver.

Glucose Sparing (Fat Utilization). The 180 g of glucose per day produced by gluconeogenesis in the liver and kidneys during fasting supplies 720 kcal: 180 g/day × 4 kcal/g = 720 kcal/day. As described later in this chapter, normal total energy expenditure for an average adult equals 1500 to 3000 kcal/day. Accordingly, gluconeogenesis cannot supply all the body's energy needs. The following essential adjustment must therefore take place during the transition from the absorptive to the postabsorptive state: Most organs and tissues markedly reduce their glucose catabolism and increase their fat utilization, the latter becoming the major energy source. This metabolic adjustment, termed **glucose sparing**, "spares" the glucose produced by the liver for use by the nervous system.

The essential step in this adjustment is lipolysis, the catabolism of adipose-tissue triacylglycerol, which liberates glycerol and fatty acids into the blood. We described lipolysis in the previous section in terms of its importance in providing *glycerol* to the liver for conversion to glucose. Now, we focus on the liberated *fatty acids*, which circulate bound to plasma albumin. (Despite this binding to protein, they are known as free fatty acids in that they are "free" of glycerol.) The circulating fatty acids are metabolized by almost all tissues, excluding the nervous system. They enter the Krebs cycle by way of acetyl CoA and are catabolized to carbon dioxide and water (Chapter 5), thereby providing energy.

The liver also catabolizes fatty acids to acetyl CoA. The liver is unique, however, in that most of the acetyl CoA it forms from fatty acids during the postabsorptive state, particularly during prolonged fasting, does not enter the Krebs cycle but is processed into three compounds collectively called **ketones** (or ketone bodies). The reader should distinguish ketones from keto acids, which are metabolites of amino acids. Ketones are released into the blood and provide an important energy source during prolonged fasting for the many tissues capable of oxidizing them via the Krebs cycle. One of the ketones is acetone, some of which is exhaled and accounts for the distinctive breath odor of individuals undergoing prolonged fasting or, as we shall see, suffering from severe untreated diabetes mellitus.

The net result of fatty acid and ketone utilization during fasting is provision of energy for the body and sparing of glucose for the brain. Moreover, an important change in brain metabolism with prolonged fasting also occurs. Many areas of the brain are capable of utilizing ketones for energy, and so as these substances begin to build up in the blood after the first few days of a fast, the brain begins to utilize them, as well as glucose, for its energy source. The survival value of this phenomenon is very great; when the brain greatly reduces its glucose requirement by utilizing ketones, much less protein breakdown is required to supply the amino acids for gluconeogenesis. Accordingly the protein stores will last longer, and the ability to withstand a long fast without serious tissue disruption is enhanced.

Table 18-2 summarizes the events of the postabsorptive period. The combined effects of glycogenolysis, gluconeogenesis, and the switch to fat utilization are so efficient that, after several days of complete fasting, the plasma glucose concentration is reduced by only a few percent. After 1 month, it is decreased only 25 percent.

ENDOCRINE AND NEURAL CONTROL OF THE ABSORPTIVE AND POSTABSORPTIVE STATES

We now turn to the endocrine and neural factors that control and integrate these metabolic pathways and transformations. As before, the reader should constantly refer to Figures 18-1 and 18-2. We shall focus primarily on the following questions, summarized in Figure 18-3, raised by the previous discussion: (1) What controls net anabolism of protein, glycogen, and triacylglycerol in the absorptive phase, and net catabolism in the postabsorptive phase? (2) What induces primarily glucose utilization by cells for energy during the absorptive phase, but fat utilization during the postabsorptive phase?

TABLE 18-2 SUMMARY OF NUTRIENT METABOLISM DURING THE POSTABSORPTIVE PERIOD

1. Glycogen, fat, and protein syntheses are curtailed, and net breakdown occurs.

2. Glucose is formed in the liver both from the glycogen stored there and by gluconeogenesis from blood-borne lactate, pyruvate, glycerol, and amino acids. The kidneys also perform gluconeogenesis during a prolonged fast.

3. The glucose produced in the liver (and kidneys) is released into the blood, but its utilization for energy is greatly reduced in muscle and other nonneural tissues.

4. Lipolysis releases adipose-tissue fatty acids into the blood, and the oxidation of these fatty acids and of ketones produced from them by the liver provides most of the body's energy supply.

5. The brain continues to use glucose but also starts using ketones as they build up in the blood.

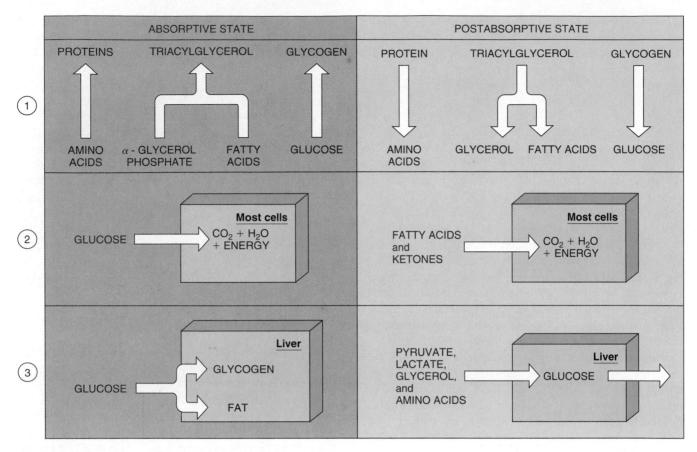

FIGURE 18-3

Summary of critical points in transition from absorptive state to postabsorptive state. The phrase "absorptive state" could be replaced with "actions of insulin," "postabsorptive state" with "results of decreased insulin."

(3) What drives net glucose uptake by the liver during the absorptive phase, but gluconeogenesis and glucose release during the postabsorptive phase?

The most important controls of these transitions from feasting to fasting, and vice versa, are two pancreatic hormones—insulin and glucagon. Also playing a role are the hormone epinephrine, from the adrenal medulla, and the sympathetic nerves to liver and adipose tissue.

Insulin and glucagon are peptides secreted by the **islets of Langerhans**, clusters of endocrine cells in the pancreas. Appropriate histological techniques reveal four distinct types of islet cells, termed A (or alpha), B (or beta), D (or delta), and F (or PP) cells, each of which secretes a different hormone. The **beta cells** are the source of insulin, and the **alpha cells** of glucagon. There are two other pancreatic hormones, somatostatin and pancreatic polypeptide, secreted by the delta cells and the PP cells, respectively, but the functions of these two pancreatic hormones are not known.

Insulin

Insulin is the most abundant hormone secreted by the islets and is the single most important controller of organic metabolism. Its secretion, and hence plasma concentration, are increased during the absorptive state and decreased during the postabsorptive state. For simplicity, insulin's many actions are often divided into two broad categories: (1) metabolic effects on carbohydrate, lipid, and protein synthesis; and (2) growth-promoting effects on DNA synthesis, cell division, and cell differentiation. This section deals with the metabolic effects; the growth-promoting effects are described later in this chapter in the section on growth.

Insulin's major targets are muscle (both cardiac and skeletal), adipose tissue, and liver, and the most important responses of these targets are summarized in Figure 18-4. Compare this figure to Figure 18-1 and you will see that these responses to insulin are the same as the events of the absorptive-state pattern. Conversely, the effects of a reduction in plasma insulin are the same as the events of the postabsorptive pattern in Figure 18-2.

What are the biochemical sequences of events that lead to the responses summarized in Figure 18-4? The first step in all the sequences is the binding of insulin to specific receptors on the outer surface of the plasma membrane of its target cells. As noted in Chapter 7, the insulin-

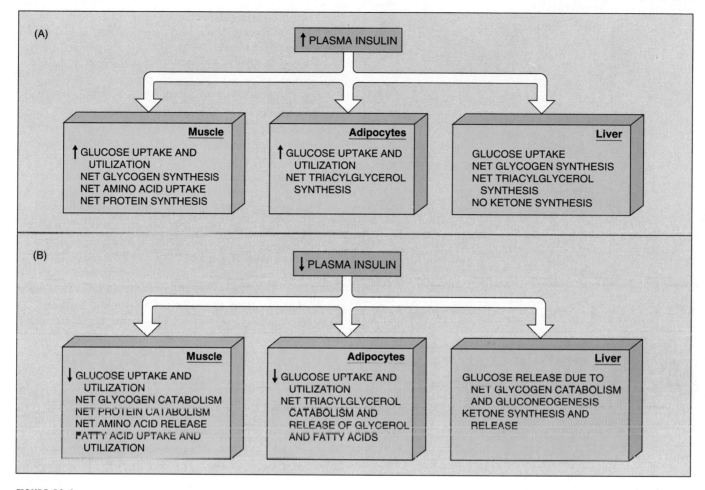

FIGURE 18-4

Summary of overall target-cell responses to an increase (A) or decrease (B) in the plasma concentration of insulin. The biochemical events that underlie these responses are given in Figure 18-5.

activated receptor is a tyrosine kinase enzyme, which catalyzes its own phosphorylation using ATP. This autophosphorylation is necessary for the insulin receptor to trigger the next steps in the sequences leading to the cell's responses, that is, to initiate the signal transduction mechanisms (Chapter 7).[1] In some cases, the insulin receptor inhibits adenylyl cyclase, thereby reducing the intracellular cyclic AMP concentration, but in most cases the signal transduction mechanisms remain unclear, involving as yet unidentified second messengers.

Whatever the signal transduction mechanisms are, the final steps of the sequences leading to the cell's responses are changes in the target-cell's membrane transport and/or enzymes, to which we now turn. It is important here not to lose sight of the forest for the trees: The essential information (the "forest") to understand about insulin's actions is

the target cells' ultimate responses, that is, the material summarized in Figure 18-4; the following sections, summarized in Figure 18-5, attempt merely to show some of the specific biochemical reactions (the "trees") that underlie these ultimate responses.

Effects on Muscle and Adipose Tissue. Glucose enters most cells of the body by the carrier-mediated mechanism that we described in Chapter 6 as facilitated diffusion. Glucose transport is unique in muscle and adipocytes (and a few other cell types), however, in that the glucose transporter is responsive to insulin. This hormone causes glucose-transport proteins stored in the cytoplasm to be inserted in the plasma membranes of these cells. This causes greater glucose entry, which then increases this sugar's availability for all the reactions in which it participates in these cells (Figure 18-5): In muscle, the most important are glycolysis and glycogen synthesis; in adipose tissue, they are syntheses of fatty acids and α-glycerol phosphate, which then combine to form triacylglycerol.

---

[1]There is still controversy, however, as to whether all biological responses to insulin require activation of insulin receptor tyrosine kinase and receptor autophosphorylation.

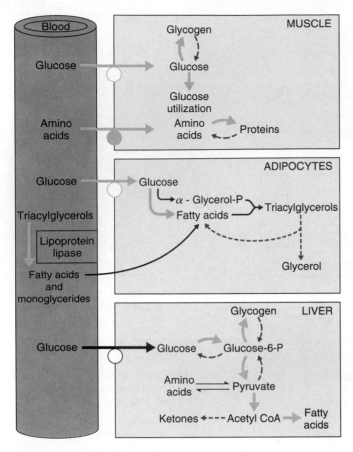

FIGURE 18-5

Key biochemical events that underlie the responses of target cells to insulin summarized in Figure 18-4. Each green arrow denotes a process stimulated by insulin, whereas a dashed red arrow denotes inhibition by insulin. All these effects, except for those exerted on the transport of glucose and amino acids, are mediated by insulin-dependent enzymes. The bowed arrows, as described in Chapter 5, denote pathways whose reversibility is mediated by different enzymes. For simplicity we do not show the multiple steps in liver between pyruvate and glucose by which insulin inhibits gluconeogenesis while stimulating glucose utilization (see Chapter 5 for a review of the biochemical steps in these pathways).

But insulin favors glycolysis and net synthesis of glycogen and triacylglycerol not just by its effects on glucose *transport*. Insulin can also alter the activities and/or concentrations of the *enzymes* involved in the metabolic pathways of these substances. (For simplicity in these descriptions, when we refer to stimulation and inhibition we will not specify whether it is enzyme activity or enzyme concentration that is being altered.)

Glycogen synthesis in muscle provides an excellent example (Figure 18-5, top right): Increased glucose transport stimulates glycogen synthesis by increasing glucose availability, but in addition insulin increases the activity of the enzyme (glycogen synthase) catalyzing the rate-limiting step in glycogen synthesis and inhibits the enzyme (glycogen phosphorylase) that catalyzes glycogen catabolism. Thus, insulin favors glucose transformation to glycogen in muscle by a triple-barreled effect!

The situation for triacylglycerol metabolism in adipocytes is analogous to that for carbohydrate (Figure 18-5): The stimulation by insulin of glucose transport into adipocytes provides precursors for the synthesis of triacylglycerols, but insulin also stimulates the intracellular enzymes that catalyze fatty acid synthesis, and very importantly, it inhibits the intracellular lipase that catalyzes triacylglycerol breakdown. Again there is a triple-barreled effect favoring, in this case, triacylglycerol storage in adipocytes. Actually there is a four-barreled effect, for insulin also stimulates lipoprotein lipase in the endothelial cells of adipose-tissue capillaries; recall that this enzyme catalyzes the breakdown of plasma triacylglycerols and releases fatty acids that can then enter the adipose-tissue cells and be built into triacylglycerol there. The reader must remember to distinguish lipoprotein lipase, which is on the surface of endothelial cells and promotes fat *storage*, from the completely different intracellular lipase that mediates lipolysis, thereby favoring fat *mobilization*.[2]

And similarly for protein in muscle (Figure 18-5): First, insulin stimulates the active transport system that moves amino acids into muscle cells, thereby making more amino acids available for protein synthesis. But this hormone also stimulates some of the ribosomal enzymes that mediate the synthesis of protein from these amino acids and inhibits the enzymes that mediate protein catabolism.

Effects on Liver. Some of insulin's effects on carbohydrate and lipid metabolism in liver are the same as those seen in muscle and adipocytes. Thus, in liver insulin favors both net glycogen synthesis and net triacylglycerol synthesis through the same profile of enzyme stimulation and inhibition described above for muscle and adipocytes.

There are, however, several aspects of insulin's actions on liver that are different from those on the other targets and determine whether the liver will take up or release glucose. First, glucose production—gluconeogenesis—is an activity limited to the liver (and the kidneys), and it is abolished by insulin, which inhibits critical enzymes that mediate the gluconeogenic pathways. Thus, the insulin-stimulated liver does not release glucose but rather takes it up. Indeed, it takes it up in very large quantities despite a second important difference between liver and insulin's

---

[2]The intracellular lipase that is affected by insulin (and other hormones) is often called hormone-sensitive lipase. This can be confusing because, as we have seen, endothelial-cell lipoprotein lipase is also sensitive to hormones.

other two major targets: The facilitated-diffusion glucose transporter in liver, unlike that in muscle and adipocytes, is *not* influenced by insulin.

How, then, does insulin cause the marked uptake of glucose? First, recall two facts from previous chapters: (1) Facilitated diffusion into a cell, although carrier-mediated, is downhill transport and is dependent upon a concentration difference across the plasma membrane (Chapter 6); and (2) the first step in the intracellular metabolism of glucose is its phosphorylation to glucose 6-phosphate (Chapter 5). Insulin stimulates the enzyme (glucokinase) in liver that catalyzes this first metabolic step and inhibits the enzyme (glucose-6-phosphatase) that removes the phosphate, and this keeps the cytosolic glucose concentration low, resulting in a large concentration gradient favoring glucose movement into the liver cells.

Finally, recall that ketone formation is another process limited to the liver. Insulin inhibits this process in a variety of ways.

Effects of Decreases in Plasma Insulin Concentration. A decrease in plasma insulin concentration, by eliminating or reducing insulin's effects, will bring about results just opposite those described in the previous two sections. (1) net protein catabolism in muscle due to less entry of amino acids into muscle cells, decreased activity of the enzymes mediating protein synthesis, and less inhibition of the enzymes mediating protein catabolism; (2) net glycogen catabolism in all target cells due to less glucose entry into cells, decreased activity of the enzyme mediating glycogen synthesis, and less inhibition of the enzyme mediating glycogen catabolism; (3) net fat catabolism in adipose tissue due to less entry of glucose into adipose-tissue cells, decreased activity of the enzymes mediating fat synthesis, and less inhibition of the enzyme mediating lipolysis; (4) decreased glycolysis due to less entry of glucose into muscle and adipose tissue (and several other tissues) and decreased activity of the glycolytic enzymes; (5) increased utilization of fatty acids and ketones by many cells due to increased availability of these substances secondary to lipolysis and to ketone synthesis by the liver; and (6) gluconeogenesis and release of glucose by the liver due to less inhibition of the gluconeogenic enzymes.

We have now given a major part of the answers to the three questions posed on page 607 in that a *decrease* in plasma insulin concentration is largely (but not solely, as we shall see) responsible for the metabolic transformations that occur in going from the absorptive phase to the postabsorptive phase: Thus, effects 1, 2, and 3 in the above paragraph help explain the shift from net anabolism to net catabolism, effects 4 and 5 help explain the shift from glucose utilization to fatty acid and ketone utilization for en-

ergy,[3] and effect 6 helps explain the appearance of gluconeogenesis. With the next meal, the plasma insulin concentration increases as a result of increased insulin secretion and plays an important role in reversing all these transformations, that is, helps restore the metabolic profile of the absorptive phase.

Control of Insulin Secretion. The most important control of insulin secretion is the glucose concentration of the blood flowing through the pancreas, a system requiring no participation of nerves or of other hormones. An increase in blood glucose concentration stimulates insulin secretion, whereas a decrease inhibits secretion. The feedback nature of this system is shown in Figure 18-6: The rise in plasma glucose concentration following a meal stimulates insulin secretion, and the insulin stimulates entry of glucose into muscle and adipose tissue, as well as net uptake, rather than net output, of glucose by the liver. These effects reduce the blood concentration of glucose, thereby removing the stimulus for insulin secretion, which returns to its previous level.

There are numerous insulin-secretion controls other than plasma glucose concentration (Figure 18-7). One is the plasma concentration of certain amino acids, an elevated amino acid concentration causing enhanced insulin secretion. This is another negative-feedback control: Amino acid concentrations increase after ingestion of a protein-containing meal, and the increased plasma insulin stimulates uptake of these amino acids by muscle (and other cells as well).

There are also important hormonal controls over insulin secretion. For example, one of the hormones—glucose-dependent insulinotropic peptide (GIP, also termed gastric inhibitory peptide)—secreted by the gastrointestinal tract (Chapter 17) in response to eating stimulates the release of insulin. This provides an "anticipatory" (or feedforward) component to glucose regulation during ingestion of a meal; that is, insulin secretion will rise earlier and to a greater extent than it would if plasma glucose were the only controller.

Finally, the autonomic neurons to the islets of Langerhans also influence insulin secretion. Activation of the parasympathetic neurons, which occurs during ingestion of a meal, stimulates secretion of insulin and constitutes a second type of anticipatory regulation. In contrast, activa-

---

[3]The decreased glycolysis in muscle associated with a low plasma insulin concentration is only partly due to the loss of insulin's *direct* actions on glucose uptake and glycolytic enzymes. A second important contributor is the interaction called the glucose-fatty acid cycle: As fatty acid utilization increases in muscle, metabolites generated in the process themselves inhibit glycolysis and, ultimately, glucose uptake. Thus, muscle glucose utilization is controlled by insulin both directly and indirectly, the latter via insulin's actions on adipose tissue.

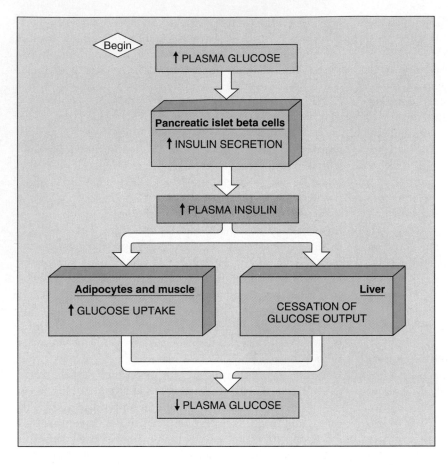

FIGURE 18-6

Negative-feedback nature of plasma glucose control over insulin secretion.

FIGURE 18-7

Major controls of insulin secretion. GIP = glucose-dependent insulinotropic peptide, a gastrointestinal hormone.

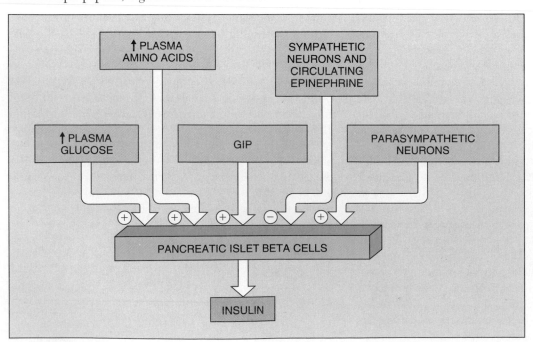

tion of the sympathetic neurons to the islets or an increase in the plasma concentration of epinephrine (the hormone secreted by the adrenal medulla) inhibits insulin secretion. The significance of this relationship for the body's response to low plasma glucose (**hypoglycemia**), stress, and exercise—all situations in which sympathetic activity is increased—will be described later in this chapter.

To repeat, insulin unquestionably plays the primary role in controlling the metabolic adjustments required for feasting or fasting, but other hormonal and neural factors also play significant roles. They all oppose the action of insulin in one way or another and are known as **glucose-counterregulatory controls**. Of these, the most important is glucagon.

Glucagon

As noted earlier, **glucagon** is the peptide hormone produced by the alpha cells of the pancreatic islets. The major physiological effects of glucagon are all on the liver.[4] Glucagon binds to receptors in the plasma membrane of liver cells, leading to the activation of adenylyl cyclase and generation of cyclic AMP in the cells. Cyclic AMP in turn activates cAMP-dependent protein kinase, which phosphorylates enzymes that mediate the effects of glucagon. All these effects on the liver are opposed to those of insulin (Figure 18-8). (1) increased glycogen breakdown; (2) increased gluconeogenesis; and (3) synthesis of ketones. Thus, the overall results of glucagon's effects are to increase the plasma concentrations of glucose and ketones, which are important for the postabsorptive period.

From a knowledge of these effects, one would logically suppose that glucagon secretion should increase during the postabsorptive period and prolonged fasting, and such is the case because a major stimulus for glucagon secretion is hypoglycemia. The adaptive value of such a reflex is obvious: A decreasing plasma glucose concentration induces increased release of glucagon which, by its effects on metabolism, serves to restore normal blood glucose concentrations by glycogenolysis and gluconeogenesis while at the same time supplying (if the fast is prolonged) ketones for cell utilization. Conversely, an increased plasma glucose concentration inhibits glucagon's secretion, thereby helping to return the plasma glucose concentration toward normal.[5]

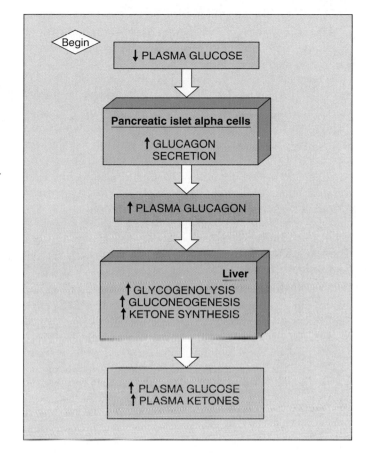

FIGURE 18-8
Negative-feedback nature of plasma glucose control over glucagon secretion.

Thus, during the postabsorptive state plasma insulin concentration is low and plasma glucagon concentration is high, and this combined change accounts almost entirely for the transition from the absorptive to the postabsorptive state. Said in a different way, this shift is best explained by a rise in the glucagon/insulin ratio in the plasma.

Thus far, the story is quite uncomplicated: The beta cells and alpha cells of the pancreatic islets constitute a push-pull system for regulating plasma glucose by producing two hormones—insulin and glucagon—whose actions and major controlling input are just the opposite of each other. However, we must now point out a complicating feature: A second major control of glucagon secretion is the plasma amino acid concentration acting directly on the alpha cells, and in this regard the effect is identical to rather than opposite that for insulin: Glucagon secretion, like insulin secretion, is stimulated by a rise in plasma amino acid concentration. Therefore, absorption of a mixed protein-carbohydrate meal is accompanied by a rise in the plasma concentrations of both insulin and glucagon. However, the insulin rise is relatively much larger than the

[4]Glucagon in very large concentrations also acts on adipose tissue to stimulate lipolysis, but this effect probably does not occur physiologically.
[5]The mechanism by which changes in plasma glucose concentration act on the islets to alter glucagon secretion is controversial. It has been proposed that the A cells are controlled not by glucose per se but by insulin, that is, that an increase in insulin directly inhibits glucagon secretion, whereas a decrease in insulin removes the inhibition, resulting in increased secretion. Another proposal is that some substance other than insulin—possibly GABA—is coreleased with insulin from the B cells and acts locally to inhibit glucagon secretion. Pancreatic somatostatin, released from nearby D cells, may also inhibit glucagon secretion.

glucagon rise because the postingestion increases in blood glucose and amino acids work together to stimulate insulin secretion, whereas they tend to counteract each other so far as glucagon secretion is concerned.

The secretion of glucagon, like that of insulin, is controlled not only by the plasma concentrations of glucose and amino acids but also by neural and hormonal inputs to the islets (Figure 18-9). For example, the sympathetic nerves to the islets stimulate glucagon secretion—just the opposite of their effect on insulin secretion. The adaptive significance of this relationship for exercise and stress will be described subsequently. Interestingly, the parasympathetic nerves also stimulate glucagon secretion.

Epinephrine and Sympathetic Nerves to Liver and Adipose Tissue

As noted earlier, epinephrine and the sympathetic nerves to the pancreatic islets inhibit insulin secretion and stimulate glucagon secretion. In addition, epinephrine also affects nutrient metabolism directly (Figure 18-10). Its major direct effects include stimulation of (1) glycogenolysis in both the liver and skeletal muscle, (2) gluconeogenesis in the liver, and (3) lipolysis in adipocytes. Activation of the sympathetic nerves to the liver and adipose tissue elicits essentially the same responses by these organs as does circulating epinephrine.

Thus, enhanced sympathetic nervous system activity exerts effects on organic metabolism—increased plasma concentrations of glucose, glycerol, and fatty acids—that are opposite those of insulin.

As might be predicted from these effects, hypoglycemia leads reflexly to increases in both epinephrine secretion and sympathetic-nerve activity to the liver and adipose tissue. This is the same stimulus that, as described above, leads to increased secretion of glucagon, although the receptors and pathways are totally different. When the plasma glucose concentration decreases, glucose receptors in the central nervous system initiate the reflexes that lead to increased activity in the sympathetic pathways to the adrenal medulla, liver, and adipose tissue. The adaptive value of the response is the same as that for the glucagon response to hypoglycemia: Blood glucose returns toward normal, and fatty acids are supplied for cell utilization.

How important is the sympathetic nervous system in the acute compensatory response to hypoglycemia? The present view is that this system is less important than glucagon but nevertheless contributes to bringing plasma glucose back toward normal.

In contrast to its increase during *acute* hypoglycemia, sympathetic nervous system activity decreases during prolonged fasting or ingestion of low-calorie diets; the adaptive significance of this change is discussed later in this chapter.

FIGURE 18-9

Major controls of glucagon secretion. Note that the sympathetic and parasympathetic nerves to the pancreatic alpha cells both stimulate glucagon secretion.

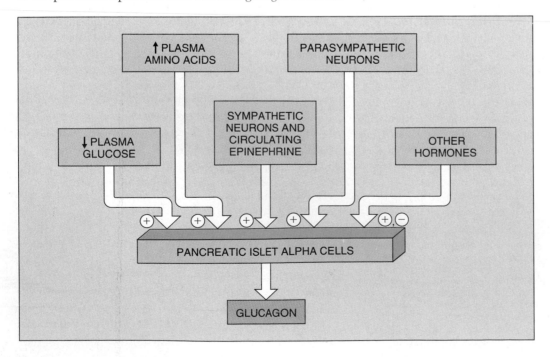

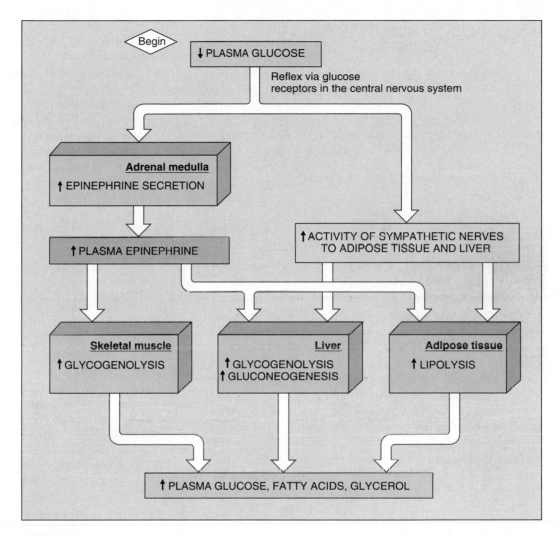

FIGURE 18-10

Participation of the sympathetic nervous system in the response to a low plasma glucose concentration (hypoglycemia). Glucose receptors in the liver (not shown) may also participate in this reflex. (Glycogenolysis in skeletal muscle contributes to increased plasma glucose by releasing lactate and pyruvate, which are converted to glucose in the liver.)

Other Hormones

In addition to the three hormones already described in this section, there are many others—cortisol, growth hormone, thyroid hormones, sex steroids, vasopressin, angiotensin, and still more—that have various effects on organic metabolism. The secretion of these hormones, however, is not primarily keyed to the transitions between the absorptive and postabsorptive states.[6] Instead, their secretion is controlled by other factors, and these hormones are for the most part involved in homeostatic processes described elsewhere in this book. Nonetheless, the effects of cortisol and growth hormone on nutrient me-

tabolism warrant description here for two reasons: (1) Though the plasma concentrations of these two hormones do not usually change in accord with the absorptive and postabsorptive states, their *basal* plasma concentrations play physiological roles in determining the body's normal responses to these states; (2) an excess of either hormone produces important abnormalities in nutrient metabolism.

Cortisol. Cortisol, the major glucocorticoid produced by the adrenal cortex, plays an essential "permissive" role in the adjustments to fasting. We have described how fasting is associated with stimulation of both gluconeogenesis and lipolysis; however, neither of these critical metabolic transformations occurs to the usual degree in a person deficient in cortisol. In other words, the plasma cortisol

---

[6]Some people do show a small burst of growth hormone secretion several hours after a meal, but it is unlikely that this change contributes significantly to postabsorptive adaptations.

TABLE 18-3 EFFECTS OF CORTISOL ON ORGANIC METABOLISM

1. Basal concentrations are permissive for stimulation of gluconeogenesis and lipolysis in the postabsorptive state
2. Increased plasma concentrations cause:
   a. Increased protein catabolism
   b. Increased gluconeogenesis
   c. Decreased glucose uptake by cells
   d. Increased triacylglycerol breakdown

Net result: Increased plasma concentrations of amino acids, glucose, and free fatty acids

level need not *rise* during fasting and usually does not, but the presence of even small amounts of cortisol in the blood somehow maintains the concentrations of the key liver and adipose-tissue enzymes required for gluconeogenesis and lipolysis. Therefore, in response to fasting, people with a cortisol deficiency develop hypoglycemia serious enough to interfere with brain function.

Moreover, cortisol can play more than a permissive role when its plasma concentration does increase, as occurs during stress (Chapter 20). In high concentration, cortisol elicits many metabolic events ordinarily associated with fasting (Table 18-3). Clearly, here is another hormone, in addition to glucagon and epinephrine, that can exert actions opposite those of insulin. Indeed, persons with very high plasma levels of cortisol, due either to abnormally high secretion or to cortisol administration for medical reasons (Chapter 20), develop symptoms similar to those seen in individuals with insulin deficiency.

Growth Hormone. The primary physiological effects of growth hormone are to stimulate both growth and protein anabolism. Compared to these effects, those it exerts on carbohydrate and lipid metabolism are minor. Nonetheless, as is true for cortisol, either severe deficiency or marked excess of growth hormone does produce significant abnormalities in lipid and carbohydrate metabolism. Growth hormone's effects on these nutrients are similar to those of cortisol and opposite those of insulin. Growth hormone (1) renders adipocytes more responsive to lipolytic stimuli; (2) increases gluconeogenesis by the liver; and (3) reduces the ability of insulin to cause glucose uptake by peripheral tissues. These are often termed growth hormone's "anti-insulin effects."

Summary

To a great extent insulin may be viewed as the "hormone of plenty." Its secretion and plasma concentration are increased during the absorptive period and decreased during postabsorption, and these changes are adequate to cause most of the metabolic changes associated with these periods. In addition, opposed in various ways to insulin's effects are the actions of four major glucose-counterregulatory controls—glucagon, epinephrine and the sympathetic nerves to the liver and adipose tissue, cortisol, and growth hormone (Table 18-4). Glucagon and the sympathetic nervous system are activated during the postabsorptive period (or in any other situation with hypoglycemia) and definitely play roles in preventing hypoglycemia, glucagon being the more important. The rates of secretion of cortisol and growth hormone are not usually coupled to the absorptive-postaborptive pattern; nevertheless, their presence in the blood at basal concentrations is necessary for normal adjustment of lipid and carbohydrate metabolism to the postabsorptive period, and excessive amounts of either hormone cause abnormally elevated plasma glucose concentrations.

TABLE 18-4 SUMMARY OF GLUCOSE-COUNTERREGULATORY CONTROLS*

	Glucagon	Epinephrine	Cortisol	Growth hormone
Glycogenolysis	X	X		
Gluconeogenesis	X	X	X	X
Lipolysis		X	X	X
Inhibition of glucose uptake			X	X

* All the processes listed on the left—glycogenolysis, gluconeogenesis, lipolysis, and inhibition of glucose uptake—are opposed to insulin's actions and are stimulated by one or more of the glucose-counterregulatory hormones in the table. An X indicates that the hormone stimulates the process; no X indicates that the hormone has no major physiological effect on the process. Epinephrine stimulates glycogenolysis in both liver and skeletal muscle, whereas glucagon does so only in liver.

FUEL HOMEOSTASIS IN EXERCISE AND STRESS

During exercise large quantities of fuels must be mobilized to provide the energy required for muscle contraction. As described in Chapter 11, these fuels include plasma glucose and fatty acids, as well as the muscle's own glycogen.

The plasma glucose used during exercise is supplied by the liver, both by breakdown of its glycogen stores and by gluconeogenesis—conversion of pyruvate, lactate, glycerol, and amino acids into glucose. The glycerol is made available to the liver by a marked increase in adipose-tissue lipolysis with a resultant release of glycerol and fatty acids into the blood, the fatty acids serving along with glucose as a fuel source for the exercising muscle.

What happens to blood glucose concentration during exercise? It changes very little in short-term, mild to moderate exercise and may increase slightly with strenuous short-term activity. However, during prolonged exercise (Figure 18-11), more than 90 min, plasma glucose concentration decreases, sometimes by as much as 25 percent. These relatively minor changes in blood glucose in the presence of marked increases in glucose utilization clearly demonstrate that glucose output by the liver must increase approximately in proportion to the increased utilization, at least until the later stages of exercise when it begins to lag somewhat.

The metabolic profile seen in an exercising individual—increases in hepatic glucose production, triacylglycerol breakdown, and fatty acid utilization—is similar to that seen in a fasting person, and the controls are also the same: Exercise is characterized by a fall in insulin secretion and a rise in glucagon secretion (Figure 18-11), plus increased activity of the sympathetic nervous system. In addition, cortisol and growth hormone are also secreted in increased amounts. All these events tend to increase plasma glucose, balancing the glucose-lowering effect caused by increased muscle glucose utilization.

What triggers increased glucagon secretion and decreased insulin secretion during exercise? One signal during prolonged exercise is the modest decrease in plasma glucose that occurs; this is the same signal that controls the secretion of these hormones in fasting. A second input—independent of plasma glucose concentration—is increased circulating epinephrine and enhanced activity of the sympathetic neurons supplying the pancreatic islets; this output is mediated by the central nervous system as part of the neural response to exercise. Thus, the increased sympathetic nervous system activity characteristic of exercise not only contributes directly to fuel mobilization by acting on the liver and adipose tissue but contributes indirectly by inhibiting the secretion of insulin and stimulating that of glucagon.

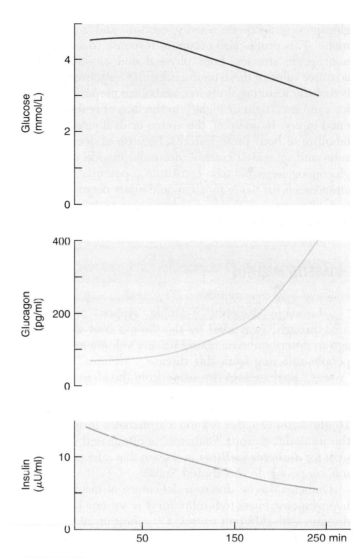

FIGURE 18-11

Plasma concentrations of glucose, glucagon, and insulin during prolonged (250 min) moderate exercise at a fixed intensity. (*Adapted from Felig and Wahren.*)

One component of the response to exercise is quite different from fasting: In exercise glucose uptake and utilization by the muscles is increased, whereas in fasting it is markedly reduced. How is it that, during exercise, the movement of glucose, via facilitated diffusion, into muscle can remain high in the presence of reduced plasma insulin and increased plasma concentrations of cortisol and growth hormone, all of which decrease glucose uptake by skeletal muscle? By an as yet unidentified mechanism, muscle contraction causes, as does insulin, migration of intracellular stores of glucose transporters to the plasma membrane.

Exercise is not the only situation characterized by the neuroendocrine profile of decreased insulin and increased

There are several factors that combine to cause NIDDM. One major problem is target-cell hyporesponsiveness to insulin, termed *insulin resistance*. Insulin's target cells do not respond adequately to circulating insulin because of alterations either in the insulin receptors and/or some intracellular process occurring after receptor activation. Obesity accounts for much of this insulin resistance in NIDDM, for obesity in any person—diabetic or not—induces some degree of insulin resistance, particularly in adipose tissue cells. However, additional components of insulin resistance, not related to obesity and not yet understood, also usually occur with NIDDM.

As a result of target-cell hyporesponsiveness to insulin, plasma glucose increases. Note, however, that this rise will stimulate the pancreatic beta cells to secrete additional insulin, and the resulting increase in plasma insulin concentration will tend to overcome the target-cell hyporesponsiveness. Thus, significant NIDDM emerges only when the insulin resistance exceeds the ability of the beta cells to compensate by secreting more insulin. Until recently it was thought that the beta cells were entirely normal in NIDDM unless they became "exhausted" by their persistent hypersecretion of insulin. Recently, however, it has become clear that most people with NIDDM not only have insulin hyporesponsiveness but also have a defect in the ability of their beta cells to secrete insulin in response to a rise in plasma glucose concentration.

Thus, NIDDM is a multifactorial disease: Insulin resistance is the primary factor inducing hyperglycemia, but an as yet unidentified defect in beta-cell function prevents these cells from responding to the hyperglycemia in normal fashion. In contrast, other persons who are obese (and therefore have some degree of insulin resistance) but who have normal beta cells do not develop NIDDM because their beta cells are able to secrete enough insulin to get the job done.

The major therapy for obese persons with NIDDM is dietary—caloric reduction, which eliminates the insulin resistance caused by obesity. An exercise program also is useful, because insulin responsiveness is increased by frequent endurance-type exercise, independent of changes in body weight. This may reflect the fact that training causes a substantial increase in the total number of plasma-membrane glucose transporters in both muscles and adipocytes.

If plasma glucose concentration is not adequately controlled by a program of diet and exercise, then the use of drugs is warranted. The most commonly used family of orally active agents is the *sulfonylureas*, which lower plasma glucose mainly by acting on the beta cells to stimulate insulin secretion.

Unfortunately, people with either IDDM or NIDDM tend to develop a variety of chronic abnormalities, including atherosclerosis, small-vessel and nerve disease, suscep-

tibility to infection, and blindness. The factors responsible are still unclear, but it is hypothesized that elevated plasma glucose contributes directly or indirectly to some, if not all, of these abnormalities.

This discussion of diabetes has focused on insulin, but it is now clear that the hormones that elevate plasma glucose concentration may contribute to the severity of the disease. Glucagon is quite important in this regard. Since glucagon secretion is inhibited by an elevated plasma glucose level, one would expect to find a low plasma glucagon concentration in diabetic persons. However, most diabetics, particularly those with IDDM, have plasma glucagon concentrations that are either increased or unchanged.[9] This absolute or relative glucagon excess contributes to the metabolic dysfunction typical of diabetes.

Finally, as we have seen, all the systems that raise plasma glucose concentration are activated during stress, which explains why stress exacerbates the symptoms of diabetes. Since diabetic ketoacidosis itself constitutes a severe stress, a positive-feedback cycle is triggered in which a marked lack of insulin induces ketoacidosis, which elicits activation of the glucose-counterregulatory systems, which worsens the ketoacidosis.

HYPOGLYCEMIA AS A CAUSE OF SYMPTOMS

As we have seen, "hypoglycemia" means a low plasma glucose concentration. Plasma glucose concentration can drop to very low values during fasting in individuals with several types of disorders. This is termed *fasting hypoglycemia*, and the relatively uncommon disorders responsible for it can be understood in terms of the regulation of blood glucose concentration. They include (1) an excess of insulin due to an insulin-producing tumor, a drug that stimulates insulin secretion, or the taking of too much insulin by a diabetic; and (2) a defect in one or more of the glucose-counterregulatory systems, for example, inadequate glycogenolysis and/or gluconeogenesis due to liver disease, glucagon deficiency, or cortisol deficiency.

Fasting hypoglycemia causes many symptoms, some of which—hunger, increased heart rate, tremulousness, weakness, nervousness, and sweating—are accounted for by activation of the sympathetic nervous system caused reflexly by the hypoglycemia. Other symptoms, such as headache, confusion, uncoordination, and slurred speech are direct consequences of too little glucose reaching the

---

[9]From the material given in footnote 5 the most likely explanation can be deduced: If hypoglycemia stimulates glucagon secretion *indirectly* via insulin or some substance coreleased with insulin, then one would expect the defect in insulin secretion associated with diabetes to result in less inhibition of glucagon secretion.

brain. More serious brain effects, including convulsions and coma, can occur if the plasma glucose concentration becomes low enough.

In contrast, low plasma glucose concentration has *not* been shown to routinely produce either acute or chronic symptoms of fatigue, lethargy, loss of libido, depression, or many other symptoms for which the lay press frequently holds it responsible. Despite this, a large number of persons who suffer from such symptoms, particularly several hours after eating, have been told or have assumed that the symptoms are due to "reactive" hypoglycemia. Few of these people have ever had their blood glucose concentrations measured at the time of the symptoms, and the blood sugar is usually within the normal range in those cases where measurements have been made. For all these reasons, most experts believe that most of the symptoms popularly ascribed to reactive hypoglycemia have other causes.

REGULATION OF PLASMA CHOLESTEROL

n the previous sections, we described the flow of lipids to and from adipose tissue in the form of fatty acids and triacylglycerols complexed with proteins. One very impor-

tant lipid—**cholesterol**—was not mentioned earlier because it, unlike the fatty acids and triacylglycerols, serves not as a metabolic fuel but rather as a precursor for plasma membranes, bile salts, steroid hormones, and other specialized molecules. Thus, cholesterol has many important functions in the body. Unfortunately, it can also cause problems. Specifically, high plasma concentrations of cholesterol enhance the development of ***atherosclerosis***, the arterial thickening that leads to heart attacks, strokes, and other forms of cardiovascular damage (Chapter 14).

A schema for cholesterol metabolism is illustrated in Figure 18-13. The two sources of cholesterol are synthesis within the body and dietary intake. Almost all cells can synthesize some of the cholesterol required for their own plasma membranes, but most cannot do so in adequate amounts and depend upon receiving cholesterol from the blood. This is also true of the endocrine cells that produce steroid hormones from cholesterol. Thus, most cells *remove* cholesterol from the blood. In contrast, the liver and cells lining the gastrointestinal tract can produce large amounts of cholesterol, most of which *enters* the blood. Dietary cholesterol comes from animal sources, egg yolk being by far the richest in this lipid (a single egg contains about 250 mg of cholesterol). Not all ingested cholesterol is absorbed into the blood, however, much of it simply

FIGURE 18-13

Metabolism of cholesterol.

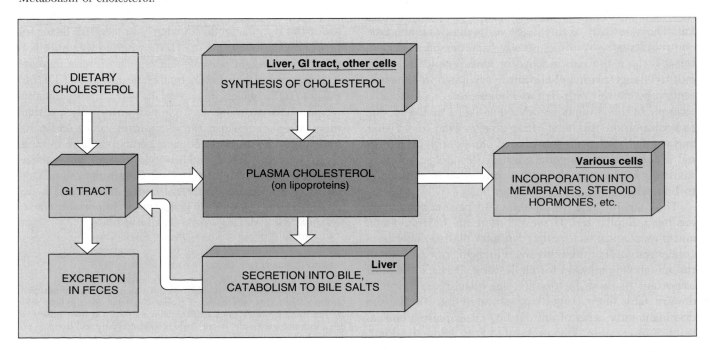

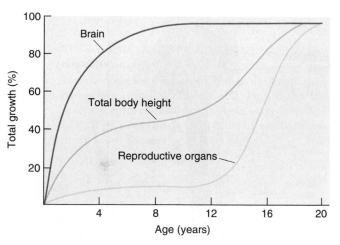

FIGURE 18-15

Relative growth in brain, total body height (a measure of long bone and vertebral growth), and reproductive organs. Note that brain growth is nearly complete by the age 5, whereas maximal height and reproductive-organ size are not reached until the late teens.

On the other hand, the final height a child reaches cannot be increased beyond the genetically determined maximum by the child eating more than adequate vitamins, protein, or total calories. Overfeeding produces obesity, not growth.

Sickness can also stunt growth, but if the illness is temporary, the recovered child manifests a remarkable growth spurt ("catch-up" growth) that rapidly brings him or her up to the normal height expected for his or her age.

HORMONAL INFLUENCES ON GROWTH

The hormones most important to human growth are growth hormone, thyroid hormones, insulin, testosterone, and estrogens, all of which exert widespread effects. In addition to all these hormones, there is a huge group of peptide **growth factors** (for example, nerve growth factor), each of which is highly effective in stimulating differentiation and/or cell division of certain cell types. The general term for a chemical that stimulates cell division is a **mitogen**. There are also peptide **growth-inhibiting factors** that modulate growth by inhibiting cell division in specific tissues. Numbering more than 60 at present, these growth factors and growth-inhibiting factors are usually produced by multiple cell types rather than by discrete endocrine glands. Indeed, many of them are produced and released in the immediate vicinity of their sites of action and so are categorized as paracrine and autocrine agents. Some, however, may enter the blood and function as hormones. In any case, their secretion is often controlled by hormones.

The physiology of growth factors and growth-inhibiting factors is important not just for understanding control of normal growth but also because these factors may be involved in the development of **cancer**. Thus, some **oncogenes** (genes involved in the induction of cancer, page 79) code for proteins that are identical to or very similar to growth factors, growth factor receptors, or postreceptor components of growth factor signal transduction pathways. The problem is that these proteins have lost important regulatory constraints on their activity. For example, one oncogene codes for a version of the receptor for epidermal growth factor that is always in the activated state even in the absence of the growth factor. This activated receptor imparts a continuous growth signal to the cells containing it.

The various hormones and growth factors do not all stimulate growth at the same periods of life. For example, fetal growth is largely independent of the major hormones that stimulate growth during childhood—growth hormone, the thyroid hormones, and the sex steroids.

Growth Hormone

Although growth hormone, secreted by the anterior pituitary, has little or no effect on fetal growth, it is the single most important hormone for postnatal growth. Its major growth-promoting effect is stimulation (indirect, as we shall see) of cell division in its many target tissues. Thus, growth hormone promotes bone lengthening by stimulating maturation and cell division of the chondrocytes in the epiphyseal plates, thereby continuously widening the plates and providing more cartilaginous material for bone formation.

Growth hormone excess during childhood produces **giantism**, whereas a deficiency produces **dwarfism**. However, when excess growth hormone is secreted in adults after epiphyseal closure, it cannot lengthen the bones further, but it does produce the disfiguring bone thickening and overgrowth of other organs known as **acromegaly**.

Importantly, growth hormone exerts its mitosis-stimulating (mitogenic) effect not *directly* on cells but rather *indirectly* through the mediation of a chemical messenger whose synthesis and release are induced by growth hormone. This messenger is called **insulin-like growth factor I (IGF-I)** (also known as **somatomedin C**). Under the influence of growth hormone, IGF-I is secreted by the liver and many other types of cells, and it is thought to act at these sites as a paracrine or autocrine agent. It remains controversial as to whether IGF-I also exerts some functions as a hormone, that is, as a blood-borne messenger.[11]

---

[11]The problem is that virtually all the IGF-I in plasma is tightly bound to a specific binding protein and so is unable to pass through capillaries and act on target cells. A likely hormonal effect of IGF-I is its negative-feedback inhibition of GH secretion by the anterior pituitary, as presented in Chapter 10.

Current concepts of how growth hormone and IGF-I interact on the epiphyseal plates of bone are as follows: (1) Growth hormone stimulates the chondrocyte precursor cells (prechondrocytes) and/or young differentiating chondrocytes in the epiphyseal plates to differentiate into chondrocytes; (2) during this differentiation, the cells begin both to secrete IGF-I and to become responsive to IGF-I; (3) this produced IGF-I then acts as an autocrine or paracrine agent to stimulate the differentiating chondrocytes to undergo cell division.

It is likely that a similar interplay between growth hormone and IGF-I underlies the ability of growth hormone to stimulate growth in target tissues other than bone; that is, growth hormone stimulates precursor cells to differentiate and to secrete IGF-I, and IGF-I stimulates the newly differentiated cells to undergo cell division.

The importance of IGF-I mediating the major growth-promoting effect of growth hormone is illustrated by the fact that dwarfism can be due not only to decreased secretion of growth hormone but also to decreased production of IGF-I or failure of the tissues to respond to IGF-I. For example, the short stature of Pygmies is probably due to a genetic defect in the ability to produce IGF-I in response to growth hormone.

The secretion and activity of IGF-I can be influenced by several hormones other than growth hormone and by the nutritional status of the individual. For example, malnutrition during childhood inhibits the production of IGF-I even though plasma growth hormone concentration is elevated and should be stimulating IGF-I secretion.

In addition to its specific growth-promoting effect on cell division via IGF-I, growth hormone directly stimulates protein synthesis in various tissues and organs. It does this by increasing amino acid uptake by cells, as well as by the synthesis of RNA and ribosomes. All these events are essential for protein synthesis.[12] This anabolic effect on protein metabolism facilitates the ability of tissues and organs to enlarge. Table 18-5 summarizes the multiple effects of growth hormone, all of which have been described in this chapter.

The hypothalamic hypophysiotropic hormones controlling growth hormone secretion were described in Chapter 10 (Figure 10-23). Briefly, growth hormone secretion is stimulated by growth hormone releasing hormone (GHRH) and inhibited by hypothalamic somatostatin. As a result of changes in these two signals, which are virtually 180 degrees out of phase with each other (that is, one is high when the other is low), growth hormone secretion

TABLE 18-5 MAJOR EFFECTS OF GROWTH HORMONE

1. Promotes growth: Induces precursor cells to differentiate and secrete insulin-like growth factor I (IGF-I), which stimulates cell division
2. Stimulates protein synthesis
3. Anti-insulin effects:
   a. Renders adipocytes more responsive to lipolytic stimuli.
   b. Stimulates gluconeogenesis
   c. Reduces the ability of insulin to stimulate glucose uptake

occurs in episodic bursts and manifests a striking diurnal rhythm. During most of the day, there is little or no growth hormone secreted, although bursts may be elicited by certain stimuli, including stress,[13] hypoglycemia, and exercise. In contrast, 1 to 2 h after a person falls asleep, one or more larger, prolonged bursts of secretion may occur.

In addition to the hypothalamic controls, a variety of hormones—notably the sex hormones and thyroid hormones, as described below—influence secretion of growth hormone. The net result of all these inputs is that the total 24-h secretion rate of growth hormone is highest during adolescence—the period of most rapid growth—next highest in children, and lowest in adults. Indeed, there is evidence that the decreased growth hormone secretion associated with aging is responsible, in part, for the decrease in lean-body mass, the expansion of adipose tissue, and the thinning of the skin that occur at that time.

The availability of large quantities of human growth hormone produced by recombinant-DNA technology has greatly facilitated the treatment of children with short stature due to deficiency of growth hormone. Controversial at present are the questions of whether growth hormone should be given to healthy short children who do not have growth hormone deficiency or to athletes to increase muscle mass. In addition to the ethical questions they pose, such usages are dangerous because the large amounts required can cause insulin resistance and produce diabetes.

Thyroid Hormones

The thyroid hormones (TH)—thyroxine (T_3) and triiodothyronine (T_4)—are essential for normal growth because they are required for both the synthesis of growth hormone and the growth-promoting effects of that hormone. Accordingly, infants and children with **hypothyroidism** (deficient thyroid function) manifest retarded growth due

---

[12]The similarity of growth hormone's effect on *protein* synthesis to that exerted by insulin may seem puzzling when one recalls our earlier description of the anti-insulin effects of growth hormone on *carbohydrate* and *lipid* metabolism. It has been postulated that these varied actions of growth hormone may be mediated by different receptors responding to different amino acid sequences on the large growth hormone molecule.

[13]In contrast, during childhood severe prolonged psychosocial stress may inhibit growth hormone secretion and lead to diminished growth.

to slowed bone growth. Because epiphyseal closure is delayed, bone age is decreased (that is, the bone age lags behind the child's chronological age). Growth can be restored to normal by administration of physiological quantities of thyroid hormone.

Quite distinct from its growth-promoting effect, TH is permissive for normal development of the central nervous system during fetal life and the first few months after birth. Hypothyroid infants are mentally retarded, a defect that can be completely repaired by early treatment with TH. However, if the infant is untreated for more than several months, the developmental failure is largely irreversible.

This effect on brain *development* must be distinguished from other stimulatory effects TH exerts on the nervous system throughout life, not just during infancy. A hypothyroid person exhibits sluggishness and poor mental function, and these effects are completely reversible at any time with administration of TH. Conversely, a person with an excessive secretion of TH, **hyperthyroidism,** is jittery and hyperactive.

Insulin

It should not be surprising that adequate amounts of insulin are necessary for normal growth since insulin is, in all respects, an anabolic hormone. Its stimulatory effects on amino acid uptake and protein synthesis are particularly important with regard to growth.

In addition to this general anabolic effect, however, insulin exerts specific growth-promoting effects on cell differentiation and cell division during fetal life. Insulin may also exert this effect during childhood since it can stimulate the secretion of IGF-I.

Sex Hormones

As will be described in Chapter 19, sex hormone secretion (testosterone in the male and estrogen in the female) begins in earnest at about the age of 8 to 10 and progressively increases to reach a plateau over the next 5 to 10 years. A normal pubertal growth spurt, which reflects growth of the long bones and vertebrae, requires this increased production of the sex hormones. The major growth-promoting effect of the sex hormones is to stimulate the secretion of growth hormone.

Unlike growth hormone, however, the sex hormones ultimately *stop* bone growth by inducing epiphyseal closure. The dual effects of the sex hormones explain the pattern seen in adolescence—rapid lengthening of the bones culminating in complete cessation of growth for life.

In addition to these dual effects on bone, testosterone, but not estrogen, exerts a direct anabolic effect on protein synthesis in many nonreproductive organs and tissues of the body. This accounts, at least in part, for the increased muscle mass of men compared with women.

This also is why synthetic testosterone-like agents termed **anabolic steroids** are used by athletes in an at-

---

TABLE 18-6   MAJOR HORMONES INFLUENCING GROWTH

Hormone	Principal actions
Growth hormone	Major stimulus of postnatal growth: Induces precursor cells to differentiate and secrete insulin-like growth factor I (IGF-I), which stimulates cell division Stimulates protein synthesis
Insulin	Stimulates fetal growth ? Stimulates postnatal growth by stimulating secretion of IGF-I Stimulates protein synthesis
Thyroid hormones	Permissive for growth hormone's secretion and actions Permissive for development of the central nervous system
Testosterone	Stimulates growth at puberty, at least in part by stimulating the secretion of growth hormone Causes eventual epiphyseal closure Stimulates protein synthesis
Estrogen	Stimulates the secretion of growth hormone at puberty Causes eventual epiphyseal closure
Cortisol	Inhibits growth Stimulates protein catabolism

tempt to increase their muscle mass and strength. However, it remains controversial as to how much, if at all, these agents, in men who are not testosterone-deficient to start with, increase muscle mass or improve athletic performance. Moreover, the steroids generally used have multiple toxic side effects (for example, liver damage). Although these drugs definitely have a positive effect on muscle mass and strength in women, they produce masculinization as well as the same toxic side effects as in men.

Cortisol

Cortisol, the major hormone secreted by the adrenal cortex in response to stress, can have potent antigrowth effects under certain conditions. When present in high concentration, it inhibits DNA synthesis and stimulates protein catabolism in many organs, and it inhibits bone growth. Indeed, it causes bone breakdown by inhibiting osteoblasts and stimulating osteoclasts (Chapter 16). In children, the elevation in plasma cortisol that accompanies infections and other stresses is, at least in part, responsible for the retarded growth that occurs with illness.

As we shall see in Chapter 20, cortisol and very similar steroids are commonly used medically in persons with arthritis or other inflammatory disorders. A side effect of such treatment is increased protein catabolism and bone breakdown. One must carefully distinguish cortisol-type steroids (glucocorticoids) from testosterone-type steroids (anabolic steroids).

This completes our survey of the major hormones that affect growth. Their actions are summarized in Table 18-6.

COMPENSATORY GROWTH

We have dealt thus far only with growth during *childhood*. During adult life, a specific type of regenerative organ growth, known as **compensatory growth**, can occur in many human organs. For example, after the surgical removal of one kidney, the cells of the other begin to manifest increased cell division, and the kidney ultimately grows until its total mass approaches the initial mass of the two kidneys combined. Many growth factors are known to participate in compensatory growth, but the precise signals that trigger the process are not known.

SECTION B SUMMARY

BONE GROWTH

I. A bone lengthens as osteoblasts at the shaft edge of the epiphyseal growth plates convert cartilage to bone while new cartilage is being laid down in the plate.

II. Growth ceases when the plates are completely converted to bone.

ENVIRONMENTAL FACTORS INFLUENCING GROWTH

I. The major environmental factors influencing growth are nutrition and disease.

II. Malnutrition during in utero life and infancy may produce irreversible stunting.

HORMONAL INFLUENCES ON GROWTH

I. Growth hormone is the major stimulus of postnatal growth.
   A. It stimulates the release of IGF-I from the liver and many other cells, and IGF-I then acts locally to stimulate cell division.
   B. Growth hormone also acts directly on cells to stimulate protein synthesis.
   C. Growth hormone secretion is highest during adolescence.

II. Because thyroid hormones are required for growth hormone synthesis and the growth-promoting effects of this hormone, they are essential for normal growth during childhood and adolescence. They also are permissive for brain development during infancy.

III. Insulin stimulates growth mainly during in utero life.

IV. Mainly by stimulating growth hormone secretion, testosterone and estrogen promote bone growth during adolescence, but they also cause epiphyseal closure. Testosterone also stimulates protein synthesis.

V. Cortisol in a high concentration inhibits growth and stimulates protein catabolism.

SECTION B KEY TERMS

epiphyses	growth factors
shaft	mitogen
epiphyseal growth plate	growth-inhibiting factors
osteoblasts	insulin-like growth factor I
chondrocytes	(IGF-I, somatomedin C)
epiphyseal closure	compensatory growth
bone age	

TABLE 18-7 SOME FACTORS AFFECTING THE METABOLIC RATE

Age
Sex
Height, weight, and body surface area
Growth
Pregnancy, menstruation, lactation
Infection or other disease
Body temperature
Recent ingestion of food
Prolonged alteration in amount of food intake
Muscular activity
Emotional state
Sleep
Environmental temperature
Circulating levels of various hormones, especially
  epinephrine and thyroid hormone

into account size differences, but increases markedly during pregnancy and lactation. Greater demands upon the body made by infection or other disease generally increase the BMR. However, when a person suffers wasting because of infection, the BMR may decrease below normal.

Thyroid Hormones. The thyroid hormones are the single most important determinant of BMR for any given size, age, and sex. Indeed, the BMR test was once commonly used for evaluation of thyroid hormone status but has now been superseded by more specific tests. TH increases the oxygen consumption and heat production of most body tissues, a notable exception being the brain.

This ability to increase BMR is termed a **calorigenic effect**. The mechanism of the TH calorigenic effect is presently uncertain, but the plasma concentration of TH is the major factor that "sets" the body's BMR.

Long-term excessive TH, as in persons with hyperthyroidism, induces a host of effects secondary to the calorigenic effect. For example, the increased metabolic demands markedly increase hunger and food intake; the greater intake frequently remains inadequate to meet the metabolic needs, and net catabolism of protein and fat stores leads to loss of body weight. Also, the greater heat production activates heat-dissipating mechanisms (skin vasodilation and sweating), and the person suffers from marked intolerance to warm environments. In contrast, the hypothyroid individual complains of cold intolerance.

The calorigenic effect of TH is only one of a bewildering variety of effects exerted by these hormones. With one exception—facilitation of the activity of the sympathetic nervous system (described in Chapter 10)—the functions of the thyroid hormones have all been described earlier in this chapter and are listed for reference in Table 18-8. Control of the secretion of these hormones, as well as their metabolism, is described in Chapter 10.

Epinephrine. Epinephrine is another hormone that exerts a calorigenic effect. This effect may be related to the hormone's stimulation of glycogen and triacylglycerol catabolism, since ATP splitting and energy liberation occur in both the breakdown and subsequent resynthesis of these molecules. Regardless of the mechanism, when epinephrine secretion by the adrenal medulla is stimulated, the metabolic rate rises. This accounts for part of the

TABLE 18-8 FUNCTIONS OF THE THYROID HORMONES (TH)

1. Required for normal maturation of the nervous system in the fetus and infant
    Deficiency: Mental retardation (cretinism)

2. Required for normal bodily growth because they facilitate the secretion of and response to growth hormone
    Deficiency: Deficient growth in children

3. Required for normal alertness and reflexes at all ages
    Deficiency: Mentally and physically slow and lethargic
    Excess: Restless, irritable, anxious, wakeful

4. Major determinant of the rate at which the body produces heat during the basal metabolic state.
    Deficiency: Low BMR, sensitivity to cold, decreased food appetite
    Excess: High BMR, sensitivity to heat, increased food appetite, increased catabolism of nutrients

5. Facilitates the activity of the sympathetic nervous system by stimulating the synthesis of one class of receptors (beta receptors) for epinephrine and norepinephrine
    Excess: Symptoms similar to those observed with activation of the sympathetic nervous system (for example, increased heart rate)

greater heat production associated with emotional stress, although increased muscle tone also contributes.

Food-Induced Thermogenesis.   The ingestion of food acutely increases the metabolic rate by 10 to 20 percent for a few hours after eating. This effect is known as **food-induced thermogenesis**. Ingested protein produces the greatest effect, carbohydrate and fat, less. Most of the increased heat production is secondary to processing of the absorbed nutrients by the liver, not to the energy expended by the gastrointestinal tract in digestion and absorption. It is to avoid the contribution of food-induced thermogenesis that BMR is performed in the postabsorptive state.

To reiterate, food-induced thermogenesis is the *rapid* increase in energy expenditure in response to ingestion of a meal. As we shall see, *prolonged* alterations in food intake (either increased or decreased total calories) also have significant effects on metabolic rate but are not termed food-induced thermogenesis.

Muscle Activity.   The factor that can increase metabolic rate most is altered skeletal-muscle activity. Even minimal increases in muscle contraction significantly increase metabolic rate, and strenuous exercise may raise heat production more than fifteenfold (Table 18-9). Thus, depending on the degree of physical activity, total energy expenditure may vary for a normal young adult from a value of approximately 1500 kcal/24 h to more than 7000 kcal/24 h (for a lumberjack). Changes in muscle activity also account in part for the changes in metabolic rate that occur during sleep (decreased muscle contraction), during exposure to a low environmental temperature (increased muscle contraction and shivering), and with strong emotions.

Total-Body Energy Balance

The laws of thermodynamics dictate that the total energy expenditure (metabolic rate) of the body must equal the total energy intake. We have already identified the ultimate forms of energy expenditure: internal heat production, external work, and net molecular synthesis (energy storage). The source of input is the energy contained in ingested food. Therefore:

Energy from food intake = internal heat produced
+ external work + energy stored

Our equation includes no term for loss of fuel from the body via excretion of nutrients because, in normal persons, only negligible losses occur via the urine, feces, and as sloughed hair and skin. In certain diseases, however, the most important being diabetes, urinary losses of organic molecules may be quite large and would have to be included in the equation.

Let us now rearrange the equation to focus on energy storage:

Energy stored = energy from food intake
− (internal heat produced + external work)

Thus, whenever energy intake differs from the sum of internal heat produced and external work, changes in energy storage occur; that is, the total-body energy content increases or decreases (Table 18-10).

Total-body energy content in adults is usually regulated around a relatively constant operating point. Theoretically, this constancy can be achieved through (1) adjusting metabolic energy expenditure to compensate for randomly occurring food intake, (2) adjusting food intake to changing metabolic expenditures, or (3) both. There is no question that (2) is the major means of regulating total-body energy content.

Nevertheless, there is some contribution from method 1, that is, adjustment of metabolic expenditure when food intake changes. A striking experiment documenting this phenomenon was the reduction of caloric intake in normal male volunteers from 3492 kcal/day to 1570 kcal/day for 24 weeks. These men were soldiers performing considerable physical activity, and weight loss was initially very rapid and ultimately averaged 24 percent of original body weight. However, the important fact is that the weights did stabilize at this point; that is, energy balance was reestablished despite the continued caloric intake of only 1570 kcal/day. Clearly, the metabolic rate must have decreased to the same value. The decrease was due partly to a reduction in physical activity as the men became apa-

TABLE 18-9   ENERGY EXPENDITURE DURING DIFFERENT TYPES OF ACTIVITY FOR A 70-KG (154-LB) PERSON

Form of activity	Energy kcal/h
Lying still, awake	77
Sitting at rest	100
Typewriting rapidly	140
Dressing or undressing	150
Walking on level, 4.3 km/h (2.6 mi/h)	200
Bicycling on level, 9 km/h (5.5 mi/h)	304
Walking on 3 percent grade, 4.3 km/h (2.6 mi/h)	357
Sawing wood or shoveling snow	480
Jogging, 9 km/h (5.3 mi/h)	570
Rowing, 20 strokes/min	828

about 10 to 20 per second. During shivering, the efferent motor nerves to the skeletal muscles are controlled by descending pathways under the primary control of the hypothalamus. So effective is shivering that body heat production may be increased severalfold within seconds to minutes. Because no external work is performed by shivering, all the energy liberated by the metabolic machinery appears as internal heat and is known as **shivering thermogenesis**. People also use their muscles for voluntary heat production activities such as foot stamping and hand clapping.

Thus far, our discussion has focused primarily on the muscle response to *cold;* the opposite muscle reactions occur in response to heat. Basal muscle contraction is reflexly decreased, and voluntary movement is also diminished. These attempts to reduce heat production are relatively limited, however, both because basal muscle contraction is quite low to start with and because increased body temperature acts directly on cells to increase metabolic rate.

Muscle contraction is not the only process controlled in temperature-regulating reflexes. In most experimental animals, chronic cold exposure induces an increase in metabolic rate, that is, heat production, that is not due to increased muscle activity and is termed **nonshivering thermogenesis**. Its cause is an increased secretion of epinephrine, with some contribution by thyroid hormone as well. Nonshivering thermogenesis is quite minimal, if present at all, in adult human beings, and there is no increased secretion of thyroid hormone in response to cold. Nonshivering thermogenesis does occur in infants.

Control of Heat Loss by Radiation and Conduction. For purposes of temperature control, it is convenient to view the body as a central core surrounded by a shell consisting of skin and subcutaneous tissue; we shall refer to this complex outer shell simply as skin. It is the temperature of the central core that is being regulated at approximately 37°C. As we shall see, the temperature of the outer surface of the skin changes markedly.

If the skin were a perfect insulator, no heat would ever be lost from the core. The temperature of the outer skin surface would equal the environmental temperature, and net conduction and radiation would be zero. The skin is not a perfect insulator, however, and so the temperature of its outer surface generally is somewhere between that of the external environment and that of the core.

The skin's effectiveness as an insulator is subject to physiological control by a change in the blood flow to it. The more blood reaching the skin from the core, the more closely the skin's temperature approaches that of the core. In effect, the blood vessels diminish the insulating capacity of the skin by carrying heat to the surface (Figure 18-22) to be lost to the external environment. These vessels are controlled largely by vasoconstrictor sympathetic nerves, the firing rate of which is increased in response to cold and decreased in response to heat.[17] There is also a population of sympathetic neurons to the skin whose neurotransmitters (as yet unidentified) cause active *vasodilation* in association with sweating. Certain areas of skin participate much more than others in all these vasomotor responses, and so skin temperatures vary with location.

Three *behavioral* mechanisms for altering heat loss by radiation and conduction remain to be described: changes

---

[17]In addition, the affinity of alpha-adrenergic receptors for norepinephrine, the sympathetic neurotransmitter, is increased directly by cold, and so the ability of any given rate of nerve firing to cause vasoconstriction is increased when the skin is cold.

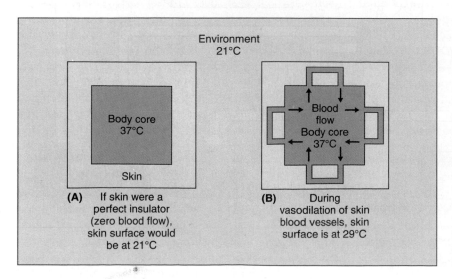

FIGURE 18-22

Relationship of skin's insulating capacity to skin blood flow. (A) If skin were a perfect insulator—in other words, if there were zero blood flow (a situation never reached in a normal person even during maximal vasoconstriction)—the temperature of its outer surface would equal that of the external environment. (B) The skin blood vessels dilate, and the increased blood flow carries heat to the body surface. In this way, the insulating capacity of the skin is reduced, and its surface temperature becomes intermediate between that of the core and that of the external environment.

in surface area, in clothing, and choice of surroundings. Curling up into a ball, hunching the shoulders, and similar maneuvers in response to cold reduce the surface area exposed to the environment, thereby decreasing heat loss by radiation and conduction. In human beings, clothing is also an important component of temperature regulation, substituting for the insulating effects of feathers in birds and fur in other mammals. The outer surface of the clothes forms the true "exterior" of the body surface. The skin loses heat directly to the air space trapped by the clothes, which in turn pick up heat from the inner air layer and transfer it to the external environment. The insulating ability of clothing is determined primarily by the thickness of the trapped air layer.

Clothing is important not only at low temperatures but also at very high temperatures. When the environmental temperature is greater than body temperature, radiation and conduction favor heat *gain* rather than heat loss. People therefore insulate themselves against such temperatures by wearing clothes. The clothing, however, must be loose so as to allow adequate movement of air to permit evaporation (see below). White clothing is cooler since it reflects more radiant energy, which dark colors absorb. Loose-fitting, light-colored clothes are far more cooling than going nude during direct exposure to the sun.

The third behavioral mechanism for altering heat loss is to seek out warmer or colder surroundings, as for example by moving from a shady spot into the sunlight. Raising or lowering the thermostat of a house or turning on an air conditioner also fits this category.

Control of Heat Loss by Evaporation. Even in the absence of sweating, there is loss of water by diffusion through the skin, which is not waterproof. A similar amount is lost from the respiratory lining during expiration. These two losses are known as **insensible water loss** and amount to approximately 600 ml/day in human beings. Evaporation of this water accounts for a significant fraction of total heat loss. In contrast to this passive water loss, sweating requires the active secretion of fluid by **sweat glands** and its extrusion into ducts that carry it to the skin surface.

Production of sweat is stimulated by the sympathetic nerves. Sweat is a dilute solution containing sodium chloride as its major solute. There are an estimated 2.5 million sweat glands spread over the adult human body, and sweating rates of over 4 L/h have been reported. The evaporation of 4 L of water would eliminate almost 2400 kcal from the body!

It is essential to recognize that sweat must evaporate in order to exert its cooling effect. The most important factor determining evaporation is the water vapor concentration of the air, that is, the relative humidity. The discomfort suffered on humid days is due to the failure of evapora-tion; the sweat glands continue to secrete, but the sweat simply remains on the skin or drips off.

Integration of Effector Mechanisms. Table 18-12 summarizes the effector mechanisms regulating temperature, none of which is an all-or-none response but a graded, progressive increase or decrease in activity. Changes in skin blood flow alone can regulate body temperature, by altering heat loss, over a range of environmental temperatures (approximately 25 to 30°C or 75 to 86°F) known as the **thermoneutral zone**. At temperatures lower than this, even maximal vasoconstriction cannot prevent heat loss from exceeding heat production, and the body must increase its heat production to maintain temperature. At environmental temperatures above the thermoneutral zone, even maximal vasodilation cannot eliminate heat as fast as it is produced, and another heat-loss mechanism—sweating—is therefore brought strongly into play. Indeed, at environmental temperatures above that of the body, heat is actually added to the body by radiation and conduction, and evaporation is the sole mechanism for heat loss. A person's ability to tolerate such temperatures is determined by the humidity and by the maximal sweating rate. For example, when the air is completely dry, an individual can tolerate a temperature of 130°C (255°F) for 20 min or longer, whereas very moist air at 46°C (115°F) is bearable for only a few minutes.

Temperature Acclimatization

Acclimatization to Heat. Changes in sweating onset, volume, and composition determine people's chronic adaptation to high temperatures. A person newly arrived in a hot environment has poor ability to do work initially; body temperature rises, and severe weakness and illness may occur. After several days, there is a great improvement in work tolerance, with little increase in body temperature, and the person is said to have acclimatized to the heat (see Chapter 7 for a discussion of the concept of acclimatization). Body temperature does not rise as much because sweating begins sooner and the volume of sweat produced is greater.

There is also an important change in the composition of the sweat, namely, a marked reduction in its sodium concentration. This adaptation, which minimizes the loss of sodium from the body via sweat, is due to increased secretion of the mineralocorticoid hormone aldosterone. The sweat-gland secretory cells produce a solution with a sodium concentration similar to that of plasma, but some of the sodium is absorbed back into the blood as the secretion flows along the sweat-gland ducts toward the skin surface. Aldosterone stimulates this absorption in a manner identical to its stimulation of sodium reabsorption in the

SECTION D. THE CHRONOLOGY OF REPRODUCTIVE FUNCTION

SEX DETERMINATION

SEX DIFFERENTIATION

Differentiation of the Gonads

Differentiation of Internal and External Genitalia

Sexual Differentiation of the Central Nervous System

PUBERTY

MENOPAUSE

SECTION D SUMMARY

SECTION D KEY TERMS

SECTION D REVIEW QUESTIONS

CHAPTER 19 CLINICAL TERMS

CHAPTER 19 THOUGHT QUESTIONS

SECTION

GENERAL TERMINOLOGY AND CONCEPTS

Before we begin detailed descriptions of male and female reproductive systems, it is worthwhile to summarize some general terminology and concepts. This brief description is for orientation, and the specifics of these processes will be dealt with in subsequent sections.

The primary reproductive organs are known as the **gonads**: the **testes** (singular *testis*) in the male and the **ovaries** in the female. In both sexes, the gonads serve dual functions: (1) **gametogenesis**, the production of the reproductive cells, termed **gametes—spermatozoa** (singular *spermatozoan*, usually shortened to **sperm**) by males and **ova** (singular **ovum**) by females; and (2) secretion of particular steroid hormones, often termed **sex hormones**. The primary sex hormones are **testosterone** in the male and **estradiol** and **progesterone** in the female.

Several comments about sex hormone terminology are useful at this point. As described in Chapter 10, testosterone belongs to a group of steroid hormones that have similar masculinizing actions and are collectively called **androgens**. Only the testes secrete significant amounts of testosterone. Other circulating androgens are produced by the adrenal cortex, but they are much less potent than testosterone and are unable to maintain male reproductive function should testosterone secretion be inadequate. Accordingly, we shall ignore them in discussing male reproduction. Estradiol—secreted in large amounts only by the ovaries—is also one of several steroid hormones, in this case hormones that have similar actions on the female reproductive tract and are collectively termed estrogens or, more commonly, simply **estrogen**. In the remainder of this chapter we shall follow the common practice of using this generic term rather than "estradiol," pointing out where relevant the situations in which an estrogen other than estradiol is produced by an extraovarian source and becomes important in the female.

The systems of ducts through which the sperm or ova are transported and the glands lining or emptying into the ducts are termed the **accessory reproductive organs**. In the female the breasts are also usually included in this category. The **secondary sexual characteristics** comprise the many external differences—hair distribution and body contours, for example—between males and females. The secondary sexual characteristics are not directly involved in reproduction.

Reproductive function is largely controlled by a chain of hormones (Figure 19-1). The first hormone in the chain is **gonadotropin releasing hormone (GnRH)**. As described in Chapter 10, GnRH is one of the hypophysiotropic hormones; that is, it is a hormone secreted by neuroendocrine cells in the hypothalamus and reaches the anterior pituitary via the hypothalamo-pituitary portal blood vessels. Accordingly, the brain is the primary regulator of the reproductive process.

Secretion of GnRH, like that of all the hypophysiotropic hormones, is triggered by action potentials in GnRH-producing hypothalamic neuroendocrine cells. These occur periodically in brief bursts, with virtually no secretion in between.[1] It is not yet known what underlies the rhythmical nature of the hypothalamic GnRH "pulse generator." This pattern of GnRH secretion is important because the anterior pituitary will not sustain a response to GnRH if the plasma concentration of this hormone remains elevated over time. The reason is that down-regulation of GnRH receptors occurs under such circumstances.

---

[1]The secretion pattern of GnRH has not been directly measured in humans because blood cannot be obtained from the hypothalomo-pituitary blood vessels in intact unanesthetized people. Its pattern has been inferred from the pattern of LH and FSH secretion from the anterior pituitary, since GnRH controls the secretion of these two hormones.

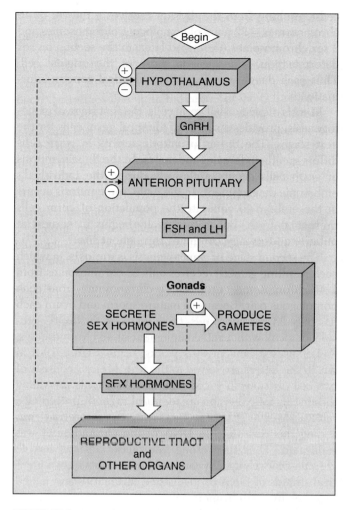

FIGURE 19-1

General pattern of reproduction control in both males and females. GnRH, like all hypothalamic hypophysiotropic hormones, reaches the anterior pituitary via the hypothalamo-pituitary portal vessels (Chapter 10). The arrow within the gonads denotes the fact that the sex hormones act locally, as paracrine agents, to stimulate gamete formation. Not shown in this introductory figure but described later is another hormone, inhibin, that is secreted by the gonads.

In the anterior pituitary, GnRH stimulates the release of the pituitary **gonadotropins—follicle-stimulating hormone (FSH)** and **luteinizing hormone (LH)**. These two protein hormones, which are produced by a single pituitary cell type, were named for their effects in the female, but their molecular structures are the same in both sexes. The two hormones act together upon the gonads, the result being gametogenesis and sex hormone secretion. In turn, the sex hormones exert many effects on all portions of the reproductive system, including the gonads from which they come and other parts of the body as well.

In addition, the steroidal sex hormones exert feedback effects on the secretion of GnRH, FSH, and LH. One other gonadal hormone—**inhibin**, which is a protein hormone—also exerts feedback effects on the anterior pituitary.

It must be emphasized that each link in this hormonal chain is essential, and malfunction of either the hypothalamus or the anterior pituitary can result in failure of sex hormone secretion and gametogenesis as surely as if the gonads themselves were diseased.

As a result of changes in the amount and pattern of hormonal secretions, reproductive function changes markedly during a person's lifetime and may be divided into the stages summarized in Table 19-1.

GENERAL PRINCIPLES OF GAMETOGENESIS

All cells at any point in gametogenesis are termed **germ cells**. These cells undergo either mitosis or the type of cell division known as meiosis. Because the general principles of gametogenesis are essentially the same in males and females, they are treated in this section, and features specific to the male or female are described later.

The first stage in gametogenesis is proliferation of the primordial germ cells by mitosis. Recall from our discussion of cell division in Chapter 4 that each nucleated human cell, *except the gametes*, contains 46 chromosomes, 23 from each parent. The two corresponding chromosomes in such a pair are said to be homologous to each other. In mitosis all the dividing cell's 46 chromosomes are replicated, and each of the two cells, termed daughter

---

TABLE 19-1   STAGES IN THE CONTROL OF REPRODUCTIVE FUNCTION

1. During the initial stage, which begins during fetal life and ends in the first year of life (infancy), GnRH, the gonadotropins, and gonadal sex hormones are secreted at relatively high levels.

2. From infancy to puberty, the secretion rates of these hormones are very low, and reproductive function in general is quiescent.

3. Beginning at puberty, hormonal secretion rates increase markedly, being stable in men but varying greatly in women during the menstrual cycle, and this ushers in the period of active reproduction.

4. Finally, reproductive function diminishes later in life as the gonads become less responsive to the gonadotropins, the ability to reproduce ceasing entirely in women.

Lumen of seminiferous tubule

Leydig cell (interstitial cell)

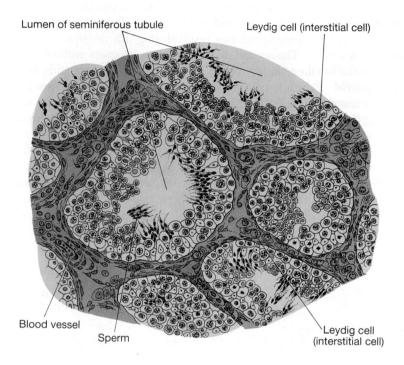

Blood vessel

Sperm

Leydig cell (interstitial cell)

FIGURE 19-3

Cross section of an area of testis. The blue areas are the seminiferous tubules, the sites of sperm production. Mature sperm from each tubule are found in the tubular lumen. This low-power magnification is only for general orientation, and the positions of the other cells in the tubules are shown in a later figure (Figure 19-8). The tubules are separated from each other by interstitial space (colored pink) that contains Leydig cells and blood vessels.

FIGURE 19-4

Section of a testis. The upper portion of the testis has been removed to show its interior. On the right, the scrotal sac covering the epididymis and vas deferens has also been removed to show these structures.

several degrees lower than normal internal body temperature. This is achieved by air circulating around the scrotum and by a heat-exchange mechanism in the blood vessels supplying the testes. In contrast to spermatogenesis, testosterone secretion can usually occur normally at internal body temperature, and so failure of testes descent does not impair testosterone secretion.

The sites of sperm formation (**spermatogenesis**) in the testes are the many tiny, convoluted **seminiferous tubules** (Figure 19-3), the combined length of which is 250 m. Each seminiferous tubule is bounded by a basement membrane and a layer of smooth-muscle cells that are responsible for peristaltic movements of the tubules. In the center of each tubule is a fluid-filled lumen containing spermatozoa. The tubular wall is composed of developing germ cells and another cell type, to be described later, called Sertoli cells.

The **Leydig cells** (also called interstitial cells), which lie in small connective tissue spaces *between* the tubules, are the cells that secrete testosterone. Thus, the sperm-producing and testosterone-producing functions of the testes are carried out by different structures.

The seminiferous tubules from different areas of a testis unite to form a network of interconnected tubes, the rete testis (Figure 19-4). Small ducts termed efferent ductules leave the rete testis, pierce the fibrous covering of

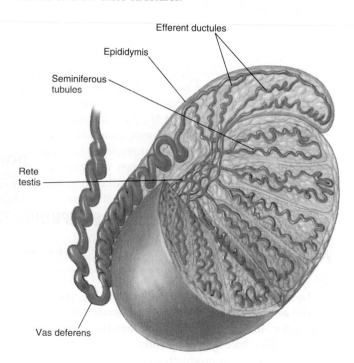

Efferent ductules

Epididymis

Seminiferous tubules

Rete testis

Vas deferens

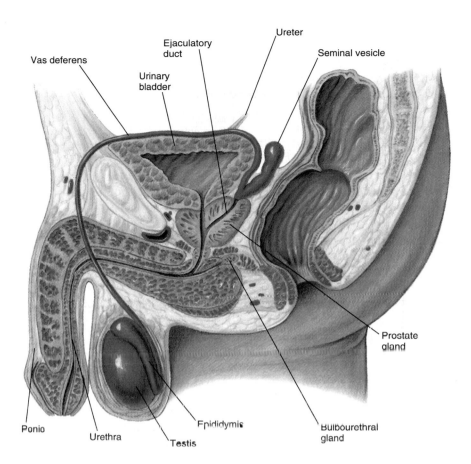

FIGURE 19-5

Anatomic organization of the male reproductive tract. This figure shows the testis, epididymis, vas deferens, ejaculatory duct, seminal vesicle, and bulbourethral gland on only one side of the body, but they are all paired structures. With the exception of the testes (the primary reproductive organs), these structures along with the prostate gland and penis constitute the accessory reproductive organs in the male. The urinary bladder and a ureter are shown for orientation but are not part of the reproductive tract. Once the ejaculatory ducts join the urethra in the prostate, the urinary and reproductive tracts have merged.

the testis, and empty into a single duct within a structure called the **epididymis** (plural *epididymides*). The epididymis is loosely attached to the outside of the testis, and the duct of the epididymis is so convoluted that, when straightened out at dissection, it measures 6 m. In turn, the epididymis draining each testis leads to a **vas** (or ductus) **deferens**, a large thick-walled tube. The vas deferens and the blood vessels and nerves supplying the testis are bound together in the **spermatic cord**, which passes through a slitlike passage, the inguinal canal, in the abdominal wall.

After entering the abdomen, the two vas deferens—one from each side—course to the back of the urinary bladder base (Figure 19-5) and become the **ejaculatory ducts**. Just at this transition, two large glands, the **seminal vesicles**, which lie behind the bladder, drain into the two vas deferens. The ejaculatory ducts then enter the substance of the **prostate gland** and join the urethra, coming from the bladder. The prostate gland is a single donut-shaped gland below the bladder and surrounding the upper part of the urethra, into which it secretes fluid through hundreds of tiny openings in the side of the urethra. The urethra leaves the prostate gland to enter the penis. The paired **bulbourethral glands**, lying below the prostate, drain into the urethra just after it leaves the prostate.

The prostate gland and seminal vesicles secrete the bulk of the fluid in which ejaculated sperm are suspended. This fluid, plus the sperm cells, constitute **semen**, the sperm contributing only a few percent of the total volume. The glandular secretions contain a large number of different chemical substances, including nutrients, buffers for protecting the sperm against the acidic vaginal secretions, and prostaglandins.[2] The function of the prostaglandins in semen is still not clear. The bulbourethral glands contribute a small volume of mucoid secretions.

In addition to providing a route for sperm from the seminiferous tubules to the exterior, several of the duct system segments perform additional functions to be described in the section on sperm transport.

SPERMATOGENESIS

The various stages of spermatogenesis are summarized in Figure 19-6. The undifferentiated germ cells, which are termed **spermatogonia** (singular *spermatogonium*) begin to divide mitotically at puberty. The daughter

---

[2]So named because it was originally thought that the prostaglandins in semen were produced by the prostate rather than at the actual site—the seminal vesicles.

struation occur. After describing the full menstrual cycle as it occurs in the absence of pregnancy, we then describe the events of pregnancy, delivery, and lactation.

ANATOMY

The female reproductive system includes the two ovaries and the female reproductive tract—two uterine tubes, a uterus, and a vagina. These structures are also termed the **female internal genitalia** (Figure 19-11A and B). In the female, unlike in the male, the urinary and reproductive duct systems are entirely separate from each other.

The ovaries are almond-sized organs in the upper pelvic cavity, one on each side of the uterus. The ends of the **uterine tubes** (also known as oviducts or fallopian tubes) are not directly attached to the ovaries but open into the abdominal cavity close to them. The opening of each uterine tube is funnel-shaped and surrounded by long, finger-like projections (the fimbriae) lined with ciliated epithe-

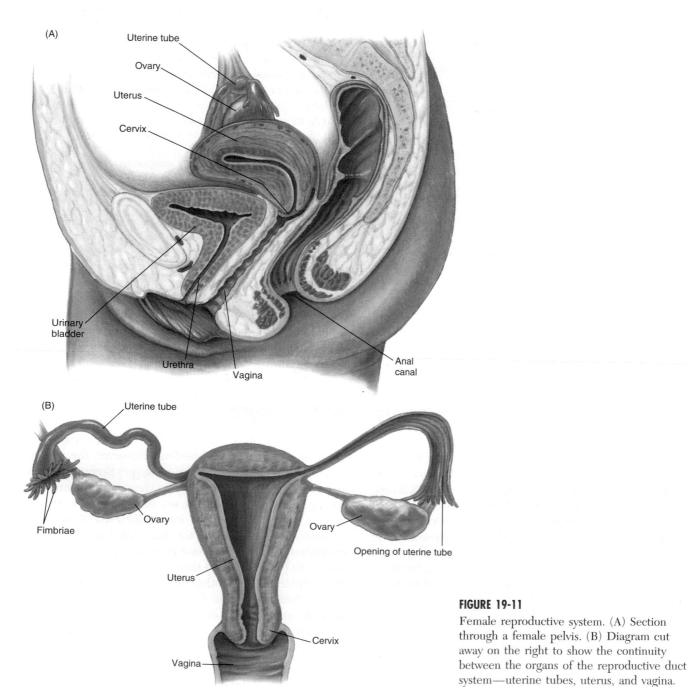

FIGURE 19-11

Female reproductive system. (A) Section through a female pelvis. (B) Diagram cut away on the right to show the continuity between the organs of the reproductive duct system—uterine tubes, uterus, and vagina.

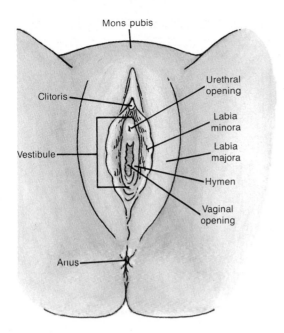

FIGURE 19-12
Female external genitalia.

lium. The other ends of the uterine tubes are attached to the uterus and empty directly into its cavity. The **uterus** is a hollow, thick-walled muscular organ lying between the urinary bladder and rectum. It is the source of bleeding during menstruation and it houses the fetus during pregnancy. The lower portion of the uterus is the **cervix**. A small opening in the cervix leads to the **vagina**, the canal leading from the uterus to the outside.

The **female external genitalia** (Figure 19-12) include the mons pubis, labia majora, labia minora, clitoris, vestibule of the vagina, and vestibular glands. The term **vulva** is another name for all these structures. The mons pubis is the rounded fatty prominence over the junction of the pubic bones. The labia majora, the female analog of the scrotum,[6] are two prominent skin folds that form the outer lips of the vulva. The labia minora are small skin folds lying between the labia majora. They surround the urethral and vaginal openings, and the area thus enclosed is the vestibule, into which the vestibular glands empty. The vaginal opening lies behind that of the urethra. Partially overlying the vaginal opening is a thin fold of mucous membrane, the hymen. The **clitoris**, the female analog of the penis, is an erectile structure located at the front of the vulva.

---

[6]The term "analog" or "homolog" used frequently in this chapter does not imply that one structure is dominant and its analog somehow an inferior imitation. It simply means that the two structures are derived embryologically from the same source and/or have similar functions.

OVARIAN FUNCTION

As noted at the beginning of this chapter, the ovary, like the testis, serves a dual purpose: (1) **oogenesis**, the production of gametes—the ova; and (2) secretion of the female steroidal sex hormones, estrogen and progesterone, as well as the peptide hormone inhibin. Before ovulation, the gametogenic and endocrine functions take place in a single structure—the follicle—and after ovulation the follicle, now without an ovum, differentiates into a corpus luteum, which has only an endocrine function. For comparison, recall that in the testes the production of gametes and the secretion of sex steroids take place in different compartments—in the seminiferous tubules and in the Leydig cells, respectively.

This section will describe the events that occur in the ovary during a menstrual cycle, and the next section will replay these events, adding the controls.

Oogenesis

First, a word about terminology is appropriate: As we shall see, the female germ cells, like those of the male, have different names at different stages of development; it is helpful to use the term **egg** to refer to the germ cells at any stage.

At birth, a female's ovaries contain an estimated total of 2 to 4 million eggs, and no new ones appear after birth. Thus, in marked contrast to the male, the newborn female already has all the germ cells she will ever have. Only a few, perhaps 400, are destined to be ovulated. All the others degenerate at some point in their development so that few, if any, remain by the time a woman reaches approximately 50 years of age. One result of this developmental pattern is that the eggs that are ovulated near age 50 are 35 to 40 years older than those ovulated just after puberty. It has been suggested that certain defects more common among children born to older women are the result of aging changes in the egg.

During early fetal development, the primitive germ cells, or **oogonia** (singular *oogonium*), a term analogous to spermatogonia in the male, undergo numerous mitotic divisions (Figure 19-13). Around the third month of fetal life, the oogonia cease dividing, and from this point on no new germ cells are generated. In the fetus, all the oogonia develop into **primary oocytes** (analogous to primary spermatocytes), which then begin a first meiotic division by replicating their DNA. They do not, however, complete the division. Accordingly, all the germ cells present at birth are primary oocytes containing 46 chromosomes, each with two sister chromatids. The cells are said to be in a state of **meiotic arrest**.

This state continues until puberty and the onset of re-

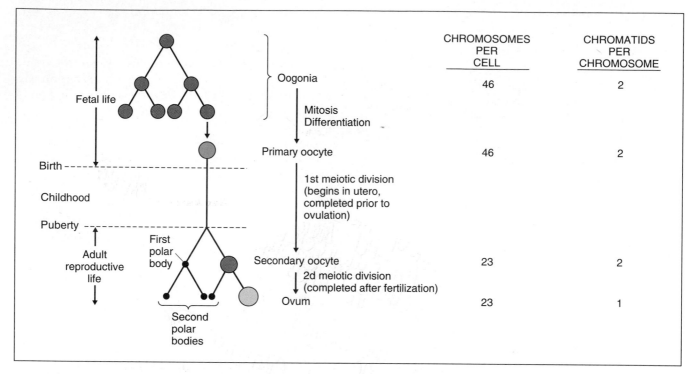

	CHROMOSOMES PER CELL	CHROMATIDS PER CHROMOSOME
Oogonia	46	2
Primary oocyte	46	2
Secondary oocyte	23	2
Ovum	23	1

FIGURE 19-13

Summary of oogenesis. Compare with the male pattern of Figure 19-6. The secondary oocyte is ovulated and does not complete its meiotic division unless it is penetrated (fertilized) by a sperm. Thus, it is a semantic oddity that the egg is not termed an ovum until after fertilization occurs. Note that each primary oocyte yields only one secondary oocyte, which can yield only one ovum.

newed activity in the ovaries. Indeed, only those primary oocytes destined for ovulation will ever complete the first meiotic division, for it occurs just before the egg is ovulated. This division is analogous to the division of the primary spermatocyte, and each daughter cell receives 23 chromosomes, each with two chromatids. In this division, however, one of the two daughter cells, the **secondary oocyte**, retains virtually all the cytoplasm. The other, termed the **first polar body**, is very small and adheres to the secondary oocyte. Thus, the primary oocyte, which is already as large as the ovum will be, passes on to the secondary oocyte half of its chromosomes but almost all of its nutrient-rich cytoplasm.

The second meiotic division occurs in a uterine tube, *after ovulation* but only if the secondary oocyte is fertilized, that is, penetrated by a sperm. As a result of this division the daughter cells each receive 23 chromosomes, each with a single chromatid. Once again, one daughter cell, now termed an ovum, retains nearly all the cytoplasm, whereas the other, termed the **second polar body**, is very small and nonfunctional. Interestingly, the first polar body also undergoes a second meiotic division at the same time

the secondary oocyte does. However, as far as is known, neither of the resulting cells nor the second polar body is fertilized, and they all eventually disintegrate. The net result of oogenesis is that each primary oocyte produces only one ovum (Figure 19-13).[7] In contrast, each primary spermatocyte produces four viable spermatozoa.

Follicle Growth

Throughout their life in the ovaries, the eggs exist in structures known as **follicles**. Follicles begin as **primordial follicles**, which consist of one primary oocyte surrounded by a single layer of cells called **granulosa cells**. Further development from the primordial follicle stage (Figure 19-14) is characterized by an increase in the size of the oocyte, a proliferation of the granulosa cells into mul-

---

[7]Since the final stage of gametogenesis—formation of the ovum—occurs only after fertilization and since fertilization occurs *outside* the ovary (in a uterine tube, as we shall see), technically the *ovaries* do not themselves produce the fully mature gametes—the ova—but only secondary oocytes; this technicality is universally ignored in talking about the ovarian function of gamete production.

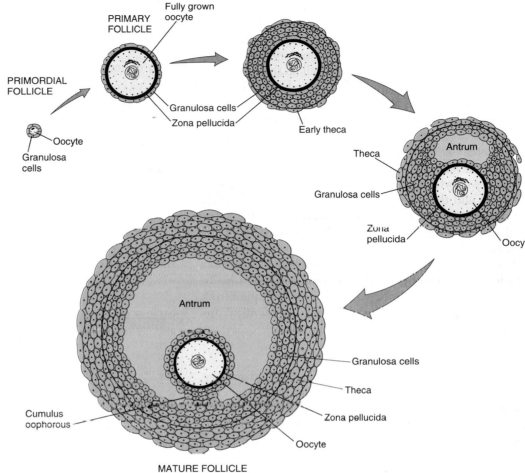

PRIMORDIAL FOLLICLE

Oocyte
Granulosa cells

PRIMARY FOLLICLE
Fully grown oocyte
Granulosa cells
Zona pellucida

Early theca

Theca
Antrum
Granulosa cells
Zona pellucida
Oocyte

Antrum
Granulosa cells
Theca
Zona pellucida
Cumulus oophorous
Oocyte

MATURE FOLLICLE

FIGURE 19-14
Development of a human oocyte (yellow) and ovarian follicle. (Adapted from Erickson et al.)

FIGURE 19-1?
Control of e
the early ar

markedly (
crucial stir
ing this ro
the numbe
their sensi
quantitati
FSH and
sensitivity

What a
the cycle?
estrogen
secretion
site of its
the amou
given amo
mus to
hence, th
period.

There
plasma c
the rising
ues (6 in
granulosa
preferen

LH Surge
The inhi
hypothal

FIGURE 1?
Summary
early and
gous path
hormone
rows in t
gens to e

tiple layers, and the separation of the oocyte from the inner granulosa cells by a thick layer of material, the **zona pellucida**. The granulosa cells secrete estrogen, small amounts of progesterone just before ovulation, and the peptide hormone inhibin.

Despite the presence of a zona pellucida, however, the inner layer of granulosa cells remains intimately associated with the oocyte by means of cytoplasmic processes that traverse the zona pellucida and form gap junctions with the oocyte. Through these gap junctions, nutrients and chemical messengers are passed to the oocyte. For example, the granulosa cells produce one or more factors that act on the oocyte to maintain it in meiotic arrest. Granulosa cells also have gap junctions with each other so the entire structure functions as a syncitium.

As the follicle grows by mitosis of granulosa cells, connective-tissue cells surrounding the granulosa cells differentiate and form layers known as the **theca**, which plays an important role in estrogen secretion by the granulosa cells, as we shall see. Shortly after this, the primary oocyte reaches full size (115 μm in diameter), and a fluid-filled space, the **antrum**, begins to form in the midst of the granulosa cells as a result of fluid they secrete.

The progression of some primordial follicles to the preantral stage occurs continuously, so that at any moment most of the follicles present are still primordial but there are always present a relatively constant number of preantral follicles. At the beginning of each menstrual cycle, 10 to 25 of these preantral follicles begin to develop into antral follicles; what causes these particular follicles to be selected is unknown. About 1 week into the cycle, a further selection process occurs: Only one follicle, the **dominant follicle**, continues to develop, and the others that had begun to enlarge undergo a degenerative process called **atresia**. The eggs in these follicles also die.

Atresia is not limited just to antral follicles, however, for follicles can undergo atresia at all stages of development. Indeed, this process begins in utero so that the 2 to 4 million follicles and eggs present at birth represent only a small fraction of those present at an earlier time in the fetus. Atresia then continues all through prepubertal life so that only 200,000 to 400,000 follicles remain when active reproductive life begins.

As the dominant follicle enlarges, mainly as a result of its expanding antrum, the granulosa cell layers surrounding the egg form a mound that projects into the antrum

the sperm head alters so that the underlying membrane-bound acrosomal enzymes become exposed to the outside, that is, to the zona pellucida. The enzymes digest a path through the zona as the sperm, using its tail, advances through this coating. The first sperm to penetrate the entire zona and reach the narrow space between the zona and the egg's plasma membrane fuses with this membrane. This sperm then slowly passes into the egg's cytoplasm, penetration being achieved not by the sperm's motility but as a result of contractile elements in the egg, which draw the sperm in.

Viability of the newly fertilized egg, now termed a **zygote**, depends upon preventing the fusion and entry of additional sperm. The mechanism of this "block to polyspermy" is as follows: The initial fusion of the sperm and egg plasma membranes triggers a reaction in which secretory vesicles located around the egg's periphery release their contents, by exocytosis, into the space between the plasma membrane and the zona pellucida. Some of these molecules are enzymes that enter the zona pellucida and cause both inactivation of its sperm-binding sites and hardening of the entire zona. This prevents additional sperm from binding to the zona and those sperm already advancing through it from continuing.

The fertilized egg completes its second meiotic division over the next few hours, and the one daughter cell with practically no cytoplasm—the second polar body—is extruded and disintegrates. The two sets of chromosomes—23 from the egg and 23 from the sperm—each become surrounded by distinct membranes and are known as pronuclei, which migrate to the center of the cell. During this period of a few hours, the DNA of the chromosomes in

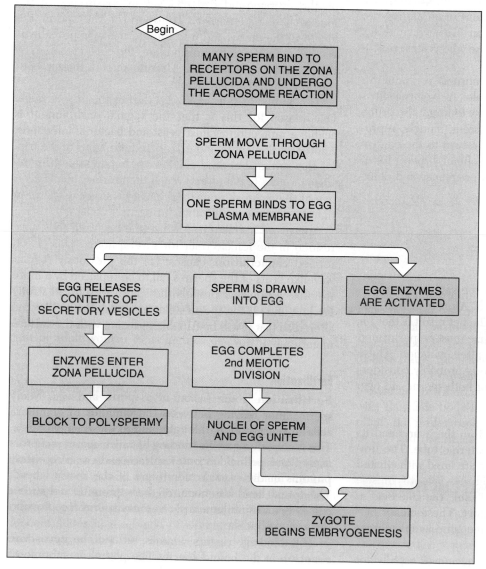

FIGURE 19-21

Events leading to fertilization, block to polyspermy, and the beginning of embryogenesis.

both pronuclei is replicated, the pronuclear membranes break down, the cell is ready to undergo a mitotic division, and fertilization, the major events of which are summarized in Figure 19-21, is complete. Fertilization also triggers activation of the ovum enzymes required for the ensuing cell divisions and embryogenesis.

If fertilization had not occurred, the egg would have slowly disintegrated and been phagocytized by cells lining the uterus. Rarely, a fertilized egg remains in the uterine tube and embeds itself in the tube wall. Such tubal pregnancies cannot succeed because of lack of space for the fetus to grow, and surgery will be necessary, unless there is spontaneous abortion, because of the risk of maternal hemorrhage. Even more rarely a fertilized egg may be expelled into the abdominal cavity where implantation may take place and proceed to term, the infant being delivered surgically. Tubal and abdominal pregnancies are termed *ectopic pregnancies*.

Early Development, Implantation, and Placentation

During its 3- to 4-day stay in the uterine tube, the **conceptus**—a collective term for the fertilized egg and all its derivatives throughout pregnancy—undergoes a number of mitotic cell divisions, a process known as **cleavage**. These divisions are unusual for mitosis in that no cell growth occurs before each division. Thus, the 16- to 32-cell conceptus that reaches the uterus is essentially the same size as the original fertilized egg.

Identical or monozygotic twins result when, at some point during cleavage, the dividing cells become com-

FIGURE 19-22

Photomicrograph showing the beginning implantation of a 9-day monkey blastocyst. [*From C. H. Heuser and G. L. Streeter, Carnegie Contrib. Embryol, 29:15 (1941).*]

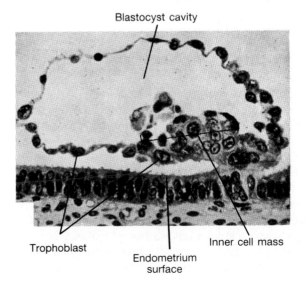

Blastocyst cavity

Trophoblast

Endometrium surface

Inner cell mass

pletely separated into two independently growing cell masses. In contrast, as we have seen, dizygotic (fraternal) twins result from two eggs being ovulated and fertilized.

After reaching the uterus, the conceptus floats free in the intrauterine fluid, from which it receives nutrients, for approximately 3 days, all the while undergoing further cell divisions. Soon the conceptus reaches the stage known as a **blastocyst**, consisting of an outer layer of cells, the **trophoblast**, an **inner cell mass**, and a central fluid-filled cavity (Figure 19-22). During subsequent development, the inner cell mass will give rise to the developing human—termed an **embryo** during the first 2 months and a **fetus** after that—and some of the membranes associated with it. The trophoblast will surround the embryo and fetus throughout development and be involved in its nutrition as well as in the secretion of several important hormones.

The period during which the zygote develops into a blastocyst corresponds with days 14 to 21 of the typical menstrual cycle. During this period the uterine lining is being prepared by estrogen and progesterone, secreted by the corpus luteum, to receive the blastocyst. By approximately the twenty-first day of the cycle, that is, 7 days after ovulation, **implantation**—the embedding of the blastocyst in the endometrium—begins. The trophoblast cells are quite sticky, particularly in the region overlying the inner cell mass, and it is this portion of the blastocyst that adheres to the endometrium and initiates implantation.

The initial contact between blastocyst and endometrium induces rapid proliferation of the trophoblast, the cells of which penetrate between endometrial cells. Proteolytic enzymes secreted by the trophoblast allow the blastocyst to bury itself in the endometrial layer. The endometrium, as well, is undergoing changes at the site of contact as the result of hormone stimulation: Increased vascularization and vascular permeability, edema, and compositional changes in the intercellular matrix and in the endometrial cells all occur. Implantation is soon completed (Figure 19-23), and the nutrient-rich endometrial cells provide the metabolic fuel and raw materials required for early growth of the embryo.

This simple nutritive system, however, is adequate to provide for the embryo only during the first few weeks, when it is very small. The structure taking over this function is the **placenta**, a combination of interlocking fetal and maternal tissues that serves as the organ of exchange between mother and fetus for the remainder of the pregnancy. The fetal portion of the placenta is supplied by the outermost layer of trophoblast cells, termed the **chorion**, and the maternal portion by the endometrium underlying the chorion. Finger-like projections, **chorionic villi**, extend from the chorion into the endometrium (Figure 19-24). The villi contain a rich network of capillaries linked to the embryo's circulatory system. The endometrium around the villi is altered by enzymes secreted from the

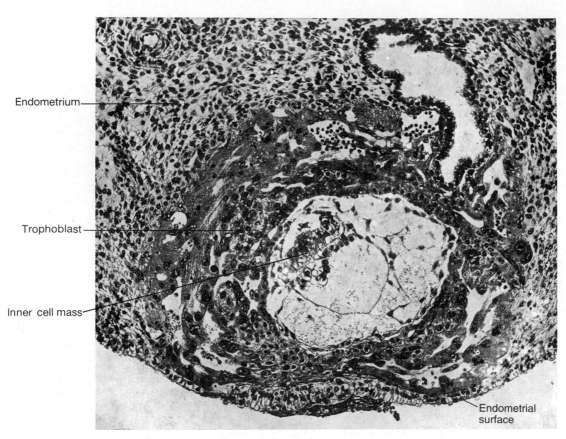

Endometrium

Trophoblast

Inner cell mass

Endometrial surface

FIGURE 19-23

Eleven-day human embryo completely embedded in the uterine lining. [*From A. T. Hertig and J. Rock, Carnegie Contrib. Embryol., 29:127 (1941).*]

cells of the villi so that each villus comes to be completely surrounded by a pool, or sinus, of maternal blood.

The maternal blood enters these placental sinuses via the uterine artery, percolates through them, and then exits via the uterine veins. Simultaneously, blood flows from the fetus into the capillaries of the chorionic villi via the **umbilical arteries** and out of the capillaries back to the fetus via the **umbilical vein**. All these umbilical vessels are contained in the **umbilical cord**, a long ropelike structure that connects the fetus to the placenta.

Five weeks after implantation, the placenta has become well established, the fetal heart has begun to pump blood, and the entire mechanism for nutrition of the fetus and excretion of its waste products is in operation. Waste products move from blood in the fetal capillaries across the cells lining the villi into the maternal blood, and nutrients move in the opposite direction. Many substances, such as oxygen and carbon dioxide, move by simple diffusion, whereas others are carried by mediated-transport mechanisms in the lining. It must be emphasized that there is an *exchange of materials* between the two bloodstreams but no actual *mingling* of the fetal and maternal blood.

Meanwhile, a space called the **amniotic cavity** has formed between the inner cell mass and the trophoblast. The epithelial layer lining the cavity is derived from the inner cell mass and is called the **amnion** (or **amniotic sac**). It eventually fuses with the inner surface of the chorion so that only a single combined membrane surrounds the fetus. The fluid in the amniotic cavity, the **amniotic fluid**, resembles the fetal extracellular fluid, and it buffers mechanical disturbances and temperature variations.

The fetus, floating in the amniotic cavity and attached by the umbilical cord to the placenta (Figure 19-25), develops into a viable infant during the next 8 months. (A description of intrauterine development is beyond the scope of this book but can be found in any standard textbook of human embryology.) Note in Figure 19-25 that only the amniotic sac separates the fetus from the uterine lumen.

Amniotic fluid can be sampled (*amniocentesis*) as early as the fourth month by inserting a needle into the amniotic cavity. A large number of genetic diseases can be diagnosed by the finding of certain chemicals either in the fluid or in cells suspended in the fluid. The chromosomes

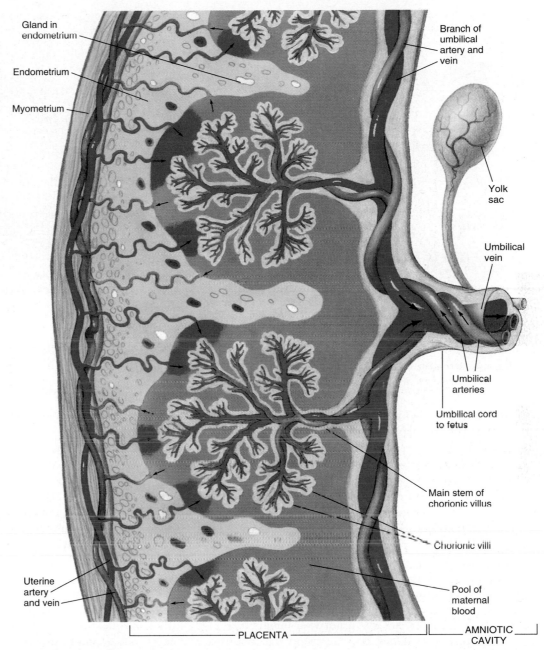

FIGURE 19-24

Interrelations of fetal and maternal tissues in formation of placenta. See Figure 19-25 for orientation of the placenta. (*From B. M. Carlson, "Patten's Foundations of Embryology," 5th ed., McGraw-Hill, New York, 1988.*)

of these cells can also be examined for diagnosis of certain disorders as well as to determine the sex of the fetus. Another technique for fetal diagnosis is ***chorionic villus sampling***. This technique, which can be performed as early as the beginning of the third month of pregnancy, involves obtaining tissue from a chorionic villus of the placenta. A third technique for fetal diagnosis is ultrasound, which provides a "picture" of the fetus without the use of x-rays.

Maternal nutrition is crucial for the fetus. ***Malnutrition*** early in pregnancy can cause certain congenital abnormalities and/or the formation of an inadequate placenta. Malnutrition retards fetal growth and results in infants with higher-than-normal death rates, reduced

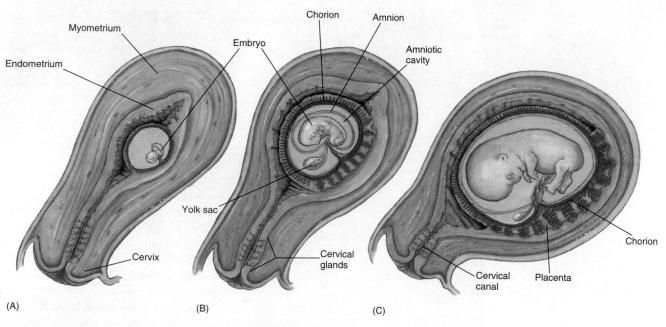

FIGURE 19-25

The uterus at (A) 3, (B) 5, and (C) 8 weeks after fertilization. Embryos and their membranes are drawn to actual size. Uterus is within actual size range. *(From B. M. Carlson, "Patten's Foundations of Embryology," 5th ed., McGraw-Hill, New York, 1988.)*

growth after birth, and an increased incidence of learning disabilities. The developing embryo and fetus are also subject to considerable influence by a host of other factors (noise, radiation, chemicals, viruses, and so on) to which the mother may be exposed. For example, drugs taken by the mother can reach the fetus via the placenta and impair fetal growth and development. In this regard, it must be emphasized that aspirin, alcohol, and the chemicals in cigarette smoke are very potent agents, as are "street drugs" such as cocaine.

It should also be recognized that, since half of the fetal genes differ from those of the mother, the fetus is in essence a foreign transplant in the mother. Why the fetus is not rejected (Chapter 20) is still not well understood.

Finally, recent evidence has suggested that approximately half of all pregnancies end in spontaneous abortion, most so early that the woman is unaware of having been pregnant.

Hormonal and Other Changes During Pregnancy

Throughout pregnancy, plasma concentrations of estrogen and progesterone remain high (Figure 19-26). Estrogen stimulates growth of the uterine muscle mass which will eventually supply the contractile force needed to deliver the fetus. Progesterone inhibits uterine motility so that the fetus is not expelled prematurely. During approximately the first 2 months of pregnancy, almost all the estrogen

and progesterone are supplied by the extremely active corpus luteum.

Recall that if pregnancy had not occurred, this gland-like structure would have degenerated within 2 weeks after its formation. The persistence of the corpus luteum during pregnancy is due to a hormone called **chorionic gonadotropin (CG),** which starts to be secreted by the trophoblast cells around the time they start their endometrial invasion. The CG gains entry to the maternal blood via the endometrial blood vessels of the placenta. The detection of CG in the mother's plasma and/or urine is used as a test of pregnancy and is positive before the next expected menstruation. This protein hormone is very similar to but not identical to LH, and it maintains the corpus luteum and strongly stimulates steroid secretion by it. Thus, the signal that preserves the corpus luteum comes from the conceptus (everything derived from the fertilized egg), not the mother's tissues.

The secretion of CG reaches a peak 60 to 80 days after the last menstrual period (Figure 19-26). It then falls just as rapidly, so that by the end of the third month it has reached a low, but definitely detectable, level that remains relatively constant for the duration of the pregnancy. Associated with this falloff of CG secretion, the placenta begins to secrete large quantities of estrogen and progesterone. The very marked increases in plasma concentrations of estrogen and progesterone during the last 6 months of pregnancy are due entirely to their secretion by the trophoblast cells of the placenta, and the corpus luteum re-

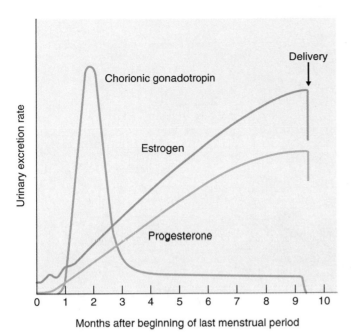

FIGURE 19-26

Urinary excretion of estrogen, progesterone, and chorionic gonadotropin during pregnancy. Urinary excretion rates are an indication of blood concentrations of these hormones.

gresses after about 3 months. Indeed, surgical removal of the ovaries during the last 7 months of pregnancy, as opposed to the first 2 months, has no effect at all upon the pregnancy.

Recall that secretion of GnRH and, hence, of LH and FSH is powerfully inhibited by high concentrations of progesterone in the presence of estrogen. Since both these steroid hormones are present in high concentration throughout pregnancy, the secretion of the pituitary gonadotropins remains extremely low. In addition, the trophoblast cells secrete large amounts of inhibin, which further contributes, via its action on the anterior pituitary, to reduced FSH secretion. The low gonadotropin levels prevent further follicle development and ovulation for the duration of the pregnancy.

An important aspect of placental steroid secretion is that the placenta has the enzymes required for the synthesis of progesterone but not those for the formation of androgens, which are the precursors of estrogen. The placenta is supplied with these androgens by the *fetal* adrenal glands via the fetal circulation, and it converts them mainly into **estriol,** the major estrogen of pregnancy.

The trophoblast cells of the placenta produce not only CG, steroids, and inhibin, but many other hormones as well, all examples of hormones produced by the conceptus (everything derived from the fertilized egg) and influencing the mother. Some of these (for example, thyroid-

stimulating hormone) are identical to hormones normally produced by other endocrine glands, whereas some are unique. One unique hormone that is secreted in very large amounts has effects similar to those of both prolactin and growth hormone. This protein hormone, **placental lactogen** (also called chorionic somatomammotropin), may play several roles in the mother—mobilizing fat for energy and stabilizing plasma glucose at relatively high levels (growth-hormone-like effects) and facilitating development of the breasts (a prolactin-like effect). In the fetus, this hormone may exert growth-promoting effects.

Some of the numerous other physiological changes, hormonal and nonhormonal, in the mother during pregnancy are summarized in Table 19-9.

One comment about fluid balance during pregnancy is necessary: Some women retain abnormally large amounts of fluid and manifest both protein in the urine and hypertension. These are the symptoms of the disease known as *toxemia of pregnancy* or eclampsia, a condition that can sometimes be controlled by salt restriction. The factors responsible for the disease are unknown.

Pregnancy Sickness. The majority of women suffer from *pregnancy sickness* (popularly called morning sickness)—nausea and vomiting—during the first three months (first trimester) of pregnancy. The exact cause is unknown, but high concentrations of estrogen, progesterone, and other substances secreted at this time are thought to act on the vomiting center (Chapter 17) in the brain. Pregnancy sickness is also associated with changes in the perception of food palatability and the presence of taste aversions.

Parturition

A normal human pregnancy lasts approximately 40 weeks. Safe survival of premature infants is now possible at about the twenty-seventh week of pregnancy, but treatment of these infants often requires heroic efforts at great costs. Delivery of the infant, followed by the placenta, the entire process being termed **parturition,** is produced by strong rhythmical contractions of the myometrium. Actually, weak and infrequent uterine contractions begin at approximately 30 weeks and gradually increase in both strength and frequency. During the last month, the entire uterine contents shift downward so that the baby is brought into contact with the cervix. In over 90 percent of births, the baby's head is downward and acts as the wedge to dilate the cervical canal when labor begins (Figure 19-27).

This dilation can occur because, during the last few weeks of pregnancy, the cervix becomes soft and flexible. The cervical softening (often termed "ripening") is largely the result of a breakup of collagen fibers. These biochemi-

TABLE 19-9 MATERNAL RESPONSES TO PREGNANCY

	Response
Placenta	Secretion of estrogen, progesterone, chorionic gonadotropin, inhibin, placental lactogen, and other hormones.
Anterior pituitary	Increased secretion of prolactin and ACTH. Secretes very little FSH and LH.
Adrenal cortex	Increased secretion of aldosterone and cortisol.
Posterior pituitary	Increased secretion of vasopressin.
Parathyroids	Increased secretion of parathyroid hormone.
Kidneys	Increased secretion of renin, erythropoietin, and 1,25-dihydroxyvitamin D_3. Retention of salt and water. *Cause:* Increased aldosterone, vasopressin, and estrogen
Breasts	Enlarge and develop mature glandular structure. *Cause:* Estrogen, progesterone, prolactin, and placental lactogen
Blood volume	Increases. *Cause:* Erythrocyte volume is increased by erythropoietin, and plasma volume by salt and water retention.
Calcium balance	Positive. *Cause:* Increased parathyroid hormone and 1,25-dihydroxyvitamin D_3.
Body weight	Increases by average of 12.5 kg, 60 percent of which is water.
Circulation	Cardiac output increases, total peripheral resistance decreases (vasodilation in uterus, skin, breasts, GI tract, and kidneys), mean arterial pressure stays constant.
Respiration	Hyperventilation (arterial P_{CO_2} decreases).
Organic metabolism	Metabolic rate increases. Plasma glucose, gluconeogenesis, and fatty acid mobilization all increase. *Cause:* Hyporesponsiveness to insulin due to insulin antagonism by placental lactogen and cortisol.
Appetite and thirst	Increase.
Nutritional RDAs	Increase.

cal changes are mediated by a variety of messengers, including estrogen and prostaglandins.

At the onset of labor or before, the amniotic sac ruptures and the amniotic fluid escapes through the vagina. When labor begins in earnest, the uterine contractions become coordinated and quite strong (although usually painless at first) and occur at approximately 10- to 15-min intervals. The contractions begin in the upper portion of the uterus and sweep downward. This coordination is made possible by the fact that the uterine smooth-muscle cells are connected to each other by gap junctions. These junctions increase markedly in number near the end of pregnancy.

As the contractions increase in intensity and frequency, the cervical canal is gradually forced open to a maximum diameter of approximately 10 cm. Until this point, the contractions have not moved the fetus out of the uterus but have served only to dilate the cervix. Now the contractions move the fetus through the cervix and vagina. At this time the mother, by bearing down to increase abdominal pressure, can help the uterine contractions to deliver the baby. The umbilical vessels and placenta are still functioning, so that the baby is not yet on its own, but within minutes of delivery both the umbilical vessels and the placental vessels completely constrict, stopping blood flow to the placenta. The entire placenta becomes separated from

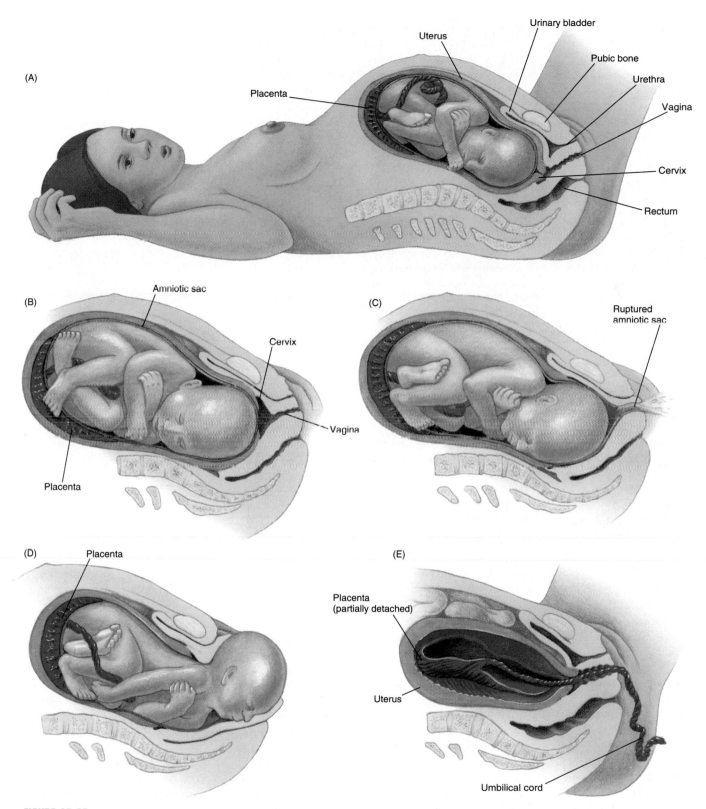

FIGURE 19-27

Stages of parturition. (A) Parturition has not yet begun. (B) The cervix is dilating. (C) The cervix is completely dilated and the fetus's head is entering the cervical canal. (D) The fetus has moved through the vagina. (E) The placenta is coming loose from the uterine wall preparatory to its expulsion.

the underlying uterine wall, and a wave of uterine contractions delivers the placenta as the **afterbirth.**

Ordinarily, parturition proceeds automatically from beginning to end and requires no significant medical intervention. In a small percentage of cases, however, the position of the baby or some maternal defect can interfere with normal delivery. The headfirst position of the fetus is important for several reasons: (1) If the baby is not oriented headfirst, another portion of its body is in contact with the cervix and is generally a far less effective wedge. (2) Because of the head's large diameter compared with the rest of the body, if the body were to go through the cervical canal first, the canal might obstruct the passage of the head, leading to problems when the partially delivered baby attempts to breathe. (3) If the umbilical cord becomes caught between the canal wall and the baby's head or chest, mechanical compression of the umbilical vessels can result. Despite these potential problems, however, many babies who are not oriented headfirst are born normally.

What mechanisms control the events of parturition? Let us consider a set of fairly well established facts:

1. The autonomic neurons to the uterus are of little importance in parturition since anesthetizing them does not interfere with delivery.
2. The smooth-muscle cells of the myometrium have inherent rhythmicity and are capable of autonomous contractions, which are facilitated as the muscle is stretched by the growing fetus.
3. The pregnant uterus near term and during labor secretes a prostaglandin that is a profound stimulator of uterine smooth-muscle contraction.
4. **Oxytocin**, one of the hormones released from the posterior pituitary, is an extremely potent uterine-muscle stimulant. It not only acts directly on uterine smooth muscle but also stimulates it to synthesize prostaglandins. Oxytocin is reflexly released as a result of input to the hypothalamus from receptors in the uterus, particularly the cervix. During pregnancy the concentration of oxytocin receptors in the uterus markedly and progressively increases as a result of estrogen stimulation and, possibly, uterine distention near term.
5. Progesterone exerts a powerful inhibitory effect upon uterine contractions by decreasing the sensitivity to estrogen, oxytocin, and prostaglandins. Shortly before delivery, the ratio of progesterone to estrogen in plasma often decreases.

These facts can now be put together in a unified pattern, as shown in Figure 19-28. Once started, the uterine contractions exert a positive-feedback effect upon themselves via both local facilitation of inherent uterine contractions and reflex stimulation of oxytocin secretion. But

what *starts* the contractions? The most tenable hypothesis at present involves both oxytocin and prostaglandin: Even though these is no dramatic change in circulating oxytocin just before the onset of labor, the increased number of oxytocin receptors in the myometrium makes the uterus so sensitive to oxytocin that contractions become coordinated and strong. The decrease in progesterone/estrogen ratio further increases responsiveness to oxytocin. Simultaneously, the increased sensitivity to oxytocin results in an increased oxytocin-induced local synthesis of uterine prostaglandin, which further stimulates uterine contractions.

The action of prostaglandin on parturition is the last in a series of prostaglandin effects on the female reproductive system we have described. They are summarized in Table 19-10.

Lactation

The secretion of milk by the breasts, or **mammary glands**, is termed **lactation**. The breasts contain ducts that branch all through the tissue and converge at the nipples (Figure 19-29). These ducts arise in saclike glands called **alveoli** (the same term is used to denote the lung air sacs). The breast alveoli, which are the sites of milk secretion, look like bunches of grapes with stems terminating in the ducts. The alveoli and the ducts immediately adjacent to them are surrounded by specialized contractile cells called **myoepithelial cells**.

Before puberty, the breasts are small with little internal glandular structure. With the onset of puberty in females, the increased estrogen causes a marked enhancement of duct growth and branching but relatively little development of the alveoli, and much of the breast enlargement at this time is due to fat deposition. Progesterone secretion also commences at puberty during the luteal phase of each cycle, and this hormone contributes to breast growth by stimulating growth of alveoli.

During each menstrual cycle, the breasts undergo fluctuations in association with the changing blood concentrations of estrogen and progesterone, but these changes are small compared with the marked breast enlargement that occurs during pregnancy as a result of the stimulatory effects of high plasma concentrations of estrogen, progesterone, prolactin, and placental lactogen. This last hormone, as described earlier, is secreted by the placenta, whereas prolactin is secreted by the anterior pituitary. Under the influence of all these hormones, both the ductal and the alveolar structures become fully developed.

As described in Chapter 10, the anterior-pituitary cells that secrete prolactin are influenced by many hormones. They are inhibited by **dopamine**, which is secreted by both the hypothalamus and the posterior pituitary. They are stimulated by one or more **prolactin releasing factors (PRF)** also secreted by both the hypothalamus and

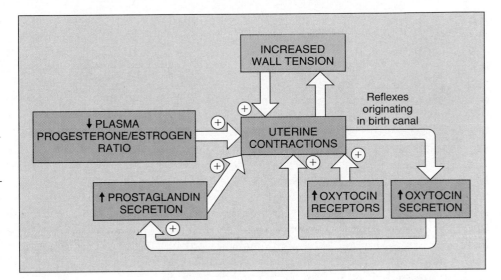

FIGURE 19-28

Factors stimulating uterine contractions during parturition. Note the positive-feedback nature of several of the inputs. Not shown in the figure is the fact that estrogen (or a decrease in the progesterone to estrogen ratio) and, possibly, uterine distention, are the cause of the increased number of oxytocin receptors in the myometrium.

the posterior pituitary. The dopamine and PRF secreted by the hypothalamus (hypophysiotropic hormones) reach the anterior pituitary by way of the hypothalamo-pituitary portal vessels, while those from the posterior pituitary arrive by way of a group of short portal vessels connecting the two lobes of the pituitary. Finally, estrogen also acts on the anterior pituitary to stimulate prolactin secretion.

Under the dominant inhibitory influence of dopamine, prolactin secretion is low before puberty. It then increases considerably at puberty in girls but not in boys, stimulated by the increased plasma estrogen concentration that occurs at this time. During pregnancy, there is a marked further increase in prolactin secretion due to stimulation

by estrogen. Despite the fact that prolactin is elevated and the breasts are markedly enlarged and fully developed as pregnancy progresses, there is no secretion of milk. This is because estrogen and progesterone, in large concentrations, prevent milk production by inhibiting this particular action of prolactin on the breasts. Thus, although estrogen causes an increase in the secretion of prolactin and acts with prolactin in promoting breast growth and differentiation, it (along with progesterone) is antagonistic to prolactin's ability to induce milk secretion. Delivery removes the source—the placenta—of the large amounts of sex steroids and thereby the inhibition of milk production.

The drop in estrogen following parturition also causes

TABLE 19-10 SOME EFFECTS OF PROSTAGLANDINS* ON THE FEMALE REPRODUCTIVE SYSTEM

Site of production	Action	Result
Late-antral follicle	Stimulate production of lytic enzymes	Rupture of follicle
Corpus luteum	Interfere with corpus luteum's hormone secretion and function	Death of corpus luteum
Uterus	Constrict blood vessels in endometrium	Onset of menstruation
	Cause changes in endometrial blood vessels and cells early in pregnancy	Facilitates implantation
	Increase contraction of myometrium	Helps initiate both menstruation and parturition

*The term "prostaglandins" is used loosely here, as is customary in reproductive physiology, to include all the eicosanoids (Chapter 7).

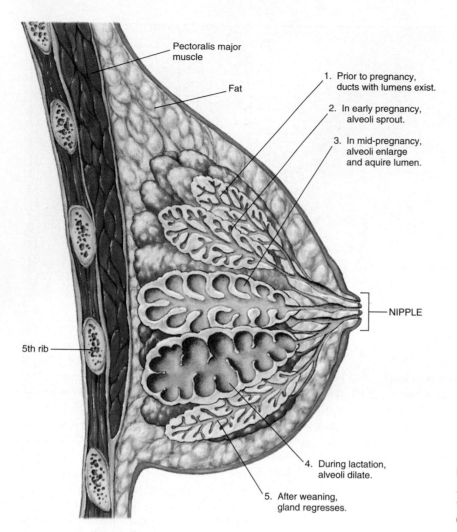

Pectoralis major
muscle

Fat

1. Prior to pregnancy,
ducts with lumens exist.

2. In early pregnancy,
alveoli sprout.

3. In mid-pregnancy,
alveoli enlarge
and aquire lumen.

NIPPLE

5th rib

4. During lactation,
alveoli dilate.

5. After weaning,
gland regresses.

FIGURE 19-29

Anatomy of the breast. The numbers refer to
the sequential changes that occur over time.
(*Adapted from Elias et al.*).

basal prolactin secretion to decrease from its peak late-pregnancy levels and after several months to return to pre-pregnancy levels even though the mother continues to nurse. Superimposed upon this basal level, however, are large secretory bursts of prolactin during each nursing period. The episodic pulses of prolactin are signals to the breasts for maintenance of milk production, which ceases several days after the mother completely stops nursing her infant but continues uninterrupted for years if nursing is continued.

The reflexes mediating the prolactin bursts (Figure 19-30) are initiated by afferent input to the hypothalamus from nipple receptors stimulated by suckling. This input's major effect is to stimulate the posterior pituitary neurons that secrete PRF.

One other reflex process is essential for nursing. Milk is secreted into the lumen of the alveoli, but the infant cannot suck the milk out of the alveoli. It must first be moved into the ducts, from which it can be sucked. This movement is called the **milk ejection reflex** (formerly called milk let-down) and is accomplished by contraction of the myoepithelial cells surrounding the alveoli. The contraction is under the control of oxytocin, which is reflexly released from posterior pituitary neurons in response to suckling (Figure 19-30), just like PRF. Higher brain centers can also exert an important influence over oxytocin release: A nursing mother may actually leak milk when she hears her baby cry or even thinks about nursing.

Another neuroendocrine reflex triggered by suckling (it may be mediated, in part, by prolactin) is inhibition of the hypothalamic-pituitary-ovarian chain at a variety of steps, with a resultant block of ovulation. If suckling is continued at high frequency, ovulation can be delayed for years. When supplements are added to the baby's diet and the frequency of suckling is decreased, however, most women will resume ovulation even though they continue to lactate. Failure to recognize this fact may result in an unplanned pregnancy.

Milk contains four major constituents: water, protein, fat, and the carbohydrate lactose (milk sugar). The alveolar

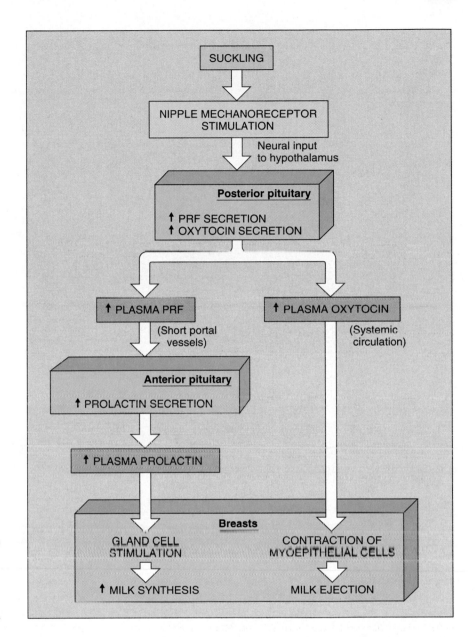

FIGURE 19-30

Major controls of the secretion of prolactin and oxytocin during nursing. In addition, the neural input to the hypothalamus may also inhibit the neurons that release dopamine from the posterior pituitary, and this would further stimulate prolactin secretion.

cells must be capable of extracting the raw materials—amino acids, fatty acids, glycerol, glucose, and so on—from the blood and building them into the higher-molecular-weight substances. Although prolactin is the single most important hormone controlling these synthetic processes, insulin, growth hormone, cortisol, and still other hormones also participate.

Milk also contains antibodies that are important for the newborn, as described in Chapter 20. Unfortunately, infectious agents, including the virus that causes AIDS (Chapter 20), can be transmitted through breast milk, as can some drugs. For example, the concentration of alcohol in breast milk is approximately the same as in maternal plasma.

Breast feeding for the first 3 to 6 months of an infant's life is advocated by the medical community. In less developed countries, where alternative formulas are often either contaminated or nutritionally inadequate because of improper dilution or refrigeration, breast feeding significantly reduces infant sickness and mortality. In the United States, effects on infant survival are not usually apparent, but the practice is economical, may reduce the severity of gastrointestinal infections, and has positive effects on the mother-infant interaction.

Contraception

About two-thirds of all American women between the ages of 15 and 44 use some method of fertility control (***contra-***

TABLE 19-11 SUMMARY OF CONTRACEPTIVE METHODS IN THE UNITED STATES*

Type and estimated percentage of use	First-year failure rate†	Advantages	Disadvantages	Comments
Surgical sterilization (vasectomy in male; tubal ligation in female) (33%)	0%	Safe, highly effective, and inexpensive over long term. Frees couples from concern associated with the use of other methods.	Requires surgery. May not be reversible.	Vasectomy is performed under local anesthesia. Tubal ligation is performed vaginally or abdominally under local or general anesthesia.
Birth control pill (oral contraceptive) (32%)	2%	Most effective reversible contraceptive. Results in lighter, more regular periods. Protects against cancer of the ovaries and uterine lining. Decreases risk of pelvic inflammatory disease, fibrocystic breast disease, and benign ovarian cysts.	Minor side effects similar to early pregnancy (nausea, breast tenderness, fluid retention) during first 3 months of use. Major complications (blood clots, hypertension) may occur in a very small number of smokers and those over 35. Controversial as to whether breast cancer is increased. Must be taken on a regular daily schedule.	Combination types contain both synthetic estrogen and progestagen. Minipill contains only progestagen and may produce irregular bleeding. Available by prescription only.
Injectable progestagens (Norplant) (Depo-Provera) (?)	1%	Long-lasting (5 yr for Norplant; 3 months for Depo-Provera).	Norplant: Prolonged menstruation; spotting. Headaches and mood changes also reported. Depo-Provera: Menstrual irregularities; ?increased risk of osteoporosis and breast cancer.	Most recently approved methods.
Intrauterine device (IUD) (3%)	5%	Once inserted, usually stays in place. Remains effective for 1–4 years.	May cause bleeding and cramping. Increased risk of pelvic inflammatory disease. If pregnancy occurs, increased risk that it may be ectopic. Must check for placement after each period. Requires annual replacement.	Available by prescription only.

ception[11]) (Table 19-11). Some forms—vasectomy, tubal ligation, vaginal diaphragms, vaginal caps, spermicides, and condoms—prevent sperm from reaching the egg. In addition, condoms significantly reduce the risk of *sexually transmitted diseases (STDs)* such as AIDS, syphilis, gonorrhea, chlamydia, and herpes.

In contrast, *oral contraceptives* are based on the fact that estrogen and progesterone can inhibit pituitary gonadotropin release, thereby preventing ovulation. One type is a combination of a synthetic estrogen and a progesterone-like substance (a progestagen or progestin). Another type is the so-called minipill, which contains only the progesterone-like substance. In actuality, oral contracep-

[11]In some usages, the term "contraception" is restricted to fertility control by the prevention of conception, that is, the union of the egg and sperm, and "abortifacient" is used to denote fertility control by interference with the pregnancy at any point beyond conception.

TABLE 19-11   SUMMARY OF CONTRACEPTIVE METHODS IN THE UNITED STATES* (continued)

Type and estimated percentage of use	First-year failure rate†	Advantages	Disadvantages	Comments
Condom (rubber, prophylactic, sheath) (17%)	10%	Protects against sexually transmitted diseases, including AIDS and herpes. May protect against cervical cancer.	Must be applied immediately before intercourse. Rare cases of allergy to rubber. May break. Blunting of sensation.	More effective when the woman uses a spermicide.
Vaginal spermicide (foams, jellies) (2%)	18% (used alone)	Available over the counter as jellies, foam, creams, and suppositories.	Messiness. Must be applied no more than 1 h before intercourse.	Best results occur when used with a condom or diaphragm.
Diaphragm (5%)	15% (with spermicide)	Can be inserted up to 6 h before intercourse.	Increased risk of urinary tract infection. Rare cases of allergy to rubber.	Use with spermicide is recommended. Available by prescription only and must be fitted. Must be left in for 6–8 h after intercourse.
Cervical cap (?)	15% (with spermicide)	Can be inserted several days before intercourse. Is smaller than a diaphragm.	Some women find it difficult to insert. Can cause an unpleasant odor.	Must be left in place for 6–8 h after intercourse but not more than 48 h.
Vaginal sponge (3%)	15%	Easy to use because spermicide is self-contained. May be inserted as much as (but no more than) 24 h before intercourse.	May be hard to remove; may fragment. May irritate vaginal lining. Higher failure rate in women who have given birth.	Must be left in for 6 h after intercourse.

*Coitus interruptus (withdrawal) and periodic abstinence from sexual intercourse around the time of ovulation (rhythm method) are not included because of their high failure rate.

†For all methods, most of the failures are due to improper or inconsistent use. It is likely that oral contraceptives, the IUD, and condoms are 99 to 100 percent effective when properly used; the others are 90 to 95 percent effective.

Source: Table adapted from University of California, Berkeley, *Wellness Letter*, 1987, and *New England Journal of Medicine*, 320:777–786, 1989.

tives, particularly the minipill, do not always prevent ovulation yet still are effective because they have other antifertility effects. For example, the progestagen component inhibits the estrogen-induced proliferation of the endometrium, making it inhospitable for implantation. In addition, the progestagen affects the composition of the cervical mucus, preventing passage of sperm through the cervix.

A newer method of delivering contraceptive progesterone-like steroids is via tiny capsules (Norplant) that are implanted beneath the skin and last for 5 years. Still more recent is the injection of yet another progesterone-like substance (Depo-Provera) every 3 months.

Not available in the United States but widely used in France and China is the drug RU 486, which has anti-progesterone activity because it binds competitively to progesterone receptors but does not activate them. Administration of RU 486, followed by a prostaglandin derivative, is an extremely effective and safe method for terminating pregnancy within 7 weeks of conception. Antagonism of progesterone's effects causes the endometrium to erode and the myometrial contractions to increase, thereby expelling the embryo.

The ***intrauterine device (IUD)***, like RU 486, also works beyond the point of fertilization. The presence of one of these small objects in the uterus somehow interferes with the endometrial preparation for acceptance of the blastocyst.

The rhythm method uses abstention from sexual inter-

estriol
placental lactogen
parturition
afterbirth
oxytocin
mammary glands
lactation

alveoli
myoepithelial cells
dopamine
prolactin releasing factor (PRF)
milk ejection reflex

SECTION C REVIEW QUESTIONS

1. Draw the female reproductive tract.
2. Describe the various stages from oogonium to mature ovum.
3. Describe the progression from a primordial follicle to a dominant follicle.
4. Name three hormones produced by the ovaries and name the cells that produce them.
5. Diagram the changes in plasma concentrations of estrogen, progesterone, LH, and FSH during the menstrual cycle.
6. What are the analogies between the granulosa cells and the Sertoli cells and between the theca cells and the Leydig cells?
7. List the effects of FSH and LH on the follicle.
8. Describe the effects of estrogen and inhibin on gonadotropin secretion during the early, middle, and late follicular phases.
9. List the effects of the LH surge on the egg and the follicle.
10. What are the effects of the sex steroids and inhibin on gonadotropin secretion during the luteal phase?
11. Describe the hormonal control of the corpus luteum and its history in a nonpregnant cycle.
12. What happens to the sex steroids and the gonadotropins as the corpus luteum degenerates?
13. Compare the phases of the menstrual cycle according to uterine and ovarian events.

14. Describe the effects of estrogen and progesterone on the endometrium, cervical mucus, and myometrium.
15. Describe the uterine events associated with menstruation.
16. List the effects of estrogen on the accessory sex organs and secondary sex characteristics.
17. List the effects of progesterone on the breasts and body temperature.
18. What are the source and effects of androgens in women?
19. How does the egg get from the ovary to a uterine tube?
20. Where does fertilization normally occur?
21. Describe the events that occur during fertilization.
22. How many days after ovulation does implantation occur, and in what stage is the conceptus at that time?
23. Describe the components of the placenta and the mechanisms of exchange between maternal and fetal blood.
24. State the sources of estrogen and progesterone during different stages of pregnancy. What is the dominant estrogen of pregnancy, and how is it produced?
25. What is the state of gonadotropin secretion during pregnancy, and what is the cause?
26. What anatomical feature permits coordinated contractions of the myometrium?
27. Describe the mechanisms and messengers that contribute to parturition.
28. List the effects of prostaglandins on the female reproductive system.
29. Describe the development of the breasts after puberty and during pregnancy and list the hormones responsible.
30. Describe the effects of estrogen on the secretion and actions of prolactin during pregnancy.
31. Diagram the suckling reflex for prolactin release.
32. Diagram the milk ejection reflex.

SECTION

THE CHRONOLOGY OF REPRODUCTIVE FUNCTION

This section treats a variety of topics that have to do, in one way or another, with sequential changes in reproductive development or function. Thus, genetic inheritance, which sets the sex of the individual—**sex determination**—is established at the moment of fertilization. This is followed by **sex differentiation**, the multiple processes in which development of the reproductive system occurs in the fetus. Then there is the maturation of the system at puberty and the eventual decline that occurs with aging.

SEX DETERMINATION

One's sex is determined by genetic inheritance of two chromosomes called the **sex chromosomes**. The larger of the sex chromosomes is called the **X chromosome** and the smaller, the **Y chromosome**. Males possess one X and one Y, whereas females have two X chromosomes. Thus, the *genetic* difference between male and female is simply the difference in one chromosome.

The reason for the approximately equal sex distribution of the population should be readily apparent: The ovum can contribute only an X chromosome, whereas half of the sperm produced during meiosis are X and half are Y. When the sperm and egg join, 50 percent should have XX and 50 percent XY. Interestingly, however, sex ratios at birth are not exactly 1:1; rather, for unclear reasons, there tends to be a slight preponderance of male births.

An easy method exists for determining whether a person's cells contain two X chromosomes, the normal female pattern. When two X chromosomes are present, only one functions; the nonfunctional X chromosome condenses to form a nuclear mass, termed the **sex chromatin**, that is readily observable with a light microscope (scrapings from the cheek mucosa are a convenient source of cells to be examined). The single X chromosome in male cells rarely condenses to form sex chromatin.

A more exacting technique for determining sex chromosome composition employs tissue culture visualization of all the chromosomes—a **karyotype**. This technique has revealed a group of genetic sex abnormalities characterized by such unusual chromosomal combinations as XXX, XXY, X, and others. The end result of such combinations is usually the failure of normal anatomical and functional sexual development.

SEX DIFFERENTIATION

It is not surprising that people with abnormal genetic endowment manifest abnormal sexual development, but careful study has also revealed individuals with normal chromosomal combinations but abnormal sexual appearance and function. In these people, sex differentiation has been abnormal, and their appearance may even be at odds with their genetic sex, that is, the presence of XX or XY chromosomes.

It will be important to bear in mind during the following description one essential generalization: The genes directly determine only whether the individual will have testes or ovaries. All the rest of sex differentiation depends upon the presence or absence of substances, such as the sex hormones, produced by the genetically determined gonads.

Differentiation of the Gonads

The male and female gonads derive embryologically from the same site in the body. Until the sixth week of uterine life, there is no differentiation of this site. In the genetic male the testes begin to develop during the seventh week. A single gene (the **SRY gene**) on the Y chromosome determines this development. In the absence of a Y chromosome and, hence, the SRY gene, testes do not develop and, instead, ovaries begin to develop at about 11 weeks.

Differentiation of Internal and External Genitalia

As far as its internal duct system and external genitalia are concerned, the fetus is capable of developing into either sex. Before the functioning of the fetal gonads, the primitive reproductive tract includes a double genital duct system—**Wolffian ducts** and **Müllerian ducts**—and a common opening for the genital ducts and urinary system to the outside. Normally, most of the reproductive tract develops from only one of these duct systems: In the male, the Wolffian ducts persist and the Müllerian ducts regress, whereas in the female, the opposite happens. The external genitalia in the two sexes and the vagina do not develop from these duct systems but from other structures at the body surface.

Which of the two duct systems and types of external genitalia develops depends on the presence or absence of fetal testes. If testes are present, they secrete (1) testosterone, from the Leydig cells under stimulation by chorionic gonadotropin secreted by the placenta, and (2) a protein called **Müllerian inhibiting factor (MIF)**, from the Sertoli cells. MIF acts as a paracrine agent to cause the Müllerian duct system to degenerate, and testosterone causes the Wolffian ducts to differentiate into the epididymis, vas deferens, ejaculatory duct, and seminal vesicle. Externally and somewhat later, under the influence of testosterone, after conversion to dihydrotestosterone, a penis forms and the tissue near it fuses to form the scrotum, into which the testes will ultimately descend, stimulated to do so by both MIF and testosterone (Figure 19-31A).

In contrast, the female fetus, lacking testes and thus testosterone and MIF, develops uterine tubes and a uterus from the Müllerian system as well as a vagina and female external genitalia from the structures at the body surface (Figure 19-31B). A female gonad need not be present for the female organs to develop; in other words, female development will occur automatically unless stopped from doing so by the presence of secretions from functioning testes.

There is a variety of conditions in which normal sex differentiation does not occur. For example, in the syn-

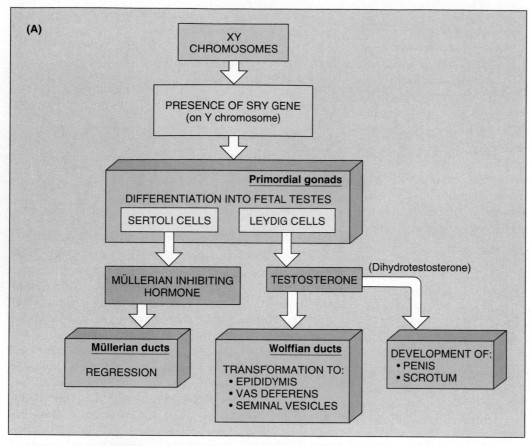

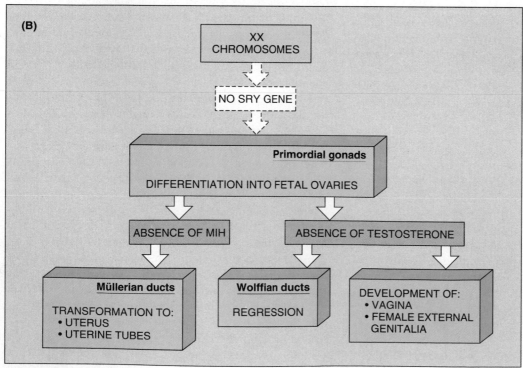

FIGURE 19-31

Sex differentiation. (A) Male. (B) Female.

drome known as *testicular feminization* (or androgen insensitivity syndrome), the person's genetic endowment is XY and testes are present, but he has female external genitalia, a vagina, and no internal duct system at all. The problem causing this is a lack of androgen receptors due to a genetic defect. The fetal testes differentiate as usual, and they secrete both MIF and testosterone. MIF causes the Müllerian ducts to regress, but the inability of the Wolffian ducts to respond to testosterone also causes them to regress, and so no duct system develops. The tissues that give rise to external genitalia (and the vagina, in the female) are also unresponsive to testosterone, and so female external genitalia and a vagina develop rather than male structures.

Sexual Differentiation of the Central Nervous System

In humans and other primates there are no inherent male-female differences in the ability of the hypothalamus to secrete GnRH in response to neuronal or hormonal inputs. For example, administration of large amounts of estrogen to castrated male monkeys elicits LH surges indistinguishable from those shown by females.

The situation may be different for sexual *behavior*, however, in that differences in the brain may be formed during development. For example, genetic female monkeys given testosterone during late fetal life manifest evidence of masculine sex behavior (mounting, for example) as adults.

In this regard, a potentially important difference in brain anatomy has recently been reported for people: The size of a particular nucleus (neuronal cluster) in the hypothalamus is more than twice as large in men as in women. Interest in this difference soared when a subsequent study showed that the nucleus is also more than twice as large in heterosexual men as in homosexual men. A similar sexually dimorphic area exists in rats, in which it is known to be involved in male-type sexual behavior and is influenced during development by testosterone. Evaluation of the meaning of these findings for the genetics and hormone dependency of sexual behavior and gender preference will await much more research. Another relevant human study that has gained much attention reported that 52 percent of identical twin brothers of gay men also were gay, compared to 22 percent of fraternal twins and 11 percent of genetically unrelated (adoptive) brothers.

PUBERTY

Puberty is the period, usually occurring sometime between the ages of 10 and 14, during which the reproductive organs, having differentiated many years earlier in utero, mature and reproduction becomes possible.

In the female, GnRH, the pituitary gonadotropins, and estrogen are all secreted at very low levels during childhood. Accordingly, follicle maturation and menstrual cycles do not occur, the female accessory sex organs remain small and nonfunctional, and there are minimal secondary sex characteristics. The onset of puberty is caused, in large part, by an alteration in brain function that raises secretion of GnRH. This hypophysiotropic hormone in turn stimulates secretion of pituitary gonadotropins, which stimulate follicle development and estrogen secretion. Estrogen, in addition to its critical role in follicle development, induces the striking changes in the accessory sex organs and secondary sex characteristics associated with puberty.

The picture for the male is analogous to that for the female. Increased GnRH secretion at puberty causes increased secretion of pituitary gonadotropins, which stimulate the seminiferous tubules and testosterone secretion. Testosterone, in addition to its critical role in spermatogenesis, induces the pubertal changes in the accessory reproductive organs, secondary sex characteristics, and sex drive.

The mechanism of the brain change that results in increased GnRH secretion at puberty remains unknown.[12] Whatever the mechanism, the process is not abrupt but develops over several years, as evidenced by slowly rising plasma concentrations of the gonadotropins and testosterone or estrogen.

It should be recognized that the maturational events of puberty usually proceed in an orderly sequence but that the ages at which they occur may vary among individuals. In girls, the onset of breast development is usually the first event, beginning at an average age of 11, although pubic hair may, on occasion, appear first. **Menarche**, the first menstrual period, is a later event (average of 12.3 years) and occurs almost invariably after the peak of the total-body growth spurt has passed.

In boys, the first sign of puberty is accelerated growth of testes and scrotum. Pubic hair appears a trifle later, and axillary and facial hair still later. Acceleration of penis growth begins on the average at 13 years and is complete by 15.

Some children with brain tumors or other lesions of the hypothalamus may undergo precocious puberty, that is, sexual maturation at an unusually early age, sometimes within the first 5 years of life. The youngest mother on record gave birth to a full-term, healthy infant by caesarean section (abdominal incision) at 5 years, 8 months.

---

[12]One proposed candidate for the trigger is a decrease in secretion of the hormone melatonin by the pineal gland, but there is no convincing evidence for this hypothesis in humans. Another theory is that the brain becomes less sensitive to the negative feedback effects of gonadal hormones at the time of puberty.

MENOPAUSE

Around the age of 50, on the average, menstrual cycles become less regular. Ultimately they cease entirely, and this cessation is known as the **menopause**. The phase of life beginning with menstrual irregularity and culminating in menopause is known as the **climacteric**, the counterpart of puberty. It involves numerous physical and emotional changes as sexual maturity gives way to cessation of reproductive function.

Menopause and the irregular function leading to it are caused by ovarian failure. The ovaries lose their ability to respond to the gonadotropins, partly because of a decreasing number of follicles and partly because the remaining follicles are hyporesponsive. That the hypothalamus and anterior pituitary are functioning relatively normally is evidenced by the fact that the gonadotropins are secreted in greater amounts in response to the decreasing plasma estrogen levels.

Although some ovarian secretion of estrogen generally continues beyond menopause, as does peripheral conversion of adrenal androgens to estrogen, plasma estrogen gradually diminishes until it is inadequate to maintain the estrogen-dependent tissues. The breasts and genital organs gradually atrophy to a large degree. Thinning and dryness of the vaginal epithelium can cause sexual intercourse to be painful. Marked decreases in bone mass and strength, termed *osteoporosis*, may occur because of bone resorption and can result in bone fractures (Chapter 16). Sex drive frequently stays the same and may even increase. The hot flashes so typical of menopause are accompanied by dilation of the skin arterioles, a feeling of warmth, and marked sweating, but why estrogen deficiency causes this is unknown. Another aspect of menopause is its relationship to cardiovascular diseases. Women have much less coronary artery disease than men until after the menopause, when the incidence becomes similar in both sexes (see Chapter 18 for estrogen's effects on plasma cholesterol).

Most of the symptoms associated with menopause, as well as the increases in osteoporosis and coronary artery disease, can be reduced by the administration of estrogen. The desirability of such administration is controversial, however, because of the fact that estrogen administration definitely increases the risk of developing uterine (endometrial) cancer and, possibly, breast cancer as well. This risk of cancer can be reduced, however, by administration of a progestagen along with estrogen, but there is some question as to whether the progestagen might eliminate some of estrogen's protective effect against coronary artery disease. Because of these complexities, quantitation of the competing risks and benefits of estrogen replacement therapy, with and without added progestagen, must await the completion of the large controlled studies presently underway in postmenopausal women.

Changes in the male reproductive system with aging are less drastic than those in women. Once testosterone and pituitary gonadotropin secretions are initiated at puberty, they continue, at least to some extent, throughout adult life. There is a steady decrease, however, in testosterone secretion, beginning at about the age of 40, which apparently reflects slow deterioration of testicular function and, as in the female, failure of the gonads to respond to the pituitary gonadotropins. Along with the decreasing testosterone levels, both sex drive and capacity diminish, although many men continue to be fertile in their seventies and eighties.

With aging, some men manifest increased emotional problems, such as depression, and this is sometimes referred to as "male menopause" (or male climacteric). It is not clear, however, what role hormone changes play in this phenomenon.

SECTION D SUMMARY

SEX DETERMINATION AND SEX DIFFERENTIATION

I. Sex is determined by the two sex chromosomes: Males are XY, and females are XX.

II. A gene on the Y chromosome is responsible for the development of testes. In the absence of a Y chromosome, testes do not develop and ovaries do instead.

III. When a functioning male gonad is present to secrete testosterone and MIF, a male reproductive tract and external genitalia develop. In the absence of testes, the female system develops.

PUBERTY

I. At puberty, the hypothalamic-anterior-pituitary-gonadal chain of hormones becomes active as the result of a change in brain function that permits increased secretion of GnRH.

II. In girls the first sign of puberty is either the beginning of breast development or appearance of pubic hair. In boys it is acceleration of growth of the testes and scrotum.

MENOPAUSE

I. Around the age of 50, a woman's menstrual periods

become less regular and ultimately disappear—menopause.

    A. The cause of menopause is a decrease in the number of ovarian follicles and their hyporesponsiveness to the gonadotropins.

    B. The symptoms of menopause are largely due to the marked decrease in plasma estrogen concentration.

II. Men show a steady decrease in testosterone secretion after age 40 but generally no complete cessation of reproductive function.

SECTION D KEY TERMS

sex determination	Wolffian ducts
sex differentiation	Müllerian ducts
sex chromosomes	Müllerian inhibiting factor (MIF)
X chromosome	puberty
Y chromosome	menarche
sex chromatin	menopause
karyotype	climacteric
SRY gene	

SECTION D REVIEW QUESTIONS

1. State the genetic difference between males and females and a method for identifying genetic sex.

2. Describe the sequence of events, the timing, and the control of the development of the gonads and the internal and external genitalia.

3. What is the state of gonadotropin and sex hormone secretion before puberty?

4. What is the state of estrogen and gonadotropin secretion after menopause?

5. List the hormonal and anatomical changes that occur after menopause.

CHAPTER 19 CLINICAL TERMS

vasectomy	malnutrition
castration	toxemia of pregnancy
impotence	pregnancy sickness
dysmenorrhea	contraception
premenstrual syndrome (PMS)	sexually transmitted
ectopic pregnancies	diseases (STDs)
amniocentesis	oral contraceptives
chorionic villus sampling	intrauterine device

in vitro fertilization   testicular feminization
osteoporosis

CHAPTER 19 THOUGHT QUESTIONS

(Answers are given in Appendix A.)

1. What symptom will be common to a person whose Leydig cells have been destroyed and to a person whose Sertoli cells have been destroyed? What symptom will not be common?

2. A male athlete taking large amounts of an androgenic steroid becomes sterile (unable to produce sperm capable of causing fertilization). Explain.

3. A man who is sterile is found to have no evidence of demasculinization. He has an increased blood concentration of FSH and a normal plasma concentration of LH. What is the most likely basis of his sterility?

4. If you were a scientist trying to develop a male contraceptive acting on the anterior pituitary, would you try to block the secretion of FSH or that of LH? Explain the reason for your choice.

5. A 30-year-old man has very small muscles, a sparse beard, and a high-pitched voice. His plasma concentration of LH is elevated. Explain the likely cause of all these findings.

6. There are disorders of the adrenal cortex in which excessive amounts of androgens are produced. If this occurs in a woman, what will happen to her menstrual cycles?

7. Women with inadequate secretion of GnRH are often treated for their sterility with drugs that mimic the action of this hormone. Can you suggest a possible reason that such treatment often is associated with multiple births?

8. Which of the following would be a signal that ovulation is soon to occur: the cervical mucus becoming thick and sticky, an increase in body temperature, a marked rise in plasma LH?

9. The absence of what phenomenon would interfere with the ability of sperm obtained by masturbation to fertilize an egg in a test tube?

10. If a woman 7 months pregnant is found to have a marked decrease in plasma estriol but a normal plasma progesterone for that time of pregnancy, what would you conclude?

11. What types of drugs might you work on if you were trying to develop one to stop premature labor?

12. If a genetic male failed to produce MIF during in utero life, what would the result be?

13. Could the symptoms of menopause be treated by injections of FSH and LH?

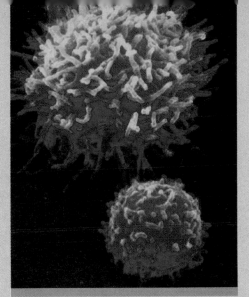

CHAPTER
20

DEFENSE MECHANISMS OF THE BODY

SECTION A. IMMUNOLOGY: DEFENSES AGAINST FOREIGN MATTER

CELLS MEDIATING IMMUNE DEFENSES

NONSPECIFIC IMMUNE DEFENSES

Defenses at Body Surfaces

Inflammation

   Vasodilation and increased permeability to protein

   Chemotaxis

   Killing by phagocytes

   Complement

   Tissue repair

Interferon

SPECIFIC IMMUNE DEFENSES

Overview

Lymphoid Organs and Lymphocyte Types

   Lymphoid organs

   Lymphocyte origins

Functions of B Cells and T Cells

Lymphocyte Receptors

   B-cell receptors

   T-cell receptors

Antigen Presentation to T Cells

   Presentation to helper T cells

   Presentation to cytotoxic T cells

NK Cells

Development of Immune Tolerance

Antibody-Mediated Immune Responses: Defenses Against Bacteria, Extracellular Viruses, and Toxins

   B-cell recognition and activation

   Antibody secretion

   The attack: Effects of antibodies

   Active and passive humoral immunity

   Summary

Defenses Against Virus-Infected Cells and Cancer Cells

   Role of cytotoxic T cells

   Role of NK cells and activated macrophages

   Immunotherapy against cancer

SYSTEMIC MANIFESTATIONS OF INFECTION

FACTORS THAT ALTER THE BODY'S RESISTANCE TO INFECTION

AIDS

Antibiotics

HARMFUL IMMUNE RESPONSES

Graft Rejection

Transfusion Reactions

Allergy (Hypersensitivity)

   Immediate hypersensitivity

Autoimmune Disease

Excessive Inflammatory Responses to Microbes

SECTION A SUMMARY

SECTION A KEY TERMS

SECTION A REVIEW QUESTIONS

SECTION B. NONIMMUNE METABOLISM OF FOREIGN CHEMICALS

ABSORPTION

STORAGE SITES

EXCRETION

BIOTRANSFORMATION

SECTION B SUMMARY

SECTION B KEY TERMS

SECTION B REVIEW QUESTIONS

SECTION C. HEMOSTASIS: THE PREVENTION OF BLOOD LOSS

FORMATION OF A PLATELET PLUG

BLOOD COAGULATION: CLOT FORMATION

ANTICLOTTING SYSTEMS

Factors That Oppose Clot Formation

The Fibrinolytic System

ANTICLOTTING DRUGS

SECTION C SUMMARY

SECTION C KEY TERMS

SECTION C REVIEW QUESTIONS

SECTION D. RESISTANCE TO STRESS

FUNCTIONS OF CORTISOL IN STRESS

FUNCTIONS OF THE SYMPATHETIC NERVOUS SYSTEM IN STRESS

OTHER HORMONES RELEASED DURING STRESS

SECTION D SUMMARY

SECTION D KEY TERMS

SECTION D REVIEW QUESTIONS

CHAPTER 20 CLINICAL TERMS

CHAPTER 20 THOUGHT QUESTIONS

SECTION

IMMUNOLOGY: DEFENSES AGAINST FOREIGN MATTER

mmunology is the study of the physiological responses by which the body destroys or neutralizes foreign matter, both living and nonliving. In distinguishing "self" from "nonself," immune responses (1) protect against infection by **microbes**—viruses, bacteria, fungi, and parasites; (2) isolate or remove nonmicrobial foreign substances; and (3) destroy cancer cells that arise in the body, a function known as **immune surveillance**.

Immune defenses (also termed simply immunity) can be classified into two categories—nonspecific and specific—which interact with each other. **Nonspecific immune defenses** protect against foreign substances or cells without having to recognize their specific identities. **Specific immune defenses** depend upon recognition of the substance or cell to be attacked.

Before introducing the cells that participate in immune defenses, let us first look at the microbes we shall be most concerned with in this chapter—bacteria and viruses. These are the dominant infectious organisms in the United States and other industrialized nations. On a global basis, however, infection with parasitic protozoans (malaria, for example) or worms are responsible for considerable illness and mortality. For example, over 600 million people presently suffer from malaria.

Bacteria are unicellular organisms (prokaryocytes, Chapter 3) that have an outer coating, the cell wall, in addition to a plasma membrane, but no intracellular membrane-bound organelles. Infectious bacteria may replicate at their initial site of entry or they may travel via the blood or lymph to other areas before significant replication occurs. Bacteria can damage tissues at their sites of replication, or they can release into the extracellular fluid toxins that are carried by the blood and disrupt physiological functions in other parts of the body.

Viruses are essentially nucleic acids surrounded by a protein coat. Unlike bacteria, which can carry out metabolic activity and replicate independent of other cells, viruses lack both the enzyme machinery for energy production and the ribosomes essential for protein synthesis. Thus, they cannot multiply by themselves but must "live" inside other cells whose biochemical apparatus they make use of. The viral nucleic acid directs the host cell to synthesize the proteins required for viral replication, with the required nucleotides and energy sources also being supplied by the host cell.

The effect of viral habitation and replication within a cell depends on the type of virus. Some viruses (the common cold virus, for example), after entering a cell, multiply rapidly, kill the cell, and then move on to other cells. Others, such as the virus that causes genital herpes, can lie dormant in infected cells before suddenly undergoing the rapid replication that causes cell damage. Still others, termed slow viruses, replicate inside their host cells very slowly, and the viral nucleic acid may even become associated with the cell's own DNA molecules, replicating along with them and being passed on to the daughter cells during cell division. Such a virus [the one that causes AIDS (acquired immune deficiency syndrome), for example] may remain in the cell or the cell's offspring for many years, replicating very slowly until it reaches numbers that cause disease. Finally, certain viruses cause transformation of their host cells into cancer cells.

CELLS MEDIATING IMMUNE DEFENSES

The cells that carry out immune responses are collectively termed the **immune system**, but they do not constitute a "system" in the sense of anatomically connected organs like the gastrointestinal or urinary system. Rather, they are a diverse collection of cells found both in the blood and in tissues throughout the body. The major cell types are listed in Table 20-1, along with their sites of production. Because of the large number of cells and the far larger number of chemical messengers that participate in immune responses, a miniglossary defining the cells and messengers discussed in this chapter is given at the end of Section A (Table 20-12).

The most numerous of the immune-system cells are the **leukocytes**. Their anatomy, origin in the bone marrow, and distribution in blood were described in Chapter 14, Section A, and should be reviewed at this time. Unlike erythrocytes, the leukocytes use the blood mainly for transportation and leave the circulatory system to enter the tissues and function there. In this regard, the lymphocytes are the most complex of the leukocytes, and we shall delay until a subsequent section the description of the var-

TABLE 20-1 CELLS MEDIATING IMMUNE RESPONSES

Name	Site produced
Leukocytes (white blood cells)	
Neutrophils	Bone marrow
Basophils	Bone marrow
Eosinophils	Bone marrow
Monocytes	Bone marrow
Lymphocytes	Bone marrow, thymus, and peripheral lymphoid organs
B cells	
T cells	
Cytotoxic T cells	
Helper T cells	
Suppressor T cells	
NK cells	
Plasma cells	Peripheral lymphoid organs; differentiate from B lymphocytes during immune responses
Macrophages	Almost all tissues and organs; differentiate from monocytes
Mast cells	Almost all tissues and organs; differentiate from bone marrow cells

ious classes and subclasses of lymphocytes, their origins, migrations, and major organs of residence—the lymphoid organs.

Plasma cells are not a distinct cell line but differentiate from a particular set of lymphocytes (the B lymphocytes) during immune responses. Despite their name, plasma cells are not usually found in the blood but rather in the tissues in which they have differentiated from lymphocytes. The major function of plasma cells is to synthesize and secrete antibodies.

Macrophages are large cells found in virtually all organs and tissues, their structures varying somewhat from location to location. They are derived from monocytes that pass out of blood vessels to enter the tissues and become transformed into macrophages. By the time of birth, this process has already supplied the tissues with a large number of tissue macrophages that occupy fixed positions, but the migration of monocytes continues throughout life. In keeping with one of their major functions, the engulfing of particles, including microbes, macrophages are strategically placed where they will encounter their targets. For example, they are found in large numbers in the various epithelia in contact with the external environment, and in several organs they line the vessels through which blood or lymph flows.

Mast cells are also found scattered throughout many organs and tissues. They are derived from the differentiation of as yet unidentified bone marrow cells that have entered the blood and then left the blood vessels to enter the tissues, where they can undergo cell division. The most striking anatomical feature of mast cells is a very large number of secretory vesicles, and these cells secrete many locally acting chemical messengers.

The functions of all these cells are briefly listed in Table 20-2 for reference and will be described in subsequent sections.

NONSPECIFIC IMMUNE DEFENSES

The nonspecific immune defenses—those that protect against foreign matter without having to recognize its identity—include defenses at the body surfaces, the response to injury known as inflammation, and a family of antiviral proteins called interferons. Another nonspecific defense—the lymphocytes called natural killer (NK) cells—is best described later in the context of the specific immune defenses that commonly mobilize them.

TABLE 20-2 MAJOR FUNCTIONS OF CELLS MEDIATING IMMUNE RESPONSES

Neutrophils	1. Phagocytosis 2. Release chemicals involved in inflammation (vasodilators, chemotaxins, etc.)
Basophils	Have functions in blood similar to those of mast cells in tissues (see below)
Eosinophils	1. Destroy parasitic worms 2. Participate in immediate hypersensitivity reactions
Monocytes	1. Have functions in blood similar to those of macrophages in tissues (see below) 2. Enter tissues and are transformed into macrophages
B cells	1. Initiate antibody-mediated immune responses by binding specific antigens to their plasma-membrane receptors, which are immunoglobulins 2. During activation are transformed into plasma cells, which secrete antibodies 3. Present antigen to helper T cells
Cytotoxic T cells	Bind to antigens on plasma membrane of target cells (virus-infected cells, cancer cells, and tissue transplants) and directly destroy the cells
Helper T cells	Secrete cytokines that activate B cells, cytotoxic T cells, NK cells, and macrophages
Suppressor T cells	Inhibit B cells and cytotoxic T cells
NK cells	1. Bind directly and nonspecifically to virus-infected cells and cancer cells and kill them 2. Function as killer cells in antibody-dependent cellular cytotoxicity (ADCC)
Plasma cells	Secrete antibodies
Macrophages	1. Phagocytosis and intracellular killing 2. Extracellular killing via secretion of toxic chemicals 3. Process and present antigens to helper T cells 4. Secrete cytokines involved in inflammation, activation of helper T cells, and systemic responses to infection or injury (the acute phase response)
Mast cells	Release histamine and other chemicals involved in inflammation

Defenses at Body Surfaces

The body's first lines of defense against microbes are the barriers offered by surfaces exposed to the external environment. Very few microorganisms can penetrate the intact skin, and the sweat, sebaceous, and lacrymal glands all secrete antimicrobial chemicals.

The mucus secreted by the epithelial linings of the respiratory and upper gastrointestinal tracts also contains antimicrobial chemicals, but more important, mucus is sticky. Particles that adhere to it are prevented from entering the blood. They are either swept by ciliary action up into the pharynx and then swallowed, as occurs in the upper respiratory tract, or are engulfed by macrophages in the various linings.

Other specialized surface defenses are the hairs at the entrance to the nose, the cough and sneeze reflexes, and the acid secretion of the stomach, which kills microbes. Finally, a major defense against infection are the many relatively innocuous microbes normally found on the skin and other linings exposed to the external environment. These microbes suppress the growth of other potentially more dangerous ones.

Inflammation

Inflammation is the body's local response to infection or injury. Although we will concentrate mainly on the non-specific inflammation induced by the invasion of *microbes*, most of the same responses can be elicited by a variety of other injuries—cold, heat, and trauma, for example. Regardless of cause, inflammation is relatively stereotyped since a major trigger is cell or tissue injury. The function of inflammation is to destroy or inactivate foreign invaders and/or set the stage for tissue repair.

The key actors in inflammation are **phagocytes**. This term denotes any cell capable of the form of endocytosis termed **phagocytosis**, whereby particulate matter is engulfed (Chapter 6). The engulfed matter is then usually destroyed inside the phagocyte. The most important phagocytes are neutrophils, monocytes, and macrophages.

In this section, we describe inflammation as it occurs in a *nonspecific* response. We shall see later that inflammation is also an important component of many specific immune responses, in which the inflammation becomes amplified and made more effective.

The sequence of local events in a typical nonspecific inflammatory response to a bacterial infection, due say to cutting oneself with a bacteria-covered knife, is summarized in Table 20-3. The familiar manifestations of tissue injury and inflammation are local redness, swelling, heat, and pain. The events of inflammation that underlie these manifestations are induced and regulated by a large number of chemical mediators produced by the body, as summarized in Table 20-4. Any given event of inflammation, vasodilation for example, may be induced by multiple

TABLE 20-3 SEQUENCE OF EVENTS IN A LOCAL INFLAMMATORY RESPONSE TO BACTERIA

1. Initial entry of bacteria into tissue
2. Vasodilation of the microcirculation in the infected area, leading to increased blood flow
3. Marked increase in protein permeability of the capillaries and venules in the infected area, with resulting diffusion of protein and filtration of fluid into the interstitial fluid, causing swelling
4. Exit of neutrophils and, later, of monocytes from the capillaries and venules into the interstitial fluid of the infected area
5. Destruction of bacteria in the tissue either through phagocytosis or by mechanisms not requiring prior phagocytosis
6. Tissue repair

mediators, and any given mediator may induce more than one event. Based on their origins, the mediators fall into two general categories: (1) substances released into the extracellular fluid from cells that either already exist in the infected area (mast cells, for example) or enter it during inflammation (neutrophils, for example); and (2) peptides (kinins, for example) generated in the infected area by the enzymatic splitting of proteins that circulate in the plasma. The stimuli for the release or generation of the mediators are microbial chemical substances or chemicals released by tissue cells that have interacted with and/or been damaged by the microbes.

Let us now go step by step through the process summarized in Table 20-3, assuming that the bacterial infection is localized to the tissue just beneath the skin and that the bacteria have not entered the blood. If entry into the blood or lymph were to occur, then similar inflammatory responses would take place in any other tissue or organ invaded by the blood-borne or lymph-borne bacteria. Also, microbes can be phagocytized by neutrophils and monocytes in the blood itself.

Vasodilation and Increased Permeability to Protein. A variety of chemical mediators dilate most of the microcirculation vessels in an infected and/or damaged area. The mediators also cause the local capillaries to become quite permeable to proteins by inducing the capillary endothelial cells to contract, opening spaces between them.

The adaptive value of these vascular changes is twofold: (1) The increased blood flow to the inflamed area—which accounts for the redness—increases the delivery of leukocytes; and (2) the increased capillary permeability to protein ensures that the plasma proteins that participate in

TABLE 20-4 SOME IMPORTANT LOCAL INFLAMMATORY MEDIATORS

Mediator	Source
Kinins	Plasma proteins
Complement	Plasma proteins
Products of blood clotting	Plasma proteins
Histamine	Mast cells
Eicosanoids	Many cell types
Platelet-activating factor	Many cell types
Interleukin 1, tumor necrosis factor, interleukin 6, and other cytokines	Monocytes, macrophages, lymphocytes, and several nonimmune cell types
Lysosomal enzymes, nitric oxide, and other oxygen-derived substances	Neutrophils and macrophages

inflammation—many of which are normally restrained by the intact capillary endothelium—can gain entry to the area.

As described in Chapter 14, the vasodilation and increased permeability to protein cause net filtration of plasma into the interstitial fluid and the formation of edema. This accounts for the swelling in an inflamed area, which is simply a consequence of the changes in the microcirculation and has no known adaptive value of its own.

Chemotaxis. Within 30 to 60 min of the onset of inflammation, circulating neutrophils begin to stick to the luminal surface of the endothelium of the capillaries and venules in the infected area. This occurs because several inflammatory mediators stimulate the endothelial cells to express on their surface "adhesion molecules," which can bind to other adhesion molecules displayed on the surface of the circulating neutrophils. A narrow projection of the neutrophil is then inserted into the space between two endothelial cells, and the entire neutrophil squeezes through the capillary wall and into the interstitial fluid. In this way, huge numbers of neutrophils migrate into the inflamed area and move toward the microbes.

But movement of leukocytes from the blood into the damaged area is not limited to neutrophils. Monocytes follow later and once in the tissue undergo the anatomical and functional changes that transform them to macrophages. Meanwhile, some of the macrophages already present in the tissue may become active.

The entire process whereby various phagocytes are attracted to the vicinity of invading microbes is known as **chemotaxis**, and any chemical mediator that can cause it is termed a **chemotaxin**.

Killing by Phagocytes. The initial step in phagocytosis is contact between the surfaces of the phagocyte and microbe. Such contact is not itself always sufficient to trigger engulfment, particularly with those bacteria that are surrounded by a thick polysaccharide capsule. As we shall see, chemical factors produced by the body can bind the phagocyte tightly to the microbe and markedly enhance phagocytosis. Any substance that does this is known as an **opsonin**, from the Greek word that means "to prepare for eating."

As the phagocyte engulfs the microbe (Figure 20-1), the internal, microbe-containing sac formed in this step is called a **phagosome**. The microbe remains in the phagosome, a layer of plasma membrane separating it from the phagocyte's cytosol. The phagosome membrane then makes contact with one of the phagocyte's lysosomes, which are filled with a variety of hydrolytic enzymes, the membranes of the two structures fuse, and the combined vesicles are now called the **phagolysosome**. Inside the phagolysosome, the microbe's macromolecules are broken down by the lysosomal enzymes. In addition, enzymes found in the phagolysosome membrane produce **nitric oxide** (from the amino acid arginine, Chapter 8), as well as hydrogen peroxide and other oxygen derivatives, all of which are extremely destructive toward macromolecules.

Intracellular destruction is not the only way phagocytes can kill microbes. The phagocytes also release their antimicrobial hydrolytic enzymes and oxygen derivatives into the *extracellular* fluid, where these chemicals can destroy the microbes without prior phagocytosis. (As we shall discuss later, these chemicals can also damage normal tissue.)

The phagocytes also secrete still other substances into the extracellular fluid (Figure 20-2), which function as in-

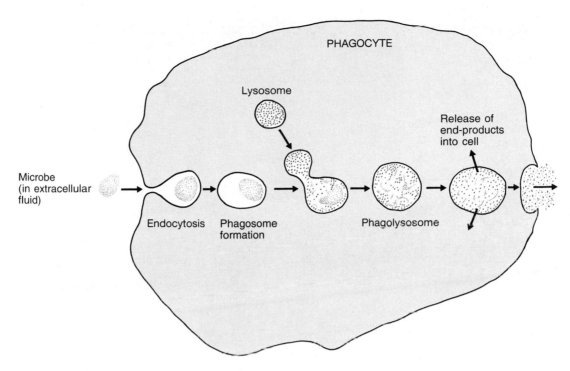

FIGURE 20-1

Phagocytosis and intracellular digestion of a microbe. The microbe is taken into the cell by endocytosis, and a membrane-bound phagosome is formed inside the phagocyte. The phagosome then merges with a lysosome, which brings together the digestive enzymes of the lysosome and the contents of the phagosome. After digestion has taken place in the phagolysosome, the end products are released to the outside of the cell by exocytosis or used by the cell for its own metabolism.

flammatory mediators. Thus, positive feedback occurs such that when more phagocytes enter the area and encounter microbes, more inflammatory mediators are released to bring in more phagocytes.

Complement. The family of proteins known as **complement** provides another means for killing microbes without prior phagocytosis. Certain of the complement proteins always circulate in the blood in an inactive state. Upon activation of one of the group in response to infection or damage, there occurs a cascade in which this active protein activates a second complement protein, which activates a third, and so on. In this way, multiple complement proteins are generated in the extracellular fluid of the infected areas from inactive precursors that have entered from the blood. Since this system consists of at least 20 distinct proteins, it is extremely complex, and we shall identify the roles of only a few of the individual proteins.

Five of the active proteins generated in the complement cascade form a complex, the **membrane attack complex (MAC)**, which embeds itself in the microbial plasma membrane. In this manner, channels are created in the membrane, making it leaky. Water and salts enter the microbe, which disrupts the intracellular ionic environment and kills the microbe.

In addition to supplying a means for direct killing of microbes, the complement system serves other important functions in inflammation (Figure 20-3). Some of the activated complement molecules along the cascade cause, either directly or indirectly by stimulating the release of other inflammatory mediators, vasodilation, increased capillary permeability to protein, and chemotaxis. Also, one of the complement molecules—C3b—acts as an opsonin to attach the phagocyte to the microbe (Figure 20-4).

As we shall see later, antibodies, a class of proteins secreted by lymphocytes, are required to activate the first protein (C1) in the full sequence known as the classical complement pathway, but lymphocytes are not involved in nonspecific inflammation. How, then, is the complement sequence initiated during nonspecific inflammation? The answer is that there is an **alternate complement pathway**, one that is not antibody-dependent and bypasses C1. The alternate pathway is initiated as the result of complex interactions between complement molecules beyond C1, several other plasma proteins, and polysaccharides on the surface of the foreign particles. The alternate pathway

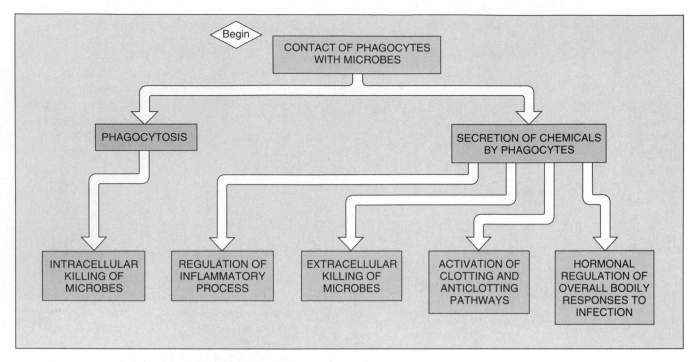

FIGURE 20-2

Role of phagocytes in nonspecific immune responses.

plugs into the classical pathway at the point of formation of C3b. Not all microbes have a surface conducive to initiating the alternate pathway.

Tissue Repair. The final stage of inflammation is tissue repair. Depending upon the tissue involved, multiplication of organ-specific cells by cell division may or may not occur during this stage. For example, liver cells multiply but neurons do not. In any case, fibroblasts (a type of connective-tissue cell) in the damaged area divide rapidly and begin to secrete large quantities of collagen. These events are brought about by chemical mediators, particularly a group of locally produced growth factors, for example, fibroblast growth factor.

FIGURE 20-3

Functions of complement proteins. The effects on blood vessels and chemotaxis are exerted both directly by complement molecules and indirectly via other inflammatory mediators (for example, histamine) whose release the complement molecules stimulate.

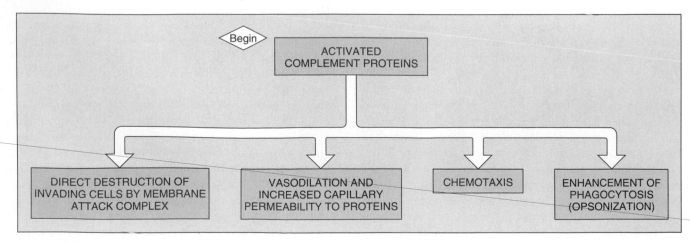

EXTRACELLULAR FLUID

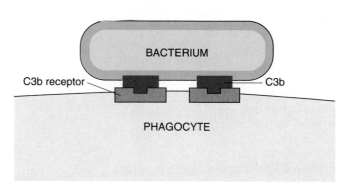

FIGURE 20-4

Function of complement C3b as an opsonin. One portion of this complement molecule binds nonspecifically to the surface of the microbe, whereas another portion binds to specific receptor sites for it on the plasma membrane of the phagocyte. The structures are not drawn to scale.

Interferon

Interferon refers collectively to a family of three proteins that *nonspecifically* inhibit viral replication inside host cells. In response to infection by a virus, various cell types secrete interferon into the extracellular fluid. Interferon then binds to plasma membrane receptors on nearby cells, whether they are infected or not (Figure 20-5). It also enters the circulation and reaches cells at far-removed

sites. Thus cells that can synthesize interferon provide it to cells that cannot.

How does interferon prevent viral replication? Its binding to the plasma membrane triggers the synthesis of several enzymes by the cell. If the cell is infected or eventually becomes infected, these enzymes block the synthesis of proteins the virus requires for replication. It must be reemphasized that interferon is not specific. Many, but not all, viruses induce interferon synthesis, and interferon in turn can inhibit the multiplication of many kinds of viruses.

SPECIFIC IMMUNE DEFENSES

Overview

Lymphocytes mediate specific immune defenses. Unlike nonspecific defense mechanisms, lymphocytes must recognize the specific foreign matter to be attacked. Any foreign molecule that can trigger a specific immune response against itself or the cell bearing it is termed an **antigen**.[1] Most antigens are either proteins or very large polysaccharides. The term "antigen" does not denote a specific struc-

---

[1]Terminology can be confusing here. Technically, a molecule that induces a specific immune response is an *immunogen*, whereas "antigen" refers to the ability of a molecule to react with the products of the response, particularly antibodies. Despite this, "antigen" is commonly used interchangeably with "immunogen," and we have adopted this practice.

FIGURE 20-5

Role of interferon in preventing viral replication. (A) Several cell types, when infected with virus, secrete interferon, which enters the interstitial fluid and blood and binds to interferon receptors on adjacent or far-removed cells (B). This induces synthesis of proteins (C) that inhibit viral replication should virus enter the cell (D). We have shown two cells acted upon by interferon to denote the amplification effect here: The interferon secreted by a single cell can stimulate many cells to produce antiviral proteins.

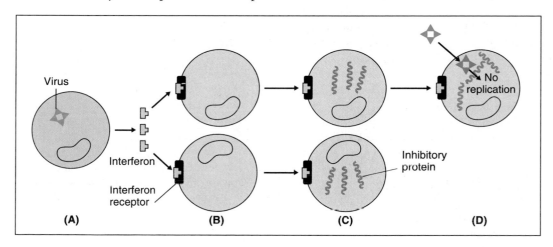

ture in the way that anatomical terms like "microtubule" and "integral membrane protein" do. Rather it is a functional term; that is, any molecule, no matter what its function may otherwise be, that can induce a specific immune response is by definition an antigen. It is the ability of lymphocytes to distinguish one antigen from another that confers specificity upon the immune responses in which they participate.

A common example of an antigen is ragweed pollen, the antigen that causes the specific immune response we know as hay fever. In other cases the antigen is part of the surface of a cell—microbe, virus-infected body cell, tumor cell, or transplanted cell—that appears in the body. The reason for saying "appears in" rather than "enters" is that, as we shall see, body cells, themselves, produce the "foreign" molecules that act as antigens on tumor cells and virus-infected cells. These molecules are foreign in the sense that they are not present in normal cells. As we shall see, normal cells can be transformed in still other ways and, as a result, possess components that can serve as antigens.

A typical specific immune response can be divided into three stages: (1) antigen encounter and recognition by lymphocytes, (2) lymphocyte activation, and (3) the attack.

1. A lymphocyte programmed during its development to "recognize" a specific antigen encounters it, and the antigen becomes bound to receptors specific for that antigen on the outer surface of the lymphocyte's plasma membrane. This binding is the physicochemical meaning of the word "recognize." Accordingly, the ability of lymphocytes to distinguish one antigen from another is determined by the nature of the plasma-membrane receptors the lymphocytes have.
2. Binding of antigen by receptor is the trigger for lymphocyte activation. The lymphocyte undergoes a cell division, and the two resulting daughter cells then also divide, even though only one of them still has the antigen combined with it, and so on. In other words, the original binding of antigen by a single lymphocyte specific for that antigen triggers multiple cycles of cell divisions to occur. As a result, many lymphocytes are formed that are identical to the one that started the cycles and can recognize the antigen. These progeny then differentiate into cells that serve multiple functions, depending upon the lymphocyte type. With few exceptions, this process of cell division and differentiation, termed **lymphocyte activation**, requires interaction, via chemical messengers, between one type of lymphocyte—helper T cells—and the "effector" lymphocytes—B cells and cytotoxic T cells—that continue the responses into the attack phase.
3. The activated effector lymphocytes launch an attack against all antigens of the kind that initiated the im-

mune response. B cells do so indirectly by secreting antibodies, which then recruit and guide other molecules and cells to perform the actual attack. In contrast, cytotoxic T cells directly attack and kill the cells bearing the antigens. It is essential to understand that, theoretically, it takes only one or two antigen molecules to *initiate* the specific immune response that will then result in an attack on all of the other antigens of that specific kind in the body.

Lymphoid Organs and Lymphocyte Types

Our first task is to describe how lymphocytes arise and the organs and tissues in which they come to reside. Then we describe the various types alluded to in the overview and summarized in Tables 20-1 and 20-2.

Lymphoid Organs. Like all leukocytes, lymphocytes circulate in the blood. At any moment, however, the great majority of lymphocytes are not in the blood but in a group of organs and tissues collectively termed the **lymphoid organs**. These are subdivided into primary lymphoid organs and peripheral lymphoid organs.

The **primary lymphoid organs** are the bone marrow and thymus. These organs supply the peripheral lymphoid organs with mature lymphocytes already programmed to perform their functions. The bone marrow and thymus are not normally sites at which specific immune responses occur.

The **peripheral lymphoid organs** are the lymph nodes, spleen, tonsils, and lymphocyte accumulations in the linings of the intestinal, respiratory, genital, and urinary tracts. It is in the peripheral lymphoid organs that lymphocytes are stimulated to participate in specific immune responses.

We have stated that the bone marrow and thymus supply lymphocytes to the peripheral lymphoid organs. Most of the lymphocytes in the peripheral organs are not, however, cells that originated in the primary lymphoid organs. The explanation is that, once in the peripheral organ, a lymphocyte can undergo cell division to produce additional identical lymphocytes, which in turn undergo cell division, and so on. In other words, all lymphocytes are *descended* from ancestors that were produced in the bone marrow or thymus but may not themselves have arisen in these organs.

(A distinction must be made between the "lymphoid organs" and the "lymphatic system," described in Chapter 14. The latter is a network of lymphatic vessels and the lymph nodes found along these vessels. Of all the lymphoid organs, only the lymph nodes also belong to the lymphatic system.)

There are no anatomical links, other than via the cardiovascular system, between the various lymphoid organs.

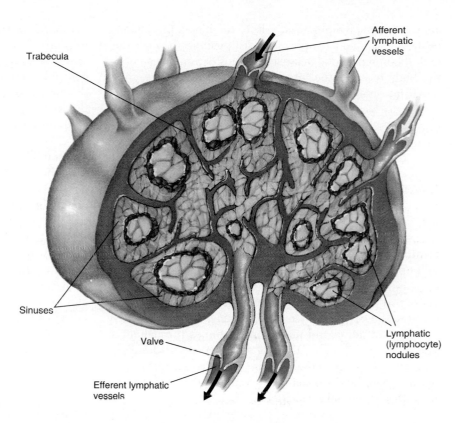

FIGURE 20-6

Anatomy of a lymph node.

Let us look briefly at these organs excepting the bone marrow, which was described in Chapter 14.

The **thymus** lies in the upper part of the chest. Its size varies with age, being relatively large at birth and continuing to grow until puberty, when it gradually atrophies and is replaced by fatty tissue. Before its atrophy, the thymus consists mainly of lymphocytes that will eventually migrate via the blood to the peripheral lymphoid organs. It also contains endocrine cells that secrete a group of hormones that exert a still poorly understood regulatory effect on the peripheral lymphocytes of thymic origin.

Recall from Chapter 14 that the fluid flowing along the lymphatic vessels is called lymph, which is interstitial fluid that has entered the lymphatic capillaries and is being routed to the large lymphatic vessels that drain into systemic veins. During this trip, the lymph flows through **lymph nodes** scattered along the vessels. Lymph, therefore, is the route by which lymph-node cells encounter the materials that trigger their immune responses. Each node is a honeycomb of lymph-filled sinuses (Figure 20-6) with large clusters of lymphocytes between the sinuses. There are also many macrophages and, as is the case with other peripheral lymphoid organs, cells that are distinguishable from macrophages but carry out macrophage-like functions. For simplicity, these cells are included in our use of the term "macrophages."

The **spleen** is the largest of the lymphoid organs and lies in the left part of the abdominal cavity between the

stomach and the diaphragm. In essence, the spleen is to the circulating blood what the lymph nodes are to the lymph. Blood percolates through the vascular meshwork of the spleen's interior, and large collections of lymphocytes and macrophages are found in the spaces of the meshwork. The macrophages of the spleen, in addition to interacting with lymphocytes, also phagocytize aging or dead erythrocytes.[2]

The **tonsils** are a group of small, rounded organs in the pharynx. They are filled with lymphocytes and macrophages and have openings ("crypts") to the surface of the pharynx. Their lymphocytes respond to microbes that arrive by way of ingested food as well as inspired air. Similarly, the lymphocytes in the linings of the various tracts exposed to the external environment respond to infectious agents that penetrate into these linings from the lumen of the tract.

Finally, we must describe the source of the lymphocytes in blood. Some are cells on their way from the bone marrow or thymus to the peripheral organs, but the vast majority are cells that are participating in lymphocyte traffic between the peripheral lymphoid organs, blood, lymph, and all the tissues of the body. Lymphocytes from the peripheral lymphoid organs constantly enter the lymph and

---

[2]In the fetus, the spleen is an important organ for forming all types of blood cells, but in the adult only lymphocytes are formed there.

are carried, via lymphatic vessels, to the blood. Simultaneously, some blood lymphocytes are pushing through the endothelium of blood-vessel capillaries or venules all over the body to enter the interstitial fluid. From there, they move into lymphatic capillaries and along the lymphatic vessels to lymph nodes. They may then leave the lymphatic vessels to take up residence in the node. This recirculation is going on all the time, not just during an infection. It greatly increases the likelihood that any given lymphocyte will encounter the target it is specifically programmed to recognize.

Lymphocyte Origins. The multiple populations and subpopulations of lymphocytes are summarized in Tables 20-1 and 20-2. The **B lymphocytes**, or simply **B cells**, mature in the bone marrow and then are carried by the blood to the peripheral lymphoid organs. This overall process of maturation and migration continues throughout a person's life. All generations of lymphocytes that subsequently arise from these cells by cell division in the peripheral lymphoid organs will be identical to the parent cells, that is, will also be B cells.

In contrast to the B cells, other lymphocytes leave the bone marrow in an immature state during fetal and early neonatal life. They are carried to the thymus and mature in this organ before heading on to the peripheral lymphoid organs. They constitute the second major class of lymphocytes, the **T lymphocytes** or **T cells**. Like B cells, T cells also undergo cell division in peripheral lymphoid organs, the offspring being identical to the original T cells.

In addition to the B and T cells, there is a third population of lymphocytes that are large and granular and include the **natural killer cells (NK cells)**. These cells arise in the bone marrow, but their precursors and life history are still unclear. As we shall see, NK cells, unlike B and T cells, do not manifest specificity for antigens.

Functions of B Cells and T Cells

B cells, upon activation by antigen, differentiate into plasma cells, which secrete **antibodies**. These proteins then travel all over the body to reach antigens of the kind that stimulated that particular immune response. They combine with the antigens and guide an attack (by phagocytes, complement, or NK cells, as we shall see) that eliminates the antigens or the cells bearing them. Antibody-mediated responses are also called humoral responses, the adjective "humoral" denoting communication by way of soluble chemical messengers, antibodies in this case, in the blood.

There are multiple functional subsets of T cells, termed **cytotoxic, helper**, and **suppressor T cells**.[3] Cytotoxic T cells are, themselves, "attack" cells. They travel to the location of antigen-bearing cells, bind to them via the antigen and directly kill them, via secreted chemicals, without the intermediation of antibodies.[4] It is worth emphasizing the important geographical difference in antibody-mediated responses and responses mediated by cytotoxic T cells. In the former case, the B cells remain in whatever location the recognition and activation steps occurred and send their antibodies forth, via the blood, to seek out antigens or antigen-bearing cells identical to those that triggered the response. In the responses mediated by cytotoxic T cells, the cells themselves must enter the blood and seek out the targets.

Antibody-mediated responses have an extremely wide diversity of targets and are the major defense against bacteria, viruses, and other microbes in the extracellular fluid, and against toxic molecules (toxins). In contrast, the direct killing of cells carried out by cytotoxic T cells occurs with a more limited number of targets, specifically the body's own cells that have become cancerous or infected with viruses.

We have now assigned roles to the B cells and cytotoxic T cells. What roles do the other two classes of T cells perform? Suppressor T cells inhibit the function of both B cells and cytotoxic T cells. Suppressor T cells are still poorly understood, and thus we shall have relatively little to say about them in this chapter. Helper T cells help activate both B cells and cytotoxic T cells. The helper T cells go through the usual first two stages of the immune response in that they must combine with antigen and then undergo activation. Once activated, however, they do not direct an attack against antigens but instead secrete protein messengers that act on B cells and cytotoxic T cells that have also bound antigen. This is a very important point: With only a few exceptions, the binding of antigen by a B cell or T cell is usually not enough to cause activation of the cell; a second signal—messengers secreted by helper T cells—is also required.

One important note on terminology is appropriate: Protein chemical messengers secreted by lymphocytes are **lymphokines**, and those secreted by monocytes and mac-

---

[3]Another way to categorize T cells is not by function but rather by the presence of certain proteins, particularly those called CD4 and CD8, in their plasma membranes. Cytotoxic T cells and suppressor T cells have CD8 and so are also commonly called CD8 cells; helper T cells have CD4 and so are also commonly called CD4 cells.

[4]Responses mediated by cytotoxic T cells are sometimes termed cell-mediated responses. Unfortunately this can be confusing since the term is also used to refer to a particular category of immune response—delayed hypersensitivity—in which mainly helper T cells and macrophages participate.

rophages are termed **monokines**. However, because certain of these messengers are secreted by both lymphocytes and monocytes or macrophages, as well as by several other nonimmune cell types—notably fibroblasts and endothelial cells—the term **cytokines** is generally used to include all protein messengers that regulate immune responses.[5] We shall use this term exclusively. (To avoid confusion, it should be recognized that antibodies are not classified as cytokines.)

---

[5]The suffix-*kine*, derived from the Greek word for "action," indicates the function of these proteins in activating cells of the immune system. The prefix used indicates the cell that secretes the protein, the prefix *cyto-* denoting any cell.

The cytokines exert many local effects on the cells of the immune system, and some also circulate in the blood to have hormone-like effects on organs and tissues involved in host defenses. They are also important inflammatory mediators. There are presently more than 20 known cytokines [including 12 interleukins, 4 colony-stimulating factors (Chapter 14), 3 interferons, and 2 tumor necrosis factors], and each usually has multiple target cells and actions. We will, of necessity, limit our discussions in the rest of this chapter to only a few of them.

Figure 20-7 summarizes the basic interactions among B, cytotoxic T, and helper T cells presented in this section.

Lymphocyte Receptors

As stated earlier, the ability of lymphocytes to distinguish

FIGURE 20-7

Summary of roles of B, cytotoxic T, and helper T cells in immune responses. Suppressor T cells, not shown in the figure, can inhibit B-cell and cytotoxic T-cell responses.

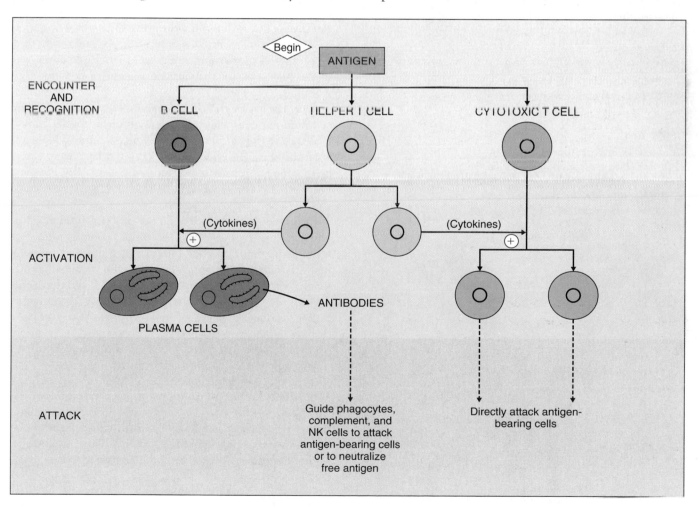

one antigen from another is determined by the lymphocytes' receptors.

B-Cell Receptors. We need to restate one fact and add a new one before describing B-cell receptors. The old fact is that after activation, B cells proliferate and differentiate into plasma cells, which secrete antibodies. The new one is that the plasma cells derived from a particular B cell can secrete only one particular antibody. Now for the receptor: Each B cell always displays on its plasma membrane copies of the particular antibody its plasma cell progeny are able to produce. This surface protein (glycoprotein, to be more accurate) acts as the receptor for the antigen specific to it. Since all antibodies are categorized as **immunoglobulins**, B-cell receptors are immunoglobulins. (The receptors are technically not themselves antibodies since only *secreted* immunoglobulins are termed antibodies.)

Each immunoglobulin molecule is composed of four interlinked polypeptide chains (Figure 20-8). The two long chains are called heavy chains, and the two short ones, light chains. There are five major classes of immunoglobulins, determined by the amino acid sequences in the heavy chains. The classes are designated by the letters A, D, E, G, and M after the symbol Ig for immunoglobulin: IgA, IgD, and so on.

As illustrated in Figure 20-8, immunoglobulins have a "stem," called the **Fc** portion and comprising the lower

FIGURE 20-8

Immunoglobulin (antibody) structure. The Fc portions are the same for all immunoglobulins of a particular class. Each "prong" contains a single antigen-binding site. The links between chains represent disulfide bonds.

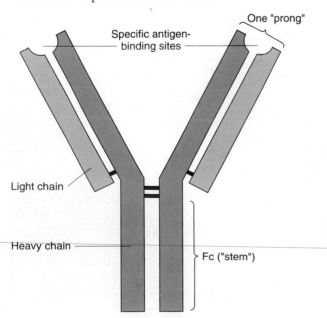

half of the two heavy chains, and two "prongs," each containing one **antigen binding site** (also termed antibody combining site)—the amino acid sequences that bind antigen. The amino acid sequences of the Fc portion are identical for all immunoglobulins of a single class (IgA, IgD, and so on). In contrast, the amino acid sequences of the antigen binding sites vary from immunoglobulin to immunoglobulin in a given class (and are termed the "variable regions"). Thus, each class contains thousands, or even millions, of unique immunoglobulins, each capable of combining with only one specific antigen or, in some cases, several antigens whose structures are very similar. The interaction between an antigen and an immunoglobulin is analogous to the lock-and-key interactions that apply generally to the binding of ligands by proteins.

Any given B cell or clone of identical B cells produces receptors—plasma membrane immunoglobulins—with unique antigen binding sites. Thus, the body has armed itself with small clones of millions of different B cells in order to ensure that receptors will exist that are specific for the vast number of different antigens the organism *might* encounter during its lifetime. The immunoglobulin that any given B cell (and all of its plasma-cell progeny) can produce was determined during the cell's maturation in the bone marrow. Diversity arose as the result of a unique series of rearrangements in the multiple DNA segments that code for the variable regions of the immunoglobulins.

One last point should be mentioned: B-cell receptors can bind antigen whether the antigen is a free individual molecule dissolved in the extracellular fluid or whether it is on the surface of a foreign cell. In the later case, the B cell becomes linked to the foreign cell via the complex between B-cell receptor and surface antigen.

T-Cell Receptors. T cells do not produce immunoglobulins, and so T-cell surface receptors for antigen are not immunoglobulins. Rather they are two-chained proteins that, like immunoglobulins, have specific regions that differ from one T cell to another. As in B-cell development, multiple DNA transformations occur during T-cell maturation, leading to clones of millions of distinct T cells—distinct in that each cell and its offspring possess receptors of a single specificity. For T cells, this maturation occurs during their residence in the thymus.

In addition to their general structural differences, the B- and T-cell receptors differ in a much more important way: The T-cell receptor cannot combine with antigen unless the antigen is first complexed with certain of the body's own plasma-membrane proteins. The T-cell receptor combines with the entire complex of antigen and body (self) protein.

The self plasma-membrane proteins that must be complexed with the antigen in order for T-cell recognition to

TABLE 20-5   MHC RESTRICTION OF THE LYMPHOCYTE RECEPTORS

Cell type	MHC restriction
B	None
Helper T	Class II, found only on macrophages, B cells, and several other cell types (dendritic cells and keratinocytes)
Cytotoxic T and suppressor T	Class I, found on all nucleated cells of the body
NK	None

occur are a group of proteins coded for by genes known as the **major histocompatibility complex (MHC)** and therefore called **MHC proteins**.[6] Since no two persons other than identical twins have the same MHC genes,[7] no two individuals have the same MHC proteins on the plasma membranes of their cells. MHC proteins are, in essence, cellular "identity tags," that is, genetic markers of biological individuality.

The MHC proteins are often termed "restriction elements" since, as we have seen, the ability of a T cell's receptor to recognize an antigen is restricted to situations in which the antigen is complexed with an MHC protein. There are two classes of MHC proteins: I and II. Class I proteins are found on the surface of virtually all nucleated cells of a person's body, that is, virtually all cells but erythrocytes. Class II proteins are found only on the surface of macrophages, B cells, and several macrophage-like cells—dendritic cells, which are found in virtually all tissues but the brain, and keratinocytes, a common cell in the skin. The different subsets of T cells do not all have the same MHC requirements (Table 20-5): Cytotoxic and suppressor T cells require antigen to be associated with class I proteins, whereas helper T cells require class II proteins.

At this point you might well ask: How do antigens, which are foreign, end up on the surface of the body's own cells complexed with MHC proteins? The answer is provided by the process known as **antigen presentation**, to which we now turn.

Antigen Presentation to T Cells

To repeat, T cells can bind antigen only when the antigen appears on the plasma membrane of a host cell complexed with the cell's MHC proteins. Cells bearing these complexes therefore function as **antigen-presenting cells (APCs)** for T cells.

Presentation to Helper T Cells. Since helper T cells require class II MHC proteins and since these proteins are found only on macrophages, B cells, and the macrophage-like dendritic cells and keratinocytes, only these cells can function as APCs for helper T cells. The function of the macrophage as an APC for helper T cells is easiest to visualize (Figure 20-9A) since the macrophage forms, in essence, a link between nonspecific and specific responses. After a microbe or noncellular antigen has been phagocytized or pinocytized by a macrophage in a *nonspecific* response, it is partially broken down into smaller peptide fragments by proteolytic enzymes. The resulting fragments then bind *inside* the cell to class II MHC proteins synthesized there. The fragments actually fit into a groove in the center of the MHC proteins. The fragment-MHC complex is then transported to the cell surface where it is displayed in the plasma membrane. It is to this entire complex on the cell surface that a specific helper T cell can bind.

It is presently thought that antigen hydrolysis and binding of the fragments to the class II MHC proteins occur in the endocytosed vesicles. Note that it is not the intact antigen but rather the peptide fragments, termed antigenic determinants or **epitopes**, of the antigen that are complexed to the MHC proteins and presented to the T cell. Despite this, it is customary to refer simply to "antigen" presentation. More than one epitope can be formed from a given antigen.

---

[6]The term "histocompatibility" means "tissue compatibility." It refers to the fact that the likelihood that a tissue transplant from one person to another will be compatible is often evaluated by testing how closely the two individuals' MHC proteins match. In humans, the MHC proteins are termed HLA proteins, for "human leukocyte antigens," because they were first discovered on leukocytes. We prefer to use the term "MHC proteins" because of its universal biological applicability, as well as to avoid the incorrect impression that the proteins are found only on leukocytes.

[7]The MHC system of genes is extremely polymorphic, having multiple alternative forms or alleles (Chapter 4) of each gene. For example, there are at least 50 distinct alleles of one of the genes.

longed period of exposure and activation required by B cells and cytotoxic T cells. Why then do we deal with them in the context of *specific* immune responses? Because, as we shall see, their participation in an immune response is greatly enhanced by cytokines secreted by helper T cells activated during specific responses.

Development of Immune Tolerance

Our basic framework for understanding specific immune responses requires consideration of one more crucial question: How does the body develop what is called **immune tolerance**—lack of immune responsiveness to *self-components*? This may seem to be a strange question given our definition of an antigen as a *foreign* molecule that can generate an immune response. In essence, however, we are now asking how it is that the body "knows" that its own molecules—particularly proteins—are not foreign.

Recall that the huge diversity of lymphocyte receptors is ultimately the result of multiple random DNA recombination processes. It is virtually certain, therefore, that in each person clones of lymphocytes would have emerged with receptors that could bind to that person's own proteins. The existence and functioning of such lymphocytes would, of course, be disastrous because such binding would launch an immune attack against the cells expressing these proteins; that is, the person's own (self) proteins would act as antigens. There are at least two mechanisms, termed clonal deletion and clonal inactivation, that explain why *normally* there are no active lymphocytes that respond to self-components.

First, during in utero and early postnatal life, T cells are exposed to a potpourri of self proteins in the thymus. There, those T cells that have receptors capable of binding self proteins are destroyed by an unknown mechanism. This process is termed **clonal deletion** (also called negative clonal selection).

But clonal deletion does not fully explain immune tolerance. It is very likely, for example, that some proteins in the body do not make their way to the thymus during development, and so T cells capable of binding to these proteins would not be destroyed. A second process, termed **clonal inactivation** (or clonal anergy) acts not in the thymus but in the periphery and somehow *inactivates* potentially self-reactive lymphocytes instead of killing them.

To summarize, the body normally does not launch a specific immune attack against its own proteins because it has no T cells able to bind to these proteins. Such lymphocytes did exist in the body at one time but were either destroyed or inactivated.

This completes our framework for understanding specific immune responses. The next two sections utilize this

framework in presenting typical responses from beginning to end, fleshing out the interactions between lymphocytes and describing the attack mechanisms used by the various pathways.

Antibody-Mediated Immune Responses: Defenses Against Bacteria, Extracellular Viruses, and Toxins

A classical antibody-mediated response is one that results in the destruction of bacteria. The sequence of events, which would be quite similar to the response to a virus in the extracellular fluid, is summarized in Table 20-6 and Figure 20-11.

B-Cell Recognition and Activation. The story starts in the same way as for nonspecific responses, with the bacteria penetrating one of the body's linings and entering the interstitial fluid. The bacteria then enter the lymphatic system and/or bloodstream and are carried to the lymph nodes and/or the spleen, respectively. There a B cell specific for an antigen on the bacterial surface binds to the antigen via the B cell's plasma membrane immunoglobulin receptor.[9]

In a few cases (notably bacteria with polysaccharide capsules), this binding is all that is needed to trigger B-cell activation. For the great majority of antigens, however, binding is not enough, and signals in the form of cytokines released into the interstitial fluid by helper T cells near the antigen-bound B cells are also needed.

But for helper T cells to be brought into play and secrete cytokines, they must bind to a complex of antigen and class II MHC protein on an antigen-presenting cell (APC). Let us assume that in this case the APC is a macrophage that has phagocytized one of the bacteria, hydrolyzed its proteins into peptide fragments, complexed them with class II MHC proteins, and displayed the complexes on its surface. A helper T cell specific for the complex then binds to it, beginning the activation of the helper T cell. Moreover, the macrophage helps this activation process in a second way: It secretes IL-1.

So far this has all been review. Now we begin new material. IL-1 stimulates the helper T cell to enlarge, to secrete another cytokine named **interleukin 2 (IL-2)**, and to express the receptor for IL-2. This messenger, acting as an autocrine agent, then further stimulates the helper T cell (Figure 20-11). The cell divides, beginning the mitotic cycles that lead to formation of a clone of activated helper T cells, and these cells then release not only IL-2 but sev-

---

[9]In our scenario, B cells bind directly to antigen with no intermediation of macrophages. It is likely that, in many cases, a macrophage first phagocytizes the antigen-bearing foreign cell, processes the antigen, and presents it on the surface of the macrophage. But, unlike the story for antigen presentation to T cells, any antigen presentation to B cells by macrophages would not involve complexing of the antigen to MHC proteins.

> **TABLE 20-6 SUMMARY OF EVENTS IN ANTIBODY-MEDIATED IMMUNITY AGAINST BACTERIA**
>
> 1. In peripheral lymphoid organs, bacterial antigen binds to specific receptors on the plasma membrane of B cells.
> 2. Simultaneously, antigen-presenting cells (for example, macrophages) (APCs) present to helper T cells processed antigen complexed to MHC Class II proteins on the APCs and secrete IL-1, which acts on the helper T cells.
> 3. In response, the helper T cells secrete IL-2, which activates the helper T cells to proliferate and secrete IL-2 and other cytokines. These activate the antigen-bound B cells to proliferate and differentiate into plasma cells. Certain B cells differentiate into memory cells rather than plasma cells.
> 4. The plasma cells secrete antibodies specific for the antigen that initiated the response, and the antibodies circulate all over the body via the blood.
> 5. Antibodies combine with antigen on the surface of the bacteria anywhere in the body.
> 6. Presence of antibody bound to antigen facilitates phagocytosis of the bacteria by neutrophils and macrophages. It also activates the complement system, which further enhances phagocytosis and can directly kill the bacteria by the membrane attack complex.

eral other cytokines (for example, **interleukin 6**) as well.

It is these cytokines, along with IL-2, that provide the additional signals required to activate nearby antigen-bound B cells to proliferate and differentiate into plasma cells, which then secrete antibodies.

Thus, as shown in Figure 20-11, we are dealing with a series of protein messengers interconnecting the various cell types, the helper T cells serving as the central coordinator. The macrophage releases IL-1, which acts on the helper T cell to stimulate release of IL-2, which stimulates the helper T cell to multiply, the activated progeny then releasing still other cytokines that, along with IL-2, activate antigen-bound B cells. Some of the B-cell progeny do not differentiate into plasma cells but instead become **memory cells** (Figure 20-11), ready to respond vigorously should the antigen ever reappear at a future time. In other words, the proliferation triggered by a first exposure to an antigen results in a long-lasting expansion of the clone of B cells specific for that antigen.

The example we have been using employed a macrophage as the APC to helper T cells. Recall, however, that this role can also be served by B cells. Moreover, B cells can also secrete the IL-1 required for activation of the helper T cells. The binding of the helper T cell to the antigen-bound B cell ensures maximal stimulation of the B cell by the cytokines secreted by that helper T cell and any of its progeny that remain nearby.[10]

---

[10]Some experts believe that even when a macrophage acts as the APC, the helper T cells activated by this process then bind to antigen-bound B cells, thereby reducing the distance over which the cytokines secreted by the helper T cell must act.

Antibody Secretion. Plasma cells produce thousands of antibody molecules per second before they die in a day or so. We mentioned earlier that there are five major classes of antibodies. The most abundant are the **IgG** antibodies, also commonly called **gamma globulin**. They and **IgM** provide the bulk of specific immunity against bacteria and viruses in the extracellular fluid. **IgE** antibodies mediate allergic responses and participate in defenses against multicellular parasites. **IgA** antibodies are secreted by plasma cells in the linings of the gastrointestinal, respiratory, and genitourinary tracts. IgA antibodies generally do not circulate but act locally in the linings or on their surfaces. They are also secreted by the mammary glands and hence are the major antibodies in milk. The functions of **IgD** are still unclear.

In the kind of infection we've been describing, the secreted antibodies—mostly IgG and IgM—enter the blood, which carries them from the peripheral lymphoid organ in which recognition and activation occurred to all tissues and organs of the body. At sites of infection, the antibodies leave the blood (recall that nonspecific inflammation has already made capillaries leaky at these sites) and combine with the type of bacterial surface antigen that initiated the immune response (Figure 20-11). These antibodies then direct the attack against the bacteria to which they are now bound.

Thus, immunoglobulins play two distinct roles in immune responses: (1) During the initial recognition step, those on the surface of B cells bind to antigen brought to them; and (2) those secreted by the plasma cells seek out and bind to bacteria bearing the same antigens, "marking" them as the targets to be attacked.

TABLE 20-7 SOME IMPORTANT CYTOKINES SECRETED BY HELPER T CELLS AND THEIR LOCAL ACTIONS

1. Interleukin 2
   a. Acts as an autocrine agent to stimulate its cells of origin, helper T cells, to proliferate and secrete other cytokines.
   b. Stimulates the proliferation and differentiation of B cells and cytotoxic T cells.
   c. Activates macrophages and enhances the killing properties of cytotoxic T cells and NK cells.
2. Interleukin 6 and several other cytokines stimulate B-cell proliferation and differentiation into antibody-secreting plasma cells.
3. Gamma interferon activates macrophages and enhances the killing properties of cytotoxic T cells and NK cells.

fever is often beneficial, in that an increase in body temperature enhances many of the protective responses described in this chapter.

Decreases in the plasma concentrations of iron and zinc occur in response to infection and are due to changes in the uptake and/or release of these trace elements by liver, spleen, and other tissues. The decrease in plasma iron concentration has adaptive value since bacteria require a high concentration of iron to multiply. The role of the decrease in zinc is not known. The decrease in appetite characteristic of infection may also deprive the invading organisms of nutrients—particularly minerals—they require to proliferate.

Another adaptive response to infection is the secretion by the liver of a group of proteins known collectively as **acute phase proteins**. These proteins exert a large array of adaptive effects on the inflammatory process, immune cell function, and tissue repair.

Another response to infection, release of neutrophils and monocytes by the bone marrow, is of obvious value. Finally, there is release of amino acids from muscle, and these amino acids provide the building blocks for the synthesis of proteins required to fight the infection and for tissue repair.

All these responses and many others not listed are elicited by one or more of the cytokines released from stimulated macrophages. Thus, IL-1, TNF, and IL-6, all of which serve *local* roles in immune responses, also serve as

TABLE 20-8 SUMMARY OF HOST RESPONSES TO VIRUSES

	Main cells involved	Comment on action
Nonspecific defenses		
Anatomical barriers	Body surface linings	Physical barrier; antiviral chemicals
Inflammation	Tissue macrophages	Phagocytosis of extracellular virus
Interferon	Multiple cell types after viruses enter them	Interferon nonspecifically prevents viral replication inside host cells
Specific defenses		
Antibody-mediated	Plasma cells derived from B cells secrete antibodies	Antibodies neutralize virus and thus prevent viral entry into cell
		Antibodies activate complement, which leads to enhanced phagocytosis of extracellular virus
Direct cell killing	Cytotoxic T cells, NK cells, and activated macrophages	Via secreted chemicals, destroy host cell and thus induce release of virus into extracellular fluid where it can be phagocytized

hormones to elicit far-flung responses such as fever (Figure 20-17).[12] This is a good place to review the various functions of macrophages in immune responses (Table 20-9).

Several other cytokines also participate. For example, **colony-stimulating factors**, which are secreted by macrophages, lymphocytes, endothelial cells, and fibroblasts, provide the stimulus to the bone marrow to produce more neutrophils and monocytes (Chapter 14).

FACTORS THAT ALTER THE BODY'S RESISTANCE TO INFECTION

There are many factors that determine the body's capacity to resist infection. We offer here only a few examples.

Protein-calorie malnutrition is, worldwide, the single greatest contributor to decreased resistance to infection. Deficits of specific nutrients other than protein can also lower resistance to infection.

A preexisting disease, infectious or noninfectious, can also predispose the body to infection. People with diabetes, for example, have a propensity to numerous infections, at least partially explainable on the basis of defective leukocyte function. Moreover, any injury to a tissue lowers its resistance, perhaps by altering the chemical environment or interfering with the blood supply.

A growing body of evidence has also documented that both stress and a person's state of mind can either enhance or reduce resistance to infection (and cancer). The physiological links among stress, state of mind, and resistance are only now being determined, and the entire question is being given great impetus by the emerging field of psychoneuroimmunology. Until recently, the tendency was to treat the immune system, on the one hand, and the nervous and endocrine systems, on the other, as entirely separate. It is now clear, however, that lymphoid tissue is innervated and that the cells mediating immunity possess receptors for many neurotransmitters and hormones. Conversely, many of the cytokines released by immune cells have important effects on the brain and endocrine system. Moreover, lymphocytes secrete several of the same hormones produced by endocrine glands. It seems certain, therefore, that the nervous and endocrine systems interact with the immune system in important ways. For example, it has been shown that the production of antibodies can be altered by psychological conditioning in much the same way as other body functions. Some possible mediators of the effects of stress on immune responses are discussed in Section C of this chapter.

Resistance to infection will also be impaired if one of the basic resistance mechanisms itself is deficient, as, for example, in people having a genetic deficiency in antibody synthesis. These individuals experience frequent and sometimes life-threatening infections that can be prevented by regular replacement injections of gamma globulin. Another genetic defect is combined immunodeficiency, which is an absence of both B and T cells. If untreated, infants with this disorder usually die within their first year of life from overwhelming infections. Combined immunodeficiency can be cured by a bone-marrow transplantation which supplies both B cells and cells that will migrate to the thymus and become T cells.

---

[12]A remarkable recent finding is that certain bacteria known to be highly virulent respond to IL-1 with increased proliferation. Thus, the bacteria have "captured" a host defense mechanism for their own purposes.

TABLE 20-9   ROLE OF MACROPHAGES IN IMMUNE RESPONSES

1. In nonspecific inflammation, phagocytize particulate matter, including microbes. Also secrete antimicrobial chemicals and protein messengers (cytokines) that function as local inflammatory mediators. The inflammatory cytokines include IL-1 and TNF.

2. Process and present antigen to helper T cells.

3. Secrete IL-1, which stimulates helper T cells to secrete IL-2 and to express the receptor for IL-2.

4. During specific immune responses, perform same killing and inflammation-inducing functions as in (1) but are more efficient because antibodies act as opsonins and because the cells are transformed into activated macrophages by IL-2 and gamma interferon, both secreted by helper T cells.

5. Secrete IL-1, TNF, and another cytokine, IL-6, which mediate many of the systemic responses to infection or injury.

ple, zidovudine in HIV infections), there are no antibiotics presently in common use against viruses.

Antibiotics exert a wide variety of effects, but the common denominator is interference with the synthesis of one or more of the bacterium's essential macromolecules. Antibiotics must not be used indiscriminately. For one thing, they may exert toxic effects on the body's cells as well as the bacteria. A second reason for judicious use is the problem of drug resistance. Most large bacterial populations contain a few mutants that are resistant to the drug. These few are capable of multiplying into large populations resistant to the effects of that particular antibiotic. Perhaps even more important, resistance can be transferred from one microbe directly to another previously nonresistant microbe by means of genes ("resistance genes") passed between them. A third reason for the judicious use of antibiotics is that these agents may actually contribute to a new infection by eliminating certain species of relatively harmless bacteria that ordinarily prevent growth of more dangerous ones.

HARMFUL IMMUNE RESPONSES

Until now, we have focused on the mechanisms of immune responses and their *protective* effects. In this section we shall see that immune responses can be harmful to the body.

Graft Rejection

The major obstacle to successful transplantation of tissues and organs is that the immune system, of course, recognizes the transplants, called grafts, as foreign and launches an attack against them. This is termed *graft rejection*. Although antibodies play some role, cytotoxic T cells are mainly responsible for graft rejection.

Except in the case of identical twins, the class I MHC proteins on the cells of a graft differ from the recipient's. So do the class II molecules present on the macrophages present in the graft (recall that virtually all organs and tissues have macrophages). Accordingly, the MHC proteins of both classes are recognized as foreign, and the cells bearing them are destroyed by the recipient's cytotoxic T cells with the aid of helper T cells.[16]

Some of the tools aimed at reducing graft rejection are radiation and drugs that kill actively dividing lymphocytes

and thereby decrease the host's T-cell population. The single most effective drug, however, is **cyclosporin,** which does not kill lymphocytes but rather blocks the production of IL-2 and other cytokines by helper T cells. This eliminates a critical signal for proliferation of the cytotoxic T cells.

Adrenal corticosteroids (Chapter 10) in large doses are also used to reduce the rejection. Their possible mechanisms of action are described in Section D.

Transfusion Reactions

Transfusion reactions, the illness caused when erythrocytes are destroyed during blood transfusion, are a special example of tissue rejection, one that illustrates the fact that antibodies rather than cytotoxic T cells can sometimes be the major factor in rejection. Erythrocytes do not have MHC proteins, but they do have plasma-membrane proteins and carbohydrates that can function as antigens when exposed to another person's blood. There are more than 400 erythrocyte antigens, but the ABO system of carbohydrates is the most important for transfusion reactions.

As described in the section on blood types in Chapter 14, some people have the gene that results in synthesis of the A antigen,[17] some have the gene for the B antigen, some have both genes, and some have neither gene. The erythrocytes of those with neither gene are said to have O-type erythrocytes. Accordingly, the possible blood types are A, B, AB, and O (Table 20-10).

Type A individuals always have anti-B antibodies in their plasma. Similarly, type B individuals have plasma anti-A antibodies. Type AB individuals have neither anti-A nor anti-B antibody, and type O individuals have both. These antierythrocyte antibodies are called **natural antibodies**. It is thought that they are induced early in life by antigens very similar to A and B on the surface of intestinal bacteria.

With this information as background, we can predict what happens when a type A person is given type B blood. There are two incompatibilities: (1) The recipient's anti-B antibody causes the transfused cells to be attacked, and (2) the anti-A antibody in the transfused plasma causes the recipient's cells to be attacked. The latter is generally of little consequence, however, because the transfused antibodies become so diluted in the recipient's plasma that they are ineffective in inducing a response. It is the destruction of the transfused cells by the recipient's antibodies that produces the problems.

Similar analyses show that the following situations

---

[16]There is an interesting problem here concerning antigen presentation. To be recognized by the host's cytotoxic T cells, the *graft's* MHC proteins should theoretically by complexed with the *host's* MHC proteins on *host* antigen-presenting cells. It is not clear whether (and how) this really occurs or whether foreign MHC proteins are so strongly antigenic that they can be recognized without such complexing.

[17]Genes, of course, do not code directly for carbohydrates; rather they code for the particular enzymes that catalyze formation of the carbohydrates.

TABLE 20-10 HUMAN ABO BLOOD GROUPS

| Blood group | Percent° | Antigen on RBC | Genetic possibilities | | Antibody in blood |
			Homozygous	Heterozygous	
A	42	A	AA	AO	Anti-B
B	10	B	BB	BO	Anti-A
AB	3	A and B	—	AB	Neither anti-A nor anti-B
O	45	Neither A nor B	OO	—	Both anti-A and anti-B

°In the United States.

would result in an attack on the transfused erythrocytes: a type-B person given either A or AB blood; a type A person given either type B or AB blood; a type O person given A, B, or AB blood. Type O people are, therefore, sometimes called universal donors, whereas type AB people are universal recipients. These terms are misleading, however, since besides those of the ABO type, there are a host of other erythrocyte antigens and plasma antibodies against them. Therefore, except in a dire emergency, the blood of donor and recipient must be tested for incompatibilities directly by the procedure called **cross-matching**. The recipient's serum is combined on a glass slide with the prospective donor's erythrocytes (a "major" cross-match), and the mixture observed for rupture (hemolysis) or clumping (agglutination) of the erythrocytes. In addition, the recipient's erythrocytes can be combined with the prospective donor's serum (a "minor" cross-match)

Another group of erythrocyte membrane antigens of medical importance is the Rh system of proteins. There are more than 40 such antigens, but the most strongly antigenic one is termed Rh_o (also called D), known commonly as the **Rh factor** because it was first studied in rhesus monkeys. Human erythrocytes either have the antigen (Rh-positive) or lack it (Rh-negative). About 85 percent of the United States population is Rh-positive.

The Rh system follows the classical immunity pattern in that no one has anti-Rh antibodies unless exposed to Rh-positive cells from another person. This can be a problem if an Rh-negative person is subjected to multiple transfusions with Rh-positive blood, but its major importance is in the mother-fetus relationship. When an Rh-negative mother carries an Rh-positive fetus, some of the fetal erythrocytes may cross the placental barriers into the maternal circulation, inducing her to synthesize anti-Rh antibodies. Because this occurs mainly during separation of the placenta at delivery, a first Rh-positive pregnancy rarely offers any danger to the fetus since delivery occurs before the antibodies are made by the mother. In future pregnancies, however, these antibodies will already be present in the mother and can cross the placenta to attack and hemolyze the erythrocytes of an Rh-positive fetus. This condition, which can cause an anemia severe enough to cause death of the fetus in utero or of the newborn, is called **hemolytic disease of the newborn**. The risk increases with each Rh-positive pregnancy as the mother becomes more and more sensitized.

Fortunately, this disease can be prevented by giving an Rh-negative mother human gamma globulin against Rh-positive erythrocytes within 72 h after she has delivered an Rh-positive infant. These antibodies bind to the antigenic sites on any Rh-positive erythrocytes that might have entered the mother's blood during delivery and prevent them from inducing antibody synthesis by the mother. The administered antibodies are eventually catabolized.

You may be wondering whether ABO incompatibilities are also a cause of hemolytic disease of the newborn. For example, a woman with type O blood has natural antibodies to both the A and B antigens. If her fetus is type A or B, this theoretically should cause a problem. Fortunately, it usually does not, partly because the A and B antigens are not strongly expressed in fetal erythrocytes and partly because the natural antibodies are of the IgM type, which do not readily cross the placenta.

Allergy (Hypersensitivity)

Allergy or **hypersensitivity** refers to certain diseases in which immune responses to environmental antigens cause inflammation and damage to the body itself. Antigens that cause allergy are termed **allergens**, common examples of which include those in ragweed pollen and poison ivy. Most allergens themselves are relatively or completely harmless, and it is the immune responses to them that cause the damage. In essence, then, allergy is immunity gone wrong, for the response is inappropriate to the stimulus.

To develop a particular allergy, a genetically predisposed person must first be exposed to the allergen. This

BIOTRANSFORMATION

The metabolic alteration—biotransformation—of foreign molecules occurs mainly in the liver but to some extent also in kidney, skin, placenta, and other organs. A large number of distinct enzymes and pathways are involved, but the common denominator of most of them is that they transform chemicals into more polar, less lipid-soluble substances. One consequence of this transformation is that the chemical may be rendered less toxic, but this is not always so. The second, more important, consequence is that the chemical's tubular reabsorption is diminished and urinary excretion facilitated. Similarly, for substances handled by biliary secretion, gut absorption of the metabolite is less likely so that fecal excretion is also enhanced.

The hepatic enzymes that perform these transformations are called the **microsomal enzyme system (MES)** and are located mainly in the smooth endoplasmic reticulum. One of the most important facts about this enzyme system is that it is easily inducible; that is, the number of these enzymes can be greatly increased by exposure to a chemical that acts as a substrate for the system. For example, chronic overuse of alcohol results in an increased rate of alcohol catabolism because of induction of the microsomal enzymes. This accounts for much of the tolerance to alcohol, that is, the fact that increasing doses must be taken to achieve a given magnitude of effect.

The hepatic biotransformation mechanisms vividly demonstrate how an adaptive response may, under some circumstances, turn out to be maladaptive. These enzymes all too frequently "toxify" rather than "detoxify" a drug or pollutant. In fact, many foreign chemicals are quite nontoxic until the liver enzymes biotransform them. Of particular importance is the fact that many chemicals that cause cancer do so only after biotransformation. For example, a major component of cigarette smoke is transformed by the MES into a carcinogenic compound. Individuals with a particularly highly inducible MES have a twenty- to forty-fold higher risk of developing lung cancer from smoking.

The MES can also cause problems in another way because it evolved primarily not to defend against foreign chemicals, which were much less prevalent during our evolution, but rather to metabolize *endogenous* substances, particularly steroids and other lipid-soluble molecules. Therefore, the induction of these enzymes by a drug or pollutant increases metabolism not only of that drug or pollutant but of the endogenous substances as well. The result is a decreased concentration in the body of the normal substance, resulting in its possible deficiency.

Another fact of importance concerning the MES is that whereas certain chemicals induce it, others inhibit it. The presence of such chemicals in the environment could have deleterious effects on the system's capacity to protect against those chemicals that it transforms. Just to illustrate how complex this picture can be, note that any chemical that inhibits the microsomal enzyme system may actually confer protection against those other chemicals that must undergo transformation in order to become toxic.

SECTION B SUMMARY

I. The concentration of a foreign chemical in the body depends upon degree of exposure to the chemical, its rate of absorption across the GI tract, lung, skin, or placenta, and its rates of storage, biotransformation, and excretion.

II. Biotransformation occurs in the liver and other tissues and is mediated by multiple enzymes, notably the microsomal enzyme system (MES). Its major function is to make lipid-soluble substances more polar (less lipid-soluble), thereby decreasing renal tubular reabsorption and increasing excretion.

   A. This system can be induced or inhibited by the chemicals it processes and by other chemicals.

   B. It detoxifies some chemicals but toxifies others, notably carcinogens.

SECTION B KEY TERMS

biotransformation   microsomal enzyme system (MES)

SECTION B REVIEW QUESTIONS

1. Why is the urinary excretion of lipid-soluble substances generally very low?

2. What are two functions of biotransformation mechanisms?

3. What are two ways in which activation of biotransformation mechanisms may actually cause malfunction?

HEMOSTASIS: THE PREVENTION OF BLOOD LOSS

Elimination of bleeding is known as **hemostasis** (don't confuse this word with "homeostasis"). Physiological hemostatic mechanisms are most effective in dealing with injuries in small vessels—arterioles, capillaries, venules—which are the most common source of bleeding in everyday life. In contrast, the bleeding from a medium or large artery is not usually controllable by the body. Venous bleeding is less dangerous because veins have low blood pressure. Indeed, the drop in pressure induced by raising the bleeding part above the heart level may stop hemorrhage from a vein. In addition, if the venous bleeding is into the tissues, the accumulation of blood may increase interstitial pressure enough to eliminate the pressure gradient required for continued blood loss. Accumulation of blood in the tissues can occur as a result of bleeding from any vessel type and is termed a *hematoma*.

When a blood vessel is severed or otherwise injured, its immediate inherent response is to constrict (the mechanism is unclear). This short-lived response slows the flow of blood in the affected area. In addition, this constriction presses the opposed endothelial surfaces of the vessel together, and this contact induces a stickiness capable of keeping them "glued" together against high pressures.

Permanent closure of the vessel by constriction and contact stickiness occurs only in the very smallest vessels of the microcirculation, however, and the staunching of bleeding ultimately is dependent upon two other processes that are interdependent and occur in rapid succession: (1) formation of a platelet plug, and (2) blood coagulation (clotting). The blood platelets are involved in both processes.

FORMATION OF A PLATELET PLUG

The involvement of platelets in hemostasis requires their adhesion to a surface. Although platelets have a propensity for adhering to surfaces, they do not adhere to the normal endothelial cells lining the blood vessels. However, injury to a vessel disrupts the endothelium and exposes the underlying connective-tissue collagen molecules—fibrous proteins that constitute a major component of the interstitial matrix. Platelets adhere to collagen, an event facilitated by **von Willebrand factor (vWF)**, a plasma protein secreted by endothelial cells and platelets. This protein forms a bridge between the damaged vessel wall and the platelets: It binds to collagen, and then platelets bind to it.[18]

Adhesion triggers the platelets to release the contents of their secretory vesicles ("granules"), which contain a variety of chemical agents. Many of these agents, including adenosine diphosphate (ADP) and serotonin, then act locally to induce changes in the surface of the platelets, causing new platelets to adhere to the old ones. Termed **platelet aggregation**, this self-perpetuating (positive-feedback) process rapidly creates a **platelet plug** inside the vessel.

Chemical agents in the platelets' secretory granules are not the only stimulator of platelet aggregation. In addition, adhesion of the platelets to collagen induces the synthesis, from arachidonic acid in the platelet plasma membrane, of **thromboxane A_2**, a member of the eicosanoid family (Chapter 7). This substance is released into the extracellular fluid and acts locally to further stimulate platelet aggregation and secretion of platelet granules (Figure 20-20).

Fibrinogen, a plasma protein whose crucial role in blood clotting is described in the subsequent section, also participates in the formation of platelet plugs. It does so by forming bridges between platelets. The binding sites for fibrinogen on the platelet plasma membrane somehow become exposed as platelet aggregation proceeds.

The platelet plug can completely seal small breaks in blood vessel walls. Its effectiveness is further enhanced by another property of platelets—contraction. Platelets contain a very high concentration of actin and myosin, which are stimulated to contract in aggregated platelets. This results in a compression and strengthening of the platelet plug.[19]

While the plug is being built up and compacted, the vascular smooth muscle in the vessels around it is being stimulated to contract (Figure 20-20), thereby decreasing the blood flow to the area and the pressure within the damaged vessel. This vasoconstriction is the result of platelet activity, for it is mediated by thromboxane A_2 and by several chemicals contained in the secreted platelet granules.

---

[18]vWF serves a second function in clotting: It acts as a binding protein for one of the other proteins—factor VIII—involved in clotting and described later in the text.

[19]In a test tube this contraction and compression are termed clot retraction.

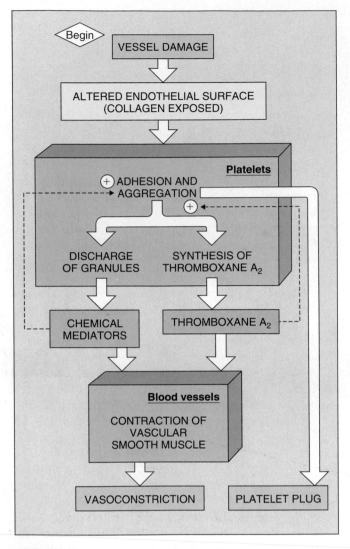

FIGURE 20-20

Sequence of events leading to vasoconstriction and formation of a platelet plug following damage to a blood-vessel wall. Note the two positive feedbacks in the pathways.

Once started, why does the platelet plug not continuously expand, spreading away from the damaged endothelium along intact endothelium in both directions? One important reason involves the ability of the adjacent intact endothelial cells to synthesize and release the eicosanoid known as **prostacyclin** (also termed prostaglandin I_2, **PGI$_2$**), which is a profound inhibitor of platelet aggregation. Thus, whereas stimulated *platelets* possess the enzymes that produce thromboxane A_2 from arachidonic acid, normal *endothelial cells* contain a different enzyme, one that converts intermediates formed from arachidonic acid not to thromboxane A_2 but to PGI$_2$ (Figure 20-21). In addition to PGI$_2$, the endothelial cells also release **nitric oxide**, which is not only a vasodilator (recall that nitric oxide is endothelium-derived relaxing factor) but also an inhibitor of platelet aggregation.

To reiterate, the platelet plug is built up extremely rapidly and is the primary sealer of breaks in vessel walls. In the following section, we shall see that platelets are also absolutely essential for the next, more slowly occurring, hemostatic event, blood coagulation.

BLOOD COAGULATION: CLOT FORMATION

Blood coagulation (clotting) is the transformation of blood into a solid gel termed a **clot** or **thrombus** and consisting mainly of a protein polymer known as **fibrin**. Clotting occurs locally around the original platelet plug and is the dominant hemostatic defense. Its function is to support and reinforce the platelet plug and to solidify blood that remains in the wound channel.

The events leading to clotting are summarized, in very simplified form, in Figure 20-22. These events, like plate-

FIGURE 20-21

Platelets produce thromboxane A_2 (TXA$_2$), whereas normal endothelium adjacent to a platelet plug produces prostaglandin I_2 (PGI$_2$) from platelet and endothelial-cell arachidonic acid, and this eicosanoid inhibits platelet aggregation. Nitric oxide, NO, also secreted by the endothelial cells, does the same thing as PGI$_2$. Thus, PGI$_2$ and NO prevent spread of platelet aggregation from the damaged site.

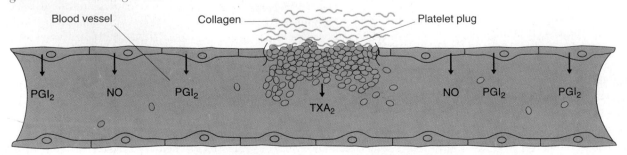

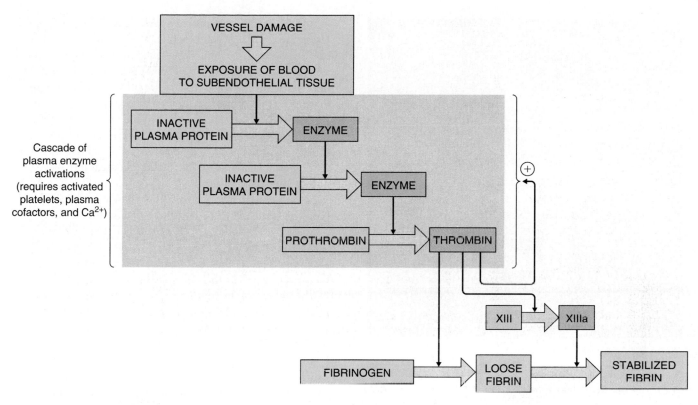

FIGURE 20-22

Simplified diagram of the clotting pathway. The pathway leading to thrombin is denoted by two enzyme activations, but the story is actually much more complex (as will be shown in Figures 20-24 and 20-25). Note that thrombin has three different effects—generation of fibrin, activation of factor XIII, and positive-feedback on the cascade leading to itself.

let aggregation, are initiated when injury to a vessel disrupts the endothelium and permits the blood to contact the underlying tissue. This contact initiates a locally occurring sequence or "cascade" of chemical activations. At each step of the cascade, an inactive plasma protein, or "factor," is converted (activated) to a proteolytic enzyme, which then catalyzes the generation of the next enzyme in the sequence. Each of these activations results from the splitting of a small peptide fragment from the inactive plasma protein precursor, thus exposing the active site of the enzyme. It should be noted, however, that several of the plasma protein factors, following their activation, function not as enzymes but rather as cofactors for the enzymes.

To reduce the risk that you might "lose sight of the forest for the trees" immediately, Figure 20-22 gives no specifics about the cascade until the point at which a plasma protein, **prothrombin**, is converted to an enzyme called **thrombin**. Thrombin then catalyzes a reaction in which several polypeptides are split from molecules of the large rod-shaped plasma protein **fibrinogen**. The still large fibrinogen remnants then bind to each other to form fibrin. The fibrin, initially a loose mesh of interlacing

strands, is rapidly stabilized and strengthened by enzymatically mediated formation of covalent cross-linkages. This chemical linking is catalyzed by an enzyme known as factor XIIIa, which is formed from the plasma protein inactive factor XIII in a reaction also catalyzed by thrombin.

Thus, thrombin catalyzes not only the formation of loose fibrin but also the activation of factor XIII, which will stabilize the fibrin network. But thrombin does even more than this: It exerts a profound positive-feedback effect on its own formation. It does this by activating several proteins in the cascade and also by activating platelets. (We'll talk about platelet activation and its significance for clotting in the next paragraph). Therefore, once thrombin formation has begun, reactions leading to much more thrombin generation are brought into play by this initial thrombin. We will make use of this crucial fact later when we describe the specifics of the cascade leading to thrombin.

In the process of clotting, many erythrocytes and other cells are trapped in the fibrin meshwork (Figure 20-23), but the essential component of the clot is fibrin, and clotting can occur in the absence of all cellular elements except platelets. Platelets are essential because some of the

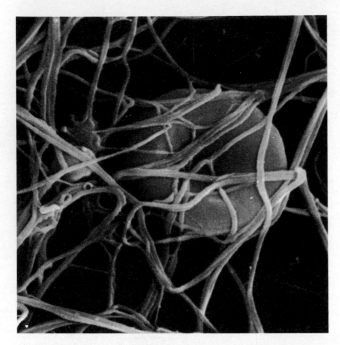

FIGURE 20-23
Scanning electron micrograph of an erythrocyte enmeshed in fibrin. (*Courtesy of Elia Kairinen, Gillett Research Institute.*)

cascade reactions take place mainly on the surface of platelets. To participate, the platelets themselves must be activated, which occurs very early in the clotting response; as noted above, thrombin is an important stimulator of this activation. The activation causes the platelets to display specific plasma-membrane receptors that bind several of the clotting factors. The activated platelets also display particular phospholipids, called **platelet factor (PF)**, which functions as a cofactor in the steps mediated by the bound factors.

One more generalization about the clotting cascade should be noted: Plasma calcium is required at various steps. However, calcium concentration in the plasma can never get low enough to cause clotting defects because death would occur from muscle paralysis or cardiac arrythmias before such low concentrations were reached.

Now we present the specifics of the early portions of the clotting cascade, those leading from vessel damage to the prothrombin-thrombin reaction. Until very recently, it had been thought that there were *two* mechanisms by which exposure of the blood to subendothelial tissue could initiate the cascade and that these mechanisms gave rise to two completely independent, parallel pathways which merged at the step before the prothrombin-thrombin reaction. These are called (1) the **intrinsic pathway**, so named because everything necessary for it is *in* the blood;

and (2) the **extrinsic pathway**, so named because a cellular element *outside* the blood is needed. We will first present this "classical" dual view (many tests of clinical bleeding disorders require an understanding of it) and then describe how, in fact, the two pathways function in an integrated way. Figure 20-24 will be an essential reference for this entire discussion. Also, Table 20-13 is a reference list of the names of and synonyms for the substances in these pathways.

The first plasma protein in the classical intrinsic pathway (upper left of Figure 20-24) is called factor XII. It can become activated to factor XIIa when it contacts certain types of surfaces, including the collagen fibers underlying damaged endothelium.[20] Factor XIIa then catalyzes the activation of factor XI to factor XIa, which activates factor IX to factor IXa. This last factor then activates factor X to factor Xa, which is the enzyme that converts prothrombin to thrombin. Note in Figure 20-24 that another plasma protein—factor VIIIa, the activated form of factor VIII—serves as a cofactor (not an enzyme) in the factor IXa-mediated activation of factor X. The importance of factor VIII is emphasized by the fact that the disease **hemophilia,** in which excessive bleeding occurs, is usually due to a genetic absence of this factor. In a smaller number of cases hemophilia is due to an absence of factor IX.

Now we turn to the extrinsic pathway for initiating the clotting cascade (upper right of Figure 20-24). This pathway begins with a protein called **tissue factor**, which is *not* a plasma protein. It is located instead on the outer plasma membrane of various tissue cells, including fibroblasts and other cells in the walls of blood vessels below the endothelium (tissue factor is *not* normally found on endothelial cells or blood cells). The blood is exposed to subendothelial cells when vessel damage disrupts the endothelial lining, and tissue factor then binds a plasma protein, factor VII, which becomes activated to factor VIIa. The complex of tissue factor and factor VIIa on the plasma membrane of the cell then catalyzes the activation of factor X. In addition, it catalyzes the activation of factor IX, which can then help activate more factor X by plugging into the intrinsic pathway.

In summary, theoretically clotting can be initiated either by the activation of factor XII or by the appearance of the tissue factor-factor VIIa complex. The two paths merge at factor Xa, which then catalyzes the conversion of

---

[20]The contact activation of factor XII is a complex process that requires not only collagen but also the participation of several other plasma proteins. Contact activation also explains why blood coagulates when it is taken from the body and put in a glass tube. This has nothing whatever to do with exposure to air, as popularly supposed, but happens because the glass surface induces the activation of factor XII and aggregation of platelets, as does a damaged vessel surface. A silicone coating markedly delays clotting by reducing the activating effects of the glass surface.

TABLE 20-13 OFFICIAL INTERNATIONAL COMMITTEE DESIGNATIONS FOR CLOTTING FACTORS ALONG WITH SYNONYMS MORE COMMONLY USED AT PRESENT

Factor I (fibrinogen)

Factor Ia (fibrin)

Factor II (prothrombin)

Factor IIa (thrombin)

Factor III (tissue factor, tissue thromboplastin)

Factor IV (Ca^{2+})

Factors V, VII, VIII, IX, X, XI, XII, and XIII are the inactive forms of these factors; the active forms add an "a" (for example, factor XIIa). There is no factor VI.

Platelet factor

FIGURE 20-24

Classical view of two independent pathways—called intrinsic and extrinsic—leading to the generation of thrombin. In the extrinsic pathway, tissue factor is a receptor for plasma factor VII, which becomes activated after binding to it. Factors VIIIa and Va act as cofactors, not enzymes. Activated platelets participate in the formation of factor Xa and thrombin. You might think that factors IX and X were accidentally transposed in the intrinsic pathway, but such is not the case; the order of activation really is XI, IX, and X. For the sake of clarity, the roles of calcium are not shown. As described in the text (and illustrated in Figure 20-25), factor XII and the contact activation step probably play little, if any, role in blood clotting in the body. The extrinsic pathway is usually the initiator, and the thrombin generated initially by it then recruits the intrinsic pathway by activating factors XI, VIII, and V, as well as platelets (not shown).

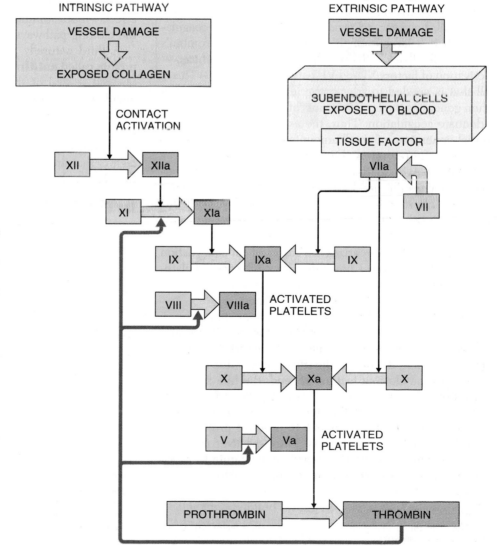

TABLE 20-14 ACTIONS OF THROMBIN

Procoagulant	Cleaves fibrinogen to fibrin
	Activates clotting factors XI, VIII, V, and XIII
	Stimulates platelets to display platelet factor and specific receptors for several clotting proteins
Anticoagulant	Activates protein C, which deactivates clotting factors VIII and V

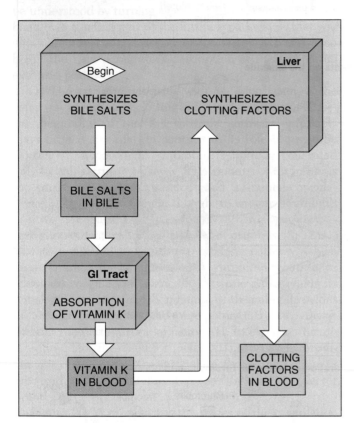

FIGURE 20-26
Roles of the liver in clotting.

increases the ability of t-PA to generate plasmin from plasminogen. Thus, fibrin is an important initiator of the fibrinolytic process that leads to its own dissolution.[24]

The secretion of t-PA is the last of the various anticlotting functions exerted by endothelial cells that we have mentioned in this chapter. They are summarized in Table 20-15.

ANTICLOTTING DRUGS

Various drugs are used clinically to prevent or reverse clotting, and a brief description of these actions serves as a review of key clotting mechanisms. One of the most common uses of these drugs is in the prevention and treatment of myocardial infarction (heart attacks), which,

---

[24]Plasminogen activators are normally involved not only in fibrinolysis but also in a host of other physiological processes, including tissue repair, ovulation, fertilization, and cell proliferation.

TABLE 20-15 ANTICLOTTING ROLES OF ENDOTHELIAL CELLS

Action	Result
Synthesize and release PGI$_2$ and nitric oxide	These inhibit platelet aggregation
Bind thrombin, which then activates protein C	Active protein C inactivates clotting factors VIII and V
Display heparin molecules on the surfaces of their plasma membranes	Heparin binds antithrombin III, and this molecule then inactivates thrombin and several other clotting factors
Secrete tissue plasminogen activator	Tissue plasminogen activator catalyzes the formation of plasmin, which dissolves clots

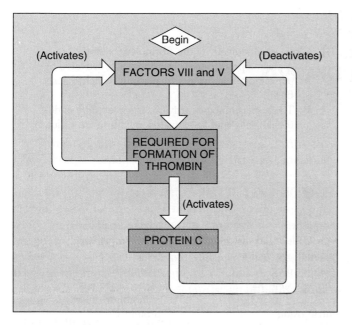

FIGURE 20-27
Thrombin activates factors VIII and V directly but deactivates them indirectly via protein C. Thus, it exerts both stimulatory and inhibitory effects on its own formation. (To activate protein C, thrombin must first bind to a thrombin-receptor, thrombomodulin, on endothelial cells, and this binding eliminates thrombin's procoagulant effects.)

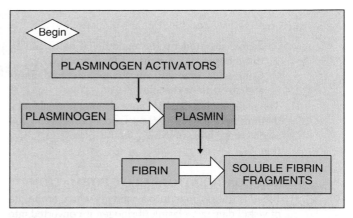

FIGURE 20-28
Basic fibrinolytic system. There are many different plasminogen activators and many different pathways for bringing them into play.

as described in Chapter 14, is often the result of abnormal clotting in an atherosclerotic coronary vessel.

Aspirin inhibits the cyclooxygenase enzyme in the eicosanoid pathways that generate prostaglandins and thromboxanes (Chapter 7). Since thromboxane A_2, produced by the platelets, is important for platelet aggregation, aspirin reduces both platelet aggregation and the ensuing coagulation. Importantly, low doses of aspirin inhibit platelet cyclooxygenase but not endothelial-cell cyclooxygenase, and so the formation of prostacyclin—the prostaglandin that opposes platelet aggregation—is not impaired. It has been demonstrated that the taking of one aspirin every other day for several years by men with no previous history of heart disease reduces the incidence of heart attacks by 50 percent.

Drugs that interfere with the action of vitamin K, which is required for synthesis of clotting factors by the liver, are collectively termed ***oral anticoagulants***.

Heparin, the naturally occurring endothelial-cell cofactor for antithrombin III, can also be administered as a drug, which then binds to endothelial cells. In addition to its role in the action of antithrombin III, heparin also inhibits platelet function.

In contrast to aspirin, the oral anticoagulants, and heparin, all of which *prevent* clotting, the fourth type of drug—plasminogen activators—dissolves a clot *after* it is formed and is termed ***thrombolytic therapy***. Intravenous administration of recombinant t-PA or a proteolytic drug called streptokinase within a few hours after myocardial infarction significantly reduces myocardial damage and mortality.

SECTION C SUMMARY

I. The initial response to blood-vessel damage is vasoconstriction and the sticking together of the opposed endothelial surfaces.

II. The next events are formation of a platelet plug followed by blood coagulation (clotting).

FORMATION OF A PLATELET PLUG

I. Platelets adhere to exposed collagen in a damaged vessel and release the contents of their secretory vesicles.

A. These substances help cause platelet aggregation.

B. This process is also enhanced by von Willebrand

tion because, at 18 pM, all the binding sites are occupied (the system is saturated) and there are no further binding sites available.

4-5. Phosphoprotein phosphatase removes the phosphate group from proteins that have been covalently modulated by protein kinase. Without phosphoprotein phosphatase, the protein could not return to its unmodulated state and would remain in its activated state. The ability to decrease as well as increase protein activity is essential to the regulation of physiological processes.

4-6. Nucleotide bases in DNA pair, A to T, and G to C. Given the base sequence of one DNA strand as

A-G-T-G-C-A-A-G-T-C-T

the corresponding strand of DNA would be

T-C-A-C-G-T-T-C-A-G-A

and the sequence in mRNA transcribed from the first strand would be

U-C-A-C-G-U-U-C-A-G-A

(Recall that uracil U replaces thymine T in RNA.)

4-7. The triplet code GTA will be transcribed into mRNA as CAU, and the anticodon in tRNA corresponding to CAU will be GUA.

4-8. If the gene were composed only of the triplet exon code words, it would be 300 nucleotides in length since a triplet of 3 nucleotides codes for one amino acid. However, because of the presence of intron segments, which account for 75 to 90 percent of the nucleotides in a gene, the gene would be between 900 and 2700 nucleotides long. Thus, the exact size of a gene cannot be determined by knowing the number of amino acids in the protein coded by the gene.

4-9. Tubulin is the protein that polymerizes to form microtubules. Tubulin monomers become linked together in a spiral that forms the walls of the hollow microtubule. Without microtubules to form the spindle apparatus, the chromosomes will not separate during mitosis. There are chemical agents in the cell that control the polymerization of tubulin at the time of mitosis and cause it to depolymerize following cell division.

4-10. A drug that inhibits DNA replication will inhibit mitosis since a duplicate set of chromosomes is necessary for cell division. Since one of the characteristics of cancer cells is their ability to undergo unlimited division, a drug that inhibits DNA replication will inhibit the multiplication of cancer cells. Unfortunately, such drugs also inhibit the division of normal cells, and this effect is particularly serious in cells that divide quickly. These include the cells that give rise to blood cells and the epithelial lining of the gastrointestinal tract. The use of such drugs must be carefully monitored to balance the damage done to normal tissues against the inhibition of tumor growth.

Chapter 5

5-1. The reactant molecules have a combined energy content of 55 + 93 = 148 kcal/mol, and the combined energy content of the products is 62 + 87 = 149. Thus, the energy content of the products exceeds that of the reactants by 1 kcal/mol, and this amount of energy must be added to A and B to form the products C and D.

The reaction is a reversible reaction since the difference in energy content between the reactants and products is small. When the reaction reaches chemical equilibrium, there will be a slightly higher concentration of reactants than products.

5-2. The maximum rate at which the end product E can be formed is 5, the rate of the slowest—rate-limiting—reaction in the pathway.

5-3. Under normal conditions, the concentration of oxygen at the level of the mitochondria is sufficient to saturate the enzyme that combines oxygen with hydrogen to form water. In the electron-transport chain, the rate-limiting reactions depend on the available concentrations of ADP and P_i, which are combined to form ATP.

If ADP and P_i concentrations are low, the rate of oxygen consumption will be low and will not be increased by increasing the oxygen concentration. In certain types of lung and circulatory diseases in which the transfer of oxygen from normal air to the blood and the delivery of blood to the tissues is impaired, the concentration of oxygen at the level of the mitochondria can become rate-limiting, and increasing the concentration of oxygen in the inhaled air will result in the delivery of more oxygen to the tissues and increase the rate of ATP formation.

5-4. During starvation, in the absence of ingested glucose, the body's stores of glycogen are rapidly depleted. Glucose, which is the major fuel used by the brain, must now be synthesized from other types of molecules. The major source of this newly formed glucose comes from the breakdown of proteins into amino acids and their conversion to glucose. To a lesser extent, the glycerol portion of fat is converted to glucose. The fatty acid portion of fat cannot be converted to glucose.

5-5. Since the Krebs cycle can function only during aerobic conditions, the catabolism of fat is dependent on the presence of oxygen. Fatty acids are broken down to acetyl coenzyme A during beta oxidation, and acetyl coenzyme A enters the Krebs cycle to be converted to carbon dioxide. In the absence of oxygen, acetyl coenzyme A cannot be converted to carbon dioxide and its increased concentration will inhibit the further beta oxidation of fatty acids.

5-6. Since the liver is the site at which ammonia is converted to urea, diseases that damage the liver can lead to an accumulation of ammonia in the blood, which is especially toxic to nerve cells. Note that it is not the liver that produces the ammonia. Ammonia is formed in most cells during the oxidative deamination of amino acids and then travels to the liver via the blood. The function of the liver is then to detoxify the ammonia by converting it to the nontoxic compound urea.

Chapter 6

6-1. (a) During diffusion, the net flux always occurs from high to low concentration. Thus it will be from 2 to 1 in A and from 1 to 2 in B. (b) At equilibrium the concentrations of solute in the two compartments will be equal: 4 mM in case A and 31 mM in case B. (c) Both will reach diffusion equilibrium at the same rate since the difference in concentration across the membrane is the same in each case, 2 mM (3 − 5) = −2, and (32 − 30) = 2. The two one-way fluxes will be much larger in B than in A, but the net fluxes are the same in both cases, although oriented in opposite directions.

6-2. The ability of one amino acid to decrease the flux of a second amino acid across a plasma membrane is an example of the competition between two molecules for the same binding site, as explained in Chapter 4. The binding site for alanine on the transport protein can also bind leucine. The higher the concentration of alanine, the greater the number of binding sites occupied by it, and the fewer available for binding leucine. Thus, less leucine will be moved into the cell.

6-3. The net transport will be out of the cell, in the direction from the higher-affinity site on the intracellular surface to the lower-affinity site on the extracellular surface. More molecules will be bound to the transporter on the high-affinity side of the membrane, and thus more will move out of the cell than into it, until the concentration in the extracellular fluid becomes large enough so that the number of bound proteins at the extracellular surface is equal to the number of bound proteins at the intracellular surface.

6-4. Although ATP is not used directly in secondary active transport, it is necessary for the primary active transport of sodium out of cells. Since it is the sodium concentration gradient across the plasma membrane that provides the energy for most secondary-active-transport systems, a decrease in ATP production, by decreasing primary active sodium transport, leading to a decrease in the sodium concentration gradient, will decrease secondary active transport.

6-5. The solution with the greatest osmolarity will have the lowest water concentration. The osmolarities are

A: 20 + 30 + 2(150) + 3(10) = 380 mOsm
B: 10 + 100 + 2(20) + 3(50) = 300 mOsm
C: 100 + 200 + 2(10) + 3(20) = 380 mOsm
D: 30 + 10 + 2(60) + 3(100) = 460 mOsm

Solution D thus has the lowest water concentration. (Recall that NaCl forms two ions in solution, and CaCl$_2$, three.)

Solutions A and C are isoosmotic since they have the same osmolarity.

6-6. Initially the osmolarity of compartment 1 is (2 × 200) + 100 = 500 mOsm, and that of 2 is (2 × 100) + 300 = 500 mOsm. The two solutions are thus isoosmotic, and there is no difference in water concentration across the membrane. Since the membrane is permeable to urea but not to NaCl, urea will diffuse from compartment 2 into compartment 1, producing an increase in the osmolarity of compartment 1, lowering its water concentration and thus causing a net flow of water into compartment 1, increasing its volume. This net movement of urea and water into compartment 1 will continue until (a) urea reaches diffusion equilibrium at a concentration of 200 mM in each compartment, and (b) the movement of water has lowered the concentration of NaCl in compartment 1 to 150 mM and raised that of NaCl in compartment 2 to 150 mM. Note that the same volume change would have occurred if there had been no urea pres-

ent in either compartment. It is only the concentration of nonpenetrating solutes, NaCl in this case, that determines the volume change, regardless of the concentration of any penetrating solutes that are present.

6-7. The osmolarities and nonpenetrating solute concentrations are:

Solution	Osmolarity, mOsm	Nonpenetrating solute concentration, mM
A	(2 × 150) + 100 = 400	2 × 150 = 300
B	(2 × 100) + 150 = 350	2 × 100 = 200
C	(2 × 200) + 100 = 500	2 × 200 = 400
D	(2 × 100) + 50 = 250	2 × 100 = 200

Only the concentration of nonpenetrating solutes, NaCl in this case, will determine the change in cell volume. Since the intracellular concentration of nonpenetrating solute is 300 mOsm, solution A will produce no change in cell volume. Solutions B and D will cause cells to swell since they have a lower concentration of nonpenetrating solutes than the intracellular fluid. Solution C will cause cells to shrink because it has a higher concentration of nonpenetrating solutes than the intracellular fluid.

6-8. Solution A is isotonic—having the same concentration of nonpenetrating solutes as the intracellular fluid (300 mM). Solution A is also hyperosmotic since its total osmolarity is greater than 300 mOsm, as is true also for solutions B and C. Solution B is hypotonic since its concentration of nonpenetrating solutes is less than 300 mM. Solution C is hypertonic since its concentration of nonpenetrating solutes is greater than 300 mM. Solution D is hypotonic (less than 300 mM of nonpenetrating solutes) and also hypoosmotic (having a total osmolarity of less than 300 mOsm).

6-9. Exocytosis is triggered by an increase in intracellular calcium concentration. Calcium ions can be actively transported out of cells by secondary countertransport coupled to the entry of sodium ions on the same transport protein. If the intracellular concentration of sodium ions were increased, the sodium concentration gradient across the membrane would be decreased, and this would decrease the secondary active transport of calcium out of the cell. This would lead to an increase in intracellular calcium concentration, which would trigger increased exocytosis.

Chapter 7

7-1. 4.4 mM. If you answered 8 mM, you ignored the fact that plasma potassium concentration is homeostatically regulated so that the doubling of input will lead to negative-feedback reflexes that oppose an equivalent increase in plasma concentration. If you answered 4 mM, you ignored the fact that homeostatic control systems cannot *totally* prevent changes in the regulated variable when a perturbation occurs. Thus, there must be *some* rise in plasma potassium concentration in this situation (to serve as the error signal for the compensating reflexes), and this is consis-

11-6. The oxidative motor units, both fast and slow, will be affected first by a decrease in blood flow since they depend on it to provide both the fuel—glucose and fatty acids—and the oxygen required to metabolize the fuel. The fast-glycolytic motor units will be affected more slowly by the decreased blood flow since they rely predominantly on internal stores of glycogen, the glucose molecules of which are anaerobically metabolized by glycolysis.

11-7. Two factors lead to recovery of muscle force. (1) Some new fibers can be formed by the fusion and development of undifferentiated satellite cells. This will replace some, but not all, of the fibers that were damaged. (2) Some of the restored force is the result of hypertrophy of the surviving fibers. The undamaged fibers must produce more force to move a given load because of the loss of supporting fibers in the accident, and these fibers are stimulated to undergo increased synthesis of actin and myosin, resulting in increases in fiber diameter and thus their force of contraction.

11-8. In the absence of extracellular calcium ions, skeletal muscle contracts normally in response to an action potential in its plasma membrane because the calcium required to trigger contraction comes entirely from the sarcoplasmic reticulum within the muscle fibers. If the motor neuron to the muscle is stimulated in a calcium-free medium, however, the muscle will not contract because the influx of calcium from the extracellular fluid into the motor nerve terminal is necessary to trigger the release of acetylcholine that in turn triggers an action potential in the muscle.

The response of smooth muscle in a calcium-free medium depends on the type of smooth muscle. Smooth muscles that depend primarily on calcium released from the sarcoplasmic reticulum will behave like skeletal muscle and respond to direct stimulation but not to nerve stimulation in the absence of extracellular calcium. Smooth muscles that rely on an influx of calcium from the extracellular fluid to trigger contraction will fail to contract in response to both types of stimuli.

11-9. The simplest model to explain the experimental observations is as follows: Upon parasympathetic stimulation, a neurotransmitter is released that binds to receptor sites on the membranes of smooth-muscle cells and triggers contraction. The substance released is not acetylcholine and does not act on ACh receptors. (Not ruled out by these observations is the possibility that the neurotransmitter acts upon some nonmuscle cells that in turn release a substance that acts upon the smooth muscle to produce contraction.)

Action potentials in the parasympathetic nerves are essential for initiating nerve-induced contraction. When the nerves were prevented from generating action potentials by blocking their voltage-sensitive sodium channels, there was no response to nerve stimulation. However, the muscle still responded to the nonmetabolized form of ACh because smooth-muscle action potentials depend on opening voltage-sensitive calcium channels, not voltage-sensitive sodium channels. ACh is the neurotransmitter released from most, but not all, parasympathetic endings. The observation that the muscle could be contracted by injecting a nonmetabolized form of ACh indicates that the smooth muscle probably has receptors for ACh and this response can be blocked by a drug that specifically blocks ACh at muscarinic receptors, the receptors for ACh on smooth muscle. When the muscarinic receptors were blocked, however, stimulation of the parasympathetic nerves still produced a contraction, providing evidence that some substance other than ACh was producing contraction. This indicates that postganglionic parasympathetic nerve endings release a substance other than ACh. It is also possible that the ending releases ACh, which acts on nicotinic receptors (these are not blocked by muscarinic drugs) located on another neuron, which then releases the non-ACh neurotransmitter that acts upon the smooth muscle.

Chapter 12

12-1. None. The gamma motor neurons are important in preventing the muscle-spindle stretch receptors from going slack, but when testing this reflex, the intrafusal fibers are not flaccid. The test is performed with a bent knee, which stretches the extensor muscles in the thigh (and the intrafusal-muscle fibers within them). The stretch receptors are therefore responsive.

12-2. The efferent pathway of the reflex arc (the alpha motor neurons) would not be activated, the effector organ (the extrafusal muscle fibers) would not be activated, and there would be no reflex response.

12-3. The drawing must have excitatory synapses on the motor neurons of both ipsilateral extensor and ipsilateral flexor muscles. Thus, there will be no reciprocal innervation.

12-4. A toxin that interferes with the inhibitory synapses on motor neurons would leave unbalanced the normal excitatory input to these neurons. Thus, the motor neurons would fire excessively, which would result in increased muscle contraction. This is exactly what happens in lockjaw as a result of the toxin produced by the tetanus bacillus.

Chapter 13

13-1. Dopamine is depleted in the basal ganglia of people having Parkinson's disease, and they are therapeutically given dopamine agonists, usually L-dopa. This treatment raises dopamine levels in other parts of the brain, however, where the dopamine levels were previously normal. Schizophrenia is associated with increased brain dopamine levels, and symptoms of this disease appear when dopamine levels are high. The converse therapeutic problem can occur during the treatment of schizophrenics with dopamine-lowering drugs when the symptoms of Parkinson's disease sometimes show as side effects.

13-2. Experiments done on anesthetized animals often involve either stimulating a brain part to observe the effects of increased neuronal activity or damaging ("lesioning") an area to observe resulting deficits. Such experiments on animals, which lack the complex language mechanisms of people, cannot help with language studies. Diseases sometimes mimic these two experimental situations, and behavioral studies of the resulting language deficits in people with aphasia, coupled with study of their brains after death, have provided a wealth of information.

Chapter 14

14-1. No. Decreased erythrocyte volume is certainly one possible explanation, but there is a second: The person might have a normal erythrocyte volume but an abnormally increased plasma volume. Convince yourself of this by writing the hematocrit equation as erythrocyte volume/(erythrocyte volume + plasma volume).

14-2. A halving of tube radius. Resistance is directly proportional to blood viscosity but inversely proportional to the *fourth power* of tube radius.

14-3. The plateau of the action potential and the contraction would be absent. You might think that contraction would persist since most calcium in excitation-contraction coupling in the heart comes from the sarcoplasmic reticulum. However, the major signal for the release of this calcium is the calcium entering across the plasma membrane.

14-4. The SA node is not functioning, and the ventricles are being driven by a pacemaker in the vicinity of the AV Node.

14-5. The person has a narrowed aortic valve. Normally, the resistance across the aortic valve is so small that there is only a tiny pressure difference between the left ventricle and the aorta during ventricular ejection. In the example given here, the large pressure difference indicates that resistance across the valve must be very high.

14-6. This question is analogous to question 14-5 in that the large pressure difference across a valve while the valve is open indicates an abnormally narrowed valve—in this case the left AV valve.

14-7. Decreased heart rate and contractility. These are effects mediated by the sympathetic nerves on the beta-adrenergic receptors in the heart.

14-8. 120 mmHg. MAP = DP + $\frac{1}{3}$(SP − DP).

14-9. The drug must have caused the arterioles in the kidneys to dilate enough to reduce their resistance by 50 percent. Blood flow to an organ is determined by mean arterial pressure and the organ's resistance to flow. Another important point can be deduced here: If mean arterial pressure has not changed even though renal resistance has dropped 50 percent, then either the resistance of some other organ or the cardiac output has gone up.

14-10. The experiment suggests that acetylcholine causes vasodilation by releasing EDRF or some other vasodilator from endothelial cells.

14-11. A low plasma protein concentration. Capillary pressure is, if anything, lower than normal and so cannot be causing the edema. Another possibility is that capillary permeability to plasma proteins has increased, as occurs in burns.

14-12. 20 mmHg/L per minute. TPR = MAP/CO.

14-13. Nothing. Cardiac output and TPR have remained unchanged, and so their product, MAP, has also remained unchanged. This question emphasizes that MAP depends on cardiac output but not upon the combination of heart rate and stroke volume that produces the cardiac output.

14-14. It increases. There are a certain number of impulses traveling up the nerves from the arterial baroreceptors. When these nerves are cut, the number of impulses reaching the medullary cardiovascular center goes to zero, just as it would physiologically if the mean arterial pressure were to decrease markedly. Accordingly, the medullary cardiovascular center responds to the absent impulses by reflexly increasing arterial pressure.

14-15. It decreases. The hemorrhage causes no immediate change in hematocrit since erythrocytes and plasma are lost in the same proportion. As interstitial fluid starts entering the capillaries, however, it expands the plasma volume and decreases the hematocrit. (This is too soon for any new erythrocytes to be synthesized.)

Chapter 15

15-1. 200 ml/mmHg.

$$\text{Lung compliance} = \frac{\Delta \text{ lung volume}}{\Delta (P_{\text{alv}} - P_{\text{ip}})}$$

$$= \frac{800 \text{ ml}}{[0 - (-8)] \text{ mmHg} - [0 - (-4)] \text{ mmHg}}$$

$$= \frac{800 \text{ ml}}{4 \text{ mmHg}} = \frac{200 \text{ ml}}{\text{mmHg}}$$

15-2. More subatmospheric than normal. A decreased surfactant level causes the lungs to be less compliant, that is, more difficult to expand. Therefore, a greater transpulmonary pressure $(P_{\text{alv}} - P_{\text{ip}})$ is required to expand them a given amount.

15-3. No.

$$\text{Alveolar ventilation} = (\text{tidal volume} - \text{dead space})$$
$$\times \text{breathing rate}$$

$$= (250 \text{ ml} - 150 \text{ ml}) \times (20 \text{ breaths/min})$$

$$= 2000 \text{ ml/min}$$

whereas normal alveolar ventilation is approximately 4000 ml/min.

15-4. The volume of the snorkel constitutes an additional dead space, and so total pulmonary ventilation must be increased if alveolar ventilation is to remain constant.

15-5. The alveolar P_{O_2} will be higher than normal, and the alveolar P_{CO_2} will be lower. If you do not understand why, review the factors that determine the alveolar gas pressures.

15-6. No. Hypoventilation reduces arterial P_{O_2} but only because it reduces alveolar P_{O_2}. That is, in hypoventilation, both alveolar and arterial P_{O_2} are decreased to essentially the same degree. In this problem, alveolar P_{O_2} is normal, and so the person is not hypoventilating. The low arterial P_{O_2} must therefore represent a defect that causes a discrepancy between alveolar P_{O_2} and arterial P_{O_2}. Possibilities include impaired diffusion, a shunting of blood from the right side of the heart to the left through a hole in the heart wall, and mismatching of air flow and blood flow in the alveoli.

15-7. Not at rest, if the defect is not too severe. Recall that equilibration of alveolar air and pulmonary capillary blood is nor-

tional binding sites in a multimeric protein

core temperature temperature of inner body

cornea (KOR-nee-ah) transparent structure covering front of eye; forms part of eye's optical system and helps focus an object's image on retina

cornification (kor-nif-ih-KAY-shun) process by which outer epithelial layer is converted to dead, horny cells

coronary pertaining to blood vessels of the heart

coronary blood flow blood flow to heart muscle

corpus callosum (KOR-pus kal-LOW-sum) wide band of nerve fibers connecting the two cerebral hemispheres; a brain commissure

corpus luteum (LOO-tee-um) ovarian structure formed from the follicle after ovulation; secretes estrogen and progesterone

cortex (CORE-tex) outer layer of organ; *see also* adrenal cortex, cerebral cortex; *compare* medulla

cortical association area region of parietal and frontal cerebral cortex; receives input from various sensory types, memory stores, and so on, and performs further perceptual processing

corticobulbar pathway (kor-tih-koh BUL-bar) descending pathway having its neuron cell bodies in cerebral cortex; its axons pass without synapsing to region of brainstem motor neurons

corticospinal pathway descending pathway having its neuron cell bodies in cerebral cortex; its axons pass without synapsing to region of spinal motor neurons; also called the pyramidal tract; *compare* noncorticospinal pathway, corticobulbar pathway

corticosteroid (kor-tih-koh-STEAR-oid) steroid produced by adrenal cortex or drug that resembles one

corticotropin releasing hormone (CRH) (kort-ih-koh-TROH-pin) hypothalamic hormone that stimulates ACTH (corticotropin) secretion by anterior pituitary

cortisol (KORT-ih-sol) main glucocorticoid hormone secreted by adrenal cortex; regulates various aspects of organic metabolism

cotransmitter chemical messenger released with a neurotransmitter from synapse or neuroeffector junction

cotransport form of secondary active

transport in which net movement of actively transported substance and "downhill" movement of molecule supplying the energy are in the same direction

countercurrent multiplier system mechanism associated with loops of Henle that creates in renal medulla a region having high interstitial-fluid osmolarity

countertransport form of secondary active transport in which net movement of actively transported molecule is in direction opposite "downhill" movement of molecule supplying the energy

covalent bond (koh-VAY-lent) chemical bond between two atoms in which each atom shares one of its electrons with the other

covalent modulation alteration of a protein's shape and therefore its function by covalent binding of various chemical groups to it

cranial nerve one of 24 peripheral nerves (12 pairs) that join brainstem or forebrain

creatine phosphate (KREE-ah-tin) molecule that transfers phosphate and energy to ADP to generate ATP

creatinine (kree-AT-ih-nin) waste product derived from muscle creatine

creatinine clearance plasma volume from which creatinine is removed by kidneys per unit time; approximates glomerular filtration rate

critical period time during development when a system is most readily influenced by environmental factors, sometimes irreversibly

cross-bridge myosin projection extending from muscle thick filament and capable of exerting force on thin filament, causing the filaments to slide past each other

cross-bridge cycle sequence of events between binding of a cross-bridge to actin, its release, and reattachment

crossed-extensor reflex increased activation of extensor muscles contralateral to a limb flexion

crossing-over process in which segments of maternal and paternal chromosomes exchange with each other during chromosomal pairing in meiosis

crystalloid low-molecular-weight solute

cumulus oophorous (QUUM-you-lus oh-oh-FOR-us) granulosa cells surrounding egg where egg projects into ovarian follicle antrum

current movement of electric charge; in biological systems, this is achieved by ion movement

cutaneous (cue-TAY-nee-us) pertaining to skin

cyclic AMP (cAMP) cyclic 3′,5′-adenosine monophosphate; cyclic nucleotide that serves as a second messenger for many chemical messengers

cyclic AMP-dependent protein kinase (KI-nase) enzyme that is activated by cyclic AMP and then phosphorylates specific proteins, thereby altering their activity; also called protein kinase A

cyclic endoperoxide eicosanoid formed from arachidonic acid by cyclooxygenase

cyclic GMP (cGMP) cyclic 3′,5′-guanosine monophosphate; cyclic nucleotide that acts as second messenger in some cells

cyclooxygenase (cy-klo-OX-ah-jen-ase) enzyme that acts on arachidonic acid and leads to production of cyclic endoperoxides, prostaglandins, and thromboxanes

cytochrome (SIGH-toe-krome) one of a series of enzymes that couples energy to ATP formation during oxidative phosphorylation

cytokine (SIGH-toe-kine) general term for protein intercellular messengers that influence cells of the immune system; secreted by macrophages and monocytes (monokine), lymphocytes (lymphokine), and other cells

cytokinesis (sigh-toe-kin-EE-sis) stage of cell division during which cytoplasm divides to form two new cells

cytoplasm (SIGH-toe-plasm) region of cell interior outside the nucleus

cytosine (C) (SIGH-toe-seen) pyrimidine base in DNA and RNA

cytoskeleton cytoplasmic filamentous network associated with cell shape and movement

cytosol (SIGH-toe-sol) intracellular fluid that surrounds cell organelles and nucleus

cytotoxic T cell (sigh-toe-TOX-ik) T lymphocyte that, upon activation by specific antigen, directly attacks a cell bearing that type of antigen and destroys it; major killer of virus-infected and tumor cells

daughter cell one of the two new cells formed when a cell divides

dead space volume of inspired air that cannot be exchanged with blood; *see* *also* anatomic dead space, alveolar dead space, total dead space

deamination (dee-am-in-A-shun) removal of amino (—NH$_2$) group from a molecule

decremental decreasing in amplitude

defecation (deaf-ih-KAY-shun) expulsion of feces from rectum

dehydroepiandrosterone (dee-hydro-epi-andro-stir-OWN) androgen hormone secreted by adrenal cortex

delta wave oscillation on electroencephalogram slower than 4 Hz; associated with sleep

dendrite (DEN-drite) highly branched extension of neuron cell body; receives synaptic input from other neurons

denervation atrophy (AT-row-fee) decrease in size of muscle fiber whose nerve supply is destroyed

dense body cytoplasmic structure to which thin filaments of a smooth-muscle fiber are anchored

deoxyhemoglobin (Hb) (dee-ox-see-HE-mo-glo-bin) hemoglobin not combined with oxygen; reduced hemoglobin

deoxyribonucleic acid (DNA) (dee-ox-see-rye-bow-new-CLAY-ik) nucleic acid that stores and transmits genetic information; consists of double strand of nucleotide subunits that contain deoxyribose

depolarize to change membrane potential value toward zero, so that cell interior becomes less negative than resting level

depression disturbance in mood characterized by pervasive sadness or loss of interest or pleasure

descending limb (of Henle's loop) segment of renal tubule into which proximal tubule drains

descending pathway neural pathways that go from the brain down to the spinal cord

desmosome (DEZ-moe-zome) cell junction that holds two cells together; consists of plasma membranes of adjacent cells linked by fibers yet separated by a 20-nm extracellular space filled with a cementing substance

diacylglycerol (DAG) (die-ace-ill-GLIS-er-all) second messenger that activates protein kinase C, which then phosphorylates a large number of other proteins

dialysis (die-AL-ih-sis) process of altering the concentration of substances in the blood by using concentration differences between plasma and a bathing solution separated by a semipermeable membrane

diaphragm (DIE-ah-fram) dome-shaped skeletal muscle sheet that separates the abdominal and thoracic cavities; principal muscle of respiration

diastole (die-ASS-toe-lee) period of cardiac cycle when ventricles are not contracting

diastolic pressure (die-ah-STAL-ik) minimum blood pressure during cardiac cycle

diencephalon (die-en-SEF-ah-lon) core of anterior part of brain; lies beneath cerebral hemispheres and contains *thalamus* and *hypothalamus*

differentiation (dif-fer-en-she-A-shun) process by which cells acquire specialized structural and functional properties

diffusion (dif-FU-shun) random movement of molecules from one location to another because of random thermal molecular motion; net diffusion always occurs from a region of higher concentration to a region of lower concentration

diffusion equilibrium state during which diffusion fluxes in opposite directions are equal, that is, net flux equals zero.

diffusion potential voltage difference created by net diffusion of ions

digestion process of breaking down large particles and high-molecular-weight substances into small molecules

dihydrotestosterone (die-hi-droh-tes-TOS-ter-own) steroid formed by enzyme-mediated alteration of testosterone; active form of testosterone in certain of its target cells

1,25-dihydroxyvitamin D$_3$ (1-25-die-hi-DROX-ee-vie-tah-min DEE-3) hormone that is formed by kidneys and is active form of vitamin D

2,3-diphosphoglycerate (DPG) (2-3-die-fos-foe-GLISS-er-ate) substance produced by erythrocytes during glycolysis; binds reversibly to hemoglobin, causing it to release oxygen

disaccharide (die-SAK-er-ide) carbohydrate molecule composed of two monosaccharides

disinhibition removal of inhibition from a neuron, thereby allowing its activity to increase

dissociation separation from

distal (DIS-tal) farther from reference point; *compare* proximal

distal convoluted tubule portion of kidney tubule between loop of Henle and collecting duct

disulfide bond R—S—S—R

disuse atrophy (AT-row-fee) decrease in size of muscle fibers that are not used for a long time

diuresis (die-u-REE-sis) increased urine excretion

diuretic (die-u-RET-ik) substance that inhibits fluid reabsorption in renal tubule, thereby increasing urine excretion

diurnal (die-URN-al) daily; occurring in a 24-h cycle

divergence (die-VER-gence) (neuronal) one presynaptic neuron synapsing upon many postsynaptic neurons; (of eyes) turning of eyes outward to view distant objects

dl deciliter; 0.1 L

DNA polymerase enzyme that, during DNA replication, forms new DNA strand by joining together nucleotides already base-paired with an existing DNA strand

dopamine (DOPE-ah-mean) biogenic amine (catecholamine) neurotransmitter and hormone; precursor of epinephrine and norepinephrine

dopamine hypothesis theory that schizophrenia is due to increased activity in dopaminergic pathways

dorsal (DOR-sal) toward or at the back

dorsal root group of afferent nerve fibers that enters dorsal region of spinal cord

double bond two covalent chemical bonds formed between same two atoms; symbolized by =

double helix molecular conformation in which two strands of molecules are coiled around each other; conformation of DNA

down-regulation decrease in number of target-cell receptors for a given messenger in response to a chronic high concentration of that messenger

dual innervation (in-ner-VAY-shun) innervation of an organ or gland by both sympathetic and parasympathetic nerve fibers

duodenum (due-oh-DEE-num) first portion of small intestine (between stomach and jejunum)

eardrum *see* tympanic membrane

ectopic focus (ek-TOP-ik) region of heart other than SA node that assumes role of cardiac pacemaker

ectopic pregnancy implantation and development of a fetus at a site other than the uterus

edema (eh-DEE-mah) accumulation of excess fluid in interstitial space

EEG arousal transformation of EEG pattern from alpha to beta rhythm during increased levels of attention

effector (ee-FECK-tor) cell or cell collection whose change in activity constitutes the response in a control system

effector macrophage *see* activated macrophage

effector protein plasma membrane protein that serves as ion channel or enzyme in signal transduction sequence; intracellular protein altered in response to activated receptor

efferent (EF-er-ent) carrying away from

efferent arteriole renal vessel that conveys blood from glomerulus to peritubular capillaries

efferent neuron neuron that carries information away from CNS

efferent pathway component of reflex arc that transmits information from integrating center to effector

egg female germ cell at any of its stages of development

eicosanoid (eye-KOH-sah-noid) general term for modified fatty acids that are products of arachidonic acid metabolism (cyclic endoperoxides, prostaglandins, thromboxanes, and leukotrienes); function as paracrine or autocrine agents

ejaculation (ee-jak-you-LAY-shun) discharge of semen from penis

ejaculatory duct (ee-JAK-you-lah-tory) continuation of vas deferens after it is joined by seminal vesicle duct; joins urethra in prostate gland

electric charge particle having excess positivity or negativity

electric force force that causes charged particles to move toward regions having an opposite charge and away from regions having a like charge

electric potential (E) (or electric potential difference) *see* potential

electric signal graded potential or action potential

electric synapse (SIN-apse) synapse at which local currents resulting from electrical activity flow between two neurons through gap junctions joining them

electrocardiogram (ECG, EKG) (ee-lek-tro-CARD-ee-oh-gram) record-

ing at skin surface of the electric currents generated by cardiac muscle action potentials

electrochemical difference force determining direction and magnitude of net charge movement; combination of electrical and chemical gradients

electrode (ee-LEK-trode) probe used to stimulate electrically, or record from, the body surface or a tissue

electroencephalogram (EEG) (eh-lek-tro-en-SEF-ah-low-gram) recording of brain electrical activity from scalp

electrogenic pump (elec-tro-JEN-ik) active-transport system that directly separates electric charge, thereby producing a potential difference

electrolyte (ee-LEK-tro-lite) substance that dissociates into ions when in aqueous solution

electromagnetic radiation radiation composed of waves with electrical and magnetic components; includes gamma rays, x-rays, and ultraviolet, light, infrared, and radio waves

electron (ee-LEK-tron) subatomic particle that carries one unit of negative charge

embryo (EM-bree-oh) organism during early stages of development; in human beings, the first 2 months of intrauterine life

emission (ee-MISH-un) movement of male genital duct contents into urethra prior to ejaculation

emotion *see* inner emotion, emotional behavior

emotional behavior outward expression and display of inner emotions

emulsification (eh-mul-sih-fih-KAY-shun) fat-solubilizing process in which large lipid droplets are broken into smaller ones

end-diastolic volume (EDV) (die-ah-STAH-lik) amount of blood in ventricle just prior to systole

endocrine gland (EN-doe-krin) group of cells that secrete into the extracellular space hormones that then diffuse into bloodstream; also called a ductless gland

endocrine system all the body's hormone-secreting glands

endocytosis (en-doe-sigh-TOE-sis) process in which plasma membrane folds into the cell, forming small pockets that pinch off to produce intracellular, membrane-bound vesicles; *see also* phagocytosis

endogenous opioid (en-dodge-en-ous OH-pea-oid) certain neuropeptides—endorphin, dynorphin, and enkephalin

endogenous pyrogen (EP) (en-DAHJ-en-us PIE-row-jen) cytokines (including interleukin 1 and probably interleukin 6 and tumor necrosis factor) that act physiologically in the brain to cause fever

endometrium (en-dough-ME-tree-um) glandular epithelium lining uterine cavity

endoperoxide *see* cyclic endoperoxide

endoplasmic reticulum (en-doe-PLAS-mik ree-TIK-you-lum) cell organelle that consists of interconnected network of membrane-bound branched tubules and flattened sacs; two types are distinguished—*granular*, with ribosomes attached, and *agranular*, which is smooth-surfaced

β-endorphin (en-DOR-fin) opioid peptide secreted by anterior pituitary; synthesized as part of pro-opiomelanocortin and cosecreted with ACTH; *see also* endorphin

endorphin an endogenous opioid; functions as neurotransmitter at synapses activated by opiate drugs and as paracrine agent and hormone

endothelium (en-doe-THEE-lee-um) thin layer of cells that lines heart cavities and blood vessels

endothelium-derived relaxing factor (EDRF) nitric oxide; secreted by vascular endothelium, it relaxes vascular smooth muscle and causes arteriolar dilation

end-plate potential (EPP) depolarization of motor end plate of skeletal-muscle fiber in response to acetylcholine; initiates action potential in muscle plasma membrane

end-product inhibition inhibition of a metabolic pathway by final product's action upon allosteric site on an enzyme (usually the rate-limiting enzyme) in the pathway

end-systolic volume (ESV) (sis-TAH-lik) amount of blood remaining in ventricle after ejection

energy ability to produce change; measured by amount of work performed during a given change

enkephalin (en-KEF-ah-lyn) peptide neurotransmitter at some synapses activated by opiate drugs; an endogenous opioid

enteric nervous system (en-TAIR-ik)

neural network residing in and innervating walls of gastrointestinal tract

enterogastrones (en-ter-oh-GAS-tronez) collective term for hormones that are released by intestinal tract and inhibit stomach activity

enterohepatic circulation (en-ter-oh-hih-PAT-ik) reabsorption of bile salts (and other substances) from intestines, passage to liver (via hepatic portal vein), and secretion back to intestines (via bile)

enterokinase (en-ter-oh-KI-nase) an enzyme in luminal plasma membrane of intestinal epithelial cells; converts pancreatic trypsinogen to trypsin

entrainment (en-TRAIN-ment) adjusting biological rhythm to environmental cues

enzyme (EN-zime) protein catalyst that accelerates specific chemical reactions but does not itself undergo net change during the reaction

enzyme activity measure of the properties of enzyme's active site as altered by allosteric or covalent modulation; affects rate of enzyme-mediated reaction

eosinophil (ee-oh-SIN-oh-fil) polymorphonuclear granulocytic leukocyte whose granules take up red dye eosin; involved in allergic responses and parasite destruction

epididymis (ep-ih-DID-eh-mus) portion of male reproductive duct system located between seminiferous tubules and vas deferens

epiglottis (ep-ig-GLOT-iss) thin cartilage flap that folds down, covering trachea, during swallowing

epinephrine (ep-ih-NEF-rin) hormone secreted by adrenal medulla and involved in regulation of organic metabolism; a biogenic amine (catecholamine) neurotransmitter; also called adrenaline

epiphyseal closure (eh-pif-ih-SEE-al) conversion of epiphyseal growth plate to bone

epiphyseal growth plate actively proliferating cartilage near bone ends; region of bone growth

epiphysis (eh-PIF-ih-sis) end of long bone

epithelial cell (ep-ih-THEE-lee-al) cell at surface of body or hollow organ; specialized to secrete or absorb ions and organic molecules; with other epithelial cells, forms an epithelium

epithelial transport molecule movement from one extracellular compartment across epithelial cells into a second extracellular compartment

epithelium (ep-ih-THEE-lee-um) tissue that covers all body surfaces, lines all body cavities, and forms most glands

equilibrium (ee-qua-LIB-rium) no net change occurs in a system; requires no energy

equilibrium potential voltage gradient across a membrane that is equal in force but opposite in direction to concentration force affecting a given ion species

erection penis or clitoris becoming stiff due to vascular congestion

error signal steady-state difference between level of regulated variable in a control system and set point for that variable

erythrocyte (eh-RITH-row-site) red blood cell

erythropoiesis (eh-rith-row-poy-EE-sis) erythrocyte production

erythropoietin (eh-rith-row-POY-ih-tin) hormone secreted mainly by kidney cells; stimulates red blood cell production; one of the hematopoietic growth factors

esophagus portion of digestive tract that connects throat (pharynx) and stomach

essential amino acid amino acid that cannot be formed by the body at all (or at rate adequate to meet metabolic requirements) and must be obtained from diet

essential element chemical substance that must be present for normal growth and function of the body

essential nutrient substance required for normal or optimal body function but synthesized by the body either not at all or in amounts inadequate to prevent disease

estradiol (es-tra-DIE-ol) steroid hormone of estrogen family; major female sex hormone

estriol (ES-tree-ol) steroid hormone of estrogen family; major estrogen secreted by placenta during pregnancy

estrogen group of steroid hormones that have effects similar to estradiol on female reproductive tract

euphorigen (you-FOR-ih-jen) drug that elevates mood

excitability ability to produce electric signals

excitable membrane membrane capable of producing action potentials

excitation-contraction coupling mechanism in muscle fibers linking plasma membrane depolarization with cross-bridge force generation

excitatory postsynaptic potential (EPSP) (post-sin-NAP-tic) depolarizing graded potential in postsynaptic neuron in response to activation of excitatory synapse

excitatory synapse (SIN-apse) synapse that, when activated, increases likelihood that postsynaptic neuron will undergo action potentials or increases frequency of existing action potentials

excretion appearance of a substance in urine or feces

exocrine gland (EX-oh-krin) cluster of epithelial cells specialized for secretion and having ducts that lead to an epithelial surface

exocytosis (ex-oh-sigh-TOE-sis) process in which intracellular vesicle fuses with plasma membrane, the vesicle opens, and its contents are liberated into the extracellular fluid

exon (EX-on) gene region containing code words for an amino acid sequence in a protein

expiration (ex-pur-A-shun) movement of air out of lungs

expiratory reserve volume (ex-PIE-ruh-tor-ee) volume of air exhaled by maximal contraction of expiratory muscles after normal expiration

extension straightening a joint

extensor muscle muscle whose activity straightens a joint

external anal sphincter ring of skeletal muscle around lower end of rectum

external environment environment surrounding external surfaces of an organism

external genitalia (jen-ih-TAH-lee-ah) (female) mons pubis, labia majora and minora, clitoris, vestibule of the vagina, and vestibular glands; (male) penis and scrotum

external work movement of external objects by skeletal muscle contraction

extracellular fluid fluid outside cell; interstitial fluid and plasma

extrafusal fiber primary muscle fiber in skeletal muscle, as opposed to modified (intrafusal) fibers in muscle spindle; also called skeletomotor fiber

extrapyramidal system *see* multineuronal pathway

by evaporation from skin and respiratory-passage lining

inspiration air movement from atmosphere into lungs

inspiratory muscles those muscles whose contraction contributes to inspiration

inspiratory neuron neuron in medulla oblongata that fires in synchrony with inspiration and ceases firing during expiration

inspiratory reserve volume maximal air volume that can be inspired above resting tidal volume

insulin (IN-suh-lin) peptide hormone secreted by B cells of pancreatic islets of Langerhans; has metabolic and growth-promoting effects; stimulates glucose and amino acid uptake by most cells and stimulates protein, fat, and glycogen synthesis

insulin-like growth factor one of a group of peptides that have growth-promoting effects

insulin-like growth factor I (IGF-I) insulin-like growth factor that mediates mitosis-stimulating effect of growth hormone on bone and possibly other tissues; also known as somatomedin C

integral protein protein embedded in membrane lipid layer; may span entire membrane or be located at only one side

integrating center cells that receive one or more signals, compare them to a physiological set point, and send out appropriate response; also called an integrator

intercalated disk (in-TER-kah-lay-ted) thickened end of cardiac muscle cell where cell is connected to adjacent cell

intercellular cleft a narrow, water-filled space between capillary endothelial cells

intercellular fluid fluid that lies between cells; also called interstitial fluid

intercostal muscle (in-ter-KOS-tal) skeletal muscle that lies between ribs and whose contraction causes rib cage movement during breathing

interferon (in-ter-FEAR-on) family of proteins that nonspecifically inhibit viral replication inside host cells; gamma interferon also activates macrophages and enhances killing ability of cytotoxic T cells and NK cells

interleukin (in-ter-LEW-kin) a family of cytokines with many effects on immune responses and host defenses

interleukin 1 (IL-1) cytokine secreted by macrophages and other cells that activates helper T cells, exerts many inflammatory effects, and mediates many of the systemic acute phase responses, including fever

interleukin 2 (IL-2) cytokine secreted by activated helper T cells that causes antigen-activated helper T, cytotoxic T, and NK cells to proliferate and increase their activity

interleukin 6 (IL-6) cytokine secreted by macrophages and other cells that increases plasma cell formation and activity; also mediates some of the acute phase responses, including probably fever

internal anal sphincter smooth-muscle ring around lower end of rectum

internal energy energy present in intramolecular bonds of organic molecules

internal environment extracellular fluid (interstitial fluid and plasma)

internal genitalia (jen-ih-TALE-ee-ah) (female) ovaries, uterine tubes, uterus, and vagina

internal urethral sphincter (you-REETH-ral) part of smooth muscle of urinary bladder wall that opens and closes the bladder outlet

internal work energy-requiring activities in body; *see also* work; *compare* external work

interneuron neuron whose cell body and axon lie entirely in CNS

interphase period of cell division cycle between end of one division and visible signs of beginning of next

interstitial cell stimulating hormone (ICSH) *see* luteinizing hormone

interstitial fluid extracellular fluid surrounding tissue cells; excludes plasma, which is extracellular fluid surrounding blood cells

interstitium (in-ter-STISH-um) interstitial space; fluid-filled space between tissue cells

interventricular septum (in-ter-ven-TRIK-you-lar) partition in heart separating right and left ventricles

intestinal phase (of gastrointestinal control) initiation of neural and hormonal gastrointestinal reflexes by stimulation of intestinal-tract walls

intestino-intestinal reflex reflex cessation of contractile activity of intestines in response to various stimuli in intestine

intracellular fluid fluid in cells; cytosol plus fluid in cell organelles, including nucleus

intrafusal fiber modified skeletal-muscle fiber in muscle spindle; also called spindle fiber

intrapleural fluid (in-tra-PLUR-al) thin fluid film in thoracic cavity between pleura lining the inner wall of thoracic cage and pleura covering lungs

intrapleural pressure pressure in pleural space; also called intrathoracic pressure

intrarenal baroreceptor pressure-sensitive juxtaglomerular cells of afferent arterioles, which respond to decreased renal arterial pressure by secreting renin

intrathoracic pressure *see* intrapleural pressure

intrinsic (in-trin-sik) situated entirely within a part

intrinsic clotting pathway intravascular sequence of fibrin clot formation initiated by factor XII or, more usually, by the initial thrombin generated by the extrinsic clotting pathway

intrinsic factor glycoprotein secreted by stomach epithelium and necessary for absorption of vitamin B_{12} in the ileum

intron (IN-trahn) region of noncoding base sequences in gene

inversely proportional relationship in which, as one factor increases by a given amount, the other decreases by a given amount

ion (EYE-on) atom or small molecule containing unequal number of electrons and protons and therefore carrying a net positive or negative electric charge

ionic bond (eye-ON-ik) strong electrical attraction between two oppositely charged ions

ionization (eye-on-ih-ZAY-shun) process of removing electrons from or adding them to an atom or small molecule to form an ion

ipsilateral (ip-sih-LAT-er-al) on the same side of the body

iris ringlike structure surrounding pupil of eye

irreversible reaction chemical reaction that releases large quantities of energy and results in almost all the reactant molecules being converted to product; *compare* reversible reaction

ischemia (iss-KEY-me-ah) reduced blood supply

ischemic hypoxia (iss-KEY-mik hi-POK-see-ah) too little blood flow to tissues to deliver adequate amounts of oxygen

islet of Langerhans (EYE-let of LAN-ger-hans) cluster of pancreatic endocrine cells; distinct islet cells secrete insulin, glucagon, somatostatin, and pancreatic polypeptide

isometric contraction (ice-so-MET-rik) contraction of muscle under conditions in which it develops tension but does not change length

isoosmotic (ice-oh-oz-MAH-tik) having the same osmotic pressure, thus the same solute particle concentration

isotonic (ice-oh-TAH-nik) containing the same number of effectively non-penetrating solute particles as cells; *see also* isotonic contraction

isotonic contraction contraction of muscle under conditions in which load on muscle remains constant but muscle shortens

isovolumetric ventricular contraction (iso-vol-you-MET-rik) early phase of systole when atrioventricular and aortic valves are closed

isovolumetric ventricular relaxation early phase of diastole when atrioventricular and aortic valves are closed

isozyme (EYE-so-zime) one of two or more enzymes that catalyze the same reaction but have slightly different structures and therefore slightly different affinities for substrate

jejunum (je-JEW-num) middle segment of small intestine

juxtaglomerular apparatus (JGA) (jux-tah-glow-MER-you-lar) renal structure consisting of macula densa and juxtaglomerular cells; site of renin secretion and sensors for renin secretion and control of glomerular filtration rate

keto acid (KEY-toe) molecule formed from amino acid metabolism and containing carbonyl (—CO—) and carboxyl (—COOH) groups

ketone (KEY-tone) product of fatty acid metabolism that accumulates in blood during starvation and in untreated diabetes mellitus; acetoacetic acid, acetone, or β-hydroxybutyric acid; also called ketone body

kilocalorie (kcal) (KILL-oh-kal-ah-ree) amount of heat required to heat 1 L water 1°C; calorie used in nutrition; also called Calorie and large calorie

kinase (KIE-nase) enzyme that transfers a phosphate (usually from ATP) to another molecule

kinesthesia (kin-ess-THEE-zee-ah) sense of movement derived from movement at a joint

kinin (KI-nin) peptide split from kininogen in inflamed area; facilitates vascular changes associated with inflammation; may also stimulate pain receptors

kininogen (ki-NIN-og-jen) plasma protein from which kinins are generated

Krebs cycle mitochondrial metabolic pathway that utilizes fragments derived from carbohydrate, protein, and fat breakdown and produces carbon dioxide, hydrogen, and small amounts of ATP; also called tricarboxylic acid cycle or citric acid cycle

L-dopa dopamine precursor; administered to patients with Parkinson's disease

lactase (LAK-tase) small-intestine enzyme that breaks down lactose (milk sugar) into glucose and galactose

lactate *see* lactic acid

lactation (lak-TAY-shun) production and secretion of milk by mammary glands

lacteal (lak-TEAL) blind-ended lymph vessel in center of each intestinal villus

lactic acid (LAK-tic) three-carbon molecule formed by glycolytic pathway in absence of oxygen; dissociates to form lactate and hydrogen ions

lactose (LAK-tose) disaccharide composed of glucose and galactose; also called milk sugar

lactose intolerance inability to digest lactose because of lack of intestinal lactase; leads to accumulation of large amounts of gas and fluid in large intestine, which causes pain and diarrhea

larynx (LAIR-inks) part of air passageway between pharynx and trachea; contains the vocal cords

latent period (LAY-tent) period lasting several milliseconds between action potential initiation in a muscle fiber and beginning of mechanical activity

lateral position farther from the midline

lateral inhibition method of refining sensory information in afferent neurons and ascending pathways whereby fibers inhibit each other, the most active fibers causing the greatest inhibition of adjacent fibers

lateral sac enlarged region at end of

each sarcoplasmic reticulum segment; adjacent to transverse tubule

law of mass action maxim that an increase in reactant concentration causes a chemical reaction to proceed in direction of product formation; the opposite occurs with decreased reactant concentration

lecithin (LESS-ih-thin) a phospholipid

lengthening contraction contraction as a load pulls a muscle to a longer length despite opposing forces generated by the active cross-bridges

lens adjustable part of eye's optical system, which helps focus object's image on retina

leukocyte (LEW-ko-site) white blood cell

leukotriene (LOO-koe-treen) type of eicosanoid that is generated by lipoxygenase pathway

Leydig cell (LIE-dig) testosterone-secreting endocrine cell that lies between seminiferous tubules of testes; also called interstitial cell

LH surge large rise in luteinizing-hormone secretion by anterior pituitary about day 14 of menstrual cycle

ligand (LIE-gand) any molecule or ion that binds to protein surface by noncovalent bonds

limbic system (LIM-bik) interconnected brain structures in cerebrum; involved with emotions and learning

lipase (LIE-pase) *see* pancreatic lipase, lipoprotein lipase

lipid (LIP-id) molecule composed primarily of carbon and hydrogen and characterized by insolubility in water

lipid bilayer a sheet consisting of two layers of phospholipid

lipolysis (lie-POL-ih-sis) triacylglycerol breakdown

lipoprotein (lip-oh-PRO-teen) lipid aggregate partially coated by protein; involved in lipid transport in blood

lipoprotein lipase capillary endothelial enzyme that hydrolyzes triacylglycerol to monoglyceride and fatty acids

lipoxygenase (lie-POX-ih-jen-ase) enzyme that acts on arachidonic acid and leads to leukotriene formation

load force acting on muscle due to weight of an object

local current flow movement of positive ions toward more negative membrane region and simultaneous movement of negative ions in opposite direction

local homeostatic response (home-ee-

carbonic anhydrase inhibitors, 558
carcinogen, 79
carcinoma, 79
cardiac angiography, 427
cardiac arrhythmias, 415, 543, 546, 744
cardiac disease, 495
cardiac pacemaker, 414
cardiopulmonary resuscitation (CPR), 470
cardiovascular disease, 622, 696
castration, 659, 660
cataract, 252
catatonia, 380
cerebellar disease, 361, 364
chill, 642
chlamydia, 688
chlorpromazine, 378
cholesterol, 470, 621–622
chorionic villus sampling, 679
chronic bronchitis, 485
chronic obstructive pulmonary disease, 484, 485, 486, 509
cigarette smoking, 470, 475, 476, 485, 508, 622, 680, 740
clasp-knife phenomenon, 364
cocaine, 208, 381, 382, 680
codeine, 212
color blindness, 257
coma, 374, 385, 606, 618, 621
combined immunodeficiency, 725
common cold, 701
constipation, 592, 595–596
contraception, 686, 687–690
convulsions, 621, 637
coronary angioplasty, 470
coronary artery disease, 469–471, 622, 696
coronary bypass, 470
coronary thrombosis, 470
cortisol deficiency, 616, 620
cortisol excess, 616
creatine phosphokinase, 469
creatinine clearance, 526–527
cretinism, 632
cross-matching, 729
cross-tolerance, 382, 383
curare poisoning, 318, 319
cyanide poisoning, 508
cyclosporin, 728
cystic fibrosis, 475

defibrillation, 470
dehydration, 559, 594, 596, 644
delayed hypersensitivity, 730
denervation atrophy, 331
Depo-Provera, 688, 689
deprenyl, 361
depression, 380, 387, 673, 696
diabetes insipidus, 532, 618

diabetes mellitus, 78, 298, 370, 470, 525, 532, 556, 607, 618–620, 627, 633, 636, 658, 725, 751
diabetic ketoacidosis (DKA), 618, 620
dialysis, 559
diarrhea, 154, 462, 530, 536, 537, 540, 543, 552, 556, 557, 592, 594, 595–596
diffuse interstitial fibrosis, 493
diffusion impairment, 509
digitalis, 468, 469
dihydrotestosterone receptor deficiency, 298
disuse atrophy, 331
disuse osteoporosis, 551
diuretics, 467, 468, 557–558
dopamine hypothesis, 380
Down's syndrome, 690
drug dependence (addiction), 378, 381–382
drug effects, at synapses, 207
drug overdose, 371, 374, 375
dumping syndrome, 586
dwarfism, 626, 627
dysmenorrhea, 672, 673
dysmetria, 361
dysplasia, 79

eating disorders, 637
echocardiography, 427
eclampsia, 681
ectopic pregnancy, 677
edema, 448, 468, 469, 557, 558, 704
Elavil, 380
electrocardiogram, 414–415
electroconvulsive therapy, 380, 385, 387
elephantiasis, 447, 469
embolism, 471
embolus, 471
emphysema, 485, 493
epilepsy, 211, 370
erythropoietin deficiency, 400, 402
excessive inflammatory responses, 732

fainting, 462, 463, 644
farsighted (hyperopia), 252
fasting, 294, 556, 602, 607, 613, 614, 616, 617, 620
fasting hypoglycemia, 620
fever, 152, 161, 162, 505, 642–644, 723–724, 725, 734
flaccid muscles, 364
forced expiratory volume, 486
forced vital capacity, 486

gallbladder disease, 565
gallstones, 589, 594–595

gastritis, 594
gene replacement therapy, 78
genetic deficiency in antibody synthesis, 725
genital herpes, 701
giantism, 626
glaucoma, 252
glucosuria, 525, 618
gonorrhea, 688
graft rejection, 726, 728, 752
growth hormone deficiency, 616, 627
growth hormone excess, 616

hallucinations, 239, 380, 381
hay fever, 708, 729, 730
headaches, 504, 595, 620, 672, 673
heart attack, 154, 467, 469–471, 593, 621, 622, 748
heart failure, 467, 468–469, 557–558
heart murmur, 420–421
heartburn, 580
heat exhaustion, 644
heat stroke, 644
Heimlich maneuver, 485, 578
hematoma, 741
hemochromatosis, 575
hemodialysis, 559
hemolytic disease of the newborn, 595, 729
hemolytic jaundice, 595
hemophilia, 744
hemorrhage, 370, 400, 444, 454–455, 456, 457, 460–462, 530, 540, 575
heparin, 749
hepatitis, 720
heroin, 229, 382
herpes virus, 182, 688, 701
high-density lipoproteins (HDL), 622
histamine test of acid secretions, 582
histotoxic hypoxia, 508
hot flashes, 696
human immunodeficiency virus, 726–727, 728
hydrocephalus, 230
hyperalgesia, 248
hypercalcemia, 546
hypercapnea, 508
hypersensitivity, 729–730
hypertension, 157, 456, 466–468, 470, 538, 558, 636, 681
hyperthermia, 637, 642, 644
hyperthyroidism, 628, 632
hypertonia, 364
hyperventilation, 492, 552, 553
hypocalcemic tetany, 334, 546
hypoglycemia, 294, 370, 606, 613, 614, 615, 616, 620–621, 627
hypotension, 460–462, 618, 637, 644, 751

hypothyroidism, 627–628, 632
hypotonia, 364
hypoventilation, 492, 509, 552, 553
hypoxemia, 508, 509
hypoxia, 508–509, 556
hypoxic hypoxia, 508

immediate hypersensitivity, 730
immune-complex hypersensitivity, 730
impotence, 657–658
in vitro fertilization, 690
inborn errors of metabolism, 77
infant mortality, 625, 687
infection, 395, 624, 629, 632, 642, 643, 644, 703, 710, 714, 715, 716–721, 723–751, 752
infertility, 690
inflammation, 163, 164, 484, 509
injectable solutions, 136–137
insufficiency of cardiac valves, 420, 421
insulin-dependent diabetes mellitus (IDDM, type 1), 618–620, 731
insulin resistance, 620
intrauterine device, 688, 689
iodine-deficient goiter, 293, 296
iron deficiency, 398, 400
ischemic hypoxia, 508

jaundice, 595
jet lag, 156

kidney disease, 467, 469, 553, 558–559
kidney stones, 558
kidney transplantation, 559

L-dopa, 361
lactate dehydrogenase, 469
lactose intolerance, 595
late-phase reaction, 730
laxatives, 595–596
leukemia, 79
Librium, 383
lidocaine, 196
lithium carbonate, 380–381
liver disease, 469, 620, 746
lockjaw, 207
loss of consciousness, 504, 508, 644
low birth weight, 625
low-density lipoproteins (LDL), 622
lower motor neuron disorder, 364
LSD (lysergic acid diethylamide), 211
lung infection, 493
lymphoma, 79

macrocytosis, 400
malaria, 700
malignant tumor, 79
malnutrition, 625, 627, 679–680, 725
mania, 380–381

masculinization of women, 279, 629
maternal malnutrition, 625, 679–680
measles, 720
Ménière's disease, 265
mental retardation, 230, 632
metabolic acidosis, 504, 505, 556, 596, 618
metabolic alkalosis, 504, 505, 556, 594
metastasis, 79
microcytosis, 400
monoamine oxidase inhibitors, 380
morphine, 212, 229, 248, 378, 382, 500
motion sickness, 265, 594
mountain sickness, 508–509
multiple sclerosis, 731
muscle atrophy, 364
muscle cramps, 334, 364
muscle spasms, 364
muscle tone, 364
muscular dystrophy, 334
mutagen, 76
mutation, 76–77
myasthenia gravis, 166, 334–335, 731
myocardial infarction, 469, 748

narcolepsy, 374
nausea, 265, 460, 594, 595, 672, 681
nearsighted (myopia), 252
"nerve gases," 319
neuron regeneration, 185
nicotine, 229
night blindness, 113
nitroglycerine, 470
non-insulin-dependent diabetes mellitus (NIDD, type 2), 618–620
nonsteroidal anti-inflammatory drugs (NSAIDS), 163–164
normocytosis, 400
Norplant, 688, 689
Novocaine (procaine hydrochloride), 196
nystagmus, 265

obesity, 467, 618, 620, 622, 626, 636–637
obsessive-compulsive disorders, 211
oncogenes, 79, 626, 715
opiate drugs, 212
oral contraceptives, 688, 689
organophosphates, 319
osteomalacia, 551
osteoporosis, 551, 696

pain, 161, 162, 250–251, 703, 734, 751
Pamelor, 380
parasitic infections, 700, 733
Parkinson's disease, 211, 360–361, 364
passive immunity, 720
penicillin, 526, 727, 730
perforated interventricular/interatrial septum, 420–421
peritoneal dialysis, 559

pernicious anemia, 400, 574
phantom limb, 239
pharmacological effects of hormones, 283–284
phenylketonuria, 77
plasma potassium changes, 543, 596
pneumothorax, 479
poison ivy, 729, 730
poliomyelitis, 182, 334, 500
polycythemia, 400
postsurgical respiratory therapy, 483
potassium-sparing diuretics, 558
precocious puberty, 695
pregnancy sickness, 681
premature delivery, 671, 681
premenstrual syndrome, 673–674
prenatal malnutrition, 625, 679–680
presbyopia, 250–252
primary hypertension, 467
procaine hydrochloride, 196
Prozac, 211, 380
pulmonary disease, 495, 499, 502, 509
pulmonary edema, 468, 493, 508

radiation damage, 185, 569
ragweed-pollen allergy, 729, 730
"reactive" hypoglycemia, 621
referred pain, 248
renal hypertension, 467, 559
respiration after surgery, 483
respiratory acidosis, 499, 556
respiratory alkalosis, 499, 556
respiratory diseases, 486–487, 552, 553
respiratory-distress syndrome of the newborn, 484
retching, 594
retrograde amnesia, 385
retroviruses, 726
rheumatoid arthritis, 731, 752
rickets, 551
rigidity, 364
rigor mortis, 312, 326
RU 486, 489
ruptured appendix, 563

sarcoma, 79
schizophrenia, 379–380
seasonal affective disorder, 296
seizures, 644
septic shock, 732
severe sweating, 462
sexually transmitted disease, 688
shock, 462
shortness of breath, 469
shunt, 493, 509
sickle-cell anemia, 399–400
sleep apnea, 372
slow viruses, 701
small-vessel disease, 620

spasticity, 364
spinal cord damage, 593
spontaneous abortion, 680
stenosis of cardiac valves, 420, 421
stimulation-produced analgesia, 248
stomach cancer, 574, 585
streptokinase, 749
stress, 154, 292, 294, 438, 470, 613, 614, 616, 617–618, 620, 627, 629, 633, 636, 725, 751–753
stroke, 211, 229, 467, 470–471, 593, 621
sulfonylurea, 620
susceptibility to infection, 620
syphilis, 688

testicular descent, failure of, 652
testicular feminization, 695
tetanus (lockjaw), 182, 207, 350, 720
thiazide, 558
tissue implantation, 185, 361

tissue transplantation, 725
tolerance, 382–384
toxemia of pregnancy, 681
transcutaneous nerve stimulation (TENS), 248
transfusion reactions, 728–729
transient ischemic attack (TIA), 470–471
transplant rejection, 726, 728
tricyclic antidepressant, 380
tumor, 78, 370
tumor suppressor genes, 79

ulcers, 574, 580, 593–594
ultrasound, 679
upper motor neuron disorder, 364
uremia, 558–559

vaccine, 720
Valium, 212, 383
vasectomy, 657, 688

vasodilator drugs, 468
ventricular fibrillation, 470
vertigo, 265
very-low-density lipoproteins (VLDL), 605
ventilation-perfusion inequality, 493, 509
virilism, 674
virus, infections, 78, 484, 680, 700–701, 707, 710, 714, 715, 721–723
vitamin deficiency, 398, 400, 592
vomiting, 462, 469, 505, 530, 543, 552, 553, 556, 557, 586, 594, 672, 681

weakness, 469, 543, 620
withdrawal, 381

x-rays, as mutagens, 76
Xylocaine (lidocaine), 196

zidovudine, 727, 728

APPENDIX

G

SUGGESTED READING

Like all scientists, physiologists report the results of their experiments in scientific journals. Approximately 1300 such journals in the life sciences publish more than 300,000 papers each year. Every physiologist must be familiar with the ever-increasing number of articles in his or her own specific field of research.

Another type of scientific writing is the review article, a summary and synthesis of the relevant research reports on a specific subject. Such reviews, which are published in many different journals, are extremely useful. Also, the American Physiological Society has a massive program of publishing comprehensive reviews in almost all fields of physiology. These reviews are gathered into a series of ongoing volumes known collectively as the "Handbook of Physiology." Another important series is the *Annual Review of Physiology*, which publishes yearly reviews of the most recent research articles in specific fields and provides the most rapid means of keeping abreast of developments in physiology.

Another type of review that is of value to the nonexpert is the *Scientific American* article. Written in a manner usually intelligible to the layperson, these articles, in addition to reviewing a topic, often present experimental data so that the reader can obtain some insight into how the experiments were done and the data interpreted. Many articles published in *Scientific American* can be obtained individually as inexpensive offprints from W. H. Freeman and Company, San Francisco, CA, 94104, which also publishes collections of *Scientific American* articles in a specific area, for example, psychobiology. Two other magazines that frequently publish excellent reviews of physiology for the nonexpert are *New England Journal of Medicine* and *Hospital Practice*. The New York Times (particularly in its Tuesday "Science" section) provides excellent coverage of physiology-related health news. Finally, in the realm of nutrition, fitness, and stress management, The University of California at Berkeley Wellness Letter, published by that university's School of Public Health, is superb; the mailing address is P.O. Box 420149, Palm Coast, FL 32142-9821.

Another level of scientific writing is the monograph, an extended review of a subject area that is broader than the review articles described above. Monographs are usually in book form and generally do not attempt to cover all the relevant literature on the topic; rather they analyze and synthesize the most important data and interpretations. At the last level is the textbook, which deals with a much larger field than the monograph or review article. Its depth of coverage of any topic is accordingly much less complete and is determined by the audience to which it is aimed.

We have restricted our suggested readings to textbooks and monographs because they are usually available in college and university libraries. Their bibliographies will serve as a further entry into the scientific literature. We list first a group of books that cover wide areas of physiology.

Cells and Neurophysiology," 21st edn., Saunders, Philadelphia, 1989.

Pickles, J. O.: "An Introduction to the Physiology of Hearing," 2d edn., Academic, San Diego, 1988.

Spillman, L., and J. S. Warner (eds.): "Visual Perception: The Neurophysiological Foundations," Academic, San Diego, 1990.

Chapter 10

Bailieue, E.-E., and P. A. Kelly: "Hormones: From Molecules to Disease," Herman, New York, 1991.

Bolander, F. F.: "Molecular Endocrinology," Academic, San Diego, 1989.

Goodman, H. M.: "Basic Medical Endocrinology," Raven, New York, 1988.

Griffin, J. E., and S. R. Ojeda: "Textbook of Endocrinology," Oxford, New York, 1988.

Greenspan, F. S.: "Basic and Clinical Endocrinology," 3d edn., Appleton and Lange, E. Norwalk, Conn. 1991.

Hedge, G. A., H. D. Colby, and R. L. Goodman: "Clinical Endocrine Physiology," Saunders, 1987.

Tepperman, J.: "Metabolic and Endocrine Physiology," 5th edn., Year Book, Chicago, 1987.

Wilson, J. D., and D. W. Foster (eds.): "Williams Textbook of Endocrinology," 7th edn., Saunders, Philadelphia, 1987.

Chapter 11

Bulbring, Edith, Alison F. Brading, Allan W. Jones, and Tadao Tomita (eds.): "Smooth Muscle," University of Texas, Austin, 1981.

Hoyle, C.: "Muscles and Their Neural Control," Wiley-Interscience, New York, 1983.

Jones, D. A., and J. M. Round: "Skeletal Muscle in Health and Disease: A Textbook of Muscle Physiology," Manchester University, Manchester, England, 1990.

Keynes, R. D., and D. J. Aidley: "Nerve and Muscle," 2d edn., Cambridge, Cambridge, 1992.

Peachy, Lee D., and Richard H. Adrian (eds.): "Handbook of Physiology: Section 10, Skeletal Muscle," American Physiological Society, Bethesda, Md., 1983.

Shepard, Roy J.: "Exercise Physiology," Decker, Philadelphia, 1987.

Squire, John: "The Structural Basis of Muscle Contraction," Plenum, New York, 1981.

————: "Muscle Design and Disease," Benjamin/Cummings, Menlo Park, Calif., 1986.

Twarog, Betty M., Rhea J. C. Levine, and Maynard M. Dewey (eds.): "Basic Biology of Muscles: A Comparative Approach," Raven, New York, 1982.

Walton, John: "Disorders of Voluntary Muscle," 5th edn., Churchill Livingstone, New York, 1988.

Woledge, Roger C., Nancy A. Curtin, and Earl Homsher: "Energetic Aspects of Muscle Contraction," Academic, New York, 1985.

Chapter 12

Brooks, V. B.: "The Neural Basis of Motor Control," Oxford, New York, 1986.

Evarts, E. V., S. P. Wise, and D. Bousfield (eds.): "The Motor System in Neurobiology," Elsevier, New York, 1985.

Kandel, E. R., J. H. Schwartz, and T. M. Jessell: "Principles of Neural Science," 3d edn., Elsevier/North-Holland, New York, 1991.

Patton, H. D., A. F. Fuchs, B. Hille, A. M. Scher, and R. Steiner (eds.): "Textbook of Physiology: Volume 1 Excitable Cells and Neurophysiology," 21st edn., Saunders, Philadelphia, 1989.

Rosenbaum, D. A.: "Human Motor Control," Academic, San Diego, 1991.

Chapter 13

Gregory, R. L.: "Odd Perceptions," Routledge, New York, 1986.

Kandel, E. R., J. H. Schwartz, and T. M. Jessell: "Principles of Neural Science," 3d edn., Elsevier/North-Holland, New York, 1991.

Kaplan, H. I., and B. J. Sadock: "Synopsis of Psychiatry: Behavioral Sciences and Clinical Psychiatry," 6th edn., Williams & Wilkins, Baltimore, 1991.

Kelner, K. L., and D. E. Koshland (eds.): "Molecules to Models: Advances in Neuroscience," American Association for the Advancement of Science, Washington, D.C., 1989.

Levitan, I. B., and L. K. Kaczmarek: "The Neuron: Cell and Molecular Biology," Oxford, New York, 1991.

Martinez, J. L., Jr., and R. P. Kesner: "Learning and Memory: A Biological View," 2d edn., Academic, 1991.

Patton, H. D., A. F. Fuchs, B. Hille, A. M. Scher, and R. Steiner (eds.): "Textbook of Physiology: Volume 1 Excitable Cells and Neurophysiology," 21st edn., Saunders, Philadelphia, 1989.

Scientific American (entire issue), "Brain and Mind," September, 1992.

Chapter 14

Beck, W. S.: "Hematology," 5th edn., MIT, Cambridge, 1991.

Berne, R. M., and M. N. Levy: "Cardiovascular Physiology," 6th edn., Mosby, St. Louis, 1992.

Mohrman, D. E., and L. J. Heller: "Cardiovascular Physiology," 3d edn., McGraw-Hill, New York, 1991.

Honig, C. R.: "Modern Cardiovascular Physiology," 2d edn., Little, Brown, Boston, 1988.

Little, R. C., and W. C. Little: "Physiology of the Heart and Circulation," 4th edn., Year Book, Chicago, 1989.

Williams, W. J., E. Beutler, A. J. Erslev, and M. A. Lichtman: "Hematology," 4th edn., McGraw-Hill, New York, 1990.

Chapter 15

Davenport, H. W.: "The ABC of Acid-Base Chemistry," 7th edn., University of Chicago, Chicago, 1978.

Levitzky, M. G.: "Pulmonary Physiology," 3d edn., McGraw-Hill, New York, 1991.

Mines, A. H.: "Respiratory Physiology," 3d edn., Raven, New York, 1992.

Staub, N. C.: "Basic Respiratory Physiology," Churchill, Livingstone, New York, 1990.

Taylor, A. E., K. Rehder, R. E. Hyatt, and J. C. Parker: "Clinical Respiratory Physiology," Saunders, Philadelphia, 1989.

West, J. B.: "Respiratory Physiology: The Essentials," 4th edn., Williams & Wilkins, Baltimore, 1989.

Crystal, R. G., and J. B. West (eds.): "The Lung: Scientific Foundations," Raven, New York, 1991.

Chapter 16

Brenner, B. M., and F. C. Rector (eds.): "The Kidney," 4th edn., Saunders, Philadelphia, 1991.

Davenport, H. W.: "The ABC of Acid-Base Chemistry," 7th edn., University of Chicago, Chicago, 1978.

Selden, D. W., and G. H. Giebisch (eds.): "The Kidney: Physiology and Pathophysiology," 2d edn., Raven, New York, 1992.

Koepen, B. M., and B. A. Stanton: "Renal Physiology," Mosby Year Book, St. Louis, 1992.

Rose, B. D.: "Clinical Physiology of Acid-Base and Electrolyte Disorders," 3d edn., McGraw-Hill, New York, 1989.

Smith, H. W.: "From Fish to Philosopher," Anchor Books, Doubleday, Garden City, N.Y., 1961.

Vander, A. J.: "Renal Physiology," 4th edn., McGraw-Hill, New York, 1991.

Chapter 17

Brooks, Frank P. (ed.): "Gastrointestinal Pathophysiology," 2d edn., Oxford, New York, 1978.

Davenport, Horace W.: "Physiology of the Digestive Tract," 5th edn., Year Book Medical Publishers, Chicago, 1982.

Granger, D. N., J. A. Barrowman, and P. R. Kvietys. "Clinical Gastrointestinal Physiology," Saunders, Philadelphia, 1985.

Johnson, L. R. (ed.): "Gastrointestinal Physiology," 3d edn., Mosby, St. Louis, 1985.

——, J. Christensen, E. D. Jacobson, and J. H. Walsh (eds.): "Physiology of the Gastrointestinal Tract," 2d edn., Raven, New York, 1987 (two volumes).

Chapter 18

Adolph, E. F.: "Physiology of Man in the Desert," Interscience, New York, 1947.

Bailieue, E.-E., and P. A. Kelly: "Hormones: From Molecules to Disease," Herman, New York, 1991.

Falkner, F., and Tanner, J. M. (eds.): "Human Growth," Plenum, New York, 1986.

Goodman, H. M.: "Basic Medical Endocrinology," Raven, New York, 1988.

Griffin, J. E., and S. R. Ojeda: "Textbook of Endocrinology," Oxford, New York, 1988.

Greenspan, F. S.: "Basic and Clinical Endocrinology," 3d edn., Appleton and Lange, E. Norwalk, Conn., 1991.

MacKowiak, P. A. (ed.): "Fever: Basic Mechanisms and Management," Raven, New York, 1991.

Vander, A. J.: "Nutrition, Stress, and Toxic Chemicals: An Approach to Environmental Health Controversies," University of Michigan, Ann Arbor, 1981.

Wilson, J. D., and D. W. Foster (eds.): "Williams Textbook of Endocrinology," 7th edn., Saunders, Philadelphia, 1987.

Chapter 19

Bailieue, E.-E., and P. A. Kelly: "Hormones: From Molecules to Disease," Herman, New York, 1991.

Carlson, B. M.: "Patten's Foundations of Embryology," 5th edn., McGraw-Hill, New York, 1988.

Goodman, H. M.: "Basic Medical Endocrinology," Raven, New York, 1988.

Griffin, J. E., and S. R. Ojeda: "Textbook of Endocrinology," Oxford, New York, 1988.

Johnson, M., and B. Everett: "Essential Reproduction," 2d edn., Blackwell, Oxford, 1985.

Tepperman, J.: "Metabolic and Endocrine Physiology," 5th edn., Year Book, Chicago, 1987.

Wilson, J. D., and D. W. Foster (eds.): "Williams Textbook of Endocrinology," 7th edn., Saunders, Philadelphia, 1987.

Yen, S. S. C., and Jaffee, R. B.: "Reproductive Endocrinology," 3d edn., Saunders, 1991.

Chapter 20

Asterita, M. E.: "The Physiology of Stress," Sciences Press, 1985.

Barrett, J. T.: "Textbook of Immunology," 5th edn., Mosby, St. Louis, 1988.

——. "Medical Immunology," F. A. Davis, Philadelphia, 1991.

Beck, W. S.: "Hematology," MIT, 5th edn., Cambridge, 1991.

Plotnikoff, N., A. Murgo, R. Faith, and J. Wybran: "Stress and Immunity," CRC, Boca Raton, La., 1991.

Roit, I.: "Essential Immunology," 6th edn., Blackwell, St. Louis, 1988.

——. "Immunology," 2d edn., Mosby, St. Louis, 1989.

Stites, D. P., and A. I. Terr: "Basic and Clinical Immunology," 7th edn., Lange, Norwalk, Conn., 1991.

Vander, A. J.: "Nutrition, Stress, and Toxic Chemicals: An Approach to Environmental Health Controversies," University of Michigan, Ann Arbor, 1981.

Williams, W. J., E. Beutler, A. J. Erslev, and M. A. Lichtman: "Hematology," 4th edn., McGraw-Hill, New York, 1990.

Adenosine triphosphate (ATP) (*Cont.*):
  metabolism in skeletal muscle, 324–325
  as a neurotransmitter, 209, 223, 225
  role of: in active transport, 127–128
    fatty acid catabolism, 104–105
    muscle contraction, 309–312, 314
    muscle fatigue, 326
    smooth muscle contraction, 340–341
  structure of, 92
  use of, in phagocytosis, 137
Adenylyl cyclase, 166–170
  and cardiac contractility, 425
ADH (*see* Antidiuretic hormone)
Adhesion molecules, 704
Adipocytes, 104
Adipose tissue, 104
  effects of sympathetic nervous system on, 614–615
  function of, in absorptive state, 603–607
  innervation of, 228
  insulin's actions on, 609–610
ADP (*see* Adenosine diphosphate)
Adrenal androgens, 279
Adrenal cortex, 274, 277
  control of, 293, 294
  hormones of, 278, 280
  production of aldosterone by, 536
Adrenal corticosteroids in graft rejection, 728
Adrenal gland, 277
Adrenal medulla, 225, 274, 277, 280
  hormones of, 277, 280
Adrenaline, 211
Adrenergic fibers, 211, 223
Adrenergic receptors (*see* Alpha-adrenergic receptors; Beta-adrenergic receptors)
Adrenocorticotropic hormone, 274, 288, 289, 294, 295
  effect of, on memory, 384
  as a neurotransmitter, 209
  in stress, 751–753
Adsorptive endocytosis, 137
Aerobic conditions, 96
Affective disorders, 380–381
Afferent arterioles, 517–519
Afferent neuron, 182, 183
Afferent pathway, 157
Affinity of protein binding sites, 57
Afterbirth, 684
Aging, 154–155
  and growth hormone, 627
  and reproductive changes in men, 696
  and reproductive changes in women, 696
  and skeletal muscle, 331–332

Agonists, 162, 163
  and receptors, 207
Agranular endoplasmic reticulum:
  fat synthesis in small intestine, 573, 574
  structure, 43, 48, 50
AIDS (*see* Acquired immune deficiency syndrome)
Air, swallowed in gastrointestinal tract, 591
Air pollution, 485
Airways, 474–476
  branching of, 476
  relation of, to blood vessels, 477
  resistance of, 484–487
Alanine, 28
  transamination of, 107–108
Albumins, 396
Alcohol, 185, 229, 383
  and antidiuretic hormone secretion, 540
  and impotence, 658
  role of, in ulcer formation, 593
Alcoholism, 211
Aldosterone, 274, 278, 280
  effect of: on sodium reabsorption, 536
    on sweat, 641–642
  inhibitors of, 558
  as a neurotransmitter, 209
  and potassium excretion, 543
  in pregnancy, 682
  release of, in stress, 753
  and renin-angiotensin system, 536, 538–539
  summary of control of, 543
Alkaline solutions, 23
Alkalosis, 552
  classification of, 556
  renal response to, 553, 555–556
  respiratory response to, 553
All-or-none, 197
Alleles, 63
Allergens, 729
Allergy, 729–730
  and hypotension, 462
Allosteric modulation:
  of enzymes, 89–90
  mechanism, 60
  of myosin, 312
  in secondary active transport, 128
Alpha-adrenergic receptors, 211
  on arterioles, 435–436
Alpha cells, 608
Alpha-gamma coactivation, 356
Alpha helix, 32
Alpha-ketoglutarate, 98
  transamination of, 107–108
Alpha rhythm, 371, 373
Alternate complement pathway, 705–706

Alveolar-blood gas exchange, 492–493
Alveolar ducts, 476
Alveolar gas pressures, 478, 491–492
Alveolar sacs, 476
Alveolar ventilation, 487–488
  dead space (*see* Dead space)
Alveoli:
  anatomy of, 476–478
  breasts, 684, 686
  lungs, 474
Alzheimer's disease, 208, 210, 211, 371, 384
Amine hormones, 276–277
Amino acids:
  absorption of, in small intestine, 571
  in absorptive state, 603–607
  active transport, 128
  catabolism, 106–110
  deamination of, 107–108
  effects of, on insulin secretion, 611–613
  essential, 108, 110–111
  extracellular and intracellular concentration, 116
  as neurotransmitters, 209, 211–212
  side chain, 29
  in small intestine, inhibition of gastric acid secretion and, 582
  synthesis of, 108–109
  structure of, 28, 29
  as substrates for glucose synthesis, 103–104, 606
  transamination of, 107–108
Amino group, 186
  ionization, 17
Aminoacyl-tRNA synthetase, 67
Aminopeptidase, 571
Ammonia, 107–108
  renal handling of, 555
Amnesia, 385
Amniocentesis, 678–679
Amnion, 678
Amniotic fluid, 678
Amniotic sac, 678, 679
Amphetamine, 378, 381
Amphipathic membrane lipids, 44–45
Amphipathic membrane proteins, 45
Amphipathic molecules, 20
Amygdala, 378
Amylase:
  pancreatic, 587
  salivary, 565, 571
Anabolic steroids, 628, 660
Anabolism, definition of, 84
Anaerobic conditions, 96
Anal sphincters, 593
Analgesics, 212
Anaphylaxis, 730
Anatomic dead space, 487, 488

Androgen-binding protein, 655
Androgens, 648
  adrenal, 274
  secretion of, by adrenal cortex, 279
  in women, 674
Androsterone, 279
Anemia, 399–400
  deficiency of vitamin B_{12}, 574
Anemic hypoxia, 508
ANF (see Atrial natriuretic factor)
Angina pectoris, 469
Angiogenesis, 437–438
Angiogenic factors, 439
Angiotensin (see Angiotensin I;
    Angiotensin II)
Angiotensin converting enzyme, 536,
    538
  blockers, in hypertension, 467–468
  inhibitors, 538
Angiotensin I, 536, 538
Angiotensin II, 275, 536, 538
  in baroreceptor reflex, 456
  in control of antidiuretic hormone
      secretion, 511
  as a neurotransmitter, 209
  production of, by lung capillaries,
      509
  as stimulus for aldosterone secretion,
      536
  and thirst, 542
  as vasoconstrictor, 436, 538
Angiotensinogen, 536, 538
  secretion of, by liver, 538
Anions, 17
Anorexia nervosa, 637
Antagonists, 162, 163
  skeletal muscle, 333
Antagonists and receptors, 207
Anterior pituitary, 274, 286
  hormones of, 274, 288–289
  in pregnancy, 682
Anterolateral system, 246, 248
Antibiotics, 727–728
Antibodies, 733
  classes of, 717
  effects of, 718–720
  in milk, 687
  secreted by plasma cells, 710
  secretion of, 717
Antibody-dependent cellular cytotoxicity
    (ADCC), 719
Antibody-mediated responses, 710, 716–
    721
Anticlotting drugs, 748–749
Anticoagulants (see Oral anticoagulants)
Anticodon, 67, 68, 69
Antidiuretic hormone (ADH), 274, 286,
    432
  control of secretion of, 540–541

effects of, on collecting ducts, 534–
    535
(See also Vasopressin)
Antigen, 707–708
  binding site, 712
  presentation of, 713–715, 732
Antigen-presenting cells (APCs), 713,
    732
  secretion of interleukin 1 by, 714
  (See also B cells; Macrophages)
Anti-inflammatory drugs in asthma, 485
Antithrombin III, 746, 748
Antrum:
  of follicle, 665
  of stomach, 580
Anus, 562
Aorta, 405
Aortic arch baroreceptor, 455
Aortic bodies, 500
Aortic pressure, 419
Aortic valves, 409
Apgar score, 690
Aphasia, 386–387
Appendix, 591–592
Appetite:
  in infection, 724, 726
  in pregnancy, 682
Aqueous humor, 250, 252
Arachidonic acid, 25, 160
  role of, in learning, 385
Arachnoid, 214
Arrhythmias, cardiac:
  and calcium, 546
  and plasma potassium, 543
Arterial baroreceptors, 455
  (See also Baroreceptors)
Arterial blood pressure, 430–432
  measurement of, 431–432
  in pregnancy, 682
  regulation of, 450–460
  relation of, to blood volume, 458–459
  (See also Mean arterial pressure)
Arteries, 404, 430–432
  and endothelium-derived natriuretic
      factor, 437
  function of, 408
Arterioles, 405, 432–437
  control of, in specific organs, 437, 438
  extrinsic controls of, 435–436
  functions of, 408, 432–434
  innervation of, 227
  local control of, 434–435
  response of, to injury, 435
  summary of controlling factors of, 437
Ascending limb of Henle's loop, 518,
    519
Ascending pathways, 236
  central control of, 244–245, 361–362
  nonspecific, 238

for somatic sensation, 245–246
  specific, 236–238
Ascending thin limb of Henle's loop,
    518
Aspartate, 209, 211
Aspirin, 161–162, 248
  as anticlotting drug, 479
  and fever, 643
Association cortex, 238–239
  role of, in motor control, 358
Asthma, 484–485, 731
Astigmatism, 252
Astroglia, 185
Atherosclerosis, 470
  and plasma cholesterol, 621
Atmospheric air, 490
Atmospheric pressure, 478
Atomic nucleus, 14–15
Atomic number, 14–15
Atomic weight, 15
Atoms, 14–15
ATP (see Adenosine triphosphate)
Atresia, 665
Atria:
  function of, 408
  secretion of atrial natriuretic factor
      by, 538, 539
Atrial contraction, 417, 418, 419
Atrial fibrillation, 420
Atrial natriuretic factor (ANF), 275,
    538, 539
  as vasodilator, 436
Atriopeptin (see Atrial natriuretic factor)
Atrioventricular (AV) node, 413, 414
Atrioventricular (AV) valves, 409
Atrium, 403
Atrophy of skeletal muscle, 331
Auditory cortex, 237, 238
Auriculin (see Atrial natriuretic factor)
Autocrine agents, 159, 160
Autoimmune disease, 730–732
Automaticity in cardiac conducting
    system, 412
Autonomic nervous system, 222–228
  dual innervation in, 226
  effects of, on heart, 427
  in exercise, 463–464
  ganglia of, 222
  neurotransmitters of, 223–226
  (See also Parasympathetic nerves;
      Parasympathetic nervous system;
      Sympathetic nerves; Sympathetic
      nervous system)
Autoreceptors, 206
AV conduction disorders, 414, 415
Axon, 181
Axon terminal, 181, 184
Axon transport, 182
AZT (see Zidovudine)

B-cell receptors, 712
B cells, 701, 702, 732
    as antigen-presenting cells, 713, 714
    functions of, 710
    origin of, 710
    receptors, 712
B lymphocytes (see B cells)
Bacteria, 700
    antibody-mediated defenses against,
        716–721
    and formation of gas in large
        intestine, 592
    in gastrointestinal tract, 563, 567
    overgrowth of, in small intestine, 591
    prokaryotic cells, 41
    size of, 41
Balance concept, 154–157
Baldness, 660
Barbiturates, 229
    effect of, on respiration, 500
Baroreceptor reflex, 455–456
    in heart failure, 468
Baroreceptors, 455
    adaptation of, 456
    in control of antidiuretic hormone
        secretion, 540, 542
    other than arterial, 456
    and sodium excretion, 535–536
    (See also Arterial baroreceptors)
Basal ganglia, 221, 352, 360–361
Basal metabolic rate, 631–632
Base:
    binding of hydrogen ions, 22
    in nucleotides, 34, 36
Base pairing, 34–36
Basement membrane, 4
    intestinal capillaries, 573, 574
Basic electrical rhythm:
    in small intestine, 590
    in stomach, 583–585
Basolateral membrane, 138, 524, 525
Basophils, 401, 701, 702
Benign tumor, 78
Bernard, Claude, 5
Beta-adrenergic agonists in asthma, 485
Beta-adrenergic blockers:
    in coronary artery disease, 470
    in hypertension, 467
Beta-adrenergic receptors:
    on arterioles, 436
    on cardiac muscle, 421, 425
    effects of thyroid hormones on, 211,
        632
Beta cells, 608
Beta oxidation, 104–105
Beta rhythm, 371, 373
Bicarbonate:
    addition of, to blood by kidneys, 554–
        556

in blood transport of carbon dioxide,
    497–499
in buffering, 552–553
extracellular and intracellular
    concentration, 116
regulation of plasma concentration by
    kidneys, 553–556
renal excretion of, 554
secretion of, in bile, 589
    by pancreas, 586–587
    by stomach, 581–582
Bile:
    composition of, 565, 589
    control of secretion of, 590
    functions of, 565
        in fat digestion and absorption,
            572–573
    secretion of, 587–590
Bile canaliculi, 587, 589
Bile pigments, 589
    and formation of gallstones, 594
Bile salts, 565
    and cholesterol, 621, 622
    enterohepatic circulation of, 589–590
    role of, in fat digestion and
        absorption, 572–573
    and vitamin K, 746, 748
Bilirubin, 396, 398, 589
    role of, in jaundice, 595
Binding sites, 56–62
    affinity, 57
    chemical specificity, 56–57
    competition, 59
    saturation, 57–59
Biogenic amines, 208–211
    (See also specific amines)
Biological rhythms, 153–154, 256
Biotransformation, 738, 740
Bipolar affective disorder (see Affective
    disorders)
Bipolar cell (retinal), 253–255
Birth control (see Contraception)
1,3-bisphosphoglycerate, 95
Bisphosphonates in prevention of
    osteoporosis, 551
Bladder (see Gallbladder; Urinary
    bladder)
Blastocyst, 677, 678
Block to polyspermy, 676
Blood, 7, 395–402
Blood-brain barrier, 229–230
Blood cells, regulation of production,
    402
Blood coagulation, 742–749
    in coronary artery disease, 470
    factors that oppose, 746
    simplified summary of, 743
Blood flow:
    distribution of, 406

summary of control of, in specific
    organs, 437
velocity of, 440
Blood groups, 728–729
Blood-testis barrier, 655
Blood vessels, 395, 477
Blood volume:
    changes in standing, 462
    in pregnancy, 682
    relation of, to arterial pressure, 458–
        459
Body-fluid compartments, 7–8
Body mass index (BMI), 636
Body of stomach, 580
Body temperature:
    circadian rhythm of, 637, 638
    increase in, as satiety signal, 634, 635
    in menstrual cycle, 673
    regulation of, 637–644
Body weight in pregnancy, 682
Bombesin, 209
Bone:
    and age, 625
    anatomy of, 547, 625
    cells, 547
    diseases of, 551
    as effector site for calcium
        homeostasis, 547
    effects of cortisol on, 627, 628
    effects of growth hormone on, 627
    effects of insulin-like growth factor I
        on, 627
    effects of sex hormones on, 628
    functions of, 547
    growth of, 625
    remodeling of, 547–548
Bone marrow, 396
    production of blood cells by, 401–402
    site of leukocyte production, 701, 708
Botulism, 319
Bowel movements, 595
Bowman's capsule, 517–519
Bowman's space, 518, 519
Boyle's law, 480–481
Bradykinin:
    in active hyperemia, 434
    and endothelium-derived relaxing
        factor, 437
    as a neurotransmitter, 209
Brain, 215–221
    blood supply of, 229–230
    control of blood flow to, 437
    effects of thyroid hormones on, 628, 632
    metabolism of, 229
    utilization of ketones by, 607
    (See also specific regions)
Brain death, 374–375
Brain dominance (see Cerebral
    dominance)

Brain self-stimulation, 377–378
Brainstem, 215–217, 219
  reticular formation, 215–216, 238
Breast feeding, 686
  advantages of, 687
  and inhibition of ovulation, 686
Breasts, 684–687
  effects of prolactin on, 274
  in pregnancy, 682
Breathing, voluntary control of, 508
  (*See also* Respiration)
Broca's area, 386, 387
Bronchi, 475, 476
Bronchioles, 475, 476
  innervation of, 227
Bronchitis, chronic, 485
Bronchodilator drugs, 485
Buffer, 552
Buffering of hydrogen ions in the body, 552–553
Bulbourethral glands, 653
Bulimia, 637
Bulk flow, 403
  across capillary walls, 442–444
Bundle branches, 413, 414
Bundle of His, 413, 414

C1, 705, 718–719, 733
C_v, 119
Ca-ATPase, 127–128
  in sarcoplasmic reticulum, 314–316
Caffeine, 229
  and acid secretion by stomach, 582
Calcitonin, 274
  in prevention of osteoporosis, 551
Calcitonin gene-related peptide, 209
Calcium:
  active transport, 128
  and arrhythmias, 546
  balance of, in pregnancy, 682
  in bone, 547
  in cardiac muscle, 416
  cytosolic concentration, 130–131
  extracellular concentration of, 116, 128
  function of, in skeletal muscle contraction, 312–315
  homeostasis of, 546–550
  hormonal controls of, 548
  and hypertension, 467
  in hypocalcemic tetany, 334
  intestinal handling of, 548
  intracellular concentration of, 116, 128
  ion, 18
  ion channels, 130–131
  renal handling of, 548
  role of: in clotting, 744, 745
    in exocytosis, 138

  in smooth muscle contraction, 340–343
  in synaptic transmission, 202, 205, 206
  as second messenger, 170–174
Calcium-binding proteins, 173–174
Calcium-channel blockers:
  in coronary artery disease, 470
  in hypertension, 467
Calcium channels:
  in cardiac muscle, 412
  role of, in action potentials, 196
  in smooth muscle, 342
Calmodulin, 173–174
  role of, in smooth muscle contraction, 340
Calmodulin-dependent protein kinase, 172–174
Caloric balance, 630–637
Calorie, 84
Calorigenic effect, 632
Calorimeter, 631
cAMP (*see* Cyclic AMP)
cAMP-dependent protein kinase, 167–170, 174
Cancer, 78–79, 626
  antigens produced by, 715
  and biological rhythms, 154
  immune defenses against, 721–723
  immunotherapy against, 723
Candidate hormones, 295–296
Cannon, Walter B., 5
Capacitation, 675
Capillaries, 405, 437–444
  anatomy of, 439–440
  in brain, 229
  bulk flow across, 442–444
  cross-sectional area of, 441
  diffusion across, 440–442
  function of, 408
  velocity of blood flow in, 440
Capillary hydrostatic pressure, 442–444
Carbamino compounds, 497
Carbohydrates:
  catabolism, 101–102
  digestion and absorption of, in gastrointestinal tract, 569–571
  energy storage, 104
  in membranes, 45
  metabolism, 109
  structure of, 23–25
Carbon:
  atomic weight of, 15
  covalent bonds, 15
Carbon dioxide:
  alveolar partial pressure of, 491
  in buffering, 552–553
  control of respiration by, 502–504, 506

  diffusion of, through membranes, 120
  formation of, 97
  molecular structure of, 16
  production of, at rest, 489
  transport of, in blood, 497–499
Carbon monoxide:
  as a neurotransmitter, 209, 212
  role of, in learning, 385
Carbonic acid, 497
Carbonic anhydrase, 497, 552
  in renal tubules, 554
  role of, in acid secretion by stomach, 582
Carbonic anhydrase inhibitors, 558
Carboxyl group, 186
  ionization, 17
Carboxypeptidase, 571, 587
Carcinogens, 79
Carcinomas, 79
Cardiac angiography, 427, 470
Cardiac arrhythmias (*see* Arrhythmias, cardiac)
Cardiac cycle, 417–421
Cardiac excitation, 413–414
Cardiac function, measurement of, 427
Cardiac muscle, 410–411
  action potentials in, 412–413
  blood supply to, 411
  characteristics of, 345
  excitation-contraction coupling, 415–416
  function of, 304
  innervation of, 410–411
  structure of, 306
Cardiac output (CO), 421–427
  control of, 426
  in exercise, 463–464
  in pregnancy, 682
Cardiopulmonary resuscitation (CPR), 470
Cardiovascular center, 216, 456
Cardiovascular reflexes, 459
Cardiovascular system, 395
  functions of components of, 408
  integration of function of, 450–460
  overall design of, 403–408
  path of blood flow through, 410
Carnitine, 110
Carotid bodies, 500
Carotid sinus, 455
Carriers, 123
Castor oil, 595
Castration, 659
Catabolism, definition of, 84
Catalyst, 84–85
Cataract, 252
Catatonia, 380
Catechol-O-methyltransferase, 211
Catecholamines, 208–211, 277
  signal transduction mechanisms for, 283

Cations, 17
Caudate nucleus, 220
C3b, 705–707
　as an opsonin, 719
CCK (see Cholecystokinin)
cdc genes, 75
Cecum, 591–592
Celiac ganglion, 223, 224
Cell, 2
　differentiation, 3, 18
　division, 73–75
　eukaryotic, 41
　organelles, 42, 48–53
　prokaryotic, 41
　shape of, 41
　size of, 40, 41
　volume of, osmotic changes in, 135–
　　137
Cell adhesion molecule (CAM), 185
Cell division cycle genes, 75
Cellulose, digestion of, in
　gastrointestinal tract, 571
Central chemoreceptors, 500, 501, 504,
　506
Central command fatigue, 326
Central nervous system (CNS), 180
　sexual differentiation of, 695
　(See also Brain; Spinal cord)
Central pattern generators, 365–366
Central thermoreceptors, 639
Centrioles, 43, 53, 74–75
Centromere, 74
Cephalic phase:
　of acid secretion, 581, 585
　role of, in pancreatic secretion, 587
Cephalic phase of gastrointestinal
　control, 578
Cerebellum, 215–217, 219
　in motor control, 361
　role of, in learning, 385
Cerebral cortex, 216, 219, 220
　lobes of 219
　　(See also specific lobes)
　motor representation in, 358, 360
　premotor area, 358–359
　primary motor cortex, 358, 359
　role of: in emotions, 379
　　in language, 386–387
　　in memory, 385
　　in motor control, 358–359
　sensory representation in, 237–238,
　　247
　supplementary motor area, 358, 359
　(See also specific regions)
Cerebral dominance, 386–387
Cerebral hemispheres, 217–219
　differences in, 386–387
Cerebrospinal fluid, 214, 215, 230
Cerebrum, 215, 217

Cervical cap, 689
Cervix, 662, 663
　dilation of, in parturition, 682
　mucus of, 671–672
　ripening of, 681
CG (see Chorionic gonadotropin)
cGMP (see Cyclic GMP)
cGMP-dependent protein kinase, 170, 174
Channel gating, 122
Channels:
　controlled by G proteins, 171–172
　as parts of receptors, 164–165
　(See also Ion channels)
Chaperones, 68
Chemical bond, 15–16
Chemical element, 14
Chemical equilibrium, 85–86
Chemical messengers, intercellular (see
　Intercellular chemical messengers)
Chemical reactions, 84–86
Chemical senses (see Smell; Taste)
Chemical specificity of protein binding
　sites, 56
Chemiosmotic hypothesis, 99–100
Chemoreceptors, control of respiration
　by, 500, 501, 504, 506
Chemotaxin, 704, 733
Chemotaxis, 704
Chest wall (see Thoracic wall)
Chewing, 565, 578
Chief cells, 581, 583
Chloride:
　ion, 17–18
　in resting membrane potential, 188,
　　190–191
Chlorpromazine, 378
Choking, 578
Cholecystokinin, 247, 526–528
　in contraction of gallbladder, 590
　enterogastrone activity, 582, 585
　as a neurotransmitter, 209
　role of, in pancreatic enzyme
　　secretion, 587, 588
Cholesterol:
　in bile, 589
　metabolism of, 621–622
　in plasma as risk factor for
　　atherosclerosis, 470
　plasma concentrations of, 622
　in plasma membrane, 44–45
　role of, in gallstone formation, 594
　structure of, 27
Choline, 110
Cholinergic fibers, 208, 223
Chondrocytes, 625
Chordae tendineae, 409
Chorion, 677
Chorionic gonadotropin (CG), 275, 680–
　681

Chorionic villi, 677, 679
Chorionic villus sampling, 679
Choroid plexuses, 230
Chromatids, 74, 75, 649, 651
Chromatin, 48, 49, 74
Chromophore, 253
Chromosomes, 48, 74
Chronic bronchitis, 485
Chronic obstructive pulmonary disease,
　485
Chylomicrons, 573, 574, 603
Chyme, definition of, 565
Chymotrypsin, 571, 587
C_i, 119
Cigarette smoking, 485
Cilia, 53
　in airways, 475
Circadian rhythm, 153
　of hormone secretion, 284
Circular muscle of gastrointestinal tract,
　568
Circulatory system, 5, 395
Citric acid, 98
Citric acid cycle (see Krebs cycle)
Class I MHC proteins, 713
　and antigen presentation, 713–715
Class II MHC proteins, 713
　and antigen presentation, 713, 714
Classical complement pathway, 718–719
Clearance, 526–527
Cleavage (of zygote), 677
Climacteric, 696
Clitoris, 663
Clonal inactivation, 716
Clonal selection, 716
Cloned DNA, 21
Clostridium botulinum, 319
Clot, 742
Clotting (see Blood coagulation)
Clotting factors, 744
　and vitamin K, 746, 748
Coagulation (see Blood coagulation)
Cobalamin (see Vitamin, B_{12})
Cocaine, 208, 381
Code words in DNA, 64
Codeine, 212
Codon, 66
Coenzyme, 87, 88
Cofactors, 87
Coitus interruptus, 689
Cold, acclimatization to, 642
Collagen in clotting, 744, 745
Collagen fibers, 4
Collateral, 181
Collecting duct system, 518, 519
　effects of ADH on, 532
Colloids in plasma, 442
Colon (see Large intestine)
Colony-stimulating factors, 275, 402

Colony-stimulating factors (*Cont.*):
  as cytokines, 711
  role of, in acute phase response, 725
Color blindness, 257
Color vision, 256–257
  opponent cells of, 257
Coma, 374, 385
Combined immunodeficiency disease, 725
Commissure, 214
Common bile duct, 566
Common hepatic duct, 566, 587
Compartments, body-fluid, 7–8
Compensatory growth, 629
Competition:
  at protein binding sites, 59
  and receptors, 162, 163
Complement, 705–706, 733
  activation of, by antibodies, 718–719
  as inflammatory mediators, 704
Compliance, 430
  (*See also* Lung compliance)
Concentration:
  definition of, 22
  as determinant of reaction direction, 85–86
  as determinant of reaction rate, 84–85
  role of, in enzyme reaction rate, 88
Conceptus, 677
Condoms, 689
  prevention of AIDS by, 727
Conducting system, 410–412
Conducting zone, 474–476
Conduction, 638, 641
Conductor (electrical), 187
Cones, 252–254
  role of, in color vision, 256–257
Conformation of proteins, 56, 60–62
Congestive heart failure:
  sodium retention in, 558
  (*See also* Heart failure)
Connecting tubule, 518, 519
Connective tissue, 4
Conscious experiences, 370, 375–377
  neural model for, 376–377
Constipation, 595
Contraception, 687–690
Contractility (cardiac muscle), 423–424, 468
Contraction:
  mechanism of, 307–319
  of muscle fiber, definition of, 307
  whole skeletal muscle, 327–334
  (*See also* Cardiac muscle; Skeletal muscle; Smooth muscle)
Contraction time, 321
Convection, 638
Convergence (of neurons), 201
Converting enzyme (*see* Angiotensin

converting enzyme)
Corona radiata, 666
Coronary angioplasty, 470
Coronary arteries, 411
Coronary artery disease, 469–471
  after menopause, 696
Coronary blood flow, 411
Coronary bypass, 470
Coronary thrombosis, 470
Coronary vessels, control of, 438
Corpus callosum, 219, 220
Corpus luteum, 666
  control of, 670–671
  hormones of, 275
  during pregnancy, 680–681
  secretion of hormones by, 670–671
Cortex, renal, 520
Corti, organ of, 261–263
Cortical association areas (*see* Association cortex)
Cortical collecting duct, 518, 519
  effect of aldosterone on, 536
  reabsorption of sodium by, 531
  as site of potassium secretion, 543
Corticobulbar pathway, 362
Corticospinal pathway, 361, 362
Corticosteroids in graft rejection, 728
Corticosterone, 278
Corticotropin (*see* Adrenocorticotropic hormone)
Corticotropin releasing hormone, 291, 293, 294
  in stress, 751, 752
Cortisol, 274, 278, 280
  anti-inflammatory effects of, 751–752
  control of secretion, 294, 295
  effects of: on growth, 627, 628
    on organic metabolism, 615–616
  effects of growth hormone on uptake of, 615–616
  functions of, in stress, 751–752
  and lactation, 687
  as a neurotransmitter, 209
  pharmacological effects of, 752
  in pregnancy, 682
  and surfactant, 484
Cotransmitter, 202, 223
Cotransport, 129, 130
Cough, 508, 703
Countercurrent multiplier system, 532–535
Countertransport, 129, 130
Covalent bonds, polar, 18
Covalent chemical bond, 15–16
Covalent modulation:
  of enzymes, 89–90
  mechanism of, 60–62
CPR (cardiopulmonary resuscitation), 470

Cramps, skeletal muscle, 334
Cranial nerves, 216, 218
  (*See also specific nerves*)
Craniosacral division of autonomic nervous system (*see* Parasympathetic nervous system)
Creatine phosphate, 324–325
Creatine phosphokinase, 469
Creatinine clearance, 526–527
CRH (*see* Corticotropin releasing hormone)
Cristae of mitochondria, 50, 52
Critical period, 153
Cross bridge:
  definition of, 307
  movement of, 307–312
Cross-bridge cycle, 311–312
Cross-matching, 729
Cross-tolerance, 382
Crossed-extensor reflex, 357–358, 365
Crossing-over, 650–651
Crystalloids, 442
CSFs (*see* Colony-stimulating factors)
Cumulus oophorous, 665, 666
Curare, 318–319
Current, 187
  decremental, 194
  local, 192–194
Cyclic AMP, 168–170, 174
Cyclic endoperoxides, 160, 161
Cyclic GMP, 170, 174
  role of, in vision, 254
Cyclin, 75
Cyclooxygenase, 160, 161
Cyclosporin, 728
Cysteine, 28
Cystic fibrosis, 476
Cytochromes, 99–100
Cytokines, 275, 733
  definition of, 711
  as inflammatory mediators, 704
  secreted by helper T cells, 724
  stimulation of ACTH release by, 751
Cytokinesis, 74
Cytoplasm, 42, 43
Cytosine, 34, 35
Cytoskeleton, 51
Cytosol, 43
Cytotoxic T cells, 701, 702, 733
  antigen presentation to, 714–715
  effect of gamma interferon on, 721, 723
  effect of interleukin 2 on, 721, 722
  functions of, 710
    in immune responses, 721–723
  in graft rejection, 728

D cells, 608
DAG (*see* Diacylglycerol)

Dalton's law, 490
Daughter cells, 73
Dead space, 487
   anatomic, 487, 488
Defecation, 567, 592–593
Defenses at body surfaces, 703
Dehydration from excessive diarrhea, 596
7-dehydrocholesterol, 550
Dehydroepiandrosterone, 279
Delayed hypersensitivity, 730
Delivery (see Parturition)
Delta cells, 608
Dendrite, 181, 184
Denervation atrophy, 331
Dense bodies, smooth muscle, 338–339
Deoxyhemoglobin, 494
   affinity of: for carbon dioxide, 499
      for hydrogen ions, 499
Deoxyribonuclease, 587
Deoxyribonucleic acid (DNA):
   chromosomes, 48
   mitochondria, 63
   polymerase, 73
   replication of, 73–74
   role of, in protein synthesis, 65–70
   storage of genetic information, 63–65
   structure of, 34–36
Deoxyribonucleotide, 34
Deoxyribose, structure of, 34
Depo-Provera, 688, 689
Depression (see Affective disorders)
Descending limb of Henle's loop, 518, 519
Descending pathways, 351, 361–364
   summary of, 363–364
   (See also specific pathways)
Desmosomes, 46, 47
Detrusor muscle, 527
Developmental acclimatization, 153
Diabetes insipidus, 532
Diabetes mellitus, 618–620
   as cause of metabolic acidosis, 556
   glucosuria in, 525
   as risk factor for atherosclerosis, 470
Diabetic ketoacidosis, 618, 619
Diacylglycerol, 170–174
Dialysis, 559
Diaphragm, 476
Diaphragm (contraceptive), 689
Diarrhea, 596
   as cause of metabolic acidosis, 556
   control of glomerular filtration rate in, 537
   in lactose intolerance, 595
Diastole, 417
Diastolic arterial pressure, 432
Diencephalon, 215, 217, 220, 221
Dietary fiber, 595

Diets, 636, 637
Diffuse interstitial fibrosis, 492
Diffusion, 116–122
   across capillary walls, 440–442
   of carbon dioxide in lungs, 492
   definition of, 116–117
   direction of, 117
   equilibrium, 117–118
   facilitated, 124–125, 131
   of gases in liquids, 490–491
   magnitude of, 117
   across membranes, 119–124, 131
   of oxygen in lungs, 492
   speed of, 117–119
   tubular reabsorption by, 525–526
Diffusion impairment, 509
Digestion, definition of, 563
Digestive system, 5
Digitalis, 468, 469
Dihydrotestosterone, 660
   and sex differentiation, 693–695
Dihydroxyacetone phosphate, 93, 95
1,25-dihydroxyvitamin D_3, 550–551
   in pregnancy, 682
   in prevention of osteoporosis, 551
   in renal disease, 559
Diphosphoglycerate, 497
   in acclimatization to high altitude, 509
2,3-diphosphoglycerate (see Diphosphoglycerate)
Directed attention, 375–376
Disaccharides, structure of, 24–25
Distal convoluted tubule, 518, 519
   reabsorption of sodium by, 531, 534
Distension of stomach, role of:
   in acid secretion, 581–582, 585
   in gastric motility, 583–585
Disulfide bond, 33
Disuse atrophy, 331
Diuresis, 532
Diuretics, 557–558
   in heart failure, 468
   in hypertension, 467
Divergence, 201
DNA (see Deoxyribonucleic acid)
Doctrine of specific nerve energies, 235
Dominant follicle, 665
Dominant genes, 63
Dopamine, 208, 209, 223, 225, 274, 277, 381
   in addiction, 382
   from adrenal medulla, 225
   as hypophysiotropic hormone, 291, 293
   influence of, on prolactin, 684
   in Parkinson's disease, 361
   from posterior pituitary, 286
   role of: in memory, 384
      in motivation, 378

in schizophrenia, 380
Dorsal columns, 246
Dorsal root, 214, 215
Dorsal root ganglion, 214, 215
Double chemical bonds, 16
Down-regulation, 162–164, 282
   of receptors, 206
Down's syndrome, 690
DPG (see Diphosphoglycerate)
Drug dependence, 381–382
Drug overdose, 371, 374
Drugs:
   psychoactive, 381–384
   tubular reabsorption of, 525
Dual innervation, 226
Ductless glands, 141
Dumping syndrome, 586
Duodenal ulcers, 593
Duodenum, 565
Dura mater, 214
Dwarfism, 626
Dynorphins, 209, 212
Dysmenorrhea, 672
Dysmetria, 361
Dysplasia, 79
Dystrophin, 334
Dystrophy, muscular, 334

Ear:
   basilar membrane, 261–262
   cochlea, 259–263
   organ of Corti, 261–263
   sound transmission in, 258–261
   structure of, 258–261
   tympanic membrane, 259, 260
   (See also Hearing)
Eating disorders, 637
ECG (see Electrocardiogram)
Echocardiography, 427
Eclampsia, 681
Ectopic pregnancy, 677
Edema, 448
   causes of, 469
   in heart failure, 468
EEG arousal, 371
Effector, 157
Effector lymphocytes, 708
Effector proteins in plasma membrane, 166, 167
Efferent arterioles, 518–520
Efferent ductules, 652
Efferent neuron, 182–183
Efferent pathway, 157
Egg, 663
Eicosanoids, 25, 160–162
   effects of, on airway resistance, 485
   in immune responses, 733
   as inflammatory mediators, 704
Ejaculation, 658

Ejaculatory ducts, 653
Ejection fraction (EF), 424
EKG (*see* Electrocardiogram)
Elastin fibers, 4
Electric potential, 187
Electric synapses, 201
Electricity, principles of, 186–187
Electrocardiogram, 414–415, 419
Electrochemical difference (gradient), 122
Electroconvulsive therapy, 380, 385, 387
Electroencephalogram, 370–372
Electrogenic pump, 190
Electrolytes, 17
Electron micrographs, 41–42
Electron microscope, 40–41
Electron transport chain, 99–100
Electrons, 14–15
    in covalent chemical bonds, 15
    in electron microscope, 41
    role of, in ion formation, 17
Elements:
    major, 14
    mineral, 14
    trace, 14–15
    (*See also* Chemical element)
Elephantiasis, 447
Embolus, 471
Embryo, 677
Emission, 658
Emotional behavior, 221, 378
Emotional experience, 221
Emotions, 378–379
    effects of: on small intestinal motility, 591
        on stomach motility, 585
    role of, in ulcer formation, 594
    and ventilation, 508
Emphysema, 485
    ventilation-perfusion inequalities in, 493
Emulsification of fat, 571–572, 574
End-diastolic volume (EDV), 417, 419
    in exercise, 466
End-plate potential (EPP), 317–318
End product inhibition, 91
End-systolic volume, 419
Endocrine disorders, 296–298
Endocrine glands, 158, 274
    definition of, 142
    in gastrointestinal tract, 568
Endocrine system, 5, 274
Endocytosis, 137, 138
    of microbes, 705
Endogenous opioids, 209, 212, 248, 249
    in addiction, 382
Endogenous pyrogen (EP), 643
Endometrium, 671
Endoplasmic reticulum:

and inositol trisphosphate, 170–171
    role of, in protein secretion, 70–71
    structure of, 42, 43, 48, 50
Endorphin, 209, 212
    effect of, on memory, 384
β-endorphin, 257, 288, 289
Endothelial cells:
    functions of, 429
    of heart, 409
    role of, in blood-brain barrier, 229
    summary of anticlotting roles of, 748
    and vascular smooth muscle, 436–437
Endothelin-1, 437
Endothelium (*see* Endothelial cells)
Endothelium-derived relaxing factor, 437
Endurance exercise, fatigue, 326
Energy:
    release of: by ATP hydrolysis, 92–93
        by glucose catabolism, 101–102
    storage of, 104
Energy balance, 633–634
Energy expenditure, 630–637
    different activities and, 633
Enkephalins, 209, 212
    effect of, on memory, 384
Enteric nervous system, 222, 575
Enterogastrones, role of, in control of acid secretion, 582, 585
Enterohepatic circulation, 589–590, 739
Enterokinase, 586–588
Entrainment, 153
Enzyme(s):
    activity of, 89–90
    characteristics of, 86–87
    concentration of, 88–91
    definition of, 86
    in plasma after myocardial infarct, 469
    protein modulation by, 61
    regulation of, 87–91
    secretion of, by pancreas, 586–587
Eosinophils, 400, 401, 701, 702, 733
    in defenses against parasites, 730
    in immediate hypersensitivity, 730, 731
Epidermal growth factor as a neurotransmitter, 209
Epididymis, 652, 653
    sperm passage through, 656
Epiglottis, 578, 579
Epilepsy, 370, 371
Epinephrine, 208, 209, 211, 225, 274, 277, 280
    from adrenal medulla, 225
    control of arterioles by, 436
    effects of: on airways, 485
        on memory, 384
        on metabolic rate, 632–633

on organic metabolism, 614–615
    functions of, in stress, 753
    as respiratory stimulant, 505, 507
    secretion of during hypoglycemia, 614–615
    stimulation of ACTH release by, 751
    in stress, 751
Epiphyseal closure, 625
Epiphyseal growth plate, 625
Epiphyses, 625
Epithelial cells, 4
    tight junctions, 46, 47
Epithelium, 4
    basolateral membrane, 138
    of gastrointestinal tract, 568–569
    luminal membrane, 138
    paracellular pathway, 138
    transcellular pathway, 138
    transport across, 138–141
Epitopes, 713
EPP (*see* End-plate potential)
Equilibria, distinguished from steady state, 150
Equilibrium potential, 189, 190, 192
Erection, 657–658
Error signal, 151, 153
    in balance, 156
Erythrocytes, 395
    breakdown of, 398
    description of, 396
    number of, in blood, 400
    production of, 398–399
    volume of, 395
Erythropoiesis in response to hemorrhage, 462
Erythropoietin, 275, 399, 400
    in acclimatization to high altitude, 509
    in pregnancy, 682
    in renal disease, 559
    in response to hemorrhage, 462
Eskimos, 642
Esophageal sphincters, 579
Esophagus, 562, 564
    function of, 564, 565
        during swallowing, 578–580
Essential amino acids, 108, 110–111
Essential elements, 14
Essential nutrients, 110–111
Estradiol, 279, 648
    conversion of testosterone to, 660
    structure of, 278
    (*See also* Estrogen)
Estriol, 681
Estrogen, 275, 648
    blood concentrations of, in menstrual cycle, 667, 668
    control of secretion of, 668
    effects of, 672–674
        on granulosa cells, 668, 669

Estrogen (*Cont.*):
  on growth, 628
  on uterus, 671–672
  feedbacks of, on pituitary and
    hypothalamus, 668–671
  influences of, on prolactin, 684
  as a neurotransmitter, 209
  in oral contraceptives, 688, 689
  ovarian secretion of, 666
  in parturition, 684, 685
  during pregnancy, 680, 681
  in prevention of osteoporosis, 551
  secretion of, by follicle, 668–669
  treatment by, after menopause, 696
Eukaryotic cells, 41
Evaporation, 638, 641
Evolution, 2, 77
Excitation-contraction coupling:
  in cardiac muscle, 415–416
  in skeletal muscle, 313–315
  in smooth muscle, 340–343
Excitatory amino acids, 209, 211
Excitatory postsynaptic potentials
  (EPSPs), 192, 203
Excitatory synapse, 201–203
Excretion of foreign chemicals, 738–739
Exercise:
  and alveolar gas diffusion, 492
  cardiovascular responses to, 463–466
  as cause of metabolic acidosis, 556
  control of ventilation in, 505–507
  and endurance, 326
  energy metabolism in skeletal
    muscles, 324–325
  and fatigue, 326–327
  fuel homeostasis in, 617–618
  high-intensity, 326
  muscle metabolism, 324–325
  and obesity, 636–637
  oxygen debt, 325
  and plasma cholesterol, 622
  in prevention of osteoporosis, 551
  skeletal muscle adaptation, 331–332
  temperature regulation in, 644
  in treatment of diabetes mellitus, 620
Exocrine glands, definition of, 141
Exocytosis, 137–138
  of microbes, 704, 705
  at neuromuscular junction, 317
  in secretion of peptide hormones,
    277, 278
Exons in mRNA, 66
Expiration, 474
  mechanism of, 482–483
Expiratory reserve volume, 485, 486
Extension at a joint, 332
External anal sphincter, 593
External environment, 4
External genitalia:

  differentiation of, 693, 694
  female, 663
External urethral sphincter, 527, 528
External work, 630
Extracellular fluid:
  acidity, 23
  composition of, 188
  as electrical conductor, 187
  as internal environment, 5
  volume of, 442
Extrinsic pathway, 744, 745
Eye:
  ciliary muscle, 250, 251
  cornea, 249–250
  cross-section of, 250
  innervation of, 224, 227, 252
  iris, 250, 252
  lens, 249–252
  movement of, 257, 258
  pupil, 250, 252
  receptor cells, 252–254
  retina, 249, 250, 253
  vitreous humor, 250, 252
  zonular fibers, 250, 251
  (*See also* Vision)

F cells, 608
Facilitated diffusion, characteristics of,
  124–125, 131
Factor I (*see* Fibrinogen)
Factor Ia (*see* Fibrin)
Factor II (*see* Prothrombin)
Factor IIa (*see* Thrombin)
Factor III (*see* Tissue factor)
Factor IV (*see* Calcium)
Factor IX, 744, 745, 747
Factor IXa, 744, 745, 747
Factor V, 746, 747
Factor Va, 746, 747
Factor VII, 744, 745, 747
Factor VIIa, 744, 745, 747
Factor VIII, 744–747
Factor VIIIa, 744, 745, 747
Factor X, 744, 745, 747
Factor Xa, 744, 745, 747
Factor XI, 744–747
Factor XIa, 744, 745, 747
Factor XII, 744–747
Factor XIIa, 744, 745, 747
Factor XIII, 743
Factor XIIIa, 743
FAD (*see* Flavine adenine dinucleotide)
FADH$_2$ (*see* Flavine adenine
  dinucleotide)
Fainting, 462
Fallopian tubes (*see* Uterine tubes)
Farsighted (*see* Hyperopia)
Fasciculus cuneatus, 246
Fasciculus gracilis, 246

Fast-glycolytic fibers, skeletal muscle,
  327–328
Fast-oxidative fibers, skeletal muscle,
  327, 328
Fasting, 602
Fasting hypoglycemia, 620
Fat, 25
  catabolism, 104–105, 109
  digestion and absorption of, in small
    intestine, 571–574
  as energy storage, 104
  metabolism of, in postabsorptive state,
    604, 606–607
  as stimulus for gallbladder
    contraction, 590
  storage of, in adipose tissue, 104
  synthesis of, 105–106
    in absorptive state, 603–607
  (*See also* Fatty acids; Lipids;
    Triacylglycerol)
Fat-soluble vitamins, 110–111
Fatigue:
  central command, 326
  of skeletal muscles, 326–327
Fatty acids:
  absorption of, in small intestine, 572–
    574
  catabolism, 104–105
  essential nutrients, 110
  metabolism of, in muscle during
    exercise, 325
  and plasma cholesterol, 622
  in small intestine: inhibition of gastric
    acid secretion, 582
    inhibition of gastric emptying, 582,
    586
  structure of, 25, 27
  synthesis of, 105–106
    from amino acids, 108
    synthesis from glucose, 603–607
Fc, 712
  binding of, to phagocytes, 719
  binding of complement to, 719
Feces:
  color of, 589
  composition of, 563, 593
  sodium excretion in, 530
  water excretion in, 530
Feedforward regulation, 152–153
Fermentation, 94
Ferritin, 398
  role of, in iron absorption, 575
Fertilization, 675–677
Fetal adrenal glands, 681
Fetus, 677
  at different times of pregnancy, 680
FEV$_1$, 486
Fever, 642–644
  in infection, 723–724, 726

Fiber:
muscle, 304
in vegetable matter, 571
Fiber types, skeletal muscle, 327, 328
Fibrin, 742
Fibrinogen, 396, 743, 745, 747
in formation of platelet plug, 741
Fibrinolytic system, 746–749
Fibroblast growth factor, 706
Fibroblasts in tissue repair, 706
Fight-or-flight response, 226, 618, 753
Filtered load, 524
Filtration across capillary walls, 443–444
First messengers, 164
First-order neuron, 222
Flatus, 592
Flavine adenine dinucleotide (FAD), 87–88
role of: in fatty acid catabolism, 104–105
in Krebs cycle, 97–99
in oxidative phosphorylation, 98–100
Flexion at a joint, 332
Flexion reflex, 357
Flow autoregulation, 434, 435
Fluid endocytosis, 137
Fluid-mosaic model of membrane, 45–46
Flux:
definition of, 117
net, 117–118
Folic acid in erythrocyte formation, 398
Follicle (ovarian):
control of development, 668–669
dominant, growth of, 665
growth of, 664–666
secretion of estrogen by, 668, 669
Follicle-stimulating hormone (FSH), 274, 288, 289, 649
blood concentrations in menstrual cycle, 667
control of secretion of, 292, 293
effect of, on Leydig cells, 658, 659
effects of estrogen on, 668–671
inhibition of, by inhibin, 658, 659
during pregnancy, 681
during puberty, 695
Follicular phase, 666
Food-induced thermogenesis, 633
Food intake, control of, 634–637
Food poisoning, 319
Forced expiratory volume in 1 s, 486
Forced vital capacity (FVC), 486
Forebrain, 215, 217–221
Foreign chemicals, 738
Fovea centralis, 250, 257
Free-running rhythm, 153
Frequency-tension relation, 322–323

Frequency (wave), 249
Frontal lobe, 219–221
Fructose, 604
absorption of, in small intestine, 571
structure of, 25
Fructose 1,6-diphosphate, 95
Fructose 6-phosphate, 95
FSH (see Follicle-stimulating hormone)
Fumarate, 98
Functional residual capacity, 477
Functional site on protein, 60, 61
Functional units, 3, 4
Fundus of stomach, 580
Fused-vesicle channels, 439
FVC (see Forced vital capacity)

G₁, 74–75
G₂, 74–75
G proteins, 165 166
controlling ion channels, 171–172
Galactose, 604
absorption of, in small intestine, 571
structure of, 24
Galanin, 209
Gallbladder, 562, 564, 566
concentration of bile in, 500
function of, 564, 565
innervation of, 228
Gallstones, 594–595
Gametes, 648
Gametogenesis, 648
general principles of, 649–651
Gamma-aminobutyric acid (GABA), 209, 211, 382
effect of, on memory, 384
Gamma globulin, 717
in passive immunity, 720
Gamma interferon, 721, 723, 733
summary of effects of, 724
Ganglion, 214
autonomic, 223
collateral, 223
(See also specific ganglia)
Ganglion cell (retinal), 253, 255–256
Gap junctions:
in cardiac muscle, 410
in smooth muscle, 344
structure of, 46–48
Gas, intestinal (see Flatus)
Gases:
exchanges in alveoli and tissues, 488–494
as neurotransmitters, 209, 212
in plasma, 397
Gastric inhibitory peptide (see Glucose-dependent insulinotropic peptide)
Gastric phase:
of acid secretion, 581–582, 585

of gastrointestinal control, 578
role of, in pancreatic secretion, 587
Gastrin, 275, 576, 577
as a neurotransmitter, 209
role of: in acid secretion by stomach, 581–582, 585
in stomach motility, 585
Gastroileal reflex, 591
Gastrointestinal reflexes, 575–576
Gastrointestinal system, 562–563
Gastrointestinal tract, 562–563
and calcium homeostasis, 548
digestion and absorption of:
carbohydrates, 569–571
fat, 571–574
proteins, 571
effect of 1,25-dihydroxyvitamin D₃ on, 550–551
and hormones, 275, 576–578
satiety signals from, 634, 635
structure of wall, 567–569
volume of secretions, 567
GDP (see Guanosine diphosphate)
Gene, definition of, 63
Gene cloning, 77–78
Genes, mutation of, 75–77
Genetic code, 64–65
Genetic information, 63
expression of, 73 78
Genome, 63
Germ cells, 649
GFR (see Glomerular filtration rate)
GH (see Growth hormone)
GHRH (see Growth hormone releasing hormone)
Gᵢ protein, 169
Giantism, 626
GIP (see Glucose-dependent insulinotropic peptide)
Glands, characteristics of, 141–142
Glaucoma, 252
Glial cell, 185
Globin, 396
Globulins, 396
Globus pallidus, 220
Glomerular capillaries, 517–519
Glomerular capillary blood pressure, 523
Glomerular filtration rate (GFR), 520, 522–524
control of, 536, 537
increase in, by atrial natriuretic factor, 538
measurement of, 526–527
Glomerulus, 517–519
Glottis, closure of, during swallowing, 578
Glucagon, 275, 608
control of secretion of, 613–614
in diabetes mellitus, 620

Glucagon (*Cont.*):
  effects of, 613–614
  as a neurotransmitter, 209
  release in stress, 753
  as satiety signal, 634, 635
Glucocorticoids, 278–279
  as neurotransmitters, 209
Gluconeogenesis, 606–607
  effects of cortisol on, 615–616
  effects of epinephrine on, 614–615
  effects of glucagon on, 613
  effects of growth hormone on, 616
Gluconeogenic pathway, 103–104
Glucose:
  absorption of, in small intestine, 571
  in absorptive state, 603–607
  in brain, 229
  catabolism of, 101–102
  conversion of, to fat, 106
  effects of, on insulin secretion, 611–613
  effects of growth hormone on uptake of, 616
  extracellular and intracellular concentrations of, 116
  facilitated diffusion of, 124
  glycolytic breakdown of, 93–96
  as satiety signal, 634, 635
  sources of, in postabsorptive state, 606–607
  storage of, as glycogen, 102–103
  structure of, 24
  tubular reabsorption of, 525
Glucose 6-phosphate, 95, 102, 103
Glucose-counterregulatory controls, 613, 616
Glucose-dependent insulinotropic peptide (GIP), 275, 576, 577
  effect of, on insulin secretion, 611, 612
Glucose sparing, 606–607
Glucose transporters, effects of insulin on, 609–610
Glucosuria, 525
Glutamate, 209, 211
  effect of, on memory, 384
Glutamic acid, 28
  oxidative deamination of, 107–108
Glycerol:
  as source of glucose, 606
  structure of, 25, 27
  as substrate for glucose synthesis, 103–104
α-glycerol phosphate, 603
  role of, in fat synthesis, 106
Glycine, 209, 211
Glycocholic acid, 572
Glycogen:
  metabolism of, in muscle during

exercise, 325, 326
  storage of, 102–103
  structure of, 25, 26
  synthesis of, 103–104
    in absorptive state, 603–607
Glycogenolysis:
  effects of epinephrine on, 614–615
  effects of glucagon on, 613
  in postabsorptive state, 606
Glycolysis, 93–98, 101, 109
  characteristics of, 96
  pathway, 96
  in skeletal muscle, 325
Glycoproteins, 31
GnRH (*see* Gonadotropin releasing hormone)
G$_o$, 74–75
Goiter (*see* Iodine-deficient goiter)
Goldman equation, Appendix D, 189
Golgi apparatus:
  role of, in protein secretion, 70–71
  structure of, 42, 43, 49, 51
Golgi tendon organ, 357
Gonadotropic hormones, 274, 288, 289, 649
  (*See also* Follicle-stimulating hormone; Luteinizing hormone)
Gonadotropin releasing hormone (GnRH), 292, 293, 648–649
  effects of estrogen and progesterone on, 668–671
  during puberty, 695
  in male, 658
  as a neurotransmitter, 209
  during pregnancy, 681
Gonadotropins, (*see* Gonadotropic hormones)
Gonads, 648
  effects of gonadotropic hormones on, 274
  hormones of, 275, 279–280
Graded potentials, 191–195, 235, 370
Graft rejection, 728
Gram atomic mass, 15
Granular endoplasmic reticulum, structure of, 43, 48, 50
Granulosa cells, 664, 665
  effects of, on oogenesis, 669
  secretion of estrogen by, 668–669
  summary of functions of, 671
Gravity, effects of, on cardiovascular function, 462–463
Gray matter (of spinal cord), 214, 215
Ground substance, 4
Growth, 624–630
  effect of testosterone on, 660
  effects of thyroid hormones on, 632
  environmental factors influencing, 625–626

hormonal influences on, 626–629
  summary of hormonal effects on, 628
Growth cone, 185
Growth factors, 185, 275, 626
  in tissue repair, 706
Growth hormone (GH), 274, 288, 289
  circadian rhythm of, 284
  control of secretion of, 294–295, 297
  effects of: on carbohydrate and lipid metabolism, 616
    on growth, 626–627
    on protein metabolism, 627
  and lactation, 687
  release in stress, 753
  secretion of, 627
Growth hormone releasing hormone (GHRH), 291, 293–295, 297, 627
  as a neurotransmitter, 209
Growth-inhibiting factors, 626
G$_s$ protein, 166, 167
GTP (*see* Guanosine triphosphate)
GTPase cycle, 166
Guanine, 34, 35
Guanosine diphosphate (GDP), 166
  role of, in Krebs cycle, 97–99
Guanosine triphosphate (GTP), 166
  role of, in Krebs cycle, 97–99
Guanylyl cyclase, 170

H-ATPase, 127–128
  in stomach, 582, 583
H zone, 306, 308, 309
Habituation, 375
Hair cells, 261–263
  sensitivity of, 238
Hallucinations, 239, 381
Harvey, William, 403
HCl (*see* Hydrochloric acid)
Hearing, 257–263
  neural pathways in, 263
  normal range, 258
  role of hair cells in, 261–263
  (*See also* Ear; Hair cells)
Heart, 395
  anatomy of, 409–411
  as endocrine gland, 275
  innervation of, 224, 227
Heart attack (*see* Myocardial infarct)
Heart failure, 468–469
  congestive, 558
Heart-lung apparatus, 422–423
Heart murmurs, 420
Heart rate (HR), 413
  control of, 421–422
  in exercise, 463–464, 466
Heart sounds, 419, 420
Heartbeat coordination, 411–416
Heartburn, 580

Heat:
    acclimatization to, 641–642
    energy as, in chemical reactions, 84
    control of production of, 639–640
    and thermal motion, 116
Heat exhaustion, 644
Heat gain, mechanisms of, 638
Heat loss:
    control of, 640–641
    mechanisms of, 638
Heat stroke, 644
Heavy chains, 712
Heimlich maneuver, 485, 486, 578
Helicobacter pylori, 594
Helper T cells, 701, 702, 733
    antigen presentation to, 713–714
    functions of, 710
    interaction of, with cytotoxic T cells,
        721–723
    target of HIV, 727
Hematocrit, 395
Hematoma, 741
Hematopoietic growth factors (HGFs),
    402
Heme, 396, 398
Hemodialysis, 559
Hemoglobin, 396
    carriage of oxygen by, 494
    saturation of, 494–497
Hemolytic disease of the newborn, 729
Hemophilia, 744
Hemorrhage, 400
    arterial baroreceptor reflex in
        response to, 457
    cardiovascular responses to, 460–462
    effect of, on arterial pressure, 454–
        455
    fluid shifts in response to, 460–461
Hemostasis, 741–749
Heparin, 746, 749
Hepatic portal vein, 569
Hepatocytes, 589
Hering-Breuer inflation reflex, 500
Heroin in brain, 229
Herpes virus, 182
Heterozygote, 63
Hexoses, 24
HGFs (*see* Hematopoietic growth
    factors)
High-affinity protein binding sites, 57–
    58
High altitude, acclimatization to, 508–
    509
High-density lipoproteins (HDL), 622
High-intensity exercise and fatigue, 326
Hippocampus, 385
Histamine, 733
    effects of, on airway resistance, 485
    and endothelium-derived relaxing

factor, 437
    in immediate hypersensitivity, 730
    as inflammatory mediator, 704
    as a neurotransmitter, 208, 209
    role of, in gastric acid secretion, 582
Histotoxic hypoxia, 508
HIV (*see* Human immunodeficiency
    virus)
Homeostasis, 4–7, 150
    and aging, 156–157
    and biological rhythms, 154
Homeostatic control systems, 5, 150
    components of, 157–162
    general characteristics of, 150–155
    (*See also* Local homeostatic
        responses)
Homeothermic animals, 637
Homosexuality, 695
Homozygote, 63
Hormone(s), 158, 247
    and the blood-brain barrier, 277–278
    categories of, 281
    control of secretion of, 284–286
    endocrine gland secretion of, 141
    mechanisms of action of, 282–284
    metabolism and excretion of, 281–282
    pharmacological effects of, 283–284
    structures and synthesis of, 276–281
    transport of, in blood, 280–281
Hormone receptors, 282
Hot flashes, 696
Human immunodeficiency virus (HIV),
    726
Hydrocephalus, 230
Hydrochloric acid (HCl):
    functions of, in stomach, 565
    secretion of, by stomach, 581–582
Hydrogen:
    atomic weight of, 15
    covalent bonds, 15
Hydrogen bonds, 19
Hydrogen ion(s):
    buffering of, 552–553
    concentration of, 22–23
    homeostasis of, 552–556
    role of, in oxidative phosphorylation,
        99–100
    sources of gain and loss, 552
    transport of, in blood, 499
    tubular secretion of, 554–556
    (*See also* Acidity)
Hydrogen-ion concentration and carbon
    dioxide, 502
Hydrolysis, 20
    of ATP, 92
Hydrophilic molecules, 20
Hydrophobic molecules, 20
Hydrostatic pressure, 406
Hydroxyapatite, 547

Hydroxyl group, 18
17-Hydroxyprogesterone, 279
5-Hydroxytryptamine (*see* Serotonin)
Hymen, 663
Hyperalgesia, 248
Hypercalcemia, 546
Hypercapnia, 508, 509
Hyperemia, 434
Hyperopia, 252
Hyperosmotic solutions, 136
Hyperresponsiveness (hormonal), 298
Hypersecretion (hormonal), 297–298
Hypersensitivity (allergy), 729–730
Hypertension, 466–468
    and renin, 538
    as risk factor for atherosclerosis, 470
    use of diuretics in, 558
Hyperthermia, 642, 644
Hyperthyroidism, 628
Hypertonia, 364
Hypertonic solutions, 135, 136
    effects of, on fluid absorption by
        small intestine, 590
    in small intestine: inhibition of gastric
        acid secretion, 582, 585, 586
    inhibition of gastric emptying, 582,
        585, 586
Hypertrophy of skeletal muscle, 331
Hyperventilation, 492
Hypocalcemia, 546
Hypocalcemic tetany, 334, 546
Hypoglycemia, 613, 620–621
Hypoosmotic solutions, 136
Hypophysiotropic hormones, 274, 287–
    296
Hyporesponsiveness (hormonal), 296,
    298
Hyposecretion (hormonal), 296–297
Hypotension, 460–462
Hypothalamic releasing hormones (*see*
    Hypophysiotropic hormones)
Hypothalamo-pituitary portal vessels,
    286, 287, 290
Hypothalamus, 215, 219–221
    as endocrine gland, 274, 276, 285
    and erection, 657
    glucose receptors in, 614, 615
    and hormone secretion, 286–296
    in motivation, 378
    osmoreceptors in, 541
    and precocious puberty, 695
    relation of, to anterior pituitary, 287
    role of, in emotions, 378–379
    and temperature regulation, 639
Hypothyroidism, 627
Hypotonic solutions, 135, 136
Hypoventilation, 492
    as cause of hypoxic hypoxia, 509
Hypoxemia, 508

Hypoxia, 508–509
Hypoxic hypoxia, 508, 509

I band, 306–308
IgA, 717, 733
    in mother's milk, 720
IgD, 717, 733
IgE, 717, 733
    in immediate hypersensitivity, 730, 731
IGF-I (*see* Insulin-like growth factor I)
IgG, 717, 733
    transfer across placenta, 720
IgM, 717, 733
Ileocecal sphincter, 592
Ileum, 565
    role of, in vitamin B_{12} absorption, 574
Immediate hypersensitivity, 730, 731
Immune-complex hypersensitivity, 730
Immune defenses:
    nonspecific (*see* Nonspecific immune defenses)
    specific (*see* Specific immune defenses)
Immune responses:
    harmful, 728–732
    summary of cells involved in, 732–733
    summary of chemical mediators involved in, 733–734
Immune surveillance, 700
Immune system, 5, 701–702
    effects of cortisol on, 751–752
Immune tolerance, 716
Immunogen, 707
Immunoglobulins, 734
    as B-cell receptors, 712
    functions of, 717
    structure of, 712
Immunology, 700
Implantation, 677
Impotence, 657
In vitro fertilization, 690
Inborn errors in metabolism, 77
Infection:
    factors that alter resistance to, 725
    systemic responses to, 723–726
Inferior cervical (stellate) ganglion, 223, 224
Inferior mesenteric ganglion, 223, 224
Inferior vena cava, 405
Infertility, 690
Inflammation, 703–707
    excessive, 732
    mediators of, 703, 704
    summary of events in, 703
Inflammatory mediators, 703, 704
Inguinal canal, 653

Inhibin, 275, 649
    effect of, on FSH secretion, 658, 659
    feedback on anterior pituitary, 668, 671
    ovarian secretion of, 666
    during pregnancy, 681
Inhibitory postsynaptic potentials (IPSPs), 192, 203
Inhibitory synapse, 201, 203
Initial segment, 181, 205
Inner cell mass, 677, 678
Inner emotions, 378
Inositol, 110
Inositol trisphosphate (IP_3), 170–174
Insensible water loss, 530, 641
Inspiration, 474
    mechanism of, 481–482
Inspiratory reserve volume, 486
Insufficiency, 420
Insulator (electrical), 187
Insulin, 275, 608
    control of secretion of, 611–613
    effects of, 608–611
        on growth, 628
    inhibition of release of, in stress, 753
    and lactation, 687
    mechanism of action of, 608–609
    as a neurotransmitter, 209
    resistance to, 620
    as satiety signal, 634, 635
Insulin-dependent diabetes mellitus (IDDM), 618
    as autoimmune disease, 731
Insulin-like growth factor I (IGF-I), 274, 289
    effects of, on bone and growth, 626–627
Insulin-like growth factors, 275
Insulin resistance, 620
Integral membrane proteins, 45
Integrating center, 157
Integration, role of:
    neurons in, 201
    synapses in, 203–205
Integumentary system, 5
Intercalated disks, 410
Intercellular chemical messengers, 159–162
Intercellular clefts (in capillaries), 439
Intercellular fluid, 7
    (*See also* Interstitial fluid)
Intercostal muscles, 476
Interferon(s), 275, 707, 734
    as cytokines, 711
    as a neurotransmitter, 209
Interleukin 1, 721, 722, 734
    and activation of helper T cells, 714
    and fever, 643–644
    as a neurotransmitter, 209

    role of, in acute phase response, 724–726
    in septic shock, 732
    stimulation of ACTH release by, 751
Interleukin 2, 734
    effect of: on B cells and helper T cells, 716–717
        on cytotoxic T cells, 721, 722
        on NK cells and macrophages, 723
    in immunotherapy, 723
    role of, in acute phase response, 724–726
    summary of effects of, 724
Interleukin 6, 734
    effect of, on B cells, 717
    and fever, 643
    role of, in acute phase response, 724–726
    summary of effects of, 724
Interleukins, 275
    as cytokines, 711
    in exercise, 644
    as hematopoietic growth factors, 402
    as inflammatory mediators, 704
Intermediate filaments, 52–53
Internal anal sphincter, 593
Internal environment, 4–7
    as extracellular fluid, 5
Internal genitalia:
    differentiation of, 693, 694
    female, 662
Internal urethral sphincter, 527
Internal work, 630
Interneuron, 183–184
    role of, in motor control, 352
Interphase, 74
Interstitial fluid, 7
    protein concentration in, 442–444
    as reservoir for plasma, 442
    (*See also* Intercellular fluid)
Interstitial hydrostatic pressure, 442–444
Intestinal phase:
    of acid secretion, 582, 585
    of gastrointestinal control, 578
Intestino-intestinal reflex, 591
Intracellular fluid, 7, 43
    composition of, 188
    as electrical conductor, 187
Intrapleural fluid, 477
Intrapleural pressure, 479
Intrarenal baroreceptors, 538, 539
Intrauterine device, 688
Intrinsic factor, 398, 574
Intrinsic pathway, 744, 745
Introns in mRNA, 66
Inulin, 526
Involuntary actions, 351–352
"Involuntary" nervous system, 226
Iodine and thyroid hormones, 276

Iodine-deficient goiter, 293
Ion channels:
  gating, 122
  mechanosensitive, 122
  messenger linked, 122
  in receptor potentials, 235
  role of: in action potentials, 194–196
    in synaptic potentials, 202–203
  voltage-sensitive, 122
  (See also Channels; Membrane)
Ionic bond, 20
Ions, 17–18
IP₃ (see Inositol trisphosphate)
Iron, 396
  absorption of, by small intestine, 575
  balance of, 399
  in erythrocyte formation, 398
  in infection, 724, 726
Iron deficiency, 398
Irreversible reactions, 85, 86
Ischemic hypoxia, 508
Islets of Langerhans, 608
Isocitrate, 98
Isometric contraction, 320–321
Isoosmotic solutions, 136
Isotonic contraction, 320–321
Isotonic saline, 136
Isotonic solutions, 135, 136
Isovolumetric ventricular contraction, 417–419
Isovolumetric ventricular relaxation, 417–419
Isozymes of smooth muscle myosin, 340–341

Jaundice, 595
Jejunum, 565
Jet lag, 154
Joint position, awareness of, 246
Joint receptors in control of ventilation, 505, 507
Juxtaglomerular apparatus, 520, 521
Juxtaglomerular cells, 520, 521, 538, 539

Kallikrein, 434
Karyotype, 693
Keto acids, 107–108
  in absorptive state, 603, 605
Ketoacidosis, 618, 619
Ketone bodies (see Ketones)
Ketones, 607
  as cause of metabolic acidosis, 556
  effects of glucagon on synthesis of, 613
Kidneys:
  basic processes of, 520–527
  and calcium homeostasis, 548
  control of blood flow to, 437
  diseases of, 558–559

energy derived by, from fat catabolism, 104
excretion of urea by, 108
glucose formation by, 103–104
formation of 1,25-dihydroxyvitamin D₃ by, 550–551
functions of, 517
hormones of, 275
in pregnancy, 682
role of, in hydrogen-ion homeostasis, 553–556
secretion of renin by, 536, 538
structure of, 517–520
Kilocalorie, 84, 631
Kinesthesia, 247
Kininogen, 434
Kinins, 734
  as inflammatory mediators, 704
Knee jerk (see Stretch reflex)
k_p, 119
Krebs cycle, 93, 94, 101, 109
  pathway, 96–99
  role of, in glucose catabolism and synthesis, 96–97

L-dopa, 361
Labia majora, 663
Labia minora, 663
Lacrymal glands:
  antimicrobials in, 703
  innervation of, 224, 228
Lactase, 595
Lactate:
  formed during glycolysis, 94–96
  role of, in glucose synthesis, 103–104
    in muscle fatigue, 326
  as source of glucose, 606
Lactate dehydrogenase, 469
Lactation, 684–687
Lacteals, 569, 573, 574
Lactic acid, 556
  (See also Lactate)
Lactose intolerance, 595
Lamina propria, 568
Language, 184
Large intestine, 562, 564
  absorption of salt and water, 592
  anatomy of, 591–592
  effects of aldosterone on, 536
  function of, 564, 567
  innervation of, 224, 228
  motility, 592–593
Larynx, 474, 475
Late-phase reaction, 730, 731
Latent period, 321
Lateral geniculate nucleus, 255, 256
Lateral inhibition, 242–244
Lateral sacs of sarcoplasmic reticulum, 314–316

Lateral traction, 484, 485
Law of mass action, 86
Law of the intestine, 591
Laxatives, 595–596
Learned reflex, 157
Learning, 221, 384–386
Lecithin in bile, 589
Length-tension relation:
  in cardiac muscle, 423
  in skeletal muscle, 323–324
Lengthening contraction, 320
Leucine, 28
Leukemias, 79
Leukocytes, 395, 400, 402, 701
  distribution of, in blood, 400
Leukotrienes, 160, 161
  in inflammation, 734
Lever action of muscles, 332–334
Leydig cells, 652
  effect of LH on, 658, 659
LH (see Luteinizing hormone)
LH surge, 668
  cause of, 669, 670
  effects of, on ovarian function, 670
Lidocaine, 196
Ligand, 56
Light, 249
Light adaptation, 254
Light chains, 712
Limbic system:
  functions of, 219
  in motor control, 363
  in olfactory pathways, 267
  in perceptual processing, 238
  role of, in emotions, 378, 379
  structure of, 221
Linoleic acid, 110
Linolenic acid, 110
Lipase, 574
Lipid bilayer (see Membrane)
Lipids:
  as electrical insulators, 187
  membrane, 44–45
  phospholipids, 26, 27
  steroids, 26–27
  structure of, 23, 25–27
  triacylglycerol, 25, 27
  (See also Fat)
Lipolysis:
  effects of cortisol on, 615–616
  effects of epinephrine on, 614–615
  effects of growth hormone on, 616
  in postabsorptive state, 606
β-lipoprotein, 288, 289
Lipoprotein lipase, 605
Lipoproteins, 622
β-lipotropin, 274
Lipoxygenase, 160, 161
Liter, 22

Multineuronal pathways, 216, 219
Multinucleated cells, 304
Multiple sclerosis, 731
Multisynaptic pathways (see
    Multineuronal pathways)
Multiunit smooth muscles, 344–345
Muscarinic receptors, 208, 225, 226
Muscle:
    characteristics of, 345
    and cramps, 364
    effects of, on metabolic rate, 633
    fiber, 304
    functions of, 304
        in absorptive state, 603–607
    insulin's actions on, 609–610
    receptors, in control of ventilation,
        505, 507
    spasms, 364
    thick filaments, 52–53
    tone, 364
    types of, 304
    versus muscle fiber, 304
    (See also Cardiac muscle; Skeletal
        muscle; Smooth muscle)
Muscle spindle, 354–355
Muscular dystrophy, 334
Muscularis externa, 568
Muscularis mucosa, 568
Musculoskeletal system, 5
"Mushrooms," 381
Mutagens, 76
Mutation, 75–77
Myasthenia gravis, 164, 334–335, 731
Myelin, 182, 198, 214, 222, 235
Myelin formation and Vitamin B_{12}, 398
Myeloid stem cell, 401
Myenteric plexus, 568, 575
Myoblasts, 304
Myocardial infarct, 469–471
    use of anticlotting drugs in, 748–749
Myocardium, 409
Myoepithelial cells, 684
Myofibrils, 305–309
Myogenic response, 435
Myogenic tone, 433
Myoglobin, 327–328
    in acclimatization to high altitude, 509
Myometrium, 671
Myopia, 252
Myosin, 52
    ATPase, 309–312
    location, 305
Myosin light-chain kinase, 340
Myotatic reflex (see Stretch reflex)

Na (see Sodium)
NAD+ (see Nicotinamide adenine
    dinucleotide)
NAD$^+$ (see Nicotinamide adenine

dinucleotide)
Na,K-ATPase, 127–130
    in resting membrane potential, 190
Natural antibodies, 728, 734
Natural killer cells (see NK cells)
Natural selection, 2, 77
Nearsighted (see Myopia)
Negative balance, 156
Negative feedback, 150, 152
Negative nitrogen balance, 110
Nephron, 517, 518, 520
Nernst equation, Appendix D, 189
Nerve(s), 180, 214, 222
    cranial, 216, 218
    spinal, 215
    (See also specific nerves)
Nerve cells, 3
    (See also Neuron)
Nerve fiber, 181
Nerve gases, 319
Nerve growth factor, 185
Nerve tissue, 4
Nervous system, 5, 180
    (See also Autonomic nervous system;
        Central nervous system; Enteric
        nervous system; Peripheral
        nervous system)
Net flux, 117–118
Net glomerular filtration pressure, 523
Neural development, 185
Neural implantation, 185
Neural regeneration, 185
Neuroblast, 185
Neuroeffector communication, 212–213
Neuroeffector junction, 212–213
Neuroglia, 185
Neurohormones, 159, 160, 276
Neurokinin, 209
Neuromodulators, 207–208
    (See also Neurotransmitters)
Neuromuscular junction, 315–319
Neuron, 181
    afferent, 182, 183
    anatomy of, 181
    efferent, 182–183
    functional classes of, 182–184
    ionic composition of, 188
    polymodal, 238
    postsynaptic, 184
    presynaptic, 184
    repair of, 185
    (See also Motor neuron)
Neuropeptide Y, 209
Neuropeptides, 209, 212, 223
Neurotensin, 209
Neurotransmitters, 159, 184, 202, 207–
    212
    of autonomic nervous system, 223–
    226

role of, at synapses, 202
    (See also specific neurotransmitters)
Neutral solution, 23
Neutrons, 14–15
Neutrophils, 401, 701, 702, 733
    release of, during infection, 724, 726
Niacin, 87
Nicotinamide adenine dinucleotide, 87–
    88
    role of: in fatty acid catabolism, 104–
        105
    in fatty acid synthesis, 106
    in glycolysis, 94–96
    in Krebs cycle, 97–99
    in oxidative phosphorylation, 98–
        100
Nicotine, 229
Nicotinic receptors, 208, 225, 226
    at neuromuscular junction, 317
Nitric oxide:
    as defense, against microbes, 704
    as endothelium-derived relaxing
        factor, 437
    in hemostasis, 742
    as a neurotransmitter, 209, 212
    role of: in erection, 657
    in learning, 385
Nitrogen covalent bonds, 15
Nitroglycerin, 470
NK cells, 701, 702, 733
    in antibody-dependent cellular
        cytotoxicity, 719
    in defenses against viruses and
        cancer, 723
    function of, 715
    origin of, 710
Nociception (see Pain)
Nociceptors, 248
Node of Ranvier, 182, 235
Noncholinergic, nonadrenergic nerves,
    485
Noncorticospinal pathways, 361–363
Non-insulin-dependent diabetes mellitus
    (NIDDM), 618
Nonpenetrating solutes, 135
Nonpolar molecules, 19
    membrane permeability of, 119–120
Nonshivering thermogenesis, 640
Nonspecific immune defenses, 700,
    702–707
Nonsteroidal anti-inflammatory drugs
    (NSAIDs), 161–162
Norepinephrine, 208, 209, 211, 225, 274
    from adrenal medulla, 225, 277, 280
    and autonomic nervous system, 223–
    226
    control of arterioles by, 435–436
    effects of, on cardiac contractility,
    425

Norepinephrine (Cont.):
  receptor types, 211, 226
  role of, in motivation, 378
Normocytosis, 400
Norplant, 688, 689
Novocaine, 196
Nuclear envelope, 43, 48–49, 74
Nuclear pores, 43, 48–49, 67
Nucleic acids, structure of, 23, 34–36
Nucleolus, 43, 48–49
Nucleotide base pairing, 34–36, 65
Nucleotide triphosphates, 65
Nucleotides, structure of, 34–35
Nucleus:
  atomic, 14
  cell, 42, 43, 48–49
Nucleus (neural), 214
  (See also specific nuclei)
Nucleus accumbens, 383
Nutrients:
  in plasma, 397
  summary of metabolism of: in
    absorptive state, 606
    in postabsorptive state, 607

Obesity, 636–637
  as risk factor for hypertension, 467
Obligatory water loss, 533
Occipital lobe, 219, 220
Ohm's law, 187
Olfaction (see Smell)
Olfactory mucosa, 266, 267
Olfactory nerve, 218
Oligodendroglia, 182, 185
Olive oil, 622
Oncogenes, 79, 626
  coding of, for new antigens, 715
Oogenesis, 663–664
Oogonia, 663, 664
Operating point, 150
Opsin, 253
Opsonin, 704, 719, 734
Optic nerve, 218, 250, 256
Optimal muscle length, 323
Oral anticoagulants, 749
Oral contraceptives, 688, 689
Organ of Corti, 261–263
Organ systems, 3, 4
  functions of, 5
Organic chemistry, 23
Organic metabolism in pregnancy, 682
Organophosphates, 319
Organs, 3, 4
Orgasm:
  in female, 675
  in male, 658
Orienting response, 375
Osmolarity, 132
Osmole, 132

Osmoreceptors in control of antidiuretic
    hormone secretion, 541, 542
Osmosis, 131–137
  diffusion of water, 131–132
Osmotic diuresis, 532
  in diabetes mellitus, 619
Osmotic pressure, 134–135
Osteoblasts, 547, 625
Osteoclasts, 547
Osteocytes, 547
Osteoid, 547
Osteomalacia, 551
Osteoporosis, 551
  after menopause, 696
Ovarian hormones, sites of secretion of,
    666
Ovaries, 648
  control of function of, 666–671
  function of, 663–666
  hormones of, 275
Oviducts (see Uterine tubes)
Ovulation, 661, 666
  inhibition of, by breast feeding, 686
Ovum transport, 675
Oxaloacetate, 97, 98
  role of, in glucose synthesis, 103
Oxidative deamination of amino acids,
    107–108
Oxidative phosphorylation, 93, 94, 97
    101, 109
Oxidative skeletal muscle fibers, 327
    328
Oxygen:
  alveolar partial pressure of, 491
  consumption of, at rest, 489
  content of, in blood, 494
  control of respiration by, 500–502
  covalent bonds, 15
  diffusion of, through membranes,
    120
  effects of, on pulmonary blood
    vessels, 493
  in peroxisomes, 51
  role of, in oxidative phosphorylation,
    98–100
  transport of, in blood, 494–497
Oxygen-carrying capacity, 494
Oxygen debt, 325
Oxygen-hemoglobin dissociation curve,
    494–495
Oxytocin, 246, 286
  in milk ejection reflex, 686, 687
  as a neurotransmitter, 209
  in parturition, 684, 685

P wave, 415
Pacemaker potentials, 192, 198–199
  in cardiac conducting system, 413
  in smooth muscle, 342

Pacemakers in biological rhythms, 154
Pain, 243, 246, 248–249
  and antidiuretic hormone secretion,
    541
  blood pressure response to, 459
  descending control of, 244
  prostaglandins and, 248
  referred, 248
  and ventilation, 508
Pancreas, 562, 564, 566
  functions of, 564, 565
  gastrointestinal secretions, 586–587
  hormones of, 275
  innervation of, 228
  volume of secretions, 567
Pancreatic duct, 566
Pancreatic polypeptide, 275, 608
  as a neurotransmitter, 209
Papillary muscles, 409
Paracellular pathway, 138
Paracrine agents, 159, 160
Paradoxical sleep, 372, 374
Parasympathetic nerves:
  in baroreceptor reflex, 456
  control of arterioles by, 436
  effects of: on airways, 485
    on heart rate, 421–422
    on insulin secretion, 611, 612
    on salivary glands, 578
  in exercise, 463–464
  role of: in erection, 657
    in gastric emptying, 585–586
Parasympathetic nervous system, 223
    228
  acetylcholine and, 223
  control of hormone secretion by,
    284–285
  ganglia of, 223
Parathormone (see Parathyroid
    hormone)
Parathyroid glands, 274
  in pregnancy, 682
Parathyroid hormone, 274
  effects of, 548–549
  in pregnancy, 682
Parietal cells, 581–583
Parietal lobe, 219, 220
Parietal pleura, 477
Parkinson's disease, 211, 360–361
Parotid salivary glands, 562
Partial pressure, 489–490
  in alveoli, blood, and cells, 490,
    492
Parturition, 681–684
  causes of, 684, 685
  stages of, 683
Passive immunity, 720
Pathways:
  ascending, 236–238

Pathways (*Cont.*):
  descending, 351, 361–364
  long neural, 216, 219
  multineuronal, 216, 219
  neural, 214
  (*See also* Motor control systems;
    Sensory systems, neural pathways
    in)
Peanut oil, 622
Pelvic inflammatory disease, 688
Pelvis, renal, 518
Penicillin:
  allergy to, 730
  excretion of, 739
Penis, mechanoreceptors on, 657
Pentoses, 24
Pepsin, 565
  activation of, 582–583
Pepsinogen, 580, 582–583
  secretion of, 583
Peptide(s), 30
  absorption of, in small intestine, 571
  as neurotransmitters, 209, 212
  in stomach, role of, in acid secretion,
    581–582, 585
  (*See also* Protein)
Peptide bond, 30
Peptide hormones, 277–278
  signal transduction mechanisms for,
    283
Perception, 234, 238–239
Perforin, 721, 722, 734
Pericardium, 409
Peripheral chemoreceptors, 500, 501,
    504, 506
  in acclimatization to high altitude, 509
Peripheral lymphoid organs, 708
  site of lymphocyte production, 701,
    708
Peripheral membrane proteins, 45
Peripheral nervous system, 180, 221–
    228
  divisions of, 222
  (*See also* Autonomic nervous system)
Peripheral thermoreceptors, 639
Peripheral veins, 444
Peristalsis:
  definition of, 579
  in esophagus, 579
  secondary, 579
  in stomach, 583–584
Peritoneal dialysis, 559
Peritubular capillaries, 520
Permeability of plasma membrane, 116
Permeability constant, 119
Permissiveness, 282
Pernicious anemia, 400
Peroxisomes, 43, 51
Peyote, 381

PGE (*see* Prostaglandins)
PGI$_2$ (*see* Prostacyclin)
PH (*see* Parathyroid hormone)
pH, definition of, 22
Phagocytes, 703
  killing by, 704–706
  secretion by, 704–706
Phagocytosis, 137, 703
  effects of antibodies on, 719
Phagolysosome, 704, 705
Phagosome, 704, 705
Phantom limb, 239
Pharmacological effects of hormones,
    283–284
Pharynx, 474, 475, 562, 565
Phase shift, 153–154
Phencyclidine, 211
Phenylalanine, 28
Phenylketonuria, 77
Phosphate:
  extracellular and intracellular
    concentration, 116
  as renal tubular buffer, 554–555
  parathyroid hormone effects on
    excretion of, 548
Phosphatidylinositol bisphosphate, 170–
    171
Phosphodiesterase, 168
Phosphoenopyruvate, 95, 103
3-phosphoglyceraldehyde, 93, 95
2-phosphoglycerate, 95
3-phosphoglycerate, 95
Phospholipase A$_2$, 160–162
Phospholipase C, 170–171
Phospholipids:
  and eicosanoids, 160–162
  in membranes, 44–45
  in surfactant, 483
  structure of, 26, 27
Phosphoprotein phosphatase, 61
Phosphorylation of proteins, 60–62
Photopigments, 252–254
Photoreceptors:
  mechanism of, 240
  (*See also* Cones; Rods)
Physiologic dead space (*see* Dead space)
Pia mater, 214
Pineal gland, 275, 295–296
Pinocytosis, 137
PIP$_2$ (*see* Phosphatidylinositol
    bisphosphate)
Pituitary gland, 286, 287
Placenta, 677–680
  hormones of, 275
  production of hormones by, 680–681
Placental lactogen, 275, 681
Plant proteins in diet, 110
Plasma, 7, 395, 396
Plasma cells, 701, 702, 710, 733

Plasma cholesterol (*see* Cholesterol)
Plasma electrolytes, 397
Plasma membrane, 42–48
  as electrical insulator, 187
  (*See also* Membrane)
Plasma nutrients, 397
Plasma proteins, 396, 397
  and bulk flow across capillaries, 442–
    444
  concentration of, 442–444
Plasma volume, 395, 442
Plasma waste products, 397
Plasmin, 746, 749
Plasminogen, 746, 749
Plasminogen activators, 746–747
Plasticity, 386
Platelet-activating factor, 734, 744, 745
  in immediate hypersensitivity, 730
  as inflammatory mediator, 704
Platelets, 395, 402
  activation of, 744, 745, 747
  adhesion, 741
  aggregation of, 741
  contraction of, 741
  plug, 741
  role of, in clotting, 743–745, 747
Pleura, 476
Pleural sac, 476
Pluripotent stem cells, 401–402
Pneumothorax, 479
Podocytes, 519
Polar bodies, 664
Polar covalent bonds, 18
Polar molecules, 18–20
  membrane permeability of, 119–120
Polio virus, 182
Poliomyelitis, 500
Polycythemia, 400
Polymers, 24
Polymorphonuclear granulocytes, 400,
    401
Polypeptides, 30
Polysaccharides, structure of, 25, 26
Polyunsaturated fatty acids, 25, 27
Pons, 215, 217
  and respiration, 500
Pool, 155
Positive balance, 156
Positive feedback, 151
Positive nitrogen balance, 110
Postabsorptive state, 602, 606–607
  endocrine and neural control of, 607–
    616
Posterior pituitary, 286
  hormones, 274, 286
  in pregnancy, 682
Postganglionic fiber, 223
Postsynaptic neuron, 184
Postsynaptic potentials, 192, 201–203

Postsynaptic potentials (*Cont.*):
  interaction of, 203–205
  (*See also* Excitatory postsynaptic
    potentials; Inhibitory postsynaptic
    potentials)
Postural reflexes, 365
Posture:
  descending control of, 362–363
  maintenance of, 364–365
Potassium:
  in action potentials, 194–196
  and arrhythmias, 543
  in control of aldosterone secretion,
    543
  equilibrium potential, 189–190
  extracellular and intracellular
    concentration of, 116
  ion, 18
  primary active transport, 127–128
  regulation of, 543–545
  in resting membrane potential, 188–
    190
  secretion of, by large intestine, 502
Potassium-sparing diuretics, 558
Potential difference, 187, 192
  (*See also* Membrane potentials)
Potentiation of gastrointestinal tract
    hormones, 577
PP cells, 608
Precapillary sphincters, 440
Precocious puberty, 695
Preganglionic fiber, 223
Pregnancy, 675–690
  heartburn during, 580
  hormone changes during, 680–681
  maternal responses to, 682
Pregnancy sickness, 681
Pregnenolone, 279
Prehormone, 212
Premenstrual syndrome, 673
Preprohormones, 212, 277, 278
Presbyopia, 252
Pressure(s), 406
  in vascular system, 430
Presynaptic neuron, 184
Presynaptic synapses, 206, 244
Primary active transport, 127–128, 131
Primary afferent, 222
Primary hypertension, 467
Primary lymphoid organs, 708
Primary oocytes, 663, 664
Primary spermatocytes, 654
Primordial follicles, 664, 665
Procaine hydrochloride, 196
Product, enzyme, 86
Progestagens:
  as contraceptives, 688
  treatment with, after menopause, 696
Progesterone, 275, 279, 648

blood concentrations of, in menstrual
    cycle, 667, 668
  effects of, 672–674
    on uterus, 671–672
  feedback of, on hypothalamus, 668,
    671
  influence of, on prolactin, 684
  as a neurotransmitter, 209
  ovarian secretion of, 666
  in parturition, 684, 685
  during pregnancy, 680, 681
Progestin (*see* Progestagens)
Prohormones, 212, 277, 278
Prokaryotic cells, 41
Prolactin, 274, 288, 289
  actions in male, 660
  control of secretion of, 292, 293
  effects of, on breasts, 684–685
  as a neurotransmitter, 209
  release of, in stress, 753
Prolactin releasing factor (PRF), 274,
    286, 684
  during lactation, 686, 687
Proliferative phase, 671, 672
Proline, 28
Promoter sites, 66
Proofreading, 75
Proopiomelanocortin, 288, 289
Proprioception, 247
Prostacyclin:
  in hemostasis, 742
  as vasodilator, 437
Prostaglandins, 160, 161
  cause of dysmenorrhea by, 672
  effect of, on corpus luteum, 671
  and fever, 643
  as inflammatory mediators, 734
  in menstruation, 672
  as neurotransmitters, 209
  in parturition, 684, 685
  summary of effects of, on female
    reproductive system, 685
Prostate gland, 653
Proteases, 106
Protein(s):
  activity, 59–62
  allosteric modulation of, 60
  amino acid sequence, 30
  binding sites, 56–62
  catabolism of, 106–110
    in postabsorptive state, 606
  conformation, 31–34
  conformation of binding sites, 56–57
  covalent modulation, 60–62
  digestion of, by pepsin, 583
  digestion and absorption of, in
    gastrointestinal tract, 571
  energy storage, 104
  extracellular and intracellular

concentration of, 116
  functions of, 56
  increased permeability to, in
    inflammation, 703–704
  membrane, 45
  membrane channels, 120–121
  posttranslational processing, 68–70
  regulation of synthesis of, 72–73
  secretion of, 70–72
  as source of glucose, 606
  stimulation of acid secretion, 581–582
  structure of, 29–34
  synthesis of, 65–70
    in absorptive state, 603–607
    role of essential amino acids in, 108
  (*See also* Binding sites; Peptide)
Protein C, 746, 748
Protein-calorie malnutrition, 725
Protein kinase A (*see* cAMP-dependent
    protein kinase)
Protein kinase C, 170–171, 174
Protein kinase G (*see* cGMP-dependent
    protein kinase)
Protein kinases, 165
  role of, in covalent modulation, 61
  (*See also specific protein kinases*)
Prothrombin, 743–745, 747
Protons, 14–15
Proximal convoluted tubule, 518, 519
Proximal straight tubule, 518, 519
Proximal tubule, 518, 519
Prozac, 211, 380
Psilocybin, 211, 381
Psychoneuroimmunology, 725
PTH (*see* Parathyroid hormone)
Puberty, 695
Pulmonary (term), 474
Pulmonary arterial pressure, 454
Pulmonary arteries, 405
Pulmonary circulation, 403–404
  in expiration, 482–483
  in inspiration, 481–482
  pressures in, 420, 477–479
  (*See also* Alveolar gas pressures;
    Intrapleural pressure)
Pulmonary edema, 468
Pulmonary stretch receptors, 500
Pulmonary surfactant (*see* Surfactant)
Pulmonary trunk, 405
Pulmonary valves, 409
Pulmonary vascular resistance, 454
Pulmonary veins, 405
Pulse pressure, 431
  and arterial baroreceptors, 455–456
  in exercise, 466
Pumps (*see* Active transport; Mediated
    transport)
Purines, 34, 36
Purkinje fibers, 413, 414

Putamen, 220
Pyloric sphincter, 583, 584
Pyramidal cell of cerebral cortex, 219
Pyramidal system, 362
Pyrimidines, 34, 36
Pyruvate, 95
  role of, in glucose synthesis, 103–104
    in glycolysis, 93
  as source of glucose, 606
Pyruvic acid (see Pyruvate)

QRS complex, 415

Radiation, 638, 641
  effects of: on gene mutation, 76
    on neural development, 185
Ragweed pollen, 708
Random coil, 32
Rate limiting reaction, 90–91
RDAs, 682
Reabsorption (see Tubular reabsorption)
Reaction rate, 84–85
  enzyme-mediated, 88–91
Reactive hyperemia, 435
Reactive hypoglycemia, 621
Receptive field, 236
  regional sensitivity of, 241–242
  size and overlap of, 241–242
Receptive relaxation of stomach, 583
Receptor activation, 164
  effects of, on channels, 174
Receptor potential, 192
Receptors:
  binding sites, 162–164
  for chemical messengers, 184, 202,
    206–207
  containing channels, 164–165
  and G proteins, 165–166
  for hormones, 282
  in reflexes, 157
  sensory, 183, 234–236
    chemoreceptors, 266
    hair cells (see Hair cells)
    (See also specific type)
  specificity of, 234–235, 240
Recessive genes, 63
Reciprocal innervation, 226, 355
Recombinant DNA, 77–78
Recruitment:
  of motor units, 330
  of sensory units, 241
Rectum, 562, 564, 567, 591–592
  function of, 564, 567
Red skeletal muscle fibers, 327
Reflex, 157–158
  monosynaptic, 355
  polysynaptic, 355
  (See also specific reflex)
Reflex arc, 157–158

Refractory periods, 197
  of heart, 416
Regulatory site on protein, 60, 61
Relaxation of muscle fiber, definition of,
    307
Relaxin, 275
Releasing factors (see Hypophysiotropic
    hormones)
REM sleep (see Paradoxical sleep)
Renal clearance, 526–527
Renal corpuscle, 517–519
Renal cortex, 520
Renal hypertension, 467, 559
Renal medulla, 520
Renal pelvis, 518, 520
Renal processes, 520–527
Renal sympathetic nerves, effects of:
  on glomerular filtration rate, 537
  on renin secretion, 538, 539
Renin, 275, 536, 538
  control of secretion of, 538–539
  in pregnancy, 682
  in renal disease, 559
Renin-angiotensin system, 536, 538
Reproduction, stages in the control of,
    649
Reproductive function, male, hormonal
    control of, 658–660
Reproductive system, 5
  female, anatomy of, 662
  male, anatomy of, 651–653
Residual volume, 485, 486
Resistance, 406–407
  of airways, 484–487
Resistance (electrical), 187
Respiration, 474
  control of, 500–508
  control center for, 216
  in pregnancy, 682
Respiratory acidosis, 556
Respiratory alkalosis, 556
Respiratory bronchioles, 475, 476
Respiratory distress syndrome of the
    newborn, 484
Respiratory pump, 445–446
Respiratory quotient (RQ), 488
Respiratory system, 5
  functions of, 474
  organization of, 474–479
  role of, in hydrogen-ion homeostasis,
    553
Respiratory zone, 475, 476, 478
Resting potential, 187–192
Resting tidal volume, 485, 486
Restriction elements (see MHC
    proteins)
Restriction nucleases, 77–78
Restrictive lung diseases, 486–487
Retching, 594

Rete testis, 652
Reticular fibers, 4
Reticulocytes, 397
Retinal, 253
Retrograde amnesia, 719
Retrovirus, 726
Reversible reactions, 85, 86
Rh factor, 729
Rheumatoid arthritis, 731
Rhodopsin, 253
Rhythm method, 689
Rhythms, biological (see Biological
    rhythms)
Riboflavin, 87
Ribonuclease, 587
Ribonucleic acid (RNA):
  enzymatic action, 86
  messenger RNA, 65–70
  mRNA splicing, 66
  polymerase, 65–66
  ribosomal RNA, 67
  role of: in protein synthesis, 65–70
    in transcription, 65–67
  structure of, 35–36
  transfer RNA, 67, 68
Ribose, 34–35
Ribosomal RNA (rRNA), 67
Ribosomes, 43, 48, 50
  role of, in protein synthesis, 67, 69
  structure of, 67, 69
Rickets, 551
Rigidity, 364
Rigor mortis, 312
RNA (see Ribonucleic acid)
Rods, 252–254
  sensitivity of, 238
rRNA (see Ribosomal RNA)
RU 486, 689

S phase of cell division, 74–75
SA node, effects of autonomic nerves
    on, 421–422
Saccades, 257
  in REM sleep, 372
Saccule, 263, 265
Saliva, 565
  secretion of, 578
Salivary glands:
  effects of aldosterone on, 536
  function of, 564, 565
  innervation of, 224, 227
  volume of secretions of, 567
Salt:
  and hypertension, 467
  total-body balance of, 530
Salt appetite, 542
Saltatory conduction, 198
Sarcomas, 79

Sarcomere, 305, 308
Sarcoplasmic reticulum, 314–316
  function of, in cardiac muscle, 416
  role of, in contraction duration, 322
  in smooth muscle, 341
Satellite cells, 304
Satiety signals, 634–636
Saturated fatty acid, 25, 27
  and plasma cholesterol, 622
Saturation:
  of enzymes, 88
  of protein binding sites, 57–59
  of receptors, 162, 163
Schizophrenia, 379–380
Schwann cell, 182, 222
Scrotum, 651, 653
Sebaceous glands, antimicrobials in, 703
Second messengers, effects of, 174
Secondary active transport, 128–131
  role of Na,K-ATPase in, 128–130
Secondary oocytes, 664
Secondary peristalsis, 579
Secondary sex characteristics, 648
  effects of testosterone on, 660
Secondary spermatocytes, 654
Secretin, 275, 526–528
  enterogastrone activity, 582, 585
  as a neurotransmitter, 209
  potentiation of CCK, 477
  role of, in pancreatic bicarbonate
    secretion, 587, 588
  stimulation of bicarbonate secretion
    by bile ducts, 589
Secretion:
  definition of, 563
  by exocytosis, 137–138
  (See also Tubular secretion)
Secretions:
  gastrointestinal tract, 567
  of glands, 141–142
Secretory phase, 671, 672
Secretory vesicles, 49
  and peptide hormones, 277, 278
Segmentation in small intestine, 590–
  591
Semen, 653
Semicircular canals, 263
Seminiferous tubules, 652
  effect of FSH on, 658, 659
Sensation, 234, 238–239
Sensorimotor cortex, 352, 358
Sensory information, 234
Sensory receptors (see Receptors,
  sensory)
Sensory systems, 234
  acuity of, 241
  general principles of, 245
  information processing in, 239
  neural pathways in, 236–238

parallel pathways in, 239
Sensory unit, 236
Septic shock, 732
Serine, 28
Serosa, 568
Serotonin, 209, 210, 381
Sertoli cells:
  effect of FSH on, 658, 659
  functions of, 655–656
  secretion of Müllerian inhibiting
    factor by, 693
Serum, 396
Set point (see Operating point)
Sex chromatin, 603
Sex chromosomes, 693, 695
Sex determination, 692, 693
Sex differentiation, 692–695
Sex drive:
  effects of testosterone on, 660
  after menopause, 696
Sex hormones, 648
  effects of, on growth, 628
  inhibition of release of, in stress, 753
  during puberty, 695
Sexual response, female, 674–675
Sexually transmitted diseases, 688, 689
Shivering, 639
Shivering thermogenesis, 640
Shock:
  cardiovascular, 462
  septic, 732
Short-loop negative feedback, 293–294
Short portal vessels, 286, 287
Short reflexes in gastrointestinal tract,
  576
Shortening velocity, skeletal muscle
  control of, 330–331, 333–334
Shunt, 509
Sickle-cell anemia, 399–400
Side chain of amino acids, 28, 29
Sigmoid colon, 592
Signal sequence, 70
Signal transduction mechanisms, 164–
  176
Single-unit smooth muscles, 344–345
Sinoatrial node (SA), 411
Sister chromatids, 74, 75, 649, 650
Skeletal muscle:
  action potentials in, 313–320
  activity of, during sleep, 371–373
  adaptation of, 331–332
  and aging, 331–332
  characteristics of, 345
  contractile mechanism, 307–319
  control of arterioles in, 437
  control of muscle tension by, 329
  control of shortening velocity by,
    330–331, 333–334
  and cramps, 334

damage to, 304
differentiation, 304
diseases of, 334–335
energy derived from fat catabolism,
  104
energy metabolism, 324–325
excitation-contraction coupling, 313–
  315
extrafusal fibers, 354
and fatigue, 326–327
fiber types, 327, 328
frequency-tension relation, 322–323
function of, 340
glycogen storage, 102
and hypocalcemic tetany, 334
innervation of, 222
intrafusal fibers, 354
length-tension relation, 323–324
load-velocity relation, 324
mechanics of single fiber contraction,
  320–324
motor units, 316–317
muscular dystrophy, 334
myasthenia gravis, 334–335
optimal muscle length, 323
role of calcium, 313–315
sarcoplasmic reticulum, 314–316
shortening velocity, 324
skeletomotor fibers, 354
spindle fibers, 354
strength, 329–330
structure of, 304–307
summary of excitation-contraction
  coupling events, 319
transverse tubules, 314–316
whole muscle contraction, 327–334
Skeletal-muscle pump, 445–446
Skin:
  control of blood flow to, 437
  functions of, 5
  innervation of, 227, 228
  and temperature regulation, 640
Skull, 214
Sleep, 371–374
  neural substrates of, 372–374
Sleep apnea, 372
Sliding-filament model of contraction,
  307–312
Slow channels, 412
Slow-oxidative fibers, skeletal muscle,
  327, 328
Slow viruses, 701
Small intestine:
  epithelial replacement, 569
  function of, 564, 567
  inhibition of digestion in, by gastric
    acid, 582, 585
  innervation of, 224, 228
  motility, 590–591

Small intestine (*Cont.*):
  regulation of gastric acid secretion, 582, 585
  regulation of gastric emptying, 584–586
  secretions, 590
  surface area, 569
  volume of secretions, 562, 564, 565, 567
Smell, 266, 267
  representation of, in brain, 238
  sensitivity of, 239
Smooth muscle:
  actin and myosin, 338–339
  action potentials in, 342
  characteristics of, 345
  excitation-contraction coupling, 340–343
  function of, 304
  hormonal stimulation of, 342
  innervation of, 342–343
  response of, to stretch, 343
  role of calcium, 340–341
    in contraction, 340–341
  structure of, 306, 338–339
  tension, 338
  tone, 341
  types of fibers, 343–345
Sneeze, 508, 703
Sodium:
  absorption of, by small intestine, 575
  in action potentials, 194–196
  active transport across epithelia, 139–140
  basic renal processes for, 530–535
  content of sweat, 641
  control of tubular reabsorption of, 536, 538–539
  equilibrium potential, 189–190
  extracellular and intracellular concentration, 116
  and hypertension, 467
  ion, 17–18
  Na,K,2Cl cotransporters, 531, 533
  Na,K-ATPase pumps, in tubular sodium reabsorption, 530, 531
  primary active transport, 127–128
  renal regulation of, 535–539
  in resting membrane potential, 188–190
  retention of, in heart failure, 468
  role of, in secondary active transport, 128–130
  total-body balance of, 530
  tubular reabsorption of, 530–532
Sodium-calcium exchanger, 130
Soft palate, elevation of, during swallowing, 578
Solubility of molecules, 20

Solutes, 20
Solutions, 20–21
Solvent, 20
Somatic nervous system, 222
Somatic receptors, 237
Somatic sensation, 245–249
  receptors for, 245
  sense of posture and movement, 247
  (*See also specific type*)
Somatomedin C (*see* Insulin-like growth factor I)
Somatosensory cortex, 237, 246, 358, 359
Somatostatin (SS), 275, 291, 293
  in control of growth hormone, 294–295, 297
  effect of, on growth hormone secretion, 627
  as a neurotransmitter, 209
  from pancreas, 608
Somatotropin (*see* Growth hormone)
Sound, 258, 259
Spasticity, 364
Specialized cell types, 2, 3
Specific immune defenses, 700, 707–723
  overview, 707–708
Specificity of receptors, 162, 163
"Speed," 381
Speed of muscle shortening, 324
Sperm, 648
  anatomy of, 655
  capacitation of, 675
  transport of, 656–658
    in female, 675
Spermatic cord, 653
Spermatids, 654
Spermatogenesis, 652–655
Spermatogonia, 653
Spermatozoa, 648
Spermicides, 689
Sphincter of Oddi, 566, 590
Spinal cord, 214–217
Spinal nerves, 215
Spindle fibers, 74–75
Spinocerebellar tracts, 246
Spinothalamic tract, 246
Spleen, 709
SRY gene, 693, 694
SS (*see* Somatostatin)
Stable balance, 156
Starch:
  digestion of, in gastrointestinal tract, 571
  structure of, 25
Starling forces (capillary), 442–444
Starling's law of the heart, 422–423
States of consciousness, 370–375
  altered, 379–384

neural substrates of, 372–374
  (*See also specific state*)
Steady state, 150
Stellate (inferior cervical ganglion), 223, 224
Stenosis, 420
Sterilization, 688
Steroid hormones, 278–280
  mechanisms of action of, 283
Steroids:
  diffusion of, through membranes, 120
  in plasma membrane, 44
  structure of, 26–27
Stimulation-produced analgesia, 248
Stimulus, 157, 234
  coding of: for duration, 243–244
    for intensity, 240–241
    for location, 241–243
    for type, 240
  modality, 240
Stomach, 562, 564
  absorption from, 565
  acid secretion in, 581–582
  anatomy of, 580
  function of, 564, 565
  innervation of, 224, 227
  motility, 583–586
  pepsin secretion by, 582–583
  pyloric sphincter, 583, 584
  ulcers, 593–594
  volume of secretions, 567
Storage sites for foreign chemicals, 738, 739
"STP," 381
Streptokinase, 749
Stress:
  and biological rhythms, 154
  as controller of cortisol secretion, 294
  definition of, 751
  in diabetes mellitus, 620
  and food intake, 635
  fuel homeostasis in, 617–618
  hormones released during, 751, 753
  and plasma cholesterol, 622
  resistance to, 751–753
  and resistance to infection, 725
  as risk factor for atherosclerosis, 470
Stretch reflex, 183–184, 354–356, 365
Striated muscles, 305
  (*See also* Cardiac muscle; Skeletal muscle)
Stroke, 229
  in atherosclerosis, 470
  in hypertension, 467
  and plasma cholesterol, 621
Stroke volume (SV), 417, 419
  control of, 422–427
  in exercise, 463–464, 466
Strong acids, 22

Subarachnoid space, 214, 230
Subatomic particles, 14–15
Subcortical nuclei, 220, 221
Sublingual salivary glands, 562
Submandibular salivary glands, 562
Submucosa, 568
Submucus plexus, 568, 575
Substance P, 209, 212, 248
Substrate, 61
  enzyme, 86
Substrate phosphorylation in glycolysis,
    94
Succinate, 98
Suckling reflexes, 687
Sucrose, structure of, 24–25
Sulfate, product of amino acid
    catabolism, 108
Sulfonylureas, 620
Summation:
  of muscle tension, 322
  spatial, 193, 204
  temporal, 193, 204
Superior cervical ganglion, 223, 224
Superior mesenteric ganglion, 223, 224
Superior vena cava, 405
Supersensitivity, 162
Suppressor T cells, 701, 702, 733
  functions of, 710
Suprachiasmatic nucleus, 256
  role of, in states of consciousness, 374
Surface tension, 483
Surfactant, 476, 483, 484
Swallowing, 578–580
  of air, 591
  control center for, 216
Swallowing center, 578
Sweat:
  antimicrobials in, 703
  during heat acclimatization, 641–642
Sweat glands, 641
  effects of aldosterone on, 536
  innervation of, 228
Sweating, renal response to, 541–542
Swelling, 704
Sympathetic nervous system, 223–228
  acetylcholine and, 223
  in baroreceptor reflex, 456
  control of arterioles by, 435–436
  control of hormone secretion by,
    284–285
  effects of: on adipose tissue and liver,
    614–615
    on contractility, 423–425
    on heart rate, 421–422
    on insulin secretion, 611, 612
    on lymph flow, 448
    on salivary glands, 578
    on veins, 445
  effects of thyroid hormones on, 632
  in exercise, 463–464

functions of, in stress, 753
ganglia of, 223, 224
in hypertension, 467
norepinephrine and, 223
role of, in ejaculation, 658
  in erection, 657
  in gastric emptying, 585, 586
  in temperature regulation, 639–
    640
Sympathetic trunks, 223, 224
Synapse(s), 184, 201–203
  activation of postsynaptic cell, 203–
    205
  chemical, 201–203
  drugs and diseases at, 207
  effectiveness of, 205–207
  electric, 201
  excitatory, 201–203
  functional anatomy of, 201–202
  inhibitory, 201, 203
  interaction of, 203–205
  neurotransmitter release from, 202,
    205–207
  presynaptic, 206, 244
Systemic arterial pressure (see Arterial
    blood pressure)
Systemic circulation, 404
  pressures in, 419
Systemic manifestations of infection,
    723–726
Systole, 417
Systolic arterial pressure, 431

T_3 (see Triiodothyronine)
T_4 (see Thyroxine)
T-cell receptors, 712–713
T cells, 701, 702, 733
  functions of, 710
  origin of, 710
  receptors, 712–713
  subsets of, 710
  (See also Cytotoxic T cells; Helper
    T cells; Suppressor T cells)
T lymphocytes (see T cells)
T tubule (see Transverse tubules)
T wave, 415
Target cells, 159, 274
Taste, 266–267
  representation of, in brain, 237, 238
Taste buds, 266
Taurine, 209
Teleology, 2
Temperature:
  in control of ventilation, 505, 507
  as determinant of reaction rate, 84–
    85
  effects of: on hemoglobin saturation,
    496–497
    on protein conformation, 60
  role of, in enzyme reaction rate, 88

sensation of, 243, 246–248
  and thermal motion, 116
  (See also Body temperature)
Temperature-regulating reflexes, 638–
    641
Temperature regulation (see Body
    temperature)
Temporal lobe, 219, 220
Tendons, 304, 305
Tension:
  muscle, 320, 329–330
  smooth muscle, 341
Terminal bronchioles, 476
Termination code words, 64
Testes, 648
  descent of, 651–652
  hormones of, 275
Testicular feminization, 695
Testosterone, 275, 279, 648
  during aging, 696
  binding of, to androgen-binding
    protein, 655
  effect of LH on secretion of, 658,
    659
  effects of, 659–660
    on growth, 628
    on protein metabolism, 628
  and erythropoietin, 399
  mechanism of action of, 660
  as a neurotransmitter, 209
  role of, in spermatogenesis, 658, 659
  and sex differentiation, 693, 694
  structure of, 278
Tetanus (lockjaw), 182, 207, 350
Tetanus (skeletal muscle), 322–323
Tetany, 546
Tetrad, 650
Thalamus, 215, 219–221
  role of, in EEG, 370
Theca, 665
  production of androgens by, 668–669
Thermoneutral zone, 641
Thermoreceptors, 639
Thiazides, 558
Thick ascending limb of Henle's loop,
    518
  reabsorption of sodium by, 531, 534
Thick filaments, 305–309
  smooth muscle, 338–339
Thin filaments:
  skeletal muscle, 305–310, 313
  smooth muscle, 305–310, 338–339
Thirst, 542, 543
  in pregnancy, 682
Thoracic wall, 476
Thoracolumbar division of autonomic
    nervous system (see Sympathetic
    nervous system)
Thorax, 476
Threshold, 196–197

Thrombin, 743–745, 747
    positive feedback effects of, 745–747
    stimulation of protein C by, 746, 748
    summary of actions of, 748
Thrombolytic system (see Fibrinolytic system)
Thrombolytic therapy, 749
Thromboxane A2, 741, 742
Thromboxanes, 160, 161
Thrombus, 742
Thymine, 34, 35
Thymopoietin, 275
Thymosin as a neurotransmitter, 209
Thymus:
    anatomy of, 709
    clonal selection in, 716
    as endocrine gland, 275
    as site of lymphocyte production, 701, 708
Thyroglobulin, 276
Thyroid gland, 274, 276
    control of, 293
Thyroid hormones, 276–277
    actions of, on protein synthesis, 283
    effects of: on growth, 627–628
        on metabolic rate, 632
    functions of, 632
    release of, in stress, 753
Thyroid-stimulating hormone, 274, 288, 289
Thyrotropin (see Thyroid-stimulating hormone)
Thyrotropin releasing hormone, 292, 293
    as a neurotransmitter, 209
Thyroxine, 274, 276
Tidal volume, 485, 486
Tight junctions:
    role of, in epithelial transport, 137
    structure of, 46, 47
Tissue factor, 744–747
Tissue plasminogen activator, 747, 749
Tissue repair, 706
Tissue thromboplastin (see Tissue factor)
Tissues, 3
Titin filaments, 306, 308
T_m-limited transport mechanisms, 525
Tolerance, 381–384
Tone, smooth muscle, 341
Tonsils, 709
Total blood carbon dioxide, 498
Total energy expenditure, 630
Total peripheral resistance (TPR):
    as determinant of mean arterial pressure, 450–454
    in exercise, 463–464, 466
Touch-pressure, 226–229, 246–247
Toxemia of pregnancy, 681
Toxins, neutralization of, by antibodies, 719, 720

Trace elements, 14–15
Trace metals:
    absorption of, by small intestine, 575
    in bile, 589
Trachea, 474–476
Tract, 214
Transamination of amino acids, 107–108
Transcellular epithelial transport, 524
Transcellular pathway, 138
Transcription of genetic message, 65–67
Transcutaneous electric nerve stimulation (TENS), 248
Transduction, 234, 235
Transfer RNA (tRNA), 67, 68
Transferrin, 398
Transfusion reactions, 728–729
Transient ischemic attacks (TIAs), 470–471
Translation of genetic message, 67–70
Transmembrane potential (see Membrane potentials)
Transmembrane proteins, 45
Transport maximum, 525
Transporters, 123–124
Transpulmonary pressure, 479
Transverse tubules, 314–316
    function of, in cardiac muscle, 416
TRH (see Thyrotropin releasing hormone)
Triacylglycerol:
    in absorptive state, 603–607
    catabolism of, 104–105
    metabolism of, in postabsorptive state, 606–607
    structure of, 25–27
    synthesis of, 105–106
    (See also Fat; Fatty acids; Glycerol)
Tricarboxylic acid cycle (see Krebs cycle)
Tricuspid valve, 409
Tricyclic antidepressants, 380
Triiodothyronine, 274, 276
Triplet code, 64
tRNA (see Transfer RNA)
Trophoblast, 677, 678
    production of hormones by, 680–681
Tropic hormones, 286
Tropomyosin, 313
Troponin, 313
    role of, in summation and tetanus, 322–323
Trypsin, 571, 587, 588
Trypsinogen, 587, 588
TSH (see Thyroid-stimulating hormone)
Tubal ligation, 688
Tubular metabolism, 526
Tubular reabsorption, 520, 522, 524–526
    of sodium, 530–532
        control of, 536, 538–539
    of water, 530–532
Tubular secretion, 521, 522, 526

Tubule, renal, 517
Tubulin, 52–53
Tumor(s), 78
    and angiogenic factors, 439
Tumor necrosis factor (TNF), 275, 734
    as cytokine, 711
    and fever, 643
    as killer of cells, 723
    in septic shock, 732
Tumor suppressor genes, 79
Twins:
    dizygotic, 666, 677
    monozygotic, 677
Twitch contraction, 321
Type I alveolar cells, 476
Type II alveolar cells, 476
Tyrosine as source of biogenic amines, 208, 210
Tyrosine kinases and receptors, 165

Ulcers, 593–594
    role of Helicobacter pylori in, 594
Ultrafiltrate, 442
Umbilical arteries, 678, 679
Umbilical cord, 678, 679
Umbilical vein, 678, 679
Unsaturated fatty acids, 25, 27
    and plasma cholesterol, 622
Up-regulation, 162–164, 282
    of receptors, 206
Uphill transport (see Active transport)
Upper esophageal sphincter, 579, 580
    role of, in vomiting, 594
Upright posture, cardiovascular response to, 462
Uracil, 35
    base pairing, 65
Urea, 603
    structure of, 108
    synthesis of, 108
    tubular reabsorption of, 525
Uremia, 558–559
Ureter, 520, 521
Urethra, 520, 521
Urethral sphincters, 527–528
Urinary bladder, 520, 521, 527
    innervation of, 224, 228
Urinary system, 5
    structure of, 517–520
Urination (see Micturition)
Urine, color of, 589
Urine concentration, 532–535
Uterine motility, 274
Uterine tubes, 662
Uterus, 662, 663
    changes of, in menstrual cycle, 671–672
    contractions of, in parturition, 681–684
    at different times of pregnancy, 680

Uterus (Cont.):
    effects of estrogen and progesterone on, 671–672
    innervation of, 228
Utricle, 263, 265

Vaccine, 720
Vagina, 662, 663
Vaginal spermicide, 689
Vaginal sponge, 689
Vagus nerve, 218, 224
Valves in veins, 445–446
van der Waals, forces, 31–33, 56
Varicosities, autonomic nerves, 342
Varicosity of nerve fiber, 181
Vas deferens, 652, 653
    sperm storage in, 656
Vasa recta, 520
Vascular reactivity, 751
Vascular system, 395
    pressures in, 430
Vasectomy, 657, 688
Vasoactive intestinal peptide.
    effect of, on airway resistance, 485
    as a neurotransmitter, 209
Vasoconstriction, 433
    and capillary pressure, 444
    in hemostasis, 742
Vasodilation, 433
    and capillary pressure, 444
    in inflammation, 703–704
Vasodilator drugs:
    in heart failure, 468
    in hypertension, 467
Vasopressin, 274, 286
    in baroreceptor reflex, 456
    effect of, on memory, 384
    as a neurotransmitter, 209
    in pregnancy, 682
    release in stress, 753
    stimulation of ACTH release by, 751
    as vasoconstrictor, 436
    (See also Antidiuretic hormone)
Veins, 405, 444–446
    effects of sympathetic nerves on, 445
    function of, 408
    innervation of, 227
Velocity of muscle shortening, 324
Venous pressure, 445–446
Venous return, 423, 444–446
    identity with cardiac output, 446
Venous valves, 445–446
Ventilation, 480–488
    control of, in exercise, 505–507
    protective reflexes in control of, 507–508
    voluntary control of, 508
Ventilation-perfusion inequalities, 493
    as cause of hypoxic hypoxia, 509
Ventral root, 214, 215

Ventricles:
    cardiac, 403, 408
    cerebral, 215, 217, 220, 230
Ventricular ejection, 417–419
Ventricular fibrillation, 470
Ventricular filling, 417–419
Venules, 405
    function of, 408
Vertebral column, 214
Vertigo, 265
Very-low-density lipoproteins (VLDL), 605
Vestibular apparatus, 263
Vestibular system, 263–266
    control of eye muscles, 265
    dysfunction of, 265–266
    role of, in posture, 265
    stimuli sensitive to, 263–265
    structure of, 263–265
Vestibule, 663
Vibration, sensation of, 246
Villi, structure of, 569
Viruses, 700–701
    antigens produced from, 715
    cancer, 79
    immune defenses against, 721–723
    inhibition of replication of, by interferon, 707
    neutralization of, by antibodies, 719, 720
    size of, 41
    summary of host responses to, 724
Visceral blood flow, control of, 437
Visceral pleura, 476–477
Viscosity, 407
Visible spectrum, 249
Vision, 240–257
    for different distances, 250
    neural coding of, 254–256
    neural pathways of, 254–256
    optics of, 249–252
    (See also Color vision; Eye)
Visual cortex, 237, 238, 255, 256
Visual field, 256
Vital capacity, 486
Vital force, 2
Vitalism, 2
Vitamin(s):
    absorption of: by large intestine, 592
        by small intestine, 573–574
    B complex, 111
    B12: absorption, 574
        in erythrocyte formation, 398
    C, tubular reabsorption of, 525
    D₃, 549–550
    definition of, 87
    essential nutrients, 110–111
    fat-soluble, 110–111
    K, 746, 748
    niacin, 87

    riboflavin, 87
    water-soluble, 110–111
Vocal cords, 474, 475
Voltage-sensitive channels, 122
Voluntary actions, 351–353, 363
Vomiting, 594
    as cause of metabolic alkalosis, 556
    control center for, 216
Vomiting center, 594
von Willebrand factor (vWF), 741
Vulva, 663

Waking state, 371
Walking, 365–366
Waste products in plasma, 397
Water:
    absorption of, by small intestine, 574–575
    basic renal processes for, 530–535
    concentration of, 132–134
    diffusion of, 131–137
    essential nutrient, 110–111
    mechanism of tubular reabsorption, 530–532
    molecular structure of, 16–17
    movement of, across epithelia, 139–141
    product of oxidative phosphorylation, 98–100
    properties of, 19–20
    renal regulation of, 540–541
    total-body balance of, 529–530
    (See also Osmosis)
Water diuresis, 532
Water-soluble vitamins, 110–111
Wavelength, 249
Weak acids, 22
Wernicke's area, 386, 387
White blood cells (see Leukocytes)
White matter (of spinal cord), 214, 215
White skeletal muscle fibers, 327
Windchill index, 638
Withdrawal, 381–382
Withdrawal reflex, 357
Wolffian ducts, 693, 694
Working memory, 384

X chromosome, 693
Xylocaine, 196

Y chromosome, 693
Yolk sac, 679

Z line, 306, 307, 308
Zidovudine, 727
Zinc in infection, 724, 726
Zona pellucida, 665
Zygote, 676
Zymogens, 583